CW01150752

ROUTLEDGE HANDBOOK OF SPORT, LEISURE, AND SOCIAL JUSTICE

This is the first book to explore in breadth and in depth the complex intersections between sport, leisure, and social justice.

This book examines the relations of power that produce social inequalities and considers how sport and leisure spaces can perpetuate those relations, or act as sites of resistance, and makes a powerful call for an activist scholarship in sport and leisure studies. Presenting original theoretical and empirical work by leading international researchers and practitioners in sport and leisure, this book addresses the central social issues that lie at the heart of critical social science – including racism, sexism, homophobia, transphobia, ableism, religious persecution, socio-economic deprivation, and the climate crisis – and asks how these issues are expressed or mediated in the context of sport and leisure practices. Covering an incredibly diverse range of topics and cases – including sex testing in sport; sport for refugees; pedagogical practices in physical education; community sport development; events and human rights; and athlete activism – this book also surveys the history of sport and social justice research, as well as outlining theoretical and methodological foundations for this field of enquiry.

The *Routledge Handbook of Sport, Leisure, and Social Justice* is an indispensable resource for any advanced student, researcher, policymaker, practitioner, or activist with an interest in the sociology, culture, politics, history, development, governance, media and marketing, and business and management of sport and leisure.

Stefan Lawrence is Senior Lecturer in sport business management at Leeds Beckett University, UK. Stefan has published widely on sport and leisure and their relationship to social justice and digital cultures respectively. He is a member of the editorial boards for *Leisure Sciences*, *Leisure Studies* and *Managing Sport and Leisure*, and is a Principal Fellow of Advance HE.

Joanne Hill is Senior Lecturer in physical education and sport sociology at the University of Bedfordshire, UK, where she is also Co-Deputy Director for the Institute of Sport and Physical Activity Research. She researches the impact of the social construction of the body, gender and ethnicity on physical activity and sport engagement; and critical pedagogies/social justice in physical education and higher education, using participatory and creative methods.

Rasul Mowatt is a Professor and Researcher who studies social justice and the geographies of race. He is Head of the Department of Parks, Recreation and Tourism Management at North Carolina State's College of Natural Resources, USA. Before joining NC State, Rasul served on Indiana University's faculty for 15 years and previously taught at the University of Illinois, Urbana-Champaign. He is president of The Academy of Leisure Sciences, co-editor of *Leisure Sciences*, and founding editor of *Recreation, Parks and Tourism in Public Health*.

ROUTLEDGE CRITICAL PERSPECTIVES ON EQUALITY AND
SOCIAL JUSTICE IN SPORT AND LEISURE

Series editors
Kevin Hylton
Leeds Beckett University, UK
Jonathan Long
Leeds Beckett University, UK

This series presents important new critical studies that explore and explain issues relating to social justice and equality in sport and leisure. Addressing current debates and examining key concepts such as inclusion and exclusion, (anti)oppression, neo-liberalism, resistance, merit(ocracy), and sport for all, the series aims to be a key location for scholars, students and policy makers interested in these topics.

Innovative and interrogative, the series will explore central themes and issues in critical sport and leisure studies, including: theory development, methodologies and intersectionality; policy and politics; 'race', ethnicity, gender, class, sexuality, disability; communities and migration; ethics and morals; and media and new technologies. Inclusive and transdisciplinary, it aims to showcase high quality work from leading and emerging scholars working in sport and leisure studies, sport development, sport coaching and PE, policy, events and health studies, and areas of sport science that consider the same concerns.

Available in this series:

FAMILIES, SPORT, LEISURE AND SOCIAL JUSTICE
From Protest to Progress
Edited by Dawn E. Trussell and Ruth Jeanes

SPORT AS SOCIAL POLICY
Midnight Football and the Governing of Society
David Ekholm and Magnus Dahlstedt

CREATIVE AND INCLUSIVE RESEARCH METHODS IN SPORT, PHYSICAL ACTIVITY AND HEALTH
Understanding British Chinese Children's Experiences
Bonnie Pang

ROUTLEDGE HANDBOOK OF SPORT, LEISURE, AND SOCIAL JUSTICE
Edited by Stefan Lawrence, Joanne Hill, and Rasul Mowatt

For more information about this series, please visit: https://www.routledge.com/Routledge-Critical-Perspectives-on-Equality-and-Social-Justice-in-Sport/book-series/RCPESJSL

ROUTLEDGE HANDBOOK OF SPORT, LEISURE, AND SOCIAL JUSTICE

Edited by
Stefan Lawrence, Joanne Hill, and Rasul Mowatt

Routledge
Taylor & Francis Group
LONDON AND NEW YORK

Designed cover image: Getty Images / Michael Duva

First published 2024
by Routledge
4 Park Square, Milton Park, Abingdon, Oxon OX14 4RN

and by Routledge
605 Third Avenue, New York, NY 10158

Routledge is an imprint of the Taylor & Francis Group, an informa business

© 2024 selection and editorial matter, Stefan Lawrence, Joanne Hill, and Rasul Mowatt; individual chapters, the contributors

The right of Stefan Lawrence, Joanne Hill, and Rasul Mowatt to be identified as the authors of the editorial material, and of the authors for their individual chapters, has been asserted in accordance with sections 77 and 78 of the Copyright, Designs and Patents Act 1988.

All rights reserved. No part of this book may be reprinted or reproduced or utilised in any form or by any electronic, mechanical, or other means, now known or hereafter invented, including photocopying and recording, or in any information storage or retrieval system, without permission in writing from the publishers.

Trademark notice: Product or corporate names may be trademarks or registered trademarks, and are used only for identification and explanation without intent to infringe.

British Library Cataloguing-in-Publication Data
A catalogue record for this book is available from the British Library

Library of Congress Cataloging-in-Publication Data
Names: Lawrence, Stefan, editor. | Hill, Joanne, editor. | Mowatt, Rasul A., editor.
Title: Routledge handbook of sport, leisure, and social justice / edited by Stefan Lawrence, Joanne Hill and Rasul Mowatt.
Other titles: Handbook of sport, leisure, and social justice
Description: Abingdon, Oxon ; New York, NY : Routledge, 2024. | Series: Routledge critical perspectives on equality and social justice in sport and leisure | Includes bibliographical references and index. |
Identifiers: LCCN 2023052122 | ISBN 9781032485607 (hardback) | ISBN 9781032485645 (paperback) | ISBN 9781003389682 (ebook)
Subjects: LCSH: Sports--Sociological aspects. | Physical education and training--Sociological aspects. | Recreation--Sociological aspects. | Leisure--Sociological aspects. | Social justice. | Human rights.
Classification: LCC GV706.5 .R679 2024 | DDC 306.4/83--dc23/eng/20231213
LC record available at https://lccn.loc.gov/2023052122

ISBN: 978-1-032-48560-7 (hbk)
ISBN: 978-1-032-48564-5 (pbk)
ISBN: 978-1-003-38968-2 (ebk)

DOI: 10.4324/9781003389682

Typeset in Times New Roman
by SPi Technologies India Pvt Ltd (Straive)

CONTENTS

List of contributors   *x*

PART I
Historicising and theorising social justice in sport and leisure   **1**

1 Sport, leisure, and social justice at the neoliberal moment: challenges for integrity and activist scholarship   3
 Stefan Lawrence, Joanne Hill, and Rasul Mowatt

2 Contrasting approaches to social justice in sport   18
 Jim Lusted

3 Heritage, public history, and social justice in sport and leisure   33
 Matthew L. McDowell

4 Sport, leisure, and social justice in the age of precarity and prosumption   45
 Spencer Swain

PART II
Sex, gender, and sexualities   **57**

5 Women, sport, and activism: an international perspective   59
 Celia Valiente

6 Sport, masculinities, and homosexualities: why inclusive masculinity
   theory can be considered dangerous for queer sportspeople   71
   Richard Pringle

7 The invisibility of trans men in sport and sporting spaces   85
   Abby Barras

8 Sex-testing and discrimination in sport: upholding an uneven
   playing field   99
   Grace Athanas-Linden

9 Doing and undoing gender in physical education and youth sport:
   the potential for practice   114
   Hannah Kettley-Linsell and Joanne Hill

PART III
'Race', forced migration, and religion   **129**

10 Social justice, sport, leisure, and racism in the United States   131
   Adam Love, Steven N. Waller, Ashley Gardner, and Chermaine Cole

11 Race, social justice, leisure, and sport in Brazil: a critical perspective in
   defence of anti-racism   145
   *Lennon Giulio Santos de Farias, Neilton de Sousa Ferreira Júnior,
   Léo Barbosa Nepomuceno, Eduardo Vinícius Mota e Silva,
   Luciana Venâncio, Luiz Sanches Neto, and Henrique Antunes Cunha Júnior*

12 Sport and social justice for refugees: advocating for leisure activities
   as a basic human need   157
   Mark Doidge

13 Mental health, Drapetomania, and professional football: a memorial
   to Dalian Atkinson   170
   Colin King

14 Christianity, sport, and social justice   178
   David Torevell

15 Race, social justice, and children's everyday leisure geographies   192
   Utsa Mukherjee

PART IV
Physical education, young people, and families   **203**

16 Families, advocacy, and social justice in youth sport   205
  Ruth Jeanes and Dawn Trussell

17 Teaching for social justice through physical education   219
  Rod Philpot, Wayne Smith, Richard Pringle, Alan Ovens, and Göran Gerdin

18 Legitimate embodiment in formal education: imagery in physical education textbooks   236
  Ana Rey-Cao and Alba González-Palomares

19 Chinese government's modern governance and the challenges to social justice in school sports   251
  Honglu Zhang

20 Teaching for social justice through physical education in the context of US legislation and policies against critical race theory   264
  Micah J. Dobson

21 School physical education and social justice: what are we doing in Brazil?   280
  Isabel Porto Filgueiras, Elisabete dos Santos Freire, Bruno Freitas Meireles, Ewerton Leonardo da Silva Vieira, Bruna Gabriela Marques, Graciele Massoli Rodrigues, Luiz Sanches Neto, and Luciana Venâncio

PART V
Sport, development, and community   **293**

22 Equality and social justice in sport for development and peace   295
  Simon C. Darnell and Rob Millington

23 Sport for development: a troubling past to a brighter future?   308
  Michael Sup

24 Implementing service-learning for social change in sport management curricula   321
  Michael B. Edwards, Kimberly A. Bush, and J. Lin Dawson

25 Community sport development: where sport development
and social justice meet 334
Janine Partington and Dan Bates

26 Sport, Physical Education (PE) and Sport-for-All (SfA) programmes:
intersectional perspectives from Cyprus and Greece 349
Foteini Papadopoulou and Symeon Dagkas

27 Socioeconomic status in sport and leisure engagement 363
Adam Gemar

28 Addressing power dynamics in disability sport studies:
emancipatory participatory principles for social justice research 376
Damian Haslett

29 Sport and crime reduction 390
Peter R. Harris

PART VI
Elite sport, activism, and media 403

30 English football, safe standing, and social movements:
an eventful sociology of fan activism 405
Mark Turner

31 Branding social justice in sport 419
Antonio S. Williams, Tanya K. Jones, Kelly J. Brummett, and Zack P. Pedersen

32 National anthems and athlete activism 431
Keith D. Parry, Daryl Adair, and Jamie Cleland

33 Sport, the media, and athlete activism: 'just shut up and play' 446
Steph Doehler

34 Social media and online activism in women's rugby:
From #IAmEnough to #ICare 459
Ali Bowes and Alex Culvin

35 The five groups of environmental sports activists: a complex medley 471
Toby Miller

PART VII
Future directions and research methods for social justice   **489**

36 Research methods for sport, leisure, and social justice   491
Ian Jones and Jayne Caudwell

37 Arts-based research and social justice in sport and leisure   504
David Carless and Kitrina Douglas

38 Participatory research in sport, leisure, and forced migration: where is the social justice?   518
Chris Webster and Robyn Smith

39 Indigenous methodologies for sport, leisure and social justice research: a Pacific studies perspective   531
Gina Hawkes

40 Research integrity and ethics in sport social justice research: safe practice   544
Christina Philippou

41 Intersectional scholarship on sport and leisure: trends, tensions, and promising directions   556
Prisca Bruno Massao and Mari Haugaa Engh

Index   *570*

CONTRIBUTORS

Daryl Adair is Associate Professor of sport management in the Business School, University of Technology Sydney, Australia. His research has encompassed sport history, sociology, politics, media, and management. His recent interests are gender relations in sport, race and ethnicity in sport, and drugs in sport.

Grace Athanas-Linden received her MS in sport business from the School of Sport, Tourism and Hospitality Management at Temple University, USA, in May 2021. She presented her Master's project work, "Sex-Segregation: The Continuation of Historical Inequities", at the Women in Sport and Exercise (WISE) 2021 conference. While at Temple University, Grace worked as a Research Assistant for the Sport Industry Research Center and as a summer Research Assistant for the Center for Sport, Peace, and Society at the University of Tennessee, USA.

Abby Barras (she/her) is a Critical Social Scientist and Lecturer in the School of Humanities and Social Sciences at the University of Brighton, UK. Her qualitative research interests and expertise centre around gender, sport/exercise inequalities, LGBTQ+ communities, transfeminist theory, and the body/embodiment. Abby is currently writing a book for Routledge called *Transgender and Non-Binary People in Everyday Sport: A Trans Feminist Approach to Improving Inclusion* (Routledge 2025) based on her PhD findings.

Dan Bates is Senior Lecturer at Leeds Beckett University, UK. His research and consultancy work covers several aspects of sport for development theory and practice, with a specific focus on community models of delivery, power and governance, and qualitative evaluation methodologies.

Ali Bowes is Senior Lecturer in the sociology of sport at Nottingham Trent University, UK. Ali serves on the editorial boards of both *Sociology of Sport Journal* and *Managing Sport and Leisure*. Ali is the co-editor of *The Professionalisation of Women's Sport* (Emerald Publishing 2021) and *Women's Football in a Global, Professional Era* (Emerald Publishing 2021).

Contributors

Kelly J. Brummett is a PhD student at Indiana University Bloomington, USA. Her research interest is athlete branding, specifically college student–athlete name, image, and likeness and the intersection of law, media, and social justice. She earned her undergraduate degree in economics and management and MBA from the University of South Florida. Prior to pursuing her PhD, Kelly spent 15 years working in intercollegiate athletics, most recently at the National Collegiate Athletics Association (NCAA).

Kimberly A. Bush is Associate Department Head and Community Program Coordinator at North Carolina State University, USA. She teaches sport management classes, where she strives to foster an ethic of care in her classroom and exhibits dedication to the scholarship of teaching and learning around justice, equity, diversity, and inclusion.

David Carless is a Qualitative Researcher in social science and health. His arts-based, autoethnographic and narrative collaborations have been published online, in journal articles, books and invited chapters. David works at the University of the West of Scotland and is an Honorary Professor at the University of Edinburgh, UK.

Jayne Caudwell is Associate Professor of social sciences, gender and sexualities in the Department of Social Sciences and Social Work at Bournemouth University, UK. Her work is concerned with sport and leisure cultures, feminist theory and activism, LGBTQ+ inclusion, and qualitative research methodologies.

Jamie Cleland is Senior Lecturer in sport and management at the University of South Australia, Australia. His research primarily focuses on contemporary social issues in sport and society, including terrorism and security, match official abuse, sexuality, masculinity, homophobia, violence, race, and athlete and fan activism.

Chermaine Cole is a clinical assistant professor in the Department of Kinesiology and Health at Georgia State University. Her primary research interests include exploring the career mobility patterns of African American female park and recreation professionals and the factors that influence their progression in leadership positions.

Alex Culvin is Senior Lecturer in sports business at Leeds Beckett University, UK. Alex works in player and union relations at FIFPro, the global union of professional footballers. Alex is the co-editor of *Women's Football in a Global, Professional Era* (Emerald Publishing 2021) and *The Professionalisation of Women's Sport* (Emerald Publishing 2021).

Henrique Antunes Cunha Júnior teaches African urbanism as Visiting Professor at the Federal University of Bahia, Brazil. He has a PhD in engineering and academic distinction – super thesis – as full professor from the University of São Paulo. He supervised 31 PhD dissertations within the systemic complexity and transdisciplinarity theory in its African version.

Symeon Dagkas is Provost at St Mary's University, Twickenham, UK, and is responsible for academic development matters, research, staff workload, and performance. He joined St Mary's in 2018 from Canterbury Christ Church University where he was the Head of the School of Human and Life Sciences. He has also served as Director of Research and Deputy Associate Dean, Research at the University of East London and Head of the Sport Pedagogy Department in the School of Education, at Birmingham University where he spent 13 years in various roles.

Contributors

Simon C. Darnell is Associate Professor and Director of the Centre for Sport Policy Studies in the Faculty of Kinesiology and Physical Education at the University of Toronto, Canada. He researches the relationships between sport, international development and peacebuilding; environmental sustainability in sport-for-development, and social activism in sport culture.

J. Lin Dawson is Dean of the School of Exercise Science and Collegiate Athletics at Saint Augustine's University, USA. Dawson played for ten years for the New England Patriots. Dawson holds an MBA and a PhD in Organisational Leadership.

Micah J. Dobson is Assistant Professor of recreation management and leisure studies at Shaw University, USA. His primary areas of focus are racial/social justice in teaching, diversity, and inclusion in sport management, gender equity in leisure studies, and infusing self-advocacy into physical education and health education.

Steph Doehler is a Sport Sociologist in the School of Education, Childhood, Youth and Sport at the Open University, UK. Her scholarly interests revolve around athlete activism and sports communication. She has presented at various global conferences and serves as a peer-reviewed for several esteemed publications.

Mark Doidge is Reader in the School of Sport, Exercise and Health Sciences at Loughborough University, UK. His research focuses on social activism among football fans, environmentalism, anti-racism, and supporting refugees.

Kitrina Douglas is a video/ethnographer, storyteller, song-writer, performer, researcher, and narrative scholar whose research spans the arts, humanities, and social sciences working to make research findings more accessible and democratic. With David Carless she produces and edits the online series of programmes called, "Qualitative Conversations" available on YouTube (www.youtube.com/channel/UCkWCTy8bNOY6JlvX_yg-Uig).

Michael B. Edwards is Associate Professor of community sport at North Carolina State University, USA. His research interests centre on access to physical activity and sport and sport's impact on community health, development, and wellbeing as well as how practices and policies related to sport can build sustainable capacity for health development.

Mari Haugaa Engh is Lecturer in the School of Social Sciences at the University of KwaZulu-Natal, South Africa. Mari is an inter-disciplinary gender studies scholar, with expertise in gender, sexuality, sport, and migration. She has published widely about African women's football, sports labour migration, and gender and sexualities in sport.

Ashley Gardner is an assistant professor of instruction in the Department of Sport and Recreation Management at Temple University. Her research explores the lack of racial diversity in sport organizations and governing bodies to identify the ways racial inequity is (re)produced in sport structures

Lennon Giulio Santos de Farias has a graduation degree in physical education from the Federal University of Ceará, Brazil. He is a member of the Physical Activity and Sports Psychosocial Studies Group.

Contributors

Isabel Porto Filgueiras is Professor at São Judas University, Brazil, and leads the Research Group on Physical Education Teacher Education and Critical Pedagogies. She worked as a teacher in schools before lecturing in higher education. She has a Master's degree and a PhD in education from the University of São Paulo, Brazil.

Adam Gemar is Lecturer in the Department of Social and Political Sciences at the University of Cyprus. Adam's research revolves around sociological understandings of sport, culture, religion, and their intersections with social inequalities.

Göran Gerdin is Associate Professor in the Department of Sport Science at Linnaeus University, Sweden. His research focuses on how issues of gender, bodies, spaces, pleasures, inclusion, equity and social justice shape teaching practice and student experience in school physical education and teacher education.

Alba González-Palomares is Assistant Professor in the Faculty of Education at Salamanca University, Spain. Her research focuses on the social aspects surrounding physical education in schools and in sports. She is the author of various publications both nationally and internationally related to visual literacy and co-educational practices in physical education.

Peter R. Harris spent 18 years as a youth worker before completing an ESRC-funded PhD in Criminology. He has presented at national and international conferences on the issue of youth violence and masculinity and has produced several published works in the area of youth work and youth crime.

Damian Haslett is Programme Manager for Public and Patient Involvement (PPI) at University College Cork, Ireland. Damian's research background has combined thinking from critical psychology and disability studies with a focus on sport, disability, and social activism. He has worked on a variety of collaborative projects including research underpinned by emancipatory participatory principles and values.

Gina Hawkes is a Qualitative Social Scientist whose work spans anthropology, human geography, and sport and leisure studies. She is interested in diverse qualitative methodologies and knowledge systems, decolonial and other socially just approaches to sport and leisure, and the connections between humans and nature in outdoor 'play' spaces.

Ruth Jeanes is Professor and Head of the School of Curriculum, Teaching and Inclusive Education at Monash University, Australia. She is a sociologist whose research examines inequity, discrimination and social justice within community sport. Ruth has published extensively with her research work examining gender relations in community sports clubs and the growth of informal sport participation amongst multicultural young people.

Ian Jones is Associate Professor in Sport at Bournemouth University, UK. His key interests are in the areas of social identity and group belonging, and research methods. He is author of *Research Methods for Sports Studies* (Routledge 2022) *and Qualitative Research in Sport and Physical Activity* (SAGE 2012). He is also a managing editor of the *Journal Leisure Studies*.

Tanya K. Jones is Faculty Member on the flagship campus in the School of Public Health at Indiana University-Bloomington, USA.

Contributors

Neilton de Sousa Ferreira Júnior is Adjunct Professor at the Federal University of Viçosa, Brazil, and member of the Olympic Studies Group and the Brazilian College of Sports Sciences' Ethnic-Racial Relations Group. He researches ethnic-racial relations in physical education and modern sport.

Hannah Kettley-Linsell is Research Associate at Imperial College London, UK. Her research interests centre on equality, diversity, and inclusion in education. She has a particular interest in social justice, with recent work focused on gender diversity within physical education.

Colin King is Head Coach at Black and Asian Coaches Association, UK.

Adam Love is Associate Professor in the Department of Kinesiology, Recreation, and Sport Studies at the University of Tennessee, Knoxville, USA. His research investigates issues of racial and gender ideology, focusing on ways in which sport and physical activity programmes, organisations, and institutions can operate in a more ethical, just, open, democratic, and accessible way.

Jim Lusted is Lecturer in sport and fitness at The Open University, UK. He has undertaken numerous research projects with sport organisations related to social inequalities in sport spanning two decades. More recently, Jim has focused his research on racialised inequalities in sport coaching contexts.

Bruna Gabriela Marques is Professor at the stricto sensu graduate programmes in physical education and in ageing sciences at São Judas University, Brazil. She is experienced in the physical education field, researching on ageing, public health, and health education.

Prisca Bruno Massao is Associate Professor in the Institute of Social Sciences, Religion and Ethics at Inland Norway University of Applied Sciences, Norway. Massao's areas of research include sport and education sociology with gender, race, and racism as her speciality where she has published widely both in English and Norwegian.

Matthew L. McDowell is Lecturer of sport policy and management at the University of Edinburgh, UK. He has written extensively on the history of football, surfing, curling, and sporting events, and teaches sport history and heritage. He is a former Chair of the British Society of Sports History.

Bruno Freitas Meireles is a Physical Education Teacher, School Manager and Teacher Educator. His research emphasises Paulo Freire's dialogical framework to investigate the continuing education of physical education teachers.

Toby Miller is Visiting Professor at the Universidad Complutense de Madrid, Spain, Professor and Chair at the Universidad de la Frontera, and Research Professor, Graduate Division at the University of California, Riverside, USA.

Rob Millington is Assistant Professor in sport and social change and sport for development and peace. His research focuses on how international NGOs such as the United Nations and the International Olympic Committee mobilise sport for development in policy and practice in both historical and contemporary contexts. More recently, his work has focused on the environmental component and sustainable development, to consider what role, if any, sport can play in an environmental context and in meeting sustainable development objectives, including the Sustainable Development Goals.

Utsa Mukherjee is Lecturer in education at Brunel University London, UK. His research is located at the intersection of childhood studies and leisure studies, with a focus on questions around social inequalities and identities.

Léo Barbosa Nepomuceno is Adjunct Professor at the Institute of Physical Education and Sports, Federal University of Ceará, Brazil. He is also a member of the Laboratory for Qualitative Health Research and Assessment at the graduate programme in collective health.

Luiz Sanches Neto is Vice-Coordinator of the professional Master's programme in physical education and Adjunct Professor at the Institute of Physical Education and Sports, Federal University of Ceará, Brazil. He leads the Research Group on School Physical Education and Collaborative Educative Processes and is an ISATT member.

Alan Ovens is an Associate Professor and Discipline Leader of the Sport, Health and Physical Education Discipline Group. His research focusses on the interacting themes of education, wellbeing and human movement.

Foteini Papadopoulou is Lecturer in the Sport Department at the Metropolitan College in Athens, Greece. Foteini holds extensive professional experience in the fields of Sport, PE and Sport-for-All and in CPD relevant to their role in tackling social disadvantage, youth disaffection and on sociological issues of body image.

Keith D. Parry is Head of the Department of Sport and Event Management at Bournemouth University, UK, and Adjunct Fellow of Western Sydney University, Australia. His research interests are primarily focused on identity, sport and in/exclusion and how both traditional and newer, online media formats are used to present and discuss these subjects.

Janine Partington is Senior Lecturer at Leeds Beckett University, UK. Prior to this she worked in community sport development within local government and charitable organisations. Her PhD examines the changing role of local government in sport development, with broader academic interests centring on sport and 'community', and global sport policy.

Zack P. Pedersen is Assistant Professor at Texas Tech University, USA, specialising in communication and media, with a focus on quantitative and qualitative social research. His expertise lies in branding, marketing, and consumer behaviour.

Christina Philippou is Principal Lecturer at the University of Portsmouth, UK. Her research focuses on forensic accounting, and finance, governance, ethics, and corruption in sport. Prior to academia, she worked as a forensic accountant where she conducted a number of financial crime and regulatory breach investigations and compliance work.

Rod Philpot is Senior Lecturer in the Faculty of Education and Social Work at the University of Auckland, New Zealand. He is a critical qualitative researcher whose research focuses on issues of social justice and pedagogies for social justice in physical education teacher education and school health and physical education.

Richard Pringle is Professor of the sociology of sport, health and physical education at Monash University, Melbourne, Australia. He is a critical qualitative researcher who examines diverse sociocultural, pedagogical, and theoretical issues associated with sport, exercise, health, physical education, bodies, sexualities and genders.

Ana Rey-Cao is a tenured Lecturer in the Faculty of Education and Sport at Vigo University, Spain. Her research focuses on the social aspects surrounding body culture. Among her research features the analysis of stereotypes in physical education textbooks. She has transferred the knowledge to didactic materials for visual literacy.

Graciele Massoli Rodrigues is Vice-Coordinator of the stricto sensu graduate programme in physical education at São Judas University, Brazil, and Professor at the Higher School of Physical Education in Jundiaí, Brazil. She researches inclusion and diversity in physical education and leads the Study Group on Physical Education and People with Disabilities.

Elisabete dos Santos Freire is Professor and Coordinator of the stricto sensu graduate programme in physical education at São Judas University, Brazil. She has been researching on knowledge in school physical education classes and teachers' inquiry. She leads the group Dialogues: Physical Education, School and Curriculum and is an ISATT member.

Eduardo Vinícius Mota e Silva coordinates physical education undergraduate programmes at the Institute of Physical Education and Sports, Federal University of Ceará, Brazil. He has a PhD in human development and technology and Master's in physical education from São Paulo State University.

Ewerton Leonardo da Silva Vieira teaches in the state education network. He has a Master's degree in physical education from the Federal University of Rio Grande do Norte, Brazil. He was a temporary lecturer at the Federal Institute of Education, Science and Technology where he led the Academy & Football extension project as a teacher–researcher.

Robyn Smith is Doctoral Researcher at Brunel University London, UK. She utilises participatory approaches to explore the sport and leisure experiences of refugee and immigrant youth in the UK and Canada. Her research interests include race, ethnic, and diasporic studies in youth leisure; sport for development, refugee youth wellbeing; and participatory methodologies.

Wayne Smith is Associate Professor (Honorary) at the University of Auckland, New Zealand. He has lectured in HPETE for the past 30 years. His research contributions have been in critical pedagogy in physical education and skill learning. His most recent research has focused on pedagogies for social justice in HPE.

Michael Sup is Assistant Professor of Instruction in the Department of Recreation and Sport Pedagogy at Ohio University, USA. Michael's doctoral degree was in Curriculum and Instruction with a concentration of Educational Leadership and Critical Studies in the field of Sport and International Development.

Contributors

Spencer Swain is Senior Lecturer in youth, society, and education at York St. John's University, UK. He is a sociologist with a social and political theory background. He researches the sociology of culture and leisure; migration and diaspora; sports management and development; and inequalities within education.

David Torevell is Honorary Senior Research Fellow at Liverpool Hope University, UK and Visiting Professor at Mary Immaculate College, Limerick, Ireland.

Dawn Trussell is Professor in the Department of Sport Management at Brock University, Canada. Dawn was awarded a Chancellor's Chair for Research Excellence (2021–2024) for her work on allyship and activism in sport. Her research focuses on issues of social justice within community sport and is funded by the Social Sciences and Humanities Research Council of Canada and Sport Canada.

Mark Turner is Senior Lecturer in sport sociology at Manchester Metropolitan University, UK. His research examines the regulation and governance policies of football supporters. His work applies relational sociology to the study of social movements, within different sport and leisure contexts.

Celia Valiente is Professor of sociology at the Universidad Carlos III de Madrid, Spain. Her main research interests are the women's movement, sports, and gender policies in Spain from a comparative perspective. Her research on sports has been published by *International Journal of the History of Sport*; *International Review for the Sociology of Sport*; *Managing Sport and Leisure*; and *Sport in Society*.

Luciana Venâncio coordinates the professional Master's programme in physical education and is Adjunct Professor at the Institute of Physical Education and Sports, Federal University of Ceará, Brazil. She leads the Research Group on School Physical Education and Relationships to Knowledge and is an ISATT member.

Steven N. Waller is Professor in the Department of Kinesiology, Recreation, and Sport Studies at the University of Tennessee, Knoxville, USA. His areas of research include institutional evil and structural barriers to career advancement for minorities and women in recreation and sport organisations.

Chris Webster completed his PhD at Leeds Beckett University, UK, and is now an independent community researcher based in Leeds. Chris' research and activism is focused around borders, forced migration and leisure spaces.

Antonio S. Williams is interim Assistant Dean for Doctoral Research and Education Growth and Elevation Beinner Family Professor in Sports Marketing and Management, and Associate Professor in the School of Public Health at Indiana University-Bloomington, USA.

Honglu Zhang is an expert in sports history and the Olympics. Her research focuses on the governance of Olympic education, analysing stakeholder involvement and student responses. Interested in power dynamics, she explores social justice, school sport, migrants, and traditional cultural play. Dr Zhang currently serves as a community advisor in New Zealand, using sports and physical education to empower and engage Asian communities, promoting inclusivity, and participation.

PART I

Historicising and theorising social justice in sport and leisure

1
SPORT, LEISURE, AND SOCIAL JUSTICE AT THE NEOLIBERAL MOMENT

Challenges for integrity and activist scholarship

Stefan Lawrence, Joanne Hill, and Rasul Mowatt

Over the last decade or so the prominence of sport and leisure industries in mainstream socio-cultural–political debate has become increasingly salient. This (re)new(ed) visibility, after a notable absence of activism in elite sport, has coincided with broader societal shifts towards a greater and more public engagement with issues of widening inequality across the globe. Where once we were implored to keep 'politics out of sport', the impossibility and implausibility of that statement now must surely be plain for all to see. The cultural cachet of sport and leisure has helped bring matters front and centre that may otherwise have remained hidden. From *Black Lives Matter* and *Refugees Welcome* to the *Rainbow Laces* and *#WeThe15* campaigns, sport and leisure arenas – and the many celebrity personalities that reside within their realms – have leveraged their status to raise awareness on several fronts such as White supremacy, racism, patriarchy, sexism, homophobia, transphobia, xeonophobia, ableism, sportswashing, religious persecution, socio-economic deprivation, to name a few. Social justice, at least as term and concept, then is no longer a debate that is being had simply on the left of the political spectrum; it has become the defining cultural debate of the immediate post-COVID-19 moment. This context, which justifies the need for this handbook, has greatly influenced the perspectives and contributions found within it.

Such a dramatic shift over a relatively short period of time has meant that socially scientific disciplines and discourses (sociology and cultural studies, in particular) have stepped out from the academic shadows and into mainstream media and political discourse. Critical Race Theory (CRT), for instance, has drawn scathing attacks from conservatives in both the UK and the USA (Lawrence & Hylton, 2022), which in and of itself speaks to the impact that its major tenets are having on those that defend the status quo. Before we are overwhelmed by some glorious homily of absolute social improvement, however, we must remember that what has sparked such an awakening in the first place are serious affronts on the social and political progress made in liberal democracies, over the last few decades. Sport and leisure spaces have been sites that have not been immune to such events. In some respects, they have reflected and catalysed a resurgence of dominant hegemonies and social inequalities as much as they have led resistances. While there has been much positive and intentional action, the last few years or so have seen a rise in reports of hate crime, anti-immigration rhetoric, domestic violence, transphobia, cuts to disability support allowances, and the mainstreaming of White nationalist and separatist groups.

The current milieu, with which the chapters in this handbook, authored by an international cast of contributors, engage with, is a cause for both concern and optimism. While some contributions document professional sport others are writing about sport and leisure in the everyday. Nonetheless, regardless of the topic, they and we are writing against a sombre socio-historical moment: despite the implementation of legal frameworks such as Title IX in the United States and the Equality Act 2010 in the United Kingdom, egregious violations of the rights of individuals persist. The recent reversal of Roe vs Wade by the US Supreme Court in June 2022 and the UK Conservative government's reluctance to reject the option of exiting the European Convention on Human Rights (ECHR) for the purpose of deporting asylum seekers to Rwanda are but two examples of such violations. Thus, it is imperative for scholars of sport and leisure to undertake further critical explorations of the role that sport and leisure play in contemporary cultures, in the hope we might tip the balance in favour of those working for human dignity, egalitarianism, and a compassionate humanist politics.

To that end, the introductory chapter to this handbook will help set the context for the chapters that follow by calling for a greater and urgent reflection on what is meant by the term 'social justice' and how sport and leisure scholars and practitioners might mobilise it. Just as the term 'feminism' is relatively unsatisfactory, given that myriad different strands exist with differing and competing approaches to dismantling patriarchy, social justice too has become an increasingly vague and rather woolly term. We must, as we argue throughout the rest of this chapter, move away from the notion that simply doing research on or with, say, refugees and asylum seekers or 2SLGBTQIA+ people is social justice work simply because these groups have been historically marginalised in sport and leisure spaces. The textual boundaries, axiologies, and underlying presuppositions of social justice when working with such groups, we argue, need to feature in research practices with a greater precision and clarity. Therefore, our first move, below, is to outline the definition of social justice we promote throughout the handbook.

What is social justice?

Social justice, in its most conventional sense, is a term that has tended to refer to an interventionist approach to matters of socioeconomic inequality, in the form of economic redistribution, cultural recognition, and political representation (Fraser, 1999), which advocates hope will facilitate a fairer and more equitable society. If structures and systems of justice are what exist (or what should exist) within institutions, then social justice work is the social, cultural, economic, and political response to the failures of those structures, the protest of absence in those structures, and the radical desire to catalyse new and alternative systems, institutions and policies. It is from this critical definition and tradition we invite readers to take their steer in reading and interpreting the various mobilisations and usages of the term 'social justice' in the handbook.

However, not only are the sociolinguistics of the term important, so too are its politics.

Historically, with its emphasis on social reformism and obvious ties to egalitarianism, social justice has been linked most prominently to groups who occupy the political space often and reductively referred to as 'the left'. This leftist hue that has very much coloured more conventional discourses and definitions of social justice. When we interrogate it further, it reveals itself to be influenced heavily, to differing degrees, by left libertarianism[1] and/or social democracy (which are related but distinct ideologies), and their shared ideals, such as individual freedom, opposition to unregulated capitalisms, social equality, anti-authoritarianism, the 'common good', and collective ownership of property and natural resources. Such approaches have influenced strongly much of the political ire in sport and leisure studies scholarship advocating for social justice – although this corpus rarely nor intentionally marks itself out as being of 'the left' nor necessarily as being influenced by political theory.

In more recent times though, social justice has become hard to caricature as a set of ideals held exclusively by social progressives who do their work in the third sector, at and for not-for-profit organisations. Indeed, Williams (2015) notes more and more groups on 'the right' of the political spectrum – a collective often imagined to be more pro-business and traditionalist than those of 'the left' – have embraced support for social causes such as gay marriage and non-racist action, which very much align with more 'conventional' interpretations of social justice. The Centre for Social Justice in the UK, for instance, was founded as a centre-right think tank, by, among others, Conservative MP Sir Iain Duncan Smith – who served as Secretary of State for Work and Pensions in the UK between 2010 and 2016. During this time, he is often regarded as a leading figure in welfare reform, including: the introduction of the controversial Universal Credit system; reducing the maximum time claimants could receive Jobseeker's Allowance; the introduction of a benefits cap; and claiming individuals should take more responsibility for their personal circumstances. His approach to social justice then very much rejects structural notions of poverty and inequality, which is an explanation favoured by the left (Bramley, 2005). Understanding the particulars of this approach to social justice, and marking it out as distinct from other approaches, is important for social justice work in sport and leisure for reasons we will continue with below.

Les Back's (2022) notion of 'diversity conservatism' is especially useful to help capture the ways in which the term social justice and what is believed to be 'socially just' has manifested and evolved within the realms of the UK Conservative and Unionist Party. By using this term, Back is capturing a worldview that we suggest has come to dominate on the 'right' of politics, which supposes the recent successes and ascension of women, 2SLGBTQIA+ people and ethnic minorities in public life is validation of the emancipatory potential of free-market individualism and, what he calls, late Thatcherism. From this position, we are asked to understand the term 'socially just' to refer to the earned benefits accrued from exercising economic freedom within the capitalist order. Such a conception of social justice follows neatly in the tradition of the high priest of neoliberal economics (whose ideas we will explore further below), and macro-economic advisor to Margaret Thatcher and Ronald Reagan, Milton Friedman (1975) and his claim that "[a] society that puts equality before freedom will get neither. A society that puts freedom before equality will get a high degree of both". The Friedman doctrine differs from the leftist approaches commonly deployed in sport and leisure scholarship. The latter places a strong focus on social justice as a universal right, one unrelated to merit, and which favours a fair redistribution of resources, while the former views the most just and fair society as one that provides individuals access to the free market because it believes it to be a driver of (economic) freedom.

We also see a shift in the willingness of sport and leisure industries, too, which until relatively recently were reluctant to advocate for social justice agendas. This turn, has partly come in the form of brand advocacy delivered through public relations campaigns emanating at for-profit organisations, as well as in the form of a public and social policy environment that is awash with the phraseology of equality, diversity, and inclusion. Increasingly, forms of collective activism have become commandeered by sport and leisure-based agencies that have advanced a public–political campaign that becomes a part of the influencing discourse for the rest of the population that consume the "social justice" commercial, "social justice" branded product, or the "social justice" brand ambassador (Erickson, 2011). Nike, Patagonia, Ben & Jerry's, and Smart Water are just some of the companies that have galvanised public desire for progressive stances on social, cultural, and environmental matters. The aligning of brand identity through digital media content with 'socially just' values means what social justice is and how it is being used and by whom is increasingly multifaceted.

The Qatar FIFA World Cup 2022 was a particularly pertinent example of the competing definitions, applications, and the role of social justice within sport and leisure, in an ever more globalised, culturally diverse sporting and leisure ecosystem. A unique set of challenges were presented to those engaged in social justice work by events at the 2022 FIFA World Cup in Qatar, not least because it was a global media spectacle at which several colliding rights issues surfaced. On the one hand, criticisms emanating from liberal democracies challenged the sovereignty of the Qatari state and its human rights record, especially accusations of modern slavery, restrictions on free speech, and its exercising of soft power through football. On the other hand, during the tournament, Qatari officials complained of an underlying Islamophobia and mobilisations of racist tropes in liberal media coverage, most commonly in relation to the state's position on 2SLGBTQIA+ rights. The event sparked a polarising debate on the balance between cultural sensitivity, religious belief, and universal human rights, as well as the suitability of sports mega events in promoting a politics of inclusion.

The seemingly near universal acceptance of social justice as being an inherently 'good' and/or worthwhile aspiration, as we have begun to unfold, has not translated naturally into a working consensus vis-à-vis what social justice is, why or when it should be pursued nor does it offer any guidance to sport and leisure students, scholars, practitioners, and/or policy makers about how they might go about achieving it and to what degree. Simply put, 'social justice', its ideals, values, and goals, are becoming increasingly muddled by the moral relativism emerging at the nexus of geopolitical debate, globalised media discourse, and, most significantly, the enduring neoliberalisation of sport and leisure industries. We go on to pay specific attention to the latter given, for us, it is a key technology in shaping contemporary social justice discourse.

Social justice and the neoliberal moment

Neoliberalism, the dominant political and economic system operative across Western liberal democracies since the early-1980s, has very much shaped debates that surround the politics of social justice. Sport and leisure industries, too, have certainly not escaped its clutches (Andrews & Silk, 2012; Fletcher et al., 2016) and have been shifting operations to better align with those of the neoliberal model since the 1980s and early 1990s. The English Premier League (EPL), historically, is an example of the neoliberal model *par excellence* even more so than the National Football League (NFL), based in the canon of capitalism, the United States. Since its inception in 1992, very little external regulation of the EPL and its affairs from the UK government has occurred and its own governance processes have been extremely reluctant to self-impose regulatory oversight of the internal market, in terms of player transfers and salaries nor employment and recruitment practices relating to managers or executives (Morrow, 2023). This weddedness to neoliberal principles is confounded by the EPL's unease at the UK government's plan to introduce an independent regulator for professional clubs in the English football pyramid, following recommendations from the Fan-Led Review of Football Governance, which was driven by Conservative MP, Tracey Crouch.

But what is neoliberalism? How does it function? And why is it relevant to a handbook on sport, leisure, and social justice? As Rose (2022) notes, "neoliberalism refers to political economic policies ... where the dominant logic of free markets has become a guide for all human decisions" (p. 1). At its core, therefore, according to most basic definitions, it is an approach that prefers free-market capitalism, systematic deregulation, and an overall reduction in government spending. But most fundamentally, this approach is firmly political – not economic – despite its work in all fiscal and fiduciary matters. Neoliberalism's major tenets advocate for low/no taxation, laissez-faire free-market economics, individual liberty, privatisation of public assets, a reduction in the size of the state and how much it borrows/spends (Heywood, 2021). As such, neoliberalism instigates a series of measures that call for austerity of public and social services to those most in need, a shifting of those resources to private entities, and the loosening up of regulation and taxation of those private entities. In the US, for instance, public access to and financial support for youth recreational sports is defunded while privately operated competitive youth sports leagues have flourished.

For our purpose, specifically, it is important to remember that the drive for capital (the accumulation thereof) is guided by two operations: extraction and dispossession. And the hastening of this drive was given greater form and function under the regimes of Thatcher and Reagan during the 1980s. The suppression of mass strikes and the living wage, the termination of key social services and poverty-elimination initiatives, as well as the repression of social activism and organisation in response to such aggravations, have collectively led to a maximisation of extraction and dispossession. This new form of global capitalism required an anti-democratisation of society because domination is the mode of governance.

The neoliberal approach as a political technology then is one of governance, specifically, a way to govern. There is a market-orientation to the policies that come forth from such a political approach, but it is important for this to be seen and understood as an outcome rather than its intent. While the three preferences listed above are the typical aspects of what comprises neoliberalism, we argue that it is reduction in government spending that is the true intent of neoliberalism. Oncescu and Fortune (2023) highlighted the ways that neoliberalism influences and impacts municipal recreation practitioners' decision-making where low-income users are on the outside of the mission of programming (and finding ways to aid those populations through subsidies or fee assistance is either obstructed or difficult). Neoliberalism most assuredly produces austerity, and austerity ushers in mass poverty that in turn brings forth various forms of mass incarceration (e.g. death penalty, prison, detention, over-sentencing, widespread arrests, and mass surveillance). These connections are not leaps in logic. To advance the profiteering in the private sector, resources that are in or would ever be considered in the public sector must be reduced (austerity). To advance that reduction (for profiteering) in the public sector, those populations that are dependent on civil and social welfare will suffer while suffering further from lower wage work (poverty). To advance the removal of welfare, law enforcement is necessary for social control (mass incarceration).

Neoliberalism then is a carceral logic and situating it as such means that through its governance, we are continuously shaped by ideas and practices of imprisonment, containment, and restriction. So, in the realm of the concepts of sport, leisure, and social justice, which are philosophically grounded in perceived freedom and self-expression, the presence or influence of carceral logic is troubling. That is because, in tandem with the drive for the accumulation of capital that is guided by extraction and dispossession, neoliberalism produces surplus populations. Populations that are surplus because they have been forced to move from their lands and properties. Such a system cannot be considered socially just by any definition. That is because people are deemed of such little worth that they can be readily replaced and are thus placed in a holding pattern on the periphery of cities, neighbourhoods of significance, public parks (enforced like private parks), and sports and leisure programming as temporary staff but never as participants. In their state as surplus populations, these people have looked to activism but also to self-sufficiency for their basic and pro-social needs. No longer able to look to government, non-profits, or other concerned citizens, populations have created opportunities for sport and leisure for themselves (Golob & Giles, 2015). In favelas, shantytowns, rural towns, and public housing units, the freest expression of sport and leisure may actually reside albeit without the innovations of technology and equipment that come with more commodified forms of sport and leisure in wealthier settings. And even inside those wealthier settings, there are examples of push-back that disrupt the social acceptance and consent that society has given to the status-quo through forms of protest.

It is no surprise that in the 2010s and 2020s the UK and the US, just as they did in the 1970s and 1980s, have taken the lead on expanding the reach but also the body of thought on neoliberalism. Because leisure (and sport) serves economic interests and revenue generation, happiness and well-being measurements dominate research publications and funding. While there is money to be made in the professional settings of leisure, leisure has no market value as an area of study in the university (Fletcher et al., 2016; Rose & Dustin, 2009). With its history and philosophy grounded in the other matters that are beyond providing programming for a consumer base, leisure is far too problematic to remain as simply an area of study. Knowledge production is an important ground of contestation as it can lead to complacency through social control or protest through social enlightenment. Vocational learning appears to lean in favour of the former rather than the latter, making the production of learning materials like this handbook vital.

But this is not advocating for a need (of the history and philosophy) of sport and leisure but instead of the history and philosophy of leisure (and sport as a form thereof) that emphasises the social good, borne out of a response to poverty and social decay, the provisions for those most in need. What is needed is the learning of leisure that is attentive "to the pressing issues at any given time, and the potential role of leisure in" those pressing issues (Fletcher et al., 2016, p. 302). Thus, any handbook that professes to link sport, leisure, and social justice, and consider them as one, must also link to the process of knowledge production and the translation of such knowledge into meaningful action. The handbook's final section does this in more detail; however, it would be remiss of us not to begin this conversation here by engaging a key enabler of action research such as activist-scholarship.

Activist-scholarship and the public sociology of sport and leisure

Activist-scholarship, and by association social justice work, is in large part a practice of disruption and deconstruction. At its most fundamental level, Dillard (2008, p. 279) suggests that activist-scholarship is a political response to the notion of research for research's sake, "mandating research and educational practice that are concrete physical actions in service to community and beyond solely researcher theorizing". In other words, as Ladson-Billings and Donnor (2008, p. 74) note,

> scholars who take on the challenge of moral and ethical activist work cannot rely solely on others to make sense of their work and translate it into usable form ... scholars must also engage new forms of scholarship that make translations of their work more seamless.

Activist-scholarship is, then, not a mere standpoint of opposition to Western epistemologies, but is an ethical, pragmatic, and moral approach to research in and of itself. That is, in being committed to social justice, and in acknowledging "research is always already moral and political" (Denzin and Lincoln, 2008, p. ix), scholarship can develop as a means to achieve greater human liberation from oppressive systems, discourses and knowledges. Activist-scholarship (or scholar-activism) might also be named as "politically engaged scholarship" (Sudbury & Okazawa-Rey, 2015), "socially engaged research" (Tungohan et al., 2019), public sociology (Burawoy, 2005) or being a public intellectual (Said, 2012), and to be defined as the promotion of social or political change through shared goals with community partners. Sudbury and Okazawa-Rey (2015, p. 3) phrase it such: "The production of knowledge and pedagogical practices through active engagements with, and in the service of, social movements".

Activist-scholarship as a composite term means not separating out 'activism' and 'scholarship' from one another; that activism is not 'on the side' of the more important scholarship. Activist-scholars speak truth to power, maintaining distance from official or institutional bodies, taking sides, and do not aim for neutrality. Indeed, activist-scholarship has argued back against concerns that it is not objective, by pointing out that community activists would not accept research that is uncredible and/or illegitimate (Tungohan et al., 2019). Subjectivity might cause concerns regarding intellectual rigour amid social justice movements, politics, and elitist neoliberal universities. Sudbury and Okazawa-Rey (2015, p. 2) ask:

> Can good scholarship be politically engaged? ... What are the political imperatives to attempt this work, and how are these imperatives shaped by our relative power and privilege as academics? ... What are the costs of such politically engaged scholarship? What are the costs of not attempting it?

For some, sociology that claims objectivity and detachment stands on the backs of marginalised scholars who were more often the ones doing applied research (Romero, 2020). We focus now on activist-scholarship and public sociology in sport to pick up on some central issues. For consistency we refer to 'activist-scholarship'.

What does activist-scholarship look like in the neoliberal moment?

Knowledge and teaching

Speaking to university sport sociology lecturers and professors at North American Society for the Sociology of Sport (NASSS), Cooky (2017) said "we are all public sociologists" because of our teaching roles. Education has been a fruitful field for activist-scholarship and social justice methodologies in which the co-construction of meaning with practitioners can support educators' opening up of knowledge of White privilege, race hierarchy, and colour-blindness.

In Physical Education (PE) research and teacher education, activism is framed as having an impact on pre-service teachers and in-service teachers – due to the close connection between social justice and critical pedagogies – through enhancing their critical pedagogical knowledge and critical content knowledge to subsequently make a difference for their own students (Hill et al., 2022). In these fields, it is relatively easy to see the ongoing journey of impact on publics and participants, or the next generation of students and athletes. Some research on education policy acknowledges the need to make changes at regional or national levels (Landi et al., 2021), although specific impact may be difficult to measure.

It is not always straightforward to encourage students to believe in the need for change and to make change. The impact of social justice knowledge on undergraduate sport and leisure students is, according to Pringle and Falcous (2018), not always positive and attempts may backfire as found in the strong student push-back reported by Devís-Devís and Sparkes (2003) and Shelley and McCuaig (2018). Tinning's (2002) call for a modest pedagogy suggests small steps; a linear trajectory to success is not realistic (Pringle et al., 2018). Evidence that personal and professional experiences such as placements do have an impact on social justice knowledge and disposition (Hill et al., 2022) demonstrates ways in which 'show, don't tell' can support students' appreciating the imperative of social justice. Activism might not go beyond higher educational institutions but support justice for those within institutions, such as campaigns to change sexual abuse policy and procedure (Walton-Fisette, 2018). By disrupting processes of difference-making and discrimination in the classroom, "I can use my positionality [as a student, scholar, someone who benefits from discriminatory systems] for meaningful change [and translate complex theories] in ways that enable undergraduate students to relate, connect, and understand" (Calow, 2022, p. 6).

Methodologies

Methods for generating social justice knowledge are widespread: centring the voices of participants and communities as an ethical practice. An epistemology based on an ethics of care, of doing meaningful work, is a way to be "connected ... back to the set of historic, structural and economic relations in which they are situated" (Jackson et al., 2020, p. 438) and to avoid descriptive work. Activist-scholarship may align with disruption of standard methodologies and challenges to accepted ethical practice. Participatory action research, and more recently the concept of co-production, are go-to methodologies for centring community interests, involving participants in the design, conduct and outcomes of research. Auto-ethnography and story as methods have enabled researchers to become embedded in participants' lives. New materialist ways of knowing and producing knowledge have also, it is claimed, offered awareness of the entanglement of the body, the researcher's presence, the way a researcher selects and interacts with methods and theories, that should be considered when thinking of the purpose and impact of research (Thorpe et al., 2020). All these methods may challenge university and funder requirements to use established or legitimised methods (Pringle et al., 2018). Notwithstanding critiques of new materialism as colonialist (Pang, 2022), claims by new materialist scholars about different ways of looking at knowledge and experience afresh (Thorpe et al., 2020) echo CRT methodologies (Hylton, 2012). CRT supports epistemologies that do not centre White methods and voices, pushing back against the exclusion of race and gender in dominant "social and political developments and landmarks in knowledge and dominant paradigms" (Hylton, 2010, p. 342). Hylton (2012) makes an explicit call for activist-scholars to articulate the impact of their work on challenging negative racialised relations, which would also challenge the homogenisation of marginalised voices.

Qualitative methods are common in sport sociology and cultural studies, and this has been offered as a reason why those fields have had only a very humble impact in policy terms

(Pringle & Falcous, 2018). Social change might be more thoroughly realised with greater involvement of quantitative and mixed method research and ways of thinking differently. Pringle and Falcous (2018) give the example of medical knowledge on concussion leading to changes in game play, where quantitative evidence was given greater weight by policy makers (perhaps being more easily translated into policy briefs by researchers?). Quantitative and mixed method research might suggest more complex interdisciplinary teams:

> In the interests of pursuing social justice it may be of value within the sociology of sport to re-evaluate our epistemological and/or methodological hierarchies and be prepared and cross bridges between quantitative and qualitative research and the humanities and science.
>
> (Pringle & Falcous, 2018, p. 270)

Audience

Activist-scholarship means not relying on others to use scholars' ideas to take on the social justice agenda but scholars doing this work or being involved in the activism themselves. Social justice work necessarily engages with politicised topics, so public sociologists come under attack (as distanced ivory tower intellectuals). Where there is "ongoing distrust of sports people for intellectuals" who often debunk myths and accepted cultures in sport (Bairner, 2009, p. 127) then scholars need to think about how to translate work for a public – in the sense of the language required – or better to "co-construct knowledges and participate collaboratively in the processes of translation" (Cooky, 2017, p. 6). Cooky's point here further challenges a top-down approach that knowledge is something that scholars pass on to 'on the ground' activists. Of course, suggesting that activism has to be 'on the ground' might exclude research on national and international media, mega-events and so on. Donnelly (2015) picks out examples of distributive research on stacking, sport media representation, and ethnic underrepresentation that have slowly 'leaked' from the academy to the public, and notes that more timely communication might be a way to get to the public and those who can make a difference more quickly. Influencing public and policy at local or national levels, as Bairner (2009) recounts, requires close relations with individuals in the community or organisation; a 'publish and hope' approach to disseminating research does not work. Instead, being involved with publics and being active with them over time, as per Burawoy's (2005) organic public sociology, has greater visibility and impact. Examples of ongoing events or projects include Bournemouth University and the University of Brighton's Football 4 Peace versus Homophobia project (Caudwell & Spacey, 2018) that "achieved awareness raising of homophobia, biphobia and transphobia within student and local/national LGBT+ communities" (Caudwell, 2022, p. 342). This project also indicates the value of providing space (as a site for research, and for activism) for groups or individuals ostracised or outright banned from sport and leisure spaces.

The impact of scholars can also be affected by department and career stage that affect our ability to do the work, how the work is received and valued, and who our audiences are (Walton-Fisette, 2018). Barriers to activist-scholarship might include push-backs against a 'politically correct' intellectualism where, in the UK for one, free-speech rules for universities and the concept of 'cancel culture' have been used to critique, for instance, trans-supportive scholarship in sport and physical activity (see also dos Santos Freire et al. (2024) for discussion of Brazilian critical pedagogy under right-wing governments). Activist-scholarship may come up against national security-related concerns from right-wing governments (Sudbury & Okazawa-Rey, 2015), and sport activist-scholarship may be no different. In relation to the Qatar 2022 FIFA World Cup, Sochi Games 2014, and Beijing Games 2008 and 2022, intervention at these events to advance anti-homophobia activism and scholarship have been regarded with suspicion. Such initiatives were perceived to inject politics into sports and divert attention from the ostensible entertainment value and reputedly efficient management of these events.

Not all social justice scholarship is activism; the editorial for a recent special issue on social justice in sport communication research (Jackson et al., 2020) calls for research questions, lenses and foci on participants and organisations beyond the academy, indicating that it is not always the case that sport communication research, and relatedly sport and leisure research per se, has attempted to influence practice through activism. Simply researching and finding prevalence of injustice, abuses and representational disparities is not enough. Echoing Jackson et al. (2020) and their call for a disposition towards social justice, Pringle et al. (2018, p. 9) highlight arguments that social change takes time and occurs in relation to "dynamic and ubiquitous webs of knowledge/power/materials relationships; webs that remain outside of individual or researcher control". Identity transformation might occur over time as scholars shift through feelings of "that's not fair" (Hill et al., 2022, p. 6), emotional commitments, and a disposition towards activism. It is the audience, then, that is crucial in turning social justice scholarship into activist scholarship.

However, as Stephens and Bagelman (2023) have pointed out, the impact agenda within neoliberal universities can lead to distrust of the idea of activism among scholars. There are intense requirements to demonstrate influence on the public, policy makers and practitioners, to evidence impact beyond academic discourse to meet neoliberal performance metrics, funding requirements, and research 'excellence' exercises. While this could be a sign that activism is becoming more acceptable in scholarship, equally the fight for funding means that scholars' time may be taken up with 'easy win' publications where measurable impact, H-indexes, and citation counts are valued over slower, radical, critical, or community-aligned work that requires time and resources to build relationships (Sudbury & Okazawa-Rey, 2015). We know personally of colleagues who have received feedback on publications that social justice writing reads 'too much' like political activism (see also Tinning, 2013, on the reception of critical and sociocultural paradigms in health research). Somewhere between lofty aspirations and despair, between privilege and precarity, sport activist-scholars might be 'happy to be unspectacular': "it is in this embracing of modesty and contingency which promises neither emancipation nor succumbs to domination that we see the scholar activist as a figure of political possibility"(Stephens & Bagelman, 2023, p. 15).

A key feature of activist-scholarship as we see it then is that of research and researcher integrity – a concept that itself is deeply connected to the notions of rectitude, responsibility, transparency, and accountability. The question that this sets us up to consider is, how best to engage with the neoliberal order? Or is this a futile act if we want to maintain a sense of integrity in activistic-scholarly work orientated towards social justice outcomes? In the following section we explore some of the tensions the neoliberal moment presents for social justice work and offer some potential political frameworks through which we might operate. We do this by broadening our focus from scholarship within the academy to the sport and leisure sector more broadly in the spirit of praxis.

Searching for integrity

One of the apparent triumphs of neoliberalism, particularly in its manifestation within the realms of sport and leisure, is the emergence of multinational sport and leisure conglomerates. These entities, with their reach and global influence, have acquired a potential to leverage social justice agendas and actors in ways that would have been unimaginable as recently as half a century ago. In turn and owing much to the economic expansion of sport and leisure industries more broadly, as well as consumer markets more expectant of justice, equity, diversity, and inclusion (JEDI), an entire sector has clearly emerged within sport and leisure industries. While this sector has begun to offer EDI (equity, diversity, and inclusion in the UK), and JEDI (justice, equity, diversity, and inclusion in the US), solutions in the form of audits, consultation services, conferences and events, and promotional/educational materials, some in this sector have also sought to capitalise on the notion that organisational diversity is associated with improved financial performance, good corporate governance, openness to change, and recruiting the best talent (Fletcher & Hylton, 2018). Given neoliberalism enhances the ways that individuals can commodify themselves, thereby allowing sport and leisure consumerism to run rampant outside of the neoliberal workplace (McDonald et al., 2008), myriad JEDI professionals can now be found selling their labour to fill vacancies at or provide services to professional sports clubs, leisure venues, local governments, and a host of private employers.

For some, this might indicate a glorious shift away from regressive thinking, a welcome reimagining of sport and leisure as more inclusive industries, ones which are embracing globalisation fully, if only to capture new and emerging markets. For proponents of neoliberalism, the system is doing what it is designed to do: the 'invisible hand of the market' is recognising gaps in provision and consumer demand, and, in turn, creating jobs to serve these new and more ethically attuned markets. For some socially enterprising organisations and individuals, few ethical questions need to be asked before selling JEDI solutions. Such a belief is rooted in the claim that "[o]ne of the great mistakes is to judge policies and programs by their intentions rather than their results" (Friedman, 1975). For neoliberal social justice work, the (profit) motive for doing social justice work is wholly negated if the outcome of such work is a social justice dividend.

We, however, advise adopting a more critical approach and suggest a more cautionary engagement is needed with the motives of what might be called the neoliberal social justice industries. That is because neoliberal social justice work at its core is guided (if not defined) by an ideological belief in elevating individual economic freedom – and capitalising on it – over all else. The issue of course is that any social justice dividend – such as the right to be treated fairly in the workplace, regardless of sex, 'race', disability status, sexuality, age, or any other characteristic (Long, Fletcher, & Watson, 2017) – derived from neoliberal approaches will always remain secondary to the realising of surplus value, which produces surplus populations. Relying overly on 'the business case' will do nothing to counter and challenge the reductivist neoliberal mantra that "human beings are ... accountable for their predicament or circumstances according to the workings of the market as opposed to finding faults in larger structural and institutional forces" (Wilson, 2007, p. 97). Whichever way it is sliced, prioritising profit over people subjugates the moral and humanist case for social justice against financial objectives.

We caution those who strive for social justice amidst the neoliberal moment and present four specific concerns and recommended responses to maintain an integrity approach:

1. First, we must be mindful that the so-called (J)EDI sector lacks clear and agreed-upon goals and/or motives, relying instead on vague and amorphous slogans like 'promote diversity' or 'no to racism'. To preserve integrity, taglines and headlines must be accompanied by interventions and policies that have concrete outcomes for the populations they are intended to serve. They must not be reduced to mere marketing ploys designed to elicit superficial engagement.
2. Second, we must recognise that influential stakeholders often promote very specific discourses of social justice, utilising them for their own purposes, which may or may not align with the interests of historically marginalised groups and peoples, as well as to create new markets and industries. Social justice work is not concerned with prioritising one group's needs over another. It is, however, interested in acknowledging the severity and urgency of the needs of all disempowered groups in a manner that also recognises difference (see Fraser, 1999).
3. Third, we must acknowledge that the current (J)EDI sector is fragmented and disparate, owing largely to the professionalisation and proliferation of the sport and leisure industries. (J)EDI professionals are often scattered across private, public, and charitable organisations, all working to different and often conflicting agendas and targets, often for relatively low pay or in voluntary roles. Leaders in sport and leisure must embed the principles of social justice within an entire organisation, properly resource it, impose targets for accountability, and avoid creating (J)EDI silos that are separate from other areas of a group, organisation, or business.
4. Lastly, where corporate cultures and principles as well as the profit-motive have pervaded most deeply and bullishly, some sport and leisure organisations and (J)EDI workers have either wilfully or reluctantly displayed characteristics such as (humble)boastfulness, self-congratulation, and a lack of reflexivity. An integrity approach avoids such criticisms by doing social justice work not for personal or organisational gain but emphasising a moral and ethical dividend for others that is humble, reflective and understated. Social justice work is not a self-reflexive vanity project that is self-indulgent and superfluous: it strives for meaningful, material change and is done first and foremost to respond to the self-determined needs of historically marginalised groups and peoples.

It is of the utmost importance we acknowledge the problems, tensions, and contradictions presented by neoliberalism for social justice work, given we have argued that the former (despite what its advocates claim) does not foster the prosperity of markets to deliver social justice dividends, but rather to hasten an increase in returns by any means necessary – even if it requires the use of militaristic force and intellectual coercion. Considering the dwindling availability of resources amidst a testing post-global pandemic context in which many social justice scholars and practitioners find themselves, we present an integrity approach - as well as this introductory chapter and handbook in its entirety - as a resource to navigate contradictory economic and cultural conditions.

Conclusion

It is with great pleasure, and yet, also with a sense of trepidation, that we have traced the socio-historical context and discursive variations of social justice in this introductory chapter's call to critically revisit the assumptions, presuppositions, and Tacit politics of sport and leisure social justice research and practice. Pleasure, because there is a mass of people who are working to reduce inequalities; and, trepidation, because this work is hard and fraught with challenges. To attempt to navigate such tricky terrain then, we suggest, it is first and foremost necessary to return to asking fundamental questions about social justice research and practice that probe the philosophical and political tensions that are inevitably embedded in our work and the work of others. As we go about our work in social justice, we should be attuned to the ways in which certain words and concepts are deployed, to the assumptions that underlie them and be mindful of the ways in which these assumptions are instrumental in a larger system of power and privilege.

It is through this process of reflection and critical rereading that it is possible to reveal the hidden structures of power and privilege that shape our thinking and our understanding of the world. By making these structures visible, it becomes possible to challenge them, and to work towards a more just and equitable society. In this way, the introductory chapter serves not only as a precursor to the rest of the handbook, which positions this handbook within a particular time and space, but also as an invitation to engage in a process of critical reflection as well as transformative action. Through this process, we can begin to unravel the complex web of power and privilege that underlies the study of sport, leisure and social justice, and work towards a more just and equitable future for all.

Note

1 Left libertarianism must not be confused with right libertarianism, which diverges along mainly economic lines in terms of the consequences of capitalism, the free market, individual ownership of capital and resource, and private property.

References

Andrews, D. L., & Silk, M. L. (2012). *Sport and neoliberalism*. Philadelphia: Temple University Press.

Back, L., Keith, M., Shukra, K., & Solomos, J. (2022). *The unfinished politics of race*. Cambridge: Cambridge University Press.

Bairner, A. (2009). Sport, intellectuals and public sociology: Obstacles and opportunities. *International Review for the Sociology of Sport*, 44(2–3), 115–130. https://doi.org/10.1177/1012690209338439

Bramley, G. (2005). Structure rather than behaviour: On the causes of poverty. *British Politics and Policy at LSE*. Retrieved from https://blogs.lse.ac.uk/politicsandpolicy/what-causes-poverty/

Burawoy, M. (2005). For public sociology. *American Sociological Review*, 70(1), 4–28. https://doi.org/10.1177/000312240507000102

Calow, E. (2022). Activism for intersectional justice in sport sociology: Using intersectionality in research and in the classroom. *Frontiers in Sports and Active Living*, 4(2). https://doi.org/10.3389/fspor.2022.920806

Caudwell, J. (2022). Queering indoor swimming in the UK: Transgender and non-binary wellbeing. *Journal of Sport and Social Issues*, 46(4), 338–362. https://doi.org/10.1177/01937235211043648

Caudwell, J., & Spacey, G. (2018). Football 4 peace versus (v) homophobia: a critical exploration of the links between theory, practice and intervention. In H. Larsson, G. Gerdin, & R. Pringle (Eds), *Critical research in sport, health and physical education: How to make a difference* (pp. 39–51). London: Routledge. doi: 10.4324/9780203702598-3

Cooky, C. (2017). "We cannot stand idly by": A necessary call for a public sociology of sport. *Sociology of Sport Journal*, 34(1), 1–11. https://doi.org/10.1123/ssj.2016-0156

Denzin, N., & Lincoln, Y. (2008). Preface. In N. K. Denzin, Y. S. Lincoln, & L. T. Smith (Eds), *Handbook of critical and indigenous methodologies*. Thousand Oaks, CA: Sage.

Devís-Devís, J., & Sparkes, A. C. (2003). Burning the book: A biographical study of a pedagogically inspired identity crisis in physical education. *European Physical Education Review*, 5(2), 135–152. https://doi.org/10.1177/1356336x990052005

Dillard, C. B. (2008). When the ground is black, the ground is fertile: Exploring endarkened feminist epistemology and healing methodologies of the spirit. In N. K. Denzin, Y. S. Lincoln, & L. T. Smith (Eds), *Handbook of critical and indigenous methodologies* (pp. 277–292). Thousand Oaks, CA: Sage.

Donnelly, P. (2015). Assessing the sociology of sport: On public sociology of sport and research that makes a difference. *International Review for the Sociology of Sport*, 50(4–5), 419–423. https://doi.org/10.1177/1012690214550510

dos Santos Freire, A., et al. (2024). School physical education and social justice: What are we doing in Brazil? In S. Lawrence, J. Hill, & R. Mowatt (Eds), *Routledge handbook of sport, leisure, and social justice*. Routledge.

Erickson, B. (2011). Recreational activism: politics, nature, and the rise of neoliberalism. *Leisure Studies*, 30(4), 477–494. https://doi.org/10.1080/02614367.2011.594078

Fletcher, T., Carnicelli, S., Lawrence, S., & Snape, R. (2017). Reclaiming the 'L' word: Leisure studies and UK higher education in neoliberal times. *Leisure Studies*, 36(2), 293–304. https://doi.org/10.1080/02614367.2016.1261182

Fletcher, T., & Hylton, K. (2018). 'Race', ethnicity and whiteness in the governance of the events industry. *Journal of Policy Research in Tourism, Leisure and Events*, 10(2), 164–179. https://doi.org/10.1080/19407963.2017.1406676

Fraser, N. (1999). Social justice in the age of identity politics: Redistribution, recognition, and participation. *Culture and Economy after the Cultural Turn*, 1, 25–52.

Friedman, M. (1975). Living within our means: Milton Friedman interview. [television broadcast] 7 December. Hoover Institution Digital Collections. Available at: https://calisphere.org/item/04b4cbdace7d3f6278e60489c0060d96/ [Accessed 12 January 2024].

Golob, M. I., & Giles, A. R. (2015). Multiculturalism, neoliberalism and immigrant minorities' involvement in the formation and operation of leisure-oriented ventures. *Leisure Studies*, 34(1), 98–113. https://doi.org/10.1080/02614367.2014.962589

Heywood, A. (2021). *Political ideologies: An introduction*. New York: Bloomsbury Publishing.

Hill, J., Walton-Fisette, J. L., Flemons, M., Philpot, R., Sutherland, S., Phillips, S., Flory, S. B., & Ovens, A. (2022). Social justice knowledge construction among physical education teacher educators: The value of personal, professional, and educational experiences. *Physical Education and Sport Pedagogy*, 1–13. https://doi.org/10.1080/17408989.2022.2123463

Hylton, K. (2010). How a turn to critical race theory can contribute to our understanding of "race", racism and anti-racism in sport. *International Review for the Sociology of Sport*, 45(3), 335–354. https://doi.org/10.1177/1012690210371045

Hylton, K. (2012). Talk the talk, walk the walk: Defining critical race theory in research. *Race Ethnicity and Education*, 15(1), 23–41. https://doi.org/10.1080/13613324.2012.638862

Jackson, D., Trevisan, F., Pullen, E., & Silk, M. (2020). Towards a social justice disposition in communication and sport scholarship. *Communication and Sport*, 8(4–5), 435–451. https://doi.org/10.1177/2167479520932929

Ladson-Billings, G., & Donnor, J. K. (2008). Waiting for the call: The moral activist role of critical race theory scholarship. In N. K. Denzin, Y. S. Lincoln, & L. Tuhiwai Smith (Eds), *Handbook of critical and indigenous methodologies* (pp. 61–83). Thousand Oaks, CA: Sage.

Landi, D., Walton-Fisette, J. L., & Sutherland, S. (2021). Physical education policy research in the United States: Setting a new orientation. *Quest*, 73(1), 45–62. https://doi.org/10.1080/00336297.2020.1866042

Lawrence, S., & Hylton, K. (2022). Critical race theory, methodology, and semiotics: The analytical utility of a "race" conscious approach for visual qualitative research. *Cultural Studies ↔ Critical Methodologies*, 22(3), 255–265. https://doi.org/10.1177/15327086221081829

Long, J., Fletcher, T., & Watson, B. (Eds). (2017). *Sport, leisure and social justice*. London: Routledge.

McDonald, M., Wearing, S. L., & Ponting, J. (2008) Narcissism and neo-liberalism: Work, leisure and alienation in an era of consumption. *Loisir et Société / Society and Leisure*, 30(2), 489–510.

Morrow, S. (2023). *Football clubs: Who are the people? The people's game? Football, finance and society*. Cham: Springer International Publishing.

Oncescu, J., & Fortune, M. (2023). Neoliberalism's influence on recreation access provisions: Municipal recreation practitioners' perspectives. *Journal of Leisure Research*, 54(1), 89–108. https://doi.org/10.1080/00222216.2022.2044942

Pang, B. (2022). The postmonolingual turn: Rethinking embodiment with New Confucianism in bodily education and research. *Sport, Education and Society*, 27(8), 893–905. https://doi.org/10.1080/13573322.2021.1953461

Pringle, R., & Falcous, M. (2018). Transformative research and epistemological hierarchies: Ruminating on how the sociology of the sport field could make more of a difference. *International Review for the Sociology of Sport*, 53(3), 261–277. https://doi.org/10.1177/1012690216654297

Pringle, R., Larsson, H., & Gerdin, G. (2018). Introduction: Are we making a difference?. In *Critical Research in Sport, Health and Physical Education* (pp. 1–24). New York: Routledge.

Romero, M. (2020). Sociology engaged in social justice. *American Sociological Review*, 85(1), 1–30. https://doi.org/10.1177/0003122419893677

Rose, J. (2022). Neoliberalism and its (leisure) discontents. *Leisure Sciences*, 1–7. https://doi.org/10.1080/01490400.2022.2098881

Rose, J., & Dustin, D. (2009). The neoliberal assault on the public university: The case of recreation, park, and leisure research. *Leisure Sciences*, 31(4), 397–402. https://doi.org/10.1080/01490400902988333

Said, E. W. (2012). *Representations of the Intellectual*. New York: Vintage.

Shelley, K., & McCuaig, L. (2018). Close encounters with critical pedagogy in socio-critically informed health education teacher education. *Physical Education and Sport Pedagogy*, 23(5), 510–523. https://doi.org/10.1080/17408989.2018.1470615

Stephens, A. C., & Bagelman, J. (2023). Towards scholar-activism: Transversal relations, dissent, and creative acts. *Citizenship Studies*, 1–18. https://doi.org/10.1080/13621025.2023.2171251

Sudbury, Julia, & Okazawa-Rey, Margo (2015). *Activist scholarship: Antiracism, feminism, and social change*. New York: Routledge.

Thorpe, H., Brice, J., & Clark, M. (2020). A lively introduction: New materialisms, feminisms, and moving bodies. In H. Thorpe, J. Brice, & M. Clark (Eds), *Feminist new materialisms, sport and fitness* (pp. 1–27). https://doi.org/10.1007/978-3-030-56581-7_1

Tinning, R. (2002). Toward a "modest pedagogy": Reflections on the problematics of critical pedagogy. *Quest*, 54, 224–240. https://doi.org/10.1080/00336297.2002.10491776

Tinning, R. (2013). 'I don't read fiction': Academic discourse and the relationship between health and physical education. *Sport, Education and Society*, January 2014, 1–12. https://doi.org/10.1080/13573322.2013.798638

Tungohan, E., Levac, L., & Price, K. (2019). Introduction to dialogues section on socially engaged research and teaching in political science. *Politics, Groups, and Identities*, 8(1), 160–163. https://doi.org/10.1080/21565503.2018.1564058

Walton-Fisette, T. (2018). Metaphorically 'Taking a Knee': Pausing, reflecting, acting. *Sociology of Sport Journal*, 35(4), 293–300. https://doi.org/10.1123/ssj.2018-0024

Williams, B. (2015). Conservatism and social justice in theory. In *The evolution of conservative party social policy* (pp. 54–77). London: Palgrave Macmillan. https://doi.org/10.1057/9781137445810_4

Wilson, B. M. (2007). Social justice and neoliberal discourse. *Southeastern Geographer*, 47(1), 97–100. https://doi.org/10.1353/sgo.2007.0016

2
CONTRASTING APPROACHES TO SOCIAL JUSTICE IN SPORT

Jim Lusted

Introduction

The high-profile coverage of campaigns in sport that align to the idea of social justice – like the recent 'taking a knee' protest by professional athletes against global racial inequalities – indicates that sport remains a key player in struggles against injustice. At the same time the mixed reception of social justice claims from sports fans, athletes, administrators, even key power holders, and the changes that are (or are not) prompted because of them, can offer insight on the debates (and disagreements) about social justice in contemporary societies. Closer scrutiny of the nature of these social justice claims both *in* and *through* sport can help begin to make sense of the various ways in which the term is understood – and, crucially, why such campaigns seem to generate increasing controversy and often fail to prompt significant changes.

We increasingly hear about social justice being a core principle among sport organisations and sport scholars. The term is frequently used as if there is some assumed consensus over what it means. For example, social justice is often found in strategic documents, policies, and action plans, but what does the term actually mean when it is being used? It is rarely defined or explicitly examined in sport policy discourse, leading to the term signalling quite different meanings within sport stakeholders – such as the aims of various schemes aligned to social justice, what their outcomes might be, and how best they might be achieved. For this reason, there is a need to consider the different perspectives that inform debates about what people consider a 'just' society to be like – and even whether justice can or should be a feature of a society at all.

This imprecise use of the term is similarly evident in much of the academic research in sport, which often calls upon 'social justice' without any real conceptual discussion . A small body of work – including a previous collection on sport and social justice (Long, Fletcher & Watson, 2017a) – has begun to critically interrogate notions of social justice in a sports context. Wetherly et al. (2017, p. 15) note that "leisure and sport scholars have sometimes played fast and loose with notions of social justice, using it, and similar terms, to justify positions without proper consideration of what is entailed". One consequence of this imprecise use of the term is that it can paint an overly simplistic account of social justice claims in and through sport, as if all that is needed is everyone to pull together and 'implement' some assumed set of principles. As has been suggested elsewhere, such a presumed consensus around the term implies that:

> the problem of social justice would be limited to one of social engineering—ways of organizing social institutions to ensure that the individuals, groups, and organizations that make up society act in "just" ways in accordance with the rules of "absolute, true, and universal" social justice.
>
> (Almgren, 2017, p. 1)

The aim of this chapter is therefore to extend some of these preliminary discussions about the concept of social justice in a sport setting to provide the reader with an introductory, critical interrogation of some of the contrasting ways in which the term has been theorised and understood. In doing this, this chapter will consider how such varied interpretations can help make some sense of the controversies and limitations of social justice claims made in and through sport. The 'schools of thought' that have been selected for review here are labelled as follows: social justice sceptics, libertarian social justice, Rawlsian social justice, justice through recognition, and then concluding with the 'integrated' theory of social justice proposed by Nancy Fraser (1995, 2000, 2007). I will argue that this integrated approach is a potentially fruitful avenue to pursue because it offers a resolution to some of the core limitations noted in other theoretical positions. Moreover, the use of Fraser's integrated theory has largely been ignored by sport scholars. This is notable given the potential it has to aid the critical interrogation of social justice claims in sport, given the limited change they appear to have prompted in recent years, and the ongoing experiences of exclusion and discrimination felt by minoritised populations in sport.

What is social justice?

As one of the central claims of this chapter is that the term social justice is generally used with imprecision and assumed understanding across both sport policy circles and sport scholarship, it is probably wise to immediately try to address some grounding principles of the term. Even this is not a straightforward task. In the preface to his seminal text on social justice, philosopher David Miller notes the widespread tensions around the use and meaning of the term. It is worth reproducing here in full as it encapsulates the position taken in this chapter:

> Social justice is an idea that is central to the politics of contemporary democracies. Not everybody is for it. Some believe that the pursuit of social justice is a snare and a delusion and that we should be guided by other ideals – personal freedom for instance. Among those who support it, it is not at all clear what the idea means. Often it seems little more than a rhetorical phrase used to add luster [sic] to some policy or proposal that the speaker wants us to support. People may be committed to social justice in the abstract, and yet disagree bitterly about what should be done about some concrete social problem such as unemployment. This increases our suspicion that the term may have emotive force, but no real meaning beyond that. It looks as though we are giving an argument in favour of a political measure when we say that it will promote social justice, but perhaps we are doing no more than emphatically expressing our support.
>
> (Miller, 2001, p. ix)

With this in mind, attempting even a basic introduction to the term is fraught with difficulty, given the widely contested and ambiguous ways in which social justice is understood. Perhaps that is a reason why it is so rarely clearly discussed in policy and academia. Indeed, as Miller implies above, there are even some – like the economist and philosopher Friedrich von Hayek – who challenge the very premise of the term, referring to social justice as a 'mirage' that has little explanatory value (see Ikeda, 2013; Swift, 2019). I will discuss this and other 'sceptical' positions later in this chapter, but we should not underestimate their influence on contemporary politics and attitudes towards social justice campaigns, including those in sport.

When we talk of social justice, what are we broadly referring to? We might usefully begin by separating out the two words that make up the term, taking the second of the two words, 'justice' first and then making sense of what the specific type of justice is being described when the term 'social' is added. A normative picture of justice might conjure up an image of a court of law or a trial taking place, the outcome of which might be described as either 'justice being served' or a 'miscarriage of justice' depending on the interpretation of the verdict. A dictionary definition of justice follows this visualisation, as "[the] maintenance of what is just or right ... assignment of deserved reward or punishment; giving of due deserts" (Oxford English Dictionary, 2022). Here, the term justice seems to be about ensuring people 'get what they deserve', often in the context of law-breaking, with the victim receiving justice through the punishment or sanctions that are duly placed on the perpetrator.

The type of justice characterised above broadly falls into the category of what is termed 'retributive' or legal justice, which concerns itself with according 'blame and punishment' to people due to their actions within an agreed legal framework (Smilansky, 2006), hence its association with criminal justice and law. Notions of 'maintaining what is right' and ensuring that people get what they deserve extend well beyond this legal sphere. What about considerations of whether members of a society get what they deserve more broadly? What about people who, perhaps through no obvious fault of their own, end up on the receiving end of social burdens as associated with poverty, racism, sexism, ablism, homophobia, or other commonly recognised social inequalities? How are such benefits and burdens of a society distributed across individuals and social groups? Considerations of this kind tend to be termed 'distributive' justice as they refer to claims related to how such resources are allocated across a population or society. In addition, are social groups always viewed as equals, with the same status and worth as others? This idea is broadly conceptualised as 'representational' justice. In both cases, the term 'social' is added to the term 'justice' to indicate interest in the extent to which the historic, contemporary, and future distribution of privileges and disadvantages, and the varied recognition of people's differences that are obtained from access to resources like power, or inherited wealth might be considered 'just' or fair, based on what one might deserve over someone else.

Taking this idea of distribution further, we can return to Miller (2001) for a widely cited definition of social justice, who notes that the term broadly describes a situation where

> each person gets a fair share of the benefits, and carries a fair share of the responsibilities, of living together in a community. . . Social justice tells us how different types of goods and bads should be distributed across a society.
>
> (pp. 3–5)

How such things are *and should be* distributed – both in the past and present – are the subject of much debate and form the basis of many of the differences between key theoretical positions on social justice that are surveyed later in this chapter.

Social justice in and through sport

Is there a more high-profile site where social justice claims are so regularly 'played out' than the world of sport? Some of the most iconic and recognisable moments of protest and resistance against a variety of social injustices over the years have been set against the backdrop of sporting events such as the tragic suffragette protest by Emily Davison at the 1913 Epson Derby and the Black power salutes of US athletes John Carlos and Tommy Smith at the 1968 Munich Olympic Games. More recently sportspeople at events across the world have 'taken the knee' as a symbol of solidarity to racial justice claims, sparked by the murder of Black American George Floyd by a US police officer. The global popularity and media coverage enjoyed by professional sports and their celebrity-status athletes – with the capacity to cut through into mainstream popular culture and national politics – means that sport has become an important site *through* which social justice claims are made.

Such claims are by no means universally supported. Take, for example, the estimated 31 million people in the United Kingdom (UK) who tuned into watch the UEFA Euro 2021 men's football final match between England and Italy – nearly half the total population (Waterson, 2021). Most of these viewers would have observed all 22 players from both teams crouching down to 'take the knee' – a signal of their support for wider campaigning against racial injustice. While the England team collectively backed the movement, at a previous match in the tournament only five Italian players made the gesture, and it was reported that the squad members had different views about taking the knee (Giuffrida, 2021). Similar gestures have been made by players at the start of professional football matches in England since 2020, being met with a range of responses that included, at some grounds, a substantial group of fans 'booing' to show their disagreement (Sky Sports, 2021).

Increasingly, there are also claims made about the need for greater social justice *within* sport itself. These arguments foreground the notion that historic and contemporary structures, cultures, institutions, and practices of sport are themselves unjust and in need of reform (Long, Fletcher, & Watson, 2017b). Whether it be highlighting the barriers to opportunities to participate – on and off the field of play – or being locked out of decision-making at the highest levels of sport organisations. In recent years a whole raft of sport policies, strategic documents, action plans and campaigns that refer at least in some way to social justice claims have emerged across many national settings including the UK. Some of these have included standards or codes that sport organisations have expected to meet or work towards, such as The UK Equality Standard for Sport (Sports Council Equality Group, 2022) and the Code for Sports Governance (Sport England, 2021). These types of 'top-down' policies have been shown to be sometimes resisted by local sport organisations and, perhaps in part because of such resistance, have had limited impact (Lusted, 2009, 2014).

As the mixed reaction to social justice claims both in and through sport suggest, there is by no means any general consensus about the nature and legitimacy of them – nor indeed what the basis of these claims are and what might need to change for them to be met. Far too often, however, the term is used so loosely and rhetorically in sport discourse to imply the exact opposite. Elsewhere I have used the phrase the 'equality consensus' in sport to describe a similar kind of unquestioning, unspoken assumption that everyone knows or agrees what a term like social equality represents – with problematic consequences (Lusted, 2017). For example, there are multiple reasons why sport might engage with issues associated with equality and social justice; such engagement may be underpinned by a moral purpose, but it might also equally be driven by cruder business interests (such as brand/PR management) or compliance with legislation or political pressure (Lusted, 2012; see also Ahmed, 2012). We might argue that a similar problematic 'consensus' exists around the use of the term social justice within sport too.

This simplistic 'consensus' that exists in sport hides the more complex and often contradictory relationship between sport and social inequalities and the associated struggles for power and legitimacy between different groups. On the one hand, sport has been viewed as having a 'mythopoeic' capacity to be an inherent 'force for good' (Coalter, 2007). It is often seen as a progressive vehicle that can deliver a whole range of non-sporting, social objectives – like community cohesion and inclusion – that are much less likely to be achieved in other social settings. On the other hand, sport has been consistently shown to be socially exclusive, reproducing forms of discrimination and disadvantage. This can be evident throughout the history of sport – this seemingly contradictory role is summarised well by Darnell and Millington (2019) in their critical discussion of the ways that sport has contributed to wider social change and development. They note that sports like cricket and baseball have historically been cultural practices that have aided the colonial rule of Western nations while simultaneously offering site for the oppressed to resist imperial domination by "beating colonizers at their own sports" and helping to inspire anti-colonial movements (Darnell & Millington, 2019, p. 177). This highlights the overly simplistic ways in which sport is often associated with social justice.

Assessing the competing theories of social justice

Given the huge amount of writing on the concept of social justice – notably in the field of political philosophy but increasingly across the range of social sciences – it is a somewhat daunting task to seek to offer a succinct, authoritative summary of the main competing theories or 'schools of thought' related to social justice. Wetherly et al. (2017) have tried something similar in a sport context and noted the scale of such a task and the limitations in presenting an authoritative overview. They chose to follow the distinction proposed by Sandel (2007) who identifies two positions associated with laissez-faire neoliberalism and liberal/social democratic fairness. In their chapter, they focus attention only on social justice approaches associated with fairness. They argue that this is justified "because it is debateable whether [laissez-faire] neoliberalism should be considered as an approach to social justice" (Wetherly et al. 2017, p. 17).

I want to argue here against the position taken by Wetherly et al. (2017) – that understanding these alternative positions are, in fact, essential to be able to examine the nature of social justice claims in and through sport and, crucially, the varied reception to them. There is a need to widen the theoretical examination of social justice in sport to examine approaches that contrast with the distributive justice-as-fairness Rawlsian approach – including those that take a laissez-faire, neoliberal political position. Moreover, a broader consideration of the key approaches to social justice – and the differences between them – can help inform those researching issues related to social justice in sport.

In total, five different schools of thought are presented in this chapter. Getting the balance between being sufficiently introductory and accessible (for readers new to these approaches), while avoiding over-simplifying what are complex and deeply theorised positions (for readers already familiar with them) has been challenging. What follows is therefore not meant to represent an authoritative or even particularly representative survey of social justice theories (readers may find Campbell's (2010) extended discussion of social justice more up to this task). They are, however, discussed in a relatively logical sequence in that each subsequent theory can be seen to critique or develop in some way that of the previous approach/es. They are also selected because, taken together, they provide the theoretical terrain upon which Nancy Fraser's particular take on social justice has emerged. I will attempt to show that this approach warrants more detailed consideration because it offers a holistic, integrated framework that can resolve some of the limitations of these other conceptions of justice.

Social justice sceptics

Our journey starts with a focus on those who reject the very legitimacy of a concept of social justice. To repeat, such positions in relation to social justice may have not received much scrutiny in the field of sport studies, but they warrant inclusion not least because they may help make sense of some of the current criticisms of social justice campaigns, movements, and associated claims. The sceptics discussed below reflect radical positions on both ends of the traditional political spectrum of 'right' and 'left' – and while they agree on the invalidity of the concept of social justice, they do so for very different reasons.

The first position of scepticism can be traced to traditional Marxist thought, whereby social justice is viewed as an extension of capitalist and, more recently, neoliberal ideology and control. As Campbell (2010, pp. 163–164) suggests, "Marx's contention [is] that rights and justice are essentially bourgeois ideas which reinforce the ideology of capitalist economic organisation". This mirrors a classical Marxist interpretation of sport, which points to its inherent capacity to promote capitalist interests and class exploitation (Brohm, 1978). The argument here is that while the structural base of a society is fundamentally exploitative, any attempt to seek social justice *within* such conditions – and institutions such as sport – is necessarily restrictive. Thus, social justice movements and associated claims for progressive reform are viewed as mechanisms of false consciousness that serve to obscure the proletariat from their ongoing exploitation and genuine interests (Nguyen, 2021). This also informs the Marxist critique of social justice theories themselves – that are said to be informed by, and products of, capitalist systems of production and exploitation. It is well beyond the limits of this chapter to explore the complexities of Marxist interpretations of social justice (Cole, 2003 and Nguyen, 2021 offer useful starting points for further reading), but it should be noted that while Marxist ideas might provide a highly sceptical critique of social justice movements and theories, Marxist social theory more broadly has informed much of the writing on social justice, particularly those that emphasise the radical re-allocation of power and resources (Campbell, 2010). It is also important to note here the influence of neo-Marxist (particularly Gramscian) ideas in foregrounding a more interventionist approach to social justice, and a greater recognition of the potential for cultural practices such as sport to prompt wider social change (Carrington & McDonald, 2009).

The contrasting sceptical position can be well illustrated in the work of political philosopher Friedrich von Hayek (Hayek, 2012; Hayek & Caldwell, 2014). A radical libertarian and advocate of free-market economics, his ideas are said to have heavily influenced the emergence of 'new right' neoliberalist politics, led by Margaret Thatcher in the UK and Ronald Reagan in the USA (Swift, 2019). Hayek famously described social justice as a 'mirage', a term that is effectively meaningless in that, in his view, it was simply wrong to suggest that a society could either be viewed as 'just' or 'unjust'. In his view, justice could only be understood in relation to individual actions and decisions – and any attempts to extrapolate such actions into broader social processes or at a 'society' level rendered the concept 'fraudulent' (Hayek, 2012, p. xii). Hayek also took the view that attempts by a government or state to pursue policies aimed at promoting social justice fundamentally interfered with individual freedoms (which he saw as being the fundamental concern for any government). In any case, the challenge of agreeing how the benefits and burdens of a society should be 'justly' allocated could never be reasonably resolved.

So, whether it be simply another tool of capitalist exploitation, or a concept that is fundamentally flawed and akin to a 'mirage', I have introduced two different schools of thought that advocate for the ontological impossibility of a socially 'just' society. These sceptical positions require much greater consideration than we have so far seen in sport and leisure studies as they have the potential to more deeply examine the resistance to, rejection of, and even the limited impact of social justice claims in and through sport. For example, Hayek's simple rejection of the premise of social justice may offer a theoretical lens with which to make sense of those who 'boo' the taking of the knee, for example (see Serazio & Thorson, 2020) – while the Marxist position can help aid an understanding of why social inequalities remain so stubbornly stable across sport, informing a view of sport policy associated with social justice as a rhetorical, gestural 'window-dressing' exercise by sport organisations and power holders.

Libertarian social justice – the inevitability of inequalities

A libertarian approach to social justice can be identified in some of the writings of von Hayek – with the exception being that rather than dismiss out of hand the notion of social justice, other libertarian writers have taken on the challenge of trying to sketch out some basic principles of what a socially just society might look like – albeit with a very strong focus on individual actions. The writer most associated with this school of thought is Robert Nozick, in particular the thesis he laid out in *Anarchy, State and Utopia* (Nozick, 2013), first published in 1974. Nozick's work represents a modern libertarian political philosophy that has gained particular prominence in modern US politics and spread to shape many other national political contexts including the UK.

Nozick draws upon core libertarian principles and a laissez-faire approach that, like Hayek, prioritises the protection of individual rights and freedoms, above all other claims, albeit firmly situated within a capitalist economic system. There is also agreement with Hayek that the involvement of government and other social institutions in people's lives should be kept to a minimum because invariably such state intervention is said to constrain or interfere with an individual's rights and freedoms. Of particular concern is the state's potential capacity to shape the distribution of resource across a society. Nozick argues that any such attempt at redistribution (such as through progressive tax measures or means-tested benefits) is essentially unjust. He suggests this is the case because individuals should be free to pursue their own material interests within a broader capitalist system of production. Provided the accrual of goods, resources, wealth, and so on are gained legitimately, an individual should have the right to 'own' such advantages or benefits. This position effectively argues that social inequalities between people – at least in terms of ownership of property, wealth, etc. – while not perhaps an ideal situation is nonetheless 'just' or fair. For the state or other social institutions to take away such (fairly gained) advantages would simply be *unfair*. In sport, this can be seen perhaps in the organisational response to calls for reform of professional sports such as English football clubs, in the wake of ever widening financial gaps between clubs and leagues. A recent fan-led review into football governance proposing independent regulation and greater re-distribution of wealth across the leagues has been opposed by the English Premier League (Conn, 2021). This school of thought is often termed justice as 'entitlement' as it proposes the view that we should be entitled to claim advantages over others – provided we have legitimately 'earned' them. In addition, there should be no limits or influence placed on how such advantages should manifest themselves, nor the consequences (such as social inequalities) that might come from them. It is for the capitalist free-market to decide. Swift summarises:

> as long as people's property rights are respected, which means no coercive stage action except that which is necessary for the protection of property rights, whatever distribution results, however unequal it may be, is just.
>
> (Swift, 2019, p. 34)

While such an approach may not chime with many of the normative assumptions people may have when they think about social justice, there is merit in exploring how this modern libertarian view might not only inform sport discourse but also help to explain the persistence – and acceptance – of social inequalities in sport and leisure settings. Here in particular, these libertarian perspectives seek to avoid at all costs any state or institutional intervention or 'manipulation' of historic patterns of resource distribution and benefits. For example, elsewhere I have shown how this commitment to sheltering sport from overt political interference or policy intervention has been called on by power holders in sport to resist policy changes associated with social equality (Lusted, 2009, 2018). Another example might be the additional funding of women's sports that remains highly contested and resisted, with huge inequalities in financial support between many male and female sports often justified in a range of different ways (Wicker, 2019).

Rawlsian social justice – justice as fairness

Earlier I suggested that there existed some kind of unwritten, assumed consensus in both sport and leisure policy and practice and sport and leisure scholarship as to what is meant when the term social justice is called upon. It is fair to say that the closest approach to this normative position can be found in the hugely influential work of John Rawls and his interpretation of justice as fairness. Rawls' core position is outlined in his book *A Theory of Justice* published originally in 1971 (Rawls, 1999), and his work (in)directly informs most sport scholarship in this area. Articles including Wetherly et al. (2017), Meir and Fletcher (2020) and Schweiger (2014) draw directly upon a Rawlsian approach in their various discussions of social justice and sport.

Several elements of Rawls' conception separate it from libertarian approaches. The first is that, politically, they take different views on the role of the state and social institutions, and on people's obligations to others. Whereas the libertarian view prioritises individual freedoms and agency, meaning society ought to be an aggregate of autonomous individuals, Rawls advocates a position akin to long standing conceptions of a social contract – that is, a society consists collectively of people who have both formal (i.e. legal) and informal (i.e. social norms) mutual obligations towards each other that require co-operation (Swift, 2019). In this respect, Rawls' approach has been associated with liberal and social democratic political positions (von Platz, 2016). He argues that a just society is one that works towards a fair allocation of benefits and burdens across a society. A hypothesis is used to inform what Rawls terms the 'original position' from which the structural basis of a society should be formed. This proposes that were people not to know what type of 'talents' they may be blessed with, nor the social position they would be born into (i.e. one of advantage or disadvantage), people would logically choose to enter a society where such social 'goods' and 'bads' are distributed as fairly and equally as possible. Rawls terms this the 'veil of ignorance' which forms the structural basis of procedural fairness (Rawls, 1999).

One of the more important claims drawn from a Rawlsian approach is that social justice is located in the basic structure of a society and its major institutions – above and beyond individual actions (Rawls, 1999). This leads to the view that there is a central role for the state and other social institutions to play in 'managing' the distribution of resources to ensure such allocation is fair and equitable (Miller, 2001). This includes ensuring there are equal opportunities for everyone to seek to achieve the types of skills, knowledge and experience through education, occupation and other avenues required to lead a fulfilling life. To ensure such opportunities are not skewed to those with greater access to wealth, power, prestige, and so on, Rawls advocates for the 'difference principle' – that unequal treatment of people and the re-allocation of resources is acceptable and may be necessary, but only on the basis that it 'maximises' opportunities for the worst off in a society (Wetherly et al., 2017). For example, progressive taxation policy enables the re-distribution of wealth across a society, with high earners paying more of their income in tax than others.

There are significant parallels with this approach and the historical development of sporting structures and governance insofar as sport's codification is an acknowledgement that certain rules and regulations enforced by a governing body is mutually beneficial for all participants. One might only look to the sense of moral outrage caused by footballers diving, an athlete's use of illicit drugs or referees as a legal requirement in Mixed Marital Arts to understand the extent to which sport acknowledges a duty to the collective. The extension and deeper implementation of these principles might then be seen as the natural conclusion to processes of codification. From this, we can also identify several connections between some of these core principles of social justice as fairness to the rhetoric of sport policy discourse, particularly given the liberal idea of equality of access and opportunity underpins many of the approaches taken to tackling inequalities in sport and increasing diversity (Lusted & Fielding-Lloyd, 2017). There is certainly the potential for sport scholars to explore more deeply the underlying associations between a Rawlsian analysis of social justice and contemporary sport and leisure policy associated with equality, diversity, and inclusion given the extent to which sporting ideals are linked so irrevocably the idea of fairness and, more recently, connected to wider government agendas and intervention in sport.

Social justice through recognition

Although the Rawlsian approach to social justice is arguably the closest perspective to how the term is broadly used in sport policy and scholarship, in recent years there have been several attempts across social science disciplines to critique this thesis. One of the most influential of these has been led by feminists including the work of Iris Marion Young, notably *Justice and the Politics of Difference* (2011) (see also her early thoughts on the exclusion of women in sport, Young, 1979). This feminist critique of Rawls' approach is in part a disciplinary one, in that it adopts a more critical sociological lens on social justice as opposed to the political philosophy that has informed most writing on the concept, including Rawls' own approach (Campbell, 2010). The critique rests on two key areas. The first is that the hypothetical 'veil of ignorance' is considered too impartial because it implies a neutral 'starting point' within the structural basis of a society. Young argues that this type of assumed social position is unrealistic and fails to consider the long-standing power relationships between social groups in a society including those related to gender (Maboloc, 2015). She argues that the influence of cultural differences across a population in contributing to injustices are not properly recognised in a Rawlsian theory (Young, 2011). For example, returning to our earlier discussion of sport and codification, Young might point to the role played by male hegemony in the historical and ongoing shaping of such a process which has led to a historical prioritisation of male sport participation and the restriction and patriarchal control of female participation.

Relatedly, the second area of critique lies in the notion of distributive justice – that is debates that relate to the allocation and re-allocation of social resources. Debates around such (re)distribution are shown to be too narrowly focused on mainly economic-related resources at the neglect of other disparities between groups of people that can create unjust outcomes. Again, the argument here is that issues of power and cultural representation are insufficiently considered when discussing the distribution of benefits and burdens in a society. As Young notes:

> instead of focusing on distribution, a conception of justice should begin with the concepts of domination and oppression. Such a shift brings out issues of decision making, division of labor, and culture that bear on social justice but are often ignored in philosophical discussions.
>
> (Young, 2011, p. 3)

In short, Young argues that a fair distribution of resources *in itself* is not sufficient for a just society – particularly for social groups who have been historically disenfranchised, subjected to structural oppression, misrepresentation, and their differences to others de-valued and not legitimately recognised. This is also reflected in other critical social theories such as Critical Race Theory, which points to the limits of resource distribution, and instead argues for a deconstruction of the power-wealth couplet to expand our understanding of how power and privilege is often located in racialisation. Such a position is closely aligned to identity politics, that is, movements and social justice claims that centre around correcting the previous injustices felt by members of minoritised and oppressed social groups – including those defined by gender, race or ethnicity, sexual orientation, and disability.

Arguably, it is this focus on recognition, representation and empowerment that informs many of the contemporary social justice claims (but not always policy responses) in and through sport and leisure today. Certainly, the Black Lives Matter movement has highlighted the ongoing racial injustice in both sport and wider society is clearly derived from this focus on identity politics and away from a narrow Rawlsian emphasis on resource redistribution. Such claims made through an identity lens can also be shown to create controversy and be the subject of counter, false-equivalence identity claims (i.e. 'white lives matter') or even be co-opted by elites for their own hegemonic purposes (Táíwò, 2022). Eschmann et al. (2021), for example, highlight the contested nature of these claims in their analysis of the #BoycottNike movement that emerged following an advertisement by multi-national corporation Nike that sought to brand-identify with Kaepernick's 'taking the knee' gesture. Such co-option was seen on one hand to help re-frame and popularise Kaepernick's stance against racial injustice, while at the same time provoking more overt resistance to racial justice claims, as seen in the social media hashtag that emerged (Eschmann et al., 2021).

Towards an integrated theory of social justice for sport

The previous survey of some quite contrasting approaches to social justice leads us to consider an integrated approach to social justice, which I will argue has the potential to offer sport policy makers and social justice campaigners a useful blueprint from which to challenge injustice and pursue progressive change in and through sport. I draw on the work of Nancy Fraser, notably her 1997 thesis entitled *Justice Interruptus: Critical Reflections on the "Postsocialist" Condition* (1997), which questioned the change in emphasis from material re-distribution to cultural representation and recognition in social justice theorising.

Fraser directly critiques the work of Iris Marion Young and her attempt to prioritise recognition over redistribution in several articles (including Fraser 1995, 2000) which effectively argue that while such claims around cultural recognition are required elements towards a more just society – particularly for minoritised, disempowered groups, the shift towards identity politics had side-lined prior claims regarding the redistribution of resources. In simple terms, while Fraser's integrated approach appreciates the analytical separation of these contrasting claims, she views both as equally important to the overall goal of social justice claims, with neither taking priority (Lovell, 2007). Social justice cannot be achieved without due consideration of both, as Lovell articulates:

> Access to economic capital does not in and of itself command recognition. 'New money' may be discounted within traditional status orders; and on the other hand a lessening of inequality through measures of redistribution to individuals and communities may not on its own secure the ability among the dominated to command respect, but may provoke resentment and a deepening of misrecognition.
>
> (Lovell, 2007, p. 72)

It is difficult to convey Fraser's critique of previous social justice theorising within the space available in this chapter. A good starting point is her article 'Rethinking Recognition' that does this in a succinct and accessible way (Fraser, 2000). In it, Fraser argues that while the shift towards recognition of cultural difference is an important and legitimate area of social justice claims, its prioritisation has led to two key problems. First, it has caused the 'displacement' of discussions around re-distribution, with identity politics "largely silent on the subject of economic inequality" (Fraser, 2000, p. 109) and, in many cases, avoids or misunderstands the material basis (or influence) of such misrecognition. Second, Fraser notes that political movements that centre around identity claims have the potential to reify (make 'real' or generalise) the nature of social groups such as gender, ethnicity, and sexuality. As Fraser puts it herself, this reification can "impose a single, drastically simplified group-identity which denies the complexity of people's lives, the multiplicity of their identifications and the cross-pulls of their various affiliations" (2000, p. 112). One might see such tensions here in equality policies in sport, particularly those that are traditionally elitist such as cricket. For example, the content of 2021 Equality, Diversity and Inclusion Plan for the England and Wales Cricket Board (ECB, 2021) focuses largely on recognition of the importance of diversity and equitable representation – but is largely absent of any discussion around the re-distribution of financial resources across the game.

Fraser's proposed solution to these perceived inadequacies of the cultural recognition/identity politics, is found in her concept of 'participatory parity' (2007, see also Rozaitul et al. 2017 for a useful summary). Social justice can only be achieved if all people within a society can interact with each other as peers and equals and, importantly, "injustice claims of whatever kind are to be validated only if the practices they target can be shown to diminish or obstruct the possibilities for equal participation in social life" (Lovell, 2007, p. 69). For this parity to be possible, (at least) two core social conditions must exist – people must have sufficient access to material resources to enable their full participation *and* that all people (and their cultural differences) are held in equal status, esteem and worth. Without both of these conditions, Fraser argues there will never be participatory parity across a society, and thus injustices will remain unchallenged. Going back to the example of cricket, while the sport might value diversity and create a more inclusive, welcoming environment for all, if people do not have the spare time or income available to support their participation there is likely to be limited progress towards a more socially just sport.

Fraser's approach is starting to be considered in sport scholarship, particularly by feminist approaches to the examination of sport. The integrated approach to social justice is noted in Watson and Scraton's (2017) account of the material and cultural considerations in sport feminism. Jakubowska (2018) and Rozaitul et al. (2017) have both made useful attempts to apply Fraser's conceptual framework to examine the experiences of women accessing leadership roles in Polish sport and those of Muslim women in UK sport and physical activity respectively. But these are certainly isolated examples, and there is the potential for sport scholars to more deeply consider the value and application of Fraser's integrated thesis on justice for a whole range of research questions about sport and social justice claims – and not only on the study of gender.

A starting point here may be to follow the approach taken by the above studies by centralising the concept of participatory parity in attempting to evaluate claims related to social justice in sport. That is, to what extent do policy interventions, initiatives and wider rhetorical claims about achieving social justice in and through sport create the conditions for all people to simultaneously be held in equal status, esteem, and worth, while also having the material resources to enable their full participation on a par with others? Can the notion of participatory parity help to explain why such initiatives seem to have limited long-term impact and fail to disrupt existing social structures in sport? There is the need for sport policy makers to take more careful consideration of the ways in which they design such policy interventions and action plans, noting the pitfalls that can occur within social movements that fail to adopt a more integrated, holistic approach to promoting social justice. There is a fruitful line of analysis to explore as to whether Fraser's core requirements of participatory parity, that includes both material redistribution *and* cultural recognition are evident in contemporary sport policies and, if not, how such policies can be designed to meet these integrated requirements for social justice.

Conclusion

This whistle-stop tour of some key schools of thought related to social justice has aimed to introduce the reader to some of the key debates and disagreements within the theorising of social justice. In providing basic overviews of the approaches I have termed social justice sceptics, libertarian social justice, Rawlsian social justice, justice through recognition and, finally, an integrated approach to social justice, I have tried to illustrate how each might aid the critical investigation of social justice claims in sport. I have also indicated that Fraser's integrated approach to social justice has the potential to resolve some of the criticisms and limitations of previous conceptions – and offers a promising theoretical and conceptual framework for sport scholars to be guided by in their critical interrogation of social justice issues in sport. There is also the potential for the integrated approach to inform future policy and practice within sport organisations, as they seek to find better ways to tackle inequalities in sport settings. There is certainly an argument to be had that attempts so far to promote social justice in sport have largely failed to fully appreciate, or engage with, the core causes of injustice:

> If inequalities are to cease to be of significance, and if promises of social justice, such as 'sport for all' are to be realised, then the analysis of policy needs to be related to broader relations of power in the culture of both sport and society.
>
> (Meir & Fletcher 2020, p. 251)

It has been noted that the very nature of sporting structures and cultures – including the prioritisation of competition, winners and losers and the increasingly aggressive commodification of both elite sport and our own leisure lives might render sport as an unsuitable arena from which to promote social justice (Wetherly et al., 2017). There is room for optimism, however. The cultural significance of sport – with its capacity to cut through into mainstream political discourse and, more locally, the potential it has to shape community cohesion and development, means that the struggle for social justice is as merited in a sport context as any other social setting.

References

Ahmed, S. (2012). *On being included*. Durham, NC: Duke University Press.
Almgren, G. (2017). *Health care politics, policy, and services: A social justice analysis*. New York: Springer Publishing Company.
Brohm, J-M. (1978) *Sport: A prison of measured time*. London: Ink Links.
Campbell, T. (2010). *Justice*, 3rd ed. Basingstoke: Palgrave Macmillan.
Carrington, B., & McDonald, I. (eds) (2009). *Marxism, cultural studies and sport*. London: Routledge.
Coalter, F. (2007). *A wider social role for sport: Who's keeping the score?* London: Routledge.
Cole, M. (2003). Might it be in the practice that it fails to succeed? A Marxist critique of claims for postmodernism and poststructuralism as forces for social change and social justice. *British Journal of Sociology of Education*, 24(4), 487–500.
Conn, D. (2021). Crouch review a genuine landmark for football with possibility of real change. *The Guardian* [online]. Available at: www.theguardian.com/football/2021/nov/25/crouch-review-a-genuine-landmark-for-football-with-possibility-of-real-change. Accessed 12 May 2022.
Darnell, S., & Millington, R. (2019). Social justice, sport, and sociology: A position statement. *Quest*, 71(2), 175–187.
England and Wales Cricket Board. (2021). *Equity, Diversity and Inclusion Plan*. [online] Available at: https://resources.ecb.co.uk/ecb/document/2021/11/26/fcc98918-3246-4d5c-9d8c-ccee2dc193ba/ECB-EDI-Action-Plan-2021.pdf. Accessed 21 June 2022.
Eschmann, R., Groshek, J., Li, S., Toraif, N., & Thompson, J. G. (2021). Bigger than sports: Identity politics, Colin Kaepernick, and concession making in #BoycottNike. *Computers in Human Behavior*, 114, 106583, 1–11.
Fraser, N. (1995). Recognition or redistribution? A critical reading of Iris Young's justice and the politics of difference. *Journal of Political Philosophy*, 3(2), 166–180.
Fraser, N. (2000). Rethinking recognition. *New Left Review*, 3, 107–120.
Fraser, N. (2007). Feminist politics in the age of recognition: A two-dimensional approach to gender justice. *Studies in Social Justice*, 1(1), 23–35.
Giuffrida, A. (2021). Italy undecided over taking knee at Wembley, but Alaba says Austria will. *The Guardian* [online]. Available at: www.theguardian.com/football/2021/jun/25/italy-will-not-take-knee-at-wembley-after-criticism-over-rome-shambles-euro-2020. Accessed 11 February 2022.

Hayek, F. (2012). *Law, legislation and liberty, volume 2: The mirage of social justice* (Vol. 2). Chicago: University of Chicago Press.

Hayek, F., & Caldwell, B. (2014). *The road to serfdom: Text and documents: The definitive edition*. London: Routledge.

Ikeda, Y. (2013). Friedrich Hayek on social justice: Taking Hayek seriously. *History of Economics Review*, 57(1), 32–46.

Jakubowska, H. (2018). Poland: Underrepresentation and misrecognition of women in sport leadership. In A. Elling, J. Hovden, & A. Knoppers (eds) *Gender diversity in European sport governance*. London: Routledge. 59–69.

Long, J., Fletcher, T., & Watson, B. (2017a). *Sport, leisure and social justice*. London: Routledge.

Long, J., Fletcher, T., & Watson, B. (2017b). Introducing sport, leisure and social justice. In J. Long, T. Fletcher, & B. Watson (eds) *Sport, leisure and social justice*. London: Routledge. 1–14.

Lovell, T. (2007). Nancy Fraser's integrated theory of justice: A 'sociologically rich' model for a global capitalist era? In T. Lovell (ed.) *(Mis) recognition, social inequality and social justice*. London: Routledge. 78–99.

Lusted, J. (2009). Playing games with 'race': Understanding resistance to 'race' equality initiatives in English local football governance. *Soccer & Society*, 10(6), 722–739.

Lusted, J. (2012). Selling race equality to sport organisations: Challenges and limitations. In D. Hassan & J. Lusted (eds) *Managing sport: Social and cultural perspectives*. London: Routledge. 90–107.

Lusted, J. (2014). Equality policies in sport: Carrots, sticks and a retreat from the radical. *Journal of Policy Research in Tourism, Leisure and Events*, 6(1), 85–90.

Lusted, J. (2017). Understanding the varied responses to calls for a 'Rooney rule' in English football. In D. Kilvington & J. Price (eds) *Sport and discrimination*. London: Routledge. 56–70.

Lusted, J. (2018). A critical realist morphogenetic approach to researching sport policy: Reflections on a large-scale study of policy implementation in grassroots English football. *International Journal of Sport Policy and Politics*, 10(4), 705–719.

Lusted, J., & Fielding-Lloyd, B. (2017). The limited development of English women's recreational cricket: A critique of the liberal "absorption" approach to gender equality. *Managing Sport and Leisure*, 22(1), 54–69.

Maboloc, C. R. (2015). Difference and inclusive democracy: Iris Marion Young's critique of the Rawlsian theory of justice. *Social Ethics Society Journal of Applied Philosophy*, 1(1), 19–36.

Meir, D., & Fletcher, T. (2020). The physical education and sport premium: Social justice, autonomy and school sport policy in England. *International Journal of Sport Policy and Politics*, 12(2), 237–253.

Miller, D. (2001). *Principles of social justice*. Cambridge, MA: Harvard University Press.

Nguyen, M. H. (2021). Friedrich Engels's critique of the nature of social justice under capitalism. *International Critical Thought*, 11(1), 76–82.

Nozick, R. (2013). *State and utopia anarchy*. New York: Basic Books.

Oxford English Dictionary. (2022). *Justice* [online]. Available at: www.oed.com/view/Entry/102198. Accessed 10 February 2022.

von Platz, J. (2016). Social cooperation and basic economic rights: A Rawlsian route to social democracy. *Journal of Social Philosophy*, 47(3), 288–308.

Rawls, J. (1999). *A theory of justice: Revised edition*. Boston, MA: Harvard University Press.

Rozaitul, M., Dashper, K., & Fletcher, T. (2017). Gender justice? Muslim women's experiences of sport and physical activity in the UK. In J. Long, T. Fletcher, & B. Watson (eds) *Sport, leisure and social justice*. London: Routledge. 70–83.

Sandel, M. J. (ed.). (2007). *Justice: A reader*. Oxford: Oxford University Press.

Schweiger, G. (2014). Social justice and professional sports. *International Journal of Applied Philosophy*, 28(2), 373–389.

Serazio, M., & Thorson, E. (2020). Weaponized patriotism and racial subtext in Kaepernick's aftermath: The anti-politics of American sports fandom. *Television & New Media*, 21(2), 151–168.

Sky Sports. (2021). Burnley captain Ben Mee critical of fans who booed players taking a knee. *Sky Sports* [online]. Available at: www.skysports.com/football/news/11708/12385206/burnley-captain-ben-mee-critical-of-fans-who-booed-players-taking-a-knee. Accessed 11 February 2022.

Smilansky, S. (2006). Control, desert and the difference between distributive and retributive justice. *Philosophical Studies*, 131(3), 511–524.

Sport England. (2021). *A Code for Sports Governance* [online]. Available at: https://sportengland-production-files.s3.eu-west-2.amazonaws.com/s3fs-public/2021-12/A%20Code%20for%20Sports%20Governance.pdf?VersionId=Q0JD6BVXB.VgwbGEacG0zWsNPiWcGDHh. Accessed 11 May 2022.

Sports Council Equality Group. (2022). *Equality Standard for Sport* [online]. Available at: https://equalityinsport.org/equality-standard-for-sport/. Accessed 11 May 2022.

Swift, A. (2019). *Political philosophy: A beginners' guide for students and politicians*. London: Wiley.

Táíwò, O. (2022). *Elite capture: How the powerful took over identity politics (and everything else)*. Chicago, IL: Haymarket Books.

Waterson, J. (2021). Euro 2020 final attracts estimated 31 million TV audience in UK. *The Guardian* [online]. Available at: www.theguardian.com/media/2021/jul/12/euro-2020-final-attracts-estimated-31-million-tv-audience-in-uk-diana-funeral. Accessed 11 February 2022.

Watson, B., & Scraton, S. (2017). Gender justice and leisure and sport feminisms. In J. Long, T. Fletcher, & B. Watson (eds) *Sport, leisure and social justice*. London: Routledge. 43–57.

Wetherly, P., Watson, B., & Long, J. (2017). Principles of social justice for sport and leisure. In Long, J. Fletcher, T. & Watson, B. (eds) *Sport, leisure and social justice*. London: Routledge. 15–27.

Wicker, P. (2019). Public expenditure on women's sport and gender equality among recipients of public expenditure in European sport. In N. Lough & A. Geurin (eds) *Routledge handbook of the business of women's sport*. London: Routledge. 204–216.

Young, I. (1979). The exclusion of women from sport: Conceptual and existential dimensions. *Philosophy in Context*, 9, 44–53.

Young, I. M. (2011). *Justice and the politics of difference*. Princeton, NJ: Princeton University Press.

3
HERITAGE, PUBLIC HISTORY, AND SOCIAL JUSTICE IN SPORT AND LEISURE

Matthew L. McDowell

Introduction

In relation to this collection's theme of sport, leisure, and social justice, this chapter will examine issues regarding the heritage and public history of sport – specifically with regard to the United Kingdom, but also in relation to elsewhere, notably the United States. Heritage is a ubiquitous feature of the sport and leisure industries, and participants in sport and leisure both consciously and unconsciously interact with it. In society at large, heritage is continually contested and debated ground; and, whilst sport and leisure might at first appear to have avoided the controversies consuming heritage in other sectors, it is actually reflective of many of these tensions. No statues of controversial sporting heroes have yet been dragged into harbours, and discourses around items stolen from different parts of the British Empire have yet to seriously be discussed within the sport and leisure industry. However, the controversies which surround modern sport, and its existence as a leisure industry within capitalism, are never far from any conversation about sporting heritage, as are the discussions about which communities are represented (and which are excluded) within this heritage.

Heritage and public history have a complicated relationship with 'social justice'. In the academic sense, 'social justice' has not been used particularly much in 'heritage'. When it has, it has typically been the term as defined by Nancy Fraser (1999), who believed that recognition of large collective identities (for instance, 'working class') oversimplified a complex set of lives and identities, and thus served to further exacerbate differences, rather than act as something truly inclusive. Fraser's model has been used in a variety of academic applications: towards discussing the heritage of Australia's Aboriginal communities (Smith, 2010), to critique the distinction between social justice- and human rights-based mediations on heritage (Baird, 2014), and in 'action' heritage amongst schoolchildren, homeless residents, and other groups in Sheffield and Rotherham (Johnston & Marwood, 2017). Indeed, perhaps the main question with heritage is '*whose* history/heritage is being discussed?' This is as much about what is said as what is *not*: for instance, the 2007 bicentenary of the Abolition of the British Slave Trade Act in the UK largely became a celebration of white heroes such as William Wilberforce, and an exclusion of (usually minority) voices who were more critical about Britain's role in Empire (Moody, 2015). The lack of maturity of 'sport heritage' as an idea, and the increasing use of heritage as 'leisure' rather than 'education', mean that sport has only recently begun to grasp at these dilemmas.

Definitions of heritage and public history

Heritage is indelibly related to history. However, the bond between the two is a contentious one. At least some debates about 'heritage' begin with definitions of the term. In an academic sense, it is North American-based scholars (at least in sport) who dominate discussion on it. Indeed, in the context of sport, Gregory Ramshaw (2020) paraphrases a variety of definitions towards that end, including that of Emma Waterton and Steve Watson (2015), who describe heritage as 'a version of the past received through objects and display, representations and engagement, spectacular locations and events, memories and commemorations, and the preparations of places for cultural purposes and consumption'. Dallen Timothy (2008) argues that heritage is 'what we inherit from the past and use in the present day'. Ramshaw's (2020) own definition of sport heritage is 'the recognition and use of the sporting past as a means of addressing or illuminating a variety of contemporary social, cultural, and economic processes and practices'. It is this relationship with contemporary audiences where the problem often lies; heritage is meant to interpret the past in the context of the present – an opposite tendency from academic history, whereby historians are expected to examine the past on its own terms. Indeed, Ramshaw (2020, p. 2) believes that historians castigate heritage as 'bad history'. This author would argue that heritage must be understood not just as a collection of historical assets but as a *performance* by the individuals, groups, and organisations which stress it, and some understanding of how audiences are likely to interpret it.

Thus, the working definition for this chapter is that heritage is history interpreted for the public: it functions as a public record of the history of people, places, and organisations, and can be used towards a variety of ends, including education, community and public relations, and commerce.

The term 'public history' is also frequently used. In 1978, Robert Kelley defined public history as 'the employment of historians and the historical method outside of academia: in government, private corporations, the media, historical societies and museums, even in private practice' (p. 16). A more recent definition from Faye Sayer, in 2019, emphasised a more dynamic definition involving non-historians: she stated that public historians were 'individuals, usually trained historians, who work in either a professional or academic capacity and who engage in the practice of communicating the past to the public' (p. 2).

Ramshaw (2020) uses three typologies to describe different kinds of sporting heritage. The first is 'tangible immovable', and typically refers to structures such as stadia, parks, and sporting venues, but can include 'permanent' items of manmade landscape such as statues. The second category is 'tangible movable' heritage, which includes items in museums, archival material, and even the people within organisations who have knowledge of its history. The third is 'intangible sport heritage' – what one cannot physically take with them, and does not exist in any physical form – which might feature the continual transmission of knowledge, but might also have elements which hint at power within organisations and amongst individuals: the moral ownership of traditions, the presence of business and managerial cultures, the number of championships won, etc. When most people think of 'heritage', it is likely they are thinking of 'tangible immovable' and 'tangible movable' heritage: what can be seen, what can be touched, what can be experienced by the consumer of sport.

UK sport heritage and academic history

When participants in sport make a conscious decision to engage with heritage, it is likely they first head to the museum, perhaps the most acknowledged 'tangible movable' element of heritage. Much like attending sporting events, inclusive of travel to them, it can be said attending museums is a form of leisure. In 2000, Malcolm Foley and Gayle McPherson noted a shift in the broader UK museum sector: here, the *educational* functions of the museums were shifting towards more explicitly *leisure*-based ones, with attendees of museums increasingly treated, and acting, like tourists. The history of sport and leisure is often a part of local history displays, though not usually the primary one, with exhibits often tucked away in more distant corners of the building. The 'history of leisure', as such, is rarely catered for within its own institutions, though there are notable exceptions, such as Bradford's National Science and Media Museum, and the much smaller Museum of Childhood in Edinburgh, a museum dedicated to toys (Museums and Galleries Edinburgh, 2022; Science and Media Museum, n.d.-b).

At least superficially, sport is far more visible. The UK, in comparison to the US, has been slower to develop a clear sector for sport heritage. According to Justine Reilly (2015), the UK's first museum specifically created for sport's was the Marylebone Cricket Club's in 1953; in 1977 and 1983 respectively, the Wimbledon All England Tennis Club and the World Rugby Museum at Twickenham were created. By contrast, the most popular sport played by men in the UK, football, did not have its National Football Museum open until 2001 in Preston; the museum moved to Manchester in 2012 to increase its display space (Johnes & Mason, 2003; Moore, 2013, 2021). Beyond these major museums, as well as the National Horse Racing Museum at Newmarket, the UK's sporting heritage is a disparate archipelago of different organisations' collections, personal collections, and local museums, some of which advertise themselves as sporting collections, and some which do not. Reilly, in 2014, additionally highlighted a lack of quantifying what existed; hence, when she graduated, she created Sporting Heritage, a new community interest company, which has since attempted to act as an umbrella organisation for UK sport heritage and interested professionals (Reilly, 2014; Sporting Heritage, n.d.-c).

The coalescing of 'sport heritage' is, to some extent, made possible by the exact same process which currently funds sport: the National Lottery (Houlihan & Lindsey, 2013). Since its inception in the mid-1990s, the Heritage Lottery Fund has been a significant facilitator of heritage/public history projects on sport (Reilly, 2015). In addition to this, other funding has encouraged partnerships between heritage practitioners, sporting organisations, and academic historians, most notably collaborative doctoral partnerships initiated between Sporting Heritage and the Arts and Humanities Research Council (AHRC). 'Public' money being used for community history projects on sport has meant a shift towards different kinds of projects: one such project, leading up to the run-up to the 2014 Commonwealth Games in Glasgow, sought to explicitly engage schoolchildren in Glasgow's South Side with less celebrated and publicly discussed elements regarding the local history of sport, an attempt to create connections with local sporting organisations (Haynes, 2020). In a 2021 interview, Reilly discussed how, in the wake of threats against the England men's football team's Black players after EURO 2020, she believed that the heritage of UK sport had hitherto not acknowledged the presence of minority athletes, and that Sporting Heritage, with the help or an advisory committee, would seek to highlight appropriate stories and collections. She also discussed audiences regarding acknowledging neurodiversity when creating cultural spaces and heritage displays (Mulla, 2021). Ten years ago, disability, inclusive of Paralympics and parasport, was noted as poorly served by heritage (Brittain, Ramshaw, & Gammon, 2013).

These developments have been mirrored by the integration of sport heritage into the curricula of UK undergraduate and postgraduate sport/event management degrees (McDowell, 2023), a move long presaged by developments in the US (Kohe, 2018; Kohe, Smith, & Hughson, 2023; Pfleegor & Seifried, 2013). The relationship between sport heritage and academic history, however, has germinated slowly, and remains a tense one. Some of this has to do with time and money. The main scholarly body for academic historians of sport, the British Society of Sports History (BSSH), in the early to mid-2010s utilised a programme of regional networks to facilitate dialogue between academic historians, heritage practitioners, and members of the community. However, due the shifting commitments of the individuals involved, these networks have since been discontinued.[1] In the longer term, however, there is a concern amongst academic historians of sport that the aim of heritage is to *celebrate* sport without attempting to interrogate sport's existence as a social and political institution. At least part of the issue here is that most UK sport museums sit under the aegis of what Murray Phillips (2012), in his typology of sport museums describes as 'corporate museums': collections owned by, operated under and housed within sporting organisations. In many cases, the content in and messages broadcasted by these corporate museums can reflect organisational branding, marketing, and commodification (Appel, 2015; Ramshaw & Gammon, 2010). Heritage practitioners counter that their audiences are different to those of academic historians: that most practitioners agree with efforts to tell nuanced versions of the history of sport, but within a more dynamic athlete/supporter culture which prioritises lived experience, oral testimony, and material culture over the written word – the latter the basis of most academic historical research on sport (Moore, 2013; Vamplew, 1998, 2004). There has been debate on the nature of archives of sites which reinforce power within and outside organisations; to some extent, oral history techniques common in the field of heritage have been useful at liberating historical research on sport from archival documents which marginalise the contributions of women and minorities (Booth, 2006; Johnes, 2007; Skillen & Osborne, 2015). Lisa Taylor (2023) has noted how oral histories of women in British rowing have worked to undermine the narrative of a deeply gendered official archive which prioritises men's achievements in the Olympics and the annual Henley regatta. Paul Ian Campbell's 2016 monograph on the late twentieth-/early twenty-first century history of African-Caribbean football in the East Midlands foregrounded ethnographic research. In turn, academics have become reliant on heritage/public history publications for addressing gaps in their own research, most notably the Played in Britain series under editor Simon Inglis, a series of books on the history/heritage of the UK's sporting built environment (Played in Britain, n.d.-a). Two titles in the series, *The British Olympics* and *Played in Liverpool*, have been authored by academic historians: Martin Polley (2011) and Ray Physick (2007), respectively.

The performance of heritage

Performance is at the heart of heritage: from re-creations of archaeological sites to historical re-enactment by enthusiasts (as a form of education, a political statement, or leisure), and many other forms (Haldrup & Bærenholdt, 2015). This form of 'intangible heritage' is frequently performed in the context of sport: for example, at Olympic ceremonies and other sporting events. Catherine Baker (2015) believes that the opening of the 2012 (Summer) Olympics in London, a spectacle put together by British screen titans Danny Boyle and Frank

Cottrell Boyce, functioned as a giant performance of public history for a global television. Only this performance, too, had at its heart issues of power and decision-making about *what* and *whose* history gets discussed: the need to tell a story of a diverse, modern Britain that hinted at radical elements of history, whilst papering over details of the UK's historic involvement with Empire and the slave trade, and the contemporary reality of structural racism, bigotry, and (in the case of the Conservative-Liberal Democrat government of the period) brutal austerity. This event, then, a much-celebrated event amongst UK political and media commentators even a decade later, was remarkably un-prescient about the future direction of politics and culture in the UK (Evans, 2021; Heritage, 2019).

It was an event, after all, held under the auspices of the International Olympic Committee (IOC), an organisation which explicitly uses a mythical Greek past as a basis for its modern-day Olympics (Golden, 2012). This was a mythical past beloved by Britain's first attendees of the modern Olympics in 1896 in Athens, a past convincing to the elitist, Oxbridge-educated administrators of British sport who saw what they wanted to see in the ancient Greeks: gentleman amateurs who played for love of sport (Carter, 2021). The past has since been discredited; but, to the IOC, it remains an intangible heritage to build upon, and it sidesteps having to discuss the origins of more contemporary elements of the modern Olympics. This includes the 1908 creation of an Olympic marathon at White City, London, with the distance 26 miles 385 yards the first to be standardised for such a competition (it was certainly not a distance created on a battlefield in ancient Greece), and more unsettlingly the creation of the torch relay for the 1936 Olympics in Berlin, an opportunity for Nazi Germany to make a desired connection to ancient Greek culture explicit (Large, 2012; Polley, 2009). Particularly in the latter case, established Olympic heritage recycles dangerous myths: the IOC's website in December 2021 might have acknowledged that 1936 was the first use of 'modern torches' at the Olympics, but this is backgrounded against a phrase at the top of the page stating that the relay is 'a modern invention inspired by practices from ancient Greece' (IOC, 2021). Official heritage, here, can act as a steer against accountability, and can replicate regressive ideologies (Rider & Wamsley, 2012).

The IOC is not the only institution to mythologise history in service of political aims. One case of this is Ireland's Gaelic Athletic Association (GAA), the governing body of Irish football and hurling. Both sports were codified in the late nineteenth century, but hurling existed (in some form) for centuries; these 'traditions' were modernised to 'reclaim' Irish history, and to symbolically resist British colonisers and their sports – association football, rugby, and cricket (Rouse 2015). The GAA's sites themselves represent the heritage of modern Ireland; the GAA's national stadium, Croke Park in Dublin (also the site of the GAA's museum), was itself the location of killings by British forces on 21 November 1920 ('Bloody Sunday'); the GAA's grounds are named after figures from the Irish War of Independence and the Irish Civil War (Cronin, 1998, 2012). Here, heritage emphasises a radical tradition. The GAA's own heritage tells a different tale than England's Rugby Football Union (RFU), which has invested a great deal in the largely discredited historical myth of former pupil of Rugby School William Webb Ellis single-handedly creating the game: from statues, cups, and even to the opening ceremony of the 2015 men's Rugby World Cup in England, which featured a dramatisation of Webb Ellis's creation of the sport (World Rugby, 2015). It is a powerful story which markets rugby union as a game not played by working-class men from Huddersfield, or succeeded in by men (and women) from Pacific islands, but as the unique preserve of elite English men and boys (Smith, 2012). The World Rugby Museum has only recently begun to include more material on women's rugby in its collections and displays (Furse & Mason, 2023).

The 'past' in the present

Heritage is important for athletes, supporters, clubs, and organisations, *and critics* of sport. It serves as a reference point for shared experiences, identities, and values under a given banner, place, and time. It is something that participants (or, in the neoliberal sense, customers) interact with every day, and it tells a story about where participants came from, where they are at, and where they might be heading – and who *controls* and *monetises* these pasts, presents, and futures. When examining the role of heritage in sport, it is important to critically engage with issues such as representation, marginalisation, and power dynamics within and between communities. Therefore battles over heritage are often vicious: they typically reflect contemporary political realities and struggles.

At English football grounds, statues arguably represent figures of consensus rather than controversy; the subjects are often famous footballers and managers themselves. Why these statues have been erected, however, depends on who funds their construction. Owners, widely disliked figures, often help fund them as an olive branch to their supporters; but, in other instances (notably the construction of Thierry Henry's statue in front of Arsenal's Emirates Stadium), statues are designed explicitly with the global marketing appeal of a club in mind. At the same time, statues can also be used by supporters as a focal point towards voicing *dis*satisfaction about the direction of the club – and quite often, references are made to the club's *tradition*, and to present matters representing some kind of betrayal of the subject depicted in the statues (Stride, Wilson, & Thomas, 2013; Thomas & Stride, 2013). These are not just arguments over club policy; they represent public discussions about identities, class, capitalism, and many other causes associated with social justice.

Whilst heritage is obviously about more than built environment, it is likely that, for one to acknowledge that sporting 'heritage' exists within a place, and amongst certain people, some physical reminder is needed of *why a place*, or *why someone from that place*, is relevant. Famous athletes in England, for instance, much like other famous historical figures, often have their achievements denoted through official blue plaques assigned and designed by English Heritage. Dedications such as this, in terms of gender, race, class, and sexuality, are not evenly or proportionately distributed. Mercedes Gleitze may have, in 1927, become the first known woman to swim across the English Channel, but a blue plaque acknowledging this significant feat was not placed on her former home in Brighton until January 2022. Her family were unaware of her achievements until her death, 40 years previous to the unveiling of the blue plaque (Wilkins, 2022). In this vein, a campaign group called the Blue Plaque Rebellion was set up in 2017 by journalist Anna Kessel and the Women's Sport Trust to combat this imbalance; it worked with English Heritage, sport organisations, and local government to raise awareness of women's historical sporting contributions. Blue Plaque Rebellion also featured experts in academic sport history amongst its supporters, notably Professor Martin Polley, Professor Dave Day, and Dr Lisa Taylor (Blue Plaque Rebellion, 2017; Blue Plaque Rebellion, n.d.).

The continuous discussion of *who* gets represented, and *why*, indicates sport heritage is not isolated from the world around it, and needs to be seen in the context of contemporary (and historic) debates on history, representation, and power. After the killing of George Floyd by police in Minneapolis in May 2020, UK protestors, including those in the British iteration of the #blacklivesmatter movement, sought to redress historical wrongs by dragging a statue of Edward Colston into Bristol's harbour. Colston, celebrated in Bristol as a merchant philanthropist, made his money from direct involvement in the human slave trade in the late seventeenth and early eighteenth centuries, and his harbourside statue had long been a source of controversy. Public figures, notably broadcaster and historian David Olusoga (2020), believed that this was long overdue (in concert with the removal of Colston's ubiquitous name from Bristol locales), and was in fact not the *destruction* of history, but the *making* of it. The reaction was swift. In response to Colston's toppling from the plinth, a campaign group called Save Our Statues was initiated. Far-right figures such as Stephen Yaxley-Lennon (commonly referred to as 'Tommy Robinson') vowed to defend statues with street armies, particularly after the phrase 'Churchill is a Racist' was graffitied onto the Westminster statue of the late Prime Minister days after Colston was pulled down (Sabbagh, 2020). This conflict was not just fought in the UK's cities: in 2020, the National Trust (of England, Wales, and Northern Ireland) published a report into its properties' relationships with historic wealth from the trade. The uproar was enormous: the report's editors received death threats, the Trust was criticised by right-wing Conservative MPs for injecting 'politics' and a 'woke agenda' into its remit, and in October a well-funded reactionary protest group known as Restore Trust secured some seats on the National Trust's council (Hinsliff, 2021; Huxtable et al., 2020; ThirdSector, 2021).

The removal of statues of historical figures, like the erection of them, are reflective of the continual negotiation of a troubled past in the gaze of a changing present (von Tunzelmann, 2021). Here, it is worth discussing cases where statues of figures connected to sport have been either moved or destroyed when evidence has emerged of the cover-up of crimes. Joe Paterno was one of the most successful American football head coaches in US university history during his time at Pennsylvania State University (1966–2011); once evidence emerged about his protecting a coach accused of the sexual abuse of players, a sculpture of Paterno located in the centre of campus inscribed with the words 'Educator. Coach. Humanitarian' was removed in 2012, to tears from onlookers (Snyder, 2020). To this day, no one knows where the statue resides, or if it even still exists. In the UK, it was a patron and sponsor of sport and physical activity whose statues were quietly removed with little fanfare or tears. Sculptural representations of and plaques honouring the BBC television presenter Jimmy Savile – well-known for his philanthropy, charity-fundraising marathons, and encouragement of exercise and physical activity – were quietly moved from many local government leisure centres (most notably a wooden-carved sculpture in Glasgow's Scotstoun Leisure Centre) and were quickly destroyed after his 2012 death, when countless victims of child sexual abuse made claims against Savile (Rudd, 2012). Increasingly, actions such as this echo in the continuing investigations of historic sexual abuse at UK football clubs: for instance, in January 2022 Southampton Football Club stated that they were considering taking down the statue of former manager Ted Bates which stood in front of their ground at St Mary's Stadium. Bates was accused of ignoring complaints about former youth coach Bob Higgins, who was jailed in 2019 after being convicted of sexually abusing boys whilst employed at Southampton and Peterborough United (Sheldon & Taylor, 2022). By May 2022, however, the club ruled that they were not removing the statue; one survivor believed that the club feared a backlash from supporters (Fishwick, 2022).

The fate of statues of Paterno and Savile are reminders that, whilst heritage is ostensibly *about* the past, it continually reflects the power dynamics of the *present*: both the present at the time statues were created, and their continuing existence in the present. Edward Colston's statue was not built until 1895, almost two centuries after Colston lived, and about 60 years after the UK abolished slavery; it was constructed to reflect the politics of late nineteenth-century Bristol, a city still heavily dependent upon imperial trade (Morgan, 1998). Protestors in

Bristol almost certainly drew their inspiration both from protests in England and South Africa against the continued statuary presence of imperialist hero Cecil Rhodes on university campuses, and from the removal and/or destruction of statues honouring 'Confederate' (hereafter referred to as 'rebel') war heroes from the US Civil War (1861–1865) (Drayton, 2019). After a spike in the 1900s, many statues honouring rebel leaders continued to be built, including ones whose erections also spiked with the formal desegregation of institutions during the 1960s, and the 2008 election and inauguration of Barack Obama, the US's first Black president. In the former case, the 'honouring of heritage' even included, after the desegregation of schools, the naming of such schools after rebel leaders and heroes (Best, 2020). These statues and naming ceremonies, then, were almost certainly intended as a political statement about the present.

The redressing of history? Some examples from Glasgow

Relevant to this collection, how might we use heritage and public history in the context of social justice now, and as a means of redressing the past? It is beyond the remit (and beyond the expertise and practice of this author) to discuss how we might 'decolonise' UK sport museums and grounds. Colonial plunder has formed the backbone of many venerated collections in the UK museum sector, most notably the British Museum (Hicks, 2020). This phenomenon has yet to be quantified regarding sport. However, as David Kennedy (2023) has recently noted regarding Merseyside football, separating the heritage of Everton and Liverpool FCs from the global chattel slave trade is practically impossible – inclusive of the fortunes of their founders and early shareholders, and the industries that early footballers and supporters were employed in. How sporting institutions which date from the period tell this particular story of proximity to and benefit from Empire will be watched closely in the coming years.

For the foreseeable future, it is also likely that corporate museums will dominate sport heritage. In the past ten years, museums which sit in the public sector have held exhibits on sport: the Scottish National Portrait Gallery in Edinburgh, in the mid-2010s, housed the exhibit 'Playing for Scotland: The Making of Modern Sport', whilst in the early 2010s – in the run-up to the Commonwealth Games – the Kelvingrove Museum hosted 'More than a Game: How Scotland Shaped World Football', an exhibit which itself was on loan from the Scottish Football Museum (McBrearty, 2013). The latter example is likely the rule rather than the exception: sport is likely to be in charge of telling its own stories for a long time.

But even here, there are potential ways forward. Olivette Otele (2020) recently noted that 'African Europeans' are not a new presence in Europe, despite the emergence of a scientific racism (in conjunction with the rise of overseas empires) which denied their existence, and commented on their novelty and un-belonging into the present day. One person discussed at the 'More than a Game' exhibition was Andrew Watson, an early figure in Scottish football that was barely touched by academia, and has only subsequently (and briefly) been acknowledged by this author (2013) and Tony Talburt in a 2017 book on him. Andrew Watson is believed to have been the first Black men's football international in the United Kingdom; he captained Scotland to victory against England in 1881, and played for Glasgow's Queen's Park and London's Corinthians, clubs typically reserved for educated gentlemen. Watson was born in Guyana in 1856; his mother was Black, and his father was a Scottish sugar plantation owner who, until 1835, owned slaves. Andrew inherited his father's wealth, and attended private school in England, and later the University of Glasgow. Watson is better covered in public discourse than he is in academia; it was Ged O'Brien of the Scottish Football Museum who first discussed him in the public domain, and others took note, including Malik Al Nasir, a poet from Liverpool who used Watson (a distant cousin) as a means of exploring his own Guyanese roots. Commuters taking a train through Glasgow's South Side see Watson's likeness on a mural near Mount Florida train station, not far from Hampden Park (Al Nasir, 2020; Collins, 2020).

There is a danger in Watson being used like US baseball's Jackie Robinson: an exception to the rule, and a poor barometer on white Scots' progress towards an anti-racist future. And, given that this is Glasgow, the city's major football clubs, Celtic in particular, provide relevant examples of how migrants and their descendants use football to articulate their heritage (Kelly & Bradley, 2019). But, for Glasgow, is the acknowledgement of Watson part of a much larger reckoning? At the 2014 Commonwealth Games in the city (held in the year of Scotland's own independence referendum), one notable venue in the Merchant City (so named after businessmen who made their wealth from slave plantations in the Americas) formed part of the official cultural programme for the Games. This venue was the Empire Café, a hub created by architect Jude Barber and poet Louise Welsh to feature historians, poets, artists, and others with the expressed purpose of discussing Glasgow's relationship with slavery (Spooner, 2014; Welsh, 2014). As ever, 'outcomes' from such projects are far more relevant than discussion: in this case, how does being educated about Glasgow's relationship with slavery destroy racism in the present day? That remains to be seen. It does, however, allow for the opportunity of using sport – even sporting events with an explicitly imperialist past – as a means of being able to build frameworks and networks for future fights. It is an opportunity to use heritage critically, rather than in a celebratory fashion.

Conclusion

This chapter is far from a thorough examination of sport heritage and public history in the UK. It does, however, provide an overview of some of the issues involved in preserving and interpreting the sporting past in the UK. It also ties this preservation and interpretation to contemporary debates on British history, with the note that any attempt at interpreting the past at some level reflects 'politics' or 'identity politics': terms often used by right-wing critics of attempts to critique the past, despite their own attempts to muzzle dissent reflecting some kind of deeply politicised understanding of it. On both the academic and practitioner end, there is an increasing amount of interest in sport heritage as a form of leisure; and, whilst sport heritage at first appears to enjoy little of the controversies that have dominated UK press discourse, it too is reflective of these tensions. This author predicts that, in the coming years, these public debates over how we preserve the sporting past will increasingly end up spilling over into the public domain, and that both academics and practitioners will need to fully consider these issues when designing (and critiquing) heritage designed for diverse users. Accordingly, it is also hoped that this chapter has shown some examples of how heritage can possibly be used to begin to add nuance to and even subvert established narratives of history.

Note

1 The author was the organiser of the BSSH's Scottish network from 2013 through 2017, and the UK Chair of the BSSH from 2017 to 2019.

References

Al Nasir, M. (2020) Searching for my slave roots. *BBC*, July, www.bbc.co.uk/news/extra/3k9u8lh178/Searching_for_my_slave_roots, accessed 30 January 2022.

Anon. (2021) National Trust members narrowly reject motions from protest group at annual general meeting. *ThirdSector*, 1 November, www.thirdsector.co.uk/national-trust-members-narrowly-reject-motions-protest-group-annual-general-meeting/governance/article/1732010, accessed 28 January 2022.

Anon. (2022) Museum of Childhood. *Museums and Galleries Scotland*, www.edinburghmuseums.org.uk/venue/museum-childhood, accessed 31 August 2022.

Anon. (n.d.-a) About us. *Played in Britain*, www.playedinbritain.co.uk/about-us.php, accessed 30 January 2022.

Anon. (n.d.-b) Science and Media Museum. www.scienceandmediamuseum.org.uk/, accessed 31 August 2022.

Anon. (n.d.-c) Who we are. *Sporting Heritage*, www.sportingheritage.org.uk/content/what-we-do/about-us/who-we-are, accessed 30 January 2022.

Appel, H. H. (2015) 'Proper museum' or branding platform? Club museums in England? *Soccer & Society* 16(2–3): 294–306.

Baird, M. F. (2014) Heritage, human rights, and social justice. *Heritage & Society* 7(2): 139–55.

Baker, C. (2015) Beyond the island story? The opening ceremony of the London 2012 Olympic Games as public history. *Rethinking History* 19(3): 409–28.

Best, R. (2020) Confederate statues were never really about preserving history. *FiveThirtyEight*, 8 July, https://projects.fivethirtyeight.com/confederate-statues/, accessed 26 January 2022.

Blue Plaque Rebellion (2017) Introduction to the Blue Plaque Rebellion, 14 October, www.womenssporttrust.com/blue-plaque-rebellion/, accessed 26 January 2022.

Blue Plaque Rebellion (n.d.) Who is behind the Blue Plaque Rebellion, www.blueplaquerebellion.com/who-is-behind-the-blue-plaque-rebellion/, accessed 26 January 2022.

Booth, D. (2006) Sites of truth or metaphors of power? Refiguring the archive. *Sport in History* 26(1): 91–109.

Brittain, I., Ramshaw, G., & Gammon, S. (2013) The marginalisation of Paralympic heritage. *International Journal of Heritage Studies* 19(2): 171–85.

Campbell, P. I. (2016) *Football, ethnicity and community; the life of an African-Caribbean football club*. Oxford: Peter Lang.

Carter, A. (2021) 'At home at Oxbridge': British views of ancient Greek sport 1749–1974. *Sport in History* 41(2): 280–307.

Collins, M. (2020) The incredible story of Andrew Watson, the First Black International Footballer. *Vice*, 1 October, www.vice.com/en/article/akzbxz/andrew-watson-first-black-international-footballers, accessed 30 January 2022.

Cronin, M. (1998) Enshrined in blood: The naming of Gaelic Athletic Association grounds and clubs. *The Sports Historian* 17(2): 90–104.

Cronin, M. (2012) Croke Park: Museum, stadium and shrine for the nation. In M. G. Phillips (ed.) *Representing the sporting past in museums and halls of fame*. New York: Routledge, pp. 91–106.

Drayton, R. (2019) Rhodes must not fall? Statues, postcolonial 'heritage' and temporality. *Third Text* 33(4–5): 651–66.

Evans, T. (2021) How London 2012's Olympic opening ceremony found meaning in a divided nation. *The Independent*, 22 July.

Fishwick, B. (2022) Southampton FC rule Ted Bates statue will stay outside St Mary's Stadium. *Southern Daily Echo*, 28 May 2022.

Foley, M. & McPherson, G. (2000) Museums and leisure. *International Journal of Heritage Studies* 6(2): 161–74.

Fraser, N. (1999) Social justice in the age of identity politics. In L. Ray & A. Sayer (eds) *Culture and economy after the cultural turn*. Thousand Oaks CA: Sage, pp. 25–52.

Furse, L. & Mason, D. (2023) Women in the World Rugby Museum archive in three case studies. *Sport in History*. 43(3): 274–92.

Golden, M. (2012) The Ancient Olympics and the modern: Mirror and mirage. In H. J. Lenskyj and S. Wagg (eds) *The Palgrave handbook of Olympic studies*. London: Palgrave Macmillan, pp. 15–25.

Haldrup, M. & Bærenholdt, J. O. (2015) Heritage as performance. In E. Waterson & S. Watson (eds) *The Palgrave handbook of contemporary heritage research*. London: Palgrave Macmillan, pp. 52–67.

Haynes, R. (2020) From sporting past to future well-being: Sport heritage and intergenerational learning in Glasgow. *Sport in History* 40(2): 257–77.

Heritage, S. (2019) The London Olympics opening ceremony: A moment of optimism that destroyed the decade. *The Guardian*, 26 December.

Hicks, D. (2020) *The Brutish museums: The Benin bronzes, colonial violence and cultural restitution*. London: Pluto Press.

Hinsliff, G. (2021) Cream teas at dawn: Inside the war for the National Trust. *The Guardian*, 16 October.

Houlihan, B. & Lindsey, I. (2013) *Sport policy in Britain*. London: Routledge.

Huxtable, S.-A. et al. (2020) *Interim report on the connections between colonialism and properties now in the care of the National Trust, including links with historic slavery*. Swindon: National Trust.

IOC (2021) The Olympic torch relay. https://olympics.com/en/olympic-games/olympic-torch-relay, accessed 6 December 2021.

Johnes, M. (2007) Archives, truths, and the historian at work: A reply to Douglas Booths 'Refiguring the Archive'. *Sport in History* 27(1): 127–35.

Johnes, M. & Mason, R. (2003) Soccer, public history and the National Football Museum. *Sport in History* 23(1): 115–31.

Johnstone, R. & Marwood, K. (2017) Action heritage: Research, communities, social justice. *International Journal of Heritage Studies* 23(9): 816–31.

Kelley, R. (1978) Public history: Its origins, nature, and prospects. *The Public Historian* 1(1): 16–28.

Kelly, J. & Bradley, J. M. (2019) Celtic FC's 1967 Lisbon Lions: Why the European Cup victory of the first club from Britain was a defining moment for the Irish diaspora in Scotland. *Soccer & Society* 20(7–8): 1041–55.

Kennedy, D. (2023) Merseyside football and the slave trade. *Soccer and Society* 24(6): 883–95.

Kohe, G. Z. (2018) Running with the ball? Making a play for sport heritage archives in higher education contexts. *International Journal of Heritage Studies* 24(3): 256–69.

Kohe, G. Z., Smith, J., & Hughson, J. (2023) #hoops #basketballhistory @Hoops_Heritage: Examining possibilities for basketball heritage within the context of higher education, critical museology and digital redirections. *Sport in History* 43(3): 354–77.

Large, D. C. (2012) The Nazi Olympics: Berlin 1936. In H. J. Lenskyj & S. Wagg (eds) *The Palgrave handbook of Olympic studies*. London: Palgrave Macmillan, pp. 60–71.

McBrearty, R. (2013) *More than a Game: How Scotland shaped world football*. Glasgow: Glasgow Museums.

McDowell, M. L. (2023) Sport (tourism and) heritage, undergraduate sport management degrees, and remote teaching: A view From Scotland. *Sport Management Education Journal* 17(2): 158–63.

Moody, J. (2015) Heritage and history. In E. Waterson & S. Watson (eds) *The Palgrave handbook of contemporary heritage research*. London: Palgrave Macmillan, pp. 113–28.

Moore, K. (2013) Sport history, public history, and popular culture: A growing engagement. *Journal of Sport History* 40(1): 39–55.

Moore, K. (2021) Triumph in austerity? The National Football Museum for England, 2008 to 2017. *Soccer & Society* 22(6): 677–91.

Morgan, S. (1998) Memory and the merchants: Commemoration and civic identity. *International Journal of Heritage Studies* 4(2): 103–13.

Mulla, I. (2021) How sporting heritage can tell us so much about today and why it needs to be more diverse. *Yorkshire Post*, 12 August.

Olusoga, D. (2020) The toppling of the Edward Colston statue is not an attack on history. It is history. *The Guardian*, 8 June.

Otele, O. (2020) *African Europeans: An untold history*. London: Hurst & Company.

Pfleegor, A. G. & Seifried, C. S. (2013) Is building new the only option? A teaching approach to heritage management. *Sport Management Education Journal* 6(1): 32–42.

Phillips, M. G. (2012) Introduction: Historians in sport museums. In M. G. Phillips (ed.) *Representing the sporting past in museums and halls of fame*. New York: Routledge, pp. 1–26.

Physick, R. (2007) *Played in Liverpool: Charting the heritage of a city at play*. English Heritage.

Polley, M. (2009) From Windsor Castle to White City: The 1908 Olympic marathon route. *The London Journal* 34(2): 163–78.

Polley, M. (2011) *The British Olympics: Britain's Olympic heritage 1612–2012*. English Heritage.

Ramshaw, G. (2020) *Heritage and sport: An introduction*. Bristol: Channel View Publications.

Ramshaw, G. & Gammon, S. (2010) On home ground? Twickenham stadium tours and the construction of sport heritage. *Journal of Heritage Tourism* 5(2): 87–102.

Reilly, J. (2014) Sport, museums and cultural policy. Unpublished PhD thesis, University of Central Lancashire.

Reilly, J. (2015) The development of sport in museums. *International Journal of the History of Sport* 32(15): 1778–83.

Rider, T. C. & Wamsley, K. B. (2012) Myth, heritage and the Olympic enterprise. In H. J. Lenskyj & S. Wagg (eds) *The Palgrave handbook of Olympic studies*. London: Palgrave Macmillan, pp. 289–303.

Rouse, P. (2015) *Sport & Ireland: A history*. Oxford: Oxford University Press.

Rudd, A. (2012) Jimmy Savile: Memorials across the country taken down in wake of sex abuse claims. *Daily Mirror*, 10 October.

Sabbagh, D. (2020) Campaigners fear far-right 'defence' of statues such as Churchill's. *The Guardian*, 10 June 2020.

Sheldon, D. & Taylor, D. (2022) Southampton considering taking down Ted Bates' statue at St Mary's. *The Athletic*, 20 January, https://theathletic.com/3080123/2022/01/20/southampton-considering-taking-down-ted-bates-statue-st-marys/, accessed 27 January 2022.

Skillen, F., & Osborne, C. (2015) It's good to talk: Oral history, sports history and heritage. *International Journal of the History of Sport* 32(15): 1883–98.

Smith, L. (2010) Ethics or social justice? Heritage and the politics of recognition. *Australian Aboriginal Studies* 2: 60–68.

Smith, J. (2012) Discredited class-war fable or priceless promotional asset? The duality of Rugby Union's William Webb Ellis foundation myth. In J. Hill, K. Moore, J. Wood (eds) *Sport, history, and heritage: Studies in public representation*. Croydon: Bowdell and Brewer, pp. 19–32.

Snyder, A. (2020) 'Sue has it.' 'Check the meat lab.' Search for the Joe Paterno statue. *The Athletic*, 19 June, https://theathletic.co.uk/1878300/2020/06/19/where-is-the-joe-paterno-statue-penn-state-football-search/, accessed 17 August 2020.

Spooner, R. (2014) Sport, slavery, & sciences: The Commonwealth Games gets an Empire Café. *Bad History* 3(3): 8–13.

Stride, C., Wilson, J. P., & Thomas, F. (2013) Honouring heroes by branding in bronze: Theorizing the UK's football statuary. *Sport in Society* 16(6): 749–71.

Talburt, T. (2017) *Andrew Watson: The world's first Black superstar*. Hertford: Hansib Publications.

Taylor, L. (2023) Confronting silences in the archive: Developing sporting collections with oral histories. *Sport in History* 43(3): 293–306.

Thomas, F. & Stride, C. (2013) The Thierry Henry statue: A hollow icon? In D. Sandle et al. (eds) *Fields of vision: The arts in sport*. Brighton: Leisure Studies Association, pp. 33–52.

Timothy, D. J. (2008) *Cultural heritage and tourism: An introduction*. Bristol: Channel View Publications.

von Tunzelmann, A. (2021) *Fallen idols: Twelve statues that made history*. New York: Harper.

Vamplew, W. (1998) Facts and artefacts: Sports historians and sports museums. *Journal of Sports History* 25(2): 268–82.

Vamplew, W. (2004) Taking a gamble or a racing certainty: Sports museums and public sports history. *Journal of Sport History* 31(2): 177–91.

Waterton, E. & Watson, S. (2015) Heritage as a focus of research: Past, present and new direction. In E. Waterton & S. Watson (eds) *The Palgrave handbook of contemporary heritage research*. London: Palgrave Macmillan, pp. 1–17.

Welsh, L. (ed.) (2014) *Yonder Awa: Poetry from the Empire Café*. Glasgow: Collective Architecture.

Wilkins, C. (2022) Blue plaque unveiled to honour the first British woman to swim the Channel. *ITV News Meridien*, 24 January, www.itv.com/news/meridian/2022-01-24/blue-plaque-unveiled-to-honour-the-first-british-woman-to-swim-the-channel, accessed 26 January 2022.

World Rugby (2015) Rugby World Cup: Opening ceremony intro, 18 September, www.youtube.com/watch?v=Z3Mbd9W9u50, accessed 27 January 2022.

4
SPORT, LEISURE, AND SOCIAL JUSTICE IN THE AGE OF PRECARITY AND PROSUMPTION

Spencer Swain

Introduction

Power, a concept central to the notion of social justice, has been the subject of scholarly interest for many social and political thinkers since the Italian philosopher Niccolo Machiavelli (2003 [1513]) introduced the phrase into the cultural lexicon at the beginning of the sixteenth century. In the intervening years, definitions have sought to understand power as the capacity of an individual or institution to influence the actions, beliefs, or conduct of others. Consequently, such thinking has resulted in two distinct yet radically different understandings. The first focuses on power from a personal perspective, connecting with the idea of individual agency to narrate interpersonal conflict whereby people in authority control the opinions and behaviours of others (Lukes, 2005). This micro-sociological account exposes how power manifests through various forms of interpersonal interaction, whether in corporate environments or through the techniques used by sports managers and coaches to exert influence over their players through inspiring half-time team talks or fine systems (Law & Bloyce, 2019). The second understands power as a form of authority that aligns with social structures to help legitimise, normalise and control behaviour (Castells, 2016). This macro-sociological account explains how power instils a sense of discipline through regulating and normalising behaviour to comply with the wishes of elites. Such thinking, led by the French social theorist Michel Foucault (1970), has sought to expose the ubiquity of power as a productive force used to increase efficiency and organise the population around tasks such as work or reproduction.

However, social theorists, such as the British sociologist Anthony Giddens have questioned this dichotomy between structure and agency by blending the two. In his theoretical work on structuration, Giddens (1986) argues that just as social structures influence an individual's autonomy, these very same social structures are maintained and adapted through an individual's agency. Such thinking exposes how modalities of power are established, challenged, and reformed as they impact members of society who adapt and contest such structures. This rationale helps articulate how methods of exercising power are constantly in flux, being created and renewed to align with changes in political thinking that influence the structure of economic and social policies. The context behind this insight exposes how the implementation of power changes to adapt to service different societal systems. This point is documented by Zygmunt Bauman, who explains how the strategies involved in controlling populations have evolved from the production-based principles of industrial society to the post-industrial setting of a consumer society (Bauman & Haugaard, 2008). Through this lens, power is understood as an entity open to transformation. One that helps us better understand leisure's relationship with social justice, namely how oppressive power structures challenge the quest for equity, diversity, and inclusion. Here, past wrongs can be connected to ongoing conflicts within the present, showing how sport and leisure represent a site in social life where inequalities are exposed, challenged, and contested, repeating themselves cyclically (Riches, Rankin-Wright, Swain, & Kuppan, 2017). Through this lens, this chapter seeks to define social justice as a movement that is agile as opposed to static by exposing how structural inequalities manifest through power dynamics open to reformulation and the subsequent need for progressive movements to adapt to such changes.

A contemporary example is the Black Lives Matter movement and how it has used the media influence of sport and the celebrity of athletes like Lebron James and Colin Kaepernick to challenge racism and police brutality towards people of colour. Building upon the work of the Civil Rights movement in the 1960s and the Black Nationalist writings of thinkers like Marcus Garvey and the UNIA movement in the early 1900s (Christian, 2008), these player activists have sought to challenge racialised oppression by seeking equal opportunities and treatment within society. Nevertheless, there are distinct differences in how such movements have enacted this call for justice and the techniques used by ruling elites to subvert such challenges. This perspective can be seen in how both the Civil Rights Movement and the UNIA[1] focused their efforts on challenging social injustices enacted through scientific racism that plagued the legislative and administrative structures of the United States. Such structural racism and its cancerous growth within the United States legal system saw the propagation of racialised segregation through Jim Crow laws that separated sports arenas and leisure spaces such as swimming pools on the classification of 'race' (Carrington, 2010; Mowatt, 2017). This led Civil Rights leaders to call for social reforms, enacting legislative and administrative changes to the constitution that challenged the instrumentalised rationalities of white superiority. In short, this approach sought to change attitudes by changing the law, which, in turn, it was hoped would bring about equality.

In contrast, the Black Lives Matter movement has sought to expose the insidious workings of cultural racism that use the hyperbolic function of the media to portray people of colour as deviants and vagabonds. The context behind such thinking exposes how such communities continue to find themselves subjugated to racial oppression, a point seen in the brutal murders of George Floyd and Breonna Taylor. Moreover, the cruelty of such murders has sought to expose the legacy of scientific racism and its impact on the lives of people of colour, whereby despite being seen as equal within the doctrine of the law, such incidents serve to expose how this does not translate into cultural attitudes. Here, the cultural significance of sport has been mobilised to highlight the complexity of such racial discrimination, communicating the plight and lived experiences of people of colour to consumers worldwide who follow the athletes who protest such treatment. As a result, sport's position as a global commodity has helped to galvanise support by educating consumers about the lived experiences of people of colour and the injustices they face. However, at the same time, these same sports stars find themselves open to a new form of attack from the political right, portraying such protests as unpatriotic and ungrateful to the fans who pay to watch them (Edwards, 2017; Trimbur, 2019). This situation exposes the consumer dynamics associated with power in modern society, demonstrating how the fight for social justice has transitioned from changing the legislative dogma of social institutions to controlling the media optics put before the consumer and the message this portrays.

To this end, this chapter seeks to provide a detailed overview of existing theories on power, starting with the epoch of modernity and the systemic workings of power in industrial societies through Foucault's (1977, 1991) idea of panoptic surveillance. From here, the discussion introduces the work of the late social theorist Zygmunt Bauman and his reconceptualisation of power. This idea connects power to the idolatry of consumer-based economics and a shift towards excessive personal freedom that has seen the state retreat from people's daily lives (Bauman, 2006). Here, sport and leisure are no longer seen to solely represent a site in social life used to instil disciplinary control. But rather a cultural space used by citizens to look at the actions of significant others, that is, celebrities, style gurus, or elite athletes who saturate the public consciousness (Swain, 2019). This system, it is argued, highlights how post-industrial societies have moved away from disciplinary control to a subversive form of seduction driven by an economic model that exudes uncertainty and the need to follow the example of others. In short, power is no longer enacted solely from the top down but increasingly from the bottom up (Bauman, 2000).

Power as authority: The transition from feudalism to modernity

The epoch of modernity commonly associated in sociological discourse with industrialism emerged from an event known as the Enlightenment that occurred in Western Europe during the mid-eighteenth century.[2] At its core, the Enlightenment represented an intellectual and philosophical movement that brought about considerable change, most notably through its values of championing the sovereignty of reason and exploring the social world through the human senses instead of spirituality and divinity. Such thinking, in turn, led to the principles of science and reason supplanting religion as the dominant authority used to explain social phenomena and instigate a separation between the state and the church (Bauman, 1988). Importantly, for the upcoming discussion, this change saw the emergence of many social institutions that we take for granted today. These include parliamentary democracy and constitutional sovereignty, the judicial system, economic and financial structures such as banks, and the idea of territorial sovereignty that eventually gave birth to the nation-state (Giddens, 1991, 1998). In sports and leisure, these changes have been documented through concepts such as parliamentarisation and sportisation. These terms are taken from the figurational sociology of Norbert Elias (2000) to explain the emergence of governing organisations and the subsequent implementation of rules, leagues and codes of conduct designed to civilise previously disorganised games (Cock, 2018; Mierzwinski, Cock, & Velija, 2019).

The arrival of such bureaucracy constructed through the rationality of reason brought an end to the feudal order that had implemented traditional methods of imposing power based on the divine rights of the Monarchy and the implementation of physical acts of violence to justify divine opulence (Foucault, 1977). This traditional approach to maintaining order can be seen in the emblematic use of gladiatorial games within ancient Roman society and the role of sport in symbolically affirming the relationship between Emperors and their Gods. Here, deciding who should die or be spared in gladiatorial contests helped confirm the Emperor's position as a messenger to the Gods, as someone who could do their bidding and speak for them on Earth (Spracklen, 2011). Analysing such power relations through the prism of social justice exposes how leisure in traditional societies centred on implementing power by harnessing the mystique of the spiritual world. This perspective is communicated poignantly by Giulianotti (2015), who explains the role of mob football in the Middle Ages as a spiritual event constructed around the belief that the winning team would carry favour with God and bless their village with a good harvest. Interestingly, from the point of view of the relationship between power and social justice, such a system exposes how tradition, in the form of long-standing beliefs and practices, elevated specific individuals, such as the Monarch or tribal chief, above others in society, forging a theocracy whereby one's association with religious customs and traditions symbolised power.

However, the power structures associated with feudalism began to disintegrate around the middle of the eighteenth century. The first of these challenges came from the emergence of science as a disciplinary system that had started supplanting religion as the dominant authority to explain social phenomena. An example was the emergence of scientific disciplines like geology to rationalise environmental catastrophes, such as the 1755 Lisbon earthquake. Similarly, as science supplanted spirituality, calls grew louder for an equal distribution of power and wealth within society, culminating in the French revolution of 1793 that saw the theocratic link between Monarchy and God broken with the execution of King Louis XVI by the proletariat-led French National Convention. Subsequently, early modern societies found themselves in a state of transition due to the decline of religious authority (Bauman, 1991), creating a state of anomie (Durkheim, 1997 [1893]), whereby in the face of the declining role of religion in the public sphere, individuals lacked the ethical and emotional guidance needed to govern their lives. Furthermore, these populations also faced extreme uncertainty, characterised by the German philosopher Erich Fromm (2001) as a form of 'negative freedom' whereby men and women were stripped of their communal togetherness and forced to embrace a feeling of moral aloneness without the doctrine of religion to guide them. Subsequently, modern societies sought to construct structures to enforce order and implement power to counteract such insecurities (Swain, 2017b) through a method of public administration that neatly mirrored scientific methods of investigation used to document the natural world. In so doing, these rationalities sought to counteract ambivalence by suppressing:

> everything ambiguous, everything that sits astride the barricade and thus compromises the vital distinction between inside and outside. Building and keeping order means making friends and fighting enemies. First and foremost, it means purging ambivalence.
> (Bauman, 1991, p. 24)

Consequently, such logic sought to organise society around bureaucratic reason, a method of organisation that replaced the spiritual guidance of religion (Bauman, 1988).

This change has led many social theorists working within the theoretical tradition of the Frankfurt School of critical theory (see Adorno & Horkheimer, 1997; Spracklen, 2009) to position modernity as an ambivalent project. Here, such ambivalence stems from promoting the enlightened virtues of liberty and democracy that instigated a break from the serfdom of feudalism. While simultaneously invoking a totalitarian attitude that has sought to order the world around the ideological views of its architects (white, middle-class men) (Bottomore, 2002).

Modernity and the panopticon: Sport and leisure as a site of discipline

This purging of ambivalence connects with the ideas of the French philosopher Michel Foucault (1970), who wrote about how 'technologies of power' operate ubiquitously to control individuals from afar through a technique that he would later term governmentality (Foucault, 1991). Central to such thinking is a focus on how governments and other forms of the state apparatus, like prisons and schools, implement power psychologically by entwining citizens within a 'web of power' built around discourse patterns. Such communication and debate help to control, judge, and normalise the actions of citizens by allowing power to reach "into the very grain of individuals, touching their bodies and inserting itself into their actions and attitudes, their discourses, learning processes and everyday lives" (Foucault, 1977, p. 39). This idea exposes how state institutions normalise behaviours that conform to their ideologies, creating rationalities that guide and control the population's behaviour. At the centre of this method is an apparatus known as the panopticon, a term first brought into the academic idiolect by the British philosopher Jeremy Bentham (2009 [1791]) in his writings on penology and the criminal justice system. Bentham explained how the panopticon represented a circular prison controlled through a central guard tower, blinding lights, and observable detainment cells, allowing correctional officers to view prisoners without inmates knowing. Paramount to this method of control was the need to instil discipline through surveillance, ensuring institutionally verified behaviours were followed due to inmates being unaware if their actions were being observed. The effect of such a system served to structure inmates' behaviour into a pattern set by the rationalities of the prison authorities, creating a normalising gaze that socialised inmates into behaviours deemed appropriate by those in charge. This method of control interested Foucault (1977, p. 201), who applied this thinking to explain how state institutions disciplined their citizens through the constant spectre of surveillance, a method that he argued helped to induce "a state of conscious and permanent visibility that assures the automatic functioning of power". Thus, helping to normalise expectations and create a population of 'docile bodies' disciplined to act in a manner endorsed by the bureaucratic rationalities of state institutions.

Within leisure studies, panoptic power structures have been understood to represent a 'technology of dominance' used to exclude, classify, regulate and normalise behaviour (Lang, 2010). The work of Kirk (1998) and Hargreaves (1986), in particular, has been pivotal in taking Foucault's ideas and applying them to physical education settings, explaining how teachers use surveillance to control students through disciplinary tactics designed to instil institutionally appropriate behaviours. This approach focuses on the 'teacher's gaze' and its influence in getting students to behave appropriately for fear of being punished for not conforming to the type of behaviour legitimised in the cultural sphere of the gymnasium and the broader school. At the same time, it is also documented how such rationalities encourage behaviours centred around competitiveness and obedience, designed to discipline young people into the behaviours coveted by capitalist societies. Scholars writing in sports coaching have also used Foucault's ideas to explain coach-athlete relations (Lang, 2015). Here, the use of surveillance by coaches has been documented to enhance their athlete's performances, culminating in tactics designed to instil a feeling of constant surveillance within the psyche of their charges to improve performances (Markula & Pringle, 2006). Moreover, such insights document the ambivalence associated with modernity (Swain, 2019) in how such tactics have been shown to have had a tremendous impact on athlete performance by disciplining many to become world-class competitors. However, at the same time, it can be argued that such legislative systems have forged an environment whereby the authoritative power exercised by coaches, namely in the form of sexual abuse and issues regarding athlete well-being has gone unchecked, causing those experiencing such trauma to normalise such behaviour (Webb & Macdonald, 2007).

Such insights help us better understand the relationship between power and social justice within the epoch of modernity, exposing modernity's need to control nature, create hierarchical bureaucracies, implement rules and regulations, exercise control and remove personal insecurities, to make the chaotic aspects of human life that appeared in early modern societies seem both ordered and familiar. Yet, this same disciplinary gaze enacted by state institutions is also problematic, as the rationalities it sought to maintain promoted the interests of its architects – white, cis-gendered, middle-class men. An example of such thinking and its impact on social justice within the arena of sport can be seen in boxing, where a 'colour line' was erected in the early 1900s to divide fighters using the pseudo-science of 'race' to attribute genetic differences and behavioural characteristics to a person's skin colour. This approach documents how baseless claims built upon empirically impoverished science were rationalised by the institutions of modernity to divide professional sport on the categorisation of 'race' (Hylton, 2009; Ratna, 2015). Similarly, women's engagement in sports, physical activity, and male-dominated recreational activities have been policed by the same institutional bureaucracy, positioning such behaviours as an affront to social expectations of femininity. The consequences have led to women being excluded or marginalised from sporting activities, physical education lessons, and clubhouses due to the expectation that their behaviour conforms to feminine cultural tropes of submissiveness and passivity (Scraton, 1992; Flintoff, Fitzgerald, & Scraton, 2008).

Liquid modernity: From discipline to seduction

While Foucault's work on panopticism has garnered interest, his ideas have also been critiqued within contemporary social theory, namely by theorists who have sought to chart a change in the constitution of modernity (Beck, 1992; Bauman, 2000; Giddens, 1991) and the impact this has had on the workings of power. For example, Zygmunt Bauman (2006) investigates how the structural workings of power have changed in the period he refers to as liquid modernity, whereby the economic base of Western democracies has transformed from being centred around industrialism and production to now being consumer-orientated. Within leisure, this can be observed in the emergence of privatised industries run to maximise profits through selling products to consumers in a global marketplace. An example is the English Premier League, which has a global fanbase and private television contracts for exclusive broadcasting rights. This level of commercialisation shows how the leisure industries are no longer solely controlled by public sector organisations but instead open to free-market forces and the vast revenue streams they can sustain (Chadwick, Parnell, Anagnostopoulos, & Widdop, 2018). Bauman (2007) attributes this transformation to three pivotal events. The first is the emergence of New Right economic policies championed by thinkers such as Milton Freidman and Friedrich Von Hayek, which led the US Federal Reserve and many European governments to abandon Keynesian welfare strategies during the 1980s (Bauman, 2000). This ideology has seen the welfare system stripped back and sold off to private companies (a shadow state, so to speak) who run services around the motive of profit instead of any perceived benefits to society (Blackshaw, 2005; Swain, Lashua, & Spracklen, 2021). Examples of this change in leisure provision can be seen in the proliferation of corporate gym companies that have saturated the fitness industry at the expense of public-owned facilities that successive right-wing governments in the UK have sold off through compulsory competitive tendering (CCT).[3]

Second, Bauman (2000) explains how such policies have created a culture of excessive individualism initiated by the scaling back of the welfare state, which has placed a greater emphasis on individual responsibility. As a result, members of the polis find themselves increasingly left to their own devices by managing personal risk through consuming, emphasising individual decision-making and forward-thinking (Smith, 1999; Swain, 2017b). The precarity involved in deciphering information provided by 'experts' and 'expert systems' underlines how fluid and forward-thinking liquid modern consumers have to be to manage their lives, highlighting how such excessive freedom can lead to a crisis in personal security and the need to look to others, namely celebrity role models for guidance (Bauman 2007). Lawrence (2016) provides an example of this in his research on racialised male body image that explores how white men exercise a sense of embodied control over their bodies by reaffirming their jurisdiction and supremacy by looking to white masculine male bodies in men's health magazines. Similarly, Swain (2021b) has attributed this social climate to the political success of former elite athletes such as Vitali Klitschko and Manny Pacquaio by theorising how the precarity associated with consumer capitalism has led the electorate to seek security in the strength projected by such sporting celebrities.

Finally, capitalism in liquid modernity has become truly global, with multinational corporations no longer being welded to the nation-state, as in industrial modernity, but instead free to conduct their operations across borders, reducing the Government's ability to regulate them in the process (Bauman, 2000). In addition, technological advancements in communications and media have allowed cultural flows of information to cross borders, permitting consumers in different countries to access media and sports from all over the globe. This point is evidenced in how sporting celebrities are no longer tied to local or national geographies but instead genuinely global in their appeal, allowing them to become global icons backed by major sports companies who invest heavily to have such personalities endorse their products in the hope of spreading their brand into new markets (Gilchrist, 2004). Furthermore, this same process of global commodification is seen in leisure cultures such as hip-hop, which has seen both the sounds and the styles associated with such music spread far beyond the inner-city conurbations of the United States where it first emerged. The cultural impact of such music has led to the forging of distinct syncretic sounds, whether within First Nation communities in Canada (Lashua, 2006) or among inner-city grime artists in the United Kingdom (Swain, 2018).

The viewer society, synopticism, and the rise of the prosumer

To understand this change in power and its impact on methods of social control, Bauman (2000) engages with the psychoanalytical work of Sigmund Freud and his notion of the 'pleasure principle', which he uses to explain the shift away from the disciplinary methods associated with the 'reality principle' that provide the foundation for Foucault's writings on panopticism. Here, Bauman articulates how the change to a consumer-orientated economic system has reconceptualised the relationship between the state and its citizens entirely, from a model centred on disciplining the population around the principles of a production-based economy grounded on social classifications of work (i.e. the working class/middle class, etc.). To a system characterised by excessive freedom, permitting individuals to manage their lives through the procurement of information. In other words, the security provided by the command and control systems implemented by the state in industrial capitalism has been dismantled for the most part and replaced by a consumer-orientated system that permits individuals the freedom to choose (Bauman, 2006). This shift towards a more libertarian approach at the same time highlights a dichotomy in how liquid modern consumers trade security for freedom, articulated through a mentality that promotes a message that:

> Security is disempowering, disabling, breeding the resented 'dependency' and altogether constraining the human agents' freedom. What this passes over in silence is that acrobatics and rope-walking without a safety net are an art few people can master and a recipe for disaster for all the rest. Take away security, and freedom is the first casualty.
> (Bauman & Tester, 2001, p. 52)

This insight exposes the complexity of freedom, not solely as an ontological entity but rather as a relational concept, connecting with philosophical debates led by thinkers such as Erich Fromm (2001), who sought to expose how human beings resent the unbridled freedoms of unregulated capitalism (Swain, 2021a). Bauman (2000) explains how such anxieties mirror those experienced in early modern societies when religious rationalities disintegrated in the face of scientific exploration and elucidates how a similar feeling of fear and uncertainty is now characterising liquid modern life. This perspective, in turn, is used to narrate the psychological impact of the welfare state's scaling back on individuals, leaving them alone to decipher information and make forward-orientated consumer decisions (Bauman, 2005).

This situation resonates with the Norwegian Criminologist Thomas Mathiesen's (1997) work on 'the viewer society', an idea that explains how the disciplinary system of the panopticon has been replaced in post-industrial consumer societies by the synopticon. The synopticon represents a system of power that encourages the consumer masses to watch the actions of the few, namely celebrity-style icons who saturate the public consciousness through various mediums, such as mass and social media. Bauman (2005) uses Mathiesen's analogy to articulate how liquid modern individuals find themselves trapped within the workings of the synopticon due to the need to find role models to help interpret the vast swathes of information they have to process daily. Through this system, individuals try to alleviate the insecurity of making choices by gravitating towards role models like celebrities, lifestyle gurus, and social media personalities who can advise and guide their choices. A point articulated below:

> It is now your task to watch the swelling ranks of Big Brothers and Big Sisters, and watch them closely and avidly, in the hope of finding something useful for yourself: an example to imitate or a word of advice about how to cope with your problems, which, like their problems, need to be coped with individually and can be coped with only individually.
> (Bauman, 2000, p. 30)

This shift in power structures has impacted the area of sport and leisure, which is no longer seen solely as a site used to discipline the population into socially desirable behaviours. But instead, as a site in social life that provides the role models through which power now operates through the spectre of 'precarization' (contingency) that characterises liquid modern society and forces members of the public to look to such role models when consuming (Bauman, 2005; Swain, 2019).

This situation connects with the idea of the prosumer, a term coined by the American futurologist Alvin Toffler (1980) to refer to those who consume and produce value, either for self-consumption or consumption by others, and in turn, receive implicit or explicit incentives from corporate organisations for doing so (Ritzer, Dean, & Jurgenson, 2012). Interestingly, this concept documents the position of elite athletes as consumer role models that ordinary members of the public look to when helping them choose how best to navigate their lives (Bond et al., 2021). Contemporary research in this area by Hylton and Lawrence (2015) has sought to expose the impact of celebrity culture on the identity formation of white men by analysing how such consumers conceptualise body image by looking to examples in the form of the footballer Cristiano Ronaldo. This insight discloses how the synoptic method of watching those in the public eye plays a pivotal role in helping to construct a sense of personal style and body image. In other areas of leisure, this is seen most notably in the form of YouTube influencers and lifestyle bloggers who use social media to provide advice to their followers on a whole range of personal issues, from health and fitness to tourism and travel (Ritzer & Jurgenson, 2010; Swain, 2017a).

Adiaphorization: Exclusionary power and social justice

This transformation in power structures raises questions regarding how movements seeking to enact social justice can disrupt such a system. At the centre of this move to counteract calls for increasing collectivism is the concept of adiaphorization, a term used to describe the process whereby moral questions regarding the role of social institutions in the well-being of citizens are ignored in favour of individual consumer practices (Bauman, 2008). Under this system, the disadvantaged or 'flawed consumers' of liquid modern societies, a term used to incorporate the remnants of the working class, women, people with (dis)abilities or migrant communities, find the blame for their situation placed firmly onto themselves. This mindset conforms to the neoliberal doctrine of individualisation centred on consuming and personal responsibility, thereby causing the inequalities and high levels of destitution seen in contemporary society to be attributed to personal shortcomings in managing individual agency, as opposed to structural disparities in resource allocation and the endemic poverty this facilitates (Bauman, 2000; Swain, 2021a). The use of this systemic form of exclusionary power exposes how the underrepresentation of marginalised groups in sport and leisure and the health disparities that emerge from such exclusion (obesity and mental health) is linked to the inability of individuals to select "the right commodities" (Bauman, 2006, p. 86) to consume. Subsequently, a narrative has emerged that seeks to blame bad individual decision-making rather than the dismantling of social welfare programmes designed to prevent such injustices from occurring.

This reconceptualisation of whom to blame for inequality and personal suffering exposes how synoptic power maintains its control by decentralising accountability away from political elites by making such issues an individual rather than a societal matter (Bowling & Westenra, 2020). An example of this subversion of institutional responsibility and hyper-individualism can be seen in the academic literature on doping in sports, whereby the blame for athletes using performance-enhancing drugs is placed firmly at the door of the athletes themselves as opposed to the hyper-commercialised social structures influencing the cultural sphere of sport (Houlihan, 2016). This individualised perspective is evidenced in the proliferation of psychological explanations used to explain doping, whether that be through the language of burnout, anxiety, or perfectionism, all of which promote individualised causes and solutions that overlook, or are not aware of, broader social, economic, and political forces (Waddington, 2005). The problem with this approach is that the social structures that impact the propensity of athletes to dope, such as sports offering a way out of poverty-stricken neighbourhoods, or the increased commercialisation of sport that makes an athlete's success fund entire sports science teams, promoters and marketing agencies, become overlooked. Subsequently, the public never questions how modern sports' commercialised and professionalised dynamics have led to a proliferation in doping, whether by enticing a poor athlete to take a steroid to enhance their performance in the hope of gaining a sponsor and a way out of the ghetto, or a nutritionist who might prescribe a banned substance to an athlete in the hope of them winning a competition and frequenting their services again (Spracklen, 2014). Such examples highlight the condition of adiaphorization that haunts liquid modern societies by diverting questions of inequality and injustice away from social structures and instead onto the individual.

Conclusion

This chapter provides insight into the relationship between power and social justice through the lens of sport and leisure. First, this chapter has sought to explore the systemic workings of power as a form of authority within industrial modernity, unpacking research that has positioned sport and leisure as a mechanism of disciplinary power built around panoptic surveillance. From here, this chapter introduced a more nuanced perspective of power that has gained traction within the writings of the late Polish sociologist Zygmunt Bauman who wrote about an evolution in the cultural landscape of modernity, connecting contemporary debates on social control to ideas regarding precarity, excessive individualism, and synopticism. This line of investigation has sought to expose how increased levels of individualisation and celebrity culture instrumentalise consumer solutions to members of the polis looking to alleviate the uncertainty they experience in their daily lives. The dynamics expose how sport and leisure no longer solely represent a site of disciplinary control whereby the few watch the actions of the many (panopticism) but rather as a commercialised arena in which the many now watch the actions of the few (synopticism). The concepts introduced here are designed to invoke debate and get scholars thinking about how power can be understood differently and how societal transformations can lead to new systems of power emerging.

Notes

1 United Negro Improvement Association – a large Pan-African political movement that sought the strengthening of social, economic, and cultural ties between black communities in Africa, the Caribbean, and the Americas.
2 The exact date referring to the start of 'The Enlightenment' is debated; however, there is a consensus that it took place within the mid-eighteenth century.
3 Compulsory Competitive Tendering – an initiative whereby local authorities were forced to open in-house services, such as leisure and sport services, to private competition in the 1980s to cut costs and improve value for money.

References

Adorno, T. & Horkheimer, M. (1997) *Dialectic of enlightenment: Philosophical fragments*. New York: Verso.
Bauman, Z. (1988) *Modernity and the Holocaust*. Ithaca: Cornell University Press.
Bauman, Z. (1991) *Modernity and ambivalence*. Ithaca: Cornell University Press.
Bauman, Z. (2000) *Liquid modernity*. Cambridge: Polity.
Bauman, Z. (2005) *Liquid life*. Cambridge: Polity.
Bauman, Z. (2006) *Liquid fear*. Cambridge: Polity.
Bauman, Z. (2007) *Liquid times: Living in an age of uncertainty*. Cambridge: Polity.
Bauman, Z. (2008) *Does ethics have a chance in a world of consumers?* Cambridge, MA: Harvard University Press.

Bauman, Z. & Haugaard, M. (2008) Liquid modernity and power: A dialogue with Zygmunt Bauman. *Journal of Power*. 1(2), pp. 111–130.

Bauman, Z. & Tester, K. (2001) *Conversations with Zygmunt Bauman*. Cambridge: Polity.

Beck, U. (1992) *Risk society: Towards a new modernity*. London: Sage.

Bentham, J. (2009) *Panopticon: Or the inspection house* (1791). Montana: Kessinger Publishing.

Blackshaw, T. (2005) *Zygmunt Bauman*. London: Routledge.

Bond, A., Widdop, P., Cockayne D., & Parnell, D. (2021) Prosumption, networks and value during a global pandemic: Lockdown leisure and COVID-19. *Leisure Sciences*. 43(1–2), pp. 70–77.

Bottomore, T. (2002) *The Frankfurt school and its critics*. New York: Routledge.

Bowling, B. & Westenra, S. (2020) 'A really hostile environment': Adiaphorization, global policing and the crimmigration control system. *Theoretical Criminology*. 24(2), pp. 163–183.

Carrington, B. (2010) *Race, sport and politics: The sporting black diaspora*. Washington DC: Sage.

Castells, M. (2016) A sociology of power: My intellectual journey. *Annual Review of Sociology*. 42(1), pp. 1–19.

Chadwick, S., Parnell, D., Anagnostopoulos, C., & Widdop, P. (2018) *Routledge handbook of football business and management*. London: Routledge.

Christian M. (2008) Marcus Garvey and African unity: Lessons for the future from the past. *Journal of Black Studies*. 39(2), pp. 316–331.

Cock, S. (2018) Doing developmental research as a figurational sociologist: A case study on the long-term sportization of swimming. In: Malcolm, D. & Velija, P. (eds) *Figurational research in sport, leisure and health*. London: Routledge, pp. 87–101.

Durkheim, E. (1997) *The division of labour in society*. Trans. W. D. Halls, Intro. Lewis A. Coser. New York: Free Press, pp. 39–60.

Edwards, H. (2017) *The revolt of the black athlete*. Champaign, IL: University of Illinois Press.

Elias, N. (2000) *The civilising process: Sociogenetic and psychogenetic investigations*. Oxford, England: Blackwell.

Flintoff, A., Fitzgerald, H., & Scraton, S. (2008) The challenges of intersectionality: Researching difference in physical education. *International Studies in the Sociology of Education*. 18(2), pp. 73–85.

Foucault, M. (1970) *The order of things*. London: Routledge.

Foucault, M. (1977) *Discipline and punish: The birth of the prison*. London: Pantheon Books.

Foucault, M. (1991) Disciplines and sciences of the individual. In: P. Rabinow (ed.) *The Foucault reader: An introduction to Foucault's thought*. London: Penguin, pp. 169–257.

Fromm, E. (2001) *The fear of freedom*. London: Routledge Classics.

Giddens, A. (1986) *The constitution of society: Outline of the theory of structuration*. Los Angeles: University of California Press.

Giddens, A. (1991) *Modernity and self-identity: Self and society in the late modern age*. Cambridge: Polity.

Giddens, A. (1998) *Conversations with Anthony Giddens: Making sense of modernity*. Cambridge: Polity.

Gilchrist, P. (2004) Local heroes and global stars. In Allison, L. (ed.) *Global politics of sport*. London: Routledge, pp. 118–139.

Giulianotti, R. (2015) *Sport: A critical sociology* (2nd Ed.). Cambridge: Polity.

Hargreaves, J. (1986) *Sport, power and culture*. Cambridge: Polity Press.

Houlihan, B. (2016) Doping in sport. In. Houlihan, B. & Malcolm, D. (eds) *Sport and society* (3rd Ed.). London: Sage, pp. 342–362.

Hylton, K. (2009) *Race and sport: Critical race theory*. London: Routledge.

Hylton, K. & Lawrence, S. (2015) Reading Ronaldo: Contingent whiteness in the football media. *Soccer & Society*. 16 (5–6), pp. 765–782.

Kirk, D. (1998) *Schooling bodies: School practice and public discourse 1880-1950*. London: Leicester University Press.

Lang, M. (2010) Surveillance and conformity in competitive youth swimming. *Sport, Education and Society*. 15(1), pp. 19–37.

Lang, M. (2015) Touchy subject: A Foucauldian analysis of coaches' perceptions of adult–child touch in youth swimming. *Sociology of Sport Journal*. 32(1), pp. 4–21.

Lashua, B. D. (2006) "Just another native?" Soundscapes, chorasters, and borderlands in Edmonton, Alberta, Canada. *Cultural Studies – Critical Methodologies*. 6(3), pp. 391–410.

Law, G. & Bloyce, D. (2019) 'Pressure to play?' A sociological analysis of professional football managers' behaviour towards injured players. *Soccer & Society*. 20(3), pp. 387–407.

Lawrence, S. (2016) Racialising the "great man": A critical race study of idealised male athletic bodies in Men's Health magazine. *International Review for the Sociology of Sport.* 51(7), pp. 777–799.

Lukes, S. (2005) *Power: A radical view.* London: Palgrave Macmillan.

Machiavelli, N. (2003) *The prince.* London: Penguin.

Markula, P. & Pringle, R. (2006) *Foucault, sport and exercise: Power, knowledge and transforming the self.* London: Routledge.

Mathiesen, T. (1997) The viewer society: Michel Foucault's panopticon revisited. *Theoretical Criminology.* 1(2), pp. 215–234.

Mierzwinski, M., Cock, S., & Velija, P. (2019) A position statement on social justice, physical education and bullying: A figurational sociological perspective. *Quest.* 71(2), pp. 215–226.

Mowatt R. A. (2017) A critical expansion of theories on race and ethnicity in Leisure Studies. In Spracklen, K., Lashua B., Sharpe E., & Swain S. (eds) *The Palgrave handbook of leisure theory.* London: Palgrave Macmillan, pp. 577–594.

Ratna, A. (2015) Sport and South Asian diasporas: Playing through time and space. *International Review for the Sociology of Sport.* 50(6), pp. 747–750.

Riches, G., Rankin-Wright, A., Swain, S., & Kuppan, V. (2017) Moving forward: Critical reflections of doing social justice research. In. Long, J., Fletcher, T., & Watson, B. (eds) *Sport, leisure and social justice.* London: Routledge, pp. 209–221.

Ritzer, G. & Jurgenson, N. (2010) Production, consumption, prosumption: The nature of capitalism in the age of the digital "prosumer." *Journal of Consumer Culture.* 10(1), pp. 13–36.

Ritzer, G., Dean, P., & Jurgenson N. (2012) The coming of age of the prosumer. *American Behavioral Scientist.* 56(4), pp. 379–398.

Scraton, S. (1992) *Shaping up to womanhood: Gender and girls' physical education.* Buckingham: Open University Press.

Smith, D. (1999) *Zygmunt Bauman: Prophet of postmodernity.* Cambridge: Polity.

Spracklen, K. (2009) *The purpose and meaning of leisure: Habermas and leisure at the end of modernity.* Basingstoke: Palgrave.

Spracklen, K. (2011) *Constructing leisure: Historical and philosophical debates.* Basingstoke: Palgrave.

Spracklen, K (2014) *Exploring sports and society: A critical introduction for students.* Basingstoke. Palgrave.

Swain, S. (2017a) Leisure in the current interregnum: Exploring the social theories of Anthony Giddens and Zygmunt Bauman. In Spracklen, K., Lashua, B., Sharpe, E., & Swain, S. (eds) *The Palgrave handbook of leisure theory.* Basingstoke: Palgrave, pp. 799–816.

Swain, S. (2017b) The Khat controversy: Dark leisure in a liquid modern world. *Annals of Leisure Research.* 20 (5), pp. 610–625.

Swain, S. (2018) Grime music and dark leisure: Exploring grime, morality and synoptic control. *Annals of Leisure Research.* 21 (4), pp. 480–492.

Swain, S. (2019) Sport, power and politics: Exploring sport and social control within the changing context of modernity. *International Journal of the Sociology of Leisure.* 2(4), pp. 385–402.

Swain, S. (2021a) Voices from the margins: Khat-chewing, devotional leisure and ambivalence in the British-Somali diaspora. In: De Martini-Ugolotti, N. & Caudwell, J. (eds) *Leisure and forced migration: Reframing critical analysis of lives lived in the asylum system.* London: Routledge, pp. 139–154.

Swain, S. (2021b) Pugilism, power, and the cultural politics of celebrity: Charting Vitali Klitschko's rise from Heavyweight Champion to Mayor of Kiev. *Journal of Global Sport Management.* doi: 10.1080/24704067.2021.1991829

Swain, S., Lashua, B., & Spracklen, K. (2021) Khat-chewing, moral spacing and belonging: Sociological insights into the cultural space of the *mafrish* in the leisure lives of older and middle-aged British-Somali males. *International Journal of the Sociology of Leisure.* 4(3), pp. 1–22.

Toffler, A. (1980) *The third wave.* New York: William Morrow.

Trimbur, L. (2019) Taking a knee, making a stand: Social justice, Trump America, and the politics of port. *Quest.* 71(2), pp. 252–265.

Waddington, I. (2005) Changing patterns of drug use in British sport from the 1960s. *Sport in History.* 25(3), pp. 472–496.

Webb, L. A. & Macdonald, D. (2007) Techniques of power in physical education and the underrepresentation of women in leadership. *Journal of Teaching in Physical Education.* 26(1), pp. 279–297.

PART II

Sex, gender, and sexualities

5
WOMEN, SPORT, AND ACTIVISM
An international perspective

Celia Valiente

The best known examples of elite athletes' activism were undertaken by men, including Tommie Smith, John Carlos, Muhammad Ali, and more recently US American football player Colin Kaepernick and the players of the National Basketball Association (NBA) protesting against racism. However, women have also a long history of activism, including high-profile sporting women such as US tennis champion of the 1960s and 1970s Billie Jean King, US tennis champions from the 2000s onwards Venus and Serena Williams (Tredway, 2019), US soccer[1] champions mainly from the 2010s onwards Megan Rapinoe (Cooky & Antunovic, 2020), and players of the Women's National Basketball Association (WNBA) fighting against racism (Cooky & Antunovic, 2020).

Although professional male athletes' activism has received most attention by mass media and academic studies, there is no reason to ignore women athletes' activism (Cooky & Antunovic, 2020; Kitching et al., 2022). This chapter maps and reviews scholarly literature on women elite athletes' activism since the late-1960s mainly (but not exclusively) in Western countries.[2] By activism I mean individual and collective efforts made in public to advance (or impede) social change within or outside sport. I decided to start this review in the late-1960s because in many Western countries, the second wave of the women's movement appeared around that moment. This second wave of women's activism demanded, among other things, women's access to education, paid employment and politics, and women's reproductive rights (Ferree & Mueller, 2004). Although this second wave initially did not include the demand of women's full inclusion in the world of sport, some female elite athletes' activism dated from that moment. Gender equality in sport became a goal of the women's movement in subsequent decades, and in some countries only very recently.

In general and with exceptions, when deciding which works to review, I selected them if the main topic (or one of the main topics) is female high-profile athletes' activism, regardless of the institutional affiliation of their authors (departments of sport sciences, sociology, or others). When assessing existing research, I highlight the contribution made by scholarly works rather than pinpointing their limitations. Most (but not all) authors whose research is reviewed here are women and they happen to be feminist, in the sense that they think that gender inequality exists, is wrong, and should be reversed.

The topic under review here has received some scholarly attention but mainly in the English-speaking world. The United States is the case study most analysed, and an excellent literature review on this case already exists (Cooky, 2018). Although this chapter mainly reviews works in English, I have made every effort to analyse women's top athletes' activism beyond the United States. In spite of this effort, and inevitably, the United States and some sports (tennis and football) are considerably more covered than others. This imbalance does not mean that some countries and sports are more important than others. This imbalance simply reflects the fact that for some countries and sport there is more research.

This chapter argues that activism undertaken by women and men high-profile athletes differs regarding the (i) goals, (ii) location, and (iii) tactics. (i) As for goals of the mobilisation, female top-ranked athletes' activism is peculiar for its demand of gender equality within sport along with other social justice objectives within or outside sports. (ii) As regards the location of protests, individual sports are probably more central to elite female athletes' activism than male athlete activism, as tennis is the most lucrative sport for women athletes who excel. Thus, women's tennis attracts media attention, top female players' activists are well-known, and analysts have studied them. (iii) With respect to tactics, female elite athletes resort less to confrontational tactics than male world-class athletes, as is the case of women's activism in general.

This chapter is organised in six parts. The first, second, and third parts review the goals, location, and tactics of female high-profile athletes' activism respectively. The fourth part presents research on male allies of women top-ranked athletes' mobilisation. The fifth part examines what we know about outcomes of female elite athletes' activism. The sixth part draws a conclusion and identifies future directions for research.

Goals

Histories of sport in Western countries show that contemporary sports developed mainly in the nineteenth and twentieth centuries as activities for boys and men, who trained and competed. With exceptions, women were forbidden in this part of society. Consequently, the first women who mobilised regarding sport fought for the right to participate (Hargreaves, 1994, 2000; Valiente, 2019, 2020b). The demand of inclusion was not only advanced at the national and international levels by women sporting pioneers but also by more recent cohorts until all sports be open to girls and women (Cahn, 2015; Hall, 2016; Lenskyj, 2013).

In past and present decades, female athletes have demanded not only the right to participate in sports but also an improvement of the conditions under which they train and compete. These conditions comprise, among other things, access to facilities, high-quality coaches, and resources to travel and compete (Hall, 1995; Steidinger, 2020).

In past and present times, women elite athletes have demanded better pay and, in some cases, equal pay. This economic demand is understandable, since elite champions have highly demanding but very short sporting careers. During these careers world-class athletes train and compete incessantly, and very often they do not prepare themselves for the moment when their sporting careers end. For instance, in women's and men's tennis, up to 1968, only amateur (that is, non-paid) players were allowed to take part in major tournaments. Thus, major tournaments did not pay participants. The Open era began in 1968, when amateur and professional tennis players were allowed to participate in all types of contests.

Subsequently, prize money was permitted. Billie Jean King and other high-profile women players demanded vocally to tennis governing bodies not only equal prize money but also an equal number of high-profile tournaments (Tredway, 2019). More (or equal) prize money and a higher number of contests are also central demands advanced by female athletes in other sports such as golf (Kitching et al., 2022) and football/soccer (Cooky & Antunovic, 2020) (see below).

Pregnancy affects women but not men, and women elite athletes have requested that sporting careers are organised in a way that makes possible the combination of maternity and elite sport. For example, Serena Williams has demanded that female tennis players retain their ranking during maternity leave (Steidinger, 2020).

Goals related to sexuality and violence have been pursued recently by women athlete activists. They have denounced sexual harassment and abuse against sporting girls and women (and to a lesser extent sporting boys and men). Top-ranked women athletes have also requested opportunities and respect for female athletes who are not heterosexual (Hall, 1995; Hargreaves, 2000; Steidinger, 2020).

In demanding the right to participate in sports, and train and compete in the same conditions as men, not being penalised for maternity, and not being predated sexually, women athletes' activism is necessarily different from men athletes' activism. But this is not the case in other regards. In their activism, both women and men athletes have advanced similar claims related to social causes in and out of sport. For example, tennis champions Venus and Serena Williams have consistently denounced racism in the top tennis circuit. Additionally, Serena Williams has actively mobilised in favour of improvement of police behaviour, prison reform and prisoners' rights, as these phenomena disproportionately affect African Americans (Tredway, 2020). Similarly, from 2014 onwards, players of the WNBA have organised protest actions against racial inequality and police brutality as part of the social movement #BlackLivesMatter (Cooky & Antunovic, 2020).

Elite sport is organised explicitly around the principle that all individuals can be classified as women or men. Gender segregation is mandatory, as men compete against men and women against women. Thus, the question of who is a woman and who is subsequently allowed to compete against women has been and is going to be a central and contested question. Starting in the 1930s, elite sport has a long history of attempts to answer this question by classifying all individuals as women or men using a variety of methods, including, among others, physical examination, chromosome analysis, and study of testosterone levels. These various methods have been utilised in the past and present decades to survey self-defined women athletes, in order to impede that men pretend to be women, compete against women and win. Elite sport has also a history of self-defined women athletes who have contested this surveillance policy. The most famous case of an athlete activist in this sense is South African middle-distance runner Caster Semenya, who won two 800 metres Olympic gold medals (London 2012 and Rio 2016) and three World Championships (2009, 2011, 2017). Semenya is an intersex woman with a naturally high level of testosterone. In 2009 she was made to undergo a sex verification test, which she passed. In 2018, World Athletics mandated a maximum threshold level of testosterone for female runners. To comply with this mandate, Semenya would have to take medication to lower her testosterone levels. She refused and appealed to various bodies including the European Court of Human Rights. Her refusal meant that she did not compete in various elite events including the 2020 Tokyo Olympic Games (Cooky & Dworkin, 2018; Schultz, 2021; Wheaton et al., 2020).

Location

Individual sports are possibly more central a location for women athletes' activism than men athletes' activism. This is so because the women's sport that has the highest profile and is best paid is tennis. Although tennis is played in two ways (singles and doubles), tennis is generally considered an individual sport. Therefore, it is not surprising that activists have appeared among top-ranked women players, and that these women are very well-known. For instance, such is the case of US tennis champions Billie Jean King and Venus and Serena Williams (Tredway, 2020).

Women's team sports have also been the site of women's activism. For example, in 2016, the United States Women's National Soccer Team (USWNT) filed a wage discrimination complaint with the Equal Employment Opportunity Commission alleging that female footballers were paid less than male footballers. On the same grounds, in 2019, the USWNT filed a lawsuit against US Soccer Federation (Cooky & Antunovic, 2020) (see below).

Long ago, social movement scholars showed that at some point in the development of social movements, formal organisations are usually created to sustain the mobilisation (della Porta & Diani, 2020; Snow et al., 2019). There are also some examples of this process in women athletes' activism. In 1973, Billie Jean King and over 60 other elite tennis players founded an organisation called the Women's Tennis Association (WTA) to defend women players' interests and manage a vibrant tennis tour (the WTA tour). In this way, a new location of sport activism was created: a one-sport organisation (Tredway, 2020).

Multi-sport organisations have also been formed by women athletes, former athletes, and other women's sport activists to improve the status of women in sport. In 1974, tennis champion Billie Jean King founded the Women's Sports Foundation (WSF) to promote sport and physical activity for girls and women. The WSF is a non-profit organisation based in the United States with projects focused on educating the public on the benefits of sport, funding female athletes to reach their full potential, advocating changes in public policies to encourage women's participation in sport, and funding research that improves female sport. The WSF is sustained mainly by members' fees, private donations, and corporate sponsors (Comeau & Church, 2010; Hall, 1997; Women's Sports Foundation, n.d.). In this respect, the WSF is different from multi-sport organisations of other countries that pursue similar goals but are financially sustained mainly or entirely with state money. This is the case, for instance, for the Canadian Association for the Advancement of Women in Sport (CAAWS), which was founded in 1981 and rebranded to Canadian Women & Sport in 2020 (Comeau & Church, 2010; Hall, 1997; Canadian Women & Sport, n.d.).

As elite sport is organised around national and international contests, it is not surprising that women's sport advocates have founded international organisations and have organised (or participated in) international conferences to advance the status of women's sport. In 1994, the first World Conference on Women and Sport was held in Brighton, United Kingdom. Organised by the British Sports Council and supported by the International Olympic Committee and the British Council, the conference was targeted mainly to sport policy and decision makers at the national and international levels. Some former top-performance women athletes were highly involved in the organisation of the conference. It was attended by over 280 delegates from above 80 countries on five continents. The conference elaborated the 1994 Brighton Declaration on Women and Sport comprising ten principles towards women's full inclusion in all aspects of the world of sport. The conference established the International Working Group on Women and Sport, which, among other activities, has monitored the response to the Brighton Declaration, and has called a world conference on women and sport every four years ever since. The Brighton Declaration was updated in 2014 to embrace not only sport but also physical activity (the Brighton plus Helsinki 2014 Declaration) (International Group on Women and Sport, 2014) and has over 550 signatories. The Brighton Declaration and other documents emanated from the aforementioned subsequent conferences are tools to be used by women's sport activists to advance their claims (Hargreaves, 1999, 2000; Matthews, 2018, 2021).

The internet is increasingly a location for women athletes' activism. Since the 1970s, scholars have studied the treatment of female sports by conventional media, such as newspapers, magazines, television, and radio. This scholarship generally shows that the media cover women's sports minimally. When mass media report on female sports, female athletes are usually sexualised and trivialised, in the sense that media often note high-performance women athletes' body appearance, clothing, and private lives, and considerably less about their athletic practice and achievements (Bernstein, 2002; Cooky et al., 2015). The advent of social media, blogs, and the internet in general offers women athletes and fans the possibility to produce and disseminate content that challenges stereotyped presentations of female sports that abound in mainstream media. In this case, the internet has a formidable potential for activism. But this potential has to be realised, since on-line coverage of women's sports often reproduces stereotypical views on sporting females. Sometimes, this is even the case of women athletes' self-created content (Antunovic & Hardin, 2012).

Recent research shows that some women athletes are utilising the aforementioned potential of social media. A study of social media profiles of 26 Muslim sportswomen with diverse sporting practices (from non-competitive to competing at the local, national, and international levels) from 11 developed and developing countries documents that these sporting women challenge dominant discourses of Muslim women as passive victims in need of salvation. Through digital activism, these Muslim women athletes portray themselves as athletically active and strong. They demand sport policies that permit them full inclusion in the sport world, for instance, by allowing them to train and compete in clothing compatible with their faith (Ahmad & Thorpe, 2020).

Tactics

As it is the case of all social movements, when advancing their claims, women elite athletes can use a repertoire of non-confrontational and confrontational tactics. Although the line between the two types of tactics is not clear-cut, non-confrontational tactics are usually defined as those that are not threatening. In contrast, confrontational tactics are disruptive devices that attempt to destabilise the status quo and include, among others, litigation, strikes, boycotts to sport contests and the use of violence (della Porta & Diani, 2020; Snow et al., 2019).

The case of women's professional football in Spain can support this point. In the late 2010s, Spanish female footballers mobilised collectively requesting an improvement in the conditions under which they train and compete. These athletes made public statements to the mass media, sport managers and politicians affirming politely that they acknowledged that the technical and economic level of men's football is considerably higher than that of women's football. Spanish women footballers publicly stated that they were not asking for equal pay or any other type of equality in comparison with men's footballers but only an improvement of women footballers' conditions. Only when women footballers assessed that these non-confrontational tactics were not leading to satisfaction of their demands, did they threaten to use (and eventually used) a confrontational tactic *par excellence*: a strike. During a weekend of November 2019, they did not participate in any match of the top league (Valiente, 2022).

Cases of use of confrontational tactics exist and are rather visible because of the media attention that these tactics attract. In protest against alleged racism of the Indian Wells tennis tournament, Venus and Serena Williams boycotted that competition from 2002 onwards. Serena Williams started taking part in this contest again in 2015 and Venus Williams in 2016 (Tredway, 2020). Another example is the aforementioned mobilisation by US professional women footballers requesting equal pay in comparison with male footballers that included in 2016 a wage discrimination complaint with the Equal Employment Opportunity Commission and in 2019 a lawsuit against the US Soccer Federation (Cooky & Antunovic, 2020). Notwithstanding these and other cases of use of confrontational tactics, in comparison with male athletes, women athletes have utilised confrontational tactics less than men, as is the case of women's movements in general.

When deciding whether a tactic is confrontational or non-confrontational, context is everything. Two examples serve to illustrate this point. In some religions such as Catholicism, the act of kneeling is a sign of reverence and respect. Kneeling is part of the ritual and is done in the most important celebration (the mass) and in many other ceremonies. In contrast, when in recent years US elite athletes have protested the national anthem denouncing racism and oppression of other disadvantaged groups, kneeling has been seen as a major confrontational tactic. On the other hand, when track and field women athletes from the West compete in shorts, they are simply following a mainstream sport dress code. This was different for Hassiba Boulmerka, a former runner from Algeria. In the 1,500 metres, she was world champion in 1991 (Tokyo) and 1995 (Gothenburg), and Olympic gold medallist (Barcelona 1992). For running in shorts and not being veiled in public, she received life threats from Islamic fundamentalists. These threats led her to live in Europe under protection (Fundación Princesa de Asturias, n.d.; Hargreaves, 1994, 2000).

Allies

Activists benefit from allies to advance their claims. Men outnumber women among those who occupy the highest positions in sport management (Burton & Leberman, 2017; Elling et al., 2019). Thus, women athlete activists sometimes (or often) attempt to find male allies among sport decision makers to support their claims (Steidinger, 2020). In this regard, women athlete activists are not different from other women's rights activists of past and present times (Valiente, 2017, 2020a). For example, in the nineteenth and twentieth centuries, some states conferred the right to vote to men (or rather, to some groups of men) but not to women. In various Western countries, female suffrage was later achieved thanks to women's mobilisation and the support of some male allies, as all politicians at that time were men (Paxton et al., 2021).

Male supporters of claims advanced by women athlete activists are not limited to sport decision makers, as fans can also play an important role in this regard. For example, the USWNT won the Women's World Cup of football in 2019. During the celebration ceremony, the crowd chanted "Equal pay" and "Pay them" to the US Soccer Federation President to support this claim advanced by the US women's national team (Cooky & Antunovic, 2020).

Acting publicly in this way, fans amplify athletes' claims and send cues to sport managers about the importance of these demands.

Granted, fans can act as allies of women athletes' activism but also as ambivalent spectators and even as main opponents. A study analysed the reactions by users of Colin Kaepernick and Megan Rapinoe's public Facebook pages after the two athletes protested the US national anthem (the former denouncing racism and the latter condemning racism and the oppression of the LGTB community). Although both athletes explained that their mobilisation was not against the United States or the military but in favour of oppressed minorities, their protests were criticised by many fans as un-patriotic and un-American (Schmidt et al., 2019). Similarly, football fans reacted in social media to Megan Rapinoe's comment that she would reject the invitation to visit the White House (and President Trump) if the US women's national soccer team won the 2019 Women's World Cup. Fans' comments varied widely ranging from full approval to severe condemnation. This wide variety is understandable if taken in mind that sport fans form an internally heterogeneous group (Gallagher et al., 2022).

Outcomes

If one compares the situation of women's sport in Western countries in the late-1960s (the initial moment covered by this review chapter) and now, one would easily conclude that an enormous progress has taken place. Sports are now open to women, and women's participation in sport (amateur and professional) has remarkably increased. For instance, in the 1964 Tokyo Olympic Games, women accounted for only 13 per cent of athletes and competed in only seven sports. For the first time in the Olympic Games in London in 2012, women competed in all sports. In the 2020 Tokyo Olympics Games, women accounted for 48 per cent of athletes (International Olympic Committee, 2021; Zafra et al., 2021).

It is safe to affirm that at least part of this progress at the national and international levels has been caused by women athletes' mobilisation on behalf of women in sport. However, when assessing exactly which part of the progress is due to women athletes' mobilisation, analysts face a monumental challenge pervading social sciences, that is, the difficulty of disentangling the impact of the factor under analysis (women athletes' activism) from the impact of other causal factors. We know that, in some cases, progress in favour of gender equality in sport was caused by initiatives undertaken by politicians autonomously rather than athletes' activism. In these cases, states act as gender equality activists, to use the language coined by political scientist Jennifer Piscopo (2015). For example, since 2014 in Spain, sport policy makers of the central state level imposed a gender quota of three women (or 33 per cent) of board members of national sport federations which apply for state funding (Valiente, 2021). This gender quota made the proportion of board members increase from 12 per cent in 2013 (the year prior to the establishment of the quota) to 28 per cent in 2019 (author's calculation based on data from Consejo Superior de Deportes, 2014–2020).

An assessment of outcomes obtained thanks to women athletes' activism would be incomplete if ignoring that often athletes' activism pursuing goals within sport is a high-risk activity. Especially if athletes use confrontational tactics, athlete activists risk being expelled from the very sport in which they excel. For instance, in the early 1970s, world-class tennis player Billie Jean King and other high-profile female tennis players mobilised in favour of equal pay, and risked being prohibited from participating in principal tennis championships (Tredway, 2019).

Athletes' activism is also usually high-risk behaviour when athletes mobilise pursuing goals outside sport. Athletes undertaking charity work are praised. However, when athletes use their sporting status to claim social justice outside sport, athletes are often severely reprimanded and reminded that the sport field is no place for political demands but to play and excel athletically. For their activism, athlete activists have faced dramatic and detrimental consequences in their personal and sporting lives, as the cases of Tommie Smith, John Carlos, Muhammad Ali, and many others prove (Kaufman, 2008).

Even in the absence of high risks, athletes' activism has often important costs. For example, boycotting a tournament involves forgoing the opportunity to earn money and points necessary to maintain or improve a position within rankings. Boycotting a tournament may involve isolation and criticism from other athletes who do not boycott the tournament (Kitching et al., 2022). Activism may also impact negatively on athletic performance, as activist athletes do not focus exclusively on their sporting careers but dedicate attention, time, and energy to mobilisation (Kitching et al., 2022).

Undoubtedly, activism has rewards attached to it. Otherwise, athletes' activism would not exist. If women athlete activists achieve some of their goals within sport, such as more prize money, they would benefit from such gains, provided that they win tournaments. On the other hand, if the status of women's sport is improving, athlete activists obtain the personal satisfaction of being part of this improvement process (Kitching et al., 2022). But the low number of athlete activists probably is explained by the fact that costs outnumber rewards.

Scholars nearly always positively assess top-ranked women athletes' activism. Various reasons explain this approving tone of the research. For sure, many women top athletes are admirable individuals with a personal history of effort, persistence, and courage. Goals pursued by women athletes in their activism are laudable, including aims such as gender equality and end of racism. But it is important to remember that women athletes and former athletes have also mobilised around not so praiseworthy goals (to say the least). This is arguably the case with Margaret Court, a former tennis world champion in the 1960s and 1970s, later a Christian minister and "the most decorated player in the history of tennis, male and female" (Tredway, 2020, p. 141). In the 1990s, Court initiated a long and sustained homophobic activism in and out of sport that continued well into the second decade of this century (Tredway, 2020).

Conclusion

Thanks to research elaborated by scholars from different academic disciplines, we now know that in Western countries since the late-1960s, some high-profile female athletes and ex-athletes have acted as activists. In comparison with men athletes' activism, women athletes' activism is more centred on gender equality issues within and beyond sports, individual sports are more often a location for activism, and confrontational tactics are less utilised.

The findings of existing scholarship suggest four avenues for development of research on the topic under review here: the use of innovative ways to gather primary data; quantitative studies with a large number of cases; the interrogation of the difference between activism and philanthropy; and studies beyond the English-speaking world.

Regarding the use of innovative ways to gather primary data, works assessed in this chapter were based on standard secondary data such as bibliography, press clippings and on-line news outlets. Given the difficulties of accessing world-class women athletes, especially in high-profile sports (Lenskyj, 2013), scholars have relied primarily on sources already available, such as athletes' autobiographies or statements to the media (mainstream and on-line). Nonetheless, some researchers have managed to interview top-ranked athletes (Tredway, 2020). Moreover, at times, scholars have used ingenious methods to generate primary data for their research. For example, Tredway (2020) analysed social activism in women's tennis with various sources, including athletes' answers to her questions, as she had gained accreditation to access press conferences. In this way, Tredway gathered information necessary to answer the research questions of her study. The use of ingenious and innovative ways to gather primary data is strongly recommended to further investigate women athletes' activism.

As for the elaboration of quantitative studies with a large number of cases, nearly all works reviewed here have been undertaken with qualitative methods and are based on single case studies or a limited number of cases. This is understandable and reflects the newness of the field (of studies on women elite athletes' activism). Probably, if scholars continue studying the topic, the field will be eventually mature enough for the next step of scholarly research: quantitative methods using a large number of cases. This is in fact what has happened in other areas of gender studies. For example, from the 1970s onwards, 'women and politics' analyses were being developed as researchers analysed single or a small number of cases. It was only in the first decade of the twenty-first century when enough knowledge on single or very few cases was accumulated for gender scholars to study issues with quantitative methods and using a large number of cases (Valiente, 2018).

Concerning the interrogation of the difference between activism and philanthropy, it is not a principal object of study in the literature on social movements. But this difference is crucial to understand women (and men) athletes' efforts to produce social change, since, as stated before, charity work by athletes is generally praised while activism is highly contested (Kaufman, 2008). Furthermore, it is often the case that athletes of both sexes establish charity foundations once their athletic careers end, and some athletes also do so during their sporting trajectories. For example, Cathy Freeman, a former sprinter, is an Indigenous woman from Australia who was Olympic gold medallist (400 metres, Sydney 2000) and Olympic silver medallist (400 metres, Atlanta 1996) (Hargreaves, 2000). After her retirement from athletics, in 2007, she founded the Cathy Freeman Foundation to support education of Aboriginal children in her country (Cathy Freeman Foundation, n.d.). This and other cases suggest that rather than two opposites, activism and charity work are both examples of athletes' and former athletes' efforts to improve the world in which they live. The analysis of athletes' activism and charity work would be a contribution not only to the knowledge on sporting women's activism but also to the broader field of social movement studies.

Finally, as the references by this chapter make clear, research on elite women athlete activists covers mainly English-speaking countries. We know virtually nothing about the topic for other Western countries. I close this chapter exhorting scholars to analyse that part of the world.

Notes

1 In this chapter, the terms 'soccer' and 'football' are used synonymously to name the same sport. The former is used when referring to the United States and the latter to all other countries.
2 To avoid repetitions, women (or female) elite athletes are also called world-class (or high-profile, or top-ranked) athletes, or simply athletes.

References

Ahmad, N., & Thorpe, H. (2020). Muslim sportswomen as digital space invaders: Hashtag politics and everyday visibilities. *Communication & Sport*, 8(4–5), 668–691. https://doi.org/10.1177/2167479519898447

Antunovic, D., & Hardin, M. (2012). Activism in women's sports blogs: Fandom and feminist potential. *International Journal of Sport Communication*, 5(3), 305–322. https://doi.org/10.1123/ijsc.5.3.305

Bernstein, A. (2002). Is it time for a victory lap?: Changes in the media coverage of women in sport. *International Review for the Sociology of Sport*, 37(3–4), 415–428. https://doi.org/10.1177/101269020203700301

Burton, L. J., & Leberman, S. (Eds) (2017). *Women in sport leadership: Research and practice for change*. Abingdon: Routledge.

Cahn, S. K. (2015). *Coming on strong: Gender and sexuality in women's sport* (2nd ed.). University of Illinois Press.

Canadian Women & Sport. (n.d.). Our story. Retrieved 2 July 2021, from www.caaws.ca

Cathy Freeman Foundation. (n.d.). About us. Retrieved 16 July 2021, from www.cathyfreemanfoundation.org.au

Comeau, G. S., & Church, A. G. (2010). A comparative analysis of women's sport advocacy groups in Canada and the United States. *Journal of Sport and Social Issues*, 34(4), 457–474. https://doi.org/10.1177/0193723510387053

Consejo Superior de Deportes. (2014–2020). *Annual reports 2013–2019*. Retrieved from www.csd.gob.es

Cooky, C. (2018). Women, sports, and activism. In C. Cooky & M. A. Messner (Eds), *No slam dunk: Gender, sport, and the unevenness of social change* (pp. 70–90). Rutgers University Press.

Cooky, C., & Antunovic, D. (2020). "This isn't just about us": Articulations of feminism in media narratives of athlete activism. *Communication & Sport*, 8(4–5), 692–711. https://doi.org/10.1177/2167479519896360

Cooky, C., & Dworkin, S. L. (2018). Policing the boundaries of sex: A critical examination of gender verification and the Caster Semenya controversy. In C. Cooky & M. A. Messner (Eds), *No slam dunk: Gender, sport, and the unevenness of social change* (pp. 37–53). Rutgers University Press.

Cooky, C., Messner, M. A., & Musto, M. (2015). "It's dude time!" A quarter century of excluding women's sports in televised news and highlight shows. *Communication & Sport*, 3(3), 261–287. https://doi.org/10.1177/2167479515588761

della Porta, D., & Diani, M. (2020). *Social movements: An introduction* (3rd ed.). Wiley Blackwell.

Elling, A., Hovden, J., & Knoppers, A. (Eds). (2019). *Gender diversity in European sport governance*. Routledge.

Ferree, M. M., & Mueller, C. M. (2004). Feminism and the women's movement: A global perspective. In D. A. Snow, S. A. Soule, & H. Kriesi (Eds), *The Blackwell companion to social movements* (pp. 576–607). Blackwell.

Fundación Princesa de Asturias. (n.d.). Hassiba Boulmerka, Premio Príncipe de Asturias de los Deportes 1995 [Hassiba Boulmerka, 1995 Princess of Asturias Sports Prize]. Retrieved July 16, 2021, from http://www.fpa.es/

Gallagher, H. F., Wright, C., & Kassing, J. W. (2022). "I'm not going to the f***ing White House": Fan discourse about Megan Rapinoe during the 2019 FIFA Women's World Cup. In R. Magrath (Ed.), *Athlete activism: Contemporary perspectives* (pp. 144–154). Routledge.

Hall, M. A. (1995). Women and sport: From liberal activism to radical cultural struggle. In S. Burt & L. Code (Eds), *Changing methods: Feminists transforming practice* (pp. 265–299). Broadview Press.

Hall, M. A. (1997). Feminist activism in sport: A comparative study of women's sport advocacy organizations. In A. Tomlinson (Ed.), *Gender, sport and leisure: Continuities and challenges* (pp. 217–250). Meyer & Meyers.

Hall, M. A. (2016). *The girl and the game: A history of women's sport in Canada* (2nd ed.). University of Toronto Press.

Hargreaves, J. (1994). *Sporting females: Critical issues in the history and sociology of women's sports*. Routledge.

Hargreaves, J. (1999). The "women's international sports movement": Local-global strategies and empowerment. *Women's Studies International Forum*, 22(5), 461–471. https://doi.org/10.1016/S0277-5395(99)00057-6

Hargreaves, J. (2000). *Heroines of sport: The politics of difference and identity*. Routledge.

International Group on Women and Sport. (2014). *Brighton plus Helsinki 2014 Declaration on Women and Sport*. Retrieved from https://iwgwomenandsport.org/wp-content/uploads/2019/03/Brighton-plus-Helsinki-2014-Declaration-on-Women-and-Sport.pdf

International Olympic Committee. (2021). *Factsheet: Women in the Olympic Movement, 09 December 2021*. Retrieved December 31, 2021, from https://stillmed.olympics.com/media/Documents/Olympic-Movement/Factsheets/Women-in-the-Olympic-Movement.pdf

Kaufman, P. (2008). Boos, bans, and other backlash: The consequences of being an activist athlete. *Humanity & Society*, 32(3), 215–237. https://doi.org/10.1177/016059760803200302

Kitching, N., Bowes, A., & MacLaren, M. (2022). Online activism and athlete advocacy in professional women's golf: Risk or reward? In R. Magrath (Ed.), *Athlete activism: Contemporary perspectives* (pp. 181–192). Routledge.

Lenskyj, H. J. (2013). *Gender politics and the Olympic industry*. Palgrave Macmillan.

Matthews, J. J. K. (2018). Tensions and future directions for the women and sport movement. In L. Mansfield, J. Caudwell, B. Wheaton, & B. Watson (Eds), *The Palgrave handbook of feminism and sport, leisure and physical education* (pp. 181–199). Palgrave Macmillan.

Matthews, J. J. K. (2021). The Brighton Conference on women and sport. *Sport in History*, 41(1), 98–130. https://doi.org/10.1080/17460263.2020.1730943

Paxton, P., Hughes, M. M., & Barnes, T. D. (2021). *Women, politics, and power: A global perspective* (4th ed.). Rowman & Littlefield.

Piscopo, J. (2015). States as gender equality activists: The evolution of quota laws in Latin America. *Latin American Politics and Society*, 57(3), 27–49. https://doi.org/10.1111/j.1548-2456.2015.00278.x

Schmidt, S. H., Frederick, E. L., Pegoraro, A., & Spencer, T. C. (2019). An analysis of Colin Kaepernick, Megan Rapinoe, and the National Anthem Protest. *Communication & Sport*, 7(5), 653–677. https://doi.org/10.1177/2167479518793625

Schultz, J. (2021). Good enough? The "wicked" use of testosterone for defining femaleness in women's sport. *Sport in Society*, 24(4), 607–627. https://doi.org/10.1080/17430437.2019.1703684

Snow, D. A., Soule, S. A., Kriesi, H., & McCammon, H. (Eds). (2019). *The Wiley Blackwell companion to social movements*. John Wiley & Sons.

Steidinger, J. (2020). *Stand up and shout out: Women's fight for equal pay, equal rights, and equal opportunities in sport*. Rowman & Littlefield.

Tredway, K. (2019). The original 9: The social movement that created women's professional tennis, 1968-73. In R. J. Lake (Ed.), *Routledge handbook of tennis: History, culture and politics* (pp. 411–421). Routledge.

Tredway, K. (2020). *Social activism in women's tennis: Generations of politics and cultural change*. Routledge.

Valiente, C. (2017). Male allies of women's movements: Women's organizing within the Catholic Church in Franco's Spain. *Women's Studies International Forum*, 62, 43–51. https://doi.org/10.1016/j.wsif.2017.03.004

Valiente, C. (2018). Gender and political sociology. In W. Outhwaite, & S. P. Turner (Eds), *The Sage handbook of political sociology* (Vol. 1, pp. 143–156). Sage.

Valiente, C. (2019). Sport and social movements: Lilí Álvarez in Franco's Spain. *International Review for the Sociology of Sport*, 54(5), 622–646. https://doi.org/10.1177/1012690217733679

Valiente, C. (2020a). Feminist mobilizations within organized religions in Western Europe. In C. Flesher Fominaya, & R. A. Feenstra (Eds), *Routledge handbook of contemporary European social movements* (pp. 185–195). Routledge.

Valiente, C. (2020b). Women pioneers in the history of sport: The case of Lilí Álvarez in Franco's Spain. *International Journal of the History of Sport*, 37(1–2), 75–93. https://doi.org/10.1080/09523367.2020.1722645

Valiente, C. (2021). The impact of gender quotas in sport management: The case of Spain. *Sport in Society*, 25(5), 1017–1034. https://doi.org/10.1080/17430437.2020.1819244

Valiente, C. (2022). Elite athlete activism for gender equality in sport: Women's football in Spain. In R. Magrath (Ed.), *Athlete activism: Contemporary perspectives* (pp. 109–119). Routledge.

Wheaton, B., Mansfield, L., Caudwell, J., & Watson, R. (2020). Caster Semenya: The surveillance of sportswomen's bodies, feminism and transdisciplinary research. In C. A. Taylor, C. Hughes, & J. B. Ulmer (Eds), *Transdisciplinary feminist research: Innovations in theory, method and practice* (pp. 116–123). Routledge.

Women's Sports Foundation. (n.d.). Who we are. Retrieved July 29, 2021, from www.womenssportsfoundation.org/who-we-are/

Zafra, M., Villaescusa, L., Alonso, A., Iguacel, J. A., Sevillano, L., & Clemente, Y. (2021, July 23). De Tokio 1964 a Tokio 2020: Misma sede, distinta competición [From Tokyo 1964 to Tokyo 2020: Same place, different competition]. *El País*.

6
SPORT, MASCULINITIES, AND HOMOSEXUALITIES

Why inclusive masculinity theory can be considered dangerous for queer sportspeople

Richard Pringle

The performance of genders and sexualities, as entangled discursive/material constructions, are never static but undergo periods of change in differing directions, contexts, time periods and within individuals. In the current era, within sporting contexts in Western liberal democracies, we *appear* to be in the midst of a progressive epoch with respect to how sporting masculinities and femininities are performed (McCormack & Anderson, 2014; Toffoletti & Palmer, 2019). In recent decades, as an example, there have been considerable transformations in the acceptance and celebration of female athleticism (Cooky & Messner, 2018). These transformations are reflected in the increased female participation rates in an increasingly diverse range of sports.

These changes, although seemingly dramatic, have eventuated through the hard-fought action of feminist activists over many decades. Although positive changes have occurred, gender inequities in sport still remain with significant differences, for example, in professional salaries, sport withdrawal rates, and inequitable media coverage (e.g. Mansfield, Caudwell, Wheaton, & Watson, 2018; Toffoletti & Palmer, 2019). Moreover, recent research reveals that female sport participants can face harassment in clubs, trivialisation of performances, sexualisation in media representations and be subject to violence, racial abuse and homophobic prejudice in a manner that subjugates, harms, limits sport participation and constrains the performance of femininities in a relatively narrow manner (e.g. Ohlert, Seidler, Rau, Rulofs, & Allroggen, 2018; Pavlidis, 2018; Spaaij, Knoppers, & Jeanes, 2020). These existing issues highlight that it is still not time for a victory lap of feminist celebration (Bernstein, 2002). Although we may welcome the broadly 'progressive' shift in female sport, there is still a need for on-going feminist activism and advocacy as "gender relations remain a powerful and obdurate force in all societies and cultures" (Mansfield, et al., 2018, p. 5).

There is also evidence to suggest that a progressive shift in the performance of sporting masculinities is occurring. This evidence suggests that many young straight men are performing a more respectful or *inclusive* form of masculinity that rejects violence and bullying while also being pro-feminist and gay friendly (McCormack & Anderson, 2014). Scholars have long recognised that homonegativism[1] is a "central organizing principle for our cultural definition of manhood" (Kimmel, 2010, p. 277). The proponents of inclusive masculinity theory (IMT) have, correspondingly, suggested that the apparent softening in contemporary masculinities is tied to a progressive shift in the acceptance of diverse sexualities; of which there is accumulating evidence.

The media periodically reports, for example, on the 'coming out' of elite athletes such as Josh Cavallo (football), Carl Nassib (NFL) or Megan Rapinoe (football) and often with reports of how the coming out process made the athlete a better and more satisfied person (Manasan, 2021). The increased acceptance of diverse sexualities is also reflected in various statistical claims, such as the recent headline that proclaimed: "At least 186 out LGBTQ athletes at the Tokyo Summer Olympics, by far a record: there were more out LGBTQ athletes in Tokyo than all the previous Summer Olympics combined" (Outsports, 2021). Or the assertion that since 2019 an additional six countries have legalised same-sex marriage which currently brings the total number of countries to 31. Caudwell (2015) reflects: "In many ways, it is easy to explain the recent shifts in the UK's media and statutory response to same-sex sexuality through notions of progress, equality and perhaps affect" (p. 244). Caudwell counters, however, by arguing that the narrative of apparent progress and equality is problematic as it acts to conceal a rife of serious problems associated with homonegativism. She states that although there is increased visibility of some LGBTIQ+ sexualities, messy or non-normative sexualities still "do not feature positively within public celebrations of sexuality and sport" (p. 244).

More pointedly, the adverse health and social impacts of homonegativism are still of concern in the current period. Indeed, little has changed from Eve Sedgwick's (1993) matter-of-fact observation from nearly 30 years ago:

> I think everyone who does gay and lesbian studies is haunted by the suicides of adolescents. To us, the hard statistics come easily: that queer teenagers are two to three times likelier to attempt suicide, and to accomplish it, than others; that up to 30 percent of teen suicides are likely to be gay or lesbian; that a third of lesbian and gay teenagers say they have attempted suicide; that minority queer adolescents are at even more extreme risk … The knowledge is indelible, but not astonishing to anyone with a reason to be attuned to the profligate way this culture has of denying and despoiling queer energies and lives.
>
> (p. 1)

Recent evidence from various sources reveal that concern about LGBTIQ+ self-harm is still warranted. For example a large-scale American study by Painter, Scannapieco, Blau, Andre, and Kohn (2018) involving 3208 LGBTIQ+ and non- LGBTIQ+ youth concluded that: "This study represents a national picture of LGBTQ mental health status which should set off alarms for all social service providers" (p. 232). Of great concern was the finding that "LGBTQ youth were 3 times more likely to have self-harmed or attempted suicide" (p. 232) in comparison to non- LGBTIQ+ youth, and, most importantly, that "these mental health disparities are frequently explained by LGBTQ-specific experiences" (p. 224). The evidence that rates of self-harm and suicide have not changed in over three decades and that these rates can be "explained" by life experiences connected to issues related to LGBTIQ+ appears to stand in clear opposition to the simplistic narrative of 'progress' towards acceptance of homosexualities. There is even evidence of a regressive shift with reports that hate crimes against queer people have increased in recent years in the UK (Chao-Fong, 2021).

Within this chapter I expand on Caudwell's argument to suggest that the narrative of progress towards acceptance of diverse sexualities is not only too simplistic but can also be *dangerous* as it detracts from the difficult work of challenging aspects of homonegativism. I focus my attention on Anderson's (2009) theory known as IMT and the associated empirical work examining sexualities and sporting contexts. I focus on this research for three reasons: (i) this work has gained significant academic attention in the last decade; (ii) the findings and conclusions derived from IMT reinforce a narrative that homonegativism is no longer a serious social concern (despite the very clear set of mental health disparities between people who identify as queer or straight), and (iii) these findings stand in stark opposition to sexualities research as underpinning by virtually any other theoretical perspective. IMT researchers, for example, overwhelmingly find decreasing or near non-existent rates of homonegativism in various sport settings. In contrast:

> researchers informed by alternative theoretical lenses like queer theory (Sykes, 2011), binary theorising (Phipps, 2021), positivism (Denison & Kitchen, 2015; Denison et al., 2021), new materialism (Landi, 2019) and sociological perspectives (De Boise, 2015; Storr et al., 2021) continue to identify concerns related to LGBT+ discrimination.
> (Storr, Jeanes, Rossi, & lisahunter, 2022, p. 93)

Moreover, a recent systematic review of homonegativity and sport concluded that the "results ultimately highlight the need for greater awareness of issues related to sexuality and gender stereotypes within sporting contexts, particularly those that involve male athletes, which seem to adhere strongly to the prescriptions of patriarchy and hegemonic masculinity" (Rollè, Cazzini, Santoniccolo, & Trombetta, 2021. p. 21).

In drawing from Deleuze and Guattari's (1988) interest in wanting to know what something 'does', as opposed to 'is', in this chapter I examine the question what does IMT 'do' in specific relation to issues of social justice as concerned with sexualities? Deleuze and Guattari were interested to understand how objects and ideas influence each other and what these interactions *do* or *produce*. Their underpinning philosophy was not to reveal what is already known but to create new ways of thinking and feeling that they hoped would spur critical reflection and create potential change. In a similar light, I am not interested in examining the theoretical intricacies or shortcomings of IMT (e.g. see De Boise, 2015; O'Neill, 2015), but I am interested in how IMT influences research directions, research interpretations, understandings of homosexualities, political actions and, of course, the impact of homonegativism on queer people.

My understanding of social justice draws from Foucault's (1987) concern to minimise harmful relations of power. Foucault did not believe that humans can escape the workings of power – as relations of power exist between all humans – or that power is inherently bad or good. Yet he was concerned about power relations that work to unfairly control and harm individuals. Foucault states:

> I do not think that a society can exist without power relations, if by that one means the strategies by which individuals try to direct and control the conduct of others. The problem, then, is not to try to dissolve them in the utopia of completely transparent communication but to acquire the rules of law, the management techniques, and also the morality, the ethos, the practice of the self, that will allow us to play these games of power with as little domination as possible.
> (1987, p. 298)

In this chapter, given the topic of examination, I connect the pursuit of social justice with concern to minimise harmful relations of power that restrict and damage the lives of queer people. I shape this chapter in response to one prime question: how does research underpinned by IMT shape the workings of social justice as concerned with homonegativism? I acknowledge that this question cannot be answered definitively, yet I examine this question, and acknowledge my biases, to encourage greater critical thinking about the influence of IMT.

What is IMT and how does it shape researchers' conclusions?

Denzin (2018) suggests that within the 'eight moment' of qualitative research that the "criteria for evaluating critical qualitative work are moral and ethical" (p. 17). This turn to ethics is overtly political. Denzin (2018) explains:

> The moral ethnographer-as-performer takes sides, working always on the side of those who seek a genuine grassroots democracy. Accordingly, this ethics asks that interpretive work provide the foundations for social criticism, and social action. These texts represent calls to action.
>
> (p. 19)

This moral turn in qualitative research underpins my concern for examining research as underpinned by IMT: specifically, the knowledge this research produces and the social actions that stem from this knowledge. In the first place, I am interested in how inclusive masculinity theory shapes the researcher's interpretations. It is my critical contention that the underpinning tenets of IMT closely shape the conclusions drawn in a somewhat circular fashion.

To develop this argument, I discuss my earlier concerns with the concept of hegemonic masculinity: I do this to develop the argument that the prime theoretical weaknesses of inclusive masculinity mirror the theoretical weaknesses of hegemonic masculinity. That is, that IMT is a quasi-structuralist model that rests on a generalised understanding of a pre-existing gender/sexuality 'order' and that this order is assumed to *determine* gender performances and relationships. More importantly, that this pre-existing understanding of the gender/sexuality order overwhelmingly mirrors the conclusions drawn by IMT researchers. But first I retrace my concerns with the concept of hegemonic masculinity.

My doctoral research examined the place of rugby union in shaping men's understandings of masculinities in Aotearoa New Zealand (Pringle, 2003). My initial concern for undertaking this research was shaped by my beliefs that rugby was an inescapable social force for males that encouraged problematic ways of performing masculinity. I specifically viewed rugby as an influential institution that promoted sexism, homophobia, and dangerous expressions of masculinity. My thinking had been shaped in part by earlier sporting research that had drawn on the concept of hegemonic masculinity (e.g. Bryson, 1990; Messner & Sabo, 1994; White & Young, 1997). Given the dominance of this theory, it was not surprising that I initially worked under its guise.

Yet through critically engaging with this theory – or what Hall (1996) called "wrestling with the angels" – I found that this theory could not explain the complexities and contradictions of my research participants' lived experiences. My research participants were telling me on the one hand, how they loved the bruising nature of rugby, and knocking others to the ground, how being good at rugby gave them manly status, how excessive drinking with the boys could be boisterous fun, and how they would, at times, talk about women or homosexuals in a disparaging manner (see Pringle, 2003). In other words, their values and actions seemed to match the recognised traits of hegemonic masculinity. On the other hand, however, they would broadly talk with concern about injuries, respect for their opposition, the need to look after their bodies, their dislike of drinking too much, their support of liberal feminist views, and their desire to be good partners and fathers. They further expressed that it was through their diverse rugby experiences that they also questioned and, at times, rejected particular understandings of masculinity. Through suffering significant injuries in rugby, as an example, many of my interviewees stated that they questioned the expectation that men should tolerate pain stoically (Pringle & Markula, 2005). It became apparent that the concept of hegemonic masculinity could not represent the complexities and contradictions of my participants' social relationships, understandings of social issues, and lived rugby experiences.

Other researchers were also raising concerns with the workings of hegemony theory. Tomlinson (1998) raised issue with how the theory tended to represent the workings of power within sport as an "all-or-nothing model" (p. 237); that is, sport was either portrayed as supporting *or* resisting hegemonic masculinity. Miller (1998) similarly raised issue with how the theory had difficulty explaining "the times when men are not being men, when their activities might be understood as discontinuous, conflicted, and ordinary, rather than interconnected, functional, and dominant" (p. 433). Berggren (2014) aptly noted that the prime contradiction revolves around 'masculinity' as an overarching structure that broadly shaped masculinities and the realities – and stark differences – of men's messy lived experiences. Donaldson (1993) simply concluded that that theory is "as slippery and difficult as the idea of masculinity itself" (p. 644).

I suggest that these slippery problems related to the prime *tenets* of hegemonic masculinity: that is, the assumption that the gender order is *structured* in a particular manner. And that this prime understanding of an assumed gender order – when combined with the notion that the ruling classes shape the production of gender ideologies – results in an inevitable and circular conclusion: that is, that the conclusion affirms the ontological assumptions that underpin hegemonic masculinity.

Given that performances of genders and sexualities are never static and that significant changes to the gender/sexuality 'orders' have taken place in the last three decades, it is now easier to see that the concept of hegemonic masculinity appears dated or "too modernist, structuralist and deterministic" (Waling, 2019, p. 93) and, relatedly, limited for understanding the complexities and contradictions of lived masculinities. Yet, it was through my early experience of viewing rugby union through a hegemonic masculinity lens that I recognised the dangers of research that is too theoretically driven. In the following, I raise speculative concern that similar problems exist with research that draws on IMT.

Inclusive masculinity theory: Some theoretical concerns

Eric Anderson's theorising on inclusive masculinity was first introduced in detail in his 2009 text *Inclusive masculinity: the changing nature of masculinities*. His theory was developed in response to qualitative research findings within male sport settings that revealed that social dynamics were "not predicated on homophobia, stoicism or a rejection of the feminine" (Anderson & McCormack, 2018, p. 547). Moreover, he suggested that these young men – typically university educated – had gay friends, rejected violence and bullying, and accepted various feminine artefacts or performances. Anderson provided welcome attention to the changing nature of masculinities and the notion that masculinities are not inherently problematic. Moreover, Anderson and McCormack suggested that "hegemonic masculinity could not account for the social dynamics of these male peer groups" (p. 547). As a counter to the tenets of hegemonic masculinity, Anderson (2009) developed the notion of inclusive masculinity.

IMT draws reductively on the notion that homophobia is the "most important policing agent of masculinity" (Anderson, 2009, p. 8) yet overlooks that there are multiple axes of power that shape performances and understandings of masculinity in substantial ways. For example, the theory "actively rejects engagement with feminist methodology and pedagogy, and ignores men's interactions with women" (Waling, 2019, p. 94). Yet, feminist thinking is an omnipresent influence within men's lives and most straight or gay men have close connections with women and girls that shape their performances of masculinities. In contrast, IMT directs research attention to focus primarily on men's relationships in homosocial contexts and with a focus on homosexuality. This narrow focus is underpinned by the prime belief that within homophobic societies, men fear being 'homosexualised' or being identified as homosexual. Anderson calls this fear "homohysteria" (p. 8). Yet very little evidence is provided to substantiate the claim that straight men actually *fear* being identified as homosexual or that this might be a significant problem for many cis-gendered men.[2]

Anderson (2009) further asserts that the conditions that once produced homohysteria have decreased so that males no longer fear being homosexualised and, relatedly, the hegemonic form of masculinity is no longer culturally dominant. These developments have allegedly allowed the growth of an oppositional form of masculinity called *inclusive masculinity*, which celebrates or at least accepts the principles of feminism and gay rights. Anderson explains further that given the existence of "two oppositional masculinities, each with equal influence, co-existing within one culture" (p. 93) that the concept of hegemonic masculinity is no longer an appropriate tool for analysing contemporary masculinities. Yet Anderson and McCormack (2018) do not outrightly reject the concept of hegemonic masculinity or its broad theoretical workings, as they contend:

> that in homohysteric cultures, men's behaviours are severely restricted, and archetypes of masculinity are stratified, hierarchically, with one hegemonic form of masculinity being culturally exalted – just as Connell (1995) described happening in the 1980s and early 1990s ... As such, IMT values Connell's theorizing regarding the multiplicity of masculinities and their social organisation in homohysteric cultures ...
> (Anderson & McCormack, 2018, p. 548)

This is a key point, as proponents of IMT may assert that there is no longer a dominant or hegemonic form of masculinity, yet the theory fundamentally draws on a framework of thinking that is similar to hegemonic masculinity: IMT, relatedly, suffers some of the same theoretical criticisms. That is, the theory can be understood as quasi-structuralist and deterministic: as men's performances are primarily believed to be shaped or determined in relation to broader social *structures* concerned with the acceptance of rejection of diverse sexualities. To work within this quasi-structuralist theory, one needs to accept that homonegativism is primarily a problem of the past. It is *my contention*, that this ontological belief shapes the conclusion drawn by IMT researchers.

Inclusive masculinity theory: Some empirical concerns

In this section I draw on IMT research that has examined sportsmen's close/intimate contact with other male athletes to raise concern with the respective conclusions. Researchers who draw from IMT paint a picture that homonegativism has declined to such a point that sportsmen routinely kiss and cuddle each other (Anderson, Ripley, & McCormack, 2019), sleep/spoon each other (Anderson & McCormack, 2015), can even gain status from being identified as homosexual (McCormack, 2012), and can indulge in sexual activity with other males with little concern about stigmatisation (Scoats, Joseph, & Anderson, 2018). Large scale survey evidence and in-depth interviews from IMT researchers in the US, for example, suggest that 40 per cent of men kiss their male friends on the cheeks and 10 per cent lip kiss (Anderson et al., 2019). Anderson and McCormack's (2015) in-depth interview study with 40 student–athletes at a British university similarly found an expansion of accepted masculine behaviours:

> In addition to sharing a bed with friends and acquaintances, our participants are able to engage in prolonged acts of homosocial tactility – namely cuddling and spooning – while simultaneously professing love for their friends ... it is our contention that labelling these behaviours as queer or transgressive is problematic as they have become *normative* among British youth.
>
> (p. 223)

While sleeping or spooning with male friends (in a non-sexual manner), the research participants in Anderson and McCormack's (2015) study suggested that they were not concerned about getting an erection. One participant stated: "I've woken up with one before. We all have. If we're fully awake, then we'll banter about it", he said. "All the boys piss themselves, maybe saying something 'happy to see me' or whatever. We love it" (p. 223). The broad picture painted by this research is that homophobia has rapidly declined to such an extent that men can now participate in a range of close contact/intimate activities with other males with little concern. Scoats et al. (2018) concluded:

> Similar to other research showing that men are able to engage in what were once stigmatized sexual or semi-sexual behaviours ... these men were able to have bromances, view gay porn, engage in semi-sexual activity with other men, and consent to hypothetical (and sometimes actual) MMF threesomes; all without challenge to their straight identities.
>
> (p. 44)

Anderson and McCormack conclude that this expansion of masculine performances "is best explained by changing levels of homohysteria, as described by inclusive masculinity theory" (2015, p. 224). In other words, these broad findings are used to suggest that IMT should not be considered as simply a *theory* but as evidential fact. They conclude by reciting the fundamental tenets of IMT:

> In the homohysteric 1980s and 1990s, cuddling and other forms of homosocial tactility were socially coded as "gay" and therefore avoided. But as homohysteria began to decline, men were able to associate themselves with behaviours traditionally coded as feminine ... Significantly, as men engaged in restricted forms of homosocial tactility, the association with homosexuality was further eroded.
>
> (Anderson & McCormack, 2015, p. 224)

A question of importance, however, is to what extent has broad attitudes towards homonegativism changed. In my own research with Erik Denison (Pringle & Denison, 2021), we have sought to understand sportsmen's views on homosexuality and close intimacy with other sportsmen. We conducted surveys with 139 British rugby players and conducted focus group interviews with players from eight British clubs. Our results support some of the findings from the IMT researchers but with some very significant differences. Our results illustrate that these male rugby players did, at times, kiss their male teammates and they would also tell their mates that they love them. Yet these kisses, hugs, and expressions of love typically occurred after they had been drinking alcohol, and it was strictly performed without any hint of romance or sexual interest: as the following transcripts reveal:

Louis:	Yeah, when you're drunk, you kind of do it but not in like a … You don't do it regularly, you just kind of go when you're drunk "oh I love you mate", and you give them a big kiss.
Kevin:	Yeah.
Thomas:	Banter at uni is like "oh I love you, but yeah we're so straight" to kiss each other like that.
Louis:	Yeah. It's more at night when you're absolutely hammered. If you're like paralytically drunk at uni.
Richard Pringle:	Okay, the context, you might have a kiss, but usually you're drunk – It's not a romantic thing? It's not, "come on baby!"
Kevin:	No, no, no.
Louie:	It's more to show people like "yeah we're such good mates we're kissing".
Richard Pringle:	Okay. So, it's done in a heterosexual way? Okay. If it was done in a homosexual way, how would that be received?
Louie:	What, if someone like kissed me?
Richard Pringle:	Yeah, kissed you on the lips and said "I actually …"
Thomas:	I'd politely decline.
Louie:	I'd be like, "what the fuck". I might punch you in the face.
Thomas:	You'd just be a bit confused, like "mate I'm not interested in that".

This transcript excerpt from a focus group reveals that within a particular context – in drunken celebration mode – these men could express affection for each other via kisses and hugs. Yet, these kisses could only be performed if there was no hint of homosexual attraction. As Thomas expressed: "Oh I love you, but yeah we're so straight". Louie, one of the participants, even suggested that he might punch a teammate if he expressed homosexual desire for him. Hence, we concluded that although there appears to be increased ability for men to hug or kiss each other, these changes did not necessarily reflect a significant erosion of homonegativism. Indeed, the talk of violence towards a player who expressed same-sex attraction is highly homonegative and of concern.

Ralph and Roberts' (2020) investigation of homosocial intimacy among young Australian men drew similar conclusions to Pringle and Denison (2021), they concluded:

> While our findings confirm the prevalence of homosocial kissing … such behaviours was not described as an authentic display of platonic affection and was still subjected to homohysteric policing … Behaviours beyond hugging were described as socially

acceptable only if thought a joke, a dare, a celebratory gesture, a gesture of support, or for the attracting of women's attention – that is, *anything* but genuine displays of affection.

(p. 16)

Ralph and Roberts (2020) conclude that increased acceptance of kissing or hugging between men does not necessarily provide "evidence of declining homohysteria" (p. 16). Indeed, they asserted that "homosocial intimacy remains governed by homohysteric sentiment" (p. 16). This conclusion is in direct opposition to those drawn by the IMT theorists (e.g. Anderson & McCormack, 2015; Anderson, et al., 2019; McCormack, 2012; Scoats et al., 2018) and calls into question the alleged decline in homonegativism.

A similar case of an oppositional conclusion relates to Cleland's (2019) research on "Britain's first openly gay football referee: The story of Ryan Atkin" (p. 125). Cleland, draws from IMT, to detail how Ryan Atkin's 'coming out' story was a positive experience that provides "empirical evidence of decreasing levels of homophobia in the culture of football" (p. 140). He adds: "In the case of Atkin, the evidence available in his story so far is that in the culture of refereeing in men's football, various forms of masculinity and sexuality retain *equal* cultural value among a number of key stakeholders" (p. 140; italics added for emphasis). In other words, Cleland is drawing from one of the key tenets of IMT to suggest that there is no longer a dominant or hegemonic form of masculinity and diverse sexualities are equally accepted. He then draws on Anderson's (2009) influential text to assert "behaviors that once would have led to homosexual suspicion and stigmatization no longer pose a significant threat to heterosexual identity" (p. 141). Cleland concludes by making the bold and generalised statement alleging that "the publication of articles in support of LGBT men and women involved in sport like those focused on Ryan Atkin means that homophobia continues to be stigmatized and challenged rather than their sexuality" (p. 141). Hence, he suggests that the current climate towards homonegativism has completely inverted.

In sharp contrast, however, a recent news article quotes Atkins on the problems of homophobic abuse in UK football. Atkins' words are in direct opposition to what Cleland has concluded: "It (homonegativism) has to be stamped out and addressed … There is still a lot of work to be done" (BBC sport, 2019). He added:

It can sometimes be slightly disheartening to think that there are other people who are LGBT who don't feel that it's the right time for them or have the confidence to come out. I often speak to people who are not out in sport, and ask them, 'What are your fears?' You get a mixture of responses about why they wouldn't choose or won't come out. I'm just hopeful that, as time progress, and especially within football, the culture is slowly changing.

(BBC Sport, 2019: https://www.bbc.com/sport/football/50489826)

Atkins accordingly expressed his dismay that homonegative abuse was a still a problem in football, that LGBTIQ+ people feared coming out and that the culture was only "slowly changing".

A perusal of various newspaper articles on gay referees further reveal that homophobia is still of major concern. A *Belfast Telegraph* headline reads: "NI's first openly gay football referee Ryan Hanna: 'I was victim of vile homophobic slurs … and the Irish FA did nothing about it'" (McNeilly, 2021). Whereas, a headline from *The Guardian* reads: "Gay referee in Spain receives death threats after return to football: Jesús Tomillero, who quit in May but later reversed decision, says he is 'really, really scared' but will carry on refereeing" (Jones, 2016). Tomillero was scared as he had received threats via social media, that stated: "You son of a bitch. You messed with the club. We'll kill you with AIDS, you faggot", and "Not long left to live, faggot". Another news headline similarly talks of homophobic death threats to a gay referee: "I've received homophobic abuse and death threats, reveals referee James Child" (Laybourne, 2021). Child, a professional rugby league referee, stated: "I do receive my fair share of abuse and had a couple of death threats over the last few years which were referred to the police" (Laybourne, 2021). Another *Guardian* (2015) headline reads: "NBA referee Bill Kennedy comes out as gay after Rajon Rondo confrontation". The article reveals that Kennedy was the target of a homophobic slur from NBA player Rondo and he came out to illustrate that "you must allow no one to make you feel ashamed of who you are".

The evidence I have discussed in relation to sportsmen's intimacies/kissing and homonegativism/referees, counters the optimistic conclusions drawn by IMT researchers and suggests, at the least, that there is a need for caution in reaching any broad conclusion about the alleged decreases in homonegativism. Yet the 'reality' of greatest concern is the overwhelming epidemiological data related to the higher suicide and self-harm rates amongst queer people. A recent meta-analysis of 44 studies, for example, found "a clear link between various types of minority stressors and suicidal ideation and suicide attempts among LGBT adolescents and young adults" (de Lange, Baams, van Bergen, Bos, & Bosker, 2022). This recent epidemiological evidence calls out for the problems of homonegativism to be actively challenged. The following section, however, reveals that research underpinned by IMT encourages a belief that homonegativism is no longer of prime social concern.

What does IMT research do for the political promotion of queer people?

The research stemming from IMT paints an overly optimistic *interpretation* of the apparent changes in acceptance of diverse sexualities to the detriment of concern about the impact of homonegativism. A quick perusal of academic article titles, from IMT researchers, provide the distinct impression that concern or fear of homosexuality is fading and fading fast:

"On the doorstep of equality: Attitudes towards gay athletes among academy level footballers" (Magrath, Anderson, & Roberts, 2015);
"The declining significance of homophobia" (McCormack, 2012);
"It's just not acceptable anymore: The erosion of homophobia and the softening of masculinity at an English sixth form" (McCormack & Anderson, 2010);
"Relaxing the straight male anus: Decreasing homohysteria around anal eroticism" (Branfman, Stiritz, & Anderson, 2018);
"Changing the Game: Sport and a Cultural Shift away from Homohysteria" (Magrath, Anderson, & Bullingham, 2014)
"'I don't mind watching him cum': Heterosexual men, threesomes, and the erosion of the one-time rule of homosexuality" (Scoats, et al., 2018).

My concern with the representational image from IMT researchers is that homonegativism is no longer of serious social concern as we are allegedly on the 'doorsteps of equality' as it is 'not acceptable anymore'. Although the acceptance of diverse sexualities has increased, it is clear that the adverse impact of homonegativism is not an all or nothing reaction. That is, a gay sportsman could be aware that the majority of his team, school class or work colleagues may be more accepting of diverse sexualities, yet he/they may also be aware that a smaller percentage of people still view homosexuality as unnatural, perverse, abhorrent, or immoral and that the revelation of one's sexuality might, therefore, result in abuse, rejection, isolation, or violence. Hence, although the rates of homonegativism may be declining, this is not reflected in a decrease in the rates of mental health issues, self-harm, or suicide amongst queer people. These rates have not shown a decline in over thirty years (de Lange, et al., 2022; Painter, et al., 2018).

IMT researchers are also having a *direct* impact on the politics of homonegativism. Written evidence was submitted to the UK House of Commons (2017) investigation into *Homophobia in Sport* by Eric Anderson, Jamie Cleland, Rory Macgrath, and Rachel Bullingham. Within their executive summary they state:

> Although the foundation of men's sport in the 19th and 20th centuries is based on male homophobia, radical changes in decreasing antipathy toward sexual minorities has restructured sporting culture in the last 20 years, making it mostly inclusive of sexual minorities ... Research on lesbians in sport shows highly inclusive and supportive cultures.
> (Anderson, Cleland, Macgrath & Bullingham, 2016, p. 2)

They further explain within their report that the absence of openly gay men in "football, or other masculinised sports, is not evidence of homophobia" (p. 2). In contrast, they suggest that this absence can be explained by gay men's personal choices to participate in other individual or aesthetic sports. Their submission also states that when "gay and lesbian athletes come out of the closet in sport today, they are met with open-arms, celebration and often times increased cultural capital" (p. 8). Their submission to the parliamentary investigation into homophobia and sport via The Culture, Sport and Media Committee, as appointed by the House of Commons, was designed to prevent any form of political actions towards challenging homonegativism. It is in this light, that I conclude that IMT research is dangerous as it actively tries to thwart action to challenge the harms of homonegativism.

Conclusion

Within this chapter I have argued that the narrative of progress towards acceptance of diverse sexualities is simplistic and potentially *dangerous* as it detracts from the difficult work of challenging aspects of homonegativism. I have provided evidence to illustrate how IMT researchers prop up this simplistic narrative through drawing conclusions that match, in circular fashion, the tenets of their underpinning quasi-structuralist and deterministic theory. I have also provided evidence to illustrate that differing researchers – that have examined the same phenomena as IMT researchers (i.e. sportsmen kissing each other or gay referees and homonegativism) – have drawn oppositional conclusions to suggest, at the very least, that there is a need for caution before drawing any broad conclusion about the alleged decrease in homonegativism. Yet rather than heeding caution, I have provided evidence to illustrate that leading IMT researchers are actively trying to challenge the need for political action against homonegativism (see Anderson et al., 2016). In this manner, I conclude that research underpinned by IMT is dangerous as it ignores the very real harms of homonegativism that are manifested in the realities that queer teenagers are two to three times likelier to attempt suicide than others. Thus, in relation to my prime research question: 'what does IMT do?', I suggest it has a tendency to induce political apathy and stall social justice as the research findings discourage belief that there is a need to minimise harmful relations of power between queer and straight people. In contrast, I argue that there is still a need for activism to garner support for diverse sexualities.

Notes

1 I use the term 'homonegativism' – which simply means negative attitudes towards homosexuality – rather than homophobia. Standard definitions of homophobia relate to people who *fear* or dislike homosexuals. People feel fear when they are frightened, in danger or in pain. Yet, in this light, the word homophobia does not seem apt, as it suggests that LGBTIQ+ people frighten, scare, or hurt other (straight) people. The term homonegativism was first coined by Hudson and Ricketts (1980) as they regarded the term homophobia as lacking credibility in its presumption of motivation.
2 Homosexuality obsessive-compulsive disorder (HOCD) is defined as the fear of being or becoming homosexual. HOCD is not officially classified in the *Diagnostic and Statistical Manual of Mental Disorders* yet it is accepted by some, in the psychological healthcare community, as a form of OCD. It is, nevertheless, an apparently rare form of mental illness and is poorly examined or understood.

References

Anderson, E. (2009). *Inclusive masculinity: The changing nature of masculinities*. London: Routledge.
Anderson, E., & McCormack, M. (2015). Cuddling and spooning: Heteromasculinity and homosocial tactility among student-athletes. *Men and Masculinities*, 18(2), 214–230.
Anderson, E., & McCormack, M. (2018). Inclusive masculinity theory: Overview, reflection and refinement. *Journal of Gender Studies*, 27(5), 547–561.
Anderson, E., Cleland, J., Macgrath, R., & Bullingham, R. (2016). *Homophobia in sport: Research, evidence and speculation*. Submitted to House of Commons: Culture, Media and Sport Committee: Homophobia in Sport. https://committees.parliament.uk/committee/378/digital-culture-media-and-sport-committee/news/105005/homophobia-in-sport-committee-announces-report-publication/~/link/2d6d37cd388a44b3aaaa6d368e45c3ed.aspx
Anderson, E., Ripley, M., & McCormack, M. (2019). A mixed-method study of same-sex kissing among college-attending heterosexual men in the US. *Sexuality & Culture*, 23(1), 26–44.
BBC Sport. (2019, 22 November). Ryan Atkin: From linesman to champion – First openly gay referee on experiences. BBC. https://www.bbc.co.uk/sport/football/50489826
Berggren, K. (2014). Sticky masculinity: Post-structuralism, phenomenology and subjectivity in critical studies on men. *Men and Masculinities*, 17(3), 231–252.
Bernstein, A. (2002). Is it time for a victory lap? Changes in the media coverage of women in sport. *International Review for the Sociology of Sport*, 37(3–4), 415–428.
Branfman, J., Stiritz, S., & Anderson, E. (2018). Relaxing the straight male anus: Decreasing homohysteria around anal eroticism. *Sexualities*, 21(1–2), 109–127.
Bryson, L. (1990). Challenges to male hegemony. In M. A. Messner and D. F. Sabo (Eds), *Sport, men, and the gender order: critical feminist perspectives* (pp. 173–184). Champaign, IL: Human Kinetics.
Caudwell, J. (2015). Sexualities and sport. In R. Giulianotti (Ed.), *Routledge handbook of the sociology of sport* (pp. 240–250). London: Routledge.
Chao-Fong, L. (2021, December 3). Recorded homophobic hate crimes soared in pandemic, figures show. *The Guardian*. https://www.theguardian.com/world/2021/dec/03/recorded-homophobic-hate-crimes-soared-in-pandemic-figures-show
Cleland, J. (2019). Britain's first openly gay football referee: The story of Ryan Atkin. In Rory Magrath (Ed.), *LGBT athletes in the sports media* (pp. 125–146). Cham: Palgrave Macmillan.
Connell, R. W. (1995). *Masculinities*. St Leonards: Allen & Unwin.
Cooky, C., & Messner, M. A. (2018). *No slam dunk*. New Brunswick, NJ: Rutgers University Press.

De Boise, S. (2015). I'm not homophobic, "I've got gay friends": Evaluating the validity of inclusive masculinity. *Men and Masculinities*, *18*(3), 318–339.

Deleuze, G., & Guattari, F. (1988). *A thousand plateaus: Capitalism and schizophrenia*. Minneapolis and London: Bloomsbury Publishing.

Denison, E., & Kitchen, A. (2015). Out on the Fields. *The First International Study on Homophobia in Sport*. http://www.outonthefields.com/wp-content/uploads/2016/04/Out-on-the-Fields-Final-Report.pdf

Denison, E., Bevan, Nadia, & Jeanes, Ruth (2021). Reviewing evidence of LGBTQ+ discrimination and exclusion in sport, *Sport Management Review*, *24*(3), 389–409. https://doi.org/10.1016/j.smr.2020.09.003

Denzin, N. K. (2018). *The qualitative manifesto: A call to arms*. New York: Routledge.

Donaldson, M. (1993). What is hegemonic masculinity? *Theory and Society*, *22*(5), 643–657.

Foucault, M. (1987). The ethic of care for the self as a practice of freedom. In J. Bernauer and D. Rasmussen (Eds), *The final Foucault* (pp. 1–20), Cambridge, MA: The MIT Press.

The Guardian. (2015, 15 December). NBA referee Bill Kennedy comes out as gay after Rajon Rondo confrontation. https://www.theguardian.com/sport/2015/dec/14/nba-referee-bill-kennedy-comes-out-as-gay-after-rajon-rondo-confrontation

Hall, S. (1996). Cultural studies and its theoretical legacies. *Stuart Hall: Critical Dialogues in Cultural Studies*, *262*(275), 596–634.

Hudson, W. W., & Ricketts, W. A. (1980). A strategy for the measurement of homophobia. *Journal of Homosexuality*, *5*(4), 357–372.

Jones, S. (2016, 14 September). Gay referee in Spain receives death threats after return to football: Jesús Tomillero, who quit in May but later reversed decision, says he is 'really, really scared' but will carry on refereeing. *The Guardian*. https://www.theguardian.com/world/2016/sep/13/gay-referee-in-spain-receives-death-threats-after-return-to-football

Kimmel, M. S. (2010). Masculinity as homophobia: Fear, shame, and silence in the construction of gender identity. In S. R. Harper, & F. Harris III (Eds), *College men and masculinities: Theory, research, and implications for practice* (pp. 23–31). San Francisco: Jossey-Bass.

de Lange, J., Baams, L., van Bergen, D. D., Bos, H. M., & Bosker, R. J. (2022). Minority stress and suicidal ideation and suicide attempts among LGBT adolescents and young adults: A meta-analysis. *LGBT Health*, *9*(4), 222–237.

Landi, D. (2019). Queer men, affect, and physical education. *Qualitative Research in Sport, Exercise and Health*, 11(2), 168–187. doi: 10.1080/2159676X.2018.1504230

Laybourne, I. (2021, February 25). I've received homophobic abuse and death threats, reveals referee James Child. *Yahoo!Sports*. https://sports.yahoo.com/ve-received-homophobic-abuse-death-102936512.html

Magrath, R., Anderson, E., & Bullingham, R. (2014). Changing the game: Sport and a cultural shift away from homohysteria. In Eric Anderson & Jennifer Hargreaves (Eds), *Routledge handbook of sport, gender and sexuality*. London: Routledge.

Magrath, R., Anderson, E., & Roberts, S. (2015). On the door-step of equality: Attitudes toward gay athletes among academy-level footballers. *International Review for the Sociology of Sport*, *50*(7), 804–821.

Manasan, A. (2021, April 11). Coming out 'made me a better, more full person,' says US soccer star Megan Rapinoe. *The Sunday Magazine*. http://www.cbc.ca/radio/sunday/the-sunday-magazine-for-november-29-2020-1.5817667/coming-out-made-me-a-better-more-full-person-says-u-s-soccer-star-megan-rapinoe-1.5819650

Mansfield, L., Caudwell, J., Wheaton, B., & Watson, B. (Eds). (2018). *The Palgrave handbook of feminism and sport, leisure and physical education*. London: Palgrave Macmillan UK.

McCormack, M. (2012). The positive experiences of openly gay, lesbian, bisexual and transgendered students in a Christian sixth form college. *Sociological Research Online*, *17*(3), 229–238.

McCormack, M., & Anderson, E. (2010). 'It's just not acceptable any more': The erosion of homophobia and the softening of masculinity at an English sixth form. *Sociology*, *44*(5), 843–859.

McCormack, M., & Anderson, E. (2014). The influence of declining homophobia on men's gender in the United States: An argument for the study of homohysteria. *Sex Roles*, *71*(3), 109–120.

McNeilly, C. (2021, December 2). NI's first openly gay football referee Ryan Hanna: 'I was victim of vile homophobic slurs … and the Irish FA did nothing about it'. *Belfast Telegraph*. https://www.belfasttelegraph.co.uk/news/northern-ireland/nis-first-openly-gay-football-referee-ryan-hanna-i-was-victim-of-vile-homophobic-slurs-and-the-irish-fa-did-nothing-about-it-41113114.html

Miller, T. (1998). Commodifying the male body, problematizing "hegemonic masculinity?". *Journal of Sport and Social Issues*, *22*(4), 431–446.

Messner, M. A. and Sabo, D. (1994). *Sex, violence & power in sports*. Freedom, CA: Crossing.

Ohlert, J., Seidler, C., Rau, T., Rulofs, B., & Allroggen, M. (2018). Sexual violence in organized sport in Germany. *German Journal of Exercise and Sport Research*, *48*(1), 59–68.

O'Neill, R. (2015). Whither critical masculinity studies? Notes on inclusive masculinity theory, postfeminism and sexual politics. *Men and Masculinities*, *18*(1), 100–120.

Outsports. (2021). At least 186 out LGBTQ athletes at the Tokyo Summer Olympics, by far a record. https://www.outsports.com/olympics/2021/7/12/22565574/tokyo-summer-olympics-lgbtq-gay-athletes-list

Painter, K. R., Scannapieco, M., Blau, G., Andre, A., & Kohn, K. (2018). Improving the mental health outcomes of LGBTQ youth and young adults: A longitudinal study. *Journal of Social Service Research*, *44*(2), 223–235.

Pavlidis, A. (2018). Making "space" for women and girls in sport: An agenda for Australian geography. *Geographical Research*, *56*(4), 343–352.

Phipps, C. (2021). Thinking beyond the binary: Barriers to trans* participation in university sport. *International Review for the Sociology of Sport*, *56*(1), 81–96.

Pringle, R. (2003). *Doing the damage? An examination of masculinities and men's rugby experiences of pain, fear and pleasure* (Doctoral dissertation, The University of Waikato).

Pringle, R. & Denison, E. (2021). "A critical examination of homo-negative language use and the pragmatics of inclusion and exclusion of gay rugby players." Presented to *17th International Pragmatics Conference*, Winterthur, Switzerland (27 June to 2 July).

Pringle, R., & Markula, P. (2005). No pain is sane after all: A Foucauldian analysis of masculinities and men's rugby experiences of fear, pain, and pleasure. *Sociology of Sport Journal*, *22*(4), 472–497.

Ralph, B., & Roberts, S. (2020). One small step for man: Change and continuity in perceptions and enactments of homosocial intimacy among young Australian men. *Men and Masculinities*, *23*(1), 83–103.

Rollè, L., Cazzini, E., Santoniccolo, F., & Trombetta, T. (2021). Homonegativity and sport: A systematic review of the literature. *Journal of Gay & Lesbian Social Services*, *34*(1), 86–111.

Scoats, R., Joseph, L. J., & Anderson, E. (2018). 'I don't mind watching him cum': Heterosexual men, threesomes, and the erosion of the one-time rule of homosexuality. *Sexualities*, *21*(1–2), 30–48.

Sedgwick, E. K. (1993). Queer and now. In *Tendencies* (pp. 1–20). Durham, NC: Duke University Press.

Sykes, H. J. (2011). *Queer bodies: Sexualities, genders, & fatness in physical education*. Peter Lang Publishing.

Spaaij, R., Knoppers, A., & Jeanes, R. (2020). "We want more diversity but …": Resisting diversity in recreational sports clubs. *Sport Management Review*, *23*(3), 363–373.

Storr, R., Jeanes, Ruth, Spaaij, Ramón & Farquharson, Karen (2021). "That's where the dollars are": understanding Why community sports volunteers engage with intellectual disability as a form of diversity. *Managing Sport and Leisure*, *26*(3), 175–188. https://doi.org/10.1080/23750472.2020.1730226

Storr, R., Jeanes, R., Rossi, T., & lisahunter. (2022). Are we there yet? (Illusions of) Inclusion in sport for LGBT+ communities in Australia. *International Review for the Sociology of Sport*, *57*(1), 92–111.

Toffoletti, K., & Palmer, C. (2019). Women and sport in Australia—New times? *Journal of Australian Studies*, *43*(1), 1–6.

Tomlinson, A. (1998). Power: Domination, negotiation, and resistance in sports cultures. *Journal of Sport and Social Issues*, *22*(3), 235–240.

Waling, A. (2019). Rethinking masculinity studies: Feminism, masculinity, and poststructural accounts of agency and emotional reflexivity. *The Journal of Men's Studies*, *27*(1), 89–107.

White, P. & Young, K. (1997). Masculinity, sport, and the injury process: A review of Canadian and international evidence. *Avante*, *3*(2), 1–30.

7
THE INVISIBILITY OF TRANS MEN IN SPORT AND SPORTING SPACES

Abby Barras

Introduction

In December 2022, after six years of campaigning, by the Scottish National Party, Gender Recognition Reform (Scotland) Bill was passed by the Scottish parliament by 86 votes to 39 (Morton & Seddon, 2023). The proposals of the Bill were designed to streamline and make easier the process of a person changing their legal gender in Scotland, for example by lowering the minimum age that someone can apply from 18 to 16, although stipulating that 16- and 17-year-olds would need to have lived as their acquired gender for six months rather than three.

The process of gender recognition (which for those who wish to, involves applying for a Gender Recognition Certificate) has been criticised by trans people and campaigners for reform since its introduction within the Gender Recognition Act (GRA, UK, 2004) as unnecessarily bureaucratic, intrusive, and demeaning (Barras, 2021). But by 16 January 2023, the UK government had, for the very first time since its inception in 1998 (Scotland Act, 1998), invoked what is called section 35 of the Scotland Act to block and veto the bill (Clear, 2023). The purpose of this veto is to prevent the Bill from becoming law, on the grounds it would affect equality law for the whole of the UK.

The Bill was opposed by the Scottish Conservatives, and others, including the organisation Fair Play for Women, a well-known organisation who according to their website are 'a campaigning and consultancy group which raises awareness, provides evidence and analysis, and supports policy-makers to protect the rights of women and girls in the UK' (Fair Play for Women, 2024). In December 2023, the Scottish ministers confirmed they were abandoning their legal challenge against the UK government veto of gender recognition reforms (BBC, 2023). Although the Bill does not introduce new rights for trans people and simply means that they can have better access to their human rights, the bill meant Scotland would have been the first part of the UK to introduce a self-identification system for anyone who wanted to change their gender. It is this aspect of the self-identification which is challenged by those who oppose it, by claiming it could be exploited by predators and putting women and girls at risk. Writing in the *Daily Mail*, gender critical feminist Julie Bindel claimed "predatory men using the cloak of gender self-identification could present themselves as female and find their way into women's changing rooms in shops and sports facilities" (Bindel, 2022, n.p.). The historical pathologising of many trans people within legal discourses has made the ethics and politics of self-definition for trans people unnecessarily fraught, and thus especially important for their own agency within research, the law and in daily life (Burns, 2018; White & Newbegin, 2021).

On 9 August 2021, Professor Kathleen Stock, a prominent voice in the gender critical feminist movement in the UK and former Professor of Philosophy at the University of Sussex tweeted:

> A million quid footed by taxpayer to lobby for males in women's prisons, sport, changing-rooms, prizes, shortlists; for the policing of speech about biological sex; for fanning flames of social division and saying there should be #nodebate about it.

In response, Freddy McConnell, writer, journalist and activist, tweeted:

> Why are you obsessed with trans people? Why do you talk about us in such offensive and inaccurate ways? Trans people use appropriate spaces/services thanks to the Equality Act, not Stonewall. Maybe stop letting your bigotry fan flames of social division? Get a new hobby?

Freddy followed this with a second tweet saying: "Has Kathleen ever been known to acknowledge trans men, let alone engage with us on respectful terms?"

To state that gender critical feminists such as Professor Stock have paid little attention to trans men (and non-binary people) generally, never mind in sport and sporting spaces, is not an exaggeration. Freddy's tweet offered a shrewd observation about how the presence of trans men in public life generally as well as in sport and sporting spaces is frequently overlooked by gender critical feminists. In turn this oversight leads to an important conversation about how trans men's perspectives and experiences are also an opportunity for challenging inequalities in sport.

The spaces which Stock tweeted about – women's prisons, sport, and changing rooms – are never discussed in relation to the trans men (or non-binary people) who use them. In fact, why are trans men as Freddy asked, not acknowledged in discussions generally, or in wider discourses about trans people in sport? The one topic of discussion which does draw comment from the gender critical feminist quarter is on trans pregnancy (Conaghan, 2018), though this is beyond the scope of this chapter to explore further. In the UK, trans people are legally entitled to use spaces such as changing rooms and toilets due to the 2010 Equality Act. Whilst conversations transgender women are frequently framed as being interlopers in cisgender women's spaces, transgender men (and non-binary people) are noticeably absent. In fact, in research regarding trans people's inclusion in sport, transgender men hardly feature at all.

By drawing on some of the existing literature about trans men in sport and sporting spaces, this chapter considers why this might be. It aims to highlight how the prevalence of hegemonic masculinity which is so embedded in sport serves to produce inequalities for many people, both trans and cis. This chapter considers the place and role of trans men's voices and lived experiences in sport, and why their being overlooked by gender critical feminists highlights a missed opportunity for challenging inequalities in women's sports. Before doing so, some definitions of the commonly used terms in this chapter are provided.

Transgender and non-binary

The term 'transgender' (and the frequently abbreviated 'trans' which this chapter uses) is an umbrella term for people whose gender identity or presentation does not match the sex they were assigned at birth (Pearce, Steinberg, & Moon, 2019). It can refer to people who identify as trans men (people who were assigned female at birth but identify as men), trans women (people who were assigned male at birth but identify as women), or those who identify as non-binary (those who do not identify solely as either male or female, some or all of the time). It is important to recognise that the term non-binary is a valid gender identity in its own right. The term trans covers a variety of experiences, expressions, and identities including gender queer, gender fluid, and gender non-conforming, though it is not limited to these descriptions and an individual may use terms inter-changeably. For example, a person may identity as gender-queer but not necessarily as trans (Richards, Pierre-Bouman, & Barker, 2017).

Gender critical feminism

The term 'gender critical feminist' is a recent upcycle of the term 'TERF' (trans-exclusionary radical feminist). Many gender critical feminists claim the term 'TERF' is a slur, despite it being a largely accurate description of their beliefs and instead prefer the term 'gender critical feminist'. Gender critical feminists are frequently set in opposition in the media against trans people

> on a seemingly unrelenting path of mutual antagonism … trans rights have been pitted against sex-based rights for "real" women, with conflict forever spiralling into charge and counter charge of hate speech and silencing, and into bitter social media wars.
>
> (Hines, 2019, p. 155)

As this chapter will detail later, trans men are already participating in sport at both elite and recreational levels. Yet trans men/masculine presenting people are also themselves subject to policing and gendered assumptions about their bodies from others in sporting spaces and communities, as well as concerns about safety and passing (Abelson, 2014; Barras & Frith, 2023; Caudwell, 2014; Farber, 2017).

Sport

For the purposes of this chapter, the term 'sport' is used as a catch-all to describe physical activity and exercise. It refers to sport, which is neither elite nor professional, but may still be played competitively or to a high level. 'Sporting spaces' refers to the areas where physical activity, sport or exercise takes place, such as the football field, as well as associated areas, in particular, changing rooms (Barras, Frith, Jarvis, & Lucena, 2021).

Methods

The basis for this chapter originated from a theme explored in the author's PhD research, in which she examined the lived experiences of trans and non-binary adults in everyday sport and physical exercise in the UK (Barras, 2021). This chapter's approach is to draw on four key pieces of research from the academic literature in the area of trans men's experiences of participation in sport, as opposed to a narrow empirical piece. However, some empirical data is cited where necessary for drawing attention to a specific experience. This is because whilst this chapter looks more towards a small sample of the literature in this area to better understand what has been written about trans men in sport, it is essential that any research which discusses trans people's lives has, where possible, an empirical connection to their lived experiences (Vincent, 2018).

The cisgender research community (to which the author belongs) must always have a commitment to not speaking for the trans community. This is because "the transgender population has been subject to a troubled history of ethically and methodologically flawed research practices [and] criticisms have been made of how trans lives have been mostly investigated, and correspondingly constructed, by cisgender people" (Vincent, 2018, p. 102). The author's intention here is to actively display solidarity with the trans community, whilst ensuring the aims of this chapter are met in keeping with its literature review approach.

Trans people in sport

There exists within the social sciences a broad range of both qualitative and quantitative research about trans people's participation in sport, though earlier research features little if any examples of trans men or of non-binary people (Erikainen et al., 2020). Much of this early research has a focus on the hypothetical trans athlete competing at elite level (Aura, 2007; Buzuvis, 2011, 2012; Cavanagh & Sykes, 2006; Donnellan, 2008; Gooren & Bunck, 2004; Reeser, 2005; Semerjian & Cohen, 2006; Sullivan, 2011; Teetzel, 2006). Despite these papers being largely supportive of inclusion for trans people in sport in principle from a human rights perspective, they mostly concern themselves with the eligibility of trans athletes to compete because they may possess an unfair competitive advantage due to immutable physiology (for trans women) and the taking of testosterone (for trans men).

As far back as 2005, Reeser noted that trans men are visibly absent from discussions regarding inclusion in sport, though the field is not without some timely contributions (Afroozeh et al., 2023; Barras & Frith, 2023; Caudwell, 2014; Farber, 2017; Klein et al., 2019; Phipps & Blackall, 2021; Saeidzadeh, 2020). This failure to acknowledge their presence in previous sporting literature renders them invisible and implies they are insignificant, yet this could not be further from the reality. Whilst it is true that trans men winning in sport rarely make headlines, and to date no trans men have competed in the modern Olympics, examples of their success at elite level exist. These examples are noteworthy because these trans men are competing in sports in which cis men traditionally excel in due to the requirement for what are considered 'masculine' physical attributes which confer an advantage over others: height and strength. Notable trans athletes include triathlete Chris Mosier, former basketball player Kye Allums, former swimmer Schuyler Bailar and boxer Patrico Manuel. It could be argued the successes of these four athletes undermine an assumption that women are inherently weaker than men, and trans men can never be as good as cis men in sport. Indeed, these examples also highlight the instability and complexity of masculinity in sport, which is clearly challenged by the inclusion of these individuals and calls into question the conflation of competitive advantage with male physiology.

Presenting the literature

The lived experience of being a trans man is often intrinsically brought into focus when they participate in sport or navigate sporting spaces. This is often due to the way sport is organised along binary lines and the prevalence of cisnormativity embedded within sport (Phipps, 2019;

Piggott, 2020). In sports settings the body is explicitly used, displayed, observed, and discussed, with bodily presentations an important aspect of the performance of cisnormative masculinity and femininity. Within these spaces,

> Both physical and social dominant forms of heterosexual masculinity and femininity can be established and/or challenged. In these areas, peoples' gendered bodies and behaviours are both scrutinised and disciplined by their peer group, with public and negative labelling for those unwilling or unable to conform to group norms.
> (Paechter, 2003, p. 71)

As previously noted, whilst trans women are frequently viewed as interlopers in cis women's spaces and in sport, trans men do attract the same amount of attention in the literature. Literature which includes a substantial contribution in this area, and which does examine trans men in spaces/sport include Caudwell's (2014) paper which examined the gendered subjectivities of two young trans men and their inclusion in sport; Klein, Paule-Kobaa and Krane's (2019) paper which presents a case study of a trans male college athlete as he transitions from the women's to the men's team; Farber's (2017) work on trans men in online fitness forums and Afroozeh et al.'s work (2023) which draws on cultural cisgenderism to analyse the sporting experiences of twelve trans men in Iran and their experiences of women's sport environments, and the extent to which it is embedded into Iranian culture.

Caudwell (2014) drew on three semi-structured interviews with two young trans men, Finn and Ed, for her paper. In this paper Caudwell notes how their narratives provide "valuable testimonies on transgender and transgender and sport: more specifically, their experiences of school sport, their embodied subjectivities, transitioning and sport participation" (Caudwell, 2014, p. 398). One aspect of Caudwell's findings is that both Finn and Ed self-identify not as trans men but as male, but that neither Finn nor Ed imagined participating in organised men's sport, a place they found to be unsafe for them. In addition, they did not aspire to heterosexual masculinity "in order to produce their embodied masculinity/masculine subjectivity" (Caudwell, 2014, p. X).

Farber's (2017) paper is based on a content analysis of a Reddit message board about transgender men's fitness and interviews with eight transgender men. Participants were asked about their experiences with fitness, transitioning and involvement in online communities, asking "How might transgender men engage with and reshape cultural associations and institutional hierarchies of biological male sex, masculinity and muscular embodiment?" (Farber, 2017, p. 256). Farber examines what they see as the "coalescing digital and physical worlds of sex, gender and fitness" (Farber, 2017, p. 255). Farber (2017, p. 256), argues that fitness is a "trans practice", or means through which people may modify their bodies, personal identifications and genders, and that Transgender men engage in strategic fitness habits to pursue their ideals of the 'male' and 'masculine' body, illuminating both the stronghold and malleability of sex and gender norms.

Like those in Caudwell (2014) the individuals in Farber's research highlighted that masculinity is not always tied to maleness, rather that individuals were able to construct their own version of masculinity within sport and sporting spaces. Farber notes, as this chapter does, that research so often focuses on cisgender people that the lived experiences of trans people is missed. More importantly, by seeking to understand how trans people navigate sport and sporting spaces, a better understanding of sports' relationship to gender can be made. In this way, the trans men in all these papers felt themselves to be more masculine through fitness and describing their experiences in gyms. As Farber concluded, "they upheld the 'traditional' linkage between male bodies, masculinity, strength and muscularity, [and] they also remapped linear associations between cisgender men, masculinity and muscularity" (Farber, 2017, p. 258).

Klein, Paule-Kobaa and Krane's 2019 paper presents a case study of a trans male college athlete as he transitions from the women's to the men's team, framing their study through a trans feminist lens. The authors contribution is significant not only because the student is a trans man, but also because previous studies are retrospective accounts (e.g., Hargie et al., 2017; Lucas-Carr and Krane, 2012; Semerjian and Cohen, 2006).The authors found that whilst there was evidence of (trans) identities being socially accepted, essentialist understandings of sex and gender remained prevalent in sport environments. Gender presentation was also policed by others in sport, with expectations that it should align with ascribed biological sex.

In Afroozeh et al., (2023) the authors draw on cultural cisgenderism to analyse the sporting experiences of twelve trans men in Iran and their experiences of women's sport environments, and the extent to which it is embedded into Iranian culture. The authors found that whilst there was evidence of (trans) identities being socially accepted, essentialist understandings of sex and gender remained prevalent in sport environments. Gender presentation was also policed by others in sport, with expectations that it should align with ascribed biological sex. A similar finding is in the study by Catherine Phipps (2021) who explored trans inclusion in the UK university sport context, particularly the experiences of one trans man who had socially but not yet medically transitioned, Phipps found that potential harassment and 'gossip' in women's sport teams may impact trans men to remove themselves from these spaces (see also Travers and Deri, 2011).

What connects the literature presented here, is the instability and complexity of hegemonic masculinity in sport, which is clearly challenged by the inclusion of these individuals, calling into question the conflation of competitive advantage with male physiology. Raewyn Connell (2005) argued that hegemonic masculinity is embodied in all men who participate in sport and physical activity, and gender identity and the characteristics of hegemonic masculinity are inextricably linked. Despite gradual gains by women in both professional and amateur sport globally, it is still largely organised both by and for men, particularly within the most popular sports, for example football, rugby, cricket and tennis, where masculinity is linked to 'socially sanctioned aggression and physical power' (Grindstaff and West, 2011, p. 865).

Trans men in sporting spaces

This was a similar experience of two of the trans men in the author's doctoral research, where an individual's masculinity often varied in relation to the sporting location they occupied, such as the gym and the weights area, and how they became privy to sexist language and behaviour in these spaces due to their passing as cis men – that is, not being read as trans by the cis men in that space.

Many sporting settings, especially certain areas of the gym like the weights area, are often viewed as masculine spaces. Joe (trans masculine/male, non-binary, water polo/rugby, pronouns they/them) said:

> I've been going to the gym once or twice a week whilst I'm off sport, and I hate it. It's horrible. I hate the gym. I hate the changing rooms, I hate the showers, I hate all of it. I hate that the men take up all of the free weights area. It's the masculinity, the horrible air of masculinity (laughs) that surrounds gyms.

Joe went on to say that when they went to the gym with their cis female rugby teammates, they had to put up with cis men staring at them and their friends. Joe found this behaviour "disgusting", because the men would "just stare at all my friends, especially when they were squatting, so they could stand behind and see their bums, and think they couldn't be seen [in the mirrors]".

As Joe became more familiar with the rules and ethos of these masculine spaces, they were able to view them as less masculine, and the cis men who occupied them were not a version of masculinity they wished to aspire to. Whilst these spaces still had to be navigated and a certain code followed to facilitate a person's use of that space, over time participants like Joe were able to use them to help construct and confirm their own gender identity and subsequent integration into that same space. Joe even poked fun at the overt (hegemonic) masculinity of these spaces, although they were able to do this precisely because they were reassured their gender identity 'matched' those of the other users.

Encounters with sexism in male sporting spaces is a common experience for many cisgender women (Giulianotti, 2016), and both sexism and homophobia remain rife within sport (Waldron, 2019). Women and girls have unquestionably been historically excluded from sport at the behest of men due to the prevalence of hegemonic masculinity, and, even when their inclusion has increased, they still often face sexism, gender stereotyping, and significantly less pay and media coverage compared to their male equivalents (Phipps, 2019). Sexism and homophobia in sport is not only experienced by trans athletes but also by those who are cis. During coverage of the 2020 Tokyo Olympics, a number of news reports (Bullens, 2021; Pruitt-Young, 2021) commented on how female athletes are facing double standards where clothing is concerned. The Norwegian women's beach handball team were fined because their shorts were too long, British Paralympian Olivia Breen was told by an official that her briefs were too short. Breen pointed to a double standard regarding athletic dress codes and questioned whether male athletes would be subjected to the same level of scrutiny. This was not the first-time clothing policies for female athletes have been unnecessarily different than for male athletes, such as the wearing of skorts for female boxers at the 2012 London Olympics (Mansfield, Caudwell, Wheaton, & Watson, 2017).

Not wanting to aspire to a particular kind of (hegemonic) masculinity was raised by Joe, when they reflected on their experiences of using a gym where cis men were not allowed to join, and how different the experience was as a trans person, because of "the way that cis men behave". Alix (29, trans masculine, personal trainer/runner, pronouns they/them) shared this view of spaces feeling masculine. Alix called the weights area in their gym "notorious … just big men down there, lifting weights … grunting … all very uncomfortable or intimidating". In addition, Joe felt as if an individual needed to be "a certain type of person" to use them. To counteract this, the trans men here constructed themselves as manlier by criticizing cis men, embodying a complex form of trans-hegemonic masculinity, undermining and challenging sporting spaces, whilst also enjoying the gender affirmation they feel when they pass well enough to use them (see the excellent 2020 article by Zara Saeidzade which examines gender practices, trans masculinity and mardānegī in contemporary Iran).

The instability of (hegemonic) masculinity and its relationship to sport and gender

The problems experienced by trans men in these spaces were felt to radiate from the cis men using them, and some of this discomfort can be understood as hegemonic masculinity. There exists a wide number of studies on hegemonic masculinity and masculine identity formation in relation to sport (Anderson, 2014; Connell, 2005; Connell & Messerschmidt, 2005; English,

2017). These works have helped to establish the link between maleness, skill, and strength as the defining characteristics of sporting masculinity in the modern industrialised West. The lived experiences of several of the people the author interviewed supported the position that hegemonic masculinity is fluid, and not fixed; rather it is relational, dependent on the person engaging with it, and can shift. It has been argued (Connell, 2005) that hegemonic masculinity is embodied in all men who participate in sport and physical activity, and gender identity and the characteristics of hegemonic masculinity are inextricably linked.

One very distinct aspect of changing rooms is the reality of encountering another person's naked body, and the possibility that, if wanting to use, for example, the shower, an individual's own naked body may be observed. For example, Harry, who played badminton, said his fellow trans men teammates could not use the showers, as they "don't want anyone else seeing that they haven't got a willy, basically" and suggested more individual cubicles with doors would be helpful. This concern of vulnerability about one's naked body was also experienced by Joe, who although they had not felt threatened in the gym, they worried someone "may notice something and accost me outside that space".

This vulnerability was both a bodily one, and one which required these participants having to "newly orientate themselves to being accountable to gender expectations for those who are sex categorised as male" (Abelson, 2014, p. 558). This was in part due to safety and in response to other (cis) men's dominating practices and the likelihood of offensive, sexist banter and even violence in these spaces. Assessing for safety and the wish to not jeopardise this safety was a genuine concern for many of the participants and was not only experienced by the trans women in this research. It was also experienced by some trans men/masculine and non-binary people, though the fear of the discovery of the visible signs of their female biography was more of concern for trans male/masculine participants. This raises questions about safety in (private) sporting spaces for many users, not just those who are cis.

A similar perspective is found in later studies, such as Abelson's (2014, 2019) research on trans men, masculinity, and spatial safety, and Schilt's (2010) study on trans men's experiences of gender inequality in working life, where she details the interactional process of "achieving social maleness" (2010, p. 48), that is, the work of being recognised as male by others. In this way trans men may gain acceptance and privileges as men, but also many "experience marginalization and discrimination if they choose to live openly as transgender" (Gottzén & Straube, 2016, p. 220).

Having to negotiate changing rooms, showers and gyms to some degree, all of which function as sites "both for the gendered display of hegemonic forms of heterosexual masculinity and for the subordination of alternatives" (Paechter, 2003, p. 47), is a common theme across this literature. In other words, it is through the repeated practice of hegemonic masculinity (and gender normativity), regardless of who is practising it, "which come to organise social life, either sustaining a patriarchal order, or challenging it in unprecedented forms" (Gottzén & Straube, 2016, p. 219). There is also the sense some of the trans masculine participants are in the privileged and unique position of experiencing both perspectives of how hegemonic masculinity works, offering an original insight into the ways it is interpreted. For example, the ways in which sporting spaces are gendered to permit easier entry to those who fit standard representations of what a cis man looks like. It could be argued that they practise masculinity more consciously than cis men due their gender identity (Abelson, 2014).

Whilst they enjoyed increased access to public spaces or found that their body afforded them a new sense of safety, their "geography of fear shifted" (Abelson, 2014, p. 558). Trans men, argued Abelson (2014), do not become immune to the threat or reality of violence (from other men) by virtue of now being seen as men. That is, these trans men now experienced a new set of fears, brought on by "the privilege of male violence" (Abelson, 2014, p. 558). This meant that for the trans men in Abelson's research, they felt that their change of position relative to women was not always a positive change because it involved the possibility of being subjected to other men's violence in a new way. This included, for example, having to negotiate interactions with men in ways they found to be sexist or homophobic, such as Joe did in the gym.

The participants in Abelson's research also identified particular bodily characteristics as important for their sense of safety. Like Harry, their perceptions of safety changed based on their own body, the space they were in, and the communities they engaged with. Abelson's research highlights similarities with both Joe and Harry, because these perceptions of safety, such as in the changing room or the showers:

> Are central to how they account for their masculine practices as they orient to their sex category and transgender status, as well as influencing how they anticipate and experience potential assessment and enforcement.
>
> (Abelson, 2014, p. 562)

It might be assumed that the very presence and the participation of trans people in these spaces subverts gender normativity and hegemonic masculinity, yet this is not always the case for some trans masculine participants. Bodies and their sex characteristics have material reality, a reality reflected in the lived experiences of Joe and Harry, highlighting that both biology and gender identity rest on social assumptions which are open to change (such as through transition) and are dependent on the cisgender gaze (such as passing). Likewise, gender socialisation on the basis of assigned sex does not automatically determine a person's gender identity.

As Ravenhill and de Visser (2017) examine in their work on gay men and masculinity, gay men, like all other men, may utilise stereotypically masculine attributes and behaviours in an attempt to accrue 'masculine capital', a term referring to the social power afforded by the display of traits and behaviours associated with hegemonic masculinity. This was the case for Alix, when they spoke about now being able to use the weights area in the gym, because they are read as male. They said:

> I've kind of ventured downstairs to the weights area, which ... you have to be a certain kind of person to go down there, but it tends to be populated by people who appear to be cis men. Um, pretty muscular, doing their thing ... I don't care anymore, and it doesn't even induce anxiety, so that's quite cool.

For those participants whose gender identity was masculine, their masculinity was sharply called into focus when they entered a sports setting, but they acknowledged the hypocrisy of policing other people's gender in these spaces. Joe used their passing privilege (being read, or 'passing' as one's preferred gender) to look out for their fellow cis female teammates. In doing this, Joe is re-essentialising hegemonic masculinity as something which can be used to stand up for their cis female teammates and intimidate the cis male users of those spaces (Bernstein-Sycamore, 2006). Alix talked about when they went swimming:

> I do go to swimming pools, when I spend time with my younger brother, but it's not generally a pleasant experience, because people will just stare at you. Which I find

bizarre, and it used to bother me, but now I enjoy staring back at people, and making them as equally uncomfortable for what they're doing.

Farber (2017, p. 262) discusses this in her paper in which she analyses trans men's experiences of masculinity via online fitness forums and their feeling about attending gyms. Farber writes:

> Gyms are not neutral spaces and particular forms of self-presentation, dress, actions and vocalizations are gendered. With cisgender men often controlling the gym space (particularly the weight room), and while many people experience 'gymtimidation', transgender men faced unique challenges in accessing and using the gym.

The trans men in these examples had genuine concerns about their own safety, but so long as they passed as cisgender (Bernstein-Sycamore, 2006), or did not disclose what Alix called their "trans heritage", they were able to utilise hegemonic masculinity to their own advantage. For example, when Alix was in the gym using the notoriously masculine weights area, they said that "I can just laugh about it [the men showing off] … it doesn't really bother me anymore". Alix has achieved the social maleness Schilt (2010) noted in her research, one which is congruent with the hegemonic masculinity on display in the gym.

In Abelson's (2014) research examining how trans men construct their masculinities in public spaces such as on public transport or in the gym, she found that respondents masculine practices changed depending on who they interacted with and the level of safety (or potential violence) they perceived. Abelson (2014, p. 549) wrote: Respondents' concerns for safety, and their masculine practices, changed according to variation in transition, physical location, audience and their physical stature.

These practices are reflected in sporting spaces because spaces are often organised in ways which presume women and men might engage in different sporting activities. For example, it is often presumed when women go to the gym, they will do cardio and muscle toning activities, whereas when men go to the gym, they will do weightlifting and muscle-building activities (Spandler et al., 2020). The way in which the gym floor is organised can reinforce these presumptions, and individuals in the literature as well as the author's study reflected upon how uncomfortable they found these 'male spaces' to be when they first started using them. Much like in male changing rooms, gendered norms and presumptions can manifest in overtly sexist and/or masculine behaviour and/or language, as Joe noted.

The spaces which gender critical feminists raise as being 'safe/unsafe' are seen only from the perspective of cis and trans women, and rarely involve any consideration of trans men and trans masculine users of these spaces. As Connell noted when writing about hegemonic masculinity as an embodied practice, masculinity tends to be something that only cis men's bodies do; yet in the examples from the literature discussed here, the participants bodies are also 'doing' masculinity on their own terms (Halberstam, 1998). Sedgewick (1995) and Halberstam (1998) have critiqued that there is a tendency within masculinity studies "that everything pertaining to men can be classified as masculinity, and everything that can be said about masculinity pertains in the first place to men" (Sedgewick, 1995, p. 12). In other words, sometimes masculinity has got nothing to do with men, much like femininity has nothing to do with women. This could mean that the values which hegemonic masculinity places on certain demonstrations of masculinity in sport (strength, speed, power) are shown to be unstable and insignificant when trans men occupy these spaces – by highlighting how trans men's bodies negotiate sport and sporting spaces, masculinity can be understood as "something that not only some specific bodies (those assigned male at birth) have or own, but as a position that is more situational and which can be deployed and activated by a variety of bodies" (Gottzén & Straube, 2016, p. 221).

Conclusion

As this chapter has shown, there are three key things which gender critical feminists may find surprising in the ways they align with their own experiences of participation in sport. First, that trans men often feel uncomfortable in sporting spaces and the way they are unnecessarily gendered; second, that it is the dominance of hegemonic masculinity in sport which is one cause of the inequalities faced by cis women and girls in sport; and third, that these are both opportunities for alliance, and not division between trans and cis people. There is also no equivalent conversation about what it means for cis men to share their (sporting) spaces with trans men, and what is missed by not considering these conversations.

There is a clear opportunity raised by this research to consider ways in which alliances can perhaps be formed with others and look towards ways to reduce hostility in practical ways in sport. After all, "one of the most distressing aspects of the hostile narrative", writes Kim Humphrey in *The Guardian* (Humphrey, 2020, n.p.), "is that it side-lines a reality of alliance". Sitting at the heart of gender critical feminism is the questioning and subsequent denial of the recognition of trans women as women, leaving non-binary, trans men, and trans masculine people disregarded on the basis they pose no 'threat' to feminism and cis women's rights (Carrera-Fernández & DePalma, 2020; Hines, 2019). Trans women can never be 'real' women because they cannot ever know what it means to be a woman biologically nor socially. From this perspective, gender critical feminists are able to deny the identities of trans women through recourse to the fixity of biological sex (Hines, 2019), and by inference, trans men can never be 'real' men. These trans men are never seen as a threat in cis women's spaces and are thus never given any consideration in these discussions.

Rather than divide women and erase their achievements in sport, the literature on trans men's experiences in sport demonstrates there is an opportunity for shared meaning and relevance with those they play sport with, including cis people. Future research with cisgender teammates could help to develop wider understandings not just of trans people's sporting experiences but those who form part of their sporting communities. This could help to foster suggestions about how to improve inclusion for people in sport generally which will lead to stronger alliances between different groups. It is also important to listen to cis voices and experiences if this is to be achieved, perhaps by examining how cis and trans athletes exercise and interact alongside each other.

Trans feminist academics and activists have long been thinking of ways in which alliances can be formed between groups by looking towards shared inequalities, such as sexism and misogyny, and how they might collectively challenge these for a greater impact on change (Krane, 2019; Serano, 2013). One way to build these alliances is by encouraging all sporting organisations, not just those who position themselves as LGBTQ+ inclusive to be visibly trans inclusive, rather than wait for a trans person to ask about their policy.

Trans and feminist activists, writers and their allies, continue to counter anti-trans feminism through public debate, scholarship and policy recommendations, and this research hopes to contribute to similar opportunities for collaboration. This chapter has also revealed that the frequently overlooked narratives of trans men in sport would bring new and original perspectives to the ways in which trans people's inclusion in sport is often framed.

Gender normativity and hegemonic masculinity permeating sport often normalise the presence of homophobia, transphobia, and sexism within it.

This collaboration might include cis women who choose not to (or do not want to) conform to unrealistic beauty standards and gender normative stereotypes, wear revealing sports clothing or be subjected to other patriarchal expectations demanded of them in sports environments. This presents an opportunity of change and development for trans people's participation in sport alongside cis people, and a way to celebrate shared inequalities rather than be defined and constrained by them. Trans men's inclusion in sport offers an opportunity to interrogate those inequalities in sport which gender critical feminists believe to affect only their own inclusion. Gender critical feminism misses an opportunity to foster potential alliances with other communities, especially those who believe their own participation is being erased. This is because hegemonic masculinity is harmful to many women and girls, as it undervalues their presence in sport.

References

Abelson, M. (2014). Dangerous privilege: Trans men, masculinities, and changing perceptions of safety. *Sociological Forum, 29*(3), 549–570. https://doi.org/10.1111/socf.12103

Abelson, M. (2019). *Men in place: Trans masculinity, race, and sexuality in America*. Minneapolis, MN: University of Minnesota Press.

Afroozeh, M. S., Phipps, C., Afrouzeh, A., Mehri, A., & Alipour Asiri, Z. (2023). "The spectators ask, is it a boy or a girl? What is it?": Cultural cisgenderism and trans men's sporting experiences in Iran. *International Review for the Sociology of Sport*. https://doi.org/10.1177/10126902231162270

Anderson, E. (2014). *21st century jocks: Sporting men and contemporary heterosexuality*. London: Palgrave Macmillan.

Aura, S. (2007). "Like any other girl": Male-to-female transsexuals and professional sports. *Sports Law Journal, 14*, 95. Available at: https://heinonline.org/HOL/LandingPage?handle=hein.journals/sportlj14&div=7&id=&page=. (Accessed: 21 July 2021).

Barras, A. (2021). The lived experiences of transgender and non-binary people in everyday sport and physical exercise in the UK. Available at: https://cris.brighton.ac.uk/ws/portalfiles/portal/31240349/BARRAS_thesis.pdf. (Accessed: 20 December 2021).

Barras, A., Frith, H., Jarvis, N., & Lucena, R. (2021). Timelines and transitions: Understanding transgender and non-binary people's participation in everyday sport and physical exercise through a temporal lens. In S. Bekker, I. Costas Batlle, B. C. Clift, J. Gore, S. Gustafsson, & J Hatchard (Eds) *Temporality in qualitative inquiry: Theories, methods and practices*, pp. 57–71. London: Routledge.

Barras, A., & Frith, H. (2023). 'Cos not everyone wants to talk, they prefer to do, to move': Circuits of trans embodied pleasure and inclusion in sport and physical exercise. *Sport, Education and Society*. https://doi.org/10.1080/13573322.2023.2266755

BBC. (20 December 2023). *Scottish government abandons court case over gender law veto*. Available at: https://www.bbc.co.uk/news/uk-scotland-67773606

Bernstein-Sycamore, M. (2006). *NOBODY PASSES: Rejecting the rules of gender and conformity*. New York: Seal Press.

Bindel, J. (2022). If gutless Keir Starmer doesn't stand up for women on the trans issue, I'll never vote Labour again, writes Julie Bindel. Available at: www.dailymail.co.uk/debate/article-11577761/If-Starmer-doesnt-stand-women-trans-issue-Ill-never-vote-Labour-says-JULIE-BINDEL.html. (Accessed: 27 January 2023).

Bullens, L. (2021). Tokyo Olympics: Female athletes face double standards over uniforms. Available at: www.france24.com/en/sport/20210722-tokyo-olympics-female-athletes-face-double-standards-over-uniforms. (Accessed: 21 July 2021).

Burns, C. (2018). *Trans Britain: Our journey from the shadows*. London: Unbound.

Buzuvis, E. (2011). Caster Semenya and the myth of a level playing field. *The Modern American, 6*, 36–45. Available at: https://digitalcommons.wcl.american.edu/cgi/viewcontent.cgi?article=1136&context=tma. (Accessed: 21 July 2021).

Buzuvis, E. (2012). Including transgender athletes in sex-segregated sport: Essays from activists, coaches, and scholars, 25–31. Available at: https://digitalcommons.law.wne.edu/cgi/viewcontent.cgi?article=1248&context=facschol. (Accessed: 21 July 2021).

Carrera-Fernández, M. V., & DePalma, R. (2020). Feminism will be trans-inclusive or it will not be: Why do two cis-hetero woman educators support transfeminism? *The Sociological Review*, 68(4), 745–762. UK: SAGE. https://doi.org/10.1177/0038026120934686

Caudwell, J. (2014). [Transgender] young men: Gendered subjectivities and the physically active body. *Sport, Education and Society*, 19(4), 398–414. https://doi.org/10.1080/13573322.2012.672320

Cavanagh, S. L., & Sykes, H. (2006). Transsexual bodies at the Olympics: The International Olympic Committee's policy on transsexual athletes at the 2004 Athens Summer Games. *Body and Society*, 12(3), 75–102. https://doi.org/10.1177/1357034X06067157

Clear, S. (2023). *How the UK government's veto of Scotland's gender recognition bill brought tensions in the union to the surface.* Available at: https://theconversation.com/how-the-uk-governments-veto-of-scotlands-gender-recognition-bill-brought-tensions-in-the-union-to-the-surface-198181. (Accessed: 27 January 2023).

Conaghan, J. (2018). Sex, gender, and the trans debate. Available at: https://legalresearch.blogs.bris.ac.uk/2018/12/sex-gender-and-the-trans-debate/. (Accessed: 13 February 2022).

Connell, R. (2005). *Masculinities* (2nd ed.). Cambridge: Polity.

Connell, R. W., & Messerschmidt, J. W. (2005). Hegemonic masculinity: Rethinking the concept. *Gender and Society*, 19(6), 829–859. https://doi.org/10.1177/0891243205278639

Donnellan, L. (2008). Gender testing at the Beijing Olympics. *Sport and the Law Journal*, 1(16), 20–28. Available at: www.ul.ie/research/gender-testing-beijing-olympics-0. (Accessed: 22 July 2021).

English, C. (2017). Toward sport reform: Hegemonic masculinity and reconceptualizing competition. *Journal of the Philosophy of Sport*, 44(2), 183–198. https://doi.org/10.1080/00948705.2017.1300538

Erikainen, S., Vincent, B., & Hopkins, A. (2020). Specific detriment: Barriers and opportunities for non-binary inclusive sports in Scotland. *Journal of Sport and Social Issues*, 0(0), 1–28. https://doi.org/10.1177/0193723520962937

Farber, R. (2017). 'Transing' fitness and remapping transgender male masculinity in online message boards. *Journal of Gender Studies*, 26(3), 254–268. https://doi.org/10.1080/09589236.2016.1250618

Giulianotti, R. (2016). *Sport: A critical sociology* (2nd ed.). Cambridge: Polity Press.

Gooren, L. J. G., & Bunck, M. C. M. (2004). Transsexuals and competitive sports. *European Journal of Endocrinology*, 151(4), 425–429. https://doi.org/10.1530/eje.0.1510425

Gottzén, L., & Straube, W. (2016). Trans masculinities. *NORMA*, 11(4), 217–224. https://doi.org/10.1080/18902138.2016.1262056

Grindstaff, L., & West, E. (2011). Hegemonic masculinity on the sidelines of sport. *Sociology Compass*, 5(10), 859–881. https://doi.org/10.1111/j.1751-9020.2011.00409.x

Halberstam, J. (1998). *Female masculinity*. Durham, NC: Duke Press.

Hargie, O. D., Mitchell, D. H., & Somerville, I. J. (2017). 'People have a knack of making you feel excluded if they catch on to your difference': Transgender experiences of exclusion in sport. *International Review for the Sociology of Sport*, 52(2), 223–239. https://doi.org/10.1177/1012690215583283

Hines, S. (2019). The feminist frontier: On trans and feminism. *Journal of Gender Studies*, 28(2), 145–157. https://doi.org/10.1080/09589236.2017.1411791

Humphrey, K. (2020). Trans rights have been pitted against feminism but we're not enemies. Available at: www.theguardian.com/commentisfree/2020/jul/07/trans-rights-have-been-pitted-against-feminism-but-were-not-enemies. (Accessed: 1 December 2021).

Klein, A., Paule-Koba, A. L., & Krane, V. (2019). The journey of transitioning: Being a trans male athlete in college sport. *Sport Management Review*, 22(5), 626–639. https://doi.org/10.1016/j.smr.2018.09.006

Krane, V. (2019). *Sex, gender, and sexuality in sport: Queer inquiries*. Abingdon: Routledge.

Lucas-Carr, C. B., & Krane, V. (2012). Troubling sport or troubled by sport: Experiences of transgender athletes. *Journal of Study Sports Athletes Education*, 6(1), 21–44. https://doi.org/10.1179/ssa.2012.6.1.21

Mansfield, L., Caudwell, J., Wheaton, B., & Watson, B. (2017). *The Palgrave handbook of feminism and sport, leisure and physical education*. Basingstoke, Hampshire: Palgrave Macmillan.

Morton, B., & Seddon, P. (2023). *UK government to block Scottish gender bill*. Available at: www.bbc.co.uk/news/uk-politics-64288757?embed=true. (Accessed: 27 January 2023).

Paechter, C. (2003). Masculinities and femininities as communities of practice. *Women's Studies International Forum, 26*(1), 69–77. https://doi.org/10.1016/S0277-5395(02)00356-4

Pearce, R., Steinberg, D. L., & Moon, I. (2019). Introduction: The emergence of 'trans'. *Sexualities, 22*(1–2), 3–12. https://doi.org/10.1177/1363460717740261

Phipps, C. (2019). Thinking beyond the binary: Barriers to trans participation in university sport. *International Review for the Sociology of Sport,56*(1),81–96. https://doi.org/10.1177/1012690219889621

Phipps, C., & Blackall, C.J. (2021). 'I wasn't allowed to join the boys': The ideology of cultural cisgenderism in a UK school. *Pedagogy, Culture & Society.* https://doi.org/10.1080/14681366.2021.2000012

Piggott, L. (2020). Transgender, intersex and non-binary people in sport and physical activity: A review of research and policy, 1–37. https://doi.org/10.13140/RG.2.2.20795.64805

Pruitt-Young, S. (2021). The sexualization of women in sport extends even to what they wear. Available at: www.npr.org/2021/07/23/1019343453/women-sports-sexualization-uniforms-problem?t=1627195455928. (Accessed: 28 July 2020).

Ravenhill, J. P., & de Visser, O. R. (2017). Perceptions of gay men's masculinity are associated with their sexual self-label, voice quality and physique. *Psychology & Sexuality, 8*(3), 208–222. https://doi.org/10.1080/19419899.2017.1343746

Reeser, J. C. (2005). Gender identity and sport: Is the playing field level? *British Journal of Sports Medicine, 39*(10), 695–699. https://doi.org/10.1136/bjsm.2005.018119

Richards, C., Bouman, W. P., & Barker, M. J. (2017). *Genderqueer and non-binary genders*. Basingstoke, Hampshire: Palgrave Macmillan.

Schilt, K. (2010). *Just one of the guys?* Chicago, IL: University of Chicago Press.

Saeidzadeh, Z. (2020). "Are trans men the manliest of men?" Gender practices, trans masculinity and mardānegī in contemporary Iran. *Journal of Gender Studies, 29*(3), 295–309. https://doi.org/10.1080/09589236.2019.1635439

Scotland Act. (1998). Available at: www.legislation.gov.uk/ukpga/1998/46/section/35. (Accessed: 27 January 2023).

Sedgewick, E. K. (1995). Gosh, Boy George, you must be awfully secure in your masculinity! Available at: https://latinomasculinities.files.wordpress.com/2012/01/sedgwick-gosh-boy-george1.pdf. (Accessed: 2 July 2021).

Semerjian, T. Z., & Cohen, J. H. (2006). "FTM means female to me": Transgender athletes performing gender. *Women in Sport and Physical Activity Journal, 15*(2), 28–43. https://doi.org/10.1123/wspaj.15.2.28

Serano, J. (2013). *Excluded*. Berkeley, CA: Seal.

Spandler, H., Erikainen, S., Hopkins, A., Caudwell, J., Newman, H., & Whitehouse, L. (2020). *Non-binary inclusion in sport*. Leap Sports. Available at: https://leapsports.org/files/4225-Non-Binary%20Inclusion%20in%20sport%20Booklet.pdf. (Accessed: 3 March 2020).

Sullivan, C. F. (2011). Gender verification and gender policies in elite sport: Eligibility and "fair play". *Journal of Sport and Social Issues, 35*(4), 400–419. https://doi.org/10.1177/0193723511426293

Teetzel, S. (2006). On transgendered athletes, fairness and doping: An international challenge. *Sport in Society, 9*(2), 227–251. https://doi.org/10.1080/17430430500491280

Travers, A., & Deri, J. (2011). Transgender inclusion and the changing face of lesbian softball leagues. *International Review for the Sociology of Sport, 46*(4), 488–507. https://doi.org/10.1177/1012690210384661

UK Equality Act. (2010). Available at: www.legislation.gov.uk/ukpga/2010/15/contents. (Accessed: 27 January 2023)

Vincent, B. W. (2018). Studying trans: Recommendations for ethical recruitment and collaboration with transgender participants in academic research. *Psychology & Sexuality, 9*(2), 102–116. https://doi.org/10.1080/19419899.2018.1434558

Waldron, J. (2019). Four perspectives for understanding LGBTIQ people in sport. In V. Krane (Ed.) *Sex, gender, and sexuality in sport: Queer inquiries*, pp. 15–32. Abingdon: Routledge.

White, R. M., & Newbegin, N. (2021). *A practical guide to transgender law*. Somerset: Law Brief Publishing.

8
SEX-TESTING AND DISCRIMINATION IN SPORT
Upholding an uneven playing field

Grace Athanas-Linden

Introduction

Sex-segregated sport, upheld by sex-testing, was institutionalised in reaction to changing gender dynamics in society and the desire to enforce gender roles and a gender hierarchy (Dworkin & Cooky, 2012). At the turn of the twentieth century, women began to enter college and more women entered the workforce, causing men to become concerned that their sons would become feminine (Buzuvis, 2011; Dworkin & Cooky, 2012, Messner, 1988; Wachs, 2002). Today, sport is one of the few places in society where we "accept, expect, and even defend sex segregation as the status quo" (George, 2002, p. 1107), so ingrained is it in how sport is organised and practised (Dashper, 2012). Through segregation, sport creates and reinforces the idea of distinct, hierarchical genders, where women and girls are deemed too physically weak to participate in sport (Burton, 2015; Cohen, Melton, & Peachey, 2014; Kane, 1995).

The belief in hierarchical genders necessitates separate spaces for men and women to compete so that 'fair play' and 'equality' are upheld on the field (Kane, 1995, p. 201; McDonagh & Pappano, 2008). The rhetoric of 'fair play' is how sport governing bodies justify sex-testing (Dworkin & Cooky, 2012; Pieper, 2015, 2016). However, rather than protect women's sports, sex-testing creates and polices gender boundaries, as it is primarily weaponised against women who excel in sport and show evidence of being able to compete with men (Dworkin & Cooky, 2012; Kane, 1995). In this way, sex-testing casts doubts on women's accomplishments and discriminates against gender expansive and intersex individuals.

Laying out certain definitions now will help to clarify some of the topics discussed in this chapter. Gender identity is someone's internal sense of their gender, which can be male, female, non-binary, or anywhere on the gender spectrum (Jones, Arcelus, Bouman, & Haycraft, 2016). Cisgender individuals are those whose gender is congruous with their gender assigned at birth (based on external sex characteristics), while transgender individuals experience an incongruence between their assigned gender and their gender identity (Buzuvis, 2011; Griffin & Carroll, 2011; Jones et al., 2016). Transgender women are assigned male at birth but identify as female, while transgender men are assigned female at birth but identify as male (Griffin & Carroll, 2011). Individuals with intersex variations (referred to here as "intersex individuals/athletes") are born with atypical combinations of "sexual characteristics such as chromosomes, internal reproductive organs and [gonads], and external genitalia" (Griffin & Carroll, 2011, p. 3). These individuals may have gender identities anywhere along the spectrum.

Historical assumptions about gender

Throughout history, sport has echoed and upheld patriarchal ideas about differences between genders, namely: (1) sex and gender are binary; and (2) women are weaker and less athletic.

Sex and gender are binary

Since the eighteenth century, sex and gender have been considered binary, with males and females considered "polar opposites, both in terms of biology and societal roles" (Pieper, 2015, p. 1141). Women who deviated from the expected form of femininity by showing aggression, strength, and muscularity were said to "not be 'real' representatives of the 'weaker' sex" (Pieper, 2015, p. 1141). To maintain the ideology that men are superior to women, it is important that 'real' women are incapable of excelling in athletics (Dworkin & Cooky, 2012; Kane, 1995). Such ideas are evident in modern fears of gender transgressions. In the 1952 Olympics, Russian women helped the USSR pull ahead of Western-aligned countries, and pictures of "unapologetically strong Eastern European female athletes" raised Western fears about fading femininity, unfairness in sport, and male imposters (Pieper, 2012, p. 678). This logic – that muscular women are not 'real' women, so they may be men posing as women – leads inexorably towards the implementation of sex testing to verify which women are 'real'. In reality, American ideals of submissive and graceful women pressured female athletes to avoid gaining muscle, allowing the USSR to dominate women's gymnastics and athletics (Pieper, 2014a). Western countries characterised the Eastern European women as men because of their athletic success, upholding binary gender characteristics (Pieper, 2014a).

Such gender policing is not found solely in the past. At the 2009 World Championships, in the women's 800 metres, Caster Semenya defeated her competitors by more than two seconds (Buzuvis, 2011; Pieper, 2014a, 2015). Due to her impressive win – though slower than the world record – and her deep voice and muscular figure, her competitors accused her of being a man (Pieper, 2014a). The fact that her appearance was deemed an 'issue' – even when her win was not record-setting – shows how sex-testing policies regulate gender boundaries rather than fairness.

Women are physically weaker and less athletic

Through the 1900s, women's athletics in the United States was limited, recreational, and deemphasised competition as it was believed that strenuous exertion, especially around menstruation, was dangerous (Leong, 2018). By the mid-1900s, female physical educators had created an adapted model of sports that had very different rules from men's sports and required less exertion, bodily contact, and bodily aggression (Messner, 2002).

When Title IX was made a US law in the 1970s, it laid the foundation for women to demand equal opportunity in sports at all levels of education (Cohen et al., 2014; Leong, 2018). However, it did not change the assumption that men are superior athletes compared to women (Cohen et al., 2014; Leong, 2018). The regulations in fact allowed segregated teams if the team was selected based on competitive ability or if the sport was a contact sport

(Leong, 2018). These regulations assume that girls would not be able to make the boys' teams and therefore girls need a separate space. The contact sport exemption also assumes that girls would be injured if they played with boys. Contact sport is further held as a masculine space since there is no obligation to even provide a separate team for girls (George, 2002). In 1974, a Rhode Island District Court ruled that girls could be excluded from baseball on the basis of sex, agreeing with the assertion that girls would be injured if they were allowed to play with boys (Fields, 2001).

These ideas about the inherent lack of athleticism in those assigned female at birth also affects transgender women athletes. When Renee Richards, a transgender woman athlete playing in women's tennis in the mid-1970s, was denied entry to the 1976 US Open, the United States Tennis Association (USTA) asserted that allowing "persons not genetically female" would lead to unfairness (as cited in Pieper, 2012, p. 678). The implication is that a so-called biological woman would always lose to a so-called biological man, emphasising both a sex binary and the inferiority of female athletes. Other transgender women – such as golfer Charlotte Ann Wood in 1987 and mountain-biker Michelle Dumaresq in 2001 – also faced discrimination under the assumption that they had an inherent athletic advantage from being assigned male at birth (Buzuvis, 2011; Pieper 2014b). For example, the US Golf Association (USGA) responded to Wood's success in amateur leagues by instituting a rule that all athletes in the women's competitions be deemed "female at birth"; there was no reciprocal rule for the men's events, highlighting the belief that transgender men have a biological *disadvantage* from being assigned female at birth (Pieper, 2014b). These ideas are pulled directly from hierarchical gender norms and weaponised to discriminate against transgender athletes.

Refutation of historical assumptions

Sex-testing ignores the sex spectrum in favour of a binary

Throughout history, sport governing bodies have used different tests in an effort to clearly delineate two binary, oppositional sexes. The strong Euro-American belief in distinct sexes influences this desire of the sport governing bodies (Buzuvis, 2011). Each of those sex-tests failed to unambiguously determine sex because, as David Esptein states, "Human biology does not break down into male and female as politely as sport governing bodies wish it would" (as cited in Pieper, 2015, p. 58). The sex spectrum shows "that the sex-segregated, binary model of competition is by definition an imperfect division" (Buzuvis, 2011, p. 36). Nevertheless, sport organisations have continued to believe that sex-testing can definitively distinguish men from women (Pieper, 2015). In addition, sport officials have historically tested for sex based on single determinants, which is an unscientific view of how sex and gender are shaped. The mere fact that sport governing bodies adopted and discarded tests over time due to their flaws underlines the fact that there is not a clear line between sexes and that sport policies are influenced by political and societal assumptions. In today's understanding, there are in fact seven different factors of biological sex: chromosomes, gonads, internal organs (e.g. uterus), external genitalia, hormone production, hormone response, and secondary sex characteristics (Zomorodi, 2020). During development, the body may differentiate towards male or female in any of these categories (Zomorodi, 2020). The result is that people with intersex variations make up approximately 2 per cent of the population, the same proportion of the population as genetic redheads (Zomorodi, 2020).

Do those assigned male at birth have an advantage?

With this understanding that sex does not exist as a binary, we can turn to look at the science around whether those assigned male at birth have a biological advantage in sport.

A study examining differences in throwing ability found that differences were linked to age rather than gender; because differences linked to gender were only evident in throws using the dominant arm, it was suggested that "nonbiological factors are important in explaining the larger gender differences in throwing" (as cited in McDonagh & Pappano, 2008, p. 23). Although it is true that there are average differences between men and women, these are not categorical differences; just because the average woman is shorter than the average man, it does not mean that an individual woman is inherently shorter than every man on the team (Buzuvis, 2011; Milner & Braddock, 2016). Comparing average differences – taking a single data point (e.g. average performance or best performance) for men and women to describe the whole – reconfirms gender as two oppositional, distinct categories; if we looked at all the data points (the performance of all the men and women), we would see that women can outperform men and get a much more realistic idea of performance (Kane, 1995). The difference between the best and the worst athlete of both sexes is far greater than the difference between the average athletes in each sex (Kane, 1995). There are other biological features which are not penalised as an advantage; for instance, Michael Phelps' long arms are simply viewed as a valuable tool in his swimming success (Rogol & Pieper, 2017). It is not clear that the perceived advantage of women with heightened testosterone is any more than the advantage long arms or financial resources may provide (Jones et al., 2016). Additionally, athleticism is not directly a result of physical features, as smaller men can outperform bigger, stronger men (Buzuvis, 2011; Kane, 1995). Sport governing bodies realise this, since most sports do not stratify athletes based on physical attributes such as height or arm length (Buzuvis, 2011). Strength and speed – and performance on tasks requiring those attributes – are heavily influenced by factors such as conditioning and training (Dworkin & Cooky, 2012; Milner & Braddock, 2016). If this were not the case, there would be no point in athletes training and attempting to improve.

Hormonal levels are the most common method today of defining and 'verifying' sex (Pieper, 2015). Sport scientists have contradicted the belief that there is "no overlap between testosterone blood levels in healthy men and women" (as cited on p. 182), and explain that,

> [Testosterone] levels aren't dimorphic, but are characterized by two curves that overlap more or less depending on how you choose the women and men in the sample.
> (Jordan-Young & Karkazis, 2019, p. 185)

Furthermore, even though the average testosterone level in men is about ten times higher than the average testosterone level in women, we see an overlap of elite male and female athletic performances, rather than men outperforming women by ten times (Buzuvis, 2016). This suggests that there is not a neat advantage that testosterone offers. The relationship between androgenic hormones and athletic ability (e.g. jumping distance) has only been scantily researched, and those studies that have been conducted "fail to show consistent relationships between [testosterone] and performance" (Jones et al., 2016; Jordan-Young & Karkazis, 2019, p. 161). While some studies do find a clear correlation between speed (explosive power) and endogenous levels of testosterone, many others find no correlation between performance and endogenous testosterone levels; several have even found negative relationships, in which a higher level of endogenous (or naturally produced) testosterone is correlated to worse performance (Jordan-Young & Karkazis, 2019). One study indicated that exercise was an important factor in determining whether a high level of testosterone increased muscle mass (Jordan-Young & Karkazis, 2019). Jordan-Young and Karkazis (2019) note that while testosterone "is involved in many of the processes that underlie athletic performance ... it's neither a sufficient or even necessary ingredient" (p. 201). The limitation to testosterone's impact on athletic performance is shown through women with complete androgen insensitivity syndrome (AIS) whose bodies are unable to process testosterone and yet are "overrepresented among elite women athletes"; if testosterone were truly a deciding competitive factor, we would see women with AIS *under*-represented in elite athletics (Buzuvis, 2016; Jordan-Young & Karkazis, 2019, p. 201). The limited research on testosterone's competitive advantage is inconclusive, and certainly not clear enough to use as a basis for exclusion.

Impact

Any female athletes who do not conform to traditional ideals may be sex-tested, meaning that all women athletes (e.g. cisgender, transgender, and intersex) are affected by scrutiny and medical inquiries into their sex and gender. Sex-testing poses an ethical issue by allowing a wide variety of people (e.g. the public, media, and other athletes) to judge women's bodies (Pieper, 2016). Additionally, forcing an individual to undergo – and reveal the results of – medical procedures is deeply invasive and violates privacy, particularly for children. Questioning female athletes' sex reasserts masculine athletic superiority, reinforces a binary model of sex and gender, and discriminates against gender non-conforming individuals (Pieper, 2015).

Impact on transgender women athletes

Most sport policies regulating the participation of transgender athletes are based on "indirect, inconsistent" evidence (Jones et al., 2016, p. 712). These policies, like sex-testing and sex-segregation, presuppose a categorical, hierarchical difference between women and men. Certain policies and laws prohibit the participation of transgender athletes, explicitly assuming immutable and inherent differences between men and women. World Rugby, the international governing body of rugby, banned transgender women and girls from elite rugby in October 2020 (Mosier, n.d.). In the United States, 32 states proposed or implemented legislation regulating the participation of transgender individuals, particularly youth, in sport (Bill Track 50, 2020a, 2020b; Brassil, 2021; Ennis, 2020; Strangio, 2021; Ta, 2020). The stated rationale for these regulations is the need to protect girls' and women's sports, which comes directly from the idea that transgender women athletes (given their assignation of male at birth) have an inherent advantage over cisgender female athletes (Griffin & Carroll, 2011; Pieper, 2015). Such policies set up a structure in which transgender and cisgender individuals are inherently unequal. By making biological arguments about hierarchies of athleticism based on sex/gender, the arguments seem more legitimate and natural (Pieper, 2015).

Recent policy changes by the International Olympic Committee (IOC) and National Collegiate Athletic Association (NCAA) highlight the complex overlapping of regulations. In November 2021, the IOC issued the "IOC Framework on Fairness, Inclusion and Non-Discrimination on the Basis of Gender Identity and Sex Variations", which gives sport governing bodies the discretion to implement policies regulating the inclusion of transgender and intersex athletes and establishes ten guiding principles for the creation of inclusive policies (IOC, 2021). In January 2022, the NCAA released new guidelines that put transgender athlete participation into the hands of each sport's national governing body; if there is no national governing body, then the international federation policy would be adhered to, or in the absence of *that*, the IOC's previously established criteria would take effect (Selbe, 2022). This highlights the many layers of regulations that an athlete may be subject to. With these multi-sport organisations deferring to each sport, the wide range of athletes under their purview may be subject to radically different levels of inclusion.

Hormone regulation is perhaps the most common form of sex-testing by sport organisations today. Prior to the full implementation of the NCAA's new policy in the 2023–2024 academic year, transgender athletes had to provide documentation of sport-specific testosterone levels four weeks prior to selections for their sport's championship (NCAA, 2022). In the 2022–2023 academic year, transgender athletes additionally needed to document their testosterone levels at the beginning of their season, followed by further documentation six months later (NCAA, 2022). Spurred by the NCAA's announcement, USA Swimming released their requirements for trans women swimmers (Yurcaba, 2022). These are: (1) their blood testosterone level must be below 5 nanomoles per litre for 36 months prior to applying to compete, and (2) they must provide evidence that undergoing puberty as their sex assigned at birth does not give them an advantage over cisgender women (Yurcaba, 2022). Setting aside the burden that is placed on trans women by this second requirement, three years is the longest term demanded from any sport governing body and there is no evidence that 36 months mitigates any advantages more effectively than 24 months (Yurcaba, 2022). These policies speak to the emphasis on testosterone in determining whether an athlete belongs with their identified gender and assume that a certain hormonal range determines whether transgender women are women. This ignores the reality that many transgender individuals choose not to medically transition, and that transgender women – no matter their transitioning status – *are* women "because gender is not a fact, [rather] the various acts of gender creates [sic] the idea of gender, and without those acts, there would be no gender at all" (Butler, 1988, p. 522). To suggest otherwise – as these policies do – invalidates the experience of these individuals and excludes them.

Perhaps the most invasive requirement that sport governing policies enact is a requirement for gender-confirming surgery. World Athletics' May 2011 policy (no longer in force) dictated that transgender women athletes had to have sex re-assignment surgery and provide legal documentation of their sex, any sex-reassignment surgeries or procedures, and any post-surgery monitoring or treatment (IAAF, 2011). After this initial review, the athlete had to provide an endocrine assessment, be *provisionally* approved by the Expert Medical Panel (which can ask for further medical, scientific, or specialist assessments), and finally consent to their information being provided to those who are 'required' to review it (IAAF, 2011). Full eligibility was finally granted if the athlete complied with any prescribed medical 'treatment' prior to competing, provided evidence of having done so, and the Expert Medical Panel recommended that they be eligible (IAAF, 2011). Even after this, World Athletics could continue to monitor the athlete (IAAF, 2011). The regulations laid out a series of obstacles to transgender women athletes competing in sport, which may in and of themselves deter some athletes from attempting to compete. Surgery requirements are invasive and a violation of privacy, as they take away the athletes' autonomy to decide what transitions – if any – to undergo and force an individual to reveal their medical history to others for judgment.

There is also a clear discrepancy in the treatment of transgender women and transgender men athletes. For instance, World Athletics' current policy only requires that transgender male athletes provide a "written and signed declaration, in a form satisfactory to the Medical Manager, that his gender identity is male" (Section 3.1) while female transgender athletes have to additionally "demonstrate to the satisfaction of the Expert Panel ... that the concentration of testosterone in her serum has been less than 5nmol/L3 continuously for a period of at least 12 months" (Section 3.2.2) and keep her testosterone below that level for as long as she wishes to compete (World Athletics, 2019). Such regulations reveal a pervasive belief in the athletic inferiority of those assigned female at birth: they pose no threat to masculine athletic superiority, as it is assumed their biology will prevent them from competing at an elite level. In other words, superiority in athleticism is assumed to be based on biology while ignoring social influences, such as the discrepancy in investment in and resources for women's sports.

Increased levels of regulation also increase the barriers to participation for transgender women athletes due to the complex process for approval and temporary ineligibilities. For example, if a transgender woman swimmer wants to compete as a member of USA Swimming, she will have to comply with their requirement of diminishing her testosterone level to the required level for 36 months prior to being able to compete with her gender identity, and so potentially lose *three years* of participation. This does not consider the amount of time it might take for sport organisations to review cases and grant eligibility. Furthermore, the expense of these procedures and the cost of preparing the necessary paperwork are an additional barrier to low-income athletes. Finally, these policies demand that transgender athletes 'out' themselves: even relatively inclusive policies necessitate that the athlete reveal that they are transgender, if they have any requirements at all around 'treatment' (Teetzel, 2013). Demanding that transgender athletes make themselves known is a violation of their privacy and immediately 'others' them: they must tell the 'normal' athletic authorities that they need a special procedure to compete.

Impact on intersex female athletes

Intersex athletes' non-binary bodies blur the lines between what 'men' versus 'women' are capable of and undermines our sex-segregated system of sport (Buzuvis, 2011). Intersex women athletes – who are the only athletes 'found out' by sex-testing, since men are not sex-tested – raise similar questions of fairness as transgender women athletes; those intersex women athletes who have high hormone levels, more muscular bodies, and/or do not conform to Western ideas of femininity are particularly persecuted by efforts to regulate 'fairness'. Concerns about fairness and gender-norms lead to women who appear 'suspicious' being tested and removed from sport. When these athletes are removed from competition "the public is left with the impression that top sport performers are not carried out by 'real women', and the assumption of absolute categorical difference between women and men is left intact" (Dworkin & Cooky, 2012, p. 22). In this way, intersex female athletes are 'othered' and presented to the public as 'not women'. A conflict is set up between women without differences of sexual development (DSD) and those with DSD, reaffirming the assumption that women are lesser athletes.

One of the most well-known methods of regulating intersex athletes is to demand that they suppress elevated testosterone levels. World Athletics' current DSD Regulations state that women with endogenous testosterone over 5 nmol/L, androgen receptivity, and

XY chromosomes are ineligible to compete in certain women's international track and field events unless they artificially lower their testosterone levels (Holzer, 2020). World Athletics has instituted a policy based on normative ideas of women's bodies even though an individual's chromosomal status is irrelevant to whether high testosterone levels matter (Elsey, 2020). This policy is a return to the idea that 'real' women only have XX sex chromosomes while men have XY, and is possibly rooted in the idea that certain traits (like athleticism or aggression) are encoded in the genes. Even though both hormones and chromosomes are being used to define a woman in the athletic context, World Athletics asserts gender is a dichotomy by saying 'real' women have XX chromosomes. If 'real' women have high testosterone, there is no substantive overlap between the genders; however, if 'fake' women (with XY chromosomes) have high testosterone, then they are no longer able to compete with 'real' women. Despite the lack of scientific clarity and concerns of international human rights agencies, the Court of Arbitration for Sport (CAS), whose decision was upheld by the Swiss Federal Court (SFC), decided that the DSD Regulations were "necessary, reasonable and proportionate" and that ensuring fairness in sport is a legitimate interest that "justif[ies] serious infringements of the rights of athletes" (Elsey, 2020, para. 27). In response to Dutee Chand's case against World Athletics, the IOC set a very vague policy on hyperandrogenism (elevated levels of androgens like testosterone) in 2015 (IOC, 2015). The policy said that "rules should be in place for the protection of women in sport and the promotion of the principles of fair competition" and encouraged the national Olympic committees and federations to "revert to CAS with arguments and evidence to support the reinstatement of [World Athletics'] hyperandrogenism rules" while avoiding discrimination by letting those athletes not eligible to compete in female events compete in male events (IOC, 2015, p. 3). This policy clearly indicates that the IOC supported World Athletics' regulations but wanted to protect itself from discrimination claims. Setting aside whether such policies actually preserve fairness, it is concerning that ensuring fairness is considered more important than the right of the participants or medical ethics (Elsey, 2020). It is also clear that these regulations are not about preserving fairness in sport, since men are not tested to determine whether they have an atypically high testosterone level. If testosterone truly provides a competitive advantage, men should be tested for unusually high testosterone as well (Holzer, 2020). Evidently, hormonal policies are more about singling out women who do not conform to expectations of femininity rather than fairness.

Despite sport organisations asserting that intersex women have a 'disorder', high testosterone is not inherently a medical problem, and doctors do not lower high levels without patient complaints or impairment (Jordan-Young & Karkazis, 2019). In fact, "lowering T [testosterone] can cause significant health problems" that range from depression to osteoporosis (Jordan-Young & Karkazis, 2019, p. 199). Regulations requiring such medical interventions also raise ethical questions: should a healthy woman be required to take drugs to suppress her endogenous testosterone (Teetzel, 2013)? Individuals with intersex variations have argued for decades against such interventions because they cause "irreparable harm to sexual sensation and function" as well as "pathologize sex-atypical bodies and behavior that breaks gender norms" (Jordan-Young & Karkazis, 2019, p. 199). Regarding the harm that these regulations impose, the Office of the United Nations High Commissioner for Human Rights (OHCHR) included in a recent report that "the implementation of female eligibility regulations denies athletes with variations in sex characteristics an equal right to participate in sport and violates the right to non-discrimination more broadly" (as cited in Holzer, 2020, para. 34). Chand's lawsuit against World Athletics pointed out how suspicion-based testing denigrates athletes' dignity and self-identification (Buzuvis, 2016). Many intersex individuals only learn they have such variations later in life because interventions are done on them at a very early age and may endure trauma when their ideas about their body are disrupted by sex-testing results. The nature of this 'discovery' implies shame as being intersex automatically others and excludes them from sport (Buzuvis, 2016). Instead of protecting athletes from this harm, the rights of one group of athletes (those without intersex variations) are championed at the expense of another group of athletes (those with intersex variations), assuming that the former could not win if the latter competed (Elsey, 2020). On the other hand, "supporters of the regulations ... would say there is no right to win or to compete at the highest level when it comes to women with [DSD]" (Elsey, 2020, para. 35). This paradox allows sport organisations to implement regulations which take away the right of intersex athletes to compete in order to protect that same right for non-intersex athletes.

Impact on cisgender female athletes

While the impact of sex-testing on cisgender female athletes may be less obvious, sex-testing upholds sex-segregation and undergirds ideas about cisgender women in sport. At any time – due to physical appearance, skill, or other subjective suspicions – female athletes may be tested to see whether they are in fact 'real' women. This policing of women's bodies invades privacy even if they are not consequently barred from women's sports.

One way in which cisgender female athletes are punished for gender non-conformity is regendering. Female athletes who excel in skills or activities that are traditionally thought of as masculine are regendered, i.e. said to be a man by implying that she is too good to be a 'real' woman (Kane, 1995; Messner, 1988). The common phrase 'she hits like a boy' encapsulates this idea (Kane, 1995; Messner, 1988). Women who are regendered are made out to be exceptional and able to accomplish tasks other women cannot, thereby reinforcing the idea that men are inherently more athletic and women are incapable of possessing such skills (Kane, 1995; Messner, 1988). When a woman further breaks expectations of femininity, she is labelled a "deviant-mutant" and her status as a 'real' woman is subject to suspicion (Kane, 1995, p. 210). The threat to the gender hierarchy that these women pose is controlled by either framing them as lesbians – who are not viewed as falling into accepted gender categories – or forced to take tests to prove they are female, as previously seen (Kane, 1995). Serena Williams' muscular physique makes her more vulnerable to suspicion, and commenters online have asked whether she should identify as a woman or have 'accused' her of being transgender (Litchfield, Kavanagh, Osborne, & Jones, 2018).

Seeing women excel over men would make maintaining a gender hierarchy impossible: therefore, by segregating sport, men protect their own power (Kane, 1995). Women's sport is a "self-perpetuating phenomenon" in which women are assumed to be inferior athletes to men and so need their own sports and competitions, but then the existence of these sex-segregated events ensures that women are never given the opportunity to prove they are capable of competing against men (Leong, 2018, p. 1274). By excluding women from the realm of men's sport (enforced through sex-testing), detractors can claim that women must compete against men to truly be considered talented while ensuring that women are never given that opportunity. Women's skill can then easily be minimised while men's sport is made out to be the pinnacle of sport, comprised of the best athletes.

Intersection with race

Although a full investigation into the complex intersection between racialisation and sex-testing is not within the scope of this chapter, it is important to briefly address it here. For conciseness, this chapter will refer to 'race' when describing the way individuals are racialised.

While all women have historically faced derision for participating in sport, "black women in particular have faced hostile contempt in the West for not displaying white femininity", which is comprised of delicate, non-muscular, stereotypically White features (Pieper, 2014a, p. 1560). This preference for White femininity comes from the use of the sex binary as a tool of White supremacy and European colonisation (Elsey, 2020; Pieper, 2014a). When discussing sexual 'abnormalities', American and European medical journals referred to Black bodies more frequently than White bodies, suggesting that Black women were less sexually differentiated from men and more likely to have such ambiguous genitalia (Elsey, 2020; Pieper, 2016). The White race was overall deemed to be the most highly evolved and the most sexually differentiated (Elsey, 2020). This binary between sexually differentiated men and women was then institutionalised as a tool of colonisation to ideologically dominate cultures that accepted multiple sexes and genders by eliminating such fluidity and reorganising social relations (Pieper, 2014a). White features became seen as the most desirable or 'evolved', and any other form of femininity was denigrated.

Many racialised sex-testing controversies come from track and field. Following World War II, gender norms cemented athletics as a masculine sport, opening any women who participated to "stigmatisation as an 'amazon' or a 'muscle moll'" (Pieper 2014a, p. 1561). To adhere to ideas of White femininity in the US, White women rarely chose to compete in track and field (Pieper, 2014a). With fewer middle class White women participating in the sport, Black female athletes were given room to excel (Pieper, 2014a). Their success, however, in this masculine-gendered sport reinforced the notion that Black women were more masculine than White women and increased scepticism of their gender (Pieper, 2014a). Because of this heightened suspicion around Black female track and field athletes, World Athletics and the IOC have always been at the forefront of sex-testing.

In this context, intersex variations are viewed as 'problems' to solve: in the Global North, babies with intersex variations – who lack the ability to consent – are subjected to medical interventions to eliminate those variations (Elsey, 2020; Pieper, 2014a). Women from the Global South with intersex variations are much less likely to undergo such interventions in infancy yet are forced to go through interventions later in life to compete in sport (Elsey, 2020). The way Black women are judged is also subject to racial scrutiny – "racialized gazes around femininity ... affect who it is that looks suspicious" (Elsey, 2020, para. 22). Western, White individuals dominate sport governing bodies which make policies that force women in the Global South to physically conform to standards of Western femininity (Elsey, 2020). When the IOC's former regulations – the Stockholm Consensus – led to primarily Black and Brown athletes from the Global South having their testosterone tested, the IOC and World Athletics acknowledged the disparate impact but claimed their mandated interventions benefit athletes since the Global South is deemed to be incompetent in addressing intersex variations (Jordan-Young & Karkazis, 2019). Even the idea that intersex variations *need* to be addressed highlights the emphasis on Western femininity and exacerbates racial discrimination. The imbalance of power – culturally, socially, and economically – makes modern sex-testing a multi-faceted form of neo-colonial control.

The treatment of four athletes shows that the 'remedies' proposed by the IOC and World Athletics are about upholding the sexual binary and status quo rather than protecting fairness. According to a 2013 World Athletics report, four women between 18 and 21 years old from "rural and mountainous regions of developing countries" were determined to have high testosterone and sent to a specialist centre in France (as cited in Jordan-Young & Karkazis, 2019). Doctors determined that the high testosterone levels were caused by "chromosomal variations and internal testes" (as cited in Jordan-Young & Karkazis, 2019). While acknowledging that the women's testes had no health risk, they recommended a gonadectomy to allow them to continue playing women's sports, in addition to performing further superficial surgeries that have no impact on athletic performance such as "a partial clitoridectomy … followed by a deferred feminizing vaginoplasty and estrogen replacement therapy" (as cited in Jordan-Young & Karkazis, 2019). These incredibly invasive surgeries were utilised to 'normalise' intersex women – thereby 'othering' them – based on ideas about appropriate physiognomy for women beyond compliance with the regulations or athletic performance (Jordan-Young & Karkazis, 2019).

Racialised gender-policing takes many forms. Muscular women and Black women are both seen as more masculine, which makes it unsurprising that Serena Williams, a muscular Black female tennis player, often has her gender questioned (Litchfield et al., 2018). Anna Kournikova – who never won a professional singles tennis tournament and yet was the most sponsored female athlete in the world – constructed her own femininity in direct opposition to Serena and Venus Williams, Serena's sister and fellow tennis player (Schultz, 2005). Kournikova said at one point: "I hate my muscles. I'm not Venus Williams. I'm not Serena Williams. I'm feminine. I don't want to look like they do. I'm not masculine like they are" (as cited in Schultz, 2005, p. 346).

Kournikova in this quote equates muscularity and masculinity, implying the Williams sisters are non-women. Questioning their femininity reinforces the boundaries of appropriate (i.e. White) femininity.

We see throughout this section that Black women are more subject to suspicion and testing given the bias towards Western ideas of femininity: lean, delicate, White females are considered the norm as constructed against muscular, Black, and Brown bodies.

Efforts at inclusion

There are some promising efforts at gender inclusion. The sport governing body of Quidditch, the International Quidditch Association (IQA), allows players to self-identify and "embraces players of *all* genders and sexualities [emphasis added]" (Rulebook, 2020, p. 7). The IQA does not demand that athletes transition and instead opens participation to all. In fact, they make space for multiple genders by removing any language about identifying as either male or female and instead stating that during a Quidditch game, "a team may not have more than four players who identify as the same gender in play at the same time" out of a total of seven players in play (Rulebook, 2020, p. 12). This gender-neutral language allows the IQA to ensure that the sport is integrated on the basis of sex/gender (by holding space for different genders on the same team) without limiting what their participants' gender looks like.

Mixed roller derby has also made efforts to improve inclusion, particularly in the Women's Flat Track Derby Association (WFTDA), which most leagues follow (Pavlidis & Connor, 2016). The WFTDA's November 2015 policy states that any trans woman, intersex woman, or gender expansive individual may join a WFTDA team and that "the gender identity of any and all WFTDA participants is considered confidential and private", providing equal opportunities for both intersex and transgender athletes (Mosier, n.d., sect. Women's Flat Track Derby Association). Similarly, the Men's Roller Derby Association (MRDA):

> does not and will not differentiate between members who identify as male and those who identify as a nonbinary gender (including but not limited to genderqueer, transmasculine, transfeminine, and agender) and does not and will not set minimum standards of masculinity for its membership or interfere with the privacy of its members for the purposes of charter eligibility.
>
> (Pavlidis & Connor, 2016)

By continuing to hold themselves as 'women's/men's flat track roller derby' it is possible the WFTDA and MRDA could create informally exclusive spaces. However, both policies explicitly state that they welcome people of a variety of different genders and do not violate privacy in the form of sex-testing or body-altering procedures. The MRDA additionally attempts to stratify the league based on skill rather than gender (Pavlidis & Connor, 2016). The skill level of skaters is denoted by colours on the skater's helmet, which indicate how hard competitors may hit that skater; this is an "[attempt] to remove gender (as a restricting qualifier) and replace it with a somewhat quantitative measure of skill and ability" (Pavlidis & Connor, 2016, p. 104).

These are promising efforts at inclusion; however, one of the difficulties of writing policies concerning intersex athletes is that many intersex youths are not aware of their variations, due to interventions performed on them at a young age or simply not being informed. Policies that try to regulate their participation can out an individual as being 'atypical', which as we have already seen can be incredibly damaging when someone has grown up with a different understanding of their body and identity. For this reason, policies such as the WFTDA's that allow individuals to compete with their gender identity are the only way to keep sex-segregated sport without forcing invasive monitoring and procedures. If we accept that sport can survive without sex-testing, the next logical step is sex-integration.

Brief discussion of sex-integrated sport

To truly see inclusion and equity in sport, we must make sex-integration, based on the principles of gender equity, the default in sport. This necessitates removing the formal and informal methods of sex-segregation in sport and basing sport divisions on ability rather than gender or sex; the only reasonable exception to this is voluntary, self-segregation by marginalised groups to increase the group's participation in sport or protect them from oppression in integrated spaces (Fink et al., 2015; Kane, 1995; Leong, 2018; McDonagh & Pappano, 2008; Milner & Braddock, 2016; Travers, 2009). Cisgender women have more privilege than transgender or intersex athletes, and so must be conscious to not wield this power to marginalise these other groups. Therefore, any situation in which female athletes choose to voluntarily self-segregate must have policies that actively include transgender, intersex, and other gender non-conforming athletes (Travers, 2009).

Even setting women's sports on an equal footing (i.e. equal media coverage, equal resources, etc.) with men's would not necessarily counteract the discrimination perpetuated by sex-testing, as women's-only sport spaces – if based on a binary model of sex and gender – could perpetuate the exclusion of gender-expansive individuals (Travers, 2009). Sex-integrated sport is the only system which completely eradicates the need for sex-testing because it removes the need to regulate gender boundaries. Sex-integration threatens the traditional ideas of male superiority and causes us to rethink our notions of differences between genders (Channon, Dashper, Fletcher, & Lake, 2015). The rejection of sex differences would also help include transgender and intersex people as they would be less suspected of having a competitive advantage due to their sex characteristics. By not requiring people to classify themselves into distinct sex categories, integrated sports have the potential to be inclusive of athletes of all genders (Channon et al., 2015). Intersex and transgender athletes "would no longer be subjected to discrimination, outing, and other violations of privacy" and female athletes would be able to excel in sport without having to adhere to societal ideas about gender (Milner & Braddock, 2016, p. 112; Pieper, 2015). Furthermore, allowing men and women to be seen competing against each other would reduce assumptions that women are inherently inferior to men in sport and society (Travers, 2009). By mandating that sport be integrated, it would make clear that segregation on the basis of sex is no more acceptable than segregation on any other basis (Travers, 2009).

Conclusion

Sex-testing actively discriminates against transgender, intersex, and cisgender female athletes by upholding a gender hierarchy that privileges cisgender men and demanding invasive regulations of female athletes' bodies. This system is closely tied to our system of sex-segregated sport: sex-segregated sport requires the regulation of gender to exist, which in turn requires sex-testing to determine binary categories of sex and gender. By turning to a system of sport in which sex-integration is the default, the need for sex-testing can be eliminated, thereby removing a pervasive form of discrimination against gender non-conforming individuals.

References

Bill Track 50. (2020a, March 30). ID – H0500. www.billtrack50.com/BillDetail/1202659
Bill Track 50. (2020b, May 21). KS – HB2589. www.billtrack50.com/BillDetail/1198709
Brassil, G. R. (2021, March 29). How some states are moving to restrict transgender women in sports. *New York Times*. www.nytimes.com/2021/03/11/sports/transgender-athletes-bills.html?auth=login-email&login=email
Burton, L. J. (2015). Underrepresentation of women in sport leadership: A review of research. *Sport Management Review*, *18*(2), 155–165. https://doi.org/10.1016/j.smr.2014.02.004
Butler, J. (1988). Performative acts and gender constitution: An essay in phenomenology and feminist theory. *Theatre Journal*, *40*(4), 519. https://doi.org/10.2307/3207893
Buzuvis, E. E. (2011). Transgender student-athletes and sex-segregated sport: Developing policies of inclusion for intercollegiate and interscholastic athletics. *Seton Hall Journal of Sports and Entertainment Law*, *21*(1), 1–60.
Buzuvis, E. E. (2016). Hormone check: Critique of Olympic rules on sex and gender. *Wisconsin Journal of Law, Gender & Society*, *31*(17–2), 29–55.
Channon, A., Dashper, K., Fletcher, T., & Lake, R. J. (2015). The promises and pitfalls of sex integration in sport and physical culture. *Sport in Society*, *19*(8–9), 1111–1124. https://doi.org/10.1080/17430437.2016.1116167
Cohen, A., Melton, E. N., & Peachey, J. W. (2014). Investigating a coed sport's ability to encourage inclusion and equality. *Journal of Sport Management*, *28*(2), 220–235. https://doi.org/10.1123/jsm.2013-0329

Dashper, K. (2012). Together, yet still not equal? Sex integration in equestrian sport. *Asia-Pacific Journal of Health, Sport and Physical Education, 3*(3), 213–225. https://doi.org/10.1080/18377122.2012.721727

Dworkin, S. L., & Cooky, C. (2012). Sport, sex segregation, and sex testing: Critical reflections on this unjust marriage. *The American Journal of Bioethics, 12*(7), 21–23. https://doi.org/10.1080/15265161.2012.680545

Elsey, B. (Host). (2020, 17 September). Interview: Katrina Karkazis and Michele Krech on Gender Binaries in Sport. *Burn It All Down*. BlueWire. www.burnitalldownpod.com/episodes/interview-katrina-karkazis-and-michele-krech-on-gender-binaries-in-sport

Ennis, D. (2020, January 10). 6 states considering legislation to restrict transgender student athletes. *SB Nation Outsports*. www.outsports.com/2019/12/18/21028032/new-hampshire-washington-georgia-tennessee-missouri-restrict-transgender-athletes-sports

Fields, S. K. (2001). Cultural identity, law, and baseball. *Culture, Sport, Society, 4*(2), 23–42. https://doi.org/10.1080/713999824

Fink, J. S., Lavoi, N. M., & Newhall, K. E. (2015). Challenging the gender binary? Male basketball practice players' views of female athletes and women's sports. *Sport in Society, 19*(8–9), 1316–1331. https://doi.org/10.1080/17430437.2015.1096252

George, B. (2002). Fifty/Fifty: Ending sex segregation in school sports. *Ohio State Law Journal, 63*(4), 1107–1164.

Griffin, P., & Carroll, H. (2011). *NCAA inclusion of transgender student-athletes* (Handbook). NCAA Office of Inclusion. www.ncaapublications.com/p-4335-ncaa-inclusion-of-transgender-student-athletes.aspx

Holzer, L. (2020, September 30). The decision of the Swiss Federal Supreme Court in the Caster Semenya case: A human rights and gender analysis. *OpinioJuris*. https://opiniojuris.org/2020/09/30/the-decision-of-the-swiss-federal-supreme-court-in-the-caster-semenya-case-a-human-rights-and-gender-analysis/

International Association of Athletics Federations. (2011). *IAAF regulations governing eligibility of athletes who have undergone sex reassignment to compete in women's competition*. https://13248aea-16f8-fc0a-cf26-a9339dd2a3f0.filesusr.com/ugd/2bc3fc_476cfbfe00df48c3aa5322a29d5e11b2.pdf

International Olympic Committee. (2015). *IOC consensus meeting on sex reassignment and hyperandrogenism*. https://stillmed.olympic.org/Documents/Commissions_PDFfiles/Medical_commission/2015-11_ioc_consensus_meeting_on_sex_reassignment_and_hyperandrogenism-en.pdf

International Olympic Committee. (2021). *IOC framework on fairness, inclusion and non-discrimination on the basis of gender identity and sex-variations*. Transathlete.com. www.transathlete.com/_files/ugd/2bc3fc_483de30a599e4972b418f20994048b5a.pdf

International Quidditch Association. (2020). *IQA rulebook 2020*. Seattle, WA: Author.

Jones, B. A., Arcelus, J., Bouman, W. P., & Haycraft, E. (2016). Sport and transgender people: A systematic review of the literature relating to sport participation and competitive sport policies. *Sports Medicine, 47*(4), 701–716. https://doi.org/10.1007/s40279-016-0621-y

Jordan-Young, R. M., & Karkazis, K. A. (2019). Athleticism. In *Testosterone: An unauthorized biography*, 159–201. Harvard University Press. https://doi.org/10.1111/maq.12565

Kane, M. J. (1995). Resistance/transformation of the oppositional binary: Exposing sport as a continuum. *Journal of Sport and Social Issues, 19*(2), 191–218. https://doi.org/10.1177/019372395019002006

Leong, N. (2018). Against women's sports. *Washington University Law Review, 95*(5), 1249–1290. https://doi.org/10.2139/ssrn

Litchfield, C., Kavanagh, E., Osborne, J., & Jones, I. (2018). Social media and the politics of gender, race and identity: The case of Serena Williams. *European Journal for Sport and Society*, 143–170. https://doi.org/10.1080/16138171.2018.1452870

McDonagh, E. L., & Pappano, L. (2008). *Playing with the boys: Why separate is not equal in sports*. Oxford: Oxford University Press.

Messner, M. A. (1988). Sports and male domination: The female athlete as contested ideological terrain. *Sociology of Sport Journal, 5*(3), 197–211. https://doi.org/10.1123/ssj.5.3.197

Messner, M. A. (2002). *Taking the field: Women, men, and sports*. University of Minnesota Press.

Milner, A. N., & Braddock, J. H. (2016). *Sex segregation in sports: Why separate is not equal*. ABC-CLIO, LLC.

Mosier, C. (n.d.). Organization & governing body policy. *TRANSATHLETE.com.* www.transathlete.com/policies-by-organization

National Collegiate Athletic Association. (2022, January 19). *Board of Governors updates transgender participation policy* [Press release]. www.ncaa.org/news/2022/1/19/media-center-board-of-governors-updates-transgender-participation-policy.aspx

Pavlidis, A., & Connor, J. (2016). 'Don't be a douche': An introduction to sex-integrated roller derby. In Thorpe, H., & Olive, R. (Eds), *Women in action sport cultures: Identity, politics and experience,* 91–111. Palgrave Macmillan. https://doi.org/10.1057/978-1-137-45797-4

Pieper, L. P. (2012). Gender regulation: Renée Richards revisited. *The International Journal of the History of Sport, 29*(5), 675–690. https://doi.org/10.1080/09523367.2012.675202

Pieper, L. P. (2014a). Sex testing and the maintenance of western femininity in international sport. *The International Journal of the History of Sport, 31*(13), 1557–1576. https://doi.org/10.1080/09523367.2014.927184

Pieper, L. P. (2014b). Opening Pandora's box?: Transgender athletes and the fight for inclusion. *Sport in American History.* https://ussporthistory.com/2014/10/09/opening-pandoras-box-transgender-athletes-and-the-fight-for-inclusion/

Pieper, L. P. (2015). 'Preserving la difference': The elusiveness of sex-segregated sport. *Sport in Society, 19*(8–9), 1138–1155. https://doi.org/10.1080/17430437.2015.1096258

Pieper, L. P. (2016). *Sex testing: Gender policing in women's sports.* University of Illinois Press.

Rogol, A. D., & Pieper, L. P. (2017). Genes, gender, hormones, and doping in sport: A convoluted tale. *Frontiers in Endocrinology, 8.* https://doi.org/10.3389/fendo.2017.00251

Schultz, J. (2005). Reading the catsuit: Serena Williams and the production of blackness at the 2002 US Open. *Journal of Sport and Social Issues, 29*(3), 338–357. https://doi.org/10.1177/0193723505276230

Selbe, N. (2022, January 19). NCAA Updates Policy on Transgender Athlete Participation. *Sports Illustrated.* www.si.com/college/2022/01/20/ncaa-updates-transgender-athlete-participation-policy

Strangio, C. [@chasestrangio]. (2021, April 13). Imagine seeing 32 states try to ban trans athletes in school sports without a single currently competing trans girl athlete [Tweet]. *Twitter.* https://twitter.com/chasestrangio/status/1382087883872407555

Ta, L. (2020, February 7). Iowa bills create restrictions for transgender students playing sports and lessons on LGBT topics. *Iowa Capital Dispatch.* https://iowacapitaldispatch.com/2020/02/07/iowa-bills-create-restrictions-for-transgender-students-playing-sports-and-lessons-on-lgbt-topics/

Teetzel, S. (2013). The onus of inclusivity: Sport policies and the enforcement of the women's category in sport. *Journal of the Philosophy of Sport, 41*(1), 113–127. https://doi.org/10.1080/00948705.2013.858394

Travers, A. (2009). The sport nexus and gender injustice. *Studies in Social Justice, 2*(1), 79–101. https://doi.org/10.26522/ssj.v2i1.969

Wachs, F. L. (2002). Leveling the playing field. *Journal of Sport and Social Issues, 26*(3), 300–316. https://doi.org/10.1177/0193723502263006

World Athletics. (2019). *Eligibility regulations for transgender athletes (in force from 1 October 2019)* [Rulebook]. www.worldathletics.org/download/download?filename=ace036ec-a21f-4a4a-9646-fb3c40fe80be.pdf&urlslug=C3.5%20-%20Eligibility%20Regulations%20Transgender%20Athletes

Yurcaba, J. (2022, February 2). USA swimming announces new policy for elite transgender athletes. *NBC News.* www.nbcnews.com/nbc-out/out-news/usa-swimming-announces-new-policy-elite-transgender-athletes-rcna14606

Zomorodi, M. (Host). (2020, May 8). The biology of sex. *TedRadio Hour.* www.npr.org/programs/ted-radio-hour/852195850/the-biology-of-sex?showDate=2020-05-08

9
DOING AND UNDOING GENDER IN PHYSICAL EDUCATION AND YOUTH SPORT

The potential for practice

Hannah Kettley-Linsell and Joanne Hill

Introduction

Gender has long been a focus within physical education (PE), reflecting its historical foundations (Kirk, 2010) and contemporary practices (Metcalfe, 2018). As a subject where the body is so central to practice, PE mirrors societal norms concerning gendered bodies (Aartun et al., 2022). Traditionally, a binary male/female view of gender, perceived as biologically 'natural' has prevailed (West & Zimmerman, 1987). Taking a poststructuralist perspective, such binary gender discourses denote expected gender norms and performative acts associated with biologically sexed bodies (Butler, 1993); meaning an individual's every action is held accountable to a set of socially constructed and accepted ways to 'do' gender. In this way, the 'doing' of gender is ongoing, every-day, and unavoidable, holding members of society hostage to its (re)production (West & Zimmerman, 1987). Implicit in this binary ideology is the assumption that all individuals are cisgender, meaning their gender identity aligns with their biological sex, as prescribed by societal norms.

Following the conceptualisation of gender as a performance (Butler, 1990, 1993) or a series of acts that through repetition and reiteration are read as performing a gender expression and identity, the theory of 'doing gender' (West & Zimmerman, 1987) is useful in understanding how gender is produced and reproduced, which can be applied to PE and youth sport. The theory furthers the conceptualisation of gender as a social construction, where gender is something that people continually and actively accomplish through their performance in social interactions. West and Zimmerman (1987) suggest that many people perform gender in ways that conform to normative behaviours and activities appropriate for their gender category to display a culturally acceptable form of masculinity or femininity. Hence, the concept of doing gender refers to the process of sustaining, reproducing, and legitimising institutional arrangements and practices that are based around sex categories, perpetuating gender binaries and supporting heteronormativity. The concept of 'undoing gender' is a helpful conceptual tool for capturing when gender hierarchies and norms are challenged and gender differences are reduced in practice (Risman, 2009).

Gendered views arguably underpin many practices within PE and youth sport, influencing attitudes towards biological differences and appropriate behaviours through categorising activities as either 'masculine' or 'feminine' (Metcalfe & Lindsey, 2020), providing separate curricula (Wilkinson & Penney, 2014), and gender-segregated classes. In this way, gender norms and expectations permeate young people's experiences of PE (Fagrell et al., 2012; Sánchez-Hernández et al., 2018). The structuring of provision on gender lines sustains hierarchies in which male is valorised over female; it limits the potential for students to express themselves differently; and works to suppress or render invisible non-conforming young people (Sykes, 2011; Landi, 2018).

The notion of doing gender offers the possibility to 'undo' gender and challenge conceptions of difference and inequality. Undoing gender refers to "social interactions that reduce gender difference" (Deutsch, 2007, p. 122). We argue that undoing gender aligns with social justice efforts in PE and youth sport. While gender binaries and segregation persist in organised sport which has (many national and international governing bodies would argue) sex-based boundaries, challenging aspects of gender relations and regimes are a social justice issue for PE because stereotyping, power relations and heteronormativity contribute to dropout, bullying, marginalisation of girls' efforts, and hence affect fairness and self-actualisation. Undoing gender supports inclusion efforts in PE, characterised by valuing each young person equally, providing a meaningful and relevant curriculum through pedagogies that embrace difference, and assessing in ways that recognise diverse abilities (Walton-Fisette & Sutherland, 2018).

This chapter outlines how gender segregation and gender-typing contribute to doing gender identity. Then, drawing from PE and non-elite sport examples, we explore evidence for undoing gender, both to facilitate the active inclusion and participation of gender non-conforming and queer students and to offer all girls and boys supportive environments for self-expression.

How gender is 'done' in single-sex PE

International research concerning the social construction of gender highlights the role of schools as agencies where gender processes are developed and reproduced (Oliver & Kirk, 2015). Decisions to provide the subject in single-sex classes are underpinned by deeply held beliefs about differences in boys' and girls' attitudes, behaviours, abilities, and experiences which reinforce stereotypical expectations for girls and boys, while limiting opportunities for participation and learning (Azzarito, 2009; Hills & Croston, 2012). Scholars investigating gender norms and discourses highlight how gender norms are reinforced through a hidden curriculum (Bain, 1990), although this term has fallen out of use in recent years. The hidden curriculum encompasses elements of a student's education that are not explicitly taught, conveying implicit rules, norms, and expectations which regulate bodies and influence students' gender identities (Kirk, 1992). Neither gender equality nor gender segregation are explicitly mentioned in curriculum documents, in the UK nations at least (Gray et al., 2021), implying that curriculum makers do not prescribe specific activities for boys and girls. Instead, teachers who select gendered curricula are making these decisions for themselves, within their school contexts and shaped by their own socialisation.

In co-educational UK secondary schools, sex-segregation is a culturally accepted practice in PE (Hills & Croston, 2012). In contrast, other Western countries like Sweden, Norway, and Denmark typically embrace co-educational PE (Rønholt, 2005; Larsson et al., 2009). Nevertheless, in these countries, legislation for PE allows occasional separation based on lesson context (Annerstedt, 2008). Within the UK, co-educational PE was introduced during the 1980s and was implemented to challenge sex-based stereotyping within the subject, but it did not become the norm (Lines & Stidder, 2003). Some scholars argue that segregated programming for boys and girls can improve the quality of education and participation, as well as the success of students (e.g. Pritchard et al., 2014). Separate classes are perceived as enabling girls to participate (Murphy et al., 2014), gain confidence (Hannon & Ratliffe, 2007), and be shielded from the male gaze (Azzarito, 2009; Bréau et al., 2017). For boys, separate classes are believed to promote learning and their commitment to competitive training (Bréau & Lentillon-Kaestner, 2017).

Some religious and cultural practices, values, or circumstances mean that co-ed PE may not be possible (Benn & Dagkas, 2006), but it is not the case that co-ed PE is completely out of the question for Muslim girls (Kay, 2006; Walseth, 2013; Lleixà & Nieva, 2020), for one example. However, "to show respect for the group" single-sex PE can be a strategy for providers to "start from where girls *are*" (Oliver & Kirk, 2016, p. 6, italics theirs), alongside sensitivity to clothing requirements and changing room needs, rather than expecting Muslim girls to conform to the environment (Kay, 2006; Agergaard, 2016). Girls navigate complex intersecting systems of gender, culture, and ethnicity which influence their embodiment of faith and their engagement in physical activity, sport, and PE (Kay, 2006; Dagkas & Hunter, 2015). Thorjussen and Sisjord (2020) suggest that ethnic minority students in European contexts challenge teachers who continue to base PE curricula with majority cultures; they call for students' cultural backgrounds to be considered in curriculum design, pedagogy, and reflection, not least to diversify activity types.

Studies which have explored students' class preferences indicate that students often favour single-sex PE contexts over co-educational ones (Stidder, 2000; Timkin et al., 2019). In fact, a robust body of literature concludes that adolescent girls prefer single-sex classes in PE, indicating its positive effect on girls' learning, safety, and enjoyment levels (Hills & Croston, 2012; Hill et al., 2012; Prewitt et al., 2013; Slingerland et al., 2013). Timken et al. (2019) explored 17 girls' views of a health club approach to PE. The girls were clear in their preference for single-sex classes and felt embarrassment around boys who often made fun of them and did not include them in activities. They confided that they limited or adjusted their efforts within these classes, reflecting the findings of studies that have found higher physical activity levels among boys than among girls in co-educational classes (Williams & Hannon, 2018; Wallace et al., 2019; Vargos et al., 2021). The presence of boys elicits additional pressure on girls to exhibit a socially acceptable feminine identity (Fagrell et al., 2012; Beasley, 2013).

A smaller pool of studies has concluded that students prefer co-educational classes (Hills & Croston, 2012; Lentillon-Kaestner & Roure, 2019). Critics of sex-segregation argue that is exacerbates gender divisions and reinforces stereotypes about behaviour and abilities (Azzarito & Hill, 2013; Hill, 2015). Gerdin (2017), researching boys' experiences of PE in Sweden, found that a majority of boys in single-sex and co-educational groupings thought PE should be taught together with girls. Lentillon-Kaestner and Roure (2019) explored the effects of both contexts on 177 students; results showed that the scores across three situational interest dimensions (instant enjoyment, exploration intention, and attention demand) were higher in the co-educational context than in the single-sex context. Although some studies have shown that co-educational PE classes favour boys (e.g. Lyu & Gill, 2011; Hills & Croston, 2012) and that girls are more affected by class sex composition (Lyu & Gill, 2011), the manifestation of gender and of different masculinities and femininities changes according to groups, places, and spaces (Paechter, 2003). To this end more research is needed to fully realise how these settings impact doing gender differently. In the next section, we outline how segregation is influenced and reinforced by gender discourses concerning 'appropriate' sporting activities for girls and boys.

The gender-typing of sporting activities in PE

The practice of offering different activities to boys and to girls reinforces the gender-typing of certain movements, whereby specific ways of moving contribute to whether students are intelligible as 'normal' gendered individuals due to their performance of abiding movements. The work of Larsson and colleagues (Larsson et al., 2011, 2020) indicates that certain movements (such as those associated with games or dance) are associated with 'doing' boy or girl. This, in turn, can block students from learning certain movements, making them more difficult for students to learn because they are experienced as "not (for) me" (Larsson et al., 2020, p. 534).

Indeed, the process of doing gender raises a number of potential issues which impact the lived experiences of young people. A traditional binary vision of gender norms promotes heteronormativity as well as traditional performances of masculinity or femininity (Larsson et al., 2011, 2014). Sobal and Milgrim (2019) indicate that concepts of feminine and masculine sports are widely recognised and used as a resource for doing and redoing gender. In this way, the process of gender-typing activities can construct boundaries for exclusion and inclusion: If a sport is strongly gender-typed as masculine, girls and women may be reluctant to participate (Yi-Hsiu & Chen-Yueh, 2013). Similarly, if a sport is strongly gender-typed as feminine, boys and men may be hesitant to become or remain involved (Schmalz & Kerstetter, 2006; Lee et al., 2009). The process of gender-typing can also stigmatise individuals who attempt mixed sport participation (Schmalz & Davison, 2006).

In essence, PE is invested in constructing young people as 'normal' (Larsson et al., 2014). Boys and girls are 'invented' in the gym through a heterosexual matrix and as such, other ways of being a boy or girl are ignored (Butler, 1990; Joy & Larsson, 2019). Teachers might also make assumptions about gendered ethnicity and ascribe characteristics to minority girls and boys based on ethnic origin (van Doodewaard & Knoppers, 2018). This is a social justice issue as it restricts self-actualisation and makes risky any unconventional embodiments (e.g. Landi, 2018). As Landi (2018, p. 9) summarises, privileging the technocratic body "emphasises masculine and feminine differences in body ideals". He states that as a high school PE teacher, "I actively straightened my students along those lines". To this end, the PE curriculum can be viewed as limiting and, when paired with gender segregated classes, channels girls and boys into environments which reinforce expectations for gender performance (Hills & Croston, 2012; Metcalfe, 2018). In rewarding dominant representations of gender and regulating bodies, opportunities are limited for exploring alternative expressions of gender. Individuals who are gender non-conforming risk encountering negative social, emotional, academic and health consequences (Sykes, 2011).

'Undoing' gender in PE as a social justice action

We turn now to review research and theory that explores the idea and practice of undoing gender. Using Freire's (1987) idea of critical consciousness, educators can challenge neoliberal focus on standardised testing and measurable outcomes that, in PE, valorise cognitive knowledge of mainstream (gendered) sports and physical performance of skills. Instead they can refocus on transformational understanding – "a moment when we begin to think critically about ourselves and our identities in relation to our political circumstances" (Lynch et al., 2022, p. 5).

A social justice pedagogical position facilitates the success of all students so that all are actively engaged in learning experiences. For Walton-Fisette and Sutherland (2018, p. 463), social justice education (SJE) is in creating "a democratic environment that empowers students to actively engage in their education, understand the roles power, privilege and oppression play in their lives, and through critical reflection how they can challenge and/or disrupt the status quo". To be truly transformational, critical consciousness must involve *action* and *reflection*. Thus the role of a teacher committed to social justice and critical consciousness might be to reflect on aspects of curriculum, pedagogy and environment that are not equitable, democratic, or self-affirming; and move towards belonging, student voice, and participation – and in so doing, raise with students how they are enacting change. Under these conceptions of social justice, undoing gender can be seen as both an *action* for practitioners in their organisation of pedagogy, curriculum, and environment, and a *tool for reflection and inquiry* by young people, making gender an explicit, rather than hidden, aspect of the curriculum (Fernández-Balboa, 1993).

To conduct this review, the keywords *undo(ing)*, *challenging*, *deconstructing*, *resisting* + *gender*; or *queer(ing)*, *heteronormativity*; and *sport* or *physical education* were sought in relevant journal databases and edited collections and results collated in themes relating to the method(s) of undoing gender that they promoted. We group strategies for undoing gender in PE into four areas by what they aim to do: Tackling gender-typing with diverse activities; Mixed groups and sex integration; Pedagogies for reflection and inquiry; and Queering pedagogy.

Tackling gender-typing with diverse activities

Larsson et al. (2020, pp. 538–539) selected juggling as a movement not embedded in gender norms, finding it to be "a way of undoing gender in relation to the teacher-centred and performance-oriented approach that otherwise seems to favour boys". In one class where the teacher managed students' groupings and supported all students in understanding learning tasks, there was success in using juggling to challenge gendered movements. However, in a class that had existing strong gender norms and where the teacher allowed students to control their groupings, juggling in itself was not sufficient to challenge boys' domination or girls' restriction of movement. While encouraging young people to engage with activities usually not associated, stereotypically, with their gender, might provide a space for visibly challenging assumptions (lisahunter, 2019), there is evidence that gender norms may be affirmed in response. As Haltom (2020) argues regarding boys who baton twirl, the undoing of gender can be affected by parents' roles in framing young people's sport and physical activity participation: fathers especially were active in hiding their son's engagement in baton twirling, emphasising their sons' heterosexuality. Undoing gender, for Larsson et al. (2020), can be achieved by specifically guiding learners in the lesson objectives and helping boys and girls to "experience common learning processes" (p. 543) – so combining curricular and pedagogical undoing with classroom management and relationships. These elements of reflective practice will be further explored later in this chapter.

Mixed (co-educational) groups and sex integration

Co-ed PE has the potential to challenge stereotypes about learning, oppose discrimination, support principles of inclusion, and prepare students to engage in an integrated society (Stidder, 2000). Indeed, Hills and Croston (2012) highlighted the ability of co-ed environments to disrupt gender-based ideology, showing how girls challenged notions of male superiority, considered positive aspects of mixed-gender settings, identified similarities between boys and girls, and engaged in male-identified behaviours.

This has also been exemplified outside of school PE settings in broader sport and physical activity contexts. For example, Anderson's (2008) study of mixed-sex cheerleading illustrated how integration changed men's views of women's athleticism, which led to greater respect for female ability, helped them to befriend women and view them in a more humanised way than during their participation in male-only sports teams. Furthermore, Maclean's (2016) study of karate training revealed similar phenomena within mixed-sex clubs, where female karateka were accorded equal respect as their male counterparts. Martial arts may particularly support "level[ing] out unequal power relations between men and women by teaching women how to defend themselves and showing men that not all women are weak and unable or unwilling to fight back" (Noel, 2009, p. 34). The longer women engage in physical activity practices that challenge feminine embodiment, the more they can refigure a relationship with their body that emphasises worth, agency and capacity (Maclean, 2019). To undo gender difference, Maclean (2016) suggests how sex-integrated practice in karate also supports the development of mixed friendship "founded on mutual understanding of the other" and offers the possibility to break down views of women as sexual objects that can be fomented in men's competitive sport. The more men compete against women, the more they see that women can be good athletes (Maclean, 2016). The presence of women over time additionally helps to reduce the perception of a sport as masculine; the visibility of women in senior roles such as those with black belts in martial arts indicates that women have ownership over the activity and demonstrates their fighting superiority (Channon, 2014). Channon (2014, p. 590) calls for training to be integrated where possible:

> By encouraging behaviors which directly refute ideas about supposedly natural sex differences, integrated sports provide the chance to physically perform in ways which differ markedly from stereotypical ideals of masculinity and femininity.

There is a growing range of studies suggesting that when boys and girls play together, in activities such as korfball and quidditch (Segrave, 2016; Gubby, 2019), collaboration and teamwork become more important than gender divisions. Where girls are expected to perform well and are supported to do so, attitudes can be changed. In Hills et al.'s (2020) study of trialling mixed teams in the English Football Association under-14s, girls were welcome in training sessions but were expected to be less skilled, and only technically very skilled and "hard" girls were welcome in some teams. This indicates the importance of context in framing integrated play. Co-educational settings could positively impact the construction of gender to move away from culturally accepted norms that restrict and distress gender-diverse students, facilitating an environment which accounts for their identities and gives them positive experiences. Mixed sports in PE, such as korfball, 'may offer something different' (Gubby, 2019) through enforcing gender-integrated play; in korfball girls are better able to demonstrate their abilities and boys have to acknowledge girls' abilities. Gender-mixed activities might have potential but it can be difficult for players to drop all assumptions about gender norms and differences based on body size and ability, and as such offer more attacking or high-status positions to men (Allison & Love, 2022; Paccaud, 2022). Gubby (2019) notes that korfball (re)produces a dualist notion of gender by requesting that boys mark boys and girls mark girls.

Difficulties in long-term support for environments that contribute to undoing gender indicate the hurdles to tackle in undoing the gender regimes of PE and youth sport. As discussed earlier in this chapter, there are suggestions that gender norms for girls can best be tackled in single-sex environments where girls have control over the visibility of their bodies and the range of movements they engage in (Enright & O'Sullivan 2010). Gender differentiated curricula are an integrative form of inclusion (they enable girls to be integrated into PE structures, Penney et al., 2018), but are often based on adopting or reinforcing stereotypes: "Rather than radically changing content, integrative approaches feature adaptation to accommodate a broader range of young people within existing structures" (Penney et al., 2018, p. 1068).

Segregated classes are explained as protecting girls from boys' remarks and sexual behaviour, but "seems as if it is a way of *escaping* rather than approaching the problem of heteronormativity" (Larsson et al., 2014, p. 15, italics theirs). Post-structuralist theorising shows us that the experiences of boys and girls are more fragmented and diverse, as Scraton (2018, p. 33) summarises: "individual experiences challenge any universalistic notions of femininity and masculinity and allow for far more complex understanding of diverse and fluid gender identities". She reflects, however, that this means that undoing gender and challenging power relations through co-educational structures are not simple. Moving to co-educational groupings as a sole policy change is likely to perpetuate hegemonic masculinity unless it is accompanied by some other elements of undoing gender or queering, such as critical reflection on the part of teachers and students about their relationships, assumptions and heteronorms; or revising curricula away from gendered sports and activities. A more transgressive approach to:

> designing an inclusive curriculum requires thinking afresh about the learning that is required for a curriculum to effectively extend each student's individual physical, social and emotional capability to engage in movement and physical activity for purposes that they value and in contexts that they can relate to.
> (Penney et al., 2018, p. 1071)

Gerdin (2017) argues that "PE should be about offering young people experiences which can be transformative that will help them to see alternative identities which step outside and destabilise the traditional gender binary" (Gerdin, 2017, p. 893). This leads us into exploring calls for reflective practice and queering pedagogies, as elements of transformation.

Pedagogies for reflection and inquiry

Central to a critical or social justice pedagogy approach to challenging gender relations and stereotypes are the student–teacher relations and culturally relative pedagogies that value students' backgrounds and designing accordingly (e.g. Boyd et al., 2022) or through inquiry about physical cultures (e.g. Fisette, 2013). Some critical inquiry work embedded into or alongside a PE curriculum asks young people to draw upon popular culture in order to reflect on how gender regimes affect their lives (e.g. Oliver & Lalik, 2001; Stride, 2016). Aligning with Hills and Croston's (2012) point that heteronormative thinking can be challenged by acknowledging shared experiences amongst boys and girls, critical and reflective inquiry by young people and teachers offers the possibility to question normative ways of structuring sport and PE through illuminating and questioning what is defined as normative and transgressive. A socially critical PE will offer "transformative" experiences to "see alternative identities which step outside and destabilise the traditional gender binary" (Gerdin, 2017, p. 893).

Sánchez-Hernández et al.'s (2018) inquiry-based intervention in a co-educational secondary school football (soccer) unit used elements of cooperative learning. At the start of the unit most girls and some boys showed low engagement with football and experienced insults from peers. Students engaged in reflection on their experiences, fictional stories, jigsaw learning, and reading about or discussing elite women's football. The researchers highlight how dialogue among boys and girls enabled boys who are confident in football to listen to why some girls do not engage and to understand "the conflicts underpinning the game" (p. 817). Cooperative learning, with a focus on group learning and processing, facilitated cohesion and opportunity for leadership not just for those who were highly skilled. The study suggests that a shift away from competition in order to achieve success requires support and are quite a challenge for many students. The lack of choice in this unit was also noted as an issue, but in an activity like football that has such social baggage it is important to attempt to challenge gender relations here as well as in gender-neutral activities (those with less baggage). This paper indicates the benefit of reflection as part of pedagogy and student-centred work in PE.

Queering pedagogy

Larsson et al. (2009, p. 5) imagine how the gender order can be challenged in PE by taking action against "how the teaching constitutes gendered positions and subjectivities of certain kinds". Writing about the environment or field of PE, Fitzpatrick and McGlashan (2016) note that "straight pedagogy" should be the focus of inquiry, rather than individual identity and difference.

Alone, small pockets of resistance to the gender regime cannot overthrow dominant discourses (Gerdin, 2017). 'Tinkering' with inclusion, or talking the talk of inclusive practice without considering how student and teacher habitus has been formed in heteronormative PE fields in the past, will not result in undoing gender in any meaningful way (Fitzpatrick & McGlashan, 2016, p. 110). Acknowledging the difficulties teachers may face in attempting to challenge gender expectations, Larsson et al. (2011, p. 80) indicate that it can be more comforting to conduct a lesson within heteronormative frames; they call for teachers "not to give way to, or be anxious about, queer moments ('troublesome situations') during physical education lessons" – instead to use these moments of gender trouble to ask students to reflect and support heterogeneity.

Queering can mean to question the assumption that segregation is natural due to differences (Larsson et al., 2014). Borrowing from Sykes' (2011) definition of queering, in the sense of challenging normative behaviours and expectations, a queer PE would "not just focus on making kids healthy or skilled, but rather allow students to affirm their subjective experiences and develop activities that are suited for all students, not just the privileged few" (Landi, 2018, p. 12). Exploring and challenging heteronormativity in PE could reduce "physical threats, verbal and emotional abuse" (Joy et al., 2021, p. 673). Trans-inclusive and queer PE can be part of efforts and dialogue for social justice and inclusive PE practice as a whole or for many students who are currently alienated (Drury et al., 2022).

Using different language but similar sentiments, Larsson et al. (2014) offer three ways in which to 'teach paradoxically':

1. Create an open atmosphere for students to critically question gender stereotypes and heteronorms and for teachers to discuss how they come about.
2. Create queer situations and manage students' interruptions.
3. Equip students to challenge cultural norms and to empower them to interrupt/give space for discussion about norms.

Student-centred approaches focusing on the wishes of students are seen as essential for supporting trans students (Drury et al., 2022). Many recommendations by or for teachers assume that a school has different kit and curricula for boys and girls, and segregated classes; but does not address the underlying issue. Drury et al.'s recommendations for supporting trans students go beyond "allowing" trans students to access the kit, curriculum, and class of their chosen gender, to focus on critical reflection, whole school approaches to bullying, and reconsidering a focus on competition. Likewise, Fuentes-Miguel et al. (2022) offer insights into how trans inclusion develops over time through relationships and dialogue between teachers, students, and families – with trans students supported to share their stories in the right environment (Fuentes-Miguel et al., 2022).

That said, Fitzpatrick and McGlashan (2016) highlight how so-called 'small practices' are considered to go some way to helping teachers to attend to inclusion, reflection and power relations and hence emphasise the role of teachers, individuals, and departments in constructing many of the issues of gendering in PE (Fitzpatrick & McGlashan, 2016). This may include recruiting boys who dance into PE teacher education; using dance or gymnastics in a Sport Education season; deliberately addressing LGBTQ+ issues and homophobia; and considering relationships with students when mentioning norms of movement and appearance (Fitzpatrick & McGlashan, 2016). Likewise, mixed PE, student choice in groupings and roles; unisex or separate locker rooms; and offering alternative activities to all students (Berg & Kokkonen, 2021). By committing to small changes and reflection over time, or small acts of resistance, teachers and students may be able to shift the habitus of the PE field to one that is less invested in reproducing heteronormativity. LGBTQ+ students should not have to accommodate to existing practices, when the practices and environment themselves can be changed (Berg & Kokkonen, 2021). In this way, other theorising of PE objectives such as meaningful PE (MPE) might offer challenges to gendered PE by rooting movement in individual meanings and relevance rather than a heteronormative binary assuming girls' and boys' interests (Fletcher et al., 2021).

Research example: nurture group

We now provide a real-life example from a five-week case study in a UK secondary PE setting (Kettley-Linsell, 2017), demonstrating notable changes that supported undoing gender. PE was typically provided in single-sex classes, but each year group also contained one mixed-gender class labelled the 'nurture' group, comprising students considered to be less able by PE teachers. These nurture groups were formed in the first year of secondary school (Year 7), and most students stayed in the same group until the fourth year of secondary school (Year 10). Observational data highlighted that the only time teachers taught groups of the 'opposite' sex was during nurture group classes (never for the single-sex classes). Both male and female teachers taught the nurture groups; the male teacher provided masculine-coded sports, while the female teacher provided feminine-coded sports, but this did mean that the nurture group participated in a wider range of sports. Girls were observed playing cricket with the same competitive attitude that is often associated with boys and masculinity. When single-sex groups occasionally merged, they self-segregated, but this wasn't the case for nurture students. They readily competed with and against students of the 'opposite' gender, making segregation uncommon. Here, ability, rather than gender, defined how boys and girls perceived each other, negating male dominance. In many instances, girls exhibited just as much dominance as boys. These findings underscore the transformative impact of long-term co-educational PE settings on students' expressions of gender.

Conclusion

We argue that undoing gender is a social justice issue for PE and youth sport. Gender is 'done' in PE to produce and reproduce norms and discourses aligned with heteronormative expectations that, in line with broader sport structures, uphold masculine domination in spaces defined by the competitive and muscular moving body. Girls continue to be caught in a double standard where their enthusiastic engagement in sport is used to question their gender. This creates issues for the inclusive participation of all students, not least those who express gender in ways that challenge normative expectations. Student choice, self-actualisation, and democracy, underpinned by critical consciousness, are social justice concerns. Socially critical, transformative, and social justice pedagogies in PE should include ways to undo gender.

Gender is of course widely enacted and enforced so we would not suggest that it is easy to undo, rework, or abandon gender (Channon, 2014). Attempts to undo gender must be based in teachers' everyday lives and power relations, with space, resource, and timetabling constraints in neoliberal school environments. Undoing gender and moving towards inclusive (co-ed) PE is confounded by religious and ethnic differences; crucial to undoing gender is contextual and student-centred reflection on what is feasible and supportive of students (Thorjussen & Sisjord, 2020). Undoing gender will not be achieved in just one unit of activity. Even in PE structures that claim to be flexible and accommodating regarding gender, deeply entrenched norms and stereotypes persist; and PE teachers are apprehensive about challenging abuses in their spaces (Joy & Larsson, 2019). Heteronormative practices are upheld when LGBTQ+ young people are seen as minorities and only tolerated within a heteronormative system, rather than fully included (Fitzpatrick & McGlashan, 2016). Despite growing fluidity and acceptance among young people (lisahunter, 2019), schools and health/physical education retain strict boundaries and taboos around talking about and doing gender diversity.

Recent turns away from supporting gender diversity and self-identification in elite sport, as seen in many national and international governing bodies, suggest that attempts to challenge gender regimes are facing a renewed backlash (Travers, 2018; Cole, 2022). Increased rights have led to increased visibility for trans athletes, but this has not been universally embraced. Media outlets invoked a 'trans moral panic' which raised public concern about trans issues worldwide (Barker, 2017). Public debates and media coverage perpetuated the circulation of ideologies that construct trans and gender-diverse young people (and parents who support them) as the enemy in a politically and socially volatile environment that seeks to feed on fears of the other (manufacturing a 'culture war') as a diversion from real inequalities (Barker, 2017). Within this environment, cultures of trans-exclusionary feminism have also become more apparent, particularly in relation to the place of trans women and non-binary people within women's spaces, including sports (Hines, 2017). Overall, the anti-transgender movement breaches the equality and dignity of trans and gender non-conforming people and for this reason can be recognised as a social justice issue which often inhibits the opportunities of those who challenge the heteronormative foundations of PE and school sport.

Acknowledgements

Our thanks to the teachers and students in the observed school; and to Abby Barras for suggestions on current political and social climates.

References

Aartun, I., Walseth, K., Standal, Ø. F., & Kirk, D. (2022). Pedagogies of embodiment in physical education–A literature review. *Sport, Education and Society, 27*(1), 1–13.

Agergaard, S. (2016). Religious culture as a barrier? A counter-narrative of Danish Muslim girls' participation in sports. *Qualitative Research in Sport, Exercise and Health, 8*(2), 213–224. https://doi.org/10.1080/2159676X.2015.1121914

Allison, R., & Love, A. (2022). 'We all play pretty much the same, except...': Gender-integrated Quidditch and the persistence of essentialist ideology. *Journal of Contemporary Ethnography, 51*(3), 347–375. https://doi.org/10.1177/08912416211040240

Anderson, E. (2008). "I used to think women were weak": Orthodox masculinity, gender segregation, and sport. *Sociological Forum, 23*(2), 257–280. https://doi.org/10.1111/j.1573-7861.2008.00058.x

Annerstedt, C. (2008). Physical education in Scandinavia with a focus on Sweden: A comparative perspective. *Physical Education and Sport Pedagogy, 13*(4), 303–318.

Azzarito, L. (2009). The panopticon of physical education: Pretty, active and ideally white. *Physical Education and Sport Pedagogy, 14*(1), 19–39.

Azzarito, L., & Hill, J. (2013). Girls looking for a 'second home': Bodies, difference and places of inclusion. *Physical Education and Sport Pedagogy, 18*(4), 351–375.

Bain, L. (1990). A critical analysis of the hidden curriculum in physical education. In D. Kirk & R. Tinning (Eds) *Physical education, curriculum and culture: Critical issues in the contemporary crisis* (pp. 23–42). London: The Falmer Press.

Barker, M. J. (2017). *A trans review of 2017: The year of transgender moral panic*. The conversation. Available at: https://theconversation.com/a-trans-review-of-2017-the-year-of-transgender-moral-panic-89272 (Accessed: 31 August 2022).

Beasley, E. (2013). Navigating gender expectations for girls in co-education physical education. *Strategies: A Journal for Physical and Sport Educators, 26*, 35–37.

Benn, T., & Dagkas, S. (2006). Incompatible? Compulsory mixed-sex physical education initial teacher training (PEITT) and the inclusion of Muslim women: A case-study on seeking solutions. *European Physical Education Review, 12*(2), 181–200. https://doi.org/10.1177/1356336X06065181

Berg, P., & Kokkonen, M. (2021). Heteronormativity meets queering in physical education: The views of PE teachers and LGBTIQ+ students. *Physical Education and Sport Pedagogy, 27*(4), 368–381. https://doi.org/10.1080/17408989.2021.1891213

Boyd, K. L., Simon, M., & Dixon, C. E. (2022). Culturally relevant and sustaining pedagogies for and by Black and Latinx preservice physical education teachers. *Journal of Teaching in Physical Education, 41*(2), 212–223.

Bréau, A., & Lentillon-Kaestner, V. (2017). Les garçons face à la mixité et à la non mixité en EPS. *eJRIEPS. Ejournal de la recherche sur l'intervention en éducation physique et sport*, (40).

Bréau, A., Hauw, D., & Lentillon-Kaestner, V. (2017). Séparer les Filles et les Garçons au sein des Classes d'Education Physique et Sportive: Etat de la Question [Separating girls and boys in sports and physical education classes: Status of the issue]. *Canadian Journal of Behavioural Science/Revue Canadienne des Sciences du Comportement, 49*(3), 195–208.

Butler, J. (1990). Gender trouble, feminist theory, and psychoanalytic discourse. In L. Nicholson (Ed.) *Feminism/postmodernism* (pp. 324–340). New York: Routledge.

Butler, J. (1993). *Bodies that matter*. New York: Routledge.

Channon, A. (2014). Towards the "undoing" of gender in mixed-sex martial arts and combat sports. *Societies, 4*(4), 587–605. https://doi.org/10.3390/soc4040587

Cole, D. (2022). *South Dakota bans trans women and girls from same-gender school sports teams*. [online] CNN. Available at: www.cnn.com/2022/02/04/politics/transgender-sports-ban-south-dakota/index.html (Accessed: 31 August 2022).

Dagkas, S., & Hunter, L. (2015). 'Racialised' pedagogic practices influencing young Muslims' physical culture. *Physical Education and Sport Pedagogy, 20*(5), 547–558.

Deutsch, F. M. (2007). Undoing gender. *Gender & Society, 21*(1), 106–127.

Drury, S., Stride, A., Firth, O., & Fitzgerald, H. (2022). The transformative potential of trans*-inclusive PE: The experiences of PE teachers. *Sport, Education and Society*, 1–14. https://doi.org/10.1080/13573322.2022.2034142

Enright, E., & O'Sullivan, M. (2010). 'Can I do it in my pyjamas?' Negotiating a physical education curriculum with teenage girls. *European Physical Education Review*, *16*(3), 203–222.

Fagrell, B., Larsson, H., & Redelius, K. (2012). The game within the game: Girls' underperforming position in physical education. *Gender and Education*, *24*(1), 101–118. https://doi.org/10.1080/09540253.2011.582032

Fernández-Balboa, J.-M. (1993). Sociocultural characteristics of the hidden curriculum in physical education. *Quest*, *45*, 230–254.

Fisette, J. L. (2013). 'Are you listening?': Adolescent girls voice how they negotiate self-identified barriers to their success and survival in physical education. *Physical Education & Sport Pedagogy*, *18*(2), 184–203. https://doi.org/10.1080/17408989.2011.649724

Fitzpatrick, K., & McGlashan, H. (2016). Rethinking 'straight' pedagogy: Gender, sexuality and PE. In D. Robinson & L. Randall (Eds) *Social justice in physical education: Critical reflections and pedagogies for change* (pp. 102–121). Toronto: Canadian Scholars' Press.

Fletcher, T., Ní Chróinín, D., Gleddie, D., & Beni, S. (Eds). (2021). *Meaningful physical education: An approach for teaching and learning*. Abingdon: Routledge.

Freire, P. (1987). *Pedagogy of the oppressed*. New York: Continuum.

Fuentes-Miguel, J., Pérez-Samaniego, V., López-Cañada, E., & Devís-Devís, J. (2022). From inclusion to queer-trans pedagogy in school and physical education: A narrative ethnography of trans generosity. *Sport, Education and Society*, *28*(9), 1132–1145. https://doi.org/10.1080/13573322.2022.2073437

Gerdin, G. (2017). 'It's not like you are less of a man just because you don't play rugby': Boys' problematisation of gender during secondary school physical education lessons in New Zealand. *Sport, Education and Society*, *22*(8), 890–904. https://doi.org/10.1080/13573322.2015.1112781

Gray, S., Sandford, R., Aldous, D., Carse, N., Stirrup, J., Hardley, S., Hooper, O., & Bryant, A. (2021). A comparative analysis of discourses shaping physical education provision within and across the UK. *European Physical Education Review*, *28*(3), 575–593.

Gubby, L. (2019). Can korfball facilitate mixed-PE in the UK? The perspectives of junior korfball players. *Sport, Education and Society*, *24*(9), 994–1005. https://doi.org/10.1080/13573322.2018.1519506

Haltom, T.M. (2020). A new spin on gender: How parents of male baton twirlers (un)do gender essentialism. *Sociology of Sport Journal*, *37*(4), 283–290. https://doi.org/10.1123/SSJ.2019-0077

Hannon, J., & Ratliffe, T. (2007). Opportunities to participate and teacher interactions in co-educational versus single-gender physical education settings. *Physical Educator*, *64*(1), 11–20.

Hill, J. (2015). Girls' active identities: Navigating othering discourses of femininity, bodies and physical education. *Gender and Education*, *27*(6), 666–684.

Hill, G.M., Hannon, J.C., & Knowles, C. (2012). Physical education teachers' and university teacher educator's perceptions regarding coeducation vs. single gender physical education. *Physical Educator*, *69*(3), 265–288.

Hills, L.A., & Croston, A. (2012). 'It should be better all together': Exploring strategies for 'undoing' gender in coeducational physical education. *Sport, Education and Society*, *17*(5), 591–605. https://doi.org/10.1080/13573322.2011.553215

Hills, L. A., Maitland, A., Croston, A., & Horne, S. (2020). 'It's not like she's from another planet': Undoing gender/redoing policy in mixed football. *International Review for the Sociology of Sport*, *56*(5), 658–676. https://doi.org/10.1177/1012690220934753

Hines, S. (2017). The feminist frontier: On trans and feminism. *Journal of Gender Studies*, *28*(2), 145–157.

Joy, P., & Larsson, H. (2019). Unspoken: Exploring the constitution of masculinities in Swedish physical education classes through body movements. *Physical Education and Sport Pedagogy*, *24*(5), 491–505 https://doi.org/10.1080/17408989.2019.1628935

Joy, P., Zahavich, J.B.L., & Kirk, S.F.L. (2021). Gendered bodies and physical education (PE) participation: Exploring the experiences of adolescent students and PE teachers in Nova Scotia. *Journal of Gender Studies*, *30*(6), 663–675. https://doi.org/10.1080/09589236.2021.1937080

Kay, T. (2006). Daughters of Islam: Family influences on Muslim young women's participation in sport. *International Review for the Sociology of Sport*, *41*(3–4), 357–373. https://doi.org/10.1177/1012690207077705

Kettley-Linsell, H. (2017). The influence of power relations on gender stratification in Physical Education. Unpublished master's dissertation, University of Bedfordshire.

Kirk, D. (1992). Physical education, discourse, and ideology: Bringing the hidden curriculum into view. *Quest, 44*, 35–56. https://doi.org/10.1080/00336297.1992.10484040

Kirk, D. (2010). The 'masculinity vortex' of school physical education: Beyond the myth of hyper-masculinity. In Michael Atkinson & Michael Keher (Eds), *Boys' bodies: Speaking the unspoken* (pp. 51–72). New York: Peter Lang.

Landi, D. (2018). Toward a queer inclusive physical education. *Physical Education and Sport Pedagogy, 23*(1), 1–15. https://doi.org/10.1080/17408989.2017.1341478

Larsson, H., Fagrell, B., & Redelius, K. (2009). Queering physical education. Between benevolence towards girls and a tribute to masculinity. *Physical Education & Sport Pedagogy, 14*(1), 1–17. https://doi.org/10.1080/17408980701345832

Larsson, H., Redelius, K., & Fagrell, B. (2011). Moving (in) the heterosexual matrix. On heteronormativity in secondary school physical education. *Physical Education & Sport Pedagogy, 16*(1), 67–81. https://doi.org/10.1080/17408989.2010.491819

Larsson, H., Quennerstedt, M., & Öhman, M. (2014). Heterotopias in physical education: Towards a queer pedagogy? *Gender and Education, 26*(2), 135–150. https://doi.org/10.1080/09540253.2014.888403

Larsson, H., Nyberg, G., & Barker, D. (2020). Juggling with gender. How gender promotes and prevents the learning of a specific movement activity among secondary school students. *Gender and Education, 33*(5), 531–546. https://doi.org/10.1080/09540253.2020.1792846

Lee, J., Macdonald, D., & Wright, J. (2009). Young men's physical activity choices: The impact of capital, masculinities, and location. *Journal of Sport and Social Issues, 33*(1), 59–77.

Lentillon-Kaestner, V., & Roure, C. (2019). Co-educational and single-sex physical education: Students' situational interest in learning tasks centred on technical skills. *Physical Education and Sport Pedagogy, 24*(3), 287–300.

Lines, G., & Stidder, G. (2003). Reflections on the mixed and single-sex PE debate. In G. Stidder & S. Hayes (Eds) *Equity and inclusion in physical education* (pp. 65–90). Abingdon: Routledge.

lisahunter. (2019). What a queer space is HPE, or is it yet? Queer theory, sexualities and pedagogy. *Sport, Education and Society, 24*(1), 1–12. https://doi.org/10.1080/13573322.2017.1302416

Lleixà, T., & Nieva, C. (2020). The social inclusion of immigrant girls in and through physical education: Perceptions and decisions of physical education teachers. *Sport, Education and Society, 25*(2), 185–198. https://doi.org/10.1080/13573322.2018.1563882

Lynch, S., Walton-Fisette, J. L. & Luguetti, C. (2022). *Pedagogies of social justice in physical education and youth sport*. Abingdon: Routledge.

Lyu, M., & Gill, D. L. (2011). Perceived physical competence, enjoyment and effort in same-sex and co-educational physical education classes. *Educational Psychology, 31*(2), 247–260.

Maclean, C. (2016). Friendships worth fighting for: Bonds between women and men karate practitioners as sites for deconstructing gender inequality. *Sport in Society, 19*(8–9), 1374–1384. https://doi.org/10.1080/17430437.2015.1096249

Maclean, C. (2019). Knowing your place and commanding space: de/constructions of gendered embodiment in mixed-sex karate. *Leisure Studies, 38*(6), 818–830.

Metcalfe, S. (2018). *"Trapped": Gender, identities and PE*. Doctoral thesis, Durham University.

Metcalfe, S. N., & Lindsey, I. (2020). Gendered trends in young people's participation in active lifestyles: The need for a gender-neutral narrative. *European Physical Education Review, 26*(2), 535–551.

Murphy, B., Dionigi, R. A., & Litchfield, C. (2014). Physical education and female participation: A case study of teachers' perspectives and strategies. *Issues in Educational Research, 24*, 241–256.

Noel, H. (2009). Un-doing gendered power relations through martial arts? *International Journal of Social Inquiry, 2*(2), 17–37.

Oliver, K. L., & Kirk, D. (2015). *Girls, gender and physical education: An activist approach*. Abingdon: Routledge.

Oliver, K. L., & Kirk, D. (2016). Towards an activist approach to research and advocacy for girls and physical education. *Physical Education & Sport Pedagogy, 21*(3), 313–327.

Oliver, K. L., & Lalik, R. (2001). The body as curriculum: Learning with adolescent girls. *Journal of Curriculum Studies, 33*(3), 303–333. https://doi.org/10.1080/00220270010006046

Paccaud, L. (2022). The co-conditioning of dis/ability and gender: An intersectionality study of Powerchair Hockey. *Frontiers in Sports and Active Living, 4*(916070). https://doi.org/10.3389/fspor.2022.916070

Paechter, C. (2003). Power, bodies and identity: How different forms of physical education construct varying masculinities and femininities in secondary schools. *Sex Education: Sexuality, Society and Learning*, 3(1), 47–59.

Penney, D., Jeanes, R., O'Connor, J., & Alfrey, L. (2018). Re-theorising inclusion and reframing inclusive practice in physical education. *International Journal of Inclusive Education*, 22(10), 1062–1077.

Prewitt, S., Hannon, J., Brusseau, T., Newton, M., Shaw, J., & Summerhays, J. (2013). Effect of female only versus co-educational physical education classes on social physique anxiety in 7th grade girls. *International Journal of Secondary Education*, 1(5), 26–30.

Pritchard, T., McCollum, S., Sundal, J., & Colquit, G. (2014). Effect of the sport education tactical model on co-educational and single gender game performance. *Physical Educator*, 71(1), 132–154.

Risman, B.J. (2009). From doing to undoing: Gender as we know it. *Gender & Society*, 23(1), 81–84.

Rønholt, H. (2005). Physical education in Denmark. In U. Puhse & M. Gerber (Eds) *International comparison of physical education: Concepts, problems, prospects* (pp. 206–227). Aachen: Meyer & Meyer.

Sánchez-Hernández, N., Martos-García, D., Soler, S., & Flintoff, A. (2018). Challenging gender relations in PE through cooperative learning and critical reflection. *Sport, Education and Society*, 23(8), 812–823. https://doi.org/10.1080/13573322.2018.1487836

Schmalz, D.L., & Davison, K.K. (2006). Differences in physical self-concept among pre-adolescents who participate in gender-typed and cross-gendered sports. *Journal of Sport Behavior*, 29, 335–352.

Schmalz, D.L., & Kerstetter, D.L. (2006). Girlie girls and manly men: Children's stigma consciousness of gender in sports and physical activities. *Journal of Leisure Research*, 38, 536–557.

Scraton, S. (2018). Feminism(s) and PE: 25 years of Shaping Up to Womanhood. *Sport, Education and Society*, 23(7), 638–651. https://doi.org/10.1080/13573322.2018.1448263

Segrave, J.O. (2016). Challenging the gender binary: The fictive and real world of quidditch. *Sport in Society*, 19(8–9), 1299–1315. https://doi.org/10.1080/17430437.2015.1067783

Slingerland, M., Haerens, L., Cardon, G., & Borghouts, L. (2013). Differences in perceived competence and physical activity levels during single-gender modified basketball game play in middle school physical education. *European Physical Education Review*, 20(1), 20–35.

Sobal, J., & Milgrim, M. (2019). Gendertyping sports: Social representations of masculine, feminine, and neither-gendered sports among US university students. *Journal of Gender Studies*, 28(1), 29–44.

Stidder, G. (2000). Does sex matter? Pupil perceptions of physical education in mixed and single-sex secondary schools. *British Journal of Teaching Physical Education*, 31(3), 40–43.

Stride, A. (2016). Centralising space: The physical education and physical activity experiences of South Asian, Muslim girls. *Sport, Education and Society*, 21(5), 677–697. https://doi.org/10.1080/13573322.2014.938622

Sykes, H. J. (2011). *Queer bodies: Sexualities, genders, & fatness in physical education*. Oxford: Peter Lang.

Thorjussen, I.M., & Sisjord, M.K. (2020). Inclusion and exclusion in multi-ethnic physical education: an intersectional perspective. *Curriculum Studies in Health and Physical Education*, 11(1), 50–66. https://doi.org/10.1080/25742981.2019.1648187

Timkin, G., McNamee, J., & Coste, S. (2019). 'It doesn't seem like PE and I love it!' Adolescent girls' views of a health club physical education approach. *European Physical Education Review*, 25(1), 109–124.

Travers, A. (2018). Transgender kids and sport participation. In V. Krane (Ed.), *Sex, gender, and sexuality in sport* (pp. 163–177). Abingdon: Routledge.

van Doodewaard, C., & Knoppers, A. (2018). Perceived differences and preferred norms: Dutch physical educators constructing gendered ethnicity. *Gender and Education*, 30(2), 187–204. https://doi.org/10.1080/09540253.2016.1188197

Vargos, C., Williams, S. M., Henninger, M. L., Coleman, M. M., & Burns, R. (2021). The effects of single-sex versus co-educational physical education on American junior high PE students' physical activity levels and self-competence. *Biomedical Human Kinetics*, 13(1), 170–176.

Wallace, L., Buchan, D., & Sculthorpe, N. (2019). A comparison of activity levels of girls in single-gender and mixed-gender physical education. *European Physical Education Review*, 26(1), 231–240.

Walseth, K., (2013). Muslim girls' experiences in physical education in Norway: What role does religiosity play? *Sport, Education and Society*, 20(3), 304–322.

Walton-Fisette, J. L., & Sutherland, S. (2018). Moving forward with social justice education in physical education teacher education. *Physical Education and Sport Pedagogy*, 23(5), 461–468.

West, C., & Zimmerman, D. (1987). Doing gender. *Gender & Society*, *1*(2),125–151.

Wilkinson, S. D., & Penney, D. (2014). The effects of setting on classroom teaching and student learning in mainstream mathematics, English and science lessons: A critical review of the literature in England. *Educational Review*, *66*(4), 411–427.

Williams, S. M., & Hannon, J. C. (2018). Physical activity levels in co-educational and same-sex physical education using the tactical games model. *Physical Educator*, *75*(3), 525–545.

Yi-Hsiu, L., & Chen-Yueh, C. (2013). Masculine versus feminine sports: The effects of peer attitudes and fear of negative evaluation on sports participation among Taiwanese college students. *Review Internationale de Psychologie Sociale*, *26*(2), 5–23.

PART III

'Race', forced migration, and religion

10
SOCIAL JUSTICE, SPORT, LEISURE, AND RACISM IN THE UNITED STATES

Adam Love, Steven N. Waller, Ashley Gardner, and Chermaine Cole

From the recreational fields in parks across the United States to the elite training centres around the globe, sport is a site of deeply embedded, systemic racial inequity. At the elite level, for example, people of colour comprise more than 83 per cent of players in the National Basketball Association (NBA), yet 70 per cent of head coaches in the league are white, as are nearly 90 per cent of team presidents/CEOs (Lapchick, 2020). At the recreational level, communities remain starkly segregated, and neighbourhoods that are predominantly Black or Latino tend to lack amenities for recreation and sport (Powell et al., 2006). Such structural conditions contribute to a situation in which Black Americans engage in significantly less physical activity (Hawes et al., 2019) and have lower life expectancy (Bond & Herman, 2016) than white people. Clearly, racial inequities come at great costs to the opportunities and well-being of people of colour.

Despite such inequities, sports are frequently imagined to be apolitical contexts defined by meritocracy. The ubiquitous nature of this belief is demonstrated by the words of Nelson Mandela in a keynote speech given at the inaugural Laureus Lifetime Achievement Award ceremony: "Sport has the power to change the world. [applause] It has the power to inspire, it has the power to unite people in a way that little else does … It laughs in the face of all types of discrimination" (cited in Coakley, 2015, p. 402). Such words from someone like Mandela, who dedicated his life to fighting oppression, demonstrate the pervasiveness of what Coakley (2015) calls the Great Sport Myth – a belief that sport is inherently good, pure, and in no need of change. Such beliefs obscure a reality in which much of recreational sport takes place in highly segregated contexts, mirroring rather than challenging broader social inequalities, while leadership positions in elite sport remain disproportionately dominated by white men.

In this chapter, we emphasise the importance of understanding racism as structural and institutional in order to foster meaningful progress toward equity and social justice, while also recognising the challenges of doing so. After differentiating between a structural and individual/binary understanding of racism, we use the case of desegregating swimming pools to illustrate some of the fierce resistance that has arisen to oppose actions intended to foster equity in sport and recreation. Given the inequity that continues to define many sport and leisure contexts, diversity has too often been an afterthought in the field. However, a growing number of organisations are voicing a commitment to advancing diversity, equity, and inclusion (DEI). While doing so may represent progress from a prior tendency to ignore diversity, we discuss three cases – the National Recreation and Park Association (NRPA), the US Olympic and Paralympic Committee (USOPC), and the National Football League (NFL) – that illustrate the tendency of DEI initiatives to act as 'window dressing' when they fail to concretely name and address structural racism.

Our conception of social justice involves a commitment to working toward a world in which all people and groups are included in an equitable, respectful, and fair society (Culp, 2016). Achieving social justice involves the goal of fostering full and equitable participation in society by people from all social identity groups (Bell, 2016). In addition to thinking of social justice as a set of desired outcomes, we also consider social justice to involve a process that is democratic, participatory, collaborative, respectful of diversity, and which affirms human agency (Bell, 2016). Further, we draw insight from Theoharis (2007), who advances a vision of social justice that seeks to make issues of inequality with respect to race, class, gender, sexual orientation, and disability a focus of those in leadership positions. In this vein, resisting and challenging racial injustice in sport and recreation must entail a focus on racism as structural and institutional (Love et al., 2019). We ultimately conclude that anyone who envisions a more socially just future should focus on eliminating racist policies that reproduce structural inequality and replacing them with anti-racist policies that create more equitable sport and recreation spaces.

Understanding racism in sport and leisure

Racism is commonly thought to consist of intentional, individual acts motivated by hatred of particular racial groups. In such a mindset, racism is conceived as involving a binary distinction between 'bad' (i.e. racist) and 'good' (i.e. not racist) people. Consistent with this individualised type of framing, efforts to address racism in sport are often reduced to a strategy of identifying specific people as racists and excising them, as exemplified by the case of former Los Angeles Clippers owner Donald Sterling, who was forced to sell the franchise and banned from the NBA in 2014 after a recording in which he made insulting comments about Black people became public (Hylton & Lawrence, 2016). Bonilla-Silva (2022) labels this type of approach as "hunting for racists", which he identifies as "the sport of choice of those who practice the 'clinical approach' to race relations—the careful separation of good and bad, tolerant and intolerant Americans" (p. 15). While such efforts in cases like that of Donald Sterling may grab headlines and media attention, they often do little to address structural forms of racial inequity present in sport and recreation.

Thinking about racism as an individualised good/bad binary stifles critical consideration of the structural factors that perpetuate racial inequity. Regarding the ways in which white people react in accordance with the typical binary framing of racism, DiAngelo (2018) explains:

> Within this paradigm, to suggest that I am racist is to deliver a deep moral blow—a kind of character assassination. Having received this blow, I must defend my character, and that is where all my energy will go—to deflecting the charge, rather than reflecting on my behavior. In this way, the good/bad binary makes it nearly impossible to talk to white people about racism, what it is, how it shapes all of us, and the inevitable ways that we are conditioned to participate in it.
>
> (p. 72)

The case of former NFL coach Jon Gruden, who was fired in 2021 after emails with racist, sexist, and homophobic language became public, illustrates the predominance of such a binary understanding in public discussions of race. Gruden, when first speaking publicly about the emails nearly a full year after his firing, exclaimed: "It's shameful. But I am a good person. I believe that. I go to church. I've been married for 31 years. I've got three great boys" (Gutierrez, 2022). As Gruden's invocation of church and family demonstrate, accusations of being 'racist' lead people to focus the force of their efforts (and concurrent media attention) on questions of individual character when racism is framed as a good/bad binary.

As a more productive way of understanding and addressing racism, Kendi (2019) reminds us that 'racist' is a descriptive term, not a slur, and that:

> the only way to undo racism is to consistently identify and describe it—and then dismantle it. The attempt to turn this usefully descriptive term into an almost unusable slur is, of course, designed to do the opposite: to freeze us into inaction.
>
> (p. 9)

Conceptualising the term 'racist' as 'usefully descriptive' involves critical thinking to identify the multifarious ways in which structural racism is embedded in our society. As Kendi explains, one cannot be 'neutral' in the racism struggle, nor can there be a 'nonracist' policy: "Every policy in every institution in every community in every nation is producing or sustaining either racial inequity or equity between racial groups" (p. 18).

Ultimately, to advance equity requires a focus on understanding how racism is *structural* and *embedded in institutions* rather than a matter of individual 'good' or 'bad' actors (Bonilla-Silva, 2022). As Mills (1997) explains with respect to perpetuating racial inequity at a macro level:

> economic structures have been set in place, causal processes established, whose outcome is to pump wealth from one side of the globe to another, and which will continue to work largely independently of the ill will/good will, racist/antiracist feelings of particular individuals.
>
> (p. 36)

The importance of understanding racism as structural is underscored by Kendi (2019), who urges us to focus on eliminating racist policies, as they precede racist ideas; racist ideas develop later in order to justify racist policies and practices (Kendi, 2016).

Unfortunately, those who benefit from the status quo often go to great lengths to ensure that people do not think about racism as structural. For example, as part of a wave of legislation in the US that seeks to censor teaching about race, a recently passed law in North Dakota bans public schools in the state from teaching "the theory that racism is not merely the product of individual bias or prejudice, but that racism is systemically embedded in American society and the American legal system to facilitate racial inequality" (Baumgarten, 2021, para. 16). In attempting to mandate that students are taught to understand racism as solely a 'product of individual bias', such laws demonstrate the stakes involved in how we think about racism – and the solutions that follow from a particular line of thinking. As articulated by Carter G. Woodson, often referred to as the 'father' of Black History Month:

> When you control a man's thinking you do not have to worry about his actions. You do not have to tell him not to stand here or go yonder. He will find his 'proper place' and will stay in it.
>
> (quoted in Kendi, 2019, p. 142)

Ultimately, if we continue to understand racism as a mere result of individual bias, our actions will be limited to a strategy of "hunting for racists", obscuring the types of structural inequities that so often define sport and recreation in our society. In our forthcoming discussion, we consider ways in which sport and recreation organisations often fail to address the structural nature and effects of racism. To provide some historical grounding in our analysis, we next discuss the fierce resistance that has often met efforts to promote equity in sport and recreation spaces.

Resistance to creating equitable sport and recreation spaces

The extension of civil rights in sport and recreational spaces, and white resistance to doing so, is tantamount to understanding the US civil rights movement. The fight for equity in sport and recreation has often involved physical and policy-related violence against people of colour, African Americans in particular, to sustain segregation or impede integration. Wolcott (2012) brings to bear the point that the quest for racial equality challenged segregation at public and private amenities, such as swimming pools. As civil rights activists pushed for desegregation of public accommodations, white facility owners and patrons often believed that recreation could only be kept virtuous and safe by excluding people of colour, thus promoting a 'sterile' and pleasant vision of white leisure. In a pragmatic sense, such restrictions perpetuated racial stereotypes and inequality.

Swimming pools provoked some of the most intense fears of racial mixing among young men and women. The possibility of a racially diverse group playfully flirting with one another while dressed in swimsuits fostered white anxieties about interracial sex, manifest in a purported fear for young white women's safety. In this way, the gender-integrated nature of swimming pools frequently exacerbated racial tensions (McGhee, 2021; Wiltsie, 2007; Wolcott, 2012). White men voiced concerns about the 'cleanliness' of people of colour, paired with a belief that supposedly hypersexual Black men would act aggressively toward 'their' women, luring them away from white recreationists altogether (Wolcott, 2012). In this context, there were multiple responses to the integration of swimming pools in the twentieth century, including (a) violence against Black people who attempted to integrate private and public pools, (b) the adoption of segregationist policies at the local level, which courts tended to uphold, and (c) administrative actions, both overt and covert, to stifle the use of pools by Blacks.

One of the most notable acts of violence against Black citizens at a public aquatic facility occurred at the Fairground Park pool in St Louis, Missouri. The facility, which opened in 1911, was the largest in the nation at the time. It included a sandy beach, an elaborate diving complex, and drew approximately 10,000 swimmers annually. When a new city management team promulgated a policy to desegregate the facility in 1949, substantial backlash and bloodshed ensued. On 21 June of that year, an angry mob of more than 200 white residents encircled the pool with weapons, ranging from bats to knives, and attacked the first wave of

Black bathers that entered the pool. Throughout the day, more than 5,000 white provocateurs menaced Black swimmers at the facility (Wolcott, 2012).

Similarly, Pittsburgh, Pennsylvania, debuted a new aquatics facility at Highland Park in 1931, featuring a sandy beach with two large pools. On opening day, throngs of people came to swim at the gender-integrated facility, including Black residents, who were admitted by white pool attendants after being required to provide 'health certificates' proving they were disease-free (Wiltsie, 2007). Several Black patrons later complained to an official, who assured them access going forward. When about 50 young Black men arrived the next day, attendants admitted them to the pool. However, a larger crowd of white pool-goers harassed them, and violent opposition ensued for weeks, peaking when several hundred white youths severely beat numerous Black swimmers.

While physical violence as a means of rejecting integration served the immediate purpose of deterring Black people from using sport and recreation facilities, legally sanctioned segregationist policies often provided a more salient and pernicious solution for white people in both the southern and northern US. While Jim Crow laws that explicitly enforced racial segregation in the US largely abated after the Civil Rights Act of 1964 (Rothstein, 2017), the exclusion of Black citizens from public sport and recreation facilities continued, even in the face of lawsuits by the National Association for the Advancement of Colored People (NAACP). Moreover, in the landmark Palmer v Thompson (1971) decision, the US Supreme Court declared that a municipality could choose not to provide public amenities, such as swimming pools, as a means of avoiding desegregation (Rothstein, 2017). Illustrating this tendency, McGhee (2021) explains that many communities adopted 'drained-pool politics' when faced with desegregation mandates – if 'they' (i.e. minoritised people) needed to have access, then no one would. Subsequently, white administrators in cities such as St Louis, Pittsburgh, and Montgomery, Alabama, opted to drain and fill in pools, demolish existing aquatics facilities, and refuse to construct new pools rather than desegregate.

The geographic spaces in which we live – cities, suburbs, and towns – are often shaped by a racist history. In *The Geographies of Threat and the Production of Violence: The State and the City Between Us*, Mowatt (2022) argues that cities, as state sanctioned entities, function to "spatially racialize, genderize, and classify populations to the end of creating boundaries, enforced by laws and policies" (pp. 36–37). Subsequently, what is created are racial landscapes which depict the relationship between the social construction of racial identity and the production of place (Alderman & Modlin, Jr, 2014). Ultimately, racialised landscapes are a tangential byproduct of racially anchored social values, fear, and often strained race relations. The result is a system of racial ordering that produces a vision of what ought to be for some – segregation by geographic boundaries. This is what Trudeau (2006) labelled the "territorialized politics of belonging" (p. 422), in which places are racially bounded in ways that enforce exclusion and discrimination. In considering the social challenges and resistance associated with desegregating swimming pools, McGhee (2021) surmises that racism makes for abysmal policymaking, exacting a devastating toll on people of all races. Duany et al. (2000), in their book *Suburban Nation: The Rise and Decline of the American Dream*, provide a challenge for citizens to choose how they want their societies to be: "a society of homogenous pieces, isolated from one another in often fortified enclaves or a society of diverse and memorable neighborhoods [communities] organized into supportive towns, cities, and regions" (p. xiv). In the spirit of creating more equitable, supportive geographic spaces, we must seek to hold accountable those who broker corrupt public policy instead of those that consume it.

In his book, *How the Word is Passed*, Smith (2021) reflects on his visits to a number of monuments and landmarks that commemorate or interrogate the history of slavery and racism in varying ways. Reflecting on a trip to the National Museum of African American History and Culture with his grandparents, Smith writes:

> I think of how decades of racial violence have shaped everything we see, but sometimes I find myself forgetting its impact on those right beside me. I forget that many of the men and women who spat on the Little Rock Nine are still alive. I forget that so many of the people who threw rocks at Dr. King are still voting in our elections ... that the children who threw food at my grandmother and called her a n***** are likely bouncing their own great-grandchildren on their laps ... We tell ourselves that the most nefarious displays of racial violence happened long ago, when they were in fact not so long ago at all. These images and videos that appall our twenty-first-century sensibilities are filled with people who are still among us.
>
> (epithet removed by authors; pp. 288–289)

When thinking about inequities in our sport and recreation spaces today, we should likewise keep in mind that many of those involved in creating disparities and inequities, such as with access to swimming pools, are still making decisions and affecting public policy. In this vein, we should not assume things will necessarily 'get better' without conscious and persistent effort that agitates for progressive change. However, even administrators who had no role in creating the inequities that exist today must be pushed to take concrete, intentional action in order to create more equitable outcomes. Unfortunately, as we discuss below, diversity has too often been an afterthought in the world of sport and recreation. In cases where organisations have begun to devote attention to DEI, initiatives often fail to achieve more racially equitable outcomes.

Neglect and window dressing: Equality, diversity and inclusion in sport and recreation

Given the fierce opposition present in the history of the civil rights struggle, it may be unsurprising that sport and recreation organisations have often neglected matters of DEI. In recent years, however, many organisations have implemented programs, policies, and statements that are ostensibly intended to foster diversity. Unfortunately, many such DEI initiatives fail to give attention to racism and the need for structural change. In this way, DEI policies may serve as 'window dressing' or 'impression management' tools that help organisations craft a positive public image, despite their failure to address inequity in a meaningful way. Below, we discuss three examples – the National Recreation and Park Association (NRPA), the US Olympic and Paralympic Committee (USOPC), and the National Football League (NFL) – that illustrate the limitations of current DEI approaches in sport and recreation.

The National Recreation and Park Association and accreditation

With more than 60,000 professional members, the NRPA describes itself as the United States' "leading not-for-profit organization dedicated to building strong, vibrant, and resilient communities through the power of parks and recreation" (NRPA.org). The NRPA administratively sponsors the Commission for Accreditation of Park and Recreation Agencies (CAPRA) to provide agencies with a management system of best practices. CAPRA is the only national accreditation of park and recreation agencies and is a potentially useful measure of a department's overall quality of operation, management, and service to the community. There are currently 192 accredited park and recreation agencies in the US.

Dating back to the late 1980s, representatives from the NRPA and directors of large (i.e. serving cities of 250,000+ people) park and recreation systems in the US (a group primarily composed of white men) convened at Michigan State University to discuss creating an accreditation mechanism for the industry, similar to systems used in education, public health, and police accreditation. As a result, CAPRA was officially established in 1993 to implement and administer the accreditation process (National Recreation and Park Association, 2019). Despite a growing body of research related to racial inequity in the context of sport and recreation, the commission failed to conduct meaningful conversations related to DEI. Scholars began publishing work on the perceived barriers to occupational mobility among Black recreation and park employees (McDonald, 1983; Waller, 1989), differences in occupational category and gender of employees (Henkel & Godbey, 1977), the impact of discrimination in the workplace (Jencks, 1979), and equity issues in recreation (Dustin & Knopf, 1988; Ewert & Hollenhorst, 1990) during this time, yet there was no formal accountability in ensuring the NRPA would advocate for DEI. This lack of attention continues to foster systemic constraints and discrimination within the NRPA network. For example, resource allocation (Dahmann et al., 2010; Joassart-Marcelli, 2010) and access to parks (Gilliland et al., 2006; Rigolon, 2016; Rigolon et al., 2018) have been among the most significant detriments to communities of colour due to the negligence of the founding commission members.

Inequity is a crucial challenge facing many societies around the world, and park and recreation agencies are often in a unique position to champion efforts that advance DEI. Across the profession, however, gaps remain in understanding how systemic racism, inequitable power structures, and lack of cultural competency affect DEI and access to quality park and recreation spaces and programs. Centring equity sets a foundation for confronting these issues and ensuring that all people have access to the benefits of parks and recreation. A recent report (Roth, 2021) found that only one-third of parks and recreation agencies currently have formal DEI programs, while the most common DEI activities relate to hiring practices and policies, outlining an expressed commitment to DEI in foundational documents, and providing staff education and skill development.

Although there are no DEI standards required to achieve CAPRA accreditation, the NRPA has taken the step of publishing an *Equity Action Plan* (National Recreation and Park Association, 2021). The plan provides a framework for how the organisation is strengthening its culture and practices centred around equity and core values of trust, continuous learning, diversity, and inclusion. Specific to state affiliates, the strategy includes co-beneficial professional development opportunities, organisational change modelling, and demographic information collection. For the field at large, the plan recognises a need for targeted support for smaller agencies serving fewer than 50,000 residents, building member capacity and competency in DEI, equity best practices and peer-to-peer learning networks, and development of trusted resources. While such strategies may have promise, there are no mechanisms to ensure they are being monitored across agencies, nor are DEI standards a requirement for accreditation. As such, the existence of such initiatives may represent important progress beyond a past in which DEI has often been neglected, but DEI programs that lack enforcement mechanisms and fail to address structural racism often fail to achieve meaningful change.

The USOPC and DEI scorecards

The USOPC is the organisation responsible for overseeing National Governing Bodies (NGBs), High-Performance Management Organisations (HPMOs), and all athletes under the US Olympic umbrella. Within the US Olympic movement, a commitment toward DEI is frequently promoted through USOPC programs, initiatives, and statements. Specifically, responsibility toward the athletes and staff is demonstrated through a DEI mission statement, which reads, "The U.S. Olympic and Paralympic family embraces differences for better athletic performance and business results" (United States Olympic and Paralympic Committee, 2021). Coinciding with this commitment, the USOPC signals action by stating, "The USOPC has taken definitive steps to diversify its workforce, and the entire U.S. Olympic and Paralympic family, to better reflect the athletes we serve" (United States Olympic and Paralympic Committee, 2021). When naming the communities their workforce efforts are oriented toward, the USOPC uses the term "historically underrepresented groups", avoiding any overt mention of race or racism. This failure to specifically address racism is notable, as the actual demographic makeup of each organisation within the USOPC movement demonstrates persistent and ongoing racial inequity.

The USOPC produces DEI 'scorecards' as a mechanism for measuring the demographic makeup of its own organisation as well as each NGB and HPMO under its oversight. The specific demographic categories measured in the scorecard include women, persons with disabilities, military veterans, and people of colour. Each demographic category is given a specific percentage-based benchmark, determined using information from the US Census and other organisational data, serving as a target to reach in each category of personnel (e.g. athletes, coaches, professional staff). In particular, the benchmark for people of colour among front office staff was 25.21 per cent as of 2020, and the scorecard details each organisation's progress in reaching the benchmark.

Through analysing scorecard data from the years of 2013–2020, 30 of the 55 NGBs and HPMOs have never reached their benchmark for people of colour in front office staff. In this way, the racialised demographic data fails to demonstrate an alignment with the USOPC's ostensible commitment to diversity and inclusion presented through their rhetoric. Ultimately, while the USOPC's DEI rhetoric presents a public image of valuing diversity, the organisation continues to maintain and reproduce structural racial inequity.

The National Football League (NFL) and the Rooney Rule

As the most lucrative and most watched league in North America, the NFL holds a prominent position in the US sports landscape. For the past several decades, Black players have disproportionately populated NFL rosters, yet people of colour have held comparatively few leadership positions as head coaches and front office administrators. In response to long-standing racial inequity, the NFL promulgated the 'Rooney Rule' in 2002, which required teams to make certain affirmative efforts when hiring head coaches (Madden & Ruther, 2011). Since its initial implementation, the Rooney Rule has been expanded to include assistant coaches and senior operations positions. As of 2021, the rule requires NFL teams to interview at least two 'minority' candidates for head coach openings and at least one for second-level coaching (i.e. coordinator) openings, while also providing draft pick compensation to teams that 'develop' minorities who are hired in senior operation positions with other organisations (Harrison et al., 2021).

The Rooney Rule has certainly received positive media attention (Jones, 2020), helping the NFL brand itself as a league with a progressive commitment to social justice (Jones, 2021). However, in a league in which more than 70 per cent of players are people of colour, 27 of 32 head coaches (84.4 per cent) and 29 of 32 team CEO/presidents (90.6 per cent) were white at the beginning of the 2021 season (Lapchick, 2021). In fact, the proportion of coaching positions held by people of colour has not increased over the past decade, as 8 of 32 head coaches (25.0 pe cent) were people of colour in the 2011 season (Lapchick, 2021). As evidence that the Rooney Rule has been applied unevenly, Eugene Chung, a Korean American who played in the NFL for five years before spending ten seasons as an assistant coach, said he was told he was "not the right minority" while interviewing for NFL coaching jobs (ESPN, 2021). Overall, the NFL's lack of progress toward racial equity in leadership positions demonstrates the limited effectiveness of an initiative without active enforcement.

DEI as impression management

Sociologist Irving Goffman described how the concept of 'impression management' operates in efforts by organisations to influence the ways in which they are publicly perceived. Specifically, impression management characterises individuals and organisations as 'actors', who curate images and narratives for favourable public perceptions (DuBrin, 2010; Goffman, 1956). As part of this process, sport organisations seek to control narratives by employing opportunistic rhetoric through their media platforms, such as websites and social media channels, to shape public perceptions. As previously detailed, sport organisations such as the NRPA, USOPC, and NFL publicise numerous initiatives, programs, and statements to frame themselves as committed to DEI. However, when efforts, such as the USOPC scorecards and NFL's Rooney Rule, are not taken seriously, lack enforcement mechanisms, and do not provide tools to foster structural change, they may serve the purpose of impression management with little effect on actual organisational practices to foster equity (DuBrin, 2010; Goffman, 1956). In other words, organisations might 'show' that they are implementing policies and procedures to promote diversity, while not actually being supportive of these measures in such a way as to create systemic change (Ahmed, 2012).

As a way of interpreting the failures of sport and recreation organisations to stimulate progress through their DEI initiatives, it is necessary to understand that they are often racialised in ways that tend to privilege white people, particularly in positions of power. Throughout the sport studies literature, insights from critical race theory have been employed to shed light on how racism is embedded in many organisational settings, including Black student-athlete development (Bimper, 2017), policies and procedures perpetuating racial inequities (Cooper et al., 2017), hiring processes of NCAA head coaches (Singer et al., 2010), and the underrepresentation of people of colour working in sport organisations (Agyemang & DeLorme, 2010; Cunningham, 2021). In alignment with such work, Ray's (2019) theory of racialised organisations provides a useful lens for identifying organisational structures responsible for perpetuating racial inequity. Emerging from Ray's work is the idea of 'racialised decoupling', which refers to a gap between organisational rhetoric (e.g. diversity statements, policies) and actual organisational practices. In fact, upper-level managers often lack basic knowledge about their respective organisations' professed DEI plans, which hinders efforts to implement them in a meaningful way (Embrick, 2011). In this way, the actual organisational practices of sport and recreation organisations may be 'decoupled' from their stated commitment to diversity, resulting in the ultimate outcome of organisations that remain disproportionately white.

Fighting racism and fostering social justice in sport and recreation

Addressing racial inequity is an imperative and pressing matter, particularly in societies with increasingly diverse populations, such as the US, which is expected to have a 'majority–minority' composition by the mid-twenty-first century (Craig et al., 2018). However, those who seek to centre issues of racism in the quest for social justice face a challenging task, as issues of racial inequality are often viewed by white people as a zero-sum game in which gains by people of colour are imagined to come at the expense of white prosperity (McGhee, 2021). For instance, a growing body of research suggests that when white people are made aware of forthcoming demographic changes, they tend to shift their ideological views in a regressive, conservative direction, both for policies that are race-related (e.g. affirmative action, immigration) as well as those that are ostensibly race-neutral (e.g. oil and gas drilling, tax rates, health care, defence spending) (Craig et al., 2018). Such reactionary tendencies lead to extreme efforts by many powerbrokers to maintain a system of white dominance. As part of the aforementioned wave of efforts to censor teaching about racism in schools, a Republican legislator in Tennessee justified the need for such laws by telling a story about a white, seven-year-old girl who supposedly came home after a discussion in her classroom and asked her parents if she was racist (Richard, 2021). Such an example is representative of the efforts that white people in positions of power undertake to shield white children and parents from any discussions of racism that may cause them even slight discomfort, illustrating the challenges that lie ahead in the struggle for social justice.

A continued failure to address structural factors that perpetuate racial inequity will have dire consequences for people of all racial groups (McGhee, 2021). We live in a world with deeply embedded inequities that will not simply improve without direct, intentional interventions. As an example, the Black community owned approximately 0.5 per cent of the total wealth in the US at the time of the Emancipation Proclamation in 1863; now, more than 150 years later, that number stands at about 1 per cent (Baradaran, 2017). While sport is just one area of inequity among many in a society where white families have a median net worth 13 times greater than that of Black families (Baradaran, 2017), sport and recreation serve an important role in enhancing quality of life in communities. Because every action undertaken or policy implemented by an administrator serves to either perpetuate or challenge existing inequities, it is not possible to be neutral or simply 'not-racist' in the quest for social justice (Kendi, 2019). As such, to address racism and generate meaningful systemic change, sport and recreation organisations must move beyond ineffective DEI statements and policies that serve as 'window dressing' without enforcement mechanisms. We are caught in a cycle in which racism is often only understood in binary, individualistic terms, leading to a strategy of "hunting for racists" that seeks to identify 'good' and 'bad' people without reforming the structures that reproduce inequity (Bonilla-Silva, 2022). Ultimately, all those who envision a more just future must focus on eliminating racist policies that reproduce structural inequality and replacing them with anti-racist policies that create more equitable sport and recreation spaces.

Conclusion

In this chapter, we have highlighted ways in which deeply-seeded racial inequities continue to permeate sport and recreation in the US. Such inequities rob countless people of access to important sources of leisure, physical activity, and leadership opportunities (Hawes et al., 2019;

Powell et al., 2006), with detrimental effects on social and health-related outcomes (Bond & Herman, 2016). A more socially just future requires us to create sport and recreation spaces and systems that allow all people to participate in a full and equitable way (Bell, 2016; Culp, 2016). However, the task for those who hope to advance social justice in sport and recreation is complicated by the fact that racism is most typically framed as an individual attribute used to differentiate between 'bad' (i.e. racist) and 'good' (i.e. non-racist) people. Such a strategy of "hunting for racists" (Bonilla-Silva, 2022) tends to dominate public and mediated discussions of race, obscuring structural racial inequities. To counter this tendency, any productive path toward fostering a more just future in the field of sport, leisure, and recreation must focus on illuminating and addressing the ways in which racism is structural and embedded in institutions (Love et al., 2019). Those who benefit from the status quo, however, exert great effort to obscure the history behind structural racial inequity and to frame progress toward racial justice as a zero-sum game in which whites come out on the losing end (McGhee, 2021). Although scholars have produced a substantial body of work illustrating the socially constructed nature of race and its implications, while activists and other stakeholders have achieved important gains, our efforts toward the end of a more socially just future must be continual and ongoing. Benjamin (2016) describes race as a type of technology that "requires routine maintenance and upgrade", which drives innovators of inequity on a continual search to "embed racism deep in to the operating system" of society (p. 2227). Given this ongoing evolution of the mechanisms that drive racial inequity, our work as scholars and stakeholders committed to social justice must remain dynamic and innovative as we focus on identifying, creating, and implementing policies and practices that can produce more equitable outcomes for the benefit of all.

References

Agyemang, K., & DeLorme, J. (2010). Examining the dearth of Black head coaches at the NCAA football bowl subdivision level: A critical race theory and social dominance theory analysis. *Journal of Issues in Intercollegiate Athletics*, *3*, 35–52.

Ahmed, S. (2012). *On being included: Racism and diversity in institutional life*. Durham, NC: Duke University Press.

Alderman, D. H. & Modlinn, Jr., E. A. (2014). The historical geography of racialized landscapes. In C. E. Colten & G. L. Buckley (Eds), *North American odyssey: Historical geographies for the twenty-first century* (pp. 273–290). Lanham, MD: Rowman and Littlefield.

Baradaran, M. (2017). *The color of money: Black banks and the racial wealth gap*. Cambridge, MA: Harvard University Press.

Baumgarten, A. (2021, December 12). North Dakota's CRT ban worries professors. *Grand Forks Herald*. Retrieved from NewsBank: https://infoweb.newsbank.com/apps/news/document-view?p=WORLDNEWS&docref=news/186E3873124CE7F0

Bell, L. A. (2016). Theoretical foundations for social justice education. In A. M. Adams, L. A. Bell, D. J. Goodman, & K. Y. Joshi (Eds), *Teaching for diversity and social justice* (3rd ed., pp. 3–26). New York, NY: Routledge.

Benjamin, R. (2016). Innovating inequity: If race is a technology, postracialism is the genius bar. *Ethnic and Racial Studies*, *39*, 2227–2234. doi:10.1080/01419870.2016.1202423

Bimper, A. J. (2017). Mentorship of Black student-athletes at a predominately White American university: Critical race theory perspective on student-athlete development. *Sport, Education and Society*, *22*, 175–193. doi:10.1080/13573322.2015.1022524

Bond, M. J., & Herman, A. A. (2016). Lagging life expectancy for Black men: A public health imperative. *American Journal of Public Health*, *106*, 1167–1169. doi:10.2105/AJPH.2016.303251

Bonilla-Silva, E. (2022). *Racism without racists: Color-blind racism and the persistence of racial inequality in America* (6th ed.). Lanham, MD: Rowman & Littlefield.

Coakley, J. (2015). Assessing the sociology of sport: On cultural sensibilities and the great sport myth. *International Review for the Sociology of Sport, 50*, 402–406. doi:10.1177/1012690214538864

Cooper, J. N., Nwadike, A., & Macaulay, C. (2017). A critical race theory analysis of big-time college sports: Implications for culturally responsive and race-conscious sport leadership. *Journal of Issues in Intercollegiate Athletics, 10*, 204–233.

Craig, M. A., Rucker, J. M., & Richeson, J. A. (2018). Racial and political dynamics of an approaching "majority-minority" United States. *The ANNALS of the American Academy of Political and Social Science, 677*, 204–214. doi:10.1177/0002716218766269

Culp, B. (2016). Social justice and the future of higher education kinesiology. *Quest, 68*, 271–283. doi:10.1080/00336297.2016.1180308

Cunningham, G. B. (2021). The under-representation of racial minorities in coaching and leadership positions in the United States. In S. Bradbury, J. Lusted, & J. van Sterkenburg (Eds), '*Race', ethnicity and racism in sports coaching* (pp. 3–21). New York, NY: Routledge.

Dahmann, N., Wolch, J., Joassart-Marcelli, P., & Reynolds, K. (2010). The active city? Disparities in provision of urban public recreation resources. *Health & Place, 16*, 431–445. doi:10.1016/j.healthplace.2009.11.005

DiAngelo, R. (2018). *White fragility: Why it's so hard for while people to talk about racism*. Boston, MA: Beacon Press.

Duany, A., Plater-Zyberk, E., & Speck, J. (2000). *Suburban nation: The rise of sprawl and the decline of the American dream*. New York, NY: North Point Press.

DuBrin, A. J. (2010). *Impression management in the workplace: Research, theory, and practice*. New York, NY: Taylor & Francis.

Dustin, D. L., & Knopf, R. C. (1988). Equity issues in outdoor recreation. In *Outdoor Recreation Benchmark 1988: Proceedings of the National Outdoor Recreation Forum*, pp. 467–471.

Embrick, D. G. (2011). The diversity ideology in the business world: A new oppression for a new age. *Critical Sociology, 37*, 541–556. doi:10.1177/0896920510380076

ESPN. (2021, 22 May). Eugene Chung says he was called "not the right minority" during NFL coaching interview. *ESPN.com*. Retrieved from: https://www.espn.com/nfl/story/_/id/31490565/eugene-chung-says-was-called-not-right-minority-nfl-coaching-interview

Ewert, A., & Hollenhorst, S. (1990). Resource allocation: Inequities in wildland recreation. *Journal of Physical Education, Recreation & Dance, 61*, 32–36. doi:10.1080/07303084.1990.10604598

Gilliland, J., Holmes, M., Irwin, J. D., & Tucker, P. (2006). Environmental equity in child's play: Mapping public provision of recreation opportunities in urban neighborhoods. *Vulnerable Children and Youth Studies, 1*, 256–268. doi:10.1080/17450120600914522

Goffman, E. (1956). *The presentation of self in everyday life*. New York, NY: Doubleday.

Gutierrez, P. (2022, 30 August). Jon Gruden says emails "shameful" but I'm "good person", hope to "get another shot". *ESPN.com*. Retrieved from https://www.espn.com/nfl/story/_/id/34490318/jon-gruden-says-emails-shameful-good-person-hope-get-another-shot

Harrison, G., Kerns, C., & Stamm, J. (2021). Covering the Rooney Rule: An exploratory study of print coverage of NFL head coaching searches. *Howard Journal of Communications*. Advance online publication. doi:10.1080/10646175.2021.1999349

Hawes, A. M., Smith, G. S., McGinty, E., Bell, C., Bower, K., LaVeist, T. A., Gaskin, D. J., & Thorpe, R. J., Jr. (2019). Disentangling race, poverty, and place in disparities in physical activity. *International Journal of Environmental Research and Public Health, 16*, 1193. doi:10.3390/ijerph16071193

Henkel, D. D., & Godbey, G. C. (1977). *Parks, recreation, and leisure services employment in the public sector: Status and trends*. Arlington, VA: National Recreation and Park Association.

Hylton, K., & Lawrence, S. (2016). "For your ears only!": Donald Sterling and backstage racism in sport. *Ethnic and Racial Studies, 39*, 2740–2757. doi:10.1080/01419870.2016.1177193

Jencks, C. (1979). *Who gets ahead? The determinants of economic success in America*. New York, NY: Basic Books.

Joassart-Marcelli, P. (2010). Leveling the playing field? Urban disparities in funding for local parks and recreation in the Los Angeles area. *Environment and Planning A: Economy and Space, 42*, 1174–1192. doi:10.1068/a42198

Jones, J. (2020, May 19). NFL's Rooney Rule additions are a positive step forward, but more teeth needed. *CBSSports.com*. Retrieved from: https://www.cbssports.com/nfl/news/nfls-rooney-rule-additions-are-a-positive-step-forward-but-more-teeth-needed/

Jones, M. (2021, Dec. 30). NFL, players coalition add four more inspire change partners in fight for social justice. *USA Today*. Retrieved from: https://sports.yahoo.com/nfl-players-coalition-add-four-191717624.html

Kendi, I. X. (2016). *Stamped from the beginning: The definitive history of racist ideas in America*. New York, NY: Bold Type Books.

Kendi, I. X. (2019). *How to be an antiracist*. New York, NY: One World.

Lapchick, R. (2020). The 2020 racial and gender report card: National Basketball Association. Retrieved from University of Central Florida, The Institute for Diversity and Ethics in Sport website: https://www.tidesport.org/nba

Lapchick, R. (2021). The 2021 racial and gender report card: National Football League. Retrieved from University of Central Florida, The Institute for Diversity and Ethics in Sport website: https://www.tidesport.org/nfl

Love, A., Deeb, A., & Waller, S. N. (2019). Social justice, sport and racism: A position statement. *Quest*, *71*, 227–238. doi:10.1080/00336297.2019.1608268

Madden, J. F., & Ruther, M. (2011). Has the NFL's Rooney Rule efforts "leveled the field" for African American head coach candidates? *Journal of Sports Economics*, *12*, 127–142. doi:10.1177/1527002510379641

McDonald, J. L. M. (1983). *An analysis of the relationship among factors which may influence the occupational mobility of black personnel with recreation, parks and leisure services* (Doctoral dissertation, University of Maryland).

McGhee, H. (2021). *The sum of us: What racism costs everyone and how we can prosper together*. New York, NY: One World.

Mills, C. W. (1997) *The racial contract*. Ithaca, NY: Cornell University Press.

Mowatt, R. A. (2022). *The geographies of threat and the production of violence: The state and the city between us*. New York, NY: Routledge.

National Recreation and Park Association. (2019). *Commission for accreditation of park and recreation agencies: The national accreditation standards* (6th ed.). Retrieved from: https://www.nrpa.org/contentassets/4ecbd8c4801e494f82c38169b0aedc20/capra-national-accreditation-standards-master-document-12-8-2020.pdf

National Recreation and Park Association. (2021). Equity Action Plan. Retrieved from https://www.nrpa.org/contentassets/39a68ad8bfc5433f81c5de414d16cd7c/2021nrpaactionplan-final.pdf

Powell, L. M., Slater, S., Chaloupka, F. J., & Harper, D. (2006). Availability of physical activity-related facilities and neighborhood demographic and socioeconomic characteristics: A national study. *American Journal of Public Health*, *96*, 1676–1680. doi:10.2105/AJPH.2005.065573

Ray, V. (2019). A theory of racialized organizations. *American Sociological Review*, *84*, 26–53. doi:10.1177/0003122418822335

Richard, B. (2021, May 3). Tennessee lawmakers seek to ban critical race theory in schools. WMC. Retrieved from https://www.wmcactionnews5.com/2021/05/03/tennessee-lawmakers-seek-ban-critical-race-theory-schools

Rigolon, A. (2016). A complex landscape of inequity in access to urban parks: A literature review. *Landscape and Urban Planning*, *153*, 160–169. doi:10.1016/j.landurbplan.2016.05.017

Rigolon, A., Browning, M., & Jennings, V. (2018). Inequities in the quality of urban park systems: An environmental justice investigation of cities in the United States. *Landscape and Urban Planning*, *178*, 156–169. doi:10.1016/j.landurbplan.2018.05.026

Roth, K. (2021). Diversity, equity and inclusion in parks and recreation. *NRPA Research Reports*, 1–15.

Rothstein, R. (2017). *The color of law: A forgotten history of how our government segregated America*. New York, NY: Lightfield Publishing.

Singer, J. N., Harrison, K. C., & Bukstein, S. J. (2010). A critical race analysis of the hiring process for head coaches in NCAA college football. *Journal of Intercollegiate Sport*, *3*, 270–296. doi:10.1123/jis.3.2.270

Smith, C. (2021). *How the word is passed: A reckoning with the history of slavery across America*. New York, NY: Little, Brown and Company.

Theoharis, G. (2007). Social justice educational leasers and resistance: Toward a theory of social justice leadership. *Educational Administration Quarterly*, *43*, 221–258. doi:10.1177/0013161X06293717

Trudeau, D. (2006). Politics of belonging in the construction of landscapes: Place-making, boundary drawing and exclusion. *Cultural Geographies*, *13*, 421–443. doi:10.1191/1474474006eu366o

United States Olympic and Paralympic Committee. (2021). USOPC diversity, equity & inclusion is: Many faces, one team, one mission. Retrieved from: https://www.teamusa.org/About-the-USOPC/Diversity-Equity-Inclusion

Waller, S. N. (1989). *An analysis of perceived barriers to occupational mobility among black municipal recreation and parks employees in Michigan* (Doctoral dissertation, Michigan State University). ProQuest Dissertations and Theses Global.

Wiltsie, J. (2007). *Contested waters: A social history of swimming pools in America.* Chapel Hill, NC: University of North Carolina Press.

Wolcott, V. W. (2012). *Race, riots, and roller coasters: The struggle over segregated recreation in America.* Philadelphia, PA: University of Penn Press.

11
RACE, SOCIAL JUSTICE, LEISURE, AND SPORT IN BRAZIL

A critical perspective in defence of anti-racism

Lennon Giulio Santos de Farias, Neilton de Sousa Ferreira Júnior, Léo Barbosa Nepomuceno, Eduardo Vinícius Mota e Silva, Luciana Venâncio, Luiz Sanches Neto, and Henrique Antunes Cunha Júnior

Introduction

This chapter deals with the phenomenon of racism in the sports context and its various manifestation forms. The analyses range from denouncements of racial prejudice made by athletes, fans, and the media, to institutional expressions of racism (Farias et al., 2020). Scholars on the subject consider that racism comprises a system that organises a racial division between human beings, establishing physical but also class and geographic characteristics and differences, as defining criteria of a hierarchy that, as a rule, privileges racialised groups such as Whites (Munanga, 2004; Almeida, 2019). Although we are speaking to an Anglophonic audience, this chapter first focuses on race and racism in sport applied to the Brazilian context. The notion of social justice is entangled with race, sport, and leisure throughout this chapter.

The concept of 'natural' hierarchies between 'human races' appears in the wake of colonial development and instrumentalisation of the biological, anthropological, and psychological sciences, especially from the eighteenth century onwards, also counting on intense collaboration of European historical and philosophical thought. A consensus among the great names of modern philosophy in the idea that Blacks did not have nor were able to produce culture (Gilroy, 2007; Mbembe, 2014) converged with biological and anthropological assumptions about the 'need' of non-Whites to be protected and civilised, "because they are savages" (Odendaal, 1988).

Constitutively elastic, ambiguous, and crucial to the formation of the modern world as we know it (Mbembe, 2014), race was, as it still is, a key element in constructing and supporting epidermalised imaginaries of 'Blacksubalternity'. It comprises a rhetorical device, a delusion of modern reason which not only found fertile ground for its development within the biological and social sciences but also in literature, the arts, media, and more recently consecrates its survival through new technological convergences, responsible for what Saini (2019) identifies as *the return to race science*.

The process of *race science* marks a re-encounter of contemporary science with the assumptions of nineteenth-century science. A reunion that is distinguished by displaced techniques of racial hierarchy based on the observation of phenotypic elements to manipulate microbiological elements listed in genetic engineering. This means that the most visible face of racism only comprises the surface of a plot which relies on the exponential development of technology, in such a way that the racial hierarchy is similarly configured to organic processes. Although we know that races do not exist from a biological point of view, enthusiasts of this new technical-scientific context have made an effort to make us believe that society is organised based on biological determinations, for example Entine (2000). This condition is supported by apparently non-racist culturalist beliefs and conceptions which do nothing more than reinforce racial hierarchies by justifying 'Blackaptitude' for sports through ethnicity, followed by the very praise of sporting/athletic Blacks (Munanga, 2004; Abrahão & Soares, 2009).

Blackslavery established a strong relationship with biological assumptions, but also with the cultural setting and 'specialisation' of this group for a set of tasks. Religion would participate in this plot, offering moral justifications for the overexploitation of the Blackbody, which would find a way to redeem its 'savage' condition in intense work and in tutored life. It was in slave and colonial sociability that the very concept of the *Negro* became more complex as the current production system improved. Mbembe (2014, p. 19) argues that the thousands of people caught in the racial domination networks witnessed a functioning system in which their bodies and thoughts were elaborated from outside; an externality that transformed them into "spectators of whatever was and was not their own life".

As an aftermath of Blackslavery, *anti-Blackracism* in sport indicates (among other things) the existence of an articulation that transcends inter-personal and inter-subjective relationships to inhabit the terrain of institutional plots, in which race issues invariably intertwine with issues of class and national identity (Soares, 1999; Freitas Junior & Ribeiro, 2012). According to Darnell and Millington (2019), advocates of sport have proposed ways in which sport might support those on the social, economic, and geographic margins, even amidst widespread inequality. Both sport and leisure have been responding to various forms of inequality while pursuing social justice. This chapter helps us understand the socio-historical context and development of sport, leisure, and social justice in Brazil, and offers a contextualised review of the sport and leisure literature and how it has shaped, resisted and/or enabled social justice with an emphasis on anti-racism.

Late slavery abolishment in the Brazilian context

On the one hand, Brazil is the largest and most influential country in South America, but the reality is a country with a wide gap between rich and poor. Many of its inequity and social justice issues are related to a complex mix of factors, such as its large population of about 211 million, its ethnic and cultural diversity, class and income disparity, late slavery abolishment, unstable democracy, and political governance (Sanches Neto et al., 2021). On the other hand, Brazil was the last country to abolish Blackslavery in 1888. The period designated as post-abolition would not reserve greater opportunities for newly freed Blacks to ascend socially within the limits of formal liberal democracy, even though the historical amount of Blackresistance and organisation that emerged at the time forces us to relativise this process (Domingues, 2009).

The fact is that the Blacks and *mestizos* of this period, as well as their heirs, had to face a triple task related to the process of searching for a place in the sun in the so-called 'free societies'. Namely, the task of integration into class society, given that the access bridges to their African origins were demolished by the force of the Atlantic and of time. This is followed by the task of making *a place* out of the rubble of slavery and colonial space; a process accompanied by claims for recognition within the cultural universe of a class society that, conveniently, would not give up *race* as a containment instrument of the revolutionary contingent and the Blackascension movement (Azevedo, 1987; Fernandes, 1989).

Therefore, Blacks did not enter the bourgeois sports world in obedience to their 'aptitude' for the disciplines of the body. As in literature, cinema, science, and politics, this insertion aims to search for a repealed humanity, which could be recovered through mastery of the instruments and language of the ruling class. Fanon (2008, p. 34) explains that "all people in the midst of which an inferiority complex was born due to the burial of their cultural originality – takes a position in facing the language of the civilizing nation, that is, of the metropolitan culture". That is why sport will not only become a laboratory to reinforce racist theses, but a field of dispute to resignify the presence of Blackpeople in that society and for the very criticism of race.

Racial violence and anti-racist protest will compete (disproportionately) in the field of sporting dispute as a reflection of a broader social struggle that is invariably integrated into forms of gender and class domination. Something that must always be on our analysis horizon in this context is the fact that sport is not just a space where vices and virtues are manifested. The phenomenon in focus in its modern origin has deep relationships with the domination forms mentioned earlier. Modern sports theory makes it clear that competitive practices and their 'natural' heroes belong to the male sex (Coubertin, 2015). It also makes it clear that modern sports culture, developed within colonialist Europe, graces itself as the 'culture of all cultures', a kind of overcoming of the 'infantile stage' of the cultural practices of dominated peoples.

This leads us to the reflection that modern sport not only reflects contemporary social tensions but particularises them, and in many cases deepens, in an apparently unavoidable way, the cultural, racial, gender, and class hierarchies that sustain modernity. As an extension of this societal project, modern sport naturalises forms of separation and verification of inequalities, which are not only celebrated in the symbolic plane of the competitive rite when one national representation wins over the other, but in the concrete plane of flagrant racial divisions, gender, and class that organise the landscape of work, entertainment, and sports politics.

The modern form of sport entered both the twentieth and twenty-first centuries as a stage and laboratory for validating raciological theses linked to the assumptions of eugenics, social-Darwinism, and Western White supremacism. The interpretations extracted from the new discoveries in genetics have been able to update the concept and uses of *race* and to reestablish the bridge between the nineteenth century and the future, even though this new hierarchised engineering of the world prefers to hide in euphemisms such as *diversity* and *difference*. The fact is that the heirs of racist approaches live on in search of the racial *eldorado*, enjoying financial support for their research, as well as a relative prestige in the sports community (Entine, 2000; Saini, 2019).

This situation is even worse when it is realised that modern sports sociability at the beginning of the twentieth century had nothing to do with improving culture, but now it is an emulation and celebration of the competitive society (Huizinga, 2000). Modern sport is more and more integrated with business and econometric rationality, becoming a relatively anarchic space for the sociological categories of work and labour rights, at the same time that it is being assumed as a 'technocratic kingdom', autonomous from politics, and for that very reason, to social conventions guided by democratic principles of respect for difference. The opacity of the processes for electing leaders of national and international sports, followed by their monochromatic and masculine landscape, seems to us to be a very concrete demonstration of the long distance between the universalist and civilising discourse of sport theory and its practice (Giglio & Rubio, 2017). The scarcity of research and challenges to this system only reinforces how naturalised the racial division of sports work is.

According to Farias et al. (2020), an international look at the issue of anti-Blackracism in sport should lead us to the 'subtler' ways of maintaining the racial division mentioned earlier. This division is also established in the way international organisations deal with the South overall, giving a neocolonial and orientalist instrumentality to sports programs dedicated to the 'promotion of peace', 'development' and 'values', whose universality is not in question. The evangelistic rhetoric that accompanies these apparently well-intentioned programs not only hides unresolved problems in modern Western ideology, such as the delusional burden of 'civilising destiny', but it is also a cultural policy oriented towards the new century that aims at nothing more than maintaining the hegemony of the ruling class (Melo, 2011).

It is necessary to keep in mind that the relationship between the civilising process and sport is not given *a priori*. It refers to a dated theoretical construction counting on authors who insisted on ignoring power relations without which modern sport itself could not become hegemonic in the world. Such hegemony could only materialise through acculturation and 'modernisation' processes of autochthonous gestures. Although the success of these ventures is perfectly questionable, especially if we take into account the counter-hegemonic local appropriation forms of modern sport (Brohm, Perelman & Vassort, 2004; Domingos, 2005), we must agree, as argued by Jesus (1999, p. 8), that "the imposition of a new corporal attitude, through the assimilation of imported sports, is fully inserted in the civilizing project of the ruling class". 'Subtle' examples of the racist instrumentalisation of sport are found everywhere. They can teach us a lot about the meanings and implications of *structural racism* applied to the sports field (Almeida, 2019). But leaving the relativisation of sports colonisation for a later debate, let us return to the topic of our reflection. It is noteworthy that Brazil is currently the country with the largest Blackpopulation outside Africa. Overall, only Nigeria has a larger Blackpopulation than Brazil.

Anti-Blackracism in sport: An institutional and historical 'plot'

Although it receives little attention in Brazil, the institutional plots of containment and exclusion of Blacks have been part of the history of national sport since the early years of its formation. The fever for sports culture in Brazilian metropolises in the mid-nineteenth century was strongly guided by a modernisation concept that was clearly refractory to everything Indigenous and Black (Jesus, 1999). While European modalities found shelter from bourgeois clubs, capoeira and samba were persecuted by the state, constituting a condition that would decisively interfere in the debate on the set of cultural elements that constitute the official Brazilian identity. Far from resembling the elitist pessimism that made up the anti-sports chorus of the early twentieth century, Lima Barreto's critique of football was directed at the bourgeois form of its institution. This arrangement managed to contain the integration of Blacks into clubs for a long time, subordinating this entry to unbreakable hierarchies.

As the Blackcontingent gained space, sports institutions reoriented their containment strategies, adopting at minimum disturbing measures. In the article "Victories and defeats of mestizo football" by Freitas Junior and Ribeiro (2012, p. 304), the negative results of Brazilian campaigns in the 1950 and 1954 World Cups mobilised journalists and sports directors, selected by the then Brazilian Sports Confederation (Confederação Brasileira de Desportos – CBD), to implement a project which aimed to 'modernise' the national team with a view to participating in the 1958 World Cup in Sweden. The authors identify that "the local elites were ashamed to be represented by Blacks/mulattos, uneducated, toothless and who had great difficulties in self-control in situations of adversity".

Therefore, it was not a project oriented to the players' awareness, but, as Freitas Junior and Ribeiro (2012, p. 304) continue, an attempt to 'educate' them with a view to modifying their physical appearances, habits, cultures, and behaviours. It was only in this way that Blackathletes could represent Brazil that, in terms of ideas, would have "overcome the sociocultural backwardness – normally attributed to myths such as the mixture of races and the lack of self-control of Brazilian men". This institutional plot is also described by Corrêa (1985). Although scarce, these records allow us to locate the problem of anti-Blackracism in Brazilian sport in an everyday terrain, where institutional arbitrariness bypasses formality and registration. Hence, the difficulty that historical and sociological research encounters when trying to measure the phenomenon under study.

Although not focusing on the sports phenomenon, Fanon's (2008) intellectual work helps us to understand the relationship that Blackpeople established with the metropolis and its modern apparatus (state, school, sport, to name just a few examples), almost always taking place *from the outside in*. As obvious as it may seem, the observation that Blackpeople are always *integrating* themselves into sports is not trivial, since their reception in bourgeois sports institutions is, as a rule, mediated by *another* White person. Until recently, the athlete-institution relationship was not guided by conventional labour law but by a special regime that differentiated and distanced the athlete working class from conventional claim instruments, such as unions.

Thus, it is an issue of social justice. A certain absence of legal and political devices to defend against institutional arbitrariness and violence allows professionals in the area to go through a series of situations which would be unacceptable in other fields of action. Racial violence brings with it an aggravating factor, since it is still very little understood by professional reception and listening techniques (Tralci Filho, 2019). Once again, we are faced with a kind of *plot* that places sports professionals, and especially Blacks, in a kind of *blind spot* where the exercise of impersonality and respect is suspended.

Part of this plot is established in the celebration of a false consciousness, according to which modern sport would be like one of those systems that we judge neutral, neither good nor bad. Something like family, work, and technology. Sport would be a sufficiently equitable platform from which we can witness meritocratic justice. Following this line of reasoning widely disseminated by the academy itself, modern sport was constituted as a system open to any undertaking.

Sometimes it can serve progressive policies of recognition, as well as processes of accelerating a transfer of wealth from peripheral countries to central countries via mega-events (Brohm et al., 2004; Ouriques, 2009; Dip, 2013). The victims of this process are not restricted to sports professionals. Within the scope of capitalist mega-events are the peripheral populations, mostly Black, strategically excluded from the festivities and the 'noble' regions of the city. Such 'legacy' affects both professional sports and leisure practices. For instance, orientation towards social justice has been advocated as an integral aspect of physical education teaching, enabling students to engage with a broad range of content underpinned by ethical, political, aesthetic, theoretical-methodological, epistemological, and pedagogical principles (Sanches Neto et al., 2021).

Sports, politics, and race do not mix

The apparently hypnotic powers of sport tend to indefinitely postpone more specific investigations into the (intuitively perceived) relationship between sport and political life. Although this relationship is constantly in evidence, it is rarely systematised to the point of offering elements of mobilisation and change in unjust realities. A good example of this is when the fight against racism takes on a more systemic form, provoking a reaction in which the entire ideological complex of support for the *status quo* is mobilised, without needing to justify itself rationally or scientifically. Naturalised, the dominant discursive regime isolates the subjects of the anti-racist claim who undergo a kind of social asphyxia which is able to demoralise agendas and exhaust the energies of the struggle. There is a kind of 'sports fatalism' faithful to the maintenance of the spectacle, regardless of its victims.

Although the integration of the Blackcontingent into sport only grew in the twentieth century, it did not change the power structures established in the administrative arrangement of the sports industry developed in the nineteenth century. Nor would anything have changed in the social imagination about the *Negro*, as more optimistic voices will tell us. Guided by a liberal and nominal democratic conception of society, the idea of Blacksocial ascension through sporting talent ends up diverting attention from analytical rigour away from the production system in which sports sociability is constituted. One of the main parts of this system is the fetish responsible for turning the Black-skinned subject into a Blackperson, a body without a soul, a subhuman form abandoned by reason (Mbembe, 2014). Once formed based on this set of delusions, modern society will resort, whenever necessary, to the memory of the colony but also to the memory of the sugarcane factory, a laboratory that forged the *Negro* as a commodity-body, currency-body, mineral-body, animal, and monster (Fanon, 2008; Mbembe, 2014).

Modern sport becomes the stage for the emergence of racial injury and violence, since its spectacular form provides above all expedients of euphoria and false unanimity to its spectators/consumers, which allows racist expressions which are almost always free from punishment. The objectified relationship that the viewer establishes with the sports protagonist largely results from television reinforcement of the uncritical consumption of sports. A process that Brohm et al. (2004) call the *brutalisation* of the parties involved in the spectacle. Obviously, we do not intend here to advocate that spectator sport needs to be appreciated like works of art.

At the same time, we do not share the thesis that the phenomenon in question belongs to the field of the irrational, as in Damatta's (1982) description of football, separating it from the 'real world', in turn represented by war, the struggle for survival and work. It is necessary to take into account the fact that the sociology and history of sport have done very little with regard to the constitutive categories of modern sport. The process that led to its secularisation, rationalisation, bureaucratisation, commodification and globalisation never gave up *race*. Although the bourgeois distribution of sports is established on the basis of social class, it is race that continues to guide the model of super-exploitation and humiliation of Blackpeople.

While Blackpeople became the protagonist of the contemporary sports scene in the most diverse modalities, speculative forms about their 'race' were being perfected in the knowledge of university departments, following an accelerated process of capital movement towards 'non-productive' activities or symbolic production. So athletic performance, and especially Blackperformance, entered the 21st century as one of the most coveted economic assets. There was a new moment of racial hierarchy and the very notion of race, in which prominent Blackbodies began to reinforce the false impression of recognition through images provided by television. Abrahão and Soares (2009) identify this process in Brazilian sport based on the uses of *praise for Blackpeople* in the 1950s. Far from representing a recognition form of the humanity of the aforementioned group, the praise for performance and 'Blackaptitude' for sports, music, and the arts aimed to sediment racial hierarchies predefined in the social imagination.

The ephemeral and bipolar way in which the public approaches its sports 'stars', 'kings', 'villains' and 'monsters' leaves no doubt about the artificial and virtual character of modern sports sociability. This is not to say that the affections it produces are not harmful to the integrity of sports workers. Unlike other labour fields, sport is one of the few in which bullying/harassment is permitted, not directly, but in the form of 'incentive' by fans and coaches, among others. The conversion of Blacksports performance into merchandise is part of a reorganisation of the value production system but also of racism adapting to new social configurations. Fearing the sociocultural implications of the social ascension of Blacks through sport, the White bourgeoisie would have articulated ways to contain the emergence of a Blackbourgeoisie that could rival the former in terms of power.

In turn, the class character of such reaction regarding the permanent struggle for social justice in Brazil focused on making the rewards extracted from Blacksports work to serve the perpetuation of White power. It is worth remembering that sports equipment was once kept under the power of the local bourgeoisie, but it starts to serve any project/plot, sometimes dedicated to the deliberate exclusion of the Blackcontingent, sometimes dedicated to the containment of its political force through forms of *subordinate integration* (Ferreira Júnior & Rubio, 2019).

Then in travelling through a broader Brazilian sociocultural terrain, there is the phenomenon of the unspoken racist, characteristic of the cordial, and no less violent, formation of national subjectivity, within which the integration of Blackpeople was found – and is still found – subordinated to impressions and rhetoric anchored to the myth of racial democracy. According to Mbembe (2014), this kind of self-deception is typical of slave and colonial societies, ashamed (or proud) of the way they assert their presence in the world. It is a way of reshaping history, adapting it to more 'civilised' images of nation and sociability, which is represented in the dispute for memory and national identity, fierce in the field of historiography, the arts, literature, dramaturgy, and sports chronicle (Rodrigues Filho, 2003; Freitas Junior & Ribeiro, 2012).

The long study by Bastide and Fernandes (1959) on *Blacks and Whites in the city of São Paulo* – Southeastern Brazil – in the mid-1950s showed how the capital city's sports associations, in the figure of their associates and directors, were recalcitrant to the presence of Blacks, at the same time in which chronicles and testimonies about the 'reconciling' beauty of *mestizo* football and the 'social ascension' of Blackpeople through sports performance multiplied. The spectacle society in which we are inserted forces us to specify how the televised representation form of sports practices has influenced the general perception of reality, meaning the severity of racial violence and the lonely pain of the victimised body. First, this reflection project implies removing the arsenal of false consciences and idealised characteristics that cover the sporting phenomenon. It is only in this way can we get to the heart of the problem.

Then, we will try to take the first steps to follow, debating on racial representations in sport and its broader connections to social justice.

The problem of sport globalisation towards social justice

The globalisation of televised sports broadcasting is one of the vectors of the globalisation of goods, and is notably adept at "disguising its political character, the generalized monetization of sports 'values', fraud and cheating of all kinds" (Brohm et al., 2004, p. 2). From the side effects of this process, we highlight the aforementioned Western control of the destinies of global sport, the bourgeois and White hegemony in deliberative spaces, the racialised and rationalised distribution of sports modalities accompanied by specific policies for peripheral countries, and the devastation without (concrete recovery horizons) bodily experiences that speak of other value systems. In this context, modern sport does not only represent a phenomenon which occupies an 'empty' space, but an affirmation instrument of a determined cultural identity, under the domain of which culture hierarchisation and consequently of bodies are established (Fanon, 2008).

The idea of 'remaking' Blackcorporeality was not something new within the sport globalisation process. Regarding its presence in Africa at the beginning of the 20th century, the International Olympic Movement would not only defend that Blacks had an inferior movement body culture, but also that they needed to be disciplined in the regime of modern sports practices so that they could leave the semi-wild plane and reach the ultra-civilised plane (Coubertin, 2015). Such reasoning expresses the civilisationist and hegemonist character that constituted modern sport in detail and, to a large extent, justified its expansion. It is a condition which does not allow us to say that we are facing a force of nature which has taken root in the imagination of societies without affecting entire social ecosystems and without reinforcing predefined social conceptions and hierarchies by the force of colonialism and imperialism. All of this history counts when trying to answer the question: why is modern sport so tolerant of anti-Blackracism in Brazil and other countries?

We assume that there is no answer that addresses the complexity of the question. This is because the racial violence to which we refer is mixed with the ambiguous way in which the sports phenomenon has become popular. This fundamental ambiguity puts us before the fact that the integration of Blackpeople in modern sport in the first place does not result from a benevolent disposition of the dominant classes, but from a civilising project proposed and carried out by the dehumanised community itself (Domingos, 2005). Second, it is necessary to recognise that this integration cannot be completed in the current bourgeois configuration of sport, as in the presence of capitalist sport in colonised countries.

The ideology of sport in force is fully submitted to the 'rationality' of profit, and not only suspends any possibilities of concrete relations of recognition but also forms its participants (direct and indirect) within a regime of *brutalisation*, in which Blacks are invariably coded as proto-humans (Carrington, 2002; Brohm et al., 2004). The prototypical form has been reinforced by the raciology that guides an important part of the sports community (Entine, 2000). The racialised dualism between muscle and intelligence invariably penalises Blacks, previously represented by the strength of *Blackreasoning by Whites*, according to Mbembe (2014, p. 40), as a "prototype of a pre-human figure incapable of overcoming its own animality".

Blackpeople do not objectively exist as such but are constantly produced within the gears of capitalist accumulation. Producing Blacks as subaltern, scientific, literature, and media devices contributes to creating a social bond of accepting the racial hierarchy. Thus, an imaginary idea is created about a body entirely exposed to the will of a master (individual or collective) who strives to get the most out of his object. At the mercy of this structuring delirium, the Blackperson also becomes the name of the insult, "a symbol of the man who faces the whip and suffering on a battlefield in which *socio-racially* segmented groups and factions are opposed" (Mbembe, 2014). The condition which guarantees the uninterrupted circulation of racist gestures concerns a false impersonality of the rules of sport and their uncritical consumption, protected by the television approach.

In analysing contemporary sport, Brohm et al. (2004, n.p.) argue that "public space, reduced to a televised dream screen, is saturated with sport, to the point of compromise that politics [a privileged field of conflict resolution] is also considered as a sport". Thus configured, sport cannot therefore be an instrument of reconciliations. In the words of the authors, "the *really existing* sport is nothing but a frenzy of competition, the planetary organization of its permanent rotation in a universal calendar". It is no more than "one of the components of a time and a space made autonomous *in and by* capital". It is not a domain of democracy but of the dictatorship of the bourgeoisie, which needs to distribute some sport in a calculated way in order to survive. In this sense, the bourgeois alienation of the sports phenomenon is the alienation of most of those involved, especially Blacks. According to Fanon (2008, p. 29), this is a condition which can only be changed concretely when things "in the most materialistic sense, [take] their rightful place".

Fundamental to the Fanonian critique of culture, Blackalienation is configured within the existing relations of production, as well as in an ethical void established by post-colonial non-politics. In other words, from the moment that the Blackperson ascends to the condition of citizen in the metropolis and/or in the former colony, they start to deal with a lack of concreteness in the promises of civilisation in an uninterrupted way, by which they inherit all techniques for maintaining asymmetries between Whites and Blacks from colonialism. The condition reserved for the latter will always be that of *non-being*, fundamental to the affirmation of the White being who also learns *to be* in the negation of the *Other*. According to Fanon (2008), alienation therefore does not refer to the anti-Blackplot only, but to the way in which the White identity is configured within the same production and metropolitan culture modes. The difference lies in the fact that civilisation and nominal democracy to which we refer do not allow Blackpeople to make their descent into hell so that they can free themselves from themselves. For Mbembe's (2014), there is an epistemological interdiction that needs to be removed from the path. This prohibition is called the *Blackreasoning by Whites*. This reasoning circulates freely through the sports field, since its practice schedule is obstructed by an instrumental and reified reason, which (almost always) operates in the sense of alienation. Nevertheless, achieving social justice is only possible by confronting racism, sexism, and ultimately capitalism.

Anti-racist advocacy and teaching for social justice in physical education

There has been a proliferation of prominent Blackathletes worldwide. However, it is not a matter of representativeness that concerns us about promoting anti-racist advocacy. For instance, the experience of the Blacksoccer league in Brazil in the 1910s implies that Blackpopulations have a place to stay *a priori* which is apart from the societal places of power (Domingues, 2009). However, the institutionalised racial violence did not prevent the Blackpresence from growing in the Brazilian sports scene. This suggests that the presence of Blacks in sport and society, although progressively tolerated, is something that needs to be cultivated (but not without costs to the health of its protagonists) through different modalities of struggle (Farias et al., 2020). The problem, for that very reason, would not be in either the man or woman classified and qualified as Black, nor in the natural contradictions to the entire anti-racist struggle, but in the social order which celebrates the dehumanisation of Blackpeople in its different instances.

Then, our reflections on the condition of Blacks in contemporary sport refers to the misuses of Blackathletes' trajectories as meritocratic aiming to perpetuate racism and other social injustices. It is also important to emphasise that the integration of Blacks into professional sports in Brazilian society did not take place because of the good will of the ruling classes but because of a pragmatic need, since victory is in the foreground in the context of professional sport. Blackathletes are presented as physically superior bodies, but they create major problems when their bodies rally against social injustices (Mariante Neto et al., 2010). There is a moment – from the 1920s onwards – when the White ruling class begins to withdraw from the realm of practices to dedicate itself to organising an industry that would survive on the workforce of Blacks and the poor in Brazil. Bourgeois football starts to make use of fractions of the working class. Although such a movement did not develop without resistance on the part of the most conservative, it became inevitable due to the technical advantages that the social group – hitherto excluded – brought to the spectacle, constituting a process which can also be seen in Africa and Central America (Domingos, 2005).

Such issues are important lessons to learn; therefore, they must be taught. For Silva, Sanches Neto and Cunha Júnior (2022), there are five principles to socially just physical education teaching from an anti-racist perspective. The principles comprise teaching sports and games – with a more critical socio-cultural perspective – for understanding about the entanglements of culture, movement, body, and environment, meeting the regional and local needs. The first principle is the appreciation of the Blackeducator movement's roots; the second is the racialisation of Whiteness; the third is explaining the Blackpopulations' knowledge; the fourth is the fight against Blackepistemicide; and last but not least, the fifth principle is the specificity of Blackfeminists' thought.

Conclusion

The liberal interpretation of racism in sport seems to be right in stating that the integration of Blacks and *mestizos* in the field of sports is a strange and conflicting target, since this presence is accompanied by social ascension of the previously excluded group, which now comes to rely on important references to the constitution of one's own identity in hostile territory. However, this notion does not touch the place and role played by the ruling classes, which, in addition to the justifications of colour, claim a 'natural right' to the domination sustained through the majority occupation of the spaces of power, meaning not only through a symbolic domain, but material of the sport. Hence, the defence of the existence of a 'plot' directed to guarantee a bourgeois privilege of determining the destinies of sport, notably refractory to the manifestations of difference and demands for recognition by Blacks and women.

This plot extends to the common sense woven within the community itself, which not only resists recognising the mistakes of raciology, but also starts to return to pseudoscience at a time when genetics has made impressive scientific advances, changing the very general notion about what *race* is. Therefore, racism in sport does not only comprise a reflection of society, but a manifestation of a raciological agenda that uses cultural practices to validate old and new theses about the racial organisation of the world. Thus alienated from the cultural life of the working classes, contemporary sport then becomes a fertile ground for manifesting racism on very different scales, favouring the biopolitics of racial division of labour to the micropolitics of celebrating the dehumanisation of the racialised as being inferior. Therefore, it is a phenomenon inserted in the context of the struggle of classes and of the sexes, so that the forms of its reflection cannot lose sight of this totality.

Assumpção et al. (2010) highlight that the access pattern of the Blackpopulation and of different ethnic groups to certain sports is unequal in relation to members of the wealthier classes. Sports such as ice hockey, golf, swimming, horseback riding, tennis and motor racing are more practised by the ruling classes not as a matter of taste but as a matter of distinction (Odendaal, 1988), a condition which naturalises the anti-Blackestrangement on the part of Whites and the degree of interest by Blacks in such activities. In other words, the resolution of anti-Blackracism in sport is not just a distributive issue, since the way in which the modalities are constituted in the social imaginary is racialised and demarcated by colour lines.

At the same time, a recognition policy that is not minimally guided by the need to shake off the contaminated roots of the building – to cite a Fanonian consideration of the disalienation of the Black – will incur the same mistakes that irreprehensibly multiply in the form of branded anti-racisms and advertising pieces, skilled in exploiting the symbolic field only to add value to their products. Finally, the anti-racist task in modern sport involves a critique of its so-called universal categories and values, and the establishment of sports forms which are fundamentally rebellious to the prevailing capitalist orientation. Recognising the value of individual and collective anti-racist manifestations in sport does not prevent us from understanding their limits when it comes to confronting the class and gender structures that sustain the hierarchy and racial division of sports practices. Research aimed at the strategic establishment of these intersections is necessary so that we can propose, if necessary, another sport.

References

Abrahão, B. O. L., & Soares, A. J. (2009). Elogio ao negro no espaço do futebol: entre a integração pós-escravidão e a manutenção das hierarquias sociais. *Revista Brasileira de Ciências do Esporte*, *30*(2), 9–23. http://revista.cbce.org.br/index.php/RBCE/article/view/433

Almeida, S. (2019). *Racismo estrutural*. Pólen.

Assumpção, L. O. T., Sampaio, T. M. V., Caetano, J. N. N., Caetano Júnior, M. A., & Silva, J. V. P. (2010). Temas e questões fundamentais na sociologia do esporte. *Revista Brasileira de Ciência e Movimento*, *18*(2), 92–99. https://portalrevistas.ucb.br/index.php/RBCM/article/view/1154

Azevedo, M. M. (1987). *Onda negra, medo branco: o negro no imaginário das elites – século XIX*. Paz & Terra.

Bastide, R., & Fernandes, F. (1959). Brancos e negros em São Paulo: ensaio sociológico sobre aspectos da formação, manifestações atuais e efeitos do preconceito de cor na sociedade paulistana. *Brasiliana*.

Brohm, J.-M., Perelman, M., & Vassort, P. (2004). A ideologia do esporte-espetáculo e suas vítimas. *Le Monde Diplomatique Brasil*, 1 Jun. 2004. Retrieved from: https://diplomatique.org.br/a-ideologia-do-esporteespetaculo-e-suas-vitimas. Accessed: 30 Aug. 2022.

Carrington, B. (2002). 'Race', representation and the sporting body. Goldsmiths College.

Corrêa, L. H. (1985). Racismo no futebol brasileiro. In G. K. Dieguez (Ed.), *Esporte e poder* (pp. 31–40). Vozes.

Coubertin, P. (2015). *Olimpismo – seleção de textos*. EdiPUCRS.

Damatta, R. (1982). *Universo do futebol: esporte e sociedade brasileira*. Pinakotheke.

Darnell, S. C., & Millington, R. (2019). Social justice, sport, and sociology: a position statement. *Quest*, *71*(2), 175–187. https://doi.org/10.1080/00336297.2018.1545681

Dip, A. (2013). Com leis próprias, megaeventos criam estado de exceção. *Agência Pública*, 29 Jan. 2013. Retrieved from: https://apublica.org/2013/01/copa-do-mundo-olimpiadas-leis-estado-de-excecao/. Accessed: 30 Aug. 2022.

Domingos, N. (2005). Futebol e colonialismo, dominação e apropriação: sobre o caso moçambicano. *Análise Social*, *41*(179), 397–416. https://museudofutebol.org.br/crfb/acervo/724837

Domingues, P. (2009). Fios de Ariadne: o protagonismo negro no pós-abolição. *Anos 90*, *16*(30), 215–250. https://doi.org/10.22456/1983-201X.18932

Entine, J. (2000). *Taboo: why Blackathletes dominate sports and why we're afraid to talk about it*. Public Affairs.

Fanon, F. (2008). *Pele negra, máscaras brancas*. EdUFBA.

Farias, L. G. S., Nepomuceno, L. B., Sanches Neto, L., & Silva, E. V. M. (2020). A institucionalização do racismo contra negros(as) e as injúrias raciais no esporte profissional: o contexto internacional. *Movimento*, *26*(e26074), 1–22. https://doi.org/10.22456/1982-8918.104354

Fernandes, F. (1989). *Significados do protesto negro*. Cortez, Autores Associados.

Ferreira Júnior, N. S., & Rubio, K. (2019). Revisitando a 'raça' e o racismo no esporte brasileiro: implicações para a Psicologia Social. In: K. Rubio & J. A. O. Camilo (Eds.), *Psicologia Social do Esporte* (pp. 183–207). Laços.

Freitas Junior, M. A., & Ribeiro, L. C. (2012). Vitórias e derrotas de um futebol mestiço: reflexões sobre a questão racial no Brasil. *Emancipação*, *12*(2), 297–309. https://revistas.uepg.br/index.php/emancipacao/article/view/1845

Giglio, S. S., & Rubio, K. (2017). A hegemonia europeia no Comitê Olímpico Internacional. *Revista Brasileira de Educação Física e Esporte*, *31*(1), 291–305. https://doi.org/10.11606/1807-5509201700010291

Gilroy, P. (2007). *Entre campos: nações, culturas e o fascínio da raça*. Annablume.

Huizinga, J. (2000). *Homo ludens: o jogo como elemento na cultura*. 4th ed. Perspectiva.

Jesus, G. M. (1999). Do espaço colonial ao espaço da modernidade: os esportes na vida urbana do Rio de Janeiro. *Scripta Nova – Revista Electrónica de Geografía y Ciencias Sociales*, *45*(1), 1–14. https://revistes.ub.edu/index.php/ScriptaNova/article/view/136

Mariante Neto, F. P., Miranda, C. F.,Myskiw, M., & Stigger, M. P. (2010). Muhammad Ali, um *outsider* na sociedade americana? *Revista Brasileira de Ciências do Esporte*, *32*(2–4), 105–122. http://revista.cbce.org.br/index.php/RBCE/article/view/602

Mbembe, A. (2014). *Crítica da razão negra*. Antígona.

Melo, M. P. (2011). *Esporte e dominação burguesa no século XXI: a agenda dos Organismos Internacionais e sua incidência nas políticas de esportes no Brasil de hoje*. Tese (Doutorado em Serviço Social Esporte) – Centro de Filosofia e Ciências Humanas, Universidade Federal do Rio de Janeiro.

Munanga, K. (2004). Uma abordagem conceitual de noções de raça, racismo e etnia. In *Programa de educação sobre o negro na sociedade brasileira*, Rio de Janeiro. https://repositorio.usp.br/item/001413002

Odendaal, A. (1988). South Africa's BlackVictorians: sport, race, and class in South Africa before union. In J. A. Mangan (Ed.), *Profit, pleasure and proselytism: British culture and sport at home and abroad 1750-1914* (pp. 193–214). Cass.

Ouriques, N. (2009). Olimpíadas 2016: o desenvolvimento do subdesenvolvimento. *Motrivivência*, *21*(32–33), 126–155. https://doi.org/10.5007/2175-8042.2009n32-33p126

Rodrigues Filho, M. (2003). *O negro no futebol brasileiro*. Mauad.

Saini, A. (2019). *Superior: the return of race science*. Beacon Press.

Sanches Neto, L., Venâncio, L., Silva, E. V. M., & Ovens, A. P. (2021). A socially-critical curriculum for PETE: students' perspectives on the approaches to social-justice education of one Brazilian programme. *Sport, Education and Society*, *26*(7), 704–717. https://doi.org/10.1080/13573322.2020.1839744

Silva, I. C. C., Sanches Neto, L., & Cunha Júnior, H. A. (2022). Princípios para consolidar uma educação física escolar antirracista e tensionar a cultura esportiva contemporânea. In N. S. Ferreira Júnior & K. Rubio (Eds), *Racismo e esporte no Brasil: um panorama crítico e propositivo* (pp. 359–390). Laços.

Soares, A. J. (1999). O racismo no futebol do Rio de Janeiro nos anos 20: uma história de identidade. *Revista Paulista de Educação Física*, *13*(1), 119–129. https://doi.org/10.11606/issn.2594-5904.rpef.1999.137764

Tralci Filho, M. A. (2019). *Atleta negro, psicólogo branco: racialização e esporte na visão de profissionais de psicologia*. Tese (Doutorado em Psicologia Social) – Instituto de Psicologia, Universidade de São Paulo.

12
SPORT AND SOCIAL JUSTICE FOR REFUGEES

Advocating for leisure activities as a basic human need

Mark Doidge

As the Taliban reasserted control after the US withdrawal from Afghanistan in August 2021, the lived realities of many was witnessed by the desperate attempts to evacuate Kabul. As the US forces organised (insufficient) airlifts out of the country, video footage showed how many Afghan civilians tried to flee, including trying to cling to the wings of the plane; some falling to their death (Harding & Doherty 2021). Amongst this chaos, there were a multitude of individual stories, including ones involving sport. As the Taliban took control, they outlawed female sport, and immediately put members of female sport teams at risk for their safety. Various Afghanistan female football teams were in fear of their lives. Many fled to Pakistan and have been granted asylum around the world including Canada, Portugal, and Australia (Kvetenadze 2021). Whilst football is important to these young women, sport and leisure are not always central to people in the immediacy of seeking safety. This is reflected in government policy, which overwhelmingly focuses on education, health, housing, and employment.

Sport and leisure are important activities for refugees and asylum seekers. These activities can be beneficial for mental health by providing social interaction, whilst also being mindful and allowing participants to be 'in the moment' (Stone 2013). Mastering new skills, social relationships and environments can also help build confidence for refugees and asylum seekers, which helps develop self-efficacy and a sense of purpose (Tip et al. 2020). Sport, in particular, is a rare space where coaches and referees intervene in social activities, which means they can play a great role in providing a safe and welcoming environment (Doidge et al. 2020). Yet this needs careful management (Sterchele 2015). Sport and leisure can provide many positive benefits for all participants, including those from a refugee background. Despite these benefits, these activities should be done for their own sake. In the case of sport, we often see that projects are expected to provide other outcomes for the participants sport (what Coalter (2007) calls 'sport-plus'). As will be outlined later in the emerging literature in this area, sport is often expected to help language skills, integration, or health outcomes. Consequently, whilst this chapter outlines what impact sport and leisure can have, it first and foremost argues that these activities for refugees should just be focused on the activity itself, rather than focused on other outcomes.

The focus of this chapter will be sport, even though the main argument equally applies to leisure projects. There are two main reasons for this. One is pragmatic as the author has volunteered and researched with sport projects. The other is that sport projects (either through funding, organisers, or political direction) often have alternative outcomes imposed upon them (Coalter 2007, 2013). Whilst there is a growing body of research on leisure and forced migrants, these replicate the issues in the sport literature and have a narrow policy focus around concepts like integration and health and wellbeing (De Martini & Caudwell 2020). Leisure projects, such as music, sewing, cooking, or singing, are often done for the pleasure of doing the activity, or with an implicit social focus like sociability. It is for this reason that the argument of this chapter will be made. Sport, physical activity, and leisure activities should be done for their own sake, rather than for additional benefits or outcomes, such as inclusion, language development or skills training.

Since its inception, the discipline of sociology has been engaged in social justice (Romero 2020). Marx (1970) famously declared in the Thesis on Feuerbach that "Philosophers have hitherto only interpreted the world in various ways; the point is to change it". Jane Addams sought to use sociology to inform social work and improve the lives of people. WEB Du Bois observed that "one could not be a calm, cool, and detached scientist while Negroes were lynched, murdered and starved". Social justice, in this instance, is not merely about distribution of resources but about centring the human being, and their wants and needs. Rather than the classic conception of Rawls (1972) which addresses how rights (and duties) are distributed, this chapter follows Gerwirtz's (2001) call for a relational approach that recognises the power dynamics of social relations and how justice is mediated through them. Recognising forced migrants as human beings, and with limited social relationships in their new location, shifts the focus from what rights they have, to what needs do they want to have fulfilled; sport and leisure could be those needs.

Throughout this chapter, the word sport will be shorthand for physical activity that is broadly competitive and follows a fairly uniform set of recognised rules; this includes kickabouts in the park up to the elite game. Sport is often used as a shorthand for a variety of activities and outcomes. As Spaaij (2015, pp. 303–304) outlines in relation to the integration of refugees:

> Normative assumptions about how sport may assist the settlement of refugee and migrant youth focus on its capacity to enable new arrivals to become active and valued members of the community. However, any generalised claim that sport is a mechanism for 'good settlement' is contentious because sport is not necessarily inclusive, but is also used to differentiate and exclude.

Sport is inherently contradictory and what is beneficial, inclusive, and comforting to one person may be the opposite for another. It is not enough to assume that sport is uniform, that it has power, nor that participants are homogenous (Carter et al. 2018).

Sport has been linked to social justice since its modern origins, principally from a religious and moral perspective. Coakley (2015, p. 403) refers to the 'great sport myth' about the "pervasive and nearly unshakable belief in the inherent purity and goodness of sport". Coakley does not address sport's history, but it is here where the roots of purity, morality, and purpose of sport emerges. The roots of organised sport originated in the private schools of England and was used as a way of negotiating and controlling the schoolboys (Elias & Dunning 1986; Hargreaves 1987). From these roots, sport was a tool for training the body in a range of social and moral virtues. Muscular Christianity built on Juvenal's notion of *mens sana in corpere sano* ('a healthy mind in a healthy body') to not only instruct the middle-class schoolboys on how to act morally and socially in Victorian society. Sport, driven by the doctrine of Muscular Christianity, was also expected to instil a work ethic and discipline of the body, particularly for the working classes (Macaloon 2005). The sense that sport should have a higher moral purpose was ingrained in the mythology of modern sport since its inception.

Similar moral roots are found in the origins of the Olympics movement. Baron Pierre de Coubertin drew on the dominance of the British Empire, the centrality of sport within its education system, and historic readings of the Ancient Greek games in order to construct the Modern Olympic Games (Chatziefstathiou & Henry 2007). De Coubertin's writings and speeches outline his vision of the Olympic Movement, which was also rooted in misogyny and colonialism. De Coubertin drew on racist social Darwinism with views over certain 'races' and actively excluded women from the Games (Chatziefstathiou 2011). De Coubertin's various ideas have evolved into a pseudo-philosophical set of ideas called Olympism. Underlying these ideas are contradictory views about 'it being the taking part that counts' alongside the Olympic motto of 'faster, higher, stronger', and the valorisation of the winners through gold medals, podium finishes, and nation anthems. The International Olympic Committee (IOC) broke with the convention of national teams at the Rio 2016 games by introducing the Refugee Olympic Team (IOC 2016). Whilst only ten athletes competed, the gesture from the IOC was replicated in Tokyo 2020 with 29 participants. This still reifies elite athletic performance yet helps to elevate the individual stories of particular athletes, like Ysura Mardini, the Syrian swimmer (Michelini 2021). Whilst stories of superhuman feats can add to a particular image of refugees, they can also help to humanise them and illustrate the reasons for their seeking refuge elsewhere.

The refugee context

Refugees are a legally protected status under the UN Convention Relating to the Status of Refugees (or the 1951 Refugee Convention). A refugee is someone who has a:

> well-founded fear of being persecuted for reasons of race, religion, nationality, membership of a particular social group or political opinion, is outside the country of his (sic) nationality and is unable or owing to such fear, is unwilling to avail himself (sic) of the protection of that country; or who, not having a nationality and being outside the country of his (sic) former residence as a result of such events, is unable or, owing to such fear, is unwilling to return to it.

Effectively, the Convention individualises the status of asylum by locating it in the fear of an individual, rather than the structural factors leading to that fear. The Convention also upholds the primacy of the nation-state. Those seeking refugee status (asylum seekers), must fear for their safety in their home nation, and must leave and enter another nation in order to claim asylum. It is for this reason that asylum seekers cannot be 'illegal' as it is legal under international law to enter another country (as long as it is a signatory to the Convention) for the purposes of claiming asylum.

Due to the limited reasons permitted for claiming asylum, as well as the difficulties of crossing borders to claim asylum, millions more are internally displaced. The number of forced migrants is growing, and this will continue as climate change, war, and conflict endure. The EU and UK have become more aware of refugees since the so-called 'refugee crisis' in

2015, partly though mediatised and politicised narratives (Krzyżanowski et al. 2018). Yet 73 per cent of refugees are hosted in neighbouring countries, most of which are in the Global South (UNHCR 2021). At the end of 2021, over 82 million people were forcibly displaced, with over 26 million being refugees. The majority of these (68 per cent) originate from just five countries: Syria, Myanmar, Venezuela, Afghanistan, and South Sudan.

One-dimensional narratives of refugees and forced migrants frame media, governmental, and humanitarian responses. Across North America, the EU, UK, and Australia (ironically the location where much of the literature on refugees and sport comes from, as shall be shown below), refugees have become increasingly politicised and demonised by sections of the media and politicians (Krzyżanowski et al. 2018). For example, in the UK, successive governments from New Labour to Conservative have cut support for asylum seekers and sought to make it harder for people to claim asylum, particularly through the hostile environment policy (Goodfellow 2019; Schuster & Bloch 2005). This continues with the Illegal Immigration Bill in the UK. Consequently, refugees are marginalised in many countries, with limited opportunities for work, education, and housing, and frequently politicised and scapegoated.

The image of 'the refugee' frequently polarises around either the undeserving beneficiary of the generous hosts' welfare system, or a helpless, traumatised victim (Ludwig, 2016; Marlowe 2010: McKinnon 2008; Ong 2003). Even the identity and label of 'refugee' is one that is ascribed to the individual rather than something that is actively chosen (Zetter 1991). The image of the traumatised refugee is often amplified by media, charities, and humanitarian responses. Refugees are objects "in need of assistance, training and a host of other resettlement services, though never to speak and act of their own accord in the public" (McKinnon 2008, p. 398). The individual is reduced to a single story of their exodus and relocation, which removes their nuanced and varied life, whilst further embedding their identity as 'a refugee' (Marlowe 2010). Yet refugees are heterogenous, with numerous reasons for fleeing their homes, having undertaken a variety of journeys to seek asylum, and, more importantly, a vast array of interests, experiences and dreams that make them human. This is where sport plays its role.

If sport (and leisure) is to work for a social justice that humanises forced migrants, and recognises the relational power dynamics they operate within, then the role of ethics must play an important part. The ethical dimension affecting the position of refugees is also often overlooked (Pittaway et al. 2010). As outlined in the previous paragraphs, the image of a refugee is politicised and binary (Ludwig, 2016; Marlowe 2010: McKinnon 2008; Ong 2003). Moreover, the approach taken for refugees actively removes their agency and power. Recognising the power dynamics of working with refugees is integral to robust scholarship, as well as providing a strong ethical foundation for the participants (Doidge 2018; Mohammadi & Mashreghi 2022). Schuster (2015, p. 20) recognises that working with refugees "often feels like (is?) an exploitative relationship". Pittaway et al. (2010) reiterate the power relations within the academic-refugee dynamic. Many of the participants are structurally in a marginal position; often with fragile citizenship status and employment and housing rights.

Sport, like leisure, is one area that can work towards social justice and provide agency to the marginalised; but it is important to recognise the various power differentials inherent within sport. On the one hand, sport can provide relational opportunities to master new skills, manage emotions, and meet new people. On the other hand there are coaches who tell participants what to do, institutional power structures, or discrimination, like racism or sexism. Rarely are ethics centralised in the study of sport and it is heartening to see Spaaij et al. (2022) place ethics and power dynamics at the heart of the issue.

Research method are fundamental to the ethical management of a project. Participatory Action Research (PAR) is starting to assert itself in the field as a way of balancing out the power dynamics in the process and give the refugees a voice (Smith et al. 2023; Luguetti et al. 2022; McSweeney et al. 2022; Middleton et al., 2021; Mohammadi & Mashreghi 2022). Significantly, refugee participants have been included as co-authors in these articles, elevating their voice and shifting them from passive objects being researched into active researchers who can share their knowledge.

Given that the roots of modern sport has its foundations in the belief that sport can work for social justice and has moral, social, and individual benefits, it is unsurprising that contemporary sport for development projects also perceive wider benefits for society (Coalter 2007). There is a widespread critique of the Sport for Development sector around a number of issues such as colonialism, gender, and validity of the claims (Coalter 2013; Darnell et al. 2018; Hayhurst 2015; Schulenkorf & Adair 2014; Sugden & Tomlinson 2018). What is obvious about the sport for development sector is that invariably sport projects emerge from outside of the communities that are supposed to be benefitting. Across the literature on refugees and sport that is outlined later, the projects derive from local councils, NGOs, sport clubs, or well-meaning individuals. Rarely, is it documented how the project drew on agency of the refugee participants themselves. Returning to Pittaway et al. (2010), projects must involve their participants and actively seek their reasons for participating. For some, as with any sport project, there will be participants who dream of being picked up by Manchester United or Real Madrid. For many more, it will be to compete, and for others it will be to have fun. Locating these motivations will help centre the participants in the project and give them agency in a world that actively seeks to remove it. As this chapter seeks to argue, allowing the refugee participants to play 'for the sake of it' is fundamental to any project. Leisure projects are often more like this; not every person who joins a music workshop imagines they will play the Royal Albert Hall.

Sport and refugees

Sport cannot, and should not, tackle the structural issues that lead to forced migration. Likewise, sport should not have to have an alternative purpose for refugees; they should be allowed to play sport for their own reasons (if they wish). However, there are a growing number of projects that actively seek to engage refugee populations, particularly since 2015, and this is reflected in the literature (Spaaij et al. 2019). The majority of these studies have been undertaken in the Global North, particularly Australia (Luguetti et al. 2020, 2021; Olliff 2008; Spaaij 2012, 2015), Canada (Campbell, Glover, & Laryea 2016), Europe (McGee & Pelham 2018; Mohammadi 2019; Nobis et al. 2022; Pizzolati & Sterchele 2016; Stura 2019), South Korea (Kim et al. 2021; Park & Ok 2017) and the UK (Amara et al. 2004; Doidge et al. 2020; Smith et al. 2022). This growth in literature highlights the growing awareness of refugees in the Global North, but also illustrates a detachment from the reality of the majority of refugees, who are based in the Global South and in neighbouring countries to their home nation or who are internally displaced (UNHCR 2021). This disjuncture is reinforced with the paucity of studies based in the Global South. Only five articles specifically address sport and refugees in the Global South, one is in Indonesia (Apriadi & Juliantoro 2018) with four in Africa, with studies in Kenya (Russell & Stage 1996), Sierra Leone (Harris 2007), Tanzania (Wright 2009), and Uganda (Koopmans & Doidge 2022). In some way, this helps to explain the focus of projects (and literature) on health, integration, and barriers to participation.

As Spaaij et al. (2019) identified, three themes dominate the literature around sport and refugees: integration, barriers to participation, and health promotion. Interventions were mainly 'plus sport' (Coalter 2007; Spaaij et al. 2019) and primarily involved team sports, and particularly football. It should be noted that football is often chosen, as with global sport for development projects, because it is a popular sport (Darnell et al. 2018; Schulenkorf et al. 2016). This does not mean that it is an easy choice as football comes with existing baggage that needs to be managed carefully, particularly the competitive aspects of the game (Rookwood & Palmer 2011; Sterchele 2015). Some projects engaged in other forms of physical activity including badminton (Kim et al. 2021; Park & Ok 2017), cycling (Mohammadi 2019), dancing (Harris 2007), and table tennis (Doidge et al. 2020). Relatively few engaged within informal sport, despite its growing popularity (Jeanes et al. 2015; Wheaton et al. 2017). Consequently, there are many opportunities for projects that exist for leisure and enjoyment.

Alongside the argument of this chapter, there are many benefits to sport; the most obvious are social, psychological and health (Khan et al. 2012; Oja et al. 2015). It is for this reason that health is a dominant theme amongst the literature (Spaaij et al. 2019). Much of this is focused on the higher likelihood that refugees and asylum seekers will suffer trauma or other mental health issues (Doidge 2020; Ley et al., 2018). Even with these health benefits, sport is not the only solution. Similarly, sport can exacerbate these issues if it is not carefully managed (Doidge 2020). As with the wider political culture and bureaucracy, there is often a hostile environment for those who are perceived to be 'other', such as refugees. The focus on integration also illustrates how refugees should be integrating into a host society (which fails to recognise the various communities within that society) and also ignores the individual experiences and desires of the refugees (Agergaard 2018; Nunn et al. 2021). The policy focus on integration also ignores the various ways refugees are excluded in society, including within sport. Exclusion also manifests itself in racism, discrimination, microaggressions, and other forms of social exclusion (Spaaij 2012, 2015; Michelini et al. 2018). Refreshingly, Nobis et al. (2022) address the key aspect of integration; rather than focusing on the migrants (and why they are not part of the club); they focus on the club itself and the politics of belonging. In particular, whether migrants are even accepted as members of the sport club in the first place.

The sporting environment, generated by coaches and volunteers at sport clubs and projects, is fundamental to creating the right space for refugees (and others). The sport club can become a social focal point for refugee participants, especially if members share a common purpose or goal (Hums & MacLean 2004). Sport helps break down individuality and build new identities. Being able to enter into a sport project can help the individual to shed the refugee label that has been affixed to them, and to become a footballer, a cricketer, or a table tennis player (Doidge et al. 2020). Ultimately, activities should be fun (Koopmans & Doidge 2022), both to adapt to individuals who may be suffering from trauma, but also to ascertain their wants and interests. These benefits do not just passively emerge from the activity, but are created by the work of coaches and volunteers (Doidge et al. 2020). In some cases, this requires carefully managing the competitive aspects of sport (Sterchele 2015).

Despite some projects explicitly focusing on trauma, and using sport as a way to help some of the effects of trauma, there has been relatively little written about emotions in this field. More importantly emotions are a social and embodied experience which helps the individual locate themselves in their surroundings. Collison and De Martini Ugolotti (2021) draws on research from trauma-informed yoga classes that shifts the focus from the stereotypical image of a Muslim, female refugee body into one that is active, emotional, and embodied. This phenomenological approach is mastered beautifully in an auto-ethnographic account by

Abooali (2022) as she illustrates the embodied and sensory aspects of karate. Emotions are also important in making a distinction from the everyday experience to the sporting activity. Having pleasure or fun at sport can help alleviate the dehumanising aspects of daily life and help the individual reassert their agency and sense of self (Koopmans & Doidge 2022; Stone 2013; Webster 2022). Consequently, doing an activity one enjoys and gives oneself pleasure is a political act (Webster 2022). For this reason, refugees should not have to take part in sporting projects for reasons imposed upon them, but for its own sake.

Taking part in sport 'for its own sake'

This chapter has outlined how the majority of literature on sport and refugees is linked to the sport for development sector which invariably hopes to achieve other outcomes from participants taking part in sport. This section outlines the core argument of this chapter about taking part in sport for its own sake. It argues that refugees should be allowed to take part in sport for its own sake, rather than have additional outcomes imposed upon them. In order to do this, it reflects on the phrase 'for its own sake' and what this means for sport and participation. As outlined earlier, one of the foundational phrases of Olympism is the notion of 'it is not the winning, it is the taking part'. Whilst we can critique the contradiction from this statement to the practice of the contemporary IOC, the phrase contains an important and often-overlooked kernel of truth. Many sports participants around the world will never reach elite performance. Some may engage in competitive leagues, races or sportives in order to push themselves and develop flow (as will be outlined later). Many more will take part in five-a-side leagues, fitness classes, gyms, or park runs for the enjoyment it brings them. As a sociologist, it is not enough to reduce an activity into a purely intrinsic act, but see it as a relational activity. Sport, along with many other cultural activities, are imbued with a range of social, cultural, and economic aspects. Consequently, sports participants engage in sport for a variety of social, cultural, health and psychological reasons (Warde 2006).

As with the paradoxes contained within Olympism, there is a paradox about doing sport (or anything) for its own sake. As Champlin (1987) argues, doing something for its own sake is a paradox. Many acts are about 'means' and 'ends'. Immanuel Kant (2005 [1785]) argued that morality was an absolute good. Yet what is morality other than a socially (or theologically) proscribed set of rules? Morality only works if there are social (or theological) sanctions. Even within the moral foundations of Victorian sport, virtuous and ethical notions of 'fair play' and healthy living were grounded in Protestant notions of Christianity, earthly demonstrations of predestination, and receiving one's rewards in the afterlife. Cardinal Newman (1996 [1873]) argued that knowledge for its own sake should be the foundation of a university. Yet he contrasts the pursuit of knowledge for itself to that of a liberal notion of the university that engages in knowledge for instrumental reasons around vocational or commercial benefits. Effectively, both Kant and Newman are arguing against the social aspects of individual acts.

Yet doing something for its own sake, still brings individual psychological and social rewards. Kant argued that a good man could engage in philanthropic activity for virtue for its own sake. Yet this infers, as Camplin (1987, p. 35) argues, that "To pursue virtue for virtue's sake, nothing must count with you but virtue alone. All else must be excluded—pleasure in the happiness you bring to others, contentment, peace of mind, good nature, fellow-feeling, a sunny disposition". As with other physical and cultural activities, sport produces intense feelings and enjoyment. Physiologically, sport and physical activity improves physical health, produces endorphins, and helps with posture (Khan et al. 2012; Oja et al. 2015). Even when engaging in sport 'for its own sake' there is a personal benefit. Psychologically, there can also be a sense of personal achievement, what Csikszentmihalyi (1992, 2008) calls 'flow'. Csikszentmihalyi (2008, p. 71) states that flow is:

> a sense that one's skills are adequate to cope with the challenges at hand, in a goal-directed, rule-bound action system that provides clear clues as to how one is performing. Concentration is so intense that there is no attention left over to think about anything irrelevant, or to worry about problems. Self-consciousness disappears, and the sense of time becomes distorted. An activity that produces such experiences is so gratifying that *people are willing to do it for its own sake*, with little concern for what they will get out of it, even when it is difficult, or dangerous. [emphasis added]

Here Csikszentmihalyi argues that pleasure and a sense of achievement comes from successfully engaging in an activity, especially if it pushes the individual to feel they have achieved something, but not too much that they feel like they have failed. For those who may have experienced trauma (as some refugees will have done), this can help build a sense of personal achievement.

When we argue that something is 'for its own sake' what we are effectively saying is that we are doing it for individual needs or requirements. Malkki (2015) has identified the psychological needs individuals fulfil when they volunteer to help refugees (for example). There are many reasons people volunteer to engage in social justice projects. But there are still psychological and social benefits from doing something 'for its own sake'. There are other reasons people engage in activities 'for the sake of it'. Enjoyment and fun are important, but are missing from the literature on refugees (Koopmans & Doidge 2022). Whilst there are individual psychological factors at play for an individual to do something for its own sake, there is still a social element. As Simmel (1950) argued, many people enjoy socialising with people they enjoy being around. This sense of 'sociability' is an important part of social life, and one that the recent Covid restrictions have helped illustrate. For refugees in particular, social isolation is a structural factor of their experience, particularly in the hostile environment of the UK (see report on hotels being prisons). Separation from existing networks of solidarity, including family and friends, help isolate those seeking refuge elsewhere.

And this is where we return to refugees taking part in sport. As outlined in this chapter, much of the research around sport and refugees is embedded within the sport for development literature; a literature that is infused with sport projects trying to achieve other outcomes through the inclusion of sport (Coalter 2007, 2013). Arguing that refugees should be allowed to play sport 'for its own sake' does not preclude that there may be many benefits of playing sport (such as health, sociability, improved language skills, social and cultural capital). Likewise, it does not preclude that they may get enjoyment, mental and social wellbeing, or friendships from the activity. What this chapter seeks to do is to say that letting refugees play sport 'for its own sake' is to argue that they should have the choice in how and why they take part in sport. Some may want to compete, maybe be like Alphonso Davies and play in the Champions League and World Cup. For others, they may just want to have a kickabout with friends and switch off for an hour. Both of these, and every reason in between, are acceptable. Sport projects do not have to be for additional outcomes imposed on the participants without their voice being heard but purely to satisfy the needs of funders, project leaders, volunteers, or policymakers. Refugees do not choose to be refugees, but at least let them choose why they want to play sport.

Conclusion

There are a range of benefits to all participants in sport, including refugees. It is well known that sport provides many social, psychological and health benefits (Khan et al. 2012; Oja et al. 2015). As refugees may have a higher likelihood of trauma, sport can be a way of managing and supporting those who have undergone difficult experiences (Doidge 2020; Ley et al. 2018). Sport can be mindful and allow refugees to be in the moment and help switch themselves off from their daily lives (Stone 2013). In addition to the health benefits of sport, many projects have focussed on the role sport can play in integrating new communities (Agergaard 2018). Yet sport is not a neutral space but can exacerbate division and discrimination (Michelini et al. 2018; Nobis et al. 2021; Spaaij 2012, 2015). Consequently, projects working with refugees need to be carefully managed (Doidge et al. 2020; Sterchele 2015). The benefits that can be found are actively brought about by the coaches and volunteers and do not just passively emerge from sport itself.

When the media broadcast pictures of refugees, rarely do we see refugees as sport-loving human beings. Taking part in sport for fun is a political act in a world that is seeking to dehumanise refugees (Webster 2022). Since its inception in the nineteenth century, modern sport has been influenced by Muscular Christianity and deemed to be both pure (Coakley 2015) and functional (Elias & Dunning 1986; Hargreaves 1987). Ever since sport has been deemed to have a moral social purpose, and should be achieving something more than pleasure for its own sake. Whilst this chapter has highlighted some of the growing literature on forced migration and how sport can have a positive impact, it seeks to argue that doing sport for its own sake has to be the fundamental starting point. Centralising ethics (Doidge 2018; Spaaij et al. 2022) is crucial for research with refugees and forced migrants. In this way, their voice must be centralised and listened to. Some refugees may want to take part in sport to improve their language skills or boost their health, but for others, fun and sociability may be of more importance. Whilst this chapter finished on a reflection on the term 'for its own sake', it concluded that sport cannot do it for its own sake; the individual has a myriad of reasons why they take part in something, even if it is personal pleasure. Doing something for its own sake means that it is done for the reasons the individual wants to do them, rather than being imposed upon them by an external body. For this reason, sport projects should permit refugees to do sport for its own sake, rather than have to have a range of other outcomes like health, integration, or education. In this way, we can transform the myth that sport has to be done for some moral purpose, rather than enjoyment. And as Webster (2022) argues, this is a political act in a world that is seeking to dehumanise refugees.

References

Abooali, S. (2022). Exploring the somatic dimension for sport-based interventions: A refugee's autoethnography. *Sport in Society*, 25(3): 506–522. doi:10.1080/17430437.2022.2017814

Agergaard, S. (2018). *Rethinking sport and integration: Developing a transnational perspective on migrants and descendants in sports*. London: Routledge.

Amara, M., Aquilina, D., Argent, E., Betzer-Tayar, M., Green, M., Henry, I., et al. (2004). *The roles of sport and education in the social inclusion of asylum seekers and refugees: An evaluation of policy and practice in the UK*. Loughborough: Institute of Sport and Leisure Policy, Loughborough University and University of Stirling.

Apriadi, A., & Juliantoro, N.R. (2018). Perlindungan Hak Asasi Manusia Pengungsi Lintas Batas di Rumah Detensi Imigrasi (Rudenim) Indonesia (Studi Case: Rudenim Surabaya) [The protection of the human rights of crossborder refugees in Indonesian immigration detention facilities (Case Study: Rudenim Surabaya)]. *Journal Transborders*, 2(1): 26–43.

Campbell, G., Glover, Troy D., & Laryea, Edwin (2016). Recreation, settlement, and the welcoming community: Mapping community with African–Canadian youth newcomers. *Leisure Sciences*, 38(3): 215–231. doi:10.1080/01490400.2015.1087896

Carter, T., Doidge, M., & Burdsey, D. (2018). Something has to be done about this. In Carter, T., Burdsey, D., & Doidge, M. (Eds) *Transforming sport: Knowledge, structures, practice* 1–20 London: Routledge.

Champlin, T. S. (1987). Doing something for its own sake. *Philosophy*, 62(239): 31–47. doi:10.1017/S0031819100038560

Chatziefstathiou, D. (2011). Paradoxes and contestations of Olympism in the history of the modern Olympic Movement. *Sport in Society: Cultures, Commerce, Media, Politics*, 14(3): 332–344.

Chatziefstathiou, D. & Henry, I. (2007). Hellenism and Olympism: Pierre de Coubertin and the Greek challenge to the early Olympic movement. *Sport in History*, 27(1): 24–43.

Coakley, J. (2015). Assessing the sociology of sport: On cultural sensibilities and the great sport myth. *International Review for the Sociology of Sport*, 50(4–5): 402–406.

Coalter, F. (2007). *Sport a wider social role: Who's keeping the score?* London: Routledge.

Coalter, F. (2013). *Sport for development: What game are we playing?* London: Routledge.

Collison, C. & De Martini Ugolotti, N. (2021). Pain, faith and yoga: An intersectional-phenomenological perspective on Syrian Muslim women's experiences of resettlement in sweden. In De Martini Ugolotti, N. & Caudwell, J. (Eds) *Leisure and forced migration: Lives lived in asylum systems*, pp 121–138. London: Routledge.

Csikszentmihalyi, M. (1992). *"Flow": The psychology of happiness* (p. 6). London: Rider.

Csikszentmihalyi, M. (2008). *Flow: The psychology of optimal experience*. New York, Harper Perennial

Darnell, S., Chawansky, M., Marchesseault, D., Holmes, M., & Hayhurst, L. (2018). The state of play: Critical sociological insights into recent 'sport for development and peace' research. *International Review for the Sociology of Sport*, 53(2): 133–151.

De Martini, U. & Caudwell, J. (2020). *Leisure and forced migration: Lives lived in asylum systems*. London: Routledge.

Doidge, M. (2018). Refugees united: The role of activism and football in supporting refugees. In Carter, T., Burdsey, D., & Doidge, M. (Eds) *Transforming sport: Knowledge, structures, practice* 23–36 London: Routledge.

Doidge, M. (2020). The importance of sport in engaging refugees. In Wallis, J. & Lambert, J. (Eds) *Sport coaching with diverse populations: Theory and practice* 85–99 London: Routledge.

Doidge, M., Keech, M., & Sandri, E. (2020). 'Active integration': Sport taking an active role in the integration of refugees. *International Journal of Sport Policy and Politics*, 12(2): 305–319.

Elias, N. & Dunning, E. (1986). *Quest for excitement: Sport and leisure in the civilizing process*. Oxford: Blackwell.

Gerwirtz, S. (2001). Rethinking social justice: A conceptual analysis. Jack Demaine (Ed.), *Sociology of Education Today* (pp. 49–64). Basingstoke, GB: PalgraveMacmillan.

Goodfellow, M. (2019). *Hostile environment: How immigrants became scapegoats*. London: Verso.

Harding, L. & Doherty, B. (2021). Kabul airport: Footage appears to show Afghans falling off plane after takeoff. *The Guardian*, 16 August 2021. Available online at: www.theguardian.com/world/2021/aug/16/kabul-airport-chaos-and-panic-as-afghans-and-foreigners-attempt-to-flee-the-capital [Accessed 22 December 2021].

Hargreaves, J. (1987). *Sport, power, and culture: A social and historical analysis of popular sports in Britain*. Cambridge: Polity.

Harris, D. A. (2007). Dance/movement therapy approaches to fostering resilience and recovery among African adolescent torture survivors. *Torture*, 17, 134–155.

Hayhurst, L. (2015). Sport for development and peace: A call for transnational, multi-sited, postcolonial feminist research. *Qualitative Research in Sport, Exercise and Health*, 8(5), 424–443.

Hums, M. A. & MacLean, J. C. (2004). *Governance and policy in sport organizations*. Scottsdale, AZ: Holcomb Hathaway.

IOC. (2016). Team of Refugee Olympic Athletes (ROA) created by the IOC. Available online at: https://olympics.com/ioc/news/team-of-refugee-olympic-athletes-roa-created-by-the-ioc [Accessed 22 Dec 2021].

Jeanes, R., O'Connor, J., & Alfrey, L. (2015). Sport and the resettlement of young people from refugee backgrounds in Australia. *Journal of Sport & Social Issues*, 39: 480–500. doi:10.1177/0193723514558929

Kant, I. (2005 [1785]). *Groundwork for the metaphysics of morals*. Peterborough, ON: Broadview Press.

Khan, K., Thompson, A., Blair, S., Sallis, J., Powell, K., Bull, F., & Bauman, A. (2012). Sport and exercise as contributors to the health of nations. *The Lancet*, 380(9836): 59–64.

Kim, J., Park, S.-H., Kim, M., Kim, Y.-S., & Kim, J. (2021). A qualitative investigation of leisure engagement and health benefits among North Korean adolescent refugees. *Journal of Adolescent Research*. doi:10.1177/07435584211046260

Koopmans, B. & Doidge M. (2022). 'They play together, they laugh together': Sport, play and fun in Refugee Sport Projects. *Sport in Society special issue on sport and refugees*, 25(3) [Published online Dec 2021].

Krzyżanowski, M., Triandafyllidou, A., & Wodak, R. (2018). The mediatization and the politicization of the 'Refugee Crisis' in Europe, *Journal of Immigrant & Refugee Studies*, 16(1): 1–14.

Kvetenadse, T. (2021). Afghan girls national soccer team – Banned under the Taliban – Granted asylum with their families in Portugal. *Forbes*, 22 September 2021. Available online: www.forbes.com/sites/teakvetenadze/2021/09/21/afghan-girls-national-soccer-team-banned-under-the-taliban-granted-asylum-with-their-families-by-portugal/?sh=460cd08334b2 [Accessed 22 December 2021].

Ley, C., Rato Barrio, M., & Koch, A. (2018). "In the sport I am here": Therapeutic processes and health effects of sport and exercise on PTSD. *Qualitative Health Research* 28: 491–507.

Ludwig, B. (2016). "Wiping the refugee dust from my feet": Advantages and burdens of refugee status and the refugee label. *International Migration*, 54(1): 5–18. doi:10.1111/imig.12111

Luguetti, C., Singehebhuye, L., & Spaaij, R. (2020). Towards a culturally relevant sport pedagogy: Lessons learned from African Australian refugee-background coaches in grassroots football. *Sport, Education and Society*: 1–13. doi:10.1080/13573322.2020.1865905

Luguetti, C., Singehebhuye, L., & Spaaij, R. (2021). "Stop mocking, start respecting": An activist approach meets African Australian refugee-background young women in grassroots football. *Qualitative Research in Sport, Exercise and Health*: 1–18. doi:10.1080/2159676X.2021.1879920

Luguetti, C., Jice, Nyayoud, Singehebhuye, Loy, Singehebhuye, Kashindi, Mathieu, Adut, & Spaaij, Ramón (2023). 'I know how researchers are […] taking more from you than they give you': Tensions and possibilities of youth participatory action research in sport for development0. *Sport, Education and Society*, 28(7): 755–770. doi:10.1080/13573322.2022.2084374

Macaloon, J. (2005). *Muscular Christianity and the colonial and post-colonial world*. London: Routledge.

Malkki, L. (2015). *The need to help: The domestic arts of international humanitarianism*. Durham, NC: Duke University Press.

Marlowe, J. M. (2010). Beyond the discourse of trauma: Shifting the focus on Sudanese refugees. *Journal of Refugee Studies*, 23(2): 183–198. doi:10.1093/jrs/feq013

Marx, K. (1970). *The German ideology*. London: Lawrence and Wishart.

McGee, D., & Pelham, Juliette (2018). Politics at play: Locating human rights, refugees and grassroots humanitarianism in the Calais jungle. *Leisure Studies*, 37(1): 22–35. doi:10.1080/02614367.2017.1406979

McKinnon, S. (2008). Unsettling resettlement: Problematizing "Lost Boys of Sudan" resettlement and identity. *Western Journal of Communication*, 72(4): 397–414. doi:10.1080/10570310802446056

McSweeney, M., Hakiza, Robert, & Namukhula, Joselyne (2022). Participatory action research and visual and digital methods with refugees in Kampala, Uganda: Process, ethical complexities, and reciprocity. *Sport in Society*, 25(3): 485–505. doi:10.1080/17430437.2022.2017813

Michelini, E. (2021). The representation of Yusra Mardini as a refugee Olympic athlete: A sociological analysis. *Sport und Gesellschaft*, 18(1): 39–64.

Michelini, E., Burrmann, U., Nobis, T., Tuchel, J., & Schlesinger, T. (2018). Sport offers for refugees in Germany. Promoting and hindering conditions in voluntary sports clubs. *Society Register*, 2(1): 19–38.

Middleton, T., Schinke, R., Lefebvre, D., Habra, B., Coholic, D., & Giffin, C. (2021). Critically examining a community-based participatory action research project with forced migrant youth. *Sport in Society*. doi:10.1080/17430437.2022.2017619

Mohammadi, S. (2019). social inclusion of newly arrived female asylum seekers and refugees through a community sport initiative: The case of Bike Bridge. *Sport in Society*, 22(6): 1082–1099.

Mohammadi, S. E., & Sepandarmaz Mashreghi, S. (2022). Methodological challenges and opportunities in working within a participatory paradigm in the context of sport, forced migration and settlement: an insider perspective. *Sport in Society*, 25(3): 469–484.

Newman, J. H. (1996 [1873]). *The idea of a university*. New Haven and London: Yale University Press.

Nobis, T., Gomez-Gonzalez, C., Nesseler, C., & Dietl, H. (2022). (Not) being granted the right to belong—Amateur football clubs in Germany. *International Review for the Sociology of Sport*, 57(7): 1157–1174. doi:10.1177/10126902211061303

Nunn, C., Spaaij, R., & Luguetti, C. (2021). Beyond integration: Football as a mobile, transnational sphere of belonging for refugee-background young people. *Leisure Studies*, 41:1, 42–55, doi:10.1080/02614367.2021.1962393

Oja, P., Titze, S., Kokko, S., Jujala, U., Heinonen, A., Kelly, P., Koski, P., & Forster, C. (2015). Health benefits of different sport disciplines for adults: Systematic review of observational and intervention studies with meta-analysis. *British Journal of Sports Medicine*, 49(7): 434–440.

Olliff, L. (2008). Playing for the future: The role of sport and recreation in supporting refugee young people to 'settle well' in Australia. *Youth Studies Australia*, 27: 52–60.

Ong, A. (2003). *Buddha is hiding: Refugees, citizenship, the new America*. Berkeley, CA: University of California Press.

Park, K. & Ok, G. (2017). Social Integration of North Korean refugees through sport in South Korea. *The International Journal of the History of Sport*, 34(12): 1294–1305. doi:10.1080/09523367.2018.1430690

Pittaway, E., Bartolomei, L., & Hugman, R. (2010). "Stop stealing our stories": The ethics of research with vulnerable groups. *Journal of Human Rights Practice*, 2(2): 229–251.

Pizzolati, M., & Sterchele, D. (2016). Mixed-sex in sport for development: A pragmatic and symbolic device. The case of touch rugby for forced migrants in Rome. *Sport in Society*, 1–22. ISSN 1743-0437. doi:10.1080/17430437.2015.1133600

Rawls, J. (1972). *A theory of justice*. Oxford: Clarendon Press.

Romero, M. (2020). Sociology engaged in social justice. *American Sociological Review*, 85(1): 1–30.

Rookwood, J. & C. Palmer. (2011). Invasion games in war-torn nations: Can football help to build peace?" *Soccer & Society*, 12(2): 184–200. doi:10.1080/14660970.2011.548356

Russell, R. V., & Stage, F. K. (1996). Leisure as burden: Sudanese refugee women. *Journal of Leisure Research*, 28(2): 108–121. doi:10.1080/00222216.1996.11949764

Schulenkorf, N. & Adair, D. (Eds). (2014). *Global sport-for-development: Critical perspectives*. New York: Palgrave Macmillan.

Schulenkorf, N., Sherry, E., & Rowe, K. (2016). Sport for development: An integrated literature review. *Journal of Sport Management*, 30(1): 22–39. doi:10.1123/jsm.2014-0263

Schuster, L. & Bloch, A. (2005). Asylum policy under new labour. *Benefits*, 13(2), 115–118.

Schuster, L. (2015). The sociologist as voyeur. In K. Twamley, M. Doidge, & A. Scott (Eds) *Sociologists tales*. Bristol: Policy Press.

Simmel, G. (1950). *The sociology of Georg Simmel* (Translated & Edited by Kurt H. Wolff). Glencoe, IL: The Free Press.

Smith, R., Mansfield, L., & Wainwright, E. (2022). 'Should I *really* be here?': Problems of trust and ethics in PAR with young people from refugee backgrounds in sport and leisure. *Sport in Society*, 24(3): 434–452.

Spaaij, R., Broerse, J., Oxford, S., Luguetti, C., McLachlan, F., McDonald, B., Klepac, B., Lymbery, L., Bishara, J., & Pankowiak, A. (2019). Sport, refugees, and forced migration: A critical review of the literature. *Frontiers*, 1: 47.

Spaaij, R. (2012). Beyond the playing field: Experiences of sport, social capital, and integration among Somalis in Australia. *Ethnic and Racial Studies*, 35(9): 1519–1538.

Spaaij, R. (2015). Refugee youth, belonging and community sport. *Leisure Studies*, 34(3): 303–318.

Spaaij, R., Luguetti, Carla, & De Martini Ugolotti, Nicola (2022). Forced migration and sport: An introduction. *Sport in Society*, 25(3), 405–417. doi:10.1080/17430437.2022.2017616

Sterchele, D. (2015). De-sportizing physical activity: From sport-for-development to play-for-development. *European Journal for Sport and Society* 12(1): 97–120. doi:10.1080/16138171.2015.11687958

Stone, C. (2013). *Football: A shared sense of belonging?* Final report on the role of football in the lives of refugees and asylum seekers. Sheffield: Football United, Racism Divides.

Stura, C. (2019). "What makes us strong": The role of sports clubs in facilitating integration of refugees. *European Journal for Sport and Society*, 16(2): 128–145. doi:10.1080/16138171.2019.1625584

Sugden, J. & Tomlinson, A. (2018). *Sport and peace-building in divided societies: Playing with the enemy.* London: Routledge.

Tip, L. K., Brown, R., Morrice, L., Collyer, M., & Easterbrook, M. J. (2020). Believing is achieving: A longitudinal study of self-efficacy and positive affect in resettled refugees. *Journal of Ethnic and Migration Studies*: 1–17.

UNHCR. (2021). *Figures at a glance.* www.unhcr.org/uk/figures-at-a-glance.html [Accessed 22 December 2021].

Warde, A. (2006). Cultural capital and the place of sport. *Cultural Trends*, 15(2–3): 107–122. doi:10.1080/09548960600712827

Webster, C. (2022). The (in)significance of footballing pleasures in the lives of forced migrantmen. *Sport in Society*, 25(3): 523–536. doi:10.1080/17430437.2022.2017815

Wheaton, B., Roy, G., & Olive, R. (2017). Exploring critical alternatives for youth development through lifestyle sport: Surfing and community development in Aotearoa/New Zealand. *Sustainability*, 9(12): 1–16.

Wright, R. W. (2009). Understanding the role of sport for development in community capacity building in a refugee camp in Tanzania. Master of Science. University of Saskatchewan.

Zetter, R. (1991). Labelling refugees: Forming and transforming a bureaucratic identity. *Journal of Refugee Studies*, 4(1): 39–62.

13
MENTAL HEALTH, DRAPETOMANIA, AND PROFESSIONAL FOOTBALL
A memorial to Dalian Atkinson

Colin King

At 17 years of age, I was diagnosed with schizophrenia after being racially abused by a white football coach and I ran away from the professional game. The extract from Cartwright below (1851) therefore resonates in terms of the use of the term 'Drapetomania', the first mental health diagnosis given to Black men who ran away from slavery. It resonates as a structural racialised framework, as a pseudo-science of race applied to African communities in the context of mental health. It resonates as a theory and as a contract (Mills, 1997) between Black slave owners and African slaves that has permeated many structural relationships, particularly the context of sport (Rhoden, 2006). This chapter therefore sets out to describe and analyse its persistence and the ways in which it is embedded within the structures of sport and the lived mental health experience of Black players, particularly the manslaughter of Dalian Atkinson in 2016.

Cartwright (1851, p. 709) suggests that Black communities suffered from a particular disease, with distinct anatomical differences in skin, brain, and nerves during the period of slavery:

> If any one or more of them, at any time, are inclined to raise their heads to level with their master or overseer, humanity and their own good requires that they should be punished until they fall into that submissive state which was intended for them to occupy. They have only to be kept in that state and treated like children to prevent and cure them from running away.

Cartwright (1851) produced a symptom-based approach to race, inferiority, and abnormality. The emergence of the term Drapetomania, the "mad, run-away slave" (Cartwright, 1851, p. 707), is embedded in the current Mental Health Act 1983/2007 Section 1, based on the "disease of the mind". On a controlling level, Cartwright (1851) argues that the slave who absconds from the service of the white slave master represents the failure of the white slave owners to manage the slave. Cartwright (1851) supports his theory of Black slaves as suffering from a disease of the mind in running away from slavery in the following quotation. He writes: "Dysesthesia XEthiopis is **a** disease peculiar to negroes, affecting both mind and body" (Cartwright, 1851, p. 711).

In this chapter, I explore several important aspects of the diagnosis of Drapetomania, as a distinct form of slavery. First, the notion of "absconding from services" (Cartwright, 1851, p. 707), is supposedly caused by a disease of the mind, which can be prevented by the correct medical practice. Second, and more concerning Drapetomania is reducing the slave to "the submissive knee bender" (Cartwright, 1851, p. 709), where the slave must be kept in a position of submission to prevent from him running away. Cartwright (1851) presents the conditions that prevent rebellion: first, the inequality with their white master; second, stopped from running at night; and third, kept in a child state, with kindness to prevent running away.

The use of the word Drapetomania as a medicalised form of slavery, is used to describe the actions, theories, and models that have emerged from pseudo-scientific medical racism as shaping the race, control, and Black lives in and outside of sport (Carrington, 2010; Hylton, 2020). In today's psychiatric classification system of the DSM-5, the dark heritage of Drapetomania has led to a form of racialised 'body dimorphic disorder' (DSM-5, 2016), that has influenced both the mind and African body within the science and the management structures of sport, (King, 2004; Hawkins et al., 2017). Like my personal experiences of racial abuse (King, 2004), I analyse what is being run away from, in terms of rebellion, defiance, and Black sanity within the context of sport on several levels. First, what is implicit and explicit and second what is interpreted as running away by Black athletes. It is important to compare the constitution of slavery, mental health, and sports. They represent political and economic systems that devalue the Black body and mind (Bromberg & Simon, 1968; Metz, 2009). To this end, this chapter explores through the biographies of Black players and the manslaughter of Dalian Atkinson in 2016, whether it is possible for Black players to run away from the history of a pseudo-disease that has had devastating implications. For Dalian Atkinson, his death and his manslaughter reveals how much the lives, the body, and mind of Black men matter. As a case, it represents a powerful account of how cultural anxieties about race shape the notions of mental illness inside sports.

The framework Drapetomania as a disease of the mind that leads to a 'running away' response, particularly in the context of sport, is examined by Rhoden's (2006) book *Forty-million-dollar Slave*. Rhoden, (2006) reveals the first-person lived impact of the legacy of slavery on Black sportsmen. Rhoden (2006, p. 1) adopts the notion of 'dilemma', starting from an examination of the plantation field, and the transition to the rise of the Black athlete. Rhoden (2006) moves from slavery and sport as modes of production (see Kane, 1971; Edwards, 1983) to the link between plantation and sport. Rhoden (2006) offers a description of the plantation field, being replaced by the sports field, which is thus explored through the Black struggle for redemption, power, liberation, for freedom. The development of independent baseball, football, and sporting Leagues represents a 'running away' from the control of white owners. It represents a denunciation of being labelled a disease, "that people treat African American athletes differently than they treat African American men" (Rhoden, 2006, p. 194). This theory of 'dilemma' is an important analysis of the perception and treatment of the Black athlete (King & Bennett, 2021). The 'dilemma' presents a range of options and challenges to achieve sporting race activism for social change. The literature on sport and activism, (James, 1963; Edwards, 1983) suggests there are different forms of running away from the historical, theoretical, and medical stereotypes of Black athletes.

The work of (Darby, 2002) argues that the struggles of modern African liberation through sport are being denied. Dominant political systems of European structures, from UEFA to

FIFA, historically have created an "imperialist exploitation" (Darby, 2002, p. 170), one similar to the American model of Drapetomania. Consequently, different global spaces, and political and economic structures, reveal the complexity of the possibility of 'running away'. Bloomfield (2011) outlines the experiences of 13 African countries, from a lived experience grassroots model through the uniting of African clubs and associations. Similarly, (Armstrong & Giulianotti, 2004), focus on an analysis of violence and politics, football, and the legacy of apartheid. What resonates here is sport has the potential to empower African communities to move from 'running away', to a position of safety. The challenge is to explain what it means to 'run away from' in terms of Drapetomania is reflected in Cartwright (1851). He writes: "Mostly owing to the stupidity of mind and infeasibility of the nerves induced by the disease" (Cartwright, 1851, p. 709).

The complex range of possible meanings of what is being, 'run away from' specifically the theories of the disease of the Black mind and body from the work of (Cartwright, 1851) can be explained by the history of white psychiatry (Fernando, 2017). Fernando (2017) analyses the diagnostic frameworks of the DSM-5 (2016) and the ICD 11 (2022) that suggest that Black people are prone to schizophrenia. For (Metz, 2009) schizophrenia represents a 'Black disease', a 'protest culture', a diagnosis applied to the civil rights movement and political sports Black men. This theory has for influenced the perception of Black footballers in and outside the context of sports. The Mental Health Act 1983/2007, Section 17a, introduces a Community Treatment order which allows people to be taken back to the hospital if they fail to take their medication or 'abscond from the service'. It's legislation that has led to 90 per cent of Community Treatment Orders being used in relation to Black men (Mental Health Reform Bill, 2022). As a person sectioned under the Mental Health Act with the diagnosis 'schizophrenia', sport is a similar space that controls the Black body from running away. The temptation is to examine the 'running away' in sport (Poli, 2010) through the experiences of trafficking and of being inside football's slave trade (Hawkins, 2015).

Drapetomania and professional football

There are three thousand registered players in the English Professional Leagues, up to 35 per cent in the Premier League (Bennett, PhD study, 2021). The conditions of employment set are by mainly white owners, coaches, and managers (Bradbury, 2017). Patterns of discrimination inside the stadium, coaching and the governance of English football (King, 2004, 2021) have not been considered as a form of Drapetomania. The response to online racial abuse, the symbolic meaning of 'taking the knee'[1] (Bennet, 2021) can be interpreted as a rebellion, to being kept in a 'submissive knee bender' position. Drapetomania (Cartwright, 1851) seems more appliable to the quotation of being "kept in subjection to the white man" (Cartwright, 1851, p. 692). The literature on stacking (Melnick, 1988) or the coaching relationship, (King, 2004; Bradbury, 2017) suggests that these are similar elements of white control (Bains, 1996; Entine, 2000; Gladwell, 2006). To examine how Drapetomania operates conceptually, empirically and as a form of resistance it's important to analyse the lived reality and interpretive frameworks used by Black professional footballers.

Analysing the concept of Drapetomania offers a tool to analyse how the theories of the racialised mind and the body are controlled in sport. This control is similar to the period of slavery as governance is made visible by a culture characterised by traditionally hierarchical, white masculine power structures A culture built on similar historical racialised perceptions of sport in which "the negro is a slave by nature and cannot never be happy" (Cartwright, 1851, p. 698). Two theories of lived experience offer the interpretive models used by Black professional footballers to understand Drapetomania as the conditions inside sport that prevent the 'running away'. First, Thuram (2021) adopts the framework of the white mask from Fanon (1967). Thuram (2021) suggests behind the mask of race identity Black players understand the history of white colonial thinking. Thinking that permeates sport, a culture of control that keeps Black players from equality to a status in which they will never be treated as similar to their white owners. Second, the lived experience theory of (Barkley, 2006), offers a position to see the perception of Black men, based on fear, or what Cartwright (1851, p. 7009), suggests that Black slaves who become "sulky and dissatisfied", should be subjected to, "whipping the devil out of them" (Cartwright, 1851, p. 7009). These lived experienced theories support, Welsing, (1991) approach to Drapetomania, as a symbolism of the process of submission, a state of being treated like a child.

Drapetomania as a framework cannot always be used to understand the complex interplay of race, mental health, and rebellion in sport. The temptation is to assert through sporting literal reviews that looks at historical racism in sport, that it has led to a collective rebellion of Black players (King, 2004; Professional Football Association, 2021; Bennett, 2021). The theory of Drapetomania, the science of the physical and mental peculiarities, is useful in analysing how they deny rebellion, captured by Hoberman's (1997, p. 8) reference to the "Decades of popular scientific speculation about the special endowment of the Black athletes which have shaped entire populations". Consequently, it is more useful to conceptualise Drapetomania from Cartwright's (1851) model of:

Dysesthesia, as the control of the mind and body that prevents absconding and running away. It's contentious to assume that Black communities do not have the potential to think, to understand the conditions that have led to the control over their mind and bodies that inhibits them from 'running away'.

(Cartwright, 1851, p. 709)

It's important to understand what the metaphors of Drapetomania means as an experience of running away, compared to how it given meaning by what Thuram (2021) refers to as a response to "white thinking".

Consequently, according to Cartwright (1851, p. 692) Drapetomania, 'the running away', can be interpreted in different ways based on, "skin difference of colour that exists between the negro and White man" (p. 692). This difference in race perception can be evaluated between how white biographers and Black auto biographers construct the relationship between sport and defiance. The relationship between racism and 'running way' is articulated by Hill (1989), a white biographer, as John Barnes experience of rebellion is the moments that he does not respond to racist remarks, "kicking a banana thrown from the crowd". Barnes' first person (1999) autobiography, *What Am I, Black or Something?* exposes and analyses a more complex internal response to racism, behind the mask of race identity developed by Thuram, (2021). He sees it, denies it, and decides how he wants to respond.

Other white biographers, such as Clarkson's (2002) biography of Rio Ferdinand, avoid looking at the choices made by Black players in 'running away from racism', by focusing on Ferdinand's early life in Peckham. They fail to look at how Black players understand and respond to forms of Drapetomania, in terms of the inequality they face, how they understand and respond to the kindness to assimilate into subservient positions to white coaches

(King, 2004). Consequently, the first-hand accounts of dealing with systemic racism through Rosenoir's (2017) autobiography, *It Is Only Banter* suggests banter is a childlike relationship in which Black players are the 'servant' (Cartwright, 1851, p. 708). The term 'banter' represents the acceptable channel for racial absconding in football, it is legitimated in English professional football as a form of Drapetomania as highlighted in this quote, "if they did not prefer slavery, tranquillity and sensual enjoyment, to liberty … the organisation of their mind is such that if they had their liberty, they do not have the industry" (Cartwright, 1851, p. 694).

This idea of 'tranquillity as opposed to industry', as a choice to remain 'submissive', is articulated in the perceptions of Frank Bruno (Bruno & Mitchell, 2005; Bruno & Owens, 2017). Bruno and Mitchell (2005) describe a sequence of events that had been accumulating over several years, leading to being sectioned and compulsorily admitted to a secure ward of a psychiatric hospital under Section 3 of the 1983 Mental Health Act. The stigma of having a mental illness, 'schizophrenia' and then 'bipolar', reveals the difficulty of being unable to walk away from a sport that has pathologized the mind of Black sportsmen through the application of clinical and medicalised labels. Similarly, Mike Tyson (2015) provides a graphic account of his self-destructive responses to being entrapped in his experiences of being controlled. Tyson, (2015) explains how sport constructed him as a Black man to be feared (Barkley, 2006), his anger as reinforcing an identity as 'sulky and dissatisfied', and the need to 'punish his anger' (Cartwright, 1851, p. 709) through being sectioned under the Mental Health Act.

This aspect of internalising one's perception of being inferior can be understood as a form of Drapetomania insofar "to be frighten[ed] and panic-struck" (Cartwright, 1851, p. 709) and can be explored in the suicide of Black players, such as Justin Fashanu. Studies such as Smith's (2019) depression and suicide among elite players, and Wood et al.'s (2017) suicides in professional football in the UK, fail to explain the importance of the legacy Drapetomania. For Justin Fashanu as a form of submission, walking away, the fear of offending those who have authority over his racial and sexual identity. This form of submission, rather than becoming "rude, ungovernable and to run away" (Cartwright, 1851, p. 709), is also contextualised by the ex-professional player, Clarke Carlisle (2013), who also suffered from suicidality. Reflecting on this experience in a TV documentary, *Depression and suicide: Football's Secret Uncovered*, he explained how "it stopped him from asking for help". In *Tackling My Demons*, ex-Nottingham Forrest and Liverpool striker Stan Collymore (2004), discusses the events that led to his admission to the Priory Hospital in 1999, "I was so low I was genuinely thinking about suicide" (p. 14). Both cases of Fashanu and Collymore are illustrations of submission, 'neglecting to be protected', (Cartwright, 1851) as a form of Drapetomania. The case of Dalian Atkinson reveals the aspect of Drapetomania to be treated 'cruelly' as a feature of submission.

Drapetomania and the case of Dalian Atkinson

As a professional footballer, playing for Aston Villa and Sheffield United, Dalian Atkinson had had a successful career. He had been managed by Ron Atkinson, and he had never challenged or rebelled against his authority. After a successful career, Dalian Atkinson died on Monday 15 August 2016. At 1.30 am on Monday 15 August 2016, Dalian Atkinson, a 48-year-old Black male, became agitated and drove his girlfriend's Porsche to his father's house at Meadow Close. He was in the midst of a mental breakdown and had been shouting outside his father's house claiming to be the Messiah, demanding to be let in. A concerned neighbour called the police and PC Benjamin Monk responded. Atkinson opened the front door and confronted the officer on the drive. He was described as 'acting out of character', as

Monk used a taser to control his behaviour several times. Daliian was shocked by the Monk for 45 seconds, which was six times over the normal limit.

On falling to the ground, he was also kicked in the head. His death was described medically as 'cardiorespiratory arrest' caused by two kicks to the head. He was described in the *Judiciary Review* as "sadly lost touch with his reality and lapsed into a form of psychotic stage" (Regina v Benjamin Monk, 2021, p. 1). The analysis of the life and tragic death of Dalian Atkinson by the Police in 2016, as a case study of Drapetomania, reveals the treatment of Black players. It reveals the denial of equality, the reduction to a childlike state, the prevention of absconding and running away, and the fear of the Black body.

Atkinson represents a history of Black men who have died in mental health care (Rocky Bennett, Olaseni Lewis, Sean Rigg). Described as having a 'disease of the mind', 'sulky and dissatisfied', they all met the criteria of Drapetomania. Atkinson had been managed by Ron Atkinson, who had made racist remarks about the mind and body of Black players. Dalian's submission is one based on violence, of 'being neglected to be protected', to borrow a phrase from Cartwright (1851, p. 709). The overuse of the taser in the case of Atkinson, and the kicks to his head, suggest not only that his Black life did not matter (Hylton, 2020), but that he was forced into submission, stopped from running away, and prevented from escaping. At the same time, as suggested by Atkinson's legal team, this moment reveals that there are similar cultural behaviours in both sport and society that represent control. The manslaughter of Dalian Atkinson, and the imprisonment of PC Monk for eight years, do not address the wider implications of Drapetomania, which have contributed to the Black body and mind as a disease. These implications emerge through the Ritchie Report (1994) and the case of Christopher Clunis. Clunis was diagnosed with schizophrenia, and he murdered Jonathan Zito, a white man. Clunis was seen as big, Black, and dangerous, and his case presented the fear of the "big Black man" (Barkley, 2006) and the increased use of the diagnosis of schizophrenia (Mental Health Reform Bill, 2022), where Black men like Dalian Atkinson are now five times more likely to be compulsory detained under the Mental Health Act 1983/2007 and restrained. It reveals shocking implications of the theory of Drapetomania (Mental Health Act 1983/2007; Bennett, 2021). More Black footballers are likely to suffer similar types of restraints in football.

Conclusion

The implications of the concept of Drapetomania are useful in understanding the experiences of Black players such as Dalian Atkinson. It reveals its contribution as a process of subordination rather than a culture of rebellion and running away. For King[2] (2004), similar to Thuram (2021), behind the racial mask emerges a 'Medicalised Sporting Self' as a significant theme in the lived experiences of Black players. Whilst the concept of slavery explains how the racialised modes of production that for Rhoden (2006) transfer to sport, Drapetomania reveals the powerful implications of understanding how the mind and body of Black athletes is pathologized and how this affects the lives and careers of Black athletes. The propensity to mental illness in sports (Atkinson, 2019) is to focus on the diagnosis, as opposed to the political implications for race and racism. The tragic story of Dalian Atkinson exposes how current models of football and mental health do not address the connections between historical and discriminatory racialised processes, and their impact on mental health in relation to a diverse playing workforce. What is needed is a range of models that look at the structural, cultural, and interpersonal factors. Culturally inclusive theories that decolonialise

Eurocentric models that might have demonised Black athletes and Black communities. New models are required that examine the inter-connected aspects of mental health that unmask our fear of difference, and ultimately allow both the sporting and mental health worlds to transcend the relics of Drapetomania that remain embedded in contemporary football and sport, more broadly.

Notes

1 Michael Bennett is the Director of welfare at the Professional Footballers Association. His 2021 article "Taking the knee: Mental health, and racism in sport" looks at politics of race and mental health in this profession.
2 King's (2004) study into racism in coaching looks at how Black players have to wear the white mask, to play the white man, to be accepted into the dominant culture of race and whiteness in professional football.

References

Armstrong, G. & Giulianotti, R. (2004) *Football in Africa: Conflict, conciliation, and community*. Palgrave McMillian, Basingstoke.
Atkinson, M. (ed.) (2019) *Sport, mental illness and sociology*. Emerald Publishing Ltd, Bradford.
Bains, J. & Pate, R. (1996) *Asians can't play football*. Canongate, London.
Barkley, C. (2006) *Who's afraid of a large Black man: Race, power, fame, identity, and why everyone should read my book*. Riverhead Freestyle, New York.
Barnes, J. (1999) *The autobiography*. Headline Books, London.
Bennett, M. (2021) Behind the mask: Demedicalising race and mental health in professional football. *Lanzet Psychiatry*, 8, 264–266.
Bloomfield, S. (2011) *Africa united. How Football Explains Africa*. Canongate, London.
Bradbury, S. (2017) *Ethnic minority coaches in elite football in England: 2017 update: A report from the Sport People's Think Tank in Association with the Fare Network and the Loughborough University*. Sports People's Think Tank and the Fare network, London.
Bromberg, M.D. & Simon, F. (1968) The protest psychosis, Schizophrenia as a Black Disease Pd, Brooklyn. *Arch Gen Psychiatry*, 19, 155–196.
Bruno, F. & Mitchell, K. (2005) *Frank: Fighting back*. Yellow Jersey Press, London.
Bruno. F. & Owens, N. (2017) *Let me be Frank*. Mirror Books, London.
Carlisle, Clarke (2013) *Depression and suicide: Football's secret uncovered*. BBC. 13 July 2013.
Carrington, B. (2010) *Race, sport, and politics: The sporting Black diaspora*. Sage, London.
Cartwright, S. (1851) 'Report on the diseases and peculiarities of the Negro race.' (Originally published in 1851.) Reprinted in: A. L. Caplan, J. J. McCartney, & D. A. Sisti (eds), *Health, disease, and illness: Concepts in medicine*. Georgetown University Press, Washington, DC, pp. 28–39.
Clarkson, W. (2002) *Rio!* John Blake, London.
Collymore, S. (2004) *Tackling my demons*. HarperCollins, London.
Darby, P. (2002) *Africa Football and FIFA. Politics colonialis, and resistance*. Frank Cass, London.
DSM-5 (2016) American Psychiatric Association. (2016). *Diagnostic and statistical manual of mental disorders* (5th ed.). https://doi.org/10.1176/appi.books.9780890425596
Edwards, Harry (1983) Race In Sport: An Analysis and Some Briefly Stated Cross-Cultural Implications of the US Case. In Eric Dunning & Robert Pearton (Eds), *The Sport Process*. E. and F. Spon Ltd Publishers, London, pp. 83–124.
England and Wales Crown Court. (2021) Sentencing remarks of His Honour Judge Melbourne Inman QC: R v Benjamin Monk. Retrieved from https://www.judiciary.uk/wp-content/uploads/2021/06/R--v-Monk-Sentencing-Remarks.pdf
Entine, J. (2000) *TABOO, why Black athletes dominate sports and why we're afraid to talk about it*. Public Affairs, New York.
Fanon, F. (1967) *Black skin, White Mask*. Pluto Press, London.

Fernando, S. (2017) *Institutional racism in psychiatry and clinical psychology: Race matters*. Palgrave Macmillan, London.
Gladwell, M. (2006) *Blink, the power thinking without thinking*. Penguin, London.
Hawkins, B. J., Carter-Francique, A. R., & Cooper, J. N. (2017) *Critical race theory: Black athletic sporting experiences in the United States*. Palgrave Macmillan, New York.
Hawkins, E. (2015) *The lost boys: Inside football's slave trade*. Bloomsberg, New York.
Hill, D. (1989) *'Out of his skin' the John Barnes phenomenon*. Faber and Faber, London and Boston.
Hoberman, J. (1997) *Darwin's athletes: How sport has damaged Black America*. Houghton Mifflin Harcourt, Boston.
Hylton, K. (2020) 'Black Lives Matter' in sport …? *Equality, Diversity, and Inclusion*, 40(1), 41–48.
James, C.L.R. (1963) *Beyond the boundary*. Stanley, Paul & Co, London.
Joint Committee on the Draft Mental Health Bill. (2023) Draft mental health bill: Report of session 2022–23. UK Parliament. https://committees.parliament.uk/publications/33599/documents/182904/default/
Kane, M. (1971) An assessment of Black is best. *Sport Illustrated Magazine*, London, 72–83.
King, C. (2004) *Offside racism, playing the white man*. Berg, London.
King, C. & Bennett, M. (2021). Taking the knee, mental health, and racism in sport. *Lancet Psychiatry*, 10(8), 861–862.
Melnick, M. (1988) Racial segregation by playing position in the English football league: Some preliminary observations. *Journal of Sport and Social Issues*, 12(2), September 1988.
Metz, J. (2009) *The protest psychosis: How schizophrenia became a Black disease*. Beacon Press, Boston.
Mills, C. W. (1997) *The racial contract*. Cornell University Press, Ithaca, NY.
Poli, R. (2010) African migrants in Asian and European football: Hopes and realities. *Sport in Society*, 6, 1001–1011.
Professional Football Association (2021) *Understanding mental health*, www.thepfa.com/players/well-being/understanding-mental-health, (accessed 8 June 2021).
Rhoden, W.C. (2006) *Forty million dollar slave*. Crown Publishers, New York.
Ritchie, J. H., Dick, D., & Lingham, R. (1994) *The report of the inquiry into the care and treatment of Christopher Clunis*. HMSO.
Rosenoir, L. (2017) *'It is only banter': The autobiography of Leroy Rosenoir*. Pitch Publishing, Bournemouth.
Smith, A. (2019) Depression and suicide in professional sports work. In M. Atkinson (ed.), *Sport, mental illness, and sociology*. Emerald Publishing Limited, UK.
Thuram, L. (2021) *White thinking: Behind the mask of race identity*. Hero Press, London.
Tyson, M. (2015) *Undisputed truth: My autobiography*. HarperCollins, London.
Welsing, C. (1991) *Key to the colour*. American Press, Chicago.
Wood, S., Harrison, L. K., & Kucharska, J. (2017) Male professional footballers' experiences of mental health difficulties and help-seeking. *The Physician and Sport's Medicine*, 45, 2, 120–128.

14
CHRISTIANITY, SPORT, AND SOCIAL JUSTICE

David Torevell

As a religion active in the world, Christianity has always stood up for issues of social justice. Its sacred texts, the Old and New Testaments, include teachings and narratives which demonstrate the vital importance of treating people equally since everyone is made in the image of God. Startlingly, the writings also proclaim that the poor will inherit the Kingdom of God before the rich and privileged. The *anawim* of the Old Testament (the Hebrew word itself means 'one who is bowed down') included those who were socio-economically oppressed as well as those who were marginalised (like lepers), the powerless and the vulnerable. Jesus Himself joined this group when he "emptied himself" (Phil. 2, 7) of His Godhead and became "a servant, being born in the likeness of men" (Phil. 2, 7). The gospels record how Jesus went into the synagogue in Nazareth one Sabbath and read from the prophet Isaiah the following words:

> The Spirit of the Lord is upon me, because he has anointed me to preach good news to the poor. He has sent me to proclaim release to the captives and recovery of sight to the blind, to set at liberty those who are oppressed.
>
> (Luke 4, 18)

Every Christian, then is expected to follow this example and this is why Christians are intent on establishing a just and egalitarian society, committed to challenging injustice whenever they see it.

Sport has the potential like Christianity, to bring about a more equal and fair society. Its emphasis on teamwork, co-operation, fair play, respect, friendship, loyalty, and perseverance shows that it clearly promotes these values. Unfortunately, it often fails to do so as the Liverpool footballer Jordan Henderson's move to the Saudi Arabia Pro League side Al-Ettifaq for an estimated £700,000 a week in the summer of 2023 demonstrates. In this Gulf state human rights are infringed, and homosexuality is illegal and punishable by death. However, sport does encourage at times the coming together of all humanity, regardless of status or background, encouraging within persons and societies the goodness, resilience, and beauty it symbolises. When, therefore, sportswomen and men encounter any form of social injustice, they are equipped to challenge them in effective ways because they have been grounded in an ethical and unselfish school of formation.

This chapter explores the connections between Christianity, sport, and social justice. After a brief section on the cultural background to this relationship it outlines the foundational principles on which its philosophy is based. It then describes Martin Luther King's enduring legacy on sport before discussing Catholic Christianity's distinctive contribution to the debate. The relationship between sport and virtue is considered followed by an account of sport's engagement with contemporary debates about inclusivity, gender, and sexuality.

The cultural backdrop

Social justice is a notoriously slippery and broad concept to define and applies to a host of people and institutions – resistance fighters, politicians, teachers, lecturers, churches, religions, community development workers, and employees in a range of professions and occupations. Freebody and Finneran's summary of the three categories of the *economic*, the *social*, and the *represented* is helpful to appreciate this issue (2021). With reference to the first, although justice has been discussed philosophically since the time of Plato, the notion of social justice emerged in the nineteenth century as a largely *economic* phenomenon and consequently the preserve of the state. It would govern social lives, including living conditions, family issues, and personal health and well-being. This is still prevalent today and attention is invariably focussed on the distribution of economic resources and access to services. More recently, however, this trend has morphed into the fight for equality, specifying the *social* needs of specific groups or individuals besides their economic needs (Freebody & Finneran, 2021, p. 18); these, in turn, are frequently allied to the need for public respect to be accorded to all individuals and peoples. This entails addressing the question of *representation* – who is seen and who is centre stage when it comes to decision-making and its bearing on social/political influence? Such questions about democratic participation furnish "the stage on which struggles over distribution and recognition are played out. Establishing criteria of social belonging, thus determining who counts as a member" (quoted in Freebody & Finneran, p. 19).

The issue of representation is allied to the present-day growth of 'identity politics', a phrase which has come into fashion to signify a wide range of political positions and activities based on the shared experiences of injustice in certain social groups. This has come to be reflected sharply in the sporting world in controversies surrounding transgender persons in elite competition. The debate focuses on identity and its relationship to equality and has come about primarily because (as Rousseau foresaw) human beings tend to compare and contrast themselves justifiably to other human beings. In *Reveries of the Solitary Walker* (*Les Rêveries du Promeneur Solitaire*) Rousseau confesses how he himself became the victim of other people's evaluations (1987, pp. 55–56). So, in his *Discourse on the Origins and the Foundations of Inequality Among Men (Discours sur l'origine et les fondements de inégalité parmi les hommes)* he discusses the idea of a *sentiment de l'existence*, an identity free from the unfair accretions and prejudices of social convention and judgement (2009). Although Rousseau was, in some regard, intensely opposed to particularity, which he understood as an example of sub-social community (witnessed in his writings about the social contract whereby all individual wills are to be subordinated to the general will), he nevertheless held a deep conviction about the individual worth of each person so his views are pertinent to sport's deeply held belief in inclusive and fair participation for each member of the human race.

The desire for *public* recognition – *thymos* – and the demand for social recognition of one's identity (which governs much world politics and feelings of self-esteem today) cannot be met simply by the economic dimension of social justice. It rests on far more existential and personal concerns – the *felt need* to be *seen by others* as absolutely equal to everyone else in *all regards*. Recent gay marriage legislation would be one example of this cultural trajectory and so too would the Rainbow Laces campaign which has raised awareness for LGBTQ+ people in sport. Hegel's claim in his 1807 publication *Phenomenology of Spirit* that human history was driven by the struggle for *recognition* achieved by *universal recognition* (whereby the dignity of every human being was upheld) has now shifted towards a broader type of identity politics in the (post)modern age, which gives credence to *particular* forms of recognition in relation to tribal identity, for example, gender, sexual orientation, nationhood, race, ethnicity, disability, and so on. Although, as Fukuyama claims, the solitary dreamer does not need anyone's approval, social recognition occurred by default. Thus, the growth of identity politics gave emphasis to *individual experience within a specific social group* – for example, people of colour, disabled people, gay people, transgendered people, gypsies. Such identifiable social groupings intent on social equality would bolster their sense of solidarity with others in the same category or 'tribe' and assist their fight for justice.

However, there are two inherent dangers connected to this. First, is allowing oneself to become defined by the 'tribe' (this, of course, might not occur with due vigilance) always beneficial? Second, collective, weighty struggles for social justice might become dangerously reduced to personal, psychological problems and anxieties. This dichotomy is reflected in the use of the German words *Erfahrung*, which refers to *common* human experiences and the word *Erlebris*, which refers to the *subjective* perception of something which might not necessarily be shareable. What becomes clear in all of these struggles is the challenge and commitment, on moral grounds, to promote social justice, often against fierce odds.

The relationship between Christianity, sport, and social justice

An important and dynamic relationship has always existed between Christianity, sport, and social justice. Christianity's central teaching to love one's neighbour as oneself and thereby to enhance the common good has influenced – and has ongoing implications for – the way sport is conducted and managed, and indeed what traditionalists might argue are its fundamental values. Sporting activity exhibits values which give due weight to the dignity and inclusion of each person made in the divine image and promotes the unity and harmony of all peoples, races, religions, and cultures. These values emerged powerfully during 2022 as Beijing was hosting the Winter Olympics. China's less than impressive history of human rights has long been brought to the world's attention over the persecution of Uighur Muslims, the destruction of democracy in Hong Kong, and the 'disappearance' of the tennis player Peng Shuai. Furthermore, the successful bid by Qatar to stage the 2022 World Cup was also greeted with horror by some in view of its own poor record on human rights. But as Slot comments, "No one can kid themselves that any amount of scorn poured upon Qatar will result in a policy change and, for instance, the legalisation of homosexuality" (2022, p. 24).

Sport can, nonetheless, still be a strong and visible platform for signalling opposition to social injustice. For example, the International Olympic Committee guaranteed the rights of athletes in Beijing to express their opinions on issues of social justice, even if they did not permit this to happen while competing or when on the podium. It may also be recalled that, after qualifying for Qatar, the Denmark football team announced that its commercial partners would relinquish their advertising space on the players' training kit so it could be replaced by messaging that highlighted human rights abuses, especially the treatment and deaths of migrant workers.

The media portrayal of global sport events can assist in highlighting and helping to overcome situations of injustice. Sport's spirit of healthy competition, co-operation, and harmony can call attention to nations which blatantly flaunt such ideals. It can also be an opportunity to demonstrate the values which Christ taught making them visible across a range of individual and team events. The positive aspects of muscular Christianity are endorsed by this. For example, the virtues of loyalty, perseverance, friendship, teamwork, honesty, courage, and solidarity can be witnessed in and strengthened by sport. Its portrayal of high spiritual ideals which rests on notions of human co-operation, fairness, peace, and equal opportunities can become embedded in people's hearts and consciences whether they participate or simply spectate. Truce was the basis of the ancient Olympic Games while modern Olympism attempts to further peace and respect for all peoples on an international level (Parry, 2007, pp. 2010–2014). Athletes, particularly those who are well known, know they have a clear, social mandate to live up to such values and, when they do, become role models of virtuous behaviour, especially to the young.

I move on now to discuss an example of how securing social justice can involve struggle, and how this has impacted on sport and leisure.

Christianity and racial justice: Martin Luther King's enduring influence on sport and leisure

The struggle for race equality and black representation in sport has a rich, if somewhat depressing history and it aligns to my earlier discussion of *representation* as one facet of social justice. The historical and cultural background to this occurrence is essential to know if we are to appreciate the obstacles that black athletes continue to endure today on a global scale and often this dimension is related to religion. It is part of the same history and the same struggle. The ongoing discussion about the 'invisibility' of marginalised groups arose in light of their perception about being publicly ignored and not seen and is captured imaginatively in Ralph Ellison's influential novel *Invisible Man*. As the opening to the Prologue of the novel sets forth:

> I am an invisible man. No, I am not a spook like those who haunted Edgar Allan Poe; ... I am a man of substance, of flesh and bone, fiber and liquids – and I might even be said to possess a mind. I am invisible, understand, simply because people refuse to see me.
>
> (2016, p. 3)

The struggle for recognition is associated with this struggle for visibility.

I now focus on one historical example from the USA in the twentieth century to demonstrate how the fight for justice is inevitably a difficult one, but with the passage of time can be seen to be an immensely worthwhile one. Martin Luther King was assassinated on 4 April 1968 in Memphis. His vision for a socially inclusive society was institutionalised within the civil rights movement of the 1950s and 1960s. It was partly a quasi-ecclesial and partly a civic association reacting against racism and injustice. King believed that the American churches had failed to put into practice the Biblical mandate to prophesy deliverance to the oppressed and his political views were never wrenched from his theological ones. Certainly, in his early career he thought the movement would inaugurate a new society where famously he said, people would be judged "by the strength of their character rather than the colour of their skin". The present-day black footballers' (Raheem Sterling, Marcus Rashford and Bukayo Saka) fight against racial abuse in football is like King's and is deeply influenced and strengthened by their strong Christian beliefs and practices. Stone specialises in Pentecostal Christianity and its impact on issues relating to social justice. She argues that these three footballers are embodying the best of the black Christian tradition:

> Faith and spirituality are really at the core of their lives. ... Black Christian traditions are more about the embodiment of faith, how you live out what you say in a Sunday service, how you are attentive to the felt needs of people around you as part of your faith commitment.
>
> (quoted in Coman, 2021)

Sterling was awarded an MBE in the Queen's Honours list in 2021 for services to racial equality. Matt Baker, the national director of Sports Chaplaincy UK, says that although there are clear signs of secularisation in Western Europe, there are many people of faith in sport and countless Christians, especially in football.

There were three dominant influences on King's theology. The first was Liberal Theology, which convinced him that God acted in history; he saw his political action and protest, therefore, as being 'on the right side of history'. Second, the impact of Mahatma Gandhi on his understanding and the importance of non-violent protest. Gandhi's notion of *satyagraha* or 'love force' became embedded in his consciousness. This, he thought, would break the scourge of slavery and colonialism. The third was Henry David Thoreau, whose *On the Duty of Civil Disobedience* argued that a moral person has the right to disobey any law that is unjust. He wrote: "Under a government which imprisons any unjustly, the true place for a just man is prison" (quoted in Livingston, Schussler Fiorenza, Coakley, & Evans, 2006, p. 445). After 1967 King firmly held that unjust rulers never give up their power easily, and he began to name a whole range of issues beyond that of racial segregation in the South which were unacceptable. His resistance was not founded on humanity's ability to change unjust structures but on God's, and he never lost this hopeful faith. As he said on the eve of his death, "I may not get to the promised land, but with you I believe that we as a people will get there".

A similar influential initiative was the growth of Black theology which developed out of two strong influences. The first was African traditional religions and the second, the history of slavery. Evans quotes Hopkins about the Movement: "While white masters attempted to force their Christianity onto their black property, slaves worshipped God secretly. Out of these illegal and hidden religious practices, the 'Invisible Institution', black Christianity and black theology arose" (2006, p. 450). Hopkins claims that "For blacks, God and Jesus called them to use all means possible to pursue religiously a human status of equality" (p. 450). The America of the 1960s was a place of social unrest and turbulence due to the exclusion of people of colour from a growing economy, and what emerged was the cry for 'Black Power'. The forceful statement the Black Power Movement issued in 1966 claimed that:

> The fundamental distortion facing us in the controversy about 'black power' is rooted in a gross imbalance of power and conscience between Negroes and white Americans. ... The conscience of black men is corrupted because, having no power to implement the demands of conscience, the concern for justice is transmuted into a distorted form

of love, which, in the absence of justice, becomes chaotic self-surrender. Powerlessness breeds a race of beggars.

(quoted in Evans, p. 452)

One aspect of the contemporary *Black Lives Matter* Movement – the demand for reparations – was signalled earlier in the 1969 Black Manifesto:

We know that the churches and synagogues have tremendous wealth, and its membership in white America has profited and still exploits black people ... Underneath all of this exploitation, the racism of this country has produced a psychological effect upon us that we are beginning to shake off. We are no longer afraid to demand our full rights as a people in this decadent society.

(quoted in Evans, p. 454)

One of the most significant voices to emerge from this Movement was James Cone whose *A Black Theology of Liberation* crystallised for black Christians the way forward. He re-defined the white European definition of revelation: "Revelation is God's self-disclosure to humankind *in the context of liberation*. To know God is to know God's work of liberation on behalf of the oppressed" (quoted in Evans, p. 457). Womanist theology also emerged from this which was:

both a critical and a constructive reflection on the Christian faith based on the experience of African American women. Like Feminist theology, it criticised the patriarchal practices of the churches, the misogynist interpretations of the Bible, and androcentric theological constructions.

(p. 460)

From this grew black womanist theology, which was a critical and constructive reflection on the Christian faith based on the experience of African American women. It challenged the patriarchal dominance of the churches, the misogynist interpretations of the Bible and androcentric theological tropes. All these liberation movements constitute the historical and cultural backdrop to issues arising in sport concerning social justice for black and female players today.

A Catholic Christianity perspective: Vatican Council II and the Vatican's teaching on sport: 'Giving the best you can'

I now move on to responses to social justice by religion and sport dwelling largely on Catholic Christianity. One of the Roman Catholic documents of the Second Vatican Council (1962–1965) was devoted to social justice and was related to a wider discussion about the stance of the Church towards the modern world. *Gaudium et Spes* (Joy and Hope) saw this concern as being indelibly linked to the *dignity of the human person*:

Sacred Scripture teaches that man was created "to the image of God" ... "What is man that thou are mindful of him, and the son of man that thou dost care for him? Yet thou hast made him little less than the God, and dost crown him with glory and honor" (Ps. 8: 5–7).

(Flannery, 1998, p. 913)

A related foundational principle for understanding social justice rests on the social nature of human beings: "God did not create man a solitary being. ... by his innermost nature man is a social being; and if he does not enter into relations with others he can neither live nor develop his gifts" (pp. 913–914). This pro-social bedrock of human identity, endorsed by many people's experience during the present global pandemic, is associated with the search for truth in conscience and what constitutes the morally best for individuals and social groups: "Through loyalty to conscience Christians are joined to other men in the search for truth and the right solution to so many moral problems which arise both in the life of individuals and from social relationships" (p. 916).

The Catholic Church's strong teaching on the *common good* is allied to this sense of a person's social solidarity and interdependence with all humankind: "We are today witnessing a widening of the role of the common good, which is the sum total of social conditions which allow people, either as groups or individuals, to reach their fulfilment more fully and more easily" (p. 927). The teaching about personhood in light of this is stark: "The social order and its development must constantly yield to the good of the person, since the order of things must be subordinate to the order of persons and not the other way round" (p. 927). However, the same social order needs constant improvement and must be founded on truth, justice, and love, and grow towards a more humane equilibrium among all groupings and individuals. One section of the document is devoted entirely to social justice and this is tied to the move away from those philosophies which promote individualism and unfair treatment of others. All forms of "social or cultural discrimination in basic personal rights on the ground of sex, race, colour, social conditions, language or religion, must be curbed and eradicated as incompatible with God's designs" (p. 929). "Excessive economic and social disparity between individuals and peoples is a source of scandal and militates against social justice" (p. 930) claim the authors of the document. Those involved in sport and leisure management will be encouraged by such observations as they fulfil their corporate obligations towards securing justice by contributing to the common good "even to the point of fostering and helping public and private organisations devoted to bettering of the conditions of life" (p. 930). The more the world comes together in unity, the more widely do people's obligations transcend particular groups and gradually extend to the whole world (p. 930).

A more specific text highlighting the Catholic Church's commitment to the benefits of sport was published in 2018 with the title *Giving the Best of Yourself*. It focusses on social justice, human dignity and the common good. Section 3.8 "Equality and Respect" sums up the Church's commitment to the importance of sport nicely: "Everyone has the same right to experience and be fulfilled in multiple dimensions of culture and sport. Everyone has the same right to promote their individual capabilities as well as respect for their individual limitations" (Dicastery for Laity, Family and Life, 2018, para 3.8). Sport is an activity that can and should promote the equality of all human beings. The Catholic Church "considers sports as an instrument of education when they foster high human and spiritual ideals and when they form young people in an integral way to develop in such values as loyalty, perseverance, friendship, solidarity and peace" (para 3.8). It is "an area of our society that promotes the meeting of all humanity, and it can overcome socio-economic, racial, cultural and religious barriers" (para 3.8).

The document goes on to claim that although we are all brothers and sisters who come from the same Creator our world still faces deeply rooted inequalities and it is the task of everyone to address this reality (para 3.8). But this is primary for Christians involved in sport since it is a vitally productive space where they can seek to promote fairness and equality; without equal opportunities many different forms of aggression and conflict will find fertile terrain for growth and exploitation. However, the equality of rights in sport for every individual does not mean uniformity but respect for the multiplicity and diversity of human life in relation to disability, gender, sexual orientation, age, race, and cultural and religious backgrounds and traditions. It is understandable that there are specific differences of age in sports performance categories and that in most sports disciplines men and women do not compete against each other. As such allowing for the multiplicity of conditions, talents, and abilities and the justifiably different categories of performance, must never lead to a hierarchy of classifications or even to the airtight delimitation between different human groups. This destroys the feeling of the primary unity of the human family symbolised by the Garden of Eden pre-Fall (para 3.3).

What the Apostle Paul asks for from the Christian community as a reflection of the body of Jesus Christ should be experienced in sport:

> The eye cannot say to the hand, "I don't need you", or the head to the feet, "I don't need you". On the contrary, those parts of the body that seem to be weaker are in fact indispensable [...] If one part suffers, every part suffers with it. If one part is praised, every part rejoices with it. Now you are the body of Christ and individually members of it.
> (para 3.8)

The Para-Olympics is one inspiring example of putting St Paul's teaching into practice since it demonstrates how all sportspeople belong to the same human family.

The Vatican text shows that there are many ways sport can promote unity in society and equality between peoples. In November 2021, the Italian bishops conference and the Vatican's Sports Office held a symposium on the future of sport at the International Olympic Academy in Greece. It was entitled "Epos, Ethos, Paideia. Polis: Rethinking the sport of the future together". The Head of the Vatican's Dicastery for Laity, Family and Life, Santiago Perez de Camino, spoke about how ethical tensions can break out in sport but also how it was experiencing a transformation accelerated by the pandemic. Sport had a deep ethical dimension that could help society to start again in what could be a conscious effort to create a more inclusive and fairer society, he pointed out. What was needed was a vision to protect the inclusive value of sport, to challenge any excesses and, especially, to tailor sport to the most fragile people, thus putting social marginality back at the centre – through sport.

The document also adds that athletes and sports persons, especially those who are most renowned and enjoy celebrity status, have an unavoidable social responsibility: "You, the players, are exponents of a sports activity, which every weekend brings together so many people in the stadiums and to which social media devotes large spaces. For that reason, you have a special responsibility" (para 3.9). The authors invite athletes to "get involved with others and with God, giving the best of yourselves, spending your life for what really is worthwhile and lasts forever. Put your talents at the service of the encounter between persons, of friendship, of inclusion" (para 3.9). A previous pope, Saint John Paul II exhorted people linked to sport to "promote the building of a more fraternal and united world, thus helping to overcome situations of reciprocal misunderstanding between individuals and people" (para 3.9). Sport must always go hand in hand with solidarity because they are "called upon to radiate the most sublime values throughout society, especially the promotion of the unity of peoples, races, religions and cultures", thus helping to overcome many divisions that our world continues to experience today: "Sports can bring us together in the spirit of fellowship between peoples and cultures". They are "indeed a sign that peace is possible" (para 3.8).

Solidarity within a sports team may refer to the unity that can develop among teammates as they strive together for the same goal with such an experience providing all the participants with feelings of personal and communal esteem. Solidarity in the Christian sense, however, goes beyond simply membership of one's own team. It includes opponents who are on a different team. Similarly, there exists an intimate bond between solidarity and the common good, between solidarity and the universal destination of goods, between solidarity and equality among peoples and between solidarity and peace in the world. Sport and social justice go hand in.

Sport, culture, and virtue

The required move away from individuality to social solidarity – what Jonathan Sacks calls the shift from an 'I' culture to a 'we' culture – is summarised in his illuminating *Morality. Restoring the Common Good in Divided Times* (2020). In the final chapter he asks:

> Are we destined to live with ever more divisive politics an ever more divided societies, growing inequalities and increasing loneliness, less public regard for truth and ever more determined efforts to ban and demonise the voices with which we disagree? ... Can we change?
>
> (2020, p. 321)

His answer is, yes, we can. And the way to do this is by cultures shifting from 'I' to 'we'. The past sets us an example and he refers to his conversation with Robert Putnam, author of the acclaimed *Bowling Alone* (2000) about American culture in the twentieth century (2020, pp. 321–322) Putnam told Rabbi Sacks that in the late eighteenth century America was highly individualistic, starkly unequal, and polarised. However, at the beginning of the twentieth century, the country became more equal and more focussed on responsibilities rather than simply rights. The same cannot be said about the Trump era and its aftermath. Sacks also refers to the nineteenth century in Britain. Benjamin Disraeli wrote in 1845: "There is no community in England". But things changed and got a lot better after the devastation of two world wars as people realised co-operation was essential.

However, in order to deliver change now Sacks argues that we have to develop "eulogy virtues". This means considering the impact that one's life has on others for the good, as opposed to 'résumé virtues' which focus on the self and one's own skills, careers, and successes. Sacks argues for a renewal of 'covenantal' thinking since it asks human beings to consider the impact they have on others (p. 327). Covenantal ways of doing things emphasise what people have in common despite differences and its associated politics emphasises responsibilities to each other (p. 335). It is about "ensuring that everyone has a fair chance to make the most of their capabilities and their lives" (p. 336). "And it begins with us" (p. 336). Sport can and continues to play its part in this.

The former Governor of the Bank of England, Mark Carney, himself a Catholic, believes there is a serious crisis of values at the heart of contemporary financial capitalism. His comments have implications for the management of sport at an elite level. During his time in office, he sought to fix the 'malignant culture' he witnessed and the rampant free market mentality which produced a crisis in values. His goal was to help build an economy that worked for all. Carney's *Values(s): Building a Better World for All* (2021) recounts his invitation from the Vatican to join a group of academics, policymakers, economists, businesspeople, and charity workers to discuss the way forward for a fairer society (2021, pp. 2–4). He relates how Pope Francis shared a parable when they met:

> Our meal will be accompanied by wine. Now, wine is many things. It has a bouquet, colour and richness of taste that all complement the food. It has alcohol that can enliven the mind. Wine enriches all our senses. At the end of our feast, we will have grappa. Grappa is one thing: alcohol. Grappa is wine distilled. ... Humanity is many things – passionate, curious, rational, altruistic, creative, self-interested. ... But the market is humanity distilled. ... Your job is to turn the grappa back into wine, to turn the market back into humanity. ... This isn't theology. This is reality. This is the truth.
>
> (Carney, 2021, p. 3)

Ethical financial investment, and moral management in the sport and leisure industry, would occur only if those involved saw their task in similar ways and tried to turn the 'insipid taste of life' pressed down by competitive individualism and oppressive market forces into a far richer offering for all, Carney argued The Saudi Arabian owners of Newcastle United has a Public Investment Fund (PIF), chaired by the Crown Prince Mohammed bin Salman. Some claim they intend to have a global presence in sport far larger than merely its £244 million club investment The fund manages assets worth £355 billion and has outlined plans to increase that by another £200 billion by 2025. Amnesty International believes Saudi Arabia is using 'sports-washing' to improve its international public image in the face of its appalling human rights record (Ziegler & Slot, 2022).

The promotion of meritocracy attempts to address some of the problems Carney identified. It aims to give opportunities to others by those in power and to assist them in attaining professional and personal growth so they might be judged on their skills and competencies, not their religion, social class, race, gender, or sexual orientation. This approach has some connection to Weber's notion of the Protestant work ethic because it homes in on an individual's belief in the value of hard work to achieve prosperity, governed by a moral insistence that all individuals are equal. It is also bound up with those who oversee the flow of money and has implications for those who manage the financial culture of sport.

Meritocracy, though, is not without its critics Michael Sandel, Professor of Moral Philosophy at Harvard University, has demonstrated how an emphasis on meritocracy, championed and endorsed by many Western governments, does little to deal with issues of social injustice and may actually increase them. A triumphalist attitude, he maintains, accompanies those who gain from meritocracy which generates hubris among the winners and humiliation among the losers. He quotes from Weber's insight: "The fortunate person is seldom satisfied with the fact of being fortunate. Beyond this, he needs to know that he has a *right* to his good fortune" (2021, p. 42).

Allied to this is the notion that people get essentially what they deserve. Two consequences follow: one hubristic and one punitive. The first accords self-congratulations to the winners and the second tells the losers they are to blame for their own misfortune. Luck, chance, and acceptance of one's gifts and limitations do not come into the picture. Therefore, Sandel can persuasively conclude that during the past four decades, meritocratic assumptions have deepened their hold on the public life of democratic societies. As inequality has widened to vast proportions, the public culture has reinforced the notion that we are responsible for our fate and deserve precisely what we get. This criticism of meritocracy is worth bearing in mind as we seek to understand the issues surrounding the promotion of social justice in relation to sport.

Gender, sexuality, sport, and social justice

There has been a historical legacy of injustice in sport in relation to gender and sexuality. Managers and participants in sport and leisure activities have had opportunities to correct its sad history by policies of inclusion and non-discrimination and there are clear signs that this is now happening. Nevertheless, it is necessary to recognise the cultural pressures operating on those involved in sport at an elite level and in particular, the relationship which exists between training and performance in sport and human sexuality. Jensen's research on sporting exhibitionism is instructive:

> Societies throughout history have seen athletic practices as means of expressing, taming, celebrating, or rechannelling sexual expression. This should not surprise us, considering that both sports and sex, including abstinence from it, involve the physical body in narratives of performance and release.
> (2017, p. 525; 2019)

In an era when athleticism and sexuality are often exploitatively interlinked and which promotes aggressive consumerism, sportspeople have the opportunity to resist such trajectories rather than fall victim to them. In the present body-obsessed time we witness a decline in the integration of body, mind, and spirit so characteristic of pre-modern societies in which religion played a significant role. Those involved in the sport and leisure industries would do well to be alert to some of the dangers involved in this cultural shift (Berger, 1972; Brown, 1991; Bynum Walker, 1991; Durkheim, 1995; Mellor & Shilling, 2014). Clearly, sport has gained financial prestige and kudos by its involvement in image-making and celebrity. At a time when *image* plays a significant part in what people come to believe, strong sexualised and idealised pictures of sporting heroes often encourage a belief in their superiority making them into idols for an adoring fan base. In contrast, they can and do regularly become positive role models in numerous ways.

I now move on to how the management of and participation in sport can make a difference to sexual discrimination and use John Donnelly's play *The Pass* to illustrate the dilemmas those involved in sport sometimes experience. I offer a brief reading of the play to highlight the challenges involved and to suggest ways in which the marriage of religion and sport might assist those who experience anxiety about their sexual identity. But before looking at the text, it is important to outline the issue of *authenticity* and the role it plays in modern society. Authenticity and self-expression have come to dominate contemporary discussions about identity. This trajectory might be neatly summarised as the need for each person to develop self-confidence in order to realise their own unique potential. The Canadian philosopher Charles Taylor writes that for many individuals at the present time it is important for them to live out their own unique humanity, "as against surrendering to conformity with a model imposed on us from outside, by society, or the previous generation, or religious or political authority" (2007, p. 475). When André Gide 'came out' as a gay man in the 1920s, it was not because he no longer felt the need to maintain a *false* front but rather because he saw that front as a wrong that he was *inflicting on himself* and on others, who laboured under similar disguises. For Gide, desire, morality. and a sense of integrity came together at this moment in his life (p. 475).

Donnelly's drama *The Pass* is about two gay footballers – Jason who cannot accept his sexual orientation and Ade, who eventually does. The play focuses the audience's attention on the many opportunities presented to Jason to release himself, like Gide, from his own self-imposed imprisonment (epitomised by the claustrophobic space of the hotels rooms in which he has to live), but he never takes these chances. Certainly, the 1960s and early 1970s became a time when 'being yourself' was promulgated and this applied to sexual liberation as much as any other forms. The consequences for our social imaginary were important. As the move towards the inner self and expressiveness took hold, there was a concomitant (post)modern slide away from religion and towards what Taylor refers to as 'horizontal' ways of being, rather than regulating the self to some higher being or authority (p. 481). The seat of authority became personal integrity, allied to feelings of self-esteem and the desire for equality. Here was the unfolding dilemma: If there were a gap between what others perceived us to be and what we ourselves believed we were, there was clearly a problem. As Fukuyama claims, "The foundations of identity were laid with the perception of a disjunction between one's inside and one's outside" (2018, p. 25; Sacks, 2020, pp. 130–143). When people's sense of their own identity clashed with the role they were assigned by their surrounding culture, they were either tempted to live a lie or fight against the injustice. Jason's and Ade's unease at the situation they find themselves in as well-known footballers known by the media, becomes more pronounced as the narrative unfolds and as they feel the distance between their own sexual identity and the one other people (fans, managers, fellow team players) assume of them.

Jason's dilemma is that he is terrified his 'reputation' as a footballer will be destroyed by the disclosure that he is gay. He is well aware of his celebrity status and the admiration his figure commands on and off the pitch. He ridicules Ade's anonymity playing for an amateur football team, mockingly calling him, "Ronaldo of the marshes" (2014, p. 78). He tells Lyndsey that she cannot "begin to fathom the pressure" he's under (p. 71) to maintain his image and reputation. He wishes to be like his heterosexual teammates and his fan base, so he imitates them, becomes one of them, beginning to lose who *he* is, *authentically*, as a result. Although, as Fukuyama writes "The modern concept of identity places a supreme value on authenticity. On the validation of that inner being which is not being allowed to express itself" (2018, p. 25) in the tortuous scenario Jason finds himself in, he defies the societal trend to assert his own individuality and the need for public recognition of who he actually is, to which Fukuyama refers. His self-destructive behaviour patterns come about due to his pent-up frustration at *not being* able to be his authentic self. He convinces himself that he must *appear* as someone he is not. This is seen sharply in Jason when Lyndsey suggests he is gay. He replies, "No love, I'm not gay, what kind of word is 'gay'?" (p. 70). When such denials take place "Every situation becomes filled with dangerous occasions and the homosexual is constantly on his guard to prevent anyone from discovering his condition" (p. 26). This is heightened in Jason's bizarre decision to rent a pole dancer with whom to have sex so that his 'performance' can be filmed and then reported in the press and the public reassured that he is heterosexual. Nouwen's insights into the price gay men pay for dissembling and subterfuge is revealed he argues in the tension they feel within themselves as well as with others (1971). The gay dimension becomes a hostile enemy to be fought of at all times until one day the self cracks under the intense strain (Sullivan, 1995, pp. 3–18).

Some persuasive, recent research has shown that the 'culture' of football is no longer predominantly homophobic, but this is a contested position (Anderson 2011; Cleland, 2015,

2018; Cleland & Magrath, 2019; McGrath, 2017). Things have got a lot better for a variety of reasons. Although some religious groups still hold that homosexual relationships are not morally acceptable, there has been a fierce debate about this issue within Christianity and a softening of approach has occurred. Pope Francis said in 2020, who is he to judge homosexuals and the Anglican church allows the ordination of openly gay men and lesbians and is supportive of the relationships they form either pre or post-ordination. The Anglican bishop of Liverpool argued in 2021 for the inclusion of same-sex marriages in church. There is an interesting parallel between sport and Christianity here for both parties historically were hostile to the 'gay question' and both have moved forward to embrace a far more inclusive approach over the last 25 years or so. As the debate about human rights and social justice took hold, this inevitably impinged on sexual matters and as knowledge about sexual identities increased a more tolerant acceptance of sexual difference began. During the Olympics in Tokyo in 2021 the medal winning diver Tom Daley (who is openly gay) said "I just hope that seeing out sportspeople in all these different sports is going to help people feel less alone, feel like they can be valued and can achieve something" (Ronay, 2021, pp. 8–9; Todd, 2016). The worlds of religion and sport/leisure are now far more inclusive of diverse sexualities and the debate continues, especially with regards to transgender identities.

Conclusion

I have attempted to demonstrate the relationship between religion, sport, and social justice in this chapter by highlighting in particular Christianity's and sport's resolute historical and contemporary commitment to its moral imperative. In the various modes of countering injustice and inequality over time, emphasis was securely placed on the uniqueness, dignity, and authenticity of each human person and the virtues of resilience, teamwork, fair play, honesty, courage, and solidarity are highlighted and encouraged by both domains. Sport and religion continue in many diverse contexts to stand up for individuals and groups who feel the weight of personal, social, and cultural discrimination and sometimes hatred on social media platforms. That is why an ongoing, trans-disciplinary debate between religion, sport and social justice is paramount. The flourishing of the human person is at stake.

References

Anderson, Eric. (2011). Updating the outcome. Gay athletes, straight teams, and coming out in educationally based sports teams, *Gender and Society*, 25(2), 250–268.
Berger, Peter. (1972). *The sacred canopy: Elements of a sociological theory of religion*. New York: Anchor Books.
Brown, Peter. (1991). *Body and society*. London: Faber and Faber.
Bynum, Walker Carol. (1991). *Fragmentation and redemption: Essays on gender and the human body in medieval religion*. New York: Zone Books.
Carney, Mark. (2021). *Values: Building a better world for all*.
Cleland, Jamie. (2015). Discussing homosexuality on association football fan message boards: A changing cultural context, *International Review for the Sociology of Sport*, 50(2), 125–140.
Cleland, Jamie. (2018). Sexuality, masculinity and homophobia in association football: An empirical overview of a changing cultural context, *International Review for the Sociology of Sport*, 53(4), 411–423.
Cleland, Jamie & Magrath, Rory. (2019). Association football, masculinity and sexuality: An evolving relationship, in *The Palgrave handbook of masculinity and sport*, London: Palgrave. 307–322.

Coman, Julian. (July, 2021). God-given talent: Saka, Rashford and Sterling blaze a trail for Black British Christians, in *The Guardian*.

Dicastery for Laity, Family and Life. (2018). *Giving the best of yourself: A document about the Christian perspective on sport and the human person*. Vatican City: Dicastery for Laity, Family and Life. Available online: https://press.vatican.va/content/salastampa/en/bollettino/pubblico/2018/06/01/180601b.html (accessed on 26 July 2023).

Durkheim, Emile. (1995). *The elementary forms of religious life*. London: The Free Press.

Ellison, Ralph. (2016). *Invisible man*. London: Penguin.

Evans, Jr. James. (2006). Black theology in America, in Livingston, James, Schussler Fiorenza, Francis, with Coakley, Sarah and Evans Jr, James. *Modern Christian thought: The twentieth century*. Minneapolis: Fortress Press. 443–468.

Flannery, Austin. (1998). *Vatican II: The conciliar and post-conciliar documents*. Collegeville: Liturgical Press.

Freebody, Kelly & Finneran, Michael. (2021). *Critical themes in drama: Social, cultural and political analysis*. London: Routledge.

Fukuyama, Francis. (2018). *Identity: Contemporary identity politics and the struggle for recognition*. London: Profile Books Ltd.

Jensen, Erik. (2017). Sports and sexuality, in Edelman, R. & Wilson, W. (eds), *Oxford handbook of sports history*. Oxford: OUP. 525–539.

Jensen, Erik. (2019). Arousing cheer: Exhibitionism in men's sports from weimar to the present, in Magrath, R., Cleland, J., & Anderson, E. (eds), *The Palgrave handbook of masculinity and sport*. London: Palgrave. 39–56.

Livingston, James, Schussler Fiorenza, Francis, with Coakley, & Evans Jr, Sarah, (2006). *Modern Christian thought: The twentieth century*. Minneapolis: Fortress Press.

McGrath, Rory. (2017). *Inclusive masculinities in contemporary football: Men in the beautiful game*. London: Routledge.

Mellor, Philip & Shilling, Chris. (2014). *Sociology of the sacred: Religion, embodiment and social change*. London: Sage Pub.

Nouwen, Henri. (1971). The self-availability of the homosexual, in Oberholzer, W. D. (ed.), *Is gay good?: Ethics, theology and homosexuality*. Philadelphia: Westminster Press. 20–28.

Parry, Jim. (2007). The *religio athletae*, Olympism and peace, in Parry, J., Robinson, S., Watson, N., & Nesti, M. (eds), *Sport and spirituality: An introduction*. London: Routledge. 201–214.

Putnam, Robert. (2000). *Bowling alone*. New York: Simon and Schuster paperbacks.

Ronay, Barney. (2021). Daley uses platform for bronze and LGBTQ+ rights. *The Observer*, 8 August 2021. 8–9.

Rousseau, Jean-Jacques. (1987). *Reveries of the solitary walker*. London: Penguin.

Rousseau, Jean-Jacques. (2009). *Discourse on the origins of inequality*. Oxford: Oxford University Press.

Sacks, Jonathan. (2020). *Morality: Restoring the common good*. London: Hodder & Stoughton.

Sandel, Michael. (2021). *The tyranny of meritocracy*. London: Allen Lane.

Slot, Owen. (2022). This is sport's year of shame – it must not happen again. *The Times*. 8 January 2022.

Sullivan, Andrew. (1995). *Virtually normal. An Argument about Homosexuality*. London: Picador.

Taylor, Charles. (2007). *A secular age*. Harvard, MA: Harvard University Press.

Todd, Matthew. (2016). *Straight jacket: How to be gay and happy*. London: Bantam Press.

Ziegler, Martyn & Slot, Owen. (2022). Newcastle to be centre of global empire. *The Times*. 25 January 2022.

15
RACE, SOCIAL JUSTICE, AND CHILDREN'S EVERYDAY LEISURE GEOGRAPHIES

Utsa Mukherjee

Introduction

This chapter contributes to race-critical social justice approaches in leisure studies by focusing on racialised minority children. Therefore, it pushes the agenda of 'leisure justice research' (Henderson, 2014) into new directions by critically considering social justice with respect to leisure through the dual lens of critical race theory and the sociology of childhood. Specifically, it centres the lived experiences of racialised minority children in the Global North to rethink the current state of social justice research in leisure studies and thereby forges new avenues for research and advocacy. In doing so, I follow Henderson (2014) in conceptualising 'leisure justice research' as a way of examining the role of leisure in reproducing or resisting social inequalities as well as to reflect on how leisure can contribute to greater social justice across our societies. Recognising leisure arenas as particularly productive sites for thinking about the ways in which equity and positive social change can be realised (Riches et al., 2017), in this chapter I also aim to connect scholarship with practice, policy, and activism.

The expansive remit of social justice lends itself to fruitful dialogues with feminist, antiracist, queer, and disability scholarship, and a welcome yet belated start in that direction has already been made. The focus of this growing body of literature has been on working *with* marginalised groups, harnessing their lived experiences, and advocating on their behalf towards shared goals of emancipation and equality (Parry, Johnson, & Stewart, 2013). Nevertheless, children as leisure actors have fallen between the cracks, and their experiences of leisure have hardly been channelled to enact social justice agendas within leisure studies. The core literature in this area hardly ever mentions children in their own right.

While talking about children as a social group, it is important to clarify that, much like other social groups, children are heterogeneous and lived experiences of childhood vary both within and across time and place. Recognising this diversity, it is the leisure of racialised minority children in the Global North that forms of the basis of this chapter. In the following sections, I will build on critical literature on racially minoritised children and race-critical approaches to social justice both of which are rather thin on the ground. Indeed, as Stewart (2014, p. 326) points out, social justice leisure research can act as a "point of convergence for otherwise isolated pockets of literature". In what follows, I draw together antiracist and child-focused research from both leisure studies and childhood studies to critically survey the state of affairs in both 'pockets of literature' insofar as racialised children's leisure is concerned and thereby chart a way forward for a socially just leisure agenda for racially minoritised children. My objective here is not to produce a comprehensive review of all relevant research, but to discern patterns in the extant scholarship, unearth their underlying assumption and develop a framework for future research and advocacy.

Childhood, leisure, and social justice: thinking beyond adult-centric lenses

To date, whenever leisure scholars have theorised social justice, they have done so from an adult-centric perspective: characterising leisure as "freely chosen … experiences" (Henderson, 2014, p. 341) and situating social justice issues within the "nexus of work, income and leisure" (Wetherly, Watson, & Long, 2017, p. 16). These conceptual approaches take the adult as the default social actor whose leisure experiences form the basis for theory building and policy. This inherent adult-centrism of leisure studies marginalises children's voices and perspectives from core theoretical debates, further entrenching adult biases (Mukherjee, 2020). When children's leisure does appear in leisure publications, it is usually framed in terms of leisure's contribution to children's physical and psychological development where the interest is in the adult of tomorrow rather than the child of today (for example, see Caldwell, 2017) despite the fact that children's immersion in various forms of leisure has become synonymous with the construction of an ideal childhood in the Global North today (Frønes, 2009).

Children occupy a minority social status vis-à-vis adults within contemporary Western societies, where they are at the receiving end of unequal power relations and are consequently excluded from key decision-making processes (Mayall, 2002). Cultural ideas about who counts as a child and how they should be treated in society varies across time and place. In the contemporary Global North, as Neale (2004) points out, children are either posited as welfare dependents who are immature and ignorant and therefore cannot provide legitimate knowledge about their own lives to social researchers. Or they are seen as young citizens in their own right, who contribute to their social world, are entitled to rights, and possess legitimate knowledge that can enrich our understanding of society. Sociologists have championed the latter view, arguing that children are embedded in society and are therefore "co-builders of the social and cultural structures which make up our communities and societies" (Knutsson, 1997, p. 42). Although children and adults occupy the same social world, they do so from different social locations based largely on generational power hierarchies (Leonard, 2016). However, even within the same society, at any given time, the experiences of children differ according to their raced, classed, gendered, and other social locations. Consequently, critical analyses of children's leisure geographies necessitate close attention to how children's age-based status in interlocked with other structures of power and inequality. Throughout this chapter, my focus will be on the way age intersects with race and ethnicity within children's lived geographies.

The key tenets of social justice, such as equal rights and citizenship, equality of opportunity, and fairness of distribution, with which leisure scholars work (see Wetherly, Watson, & Long, 2017) need to be reformulated in order to fully accommodate children within leisure justice research. Children are often regarded as 'not citizens' or 'not-yet-citizens' since they lack privileges as such voting rights or obligations such as full financial responsibility (see Cockburn, 2013; Moosa-Mitha, 2005). Theories of child rights that have been derived from the 1989 United Nations Convention on the Rights of the Child (UNCRC), which includes children's right to leisure and recreational activities, also embody liberal notions of rights and citizenship (Moosa-Mitha, 2005). To critically think about children's citizenship requires us to move away from the unitary liberal model of citizenship that locates the individual as the locus of rights and responsibilities and instead embrace more inclusive approaches to citizenship where interdependence and redistribution are emphasised (Baraldi & Cockburn, 2018). Such a conceptualisation foregrounds processual and lived citizenship, where children's citizenship rights and social participation are seen as outcomes of everyday interactions and practices (Warming, 2018). Thinking from the vantage point of children's lived citizenship, calls for social justice claims that are based on difference and not sameness (Warming, 2019). This difference-centred model takes children's identity as children in the here and now as the basis for thinking about rights and citizenship, which are predicated upon belonging and inclusion in public culture (Moosa-Mitha, 2005). This resonates with Young's (1990, p. 47) contention that social justice does not mean "the melting away of differences, but institutions that promote reproduction of and respect for group differences without oppression" and is therefore wholly compatible with antiracist approaches to leisure justice research (see Floyd, 2014). I take this difference-centred model of children's citizenship as my point of entry to think about social justice and leisure in racialised minority children's everyday lives.

Pushing beyond adult-centric definitions of leisure, children's leisure in the Global North can be conceptualised in terms of three interlocking 'genres' of activities: structured or organised leisure, family-based leisure, and casual leisure (including play and screen-based leisure) (Mukherjee, 2020). Most children engage in sports as an organised recreational activity rather than in a professional capacity, and I therefore include children's sports within the folds of their structured leisure. For the rest of this chapter, I will be focusing on 'organised' and 'casual' leisure experiences of racialised minority children in the Global North.

Racialised minority children's experiences of leisure

Leisure studies has a long way to go in fully engaging with the lived experiences of racialised minority children, let alone mount social justice claims on that basis. Play is an aspect of children's leisure that has received considerable academic attention, although mostly in relation to its role in supporting the educational and psycho-social development of children. Even then, the children whose narratives form the basis of most of the play scholarship are White and middle-class, and the foundational theories of play and children's development (such as those developed by Freud, Piaget, and Vygotsky) used in this context are products of research conducted with White children in Europe (Bryan & Jett, 2018). When Floyd, Bocarro, and Thompson (2008) reviewed the top five leisure journals from across North America and Europe, they found that only 4.5 per cent (150 out of 3,369) of all published articles focused on race and ethnicity and within this crop of articles only 14 focused on children and youth. Given Floyd and his colleagues' (2008) use of the broad demographic category of children *and* youth, it is likely that the majority of these articles looked at youth rather than younger children since the former has received far more attention from leisure scholars than the latter (see Mukherjee, 2020). This dismal state of race and ethnicity focused scholarship on children's leisure has not changed much in the intervening years. In a recent integrative review of nine leisure journals, McGovern, Olschewski, and Hodge (2022) discovered that only eight articles in the last five decades had children aged six or younger as participants and a further five gathered adults' (such as parents' and teachers') reports of children's leisure. Notwithstanding this sparse literature on race, ethnicity, and children's leisure within the folds of leisure studies, there have been sporadic publications in childhood studies and cognate fields that speak to this research area. I will draw on available literature from leisure studies, childhood studies and related fields of scholarship to discern the patterns of research and underscore the need for thinking about race and social justice from the vantage point of children's everyday leisure lives.

The image of the modern child, immersed in lessons and leisure and innocent of adult prejudices, consolidated at the beginning of the twentieth century at a historical juncture when children's sentimental worth became paramount and their erstwhile role as economic actors declined with the outlawing of child labour (Zelizer, 1994). This 'sacralization' of children (Zelizer, 1994) across Western Europe and North America spurred widespread campaigns and social policy initiatives for protecting children. However, these child-saving movements centred on White children, and systematically excluded racialised others thus distancing racially minoritised children from the ideology of the modern child (Wells, 2018). For instance, starting in the nineteenth century, Indigenous children in North America were forcibly assimilated into settler religious and cultural mores, put into institutions that systematically attempted to erase Indigenous languages and cultural practices (Robinson, 2020). The bodies of racially minoritised children have been sites of structural violence and disciplinary regimes for centuries.

The echoes of this history – of how the modern idea of race and that of the innocent child in need of adult protection emerged in Europe at the same time – can be traced in the way children and their leisure cultures have been differentially framed and treated over the years along racially-charged lines. The legacies of slavery and colonialism have shaped much of the social, economic, and political structures of Western nations, and they continue to imbue the structural inequalities faced by racially marked minorities today. Consequently, children's leisure spaces in multi-ethnic and multi-racial settings reproduce these larger historical systems of power and oppression (MacNevin & Berman, 2017). These questions also implicate the way children's leisure is represented and talked about in popular culture. The modern child immersed in leisure is most frequently depicted "as white, blonde, and blue eyed, plump and angelic" (Olson, 2018, p. ix) that draw on European Romantic motifs and thereby racially encode the representational economy of children's leisure. While these whiteness-coded depictions of children's play are framed in overtly positive light, with increasing advocacy for a play-centred curriculum, these very discourses "socially construct Black boys' play as criminal, dangerous, and monstrous" (Bryan, 2020, p. 673). Similarly, a nationwide survey in the United States found that adults viewed Black girls to be less innocent, more adult-like, and less in need of protection than White girls of the same age (Epstein, Blake, & González, 2017). Indeed, Garlen (2019, p. 56) has shown that the notion of childhood innocence – which is a powerful and durable social construct bolstered by developmental psychology and popular culture – "emerged as an exclusionary social practice in the US in the 19th-century" and even today "it regulates race relations by producing a particular 'childhood' that perpetuates White supremacy". In other words, the construction of childhood innocence is an exclusionary social practice that promotes silence about the injustices that many children face, and therefore there is an urgent need to transform these dominant frameworks so that the dignity and rights of all children can be emphasised (Garlen, 2019). Building on these critiques, I argue that understanding racialised minority children's leisure experiences today and thinking about leisure justice from their perspective cannot be de-historicised, and indeed the continued legacy and traces of these historical injustices are present in the practices and discourses around children's leisure today.

Existing scholarship on racialised minority children's leisure patterns relate either to differences in levels of leisure participation or document these children's experiences of leisure. Both are crucial in arriving at a rounded understanding of how race and ethnicity inflect children's leisure geographies and to ask what social justice means in this context.

Participation: Barriers and experiences

For the last four decades, leisure researchers have played close attention to structural barriers faced by racialised minorities including migrants, diasporans and refugees in accessing leisure opportunities across societies in the Global North (see Arai & Kivel, 2009; Stodolska & Floyd, 2016). Although the focus has primarily been on adults, there have been some notable studies that have highlighted factors that preclude racially minoritised children's full participation in available leisure opportunities. One of the earliest England-wide studies of South Asian children's experiences of community play spaces found that inter-personal racist encounters, apprehensions about potential racist bullying, and lack of antiracist awareness among playworkers prompted many South Asian children to stay away from play provisions in White-majority communities (Kapasi, 2000). Even when some children did access these play projects in racially mixed settings, they tended to play separately from White children or bring along siblings and friends to play with in fear of bullying from White children. Playworkers have historically downplayed racism, invoked ideas of cultural differences, and embraced colour-blind approaches that fail to fully grasp the importance of antiracist practices in fostering racially minoritised children's sense of belonging in play facilities which are often provided by local councils or voluntary organisations. In an ethnographic study with 5-to-6-year-old children in an inner-city school in England, Connolly (1998, p. 19) encountered widespread use of racialised discourses among children that positioned British South Asian boys as "effeminate, quiet and non-physical" because of which they were not included in school football teams and fighting games. Teachers too have been known to espouse racialised notions of masculinity and leisure. It has been argued that stereotypes mounted by physical education teachers about South Asian children having "low ball skills, low coordination" and being "too frail for contact sports" that draw on pseudo-scientific ideas of race (quoted in Fleming, 1994, p. 170) have crystallised into structural barriers that continue to pattern the under-representation and low take up of sports like football among South Asian children and youth in the UK (see Burdsey, 2007; Kilvington, 2019).

Rosen's (2017) ethnographic work in an early-year setting in London provides further insights into the way different sets of values are ascribed to racialised minority children's play by both educators and other children in play setting. She cites examples of four children – two White British and two Black British – who routinely engage in imaginative plays in their daycare facility where they play act as different monster characters. On multiple occasions, the educators framed the White children's playing of monster roles as a marker of their skill, creativity, and imagination, while the same kind of monster play enacted by the Black children in the same setting elicited negative responses and these children were described as scary and potentially dangerous. These ideas were also linked to their quotidian selves outside of play in a way that was not the case with White children playing equally frenzied monsters in play settings. An educator even joked in reference to their play, that "It's gang culture already". Rosen's (2017, p. 178) findings further underline the fact that "racism ... roosts in the routine" when it comes to children's lived spaces including their ludic geographies.

In North America too, the continued exclusion and marginalisation of Black and other racialised minority children within institutional leisure settings are widely noted in the literature. Indeed, Bryan (2020) argues that while White children in the United States are usually portrayed as innocent and deserving of protection, the play of Black boys are positioned as "dangerous, inhumane, and monstrous on and beyond the playground". He goes further to theorise what he calls "school playground-to-prison pipeline" as a shorthand for thinking about the link between the criminalisation of Black boys' play and the overrepresentation of Black men in the criminal justice system in the United States.

In institutional contexts, such as early years settings, the dominant policies speak of diversity, anti-discrimination, and equality, which following Gillborn (2005, p. 493) can be described as "sanitized concepts" instead of talking about and addressing racial inequalities and racism (see MacNevin & Berman, 2017; Rosen, 2017). This directly shapes the leisure opportunities made available to children in early year settings and beyond. For example, in acknowledging the ethnic and racial diversity of children, many early years providers have turned their attention to diversifying play materials – such as racially diverse dolls, play props from diverse cultural contexts, and books that represent racial diversity – while at the same time failing to recognise and deal with the way race and ethnicity shape children's interactions among themselves and mould programme planning (MacNevin & Berman, 2017). Furthermore, it has been pointed out that alongside direct encounters with racism and barriers to participation, children from minoritised communities have historically been excluded from decision-making processes pertaining to their play spaces, provisions, and services (Kapasi, 2006). Hence, the diversification of play objects needs to be accompanied by wider conversations about structural inequalities and ways of combating them.

The way children are racialised within leisure spaces and how racial structures imbue racially minoritised children's leisure experiences is not restricted to overt or blatant forms of racism which can be named as such and addressed through existing (or new) anti-discrimination legislations and institutional policies. While racially motivated violence, stereotyping, and name-calling continue to be documented among children, including in leisure spaces, we also need to focus on racial microaggression that are everyday, routine and ordinary in their content and manifestation. In reference to racial microaggression, Delgado and Stefancic (2017, p. 2) write:

> Like water dripping on sandstone, they can be thought of as small acts of racism, consciously or unconsciously perpetrated, welling up from the assumptions about racial matters most of us absorb from the cultural heritage in which we come of age ... These assumptions, in turn, continue to inform our public civic institutions— government, schools, churches—and our private, personal, and corporate lives.

A critical race theory approach helps us realise that racial microaggression as well as obvious forms of racial violence and discrimination stem from the same deep-seated colonial and racial structures that have consolidated over time and which continue to hierarchise different groups, bestowing material and/or psychological advantages to white racial groups over those marked as racial minorities. In other words, "everyday experiences with racism are more than an individual experience, but part of a larger systemic racism that includes institutional and ideological forms" (Pérez Huber & Solorzano, 2015, p. 301). In a similar vein, leisure scholars such as Arai and Kivel (2009) have called on researchers and practitioners in the field to directly engage with the power structures and ideologies that underpin racist actions, behaviours, and policies, thereby exposing wider arrangements that produce racism and racialise leisure spaces. It is in this spirit that I have laid down the many ways in which racially minoritised children have been marginalised within or excluded from leisure spaces by White peers and adults. The way to address these issues is not to problematise White children but challenge and transform the historically constituted systems of power and oppression that produce racists structures, ideologies, and behaviour in the first place (see Bryan, 2020).

Antiracist resistance, cultural heritage, and community-building

It will be remiss to frame racially minoritised children's leisure practices solely in terms of their encounter with institutional and inter-personal racism. Racially minoritised children are not passive victims but reflexive leisure actors. A growing number of child-focused and race-critical empirical studies have shown how children challenge racist assumptions of their White peers, and build communities of solidarity and resistance with other racially minoritised children in spaces of leisure. In her study with African American mothers and children in Michigan, Winkler (2012) highlights the key role of cultural pride in resisting racism, aiding children to not internalise anti-Black stereotypes that they encounter on a daily basis. The children in Winkler's (2012) study navigate anti-Black prejudice of their peers and the messages of racial pride from their parents to arrive at their own understanding of racial boundaries in the spaces they inhabit. In their research in southern United States, Brown and Outley (2022) document how Black girls mobilise cultural leisure spaces – such as those devoted to performing arts – where they actively resist racialised gendered oppression and dehumanisation. Similarly, in my work with British Indian children in London (Mukherjee, 2023), I came across instances of children who faced racial microaggression and stereotype in leisure spaces from white peers and immediately confronted them. These experiences also strengthened the bond between racially minoritised children who often took recourse of institutional policies and structures to seek redressal and bring the perpetrator to justice (Mukherjee, 2023). Hence, we need to recognise the many ways in which racialised children mount antiracist resistance through embodied leisure activities.

Moreover, racially minoritised parents are known to mobilise leisure spaces to expose their children to cultural practices and networks linked to their ethnic and racial backgrounds. These processes illuminate a different dimension of racially minoritised children's leisure engagements and provide an important opportunity for thinking about social justice and race. For example, Lu (2001) documented the growth of Chinese schools in Chicago which operate on Sundays and cater to hundreds of mostly US-born Chinese diasporic children between the ages 4 and 13. These schools offer structured Chinese language training as well as elective courses on Chinese art, dance, and martial arts among others. The parents in the study emphasised the role of these Sunday schools in educating their children about Chinese society and culture, and instilling in them a pride about their ethnic background through an understanding of China's history and scientific achievements. Lan (2018) too found how Chinese communities in the United States have carved a space for children to learn their heritage language as well as cultural practices such as Chinese yo-yo and lion dance through after-school leisure opportunities. Relatedly, Posadas (1999) reported that leisure arenas were seized by US-born second-generation Filipino American parents to bring Filipino martial arts, dance, and music to their children's lives. Various community-based initiatives like these are centred around leisure but serve purpose that extend far beyond leisure experiences and imbue the identities of these racially minoritised children. An important example in this regard is the Black-led organisation 'Jack and Jill' in the United States that provide African American children opportunities to participate in leisure activities in a safe, all-Black environment and build friendship with other Black children (Lacy, 2007). There is a much longer history going back at least to the late nineteenth century when Black activists such as Lugenia Burns Hope raised funds and led community-based projects to create recreational facilities and playgrounds for Black children in a context where such facilities were non-existent (Carle, 2013). Recent studies contend that cutting across classes, Black parents and caregivers in the United States are increasingly enrolling their children into extracurricular programmes with an explicit view to pass on community cultural knowledge, build racial pride, and support their children to cope with racial biases, which are part of a wider process that Delale-O'Connor et al. (2020) term "racialised compensatory cultivation" of Black children through educationally focused extra-curricular activities.

In the UK, Black supplementary schools have played a similar role by creating a space for Black children to learn about Black history in free weekend classes and create community-based networks (Mirza & Reay, 2000). By offering a safe environment to Black children, these weekend schools offered an "implicit critique of the pervasive unspoken whiteness of mainstream schooling", thereby "rewriting blackness as a positive 'normative' social identity in its own right" (Mirza & Reay 2000, p. 538). More recent studies in the UK (Mukherjee & Barn, 2021; Vincent et al., 2013) have also demonstrated how leisure and cultural activities linked to minoritised communities have assumed great significance within the everyday geographies of children from these communities for whom these spaces are salient for developing a positive ethnic identity, asserting cultural pride, directing ethnic place-making, and cultivating social networks.

Another key context where children's leisure cultures have emerged as sites of anti-racism and cultural assertion is around artefacts of children's everyday leisure. Although diversifying play and reading materials alone do not undo structural and inter-personal racisms that racially minoritised children face in and beyond leisure spaces (MacNevin & Berman, 2017), it is vital that these children see people who look like them represented in toys, books, and other artefacts of everyday leisure. One of the most systematic and large-scale effort in this direction was made by Shindana Toys in the United States – a company that grew out of the Black Power movement and which launched 'Baby Nancy', a Black doll that challenged prevalent notions of beauty as Whiteness (Crittendon, Hester, & Goldberg, 2021). Just as a previous generation of children's literature and toys (such as pickaninny dolls) were embedded in anti-Blackness and promoted White supremacy, the founders of Shindana Toys in California saw their products as tools for instilling racial pride and bolstering the self-esteem of Black children while also cultivating empathy and antiracist values in other children (Crittendon, Hester, & Goldberg, 2021). *The Brownies' Book* played a similar role as the first magazine for Black children in the United States co-founded in 1920 by the sociologist W. E. B. Du Bois and which ran till 1921. These movements are still relevant today and are integral to decolonising children's leisure spaces. Indeed, given the dismal lack of representation of Black characters in children's books and magazines, the UK's first Black boys' and girls' magazines - *Cocoa Boy and Cocoa Girl* - were launched in 2020 to create an avenue for Black children to see their stories and concerns represented and a space where Black role models can be foregrounded (King, 2020). These interventions in the current state of material cultures of children's everyday leisure in the Global North hold promise for positive social change.

Conclusion

In this chapter, I have foregrounded racially minoritised children's leisure and in doing so made a case for the reformulation of social justice leisure research which is currently underpinned by adult-centric assumptions that exclude children's voices and experiences. Through a focus on children's lived citizenship and an approach to social justice predicated on difference, I have mounted a wide-ranging critique of the existing state of the field and called on leisure scholars to think more seriously and systematically about children and childhood in their research, practice, and advocacy.

The exclusion of racially marked children from much-cherished notions of childhood innocence and systems of violence and colonial extraction that have played out over centuries on the bodies of racially minoritised children are issues that leisure researchers must recognise and grapple with. Contrary to popular constructions of leisure as havens of childhood imagination and freedom, the stuff of an ideal childhood free of adult worries and injustices, the spaces of children's leisure in fact reproduce "systems of power and oppression present in the broader social context" (MacNevin & Berman, 2017, p. 827). This calls for a more historicised understanding of children's leisure as a social practice embedded in a structurally racist social formation that places a premium on Whiteness. Dealing with racially minoritised children's experiences of racist bullying and exclusion in leisure spaces can therefore never be confined to the leisure arena alone – its roots are deeper and laced in the very fabric of society that needs to be overhauled. Tinkering at the edges with anti-discrimination policies and multicultural artefacts of leisure will not be enough. What the narratives presented in this chapter have underlined is the need for structural reforms and transformation. They have equally shed light on the relevance and potency of leisure as a vehicle to challenge structural inequalities and mount transformative acts of cultural assertation and community building. Race-critical social justice approaches in leisure studies therefore need to start at the very beginning, by thinking from the time-spaces of children's leisure which has been largely absent to date. I hope the conversation in this regard starts now and includes children as key stakeholders and participants in our collective struggle to reimagine and bring into existence a socially just and inclusive leisure landscape and society at large.

References

Arai, S., & Kivel, B. D. (2009). Critical Race Theory and Social Justice Perspectives on Whiteness, Difference(s) and (Anti)racism: A Fourth Wave of Race Research in Leisure Studies. *Journal of Leisure Research, 41*(4), 459–472.

Baraldi, C., & Cockburn, T. (2018). Introduction: Lived Citizenship, Rights and Participation in Contemporary Europe. In Baraldi, C. & T. Cockburn (Eds), *Theorising Childhood: Citizenship, Rights and Participation* (pp. 1–27). Palgrave Macmillan.

Brown, A. A., & Outley, C. W. (2022). The Role of Leisure in the Dehumanization of Black Girlhood: Egypt's Story. *Leisure Sciences, 44*(3), 305–322. https://doi.org/10.1080/01490400.2018.1539686

Bryan, N. (2020). Shaking the Bad Boys: Troubling the Criminalization of Black Boys' Childhood Play, Hegemonic White Masculinity and Femininity, and the School Playground-to-Prison Pipeline. *Race Ethnicity and Education, 23*(5), 673–692. https://doi.org/10.1080/13613324.2018.1512483

Bryan, N., & Jett, C. C. (2018). "Playing school": Creating Possibilities to Inspire Future Black Male Teachers through Culturally Relevant Play. *Journal for Multicultural Education, 12*(2), 99–110. https://doi.org/10.1108/JME-04-2017-0024

Burdsey, D. (2007). *British Asians and Football: Culture, Identity, Exclusion*. Routledge.

Caldwell, L. C. (2017). Youth and Leisure. In Walker, G. J., D. Scott, & M. Stodolska (Eds), *Leisure Matters: The State and Future of Leisure Studies* (pp. 181–189). Venture Publishing.

Carle, S. D. (2013). *Defining the Struggle: National Racial Justice Organizing, 1880–1915*. Oxford University Press.

Cockburn, T. (2013). *Rethinking Children's Citizenship*. Palgrave Macmillan.

Connolly, P. (1998). *Racism, Gender Identities and Young Children: Social Relations in a Multi-Ethnic, Inner-City Primary School*. Routledge.

Crittendon, D., Hester, Y., & Goldberg, R. (2021). The Legacy of Shindana Toys: Black Play and Black Power: An Interview with David Crittendon, Yolanda Hester, and Rob Goldberg. *American Journal of Play*, *13*(2–3), 135–147.

Delale-O'Connor, L., Huguley, J. P., Parr, A., & Wang, M.-T. (2020). Racialized Compensatory Cultivation: Centering Race in Parental Educational Engagement and Enrichment. *American Educational Research Journal*, *57*(5), 1912–1953. https://doi.org/10.3102/0002831219890575

Delgado, R., & Stefancic, J. (2017). *Critical Race Theory: An Introduction* (3rd ed.). NYU Press.

Epstein, R., Blake, J., & González, T. (2017). *Girlhood Interrupted: The Erasure of Black Girls' Childhood*. Georgetown Law Center on Poverty and Inequality.

Fleming, S. (1994). Sport and South Asian youth: The Perils of 'False Universalism' and Stereotyping. *Leisure Studies*, *13*(3), 159–177.

Floyd, M. F. (2014). Social Justice as an Integrating Force for Leisure Research. *Leisure Sciences*, *36*(4), 379–387. https://doi.org/10.1080/01490400.2014.917002

Floyd, M. F., Bocarro, J. N., & Thompson, T. D. (2008). Research on Race and Ethnicity in Leisure Studies: A Review of Five Major Journals. *Journal of Leisure Research*, *40*(1), 1–22. https://doi.org/10.1080/00222216.2008.11950130

Frønes, I. (2009). Childhood: Leisure, Culture and Peers. In Qvortrup, J., W. A. Corsaro, M.-S. Honig (Eds), *The Palgrave Handbook of Childhood Studies* (pp. 273–286). Palgrave Macmillan.

Garlen, J. C. (2019). Interrogating Innocence: "Childhood" as Exclusionary Social Practice. *Childhood*, *26*(1), 54–67. https://doi.org/10.1177%2F0907568218811484

Gillborn, D. (2005). Education Policy as an Act of White Supremacy: Whiteness, Critical Race Theory and Education Reform. *Journal of Education Policy*, *20*(4), 485–505. https://doi.org/10.1080/02680930500132346

Henderson, K. A. (2014). The Imperative of Leisure Justice Research. *Leisure Sciences*, *36*(4), 340–348. https://doi.org/10.1080/01490400.2014.916971

Kapasi, H. (2000). *Asian Children Play: Increasing Access to Play Provision for Asian Children* (2nd ed.). PlayTrain.

Kapasi, H. (2006). *Neighbourhood Play and Community Action*. York: Joseph Rowntree Foundation.

Kilvington, D. (2019). Two Decades and Little Change: British Asians, Football and Calls for Action. *Soccer & Society*, *20*(4), 584–601.

King, L. (2020, June 17). Mum launches magazines for black children after being told "no one will be interested". *The Mirror*. www.mirror.co.uk/news/uk-news/mum-launches-magazines-black-children-22200101

Knutsson, K. E. (1997). *Children: Noble Causes or Worthy Citizens?* United Nations Children's Fund.

Lacy, K. R. (2007). *Blue-Chip Black: Race, Class, and Status in the New Black Middle Class*. University of California Press.

Lan, P. (2018). *Raising Global Families: Parenting, Immigration, and Class in Taiwan and the US*. Stanford University Press.

Leonard, M. (2016). *The Sociology of Children, Childhood and Generation*. Sage.

Lu, X. (2001). Bicultural Identity Development and Chinese Community Formation: An Ethnographic Study of Chinese Schools in Chicago. *Howard Journal of Communications*, *12*(4), 203–220.

MacNevin, M., & Berman, R. (2017). The Black Baby Doll Doesn't Fit the Disconnect between Early Childhood Diversity Policy, Early Childhood Educator Practice, and Children's Play. *Early Child Development and Care*, *187*(5–6), 827–839.

Mayall, B. (2002). *Towards a Sociology for Childhood: Thinking from Children's Lives*. Open University Press.

McGovern, R. A., Olschewski, E. J., & Hodge, C. J. (2022). Where Have All the Children Gone? A Review of the Presence of Children under 6 Years in Leisure Publication Outlets. *Journal of Leisure Research*, *53*(2), 290–308. https://doi.org/10.1080/00222216.2021.1916799

Mirza, H. S., & Reay, D. (2000). Spaces and Places of Black Educational Desire: Rethinking Black Supplementary Schools as a New Social Movement. *Sociology*, *34*(3), 521–544.

Moosa-Mitha, M. (2005). A Difference-Centred Alternative to Theorization of Children's Citizenship Rights. *Citizenship Studies, 9*(4), 369–388. https://doi.org/10.1080/13621020500211354

Mukherjee, U. (2020). Towards a Critical Sociology of Children's Leisure. *International Journal of the Sociology of Leisure, 3*(3), 219–239. https://doi.org/10.1007/s41978-020-00060-5

Mukherjee, U. (2023). *Race, Class, Parenting and Children's Leisure.* Bristol University Press.

Mukherjee, U., & Barn, R. (2021). Concerted Cultivation as a Racial Parenting Strategy: Race, Ethnicity and Middle-Class Indian Parents in Britain. *British Journal of Sociology of Education, 42*(4), 521–536.

Neale, B. (2004). Introduction: Young Children's Citizenship. In Neale, B. (Ed.), *Young Children's Citizenship: Ideas into Practice* (pp. 6–18). Joseph Rowntree Foundation.

Olson, D. (2018). Introduction Childhood. In Olson, D. (Ed.), *The Child in World Cinema: Children and Youth in Popular Culture* (pp. ix–xvii). Lexington Books.

Parry, D. C., Johnson, C. W., & Stewart. W. (2013). Leisure Research for Social Justice: A Response to Henderson. *Leisure Sciences, 35*(1), 81–87. https://doi.org/10.1080/01490400.2013.739906

Pérez Huber, L., & Solorzano, D. G. (2015). Racial Microaggressions as a Tool for Critical Race Research. *Race Ethnicity and Education, 18*(3), 297–320. https://doi.org/10.1080/13613324.2014.994173

Posadas, B. M. (1999). *The Filipino Americans.* Greenwood Press.

Riches, G., Rankin-Wright, A. J., Swain, S., & Kuppan, V. (2017). Moving Forward Critical Reflections on Doing Social Justice Research. In Long, J., T. Fletcher & B. Watson (Eds), *Sport, Leisure and Social Justice* (pp. 209–221). Routledge.

Robinson, M. (2020). Two-Spirit Identity in a Time of Gender Fluidity. *Journal of Homosexuality, 67*(12), 1675–1690. https://doi.org/10.1080/00918369.2019.1613853

Rosen, R. (2017). Between Play and the Quotidian: Inscriptions of Monstrous Characters on the Racialised Bodies of Children. *Race Ethnicity and Education, 20*(2), 178–191. https://doi.org/10.1080/13613324.2015.1121218

Stewart, W. (2014). Leisure Research to Enhance Social Justice. *Leisure Sciences, 36*(4), 325–339. https://doi.org/10.1080/01490400.2014.916961

Stodolska, M., & Floyd, M. F. (2016). Leisure, race, ethnicity, and immigration. In *Leisure matters: The state and future of leisure studies* (pp. 243–252). Venture Publishing, Inc.

Vincent, C., Rollock, N., Ball, S., & Gillborn, D. (2013). Raising Middle-Class Black Children: Parenting Priorities, Actions and Strategies. *Sociology, 47*(3), 427–442. https://doi.org/10.1177/0038038512454244

Warming, H. (2018). Children's Citizenship in Globalised Societies. In Baraldi, C. & T. Cockburn (Eds), *Theorising Childhood: Citizenship, Rights and Participation* (pp. 29–52). Palgrave Macmillan.

Warming, H. (2019). Trust and Power Dynamics in Children's Lived Citizenship and Participation: The Case of Public Schools and Social Work in Denmark. *Children & Society, 33*(4), 333–346. https://doi.org/10.1111/chso.12311

Wells, K. (2018). *Childhood Studies: Making Young Subjects.* Polity.

Wetherly, P., Watson, B., & Long, J. (2017). Principles of Social Justice for Sport and Leisure. In Long, J., T. Fletcher & B. Watson (Eds), *Sport, Leisure and Social Justice* (pp. 15–27). Routledge.

Winkler, E. N. (2012). *Learning Race, Learning Place: Shaping Racial Identities and Ideas in African American Childhoods.* Rutgers University Press.

Young, I. M. (1990). *Justice and the politics of difference.* Princeton University Press.

Zelizer, V. A. (1994). *Pricing the Priceless Child: The Changing Social Value of Children.* Princeton University Press.

PART IV

Physical education, young people, and families

16
FAMILIES, ADVOCACY, AND SOCIAL JUSTICE IN YOUTH SPORT

Ruth Jeanes and Dawn Trussell

Introduction

The family plays a crucial role in supporting young people's involvement in sport (Knight et al., 2016; Strandbu, Bakken, & Stefansen, 2020). Families determine the exposure young children have to opportunities that develop motor and movement skills, the value placed on sport, in addition to providing practical and emotional support necessary for children to participate in formal sport opportunities (Bailey, Cope, & Pearce, 2013; Haycock & Smith, 2014). Support from the family is paramount for talented youth athletes aspiring to elite level involvement (Dohme, Bloom, & Knight, 2021; Elliot, Drummond, & Knight, 2018; Smits, Jacobs & Knoppers, 2017). Research has also highlighted some of the problematic aspects of parental involvement in youth sport, emphasising issues with poor behaviour, including parental aggression towards coaches, volunteers and young people, and parents being over involved and placing inappropriate pressure on children to participate in sport (Elliot & Drummond, 2015; Reynolds, 2021; Sutcliffe et al., 2020).

Alongside analysis of how families and particularly parents influence involvement in sport has been a critical dialogue examining how family demographics shape young people's access and opportunities within sport. Children from low socio-economic, culturally and ethnically diverse, and single parent families are less likely to participate in sport than children from white, dual parent, middle-class families (Haycock & Smith, 2014; McMillan, McIsaac & Janssen, 2016; White & McTeer, 2012). A range of research similarly has highlighted how sport actively excludes children with minority identities including: children with disabilities (Jeanes et al., 2018), gender and sex diverse young people (Petty & Trussell, 2018), Indigenous young people (Dalton, Wilson, Evans, & Cochrane, 2015) and young people of colour (Rosso & McGrath, 2016). This chapter examines the interrelationship between families, young people's participation in sport, and social justice. We synthesise knowledge from a range of studies outlining the various ways in which diverse families are excluded and can experience social injustice within sporting contexts. We then explore an area that has received limited attention to date: the role that families play in negotiating and contesting mechanisms of exclusion and advocating for more socially just and inclusive sport communities. As this chapter will discuss, families can be at the forefront of driving changes in practice that lead to more inclusive youth sport environments and cultures. We review a small number of studies that highlight the role of families as agitators, advocates and educators who highlight inequity and injustice within youth sport. This chapter concludes by considering the implications for sports policy and practice, considering how families can be better supported to advocate for and progress social justice agendas within youth sport.

Conceptualising social justice

Whilst social justice is a frequently used term and something of a 'rallying cry', its meaning is somewhat nebulous and as a concept it is used inconsistently (Fineman, 2018). There are diverse ways of applying and conceptualising social justice that are fraught with debate. Distribution is at the heart of many social justice frameworks with Reisch (2002) suggesting that during the twentieth century there was "broad agreement in the west that a social justice paradigm must incorporate various means of achieving a fair distribution of societal goods –tangible and intangible" (2002, p. 345). Wetherly, Watson, and Long (2017) suggest equality underpins contemporary notions of social justice, with social justice concerned with "remedying social and economic disadvantages, at the expense of the 'laissez-faire' camp or neoliberalism" (p. 17) so that everyone has an equal chance at success. Hill et al. (2018) suggest "social justice is both a process and a goal" (p. 471) and outline common goals for social justice ambitions include "empowerment, equal distribution of resources and social responsibility" (p. 471). Within this chapter, we draw on feminist conceptualisations of social justice, particularly the work of Fraser (2007, 2008) and her three-dimensional concept of justice to provide the theoretical underpinning of how we understand families contribute to social justice agendas through sport. Fraser's conceptualisation of justice acknowledges socioeconomic, cultural, and political injustice. Keddie (2012) explains:

> socio-economic injustices arise when the structures of society generate maldistribution or class inequality for particular social groups, cultural injustices arise when institutionalized or hierarchical patterns of cultural value general misrecognition or status inequity for particular social groups and political injustices arise when some individuals or groups are not accorded equal voice in decision making about justice claims.
> (p. 264)

Fraser (2007) suggests that justice is centred on the principle of "parity of participation" (p. 27), when economic structures reflect an equitable distribution of material resources, there is equal cultural recognition and political spaces have equitable representation (Keddie, 2012). She argues that social justice is not possible without redistribution, recognition, and representation. The focus on recognition moves understandings of justice beyond distribution and "encompasses issues of representation, identity and difference" (p. 24). Recognition, from Fraser's perspective, considers social status and the social subordination of minority groups within society that occurs through "institutionalised patterns of cultural value [that] constitute women as inferior, excluded, wholly other or simply invisible" (p. 31). Fraser's understanding of social justice requires recognising and addressing normalised and discriminatory cultural patterns and ideologies that create patriarchal systems of power alongside the redistribution of power and resources. As this chapter illustrates, for families, encouraging greater recognition within sporting clubs of the ways in which club practices and policies marginalise diverse young people is important before redistribution of resources can occur.

Within this chapter, we also draw on aspects of critical pedagogy to conceptualise how parents advance social justice agendas within sporting clubs. Critical liberatory pedagogy aims to transform both individual understanding of oppression as well as contribute to structural conditions that produce social exclusion (Freire, 2013). Through a pedagogical process, a transformative critical educator supports learners to:

1. understand the conditions of their lives and communities,
2. engage in problem posing by questioning taken for granted assumptions about those conditions,
3. engage in dialogue to propose possible solutions,
4. develop a course of action and act collectively

(Yull, Wilson, Murray, & Parham, 2018)

As we detail in this chapter, parents supporting children in youth sport contexts can play a key role in what Freire (2013) describes as conscientisation, an educative process where oppressed and oppressors become aware of mechanisms of exclusions and the power dynamics inherent in unjust social contexts. Schenker et al. (2019) suggest teachers enact social justice pedagogies by "explicitly teaching about social justice with an aim to increase student consciousness of and capacity for addressing social justice issues" (p. 129). In the studies we examine in this chapter, parents frequently performed the role of teacher raising consciousness of inequities and exclusions with volunteers and coaches within community sport, as well as supporting education that outlined alternative possibilities.

There has been limited exploration of the role that families play in challenging social inequities within sport and advancing social justice agendas. This extends to broader social policy and social justice studies, with very few studies considering the role of the family in activism and social justice. When examining young people, studies have focused on the role of teachers as agents of social change and advocates for social justice for young people (Catone, Saunders, Perez, Harris, & Miller-Gootnick, 2017; Tompkins, Kearns, & Mitton-Kükner, 2017), but very few of these analyses extend to the family. A notable exception to the paucity of literature is Yull and Wilson's (2018) examination of the role of Black families in challenging the positioning of Black students in schools by teachers and other school staff as 'undesirable' and 'disposable'. The authors document how a parent engagement program raised awareness amongst teachers and school staff of prejudice and discrimination against Black students. Whilst parents were successful in raising awareness of discriminatory practices, the study suggests activist parents were also positioned as troublemakers who were perceived by school staff at times as "accusatory and hostile" (Yull & Wilson, 2018, p. 13). This study is valuable for illustrating the precarious position parents may place themselves in when attempting to advocate for social justice for their children and change systemic inequalities.

Social (in)justice, the family and young people's participation in sport

As noted in the introduction, families are essential for supporting young people's participation in sport (Lindstrom Bremer, 2012). However, a range of intersecting demographics heavily mediate whether families can access sporting opportunities and provide emotional, practical, and ongoing support for children. Participation statistics persistently identify culturally and ethnically diverse young people, those with disabilities, girls, LGBTIQ+ young people, Indigenous young people, and young people from low socio-economic backgrounds as participating less than traditionally dominant identities (Carroll, Witten & Duff, 2021; Denison, Jeanes, Faulkner & O'Brien, 2020; Rosso & McGrath, 2016). The lower participation rate of young people from diverse backgrounds is inextricably connected to the cultural, social, and material resources their families have available to support children's involvement in sport alongside ingrained mechanisms of exclusion that persist in community sport settings.

Various studies have documented the influence family income has on children's participation (Holt, Kingsley, Tink, & Scherer, 2011; Mchunu & Le Roux, 2010). A key aspect of socially just societies is the notion of equality of opportunity (Wetherly et al., 2017). The UN Rights of the Child Convention outlines the rights of all children to be able to access play, health, and wellbeing activities. However, socio-economic injustice is a key feature of junior sport; to paraphrase Keddie (2012) young people are "not equitably positioned in their capacity" (p. 266) to take up the benefits youth sport can offer. Participation in club-based sport for children can be costly, requiring parents to pay for membership fees, equipment and uniform costs, transportation, and specialist coaching. For many families, supporting their children's participation in sport is simply unaffordable, particularly in households with multiple children (Berger, O'Reilly, Parent, Séguin, & Hernandez, 2008). This issue is also reflective of the experiences of families in the Global South, where participation in formal sporting opportunities is frequently seen as an unnecessary luxury, that is far behind other essentials such food, health care, and education (Kay & Spaaij, 2012). For highly marginalised families in the Global South, financially supporting a child's participation in sport is not an option.

Family structure often intersects with socio-economic constraints, with sole parent families often having less disposable income available to support optional activities such as children's sport participation (Kay, 2004; Nielsen, Grønfeldt, Toftegaard-Støckell, & Andersen, 2012). Efforts within sport aimed at redistributive justice (Fraser, 2007) to address socio-economic constraints such as subsidies and reduced costs may reduce this barrier; however, studies suggest redistributive subsidy approaches can serve to stigmatise low-income families and create feeling of shame for parents who are required to 'prove' their low income status through extensive documentation (Frisby & Millar, 2002; Oncescu, Green, & Jenkins, 2021). Furthermore, studies suggest that parents in low-income families may not have had exposure to sport participation themselves, may not feel comfortable and familiar in sporting clubs, and therefore lack the social and cultural capital to support their children's participation (Holt et al., 2011; Stuij, 2015).

Socio-economic injustice particularly impacts elite level junior sport participation. Family income influences the opportunities children have to access high performance and elite level sport opportunities (Collins & Buller, 2003). Whilst children may be particularly talented, elite sport participation is expensive, requiring young people to access the best coaching, support structures, equipment, and facilities. Elite athletes across a broad range of sports have usually been raised in middle to high-income families and more often than not attended private schools that have afforded access to high-quality facilities and coaching for their sports through childhood (Houlihan, 2000; Kristiansen & Houlihan, 2017). Whilst we may believe that talent and ability are key determinants in deciding whether young people progress to elite sport, their family background is equally important in influencing their likelihood of success (Kay, 2000). Alongside financial support, several studies suggest that families of elite junior athletes are required to provide intense practical and emotional support for their children. Harwood and Knight (2015) in a review of parenting 'expertise' suggests children's progression in sport is dependent on parent's capacity to navigate the sporting system and understand how to support their children across all dimensions that contribute to elite performance. As discussed above, parents from low-income families may not have had opportunities to participate in sport themselves and therefore have limited understanding of the sporting system to be able to provide necessary support.

Further aspects of diversity also influence young people's involvement in sport and shape the capacity and willingness of families to support children's participation (Fitzgerald & Kirk, 2009; Fletcher, 2020; Kay, 2006). Fraser's (2008) understanding of cultural injustice as institutionalised patterns which value certain cultural norms over others is helpful for understanding exclusion within youth sport contexts. It is well established that the cultural norms of sport prioritise whiteness, masculinity, heteronormativity, and ability (Spaaij, Farquharson & Marjoribanks, 2015). Sport remains inherently exclusionary, with inequitable patterns of cultural recognition (Keddie, 2012), marginalising young people and families whose identities are not celebrated within dominant sporting discourses.

Racism remains prevalent within sporting contexts (Baker-Lewton, Sonn, Vincent, & Curnow, 2017; Foster & Chaplin, 2017), with studies suggesting that young people experience overt and institutional racism through their participation in sport (Farquharson et al., 2019; McHugh et al., 2019). Farquharson et al. (2019) examining junior sport clubs, cite examples where young people of colour had to endure racist taunts during competitive matches that were largely unchecked. Farquharson et al. (2019) illustrate the role coaches and volunteers in youth sport play in perpetuating racist norms and ideologies, discussing how coaches in their study gave Anglicised names to Asian and Black young people because they perceived their actual names were too difficult to pronounce and remember. Further examples include less overt displays of racism, such as coaches assuming young people will be more effective in certain playing positions or have certain capabilities (such as strength and speed), with these assumptions grounded in racial stereotypes and assumptions (Hallinan & Judd, 2009). These inequities represent a particularly complex form of cultural injustice where racial prejudice is hidden behind a seemingly strengths-based approach that appears to recognise and celebrate the talents and abilities of young people of colour, whilst simultaneously perpetuating norms established through racist assumptions (Keddie, 2012).

It is difficult for families to challenge racial injustice. In Australia for example, racial vilification laws in many youth sport contexts place the onus on the young person who has experienced racist abuse and their family to lodge a formal complaint and then proceed to a formal tribunal to have action taken against this (Farquharson et al., 2019). This process can be extremely stressful for the young person and their family in an effort to gain justice and ensure racist behaviour is appropriately recognised and disciplinary action taken against the perpetrator (such as suspension from the sport, club fines etc.). Families are often encouraged to pursue informal mediation (usually an apology from the offender) as a less stressful and 'easier' option but this approach frequently fails to acknowledge the significant negative consequences of racism on all young people or put in place mechanisms to address the broader drivers of racist cultures within sport. Racial injustice perpetuated through sport can make parents cautious of placing their children in this context, for fear of exposing them to discrimination that will have a lasting negative impact (Mansouri, Jenkins, Morgan, & Taouk, 2009).

Parents of children with disabilities experience similar injustice within sporting contexts. Access to opportunity is a fundamental part of a social justice framework, yet for many young people with disabilities sporting opportunities are not available within mainstream sports clubs (Carter et al., 2014). Families experience difficulties finding suitable sporting provision for children with disabilities in their local area, particularly when families are located in rural and semi-urban communities (Wicker & Breuer, 2014). Existing disability provision may also not cater for a disability spectrum. Community sports clubs, for example, may offer provision for young people with intellectual disabilities who require fewer adjustments to equipment and facilities than a young person with a physical disability (Storr, Jeanes, Spaaij, & Farquharson, 2021). Finding provision that meets a young person's sporting and ability needs can be difficult for families.

Where young people with disabilities are able to participate in mainstream sporting clubs, existing studies would suggest that ableism is inherent in shaping the provision offered. Studies suggest that coaches' practices are underpinned by ableist discourses that result in the devaluing of young people with disabilities in sport contexts and approaches that fail to adequately support participation (Hammond, Jeanes, Penney, & Leahy, 2019; Ives, Clayton, Brittain, & Mackintosh, 2021). Within mainstream clubs, young people with disabilities are often physically and ideologically separated from the club, with disability provision offered at different times to mainstream training and competition and young disabled people and their family rarely included in club social events (Storr et al., 2021). The experiences of young people with disabilities in sport, illustrates a lack of equality in access and resources. Fraser (2008) discusses status inequality in her understanding of social justice, pointing to the way particular groups are denied status within society. Status inequality is relevant for understanding disability discrimination within youth sport contexts. Underpinned by ableist logic, youth sport settings perpetuate status inequities that afford greater levels of status to able-bodied, high ability young people.

Research examining exclusion, sport and the family has been largely heteronormative, focusing on heterosexual parents, rarely considering gender diversity and sexuality amongst young people or parents. However, there is a growing range of research that suggests young people can encounter homophobic and transphobic bullying in youth sport contexts that, similar to racist abuse, has a profoundly negative impact on young people and their families (Petty & Trussell, 2018; Trussell, 2017; Trussell, Xing, & Oswald, 2015). An array of studies suggest that casual homophobic slurs are commonplace in youth sport (Smits, Knoppers, & Elling-Machartzki, 2021), whilst Denison et al. (2020) suggest that young people who 'come out' to their peers in sporting context experience higher levels of homophobic abuse than those who hide their sexuality. Homophobic slurs are particularly commonplace within male youth sports (Denison, Faulkner, Jeanes, & Toole, 2021), frequently dismissed as 'boys' banter' and not harmful. Smits et al. (2021) suggest that homophobic abuse is an integral part of the culture of male youth sport reflective of the heteronormative discourses that are dominant within sport settings. Whilst other forms of discrimination are rarely dealt with effectively or efficiently in youth sport contexts, studies would suggest homophobia in particular is often ignored and can be endorsed by those in positions of responsibility. Recent studies reported that junior players had frequently heard their coaches use homophobic slurs and suggested they rarely challenged players' use of phrases like 'faggot' or 'you're so gay' (Denison et al., 2021; Denison, Bevan, & Jeanes, 2021). Unsurprisingly, this form of discrimination is extremely harmful for young people's physical and mental health and leads to many LGBTIQ+ young people avoiding youth sport (Denison et al., 2020).

There are very few studies examining the experiences of transgender and non-binary young people in sport but the rigid gender binaries imposed within sport inevitably impact on how welcome transgender and non-binary young people feel within sport. Young adults who were transitioning in Jones, Arcelus, Bouman, and Haycraft's (2017) study suggest that sport was not a safe or comfortable space for them.

Michon, Keyser-Verreault, and Demers (2021), in their systematic review of the literature since 2000, outline how LGBTQI2S in sport has been vastly explored in recent years, with over 50 per cent of the studies being published since 2015. In terms of sexual orientation, most of the research has been centred on gay and lesbian athlete identities in sport and homophobia with limited attention to bisexual, pansexual, asexual, questioning, and other sexual orientations. The focus on transgender athletes remains to be overwhelming focused on their eligibility to compete, especially for trans women, with limited attention to transphobia. Michon et al.'s (2021) work is also valuable in highlighting the next priority questions for researchers including the "sporting experiences of intersex/bisexual (pansexual and asexual)/ two-spirit athletes at all levels of completion" as well as "the sporting experiences of LGBTQI2S athletes from ethnic minorities (e.g., First Nations, African-American, etc.)?"

The work of Trussell and colleagues (Trussell, 2017, 2020a, 2020b; Trussell, Kovac, & Apgar, 2018) provides a small number of studies that examine the experiences of sexually and gender diverse parents in youth sports contexts. These studies suggest that sexually and gender diverse parents consider community sport as a potentially threatening and hostile environment, a view that is supported by the literature presented in the previous section. Similar to parents of children with disabilities, or children of colour, same-sex parents are understandably reluctant to expose themselves or their children to settings where they may potentially encounter prejudice and discrimination but simultaneously want their children to have access to the many physical and social benefits that inclusive youth sport opportunities can provide (Bailey, 2005). Within Trussell et al.'s (2018) study same-sex parents commented that whilst they perceived community sport would be a hostile environment, they generally did not experience overt discrimination but pointed to various "everyday micro-aggressions" (p. 57), that were normalised practices. For example, enrolment forms requesting the details of mothers and fathers and social events that assumed traditional family formations. Trussell et al. (2018) suggest these practices, whilst small, created ongoing stigma and feelings of exclusion for LGBT+ parents and their children.

The previous section has overviewed the ways in which youth sport contexts represents sites of social injustice for diverse young people and their families. It is important to acknowledge the intersections between different forms of discrimination and recognise that some young people and their families may encounter multiple layers of social injustice. When accessible and inclusive youth sport opportunities are known to have numerous positive physical, mental, and social health benefits (Bailey, 2006), the previous section has documented how these are unevenly available to young people and families whose identities are marginalised within wider society. Youth sport is a context where there is maldistribution and inequality for particular social groups (Keddie, 2012).

The exclusionary capacity of sport is well known and recognised. Sport governing bodies globally have developed various policies, strategies and interventions seeking to promote social justice and address discrimination (Storr, 2021). However, the role that parents and families play in driving social justice agendas in youth sport has rarely been recognised within existing policies and interventions. The following section overviews an important but overlooked area, the everyday role of parents and other family member as social justice activists and educators within youth sport contexts. The limited studies available suggest that families play a crucial role in progressing social justice agendas within sport through contesting and challenging inequitable structures and processes and highlighting the potential for inclusive alternatives (Pielichaty, 2021; Trussell, 2018). In the next section we highlight how parents and families act as social justice activists by challenging the lack of access and opportunities for their children, by calling out and shining a spotlight on discriminatory practices and by providing education and guidance to coaches and volunteers to provide more inclusive and socially just spaces for all young people.

Families as Social Justice Advocates in Youth Sport

Numerous studies have documented the powerful influence parents have on encouraging and supporting young people's sport participation (Knight et al., 2016; Strandbu et al., 2020). It is extremely difficult for any child to participate in community organised youth sport without some support from their parents or caregivers. As well as providing practical support and emotional support, parents can be vital in negotiating access issues and facilitating opportunities for their children when available opportunities are limited.

Drawing on Fraser's (2007, 2008) conceptualisation of social justice, families, particularly parents, can be instrumental in highlighting a lack of resources and recognition for their children within youth sport settings. Where young people are unable to access sporting opportunities it is frequently parents who advocate for provision at their local sporting clubs, often establishing opportunities themselves to ensure their children are able to participate. Pielichaty (2021), in her ethnographic study of girls' participation in football, outlines how fathers in particular established provision for their daughters, becoming volunteers, coaches, and managers to allow their daughters to play football. Pielchaty's (2021) work is also valuable in highlighting how parents and siblings lobby for greater recognition of marginalised groups, in this context girls, within sporting structures. Parents in her study were important in continually challenging the distribution of resources and ensuring girls had equal access to facilities, funding, and equipment, alongside encouraging the club to recognise the value and importance of women and girls to their football clubs.

Jeanes et al. (2019) and Spaaij, Magee, and Jeanes (2014) similarly outline how parents of children with disabilities navigate the lack of opportunities for their child by establishing teams and programs themselves, working with clubs, sports organisations and local government to gather support, funding, and momentum for provision. Studies in other settings suggest that parents with children with disabilities are well versed in activism and advocating for disability rights (Panitch, 2012; Ryan & Cole, 2009), whilst the available limited data would suggest that this ethos transfers readily into youth sport contexts with parents prepared to pro-actively challenge limited opportunities and increase access and resources for their children (Spaaij et al., 2014). Parents in these settings become pivotal in redistribution and recognition work is essential for more socially just youth sport contexts.

Families play a further role in helping young people navigate social injustice, providing important emotional support and guidance that can help young people navigate exclusionary sporting contexts. The role families play in helping young women navigate and contest restrictive gender discourses in sporting contexts is powerfully illustrated in studies examining girls and women's sports participation in the Global South. In contexts where girls' and women's participation is tightly regulated and where public participation can result in significant stigma, families were an essential component in helping girls navigate the tensions and barriers that limited their opportunities for participation (Oxford, 2019). Oxford (2021) and Hayhurst (2013) examining the experiences of girls and women in South America and Africa outline how families both encouraged girls' participation in sport for development programs and also challenged community opposition to their participation. Stronach, Maxwell, and Taylor (2016) similarly suggest female family members provided essential encouragement and support for young women in Australian Indigenous communities, establishing opportunities and promoting participation. In these examples, families were key advocates for gender justice in youth sport, seeking to support equal citizenship and participation for young women.

Farquharson et al.'s (2019) research examining racism in junior sport suggests that parents, rather than club officials, led the way in challenging racist behaviour within youth sport settings. An example is given in this research where a young person was racially vilified during a competitive Australian Rules Football game and parents stopped the game, refusing to continue until formal action was taken. Whilst racism within youth sport often occurs unchallenged, parents in this example were vocal and decisive in illustrating they would not tolerate racist behaviour sending a clear message to youth sport officials that this behaviour needed to be addressed and acted upon. Parental advocacy and activism can therefore override ineffective discrimination policies and a lack of willingness within sport to address injustice.

Alongside advocacy and awareness raising work, existing studies would suggest that parents can be important social justice educators, providing critical and transformative educational opportunities for key actors in youth sport contexts such as volunteers and coaches. Parents raise awareness around discriminatory and limiting practices but are also well equipped to provide club volunteers with solutions for change. In this way, parents become critical educators, facilitating processes of what Freire (2013) would describe as 'conscientisation' amongst youth sport stakeholders, raising awareness of injustice and then working with youth sport stakeholders to create change. Trussell (2018) outlines how LGBTIQ+ parents encouraged volunteers and organisations to consider their heteronormative practices, suggesting changes in administration forms and policies that would lead to more inclusive environments for them and their children. Similarly, parents of children with disabilities in Spaaij et al. (2014) worked with coaches and volunteers to provide education and training to support coaches to work more inclusively with their children. This included providing coaches with an understanding of disability and how they could adjust their practices to more effectively accommodate the needs of their children. Parents, coaches, and young people engaged in processes reflective of critical pedagogy, including dialogical conversations to facilitate socially just and inclusive approaches. Yet, there are relatively few examples of the critical educational work parents may undertake within youth sport context to address social injustice and it is an area that would benefit from further exploration. We turn our attention to ways forward and important research questions in our conclusion.

Conclusion

The review presented in this chapter illustrates the ongoing inequity and lack of social justice that exists within youth sports environments. The experiences of diverse young people within youth sport settings considered in the first half of this chapter is reflective of the ongoing limited impact of policies and programs driven by sporting organisations downwards, that have attempted to create more socially just environments. Whilst top-down policies have a place, particularly in relation to regulating discriminatory behaviour in youth sport, the second half of this chapter illustrates how families draw on their own resources and understanding to advocate for their children, and can be powerful voices through which to drive changes and raise awareness of inequities and exclusionary practices that would otherwise be unseen.

The synthesis of literature here presents only an exploratory and tentative picture of the role of families as social justice advocates in youth sport; further research is needed to understand how families and parents, in particular, navigate injustice and seek to make change, particularly understanding how their knowledges and understandings could be harnessed to better inform top down policy and practices. The studies reviewed suggest, as would be anticipated, that families have a rich understanding of the ways in which particular practices in youth sport exclude them and also recognise what changes need to occur to ensure environments are welcoming and supportive for their needs. This may be around changes to coaching practice to ensure that sport participation becomes more open and available, with parents becoming critical educators for coaches and other volunteers on how to adjust and adapt their practice. Similarly, families can indicate how particular practices may not be working for them and their families and need to change.

It is equally important to emphasise that families cannot do this work alone. Trussell (2018) notes that LGBTIQ+ parents grew tired of being the advocate for LGBTIQ+ inclusion within local clubs. Research in other contexts notes that advocacy and social justice work is extremely draining for individuals considered to be in the minority group (Chen & Gorski, 2015), and the capacity for burnout in undertaking this work in youth sport contexts is high. Whilst these examples illustrate the work that families do in advocating for social justice and change, we do not wish to suggest that the responsibility for this work should be falling to them, our intention is to highlight the ways in which families do this work, the contribution it makes to supporting sporting environments that are more socially just and equitable and consider what can be taken from this understanding to improve equity and inclusion policies in the future.

It is clear that if the burden is placed on families to be the dissenting voice, to play the role of educator, to keep challenging existing practices they will become exhausted. Calling out racism as the only family of colour in a youth sport setting will eventually drain the emotional and physical resilience of the family, particularly if they continue to be the only one to raise issues, and they feel unsupported. Families need to be able to bring issues to the fore without being perceived as being troublemakers or having their concerns dismissed as individual problems rather than inherent structures issues. Furthermore, there remain broader questions surrounding who is able to engage in activism and advocacy from a marginalised position. Sport may be completely inaccessible for low income families for example, who are then not in a position to engage in bottom up advocacy, particularly when low income intersects with other marginalised identities.

Moving forward, the studies reviewed in this chapter highlight the valuable advocacy work families can undertake to contribute to more socially just youth sport environments but also the importance of sports policy makers and practitioners engaging more deeply and meaningfully with marginalised families if they wish to pursue social justice agendas. There are some examples of this process in existing literature, for example Schinke et al. (2010) drawing on participatory action research with Canadian Aboriginal families to develop a program of youth sport opportunities. However, the family has been largely ignored within policy efforts seeking to address inequity and exclusion within youth sport, yet the studies reviewed in this chapter demonstrate that families can be a rich resource in understanding how social justice ambitions can be realised. Co-designing policies, coach education, and programmes with diverse families offer productive ways to seek to address the lack of voice and recognition diverse families have within youth sporting provision and can assist in identifying informed and practical solutions to addressing discrimination within youth sport settings. Furthermore, the critical educational work diverse families engage in, informally within youth sport contexts, provides a valuable framework that can guide coach and volunteer education.

References

Bailey, R. (2005). Evaluating the relationship between physical education, sport and social inclusion. *Educational Review*, *57*(1), 71–90.

Bailey, R. (2006). Physical education and sport in schools: A review of benefits and outcomes. *Journal of School Health*, *76*(8), 397–401.

Bailey, R., Cope, E. J., & Pearce, G. (2013). Why do children take part in, and remain involved in sport? A literature review and discussion of implications for sports coaches. *International Journal of Coaching Science*, *7*(1), 56–75.

Baker-Lewton, A., Sonn, C. C., Vincent, D. N., & Curnow, F. (2017). 'I haven't lost hope of reaching out …': Exposing racism in sport by elevating counternarratives. *International Journal of Inclusive Education*, *21*(11), 1097–1112.

Berger, I. E., O'Reilly, N., Parent, M. M., Séguin, B., & Hernandez, T. (2008). Determinants of sport participation among Canadian adolescents. *Sport Management Review*, *11*(3), 277–307.

Carroll, P., Witten, K., & Duff, C. (2021). "How can we make it work for you?" Enabling sporting assemblages for disabled young people. *Social Science & Medicine*, *288*, 113213.

Carter, B., Grey, J., McWilliams, E., Clair, Z., Blake, K., & Byatt, R. (2014). "Just kids playing sport (in a chair)": Experiences of children, families and stakeholders attending a wheelchair sports club. *Disability & Society*, *29*(6), 938–952.

Catone, K., Saunders, M., Perez, W., Harris, E., & Miller-Gootnick, R. (2017). *Agency into action: Teachers as leaders and advocates for public education, communities, and social justice. Teacher Leadership & Advocacy*. Annenberg Institute for School Reform at Brown University.

Chen, C. W., & Gorski, P. C. (2015). Burnout in social justice and human rights activists: Symptoms, causes and implications. *Journal of Human Rights Practice*, *7*(3), 366–390.

Collins, M. F., & Buller, J. R. (2003). Social exclusion from high-performance sport: Are all talented young sports people being given an equal opportunity of reaching the Olympic podium? *Journal of Sport and Social Issues*, *27*(4), 420–442.

Dalton, B., Wilson, R., Evans, J. R., & Cochrane, S. (2015). Australian Indigenous youth's participation in sport and associated health outcomes: Empirical analysis and implications. *Sport Management Review*, *18*(1), 57–68.

Denison, E., Jeanes, R., Faulkner, N., & O'Brien, K. S. (2020). The relationship between 'coming out' as lesbian, gay, or bisexual and experiences of homophobic behaviour in youth team sports. *Sexuality Research and Social Policy*, *18*, 1–9.

Denison, E., Bevan, N., & Jeanes, R. (2021). Reviewing evidence of LGBTQ+ discrimination and exclusion in sport. *Sport Management Review*, *24*(3), 389–409.

Denison, E., Faulkner, N., Jeanes, R., & Toole, D. (2021). Relationships between attitudes and norms with homophobic language use in male team sports. *Journal of Science and Medicine in Sport*, *24*(5), 499–504.

Dohme, L. C., Bloom, G. A., & Knight, C. J. (2021). Understanding the behaviours employed by parents to support the psychological development of elite youth tennis players in England. *International Journal of Sport and Exercise Psychology*, *19*(6), 957–974.

Elliott, S., & Drummond, M. (2015). The (limited) impact of sport policy on parental behaviour in youth sport: A qualitative inquiry in junior Australian football. *International Journal of Sport Policy and Politics*, *7*(4), 519–530.

Elliott, S., Drummond, M. J., & Knight, C. (2018). The experiences of being a talented youth athlete: Lessons for parents. *Journal of Applied Sport Psychology*, *30*(4), 437–455.

Farquharson, K., Spaaij, R., Gorman, S., Jeanes, R., Lusher, D., & Magee, J. (2019). Managing racism on the field in Australian junior sport. In P. Essed, K. Farquharson, K. Pillay, & E. J. White (Eds), *Relating worlds of racism* (pp. 165–189). Houndmills: Palgrave Macmillan.

Fineman, M. A. (2018). Vulnerability and social justice. *Valparaiso University Law Review*, *53*, 341.

Fitzgerald, H., & Kirk, D. (2009). Identity work: Young disabled people, family and sport. *Leisure Studies*, *28*(4), 469–488.

Fletcher, T. (2020). *Negotiating fatherhood: Sport and family practices*. Cham: Palgrave Macmillan.

Foster, J. D., & Chaplin, K. S. (2017). Systemic racism in the media: Representations of Black athletes in sport magazines. In *Systemic racism* (pp. 263–283). New York: Palgrave Macmillan.

Fraser, N. (2007). Feminist politics in the age of recognition: A two-dimensional approach to gender justice. *Studies in Social Justice*, *1*(1), 23–35.

Fraser, N. (2008). Abnormal justice. *Critical inquiry*, *34*(3), 393–422.
Freire, P. (2013). *Pedagogy of the oppressed* (pp. 131–139). Abingdon: Routledge.
Frisby, W., & Millar, S. (2002). The actualities of doing community development to promote the inclusion of low income populations in local sport and recreation. *European Sport Management Quarterly*, *2*(3), 209–233.
Hallinan, C., & Judd, B. (2009). Changes in assumptions about Australian Indigenous footballers: From exclusion to enlightenment. *The International Journal of the History of Sport*, *26*(16), 2358–2375.
Hammond, A., Jeanes, R., Penney, D., & Leahy, D. (2019). "I feel we are inclusive enough": Examining swimming coaches' understandings of inclusion and disability. *Sociology of Sport Journal*, *36*(4), 311–321.
Harwood, C. G., & Knight, C. J. (2015). Parenting in youth sport: A position paper on parenting expertise. *Psychology of Sport and Exercise*, *16*(1), 24–35.
Haycock, D., & Smith, A. (2014). A family affair? Exploring the influence of childhood sport socialisation on young adults' leisure-sport careers in north-west England. *Leisure Studies*, *33*(3), 285–304.
Hayhurst, L. M. (2013). Girls as the 'new' agents of social change? Exploring the 'girl effect' through sport, gender and development programs in Uganda. *Sociological Research Online*, *18*(2), 192–203.
Hill, J., Philpot, R., Walton-Fisette, J. L., Sutherland, S., Flemons, M., Ovens, A., ... & Flory, S. B. (2018). Conceptualising social justice and sociocultural issues within physical education teacher education: International perspectives. *Physical Education and Sport Pedagogy*, *23*(5), 469–483.
Holt, N. L., Kingsley, B. C., Tink, L. N., & Scherer, J. (2011). Benefits and challenges associated with sport participation by children and parents from low-income families. *Psychology of Sport and Exercise*, *12*(5), 490–499.
Houlihan, B. (2000). Sporting excellence, schools and sports development: The politics of crowded policy spaces. *European Physical Education Review*, *6*(2), 171–193.
Ives, B., Clayton, B., Brittain, I., & Mackintosh, C. (2021). "I'll always find a perfectly justified reason for not doing it": Challenges for disability sport and physical activity in the United Kingdom. *Sport in Society*, *24*(4), 588–606.
Jeanes, R., Spaaij, R., Magee, J., Farquharson, K., Gorman, S., & Lusher, D. (2018). "Yes we are inclusive": Examining provision for young people with disabilities in community sport clubs. *Sport Management Review*, *21*(1), 38–50.
Jeanes, R., Spaaij, R., Magee, J., Farquharson, K., Gorman, S., & Lusher, D. (2019). Developing participation opportunities for young people with disabilities? Policy enactment and social inclusion in Australian junior sport. *Sport in Society*, *22*(6), 986–1004.
Jones, B. A., Arcelus, J., Bouman, W. P., & Haycraft, E. (2017). Barriers and facilitators of physical activity and sport participation among young transgender adults who are medically transitioning. *International Journal of Transgenderism*, *18*(2), 227–238.
Kay, T. (2000). Sporting excellence: A family affair? *European Physical Education Review*, *6*(2), 151–169.
Kay, T. (2004). The family factor in sport: A review of family factors affecting sports participation. In Sport England (Ed.), *Driving up participation: The challenge for sport* (pp. 39–60). London: Sport England.
Kay, T. (2006). Daughters of Islam: Family influences on Muslim young women's participation in sport. *International Review for the Sociology of Sport*, *41*(3–4), 357–373.
Kay, T., & Spaaij, R. (2012). The mediating effects of family on sport in international development contexts. *International Review for the Sociology of Sport*, *47*(1), 77–94.
Keddie, A. (2012). Schooling and social justice through the lenses of Nancy Fraser. *Critical Studies in Education*, *53*(3), 263–279.
Knight, C. J., Dorsch, T. E., Osai, K. V., Haderlie, K. L., & Sellars, P. A. (2016). Influences on parental involvement in youth sport. *Sport, Exercise, and Performance Psychology*, *5*(2), 161.
Kristiansen, E., & Houlihan, B. (2017). Developing young athletes: The role of private sport schools in the Norwegian sport system. *International Review for the Sociology of Sport*, *52*(4), 447–469.
Lindstrom Bremer, K. (2012). Parental involvement, pressure, and support in youth sport: A narrative literature review. *Journal of Family Theory & Review*, *4*(3), 235–248.
Mansouri, F., Jenkins, L., Morgan, L., & Taouk, M. (2009). *The impact of racism upon the health and wellbeing of young Australians*. Melbourne: Deakin University Press.

McHugh, T. L. F., Deal, C. J., Blye, C. J., Dimler, A. J., Halpenny, E. A., Sivak, A., & Holt, N. L. (2019). A meta-study of qualitative research examining sport and recreation experiences of indigenous youth. *Qualitative Health Research*, *29*(1), 42–54.

Mchunu, S., & Le Roux, K. (2010). Non-participation in sport by black learners with special reference to gender, grades, family income and home environment. *South African Journal for Research in Sport, Physical Education and Recreation*, *32*(1), 85–98.

McMillan, R., McIsaac, M., & Janssen, I. (2016). Family structure as a correlate of organized sport participation among youth. *PloS one*, *11*(2), e0147403.

Michon, C., Keyser-Verreault, A., & Demers, G. (2021). Review of literature on LGBTQI2S in Sport. *Gender Equity in Sport Research Hub*. https://ealliance.manifoldapp.org/read/gender-equity-in-lgbtqi2s-sport-literature-review/section/7e34f561-10d5-49f2-b166-9b1be527c1a8

Nielsen, G., Grønfeldt, V., Toftegaard-Støckel, J., & Andersen, L. B. (2012). Predisposed to participate? The influence of family socio-economic background on children's sports participation and daily amount of physical activity. *Sport in Society*, *15*(1), 1–27.

Oncescu, J., Green, L., & Jenkins, J. (2021). Exclusionary mechanisms of community leisure for low-income families: Programs, policies and procedures. *Leisure Sciences*, 1–19.

Oxford, S. (2019). "You look like a machito!": A decolonial analysis of the social in/exclusion of female participants in a Colombian sport for development and peace organization. *Sport in Society*, *22*(6), 1025–1042.

Oxford, S. (2021). The role of the primary caregiver with girls' participation in sport and leisure in socially vulnerable communities in Colombia. In D. E. Trussell & R. Jeanes (Eds), *Families, sport, leisure and social justice* (pp. 74–83). London: Routledge.

Panitch, M. (2012). *Disability, mothers, and organization: Accidental activists*. Abingdon: Routledge.

Petty, L., & Trussell, D. E. (2018). Experiences of identity development and sexual stigma for lesbian, gay, and bisexual young people in sport: "Just survive until you can be who you are". *Qualitative Research in Sport, Exercise and Health*, *10*(2), 176–189.

Pielichaty, H. (2021). *Football, Family, Gender and Identity: The Football Self*. Abingdon: Routledge.

Reisch, M. (2002). Defining social justice in a socially unjust world. *Families in Society*, *83*(4), 343–354.

Reynolds, J. F. (2021). An intervention to address youth sport parent spectator behaviors in Louisiana: Lessons for future research and social work practice. *Child and Adolescent Social Work Journal*, *38*(4), 463–474.

Rosso, E., & McGrath, R. (2016). Promoting physical activity among children and youth in disadvantaged South Australian CALD communities through alternative community sport opportunities. *Health Promotion Journal of Australia*, *27*(2), 105–110.

Ryan, S., & Cole, K. R. (2009). From advocate to activist? Mapping the experiences of mothers of children on the autism spectrum. *Journal of Applied Research in Intellectual Disabilities*, *22*(1), 43–53.

Schenker, K., Linnér, S., Smith, W., Gerdin, G., Mordal Moen, K., Philpot, R., ... & Westlie, K. (2019). Conceptualising social justice–what constitutes pedagogies for social justice in HPE across different contexts? *Curriculum Studies in Health and Physical Education*, *10*(2), 126–140.

Schinke, R., Yungblut, H., Blodgett, A., Eys, M., Peltier, D., Ritchie, S., & Recollet-Saikkonen, D. (2010). The role of families in youth sport programming in a Canadian Aboriginal reserve. *Journal of Physical Activity and Health*, *7*(2), 156–166.

Smits, F., Jacobs, F., & Knoppers, A. (2017). "Everything revolves around gymnastics": Athletes and parents make sense of elite youth sport. *Sport in Society*, *20*(1), 66–83.

Smits, F., Knoppers, A., & Elling-Machartzki, A. (2021). "Everything is said with a smile": Homonegative speech acts in sport. *International Review for the Sociology of Sport*, *56*(3), 343–360.

Spaaij, R., Magee, J., & Jeanes, R. (2014). *Sport and social exclusion in global society*. Abingdon: Routledge.

Spaaij, R., Farquharson, K., & Marjoribanks, T. (2015). Sport and social inequalities. *Sociology Compass*, *9*(5), 400–411.

Storr, R. (2021). "The poor cousin of inclusion": Australian sporting organisations and LGBT+ diversity and inclusion. *Sport Management Review*, *24*(3), 410–420.

Storr, R., Jeanes, R., Spaaij, R., & Farquharson, K. (2021). "That's where the dollars are": Understanding why community sports volunteers engage with intellectual disability as a form of diversity. *Managing Sport and Leisure*, *26*(3), 175–188.

Strandbu, Å., Bakken, A., & Stefansen, K. (2020). The continued importance of family sport culture for sport participation during the teenage years. *Sport, Education and Society*, *25*(8), 931–945.

Stronach, M., Maxwell, H., & Taylor, T. (2016). 'Sistas' and Aunties: Sport, physical activity, and Indigenous Australian women. *Annals of Leisure Research*, *19*(1), 7–26.

Stuij, M. (2015). Habitus and social class: A case study on socialisation into sports and exercise. *Sport, Education and Society*, *20*(6), 780–798.

Sutcliffe, J. T., McLaren, C. D., Benson, A. J., Martin, L. J., Arnocky, S., Shields, C., … & Bruner, M. W. (2020). Parents' moral intentions towards antisocial parent behaviour: An identity approach in youth sport. *Psychology of Sport and Exercise*, *49*, 101699.

Tompkins, J., Kearns, L. L., & Mitton-Kükner, J. (2017). Teacher candidates as LGBTQ and social justice advocates through curricular action. *McGill Journal of Education/Revue des sciences de l'éducation de McGill*, *52*(3), 677–697.

Trussell, D. E. (2017). Parents' leisure, LGB young people and "when we were coming out". *Leisure Sciences*, *39*(1), 42–58.

Trussell, D. E. (2018). Families as agents of social change and justice in communities through leisure and sport experiences. *Annals of Leisure Research*, *21*(1), 1–8.

Trussell, D. E. (2020a). Building inclusive communities in youth sport for lesbian-parented families. *Journal of Sport Management*, *34*(4), 367–377.

Trussell, D. E. (2020b). Lesbian-parented families: Negotiating the cultural narrative of heteronormativity through leisure and sport experiences. In K. Levasseur, S. Paterson, & L. Turnbull (Eds), *Thriving Mothers/Depriving Mothers: Mothering and Welfare* (pp. 243–258). Ontario: Demeter Press.

Trussell, D. E., Xing, T. M., & Oswald, A. G. (2015). Family leisure and the coming out process for LGB young people and their parents. *Annals of Leisure Research*, *18*(3), 323–341.

Trussell, D. E., Kovac, L., & Apgar, J. (2018). LGBTQ parents' experiences of community youth sport: Change your forms, change your (hetero) norms. *Sport Management Review*, *21*(1), 51–62.

Wetherly, P., Watson, B., & Long, J (2017). Principles of social justice for sport and leisure. In J. Long, T. Fletcher, & B. Watson (Eds), *Sport, Leisure and Social Justice* (pp. 15–27). London: Routledge.

White, P., & McTeer, W. (2012). Socioeconomic status and sport participation at different developmental stages during childhood and youth: Multivariate analyses using Canadian national survey data. *Sociology of Sport Journal*, *29*(2), 186–209.

Wicker, P., & Breuer, C. (2014). Exploring the organizational capacity and organizational problems of disability sport clubs in Germany using matched pairs analysis. *Sport Management Review*, *17*(1), 23–34.

Yull, D., & Wilson, M. (2018). Keeping Black children pushed into, not pushed out of, classrooms: Developing a race-conscious parent engagement project. *Journal of Black Psychology*, *44*(2), 162–188.

Yull, D., Wilson, M., Murray, C., & Parham, L. (2018). Reversing the dehumanization of families of color in schools: Community-based research in a race-conscious parent engagement program. *School Community Journal*, *28*(1), 319–347.

17
TEACHING FOR SOCIAL JUSTICE THROUGH PHYSICAL EDUCATION

Rod Philpot, Wayne Smith, Richard Pringle, Alan Ovens, and Göran Gerdin

Physical education (PE) is a mandatory school subject for many young people around the world. It is a space that is experienced in a variety of ways, making friends with those who arrive to class with attributes consistent with the practice logic of the subject and enemies of those whose identity conflicts with the beliefs and values that underpin PE practice (Evans, 1986). Although this dichotomy is simplistic and the degrees to which individual students are disabled or enabled by PE is more nuanced, a growing literature base shows that PE has been a space that can reinforce a raft of racist, sexist, and ablest beliefs as well as normalising discriminatory practices and behaviours (Fitzpatrick, 2019). Yet PE can also be delivered in a way that challenges these discriminatory beliefs. This literature provides the impetus for exploring how physical education can become an empowering space that enables young people to not only participate positively in the human movement culture, but also challenge dominant discourses about body image, health, gender, and competition. This chapter summarises scholarship that advocates and accounts for PE practices that provide a more socially just learning space, that is a space where students can develop a sensitivity toward social justice that extends beyond the classroom walls.

As a starting point, all learning in schools is situated within broader societal contexts that also do pedagogical work (Gerdin et al., 2019; Ovens et al., 2018). These contexts include government legislation such as Education Acts, national curricula, and individual school communities (Linnér et al., 2022). Conversely, policy and legislation are produced by people; by individuals and groups who exert influence and conform, and by others who challenge the status quo.

Significant changes in society do occur albeit very slowly. For example, legislation recognising same-sex marriage and affirmative action for representation of minorities have occurred in many countries. We have recently witnessed two transgender athletes, Laura Hubbard, a New Zealand weightlifter and Quinn, a member of the Canada gold medal winning women's football team, compete in the Olympic Games. While these changes have the appearance of being top-down responses to legal challenges, they also likely reflect the changing attitudes and beliefs of the people. Our point is that pedagogical work within schools and communities has a dialectical relationship with the broader social context in which it occurs. Schooling has the potential to be both influenced by, and influential on society.

Although schools and teachers work within the constraints of broader social structures, they do have agency to make PE more equitable and inclusive. School leaders can select teachers who are dispositionally oriented toward social justice. Previous research that reports on the difficulty of changing typical PE students who embody a sporting habitus (e.g. Mordal Moen & Green, 2012; Tsangaridou, 2008), has suggested that the PE community may be better to broaden the types of students that enter PE teacher education (PETE) programmes and eventually enter PE classrooms. At a classroom level, teachers do have some choice of teaching content and teaching strategies. Teaching for social justice in PE should take account of the social issues facing the specific student population of local communities and second consider who should select the content (see Enright & O'Sullivan, 2010; Oliver & Kirk, 2015).

In this chapter, we review research on teaching for social justice in PE. We begin by presenting the theoretical and contextual backgrounds that have led to the emergence of teaching for social justice in PE. Our working definition of social justice and pedagogy then serves to frame the selected literature that provides examples of teaching for social justice in PE. We conclude this chapter by offering further suggestions about what future PE practice and curricula could/should look like to strengthen the social justice agenda.

Theoretical background

Teaching for social justice focuses on the transformative possibilities of classrooms. It has emerged from the critical theories of the Frankfurt School and the neo-Marxist liberation theories of Paulo Freire (Bates, 2013; Blackmore, 2013) and has been more recently shaped by post-structuralists and neo-materialists. More than 20 years ago, Patti Lather used the metaphor of a 'big tent' to signal the need for theoretical heterogeneity in framing both research and pedagogical practices that are committed to social change (Lather, 2001). Consistent with post-structural theorising, Lather recognised that multiple theoretical tools were needed to address inequities caused by different 'isms'. Scholarship that reports on, and advocates for, socially critical pedagogies has consistently emphasised how context is constitutive of social inequities that create the need for actions based on different theoretical positions (Blackmore, 2013). For Blackmore, Lather, and other proponents of equitable education, the essence of socially critical pedagogies is the adoption of multiple teaching practices that focus on seeking to create a more socially just world.

Issues of social justice in relation to PE rose in prominence in the mid-1980s with critiques of PE and PETE curricula, and PE teachers' work (e.g. Dewar, 1990; Dodds, 1985; Fernández-Balboa, 1995; Kirk, 1986; Lawson, 1987; Tinning, 1985). Seminal books focussed on social justice in PE included *Physical Education, Sport and Schooling: Studies in the sociology of physical education* (Evans, 1986); *Physical Education, Curriculum and Culture: Critical Issues in Contemporary Crisis* (Kirk & Tinning, 1990), and *Critical Postmodernism in Human Movement, Physical Education and Sport* (Fernández-Balboa, 1997). Recent publications have built on this seminal work, including *Social Justice in Physical Education: Critical Reflections and Pedagogies for Change* (Robinson & Randall, 2016), *Critical Research in Sport, Health and Physical Education: How to Make a Difference* (Pringle, Larsson, & Gerdin, 2018), *Teaching about Social Justice Issues in Physical Education* (Walton-Fisette, Sutherland, & Hill, 2019), *Precarity, Critical Pedagogy and Physical Education* (Kirk, 2020), *Critical Pedagogies in Physical Education, Physical Activities and Health* (Stirrup & Hooper, 2021), and *Pedagogies for Social Justice in Health and Physical Education* (Gerdin et al., 2021). Despite this outpouring of critical research, the teaching of PE remains deeply connected to the repetitive teaching of sports techniques (Kirk, 2009) and strongly shaped by global neo-liberalism (McDonald, 2014). However, as the literature in this chapter will demonstrate, some teachers in some schools are enacting socially critical pedagogies.

Our use of the term 'socially critical pedagogies' in this chapter is used to capture the diversity of scholarship that is reported as critical pedagogy, social justice pedagogies, critical reflection, activist pedagogy, critical inquiry, critical action research, and transformative pedagogies. What connects these is their focus on a 'pedagogy' for social justice rather than the critique of social justice issues that may be present in schools.

What is social justice?

Social justice is a highly contestable notion that can be framed in different ways (Dowling, Fitzgerald, & Flintoff, 2012). The concept of social justice is complex, context specific, and based on individual perspectives. Our understanding of social justice is grounded in principles that are not easily reduced to a single definition. As a starting definition, social justice is the outcome of a fair and just society whereby individuals have the right to participate in political decision-making (Bell, 2007). Other key principles include freedom of expression, freedom of opportunity, and the acceptance of difference and different values and beliefs. A socially just society reflexively seeks to understand how power is distributed across society, and it actively seeks the equitable distribution of resources and the reduction or minimisation of inequity (McLaren, 2003).

The goal of *educating* for social justice therefore begins with questions of equitable access to education and who determines what a quality education involves (Brighouse, 2004). We argue that addressing these questions in a socially just society will involve *both* transforming structures that create inequity at the broader societal and institutional levels while concurrently providing socially just educational opportunities within these structures. When addressing social justice through socially critical pedagogies, teachers must navigate institutional and societal inequities and critically examine and challenge these forms of oppression.

The notion of 'pedagogy' requires a brief introduction as it is a term that is more familiar to scholars working in languages other than English (Watkins & Mortimore, 1999). Pedagogy is defined as the theory, method, and philosophy of teaching. Pedagogical research allows researchers to explore how classroom teaching can be done in different ways and understand the impact of these changes on learning. Our use of pedagogy in this chapter refers to the conscious activity of a teacher designed to enhance learning (Watkins & Mortimore, 1999). Our use of 'socially critical' as a precursor to 'pedagogy' articulates our focus on accounts of teaching for social justice and/or teaching in socially just ways. In the PE classroom, socially critical pedagogies have an emancipatory goal by helping students identify, challenge, and transform existing unequal power relations relating to physical culture, physical activity, and health (Wright, 2004). It is our belief that empowering young people to critically engage in the world of physical culture should be a key goal of PE.

The remainder of this chapter presents scholarship that articulates the ways that PE teachers address social justice issues in school PE classrooms through socially critical pedagogies. The accounts that follow are examples of practices that focus on caring for students, developing inclusive classrooms, and enacting democratic principles. Although some seminal literature is reported, these accounts are primarily restricted to scholarship from the last ten years. As such, they report on current practices in PE.

Pedagogies of care

American philosopher Nel Noddings (1992) argued that "caring is the very bedrock of all successful education" (p. 27). Pedagogies of care privilege personalised teaching strategies through which teachers focus on building relationships and knowing their students so that they can provide a trusting, supportive environment in which to facilitate learning. A pedagogy of care attends to both the learning and to the emotional needs of each of the individual students in their classrooms. Pedagogies of care are shown in the dispositions and actions of teachers when they show that they genuinely care about their students' emotional and social safety. Pedagogies of care can be defined as practices that are uniquely relational between teacher and student, which aim to foster recognition, growth, development, protection, and empowerment at the individual, community, and society level (Gordon, Benner, & Noddings, 1996). Incorporating pedagogies of care in the instructional environment can thus serve to develop students into caring citizens who can then care for themselves, others, the world, and ideas (Noddings, 2007).

Thirty years of previous PE research has shown that an ethic of care is a critical element for building trusting relationships and ultimately pedagogies for social justice in PE (see e.g. Oliver & Kirk, 2015; Rovegno & Kirk, 1995; Tinning, 2016). The earliest research for instance showed that student engagement in PE classes was dependent on the students feeling valued and cared for (see e.g. Cothran & Ennis, 1999, 2000; Ennis et al., 1997). Other research highlighted the link between teachers' caring behaviours and students' motivation and behaviour (see e.g. Larson, 2006; Larson & Silverman, 2005; Stuhr, Sutherland & Ward, 2011; Zhao & Li, 2016). Zhao and Li (2016) found that students who reported high levels of perceptions of teachers' caring behaviours were more likely to display a higher degree of positive attitudes toward PE and experience higher levels of enjoyment. Larson and Silverman (2005) reported that caring PE teachers shared a common interest in broadening relationships with their students, and they argued that physical activity/PE makes a positive difference in the lives of youth. Larson and Silverman suggested that personal biographies strongly influence teachers' attitudes towards caring. In a subsequent study on how students perceive caring teaching in PE, Larson (2006) identified 11 clusters of perceived caring teaching practices, which were further grouped into three sub-themes; 'recognise me', 'help me learn', and 'trust/respect me'. The study, importantly, points out that PE teachers have numerous opportunities to demonstrate caring teaching and that students notice when they do (Larson, 2006). Other caring teaching strategies that have been identified include treating students fairly, promoting ownership and engagement by providing choice, showing concern for students' future health, and not putting students 'on the spot' (Li & Li, 2020; Li et al., 2013; Stuhr et al., 2011). The use of physical touch has further been identified as pedagogical tool to show the students both empathy and care (Andersson et al., 2018; Caldeborg et al., 2019; Larson, 2006; McCuaig, et al., 2013).

McCuaig (2012) suggested that the field of PE has increasingly advocated for caring teacher–student relationships (also see e.g. Larson & Silverman, 2005; Owens & Ennis, 2005; Rovegno & Kirk, 1995). Similarly, Brown and Evans (2004) claimed that the potential for caring teaching in PE lies in moving beyond the "impersonal, vertical, highly regulated relationship of teacher and student toward a more personal, horizontal relationship in which there is an exchange of equals" (p. 55). This, according to Armour and Jones (1998), can lead to more meaningful and caring relationships between students and teachers in PE. Indeed, Mordal Moen et al. (2020) demonstrated that caring teaching is inevitably built on developing good relationships, and that developing such good relationships is a complex process influenced by three key elements. First, teachers have to develop knowledge about their students at a societal, group, and personal level; second, teachers have to reflect on the individual, environmental, and relational aspects required for building good relationships; and third, teachers have to implement caring teaching strategies, such as planning, caring actions, and doing 'the little things'. Drawing on Nodding's care theory, the authors argued that pedagogies of care as a social justice pedagogy is enacted when teachers use their own knowledge and knowledge about the students, together with reflection and caring teaching strategies, to arrange a learning environment that promotes inclusion and equitable outcomes for all students. Mordal Moen et al. (2020) concluded that when used in this way, a *pedagogy of care* is a crucial element in laying a foundation for pedagogies for social justice in PE.

The question of whether a pedagogy of care in itself can be considered a pedagogy for social justice remains contentious and perhaps contextual. Li and Li (2020) have recently argued that "developing students into caring individuals is one of the most important social emotional learning goals in schools" (p. 114). They further argue that too much focus in previous studies has been on caring as a means to an end and that more focus should be directed towards "caring as end in and of itself" (p. 114). Clark (2019) adds to this, suggesting that caring teaching and developing an institutional ethos of care in schooling and PE can thus be seen as a form of social justice pedagogy. While we would agree that there are contexts where a pedagogy of care is social justice focused (e.g. when there is an explicit need to care for the physical and emotional wellbeing of students), we would argue that a pedagogy of care is most often a *part* of a social justice pedagogy; that is, a foundation that builds the trust needed to engage in "pedagogies of discomfort" (Shelley & McCuaig, 2018, p. 517) that disrupt taken-for-granted practices and act on social inequities.

Pedagogies of inclusion

Pedagogies of inclusion are teaching practices designed to promote participation and equality of opportunities for students irrespective of their culture, gender, ability, origin, or ethnicity (Penney et al., 2018). The focus is on building a harmonious social environment that will hopefully endure beyond the classroom walls. The rationale for introducing pedagogies of inclusion rests on the assumption that all students have equal and universal access to certain fundamental rights, including education (Borevi, 2014, in Tolgfors 2019). Further, schools have a responsibility to prepare children to live together, peacefully within a heterogeneous society by promoting cultural competence (Grimminger-Seidenstricker & Mohwald, 2017). For many teachers, the reason for introducing pedagogies of inclusion is a perceived need to address inherent societal inequities. These are often inequalities caused by inherent differences due to ethnic, religious, gender, sexuality, nationality, language ability, physical ability, and/or culture.

The first step of a pedagogy of inclusion is to recognise the nature and causes of exclusion, discrimination, and/or prejudice. One has to begin by actively seeking to become conscious of explicit or implicit prejudices and practices that discriminate. Then one has to develop practices that seek to address this. A third and more progressive step is to look for opportunities to proactively address issues of prejudice, exclusion, and discrimination prior to and as they are enacted. This is most effective when addressed with the students themselves during the lesson. Bringing issues of this nature to the fore to be discussed in an open, honest but safe environment is most rewarding for both teachers and students.

Typically, the literature relating to pedagogies of inclusion in PE takes one of two formats. The first aims to show the connections to be made between broader societal inequities and the educational work of PE. Following this line, researchers look for ways that PE may seek to address broad inequity issues facing particular societies. A second approach looks more specifically at the very nature of PE itself seeking to critique the work it does in creating, sustaining, or promoting inequities.

Several authors have reported on the former, that is, pedagogies of inclusion that seek to address the broader social issues of particular societies. First, the social context is a primary consideration of what counts as a pedagogy of social justice (Dagkas, Benn, & Jawad, 2011; Gerdin et al., 2021). Lleixà and Nieva's (2018) research concerning the perceptions of PE teachers about the participation rates of female immigrant students in Catalonia, Spain, highlights this concern. During the period 2013–2015, immigrant students accounted for around 13.26 per cent of the total Catalonian school population (Lleixà & Nieva, 2018). This signalled the need to structure a climate that was inclusive and rich in cultural exchanges. They introduced the term 'intercultural education', which they described as being a form of pedagogy that sought intercultural interaction and exchange of information, customs, and values of different cultures. The authors reported that inclusion was more likely when teachers recognising the personal, social, and cultural individualities of immigrant students and did not see them as 'invisible', and did not try to romantically assimilate them into the dominant practices of a class. Inclusion was also more likely when teachers proactively took action to meet the needs of new immigrant students without waiting for them to reach out.

Similarly, in calling for an understanding of cultural context, Dagkas, Benn, and Jawad (2011) identified an effective pedagogy of inclusion that included flexibility regarding dress code, shared decision-making, and situation-specific policies for supporting the inclusion of specific students. A further study that investigated PE teachers' use of social justice pedagogies (Smith et al., 2021) reported how teachers focussed on inclusion by using indigenous language in their instructions and written teaching resources, small-sided games with frequent changes of partners and teammates, modifying the rules of games to focus on inclusion, and the inclusion of students in determining rules of games. Tolgfors (2019) investigated a single PE teacher's pedagogy of inclusion in support of a government initiative for social integration in Sweden. The initiative saw the Swedish government move socially disadvantaged students, most of whom were from non-Swedish ethnic and cultural backgrounds, to other schools in the city. The PE teacher used teamwork and self-regulation as inclusive initiatives and chose randomised groups and ball games that often had a learning focus of critiquing unequal power relations and stereotypical relationships. In another study Sánchez-Hernández et al. (2018) showed that cooperative learning environments provided safe spaces for pedagogies of inclusion that enable critical reflection relating to gendered embodiment.

Others have sought to address the inequities inherent within PE itself. For example, Penney et al. (2018) argue that both teachers and teacher educators fail to see or challenge practices that privilege students who are white, masculine, and of high motor skill ability. Effectively, they argue that it is the very nature of PE practice that is discriminatory and exclusionary. Their starting point for inclusion is a call for the disruption of such practices. They argue that Deluca's (2013, in Penney et al., 2018) conceptualisation of dialogical and transgressive pedagogical approaches be adopted in PE to address these exclusionary practices. In the dialogical approach the cultural complexity of society is recognised and celebrated within the PE curriculum. It aims to embrace the thinking and practice of all groups beyond the familiar to think about different ways of doing and being. In the transgressive approach, individual diversity is optimised to generate new knowledge and new learning experiences. It aims to value difference and empower individuals by sharing their uniqueness.

Penney et al. (2018) proposed that pedagogies of inclusion in PE that meet the dialogical and trangressive criteria are student-centred, and include many different ways of moving and diversity in the taught curriculum. To exemplify this they cite the work of Petrie et al. (2013) who, in their project named 'everybody counts', and Enright and O'Sullivan (2010), with their focus on girls participation in PE, as examples of pedagogies where teachers enable and support students to engage in reimagining and redesigning their PE experiences to embrace forms of movement for reasons and in ways that are meaningful to them. Similarly, O'Connor, Jeanes, and Alfrey (2016) used co-construction of the curriculum and inquiry-based learning as models of inclusion. Together these approaches advocate for a curriculum that is student-focused, student-led, and underpinned by student choice, which in turn embraces personal relevance.

Pedagogies of inclusion are socially critical pedagogies when a skilful teacher purposefully strives to increase participation and equality of opportunities for marginalised student groups. PE provides an ideal interactive learning context for inclusion and by extension social justice, when it is structured to provide learning experiences where students can participate actively in suitably modified activities and learn with and about other students with whom they may not normally associate with in their daily lives (Smith et al., 2021).

Democratic pedagogies

In this section, we broadly defined a democratic pedagogy as a deliberate and dynamic process of fostering a learning community committed to enacting democratic principles (Lynch &Ovens, 2020). In this respect, democratic pedagogies represent deliberate actions by teachers to put in place arrangements and opportunities that will bring democracy to life. By their nature, such learning communities seek inclusion, diversity, and connection, not to 'engineer consent' towards some predetermined outcomes but to respect the right of students to shape curriculum and practices in their classrooms. The curriculum that emerges from such a community is enriched by its diverse connections, and is flexible, inquiry-orientated, inclusive, and responsive to issues that are traditionally marginalised in education.

Democratic pedagogies have a strong appeal to those wishing to enact forms of teaching that are oriented to social justice, equity, and inclusion. Influenced by educationalists like John Dewey, A. S. Neill, Paulo Freire, bell hooks, and Michael Apple, democratic pedagogies are oriented towards the desire to create educational contexts in which students are immersed in the values, practices, and beliefs of democratic societies and human rights. However, it is also important to note that the meaning of democracy is both ambiguous and contested; often defined in different ways because the very definition carries different social, moral, and political agendas (Apple, 1988; Crick 2002; Gabardi, 2001).

In reviewing the literature for this section, we focussed on pedagogies oriented around the principles of creating community, sharing authority and decision-making, valuing diversity, and fostering critical agency (Apple & Beane 2007; Basu & Barton, 2010).

Reports of pedagogies of 'students as co-designers of learning' in PE align with these principles. In traditional classrooms, teachers typically make all of the key decisions and take the central role in instruction. Restructuring this around democratic principles involves rethinking both the concept of authority the forms the instruction used and the need to provide for student voice in decision making (Fitzpatrick & Pope, 2005). In terms of the authority of the teacher, the issue is not one of sharing or neutralising power, since the teacher has legal and institutional responsibilities to uphold, but how the teacher structures the learning context and uses their authority to enact democratic principles in doing so. This has been done in PE by allocating students to key responsibilities and decision-making roles (e.g. Brown, Carlson & Hastie, 2004), inviting them to reimagine and negotiate the curriculum (e.g. Enright & O'Sullivan, 2010; Guadalupe, 2015; Dunbar, 2015; Lynch & Curtner-Smith, 2019; Lynch & Sargent, 2020), or to become involved in teaching aspects of the lesson through peer-teaching (Ennis, 2013; Ovens, 2014). In general, these studies report that students engaged productively in co-designing their PE experience, with students enjoying having a voice in and ownership of how the lessons were run. Students also report finding the lessons more meaningful (Gibbons, 2009; Lynch & Curtner-Smith, 2019; Lynch & Sargent, 2020). However, while such a pedagogy can give students legitimate responsibility and power, it is also noted that it was not without its challenges. The key issue related to the need for professional development to support this approach, particularly in respect to how sharing authority should be negotiated in respect to the teacher's agenda for content and citizenship education (Browne et al. 2004).

The largest body of literature that embraces principles of democracy is 'Activist Pedagogies'. *Activism* refers to actions designed to effect social change. In relation to the context of education, an activist educator begins from a philosophical position that begins with questions of justice, democracy, and ethics with a desire to create spaces for social change (Luguetti & McLachlan, 2021). Seminal accounts of activist pedagogies incorporate principles of student co-design of learning with an explicit intention to help these girls to name and critique the meaning of their bodies (Oliver, 2001; Oliver & Lalik, 2001). The focus on girls in PE builds on longstanding research that suggests that PE is dominated by boys (Butler, 1993; Fagrel, Larsson, & Redelius, 2012; Oliver & Kirk, 2015; Parker & Curtner-Smith, 2012) and, as a result, that girls are marginalised in the subject.

More recent accounts of activist pedagogy focus on increasing the relevance of PE for girls with the ultimate goal being that they come to value a physically active life (Oliver and Kirk (2015). Kirk et al. (2018) suggest that activist pedagogies in PE aspire to help girls to identify, name and transform barriers to their physical activity enjoyment and participation "in order to increase their opportunities, interest and motivation for engaging in physical activity" (p. 234).

Activist pedagogies focus on addressing issues at the local level using local resources and are situated in local curriculum (Kirk et al., 2018). The key elements of activist pedagogies are student centred pedagogy, pedagogies of embodiment, inquiry-based education centred in action, and teachers who actively listen and respond over time to student voice in democratic ways (Lamb, Oliver, & Kirk, 2018; Luguetti, Kirk & Oliver, 2019; Walseth, Engebretsen, & Elvebakk, 2018).

The starting point in all reports of activist pedagogies is dialogue between teachers and students and between students that is designed to name inequities (Enright & O'Sullivan, 2010; Oliver, 2001), and co-construct the PE curriculum based on attempts to address these inequities. All accounts of activist pedagogies reported that this initial phase is built on a foundation of trust and mutual respect, and an ethic of care (Luguetti, Kirk, & Oliver, 2019). Many scholars have reported that both students and teachers recognise the importance of trust (Howley & O'Sullivan, 2020; Kirk et al., 2018; Oliver & Kirk, 2015). At this stage, teachers and researchers have used a range of strategies including group discussions, small focus groups, informal conversations, scrapbooking, and magazine exploration to elicit student voice that focuses on critical inquiry about bodies, identifying barriers to participation, and leads to the co-construction of subsequent PE programme content, tasks, and objectives (Guadalupe & Curtner-Smith, 2020; Oliver & Kirk, 2015).

In order to broaden the horizons of students in regard to the possibilities of PE, many activist teachers have taught a number of 'taster lessons' so that pupils could sample new and novel activities (Lamb, Oliver, & Kirk, 2018). These taster lessons provide pupils with spaces to explore alternative practices to traditional forms of PE (Kirk, et al., 2018; Walseth et al., 2018) including activities such as boxercise, yoga, tae kwon-do, body conditioning, urban orienteering, touch rugby, football, HIIT workouts, Zumba, hip hop dancing and spinning (Lamb, Oliver, & Kirk, 2018). Building on these taster lessons, activist approaches have included the co-construction of thematic units of work. These units typically move away from sports context (Lamb, Oliver, & Kirk, 2018; Walseth et al., 2018), instead including student-selected activities such as walking, fitness for football, designing your own programme, learner-centred games-based approaches, and students and teacher negotiated content and objectives (Guadalupe & Curtner-Smith, 2019).

In addition to applying the principles of democracy, activist work in PE engages adolescents in critically exploring their embodiment (e.g. Enright and O'Sullivan, 2013; Hamzeh, 2011; Oliver & Lalik, 2001). Oliver and Lalik (2004) suggest that activist teaching with girls helps them to "name the discourses that shape their lives and regulate their bodies ... [in order to support] girls' efforts to develop strategies for identifying, resisting, and disrupting forms of enculturation that threaten their health and limit their life chances" (162–163).

With respect to linking democratic pedagogies to social justice, the intention is to develop students' ability to participate in democratic processes by experiencing democratic processes in their classrooms. The second aim is to foster a critical agency that enables students to use their subject-matter knowledge to read their worlds differently, identify inequities, and act on injustice in their lives and community.

Conclusion

The PE space is not one that many would immediately associate with social justice and transformation. Although many adults likely enjoyed PE, their memories might revolve around the requirements to perform drills or skills in front of their peers, conform to rules and instructions, didactic – perhaps authoritarian – teaching styles, requirements to wear the correct uniform, and, the repeated use of competitive sporting games that produced divisions between winners and losers. As this chapter has illustrated, the early socially critical PE research tended to reveal how PE acted to entrench various sets of inequitable power relations (e.g. in relation to genders, sexualities, ethnicities, abilities, and bodies). In the last decade, however, there has been considerable growth in literature that has moved beyond critique, instead focussing on how PE is used as a space to challenge social injustices and minimise harmful relations of power and work to promote social transformation (e.g. Gerdin et al., 2021; Kirk, 2020; Robinson & Randall, 2016; Pringle, Larsson, & Gerdin, 2018; Stirrup & Hooper, 2021; Walton-Fisette, Sutherland, & Hill, 2019). In this concluding section we synthesise key findings from the literature we have reviewed in this chapter and offer ways forward for enhancing social justice in PE contexts.

Our chapter reveals that the broad principles that underpin social justice (e.g. involvement in political decisions, freedoms of opportunity and expression, and promotion of diversity and inclusion) are closely related to the teaching strategies employed within the pedagogies of care, inclusion, and democracy. These related teaching strategies, for example, primarily focus on: (i) shared power and decision-making between teachers and students (e.g. Brown & Evans, 2004; Dagkas, Benn & Jawad, 2011; Enright and O'Sullivan, 2010; Fitzpatrick & Pope, 2005; Oliver, 2001; Lynch & Ovens, 2020; Smith et al., 2021); (ii) approaches that value diversity (e.g. DeLuca, 2013; Leseth & Engelsrud, 2019; Torres & Fernández, 2015) and (iii) strategies that recognise the importance of cultural and individual differences (e.g. Apple & Beane, 2007; Basu & Barton, 2010; Dagkas, Benn, & Jawad, 2011; Leseth & Engelsrud, 2019; Torres & Fernández, 2015), and (iv) strategies to build trusting relationships and supportive learning environments (Caldeborg et al., 2019; McCuaig et al., 2013; Mordal Moen et al., 2020). Moreover, the specific tasks that teachers employ to enact these broader teaching strategies include, as key examples: having students in key decision-making roles (Browne et al. 2004; Lamb, Oliver, & Kirk, 2018; Smith et al., 2021), the use of group discussions and small focus groups (Oliver, 2001; Walseth et al., 2018), the related co-construction of PE tasks and objectives (Guadalupe & Curtner-Smith, 2020), the use of randomised groups (Tolgfors, 2019), employment of indigenous language (Smith et al., 2021), and the use of cooperative learning (Sánchez-Hernández et al., 2018) and peer-teaching tasks (Ennis, 2013; Ovens, 2014).

Overall, these accounts merge *student-centred pedagogies* with teaching/teachers that actively demonstrate care for their students and respond to student voice in democratic ways. In other words, these socially critical teaching pedagogies demonstrate the enactment of principles of quality teaching that we have long known about and that have been promoted for various school subjects. Indeed, we recognise that calls for student-centred teaching strategies have stemmed from the foundational educational and learning theorists of Piaget, Dewey, and Vygotsky. Hence, these teaching philosophies and strategies have been promoted for decades.

This recognition raises the prime question of whether the recommended socially critical pedagogies are specifically innovative and relevant for promoting social justice and transformation within the PE context? Relatedly, at this point in time, we are unsure about the effectiveness of these teaching strategies for promoting social justice, as very few researchers have specifically examined the short or long-term impact of these teaching methods on the promotion of social justice. Future research, accordingly, should examine the consequence of employing these teaching strategies with respect to their impact on student understanding of social issues and their subsequent values, beliefs and actions.

Relatedly we suggest that critical PE researchers need to provide more specific details with respect to the teaching approaches they recommend for producing social justice. For example, the literature associated with 'pedagogies of care' offered insights into how teachers can develop a trusting and supportive classroom environment in which students feel accepted and cared for and, correspondingly, how these environments can enhance student learning and motivation (Noddings, 2013). Yet the process that illustrates how the production of a caring educational environment can also result in the production of social justice is less clear. More specifically, the details of the teaching strategies required to create caring contexts that simultaneously foster social justice are absent. Yet such details are crucial if we want to encourage PE teachers to adopt strategies that promote social justice and transformation. Importantly, we should not simply accept that the production of a caring educational context will somehow result in the production of critically aware students that challenge social injustices.

From our educational experiences we are aware that if we desire to challenge existing social injustices, teachers are required to confront students' existing values, attitudes, and behaviours. Accounts within PETE that articulate strategies and the associated challenges are well documented (see e.g. Cameron, 2012; Clark, 2019; Shelley & McCuaig, 2018), yet scholarship from school PE is less common (for exceptions see Fitzpatrick & Russell, 2015; Philpot et al., 2021). PE teachers, for example, should challenge racist, sexist, or homophobic attitudes if they arise in a teaching situation and, more specifically, design lessons that actively challenge such beliefs. Yet this process of challenging such beliefs could be upsetting for some students and these students may not feel accepted, included, or cared for. Hence, the pedagogical issue of how to create a caring and inclusive educational context that also challenges injustices is a complex teaching task. We would welcome more research into understanding how pedagogies of care rub up against "pedagogies of discomfort" (Shelley & McCuaig, 2018, p. 517) so that we can understand how pedagogies of care and social activism can be mutually enacted.

In recognising the importance of detailing how specific teaching strategies can promote social justice, we have been motivated by the activist pedagogical approaches; as these approaches are specifically designed to effect students and social change. Ultimately, teaching practices need to be influenced by a critical agenda to be considered a pedagogy for social justice. Indeed, activist pedagogies promote a critical consciousness (Freire, 1970) through which students can *learn* to identify and name social problems but are also provided with strategies and tools to act upon injustices in their lives and/or communities. Oliver and Lalik (2004), as an example, designed an activist pedagogy to encourage girls to identify gendered discourses that control aspects of their lives and bodies. The aim being that once girls could identify these discourses, they were then in a position to resist and/or disrupt the power/knowledge relationships associated with these sexist discourses.

We are aware that within our chapter, we have discussed the various socially critical pedagogies separately and have perhaps run the risk of suggesting that these are models of practice that should be enacted separately and regardless of context. In contrast, we recognise the benefits of combining these pedagogies in order to produce a critical teaching arsenal with more impact. We are reminded that the emerging body of literature suggests that pedagogies of care, social inclusion, democracy, and activism are all foundations of practice (Fitzpatrick, 2013; Lamb, Oliver, & Kirk, 2018; Lynch & Curtner-Smith, 2019; Philpot et al., 2021).

The attempt to promote new styles of teaching, as particularly centred on social justice issues, is a challenge for schools, students, and teachers. Teaching for social justice through socially critical pedagogies requires teachers to recognise and reflect on the challenges for themselves and their students. Teachers in many studies have reported that the pedagogical changes are time consuming (Oliver et al., 2018). The power shift required in implementing democratic pedagogies is challenging for teachers as they fear losing control and are insecure when moving away from direct teaching (Guadalupe & Curtner-Smith, 2020; Howley & O'Sullivan, 2021) and second, they are uncertain about how to use students voice to guide their pedagogical decisions (Oliver et al., 2018). Additional challenges include the perceptions of quality PE from the administrators and colleagues. Given that PE remains predominantly teacher directed and prescribed, students take a while to believe that their voices could serve to shape their own learning experiences (Howley & O'Sullivan, 2021).

In conclusion, there is much philosophical, theoretical, and empirical work to be done in this critical research space. As a starting point, if we really want to use PE to foster social justice and transformation, we need to reconceptualise the broader aims and goals of PE within policies such as national PE curricula. If we continue to think that the 'ultimate goal' of PE, as Oliver and Kirk (2015) suggest, is to encourage pupils to value a physically active lifestyle – we wonder whether the emphasis on physical activity will overwhelm the concern with social justice? Finally, there is no-one-size-fits all socially critical pedagogy or best organisational structure that works in all contexts (Howley & O'Sullivan, 2020; Lamb, Oliver, & Kirk, 2018). At the heart of socially critical pedagogy is a commitment to social justice and providing a space to name and act on inequities (Freire, 1970). For PE teachers who come to classrooms with an emotional commitment that is coherent with teaching for social justice, the literature in this chapter suggests that there are tangible examples of socially critical pedagogies that offer a possibility of making a real difference.

References

Andersson, J., Öhman, M., & Garrison, J. (2018). Physical education teaching as a caring act—Techniques of bodily touch and the paradox of caring. *Sport, Education and Society*, *23*(6), 591–606.
Apple, M. (1988). *Teachers and texts*. New York: Routledge.
Apple, M. W., & Beane, J. A. (Eds). (2007). *Democratic schools: Lessons in powerful education*. Portsmouth, NH: Heinemann.
Armour, K. M., & Jones, R. L. (1998). *Physical education teachers' lives and careers: PE, sport and educational status*. London: Falmer Press.
Basu, S. J., & Barton, A. C. (2010). A researcher–student–teacher model for democratic science pedagogy: Connections to community, shared authority, and critical science agency. *Equity & Excellence in Education*, *43*(1), 72–87.
Bates, R. (2013). Education and social justice: A critical social theory perspective. In B. Irby, G. Brown, R. Lara-Alecio, & S. Jackson (Eds), *The handbook of educational theories* (pp. 1011–1021). Charlotte, NC: Information Age.
Bell, L. (2007). *Theoretical foundations for social justice education*. New York: Routledge.
Blackmore, J. (2013). Social justice in education: A theoretical overview. In B. Irby, G. Brown, R. Lara-Alecio, & S. Jackson (Eds), *The handbook of educational theories* (pp. 1001–1010). Charlotte, NC: Information Age Publishing.
Brighouse, H. (2004). What's wrong with privatising schools? *Journal of Philosophy of Education*, *38*(4), 617–631.
Brown, D. & Evans, J. (2004). Reproducing gender? Intergenerational links and the male PE teacher as a cultural conduit in teaching physical education. *Journal of Teaching in Physical Education*, *23*, 48–70.
Browne, T. B., Carlson, T. B., & Hastie, P. A. (2004). A comparison of rugby seasons presented in traditional and sport education formats. *European Physical Education Review*, *10*(2), 199–214.
Brubaker, N., & Ovens, A. (2012). Implementing individualized grading contracts: Perspectives of two teacher educators. In J. R. Young, L. B. Erickson, & S. Pinnegar (Eds), *Extending inquiry communities: Illuminating teacher education through self-study. Proceedings of the 9th International Conference on Self-Study of Teacher Education Practices*, Herstmonceux Castle, East Sussex, England. Provo, UT: Brigham Young University.
Butler, J. (1993). *Bodies that matter. On the discursive limits of 'sex'*. New York: Routledge.
Caldeborg, A., Maivorsdotter, N., & Öhman, M. (2019). Touching the didactic contract—A student perspective on intergenerational touch in PE. *Sport, Education and Society*, *24*(3), 256–268.
Cameron, E. (2012). DE/REconstructing my athlete-student-teacher self: A critical autoethnography of resistance in physical education teacher education (PETE). *Revue phénEPS/PHEnex Journal*, *4*(2), 1–6.
Carlson, T. B., & Hastie, P. A. (2003). The infusion of participatory democracy in a season of sport education. *ACHPER Australia Healthy Lifestyles Journal*, *51*(1), 17–20.
Cho, S. (2006). On language of possibility: Revisiting critical pedagogy. In: C. Rossatto, R. L. Allen, & M. Pruyn (Eds), *Reinventing critical pedagogy: Widening the circle of anti-oppressin education* (pp. 125–141). New York: Rowman and Littlefield.
Clark, L. (2019). The way they care: An ethnography of social justice physical education teacher education. *The Teacher Educator*, *54*(2), 145–170.

Cothran, D. J., & Ennis, C. D. (1999). Alone in a crowd: Meeting students' needs for relevance and connection in urban high school physical education. *Journal of Teaching in Physical Education, 18*(2), 234–247.

Cothran, D. J., & Ennis, C. D. (2000). Building bridges to student engagement: Communicating respect and care for students in urban high schools. *Journal of Research & Development in Education*.

Crick, B. (2002). *Democracy: A very short introduction*. Oxford: OUP.

Dagkas, S., Benn, T., & Jawad, H. (2011). Multiple voices: Improving participation of Muslim girls in physical education and school sport. *Sport, Education and Society, 16*(2), 223–239.

DeLuca, C. (2013). Toward an interdisciplinary framework for educational inclusivity. *Canadian Journal of Education, 36*(1), 305–348.

Dewar, A. (1990). Oppression and privilege in physical education: Struggles in the negotiation of gender in a university programme. In D. Kirk, & R. Tinning (Eds), *Physical education, curriculum and culture: Critical issues in contemporary society* (pp. 67–100). London: The Falmer Press.

Dodds, P. (1985). Are hunters of the functional curriculum seeking quarks or snarks? *Journal of Teaching in Physical Education, 4*, 91–99.

Dowling, F., Fitzgerald, H., & Flintoff, A. (2012). *Equity and difference in physical education, youth sport and health: A narrative approach*. New York: Routledge.

Dunbar, J. (2015). *Playful education: An autoethnographic self-study of a health and sport science academy* [Unpublished master's thesis]. The University of Auckland.

Ennis, C. D. (1999). Creating a culturally relevant curriculum for disengaged girls. *Sport, Education and Society, 4*(1), 31–49.

Ennis, C. D. (2013). Implementing meaningful, educative curricula, and assessment in complex school environments. *Sport, Education and Society, 18*(1): 115–120.

Ennis, C. D., Cothran, D. J., Davidson, K. S., Loftus, S. J., Owens, L., Swanson, L., & Hopsicker, P. (1997). Implementing curriculum within a context of fear and disengagement. *Journal of Teaching in Physical Education, 17*(1), 52–71.

Enright, E., & O'Sullivan, M. (2010). 'Can I do it in my pyjamas?' Negotiating a physical education curriculum with teenage girls. *European Physical Education Review, 16*(3), 203–222.

Enright, E., & O'Sullivan, M. (2013). "Now, I'm magazine detective the whole time": Listening and responding to young people's complex experiences of popular physical culture. *Journal of Teaching in Physical Education, 32*(4), 394–418.

Evans, J. (Ed.) (1986). *Physical education, sport and schooling: Studies in the sociology of physical education*. London: Falmer.

Fagrell, B., Larsson, H., & Redelius, K. (2012). The game within the game: Girls' underperforming position in *Physical Education*. *Gender and Education, 24*(1), 101–118.

Fernández-Balboa, J. M. (1995). Reclaiming physical education in higher education through critical pedagogy. *Quest, 47*, 91–114.

Fernández-Balboa, J. M. (1997). Physical education teacher preparation in the postmodern era: Toward a critical pedagogy. In J. M. Fernández-Balboa (Ed.), *Critical postmodernism in human movement, physical education, and sport* (pp. 121–138). Albany, NY: State University of New York Press.

Fisette, J. L., & Walton, T. A. (2013). Empowering high-school girls as media consumers/producers: Engaging in activist research through visual methods. In *Pedagogies, physical culture, and visual methods* (pp. 46–62). London: Routledge.

Fitzpatrick, K. (2013). Brown bodies, racialisation and physical education. *Sport, Education and Society, 18*(2), 135–153. https://doi.org/10.1080/13573322.2011.559221

Fitzpatrick, K. (2019). What happened to critical pedagogy in physical education? An analysis of key critical work in the field. *European Physical Education Review, 25*(4), 1128–1145.

Fitzpatrick, K., & Pope, C. (2005). Is physical education relevant? Interpersonal skills, values and hybridity. *ACHPER Australia Healthy Lifestyles Journal, 52*(3–4), 24–29.

Fitzpatrick, K., & Russell, D. (2015). On being critical in health and physical education. *Physical Education and Sport Pedagogy, 20*(2), 159–173.

Flintoff, A., & Dowling, F. (2019). 'I just treat then all the same, really'. Teachers, whiteness and (anti) racism in physical education. *Sport Education and Society, 24*(2), 121–133.

Gabardi, W. (2001). Contemporary models of democracy. *Polity, 33*(4), 547–568.

Freire, P. (1970). Cultural action and conscientization. *Harvard Educational Review, 40*(3), 452–477.

Gerdin, G., Philpot, R., & Smith, W. (2018). It is only an intervention, but it can sow very fertile seeds: Graduate physical education teachers' interpretations of critical pedagogy. *Sport, Education and Society, 23*(3), 203–215.

Gerdin, G., Philpot, R. A., Larsson, L., Schenker, K., Linner, S., Moen, K. M., Westlie, K., & Legge, M. (2019). Researching social justice and health (in) equality across different school health and physical education contexts in Sweden, Norway and New Zealand. *European Physical Education Review, 25*(1), 273–290.

Gerdin, G., Smith, W., Philpot, R., Schenker, K., Moen, K. M., Linnér, S., Westlie, K., & Larsson, L. (2021). *Social justice pedagogies in health and physical education*. Abingdon: Routledge.

Gibbons, S. L. 2009. Meaningful participation of girls in senior physical education courses. *Canadian Journal of Education, 32*(2), 222–244.

Gordon, S., Benner, P., & Noddings, N. (1996). *Caregiving: Readings in knowledge, practice. Ethics, and politics*. Philadelphia: University of Pennsylvania Press.

Gray, S., Treacy, J., & Hall, E. T. (2019). Re-engaging disengaged pupils in physical education: An appreciative inquiry perspective. *Sport, Education and* Society, *24*(3), 241–255.

Grimminger-Seidensticker, E., & Mohwald, A. (2017). Intercultural education inn physical education: Results of a quasi-experimental intervention study with secondary school students. *Physical Education and Sport Pedagogy, 22*(5), 445–458.

Guadalupe, T. (2015). *Effects of purposeful negotiation of the physical education curriculum on one teacher and a middle school minority class (girls, boys, and mixed-gender)* (Doctoral dissertation, University of Alabama Libraries).

Guadalupe, T., & Curtner-Smith, M. D. (2019). "We know what we like to do:" Effects of purposefully negotiating the curriculum on the girls in one middle school class and their teacher. *Journal of Teaching in Physical Education, 39*(2), 147–155.

Guadalupe, T., & Curtner-Smith, M. D. (2020). 'It's nice to have choices': Influence of purposefully negotiating the curriculum on the students in one mixed-gender middle school class and their teacher. *Sport, Education and Society, 25*(8), 904–916.

Hamzeh, M. (2011). Deveiling body stories: Muslim girls negotiate visual, spatial, and ethical hijabs. *Race Ethnicity and Education, 14*(4), 481–506. https://doi.org/10.1080/13613324.2011.563287

Hastie, P. A., & Buchanan, A. M. (2000). Teaching responsibility through sport education: Prospects of a coalition. *Research Quarterly for Exercise and Sport, 71*(1), 25–35.

Howley, D., & O'Sullivan, M. (2020). 'You're not going to get it right every time': Teachers' perspectives on giving voice to students in physical education. *Journal of Teaching in Physical Education, 40*(1), 166–174.

Howley, D., & O'Sullivan, M. (2021). 'Getting better bit by bit': Exploring learners' enactments of student voice in physical education. *Curriculum Studies in Health and Physical Education, 12*(1), 3–19.

Kirk, D. (1986). A critical pedagogy for teacher education: Toward an inquiry-oriented approach. *Journal of Teaching in Physical Education, 5*, 230–246.

Kirk, D. (2009). *Physical education futures*. London: Routledge.

Kirk, D. (2020). *Precarity, critical pedagogy and physical education*. New York: Routledge.

Kirk, D., & Tinning, R. (1990). *Physical education, curriculum and culture*. London: The Falmer Press.

Kirk, D., Lamb, C. A., Oliver, K. L., Ewing-Day, R., Fleming, C., Loch, A., & Smedley, V. (2018). Balancing prescription with teacher and pupil agency: Spaces for manoeuvre within a pedagogical model for working with adolescent girls. *The Curriculum Journal, 29*(2), 219–237.

Lamb, C. A., Oliver, K. L., & Kirk, D. (2018). 'Go for it Girl' adolescent girls' responses to the implementation of an activist approach in a core physical education programme. *Sport, Education and Society, 23*(8), 799–811.

Larson, A. (2006). Student perception of caring teaching in physical education. *Sport, Education and Society, 11*(4), 337–352.

Larson, A., & Silverman, S. J. (2005). Rationales and practices used by caring physical education teachers. *Sport, Education and Society, 10*(2), 175–193.

Lather, P. (2001). Ten years later: Yet again. In K. Weiler (Ed.), *Feminist engagements: Reading, resisting, and revisioning male theorists in education and cultural studies* (pp. 183–196). New York, NY: Routledge.

Lawson, H. (1987). Teaching the body of knowledge: The neglected part of physical education. *Journal of Physical Education, Recreation and Dance, 58*(7), 70–72.

Leseth, A., & Engelsrud, G. (2019). Situating cultural diversity in movement. A case study on physical education teacher education in Norway. *Sport, Education and Society*, *24*(5), 468–479.

Li, Y., & Li, W. (2020). A review of research on ethic of care in physical education and physical activity settings. *Journal of Teaching in Physical Education*, *40*(1), 109–117.

Li, W., Rukavina, P., & Foster, C. (2013). Overweight or obese students' perceptions of caring in urban physical education programs. *Journal of Sport Behavior*, *32*, 189–208

Linnér, S., Larsson, L., Gerdin, G., Philpot, R., Schenker, K., Westlie, K., Mordal Moen, K. & Smith, W. (2022). The enactment of social justice in HPE practice: How context (s) comes to matter. *Sport, Education and Society*, *27*(3), 228–243.

Lleixà, T., & Nieva, C. (2018). The social inclusion of immigrant girls in and through physical education. Perceptions and decisions of physical education teachers. *Sport, Education and Society*.

Lorente, E., & Kirk, D. (2013). Alternative democratic assessment in PETE: An action-research study exploring risks, challenges and solutions. *Sport, Education and Society*, *18*(1), 77–96.

Luguetti, C., & McLachlan, F. (2021). 'Am I an easy unit?' Challenges of being and becoming an activist teacher educator in a neoliberal Australian context. *Sport, Education and Society*, *26*(1), 1–14.

Luguetti, C., & Oliver, K. L. (2020). An activist sport approach to before-and after-school programming: Co-creating empowering possibilities with youth from socially vulnerable backgrounds. In *Before-and after-school physical activity programs* (pp. 34–44). New York: Routledge.

Luguetti, C., Kirk, D., & Oliver, K. L. (2019). Towards a pedagogy of love: Exploring pre-service teachers' and youth's experiences of an activist sport pedagogical model. *Physical Education and Sport Pedagogy*, *24*(6), 629–646.

Lynch, S., & Curtner-Smith, M. (2019). 'You have to find your slant, your groove': One physical education teacher's efforts to employ transformative pedagogy. *Physical Education and Sport Pedagogy*, *24*(4), 359–372.

Lynch, S., & Ovens, A. (2020). *Critical pedagogy in physical education*. Singapore: Springer.

Lynch, S., & Sargent, J. (2020). Using the meaningful physical education features as a lens to view student experiences of democratic pedagogy in higher education. *Physical Education and Sport Pedagogy*, *25*(6), 629–642.

McDonald, D. (2014). Is global neo-liberalism shaping the future of physical education? *Physical Education and Sport Pedagogy*, *19*(5), 494–499.

McCuaig, L. A. (2012). Dangerous carers: Pastoral power and the caring teacher of contemporary Australian schooling. *Educational Philosophy and Theory*, *44*(8), 862–877.

McCuaig, L., Öhman, M., & Wright, J. (2013). Shepherds in the gym: Employing a pastoral power analytic on caring teaching in HPE. *Sport, Education and Society*, *18*(6), 788–806.

McLaren, P. (2003). *Life in schools*. Boston, MA: Pearson/Allyn and Bacon.

Monsen, S., Cook, S., & Hannant, L (2017). Students as partners in negotiated assessment in a teacher education course. *Teaching and Learning Together in Higher Education*: Iss. 21. http://repository.brynmawr.edu/tlthe/vol1/iss21/2

Mordal Moen, K., Westlie, K., Schenker, K., Linner, S., Smith, W., Gerdin, G, Philpot, R., &c Larrson, L. (2020). Caring teaching and the complexity of building good relationships as a pedagogy of social justice in health and physical education, *Sport, Education and Society*, *25*(9), 1015–1028.

Mordal Moen, K., & Green, K. (2012). Neither shaken nor stirring: A case of reflexivity in Norwegian physical education teacher education. *Sport, Education and Society*, *19*(4), 415–434.

Muros Ruiz, B., & Fernández-Balboa, J. M. (2005). Physical education teacher educators' personal perspectives regarding their practice of critical pedagogy. *Journal of Teaching in Physical Education*, *24*, 243–264.

Noddings, N. (1984). *The false promise of the paideia: A critical review of "The Paideia Proposal"*.

Noddings, N. (1992). Social studies and feminism. *Theory & Research in Social Education*, *20*(3), 230–241.

Noddings, N. (2007). Aims, goals, and objectives. *Encounters in Theory and History of Education*, *8*, 7–15.

Noddings, N. (2013 [1984]) *Caring A Relational Approach to Ethics and Moral Education*. London: University of California Press Ltd.

O'Connor, J., Jeanes, R., & Alfrey, L. (2016). Authentic inquiry-based learning in health and physical education: A case study of 'R/Evolutionary' practice. *Physical Education and Sport Pedagogy*, *21*(2), 201–216. doi:10.1080/17408989.2014.990368

O'Sullivan, M., Kinchin, G., & Enright, E. (2010). Cultural studies curriculum in physical activity and sport. *Standards-Based Physical Education Curriculum Development*, 333–365.

Oliver, K. L. (2001). Images of the body from popular culture: Engaging adolescent girls in critical inquiry. *Sport, Education and Society*, *6*(2), 143–164. doi:10.1080/13573320120084245

Oliver, K. L., & Kirk, D. (2015). *Girls, gender and physical education: An activist approach*. New York: Routledge.

Oliver, K. L., & Kirk, D. (2016). Towards an activist approach to research and advocacy for girls and physical education. *Physical Education and Sport Pedagogy*, *21*(3), 313–327.

Oliver, K. L., & Lalik, R. (2001). The body as curriculum: Learning with adolescent girls. *Journal of Curriculum Studies*, *33*(3), 303–333.

Oliver, K. L., & Lalik, R. (2004). Critical inquiry on the body in girls' physical education classes: A critical poststructural perspective. *Journal of Teaching in Physical Education*, *23*(2), 162–195.

Oliver, K. L., & Oesterreich, H. A. (2013). Student-centred inquiry as curriculum as a model for field-based teacher education. *Journal of Curriculum Studies*, *45*(3), 394–417.

Oliver, K. L., Hamzeh, M., & McCaughtry, N. (2009). Girly girls can play games/las niñas pueden jugar tambien: Co-creating a curriculum of possibilities with fifth-grade girls. *Journal of Teaching in Physical Education*, *28*(1), 90–110.

Oliver, K. L., Luguetti, C., Aranda, R., Nuñez Enriquez, O., & Rodriguez, A. A. (2018). 'Where do I go from here?': Learning to become activist teachers through a community of practice. *Physical Education and Sport Pedagogy*, *23*(2), 150–165.

Ovens, A. (2014). Disturbing practice in teacher education through peer-teaching. In *Self-study in physical education teacher education* (pp. 87–98). Champaign, IL: Springer.

Ovens, A., Flory, S. B., Sutherland, S., Philpot, R., Walton-Fisette, J. L., Hill, J., Phillips, S., & Flemons, M. (2018). How PETE comes to matter in the performance of social justice education. *Physical Education and Sport Pedagogy*, *23*(5), 484–496.

Owens, L. M., & Ennis, C. D. (2005). The ethic of care in teaching: An overview of supportive literature. *Quest*, *57*(4), 392–425.

Parker, M. B., & Curtner-Smith, M. D. (2012). Sport education: A panacea for hegemonic masculinity in physical education or more of the same? *Sport, Education and Society*, *17*(4), 479–496.

Penney, D. (2002). *Gender and physical education: Contemporary issues and future directions*. London: Routledge.

Penney, D., Jeanes, R., O'Connor, J., & Alfrey, L. (2018). Re-theorising inclusion and reframing inclusive practice in physical education. *International Journal of Inclusive Education*, *22*(10), 1062–1077.

Petrie, K., Burrows, L., Cosgriff, M., Keown, S., Naera, J., Duggan, D. & Devcich, J. (2013). Everybody counts? Reimaging health and physical education in primary schools. *Teaching and Learning Research Initiative*.

Philpot, R., Gerdin, G., Smith, W., Linnér, S., Schenker, K., Westlie, K., Mordal Moen, K., & Larsson, L. (2021). Taking action for social justice in HPE classrooms through explicit critical pedagogies. *Physical Education and Sport Pedagogy*, *26*(6), 662–674.

Pringle, R., Larsson, H., & Gerdin, G. (Eds). (2018). *Critical research in sport, health and physical education: How to make a difference*. Abingdon: Routledge.

Robinson, D. B., & Randall, L. (Eds). (2016). *Social justice in physical education: Critical reflections and pedagogies for change*. Canadian Scholars' Press.

Rovegno, I., & Kirk, D. (1995). Articulations and silences in socially critical work on physical education: Toward a broader agenda. *Quest*, *47*(4), 447–474.

Sánchez-Hernández, N., Martos-García, D., Soler, S., & Flintoff, A. (2018). Challenging gender relations in PE through cooperative learning and critical reflection. *Sport, Education and Society*, *23*(8), 812–823.

Shelley, K., & McCuaig, L. (2018). Close encounters with critical pedagogy in socio-critically informed health education teacher education. *Physical Education and Sport Pedagogy*, *23*(5), 510–523.

Smith, W., Philpot, R., Gerdin, G., Schenker, K., Linnér, S., Larsson, L., Mordal Moen, K., & Westlie, K. (2021). School HPE: Its mandate, responsibility and role in educating for social cohesion. *Sport, Education and Society*, *26*(3), 242–254.

Stirrup, J., & Hooper, O. (Eds). (2021). *Critical pedagogies in physical education, physical activity and health*. Abingdon: Routledge.

Stuhr, P. T., Sutherland, S., & Ward, P. (2011). Care enacted by two elementary physical education teachers and their students. *International Journal of Human Movement Science*, *5*(1), 5–28.

Tinning, R. (1985). Physical education and the cult of slenderness: A critique. *ACHPER National Journal*, *107*(Autumn), 10–14.

Tinning, R. (2016). Transformative pedagogies and physical education: Exploring the possibilities for personal change and social change. In K. Ennis (Ed.), *Routledge handbook of physical education pedagogies* (pp. 299–312). Abingdon: Routledge.

Tolgfors, B. (2019). Promoting integration through physical education (2020). *Sport, Education and Society*, *25*(9), 1029–1042.

Torres, J. A., & Fernández, J. M. (2015). Promoting inclusive schools: analysis of teachers' perceptions and needs from an organizational, curricular and professional development perspective. *Interuniversity Electronic Journal of Teacher Education*, *18*(1), 177–200.

Tsangaridou, N. (2008). Trainee primary teachers' beliefs and practices about physical education during students' teaching. *Physical Education and Sport Pedagogy*, *13*, 131–152.

Walseth, K., Engebretsen, B., & Elvebakk, L. (2018). Meaningful experiences in PE for all students: An activist research approach. *Physical Education and Sport Pedagogy*, *23*(3), 235–249.

Walton-Fisette, J. L., Sutherland, S., & Hill, J. (Eds). (2019). *Teaching about social justice issues in physical education*. Charlotte: Information Age Publishing.

Watkins, C., & Mortimore, P. (1999). Pedagogy: What do we know. In *Understanding pedagogy and its impact on learning*. Sage.

Wright, J. (2004). Critical inquiry and problem solving in PE. In J. Wright, D. Macdonald, & L. Burrows (Eds), *Crtical inquiry and problem solving in physical education* (pp. 3–15). London: Routledge.

Zhao, Q., & Li, W. (2016). Measuring perceptions of teachers' caring behaviors and their relationship to motivational responses in physical education among middle school students. *Physical Educator*, *73*(3), 510.

18
LEGITIMATE EMBODIMENT IN FORMAL EDUCATION
Imagery in physical education textbooks

Ana Rey-Cao and Alba González-Palomares

Embodiment in physical education (PE) is a process through which social imaginary is embodied through corporal practices. The current hegemonic model of body culture is what Peter McLaren (1997) would classify as 'predatory culture'. A culture fashioned around the excesses of marketing and consumerism, as well as the social relationships typical of post-industrial capitalism. So obvious that its victims are immune to the revelation of its perils, becoming a field of invisibility. This chapter reveals the embodiment deemed legitimate in Spain.

Social injustice is complex in its design. Both structural and circumstantial, it is where social and economic constructions, and subjectivity and ordinary interactions, come together. This analysis focuses on issues arising from social inequalities produced by the phenomenon of cultural domination and of ethnic, racial, gender, sexuality differences, or, broadly speaking, what happens with stigmatised groups (Montané, 2015). This approach has been addressed by the paradigm of relational or cultural justice, as represented by Nancy Fraser (1997). Central to this theory of inequality is the systemic relationship between recognition, redistribution, and representation. Fraser highlights that the lack of recognition of certain groups as a result of their divergence from the hegemonic model is not merely a psychological phenomenon. It also constitutes an institutionalised social relationship that prevents equal participation in social and political life, also becoming associated with an unequal distribution of wealth. In turn, cultural or symbolic injustice is rooted in the social patterns of representation, interpretation, and communication, which leads to cultural domination over others, lack of recognition, and disrespect.

The analysis of textbook images works much in the same way as a thermometer taking the temperature of PE from a privileged position. When using a textbook, we are learning and being taught who we are, what we are expected to do, or who we can look up to as role models. Textbooks form a microcosm that selects a partial reality to offer it up as a representation of totality. This simplification has been widely established in questions of gender (González-Palomares et al., 2015a, 2017; Sánchez et al., 2017; Táboas-Pais & Rey-Cao, 2012a; Vidal-Albelda & Martínez-Bello, 2017), race (González-Palomares & Rey-Cao, 2019; Moya-Mata et al., 2018; Táboas-Pais & Rey-Cao, 2015), ethnicity (Durand, 2021; Jam et al., 2021), nationality (Bose & Gao, 2022; Canga & Cifone, 2021), sexuality (Brown & Reygan, 2019; Deckman et al., 2018; Parise, 2021), age (González-Palomares & Rey-Cao, 2017; Moya-Mata

DOI: 10.4324/9781003389682-22

et al., 2017; Rey-Cao et al., 2013; Vidal-Albelda & Martínez-Bello, 2017), somatotype (González-Palomares & Rey-Cao, 2013; Moya-Mata et al., 2016, 2018; Táboas & Rey, 2011a), class (Morales-Vidal & Cassany, 2020) and disability (González-Palomares & Rey-Cao, 2020a; González-Palomares et al., 2015b; Moya-Mata et al., 2017, 2018; Táboas-Pais & Rey-Cao, 2012b; Vidal-Albelda & Martínez-Bello, 2017). A simplification that severely harms the opportunities of groups that do not possess the hegemonic values of these variables.

The imagery in PE textbooks shows the widespread hegemonic ideological structures in photographic culture in the first decade of the twenty-first century. The contents in PE textbooks in Spain favour male sex, white, young, and non-disabled people; and two large families of corporal practices and their corresponding instrumental discourses. On the one hand, sport is linked to discourses motor efficiency; and, on the other, physical exercises (fitness) are linked to that surrounding health and appearance. PE functions as a biotechnology and a differentiation device that sustains a binaristic discourse normalising the body: healthy/unhealthy, fit/unfit, efficient/inefficient.

A review of PE would help rescue the "subjugated knowledges" (Crisorio, 2015) that Foucault (1992) identifies as the "historical contents that have been buried and disguised in a functionalist coherence or formal systemisation" and "knowledges that have been disqualified as nonconceptual or insufficiently elaborated" (p. 21). In the case of the discourse surrounding PE, these knowledges have been usurped by the cultural colonisation of the scientific discourse of positivism and the capitalist demands that derive from the production-consumption binary.

Wanted: Young, able-bodied white male who plays sport and is physically active

If we were to attempt to identify the type of student imagined through the images in PE textbooks, the concise answer would be a young, able-bodied white male who participates in sport and fitness activities in contexts of elite competition. The loose affirmation and general statements conceal the all-important detail. But we should not ignore the fact that collective imaginaries hinge on the propagation of stereotypes that are built on an amalgamation of global and all-encompassing representations of social elements which have a major impact on thought processes and ensure that the appearances that regulate life in society are repeated. But it is also possible to question the inevitability and legitimacy of these implications and make an alternative interpretation, revealing the self-instituting nature of these, institutionally so well-fashioned, hegemonic representations (Randazzo, 2012). The textbook is precisely a crystallisation of the educational institution.

To give a voice to the silenced, to speak not only of what is, of what is not, and could be included in textbook images, it is necessary to explore the archaeology of the terms that are used in the institutional discourse of PE. For this reason, a conceptual framework that foregoes terms related to the construct 'physical and sports activity' has been chosen to refer to the generic purpose of PE. These terms have traditionally been used in research that engages in dialogue with biological and biomedical sciences (Lazzarotti et al., 2010). Instead, the concepts of embodiment and corporal practices make it possible to break with hegemonic preconceptions in the context of PE to "explore the body, not only from an organic but also a symbolic, cultural and linguistic perspective" (Galak & Gambarotta, 2011, p. 932).

Embodiment and bodily practices

Embodiment refers to the concept of the body as it is taught and can be understood to be the personification of the subjectivity reflecting the ideological sedimentation of the social structure inscribed within it (McLaren, 1997). Maurice Merleau-Ponty's philosophy of chiasm (1964) allows us to imagine the duality of body and mind, of the social and the carnal, without dissolving it. The world made flesh and the flesh made world (Ralón, 2014).

The concept of embodiment has been introduced in PE precisely with the aim of broadening the focus on the body beyond the natural scientific perspective while simultaneously attending to the cultural (Aartun et al., 2020). As Hurtado and Jaramillo (2008) point out, the embodiment in PE is understood to be a process by means of which the instituted social imaginary becomes incarnate through corporal practices.

Corporal practices are deliberate expressions of embodiment. Types of action in which motricity is expressed: games, sport, dance, physical exercise, acrobatics, mindfulness practices, gestures, etc. These ways of using the body carry meaning and can be interpreted because they are related to dispositions, accessibility, and non-accessibility of the body itself (Gallo, 2012). Given that these bodily technologies pre-exist individuals themselves, they determine their activity and their identity (Cheville, 2005).

However, their presence in PE is not equitable, because the discipline has been colonised by the scientific discourse of positivism, the capitalist demands derived from the production-consumption binary, and a certain Eurocentrism (Crisorio, 2015; Moreno-Doña et al., 2018; Vicente, 2007). This discourse favours two large families of bodily practices and their corresponding, and closely interrelated, instrumental discourses: sports participation related to the discourse of motor efficiency, and physical exercise related to the discourse of healthism. The sports model is typical of the logic of Anglo-Saxon, capitalist, bourgeois bodily indoctrination.

In parallel, the mass media image of the body and its practices speaks to us suggesting an incarnation of the 'leadership body': young, handsome, dynamic, slim, athletic, jovial, muscular, and healthy. An incarnation of an enterprising subjectivity, a corporate *ethos* self-managed in accordance with the neoliberal corporate healthcare conspiracy promoted by a governing apparatus of hygiene and self-control (Fanjul et al., 2019; Leitzke & Rigo, 2020; Sánchez-Serradilla, 2016). The exaltation of fitness activities in PE contributes to the hegemony of healthism (Beltrán-Carrillo & Devís-Devís, 2019). In this context, PE causes disembodiment whereby the body is stripped of experience and transformed into a universal body that could be anybody (Amar, 2010).

From the perspective of critical pedagogy, we could ask ourselves what place in PE is occupied by the bodily practices of work, death, care, tenderness, trance or gesture-related, hedonist, domestic, introspective, local, and traditional or aggressive; or by the common practices of ordinary people as opposed to those typical of bourgeois leisure pursuits, the bodily practices of the 'diverse' population as opposed to those of the 'normal' population. Silenced or invisible bodily practices remain outside the legitimate body and do not participate in the social imaginary of a correct and healthy body (Gallo & Martínez, 2015; Moreno-Doña et al., 2018; Rey-Cao, 2020; Vicente, 2016).

A review of PE would permit the "insurrection of non-subjugated knowledge" (Crisorio, 2015), in reference to setting free the "subjugated knowledge" that Foucault (1992) identifies as "historical contents that have been buried or masked in functional coherences or formal systematisations" and "knowledges that have been disqualified as non-conceptual or insufficiently elaborated knowledges" (p. 21).

As Aartun et al. point out (2020) in their recent review of pedagogies of embodiment, the common aim of these pedagogies is to create an inclusive, fair, equitable, and empowering school subject, to minimise the harm that negative experiences in PE can have for pupils, especially pupils that are considered vulnerable individuals.[1] Bodily practices can improve the sense of positive identity when pupils are given the opportunity to think for themselves, develop resistance to unhealthy practices and make up their own choices and try putting them into practice. Pedagogies of embodiment unite critical thinking and body awareness. Critical reflection skills may also help pupils in learning how to reveal the norms, values, and power relations that underpin the hegemonic movement culture. Developing body awareness may help pupils to get to know themselves better and facilitate exploration and extension of their own capacities and boundaries.

Taking the temperature of schools: textbook imagery

One of the lines of research concerning embodiment in PE considers that the body should be addressed not only as something we have but something we are. That is, embodiment is not only brought about through bodily practices but also through cognitive knowledge of such practices. This occurs as such, for example, in campaigns promoting physical activity (Aartun et al., 2020) or in textbooks (Guimarães & García, 2014).

The school curriculum acts as a reflection of the social imaginary and is materialised through textbooks (Guichot-Reina & De la Torre-Sierra, 2020). Therefore, school textbooks are an excellent place to take the temperature of the social model shaped from school. Unsurprisingly, they were used in Spain to disseminate the ideological principles of the Franco regime (López, 2001; Martínez, 2019) and later non-conflicting and simplistic explanations surrounding the Civil War (González, 2015c). This modelling function continues to be present in contemporary society, its very normalisation and globalisation what makes it so invisible. This process constitutes one of the institutional mediation filters that contribute to the legitimation of the constructed realities inherent in the post-modern condition under late capitalism (McLaren, 1997). Hence, the relevance of research on textbooks that recognises the diversity in Europe and contributes to an examination of current threats to democratic societies posed by populist movements, the resurgence of authoritarian governments, and the improper use of digital content (Sammler, 2018).

Textbooks go beyond the dissemination of information and the development of academic skills. They play an important role in the political mediation of what is taught and the methods used to do so (Robinson et al., 2014). They choose a partial reality and offer it up as a representation of totality. Despite their biases and how they conceal asymmetric relationships, this conception of the world establishes itself as the appropriate – the natural – one (Gallardo, 2001; Gámez, 2018; González, 2015b). When using a textbook, we learn who we are, what we are expected to do, or who we can look to as role models. School manuals have a significant influence on the creation of pupils' identity and on the configuration of a legitimate imaginary (Aamotsbakken, 2006).

Specifically, textbook photographs are a privileged vantage point from which to observe the imaginary for several reasons. One is the incipient visual literacy that makes their choice less refined than the texts. A significant component of the absent and null curriculum is filtered through photographs. "Through visual language, schools prepare us for adult life and, unconsciously, pupils accept a series of values they would not accept if they were conveyed explicitly" (Acaso & Nuere, 2005, p. 219). The visual null curriculum foments the sole perspective, the construction of meanings that omit information that would make it possible to reproduce a more plural and complex perspective. Textbook photographs play mainly an illustrative role and they accompany the text and construct the meaning of complex terms via the representation of an image as if it were the whole. This can favour the creation of ideal visual imaginaries that are clichéd and simple, which make it impossible to create alternative narratives and explanations (Gámez, 2018).

Another reason that makes photographs an extremely valuable source of information is the power of the image in contemporary society. We see much more than we read: "The air we breathe is made up of oxygen, nitrogen, and images". Luengo and Blázquez (2004) adapted the phrase that Robert Guerin once related to advertising in order to demonstrate the constant presence of images in our everyday surroundings. Regardless of the cognitive significance that a photograph might acquire in terms of its characteristics (size, background, colour, focus, layout, content, detail, index reference, footnote, subtitle, etc.), research has shown that one of the main functions of photographs in textbooks is to catch the attention of the reader. Pupils notice and comment on the photographs before referring to the texts (Pozzer-Ardenghi & Roth, 2004). The effect a photograph has increases because the message is perceived as an objective reflection of reality. This is what Pericot (1987) called the 'trick of reality'. This 'trick' causes much of the content captured in images to be integrated into the brain without first passing through consciousness (Caja et al., 2002). Between the ages of 12 and 15, there is a tendency for young people to legitimate identity through images, perceiving them to be an undeniable reality (Revuelta, 2008).

Lee (2009) analysed three English textbooks at secondary education level in South Korea to explore how globalisation is reflected. These books promoted western culture, particularly American culture, by including commercial brands along with other elements related to western popular culture and arts. This specific means of reproduction is more acute because the adolescent public may lack the critical capacity necessary to process advertising content (Martínez & Sánchez, 2012), given scant visual literacy in secondary education (Pérez & Pi, 2015) and because the brand is legitimated thanks to its presence in textbooks, carriers of formal curriculum. A message is less persuasive if it is given explicitly in the form of a commercial announcement (Briñol et al., 2015). The supposed commercial neutrality of textbooks with regard to a certain brand means they have a greater capacity to condition social attitudes and values than other types of explicit advertising media (Sánchez et al., 2004).

The current hegemonic body culture disseminated in image culture is what Peter McLaren called a 'predatory culture', fashioned around the excesses of marketing and consumption and the social relations of post-industrial capitalism. So obvious that it "immunises its victims against a full disclosure of its menacing capabilities", transformed into a "field of invisibility". For this reason, it is important to "read critically the narratives that are already reading us" (McLaren, 1997, p. 113).

Embodiment in physical education textbooks in Spain

We analysed the photographs in PE textbooks over an 11-year period (González, 2015a; Táboas, 2009). From the years 2000 to 2011, we analysed 9,989 photographs from 75 PE textbooks at secondary education level (12–16-year-olds). This section sums up some of the most relevant results of the analyses.

PE textbook images show the hegemonic ideological structures disseminated in image culture in the first decade of the twenty century. Legitimate embodiment in Spain is contingent on a distinction of gender, race, disability, corporal practice. and consumption. Visual content in curricular material aimed at adolescent pupils favours: the male sex (González-Palomares et al., 2017; Táboas & Rey, 2011b; Táboas-Pais & Rey-Cao, 2012a); the white race (González et al.,

2010; González-Palomares & Rey-Cao, 2019; Táboas & Rey, 2011b; Táboas-Pais & Rey-Cao, 2015); young people (González, 2015a; Rey-Cao et al., 2013); the able-bodied (González-Palomares & Rey-Cao, 2020a; Táboas-Pais & Rey-Cao, 2012b); and two large families of corporal practices and their corresponding instrumental discourses. On the one hand, sport, linked to the discourse of motor efficiency, and on the other, physical exercises, linked to the discourse of health and appearance (González-Palomares & Rey-Cao, 2015; González-Palomares & Rey-Cao, 2013; Táboas & Rey, 2012; Táboas & Rey, 2011b; Táboas & Rey, 2010). Moreover, they represent brand consumption (González-Palomares & Rey-Cao, 2020b).

As we mentioned at the beginning of the chapter, it is the embodiment of a *young, white, able-bodied male who does sport and physical exercise*.

Man

The images included in PE textbooks reflect a clear imbalance between male and female figures, indicating the existence of a dominant male model. Men were the protagonists of 47.3 per cent of the photographs, women the protagonists of 32.9 per cent and men and women were represented together in 19.8 per cent. Joint representation was characterised in many cases by the more dynamic role of the males. However, certain publishers represented men and women almost equally, and two of them represented more women than men (Rey & González, 2017).

The photographs reveal differences[2] in the type of bodily practices linked to men and women, corresponding to the stereotypes attributed to each of the genders and summarised in Figure 18.1.

Male embodiment is characterised by participation in sports – both team and individual – in competitive settings, outdoor spaces, and at elite sporting levels.

Female embodiment is characterised by participation in individual sports, artistic activities, internalisation (yoga, tai-chi, and relaxation, among others), and fitness and physical conditioning activities, in informal and utilitarian spaces, indoor spaces, and at levels far removed from elite performance.

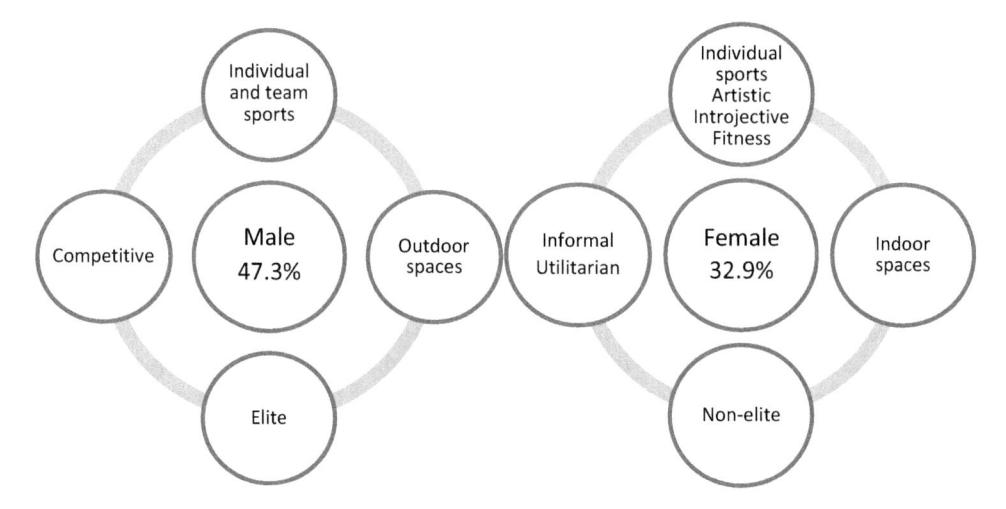

Figure 18.1 Embodiment in terms of gender.
Adapted from Rey and González (2017).

White

The images portray racial homogeneity with a majority representation of the endogroup (Western and white) and a minority representation of people from the exogroup (different to the Caucasian group). The protagonists of 87.7 per cent of the photographs were white. The images that jointly represent people from different ethnic backgrounds made up 7.2 per cent of the total. Black people were the protagonists of 3.2 per cent of the photographs, Asians 1.1 per cent and people with a native Latin American appearance, 0.1 per cent. Other ethnic groups were only represented in 0.6 per cent of the images (González-Palomares & Rey-Cao, 2019; Táboas-Pais & Rey-Cao, 2015).

People from different ethnic backgrounds to white – mainly black people – were represented in limited contexts and in accordance with racial stereotypes, mainly doing sports such as basketball and athletics, and linked to elite sports at high levels of competition. Non-whites are excluded from recreational and utilitarian scenarios and from the educational context itself (González-Palomares & Rey-Cao, 2019; Táboas-Pais & Rey-Cao, 2015). Textbooks perpetuate the use of race as a variable that legitimates the existence of differences and expectations based on racial groups.

Young

School textbooks convey an age-biased embodiment. The young body reigns supreme. Children, adolescents, and young people were present in 87.6 per cent of the photographs. The age group most ignored is the elderly, who appear in only 1.2 per cent of cases. Adults appear in 3.7 per cent of cases (González, 2015a; Rey-Cao et al., 2013). This result is understandable, given that textbooks are aimed at the adolescent population but, along with the invisibilisation of other age groups, stereotyping occurs.

- *Gender and age*. The representation of small and adolescent females is more frequent than young, adult, and elderly females. Mixed groups are more visible in childhood. In youth, adulthood, and old age, the male image prevails.
- *Age and type of bodily practice*. The probability of a person appearing engaged in a certain bodily practice depends on their age (González, 2015a). Young children and adolescents participate in team and individual sports, adults do artistic activities (such as dance) and individual sports; and the elderly do individual sports, artistic activities, and other bodily practices.

Textbook images represent the ideal of youth linked to competitive, elite-level sport. Visual content strengthens the iconic model of the young athlete. The remaining age groups are represented in other types of bodily practices, with a generalised predominance of individual sports and artistic activities that take place in non-competitive scenarios, non-sporting spaces, and in activities far removed from the sporting elite. Adults are linked to informal and utilitarian surroundings, corporal practices during leisure time or household chores.

Able-bodied

The embodiment of disabled people is ignored and stereotyped in PE textbook images. Their low profile and the symbolic disdain with which they are treated are shown by the quantity and quality of representations. Only 1.3 per cent of the photographs showed people with a disability (González-Palomares & Rey-Cao, 2020a; Táboas-Pais & Rey-Cao, 2012b).

Images perpetuate a clichéd embodiment of disability associated with a wheelchair. In 59.2 per cent of the photographs, the disability is inferred from the presence of a wheelchair. Only 5.6 per cent of the images show people with a disability participating with able-bodied people in an integrated way. They are not shown in textbooks as PE pupils in school, they do not participate in recreational or artistic activities, nor are they in the natural environment. Of the 45 images, 20 show disabled people participating in team sports (44.4 per cent); 20 in individual sports (44.4 per cent), and in the remaining five they are not taking part in physical activity (11.1 per cent). The disabled person is shown in settings of sporting success and motor excellence. Some 80 per cent of the images show elite sporting events, such as the Paralympic Games, for example; and never in educational environments (González-Palomares & Rey-Cao, 2020a; Táboas-Pais & Rey-Cao, 2012b).

The embodiment of disabled people is typical of the 'super-crip' phenomenon, that is, someone who has to overcome their impairment to achieve improbable success (Silva & Howe, 2012).

Participation in sports and physical exercise

In order to analyse the diversity of corporal practices in textbook images, the type of bodily practice in each of the photographs was identified by coding it with the indicator corresponding to the system of categories created *ad hoc* (Táboas, 2009): team sports, individual sports, artistic activities, fitness, and physical conditioning activities, in the natural environment, introspective activities (bodily awareness), games, work or everyday activities, adapted activities, and others.

Despite the diversity of possible bodily practices, the system explicitly names those that appear recurrently because, as we have mentioned, in PE discourse there are non-existent practices (care, trance, sexual, etc.) and others that are hegemonic (sport and fitness and physical conditioning exercises).

For all of the period analysed, the most recurring embodiments correspond to the efficient or fit body. In total, 46.3 per cent of the photographs show sports and 16.3 per cent, fitness activities. The remaining bodily practices are represented to a lesser extent: artistic activities, 10 per cent, activities in the natural environment, 10 per cent, games, 7 per cent, introspective bodily practices, 1.8 per cent, everyday activities, 1.8 per cent; in the work environment, 0.5 per cent, and other bodily practices, 6.3 per cent.

The analysis of the period 2006–2011 showed some changing tendencies with respect to the period 2000–2006, which we consider relevant to point out because they illustrate the peak of the fitness trend and the influence of healthism. In the period 2006–2011, sportivised embodiment continued to be predominant in all publications. Sports were the most frequent bodily practice in 11 of the 12 analysed and only one showed a greater number of fitness and physical conditioning images than sports images. But the data show a slight increase in representations of fitness with respect to the results found in the textbook photographs for the earlier period, that is, 18 per cent as opposed to 14.6 per cent (González-Palomares & Rey-Cao, 2015; Táboas & Rey, 2012). Linked to this increase, the representation of other embodiments related to bodily practices in the natural environment, artistic activities or games has decreased.

It is important to emphasise that the increase in images of fitness and physical conditioning activities that occurred during the second half of the first decade in this century is related to an increase in the number of images in the formal education context (González, 2015a).

This evolution would seem to reflect a shift towards the paradigm of physical activity for health and healthism. The main concern regarding problems of excess weight, obesity, and beauty are almost forcing PE to be instrumentalised as a fitness activity. Neoliberal logics are filtering down into school PE through the embodiment of the corporate ethos transmitted by the fitness culture: making bodies extraordinarily productive (Landa & Marengo, 2011) and handsome (Pedraza, 2011). This practical knowledge and discourses around the body and subjectivity fashion pupils' experience and self-awareness, facilitating the constitution of the modern individual (Pedraza, 2011). To paraphrase Vicente (2007), we are witnessing the reproduction of a medical-sports ethic of submission: the body, a slave to a healthy lifestyle. An instrumentalised embodiment in which bodily practices are only relevant if they get us 'fit', make us 'efficient' or make us more 'handsome'.

Branded apparel

The study carried out by Táboas-Pais and Rey-Cao (2011c) with secondary education students revealed their attention to certain brands shown in textbooks. We carried out a perception test which used photographs from PE textbooks. Some 64.3 per cent of the pupils – 56 out of 87 participants – described the clothing and the brands the male and female protagonists of the images wore: comments such as "Adidas boots, a Boss sweatshirt or Coca-Cola sponsorship" (p. 108) appear in the pupils' discourse. This interest in brands, especially branded sportswear, in their PE textbooks had not been explored previously in scientific literature, nor had it been included as a variable in prior studies on curricular materials. Brands are present to such an extent that they have been legitimated as the norm (Baudrillard, 2009).

Therefore, we included the brand variable in the study of textbooks (González-Palomares & Rey-Cao, 2020b). Of the 6,773 images from 39 textbooks analysed, 21.9 per cent – 1,441 photographs – referenced a famous brand. Of these, 93.5 per cent were related to dress – clothes or sports implements – and closely linked to competitive, high-level contexts.

PE textbooks reproduce the neoliberal logics of sport via the inclusion of sports sponsorship and the brand system in visual content related to the elite and to competition. Images of brands linked to people or spaces that illustrate examples of success, healthy lifestyles or proper behaviour implicitly convey what is considered correct, ending up legitimated as elements of an ideal lifestyle.

Conclusion

PE textbook images legitimate a limited embodiment: young, white, able-bodied person who participates in sport and physical exercise wearing branded sportswear. These images can influence pupils when it comes to choosing their bodily practices and reinforcing healthism. Women, the elderly, the disabled, and people from the exogroup do not form a part of PE's legitimate body. PE's visual discourse shows an embodiment in accordance with an instrumental rationality and the logics of the neoliberal body normalising the body as fit/unfit, efficient/inefficient. The paradigm of physical education for health (fitness) is reinforced along with the paradigm of sports efficiency. In parallel, representations of artistic practices, activities in the natural environment and games are diminished.

The embodiment upheld by PE is extremely permeable to market logics. Sports and fitness culture are devices linked to commercial practices that foment consumption and brand culture. There is a powerful element of visual penetration in fitness practices because they are more frequently present than we might think, not only in images found in the formal education but also in non-formal, informal, and instrumental education. Brand presence is inherent in competitive sport, and PE teachers could use photographs showing brands to work on responsible consumption and critical awareness with respect to the contribution of modern sport to capitalism (Perelman, 2014).

Meanwhile, there are other invisible embodiments. The results emphasise the need to visibilise and give priority to bodily practices removed from the logics of capitalism. Practices which avoid normalisation and fall under an "I can" instead of an "I must be" (Gallo, 2012, p. 840). Practices linked to the artistic, the hedonistic, the expressive, tenderness, sensitivity, filial care, self-absorption, ritual, dance, the introspective, leisure, everyday chores, and the singular.

As we have defended in other contexts (Rey-Cao, 2020), the challenge of PE is to balance objectives built on the ideal with objectives built in terms of the context. Managing chaos by searching for sustainability in the face of the dual challenges that are presented in the ternty-first century: technology/nature; violence/aggression; enjoyment/care; consumption/responsibility; local/global; sex/countersexuality and youth/aging. A meagre approach and one which is ambiguous and uncertain. But PE must contend with the end of certainty in immanent and ideal content. The alternative is a reflexive practice open to continuous questioning.

> Rethinking the body does not mean focusing solely on what it is possible to do with it, which has been carefully considered by the powers-that-be, but rather what it is that the body has been and fallen into oblivion and what the debris is that can be effectively put back together as resistance.
>
> (Amar, 2010, p. 61)

It is necessary to maintain a level of critical criteria when editing and managing visual content because the diversification of bodily culture requires a thorough review of the type of bodily practices that are visibilised and configured as reality in the microcosms of textbooks. According to Peirats et al. (2016), a possible strategy would be to resort to pedagogical advisory teams in the publishing houses who would oversee choosing visual content.

Notes

1 Moreno-Doña et al. (2018) propose using the term violated individual instead of vulnerable individual to mean that the "violated individual is so in that he/she forms a part of a system which, being characterised in a certain way, ends up violating the rights of others. The vulnerable individual, however, is a person with certain already given qualities" (p. 360).
2 All of the links that are presented in this chapter were discovered via a bivariate descriptive analysis using Pearson's chi-squared test. The concrete data can be consulted in the publications referenced.

References

Aamotsbakken, B. (2006). The relation between the model reader/-s and the authentic reader/-s. The possibilities for identification when reading curricular texts. In É. Bruillard, B. Aamotsbakken, S. V. Knudsen, & M. Horsley (Eds), *Caught in the web or lost in the textbook. Eighth International Conference on Learning and Educational Media* (pp. 99–108). Iartem: Caen, Francia.

Aartun, I., Walseth, K., Standal, Ø., & Kirk, D. (2020). Pedagogies of embodiment in physical education – a literature review. *Sport, Education and Society*. https://doi.org/10.1080/13573322.2020.1821182

Acaso, M., & Nuere, S. (2005). El curriculum oculto visual: aprender a obedecer a través de la imagen [The hidden visual curriculum: Learn to obey through images]. *Arte, Individuo y Sociedad, 17*, 207–220. https://doi.org/10.5209/ARIS.6657

Amar, M. (2010). El cuerpo des-encarnado. Apuntes para una teoría de la infancia como resistencia [The disembodied body. Notes for a theory of childhood as resistance]. *Actuel Marx, Intervenciones, 9*, 59–75. http://biopolitica.wpengine.com/wp-content/uploads/2014/01/amar_publicacion.pdf

Baudrillard, J. (2009). *The consumer society: Myths and structures*. Madrid: Siglo XXI.

Beltrán-Carrillo, V., & Devís-Devís, J. (2019). El pensamiento del alumnado inactivo sobre sus experiencias negativas en educación física: los discursos del rendimiento, salutismo y masculinidad hegemónica. [Inactive student thinking on their negative experiences in physical education: Discourses of performance, healthism and hegemonic masculinity]. *RICYDE. Revista Internacional De Ciencias Del Deporte, 15*(55), 20–34. https://doi.org/10.5232/ricyde2019.05502

Bose, P., & Gao, X. (2022). Cultural representations in Indian English language teaching textbooks. *SAGE Open, 12*(1). https://doi.org/10.1177/21582440221082102

Briñol, P., Cárcaba, M., Gallardo, I., & Horcajo, J. (2015). Forewarning of the persuasive attempt in advertising contexts. *Anales de psicología, 31*(1), 184–189. https://doi.org/10.6018/analesps.31.1.158251

Brown, A., & Reygan, F. (2019). The construction and representation of sexual and gender diversity in Namibian school textbooks: Global discourses or Southern African realities? *Journal of Namibian Studies, 25*, 31–46. https://namibian-studies.com/index.php/JNS/article/view/8326

Caja, J., Berrocal, M., & González, J. M. (2002). Un mundo lleno de imágenes [A world full of images]. *Aula de innovación educativa, 116*, 10–13. https://redined.educacion.gob.es/xmlui/handle/11162/88035

Canga, M. D., & Cifone, A. (2021). Emerging stereotypes about the target culture through popular culture and cultural heritage references in EFL textbooks. *World Journal of English Language, 11*(1), 43–51. https://doi.org/10.5430/WJEL.V11N1P43

Cheville, J. (2005). Confronting the problem of Embodiment. *International Journal of Qualitative Studies in Education, 18*(1), 85–107. https://doi.org/10.1080/09518390412331318405

Crisorio, R. (2015). La teoría de las prácticas [The theory of practice]. In R. Crisorio, L. Rocha, & A. Lescano (Coords.), *Ideas para pensar la educación del cuerpo* [Ideas for thinking about the education of the body] (pp. 14–21). La Plata: Universidad de la Plata.

Deckman, S. L., Fulmer, E. F., Kirby, K., Hoover, K., & Mackall, A. S. (2018). Numbers are just not enough: A critical analysis of race, gender, and sexuality in elementary and middle school health textbooks. *Educational Studies, 54*(3), 285–302. https://doi.org/10.1080/00131946.2017.1411261

Durand, S. (2021). Rethinking under-represented ethnicities in ELT materials through a critical discourse analysis-oriented model. *Mextesol Journal, 45*(1). https://www.mextesol.net/journal/index.php?page=journal&id_article=23342

Fanjul, C., López, L., & González, C. (2019). Adolescentes y culto al cuerpo: influencia de la publicidad y de Internet en la búsqueda del cuerpo masculino idealizado [Adolescents and body cult: The influence of Internet advertising in search of the idealised male]. *Doxa Comunicación, 29*, 61–74. https://doi.org/10.31921/doxacom.n29a3

Foucault, M. (1992). *Microfísica del poder* [Microphysics of power]. Madrid: La Piqueta.

Fraser, N. (1997). *Iustitia interrupta: Reflexiones críticas desde la posición 'postsocialista'*. [Justice interruptus: Critical reflections on the 'postsocialist' condition]. Santa Fé de Bogotá: Siglo de Hombres Editores/Universidad de los Andes.

Galak, E., & Gambarotta, E. (2011). Conquista, confirmación y construcción del cuerpo: una propuesta para el estudio de las prácticas corporales a partir de la epistemología de Pierre Bourdieu [Conquest, confirmation and construction of the concept 'body': proposals for studying corporal practices through Bourdieu's epistemology]. *Revista Brasileira De Ciências Do Esporte, 33*(4), 923–938. https://doi.org/10.1590/S0101-32892011000400009

Gallardo, I. (2001). Una aventura educativa: el uso del libro de texto hacia el siglo XXI [An educational adventure: The use of the textbook into the 21st century]. *Revista Educación, 25*(1), 81–93. https://doi.org/10.15517/revedu.v25i1.2933

Gallo, L. (2012). Las prácticas corporales en la educación corporal [Corporal practices in Corporal Education]. *Revista Brasileira de Ciências do Esporte, 34*(4), 825–843. https://doi.org/10.1590/S0101-32892012000400003

Gallo, L. E., & Martínez, L. J. (2015). Líneas pedagógicas para una Educación Corporal [Pedagogical lines for Corporal Education]. *Cadernos de Pesquisa*, *45*(157), 612–629. https://doi.org/10.1590/198053143215

Gámez, V. (2018). Análisis de la textualidad verbo-icónica de la imagen en los libros de texto de Ciencias Sociales en la etapa de Educación Primaria [Verb-icon textuality analysis of images in primary school social sciences textbooks]. *Didacticae*, *4*, 9–24. https://doi.org/10.1344/did.2018.4.9-24

González, A. (2015a). Cultura corporal y estereotipos en las fotografías de los libros de texto de educación física editados durante la Ley Orgánica de Educación [Body culture and stereotypes in photographs in physical education textbooks published during the organic law on education]. (Doctoral dissertation). Universidade de Vigo. Pontevedra.

González, B. (2015b). Libros de texto, ¿detesto la diversidad? [Textbooks, am I hindering diversity?]. In A. Mª. Trepichín, A. Arévalo, B. González, & C. Peláez (Coords.) *La subversión de los imaginarios: Tres ensayos, tres contextos* [The subversion of the imaginary: Three essays, three contexts] (pp. 21–52). México: Colegio de México. http://www.jstor.org/stable/j.ctt1c0gmmq.4

González, M. (2015c). «Tiempo de Turbulencias»: La compleja representación de la Guerra Civil española en los libros de texto de Ciencias Sociales (1970–1990) ['Times of storms': The complex portrayal of the Spanish Civil War in history textbooks (1970–1990)]. *Espacio, Tiempo y Educación*, *2*(1),163–185. https://doi.org/10.14516/ete.2015.002.001.009

González, A., Táboas, Mª. I., & Rey, A. (2010). Los libros de texto como herramientas para la promoción de una práctica físico-deportiva en igualdad: análisis comparativo de la representación racial entre los libros publicados durante la vigencia de la LOGSE y la LOE [Textbooks as tools for promoting physical activity and sport in equality: comparative analysis of racial representation in textbooks published during LOGSE and LOE]. *Cuadernos de psicología del deporte*, *10*(Suple), 31–36. http://revistas.um.es/cpd/article/view/111241/105591

González-Palomares, A., & Rey-Cao, A. (2013). Cultura corporal y estereotipos en las imágenes de los libros de texto de Educación Física publicados bajo el período de la Ley Orgánica de Educación (LOE) [Body culture and stereotypes in the images of Physical Education textbokks published under the period of the organic law of education (LOE)]. *Ágora para la educación física y el deporte*, *15*(1), 1–19. https://agora-revista.blogs.uva.es/files/2013/07/agora_15_1a_gonzalez_y_rey.pdf

González-Palomares, A., & Rey-Cao, A. (2015). Los contenidos curriculares en las fotografías de los libros de texto de Educación Física en Secundaria [Curricular contents in the photographs of secondary-level Physical Education textbooks]. *Retos*, *27*, 81–85. https://doi.org/10.47197/retos.v0i27.34352

González-Palomares, A., & Rey-Cao, A. I. (2017). Las edades en la cultura corporal: Representaciones en los libros de texto de educación física de Brasil [The ages in body culture: Representations in Brazilian physical education textbooks]. *Revista Brasileira de Educação*, *22*(71). https://doi.org/10.1590/S1413-24782017227163

González-Palomares, A., & Rey-Cao, A. (2019). Diversidad étnica y educación física: análisis de las fotografías de los libros de texto publicados durante la Ley Orgánica de Educación [Ethnic diversity and Physical Education: Analysis of the textbooks photographs published during the Organic Education Law]. *Revista Española de Educación Física y Deportes*, *426*(Esp.), 163–170. https://www.reefd.es/index.php/reefd/article/view/775/655

González-Palomares, A., & Rey-Cao, A. (2020a). The representation of disability in physical education textbooks in Spain. *Sport in Society*. https://doi.org/10.1080/17430437.2020.1828355

González-Palomares, A., & Rey-Cao, A. (2020b). Deporte, publicidad y marcas en los libros de texto de Educación Física [Sport, advertising and brands in physical education textbooks]. *Cuadernos.info*, *46*, 281–306. http://dx.doi.org/10.7764/cdi.46.1428

González-Palomares, A., Altmann, H., & Rey-Cao, A. (2015a). Estereótipos de gênero nas imagens dos livros didáticos de educação física do Brasil [Gender stereotypes in images of physical education textbooks in Brazil]. *Movimento*, *21*(1), 219–232. https://doi.org/10.22456/1982-8918.47114

González-Palomares, A., Rey-Cao, A., & Táboas-Pais, M. I. (2015b). La discapacidad en la enseñanza pública: Estudio exploratorio de los libros de texto de Educación Física de Brasil [Disability in public education: An exploratory study in Physical Education textbooks in Brazil]. *Saúde e Sociedade*, *24*(4), 1316–1331. https://doi.org/10.1590/S0104-12902015134558

González-Palomares, A., Táboas-Pais, M., & Rey-Cao, A. (2017). La cultura corporal en función del género: análisis de los libros de texto de educación física de secundaria publicados durante la ley orgánica de educación [The body culture according to gender: Analysis of secondary physical education textbooks published during education organic law]. *Educación XXI, 20*(1), 141–162. https://doi.org/10.5944/educxx1.17506

Guichot-Reina, V., & De la Torre-Sierra, A. Mª. (2020). Identidad profesional y socialización de género: un estudio desde la manualística escolar en la España democrática [Professional identity and gender socialization: A study from school textbooks in democratic Spain]. *Historia y Memoria de la Educación, 12*, 101–136. https://doi.org/10.5944/hme.12.2020.25599

Guimarães, R., & García, M. (2014). Análisis de libros de texto en Brasil y en España: una introducción al tema en el área de Educación Física [Analysis of textbooks in Brazil and Spain: An introduction to the subject in the physical education area]. *Movimento, 20*(2), http://dx.doi.org/10.22456/1982-8918.41791

Hurtado, D., & Jaramillo, L. (2008). El encarnamiento deportivizado de la educación física: sentidos que configuran la educación física como dualidad [Sporting embodiment of physical education: Dual physical education configurated by senses]. *Estudios pedagógicos, 34*(2), 99–114. http://dx.doi.org/10.4067/S0718-07052008000200006

Jam, S. Z. B., Khiabani, S. M., & Hejazi, M. (2021). Discourse representation in the images of English textbooks 'prospects' and 'visions': A semiotic analysis: The case study of ethnicity and place. *Language Related Research, 11*(6), 419–448.

Landa, M. I., & Marengo, L. G. (2011). El cuerpo del trabajo en el capitalismo flexible: lógicas empresariales de gestión de energías y emociones [The body of work in flexible capitalism: Business logic of energies and emotions management]. *Cuadernos de Relaciones Laborales, 29*(1), 177–199. https://doi.org/10.5209/rev_CRLA.2011.v29.n1.7

Lazzarotti, A., Silva, A. M., Antunes, P., Silva, A. P., & Leite, J. (2010). O termo práticas corporais na literatura científica brasileira e sua repercussão no campo da Educação Física [The term bodily practices in Brazilian scientific literature and its impact on the Physical Education field]. *Movimento, 16*(1), 11–29. https://doi.org/10.22456/1982-8918.9000

Lee, I. (2009). Situated globalization and racism: An analysis of Korean High School EFL textbooks. *Language & Literacy, 11*(1), 1–14. https://doi.org/10.20360/G2F59N

Leitzke, A., & Rigo, L. (2020). Sociedade de controle e redes sociais na internet: #saúde e #corpo no Instagram [Society of control and social media: #health and #body on Instagram]. *Movimento, 26*, e26062. https://doi.org/10.22456/1982-8918.100688

López, M. (2001). *El fenómeno ideológico del franquismo en los manuales de escolares de enseñanza primaria (1936–1945)* [The ideological phenomenon of Francoism in primary school textbooks (1936–1945)]. Manes: UNED.

Luengo, M., & Blázquez, F. (2004). *Género y libros de texto: Un estudio de estereotipos en las imágenes* [Gender and textbooks: A study of stereotypes in images]. Mérida: Instituto de la Mujer de Extremadura.

Martínez, B. (2019). La representación de la mujer en los manuales escolares de la Segunda República y del primer Franquismo (1931–1945) [The representation of women in the school manuals of the second republic and of the first franchism (1931–1945). *Investigaciones Feministas, 10*(1), 149–166. https://doi.org/10.5209/infe.62375

Martínez, E., & Sánchez, L. (2012). Communication between minors and brands on social networks. *Estudios sobre el mensaje periodístico, 18*, 589–598. https://doi.org/10.5209/rev_ESMP.2012.v18.40938

McLaren, P. (1997). *Pedagogía crítica y cultura depredadora. Políticas de oposición en la era posmoderna* [Critical pedagogy and predatory culture. Oppositional politics in the postmodern era]. Barcelona: Paidós.

Merleau-Ponty, M. (1964). *Le visible et l'invisible* [The visible and the invisible]. París: Gallimard.

Montané, A. (2015). Justicia social y educación [Social justice and education]. *Revista de Educación Social, 20*. Recuperado de https://eduso.net/res/revista/20/el-tema-colaboraciones/justicia-social-y-educacion

Morales-Vidal, E., & Cassany, D. (2020). El mundo según los libros de texto: Análisis Crítico del Discurso aplicado a materiales de español LE/L2 [The world according to textbooks: Critical discourse analysis applied to LE/L2 Spanish materials]. *Journal of Spanish Language Teaching*, 1–19. https://doi.org/10.1080/23247797.2020.1790161

Moreno-Doña, A., Toro, S., & Gómez, F. (2018). Crítica de la educación física crítica: eurocentrismo pedagógico y limitaciones epistemológicas [Criticism of critical physical education: Pedagogical eurocentrism and epistemological limitations]. *Psychology, Society, & Education*, *10*(3), 349–362. https://doi.org/10.25115/psye.v10i3.2104

Moya-Mata, I., Ros, C., & Menescardi, C. (2016). Perspectiva global de las imágenes publicadas en manuales de educación física [Global perspective of images published in physical education textbooks]. *Movimento*, *22*(4), 1277–1292. https://doi.org/10.22456/1982-8918.65304

Moya-Mata, I., Ruiz, L., Martín, J., Pérez, P., & Ros, C. (2017). La representación de la discapacidad en las imágenes de los libros de texto de Educación Física: ¿inclusión o exclusión? [Representation of disabilities in physical education textbooks image: Inclusion or exclusion?] *Retos*, *32*, 88–95. https://doi.org/10.47197/retos.v0i32.52191

Moya-Mata, I., Ros, C., & Peirats, J. (2018). ¿Qué representan las portadas de los libros de texto de Educación Física en Primaria? [What do the covers of the textbooks of Physical Education in primary represent?] *Retos*, *34*, 295–299. https://doi.org/10.47197/retos.v0i34.63412

Parise, M. M. (2021). Gender, sex, and heteronormativity in high school statistics textbooks. *Mathematics Education Research Journal*, *33*(4), 757–785. https://doi.org/10.1007/s13394-021-00390-x

Pedraza, Z. (2011). La 'educación de las mujeres': el avance de las formas modernas de feminidad en Colombia ['Education of women': The progress of modern forms of feminity in Colombia]. *Revista de Estudios Sociales*, *41*, 72–83. https://doi.org/10.7440/res43.2012.08

Peirats, J., Gallardo, I. Mª., San Martín, A., & Waliño, M. J. (2016). Análisis de la industria editorial y protocolo para la selección del libro de texto en formato digital [Analysis of the publishing industry and protocol for the selection of a suitable text book in digital format]. *Profesorado, Revista de currículum y formación del profesorado*, *20*(1), 75–89. https://recyt.fecyt.es/index.php/profesorado/article/view/49869

Perelman, M. (2014). *La barbarie deportiva: Crítica de una plaga* mundial [Sporting barbarism: A critique of a global plage]. Barcelona: Virus.

Pérez, J. M., & Pi, M. (2015). *Perspectivas 2015: El uso del audiovisual en las aulas. La situación en España* [Perspectives 2015: The use of audiovisuals in the classroom. The situation in Spain]. Barcelona: Gabinete de Comunicación y Educación de la Universidad Autónoma de Barcelona. http://www.aulaplaneta.com/wp-content/uploads/2015/09/Dossier_Perspectivas_IV_2015_100dpi.pdf

Pericot, J. (1987). *Servirse de la imagen: Un análisis pragmático de la imagen* [Using the image: A pragmatic analysis of the image]. Barcelona: Ariel.

Pozzer-Ardenghi, L., & Roth, W.-M. (2004). Making sense of photographs. *Science Education*, *89*, 219–241. https://doi.org/10.1002/sce.20045

Ralón, G. (2014). La filosofía del quiasmo: Introducción al pensamiento de Merleau-Ponty [The philosophy of chiasmus: An introduction to the thought of Merleau-Ponty]. *Diánoia*, *59*(73), 170–177.

Randazzo, F. (2012). Los imaginarios sociales como herramienta [Social imaginaries as a tool]. *Imagonautas*, *2*(2), 77–96. https://imagonautas.webs.uvigo.gal/index.php/imagonautas/issue/view/17

Revuelta, J. (2008). Pedagogía de la imagen: lectura crítica de publicidad televisiva [Image pedagogy: An educational experience on TV advertisement critical reading]. *Comunicar. Revista Científica de Educomunicación*, *31*(16), 613–621. https://doi.org/10.3916/c31-2008-03-058

Rey, A., & González, A. (2017). *Guía didáctica: El género en los ojos. Estrategias para educar con (y pese a) las fotografías de los materiales curriculares* [Didactic guide: Gender in the eyes. Strategies for educating with (and in spite of) the photographs in the curricular materials]. A Coruña: Discotrompo. https://xeneronosollos.webs.uvigo.gal/

Rey-Cao, A. (2020). La Educación Física ante el reto de la sostenibilidad. Gestionar las contradicciones del cuerpo [Physical education in the face of challenge of sustainability. Managing the body's contradictions]. In N. Puig & A. Camps (Coords.). *Diálogos sobre el deporte (1975–2020)* [Dialogues on sport (1975–2020)] (pp. 282–292). Barcelona: Inde. https://dialnet.unirioja.es/servlet/libro?codigo=768145

Rey-Cao, A., Táboas-Pais, Mª. I., & Canales-Lacruz, I. (2013). La representación de las personas mayores en los libros de texto de educación física [Representation of the elderly in Spanish Physical Education textbooks]. *Revista de Educación*, *362*, 129–153. https://doi.org/10.4438/1988-592X-RE-2013-EXT-244

Robinson, T. J., Fischer, L., Wiley, D., & Hilton, J. (2014). The impact of open textbooks on secondary science learning outcomes. *Educational Researcher*, *43*(7), 341–351. https://doi.org/10.3102/0013189X14550275

Sammler, S. (2018). Textbook research: Past achievements, current developments, future challenges. A Georg Eckert Institut researcher's view. *Didacticae*, *4*, 74–84. https://doi.org/10.1344/did.2018.4.74-84

Sánchez, L., Megías, I., & Rodríguez, E., (2004). *Jóvenes y publicidad: Valores en la comunicación publicitaria para jóvenes* [Young people and advertising: Values in advertising communication for young people]. Madrid: Injuve. http://www.injuve.es/sites/default/files/completojovenesypublicidad.pdf

Sánchez, N., Martos-García, D., & López, A. (2017). Las mujeres en los materiales curriculares: el caso de dos libros de texto de educación física [Women in curriculum materials: The case of two physical education textbooks]. *Retos*, *32*, 140–145. https://recyt.fecyt.es/index.php/retos/article/view/49344

Sánchez-Serradilla, C. (2016). *Discursos de feminidad en el estilo de vida fitness: estudio de caso de @vikikacosta en Instagram* [Discourses of femininity in the fitness lifestyle: @vikikacosta case study on Instagram. (Master's Final Project). Universidad Pompeu Fabra: Barcelona. http://hdl.handle.net/10230/27989

Silva, C. F., & Howe, P. D. (2012). The (in)validity of Supercrip representation of Paralympian athletes. *Journal of Sport and Social Issues*, *36*(2), 174–194. https://doi.org/10.1177/0193723511433865

Táboas, Mª. I. (2009). Análisis de los estereotipos corporales y de los modelos de actividad física representados en las imágenes de los libros de texto de educación física [Analysis of body stereotypes and physical activity models depicted in images in physical education textbooks]. (Doctoral dissertation). Universidade de Vigo. Pontevedra.

Táboas, Mª. I., & Rey, A. (2010). La deportivización del curriculum de educación física en las imágenes de los libros de texto de la ESO [The sportisation of the physical education national curriculum in the pictures of secondary school textbooks]. *Kronos*, *8*, 71–74.

Táboas, Mª. I., & Rey, A. (2011a). Los modelos corporales en la actividad física y el deporte: hacia una superación de los estereotipos desde la educación física escolar [Body models in sport and physical activity: Overcoming stereotypes from school physical education]. *Revista Española de Educación Física y Deportes*, *392*, 99–118. https://www.consejo-colef.es/publicaciones/archivo-revista-reefd.html

Táboas, Mª. I., & Rey, A. (2011b). Las imágenes en los libros de texto de Educación Física de la ESO: modelos corporales y actividad física [Pictures in physical education textbooks for mandatory secondary education: Body models and physical activity]. *Revista de Educación*, *354*, 293–322. https://doi.org/10.4438/1988-592X-RE-2011-354-001

Táboas, Mª. I., & Rey, A. (2011c). Las imágenes de los libros de texto de educación física: percepción y opinión del alumnado [Images in physical education textbooks: Student perception and opinion]. *Tándem. Didáctica de la Educación Física*, *36*, 103–111.

Táboas, Mª. I., & Rey, A. (2012). Los contenidos de la Educación Física en Secundaria: un análisis de las actividades físicas que se enseñan desde las imágenes de los libros de texto [The content of physical education in secondary schools: An analysis of the physical activities that are taught in the images in textbooks]. *Apunts. Educación Física y Deportes*, *107*, 45–73. https://doi.org/10.5672/apunts.2014-0983.es.(2012/1).107.04

Táboas-Pais, Mª. I., & Rey-Cao, A. (2012a). Gender differences in physical education textbooks in Spain: A content analysis of photographs. *Sex Roles*, *67*, 389–402. https://doi.org/10.1007/s11199-012-0174-y

Táboas-Pais, Mª. I., & Rey-Cao, A. (2012b). Disability in physical education textbooks: An analysis of image content. *Adapted Physical Activity Quarterly*, *29*(4), 310–328. https://doi.org/10.1123/apaq.29.4.310

Táboas-Pais, Mª. I., & Rey-Cao, A. (2015). Racial representation in physical education textbooks for secondary schools: Image content and perception held by students. *SAGE Open*, 1–11, https://doi.org/10.1177/2158244015574972

Vicente, M. (2007). La construcción de una ética médico-deportiva de sujeción: el cuerpo preso de la vida saludable [The construction of a medical and sport ethics of subjugation: The body as prisoner of 'the healthy' life]. *Salud Pública de México*, *49*(1), 71–78. http://www.scielo.org.mx/pdf/spm/v49n1/a10v49n1.pdf

Vicente, M. (2016). Bases para una didáctica crítica de la educación física [Basis for critical didactics in Physical Education]. *Apunts, Educación física y deportes*, *123*, 76–85. https://doi.org/10.5672/apunts.2014-0983.es.(2016/1).123.09

Vidal-Albelda, A., & Martínez-Bello, V. E. (2017). Representation of bodies with and without disabilities in secondary school Physical Education textbooks. *Sport in Society*, *20*(7), 957–968. https://doi.org/10.1080/17430437.2016.1221937

19
CHINESE GOVERNMENT'S MODERN GOVERNANCE AND THE CHALLENGES TO SOCIAL JUSTICE IN SCHOOL SPORTS

Honglu Zhang

Introduction

Governments play an influential role in social justice issues, either to advance or hinder them. This chapter discusses how the Chinese central government's modern governance has addressed historical and recent concerns in injustices in the areas of the public education system and school sport. Sports have long been a vehicle to either address social inequality (Darnell & Millington, 2019; Love, Deeb, & Waller, 2019) or to repress equal rights (Davis, 2007), and the same is true in China. For instance, to protect, pass on, and promote the ethnic minorities' traditional physical activities and games, since 1953, every four years, China hosts the National Traditional Games of Ethnic Minorities. The participants of these Games belong to the 55 ethnic minority groups, except the dominant Han ethnic group (which accounts for 91.11 per cent of the total Chinese population) (National Bureau of Statistics, 2021). Although the government has issued policies to direct the benefits and opportunities for all people to participate in sport, such as the 'Plan of Health China 2030' (The Communist Party of China Central Committee & the State Council, 2016) and the '14th Five-Year Plan for the Protection and Development of Persons with Disabilities' (the State Council, 2021), elite sports tend to be the priority of government support and investment of resources. For instance, in the recent four consecutive Paralympics, China dominated the medal counts of both the number of gold and the total number. However, China's elite para-sport success could be dwarfed by the limited chances of participating in adaptive sports by the more than 85 million people with disabilities in the country (Guan, 2015). Gender inequality in sport is a global problem, and Chinese women's soccer team players have received less payment and sponsors than men's soccer team, although women performed better at the international competitions (Yang, 2019). Furthermore, non-heterosexual sexual orientation is a taboo in China's elite sports. In 2021, Li Ying, a female football player and perhaps the first publicly out Chinese elite athlete, has received online trolling, and then was left out of China's Olympic squad highly likely because of her sexuality (Feng, 2021).

International academia has paid attention to the relationship between social justice and sports. The current research has investigated specific groups' experiences of sports and leisure; these groups include women, ethnic minorities, LGBTQ+, and people with disabilities (see Blauwet & Willick, 2012; Steidinger, 2020). These studies have illustrated unfairness and inequalities in school sports, elite sports, and leisure physical activities, highlighting the need for equal rights, participation, and salaries in sports worldwide. In contrast, social justice in sports seemed to be rarely discussed and examined by Chinese scholars. An exception is Fan (2004), perhaps the first analysis on justice in China's elite sport, focusing on the relationship between China's elite sport system, the training of teen athletes and the concerns of human rights violations. Since Fan's (2004) ground-breaking article on Chinese teen athletes, there is no updated research on this issue, which may be due to a two-fold factors of the strict academic censorship in the country and Chinese scholars' minimal interest in this issue. In contrast, research in both Chinese and English favoured the topics of economic, political, and cultural roles of sports (see Haugen, 2016).

In this chapter, we look into a less-studied area of government's management of sports in China, namely the school sports operated within the Chinese education system, which may differ from the relatively well-researched and highly achieved government-supported elite sport in China (Fan & Lu, 2012a, 2012b; Fan, Wu, & Xiong, 2005; Hu & Henry, 2017; Tan & Green, 2008; Zheng et al., 2019). Drawing on the empirical examples of Olympic education[1] related school sports programmes, we examine the social injustices reflected in these programmes at schools.

Sport in China has "consistently been an important government responsibility" (Zheng et al., 2018, p. 486). In China's current sports administrative system, researchers have highlighted the centralised or the top-down operation of the government, where power flows from the central level (Beijing) to local levels (counties) (Fan & Lu, 2012a, 2012b; Tan & Green, 2008; Zheng et al., 2018). In contrast to this dominant view on China's sports administration, this chapter proposes to use a hybrid rationality, combing authoritarianism and neoliberalism notions, to examine the government's authoritative and neoliberal practices that have impacted the social injustice in the education system and school sports programmes.

We divide this chapter into three sections, first, demonstrating the modern governance of Chinese government – a hybrid rationality – and discuss its influences on the education system and sport administration. The second section discusses the three situations in China's school sports, namely government's special permission to school sport related goods and services, government's unequal distribution of sports resources among schools, and unequal opportunities of sport participation among students, that were resulted from the practices of hybrid rationality. In the last section, we summarise key findings and suggestions for further research.

Chinese government's hybrid practice of authoritarianism

Scholars have debated the contemporary Chinese political-economic model, especially since the economic reforms around the late 1970s (Horesh & Lim, 2017; Ren, 2010). Some argued that China has become a neoliberal state (Li, 2017; Wang, 2011), while others argued that China is a partial neoliberal state, since it also has the legacies of state authoritarianism (Huang, 2008; Liew, 2005; Ong, 2007; Nonini, 2008). As neoliberalism has varied forms (Ball, 2012), Harvey (2007) regarded China as a strange case of neoliberalism which is marked by authoritarian control. Different terms have been used to describe the 'strange case' of China, such as a hybrid socialist-neoliberal state (Jeffreys & Sigley, 2009; Sigley, 2006), and neoliberalism with Chinese characteristics (Harvey, 2007; Peck et al., 2012), which all recognise that China has shifted from the traditional coercive administrative pole to a standpoint where neoliberal logics could be embraced. Harvey (2007) also emphasised that the central role of the state is not contradictory in the neoliberal system since state authoritarianism is key to preserve and sustain the system. Further, Peck (2010) argued that "[n]eoliberalism ... has only ever existed in 'impure' form, indeed *can* only exist in messy hybrids" (p. 7, emphasis in the original text). Neoliberalism is "a resilient, responsive and deeply reactionary credo" and "it is doomed to coexist with its unloved others, be these the residues of state socialism, developmental statism, authoritarianism, or social democracy" (Peck, 2010, p. 7). Hence, we adopt this 'impure' view on the Chinese government's hybrid socialist-neoliberal practices of modern governance. Then, we discuss the influences of a hybrid rationality of the state to social justice in the education system and sport administration.

The practices of authoritarianism and neoliberalism can be seen in the contemporary Chinese public education sector. Authoritative rationality is manifested through the government making plans for students' enrolments, assessing teachers, providing facilities and resources, and monitoring the implementation of curriculum (MoE, 2017). In particular, in the main curricula of primary and junior high schools in China, there is a subject named 'the ideological and political education', which functions as "establishing the personal authority of top leaders", "asserting power" of the Party leaders, "legitimating authoritarian rule in China" (Zeng, 2016, p. 116), and developing students to be patriots (Wang, 2012).

To develop an equal and just society is also claimed to be the central government's responsibility. In 2012, the government launched 12 core socialist values, including prosperity, democracy, civility, harmony, freedom, *equality*, *justice*, rule of law, patriotism, dedication, integrity, and friendship (emphasised by the authors). In relation to sports, social justice and equality was reflected in the policy – *Healthy China 2030*, which oversees that sport facilities, space and opportunities should be offered to all persons, regardless of their cultural and ethnic background, geographic locations, age- and gender-appropriate. The Chinese government has made improvement in social justice in the areas of income gaps and gender discriminations and the creation of a comprehensive social security system (Li, 2014). China had lower income inequality than the United States (Piketty et al., 2019).

However, in the higher education sector, the government's decisive role in students' enrolments has created significant inequality in enrolment. From 1990 to 2006, students from urban areas, especially major cities, such as Beijing and Shanghai, found it easier to get enrolled in key universities than their rural counterparts. Students from Beijing were 14 times as likely as those from the rest of the country to enrol in universities in Beijing (Yao et al., 2010, p. 853). In contrast, students from Western China had a smaller chance to even go to university (Yao et al., 2010).

Globally, the neoliberal turn in education has challenged governmental control, searched for private partnerships, and 'released' public education into the free market (Powell, 2015, 2020). Privatisation and marketisation, especially the practice of outsourcing, have been adopted in education, accompanied by the neoliberal spirits of competitiveness, freedom of choice, autonomy and decentralising the government's authority and devolving responsibilities (Sperka, 2020). In China, privatisation in education has become more diversified. There are the hybrid public–private schools, which are invested in by private sectors but remain under government ownership; there are for-profit education institutions. Mok et al. (2009) claimed in 1998 there were around 50,000 private education institutions. Private touring services or after-school education is also a type of privatisation in Chinese education. Outsourcing health and physical education is now prevalent in many countries (see Evans & Davies, 2015; Powell, 2020; Williams & Macdonald, 2015), and it is typically utilised to bring in external 'expertise' (Powell, 2020; Williams et al., 2011) or equipment (Williams et al., 2011; Williams & Macdonald, 2015).

Some have praised neoliberal practices that could incentivise public education to be more effective and economical (Dougherty & Natow, 2019; Green, 2005). Others are concerned that decentralisation and school autonomy could cause inequality among different areas (Apple, 2009; Carnoy, 1999), and students' best interests would be damaged by a profit-making aim (Kohn, 2002; Saltman, 2011). In China's educational context, neoliberal practices such as marketisation and privatisation have intensified educational inequality and widened the rural and urban gap, as well as created uneven educational resources among students from different areas (Mok et al., 2009).

We provide two examples of hybrid practices in education, *the key school system* and the outsourcing of public schools' extracurricular sports programmes. Justice in China means to distribute power, freedom, opportunity, salary, and wealth based on 'reasonable criteria' (Li, 2014). However, this 'reasonable criteria' could be opaque in the authoritative rationality, which can be seen in China's development of the *key schools*. Since the 1980s, China's education development has mirrored Deng Xiaoping's ideology of economic development – the market-oriented reform, which advocated economic competitiveness based on the strong state control (Wu, 2013). To effectively use the government's limited budget and resources for education, Deng pointed out the need for key schools and key universities. Based on ambiguous criteria, the state government nominated some schools as *key schools*, while other schools remained as regular schools (Wu, 2013). Key schools enjoy priorities in the assignment of qualified teachers, good facilities, sufficient funds, and top-performing students (Wu, 2013). However, the key school system also created educational inequalities. For instance, Fan and Song (2016) demonstrated the unequal opportunities and competition for regular schools and their students, whereby key schools had 10–20 per cent more funding than regular schools from 1978 to 1995. These issues led to the reform of the key school system and in 2006, Ministry of Education (MoE) abandoned the key school system. However, the categorisation of schools and unequal treatment among schools have not completely disappeared in China. In recent years, *the demonstration school system* has emerged in Chinese public schools and demonstrated that this system continued to (re)produce social justice concerns.

In addition, the hybrid practice of authoritarianism and neoliberalism are common to see in the extracurricular activities in Chinese public schools. Olympic education programmes for the 2008 Olympics and the 2022 Olympics provide good examples. The state government played a decisive role in designing the programme and monitoring its implementation in schools (Brownell, 2009; Mao, 2015; Zhang, 2021). In the meantime, non-public sectors were involved in the implementation at schools. For instance, during the 2008 Beijing Olympics, Johnson & Johnson partnered with the Beijing Organizing Committee for the Olympic Games (BOCOG) to initiate a Band-Aid education campaign, which worked to teach students about the values that define the Olympic movement as well as health and wound care (Sina, 2006). Indeed, outsourcing coaches is a common practice in China's school sports. The government has encouraged schools to work with outsourced sectors, such as sports clubs and coaches, to develop various sports, including football (MoE, 2017) and tennis (MoE, 2018a).

Next, we investigate how the two types of governing practices have created injustices in school sports in China's public education sector. The below empirical evidence is from Zhang's (2021) critical ethnographic research on the implementation of Olympic education (Olympic-themed activities) and winter sports in Beijing's primary schools. Beijing, as the 2022 Winter Olympic hosting city, needs to conduct educational activities around the Olympics in schools, known as the Olympic education, mainly including teaching varied winter sports and learning Olympic-related facts.

Government's special permission to the school sport related goods and services

One strategy under the hybrid rationality in Chinese school sports is the government's allowance of schools to purchase goods and services from private and not-for-profit suppliers. In terms of schools' winter sports programmes, the local government of Beijing Municipality encourages schools to work with a variety of private organisations, including private equipment companies, skiing clubs, training centres, winter sports associations (e.g. Beijing Ice Hockey Association), and other winter sports related institutions (BMBS et al., 2018). The local government further encourages schools to purchase goods and services from sports-related private suppliers by rewarding schools with funding. For example, to support the development of winter sports, Beijing government issued policy to state that the winter-sport demonstration schools can receive funding to cover various winter sports-related expenses, such as private lessons, facility hire, tickets to winter sports clubs, sports equipment, coaches, and lectures of winter sports (BMEC & Finance Bureau of Beijing, 2018).

The above example demonstrates the role of the government in supporting outsourcing the school programmes underpinned by neoliberalism – where education is positioned as a marketplace in which schools can purchase winter sports related goods and services from a range of competing private providers. Schools, as customers, had certain degrees of autonomy and freedom in choosing the commodity, in respect to the funding they get from the government. This neoliberal practice, to a degree, has been allowed in China's education system, which is primarily a state-funded and -managed public education system (He et al., 2007). However, government policy expressly 'forbids' commercial information from appearing in schools (MoE, 2018b), as a way to demonstrate that schools are still under the central planning of the government. The state resolved this inconsistent practice between authoritative and neoliberal rationalities by giving certain private winter sports organisations and suppliers special permission, and at the same time 'motivated' schools politically and financially to purchase goods and services only from these permitted organisations and suppliers. Regarding how the government decided to give which private suppliers the special permission, we could not find specific criteria or instructions from the official documents (see MoE et al., 2018; BMBS et al., 2018).

By giving the special permission to certain private winter sports organisations and suppliers, the Chinese government approved which are the 'right' private organisations for schools to work with. Indeed, when schools receive policies or announcements of sports competitions, one commonality among these documents is their requirement of using the *proper* equipment. For instance, before a winter sports competition among Beijing's primary and secondary school students, the government issues a notice that equipment can be rented or purchased from Sweep Curling Club (Haidian District Educational Commission, 2018), which sent a strong signal to the schools where they could acquire the proper equipment. The teachers of these sports programmes were also aware of the 'right' and 'approved' providers. A teacher commented, "I usually did not have much freedom to choose the equipment because district government departments would 'recommend' equipment to schools in the district" (Zhang, 2021) In this way, China's government blended authoritarian rationalities and neoliberal rationalities (i.e. privatisation, market forces, competition, consumption, choice) to promote and supervise school sports.

It may seem that all sports organisations and companies had equal opportunities to sell their products and services to schools. However, interpersonal relationship or personalised ties (关系/guan xi) is a key determinant in doing business in China. Indeed, interpersonal relationship is "the most foundational characteristic of Chinese society" (Xue et al., 2020, p. 6). A close connection with the central government is important to be the association in school sports. In China, scarce goods and opportunities are provided to individuals who have informal relationships with the government within the communist system (Manion, 1991). A coach from a floor skiing company said that "Our company has close relationship with sports bureaus and the officials, so we could have the chance to promote our equipment to more than 30 primary schools in Beijing" (Zhang, 2021).

The government's unclear selective methods for getting the special permission and the suppliers' interpersonal relationship with the government and the schools would cause fair competitions. Only the approved private sectors have access to schools, while others have no choices even if their products and services may be better. Even being successfully approved by the government, these private providers still have to compete to be chosen by schools. Their competition is usually not based on their products or services, but personal relationships with the companies. This may discourage private sectors' development and encourage corruption in the interaction between the private and the government (Adams et al., 2006). In the process of guiding schools' privatisation, schools have limited options when choosing private organisations, although each school has equal rights to choose from the state-approved organisations. However, each school's difference, students' interests and needs have failed to be recognised in nominating state-approved private sectors to develop sports.

Government's (un)equal distribution of sports resources among schools

At the school level, the government's hybrid rationality is also embedded in the implementation of the demonstration school system. This system selects certain schools be the demonstration schools, and then provided them extra financial and physical support, therefore, (re) producing education inequality among schools.

There are no specific criteria in selecting demonstration schools, and relevant policies claim that all schools could apply to become demonstration schools (see MoE, 2017, 2018a). Nevertheless, during Zhang's (2021) fieldwork, she found that only when schools have received notices or invitation to apply from the government, the schools would apply to become a demonstration school. Hence, the government have already pre-selected certain schools as they issued the policies, and schools understood the subtexts imbedded in the 'all welcome to apply' phrasing.

This system indicates the neoliberal notions of competition and freedom. Comparing to key schools' overall good performance, demonstration schools only need to focus on being good at one subject or activity. By encouraging and supporting schools to develop certain items, the government aims to build competitive schools, at least in their demonstration items. As indicated in the policy of football demonstration schools, the selected schools supposed to have the leading role or set an example for other schools (MoE, 2017). Similar phrases also appear in other policies of demonstration schools (see MoE, 2018a). Indeed, the term demonstration in Chinese means guiding, role models, which already implies that these selected schools should be better than the average. This reflects the neoliberal notion of competitiveness. The government also draws on the notion of freedom in the demonstration system. As Foucault (1982) reminded us, modern government depends on the element of freedom, as "power is exercised only over free subjects, and only insofar as they are free" (p. 790). It is impossible to force every individual to think and act in certain ways (Foucault, 1991). In relation to Chinese school sports, rather than requiring schools to develop all sports, the government allows schools to choose their demonstration items.

It is by no means that schools have full autonomy in choosing demonstration items. The central government also has authoritarian approaches in the demonstration system. In terms of sports, the central government limited schools' options of choosing demonstration items. When the government issues policies about demonstration schools, they usually list one item (e.g. football, tennis), which is the key sport the government's sport bureau focused on developing in a recent period. In this way, schools cannot but 'choose' the provided item. Besides, policies of the same item would be continually issued several times within a year or in recent consecutive years. For example, in preparing for the 2022 Winter Olympics and there were a series of 'Olympic education demonstration schools' policies since 2018 (Zhang, 2021). Different governmental organisations, such as Ministry of Education and its subordinate bodies, would issue similar policies towards the implementation of Olympic education in schools. This repetition is a strong 'suggestion' for schools to follow the government's guidelines. In these ways, the state government blended the authoritarianism and neoliberalism into the hybrid practice of the demonstration school system.

To further legitimise the practical rationality of the demonstration school system, government policies normally describe the benefits of carrying out a certain sport in school. For example, in the tennis demonstration school policy, it says, "tennis skills would improve, and students' health levels would be significantly improved. Students would have sports habits, know the importance of rules, cooperation and strong will" (MoE, 2018a, p. 2). Although these expressions did not describe the lack of winter sports or tennis as problematic, they actually govern schools to implement the policies "at a distance" (Miller & Rose, 2008, p. 16).

However, the hybrid rationality in the demonstration school system leads to the unequal distribution among schools. Schools would compete to become demonstration schools through building strong ties with the government because the selected schools would be distributed extra support and resources, financial support is one of the obvious supports. According to the 2017 policy of football demonstration school, local departments were required to provide selected schools with extra funding and policies to support the development of football in these schools (MoE, 2017). Similar preference also appeared in the 2018 policy of tennis demonstration schools (MoE, 2018a). The policy includes a guideline to support the implementation of tennis demonstration schools. It specifies several requirements/benefits for the selected schools, such as tennis courts, teachers training programmes, professional coach allocation, and specific funding (MoE, 2017). The guideline also provided prizes for schools and teachers who excel in developing tennis. Sometimes, the support for demonstration schools differs. For instance, in the provision of winter sports, the selected winter sports demonstration schools would all receive extra 500,000 RMB (equivalent to 77,000 USD) for the first year, then the government further evaluates these schools into three levels, and then provides different levels of financial support, with 250,000 RMB, 500,000 RMB, and 750,000 RMB for each level (equivalent to 38,500 USD, 77,000 USD, 115,500 USD) after that (BMEC & Finance Bureau of Beijing, 2018).

In addition to material resources, demonstration schools are given more nonmaterial resources, such as opportunities for sports events. For example, in 2018 only demonstration schools in Beijing were allowed to compete in the city's Third Winter Sports Games, even though the name of this Games seems open to every school's team (Haidian District

Educational Commission, 2018). By participating in the Games, the demonstration schools also had the opportunities to be known by the municipal officials, media, and the public.

The unclear standards for selecting demonstration schools and the extra resources and support for the demonstration schools resulted in unequal redistribution among schools. Even though fair distribution of material and nonmaterial resources, such as goods and services, access, and opportunity, is a crucial part of social justice, in practice and in the Chinese-specific context, the resources have been redistributed among Chinese schools following a hybrid rationality. Hence, schools are motivated to strive to become demonstration schools. This unequal treatment among schools could also generate an inevitable consequence that school students would have unequal access to and opportunities in school sports, which we discuss next.

Students' unequal access to school sports

In our understanding, social justice in education means that all students should have equal access to the same quality of educational processes and resources. At the government level, the Chinese central and local governments have stated in all the policies of winter sports and Olympic education that sports resources and opportunities should provide to all students, and all students can receive comprehensive development at schools (e.g. MoE et al., 2018; BMBS et al., 2018). At the school level, schools have expressed their commitment in their applications for the sports demonstration schools that they would provide winter sports equipment and learning opportunities to all students (Zhang, 2021). However, in reality, one way the demonstration schools showed the value of Olympic education was by choosing only the 'suitable' students to represent the school in sports competitions. It seems that the demonstration schools become the 'exclusive space' in which only the 'qualified' students can participate in sports.

The Winter Olympic education in the demonstration schools has been narrowed to winter sport competitions. To win the competition, the demonstration schools would organise trials to select students who are good at sports. Some schoolteachers prefer to directly select from those who are already in schools' football and basketball teams, since they view sporting techniques as transferable. For example, a teacher said, "students who are good at one sport are likely to be good at other sports, so almost all our school's floor ice hockey players are chosen from the school's football team". This short cut to form a strong winter sport team clearly derailed the purpose of the Winter Olympic education and only provided exclusive access to winter sports for limited students. The students who 'received' the so-called Winter Olympic education are those who play sports well, and they have better chances to win the glories for their schools at the winter sport competitions (Zhang, 2021). In some schools, the teachers also selected younger students to form the back-up winter sports teams. The reason behind it is that the schools can have reserved talents and be prepared for the future competitions. Students in Year 4 or 5 have less of a study burden and have more time to receive training. A teacher explained that these groups of students can receive longer training than Year 6 students and they would have better skills and "in the future, they are more likely to win more glories for the school". It seems demonstration schools were less interested in student participation in Olympic education or students' learning, while they were more interested in increasing schools' competitiveness and the 'glory' of winning.

In fact, such selection approaches contribute to schools' ambition of 'winning glory'. Foucault (1984) argued, bio-power focuses on a citizen's biological existence, such as birth, morbidity, and longevity. Bio-power seeks a productive workforce and an efficient economic system through healthy, skilled, educated populations (Dean, 2010; Markula & Pringle, 2007; Rabinow & Rose, 2006). In this case, the selection of students most likely to contribute to the productivity of the schools, namely increasing the schools' competitiveness in Olympic education.

Some Winter Olympic Education demonstration schools would organise students to participate in the Olympic-related public events, but only attractive students would be selected. For example, the selection process for a group of 40 students to perform the Olympic-themed song at a national event was like this: schoolteachers asking both male and female students to line up in the front of the classrooms and smile, and then the teachers photographed their smiling faces (Zhang, 2021). After close securitising and comparing, the 40 students who have good smiles would be selected for the event (Zhang, 2021). Apart from considering students' physical appearance, schools and teachers also tended to select groups of obedient students to perform or participate in winter sports related activities (Zhang, 2021). The schools' commitment that all students would have opportunities to participate in winter sports was not fulfilled. These selection strategies clearly led to students' unequal access to sports, facilities, and other sports-related activities.

At the same time, such a misdistribution led to misrecognition among students. As Fraser (1998) argued, "maldistribution directly entails misrecognition" (p. 6). Recognition concerns issues like disrespect, cultural imperialism, and status hierarchy (Fraser, 1998). Recognition relates to the differences among different people and requires equal respect for all participants to achieve social esteem. In other words, groups and individuals should not be marginalised and rendered as 'others'. Misrecognition in education can be found in the extent to which access to particular forms of provision privileges some groups over others (Power & Taylor, 2013). In this case, non-selected students may be misrecognised as less qualified. You (2007) argued that students in key schools had higher achievement and looked down on students who studied in non-key schools. Zhang (2021) found that in the same school, selected students felt superior to peers who failed to be selected. Most students thought that participating in Olympic education-related activities made them better than their classmates, and students in other classes and other schools (Zhang, 2021). Such superior feeling further motivated students to discriminate against students who were not in Olympic education. As a student commented, these unselected students are "noisy and bad". In the end, students did not have equal access to opportunities and resources in sports, and, most importantly, they were looked down upon, devalued in others' consciousness, and denied some of their standing as full members of their schools.

Conclusion

Sigley (2006) states: "There is no single hand, invisible or otherwise, projecting its will upon the population, on the contrary, as the governmentality literature knows well, government is a much more decentred, ad hoc and contingent affair" (p. 489). Just as the liberal government contains some forms of authoritarian governmentality (Dean, 1999; Hindess, 2001), this chapter demonstrates that non-liberal governmentality may also utilise liberal strategies. It would be fair to argue that liberal and authoritarian forms of rules are not always clearly distinguishable in modern government. We illustrate how the Chinese central and local government's hybrid administrative methods have contributed to educational injustices in school sports. We first demonstrated how China is a hybrid socialist-neoliberal society, based on a form of political rationality that employs both neoliberalism and authoritarianism.

Informed by this hybrid rationality, the central government implements two practices in school sports: privatisation and the demonstration school system. These two practices contribute to unequal distribution of resources and opportunities in Chinese education, particularly in school sports. Specifically, the government encourages schools to work with private sectors in developing school sports, while at the same time, only giving specifical permission to some private sectors to play a role in school sports. Such permission is usually given to sectors who have close relationship with the government. Schools, therefore, have limited options when purchasing goods and services from private and for-profit suppliers.

The demonstration school system also creates unequal opportunities and inequalities among schools and students. In this system, the government selects schools based on ambiguous criteria, and then provides them extra support, in terms of financial support, resources allocation, and opportunities. These unequal distributions motivate schools to strive for competitiveness, and one way in which they do so is by selecting certain students (e.g. attractive and those with sporting ability) to represent their schools in different sports or sports-related public events, which helps them stand out in the public education system. Students, therefore, are treated unfairly in many ways to engage in sporting facilities and resources. Students even marked themselves better compared to peers who failed to be selected and discriminated against them. In these ways, the moral role of education is twisted. As Fraser (1998) argued, denying "some individuals and groups the possibility of participating on a par with others in social interaction" (p. 3) is morally wrong. Overall, we argue that Chinese hybrid rationality contributes to both blatant and subtle systematic injustices in school sports.

This chapter lends further weight to exploring educational injustices in other school subjects and higher education in China. Indeed, educational injustices also happen in other aspects of schools, at least the selecting approaches also occur among other subjects. However, social justice, as a research topic, seems to be largely ignored in China. This chapter calls for more research to examine social justice and equality issues across the Chinese education system, especially in sport, leisure, and physical education areas. The role of the central government is an important perspective to consider in such research. As this chapter indicated, China's government employs a hybrid rationality and such a hybrid has produced educational injustices whether intentionally or unintentionally. Since China's economic-political model is complex and hybrid, we suggest that future researchers continuously explore the intertwined influences of authoritarianism and neoliberalism on the social justice issues.

Note

1 Each bidding city for the Olympics is required to implement Olympic education prorgammes. These prorgammes usually involves various Olympic-themed activities, such as teaching Olympic facts, making craftworks, and learning winter sports (Zhang, 2021).

References

Adams, J., Young, A., & Wu, Z. H. (2006). Public private partnerships in China: System, constraints and future prospects. *International Journal of Public Sector Management, 19*(4), 384–396. https://doi.org/10.1108/09513550610669202

Apple, M. W. (2009). *Global crises, social justice, and education*. Routledge.

Ball, S. J. (2012, March). Show me the money! Neoliberalism at work in education. In *FORUM: For promoting 3–19 comprehensive education* (pp. 23–28).

Beijing Municipal Bureau of Sport. (2018). *The first winter sports for Beijing residents* (Publication No.38).

Beijing Municipal Education Commission & Finance Bureau of Beijing. (2018). *The way to support campus winter sports in Beijing*.
Blauwet, C., & Willick, S. E. (2012). The Paralympic movement: Using sports to promote health, disability rights, and social integration for athletes with disabilities. *PM&R, 4*(11), 851–856.
Brownell, S. (2009). Beijing's Olympic education programme: Re-thinking Suzhi education, re-imagining an international China. *The China Quarterly, 197,* 44–63. https://doi.org/10.1017/S0305741009000034
Carnoy, Martin. 1999. *Globalization and educational reform: What planners need to know*. International Institute for Education Planning.
The Central Committee of the Communist Party of China & the State Council (2016). Healthy China 2030. www.gov.cn/zhengce/2016-10/25/content_5124174.htm
Darnell, S. C., & Millington, R. (2019). Social justice, sport, and sociology: A position statement. *Quest, 71*(2), 175–187. https://doi.org/10.1080/00336297.2018.1545681
Davis, T. (2007). Race and sports in America: An historical overview. *Virginia Sports & Entertainment Law Journal* 1–28.
Dean, M. (1999). *Governmentality*. Sage.
Dean, M. (2010). *Governmentality: Power and rule in modern society* (2nd ed.). Sage.
Dougherty, K. J., & Natow, R. S. (2019). Analyzing neoliberalism in theory and practice: The case of performance-based funding for higher education. *The Center for Global Higher Education*, 1–44. https://doi.org/10.7916/d8-a1kt-7p96
Evans, J., & Davies, B. (2015). Neoliberal freedoms, privatisation and the future of physical education. *Sport, Education and Society, 20*(1), 10–26. https://doi.org/10.1080/13573322.2014.918878
Fan, H. (2004). Innocence lost: Child athletes in China. *Sport in Society, 7*(3), 338–354.
Fan, H., & Lu, Z. (2012a) China's sports policy and politics in the post-Beijing Olympics era. *The International Journal of the History of Sport, 29*(1), 184–189.
Fan, H., & Lu, Z. (2012b). From Barcelona to Athens (1992–2004): 'Juguo Tizhi' and China's quest for global power and Olympic glory. *The International Journal of the History of Sport, 29*(1), 113–131.
Fan, H., & Song, L. (2016, September). Study on the imbalance reasons and the equilibrium strategy of information resources of basic education in urban and rural areas. In *2016 International Conference on Contemporary Education, Social Sciences and Humanities*, Moscow, Russia.
Fan. H., Wu, P., & Xiong, H. (2005). Beijing ambitions: An analysis of the Chinese elite sports system and its Olympic strategy for the 2008 Olympic Games. *The International Journal of the History of Sport, 22*(4), 510–529.
Feng, J. Y. (2021, June 25). *Soccer player Li Ying becomes first high-profile Chinese athlete to come out*. SupChina. https://supchina.com/2021/06/25/chinese-soccer-stars-history-making-coming-out-moment-ruined-by-homophobic-bigots/
Foucault, M. (1982). The subject and power. *Critical Inquiry, 8*(4), 777–795.
Foucault, M. (1984). Space, knowledge, and power: Interview with Paul Rabinow. In P. Rabinow (Ed.), *The Foucault reader* (pp. 239–256). Pantheon.
Foucault, M. (1991). *Discipline and punish: The birth of the prison* (A. Sheridan, Trans.). Penguin.
Fraser, N. (1998). Social justice in the age of identity politics. *Geographic thought: A praxis perspective*, 72–91.
Green, C. (2005). *The privatization of state education: Public partners, private dealings*. Routledge.
Guan, Z. X. (2015). Paralympics in China: A social approach versus an elite approach. *International Journal of the History of Sport, 32*(8), 1115–1120.
Haidian District Educational Commission. (2018). *The Third Winter Sports Competition for Primary and Secondary Schools in Beijing*.
Harvey, D. (2007). *A brief history of neoliberalism*. Oxford University Press. https://doi.org/10.1093/oso/9780199283262.001.0001
Haugen, M. B. (2016). The changing national and political role of Chinese sports: 1949–2016. *Education About Asia, 21*(2), 49–53.
He, W., Wang, X., & Yu, K. (2007). A visible hand: Government as the change agent in the transformation of management education in China. *International Journal of Management in Education, 1*(1 2), 5–20. https://doi.org/10.1504/IJMIE.2007.014374
Hindess, B. (2001). The liberal government of unfreedom. *Alternatives, 26*(2), 93–111.
Horesh, N., & Lim, K. F. (2017). China: An East Asian alternative to neoliberalism? *The Pacific Review, 30*(4), 425–442. https://doi.org/10.1080/09512748.2016.1264459

Hu, X. & Henry, I. (2017). Reform and maintenance of Juguo Tizhi: Governmental management discourse of Chinese elite sport. *European Sport Management Quarterly, 17*(4), 531–553.

Huang, Y. S. (2008). *Capitalism with Chinese characteristics: Entrepreneurship and the state*. Cambridge University Press.

Jeffreys, E., & Sigley, G. (2009). Governmentality, governance and China. In E. Jeffreys (Ed.), *China's governmentalities, governing change, changing government* (pp. 13–35). Routledge.

Kohn, A. (2002). *Education, Inc.: Turning learning into a business*. Heinemann.

Li, S. (2014, May 6). *The Government Prioritises in Tackling the Income Inequality*. Cpsnews. http://theory.people.com.cn/n/2014/0506/c384764-24981675.html

Li, Q. (2017). *The idea of governance and the spirit of Chinese neoliberalism* (Governing China in the 21st Century). Springer.

Liew, L. H. (2005). China's engagement with neo-liberalism: Path dependency, geography, and party self-reinvention. *The Journal of Development Studies, 41*(2), 331–352.

Love, A., Deeb, A., & Waller, S. N. (2019). Social justice, sport and racism: A position statement. *Quest, 71*(2), 227–238.

Manion, M. (1991). Policy implementation in the People's Republic of China: Authoritative decisions versus individual interests. *The Journal of Asian Studies, 50*(2), 253–279. https://doi.org/10.2307/2057208

Mao, W. (2015). A notable endeavour: The nature and significance of Olympic education in the pre-and post-period of Beijing's 2008 Olympic Games [Doctoral thesis, Western University]. Electronic Thesis and Dissertation Repository. https://ir.lib.uwo.ca/etd/3294

Markula, P., & Pringle, R. (2007). *Foucault, sport and exercise: Power, knowledge and transforming the self*. Routledge.

Miller, P., & Rose, N. (2008). *Governing the present: Administering Economic, social and personal life*. Polity Press.

Ministry of Education. (2017). *Selecting football demonstration schools*. www.moe.gov.cn/srcsite/A17/moe_938/s3276/201704/t20170401_301686.html

Ministry of Education. (2018a). Selecting tennis demonstration schools. www.moe.gov.cn/srcsite/A17/moe_938/s3276/201903/t20190326_375496.html

Ministry of Education. (2018b). *Jinzhi shangye guanggao shangye huodong jinru zhongxiao xuexiao he youeryuan de jinji tongzhi* [Forbid commercial information and activities in primary, secondary schools, and early childhood centers] (Publication No. 77). www.moe.gov.cn/srcsite/A06/s7053/201810/t20181012_351283.html

Ministry of Education, General Administration of Sport, & Beijing Organizing Committee for the Olympic Games. (2018). *The Olympic education plan for primary and secondary school students in Beijing 2022 Winter Olympics and Paralympics* (Publication No.10).

Mok, K. H., Wong, Y. C., & Zhang, X. (2009). When marketisation and privatisation clash with socialist ideals: Educational inequality in urban China. *International Journal of Educational Development, 29*(5), 505–512. https://doi.org/10.1016/j.ijedudev.2009.04.011

National Bureau of Statistics. (2021). Key data from the seventh national census. www.stats.gov.cn/tjsj/zxfb/202105/t20210510_1817176.html

Nonini, D. M. (2008). Is China becoming neoliberal?. *Critique of Anthropology, 28*(2), 145–176.

Ong, A. (2007). Neoliberalism as a mobile technology. *Transactions of the Institute of British Geographers, 32*(1), 3–8. https://doi.org/10.1111/j.1475-5661.2007.00234.x

Peck, J. (2010). *Constructions of neoliberal reason*. Oxford University Press.

Peck, J., Theodore, N., & Brenner, N. (2012). Neoliberalism resurgent? Market rule after the great recession. *South Atlantic Quarterly, 111*(2), 265–288.

Piketty, T., Yang, L., & Zucman, G. (2019). Capital accumulation, private property, and rising inequality in china, 1978–2015. *The American Economic Review, 109*(7), 2469–2496.

Powell, D. (2015). *'Part of the solution'?: Charities, corporate philanthropy and healthy lifestyles education in New Zealand primary schools* [Doctoral Thesis, Charles Sturt University]. UC Research Repository.

Powell, D. (2020). *Schools, corporations, and the war on childhood obesity: How corporate philanthropy shapes public health and education*. Routledge.

Power, S., & Taylor, C. (2013). Social justice and education in the public and private spheres. *Oxford Review of Education, 39*(4), 464–479.

Rabinow, P., & Rose, N. (2006). Biopower today. *BioSocieties*, *1*(2), 195–217. https://doi.org/10.1017/S1745855206040014
Ren, H. (2010). *Neoliberalism and Culture in China and Hong Kong: The countdown of time*. Routledge.
Saltman, K. J. (2011). Introduction to the first edition. In K. J. Saltman & D. A. Gabbard (Eds), *Education as enforcement: The militarization and corporatization of schools* (2nd ed., pp. 1–18). Routledge.
Sigley, G. (2006). Chinese governmentalities: Government, governance and the socialist market economy. *Economy and Society*, *35*(4), 487–508. https://doi.org/10.1080/03085140600960773
Sina. (2006, August 15). *Aoyun zhishi guatu xiang quanguo zhongxiaoxue mianfei fafang* [Handing out Olympic education posters to primary and secondary schools for free]. Sina. http://news.sina.com.cn/c/2006-08-15/09159752855s.shtml
Sperka, L. (2020). (Re)defining outsourcing in education. *Discourse: Studies in the Cultural Politics of Education*, *41*(2), 268–280. https://doi.org/10.1080/01596306.2020.1722429
The State Council (2021). *The Fourteenth Five-year Plan for the Protection and Development of the Disabled*. www.gov.cn/zhengce/content/2021-07/21/content_5626391.htm
Steidinger, J. (2020). *Stand up and shout out: Women's fight for equal pay, equal rights, and equal opportunities in sports*. Rowman & Littlefield.
Tan, T., & Green, M. (2008). Analysing China's drive for Olympic success in 2008. *The International Journal of the History of Sport*, *25*(3), 314–338.
Wang, H. (2011). *The end of the revolution: China and the limits of modernity*. Verso.
Wang, Z. (2012). *Never forget national humiliation: Historical memory in Chinese politics and foreign relations*. Columbia University Press
Williams, B. J., & Macdonald, D. (2015). Explaining outsourcing in health, sport and physical education. *Sport, Education and Society*, *20*(1), 57–72. https://doi.org/10.1080/13573322.2014.914902
Williams, B. J., Hay, P. J., & Macdonald, D. (2011). The outsourcing of health, sport and physical educational work: A state of play. *Physical Education and Sport Pedagogy*, *16*(4), 399–415. https://doi.org/10.1080/17408989.2011.582492
Wu, X. X. (2013). *School choice in China: A different tale?* Routledge.
Xue, H., Watanabe, N. M., Chen, R., Newman, J. I., & Yan, G. (2020). Football (as) guanxi: A relational analysis of actor reciprocity, state capitalism, and the Chinese football industry. *Sport in Society*, *23*(12), 2005–2030. https://doi.org/10.1080/17430437.2020.1755959
Yang, W. X. (2019). How difficult it is to reach gender equality in terms of payment. A closer look at soccer players' payment. www.thepaper.cn/newsDetail_forward_3892417
Yao, S., Wu, B., Su, F., & Wang, J. (2010). The impact of higher education expansion on social justice in china: A spatial and inter-temporal analysis. T*he Journal of Contemporary China*, *19*(67), 837–854.
You, Y. (2007). A deep reflection on the 'key school system' in basic education in China. *Frontiers of Education in China*, *2*(2), 229–239.
Zeng, J. H. (2016). Ideological and political education in China. In *The Chinese Communist Party's capacity to rule* (pp. 115–152). Palgrave Macmillan.
Zhang, H. L. (2021). *Governing Olympic education in Beijing primary schools*. [Unpublished doctoral thesis]. The University of Auckland.
Zheng, J., Chen, S., Tan, T. C., & Lau, P. W. C. (2018). Sport policy in China (mainland). *International Journal of Sport Policy and Politics*, *10*(3), 469–491.
Zheng, J., Chen, S., Tan, T-C., Houlihan, B. (2019). *Sport policy in China*. Routledge.

20
TEACHING FOR SOCIAL JUSTICE THROUGH PHYSICAL EDUCATION IN THE CONTEXT OF US LEGISLATION AND POLICIES AGAINST CRITICAL RACE THEORY

Micah J. Dobson

Foundations of social justice in physical education

Social justice is a multifaceted concept, representing both a philosophical and political theory that spotlight the idea of fairness and equality among individuals within society. It is a concept deeply rooted in the pursuit of equality of social privileges and equitable wealth opportunities within communities (Nieva Boza & Lleixà Arribas, 2021). The emergence of social justice as a distinct concept can be traced back to the 1800s, a time marked by pronounced disparities in social standing and wealth perpetuated by the prevailing social structures of the era (Howley-Rouse, 2021; Kitchener et al., 2018). This concept is foundational in addressing the social determinants of health, development, and education, focusing on the conditions and environments in which individuals are born, live, and grow. It seeks to foster a more socially aware and morally responsible society, ensuring every individual has the chance to achieve their fullest health and developmental potential. Social justice is pivotal in addressing systematic patterns of inequities. It is instrumental in creating conditions conducive to equality, participation, and tolerance, emphasising the need for diverse and inclusive learning environments.

Why address social justice via physical education

In a world grappling with escalating discrimination based on diverse social strands such as sexual orientation, gender, age, language, religion, race, and ethnicity, addressing social justice through physical education (PE) becomes a pivotal endeavour. The media often overlook the systematic inequalities affecting minority groups, perpetuating narratives that foster prejudice and harmful stereotypes (Howley-Rouse, 2021; Phillpots, 2017). For instance, in Florida, a discriminatory narrative against the LGBTQ+ group prevails, reinforcing societal divisions and inequalities (Benharris, 2022). Dominant societal groups often enjoy fundamental human rights, while the economic, political, and environmental structures seem to be aligned against the realities of minority groups. These structures and narratives underscore the urgent need for addressing social justice through avenues like PE, a powerful medium to address and mitigate these forms of social injustice (Bredemeier & Shields, 2020; Kondakci & Beycioglu, 2020).

With its inherent focus on inclusion and diversity, PE is a crucial platform to challenge and transform these inequalities. It is vital in creating a more just and equitable future for all students (Delk et al., 2022). The increasing discrimination cases and disparities in access to sports resources and programs disproportionately impact marginalised groups such as the LGBTQ+ community (Benharris, 2022). Addressing these disparities and focusing on acceptance and inclusion in PE can significantly reduce hate and discrimination, fostering a more morally responsible society and awareness of social inequalities (Papa, 2020). This approach to education, including PE and sports management, is necessary and integral in fostering a cohesive, peaceful, and secure society. It creates conditions conducive to equality, participation, and tolerance, emphasising the need for diverse and inclusive learning environments.

Social justice principles

Social justice is underpinned by three key principles: human rights, diversity, participation, equity, and access to available resources (Lynch et al., 2020). These principles are integral in understanding and addressing the holistic needs of individuals through integrated and coordinated approaches in health, social care, and education.

Access to available resources

Access to resources is a pivotal principle of social justice, encompassing many elements, including sports equipment, support networks, scholarship programs, coaching, athletic facilities, and training opportunities (Quennerstedt, 2019). This principle is foundational in ensuring that individuals from varying socioeconomic backgrounds have equitable access to these essential resources, fostering an environment of inclusivity and opportunity. However, reality often paints a different picture, with prevalent disparities in societal access to resources and services (Morison & Mavuso, 2022; Nesoff, 2022). For instance, individuals from affluent backgrounds are typically afforded the luxury of attending esteemed educational institutions and attaining higher levels of education, subsequently enjoying many opportunities post-graduation (Chung et al., 2023; Kirk & Haegele, 2019). In stark contrast, those from lower socioeconomic strata are ensnared in a cycle of limited access to lucrative opportunities and persistent disadvantage. The realm of prestigious athletic institutions and elite sports programs is no exception, often necessitating substantial financial investments in participation fees, equipment acquisitions, and specialised training.

These financial requisites act as formidable barriers for individuals from economically challenged backgrounds, curtailing their access to sports opportunities and perpetuating a cycle of disadvantage and limited access to vital resources like education for ensuing generations.

Participation and equity

Participation is a cornerstone of social justice, embodying the essence of giving every individual in society an equal voice and the opportunity to articulate their concerns and opinions.

It is about ensuring that every person plays a pivotal role in the decision-making processes that impact their living standards and forms of livelihood (Chen et al., 2020). Social injustice arises when a select few dictate pivotal decisions for the majority, and some individuals are systematically silenced and denied the chance to voice their perspectives and concerns. Equity, conversely, pertains to providing tools tailored to individuals' socioeconomic status and needs, enabling them to achieve comparable outcomes. It is a term often conflated with equality, yet it is crucial to delineate the distinct nuances between them (Pilson, 2022). While equality offers similar tools to everyone to achieve similar outcomes, equity recognises and addresses the unique needs and circumstances of specific groups or individuals (Clemens & Lincoln, 2018; Osborne, 2019). This distinction is vital as equal provisions are not always equitable due to specific groups or individuals' advanced or urgent needs. Equity considerations involve advancing policies that support overcoming systemic barriers or limitations and addressing the inherent disparities. This principle ensures that everyone can participate actively and equitably in societal processes regardless of background.

Human rights and diversity

Human rights and diversity are integral principles of social justice, interwoven to ensure the respect of every individual's legal, cultural, political, and civil rights (Barreto, 2021; Mishra, 2022). The interdependence of social justice and human rights is globally recognised by institutions like the International Criminal Court (ICC) and the United Nations, holding individuals accountable for violating these universal rights and valuing human dignity, cultural diversity, democracy, justice, fairness, equality, and the rule of law (Baiutti, 2018). Understanding and appreciating diversity and cultural differences are pivotal, as they inform the creation of inclusive policies (Baiutti, 2018). By acknowledging the unique perspectives and world views of others, we can foster open, appropriate, and effective interactions, acting for collective well-being and sustainable development. This appreciation for diversity is essential in addressing the barriers various cultural groups face and expanding opportunities for disadvantaged or marginalised groups (Craig, 2021; Page et al., 2020). Discrimination in employment based on sex, ethnicity, age, gender, and race remains a persistent problem, necessitating policies that counter such discrimination and promote diversity and social justice in society. Developing an ethnorelative perspective and critical thinking is crucial in recognising that one's point of view is not universally valid and building and maintaining significant relationships with people from different cultural backgrounds (Baiutti, 2018).

Dimensions of identity and diversity

Ethnicity, nationality, and race

Ethnicity and race, while interconnected, are distinct concepts. Race is typically associated with biological and anatomical differences, reflecting shared ancestry and physical characteristics. In contrast, ethnicity is linked to cultural expressions and identifications, encompassing national identity, heritage, and shared background (Lynch et al., 2020). Historically, individuals identifying as Black or belonging to racial minorities have encountered pervasive discrimination and marginalisation, a reality mirrored within educational settings. Many educational structures have perpetuated a Eurocentric paradigm, positioning 'Caucasian' as the normative standard and relegating other racial and ethnic identities as 'other' (Keengwe, 2022).

This Eurocentric approach to education predominantly emphasises Western ideologies and narratives, often diminishing or omitting the histories, contributions, and experiences of racial and ethnic minorities (Keengwe, 2016). Such a framework tends to present information understating the significance and value of non-Western races and ethnicities, fostering a skewed and narrow perspective.

The solution

Addressing and rectifying the implications of Eurocentric education is pivotal for integrating social justice within PE. This necessitates shifting from a predominantly white, Western-centric curriculum and pedagogy to one inclusive and reflective of diverse ethnicities and races (Meletiadou, 2022). In this endeavour, schools and physical educators should critically assess various aspects of the educational environment, including discipline policies, to ensure they do not inadvertently reinforce Eurocentric norms and expectations (Koh, 2017; Quennerstedt, 2019). Moreover, incorporating games and activities that highlight and respect the richness of Latino, African, Indigenous, Hispanic, and other marginalised cultures is essential. This approach fosters an appreciation of diversity and challenges and disrupts prevailing Eurocentric narratives. Celebrating and acknowledging the achievements of athletes from minority groups, such as John Carlos and Usain Bolt, particularly in track and field, can serve as a powerful tool to inspire and educate students about the diverse tapestry of contributions in the realm of sports (Johnson & Jackson, 2016). The emphasis on fostering an inclusive and equitable learning environment involves critically examining existing policies, practices, and curricula to identify and address any elements that may perpetuate inequalities and hinder the realisation of social justice in PE (Delgado & Stefancic, 2023). This aligns with the broader goals of social justice, aiming to create a society where every individual, regardless of their race or ethnicity, has the opportunity to thrive and realise their potential.

Gender and sexual orientation

Gender and sexual orientation, while distinct, are interconnected realms of identity. Gender is a cultural construct, often assigned based on societal norms and expectations, whereas sex is a biological classification determined by anatomical and physiological characteristics (Ferfolja & Ullman, 2019). Societal stereotypes and norms have perpetuated discriminatory practices and biases against individuals based on gender and sexual orientation, impacting their experiences and opportunities in various spheres, including PE. Sexual orientation pertains to an individual's emotional, romantic, and sexual attraction, encompassing diverse identities such as heterosexual, homosexual, bisexual, and asexual. In contrast, gender identity reflects one's internal sense of gender, which may or may not align with their assigned sex at birth (Quinlivan, 2018). The prevailing heteronormative and cisnormative structures within sports and PE have marginalised LGBTQ+ individuals, reinforcing assumptions and creating environments that are not inclusive or affirming diverse identities.

The solution

Promoting social justice within PE necessitates a commitment to addressing and dismantling these inequities and biases. Educators should critically assess and adapt their practices, curricula, and environments to be inclusive and affirming of all students, regardless of gender or sexual orientation (Siljamäki & Anttila, 2019). This involves discussing heteronormativity, homophobia, and gender diversity and ensuring that the learning environment does not perpetuate binary and exclusionary notions of gender and sex (Ferfolja & Ullman, 2019). Educators should be mindful of their students' diverse needs and experiences, considering the impact of competition, cooperation, and representation within the learning space. Activities, resources, and representations should reflect the diversity of identities and experiences, fostering a sense of belonging and respect for all students (Garland-Levett, 2016; Huber, 2021a). Educators should also consider the implications of policies and funding models on realising social justice within PE. A holistic and inclusive approach can create equitable and just learning environments, empowering all students to engage, learn, and thrive, irrespective of their gender, sexual orientation, or any other aspect of their identity.

Religion and language

Religion and language are integral components of individual and collective identity, shaping beliefs, values, and modes of communication. Religion encompasses a spectrum of beliefs and practices, with Christianity being predominant in many Western societies, influencing cultural norms and institutional structures, including the educational system (Keddie, 2020; McMillan, 2017). However, the growing diversity in religious affiliations and the increasing secularism necessitate inclusive and respectful approaches to accommodate varying beliefs and practices in educational settings, including PE (Howley-Rouse, 2021). Conversely, language is a fundamental medium of expression and interaction, reflecting and shaping cognitive processes and cultural identities. The dominance of English in countries like the United Kingdom and the United States poses linguistic diversity and inclusivity challenges, impacting non-native English speakers and those who communicate through different languages, such as Spanish, Korean, ASL, French, and German.

The solution

Promoting social justice within PE involves acknowledging and respecting students' diverse religious beliefs and languages. Educators should be attuned to their students' religious needs and accommodations, considering religious observances, attire, and dietary restrictions (Braksiek, 2022; Lee et al., 2021). They should foster an environment where diverse beliefs are recognised and valued, and students feel included and respected, irrespective of their religious affiliations. Similarly, educators should prioritise linguistic inclusivity, considering their students' linguistic needs and preferences. The curriculum and instructional approaches should be adaptable and responsive to linguistic diversity, allowing multilingual expressions and communications (Bredemeier & Shields, 2020; Leibowitz & Bozalek, 2020). This involves providing learning materials and objectives in multiple languages and creating opportunities for students to share and celebrate their languages and cultures.

Age and ability

Ability and age are pivotal considerations in PE, reflecting students' diverse competencies and life stages. Ability encompasses the range of skills and capacities individuals possess, with PE traditionally emphasising enhancing physical and motor competencies (Barber, 2016). However, students' diverse abilities, including those with disabilities, necessitate inclusive and adaptive approaches to accommodate varying needs and potentials. Age, conversely, is a determinant of physical condition and developmental stage, influencing the appropriateness and relevance of physical activities. The emphasis on youth and physical condition in sports management and PE can perpetuate age-related stereotypes and overlook the lifelong importance of physical activity.

The solution

Promoting social justice in PE involves recognising and addressing students' diverse abilities and ages. Educators should implement inclusive and adaptive curricula that consider the needs and potentials of all students, including those with disabilities (Delk et al., 2022; Lynch et al., 2020). This involves integrating disability-awareness education and disability-focused sports programs, such as goal ball and seated volleyball, and ensuring accessibility to facilities and resources. Additionally, educators should foster an age-inclusive environment that challenges age-related stereotypes and promotes lifelong physical activity. This involves selecting activities and games adaptable to different life stages and addressing community barriers that limit the participation of older populations in physical activities (Brown, 2016; Huber, 2021b). By addressing age-related stereotypes and promoting the value of physical activity across the lifespan, educators can contribute to fostering a more inclusive, equitable, and holistic approach to PE.

Historical contexts and influences

The history of teaching for social justice at historically Black Colleges and Universities

Historically Black Colleges and Universities (HBCUs) have a profound history of utilising education as a social justice conduit, a legacy deeply intertwined with their foundational principles (Johnson, 2017; Okpala & Walker, 2018). Originating during an era marked by racial segregation and profound inequalities, HBCUs have been pivotal in cultivating a sense of belonging and social consciousness among Black students, empowering them to challenge and transform societal norms. Established to counteract the severe limitations imposed on the educational opportunities available to Black individuals, HBCUs like Fisk University, Howard University, and Tuskegee University emerged as sanctuaries of intellectual pursuit and cultural affirmation (Johnson, 2017; Okpala & Walker, 2018). They have been instrumental in fostering environments that not only celebrate Black culture, intellectual achievement, and history but also illuminate the enduring struggles and resilience of the Black community. The curricula at these institutions are imbued with principles of social justice, emphasising historical challenges, the importance of activism, racial empowerment, and pride amidst systemic oppression.

The civil rights movements of the 1950s and 1960s significantly shaped the pedagogical approaches to social justice at HBCUs, transforming them into hubs of intellectual discourse and activism (Johnson, 2017; Okpala & Walker, 2018). Faculty and students at these institutions played crucial roles in combating discrimination and racial segregation, contributing to the nurturing of influential Black leaders such as John Lewis and Martin Luther King Jr. HBCUs provided pivotal spaces for organising critical dialogue, hosting civil rights conferences, and orchestrating protests against racial inequalities, thereby equipping students with the motivation, skills, and knowledge to challenge systemic racism and advocate for transformative changes (Lee et al., 2021).

However, the journey of HBCUs in championing social justice and racial equality is fraught with challenges, including persistent funding disparities, systemic barriers, and resource constraints, impacting their capacity to comprehensively address multifaceted social justice issues (Okpala & Walker, 2018). These challenges underscore the disparities in physical activity opportunities and the need for equitable improvements in the system to ameliorate these disparities (Lee & Cubbin, 2009). The societal and structural processes that hinder or prevent engagement in physical activity, especially among people of colour, necessitate dramatic systemic solutions and a redirection of focus beyond individual-level barriers (Lee et al., 2021). Despite these challenges, HBCUs continue to offer unique opportunities for collaboration and innovation. By forging alliances with other institutions, stakeholders, and community organisations, HBCUs can amplify their impact and leverage joint efforts to advance social justice through interdisciplinary approaches, global connections, and technological advancements in PE and sports management. The integration of social justice principles in health and PE curricula, as seen in New Zealand, serves as a testament to the transformative potential of education in forwarding social justice aims and advocating for more equitable communities (Fitzpatrick, 2018). The infusion of social justice principles in their curricula and their relentless pursuit of equality and empowerment amidst challenges underscore their pivotal role in shaping a more inclusive and equitable future.

Fostering inclusivity and challenging biases

Challenging biases and stereotypes

The infusion of Critical Race Theory (CRT) within sports management necessitates a profound reflection on societal biases and stereotypes perpetuating racial inequalities (Hylton, 2018; Lobato-Creekmur, 2022). It prompts coaches and administrators to confront and dismantle these biases, fostering an inclusive and unbiased environment. This involves training programs to raise awareness about unconscious biases, enhance cultural competence among staff and coaches, and provide resources to counter racial stereotypes (Lee et al., 2021). Addressing these issues proactively ensures equitable treatment and opportunities for all students, mitigating the effects of historical racialisation and racism in sports (Brown, 2016).

Incorporating diverse decision-making perspectives

The influence of CRT on policies and legislation advocates for the diversification of decision-making processes in PE and sports management (Hylton, 2018; Lobato-Creekmur, 2022). Policies fostering diversity within governing bodies, coaching staff, and athletic administrations reflect the diverse student body demographic, allowing institutions to more effectively address all students' varied needs and concerns (Rheenen, 2019). Establishing mentorship programs and leadership opportunities for marginalised and underrepresented groups is crucial in cultivating inclusive sports management structures, enabling the incorporation of diverse perspectives in decision-making processes.

Addressing disparities

CRT underscores the existence of systemic inequities within sports and PE, advocating for policies and legislation that address these disparities (Hylton, 2018). It emphasises identifying and eliminating barriers to equal sporting opportunities, allowing institutions to establish a level playing field. Policies focusing on the equitable distribution of facilities, resources, and funding ensure access to quality sporting programs for every student. Affirmative action legislation provides additional opportunities and support for historically discriminated and marginalised groups, addressing the disparities in physical activity opportunities and advocating for equitable improvements in the system (Lee & Cubbin, 2009).

Shaping inclusive environments

CRT encourages sports administrators and educators to assess the impact of race on students' experiences within sports settings, fostering environments where students from diverse racial and societal backgrounds feel supported and valued (Delgado & Stefancic, 2023; Lobato-Creekmur, 2022). The integration of CRT in sports management enables the creation of policies promoting equal participation opportunities, diverse representation in sports leadership, and equitable resource allocation. Such policies empower students to participate in sporting activities actively, develop their athletic abilities irrespective of their backgrounds, and contribute to creating more equitable schools and communities (Fitzpatrick, 2018).

Pedagogical approaches and strategies

Direct, explicit teaching

Direct and explicit teaching strategies are often driven by social justice approaches that attribute disparities in learning outcomes to methodologies that may inadvertently discriminate against and disadvantage students with diverse cultural backgrounds and varying levels of capital knowledge – skills and knowledge associated with PE (Haegele, 2019; Robinson & Randall, 2016; Wallace & Lewis, 2020; Walton-Fisette & Hill, 2020). In this context, the effectiveness of teaching methodologies is contingent upon the alignment of students' background knowledge with the school curriculum. Some students whose background knowledge aligns well with the curriculum may find conventional teaching approaches more conducive to their learning. However, for others, especially those whose cultural and social capital diverges from the predominant educational paradigms, different levels of explicit and direct teaching are crucial to establishing foundational knowledge. Direct teaching is not merely about transmitting knowledge but is deeply intertwined with recognising the diverse cultural wealth students bring into the learning environment. It's about leveraging students' rich experiences, perspectives, and insights to create a more inclusive and equitable learning environment, thereby addressing the structural and systemic inequities within educational settings. Moreover, the emphasis on direct, explicit teaching is integral to fostering an environment where every student, regardless of their background, can have an equitable opportunity to succeed. The aim is to dismantle barriers and create learning experiences that are responsive to the diverse needs of students.

Culturally responsive pedagogy

Culturally responsive pedagogy (CRP) is indeed pivotal in addressing the multifaceted needs of a diverse student body, including new immigrants and refugees. It is particularly significant in the realm of PE. Fitzpatrick (2018) elucidated that this approach is not merely about overcoming language and cultural barriers but about fostering an inclusive learning environment where diverse cultural backgrounds are acknowledged, valued, and leveraged to enhance learning experiences. CRP goes beyond the simplistic view of cultural diversity. It delves into the intricate interplay of cultural nuances, societal contexts, and individual experiences that shape the learning journey of each student. It's about recognising the rich tapestry of cultural capital that students bring into the learning environment and utilising these diverse perspectives to enrich the educational experience for all (Lee et al., 2021). Educators are the architects of the learning environment, shaping it to be inclusive, equitable, and responsive to the diverse needs of students. They are responsible for understanding the cultural contexts from which their students come and integrating this understanding into their teaching methodologies, thereby creating a learning space where every student feels valued, respected, and heard (Atkins & Duckworth, 2019). Fitzpatrick (2018) asserts CRP is about creating learning experiences that are relevant, meaningful, and empowering, allowing students to see their cultural identities as strengths and sources of empowerment.

Bicultural pedagogies

Bicultural pedagogies are integral in creating an educational environment that is reflective and inclusive of the diverse cultural tapestries that make up our societies. These pedagogies are not just about incorporating Indigenous perspectives but a holistic integration of Indigenous individuals' aspirations, experiences, knowledge, and philosophies. This ensures that the curriculum reflects the rich cultural heritage and the diverse societal fabric (Hawkins, 2018; Love et al., 2020). The essence of bicultural pedagogies lies in acknowledging and understanding the profound historical experiences of Indigenous peoples, including their experiences of discrimination, displacement, and colonisation. It's about creating a dialogue in PE that is not just informative but is transformative, fostering a deeper understanding and appreciation of Indigenous cultures, histories, and experiences (Schenker et al., 2019). This approach to teaching and learning goes beyond the conventional methods. It delves into experiential learning through dialogue in physical activities and establishing meaningful connections to wider Indigenous societies and significant places. It's about creating learning experiences enriched with cultural insights, allowing students to explore and understand the complexities of Indigenous cultures and their contributions to the broader societal context.

Active advocacy

Active advocacy within PE is a multifaceted approach that necessitates cultivating an understanding among students regarding the inherent societal structures and patterns that delineate power dynamics within various societal groups. It is a pedagogical strategy that transcends conventional teaching methodologies, focusing on the empowerment of students to discern and challenge the prevailing paradigms that perpetuate inequalities and hinder the realisation of social justice (Grimminger-Seidensticker & Seyda, 2022). Physical educators, in this context, assume a pivotal and transformative role. They are not mere conveyors of knowledge but are architects of a learning environment that is inherently conducive to the principles of social justice. They are tasked with meticulously identifying and mitigating prevailing school curricula, practices, and policies that may sustain or propagate social injustice within the educational ecosystem (Chhetri et al., 2020; Ryan & Deci, 2018).

In this endeavor, the insights provided by Watson, Jarvie, and Parker (2022), which explore sport, physical education, and social justice from various perspectives, are particularly relevant. This form of advocacy is not isolated; it is intrinsically aligned with broader principles of social justice in sports management. It underscores the imperative role of educators in dismantling systemic barriers and fostering an environment marked by inclusivity, equity, and respect for diverse perspectives. Moreover, active advocacy is about continuously reflecting and reassessing educational practices to ensure alignment with the evolving understanding of social justice.

Citizenship education

Citizenship education is integral in cultivating students who are informed, ethically responsible, and actively engaged in societal matters. This form of education is a cornerstone in fostering an understanding of civic responsibilities and political literacy, crucial components in developing individuals who are aware of and can navigate the complexities of societal structures and institutional barriers. The insights from Aguilar (2017) and Garratt and Kumar (2019) underscore the significance of this educational approach in elevating awareness of the inherent barriers within institutions and engaging students in endeavours to foster the development of social equity. With citizenship education, the emphasis is placed on the pivotal role of civic engagement and ethical responsibility. It is through such engagement and responsibility that students can actively participate in dialogues and actions aimed at addressing and mitigating societal inequalities and fostering an environment of inclusivity and equity (Levy, 2022). Integrating citizenship education within PE curricula is essential in promoting a holistic understanding of social justice, enabling students to be proactive agents of change, and advocating for equity and inclusivity within their communities.

Democratic School Process

A democratic school process values the perspectives and stories of all school community members. Barber (2016) and Richards et al. (2018) elaborate on how schools promoting open environments for discussion and student involvement in school activities cultivate democratic values, civic knowledge, and engagement. This approach is particularly relevant in sports management and PE, where diverse perspectives can enrich the learning environment and foster a sense of community and mutual respect (Harsma et al., 2022; McArthur & Ashwin, 2020). In a democratic school process, the inclusion and valuation of every school community member's diverse perspectives and narratives are paramount. This process is characterised by the cultivation of democratic values, civic knowledge, and engagement, facilitated by the creation of open environments conducive to discussion and active student involvement in various school activities. The insights provided by Barber (2016) and Richards et al. (2018) illuminate the significance of fostering such environments, emphasising their role in nurturing democratic principles and enhancing civic engagement. The incorporation of varied perspectives not only enriches the learning environment but also serves to cultivate a sense of community, mutual respect, and inclusivity. Such settings' diverse narratives and viewpoints contribute to a more holistic and enriched learning experience, fostering collaborative learning and mutual growth (Harsma et al., 2022; McArthur & Ashwin, 2020). This approach aligns with promoting a learning space where every voice is valued and heard, and every perspective is considered in shaping the educational experience.

Sports management's approach to social justice

Social justice pedagogies, originating from transformative movements such as feminism and civil rights, strive to redress social injustice and inequality, drawing extensively from Multicultural Education and other inclusive pedagogies (Richards et al., 2018). These pedagogies, deeply rooted in Paulo Freire's revolutionary educational concepts, emphasise the cultivation of ethnic identities, social actions, and a steadfast commitment to social justice (Alpert, 2020; Simcock & Lee, 2022). Freire's dialogic approaches empower the oppressed to comprehend and challenge the social constructs that shape their circumstances, advocating for an education system that values the diverse resources students bring to the learning process (Atkins & Duckworth, 2019; Carvalho, 2020). The pervasive nature of social inequalities necessitates a global focus on addressing the disparities that engender many societal issues, including health, mental well-being, and crime (Ramasubramanian et al., 2021). Approaches to social justice in sports management and PE are pivotal in fostering an environment where students and teachers actively recognise and engage with social justice principles and their societal implications (Gerdin et al., 2018; Meir & Fletcher, 2019). They encourage a critical examination and transformation of unequal power relations, making issues of privilege and power explicit and enabling students to affirm positive images and deconstruct detrimental ones (Gerdin et al., 2021).

Inclusive practices within social justice frameworks are imperative in ensuring all individuals' representation and empowerment in educational institutions' decision-making processes (Burns et al., 2019; Clark, 2019). These practices disrupt prevailing inequality patterns, fostering high expectations and confidence in students' ability to coexist harmoniously with diverse communities (Thomas et al., 2021). They emphasise the importance of incorporating students' cultural values and experiences, particularly those from marginalised groups, to counteract structural inequities and enhance the learning process (Tan, 2019; Trimbur, 2020; Wright & Richards, 2021). The intersectionality of economic, political, social, and structural factors significantly influences student achievement, necessitating the implementation of culturally responsive teaching programs to elevate the achievement levels of marginalised students (Camilletti et al., 2018; Gray et al., 2017). Integrating the culture and language of diverse student populations, such as Asian or Pasifika students, into the curriculum and co-curriculum is instrumental in enhancing their learning experiences (Ørbæk, 2021). This approach is augmented by establishing reciprocal and respectful relationships with these students, fostering an inclusive and equitable educational environment. The empirical evidence underscores the critical role of sports management in promoting social justice within educational institutions, highlighting the need for a holistic approach that integrates diverse cultural values and experiences (Lee et al., 2021). The emphasis on equitable resource allocation, diverse representation, and inclusive decision-making processes reflects the transformative potential of sports management in addressing systemic inequities and fostering social justice.

Teaching social justice amidst adversity

Teaching social justice is a transformative pedagogical approach that empowers students to engage critically and challenge systems of oppression and inequality (Chen et al., 2020; Fitzpatrick, 2018; Strunk & Locke, 2019). However, this approach often encounters significant opposition and resistance from various political entities, social institutions, and ideological frameworks, making its implementation complex. Teaching social justice inherently challenges prevailing narratives and entrenched power structures, often leading to substantial political backlash. The endeavour to integrate social justice in education, particularly in PE, can be met with attempts by politicians and policymakers to control, modify, or suppress it through legislative measures and policy alterations (Chen et al., 2020; Strunk & Locke, 2019). Educators in this context may experience mounting pressure to adhere to predetermined curricula that marginalise or entirely omit pertinent social issues and discussions on equity and justice (Gray et al., 2017). To counteract political interference and uphold the principles of social justice in education, educators need to advocate for academic freedom and autonomy relentlessly. Engaging in continuous professional development and forming alliances with like-minded educators, parents, community advocates, and organisations can fortify the resolve to integrate social justice teachings amidst adversity (D'Amico Pawlewicz & View, 2020; Lee et al., 2021). Additionally, fostering open dialogues with parents and community members can help build a supportive network that values and understands the importance of social justice in shaping holistic and equitable learning environments.

Institutional resistance can manifest in various forms, including silencing dissent, imposition of censorship, and denying essential support or resources. Influential stakeholders, school boards, and administrative bodies may attempt to stifle debates and discussions on contentious topics, fearing potential conflicts or controversies (Chen et al., 2020; Strunk & Locke, 2019). In such scenarios, educators can circumvent these challenges by establishing robust professional networks, meticulously documenting institutional bias or censorship, and seeking counsel and support from organisations dedicated to advancing social justice in education (Brown, 2016). Educators can cultivate supportive and inclusive environments by elucidating the intrinsic value of teaching social justice, primarily through PE. Emphasising the role of PE in fostering critical consciousness, resilience, and empathy can help gain institutional backing and community endorsement (Howley-Rouse, 2021). Integrating social justice principles in PE can catalyse transformative change, enabling students to understand societal structures and empower them to advocate for equity and justice.

Conclusion

In conclusion, the persistence of educational inequality is a glaring manifestation of social injustice within our educational systems, reflecting the broader inequalities ingrained in societies globally. This inequality not only hinders the realisation of the full potential of deserving students but also stifles the expression of their diverse abilities, particularly for those marginalised due to the scarcity of resources and opportunities. Therefore, governments, educational institutions, and educators must diligently integrate the principles of social justice into their curricula and teaching methodologies to address and mitigate these disparities. The intergenerational transmission of social injustice and inequality necessitates a transformative approach to education, one that is rooted in the principles of equity, inclusion, and diversity. Teaching social justice through PE is a pivotal strategy to confront and alleviate societal inequalities, emphasising uplifting disadvantaged and marginalised students. Physical educators must cultivate learning environments that are inclusive, diverse, and responsive to the needs and voices of all students, thereby contributing to the reshaping of societal norms and the reduction of social inequalities.

Education, including PE, is a cornerstone in combating various forms of social injustice. It fosters environments conducive to equality, tolerance, and active participation, laying the foundation for a more cohesive, secure, and harmonious society. The association between social justice and education is intertwined with the endeavours to counteract the reinforcing and reproducing inequalities within the educational landscape. The correlation between socioeconomic disadvantages and lower academic achievements, engagement levels, and qualification attainments underscores the pressing need for equitable educational outcomes. Addressing this formidable challenge requires a multifaceted approach, integrating culturally responsive teaching, active advocacy, bi-cultural pedagogies, and democratic school processes, as discussed throughout this chapter. Implementing such strategies in PE can catalyse transformative change, enabling students to develop a nuanced understanding of societal structures and empowering them to advocate for equity and justice.

References

Aguilar, S. J. (2017). Learning analytics: At the nexus of big data, digital innovation, and social justice in education. *TechTrends, 62*(1), 37–45. https://doi.org/10.1007/s11528-017-0226-9

Alpert, R. T. (2020). Social justice, sport, and Judaism. *Sport, Physical Education, and Social Justice*, 22–36. https://doi.org/10.4324/9781003042716-2

Atkins, L., & Duckworth, V. (2019). Theoretical conceptions of social justice and equity. *Research Methods for Social Justice and Equity in Education*. https://doi.org/10.5040/9781350015494.ch-001

Baiutti, M. (2018). Fostering assessment of student mobility in secondary schools: Indicators of intercultural competence. *Intercultural Education, 29*(5–6), 549–570. https://doi.org/10.1080/14675986.2018.1495318

Barber, W. (2016). Inclusive and accessible physical education: Rethinking ability and disability in pre-service teacher education. *Sport, Education and Society, 23*(6), 520–532. https://doi.org/10.1080/13573322.2016.1269004

Barreto, I. (2021). *Handbook of research on promoting social justice for immigrants and refugees through active citizenship and intercultural education*. IGI Global.

Benharris, L. A. (2022). The LGBTQ+ movement towards equity. *Research Anthology on Inclusivity and Equity for the LGBTQ+ Community*, 1–12. https://doi.org/10.4018/978-1-6684-3674-5.ch001

Braksiek, M. (2022). Pre-service physical education teachers' attitude toward, and self-efficacy in, inclusive physical education: Measurement invariance and influence factors. *Teaching and Teacher Education, 109*, 103547. https://doi.org/10.1016/j.tate.2021.103547

Bredemeier, B. L., & Shields, D. L. (2020). Social justice, character education, and sport. *Sport, Physical Education, and Social Justice*, 101–115. https://doi.org/10.4324/9781003042716-7

Brown, D. D. (2016). The portrayal of Black masculinity in the NFL: Critical race theory and the images of Black males. *Critical Race Theory: Black Athletic Sporting Experiences in the United States*, 217–246. https://doi.org/10.1057/978-1-137-60038-7_9

Burns, R. D., Li, L., & Brusseau, T. A. (2019). The mediating effect of physical activity on the association between cardiorespiratory endurance and mathematics performance. *International Journal of Kinesiology in Higher Education, 3*(4), 117–127. https://doi.org/10.1080/24711616.2019.1633709

Camilletti, E., Banati, P., & Cook, S. (2018). Children's roles in social reproduction: Re-examining the discourse on care through a child lens. *Journal of Law, Social Justice, and Global Development*, (21), 33–48. https://doi.org/10.31273/lgd.2018.2103

Carvalho, T. (2020). New public management and social justice in higher education. *Locating Social Justice in Higher Education Research*. https://doi.org/10.5040/9781350086784.0008

Chen, W., Li, X., John, E. P., & Hannon, C. (2020). *Actionable research for educational equity and social justice*. Routledge.

Chhetri, K., Spina, N., & Carrington, S. (2020). Teacher education for inclusive education in Bhutan: Perspectives of pre-service and beginning teachers. *International Journal of Inclusive Education*, 1–16. https://doi.org/10.1080/13603116.2020.1841840

Chung, A., Gooey, M., Jeyapalan, D., & Skouteris, H. (2023). Integrating health, social care, and education across the first 2,000 days. *Australian and New Zealand Journal of Public Health, 47*(1), 100014. https://doi.org/10.1016/j.anzjph.2022.100014

Clark, L. (2019). The way they care: An ethnography of social justice physical education teacher education. *The Teacher Educator, 54*(2), 145–170. https://doi.org/10.1080/08878730.2018.1549301

Clemens, S. L., & Lincoln, D. J. (2018). Where children play most: Physical activity levels of school children across four settings and policy implications. *Australian and New Zealand Journal of Public Health*, *42*(6), 575–581. https://doi.org/10.1111/1753-6405.12833

Craig, G. (2021). Putting the global in social justice? *The Struggle for Social Sustainability*, 237–254. https://doi.org/10.1332/policypress/9781447356103.003.0012

D'Amico Pawlewicz, D., & View, J. L. (2020). Social justice and teacher professionalism in the United States in historical perspective: Fractured consensus. *Handbook on Promoting Social Justice in Education*, 1279–1297. https://doi.org/10.1007/978-3-030-14625-2_130

Delgado, R., & Stefancic, J. (2023). *Critical race theory: An introduction* (4th ed.). NYU Press.

Delk, D. W., Vaughn, M., & Hodge, S. R. (2022). Social justice research in physical education teacher education: Contextualized in the United States. *Journal of Teaching in Physical Education*, *41*(2), 260–269. https://doi.org/10.1123/jtpe.2021-0018

Ferfolja, T., & Ullman, J. (2019). Introduction: Gender and sexuality in education and health: voices advocating for equity and social justice. *Gender and Sexuality in Education and Health*, 1–7. https://doi.org/10.4324/9781351028028-1

Fitzpatrick, K. (2018). Sexuality education in New Zealand: A policy for social justice? *Sex Education*, *18*(5), 601–609. https://doi.org/10.1080/14681811.2018.1446824

Garland-Levett, S. (2016). Exploring discursive barriers to sexual health and social justice in the New Zealand sexuality education curriculum. *Sex Education*, *17*(2), 121–134. https://doi.org/10.1080/14681811.2016.1233396

Garratt, D., & Kumar, S. (2019). Physical education, citizenship, and social justice: A position statement. *Quest*, *71*(2), 188–201. https://doi.org/10.1080/00336297.2019.1608269

Gerdin, G., Philpot, R. A., Larsson, L., Schenker, K., Linnér, S., Moen, K. M., Westlie, K., Smith, W., & Legge, M. (2018). Researching social justice and health (in)equality across different school health and physical education contexts in Sweden, Norway, and New Zealand. *European Physical Education Review*, *25*(1), 273–290. https://doi.org/10.1177/1356336x18783916

Gerdin, G., Smith, W., Philpot, R., Schenker, K., Moen, K. M., Linnér, S., Westlie, K., & Larsson, L. (2021). Conceptualizing social justice. *Social Justice Pedagogies in Health and Physical Education*, 43–56. https://doi.org/10.4324/9781003003953-3

Gray, S., Morgan, K., & Sproule, J. (2017). Pedagogy for motivation, learning, and development in physical education. *Transformative Learning and Teaching in Physical Education*, 139–158. https://doi.org/10.4324/9781315625492-10

Grimminger-Seidensticker, E., & Seyda, M. (2022). Enhancing attitudes and self-efficacy toward inclusive teaching in physical education, pre-service teachers: Results of a quasi-experimental study in physical education teacher education. *Frontiers in Education*, *7*. https://doi.org/10.3389/feduc.2022.909255

Haegele, J. A. (2019). Inclusion illusion: Questioning the inclusiveness of integrated physical education. *Quest*, *71*(4), 387–397. https://doi.org/10.1080/00336297.2019.1602547

Harsma, E., Duplat, A., & Johnson, A. P. (2022). Introduction video to volume 1 of the *International Journal of Equity and Social Justice in Higher Education*. *The International Journal of Equity and Social Justice in Higher Education*, *1*(1). https://doi.org/10.56816/2771-1803.1001

Hawkins, B. (2018). Critical research on Black sporting experiences in the United States: Athletic activism and the appeal for social justice. *Critical Research in Sport, Health and Physical Education*, 64–77. https://doi.org/10.4324/9780203702598-5

Howley-Rouse, A. (2021, March 26). *A social justice approach to education*. The Education Hub. https://theeducationhub.org.nz/a-social-justice-approach-to-education/

Huber, A. A. (2021a). Communicating social justice in teacher education. https://doi.org/10.4324/9781003036418

Huber, A. A. (2021b). Are you a teacher or what? *Communicating Social Justice in Teacher Education*, 1–17. https://doi.org/10.4324/9781003036418-1

Hylton, K. (2018). Critical race theory in sport. *Contesting 'Race' and Sport*, 1–23. https://doi.org/10.4324/9781315715476-1

Johnson, J. M. (2017). Choosing HBCUs: Why African Americans choose HBCUs in the twenty-first century. *Black Colleges Across the Diaspora: Global Perspectives on Race and Stratification in Postsecondary Education*, 151–169. https://doi.org/10.1108/s1479-358x20160000014008

Johnson, W., & Jackson, V. P. (2016). Race and racism: The Black male experience in sports. *Critical Race Theory: Black Athletic Sporting Experiences in the United States*, 153–170. https://doi.org/10.1057/978-1-137-60038-7_6

Keddie, A. (2020). Schooling and social justice through the lenses of Nancy Fraser. *Nancy Fraser, Social Justice and Education*, 40–56. https://doi.org/10.4324/9780429422461-4

Keengwe, J. (2016). *Handbook of research on promoting cross-cultural competence and social justice in teacher education*. IGI Global.

Keengwe, J. (2022). *Handbook of research on social justice and equity in education*. IGI Global.

Kirk, T. N., & Haegele, J. A. (2019). Theory of planned behavior in research examining physical activity factors among individuals with disabilities: A review. *Adapted Physical Activity Quarterly, 36*(1), 164–182. https://doi.org/10.1123/apaq.2018-0065

Kitchener, V., Williams, D., & Kilpatrick, S. (2018). Social justice and constructivist grounded theory. *Structuring the Thesis*, 225–233. https://doi.org/10.1007/978-981-13-0511-5_22

Koh, Y. (2017). A strategy to improve pre-service teachers' self-efficacy towards inclusive physical education for students with intellectual disability and autism. *International Journal of Inclusive Education, 22*(8), 839–855. https://doi.org/10.1080/13603116.2017.1412511

Kondakci, Y., & Beycioglu, K. (2020). Social justice in the Turkish education system: Issues and interventions. *Handbook on Promoting Social Justice in Education*, 309–329. https://doi.org/10.1007/978-3-030-14625-2_34

Lee, R. E., & Cubbin, C. (2009). Striding toward social justice: The ecologic milieu of physical activity. Retrieved from www.ncbi.nlm.nih.gov/pmc/articles/PMC2757772/

Lee, R. E., Joseph, R. P., Blackman Carr, L. T., Strayhorn, S. M., Faro, J. M., Lane, H., Monroe, C., Pekmezi, D., &Szeszulski, J. (2021). Still, striding toward social justice? Redirecting physical activity research in a post-COVID-19 world. *Translational Behavioral Medicine, 11*(6), 1205–1215. https://doi.org/10.1093/tbm/ibab026

Leibowitz, B., & Bozalek, V. (2020). The scholarship of teaching and learning from a social justice perspective. *Nancy Fraser, Social Justice, and Education*, 57–70. https://doi.org/10.4324/9780429422461-5

Levy, D. L. (2022). Discovering grounded theories for social justice. *Fostering Social Justice through Qualitative Inquiry*, 83–102. https://doi.org/10.4324/9781003216575-5

Lobato-Creekmur, G. (2022). Does culturally responsive teaching inherently operationalize critical race theory? *Proceedings of the 2022 AERA Annual Meeting*. https://doi.org/10.3102/1884213

Love, A., Deeb, A., & Waller, S. N. (2020). Social justice, sport, and racism. *Sport, Physical Education, and Social Justice*, 131–144. https://doi.org/10.4324/9781003042716-9

Lynch, S., Sutherland, S., & Walton-Fisette, J. (2020). The A–Z of social justice physical education: Part 1. *Journal of Physical Education, Recreation & Dance, 91*(4), 8–13. https://doi.org/10.1080/07303084.2020.1724500

McArthur, J., & Ashwin, P. (2020). Introduction: Locating social justice in higher education research. *Locating Social Justice in Higher Education Research*. https://doi.org/10.5040/9781350086784.0005

McMillan, P. (2017). Understanding physical education teachers' day-to-day practice. *Transformative Learning and Teaching in Physical Education*, 159–175. https://doi.org/10.4324/9781315625492-11

Meir, D., & Fletcher, T. (2019). The physical education and sport premium: Social justice, autonomy, and school sport policy in England. *International Journal of Sport Policy and Politics, 12*(2), 237–253. https://doi.org/10.1080/19406940.2019.1673790

Meletiadou, E. (2022). The use of student-generated videos and intercultural group assessment to promote equity, diversity, and inclusion (EDI) in higher education. *Handbook of Research on Fostering Social Justice through Intercultural and Multilingual Communication*, 24–43. https://doi.org/10.4018/978-1-6684-5083-3.ch002

Mishra, H. S. (2022). Social justice education and politics of social justice. *Politics of Education in India*, 210–218. https://doi.org/10.4324/9780429285523-21

Morison, T., & Mavuso, J. M. (2022). *Sexual and reproductive justice: From the margins to the center*. Rowman & Littlefield.

Nesoff, I. (2022). Social justice thinking. *Human Service Program Planning through a Social Justice Lens*, 1–40. https://doi.org/10.4324/9781003148777-1

Nieva Boza, C., & LleixàArribas, T. (2021). Teaching for immigrant girls' inclusion: Social justice physical education teachers' involvement with school stakeholders. *Journal of Teaching in Physical Education*, 1–9. https://doi.org/10.1123/jtpe.2021-0085

Okpala, C. O., & Walker, K. Y. (2018). *Improving the viability and perception of HBCUs*. Rowman & Littlefield.

Ørbæk, T. (2021). Bodily learning through creating dance: Student teachers' experiences from Norwegian physical education teacher education. *Frontiers in Sports and Active Living, 3*. https://doi.org/10.3389/fspor.2021.758944

Osborne, J. (2019). Rural Shakespeare and the tragedy of education. *Teaching Social Justice through Shakespeare*, 106–114. https://doi.org/10.3366/edinburgh/9781474455589.003.0010

Page, S., Holt, L., & Thorpe, K. (2020). Fostering Indigenous intercultural ability during and beyond initial teacher education. *Intercultural Competence in the Work of Teachers*, 237–254. https://doi.org/10.4324/9780429401022-18

Papa, R. (2020). *Handbook on promoting social justice in education*. Springer.

Phillpots, L. (2017). An analysis of the policy process for physical education and school sport: The rise and demise of school sport partnerships. *Understanding UK Sport Policy in Context*, 31–49. https://doi.org/10.4324/9781315084398-4

Pilson, A. (2022). Inclusive education in the post-COVID-19 world. *Being Human During COVID-19*, 132–139. https://doi.org/10.1332/policypress/9781529223125.003.0017

Quennerstedt, M. (2019). Physical education and the art of teaching: Transformative learning and teaching in physical education and sports pedagogy. *Sport, Education and Society, 24*(6), 611–623. https://doi.org/10.1080/13573322.2019.1574731

Quinlivan, K. (2018). *Exploring contemporary issues in sexuality education with young people: Theories in practice*. Springer.

Ramasubramanian, S., Riewestahl, E., & Landmark, S. (2021). The trauma-informed equity-minded asset-based model (TEAM): The six Rs for social justice-oriented educators. *Journal of Media Literacy Education, 13*(2), 29–42. https://doi.org/10.23860/jmle-2021-13-2-3

Rheenen, D. V. (2019). Race logic in American college sports. *'Race', Youth Sport, Physical Activity and Health*, 87–99. https://doi.org/10.4324/9781351122948-8

Richards, K. A., Graber, K. C., & Woods, A. M. (2018). Using theory to guide the research: Applications of constructivist and social justice theories. *Kinesiology Review, 7*(3), 218–225. https://doi.org/10.1123/kr.2018-0018

Robinson, D. B., & Randall, L. (2016). *Social justice in physical education: Critical reflections and pedagogies for change*. Canadian Scholars' Press.

Ryan, R. M., & Deci, E. L. (2018). *Self-determination theory: Basic psychological needs in motivation, development, and wellness*. Guilford Publications.

Schenker, K., Linnér, S., Smith, W., Gerdin, G., Mordal Moen, K., Philpot, R., Larsson, L., Legge, M., & Westlie, K. (2019). Conceptualizing social justice: What constitutes pedagogies for social justice in HPE across different contexts? *Curriculum Studies in Health and Physical Education, 10*(2), 126–140. https://doi.org/10.1080/25742981.2019.1609369

Siljamäki, M. & Anttila, E. (2019). Fostering intercultural competence and social justice through dance and physical education. *Dancing Across Borders*, 53–64. https://doi.org/10.4324/9781003008569-9

Simcock, P., & Lee, C. (2022). Disability, social justice and human rights: The experience of the United Kingdom. In *Human rights and social justice* (1st ed., pp. 206–228). Routledge. https://doi.org/10.4324/9781003111269-14

Strunk, K. K., & Locke, L. A. (2019). *Research methods for social justice and equity in education*. Springer.

Tan, C. (2019). Conceptualizing social justice in education: A Daoist perspective. *Compare a Journal of Comparative and International Education, 51*(4), 596–611. https://doi.org/10.1080/03057925.2019.1660144

Thomas, J. D., Uwadiale, A. Y., & Watson, N. M. (2021). Towards equitable communication of kinesiology: A critical interpretive synthesis of readability research. *Quest*, 1–19. https://doi.org/10.1080/00336297.2021.1897861

Trimbur, L. (2020). Taking a knee, making a stand. *Sport, Physical Education, and Social Justice*, 162–178. https://doi.org/10.4324/9781003042716-11

Wallace, K. O., & Lewis, P. J. (2020). Trauma-informed art and play environments. *Trauma-Informed Teaching through Play Art Narrative (PAN)*, 123–169. https://doi.org/10.1163/9789004432734_009

Walton-Fisette, J. L., & Hill, J. (2020). *Teaching about social justice issues in physical education*. Information Age Publishing Inc.

Watson, N. J., Jarvie, G., & Parker, A. (2022). *Sport, physical education, and social justice: Religious, sociological, psychological, and capability perspectives*. Routledge.

Wright, P. M., & Richards, K. A. (2021). *Teaching social and emotional learning in physical education*. Jones & Bartlett Learning.

21
SCHOOL PHYSICAL EDUCATION AND SOCIAL JUSTICE
What are we doing in Brazil?

Isabel Porto Filgueiras, Elisabete dos Santos Freire, Bruno Freitas Meireles, Ewerton Leonardo da Silva Vieira, Bruna Gabriela Marques, Graciele Massoli Rodrigues, Luiz Sanches Neto, and Luciana Venâncio

Introduction

Brazil is a country of continental dimensions, historically marked by colonisation, social inequalities, erasure of the cultures of its original peoples, economic dispossession, Black enslavement, oppression of women and the LGBTQIAPN+ population on the one hand. On the other hand, Brazilian history is also marked by the resistance of social movements and the activism of intellectuals, educators, artists, and personalities from different areas of activity who struggle to fight the power structures that produce injustice and violence.

Many Brazilian defenders of social justice were, and still are, persecuted. Paulo Freire, recognised worldwide for his theoretical formulations that support critical pedagogies, was considered subversive and exiled during the Brazilian military dictatorship government (1964–1985). Even today his work arouses attacks from neo-fascist groups which threaten the fragile advances in Brazilian democracy, education, and science. Such threats make the commitment to developing critical pedagogies in school physical education and teacher education even more urgent. Defending the freedom and rights of oppressed and marginalised groups with a view to the well-being of society and the construction of social justice is not an easy task given the global neoliberal agenda which adopts the discourse of education for all, but deepens inequalities; it promotes the erasure of cultural diversities, imposing pedagogical models and assessment standards which are external to the needs of multicultural contexts (Azzarito, 2016).

Philpot et al. (2021) argue that critical pedagogies in school physical education have in common an understanding of the socio-historical and cultural character of the human being, a commitment to social transformation, an assumption of the political character of education in relation to equity, combating discrimination, prejudices, and violence; promotion of social justice; awareness of power relations, privilege and discrimination present in societies, and an analysis of political, social, and ethical aspects of bodily practices. According to the authors, critical pedagogies are concerned with aligning curriculum, teaching, and learning to contribute to human justice, equity, democracy and freedom.

DOI: 10.4324/9781003389682-25

We understand physical education as a sociocultural and curricular component in Brazilian schools. It is a fundamental space for debate on issues that affect vulnerable groups and contribute to more democratic and fair societies. The theme of social justice in the field of school physical education in Brazil emerged during the formulation of critical pedagogies in the 1980s during the country's re-democratisation process. This movement is also noted in the United States, Canada, United Kingdom, Australia, Sweden, Norway, and New Zealand (Philpot et al., 2021). The course of critical pedagogies of school physical education in Brazil has affinities and particularities when compared to the literature produced in these countries in terms of temporality, in questioning the social function of the school in capitalist societies, and by the need to build responses to the growth of neoliberalism in public education policies (Almeida & Kirk, 2020; Kirk et al., 2019; Philpot et al., 2021). However, the dialogue and visibility of Brazilian production in the face of Anglophone initiatives remained limited due to the massive dissemination of national research in Portuguese (Almeida & Kirk, 2020).

The dialogue of Brazilian critical pedagogies with other contexts occurred, albeit sparsely, with Latin American researchers in works such as Bracht and Crisor (2003), Silva and Molina (2017), and Filgueiras and Maldonado (2020). Although the concern with the theme of social justice built in Brazil from the progressive and critical conceptual framework of social sciences and education in the last 40 years has advanced, and it is already noted that this discussion takes place at school, little is known about how the research carried out in Brazilian graduate programs has produced knowledge around themes of social justice, ethnic-racial relations, gender, sexuality, inclusion of people with disabilities and social inequality.

More recently, dialogues, comparative analyses, and collaborations between Brazilian researchers committed to critical perspectives of school physical education and international researchers have intensified. Examples of this fact can be seen in the publication of a thematic issue (both in English and Portuguese) of *Movimento* journal in 2019, which brought together productions by researchers from the United Kingdom, Australia, New Zealand, Germany, the United States, and Brazil in order to outline an overview of emerging issues of critical pedagogies in the field of physical education (Kirk et al., 2019). Further, a thematic issue of *Sport, Education and Society* journal (in English) explored collaborative perspectives by Brazilian authors on socially-just physical education-related themes (Sanches Neto et al., 2021).

In recent years, events in the area have been focused on attracting activist professors, teachers and researchers to fill this gap. For example, two editions of the School Physical Education Teacher-Researchers International Congress (*CIPPEFE*), organised in inter-institutional collaboration, already presented a debate on gender and racial prejudice as a theme in the area in its first edition in 2018. Its second edition in 2020 was entirely guided by the theme of social justice and had the participation of researchers from the English-speaking community, Chile, and Brazil in order to deepen discussions on: "Social Justice and Physical Education", "The Freirean look at the referring meanings to difference and sexuality", "Inclusive Physical Education" and "School Physical Education and Social (In)Justice: anti-racism and inequalities in the context of the pandemic", "Teaching in School Physical Education and Social Justice", and "The production of knowledge in School Physical Education". In these events, we observe works that show how Brazilian teachers and researchers have approached education for ethnic-racial relations, LGBTQIAPN+ and gender equality, class and politics, inclusion of people with disabilities, and inclusion of non-hegemonic bodily practices in the school curriculum.

The critical agenda of Brazilian physical education currently coexists with different perspectives that have adopted culture as a central reference for school physical education, configuring what has become known as the culturalist turn in the area (Costa & Almeida, 2018). The pioneering work in this turn – under Marxist influence (Castellani Filho et al., 1992) – coins the term body culture and defines the need for a critical-overcoming perspective of the curriculum, which called on teachers to commit to the social transformation of socially oppressed groups. Kunz's works (2001) – based on Paulo Freire's, the Frankfurt School's and Merleau Ponty's assumptions – also contributed to shaping the debate on critical pedagogies in Brazilian physical education.

The culturalist proposals gained prominence in Brazilian curriculum policies and pedagogical discourses, becoming present in curriculum documents from different administrative instances of national education. The concept of body culture started to be widely used in these materials, and not necessarily associated with the theoretical bases and ethical commitment of critical pedagogies. There is a continuous erasure of critical bases and the appropriation of the body culture concept by neoliberal policies in these documents. It is noticed that although the body culture concept coined in critical pedagogies has influenced Brazilian curriculum policies, the commitment to emancipation and social justice is not always present in research or in teaching practices in the area.

Given this context, in this work we seek to map how social justice has been investigated in Brazilian graduate programs in the last six years and by teachers working in Brazilian schools who participated in the 2020 edition of *CIPPEFE*, from its theoretical formulations to its development of emancipatory pedagogical practices. The aim was to describe the research and pedagogical practices engaged in social justice issues in Brazil, relating them to the international literature on the subject.

Method

We carried out an integrative literature review (Whittemore & Knafl, 2005) to map how social justice has been investigated in research carried out in postgraduate programs at Brazilian universities over the last six years and by activist teacher–researchers who participated in the 2020 edition of *CIPPEFE*. The review was conducted in the Catalog of Theses and Dissertations from the Coordination for the Improvement of Higher Education Personnel (CAPES), a database which brings together the research work developed in the country's *Stricto Sensu* Graduate Programs and 97 papers presented at *CIPPEFE* (2020).

The search in the *CAPES* Catalog was carried out in February 2023 with the term 'School Physical Education', applying the filter per year to identify the works produced between 2016 and 2022, resulting in the identification of 452 works. Then, the titles and abstracts were read. At this step the following works were excluded: 57 works (16 theses and 41 dissertations) – because they were related to investigations about school physical education from other countries, non-formal education projects, events or actions carried out in schools and surveys that only used the public and/or school space for data collection – and 327 studies that did not present characteristics common to critical pedagogies in school physical education – listed by Philpot et al. (2021), namely: theoretical foundation based on the cultural understanding of human beings and body practices, the assumption and pursuit of equity, combating discrimination, prejudice and violence, inclusion of voices and cultures of traditionally oppressed social groups and pedagogical practices committed to democratic inclusion and participation.

Regarding the 97 works presented at the *CIPPEFE* (2020) – an event whose objective was to increase the visibility of critical pedagogies to promote forms of teaching in school physical education engaged with social justice (Freire, 2017; Philpot et al., 2021) – titles and abstracts were read to identify themes related to critical pedagogies and social justice, leaving 52 works that addressed critical pedagogies and social justice. Then, the set of dissertations and theses raised in the integrative review in the *CAPES* Catalog and in the works presented at the *CIPPEFE* (2020) was organised into themes that highlight the dialogue with critical pedagogies and the promotion of social justice.

Findings

Regarding the works selected in the *CAPES* Catalog, it is noted that the research carried out in public higher education institutions represents the largest volume of studies dealing with social justice themes (56 works). Furthermore, 12 studies were carried out in graduate programs of private higher education institutions. This finding reflects the way academic research is organised in Brazil, a country in which public universities represent the largest volume of scientific production in all areas of knowledge. Unfortunately, it can be seen that this production has received recurrent attacks and funding cuts by political leaders of the extreme right-wing government that ruled the country in recent years (2019–2022) and for which critical pedagogies and social justice represent guidelines for left-wing policies.

The data also show the regional inequalities present in Brazil, as 34 works produced in universities in the Southeast region were found, which concentrates states and cities with greater economic and social development; 12 studies were developed in the Northeast region, nine in the Midwest region, seven in the South region and six in the North region. Regarding the works presented at the *CIPPEFE*, 34 communications addressed practices and knowledge produced by Brazilian teachers who work in public schools with a focus on social justice.

All the analysed production was categorised into five categories. Table 21.1 summarises the number of works found on each topic related to critical pedagogies and social justice.

Table 21.1 Works that investigated themes related to social justice in physical education at school

Categories	CAPES Theses and Dissertations Catalog		CIPPEFE works	Total
	Theses	Dissertations	Communications	
Indigenous and Black ethnic-racial relations	1	11	6	18
Rights and inclusion of people with disabilities	2	22	12	36
Knowledge of socially marginalised groups and inclusive bodily practices	2	7	13	22
Gender and sexuality issues	4	11	2	18
Critical studies on health and beauty standards	0	4	1	5

Indigenous and Black ethnic-racial relations

A total of 12 studies were found developed in Brazilian graduate programs on the theme of ethnic-racial and Indigenous relations available in the *CAPES* Catalog which discuss: (1) anti-racist practices in physical education classes at school (Silva, 2016); (2) thematisation of Indigenous bodily practices in order to break down stereotypes and prejudices against Indigenous peoples (Freitas, 2022; Reis, 2020); (3) proposals for intercultural work with a view to valuing Indigenous cultures (Gonçalves, 2020; Reis, 2020) and Afro-Brazilians (Lima, 2018; Silva Filho 2018); (4) specific knowledge and understandings produced in Indigenous schools (Leite, 2017; Paiva, 2018; Skolaude, 2019); (5) elucidation of practices for applying the laws 10,639/2003 and 11,645/2008 (Crelier, 2017; Soares, 2017) which mandates Afro-Brazilian and Indigenous history and culture teaching in the Brazilian school curriculum.

Moreover, six communications were presented at the *CIPPEFE* on this theme involving the promotion of Afro-Brazilian and Indigenous cultures, the education of teachers for anti-racist practices and the fight against racism in sports. Race is an important factor to consider in physical education, and that physical education teacher education (PETE) programs need to take steps to address issues of social justice and equity in order to create more inclusive and effective learning environments for all students. Flintoff, Dowling, and Fitzgerald (2015), Clark (2020), and Blackshear and Culp (2021) state that it is necessary to overcome the gaps between political rhetoric and practice and that racial theory can be used to elucidate the racialised experiences of Black students revealing white supremacist constructs and practices that negatively affect Black students in physical education classes.

PETE programs need to incorporate critical race theory and culturally responsive teaching practices in order to better prepare teachers to work with diverse student populations. Clark (2020) calls for a critical race pedagogy of physical education, which recognises the ways in which race and racism impact the experiences of students in physical education.

Rights and inclusion of people with disabilities in physical education classes

A total of 24 studies produced in Brazilian graduate programs were found on the theme of rights and inclusion of people with disabilities, which investigated: (1) pedagogical practices and themes from body culture in the inclusion process in physical education classes (Almada, 2017; Araújo, 2018; Frank, 2017; Gatti, 2020; Morais, 2017; Oliveira, 2022; Santos, 2018; Vilela, 2018); (2) the students' point of view on inclusion (Barbuio, 2016; Paolucci, 2022; Silva, 2022); (3) initial and continuing teacher education and the point of view of teachers in promoting the inclusion of people with disabilities in classes (Ferreira, 2016; Lopes, 2018; Morais Sobrinho, 2017; Nunes, 2018; Scarpato, 2020; Silva, 2018a; Silveira, 2020; Vicente, 2018).

On this subject, 12 communications were presented in the *CIPPEFE* which addressed strategies to guarantee the learning rights of students with disabilities in the context of remote learning required by the SARS-Cov-2 (Covid-19) pandemic protocols, teaching and learning strategies for the inclusion of students with disabilities in physical education classes, and working with differences and diversity from an inclusive perspective. Although studies on inclusion and disability represent a significant share of research on school physical education and social justice in Brazil, progress is still needed on epistemological and methodological issues (Barton, 2005; Erevelles, Grace, & Parekh, 2019).

The advancement of research in the area must consider the political dimension, equity and citizenship in emancipatory perspectives that lead to social transformation and empowerment (Barton, 2005). According to Erevelles, Grace and Parekh (2019, pp. 357) "disability remains on the fringes of radical curriculum studies – sometimes seen in an almost opportunistic way, often considered as a synonym of deviance/weakness/pathology, or conceived as the inevitable result of oppression". The authors defend the importance of expanding research on curriculum, disability, and intersectionality with gender, race, sexuality and class.

Knowledge of socially marginalised groups and inclusive bodily practices

A total of nine studies were found in the *CAPES* Catalog in this category which sought to: (1) include Capoeira and Afro-Brazilian culture in the physical education curriculum (Faria, 2018; Guimarães, 2017; Silva, 2018b); (2) discuss the potential of *Callejero* football in the inclusive and democratic participation of students (Castro, 2018; Grifoni, 2020; Moraes, 2020); (3) develop a proposal for Gymnastics for All (Francisco, 2020); (4) include the circus culture in a critical, ethical and creative perspective, valuing the freedom of bodily expressions and positioning in favour of less favoured social classes, multiculturalism, and access to the use of technological tools (Ramos, 2016; Soares, 2020).

There were seven papers on the subject presented at the *CIPPEFE*. Three focused on inserting peripheral bodily practices such as Hip-Hop, Capoeira and Circus. Six communications from activist teacher–researchers also addressed pedagogical practices aimed at the uprising of socially disadvantaged groups, the search for social justice, ecology of knowledge, and questioning of social inequalities and meritocracy typical of global capitalism through the pedagogical approach with peripheral knowledge.

In addition to McLaren's critical multiculturalism (1997), the thinking of Sousa Santos (2019) has influenced the insertion of diversified bodily practices in physical education classes, seeking social justice through curricular justice. This production dialogues with postcolonial proposals and critical theories of race and intersectionality (Azzarito, 2016). Several themes are entangled with physical education socially-just teaching, being a necessary challenge for teachers to comprehend how critically they connect with the students' lives (Venâncio et al., 2021).

Gender and sexuality issues

A total of 15 studies were located in the Master's Theses and Doctoral Dissertations Catalog in this category which discussed: (1) The participation of girls in classes (Baetta, 2017; Da Costa, 2017; Costa Júnior, 2016; Malvar, 2020; Matos, 2020; Pereira, 2020; Sá, 2020); (2) didactic experiences in dealing with bodily practices of sports, dance and circus in working with gender equality (Fernandes, 2016; Mota, 2017); (3) teacher perception of working with gender and sexuality (Conceição, 2022; Severino, 2019; Zimmermann, 2017; Zuzzi, 2016); and (4) addressing sexual diversity and homophobia in physical education classes (Aquilino, 2020; Zuanazzi, 2020).

There were two communications presented at the *CIPPEFE* on this theme which discussed: experiences of homo-affective students and teachers in the practice of *Quadrilha* – a traditional Brazilian dance – and the autobiographical experience of a teacher in teacher education. The classes of physical education can provide opportunities for promoting social justice and equality for girls, especially those who may not fit traditional gender norms. Physical education can provide a safe and supportive environment for girls to explore their physical abilities and challenge societal expectations of femininity (Cameron & Humbert, 2020). It can also serve as a platform for challenging gender and sexuality-based stereotypes and promoting inclusive and respectful attitudes towards all students (Fitzpatrick & Enright, 2016) and create inclusive spaces for LGBTQIAPN+ students (Landi et al., 2020). Thus, considering how gender-related issues underpin both teaching and learning is often seen as a taboo for physical education teachers (Lima et al., 2020).

Critical studies on health and beauty standards

There are critical studies in this category on neoliberal discourses on health, the media and standards of beauty, the investigation from the perspective of students on body patterns present in social networks (Nascimento, 2018), teacher education for problematising representations about the body (Barbosa, 2017) and development of pedagogical practices to problematise body patterns (Biscaro, 2016; Rosa, 2017). There was one communication presented on this theme at the *CIPPEFE* in which high school youth questioned the relationship between physical education and health by creating an application.

Fitzpatrick and Russell (2013) warned about the need to build critical pedagogies in the field of health, as the growing concern about obesity and sedentary lifestyle among young people has led to biologising approaches to the physical education curriculum that question critical theories for excessively reflective approaches and are poorly connected with the young people's bodily experiences. The authors defend a more embodied and experienced approach to health work which can add treatment to the markers of difference, equity and social transformation.

Brazilian studies dialogue with the international literature that discusses social justice and health. In this perspective, physical education teachers and researchers need to be careful not to give in to the self-management discourses of healthy, active and individualistic citizenship of neoliberalism which adopts biopower strategies on the efficiency of body productivity, while the poorest, Black, and women populations do not have choices for a healthy life and are also stigmatised about not making the so-called 'right' choices. For the author, critical physical education needs to give space to invisible bodies and break hegemonic discourses about the body. It needs to consider differences, interculturality, opening space for promoting and realising other identities, cultures and representations about the body, so that students find a physical education curriculum where their subjectivities are legitimised and not erased (Azzarito, 2016).

In a case study with high school physical education teachers, Alfrey and O'Connor (2020) found that the development of critical pedagogies in health and physical education requires that teachers engage in continuous cycles of action and reflection, as postulated by the concept of praxis coined by Freire (2017). Although we found many relevant themes in our literature review, it is uncertain how the research and communications presented in the *CIPPEFE* considered and promoted transformation processes in the pedagogical approach to health in a broad and critical perspective. For instance, de Oliveira et al. (2015) in Brazil and international researchers look at health from a perspective that includes social markers of difference and the integration between individual, social and ecological aspects in health education.

Conclusion

The effects of globalisation are increasing the challenges we need to face to promote social justice and equity. So, it is essential that the critical agenda of physical education in schools is expanded. There is still a gap between the curriculum anchored in critical perspectives and the curricula practised in Brazilian schools and in the international production on school physical education. Efforts have recently been made to give more visibility to academic research and the publication of teacher-researchers who seek to materialise the critical reading of the physical education curriculum in everyday school life. In order to contribute to the discussion of this theme, this work mapped how social justice has been investigated in Brazilian graduate programs in the last six years and by teachers working in Brazilian schools, as well as described the research and pedagogical practices engaged in social justice themes in Brazil, relating them to the international literature on the subject.

The analysis of studies and communications presented at the *CIPPEFE* (2020) shows that academic works and activist teacher-researchers' works seek to connect socio-critical theories – built over the last 40 years – in Brazil to promote the development of critical pedagogies. The bibliographic survey carried out in this chapter shows that the development of critical pedagogies aimed at developing the curriculum, pedagogical practices, assessment, and teacher education is ongoing. Its visibility and dialogue with international studies can be expanded so that the Brazilian critical agenda increasingly supports the guarantee of learning rights and the social emancipation of oppressed social groups.

Supported by critical pedagogical principles, physical education teachers can develop practices towards raising awareness about equality, respect for cultural diversities, combating all types of discrimination and the commitment to social justice. This kind of critically embodied pedagogy points to a praxis that proposes a reflexive action – both by students and teachers – on the world to transform it, with a view to overcoming the dehumanising injustices that have been deepened by the global neoliberal agenda.

References

Alfrey, L., & O'Connor, J. (2020). Critical pedagogy and curriculum transformation in secondary health and physical education. *Physical Education and Sport Pedagogy*, 25(3), 288–302.

Almada, R. R. (2017). *Uma proposta de ensino do goalball nas escolas: a visão dos professores e alunos* [Dissertação de mestrado, Universidade Estadual de Campinas]. http://repositorio.unicamp.br/jspui/handle/REPOSIP/321975

Almeida, F. Q., & Kirk, D. (2020). Pedagogia crítica e 'estudos sociocríticos' no Brasil e na literatura anglófona. *Perspectiva*, 38(3), 1–21.

Aquilino, S. M. (2020). *Entre jovens invisíveis e corpos silenciados: manifestações das sexualidades e a homofobia (des)veladas nas aulas de educação física* [Dissertação de mestrado, Universidade de Brasília]. https://1library.org/document/y6jgepnq-invisiveis-silenciados-manifestacoes-sexualidades-homofobia-veladas-educacao-fisica.html

de Araújo, E. V. (2018). *Dança e educação inclusiva: contribuições da dança como conteúdo da Educação Física na perspectiva da inclusão na escola* [Dissertação de mestrado]. Universidade de Pernambuco.

Azzarito, L. (2016). Permission to speak: A postcolonial view on racialized bodies and PE in the current context of globalization. *Research Quarterly for Exercise and Sport*, 87(2), 141–150. doi:10.1080/02701367.2016.1166474

Baetta, R. R. (2017). *Dança na Educação Física escolar: uma percepção de alunos e alunas* [Dissertação de mestrado]. Centro Universitário Moura Lacerda.

Barbosa, P. P. (2017). *Professores de Educação Física formados em instituições privadas e a problematização do corpo* [Dissertação de mestrado, Universidade Federal de Minas Gerais]. https://repositorio.ufmg.br/handle/1843/BUOS-AQPN7F

Barbuio, R. (2016). *Possibilidades de participação de uma aluna em condição de deficiência: focalizando a Educação Física Escolar* [Dissertação de mestrado]. Centro Universitário Moura Lacerda.

Barton, L. (2005). Emancipatory research and disabled people: Some observations and questions. *Educational Review, 57*(3), 317–327. www.tandfonline.com/doi/abs/10.1080/00131910500149325

Biscaro, M. V. (2016). *Corpo e cultura midiática: fronteiras (in)visíveis à prática pedagógica da Educação Física* [Dissertação de mestrado, Universidade Pitágoras Unopar]. https://repositorio.pgsskroton.com/handle/123456789/816

Blackshear, T. B., & Culp, B. (2021). Transforming PETE's initial standards: Ensuring social justice for Black students in physical education. *Quest, 73*(1), 22–44.

Bracht, V., & Crisor, V. R. (2003). *A educação física no Brasil e na Argentina: identidade, desafios e perspectivas*. São Paulo: Autores Associados.

Cameron, N., & Humbert, L. (2020). 'Strong girls' in physical education: Opportunities for social justice education. *Sport, Education and Society, 25*(3), 249–260.

Castellani Filho, L., Lúcia, S. C., Taffarel, C. N. Z., Varjal, E., Escobar, M. O., & Bracht, V. (1992). *Metodologia do ensino de educação física*. São Paulo: Cortez Editora.

Castro, L. E. (2018). *A construção de valores orientada pela metodologia callejera na educação física escolar* [Dissertação de mestrado, Universidade Estadual Paulista Júlio de Mesquita Filho]. https://repositorio.unesp.br/handle/11449/153734

Clark, L. (2020). Toward a critical race pedagogy of physical education. *Physical Education and Sport Pedagogy, 25*(4), 439–450. www.tandfonline.com/doi/abs/10.1080/17408989.2020.1720633

Conceição, D. M. S. (2022) *Gênero na educação física escolar: as representações das/dos docentes de educação física do Instituto Federal de Educação, Ciência e Tecnologia do Amapá (IFAP)*. [Dissertação de Mestrado. Universidade Federal do Amapá].Repositório.

Costa, M., & Almeida, F. Q. (2018). A educação física e a 'virada culturalista' do campo: um olhar a partir de Mauro Betti e Valter Bracht. *Corpoconsciência*, 1–12.

Costa Júnior, A. R. (2016). *A participação feminina na Educação Física no ensino médio: as exclusões de gênero e a pouca diversidade de conteúdos* [Dissertação de mestrado]. Universidade Federal do Rio de Janeiro.

Crelier, C. M. S. (2017). *A Educação Física Escolar e a lei 10639/03: o chão da escola X os aspectos legais* [Dissertação de mestrado, Universidade Salgado de Oliveira.].

Da Costa, S. B. (2017). *As relações entre desigualdades de gênero e autoexclusão de alunas das aulas de educação física no ensino médio* [Dissertação de mestrado Universidade Salgado de Oliveira].

Erevelles, N., Grace, E. J., & Parekh, G. (2019). Disability as meta curriculum: Ontologies, epistemologies, and transformative praxis. *Curriculum Inquiry, 49*(4), 357–372. www.tandfonline.com/doi/full/10.1080/03626784.2019.1664078

Faria, C. A. B. (2018). *História e cultura afro-brasileira nas aulas de educação física do município de Cariacica: uma proposta curricular* [Dissertação de mestrado, Faculdade Vale do Cricaré.].

Fernandes, S. C. (2016). *A educação esportiva de meninas na escola pública: experiências positivas de gênero na educação física* [Tese de doutorado, Faculdade de Educação Física da Universidade Estadual de Campinas]. https://repositorio.unicamp.br/jspui/handle/REPOSIP/304704

Ferreira, R. A. (2016). *Trabalho colaborativo na Educação Física escolar: estratégias para a formação de professores e inclusão* [Tese de doutorado, Universidade Estadual Júlio de Mesquita Filho]. https://repositorio.unesp.br/handle/11449/148798

Filgueiras, I. P., & Maldonado, D. T. (2020). Currículo e prática pedagógica de educação física escolar na América Latina (Vol. 43). CRV.

Fitzpatrick, K; Enright, E. Gender sexuality and physical education. In: *Routledge handbook of physical education pedagogies*. Routledge, 2016. p. 337–349.

Fitzpatrick, K., & Russell, D. (2013). On being critical in health and physical education. *Physical Education and Sport Pedagogy, 20*(2), 159–173. doi:10.1080/17408989.2013.8374

Flintoff, A., Dowling, F., & Fitzgerald, H. (2015). Working through whiteness, race and (anti) racism in physical education teacher education. *Physical Education and Sport Pedagogy, 20*(5), 559–570. www.tandfonline.com/doi/abs/10.1080/17408989.2014.962017

Francisco, M. F. (2020). *Ressignificação da ginástica na escola: proposta da Ginástica Para Todos na Educação Física anos iniciais* [Dissertação de mestrado, Universidade Federal de São Carlos]. https://repositorio.ufscar.br/handle/ufscar/13013

Frank, T. J. (2017). *O jogo de Fusen como recurso pedagógico na inclusão de estudantes com deficiência física severa nas aulas de Educação Física* [Dissertação de mestrado, Universidade Caxias do Sul]. https://repositorio.ucs.br/xmlui/handle/11338/3242

Freire, P. (2017). *Pedagogia do oprimido*. (63a ed.). Rio de Janeiro, São Paulo: Paz e Terra.

Freitas, S. C. (2022). *Educação Escolar Indígena, Formação de Professores e Educação Física: tensões e possibilidades para uma perspectiva intercultural na escola Pluridocente Guarani do Espírito Santo.* Dissertação de Mestrado. Universidade Federal do Espírito Santo.

Gatti, M. R. (2020). *Coensino e Educação Física escolar: perspectivas colaborativas para a inclusão de estudantes com deficiência* [Dissertação de mestrado, Universidade Federal de São Carlos]. https://repositorio.ufscar.br/handle/ufscar/13513

Gonçalves L. S. (2020). *Práticas corporais indígenas da comunidade Tenetehara-Guajajara: contribuições interculturais para a Educação Física* [Dissertação de mestrado, Universidade Federal do Maranhão]. https://tedebc.ufma.br/jspui/handle/tede/3181

Grifoni, T. (2020). *Processos educativos emergentes de uma unidade didática com o Fútbol Callejero nas aulas de Educação Física.* [Dissertação de mestrado]. Universidade Federal de São Carlos.

Guimarães, F. S. C. (2017). *A capoeira e a implementação da lei 10639/03 na educação física escolar: percepções e possibilidades* [Dissertação de mestrado, Universidade Federal do Amapá]. https://www2.unifap.br/ppgmdr/files/2018/01/L-F-C-GUIMAR%c3%83ES-A-capoeira-e-a-implementa%c3%a7%c3%a3o-da-lei-10.639-03-na-educa%c3%a7%c3%a3o-f%c3%adsica-escolar.pdf

Kirk, D., Almeida, F. Q., & Bracht, V. (2019). Pedagogia crítica da Educação Física: desafios e perspectivas contemporâneas. *Movimento (ESEFID/UFRGS), 25,* 25061.

Kunz, E. (2001). *Educação Física: ensino e mudanças.* 2. ed. Ijuí: Unijuí

Landi, D., Flory, S. B., Safron, C., & Marttinen, R. (2020). LGBTQ Research in physical education: A rising tide?. *Physical Education and Sport Pedagogy, 25*(3), 259–273.

Leite, F. F. (2017). *Saberes tradicionais Krahô: contribuições para Educação Física Indígena bilíngue e intercultural* [Dissertação de mestrado, Universidade Federal do Tocantins]. https://repositorio.uft.edu.br/handle/11612/944

Lima, L. T. G. (2018). *A inserção dos conteúdos afro-brasileiros nas aulas de Educação Física Escolar: limites e possibilidades na rede estadual de Pernambuco* [Dissertação de mestrado]. Universidade de Pernambuco.

Lima, C. E. S., Ferreira, E. C. S., Sanches Neto, L., & Venâncio, L. (2020). Breaking cultural 'taboos' about the body and gender: Brazilian students' emancipation from a thematic perspective of school physical education. *Frontiers in Education, 5*(155), 1–8. https://doi.org/10.3389/feduc.2020.00155

Lopes, B. P. L. (2018). *Esporte da escola: diálogo pedagógico na perspectiva inclusiva com supervisores do PIBID Educação Física* [Dissertação de mestrado, Universidade Federal do Rio Grande do Norte]. https://repositorio.ufrn.br/handle/123456789/30712

Malvar, A. J. M. (2020). *A participação das meninas nas aulas de educação física: dilemas de um professor no ensino do futsal* [Dissertação de mestrado, Universidade Federal de São Carlos]. https://repositorio.ufscar.br/handle/ufscar/12987

Matos, N. T. (2020). *Ontem eles jogaram, hoje é a gente professora! Os lugares das meninas na educação física e na escola* [Dissertação de mestrado, Universidade Estadual Paulista]. https://cms.ufmt.br/files/galleries/210/N031eadd1a00b91211fb38721268e8fb5d853aa56.pdf

McLaren, P. (1997). *Multiculturalismo crítico.* Instituto Paulo Freire/Cortez.

Moraes, F. D. (2020). *Educação Física Escolar ea contribuição da metodologia Callejera nos conhecimentos atitudinais.* [Dissertação de mestrado]. Universidade Federal de São Carlos.

Morais, M. P. S. (2017). *A psicomotricidade relacional como prática educativa para inclusão de adolescentes com deficiência intelectual na Educação Física escolar* [Dissertação de mestrado, Universidade Federal do Rio Grande do Norte]. https://repositorio.ufrn.br/handle/123456789/25007

Morais Sobrinho, J. (2017). *Educação Física escolar, formação permanente e inclusão: um diálogo com a diversidade* [Dissertação de mestrado, Universidade Federal do Rio Grande do Norte]. https://repositorio.ufrn.br/jspui/handle/123456789/24853

Mota, M. P. (2017). *Corpo e questões de gênero e sexualidade nas atividades circenses em uma escola de Corumbá/MS* [Dissertação de mestrado, Universidade Federal de Mato Grosso do Sul]. https://ppgecpan.ufms.br/files/2018/01/Disserta%C3%A7%C3%A3o-Mauro-Palmeira-Mota.pdf

Nascimento, E. (2018). *Dos filtros do Instagram à quadra da escola: representações sociais do corpo na perspectiva dos/as adolescentes* [Dissertação de mestrado, Universidade Federal do Vale do São Francisco]. https://rsdjournal.org/index.php/rsd/article/download/14017/12485/181423

Nunes, F. S. F. (2018). *Formação continuada na perspectiva inclusiva: o projeto Portas Abertas para a inclusão no município de Fortaleza* [Dissertação de mestrado, Universidade Estadual do Ceará]. http://bdtd.ibict.br/vufind/Record/UECE-0_d5f6d3324826283428d74c995413b3d7

Oliveira, S. S. (2022). *Impacto da pandemia nas aulas de educação física escolar em escola bilíngue para alunos surdos no contexto da Covid-19.* [Dissertação de Mestrado. Pontifícia Universidade Católica de São Paulo. https://repositorio.pucsp.br/handle/handle/29607

de Oliveira, V. J. M., Martins, I. R., & Bracht, V. (2015). Projetos e práticas em educação para a saúde na educação física escolar: possibilidades!. *Journal of Physical Education, 26*(2), 243–255. Retrieved from https://periodicos.uem.br/ojs/index.php/RevEducFis/article/view/25600

Paiva, P. W. S. C. (2018). *A compreensão da realidade dos docentes de Educação Física das escolas estaduais indígenas de Roraima* [Dissertação de mestrado, Universidade Federal de Roraima]. www.uerr.edu.br/ppge/wp-content/uploads/2019/04/13.DISSERTA%C3%87%C3%83O-PAULO.pdf

Paolucci, B. A. (2022). *'Nada sobre nós, sem nós': a produção científica da relação Educação Física escolar e inclusão entre os anos 2010-2020: uma análise acerca da percepção do aluno com deficiência.* [Dissertação de Mestrado, Universidade Federal de Goiás]. https://repositorio.bc.ufg.br/tede/handle/tede/11962

Pereira, A. C. G. (2020). *Ensaios de uma metodologia da experiência crítico-afetiva nas aulas de Educação Física: impactos sobre as relações de gênero e o empoderamento das meninas* [Dissertação de mestrado, Universidade Federal de São Carlos]. https://repositorio.ufscar.br/handle/ufscar/12988?show=full

Philpot, R., Gerdin, G., Smith, W., Linnér, S., Schenker, K., Westlie, K., ... & Larsson, L. (2021). Taking action for social justice in HPE classrooms through explicit critical pedagogies. *Physical Education and Sport Pedagogy, 26*(6), 662–674.

Ramos, B. A. (2016). *As artes circenses na educação física escolar enquanto conteúdo da cultura corporal: suas contribuições para desenvolvimento da expressão corporal e criatividade* [Dissertação de mestrado, Universidade Federal de Goiás]. https://repositorio.bc.ufg.br/tede/handle/tede/6724

Reis, P. R. (2020). *Interculturalidade e sustentabilidade: jogos e brincadeiras indígenas na Educação Física Escolar* [Dissertação de mestrado, Universidade Federal do Amazonas]. https://tede.ufam.edu.br/handle/8116

Rosa, R. C. (2017). *Educação Física no ensino médio: desvelando os sentidos do Corpo* [Dissertação de mestrado, Pontifícia Universidade Católica de Goiás]. http://tede2.pucgoias.edu.br:8080/handle/tede/3826

Sá, C. F. (2020). *Educação física e Gênero: estudo sobre a participação feminina nas aulas de Educação Física em cursos técnicos integrados ao ensino médio da educação profissional e tecnológica* [Dissertação de Mestrado]. Instituto Federal de Educação Ciência e Tecnologia de Mato Grosso.

Sanches Neto, L., Venâncio, L., Silva, E. V. M., & Ovens, A. P. (2021). A socially-critical curriculum for PETE: Students' perspectives on the approaches to social-justice education of one Brazilian programme. *Sport, Education and Society, 26*(7), 704–717. https://doi.org/10.1080/13573322.2020.1839744

Santos, T. B. (2018). *Efeito da tutoria por pares na participação de um estudante com deficiência física nas aulas de Educação Física* [Dissertação de mestrado, Universidade Federal de São Carlos]. https://repositorio.ufscar.br/handle/ufscar/9677

Scarpato, L. C. (2020). *O esporte adaptado como conteúdo da Educação Física escolar adaptada: perspectivas dos professores da rede pública de ensino da cidade de Campinas/SP* [Dissertação de mestrado, Universidade Estadual de Campinas]. http://repositorio.unicamp.br/jspui/handle/REPOSIP/347481

Severino, C. D. (2019). *A percepção dos professores sobre o ensino de Basquetebol, a participação de meninas e o uso das TICs nas aulas de Educação Física* [Tese de doutorado, Universidade Estadual Paulista]. https://repositorio.unesp.br/handle/11449/191395

Silva, E. V. M. (2016). *Ensino da história e cultura afro-brasileira por meio do atletismo: contribuições de um curso de extensão a distância para professores de Educação Física* [Tese de doutorado, Universidade Estadual Paulista 'Júlio de Mesquita Filho']. https://repositorio.unesp.br/handle/11449/136220

Silva, J. C. S. (2018a). *Os estudos sobre a pessoa com deficiência no processo de formação em nível de graduação na Educação Física brasileira: o caso da FEF/UNB* [Dissertação de mestrado, Universidade de Brasília]. https://repositorio.unb.br/handle/10482/34387

Silva, R. M. (2018b). *Entrando no jogo: reflexões sobre os saberes docentes, acadêmicos e da tradição para pensar o ensino da capoeira na escola* [Dissertação de mestrado, Universidade Federal do Rio Grande do Norte]. https://repositorio.ufrn.br/handle/123456789/25372

Silva, T. I. D. (2022). *Representações sociais de desigualdade social em contexto da educação física escolar: com a palavra os/as estudantes do ensino médio de escolas públicas e privadas de Pernambuco.* [Dissertação de Mestrado. Universidade Federal de Pernambuco.] https://repositorio.ufpe.br/handle/123456789/47217

Silva Filho, J. C. A. (2018). *Capoeira, religião e Educação Física: amálgama entre religiosidade, cultura e pessoalidade* [Dissertação de mestrado, Faculdade Unida de Vitória]. http://bdtd.faculdadeunida.com.br:8080/jspui/handle/prefix/160

Silva, M., & Molina, V. A. B. (2017). *Educación física em América Latina: currículos y horizontes formativos.* Jundiaí: Paco Editorial.

Silveira, A. A. T. (2020). *Educação Física escolar inclusiva: olhares e saberes de um grupo de professores do ensino público de Natal/RN* [Dissertação de mestrado, Universidade Federal do Rio Grande do Norte]. https://repositorio.ufrn.br/handle/123456789/29173

Skolaude, L. S. (2019). *'Educação Física não é só isso, é muito mais': uma etnografia em uma escola estadual indígena Kaingang de Porto Alegre/RS* [Dissertação de mestrado, Universidade Federal do Rio Grande do Sul]. https://lume.ufrgs.br/handle/10183/202256

Soares, D. C. (2017). *As relações étnico-raciais e as TIC na Educação Física Escolar: possibilidades para o ensino médio a partir do currículo do estado de São Paulo* [Dissertação de mestrado, Universidade Estadual Paulista]. https://repositorio.unesp.br/handle/11449/151270

Soares, F. S. (2020). *Práticas Corporais Circenses e Mídia-Educação na Educação Física Escolar* [Dissertação de mestrado]. Universidade Federal de Goiás.

Sousa Santos, B. (2019). *O fim do império cognitivo: a afirmação das epistemologias do Sul.* Autêntica.

Venâncio, L., Bruno, B. D., Silva, I. C. C., Flor, B. J. M. S., Gonçalves, Y., & Sanches Neto, L. (2021). Temas e desafios (auto) formativos para professoras de educação física à luz da didática e da justiça social. *Cenas Educacionais, 4*(e10778), 1–40. https://revistas.uneb.br/index.php/cenaseducacionais/article/view/10778

Vicente, B. I. (2018). *Educação Física Escolar e processos de exclusão: percepções de docentes de uma escola da cidade do Rio de Janeiro* [Dissertação de mestrado, Universidade Salgado de Oliveira]. www.researchgate.net/publication/344777469_Educacao_Fisica_Escolar_e_processos_de_exclusao_percepcoes_de_docentes_de_uma_escola_da_cidade_do_Rio_De_Janeiro

Vilela, I. P. (2018). *Jogos de sensibilização para aulas de Educação Física* [Dissertação de mestrado, Universidade Federal Fluminense].

Whittemore, R., & Knafl, K. (2005). The integrative review: Updated methodology. *Journal of Advanced Nursing, 52*(5), 546–553.

Zimmermann, A. P. R. C. (2017). *Dialéticas do feminino: interlocuções com professoras de educação física da rede municipal de ensino de Santa Maria (RS) sobre trabalho pedagógico* [Tese de doutorado, Universidade Federal de Santa Maria]. https://repositorio.ufsm.br/handle/1/15089

Zuanazzi, P. M. (2020). *Sexualidades, gênero e a Educação Física escolar: do silenciamento ao lugar de fala em uma produção audiovisual* [Dissertação de mestrado, Universidade Regional do Noroeste do Estado do Rio Grande do Sul.]. Repositório.

Zuzzi, R. P. (2016). *Gênero na formação de professores/as de educação física: da escolha à atuação profissional* [Tese de doutorado, Universidade Estadual de Campinas]. http://repositorio.unicamp.br/jspui/handle/REPOSIP/305030

PART V

Sport, development, and community

22
EQUALITY AND SOCIAL JUSTICE IN SPORT FOR DEVELOPMENT AND PEACE

Simon C. Darnell and Rob Millington

Introduction

The global Sport for Development and Peace (SDP) sector is the loose amalgam of organisations and stakeholders that organise, implement, and advocate for sport in the service of development and peace (see Collison et al., 2019; Giulianotti et al., 2019). In the SDP model, sport is a catalyst towards achieving non-sport goals, like gender empowerment, health promotion, social inclusion, or conflict resolution and peace building. The sector comprises a range of stakeholders, including non-governmental organisations, national and inter-governmental agencies, corporations, charitable foundations, and sport federations. All of these organisations share a general appreciation of, and support for, the role of sport in making the world a more inclusive, prosperous and peaceful place.

A host of critical approaches to SDP have emerged in recent years, which highlight the gap between the practices, ideologies, and philosophies of SDP on the one hand, and the notion of social justice on the other. These criticisms acknowledge that there are benefits that result from SDP activity, particularly the ways that SDP programs 'train' participants, especially youth, to live and subsist amidst social and material hierarchies and inequality. Yet, SDP is also rarely organised explicitly in the service of social justice, in which the purpose of SDP programs would be to build critically informed, collective action in response to injustice, and mobilise sport to challenge inequality, rather than simply navigate it (see Darnell, 2012; Hartmann & Kwauk, 2011; Hayhurst, 2016).

In this chapter, we attempt to explicate the differences between the normative approach to SDP and a social justice orientation. Following Hartmann and Kwauk's (2011) distinction between the dominant and transformative approaches, we suggest that mainstream SDP is not inherently flawed, but it is qualitatively different than a commitment to social justice. We then discuss some of the hallmarks of a more fully committed social justice orientation to SDP.

This chapter proceeds in five parts. In the next section, we provide a brief overview of the main tenets of SDP, including its historical and policy-based antecedents, and its contemporary manifestations. We then summarise some of the notable recent criticisms of SDP that exemplify its limitations in relation to social justice. The next section proposes a theoretical conception of social justice, before suggesting a series of ways in which to conceive and conceptualise a social justice approach to SDP. The conclusion proposes some future directions for work in this area.

The main tenets of SDP

Although at times framed as a new social movement (see Kidd, 2008), the concept of "sport for good" that buoys much SDP programming has a long and rich history. Most historical accounts of SDP trace its roots to the use of sport as a tool of imperialism from the eighteenth to the mid-twentieth centuries, through its use in physical education programs in nineteenth century British public schools, to the more contemporary context where sport is increasingly connected to humanitarian aid (c.f. Giulianotti & Armstrong, 2011). In the era of colonial expansion, sport became a ready tool of the assimilative practices of Empire building, whereby Western-European sports such as cricket and soccer were mobilised as part of 'civilising missions'. Physical education in the upper-class and all-male British public schools was a formative institution in this regard, where sport was viewed as a means to transform delinquent youth into upstanding young gentlemen and good soldiers of the Empire, instilling values that were "seen as required for all phases of life from warfare ... to parliamentary politics" (Allen, 2011, p. 76; see also MacAloon, 2008). The ideals of 'sport for good' were soon taken up by a range of organisations from amateur sport clubs to groups such as the Boy Scouts, the YMCA, and the Young Hebrew Association, but it was throughout the Empire that sport was mobilised in a way that parallels contemporary SDP programs (see Donnelly, 2011; Donnelly et al., 2011). In this way, physical education was a vehicle to imbue new codes of imperialist manliness – in the vein of Muscular Christianity – imparting the values of courage, strength and sportsmanship, for soldiers, missionaries and educators, while also advancing 'barbarous' and 'backward' colonial subjects and societies along the path to modernity and civility (Hokkanen & Mangan, 2006; Millington & Kidd, 2019).

It is important to note here, that much of these imperialist efforts mobilised through sport were actively resisted, even if surreptitiously (see James, 1969). In this way, sport also played an important role in percolating nationalist and anti-imperialist sentiments that would inform colonial independence movements of the post-World War II era. It is within this context that sport began to be codified within international declarations. For example, the 1948 United Nations Declaration of Human Rights affirmed the right to a standard of living adequate for health and well-being, and the right to rest and leisure (United Nations, 1948). Further, at this time, membership in international governance organisations like the UN, but also sport federations such as the International Olympic Committee (IOC) and the Fédération Internationale de Football Association (FIFA), was viewed as a means to legitimising independence movements, as were more anti-colonial efforts such as the organisation of the Games of the New Emerging Forces (GANEFO) in the 1960s (see Darby, 2005; Kidd, 2005; Millington & Kidd, 2019). Still later, the tradition of 'sport for good' informed other international development and humanitarian policies that secured the right to sport and physical activity, including the International Charter on Physical Education and Sport (1978), the International Convention of the Rights of the Child (1990), the Brighton Declaration of Women and Sport (1994), and the International Convention on the Rights of Persons with Disabilities (2006).

The 1990s would prove an impactful decade for the formalisation of sport in the development context. On the heels of boycotts of international competition with South Africa in protest of Apartheid throughout the 1980s and early 1990s, the ideals of 'sport for good' began to take on more humanitarian and entrepreneurial forms in this decade, often led by athletes directly. The efforts of four-time Olympic speed skating gold-medallist Johan Olav Koss offer a case in point in this regard. Following his successes in the 1992 and 1994 Olympics, Koss, with the aid of the Red Cross, Save the Children, and the Norwegian People's Council established Olympic Aid, which sought to initiate sport-based programs in developing countries to promote humanitarian aid, particularly for children in Bosnia and Herzegovina and Afghanistan. The program has since grown in to one of the largest, and most well-known SDP NGO, Right to Play, currently operating in 15 countries, predominantly in the global South, using "play to educate and empower children and youth to overcome the effects of poverty, conflict and disease in disadvantaged communities" (Right to Play, n.d.).

Right to Play's activities are exemplary of much of the sector. Right to Play, like other SDP organisations, approaches sport as a universal and integrative social practice (see Darnell, 2007), that can be used to overcome social and geographic divisions to promote a range of positive social development outcomes, including, but not limited to: addressing discrimination and bridging social, cultural and ethnic divides (Schulenkorf, 2010; Sugden, 2006); supporting HIV/AIDS education (Beeley et al., 2019; Forde & Frisby, 2015); promoting gender equity and empowerment (Hayhurst et al., 2014; Oxford & McLachlan, 2018); providing opportunities for people with disability (Howe, 2019); and advancing reconciliation and decolonisation in settler colonial societies (Essa et al., 2022; Gardam et al., 2019).

Indeed, there a now hundreds of SDP organisations that employ sport in pursuit of the "social good", broadly defined, across a range of sectors. These organisations include international governmental bodies like the United Nations, who have increasingly formalised the role of sport in development policies including through the Millennium Development Goals from 2000–2015, and now the Sustainable Development Goals from 2015–2030 which connect sport to *sustainable* development, including environmental protection and remediation strategies (McCullough et al., 2022; Millington & Darnell, 2020). Also relevant here are international sporting federations like the IOC and FIFA who have developed their own SDP programming and have helped to connect the hosting of the Olympic Games and FIFA World Cup to development strategies, particularly for host nations in the global South (Darnell, 2012). Finally, NGOs like the above mentioned Canadian-based *Right to Play*, as well as the Kenya-based *Mathare Youth Sport Association*, and the Norwegian-based *Kicking AIDS out* (see Coalter, 2010a) are important stakeholders. In many respects, each of these organisations have carried on the tradition of 'sport for good' outlined above, for better or worse.

Criticisms of SDP

With the above description in mind, in this section we examine some of the criticisms of SDP that have emerged in recent years. The aim here is not to denigrate the successes or benefits of SDP programs or policies but rather to illustrate a qualitative and political differentiation between the normative or popular approach to SDP and a social justice orientation.

Our distinction here is guided by Hartmann and Kwauk's (2011) conceptualisation of the dominant versus the transformative approaches to SDP. In the former, sport is organised and mobilised primarily in the service of social reproduction, and participants in SDP programs are therefore taught the skills of socialisation necessary to fit into the social, political, and economic hierarchies that characterise contemporary human life. Success in the dominant model entails, for example, SDP participants successfully competing for jobs in a scare employment market, finding membership in a team environment in ways that insulate them from racism, sexism, homophobia, or other forms of discrimination and abuse, or coming to know the Other so that cultural or racial differences can be tolerated. In the transformative model, by contrast, sport is less a form of socialisation and more a catalyst for critical pedagogy. In this model, SDP organisers, practitioners, and participants interact and communicate around the convening power of sport in order to question the causes and structures of inequality and to act in ways that challenge these forms of oppression.

Based on this distinction, it is our contention that the dominant model of SDP remains hegemonic in terms of both its ideological weight and its recurrence within the global SDP sector. Given the number of stakeholders and the shifting structure and terrain of the global SDP sector, it is not feasible here to document the number of organisations or programs that might fit into the two categories. Instead, we turn to the critical SDP research literature to examine some of the ways that scholars have deconstructed the dominant approach to SDP and highlighted its limitations in pursuing or achieving a social justice mandate.

First and foremost, SDP has been shown to have a functionalist undertone or approach that aligns with social reproduction more than social justice. In this approach, sport 'functions' as a socialising agent *a priori*, owing to its inherent positive traits and qualities, such as its role in character building, teamwork, responsibility and selflessness. Coalter (2010b, p. 296), for example, has argued that such understandings of functionalism within SDP connect to mythopoeic understandings of sport, myths that "contain elements of truth, but elements which become reified and distorted and 'represent' rather than reflect reality, standing for supposed, but largely unexamined, impacts and processes". According to Coalter (2013), such functionalist approaches have been taken up and perpetuated within SDP by 'sports evangelists' who promulgate sport's mythopoeic character, in ways that can both overstate sport's positive impact and selectively amplify its benefits through an echo-chamber of what he terms incestuous amplification. Similar critical cautions have been put forth by Giulianotti (2004), Hayhurst (2009), and Darnell (2010).

The key point with regards to the functionalist critique of SDP is that in presuming that positive benefits of sport will automatically or naturally occur, evangelists ignore both the negative forms of socialisation that can occur through sport, such as sub-cultures of violence, drug abuse, or injury, as well as the politics of the social structures into which participants are in fact being socialised. In other words, if sport's social benefit is that of its socialisation function only, then what is left unexamined is the political contestability (i.e. the inequality, exploitation, marginalisation, hierarchy) of that socialisation process. The functionalist criticism, therefore, is illustrative of the tension between the dominant and transformative approaches.

Second, SDP has been susceptible to criticisms that it is colonialist, or neo-colonialist, in its orientation and practice, or even that it is compatible with the politics of imperialism and empire (Darnell & Hayhurst, 2011; Nicholls et al., 2010). In some respects, this criticism proceeds from the post-colonial argument that the European Imperial project, which saw vast swathes of the globe conquered and controlled by European powers in the service of Empire, constructed a hierarchical system of global governance and resource distribution that affects the state of the world even today. Certainly, when applied to the processes and vectors of international development, colonialism and Empire serve to illustrate why there continues to be such disparity and inequality between the global South and North, and why development aid and efforts continue to flow along such lines (McEwan, 2009). Given the extent to which SDP is connected to the broader structures of international development policies and aid, such insights are clearly germane to SDP. In turn, and as discussed above, sport itself has a historical connection to colonialism, as one of the ways in which colonial powers asserted their cultural dominance, removed and replaced indigenous peoples, and built local consent for the European, colonial culture (Bale & Cronin, 2003; Darnell et al., 2019).

Against this backdrop, critical SDP scholars have questioned and examined the extent to which SDP policies and programs challenge and/or conform to the (post)colonial ethos. In many respects, the colonising approach to SDP has been exposed in this line of inquiry. For example, Darnell (2007) argued that when contextualised by overlapping discourses of benevolent international development and the universal benefits of sport, the testimonials of SDP volunteers demonstrate a sense of white racial superiority that draws on and confirms the dominance of colonial thinking. Similarly, Nicholls et al. (2010) concluded that the idea of a 'lack of evidence' regarding sport's efficacy within SDP was due in part to the dismissal of local forms and ways of knowing, which align with colonial ideologies in which the only true or real way of knowing was from the perspective of the European coloniser. Scholars like Hayhurst (2014) have also shown that the organisation of sport in the name of gender empowerment, and sport's connection to the 'girl effect' on a global scale, are implicated in post-colonial structures and ideologies.

More recently, critical scholars have built on the post-colonial perspective to examine SDP with respect to settler colonialism. Whereas in the global South, the de-colonial process of the 1960s meant that countries ostensibly re-gained independence from their colonial rulers, in global North countries like Canada and Australia, settler colonialism continues through to the present day. The resulting struggles of Indigenous people within contemporary settler colonial contexts have been recurring sites for SDP activity. For example, in Canada, *Right to Play* focused significant activities on Indigenous youth to support their empowerment and self-determination. However, as scholars like Arellano and Downey (2019, p. 457) have argued, despite claims to decolonisation, such programs have "unwittingly embraced 'shape-shifting' forms of settler colonialism while continuing to reinforce existing structures". This is because such programs work to create and celebrate an Aboriginal identity and subjecthood *within* the settler colonial nation, which stops well short of claiming indigenous sovereignty or nationhood in defiance of colonialism. Similar tensions have been exposed in SDP programs aimed at Indigenous people by Essa et al. (2022), Lucas and O'Connor (2021), Millington et al. (2019), Norman et al. (2019), Hayhurst et al. (2016), and Rossi and Rynne (2014).

In turn, and third, is the related critique that SDP is, in its dominant orientation and implementation, primarily a process of top-down imposition or modernisation theory in a re-packaged form. According to David Black (2017), the tension between top-down versus bottom-up approaches to development (particularly as they relate to SDP) has to do with different understandings of "the *processes and objectives* of development, and the kinds of action required to enable them" (p. 9, emphasis in original). Recognising that there is an interactive dynamic between the two (a point to which we return later), top-down development is primarily concerned with "enabling people, communities, and/or countries to better adapt, succeed and prosper in the world more or less as it is" (Black, 2017, p. 9), a perspective that aligns with Hartmann and Kwauk's (2011) dominant model of SDP. Top-down tends to be used in reference to development models and approaches that are led by relatively rich countries or organisations, and based on flows of materials, resources and expertise from the global North to South. By contrast, a bottom-up conception views development "in a more radical sense of addressing the structural roots of poverty, inequality, and marginalization, often emphasizing the need to restructure or *transform* the current order (locally, nationally, and/or transnationally)" (Black, 2017, p. 9), which is more compatible with the transformative approach to SDP.

Again, critical research has revealed evidence of a top-down orientation in the processes of SDP, in both geo-political/material ways, and experiential or ideological terms. In the former, Darnell et al. (2019) showed, through a historical analysis, that the current structuring of the global SDP sector emerged from assertions of sport's development utility made by relatively powerful actors through various processes of international relations and geo-politics. In some cases, this entailed celebrity athletes leading development activities through sport; in other cases, it was national governments asserting their foreign policy agenda through sport-based development programs (Darnell et al., 2019). In any of these instances, sport was beholden to top-down development forces, which helped to galvanise and institutionalise the SDP sector at the conclusion of the twentieth century.

In the latter, Darnell (2010) found that young Canadians serving as international volunteers in SDP tended to employ a top-down approach to development by taking their own positive sporting experiences and attempting to deliver them to Others as a form of international aid. Particularly when understood as hegemonic forms of knowledge production, these ostensibly universal understandings of sport came to constitute top-down forms of development that aimed to reproduce geographically specific and often class-based notions of sport as a universal prescription for underdevelopment. Regardless, whether geo-political or subjective and experiential, top-down development still pervades SDP activity.

In sum, in this section, we have explored some relevant critical assessments of SDP activity, all of which call into question the extent to which SDP constitutes a commitment to social justice or a process through which to achieve it. Rather, SDP has been shown, at least in its dominant form, to constitute a form of social reproduction or a means through which to socialise participants, particularly youth, into competitive social relations and structures. And yet, it is our contention that these critiques do not mean that SDP is fundamentally incompatible with social justice. In the next section, we outline what social justice means to us before discussing some of the ways to connect it to sport and SDP activity.

Conceptualising social justice

In contrast to the dominant, top-down, reproductive and/or colonial approach to development and SDP, it is our contention that it is possible to re-orient and conceptualise SDP as a commitment to, or act of, social justice, and in ways that align with the transformative approach. With that in mind, it is useful to offer some conceptualisations of what social justice is and what it means.

There is no single or absolute definition of social justice. However, as a starting point, we propose the following definition from the United States' National Association of Social Workers, which defines social justice as:

> the view that everyone deserves equal economic, political and social rights and opportunities. Social workers aim to open the doors of access and opportunity for everyone, particularly those in greatest need.
>
> (cited in Morgaine, 2014, p. 4)

Several points stand out here. One is that social justice is based on rights, as opposed to charity, a point that we have made elsewhere (Darnell & Millington, 2019) in our reflections on the sociology of sport more generally. In this sense, justice is not the benevolent delivery of resources or attention to the underserved, but rather the recognition that those in positions of inequality (materially, politically, socially) have rights to full representation and resources that are not currently being met. In this sense, justice is about an obligation to see the rights of all fulfilled, not a choice to help (or not) (also see Darnell et al., 2021).

A second point is that social justice is a broad approach or theoretical and philosophical perspective that can be applied to multiple stakeholders or groups of actors. While the example offered above applies to social workers, it can also be applied to other professions or perspectives, including sport advocates and SDP officials or practitioners. The applicability of social justice to the field of Sport for Development and Peace is in no way exclusive.

Third, it is important to recognise that while the social justice approach described here aligns with the transformative approach to SDP as outlined by Hartmann and Kwauk (2011), and to the notion of bottom-up development as spelled out by Black (2017), there is also tangible overlap with the dominant approach. In other words, the dominant approach to SDP and the social justice orientation that we are proposing here are not mutually exclusive. For example, the goal of opening doors of access and opportunity, as described in the definition above, is compatible with the dominant approach to SDP which aims to train people, usually youth, how to survive or succeed amidst structures of inequality. In this way, the point of advocating for a social justice approach to SDP is not to dismiss the dominant approach, or throw out the entire SDP model, but to advocate for its theoretical and political extension beyond charity and behaviour change, and towards transformation, social justice and activism. In this sense, a social justice approach to SDP would be concerned with supporting both the agency of participants to build success and achieve positive results, *and* challenging the structures of inequality that preclude social agents from doing so.

Before we proceed to discuss some specific ways in which to conceptualise and implement a justice approach to SDP, it is important to acknowledge that Hartmann and Kwauk have already made a valuable contribution to this by outlining some of the key elements or components of a transformative approach to SDP. In their analysis, the transformative approach requires starting from "a critique of the existing social order and its attendant power relations and social inequalities" (Hartmann & Kwauk, 2011, p. 293). Then, education and training focus on creating a shared understanding amongst participants about "the structures of power and privilege within which they are constrained" (Hartmann & Kwauk, 2011, p. 293). The role of sport in the transformative vision, then, is as a 'hook' with which to attract participants into broad discussions and educational practices about the terms of inequality and development, and to line up with other policies and programs pursuing social transformation and justice-based outcomes. Crucially, sport-based programs and activities in this paradigm are not themselves the experiences that act upon or change participants but rather sport forms the context in and through which participants act, resist and agitate for change. Similarly, coaches, leaders, program officials and stakeholders of SDP programs are not the teachers of sport and/or development but more the facilitators and enablers of a politically aware and justice-oriented community context in and from which participants seek change (Hartmann & Kwauk, 2011).

From our perspective as critical SDP scholars, that Hartmann and Kwauk (2011) have already done important heavy lifting to conceptualise a transformative approach to SDP means that there is little reason *not* to move SDP closer to a social justice orientation. In the next section, we discuss some specific ways in which we see SDP pursuing social justice.

Imagining the place and act of social justice in SDP

Given the limitations of SDP identified by critical researchers and reviewed above, in this section we discuss and posit some ways in which to move SDP beyond a process of social reproduction, and more towards a social justice orientation. In so doing, we follow the critical insights of SDP scholars but also share in the belief held by many working in this area that there remains real potential in and through SDP to pursue deep, direct, poignant, and meaningful social change. For example, despite their incisive criticism of SDP programs aimed at Indigenous people, Arellano and Downey (2019) nonetheless propose that "there remains an opportunity for sport to play an active role in the re-empowerment of indigenous communities and to act as a form of resurgence".

It should be noted that in proposing and discussing what a social justice approach to SDP might look like, we are not proposing universal programming or policy models, but rather encouraging critical reflection on the key assumptions and ideologies, and indeed the politics, of SDP. In this way, there will almost inevitably remain some work to be done by SDP stakeholders working in the field to adapt and implement a social justice perspective to their specific context.

So, what then, would a social justice approach to SDP entail, require or look like?

First, and most clearly, a social justice approach to SDP would seek social transformation, and beyond reproduction. This has been a major theme of critical SDP work, and of this chapter so far, but it bears repeating because of how fundamentally it captures the political contestability of the SDP model. While preparing youth to survive – or even thrive – amidst competitive capitalism and structures of inequality is well intentioned, and even logical given the hegemony of the capitalist model, it is qualitatively different in socio-political terms from the task or aim of questioning and challenging the structures of inequality themselves. It is this process of questioning and challenging that we suggest is crucial to SDP's social justice orientation. If committed to a social justice orientation, SDP organisations need to create and maintain space to question the underdevelopment and inequality that they seek to redress.

Admittedly, it is no small chore to switch the focus from reproduction to transformation when the forces of capital work so powerfully to maintain the current structure. For example, within the contemporary neo-liberal conjuncture, many SDP organisations are beholden to corporate funding in order to operate their programs. This corporate funding is the surplus value of the capitalist model, which corporations 'bestow' through acts of charity. Accepting and using this money, while understandable and largely justifiable on the part of SDP organisations, nevertheless perpetuates and reinforces a cycle of capitalist accumulation. It is not until this cycle and logic is challenged that SDP can move from reproduction to transformation.

Second, and relatedly, a social justice approach to SDP would extend beyond trying to solve problems, like helping poor and marginalised people, and instead develop the critical theoretical skills to examine the reasons why there is inequality and the need for development in the first place. It is here that various social science perspectives are so useful, such as critical race theory, post-colonialism, Marxism, and radical feminism, all of which help to point towards the causes of inequality, not just to proposed solutions.

As discussed above, the post-colonial perspective also remains an important tool and approach for creating and advancing an SDP praxis rooted in social justice and transformation (see Darnell & Hayhurst, 2011). Again, the post-colonial perspective insists on recognising that the current geo-political orientation of the world, in which money, expertise and power tend to be concentrated in the global North, is a product, at least in part, of the colonial enterprise. Therefore, a social justice approach to SDP would proceed from the idea that SDP is always already embedded in colonising relations and implications, and that the goal is to challenge these relations through sport. Again, as scholars like Arellano and Downey (2019) argue in relation to Indigenous people and SDP, the goal of such programs would move beyond trying to help Indigenous people fit into the contemporary structures built and secured by the colonial encounter, and aim to resist and challenge the post- and neo-colonial condition itself.

Several other features of SDP emerge if and when it is attuned to resistance in pursuit of justice, rather than conformity within relations of dominance. For example, the hierarchies within SDP practice would themselves be questioned and blurred. For Hartmann and Kwauk (2011), this means that program official and coaches are not delivering SDP to youth, but supporting and facilitating youth to challenge the structures in which they find themselves. Similarly, when put into the broader context of international development, SDP would proceed with an acute recognition of the relations of power that structure development work itself, and aim to expose and then bridge the gaps between those who are most often deemed to be the beneficiaries versus the stewards of development. As Black (2017) writes:

> part of the maturation of the field should include a better understanding of the structural differences between these two orientations; a higher degree of critical distance between top down and bottom up SFD actors and orientations, with bottom up actors better equipped to identify and challenge the ways in which much SFD programming 'naturalizes' and enables inequitable social structures and elite interests; and a closer relationship between bottom up SFD and coalitions of development actors in other development domains (e.g. health, education, disability, anti-poverty, etc.).

From this, it is also clear that a social justice and transformative orientation to SDP needs to work with people, not upon them, and to move beyond trying (only) to change the behaviour of marginalised individuals and communities, or to solicit and encourage their conformity to the hegemonic structures of social and political life. Here, a number of scholars have invoked the importance and significance of participatory research methods within the field of SDP (see Burnett, 2008; Collison & Marchesseault, 2018; Spaaij et al., 2018; Smith et al., 2021), suggesting that approaching research as a collaboration between the researchers and the researched – or collapsing these categories altogether – allows a social justice orientation to come more clearly to the fore. While participatory methods are not a panacea for challenging SDP as social reproduction (see Spaaij et al., 2018), they do offer a notable counter or rejoinder to the functionalist or positivist approach to research that can inadvertently secure the dominant model.

There are two other points that are worth raising here in relation to a social justice approach to SDP. One is that while nearly all of the stakeholders involved in the SDP sector (including critical scholars, with whom we identify) recognise and acknowledge the benefits of sport, or at least the potential thereof, a social justice orientation to SDP calls for critical reflections on, and even resistance to, the sanctity of sport itself. In this sense, while a social justice approach to SDP questions the politics of *development* and the structures of inequality to which sport attends, it also needs to question the politics of sport. Sport remains a powerful force of social reproduction despite all of the fracturing elements of life in the twenty-first century, and therefore the transformative approach to SDP will likely require resisting parts of sport culture. As a recent youth survey of SDP activity in Canada post-COVID revealed, youth's experiences with sport continue to be produced and constrained by the hierarchies of race, gender, class and ability that are embedded in sport (see Heal et al., 2021). Given this, sport cannot be relied upon to 'fix' development problems because it is part of development inequality itself. And a social justice approach to SDP will therefore need to include the ongoing sociological critique of sport (see Darnell, 2012).

Finally, and again following Arellano and Downey (2019), the real opportunity proposed by SDP may be that it offers a departure point into broader forms of social activism and political engagement. That is, if as the critical scholars reviewed in this chapter have shown, sport's organisation and mobilisation into development via SDP tends to align with reproduction, then perhaps transformation requires recognising and embracing that sport has a role to play in social and political activism and forms of resistance. The long and rich tradition of athlete activism (see Hartmann, 2003), and the connections between sport and social movements, both historically and today (see Harvey et al., 2014), show that sport-based activism may need to pick up where SDP leaves off, if the goal of such activity really is social justice and social transformation.

Conclusion

In this chapter, we have argued that a social justice approach to Sport for Development and Peace is qualitatively different than the hegemonic or dominant approach that currently underpins much of the SDP sector. Following Hartmann and Kwauk (2011), we have argued that whereas SDP tends most often to rely on sport's mythopoeic status to try and socialise participants into what are fundamentally inequitable social structures, a social justice approach would challenge the sanctity of sport and the social and political antecedents of inequality itself. To this end, we have suggested a number of possible elements or hallmarks of a social justice orientation to SDP.

Again, we recognise that the shift being described and advocated for here is significantly challenging, and perhaps even too radical to be embraced by mainstream SDP organisations, many of which are already stretched in terms of capacity, resources and time. For these reasons, it may be that critical scholars – and the readers of this collection on sport and social justice – are those who are best positioned to take on this task. Two specific actions are likely needed. One is to continue to theorise the social justice approach to SDP, by incorporating and adopting theories of social justice more clearly and specifically in relation to SDP. Two is to explore this issue empirically, by collecting data of all kinds that examine the benefits and limitations of the dominant versus transformative models. Such data-driven analyses were beyond the scope of this chapter, but if and when they are produced, they will make a vital contribution to the ongoing challenge of mobilising sport in the service of social justice around the world.

References

Allen, D. (2011). 'A man's game': Cricket, war and masculinity, South Africa, 1899–1902. *The International Journal of the History of Sport*, *28*(1), 63–80.
Arellano, A., & Downey, A. (2019). Sport-for-development and the failure of aboriginal subjecthood: Re-imagining lacrosse as resurgence in indigenous communities. *Settler Colonial Studies*, *9*(4), 457–478.

Bale, J., & Cronin, M. (Eds) (2003). *Sport and Postcolonialism*. New York: Routledge.
Beeley, P., Sanders, B., & Barkley, C. (2019). SDP and health: HIV/AIDS. In *Routledge handbook of sport for development and peace* (1st ed., Vol. 1, pp. 319–329). Routledge. https://doi.org/10.4324/9781315455174-29
Black, D. R. (2017). The challenges of articulating 'top down' and 'bottom up' development through sport. *Third World Thematics: A TWQ Journal, 2*(1), 7–22.
Burnett, C. (2008). Participatory action research (PAR) in monitoring and evaluation of sport-for-development programmes: Sport and physical activity. *African Journal for Physical Health Education, Recreation and Dance, 14*(3), 225–239.
Coalter, F. (2010a). Sport-for-development: going beyond the boundary? *Sport in Society, 13*(9), 1374–1391.
Coalter, F. (2010b). The politics of sport-for-development: Limited focus programmes and broad gauge problems? *International Review for the Sociology of Sport, 45*(3), 295–314.
Coalter, F. (2013). *Sport for development: What game are we playing?* London: Routledge.
Collison, H., & Marchesseault, D. (2018). Finding the missing voices of sport for development and peace (SDP): Using a 'Participatory social interaction research' methodology and anthropological perspectives within African developing countries. *Sport in Society, 21*(2), 226–242.
Collison, H., Darnell, S. C., Giulianotti, R., & Howe, P. D. (2019). *Routledge handbook of sport for development and peace*. Routledge.
Darby, P. (2005). The new scramble for Africa: The African football labour migration to Europe. In J. A. Mangan (Ed.), *Europe, sport, world: Shaping global societies* (pp. 217–244). Portland: Frank Cass Publishers.
Darnell, S. C. (2007). Playing with race: Right to play and the production of whiteness in 'development through sport'. *Sport in Society, 10*(4), 560–579.
Darnell, S. C. (2010). Power, politics and "sport for development and peace": Investigating the utility of sport for international development. *Sociology of Sport Journal, 27*(1), 54–75.
Darnell, S. C. (2012). Olympism in action, Olympic hosting and the politics of "sport for development and peace": Investigating the development discourses of Rio 2016. *Sport in Society, 15*(6), 869–887.
Darnell, S. C., & Hayhurst, L. M. (2011). Sport for decolonization exploring a new praxis of sport for development. *Progress in Development Studies, 11*(3), 183–196.
Darnell, S. C., & Millington, R. (2019). Social justice, sport, and sociology: A position statement. *Quest, 71*(2), 175–187.
Darnell, S. C., Field, R., & Kidd, B. (2019). *The history and politics of sport-for-development*. London: Palgrave.
Darnell, S. C., Smith, T., & Houston, C. (2021). Revisiting sport-for-development through rights, capabilities, and global citizenship. In J. Maguire, K. Liston, & M. Falcous (Eds), *The Palgrave handbook of globalization and sport* (pp. 603–626). London: Springer.
Donnelly, P. (2011). From war without weapons to sport for development and peace: The Janus-face of sport. *SAIS Review, 31*(1), 65–76.
Donnelly, P., Atkinson, M., Boyle, S., & Szto, C. (2011). Sport for development and peace: A public sociology perspective. *Third World Quarterly, 32*(3), 589–601.
Essa, M., Arellano, A., Stuart, S., & Sheps, S. (2022). Sport for indigenous resurgence: Toward a critical settler-colonial reflection. *International Review for the Sociology of Sport, 57*(2), 292–312.
Forde, S. D., & Frisby, W. (2015). Just be empowered: How girls are represented in a sport for development and peace HIV/AIDS prevention manual. *Sport in Society, 18*(8), 882–894.
Gardam, K. J., Giles, A. R., Rynne, S., & Hayhurst, L. M. (2019). A comparison of indigenous sport for development policy directives in Canada and Australia. *Aboriginal Policy Studies*.
Giulianotti, R. (2004). Human rights, globalization and sentimental education: The case of sport. *Sport in Society, 7*(3), 355–369.
Giulianotti, R., & Armstrong, G. (2011). Sport, the military and peacemaking: History and possibilities. *Third World Quarterly, 32*(3), 379–394.
Giulianotti, R., Coalter, F., Collison, H., & Darnell, S. C. (2019). Rethinking Sportland: A new research agenda for the sport for development and peace sector. *Journal of Sport and Social Issues, 43*(6), 411–437.
Hartmann, D. (2003). *Race, culture, and the revolt of the black athlete: The 1968 Olympic protests and their aftermath*. Chicago, IL: University of Chicago Press.

Hartmann, D., & Kwauk, C. (2011). Sport and development: An overview, critique, and reconstruction. *Journal of Sport & Social Issues, 35*(3), 284–305.

Harvey, J., Horne, J., Safai, P., Darnell, S., & Courchesne-O'Neill, S. (2014). *Sport and social movements: From the local to the global*. London: Bloomsbury Academic.

Hayhurst, L. M. (2009). The power to shape policy: Charting sport for development and peace policy discourses. *International Journal of Sport Policy, 1*(2), 203–227.

Hayhurst, L. M. (2014). The 'Girl Effect' and martial arts: Social entrepreneurship and sport, gender and development in Uganda. *Gender, Place & Culture, 21*(3), 297–315.

Hayhurst, L. M. (2016). Sport for development and peace: A call for transnational, multi-sited, postcolonial feminist research. *Qualitative Research in Sport, Exercise and Health, 8*(5), 420–424.

Hayhurst, L. M. C., MacNeill, M., Kidd, B., & Knoppers, A. (2014). Gender relations, gender-based violence and sport for development and peace: Questions, concerns and cautions emerging from Uganda. *Women's Studies International Forum, 47*(PA), 157–167.

Hayhurst, L. M., Giles, A. R., & Wright, J. (2016). Biopedagogies and indigenous knowledge: Examining sport for development and peace for urban indigenous young women in Canada and Australia. *Sport, Education and Society, 21*(4), 549–569.

Heal, B., Sailofsky, D., Warner, M., Darnell, S. C., & Robinson, J. (2021). *Change the game: A study focused on youth sport access, engagement and equity factors in the wake of the pandemic*. Toronto: Maple Leafs Sports and Entertainment (MLSE) Foundation.

Hokkanen, M., & Mangan, J. A. (2006). Further variations on a theme: The games ethic further adapted – Scottish moral missionaries and muscular Christians in Malawi. *The International Journal of the History of Sport, 23*(8), 1257–1274.

Howe, P. D. (2019). SDP and disability. In *Routledge handbook of sport for development and peace* (1st ed., Vol. 1, pp. 275–284). Routledge.

James, C. L. R. (1969). *Beyond a boundary*. London: Stanley Paul.

Kidd, B. (2005). Another world is possible: Recapturing alternative Olympic histories, imagining different games. In K. Young & K. Wamsley (Eds), *Global Olympics: Historical and sociological studies of the modern games* (pp. 145–160). Bangalore, India: Elsevier.

Kidd, B. (2008). A new social movement: Sport for development and peace. *Sport in Society, 11*(4), 370–380.

Lucas, R., & O'Connor, J. (2021). The representation of indigenous Australians in sport for development policy: What's the problem? *International Journal of Sport Policy and Politics, 13*(4), 587–603.

MacAloon, J. (Ed.). (2008). *Muscular Christianity in colonial and post-colonial worlds*. London: Routledge.

McCullough, B. P., Kellison, T., & Melton, E. N. (2022). *The Routledge handbook of sport and sustainable development* (1st ed.). New York: Routledge.

McEwan, C. (2009). *Postcolonialism and development*. London: Routledge.

Millington, R., & Darnell, S. C. (2020). *Sport, development and environmental sustainability*. New York: Routledge.

Millington, R., & Kidd, B. (2019). The history of SDP. In S. C. Darnell, R. Giulianotti, D. Howe, & H. Collison (Eds), *Routledge handbook sport for development and peace* (pp. 13–23). New York: Routledge.

Millington, R., Giles, A. R., Hayhurst, L. M., van Luijk, N., & McSweeney, M. (2019). 'Calling out' corporate redwashing: The extractives industry, corporate social responsibility and sport for development in indigenous communities in Canada. *Sport in Society, 22*(12), 2122–2140.

Morgaine, K. (2014). Conceptualizing social justice in social work: Are social workers "too bogged down in the trees?". *Journal of Social Justice, 4*(1), 1–18.

Nicholls, S., Giles, A. R., & Sethna, C. (2010). Perpetuating the 'lack of evidence' discourse in sport for development: Privileged voices, unheard stories and subjugated knowledge. *International Review for the Sociology of Sport, 46*(3), 249–264.

Norman, M. E., Hart, M., & Petherick, L. (2019). Indigenous gender reformations: Physical culture, settler colonialism and the politics of containment. *Sociology of Sport Journal, 36*(2), 113–123.

Oxford, S., & McLachlan, F. (2018). "You have to play like a man, but still be a woman": Young female Colombians negotiating gender through participation in a sport for development and peace (SDP) Organization. *Sociology of Sport Journal, 35*(3), 258–267.

Right to Play (n.d.). "Where we work." Retrieved from www.righttoplay.com/Learn/ourstory/Pages/Where-we-work.aspx

Rossi, T., & Rynne, S. (2014). Sport development programmes for indigenous Australians: Innovation, inclusion and development, or a product of 'white guilt'? *Sport in Society*, *17*(8), 1030–1045.

Schulenkorf, N. (2010). The roles and responsibilities of a change agent in sport event development projects. *Sport Management Review*, *13*(2), 118–128.

Smith, R., Danford, M., Darnell, S. C., Larrazabal, M. J. L., & Abdellatif, M. (2021). 'Like, what even is a podcast?' Approaching sport-for-development youth participatory action research through digital methodologies. *Qualitative Research in Sport, Exercise and Health*, *13*(1), 128–145.

Spaaij, R., Schulenkorf, N., Jeanes, R., & Oxford, S. (2018). Participatory research in sport-for-development: Complexities, experiences and (missed) opportunities. *Sport Management Review*, *21*(1), 25–37.

Sugden, J. (2006). Teaching and playing sport for conflict resolution and co-existence in Israel. *International Review for the Sociology of Sport*, *41*(2), 221–240.

United Nations (1948). Universal declaration of human rights. *UN General Assembly*.

23
SPORT FOR DEVELOPMENT
A troubling past to a brighter future?

Michael Sup

In 2002 the United Nations (UN) released the Millennium Development Goals (MDGs) as pioneering standards for raising the quality of life and championing human rights around the world (Darnell, 2013). Among these goals, several key areas were identified ranging from the eradication of extreme poverty, to nullifying the spread of HIV/AIDS as well as providing universal education for the world's poorest people (United Nations General Assembly, 2002). The UN went on to identify sport as a primary vehicle to attain these goals (Peachey & Cohen, 2016). Subsequently in 2003 the office of Sport for Development and Peace was opened (Levermore & Beacom, 2009), legitimising sport as a developmental tool (Schulenkorf & Adair, 2014).

The connection between sport and the UN stems back to 1948 and the Declaration of Human Rights which was established as a framework for international cooperation, anti-discrimination, and universal human rights (Darnell & Millington, 2019). Within this framework was a commitment to advancing health and well-being and a right to leisure which resonated with many of the social benefits connected to sports participation (Darnell & Millington, 2019). Consequently, this fusion between sport, health, and human rights helped spawn the relationship more broadly to the notion of social justice (Darnell & Millington, 2019).

Fast forward to 2019 and despite closing the office of Sport for Development and Peace, the UN still advocated the application of sport in the pursuit of the renovated 2030 Sustainable Development Goals (SDGs). Today there are 17 SDGs that still fundamentally aim to eradicate poverty, protect the planet and bring peace and prosperity to all (United Nations, 2022). The UN's SDGs further built on the initial objectives set forth by the original MDGs and still designated sport as an appropriate vehicle for achieving these goals.

In the UN's 2015 General Assembly Report, it is stated:

We recognize the growing contribution of sport to the realization of development and peace in its promotion of tolerance and respect and the contributions it makes to the empowerment of women and of young people, individuals and communities as well as to health, education and social inclusion objectives.

The above affirmation provides the platform for Sport for Development programmes (SFD) which are defined by Schulenkorf and Adair (2014) to, "engage people from disadvantaged communities in physical activity projects that have an overarching aim of achieving various social, cultural, physical, economic or health-related outcomes" (p. 3). Examples of such programming include HIV and AIDS prevention in Zambia (Njelesani, 2012); youth crime and antisocial behaviour prevention in the United Kingdom (Kelly, 2012); transnational peace-making in the Middle East (Giulianotti, 2011); and academic underachievement in the Pacific Islands (Kwauk, 2016).

While there are multiple trajectories of SFD that each target multiple SDGs, this chapter focuses on the Sport for Development and Peace (hereon SDP) movement which can be aligned with SDG 16 "Peace, Justice and Strong Institutions". This programming uses sport to target conflict-damaged societies, potentially suffering from war and violence to target peace and conflict resolutions (Giulianotti & Armstrong, 2014). Hartmann and Kwauk (2011) comment on the rapid growth of SDP organisations since the beginning of the twenty-first century, reporting that 295 organisations were registered with the International Platform on Sport for Development and Peace in 2010 (p. 284). Mwaanga and Mwansa (2014) document further evidence of SDP growth with 448 organisations involved in 2013. These organisations represent a combination of private sector, multi-national corporations, non-governmental and not-for-profit organisations (NGOs), inter-governmental and governmental organisations, professional sports teams, and smaller grassroots programmes (Giulianotti & Armstrong, 2014).

Most SDP organisations can be categorised as *sport plus* or *plus sport* models (Coalter, 2013). Sport plus programmes prioritise sport as the main activity for participants and likely have additional programming bolted on. For example, a programme might use a tournament as the main focus for participants to compete and then offer an additional workshop that targets a particular issue. The workshop is secondary to the tournament itself. Plus sport organisations then start with programming that addresses key social issues first and might use some form of sporting activity as a non-central feature of their programme (Coalter, 2013).

When further defining the types of practical sporting activities that take place within these programmes, Giulianotti (2011) offers three dominant types: (1) technical; (2) dialogical; and, (3) critical designs. A technical model is characterised as hierarchical, directive, and focused on solving a problem; a dialogical model adopts a 'training the trainers' approach and is more integrated within community social relations, providing leaders with the tools to serve their own communities; and a critical model is committed to inter-communal transformation, positioned as a facilitator for a range of diverse community groups (Giulianotti, 2011). Today the most common models are between the technical and dialogical with far fewer adopting critical designs.

Understanding SDP impact

Given the ever-expanding growth of SDP over the past two decades, a plethora of research has steadily developed seeking to understand the overall impact of SDP programming around the world (Giulianotti & Armstrong, 2014). Quests for positivist types of research typically guide monitoring and evaluation (M & E) research techniques in the field (Njelesani, 2012). Studies of this nature are usually conducted internally by SDP organisations as progress indicators to appease sponsors and other funding streams (Webb & Richelieu, 2015). These studies are typically quantitative in design and often track participation numbers and other numeric programme growth indicators as a measurement of success (Webb & Richelieu, 2015). It is well understood how these programmes are dependent on continuous funding streams that are systematically attached to the submission of positive progress reports, demonstrating programme impact and growth (Kay, 2012). This type of transactional relationship can ultimately create tension between SDP organisers and their donors (Spaaij, Oxford, & Jeanes, 2016; Webb & Richelieu, 2015).

Such measurements often result in grandiose claims of sport as a 'magic bullet' to solve societal ills (Schulenkorf & Adair, 2014). That is, a significant assumption that by merely participating in a form of organised sporting activity, this experience can cure a community of the challenges being faced. While these types of idealistic notions have drawn anecdotal criticism from scholars, there is still a significant gap in the research offering empirical and critical investigations of such programming (Burnett, 2015). In less frequent instances of programmes deploying longitudinal research methods in support of SDP programming, most examples are often individual heart-felt narratives presented by SDP organisers as evidence of their success (Hartmann & Kwauk, 2011). It is important to understand how this type of evidence can easily misconstrue the impact of development programming (Hartmann & Kwauk, 2011).

More recently there have been calls for more rigorous, interpretive, and holistic frameworks to dig deeper into understanding the SDP movement and devise progressive steps forward based upon these findings (Burnett, 2015; Spaaij, Oxford, & Jeanes, 2016). These studies have the potential to yield credible and trustworthy accounts of how SDP programmes function around the world and the potential impact they have in achieving their identified developmental goals (Darnell, Chawansky, Marchesseault, Holmes, & Hayhurst, 2016). This type of research is essential for programmes to establish a more accurate understanding of their impact, particularly concerning sociologically complex and interconnected issues such as poverty, violence, inequality, war and disease.

The lacuna in sociologically rigorous and empirical research has spurred the rise in scholarship targeting the essentialist claims of SDP (Coalter, 2013). Fundamentally, it is crucial to recognise how there is limited empirical evidence that validates the use of sport participation in achieving purported developmental goals (Kaufman, Rosenbauer, & Moore, 2015; Mwaanga & Prince, 2016; Spaaij, Oxford, & Jeanes, 2016; Svensson, Hancock, & Hums, 2016). In this sense, it has been suggested how the application of SDP programming is not only ineffective, but enhances various forms of inequality through the reproduction of oppressive ideologies and practices (Coalter, 2013; Rossi & Jeanes, 2016). For example, SDP programmes are typically Western-based/Global North organisations and are therefore likely to engender dominant hegemonic beliefs regarding class, race, gender and sexuality (Cooper, Blom, Gerstein, Hankemeier, & Indovina, 2016).

To better understand the critiques against the application of sport as a developmental tool, some scholars have applied different critical theoretical lenses to examine the SDP movement. What follows is a blend of three theoretical analyses that dig deeper beyond the surface of these fundamental criticisms. First, this section explores the imperialist and neocolonial stigma that is attached to the SDP movement. Second, a critical feminist perspective highlights the patriarchal and paternalistic footprint often reinforced by SDP programmes. The third critique is centred upon neoliberal discourse that drives the highly individualistic and egalitarian sporting fundamentalism behind SDP. Crucially, these analyses help to demonstrate these critiques in action at a variety of SDP sites around the world.

With increasing advocacy towards more critically focused and transformative programming, this chapter will conclude with recommendations for how the SDP movement could evolve beyond these critiques through the adoption of liberative pedagogies by way of programme design and implementation. In this vein, the remainder of this chapter will apply the terms 'social majority' and 'social minority' when describing the two polarised groups of people typically involved in developmental programming. 'Social majority' represents the globally proportionate number of people reflected by what have previously been labelled as 'third world', 'developing/under-developed countries', 'Global South' or 'minorities' (Esteva, Prakash, & Shiva, 2014). It is important to address the definitional contention of these traditional labels that perpetuate a coded language rationalising deficit theories (Parmar, 2009; Payne, 2005). From this point forward, it is my preference to use the term 'social majority' or 'majority world' to describe this group. 'Social majority' therefore represents the proportionately few people that hold the most economic and political power in our world (Esteva, Prakash, & Shiva, 2014). These groups have traditionally been labelled 'first world', 'developed', or 'Global North' groups.

Imperial Foundations

The universality of sport is often celebrated by social minority nations as a cross-cultural language, transcending boundaries of race, religion, gender and culture (Gilbert & Bennett, 2012). It is this essentialist notion of the power of sport that has latched itself on to the universal belief of human rights (Coalter, 2013; Darnell, 2013). However, it is important to remember that sport is neither ahistorical nor apolitical as is often presented (Millington, 2015). As such, sport has deep-rooted implications in history particularly in nations ruled by colonial governance (Darnell, 2009). In this light, the SDP movement can be strongly critiqued as a continuation of Western imperialism and neo-colonial rule (Giulianotti, 2011; Hartmann & Kwauk, 2011; Tiessen, 2011).

Before exploring some of the ways in which a post-colonial/neo-colonial lens can be applied to SDP, it is important to offer a brief definition of this theoretical lens. First, when describing colonisation, Mohanty (1988) explains it, "invariably implies a relation of structural domination, and a discursive or political suppression of the heterogeneity of the subject(s) in question" (p. 61). Stemming from the socio-political, cultural and economic impact of European domination, the purpose of a post-colonial/neo-colonial lens is to analyse how race, class, sexuality and nation interact to form social institutions and theorise the historically situated ideology that is reinforced by interlocking power relations (Hayhurst, 2011). The following section will apply a post-colonial/neo-colonial lens to flesh out some of the major critiques of SDP.

A post-colonial/neo-colonial critique argues that SDP and larger developmental enterprises carry forth institutionalised forms of imperialistic and oppressive power, immersed in Eurocentric discourses (Darnell & Kaur, 2015). Darnell and Hayhurst (2014) stress the importance in recognising how sports participation in many majority world countries is a direct legacy of European colonialisation, e.g. soccer in Africa and cricket in multiple commonwealth nations (Darnell & Hayhurst, 2014). Darnell and Hayhurst (2014) further share the example of an SDP programme in Burundi, Africa that fails to acknowledge the bloody history of ethnic conflict in this nation, which is ultimately inseparable from the legacy of colonial intervention and stewardship (p. 37).

This imperialist doctrine is most visible across SDP programmes by way of organisational structure and leadership. This is represented through hierarchal governance, that is undemocratic, and offers minimal inclusion to social majority groups or representatives (Mwaanga & Prince, 2016). The planning, design, and implementation of SDP programming is typically a centralised process, offering little to no agency to those for whom the programme is supposedly designed. In rare cases, local governance is sometimes offered limited decision-making abilities, however these are often mere tokenistic gestures of autonomy. This predominantly results in SDP programmes that essentially silence social majority groups, who have minimal control or impact over the developmental programming that has been created and oftentimes forced upon them (Mwaanga & Prince, 2016).

From a curriculum and programming perspective, many SDP organisations of the neo-colonial nature, adopt a universalised approach to development. This method decontextualises the political, economic, and social fabric of localised communities (Mwaanga & Prince, 2016). Instead of seeking to understand the historically interconnected, social, political, and economic nuanced complexities of a social majority state, SDP programmes often adopt a one-size-fits-all approach to development (Svensson, Hancock, & Hums, 2016). In their literature review of SDP organisations, Webb and Richelieu (2015) concluded this singular approach hinders the impact of SDP programming as it fundamentally fails to take into consideration the local context (p. 292).

On the ground level, this form of neo-colonialism is evidenced in some SDP programmes through the imposition of imperialist values, norms, and traditions (Levermore & Beacom, 2009). Darnell and Hayhurst (2014) offer a prime example of this imposition by way of language. Given that most SDP organisations are born from European and North American states, the dominant language in which SDP is orchestrated and conducted is in English. There is minimal expectation for SDP practitioners to learn the local language when delivering SDP projects. Rather it is the local participants themselves who are assumed to understand English. This linguistic insistence and rigid feature of SDP plays a vital role in the erasure of local contexts. Similarly Darnell and Hayhurst (2014) warn of the vernacular "lin-guicide" seldom discussed as a by-product of social science research in non-English speaking social majority states (p. 50).

A further tenant of the neo-colonial critique posits SDP programmes as paternalistic doctrines that engender a deficit-based approach to development (Sanders, 2016). In their research on an SDP programme working with Aboriginal populations, Coleby and Giles (2013) found that non-Aboriginal sources reinforced deficit discourses about participants. The authors found that the first dominant discourse determined that Aboriginal youth possessed no hope for social wellness and are prone to suicide (p. 45). The second discourse revealed the assumption that non-Aboriginal people were the sole saviours and Aboriginal people had no credit for their role in the SDP programme (p. 46). These deficit-based discourses are both damaging and harmful as they perpetuate an assumption of dependency for Aboriginal people on their non-Aboriginal neighbours.

Elsewhere, research by Tiessen (2011) found further evidence of this deficit approach in SDP and concluded that SDP programmes have the potential to reinforce 'othering' of social majority communities and states. Tiessen (2011) revealed that dominant discourse in SDP material consistently conceptualised social majority states as disadvantaged and in need of rescue from the social minority leaders of the world (p. 579). For example, Tiessen (2011) explained that online materials often presented paternalistic narratives of children regularly demonstrating an ill-conceived message that social majority states are comprised exclusively of children largely dependent on the help that only the social minority can provide (p. 580).

Tiessen (2011) also acknowledged the highly racialised undertones of some SDP rhetoric that covertly insinuated the power of the white man to rescue 'others' from their degradation (p. 581). This ties with the previously mentioned Eurocentric discourse often found in SDP programming that privileges 'Whiteness' and dominant Christian values in a hierarchal fashion, deeming anyone or anything considered 'non-White' as inferior (Nicholls, 2009). Together these findings reveal how the fangs of neo-colonial discourse are insidiously embedded within SDP from organisational structure to micro-level discourse. These examples offer a valid demonstration of the imperialist tendencies still present in SDP today.

Patriarchal undertones

Extending beyond the neo-colonial critiques outlined thus far, an added layer of a critical feminist theory posits traditional SDP programming as sites that perpetuate patriarchal ideologies, further enhancing gender inequality and heteronormative sexuality (Carney & Chawansky, 2016). Additionally, such programming simply fails to recognise the traditional Eurocentric roots of sports and how they can serve to produce and reproduce oppressive gender norms (Darnell & Hayhurst, 2014; Hayhurst, 2011). Sports, as a mirror to society, reflect a form of "soft-essentialism" that is key to understanding hegemonic gender ideology perpetuated through sports (Messner, 2011).

Once more, before delving further into these overarching critiques, it is important to offer a brief description of critical feminist theory, and why its application is particularly telling in SDP. At its core, critical feminist theory is concerned with fighting against multiple forms of inequity and oppression (De Saxe, 2016). However, the roots of critical feminist theories were born from gender inequality and the suffering of females as a result of their societal devaluation and exploitation (De Saxe, 2016). Without universalising the key components of critical feminist theory, it is crucial to recognise how this theory assumes the intersectionality of inequality and is employed as a means of deconstructing these layers (De Saxe, 2016). The next section attempts to draw connections between feminist theory and its application in critically analysing SDP.

The first major example stems from research conducted by Jeanes and Magee (2014), who present the ways in which gender norms were being established and reinforced in an SDP programme designed to empower female participants in Zambia, Africa. The primary focus of this study was to examine the impact of SDP programming from the perspectives of the programme participants themselves. From their analysis, they found a deep-rooted gendered history stemming from the imposition of Victorian values from British colonial troops (p. 138). This historical context is important to understand in developing a holistic appreciation of the gender and sport construct and how these power relations are interconnected in maintaining oppressive relations. Oftentimes, nations that have a colonial past will continue to perpetuate unequal gender relations, yet it is vital to consider the role of historically dominant Eurocentric discourse in this analysis (Hayhurst, 2011).

While many SDP programmes may be well-intentioned, often the programme organisers lack the cultural appreciation and knowledge of gender laws and customs in certain social majority states (Hayhurst, 2011). This carelessness can prove to have devastating consequences for female participants, when practitioners are unaware of the dangerous realities the participants may face as part of their lived realities. Jeanes and Magee (2014) provide further examples of this once again in their analysis of the SDP programme in Zambia. The authors found that participants faced a constant struggle with their culture, since it was forbidden for females to participate in sport. Female participants talked about the constant battle of regular participation in sport and trying to demonstrate dominant gender ideologies away from the sports field. This presented a genuine risk to their safety when returning home to their communities (Jeanes & Magee, 2014). Participants were often accused of being shameful, disrespectful, and having their sexual orientation openly challenged by members of the community (pp. 144–145). This places the programme participants in a vulnerable position about which the SDP programme organisers are typically unaware.

While it is not the intention of this section to downplay the role of SDP programming that seeks to challenge oppressive gender ideologies, it is imperative to critically examine the term 'empowerment' and its application in SDP (Hayhurst, 2011). Chawansky (2011) supports this need, stressing that in their attempts to liberate females from the shackles of unequal treatment, SDP programmes themselves often obscure the understanding of gender as a relational identity. Similar findings were discussed by Forde and Frisby (2015) who analysed the representations of gender in an SDP user manual designed to support females against HIV/AIDS. Forde and Frisby (2015) found that gender relations were aligned with hegemonic conceptions of family unit and assumed heterosexual partnerships (p. 7). Such subtle yet powerful inferences reinforce a dominant heteronormative identity, encouraging passivity and discouraging resistance against deep-rooted political disdain for non-traditional gender roles (Carney & Chawansky, 2016).

Comparable trends were found by Carney and Chawansky (2016), whose research focused on reviewing SDP academic literature and drawing upon personal work and research experiences in the field. The authors found the research base in SDP generally evades nuanced discussions of sexuality and instead focuses its M & E efforts within the boundaries of heteronormative rules (p. 291). This study concluded with a clear absence in SDP literature accounting for queer sexualities, and it could be that traditional quantitative monitoring and evaluation techniques contribute to this absence of storytelling for participants (pp. 294–295). This silence and failure to recognise the voice of multiple genders and sexual orientations serves as another strand in how the SDP movement maintains a system of patriarchy and dominant ideology of heteronormative sexuality.

Elsewhere, research conducted by Hayhurst, Giles and Wright (2016), offers an alternative perspective through their participatory action research with an SDP programme that focused on indigenous young women. The authors found this programming was designed to better equip these women for a competitive capitalist world, focusing on Eurocentric employment, post-secondary education and healthy active living by way of transformation. The authors commented on the hidden challenges for the indigenous women to succeed due to the insensitivity of the SDP programme practitioners to the socio-political factors that maintain the structural inequalities these women face in a Eurocentric society (p. 564). The authors concluded that to increase the likeliness of success in a programme like this, it must be led by Indigenous people themselves, who better understand the realities of the difficulties they face and can better navigate the broader systemic inequalities of their world (p. 565).

This range of studies suggest it is imperative to continually challenge the dominant ideas that sports can serve as a vehicle to empower female participants and marginalised groups. These assumptions fundamentally negate the colonial roots of sport participation, further perpetuating dehumanising gender norms and inequalities. Such programming not only limits opportunities for women to break from these oppressive shackles, but in some instances can further cement women's positioning as second-class citizens and subordinates to dominant male groups.

Advancing neoliberalism

As mentioned at the beginning of this chapter, one of the major fundamental critiques of the SDP movement today is centred upon a broader neoliberal agenda being advanced by the international development community. Specific to SDP, these critiques highlight the inability for programmes to purposefully identify, target and change the deep-rooted causes of underdevelopment despite the transformational abilities these programmes purport. Rather than seeking to address some of these structural issues, the majority of SDP programmes ostensibly perpetuate neoliberal logic that champions individualised behavioural transformation resulting in upward-mobility, yet makes no impact in challenging the structural inequalities at play (Darnell, 2010, Darnell, 2013). Here Darnell (2013) elaborates:

> The dominant ideology of SDP attempts (with some notable exceptions) to improve the welfare of 'Others' within the structures of merit-based achievement, or liberal egalitarianism, an orientation that in turn supports the current culture of sport and political economy development.
>
> (p. 42)

Before exploring how neoliberal ideology is manifested on the ground level, it is important to understand how the free-market politics of neoliberalism has a direct impact on SDP organisations. For example, Giulianotti and Armstrong (2014) explain how NGOs openly compete against one another for contracts awarded by large donors. This corporate structure creates a competitive marketplace based on the severity of the cases they present (Kidd, 2011). The issue evolves as SDP programmes seek to address basic human needs that are typically awarded while often failing to address the more fundamental causes of such problems in the first place (Giulianotti & Armstrong, 2014). In this way, it is the programmes that offer more of an immediate relief to development concerns that are prioritised. This funding dynamic limits the opportunities for programmes that might be engaged in any long-term development work that may have an impact on some of the core issues of inequality and injustice.

When looking closely at the structure and delivery of SDP programme curricula, it is possible to draw connections between the key messages being delivered by the programme and some of the core principles of neoliberalism (Forde, 2014). Essentially, these principles are related to SDP programming that normalise self-reliance and individualism by way of social transformation under the guise of universal global citizenship (Tiessen, 2011). Mwaanga and Prince (2016) explain, "Responsibility for learning is placed on the individual who is expected to achieve their own goals over group goals" (p. 593). However, this perspective not only imposes a divisive mentality that seeks to separate individuals from their communities, but this isolation can also result to self-blame if no actual change occurs (Mwaanga & Prince, 2016). Ultimately, this emphasis on self-interest serves as a toxin that poisons the communal nature of many social majority cultures.

This is particularly damaging to social majority populations whose cultural norms are rooted in the ideas and values of community. In their theoretical study of liberation pedagogy embedded within SDP, Mwaanga and Prince (2016) highlight how the belief system of the

Ubuntu cultural philosophy might better serve SDP programming. The Ubuntu philosophy is almost the exact opposite to the highly individualised and neo-liberal logic as it is firmly based on the non-individualistic core values of respect, compassion and understanding as the cornerstone of community (Lutz, 2009). However, these types of values and beliefs are overlooked by the majority of SDP organisations from social minority states (Mwaanga & Prince, 2016).

These messages of independence and self-reliance are usually catered to by programming that seeks to train and develop individuals for the job market. Neoliberal SDP programming of this nature were evidenced by Manzo (2012) who investigated FIFA's Football for Hope project. Manzo's study revealed how the project was implemented across several African states to combine soccer facilities with social development hubs that focused on training social entrepreneurs and local businessmen (p. 554). This type of SDP programming is typically representative of curriculum designed to train participants with skills to increase their employability and enhance their chances of securing a job, to alleviate them of their issues. This type of programming is commonly branded as 'life skill' training and is criticised for its conformist approach to perpetuating a neoliberal system (Forde, 2014). Programming of this kind neglects any form of critical thinking that seeks to deconstruct the invisible tentacles of neoliberal ideology.

Elsewhere, in their study of SDP programming in the Caribbean, Kaufman, Rosenbauer, and Moore (2015) reveal how a variety of curricula was similarly focused on the development of "soft employability skills" for youth participants (p. 178). For example, in one particular programme youth would participate in classroom-based activities that delivered sport-themed lessons in mathematics, language and computer technology. This finding speaks to the job-related training that is commonly featured in SDP programmes focused on setting young people up for future employment. From a critical perspective though, this form of training again fails to challenge some of the deep-rooted and systemic issues at play. Instead, the focus is primarily on preparing individuals to submit to the dominant neoliberal social order of equipping oneself to upwardly climb out of poverty and into the free market.

It is crucial to consider how this type of programming and curriculum design perpetuates a culture of acceptance and tolerance to a failing social and economic system. Once more, Kaufman, Rosenbauer, and Moore (2015) identify another SDP programme that claims to use soccer as a vehicle to, "inspire and mobilize communities to stop the spread of HIV in sub-Saharan Africa" (p. 179). In practical terms, this programme would use failed attempts at soccer-related drills to punish participants and relate their technical mistakes with similar erroneous judgements that can be made when it comes to HIV (e.g. unprotected sex, multiple partners, drugs and alcohol, etc.). While these teaching attempts may have the best interests of the participants at heart, this behaviourist programming is further embedding a mindset that is numb to challenging the structural inequalities present in any oppressive social majority state. Rather than encouraging participants to actively question and resist the broader macro structures that fuel the spread of HIV, these programmes foster an environment of 'self-help' by way of transformation (Forde, 2014). At best, this may indeed support an individual to recovery but will never make radical strides to eradicate this devastating disease once and for all.

The critical future of SDP

The previous sections of this chapter have attempted to synthesise some of the major critiques of the SDP movement from a blend of post-colonial/neo-colonial, critical feminist, and neoliberal perspectives. Considering this growing body of literature, an academic appeal to merge SDP programming with critical pedagogy is steadily developing (Lindsey, 2017; Mwaanga & Prince, 2016). Specifically, Mwaanga and Prince (2016) identify a new direction for SDP curricula to evolve from the current 'life-skills' training to models that encourage critical thinking skills (p. 590).

To better understand how the introduction of critical pedagogy to SDP can be of benefit, it is important to understand exactly what critical pedagogy is. As an educational framework, critical pedagogy has evolved from the tenants of critical theory to deconstruct hegemonic structures that serve to reproduce societal status quo. In the context of classroom education, Wink (2005) offers a concrete definition of critical pedagogy as the "teaching and learning that transforms us and our world for the better" (p. 67). Critical pedagogy can be further described as a cyclical process of learning, relearning, and unlearning, resulting in the unpacking of our own lived personal experiences, rethinking our histories, and rewriting our world (Wink, 2005). It is this pedagogy of transformative education that offers a lens to critically reflect, name and act on (Wink, 2005).

One of the most renowned critical pedagogues of the twentieth century – Paulo Freire – developed his ideas of critical pedagogy to combat the structural hegemonic forces in place by dominant groups in society. Through a medium of dialogue, Freire (2000) formulated a pedagogy of praxis to develop critical consciousness in the classroom through language training for impoverished groups. His method of 'praxis' involved a continuous process of action and reflection based upon contextual problem-posing, supporting oppressed groups to challenge and transform their lived realities (hooks, 1994). Giroux (2011) further describes this pedagogical process of "creating those democratic public spheres where individuals can think critically, relate sympathetically to the problems of others, and intervene in the world in order to address major social problems" (p. 13).

The educational possibilities presented through these frameworks present themselves as an opportunity with the dualistic relationship concerning SDP and its potential use as either a domineering or emancipatory vehicle. Mwaanga and Prince (2016) support the fusion of SDP with critical pedagogy claiming, "Such development of critical and analytical skills promotes the problematization of wider social, political, cultural and economic inequalities leading to critical, as opposed to prescriptive, action" (p. 590). So far, these appeals have been predominantly anecdotal in nature.

Despite the strong theoretical arguments being presented, there is minimal evidence that documents any practical attempts of this kind. While there is growing excitement around this prospect, it is important to note how there is still some scepticism that even with the infusion of liberation pedagogy, SDP programming will still be unfit to serve as a meaningful vehicle for transformative social change (Coalter, 2013).

Ultimately, there is still significant work ahead of SDP scholars and practitioners who envision a future where sports can have a crucial role to play in identifying, challenging and deconstructing the systemic forces that maintain a global structure of oppression and inequality. Coalter (2013) artistically captures this duality, coining Antonio Gramsci's notion of "pessimism of the intellect, and optimism of the will". This emotive statement can be interpreted as a need for further exploratory research within the expanding field of SDP.

References

Burnett, C. (2015). Assessing the sociology of sport: On sport for development and peace. *International Review for the Sociology of Sport*, 50(4–5), 385–390. https://doi.org/10.1177/1012690214539695

Carney, A., & Chawansky, M. (2016). Taking sex off the sidelines: Challenging heteronormativity within 'Sport in Development' research. *International Review for the Sociology of Sport*, *51*(3), 284–298. https://doi.org/10.1177/1012690214521616

Chawansky, M. (2011). New social movements, old gender games?: Locating girls in the sport for development and peace movement. In A. C. Snyder & P. Stobbe (Eds), *Critical aspects of gender in conflict resolution, peacebuilding, and social movements* (pp. 121–134). Leeds: Emerald Group Publishing Limited.

Coalter, F. (Ed.). (2013). *Sport for development: What game are we playing?* New York: Routledge.

Coleby, J., & Giles, A. R. (2013). Discourses at work in media reports on right to play's "promoting life-skills in Aboriginal youth" programme. *Journal of Sport for Development*, *1*(2), 39–52.

Cooper, J. W., Blom, L. C., Gerstein, L. H., Hankemeier, D. A., & Indovina, T. P. (2016). Soccer for peace in Jordan: A qualitative assessment of programme impact on coaches. *Journal of Sport for Development*, *4*(6), 21–35.

Darnell, S. C. (2009). *Changing the world through sport and play: a post-colonial analysis of Canadian volunteers within the 'sport for development and peace' movement* (Doctoral dissertation, University of Toronto). Retrieved from https://search-proquest-com.proxy.library.ohio.edu

Darnell, S. C. (2010). Power, politics and "sport for development and peace": Investigating the utility of sport for international development. *Sociology of Sport Journal*, *27*(1), 54–75.

Darnell, S. C. (2013). *Sport for development and peace: A critical sociology*. London: Bloomsbury.

Darnell, S. C., & Hayhurst, M. C. (2014). De-colonizing the politics and practice of sport-for-development: Critical insights from postcolonial feminist theory and methods. In N. Schulenkorf & D. Adair (Eds), *Global sport-for-development: Critical perspectives* (pp. 115–133). Basingstoke, Hampshire: Palgrave Macmillan.

Darnell, S. C., & Kaur, T. (2015). C. L. R. James and a place for history in theorizing 'sport for the development and peace sector'. *International Journal of Sport Management and Marketing*, *16*(5), 5–17.

Darnell, S. C., & Millington, R. (2019). Social justice, sport, and sociology: A position statement. *Quest*, *71*(2), 175–187. https://doi.org/10.1080/00336297.2018.1545681

Darnell, S. C., Chawansky, M., Marchesseault, D., Holmes, M., & Hayhurst, L. (2016). The state of play: Critical sociological insights into recent 'sport for development and peace' research. *International Review for the Sociology of Sport*, *53*(2), 133–151.

De Saxe, J. G. (2016). *Critical feminism and critical education: An interdisciplinary approach to teacher education*. New York, NY: Routledge.

Esteva, G., Prakash, M. S., & Shiva, V. (2014). *Grassroots post-modernism: Remaking the soil of cultures*. London: Zed Books.

Forde, S. D. (2014). Look after yourself, or look after one another? an analysis of life skills in sport for development and peace HIV prevention curriculum. *Sociology of Sport Journal*, *31*(3), 287–303. https://doi.org/10.1123/ssj.2013-0103

Forde, S. D., & Frisby, W. (2015). Just be empowered: How girls are represented in a sport for development and peace HIV/AIDS prevention manual. *Sport in Society*, *18*(8), 882–894. https://doi.org/10.1080/17430437.2014.997579

Freire, P. (2000). *Pedagogy of the oppressed* (30th anniversary ed). London: Continuum.

Gilbert, K., & Bennett, W. (2012). *Sport, peace, and development*. Champaign, IL: Common Ground Pub. LLC.

Giroux, H. A. (2011). *On critical pedagogy*. New York: Continuum International Publishing Group.

Giulianotti, R. (2011). Sport, peacemaking and conflict resolution: A contextual analysis and modelling of the sport, development and peace sector. *Ethnic and Racial Studies*, *34*(2), 207–228.

Giulianotti, R., & Armstrong, G. (2014). The sport for development and peace sector: A critical sociological analysis. In N. Schulenkorf & D. Adair (Eds), *Global sport-for-development: Critical perspectives* (pp. 115–133). Basingstoke, Hampshire: Palgrave Macmillan.

Hartmann, D., & Kwauk, C. (2011). Sport and development: An overview, critique, and reconstruction. *Journal of Sport and Social Issues*, *35*(3), 284–305. https://doi.org/10.1177/0193723511416986

Hayhurst, L. M. (2011). Corporatising sport, gender and development: Postcolonial IR feminisms, transnational private governance and global corporate social engagement. *Third World Quarterly*, *32*(3), 531–549. https://doi.org/10.1080/01436597.2011.573944

Hayhurst, L. M. C., Giles, A. R., & Wright, J. (2016). Biopedagogies and Indigenous knowledge: Examining sport for development and peace for urban Indigenous young women in Canada and Australia. *Sport, Education and Society*, *21*(4), 549–569. https://doi.org/10.1080/13573322.2015.1110132

hooks, bell. (1994). *Teaching to transgress: Education as the practice of freedom.* New York, NY: Routledge.

Jeanes, R., & Magee, J. (2014). Promoting gender empowerment through sport? Exploring the experiences of Zambian female footballers. In N. Schulenkorf & D. Adair (Eds), *Global sport-for-development: Critical perspectives* (pp. 134–154). Basingstoke, Hampshire: Palgrave Macmillan.

Kaufman, Z., Rosenbauer, B. P., & Moore, G. (2015). Lessons learned from monitoring and evaluating sport-for-development programmes in the Caribbean. In N. Schulenkorf & D. Adair (Eds), *Global sport-for-development: Critical perspectives* (pp. 173–193). Basingstoke, Hampshire: Palgrave Macmillan.

Kay, T. (2012). Accounting for legacy: Monitoring and evaluation in sport in development relationships. *Sport in Society, 15*(6), 888–904.

Kelly, L. (2012). Sports-based interventions and the local governance of youth crime and antisocial behavior. *Journal of Sport and Social Issues, 37*(3), 261–283.

Kidd, B. (2011). Cautions, questions and opportunities in sport for development and peace. *Third World Quarterly, 32*(3), 603–609. https://doi.org/10.1080/01436597.2011.573948

Kwauk, C. T. (2016). 'Let them see a different path': Social attitudes towards sport, education and development in Sāmoa. *Sport, Education and Society, 21*(4), 644–660. https://doi.org/10.1080/13573 322.2015.1071250

Levermore, R., & Beacom, A. (2009). *Sport and international development.* Basingstoke, Hampshire: Palgrave Macmillan.

Lindsey, I. (2017). Governance in sport-for-development: Problems and possibilities of (not) learning from international development. *International Review for the Sociology of Sport, 52*(7), 801–818.

Lutz, D. W. (2009). African "Ubuntu" philosophy and global management. *Journal of Business Ethics, 84*, 313–328. https://doi.org/10.1007/s10551-009-0204-z

Manzo, K. (2012). Development through football in Africa: Neoliberal and postcolonial models of community development. *Geoforum, 43*(3), 551–560.

Messner, M. (2011). Gender ideologies, youth sports, and the production of soft essentialism. *Sociology of Sport Journal, 28*(2), 151–170.

Millington, R. S. (2015). *The United Nation and sport for development and peace: A critical history* (Doctoral dissertation, Queen's University). Retrieved from https://search-proquest-com.proxy.library.ohio.edu

Mohanty, C. T. (1988). Under western eyes: Feminist scholarship and colonial discourses. *Feminist Review*, (30), 61. https://doi.org/10.2307/1395054

Mwaanga, O., & Mwansa, K. (2014). Indigenous discourses in sport for development and peace: A case study of the Ubuntu cultural philosophy in EduSport Foundation, Zambia. In N. Schulenkorf & D. Adair (Eds), *Global sport-for-development: Critical perspectives* (pp. 115–133). Basingstoke, Hampshire: Palgrave Macmillan.

Mwaanga, O., & Prince, S. (2016). Negotiating a liberative pedagogy in sport development and peace: Understanding consciousness raising through the Go Sisters programme in Zambia. *Sport, Education and Society, 21*(4), 588–604. https://doi.org/10.1080/13573322.2015.1101374

Nicholls, S. (2009). On the backs of peer educators: Using theory to interrogate the role of young people in the field of sport-in-development. In R. Levermore & A. Beacom (Eds), *Sport and international development* (pp. 156–175). Basingstoke, Hampshire: Palgrave Macmillan.

Njelesani, D. (2012). Preventive HIV/AIDS education through physical education: Reflections from Zambia. *Third World Quarterly, 32*(3), 435–452. https://doi.org/10.1080/01436597.2011.573939

Parmar, P. (2009). *Knowledge reigns supreme: The critical pedagogy of hip-hop artist KRS-ONE.* Rotterdam, NY; Boston, MA: Sense Publishers.

Payne, A. (2005). *The global politics of unequal development.* Houndmills, Basingstoke; Hampshire; New York: Palgrave Macmillan.

Peachey, J. W., & Cohen, A. (2016). Research partnerships in sport for development and peace: Challenges, barriers, and strategies. *Journal of Sport Management, 30*(3), 282–297. https://doi.org/10.1123/jsm.2014-0288

Rossi, T., & Jeanes, R. (2016). Education, pedagogy and sport for development: Addressing seldom asked questions. *Sport, Education and Society, 21*(4), 483–494. https://doi.org/10.1080/13573322.2016.1160373

Sanders, B. (2016). An own goal in sport for development: Time to change the playing field. *Journal of Sport for Development, 4*(6), 1–5.

Schulenkorf, N., & Adair, D. (Eds). (2014). *Global sport-for-development: Critical perspectives*. Basingstoke, Hampshire: Palgrave Macmillan.

Spaaij, R., Oxford, S., & Jeanes, R. (2016). Transforming communities through sport? Critical pedagogy and sport for development. *Sport, Education and Society*, *21*(4), 570–587. https://doi.org/10.1080/13573322.2015.1082127

Svensson, P. G., Hancock, M. G., & Hums, M. A. (2016). Examining the educative aims and practices of decision-makers in sport for development and peace organisations. *Sport, Education and Society*, *21*(4), 495–512. https://doi.org/10.1080/13573322.2015.1102723

Tiessen, R. (2011). Global subjects or objects of globalisation? The promotion of global citizenship in organisations offering sport for development and/or peace programmes. *Third World Quarterly*, *32*(3), 571–587. https://doi.org/10.1080/01436597.2011.573946

United Nations. (2022, May 29). *Sustainable development goals: United nations development program*. Retrieved from https://www.undp.org/sustainable-development-goals

United Nations General Assembly. (2002). *Implementation of the united nations millennium declaration: Report of the secretary-general*. Retrieved from http://www.un.org/millenniumgoals/sgreport2002.pdf?OpenElement

Webb, A. J., & Richelieu, A. (2015). Sport for development and peace snakes and ladders. *Qualitative Market Research: An International Journal*, *18*(3), 278–297. https://doi.org/10.1108/QMR-01-2014-0011

Wink, J. (2005). *Critical pedagogy: Notes from the real world* (3rd ed.). Boston, MA: Pearson/Allyn & Bacon.

24
IMPLEMENTING SERVICE-LEARNING FOR SOCIAL CHANGE IN SPORT MANAGEMENT CURRICULA

Michael B. Edwards, Kimberly A. Bush, and J. Lin Dawson

Introduction

Recent events have created an important context for high profile athletes to become more visible agents for social justice. There have been notable responses of athletes across major US sports against police violence, voter suppression laws, and in support of Black Lives Matter protests and inclusive LGBTQ+ rights helping raise public awareness whilst positioning sport at the centre of the social justice movement. Yet, the power to leverage sport for more widespread and sustainable social change has been hindered by inaction or tepid reactions from management of leagues and sport organisations that control the industry. Therefore, the interest of the overall sport industry in adopting policies and practices to facilitate social justice has been questioned. Instead, sport organisations have been criticised for using their latent power to support social change initiatives only when they align with their financial interests and diluting the power of star athletes to advocate for meaningful change. Even when providing cursory support for social justice, many prominent sport organisations continue unethical practices that consistently suppress human rights in pursuit of profits (Lee & Cunningham, 2019; McGillivray et al., 2019).

One factor contributing to the lack of commitment to social justice by sport organisations is the lack of emphasis on ethics, social issues, community development, and social justice in undergraduate sport management programs. Regardless of the level or type of sport, the foundational academic background of most sport practitioners is embedded in the American model of corporate sport management that emphasises sponsorship, ticket sales, media rights, and economic development. While curricula may provide a cursory course in social issues, the overarching theme of sport management education is to maximise capital gains above all other goals. In order for sport practitioners to understand critical social issues, identify mechanisms to address these issues, and understand the responsibility of and role for sport to promote social change, integration of theory and concepts are needed in sport management curricula that facilitates more ethical sport management practice.

Service-learning is one pedagogical approach that is potentially well suited for promoting social change practices among students. To build efficacy among practitioners to promote social change through sport, undergraduate students must be able to understand the context of society and social issues in relation to sport in order to expect them to pursue social change in their roles as practitioners. Service-learning is a form of experiential learning that emerged from Dewey's educational philosophies and provides opportunities for students to apply skills learned in the classroom to volunteer experiences that contribute to their community. Through this process, students are more likely to be exposed to cultural and social conditions different from their own, develop community attachment, and be more likely to develop professional identities related to community engagement.

The goals of this chapter are to analyse the current effectiveness of sport management education to train future practitioners to engage meaningfully in social justice and social change action and suggest that enhancements to sport management education through service-learning initiatives are needed to improve this efficacy. This chapter starts by describing how sport management practices undermine efforts to promote meaningful social change through sport and provides an overview of sport management education and its role in shaping these practices through training future managers. Next, we will discuss ways in which theory and concepts related to ethics, social issues, and social justice may be better integrated into curricula through service-learning. A background on service-learning is provided as well as specific examples of service-learning experiences in sport management programs. Finally, best practices and challenges for implementing sport management service-learning for social change outcomes are presented.

Social justice and sport

In a seemingly uneventful NFL preseason game, a quarterback took a knee during the national anthem on the back row of the team's bench area. After an observational question asked by a beat reporter, a social justice movement was born. NFL quarterback Colin Kaepernick's actions sparked a social justice fire as other notable sport superstars gave voice to other injustices.

> "I am not going to stand up to show pride in a flag for a country that oppresses black people and people of color", said Colin Kaepernick.
>
> (Wyche, 2016, para. 3)

Racial discrimination and police brutality toward people of colour have been the subjects of discussions, marches, strikes, and riots since the Emancipation Proclamation. Athletes from Moses Fleetwood Walker in the 1880s to Muhammad Ali, Jim Brown, John Carlos, and Tommie Smith in the 1960s to present-day stars like Colin Kaepernick and LeBron James have taken activist stands against racial, political, and social injustices with some common results (Carrington, 2010). They received death threats, were labelled as unpatriotic, heckled with expletives during play, experienced financial hardships, and their careers were tarnished or terminated. In most cases, the management of their teams, leagues, or sport did not support these athletes or any direct calls to action in response to social justice causes.

In major sport, and until recent events, management has often successfully deterred athlete-led protests and social action from gaining significant traction. Namely, the goals of management have been to provide cursory support through public statements while using their relationship with the media to threaten and dismantle careers of the so-called agitators or attempt to diffuse the narrative around the activists' positions until things returned to 'normal', i.e. athletes back down from a controversial stance and return to their job of playing their sport (Love, Deeb, & Waller, 2019). Because he did not back down from what NFL owners and managers portrayed as his divisive actions, Kaepernick never played again in the NFL after the 2016 season.

Traditionally sport organisations have followed a pattern of action to extinguish personal and public momentum in athlete-led social action. In many ways, the NFL's response to Kaepernick's protests followed this approach. First, high ranking organisation officials speak out and, while publicly supporting the cause, denounce what is considered 'anti-social' behaviour. Subsequently, policies are created to outlaw behaviour and to keep any other potential athlete protesters at bay. Following this action, well-known public or media figures speak about the polarising effect of the athletes' actions. The league and media focus attention on a respected peer of the protester who is used to contradict the protester(s)' actions with an opposing view and present the public outcry of fans in opposition to the athletes. The issues surrounding the original protester(s)' stance are deflected and distorted and the protester(s) is vilified in public and private spaces, limiting their ability to function as normal in society (Butterworth, 2020; Love, Deeb, & Waller, 2019).

The NFL's approach to quelling the social justice protests of Kaepernick was predictable. It followed a playbook developed over 100 years that paralleled the coercive relationship between labour and capital inherent in professional sport, where athletes are expected to be 'team players' and subservient to coaches and managers, and not empowered with individual voices (Butterworth, 2020; Love, Deeb & Waller, 2019). It also played into mainstream public perspectives where athletes should just 'shut up and play'. However, the social justice movement he started lived beyond the actions of the sport organisation and its managers. Subsequently, actions by athletes in the NBA, WNBA, and NWSL to identify and protest social injustices have been more reluctantly embraced by management, owing in some ways to the corporate consciousness of sponsors and social media exposure, the former threatening league finances and the latter circumventing league-controlled media messaging. However, social justice action continues to be led by athletes, with management only providing some level of cursory public support when it is ultimately in their financial interests or as an implicit means to preserve their influence over the social action message (Love, Deeb, & Waller, 2019). With a generational shift in public support for social justice issues, led by Generation Z, future sport managers will need to ensure their organisations are leaders in the social justice movement (Ha, 2021). However, current practices of sport management education are not always conducive to promoting socially conscious managers and are more likely to prioritise financial goals and antiquated ideas of relationships between sport organisations, athletes, and society.

Sport management education

James Mason created the first sport management graduate degree program at Ohio University in 1966 and is cited as the "father of sport management" (Stier, 2001b, p. 43). The first undergraduate sport management programs were started at St John's University and Biscayne College (now St Thomas University) (Parkhouse & Pitts, 2001). Early courses were primarily concerned with teaching maintenance processes for sport facilities as well as the organisation of sporting events (Chelladurai, 2001).

While the earliest sport management programs were broadly defined and emphasised human and social development as important outcomes of sport practice, sport management has struggled to legitimise itself both within the academy and remain relatable to practice.

Sheffield and Davis (1986) described sport management as a "pre-discipline" (p. 128), and as an emerging framework of physical education. They encouraged others to engage in scientific methods more rigorously and draw upon business and physical education. Chelladurai (1992) discussed the importance of interdisciplinary interaction and reinforced that the success of sport management relies on knowledge developed by other sub-disciplines. Discussions about drawing from other disciplines and scientific methods have been debated among scholars (Amis & Slack, 2008; Inglis, 2007). Zeigler (1987) urged sport managers to "relate significantly to the developing social science of management" (p. 22). Paton (1987) analysed the quality and quantity of management research in physical education and sport and suggested that future research be conducted in both amateur and professional sport settings. However, de Wilde, Seifried, and Adelman (2010) noted the influence of Harvard Business School's impact on the development of the field of sport management. In this sense, the focus of teaching within the sport management field became primarily focused on financial and commercial outcomes.

The field has subsequently been criticised for emphasising commercialised men's spectator sports as the dominant paradigm of sport practice and for a lack of focus on amateur and women's sports (Edwards & Welty Peachey, 2010).

The number of undergraduate sport management programs in the United States quickly grew to 167 sport management programs in the United States and 35 in other countries by 2001 (Stier, 2001a). Within an academic climate that emphasises returns based on student credit hour generation, many universities have embraced sport management as a means of capitalising on student market demand (Edwards & Welty Peachey, 2010). Thus, the field of sport management has seen even more rapid growth with high enrolment numbers in undergraduate programs (Yiamouyiannis, Bower, Williams, Gentile, & Alderman, 2013). Like many practice-oriented sciences, sport management programs are often designed to teach towards specific competencies perceived to be desired by industry, which has often been narrowly defined in commercial terms derived from the production of sport as entertainment (Edwards & Welty Peachey, 2010). In this paradigm, suggests Love, Bernstein, and King-White (2021), sport management research and teaching assumes the primacy of an industry model where athletes are considered commodities managed (or exploited) for the benefit of spectators as consumers, which, in turn, leads to financial gain for organisations. Thus, sport management students may fail to understand how the practice of sport connects to the social world or their professional roles and potential obligations as leaders in the process of social change.

An opportunity exists to integrate knowledge and skills to students on how to be social change agents in their future profession. Scholars have noted the responsibility of sport management to move beyond a focus on the sport entertainment business model that reduces participants to the role of depreciable assets to ensure the field's relevance in a changing society (Edwards & Welty Peachey, 2010; Gibson, 1993). Increasingly, stakeholders are expecting sport organisations to take on larger leadership roles related to social change and promoting progressive human rights agendas (Bush et al., 2016; McGillivray et al., 2019). Incumbent in creating ethical and responsible sport organisations will be training practitioners with a better understanding of social issues and social change processes. Light and Dixon (2007) called for professionals to participate in practices to alleviate community social challenges. They also suggested a need for creating a developmental curriculum for sport management programs. Cunningham (2014) argued scholars of sport management have a "responsibility to engage in collective action ... [to] create change" (p. 5). One pedagogical approach that may be appropriate for promoting these values in sport management students is service-learning.

Experiential education and service-learning

Experiential learning is a pedagogical approach utilised to implement social change practices with college students. It draws upon the work of John Dewey (1938/2007) and relies heavily on an 'experience' as being a critical component. Dewey (1938/2007) emphasised that learning occurs through the interaction between learner and environment in a "situation" (p. 42). In short, experiential learning is 'learning by doing' and reflecting on the experience. However, in order for experiences to be educational and positively influence future interactions, Dewey (1938/2007) noted that several components were essential: experiences should generate interest, be worthwhile intrinsically, present problems that awaken new curiosity and create a demand for information, and cover a considerable time span and be capable of fostering development over time (pp. 217–218). Dewey (1938/2007) emphasised the importance of reflective activities to allow the learners opportunities to reflect on the experience based on specific objectives (Bringle & Hatcher, 1999).

There are a variety of ways that students can engage in experiential education with service-learning being one such form. Kuh (2008) suggested that there is one practice that can be done to enhance college student success and learning:

> Make it possible for every student to participate in two high-impact activities during his or her [sic] undergraduate program, one in the first year, and one taken later in relation to the major field. The obvious choice for first-year students are first-year seminars, learning communities, and service-learning.
>
> (p. 21)

Service-learning gained momentum as pedagogical practice in higher education by the late 1980s and was seen as a separate entity from community service or volunteering (Hollander, Saltmarsh, & Slotowski, 2001). Although service-learning initially lacked a conceptual framework (Giles & Eyler, 1994), it is currently utilised frequently on campuses as a means to engage students in high impact learning activities. Service-learning is a useful way to develop socially relevant knowledge (Osborne, Hammerich, & Hensley, 1998), while providing students with opportunities to engage to help address a community need and implement knowledge and skills learned in the classroom. There are three key components to service-learning: (a) connection to course objectives, (b) service to the community, (c) structured and/or unstructured opportunities for reflection. Service-learning is a step beyond volunteering in that it involves a symbiotic relationship between campus and community (Marullo & Edwards, 2000; Zlotkwoski, 1999). It is linked to course objectives and specific course goals and intentionally integrated to meet community needs and goals (Bringle & Hatcher, 1999). It is essential that when the service-learning experience is discussed with students that it is not presented as 'volunteering' and that the difference between volunteering and service-learning is explained so students can maximally gain from this intentional learning experience.

Service-learning experiences strengthen academic learning (Conway, Amel, & Gerwien, 2009; Novak, Markey, & Allen, 2007). These experiences are also affiliated with advances in decision-making and moral reasoning (Batchelder & Root, 1994; Conrad & Hedin, 1981).

Students report that course material is reinforced and this reinforcement allows them to apply concepts to actual community situations (Wechsler & Fogel, 1995). This finding was reinforced by Kendrick (1996) who noted that students engaged in community service have a greater ability to apply course concepts when they are in new situations. Simons and Cleary (2006) noted that students who have engaged with service-learning report a higher interest in interacting with diverse people. Specifically, Eppler, Ironsmith, Dingle, and Errickson (2011) found an association with service-learning participation and reduced levels of racism. Additionally, Tomkovick, Lester, Flunker, and Wells (2008) found that if students felt the service-learning experiences during college facilitated personal development they were more likely to continue volunteering after college. Service-learning experiences have short and long-term impacts on conceptions of identity formation and beliefs about self-esteem (Jones & Abes, 2004). The service-learning experience can be so impactful that it can lead to college students working through occupational identity issues (Batchelder & Root, 1994) and seeking service-related occupations (Reed, Jernstedt, Hawley, Reber, & DuBois, 2005).

While sport management programs often include experiential learning requirements, typically in the form of internships, these initiatives are often designed primarily for students to provide operational support for sport organisations while practising specific competencies related to the management of sport facilities and the production of sport events. Only in the rare occasion that students attain internships with organisations directly involved with community development or social justice issues would these experiences provide students with service-learning opportunities. Therefore, scholars have suggested that more intentional service-learning activities be incorporated into sport management curricula.

Service-Learning as mechanism to promote social justice awareness in sport management

While long-term service-learning experiences would provide the best model for engaging students with social issues, shorter-term service-learning projects are more likely to fit within the curricular requirements of sport management undergraduate programs that are limited by inherent structural requirements (Bush et al., 2016). Projects (one of several service-learning paradigms) focus on working with communities to solve short-term problems through intentional plans while introducing students into concepts related to community engagement, social justice, and service (Morton, 1995). These programs are designed to create a space where students become exposed to local social realities and their social justice implications (Trinidad, Raz, & Magsalin, 2021). Service-learning projects seek to replace more paternalistic charity approaches by providing students with knowledge and equipping them with skills to address root causes of systemic social inequality (Einfeld & Collins, 2008). Research on service-learning projects suggests that participation has been associated with increased perceived importance of social equity, cultural competency, as well as planned community involvement (Bruening et al., 2015).

For sport management students, service-learning projects focused on community social issues may also increase social consciousness, a critical first step in developing readiness for social change and agency (Bush et al., 2016). According to Paulo Freire (1970/2000), social consciousness emerges as learners change self-centred perspectives to a more attentive awareness of the social world through specific experiences. Critical to this process is involving students in social experiences through sport that promotes a broad understanding of principles of social justice and equity (Ruiz-Montero et al., 2021). Additionally, service-learning projects may provide students with opportunities to engage with communities of practice and stakeholders beyond sport managers. Within sport management, researchers and practitioners often fail to demonstrate critical reflective perceptions of sport (Edwards, 2015; Love, Bernstein, & King-White, 2021). Tradition (even if exploitative and abusive) is sacred and change is resisted at many management levels. Service-learning projects may be one of the few opportunities for sport management students to gain perceptions critical of sport practices relative to social justice. Service-learning projects may also help sport management students develop some initial tangible skills to activate social change strategies in cooperation with organisations and communities of practice (Snelgrove & Wood, 2021). Service-learning projects may also influence students' long-term intentions to become more actively involved in social justice advocacy as individual citizens as well as in their roles as professionals (Bruening et al., 2015).

The emerging evidence of the impacts of service-learning projects in sport management has been promising. Bruening et al. (2015) examined a service-learning partnership between students and CitySport, a non-profit sport-for-development organisation working with youth in Connecticut. They found that students who participated in the project reported personal cultural and professional development along with heightened awareness of complex social issues faced by vulnerable communities. Bush et al. (2016) researched sport management student reflective experiences in College Bound, a collaboration with a local elementary school in North Carolina that focused on barriers to higher education. Students expressed how participation in the project led to a new awareness of social inequalities as well as a recognition of the importance of community engagement and social ethics in the sport profession. Students described the experience as a turning point in the development of their professional identities. Ruiz-Montero et al. (2021) found that students who participated in a project working with refugee children in Spain perceived increased prosocial competencies such as empathy, tolerance, and respect. While not project-based, Bennet, Henson, and Drane (2003) found that sport management students involved in individual short-term service-learning experiences with practitioners reported a greater sense of social responsibility due to the experience.

Best practices in implementation

The efficacy of service-learning projects to support the development of social consciousness and ethical professional identities among sport management students is not inherent. Projects must be framed within the sport-for-development paradigm, designed to facilitate social awareness and competencies as intentional outcomes, and implemented using best practices of service-learning (Bush et al., 2016). Best practices of implementation have been identified as: (a) ensuring that the experience is designed to be intellectually rich for students and to address a significant, and locally identified, community need; (b) integration of the service-learning project in course content is critical so that students can see the connections and comprehend why the experience has intellectual value; (c) a commitment to utilising time in class for students to discuss, share, and analyse experiences with peers and instructors; (d) flexibility will be critical for the students, faculty and community partner when engaging in service-learning; (e) students must be prepared and provided with instructions on how to "read experience as text"; (f) final results of the projects should be shared together by students and community partners (University of Massachusetts Amherst, n.d.).

Additionally, researchers (and practitioners) have a responsibility to be "fluent in existing research" and an additional responsibility for "our ontological entry-points and impacts"

(Patel, 2016, p. 57). As noted previously, service-learning is viewed as a high-impact activity utilised on college campuses to address social justice work. Higher education has been criticised for a lack of praise of the benefits of service-learning (Gilbride-Brown, 2008; Jones, LePeau, & Robbins, 2013; Jones, Robbins, & LePeau, 2011). As sport management educators implement service-learning projects in courses, it will be essential to stay current with literature on student identity theory and continuously examine the "process rather than a singular point of" success (Spade, 2015, p. 2). For example as noted by Lange and Stewart (2019): "an anticolonial approach (Patel, 2016) to community based learning would prioritize relationship building with the community and then center the knowledge and wisdom that pre-exists in the community".

This reframing would allow students to be in the position of learning from the community (Lange & Stewart, 2019). Additionally, it is critical to utilise tenants of theories such as critical race theory, intersectionality, and critical feminist theories that examine power dynamics between individuals and systems in our work with service-learning and social justice. Power-conscious frameworks (Linder, 2018) can help practitioners in examining their power with an intentional effort to disrupt the power imbalance between universities and students.

There are implicit challenges with implementing service-learning at the university level. Primarily, service-learning is often "viewed by faculty as 'just' an atheoretical (and time consuming) pedagogy that may be detrimental for traditional tenure and promotion committees to take seriously" (Butin, 2006, p. 474). Service-learning has received support across higher education institutions, however, it is "infrequently 'hard wired'" into institutional practices and policies (Butin, 2006, p. 475). Of important note is that service-learning is most often utilised by the most marginalised and least powerful faculty members (women, people of colour, and untenured faculty) (Antonio, Astin, & Cress, 2000). Antonio et al. also found that faculty who are in non-tenure track positions are the most likely to make community service a requirement in their courses and also most likely to advise student groups who are involved in service. In this same study, full professors were found to be generally less supportive of community service and community service graduation requirements.

Ziegert and McGoldrick (2008) identified four overarching themes that result in faculty members being hesitant or resistant to implementing service-learning in their classes. First, there is a general concern that the academic content covered in the course will be reduced or watered down due to the time needed to implement service-learning. Second, service-learning requires the faculty member to give up a feeling of control; as students are pulled from the classroom and placed with a community partner. The faculty member must trust this relationship; as the experience is less predictable than traditional classroom teaching. The community partner may have a schedule change, a budget cut or an emergency that could alter the service-learning plan. This release of control is often difficult for faculty. Third, there is a concern about the time commitment to implement service-learning in the course. Examples include: placement of students, completion of background checks, transportation arrangements, and the time spent working with students on how to interact with the community partner from both professional and pedagogical perspectives requires tremendous time. Faculty members are often weary to invest this time and place trust in this partnership. Finally, assessment of students is often a concern of faculty members; as a good portion of the engagement is outside of the direct supervision of the instructor.

Knowing there are challenges with who chooses to implement service-learning in their classes and logistical/practical considerations that lead to faculty resistance to service-learning, there are considerations for departments/colleges. First, service-learning should hold value in the promotion/tenure process. Service-learning is a powerful, yet time-consuming investment that has been associated with positive student outcomes. Service-learning is also positively associated with impacting communities. These factors should hold value for faculty as they pursue promotion/tenure. Additionally, departments/colleges should provide faculty with a systematic process for recording service-learning efforts in the community (e.g. number of students impacted, number of community members impacted, as well as any articles, presentations, or undergraduate research projects that are a result of the service-learning experience). To address logistical concerns of implementing service-learning (e.g. eliminating material), utilise service-learning as a way to enhance current course content. Additionally, faculty should be encouraged to create a contract that the community partner, instructor, and students all sign so there is a mutual understanding of the expectations for everyone involved in the experience.

Faculty can utilise changes and unpredictable moments that will occur in the experience as moments to teach the students about adaptation and resilience in practice. It will be essential to invest time in regular communication with community partners and students, particularly as challenges arise. Additionally, faculty are encouraged to communicate with leadership about their commitment to service-learning, their project ideas, and how service-learning will positively impact students enrolled in the course. Finally, faculty are encouraged to have conversations with department, college. or university communications specialists so efforts of community engagement and commitment to addressing social issues can be highlighted to institutional stakeholders. This will help celebrate accomplishments of the class/community partnership and also highlight a commitment to service-learning.

Conclusion

Although many stakeholders promote the narrative that sport is apolitical, sport has historically been intertwined with politics and, as indicated earlier in this chapter, athletes have often used their communication platforms to promote social justice activism (Carrington, 2010). However, while athletes, particularly athletes of colour, continue to lead sport's efforts to support and promote social justice activism, management along with the complicit communication framing of media partners often undermine these efforts (Butterworth, 2020; Love, Deeb, & Waller, 2019). This framing often uses the message of unity and positions athlete activists as agitators seeking to politicise sport and sow division. While management may provide tangential public support for the cause of athlete activists and, more recently, have contributed monetarily to organisations engaged in social justice work, these actions are primarily designed to diffuse athlete activism, maintain control over players' activities, and preserve their financial interests (Love, Deeb, & Waller, 2019). Management's role in undermining or resisting athlete social justice activism is emblematic of prevailing ethics in industry management that has historically reinforced societal patterns of inequality, discrimination, and power relations while facilitating numerous examples of human rights suppression (Carrington, 2010; McGillivary et al., 2019).

An important step in the process of changing the role of management to support progressive social justice activism in sport is to ensure managers develop social consciousness and professional identities that align with ethics of social justice. In this way, managers may not only be able to recognise their own responsibility to create equitable sport spaces but may be more likely to understand sport's role in communicating and advocating for the dismantling of societal structures that reproduce social injustices. While it could be argued that sport management has a moral obligation to train managers with the awareness and tools to be socially responsible (Babiak & Wolfe, 2006), there are also some significant practical reasons for future sport managers to promote social justice and create a culture of social advocacy in sport organisations. Research suggests that consumer behaviour in sport may be influenced by corporate social responsibility (Walker & Kent, 2009). Additionally, Generation Z will be one of the most important consumer groups for sport organisations in the future and are currently the largest generational cohort in the US population. In addition to being more diverse and better educated than previous generations, Generation Z is much more involved in social justice issues (Parker, Graf, & Igielnik, 2019). Parker et al. found that nearly two-thirds of Generation Z approved of athlete social justice protests in the NFL, compared to a minority of older generational cohorts. The expected prominence of Generation Z suggests that sport managers' need to align business practices and ethics more authentically with a consumer base that is more socially conscious than any previous generation or potentially lose relevance (Ha, 2021). Additionally, community stakeholders in partnership with advocacy groups are increasingly putting public pressure on sport organisations to adopt and advocate for more progressive human rights practices (McGillivray et al., 2021).

This chapter contends that incorporating service-learning projects into sport management curricula will contribute to training more socially conscious managers by exposing them to inequalities, social justice issues, and communities of practice. Although it should be noted that service-learning projects are limited in their overall efficacy to develop managers who will push for social change. Continued efforts will be necessary to change the culture of sport organisations and remove structural barriers inherent in the practice of sport management that prioritises financial outcomes and promotes hegemonic power relations. These include the need to promote members of underrepresented populations into positions of leadership in sport organisations and leagues (especially coaches and chief executives) as well increased ownership of teams and leagues by women and persons of colour. Additionally, sport governing bodies, informed by external advocacy organisational partners, must create and enforce policies that require social justice and human rights agendas in hosting agreements and league bi-laws. Finally, the adoption and embeddedness of corporate social responsibility and 'triple bottom line' goals must become the norm in sport organisations. However, despite the limitations of service-learning projects to lead to direct social justice action and the structural and cultural challenges faced by managers to change the current sport systems, service-learning projects offer some promise in contributing to social change through sport. By facilitating the development of social consciousness tied to professional identities, an important antecedent condition to individuals becoming active social advocates (Bush et al., 2016), especially early in students' educational experience, may allow sport management students to better understand social realities, integrate social justice into coursework, and eventually may support their progression from simply acknowledging social issues to more active social justice engagement in their professional careers.

References

Amis, J., & Slack, T. (2008). Organisation theory and the management of sport organisations. In B. Houlihan (Ed.), *Sport and society: A student introduction* (2nd ed., pp. 348–374). London: Sage.

Antonio, A. L., Astin, H. S., & Cress, C. M. (2000). Community service in higher education: A look at the nation's faculty. *The Review of Higher Education, 23*(4), 373–397. doi:10.1353/rhe.2000.0015

Babiak, K., & Wolfe, R. (2006). More than just a game? Corporate social responsibility and Super Bowl XL. *Sport Marketing Quarterly, 15*, 214–222.

Batchelder, T. H., & Root, S. (1994). Effects of an undergraduate program to integrate academic learning and service: Cognitive, prosocial cognitive and identity outcomes. *Journal of Adolescence*, *17*(4), 341–355.

Bennett, G., Henson, R. K., & Drane, D. (2003). Student experiences with service-learning in sport management. *Journal of Experiential Education*, *26*(2), 61–69. doi:10.1177/105382590302600203

Bringle, R. G., & Hatcher, J. A. (1999). Reflection in service-learning: Making meaning of experience. *Educational Horizons*, *23*,179–185.

Bruening, J. E., Welty Peachey, J., Evanovich, J. M., Fuller, R. D., Coble Murty, C. J., Percy, V. E., … Chung, M. (2015). Managing sport for social change: The effects of intentional design and structure in a sport-based service-learning initiative. *Sport Management Review*, *18*, 69–85. doi:10.1016/j.smr.2014.07.002

Bush, K. A., Edwards, M. B., Jones, G. J., Hook, J. L., & Armstrong, M. L. (2016). Service-learning for social change: Raising social consciousness among sport management students. *Sport Management Education Journal*, *10*(2), 127–139.

Butin, D. (2006). The limits of service-learning in higher education. *Review of Higher Education*, *29*(4), 473–498.

Butterworth, M. L. (2020). Sport and the quest for unity: How the logic of consensus undermines democratic culture. *Communication & Sport*, *8*(4–5), 452–472.

Carrington, B. (2010). *Race, sport and politics: The sporting black diaspora*. London: Sage.

Chelladurai, P. (1992). Sport management: Opportunities and obstacles. *Journal of Sport Management*, *6*, 215–219. doi:10.1123/jsm.6.3.215

Chelladurai, P. (2001). *Managing organizations for sport and physical activity: A systems perspective*. Scottsdale, AZ: Holcomb Hathaway.

Conrad, D., & Hedin, D. (1981). National assessment of experiential education: Summary and implications. *Journal of Experiential Education*, *4*(2), 6–20.

Conway, J. M., Amel, E. L., & Gerwien, D. P. (2009). Teaching and learning in the social context: A meta-analysis of service-learning's effects on academic, personal, social, and citizenship outcomes. *Teaching of Psychology*, *36*(4), 233–245.

Cunningham, G. B. (2014). Interdependence, mutuality, and collective action in sport. *Journal of Sport Management*, *28*, 1–7. doi:10.1123/jsm.2013-0152

Dewey, J. (1938/2007). *Experience and education*. New York: Simon and Schuster.

de Wilde, A., Seifried, C., & Adelman, M. (2010). The culture of history in sport management's foundation: The intellectual influence of Harvard Business School on four founding sport management scholars. *Quest*, *62*(4), 406–422.

Edwards, M. B. (2015). The role of sport in community capacity building: An examination of sport for development research and practice. *Sport Management Review*, *18*(1), 6–19.

Edwards, M. B., & Welty Peachey, J. (2010). Irreconcilable differences or vibrant habitat? An examination of sport management's perceived invasion of recreation's nest. *Sport Management Education Journal*, *4*(1), 18–30. doi:10.1123/smej.4.1.18

Einfeld, A., & Collins, D. (2008). The relationships between service-learning, social justice, multicultural competence, and civic engagement. *Journal of College Student Development*, *49*(2), 95–109. doi:10.1353/csd.2008.0017

Eppler, M., Ironsmith, M., Dingle, S., & Errickson, M. (2011). Benefits of service-learning for freshman college students and elementary school children. *Journal of the Scholarship of Teaching and Learning*, *11*, (4), 102–115.

Freire, P. (1970/2000). *Pedagogy of the oppressed*. London: Bloomsbury Academic.

Gibson, J. H. (1993). *Performance versus results: A critique of values in contemporary sport*. Albany, NY: State University of New York Press.

Gilbride-Brown, J. K. (2008) *(E)racing service-learning as a critical pedagogy: Race matters* (Unpublished doctoral dissertation). The Ohio State University, Columbus, OH.

Giles, D. E., & Eyler, J. (1994). The theoretical roots of service-learning in John Dewey: Toward a theory of service-learning. *Michigan Journal of Community Service-Learning*, *1*(1), 77–85.

Ha, W. (2021). *The impact of different types of NFL's corporate social responsibility on behavioral intentions among generation Z fans* (Doctoral dissertation). Washington State University.

Hollander, E., Saltmarsh, J., & Slotowski, E. (2001). Indicators of engagement. In L. A. K. Simon, M. Kenny, K. Brabeck, & R. M. Lerner (Eds), *Learning to serve: Promoting civil society through service-learning* (pp. 31–49). Norwell, MA: Kluwer.

Inglis, S. (2007). Creative tensions and conversations in the academy. *Journal of Sport Management, 21*, 1–14. doi:10.1123/jsm.21.1.1

Jones, S. R., & Abes, E. S. (2004). Enduring influences of service-learning on college students' identity development. *Journal of College Student Development, 45*(2), 149–166.

Jones, S. R., Robbins, C. K., & LePeau, L. A. (2011, Spring). Negotiating border crossing: Influences of social identity on service-learning outcomes. *Michigan Journal of Community Service-learning, 17*(2), 27–42.

Jones, S. R., LePeau, L. A., & Robbins, C. K. (2013). Exploring the possibilities and limitations of service-learning: A critical analysis of college student narratives about HIV/AIDS. *Journal of Higher Education, 84*(2), 213–238.

Kendrick, J. R. (1996). Outcomes of service-learning in an introduction to sociology course. *Michigan Journal of Community Service-learning, 3*, 72–81.

Kuh, G. D. (2008). *High-impact educational practices: What they are, who has access to them, and why they matter*. Washington, DC: Association of American Colleges and Universities.

Lange, A. C., & Stewart, D.-L. (2019). High impact practices. In E. S. Abes, S. R. Jones, & D.-L. Stewart (Eds), *Rethinking college student development theory using critical frameworks* (pp. 261–275). Sterling, VA: Stylus Publishing, LLC.

Lee, W., & Cunningham, G. B. (2019). Moving toward understanding social justice in sport organizations: A study of engagement in social justice advocacy in sport organizations. *Journal of Sport and Social Issues, 43*(3), 245–263.

Light, R., & Dixon, M. (2007). Contemporary developments in sport pedagogy and their implications for sport management education. *Sport Management Review, 10*(2), 159–175.

Linder, C. (2018). *Sexual violence on campus: Power-conscious approaches to awareness, prevention, and response*. Bingley, UK: Emerald Publishing.

Love, A., Deeb, A., & Waller, S. N. (2019). Social justice, sport and racism: A position statement. *Quest, 71*(2), 227–238.

Love, A., Bernstein, S. B., & King-White, R. (2021). 'Two heads are better than one': A continuum of social change in sport management. *Sport Management Review, 24*(2), 345–364, doi:10.1016/j.smr.2020.02.005

Marullo, S., & Edwards, B. (2000). From charity to justice: The potential of university-community collaboration for social change. *The American Behavioral Scientist, 43*, 895–912. doi:10.1177/000276400021955540

McGillivray, D., Edwards, M. B., Brittain, I., Bocarro, J., & Koenigstorfer, J. (2019). A conceptual model and research agenda for bidding, planning and delivering major sport events that lever human rights. *Leisure Studies, 38*(2), 175–190.

McGillivray, D., Koenigstorfer, J., Bocarro, J. N., & Edwards, M. B. (2021). The role of advocacy organisations for ethical mega sport events. *Sport Management Review, 25*(2), 1–20.

Morton, K. (1995). *The irony of service: Charity, project and social change in service-learning*. Ann Arbor, MI: Michigan Publishing, University of Michigan Library.

Novak, J. M., Markey, V., & Allen, M. (2007). Evaluating cognitive outcomes of service-learning in higher education: A meta-analysis. *Communication Research Reports, 24*(2), 149–157.

Osborne, R., Hammerich, S., & Hensley, C. (1998). Student effects of service-learning: Tracking change across a semester. *Michigan Journal of Community Service-learning, 5*(1), 5–13.

Parker, K., Graf, N., & Igielnik, R. (2019). Generation Z looks a lot like Millennials on key social and political issues. *Pew Research Center*, 17. https://www.pewsocialtrends.org/wpcontent/uploads/sites/3/2019/01/PSDT_1.17.19_generations_FULLREPORT3.pdf

Parkhouse, B. L., & Pitts, B. G. (2001). Definition, evolution, and curriculum. In B. L. Parkhouse (Ed.), *The management of sport: Its foundation and application* (pp. 2–14). Boston, MA: McGraw Hill.

Patel, L. (2016). *Decolonizing educational research: From ownership to answerability*. New York, NY: Routledge.

Paton, G. (1987). Sport management research--What progress has been made? *Journal of Sport Management, 1*, 25–31.

Reed, V. A., Jernstedt, G. C., Hawley, J. K., Reber, E. S., & DuBois, C. A. (2005). Effects of a small-scale, very short-term service-learning experience on college students. *Journal of Adolescence, 28*(3), 359–360.

Ruiz-Montero, P. J., Corral-Robles, S., García-Carmona, M., & Leiva-Olivencia, J. J. (2021). Development of prosocial competencies in PETE and sport science students. Social justice, service-learning and physical activity in cultural diversity contexts. *Physical Education and Sport Pedagogy*, 28(3), 1–15.

Sheffield, E., & Davis, K. (1986). The scientific status of sport management: An evolving disciplinary branch of study. *Quest*, 38(2), 125–134.

Simons, L., & Cleary, B. (2006). The influence of service-learning on students' personal and social development. *College Teaching*, 54(4), 307–319.

Snelgrove, R., & Wood, L. (2021). Cocreating change through sport-based social entrepreneurship. *Sport Management Education Journal*, 15(1), 57–59.

Spade, D. (2015). *Normal life: Administrative violence, critical trans politics, and the limits of law* (2nd ed.). Durham, NC: Duke University Press.

Stier, W. (2001a). The current status of sport management and athletic (sport) administration programs in the 21st century at the undergraduate and graduate levels. *International Journal of Sport Management*, 2, 60–97.

Stier, W. (2001b). Sport management: The development of sport management. *The Business of Sport*, 39–56.

Tomkovick, C., Lester, S. W., Flunker, L., & Wells, T. A. (2008). Linking collegiate service-learning to future volunteerism: Implications for nonprofit organizations. *Nonprofit Management and Leadership*, 19(1), 3–26.

Trinidad, J. E., Raz, M. D., & Magsalin, I. M. (2021). 'More than professional skills': student perspectives on higher education's purpose. *Teaching in Higher Education*, 28(6), 1–15.

University of Massachusetts Amherst. (n.d.). *Civic engagement & service-learning: Principles of best practice in service-learning*. Retrieved December 17, 2021 from https://www.umass.edu/cesl/faculty-resources/service-learning-best-practices

Walker, M., & Kent, A. (2009). Do fans care? Assessing the influence of corporate social responsibility on consumer attitudes in the sport industry. *Journal of Sport Management*, 23, 743–769.

Wechsler, A., & Fogel, J. (1995). The outcomes of a service-learning program. *NSEE Quarterly*, 20(6–7), 25–26.

Wyche, S. (2016, August 27). Colin Kaepernick explains why he sat during national anthem. Nfl.com. Retrieved December 30, 2021 from https://www.nfl.com/news/colin-kaepernick-explains-why-he-sat-during-national-anthem-0ap3000000691077

Yiamouyiannis, A., Bower, G., Williams, J., Gentile, D., & Alderman, H. (2013). Sport management education: Accreditation, accountability, and direct learning outcome assessments. *Sport Management Education Journal*, 7(1), 51–59.

Zeigler, E. F. (1987). Sport management: Past, present, future. *Journal of Sport Management*, 1, 4–24.

Ziegert, A. & McGoldrick, K. (2008). When service is good for economics: Linking the classroom and community through service-learning. *International Review of Economics Education*, 7(2), 39–56.

Zlotkwoski, E. (1999). Pedagogy and engagement. In R. Bringle, R. Games, & E. Malloy (Eds), *Colleges and universities as citizens* (pp. 9–120). Boston, MA: Allyn & Bacon.

25
COMMUNITY SPORT DEVELOPMENT
Where sport development and social justice meet

Janine Partington and Dan Bates

Once described as the cutting edge of sport development practice (Lentell, 1993), community sport development (CSD) reflects a concern for the ways in which conventional club and facility focused development often failed to realise the laudable ambition of 'Sport for All' (Hylton & Totten, 2013). Community models of practice are central to CSD, born from the realisation that externally conceived top-down sport policies and programmes have insufficiently addressed sporting and social exclusion in diverse communities (Partington & Totten, 2012; Bates & Hylton, 2021). Recent policy, programmes, and initiatives have made bold claims of 'newness' or 'doing things differently' but might more accurately be identified as a case of 'old wine in new bottles' (Haywood & Key, 1989) or 'initiativitis' (Grix, 2010). The result is that CSD practice has almost become ahistorical, with current efforts to address persistent inequalities in sport and physical activity at risk of reinventing the wheel. Existing literature in this area provides a thorough account of the ebb and flow of government intervention and interest in sport development (Houlihan & White, 2002; Coalter, 2007; Houlihan & Green, 2010). However, a dedicated and comprehensive account of CSD as a policy 'storyline' (Fisher, 2003) in its own right remains absent.

This chapter addresses this omission. In conceptualising CSD as a distinct area of sport development and charting its key developments over the past 50 years, we identify key principles and processes central to the future endeavours of policymakers and practitioners. Given the current social and economic conjuncture, building lessons learned from the past into future policy and programmes will be essential in alleviating persistent sporting and social inequalities and contributing towards the achievement of social justice. In sketching out the changing ideals and rationales underpinning community sport provision in the England, insight into how historical notions of community sport have inflected the constitution and articulation of contemporary CSD practice are illuminated. This synopsis draws upon examples of both practice and policy, past and present, to provide insight into the principles and practices that inform contemporary notions of CSD.

Furthermore, this chapter illustrates how CSD embodies principles of fairness and redistribution central to the pursuit of social justice. For Miller (2005) a socially just society is one where each person gets a fair share of the benefits of living together, and where the distribution of resources enables people to have a good life *as they see it*. Social justice can be

DOI: 10.4324/9781003389682-30

identified as the remedying of social and economic disadvantages to ensure equal access to life chances and choices (Barry, 2005), and may therefore also be referred to as distributive justice (Wetherly et al., 2017). It is this recognition that some groups in society experience unjust barriers to social and sporting participation, and that through different forms of governance inequalities in opportunity can be addressed, that the recurrent connection between CSD and social justice becomes clear.

Community sport development defined

A range of terms are often used to identify and conceptualise 'community sport', including but not limited to grassroots, mass participation, recreational sport, physical activity, sport for all, and informal sport. Such provision provides people with the opportunity to participate in sport and physical activity, whilst also potentially contributing to a range of health, social, and economic outcomes. Community sport can be delivered by voluntary, public, or commercial organisations, with projects that are local, regional, national and international in scope (Hylton & Totten, 2013). Though the variety of labels and objectives sought through community sport create conceptual ambiguity, it is the underpinning ethos and means by which these aspirations are pursued that make CSD distinct from other aspects of sport development. As will be seen throughout this chapter, this ethos is predicated on alleviating persistent inequalities in sport participation whilst also pursuing laudable ambitions of wider social justice.

Traditional sport development practice and policy is often criticised for a 'one size fits all' approach, whereby participants are expected to align with the prevailing style and culture of opportunities presented. Instead, CSD has been conceived as a better way of developing sport and physical activity opportunities for specific target populations or places, especially for those identified as underrepresented, 'hard to reach', or marginalised. As an ideal type, CSD is a "flexible, adaptable, informal, consultative, people-centred" approach to the creation of socially inclusive sporting opportunities (Hylton & Totten, 2013:122). This ambition comes from the recognition that sporting opportunities available for some are not accessible for all. However, objectives sought through CSD often go beyond participation as an end in itself. In tracing the historical developments of sport policy in the UK, Houlihan and White (2002) made the distinction between community sport provision that focuses on the 'development of sport in communities' versus provision that prioritises the 'development of communities through sport'.

Coalter (2002) suggests that the development of sport in communities largely assimilates the ideals of traditional sport development in emphasising sporting inclusion. Inclusion in sport is understood to foster desirable personal character traits which are 'transferable' to other spheres of a participant's life, potentially leading to incidental wider social outcomes through the positive socialisation of individuals (Darnell, 2007). In short, sport as an end in itself or 'sport plus' (Coalter, 2007). In contrast, projects that seek the development of communities through sport emphasise social inclusion. Alleviating barriers to participation is understood as a necessary process through which sport is used instrumentally in the promotion of wider social outcomes (Coalter, 2002). Such provision emphasises the capacity of sport to contribute to social change as part of a larger process which centres participants' experiences and needs and moves beyond just sporting inclusion (Green, 2008). This notion of CSD often draws more directly on the principles that underpin community development, not just as an alternative model of delivery but as a philosophy and process in order to utilise sport as a means to an end (Bates & Hylton, 2021). This form of provision is often identified as 'plus sport' (Coalter, 2002) and is characteristic of work pursued under the international banner of Sport for Development and Peace (SDP). The gestation and growth policy and provision surveyed in this chapter is therefore significant beyond England, given the role and position of the UK organisations in 'exporting' the use of sport for development internationally (Darnell et al., 2012).

Timeline of CSD developments in the UK

Mackintosh (2021:5) argues that "today's practice, management, and development of sport is historically, politically, and socially situated. By this we mean it is 'positioned'". What we see as CSD today has changed over time – by acknowledging these changes and the rationale for them, we can better understand how CSD as an approach can be utilised to further social justice. The timeline provided in Table 25.1 provides an overview of key policy developments and programmes that have either influenced CSD practice or been significant milestones in the establishment of CSD as a recognised form of practice in itself. The timeline should be used alongside the following sections to help readers develop an understanding of how CSD has been shaped and developed.

Pre-CSD

Many accounts of the evolution of sport policy in the UK identify an increasing convergence of sport and politics after the Second World War (see: Houlihan & White, 2002; Collins, 2010a; Jeffreys, 2012; Houlihan & Lindsey, 2013), with the publication of the Wolfenden Report in 1960 argued to mark the point at which systematic government interest in sport began. The Wolfenden Report was fundamental in establishing sport provision as an element of welfare provision, emphasising the functional value of sport to society to both individuals and communities (Bergsgard et al., 2007). It also called for the creation of a body to oversee and coordinate sport policy and funding – subsequently leading to the creation of the Sports Council in 1964. The Council's charter was both bolstered by, and consistent with, the 1975 White Paper on Sport and Recreation, which identified sport and recreation as "part of the general fabric of the social services" (recreation *as* welfare), and the Council of Europe's (1975) declaration that "every individual shall have the right to participate in sport" (recreational welfare) (Coalter, 1988). Both the White Paper and declaration emphasised the aspiration for a fair(er) distribution of sport and recreation opportunities, and focused attention on inequalities in sport participation.

Investment in facility development (the main thrust of the Sports Council work to date) had proved unsuccessful in challenging inequalities, causing the Council to [outwardly] shift its approach towards concentrating resources on specific target groups (Houlihan & White, 2002; Green, 2004; Bloyce & Smith, 2010) via the 'Sport for All' campaign which aimed to raise awareness of the benefits of sport to all ages to encourage participation. Although well intentioned, the campaign lacked impact and did not signal a real shift in Sports Council priorities from elite sport to mass participation – a recurring tension in sport policy up to the present day (Houlihan & White, 2002; Bergsgard et al., 2007; Coalter, 2007). Jeffreys (2012:147) argues that its objectives were never backed financially, and that government "intentions to use sport as an instrument of welfare policy never extended much beyond small-scale projects confined to deprived inner-city areas". Houlihan and Green (2006:233)

Table 25.1 Key milestones in the development of CSD

Year	Milestone
1960	'Wolfenden Report' published
1964	Establishment of the UK Sports Council
1972	Royal Charter awarded to the Sports Council resulting in the establishment of separate Sports Councils for England, Scotland, and Wales.
1975	White Paper on 'Sport & Recreation' and 'European Sport for All Charter' published
1977	White Paper on 'Policy for the Inner Cities' published highlighting sports contribution to tackling juvenile delinquency and urban unrest
1981	'Action Sport' programme launched targeting inner city areas
1982	Publication of 'Sport in the Community: The next ten years' strategy by the English Sports Council which marked a shift away from facility development strategies to a focus on mass participation
1984	'National Demonstration Projects' launched
1986	First 'Football in the Community' schemes established
1992	Allied Dunbar National Fitness Survey conducted – Sports Council's first serious engagement with physical activity/health agenda
1994	Establishment of the National Lottery
1995	'Sport: Raising the Game' published (DNH, 1995) with a focus on elite sport and youth sport – emphasis on 'sport for sport's sake'
1997	Election of 'New Labour' government to end 18 years of Conservative government
1999	'Policy Action Team 10 Report: The contribution of sport of the arts to neighbourhood renewal' published by the government – established 'social inclusion' as a sport policy goal and initiated the launch of Sport Action Zones in 2000.
2000	'A Sporting Future for All' national sports strategy published by New Labour with a focus on 'sport for good'
2002	'Game Plan: A Strategy for Delivering Government's Sport and Physical Activity Objectives' published outlining ambitious targets for increasing levels of physical activity in UK
2005	Award of 2012 Olympic and Paralympic Games to London
2007	Establishment of StreetGames National Charity
2008	'Playing to Win: A New Era for Sport' strategy (DCMS, 2008a) published – outlined a shift back to 'sports for sports sake' and prioritisation of funding towards elite sport and away from grassroots sport
2010	Comprehensive Spending Review announced by the new Coalition government and announcement of Big Society vision
2012	'Creating a Sporting Habit for All: A Youth Sports Strategy' published by the government – National Governing Bodies given responsibility for leading grassroots sport development
2015	'Sporting Future: A Strategy for an Active Nation' published – a return to a focus on sport and physical activity in communities, but with health as the key driver
2017	Initial 12 'Local Delivery Pilot' areas announced by Sport England
2020	Sport England financial investment in the 'Sport for Development Coalition'
2021	'Uniting the Movement' strategy published by Sport England with focus on 'whole systems change' to embed physical activity in individual lifestyles

argue 'Sport for All' in the UK has "ossified" and become "at best a symbolic status of a past concern with sport as an element of welfare". However, 'Sport for All' as an ideal built upon social justice principles has demonstrated considerable longevity and influence and is still cited extensively internationally as a policy rationale and goal (Eichberg, 2009). Despite limitations in sport policy, this period saw sport elevated to a higher political standing with recognition that sport was actually not *for all*, and that new approaches would be required to address inequalities in participation. The promotion of sport as an aspect of welfare policy along with the 'Sport for All' campaign are thus key milestones in the eventual emergence of CSD as an approach and practice.

The emergence of CSD

The election of Margaret Thatcher and a Conservative government in 1979 in the UK sounded alarm bells amongst the sport lobby due to her wholly indifferent attitude towards sport as a policy area (Coghlan, 1990; Houlihan & White, 2002; Jeffreys, 2012). Sport was viewed as "little more than a crude investment of social policy"; a potential quick fix for rising urban unrest in inner city areas and a convenient means to extend state control over the populace (Jeffreys, 2012:173). This was perhaps best evidenced by the government's move to establish Football in the Community schemes attached to Professional Football Clubs – these were presented as a move to build better relations between clubs and their communities but were mainly influenced by Thatcher's desire to tackle hooliganism (McGuire, 2008; Parnell et al., 2013). This focus on social control was at odds with the Sports Council's desire to focus on equity, but largely reflective of broader political and social shifts that ended the period of welfare expansion and instead focused attention on the externalities or collective social benefits of leisure provision (Long & Sanderson, 2001). As Coalter (2007:11) argues, "although the rhetoric of recreation as welfare was still ideologically potent, it remained politically weak and relatively marginal to core public policy developments". Spurred by the urban unrest of 1981, government investment in the Action Sport initiative therefore offered a window of opportunity in an otherwise narrowing role for [community] sport development (Lentell, 1993; Collins, 2010a).

Action Sport was significant in promoting sport development as a legitimate activity within local authorities and is widely credited as being the forerunner to subsequent CSD schemes (Houlihan & White, 2002; Coalter, 2007; Bloyce & Smith, 2010). The overall aim of Action Sport was to demonstrate that local leadership from community members could develop 'positive attitudes' amongst groups identified as problematic such as the unemployed and inner-city 'youth', as well as stimulating an increase in participation (Coalter, 2007; Bloyce & Smith, 2010). Largely at odds with the paternalistic, top-down rationale for the programme, most projects worked in local areas targeting specific groups, utilising a community-orientated approach to get to know local communities and their needs. This approach has become a fundamental aspect of CSD practice in attempting to challenge inequality and injustice through the recognition of the value of indigenous knowledge in tackling barriers to sporting and communal participation (Collins, 2010a; Hylton & Totten, 2013; Bates & Hylton, 2021).

Building on the success of the Action Sport initiative, the Sports Council launched National Demonstration Projects that targeted under-represented groups in sport such as women and minority ethnic communities. Utilising a non-facility dependent, outreach approach, the programmes were further evidence that investing in bricks and mortar alone would not address inequalities in participation. These programmes were also delivered via local authorities, and the combination of funding for these and the Action Sport initiative acted as a catalyst for the creation of specific teams of sport development officers within local authorities whose responsibilities included engaging communities in sport (Lentell, 1993; Houlihan & White, 2002; Collins, 2010a; Houlihan & Lindsey, 2013). Emerging from the early 1980s was a model of provision that, in recognition of the limitations of facility orientated policy, emphasised the importance of outreach-based programmes and the need for consultation with specific target groups; maintained a fundamental preoccupation with enabling mass participation; and espoused the notion that participation could lead to wider communal and social outcomes. In short, the principles of CSD started to emerge and become embedded within the practices of sport development officers located within local authorities.

'Sport for sport's sake'

Despite the threat to local authority sport and leisure provision from the introduction of Competitive Compulsive Tendering (an attempt by the Thatcher government to use neo-liberalist principles of marketisation to tackle perceived inefficiencies within public services by requiring local authorities to put services out to tender), many local authorities continued to invest in and support CSD programmes. However, these programmes were often viewed as "self-contained, time-restricted and project-specific activity" rather than a specific service priority (Houlihan & White, 2002:45). The increased focus on efficiency was at odds with the welfarist, redistributive principles that underpinned CSD provision. The tendering-out of sport and leisure facilities to external providers, meant that sport development services were often left marginalised within local authorities without any real strategic or political focus (Houlihan & White, 2002; Collins, 2010b). This lack of status, despite the investment into sport development programmes, impacted on the perception of sport development as a profession and recognised career path – an issue that persists to this day and which has undoubtedly influenced the often short-term and fractured nature of CSD provision in local areas.

Despite a more proactive role given to sport with the succession of John Major as Conservative party leader, government discourse remained largely concerned with elite performance and the dismissed status of sport in state schools (Jeffreys, 2012). The publication of 'Sport: Raising the Game' (DNH, 1995) largely ignored the promotion of mass participation (Coalter, 2007) suggesting instead that "sport at the highest level engages the wider community" (Department of National Heritage, 1995:34). This offered a convenient but weak justification for a shift in sport policy towards competitive sport in schools and sport-specific development and performance where the achievement of social outcomes was incidental (Lentell, 1993; McDonald, 1995; Henry, 2001). To support these new ambitions additional funding was required; The National Lottery being established in 1994 with sport included as one of five 'good causes'. Not only did this provide a significant boost for elite sport fulfilling Major's hopes of creating a 'sporting nation', it also offered real hope for further investment in community sport albeit a continuation of project-based funding as opposed to mainstream financial support.

Despite mentions of community sport in the new strategy, emphasis on target group-based provision was lost, replaced with a broader, vague focus on sports equity. Criticisms were directed at the use of 'community' in the strategy – argued to be merely a 'spray on solution' to provide a mask of legitimacy for the shift in policy towards 'sport for sport's sake' as opposed to the adoption of a real commitment to challenging inequalities in participation (Taylor, 2011; Hylton & Totten, 2013). Local authorities, then the main provider of community recreation, were largely left to their own devices but were expected along with NGBs to contribute towards sport equity (Bloyce & Smith, 2010). As Houlihan and White (2002) surmise, this period did not provide a favourable political context for CSD with the political case for additional investment into elite sport further strengthened by the poor performance of Great Britain and Northern Ireland in the 1996 Atlanta Olympic Games. However, the election of a New Labour government in 1997 offered some hope for a change in approach.

New Labour: A new impetus

Action Sport and the National Demonstration Projects provided an initial delivery model for effective community sport provision; working locally with target groups in small localities to seek wider social outcomes through sport participation (Collins, 2010a). With the election of New Labour in 1997, community sport was identified as a tool to address wider social issues and contribute to the political agenda of social inclusion and active citizenship (Coalter, 2007). As the processes of social exclusion were identified as cross-cutting, and therefore not the domain of one single government department, sport was called upon and expected to contribute to the 'joined-up' strategic rejuvenation of civil society (Houlihan & White, 2002). Mirroring the changing relationship between central and local government, Sport England adopted a more interventionist approach with the creation of the Active Communities Development Fund (ACDF), intended to build capacity and empower communities to develop programmes which addressed local issues. The ACDF focused on engaging 'more people' in 'more places' to promote equality of opportunity, increase participation, develop community sport leaders, develop community sport programmes and facilities, and improve planning for sport and recreation (Sport England, 2000).

Local government was highlighted as the preferred delivery partner for the creation of sporting opportunities with extrinsic benefits of sport, particularly in relation to the potential contribution of sporting activities in tackling social exclusion, highlighted in successive national sports strategies and policies (DCMS, 2000; DCMS/Strategy Unit, 2002; King, 2009; Collins, 2010a, 2010b; Houlihan & Lindsey, 2013; Harris & Houlihan 2014:114). Sport Development Officers (SDO) working within local government seized the opportunity to integrate sport across a wide range of policy objectives such as community safety and neighbourhood renewal, elevating the position of sport development within local government structures and facilitating an increase of inter-departmental working in addition to extending partnerships with external agencies such as health and housing providers. These partnerships opened the door for SDOs to access non-traditional funding sources such as the Neighbourhood Renewal Fund and Single Regeneration Budget (Houlihan & Lindsey, 2013). As a result of these new resources and increased political salience, the size of many sport development teams within local authorities increased, with funding for community sport development increased significantly at local level – a 'golden period' for CSD, and one which cemented the potential contribution of sport to social and community issues.

The cross-cutting role of community sport was given particular attention in the Policy Action Team 10 report to the Social Exclusion Unit (PAT 10, 1999), which assessed the role and impact sport and the arts can play in regenerating deprived areas. The findings of the report provided a clear indication that community participation and ownership are essential processes in achieving desired social outcomes through sport. Houlihan and White (2002) suggest that although PAT 10 provided greater policy coherence, it was the implementation of the Sport Action Zones (SAZ) initiative in 2000 (an element of Sport England's broader 'Active Communities' agenda) that embraced CSD over conventional sport development practice in the pursuit of social outcomes. Launched by Sport England, SAZ targeted deprived communities with the objective of providing 'help to communities to help themselves', with the overarching aim of increasing sports participation and establishing a sustainable delivery structure (Hallaitken, 2008). The SAZ demonstrated how practitioners working at a local level *with* the community through 'robust participatory consultation techniques' enabled the project to access and formulate actions based on local knowledge that would otherwise have remained unconsidered (Walpole & Collins, 2010). The initiative also highlighted the importance of engaging with non-traditional partners, which was indicative of New Labour's emphasis on partnership working and joined-up solutions to complex social issues. Hallaitken's (2008:4) report on the SAZ was unequivocal in identifying that "a bottom-up approach to developing the programme is a critical success factor" and that projects must "involve residents in programme design, delivery and review" if they are to be implemented successfully.

A second influential initiative conceived during this period was Positive Futures, Britain's largest national youth charity crime prevention programme managed by the charity Catch22 on behalf of the UK Home Office. Explicit in their assertion that their sports-based initiative is not founded on 'diversionary' or traditional sport development programme design and practice, Positive Futures describes itself as a relationship strategy that engaged young people in a 'flexible and organic' way which allows the development of trust and a locally defined development strategy (Crabbe et al., 2006). At several points in their published reports, reference is made to the "Positive Futures approach", in which staff and participants are given the flexibility and autonomy to create projects with locally defined strategic plans, forging innovative practice and partnerships (Crabbe et al., 2006:6). This way of working is evidently not limited to Positive Futures, as the value of a community development approach to sport and recreation was recognised and utilised in previous decades (Rigg, 1986; McDonald & Tungatt, 1992; Haywood, 1994). It also featured heavily in the approach advocated by StreetGames, a new national charity established in the mid-2000s which promoted 'doorstep sport' – an approach emphasising the need to offer sport at "the right time, in the right place, at the right price and in the right style" if individuals from disadvantaged communities are to be successfully engaged in sport and physical activity (StreetGames., n.d.).

Despite increased financial investment in CSD programmes, continuing dis-satisfaction with stagnating participation rates at a central government level precipitated the introduction of the Active People Survey (now the Active Lives Survey) in 2005. This would provide baseline participation data by sport and across local authority area to direct Sport England investment and to offer increased accountability on the use of public monies (Rowe, 2009). The Carter Report (2005), commissioned by the DCMS, also raised significant concerns about the lack of coordination and alignment of central and local policy for sport and argued that the local delivery system was not best placed to drive up participation levels. Consequently, the failure of local authorities to deliver increased participation or evidence the social impact of sport, combined with a lack of central government control over the policy directions taken at a local level meant that local government "fell out of favour" as primary deliverers with a new approach being identified involving an increased role for NGBs (Harris & Houlihan, 2014:114).

This change in direction was cemented in the 'Playing to Win' (DCMS, 2008a) strategy which outlined how the government aimed to capitalise on the opportunities offered by the successful bid for London to host the 2012 Olympic and Paralympic Games with increased National Lottery funding allocated to NGBs to both drive forward mass participation and support the development of elite sport. As such, financial resources available to local government to develop inclusion-based programmes reduced significantly once again – reflecting the topsy-turvy nature of political support for CSD programmes, and the tendency more broadly for political support for social justice principles to shift towards rhetoric, rather than reality.

London 2012: Medals matter

The New Labour government had provided an impetus for CSD programmes; however, London's successful bid to host the 2012 Olympic and Paralympic Games triggered an abrupt shift in policy back to 'sports for sport's sake' with politicians prioritising funding to support elite sport in the build-up to the games (Green, 2006; Coalter, 2007; Collins, 2010b). To build upon the legacy of the games, responsibility for mass participation was passed on to NGBs via the funding of Whole Sport Plans which outlined ambitious targets to drive forward mass participation by re-engaging lapsed participants and to create improved progression pathways (Collins, 2010a). This shift in policy and approach meant that financial resources previously earmarked for CSD programmes were vastly reduced. The 'no compromise' approach (which threatened funding reductions if targets were not met) taken by Sport England towards Whole Sport Plan funding pressurised NGBs to look for easy wins to increase participation rather than target 'hard to reach groups'; a shift less concerned with social justice and the alleviation of social and economic disadvantage in relation to sport participation.

Further challenges to the role of the public sector and development of CSD emerged from the global economic crisis in 2008. Whilst the New Labour government reacted to the crisis using centralised economic management (Painter, 2012), the formation of a coalition government between the Conservative and Liberal Democrat parties after the 2010 general election signalled a change in approach. Despite promises of a 'Big Society' which would empower and enable communities to influence local provision and services (Martin, 2011; Lowndes & Pratchett, 2012), significant public sector spending cuts were announced in the Comprehensive Spending Review in 2010. The much-lauded localism agenda was criticised as a "convenient rationale for fiscal retrenchment" (Painter, 2012:11), which would undermine improvements to welfare standards made under the previous government. For organisations engaged in CSD and often dependent on public sector support, the omens were not good. Outreach programmes were scaled back or cut, facilities closed (often in the most deprived communities), grant aid was reduced for voluntary and community sector organisations, and there was increased reliance on central government funding streams to prop-up 'sport for all' activities (CLOA, 2012; King, 2013; Conn, 2015; Parnell et al., 2015). Cash-strapped local authorities were forced to look for ways to reduce expenditure but continue service delivery, with many opting to outsource sport services to leisure trusts. Whilst financially attractive, these arrangements emphasised financial prudence – widening participation and challenging inequalities once again became a peripheral policy concern (Association for Public Service Excellence, 2012). The bold claims made by the London 2012 Organising Committee that the games would inspire a generation; transform the lives of young people through sport; and get more people active (DCMS, 2008b) seemed to have been forgotten in the rush to reduce expenditure.

However, as Hylton and Totten (2013) noted, CSD is not solely the domain of publicly funded sport development practitioners and whilst some organisations suffered from austerity measures, others prospered during this period. StreetGames grew in stature and become a strategic partner of Sport England, providing it with additional financial and political clout to promote doorstep sport often via the creation of national programmes which provided funding pots to support local delivery by voluntary and community organisations. In addition, Community Foundations attached to professional sports clubs grew in significance largely thanks to financial support emanating from the growing commercial strength of professional sport leagues. National programmes such as 'Premier League Kickz' were funded via broadcasting and sponsorship deals not subject to the whims of government policy or austerity measures. Having also capitalised on opportunities to 'sell' coaching programmes to schools (Powell, 2015; Parnell et al., 2016; Parnell et al., 2017), foundations were able to grow their capacity and in the absence of local authorities, often becoming the 'go to' deliverers of community sport programmes. Whilst they undoubtedly filled a gap in some areas, national programmes are often top-down and highly structured and despite the best efforts of staff on the ground are difficult to adapt to local needs – therefore only scratching the surface of deep-seated inequalities and social issues within communities.

A new era for CSD?

Having been unsuccessful in attempts to secure a mass participation legacy from the 2012 Olympic Games, there was an abrupt and largely unexpected shift in government thinking and a radical shift in policy back to 'sport for good' in 2015. The publication of 'Sporting Future: A new strategy for an active nation' (DCMS, 2015) clearly outlined a new remit for sport as part of a broader agenda for physical activity and health improvements. Five specific objectives were outlined: physical and mental health, individual and social development, and finally economic development. It was not lost on many commentators that this agenda bore much more resemblance to previous Labour policies. After almost a decade of austerity measures which had impacted significantly on their capacity to deliver sport and recreation provision (Reed, 2016), local authorities reappeared in the strategy as key delivery partners. Sport England made claims towards a new approach to fund 'who and what works' promising funding to agencies who could deliver in terms of engaging inactive members of the population, particularly women and girls, disabled people, those from lower socio-economic groups, older people, and children from 5 years old and upwards (Sport England, 2015). The promotion and development of physical activity particularly targeted at individuals classed as 'inactive' (defined as less than 30 minutes of moderate physical activity per week) rather than narrower conceptions of sport became the primary driver for funding, providing opportunities for a range of non-traditional partners such as The National Trust, The Ramblers Association, Age UK, and Girlguiding to access resources and support.

Sport England's Local Delivery Pilots (LDPs) embodied, at least at a strategic level, this desire to work differently. The LDPs adopted a whole systems approach, whereby an individual's behaviour was understood as part of a complex web of social, institutional, environmental, and policy influences (Sport England, 2021). The LDPs also stressed the centrality of working with local people, building trust over time, and working collaboratively with communities and stakeholders to co-produce desirable change (Potts et al., 2021). The programme was built on recognition of persistent inequalities in physical activity participation reflecting wider societal differences in class, race, gender, and disability. The LDPs fitted neatly with the UK government's mantra of 'levelling-up' first mooted during the 2015 national election and which stressed ambitions to tackle longstanding local and regional inequalities. 'Levelling-up' emphasised the need to take a place-based approach on the assumption that improving opportunities and raising standards of living in geographical areas would address inequalities felt by disadvantaged groups living in those areas. On the surface this mantra embodied several principles of social justice; however, critics of the policy argued that the agenda was driven by electoral calculation – designed to appeal in towns and places where the Conservative Party had traditionally fared poorly in elections, as opposed to a real desire to change deep-rooted inequalities (Tomaney & Pike, 2020; Jennings et al., 2021). Many of the successful bids for LDP funding (often lead by Public Health departments within local authorities) typified the type of area flagged up as needing to 'level up', such as "former industrial towns, ailing seaside resorts, [and] peripheral rural areas" (Jennings et al., 2021:303).

Despite this cynicism, the identification of the need to 'level up' has provided a window of opportunity for establishment of CSD approaches to the provision of sport and physical activity. The 'Levelling-up' White Paper (HM Government, 2022) details 12 levelling-up missions, two of which are narrowing the gap in Healthy Life Expectancy between the areas where it is highest and lowest, and improving the wellbeing of every area in the country. In addition, the COVID-19 pandemic which precipitated national lockdowns in the UK and other countries, further amplified disparities in access to social and environmental support for physical activity, potentially contributing to a widening gap in physical activity participation (Hasson et al., 2021). Whilst many sport providers responded to the lockdown by providing online classes and exercise programmes, individuals from disadvantaged communities often lacked the means to access these, with Hasson et al. (2021) calling for innovative, needs based and community orientated programmes to be developed supported by a commitment to improved spaces for sport and physical activity within communities.

CSD and social justice: What can we learn from 50 years of policy and practice?

This chapter has traced the gestation and development of CSD as a policy storyline distinguishable from other aspects of Sport Development. Far from often uncritical conceptions of community sport as a politically neutral endeavour, a legacy of changing political persuasions and policy narratives has continued to influence (but certainly not determine) what constitutes desirable practice in any given period. Despite claims of 'newness' and 'doing things differently', contemporary notions of desirable CSD practice are imbued with ideals and processes of the past. It is perhaps one of the failings of sport development more broadly as a profession-in-waiting that knowledge of effective CSD process and practice does not always appear to be accumulative. Shifting language, terminology, and policy have produced a 'conceptual fog' that makes agreed upon definitions challenging. Despite this ambiguity, CSD can be characterised as an appreciative and collaborative bottom-up process whereby practitioners work with communities and in cross-sector partnerships, recognising the value of local assets and the expertise of a wide range of stakeholders, to address barriers to sporting participation and alleviate social issues. A number of principles and practices characteristic of this process have been identified.

Fundamentally, CSD embodies a commitment to social justice in sport and society. From the ambitious beginnings of 'Sport for All', CSD was concerned with addressing barriers to sporting and social inclusion. This concern means that policy and practice is typically orientated towards addressing issues of fairness for communities and groups identified as disadvantaged. The development of sports facilities was identified as an ineffective way of engaging target groups and populations, catering instead for those who already had the means and inclination to participate (Houlihan & White, 2002). Instead, CSD adopts a bottom-up approach, whereby local people contribute meaningfully to the development of provision through participatory communal structures. This approach was embodied in, for example, the Sport Action Zones, during which consultation and relationship building with local people was identified as paramount (Walpole & Collins, 2010). The importance of grasping inherent power relations between the community and other stakeholders in programme development has always infused provision and given CSD a potentially radical edge (Partington &

Totten, 2012; Hylton & Totten, 2013), and contrasts more neo- or economic liberal conceptions of fairness and the role of government (Plant, 2004). Recently, Sport England's Local Delivery Pilots have been explicit in their recognition that it may be professionals' existing ways of working that create challenges to effective change, instead of communities being the source of the problem. Indeed, the notion of 'community' in CSD policy and practice continues to be understood as a complex web of social relations and resources that are essential to stimulating sustainable change (Haywood, 1994; Bates & Hylton, 2021).

As a more responsive way of confronting concerns about opportunity, equality and injustice compared to 'mainstream' Sport Development, it comes as no surprise that the ideals of CSD have endured the ebb and flow of changing political and social climates. However there are a number of ongoing challenges to the pursuit of sporting and social justice through CSD. Crucially, resources for CSD will continue to fluctuate. Sport England's commitments to the LDPs and the Sport for Development Coalition (a national charity in the UK which uses the power of sport to bring about positive social change), indicate a promising level of strategic buy-in. However, as Local Authority budgets continue to be squeezed, non-statutory expenditure will continue to be threatened. Local Authorities' reduced capacity contrasts the growth of VCS organisations, with more than 400 signatories on community sport directory (Connect Sport, 2021). Provision is no longer primarily funded publicly via local government, but increasingly reliant on third sector organisations from larger organisations such as community foundations attached to professional sports clubs down to small, locally based charities and community organisations. The breadth and scale of organisations engaged in community sport presents its own challenges, and is coupled with "increasing public, political and media scrutiny and interest in governance, ethics and integrity within community sport" (Dowling et al., 2021). Clearly there is still much work to be done on the governance and professionalisation of practice if the potential of CSD in the pursuit of social justice is to be established once and for all.

References

Association for Public Service Excellence. (2012). *Local Authority Sport and Recreation Services in England: Where next?* Manchester: ASPE.
Barry, B. (2005). *Why Social Justice Matters*. Cambridge: Polity.
Bates, D., & Hylton, K. (2021). Asset-based community sport development: Putting community first. *Managing Sport and Leisure*, 26:1–2, 133–144. doi:10.1080/23750472.2020.1822754
Bergsgard, N.A., Houlihan, B., Mangset, P., Nodland, S.I., & Rommetvadt, H. (2007). *Sport Policy: A Comparative Analysis of Stability and Change*. Oxford: Butterworth Heinemann.
Bloyce, D., & Smith, A. (2010). *Sport Policy and Development: An introduction*. Abingdon: Routledge.
Chief Leisure Officers Association. (2012). *Financial Settlements for Culture & Sport Survey Summary – June 12*. Ipswich: CLOA.
Coalter, F. (1988). *Sport and Anti-Social Behaviour: A literature review* (Research Report 2). Edinburgh: Scottish Sports Council.
Coalter, F. (2002). *Sport and Community Development: A manual*. Edinburgh: SportScotland.
Coalter, F. (2007). *A Wider Role for Sport: Who's Keeping the Score?* Abingdon: Routledge.
Coghlan, J. (1990). *Sport and British Politics since 1960*. London: The Falmer Press.
Collins, M. (2010a). The development of sport development. In M. Collins (ed.), *Examining Sports Development* (pp. 14–42). Abingdon: Routledge.
Collins, M. (2010b). From 'sport for good' to 'sport for sport's sake' – Not a good move for sports development in England? *International Journal of Sport Policy*, 2:3, 367–379. doi:10.1080/19406940.2010.519342
Conn, D. (2015, July 5). Olympic legacy failure: Sports centres under assault by thousand council cuts. *The Guardian*. Retrieved from: https://www.theguardian.com/sport/2015/jul/05/olympic-legacy-failure-sports-centres-council-cuts

Connect Sport. (2021). *Connect Sport Directory*. Retrieved from: https://www.connectsport.co.uk/directory

Crabbe, T., Bailey, G., Blackshaw, T., Brown, A., Choak, C., Gidley, B., Mellor, G., O'Connor, K., Slater, I., & Woodhourse, D. (2006). *Knowing the Score: Positive Futures Case Study Research: Final Report*.

Darnell, S. (2007). Playing with race: Right to play and the production of whiteness in "development through sport". *Sport in Society*, 10:4, 560–579. doi:10.1080/17430430701388756

Darnell, S., Field, R., & Kidd, B. (2012). *The History and Politics of Sport-for-Development: Activists, Ideologues and Reformers*. London: Palgrave.

DCMS/Strategy Unit. (2002). *Game Plan: A Strategy for Delivering Government's Sport and Physical Activity Objectives*. London: Cabinet Office.

Department for Culture, Media & Sport. (2000). *A Sporting Future for All*. London: DCMS.

Department for Culture, Media & Sport. (2008a). *Playing to Win: A new era for sport*. London: DCMS.

Department for Culture, Media & Sport. (2008b). *Before, During and After: Making the most of the London 2012 Games*. London: DCMS.

Department of Culture, Media & Sport. (2015). *A Sporting Nation: A New Strategy for an Active Nation*. London: DCMS.

Department of National Heritage. (1995). *Sport: Raising the Game*. London: DNH.

Dowling, M., Mackintosh, C., Lee, S., & Allen, J. (2021). Community sport development: Managing change and measuring impact. *Managing Sport and Leisure*, 26:1–2, 1–6. doi:10.1080/23750472.2020.1854265

Eichberg, H. (2009). Bodily democracy – Towards a philosophy of sport for all. *Sport, Ethics & Philosophy*, 3:2, 105–114. doi:10.1080/17511320903217287

Fisher, F. (2003). *Reframing Public Policy: Discursive Politics and Deliberative Practices*. Oxford: Oxford University Press.

Green, M. (2004). Changing policy priorities for sport in England: The emergence of elite sport development as a key policy concern. *Leisure Studies*, 23:4, 365–383. doi:10.1080/0261436042000231646

Green, M. (2006). From 'Sport for All' to Not About 'Sport' at All?: Interrogating sport policy Interventions in the United Kingdom. *European Sport Management Quarterly*, 6(3), 217–238.

Green, C.B. (2008). Sport as an agent for social and personal change. In V. Girginov (ed.), *Management of Sport Development* (pp. 129–145). Oxford: Butterworth Heinemann.

Grix, J. (2010). The governance debate and the study of sport policy. *International Journal of Sport Policy*, 2:2, 159–171. doi:10.1080/19406940.2010.488061

Hallaitken. (2008). *Sport Action Zone Evaluation: Final Report: Braunstone Community Association and Sport England East Midlands*.

Harris, S., & Houlihan, B. (2014). Delivery networks and community sport in England. *International Journal of Public Sector Management*, 27:2, 113–127. doi:10.1108/IJPSM-07-2013-0095

Hasson, R., Sallis, J.F., Coleman, N., Kaushal, N., Nocera, V.G., & Keith, N. (2021). COVID-19: Implications for physical activity, health disparities, and health equity. *American Journal of Lifestyle Medicine*. doi:10.1177/15598276211029222

Haywood, L. (1994). *Community Leisure and Recreation*. London: Butterworth-Heinmann.

Haywood, L., & Key, F. (1989). Community sports programmes: Old wine in new bottles. In P. Bramham, I. Henry, H. Mommaas, & H. van der Poel (eds), *Leisure and Urban Process*. London: Routledge.

Henry, I. (2001). *The Politics of Leisure Policy* (2nd ed.). Basingstoke: Palgrave.

HM Government. (2022). *Levelling-Up the United Kingdom Executive Summary*. Retrieved from: https://assets.publishing.service.gov.uk/government/uploads/system/uploads/attachment_data/file/1052046/Executive_Summary.pdf

Houlihan, B., & Green, M. (2006). The changing status of school sport and physical education: Explaining the policy change. *Sport, Education & Society*, 11:1, 73–92. doi:10.1080/13573320500453495

Houlihan, B., & Green, M. (2010). *Routledge Handbook of Sports Development*. London: Routledge.

Houlihan, B., & Lindsey, I. (2013). *Sport Policy in Britain*. Abingdon: Routledge.

Houlihan, B., & White, A. (2002). *The Politics of Sports Development: Development of sport or Development Through Sport?* Abingdon: Routledge.

Hylton, K., & Totten, M. (2013). Community sport development. In K. Hylton (ed.), *Sports Development: Policy, Process and Practice* (pp.80–126) (3rd ed.). Abingdon: Routledge.

Jeffreys, K. (2012). *Sport and Politics in Modern Britain: The Road to 2012*. Basingstoke: Palgrave Macmillan.

Jennings, W., McKay, L., & Stoker, G. (2021). The politics of levelling-up. *The Political Quarterly*, 92:2, 302–311. doi:10.1111/1467-923X.13005

King, N. (2009). *Sport Policy and Governance: Local Perspectives*. Oxford: Elsevier.

King, N. (2013). "Sport for all" in a financial crisis: Survival and adaptation in competing organisational models of local authority sport services. *World Leisure Journal*, 55:3, 215–228. doi:10.1080/04419057.2013.820503

Lentell, B. (1993). Sports development: Goodbye to community recreation? In C. Brackenridge (ed.), *Body Matters: Leisure, Images, and Lifestyles* (No. 47). Eastbourne: Leisure Studies Association.

Long, J., & Sanderson, I. (2001). The social benefits of sport: Where's the proof? In C. Gratton & I. Henry (eds), *Sport in the City: The role of sport in economic and social regeneration* (pp. 187–203). London: Routledge.

Lord Carter of Coles. (2005). *Review of National Sport Effort and Resources*. London: Sport England.

Lowndes, V., & Pratchett, L. (2012). Local governance under the coalition government: Austerity, localism and the 'big society'. *Local Government Studies*, 38:1, 21–40. doi:10.1080/03003930.2011.642949

Mackintosh, C. (2021). *Foundations of Sport Development*. Abingdon: Routledge.

Martin, S. (2011). Local government improvement prospects in England: Policies, progress and prospects. *Commonwealth Journal of Local Governance*, 8/9, May–November, 69–83.

McDonald, I. (1995). Sport for All – 'RIP'. A political critique of the relationship between national sport policy and local authority sports development in London. In S. Fleming, M. Talbot, & A. Tomlinson (eds), *Policy and Politics in Sport, Physical Education and Leisure* (LSA Publications No. 55). Eastbourne: Leisure Studies Association.

McDonald, D., & Tungatt, M. (1992). *Community Development and Sport*. London: Community Development Foundation.

McGuire, B. (2008). Football in the community: Still 'the game's best kept secret'? *Soccer in Society*, 9:4, 439–454. doi:10.1080/14660970802257481

Miller, D. (2005). What is social justice? In N. Pearce & W. Paxton (eds), *Social Justice: Building a Fairer Britain* (pp. 3–20). London: Politico's.

Painter, C. (2012). The UK coalition government: Constructing public service reform narratives. *Public Policy and Administration*, 28:1, 3–20. doi:10.1177/0952076711427758

Parnell, D., Stratton, G., Drust, B., & Richardson, D. (2013). Football in the community schemes: Exploring the effectiveness of an intervention in promoting healthful behaviour change. *Soccer in Society*, 14:1, 35–51. doi:10.1080/14660970.2012.692678

Parnell, D., Millward, P., & Spracklen, K. (2015). Sport and austerity in the UK: An insight into Liverpool 2014. *Journal of Policy Research in Tourism, Leisure and Events*, 7:2, 200–203. doi:10.1080/19407963.2014.968309

Parnell, D., Cope, E., Bailey, R., & Widdop, P. (2016). Sport policy and English primary physical education: The role of professional football clubs in outsourcing. *Sport in Society*, 20:2, 292–302. doi:10.1080/17430437.2016.1173911

Parnell, D., Spracklen, K., & Millward, P. (2017, 2017/01/01). Sport management issues in an era of austerity. *European Sport Management Quarterly*, 17:1, 67–74. doi:10.1080/16184742.2016.1257552

Partington, J., & Totten, M. (2012). Community empowerment and community sport: A case study in Rochdale. *Managing Leisure*, 17:1, 29–46. doi:10.1080/13606719.2011.638205

PAT 10. (1999). *National Strategy for Neighbourhood Renewal: Policy Action Team Audit: Report of the Policy Action Team 10: The contribution of sport and the arts*.

Plant, R. (2004). Neo-liberalism and the theory of the state: From Wohlfahrtsstaat to Rechtsstaat. *The Political Quarterly*, 75:1, 24–37. doi:10.1111/j.1467-923X.2004.620_1.x

Potts, A., Sheam, K., Frith, G., & Christy, E. (2021). Working with local people as part of a whole-systems approach to physical activity: Reflections from local delivery pilots. *Perspective in Public Health*, 141:2, 74–75. doi:10.1177/1757913920982645

Powell, D. (2015). Assembling the privatisation of physical education and the 'inexpert' teacher. *Sport, Education and Society*, 20:1, 73–88. doi:10.1080/13573322.2014.94179

Reed, A. (2016) *#cspfuture: Appraisal of the Future Role of CSPs*. London: Sport England/DCMS.

Rigg, M. (1986). *Action Sport: Evaluation Report*.

Rowe, N. (2009) The active people survey: A catalyst for transforming evidence-based sport policy in England. *International Journal of Sport Policy and Politics*, 1:1, 89–98.

Sport England. (2000) *Active Communities: An Introduction*. London: Sport England.

Sport England (2015). *In It for the Long Run.* Retrieved from: https://www.sportengland.org/our-work/local-work/local-government/in-it-for-the-long-run

Sport England. (2021). *People and Places: The Story of Doing it differently.*

StreetGames. (n.d.). *An Overview of Doorstep Sport.* Retrieved from: https://network.streetgames.org/resource/overview-doorstep-sport

Taylor, M. (2011). *Public Policy in the Community* (2nd ed.). Basingstoke: Palgrave Macmillan.

Tomaney, J., & Pike, A. (2020). Levelling up? *The Political Quarterly*, 91:1, 43–48. doi:10.1111/1467-923X.12834

Walpole, C., & Collins, M. (2010). Sports development in microcosm: Braunstone sport action zone. In M. Collins (ed.), *Examining Sports Development.* London: Routledge.

Wetherly, P. Watson, B., & Long, J. (2017). Principles of social justice for sport and leisure. In J. Long, T. Fletcher, & B. Watson (eds), *Sport, Leisure and Social Justice.* London: Routledge.

26
SPORT, PHYSICAL EDUCATION (PE) AND SPORT-FOR-ALL (SfA) PROGRAMMES

Intersectional perspectives from Cyprus and Greece

Foteini Papadopoulou and Symeon Dagkas

Introduction

Global austerity, the COVID-19 pandemic, and the worldwide economic recession have spread extensively, making social disadvantage prominent in the lives of young people. Hence, the call for the prevention and tackling of the phenomenon appears urgent (Dagkas, 2018), and it is now important to take action to prevent social disadvantage from escalating. Sport and forms of it (i.e., Physical Education (PE) and Sport-for-All (SfA)) are claimed to be a powerful way of moving forward and away from social disadvantage (Bailey, 2018; Dagkas, 2018; Hill et al., 2018). In particular, evidence suggests that PE as well as SfA can have a life-changing impact on young people who experience social disadvantage (Bailey et al., 2009; Dagkas & Hunter, 2015). Not all countries however, can achieve the desirable 'life-changing' impact (McEvoy et al., 2016). Starting from this point, PE and SfA programmes, aiming at addressing forms of social disadvantage, should be examined in depth and exclusively designed based on the disadvantaged young people's views and perceptions. There is an overarching call that seeks to draw and build upon the views of young people through the discourses of 'social disadvantage', 'PE' and 'SfA' (Toft, 2018; Zembylas, 2018 and 2020) and certainly research holds the potential to address relevant issues effectively. Furthermore, gender, social class and race/ethnicity have previously been at the core of research in social sciences and sport (Assari et.al., 2016; Booth, 2016; Azzarito & Hill, 2013), but research in locations that endure severe socio-economic crisis and recession, and on how these simultaneously impact on their interdependency and further on how these are linked to the fields of PE and SfA appears to be limited – such examples are Cyprus and Greece (Papadopoulou, 2019). Factors that illuminate issues of social disadvantage are multi-layered and incorporate not only economic, but also political, historical, geographical, social and cultural factors (Casey & Larsson, 2018; Brooks et al., 2017; Zembylas, 2017). Thus, societal fields such as the family, the school context, urban environments in different countries and how sport, PE and SfA is delivered in multifaceted contexts, play an important role in the construction of youth identities (Azzarito et al., 2017) that currently undergo significant transformations among those with social disadvantage (Azzarito &

Sterling, 2010; Quarmby & Dagkas, 2015). In parallel, young people are often called upon not only to embrace the disadvantage imposed on them but also to overcome it in order to adapt and engage effectively with the society. Research exploring social disadvantage, young people, PE and SfA would benefit from the provision of a wider focus on issues related to these topics and hence inform action research and subsequent, relevant and future interventions.

Worldwide research has widely documented and systematically develops the employment of PE along with SfA as a medium to promote pedagogies related to health and physical culture and that can address and tackle social disadvantage in contemporary societies (e.g., Bailey, 2018; Dagkas, 2016). Further, Bailey et al. (2009) highlight the term 'Sport-for-All' to be an "inclusive, generic descriptor for those structured, supervised physical activities that take place at school, and during the (extended) school day" (p. 2). In parallel, there has been a broad disposition that such SfA programmes hold the potential to influence young people positively and to counter social disadvantage (Dagkas, 2018; Walton-Fisette & Sutherland, 2018). In addition, there exists the overarching argument, and indeed perhaps the necessity, for PE and SfA to be examined through the lenses of the intersectionality of social class, gender, and race/ethnicity (Flintoff, 2018; Scraton, 2018; Azzarito and Solomon, 2005). Social disadvantage is prominent in areas that currently experience severe economic crisis and social deprivation, such as Greece and Cyprus. There are calls therefore for systematic and robust research engaging intersectionality with the focus to impact critically and further, inform hold critical impact to inform future practices and policies (Dagkas, 2016; Zembylas, 2010a,b). Hence, a holistic understanding of the implications of these differences emerges as crucial, if policies for improving the effectiveness of such programmes in tackling social disadvantage, simultaneously promote social justice (Osler, 2015).

In particular, social disadvantage in the Greek and Cypriot contexts is prominent and the two countries currently experience austerity, the COVID-19 pandemic, prolonged economic recession, social deprivation and conflict. PE and SfA programmes are often employed with the aim to maximise the claimed beneficial potential for disadvantaged young people; especially on issues of 'gender', 'race', and 'social class'. The calls of several European Union (EU) policies (e.g. FP7 (2014–2020), Erasmus+ (2024) and HORIZON 2020) support the crucial role of sport, PE and SfA, and these two countries appear to employ important elements of the suggested policies. However, research has showed that this appears to be complex and challenging due to various limitations and problems that appear in the PE curriculum and in the design and delivery of SfA programmes (Papadopoulou, 2019). Nonetheless, the current levels of social disadvantage have been established and remain persistently high, not only in Greece (e.g., The City at a Time of Crisis, 2013) and Cyprus but internationally. For example, austerity politics, wars, the COVID-19 pandemic, and the refugee crisis across the world and particularly in Greece and Cyprus have affected the lives of its populations along with children and young people disproportionately through reduced family work-incomes and cutbacks, heavy taxation, education, health services, and general welfare.

Discussing social disadvantage, PE and SfA

'Social disadvantage' is a complex term that perhaps needs to be addressed critically along with policy aspects that have been implemented to address it in recent years. 'Heavy' transitions are prominent in young people as a reflection of postmodernity and neoliberalism and the current global economic recession (Bauman, 2010). Social disadvantage can be further explored through references to the personal and social identities (e.g., discourse of embodiment, gender, race, class) during the current neoliberal era as well as to notions such as that of the term 'privilege' (Bhopal, 2018).

> Disadvantage is not as simple as it was once assumed to be. There is much more to disadvantage than low incomes and high levels of unemployment, […] Community disadvantage emerges out of the interplay between the characteristics of the residents in a community (e.g., employment, education levels, drug and alcohol use) and, over and above this, the effects of the social and environmental context in which they exist (i.e., "place effects" such as weak social networks, poor role models and a relative lack of opportunity).
>
> (Price-Robertson, 2011, p. 2)

Internationally, there is no clear definition of what exactly 'disadvantage' means or of what it comprises, although primarily it is linked with elements of 'economy', such as 'poverty' and 'unemployment and income' (Darton & Strelitz, 2003). However, factors of disadvantage appear to be similar in all resources; the most prominent are: 'poverty' (Dean, 2016); social exclusion (Chadderton & Edmonds, 2015); marginalisation; lack of employment and disengagement from education (Zembylas, 2020). In addition, Bhopal (2018) argues that in contemporary societies race constitutes a form of disadvantage when associated with privilege and whiteness.

Unemployment in Greece is about 12 per cent and the country reports the second highest unemployment rate in the EU (Statista Greece, 2022). In Cyprus, the youth unemployment rate was about 16 per cent as reported by Statista (Statista Cyprus, 2022). Similarly, children and young people who experience severe conditions such as famine and post-trauma often are refugees of war and can be included in the so-called 'disadvantaged' populations. It is striking however that even when there are initiatives to tackle these phenomena, governments and boarder agencies around the World repeatedly fail to safeguard children's rights. For example, policy decisions to detain their parents or to separate children from their parents can cause unknown consequences to the children. Although, there exist attempts to construct advantageous, beneficial, fair, and equal environments free of racism in post-racial societies, research shows that in reality social disadvantage and inequalities are prominent among populations of specific class, gender and race/ethnicity (Bhopal, 2018; Dagkas et al., 2019; Pang & Hill, 2018).

Gender norms, roles and relations influence people's susceptibility to different health conditions and diseases and affect their enjoyment of good mental, physical health and wellbeing (Wellard & Secker, 2017). They also have a bearing on people's access to and uptake of health services and on the health outcomes they experience throughout the life-course. Nonetheless, 'gender' is central to the discussion of social disadvantage since there are often misconceptions about relevant terms that constitute danger to equity and to human rights (Paechter, 2012). In parallel to gender, Dagkas and Hunter (2015) urged that immense attention should be paid to 'race' and particularly on the 'racialised' body and the way young people develop dispositions towards physical culture. Giddens and Sutton (2017) refer also to 'racialisation' as the process through which race is employed to classify people. 'Racialisation' emerges as a seminal term in the reproduction of power and inequality in contemporary societies, especially those characterised as socially disadvantaged. Racism therefore can be exhibited and imposed in the form of 'structural discrimination' – taking place on a systematic, repetitive, embedded nature within particular social structures such as schooling (Fitzpatrick & Santamaría, 2015). Further, the term 'social class' holds a particular significance when elaborating on social disadvantage and reflects major social, economic, and cultural differences in income, status, education, and lifestyle. Social classes impact perhaps on the ways in which people are treated within the societies they live and in all societal structures such as schools/teachers, families and peer groups (Evans & Davies, 2004). In particular, the dominant [in terms of power] classes are the elite and the middle class, whereas the majority of populations around the world belong to the working class. Hence, the young disadvantaged person and their 'body' is located in social classes (Wacquant, 2018). Classes such as the elite and the middle classes are often financially able to produce 'bodily' forms of high quality, since for example they are able to keep their children in 'elite' education (consequently in PE) for the longest time, release them from the need to work full or part time, and encourage them to engage in activities (such as fitness training and often participation in pre- and extra-school activities such as ballet, tennis, or horse riding); hence, these are likely to increase their acquisition of a socially valued body (Shilling, 2018). In contrast to the elite and middle classes, the working class tends to develop an instrumental relation to its body. The working class therefore develops bodies marked both by the immediate demands of 'getting by' in life, and moreover by the forms of temporary 'release' they seek from these demands (Wacquant, 2013).

Social disadvantage, PE and Sport-for-All: Policy perspectives

Within the current neoliberal policies and the attempts to construct fair, inclusive and equal social environments for all, the European Commission (2010–today) has hugely invested on children's wellbeing with policy initiatives such as the 'Investing in Children: Breaking the Cycle of Disadvantage' (2018). The specific policy (2018) argues that:

> breaking the cycle of disadvantage in early years and investing in children through a preventative approach allows reducing the risk of poverty and social exclusion. This implies not just providing children with adequate living standards: it also means helping them live up to their full potential through an integrated approach bringing them the best educational and health outcomes.

Greece and Cyprus (being members of the EU) follow the European Union's policies which are considered to be 'preventative' and address possible challenges. The prolonged refugee crisis has changed the landscape of PE, SfA, and education in these two countries; for example, refugee children are included within the state education system, although there is no particular teacher training on how to teach PE and deliver SfA to these young people. Following this, 'Investing in Children' (2018) highlights the importance of early intervention and preventative approaches. Hence, EU countries are required to:

- Support parents' access to the labour market and make sure that work 'pays' for them.
- Improve access to affordable early childhood education and care services;
- Provide adequate income support such as child and family benefits, which should be redistributive across income groups but avoid traps of inactivity and stigmatisation.
- Step up access to quality services that are essential to children's outcomes – improve access to early childhood education and care including for children under three, eliminate school segregation, enhance access to health, housing, social services.
- Support children's participation in extra-curricular activities and in services and decisions affecting children such as within social services, education, alternative care.

Currently, Cyprus and Greece are characterised not only by the economic recession but also by the COVID-19 pandemic crisis, the refugee crisis and waves of immigration from countries such as Ukraine, Afghanistan, Iran, Libya, Israel, Gaza and Syria. In Greece and Cyprus, specific policy initiatives are implemented and are in place with the aim of tackling and eliminating social disadvantage. Examples of such initiatives in Greece are:

- All refugees and migrants are entitled to state education from 'day one' although there are barriers such as the language. This is a decision of the Ministries of Education in Greece and Cyprus.
- 'Γκόλ στη Φτώχεια/Kick-out-Poverty' (2013), which utilises football as a way to tackle social disadvantage. The project is implemented by the non-governmental organisation Shedia, which supports homeless, refugees, migrants and people experiencing severe disadvantage. It is sponsored by organisations such as UEFA for Children and Stavros Niarchos Foundation as well as supported by individuals who serve as volunteers.
- 'Σέβομαι τη Διαφορετικότητα/Respect on Diversity' (British Council in Greece, 2022). 'Respect on Diversity' is sponsored by the Samsung in cooperation with the Olympic Truce organisation and the Greek Olympic Winners organisation. In brief, the project involves organising workshops and competitions with children in order to explore and elaborate constructively on the notions of respect, diversity, stopping bullying, and tolerance (British Council in Greece and International Olympic Truce Center, 2022).
- EU funded projects: Aspire (2017), Erasmus+ (2024), HEPA (2014), ZEP (2015), and BE Active/European Week of Sport (2019). For example, ASPIRE (2017) only focuses on including refugees and/or migrants and in tackling their social disadvantage through sport.
- Projects such as the project 'UrbanDig' that addresses how sport and arts can co-create urban space for the benefit of young people (Chatziefstathiou et al., 2019).
- Volunteer organisations, either supported by individual actions and/or financially supported by the Churches of Greece and Cyprus.

In Cyprus, there are similar projects that have been and are currently running to effectively tackle social disadvantage. Prominent among these are the initiatives for socially disadvantaged children named 'ZEP' (2010), 'AGO' and 'DRASE' (2014–2020). They are under the 'umbrella support' of the Cypriot Ministry of Education and are delivered at the facilities of specific schools or other indoor and outdoor facilities. Further, the EU-funded programmes such as Erasmus+, BE Active, and ASPIRE are also implemented at various locations in Cyprus. In addition, there are organisations – such as the Church of Cyprus – that support through charities socially disadvantaged young people. In addition, the Pedagogical Institute of Cyprus organises and implements seminars and workshops associated with the young people's social disadvantage within the education context where participants consist of students, teachers, and parents. However, there are currently limited seminars explicitly addressing the issues of social disadvantage through PE, SfA and overall physical activity and sport. Finally, a very significant initiative is 'Peace Players/Cyprus' (2015). 'PeacePlayers' is supported by the United Nations and constitutes the only year-round-bi-communal youth sports organisation on the island. Their aim is to:

> bring together the young people of the Greek-Cypriot and Turkish-Cypriot communities in order to 'play, learn and build meaningful friendships leaving behind generations of mistrust for a future of peace and unity'.
>
> (PeacePlayers, 2015)

Nevertheless, policy initiatives can indeed be effective in tackling and eliminating social disadvantage given certain criteria and circumstances (Price-Robertson, 2011). Stewart (2016), however, argues that policymakers who are concerned about creating and sustaining equal opportunities for all children must pay attention to children from disadvantaged family backgrounds. Morsy and Rothstein (2015) also critically note, that policymakers often resist accepting that non-school disadvantages necessarily depress outcomes – "rather, they look to better schools and teachers to close achievement gaps, and consistently come up short" (p. 4). Hence, when school improvement is not complemented by policies to narrow social class differences, students' chances of success are greatly diminished.

Research has documented that in the context of PE and SfA, disadvantage can be experienced in ways similar to those expressed within the general context of education (Azzarito et al., 2017; Zembylas, 2010a,b). Since the 1990s and as a result of this process of change and evolution, PE has been accompanied by educational reforms (Evans & Davies, 2004). All elements of PE and SfA, therefore, should not be divided but unified and orientated towards young people's learning, enjoyment, development of their critical consciousness and their overall empowerment as learners (Spaaij et.al., 2016; Freire, 1974/2010; Wellard, 2006a).

It is also important to highlight that PE and SfA share similarities and different aspects when implemented in countries other than Greece and Cyprus. For example, in Greece and Cyprus often PE takes place within the school environment and follows specific curricula, whereas SfA is implemented in specific facilities and deliver specific activities related and designed perhaps for disadvantaged young people. In Cyprus and Greece, PE and SfA share similarities and appear to be interlinked. A major reason for this is the fact that PE and SfA in Greece and Cyprus are mainly implemented in the same school *context and consist of activities from the current PE Curriculum.* eventhough they may not be 'ideal' for the disadvantaged young people. Our research in Greece and Cyprus showed that, for example, SfA activities rarely take place in facilities other than school context and are of no differrence from the ones of the PE Curriculum. Nonetheless, SfA should empower everyone and especially young people to look at sport and physical activity with mind, body, and heart wide open to safely 'build' communities that embrace social justice to be shaped in building safe and healthy communities that embrace social justice. PE and SfA appear to be the vehicle for school and communities to make their body acquire techniques and identities that characterise particular societies and the social order of these societies for addressing social disadvantage (Zembylas, 2020). In contemporary societies, 'perfection' appears to be the 'magic' word and the 'ideal' body is expected to be slim, slender, toned, and athletic. Hence, 'hierarchies of the body' develop in PE and SfA – overall in schools – and perhaps lead to discriminations based on notions such as 'body-ability', 'body-gender', 'body-class', 'body-ethnicity', 'body-size', 'body-shape'. and 'body-weight'. Consequently, these hierarchies can mean that, while some bodies are regarded as 'perfect' for the lesson, others that are seen as not conforming to the 'body ideal', may perceived as less worthy (Wellard, 2006a, 2012).

Hence, the role of PE and SfA in tackling social disadvantage among young people should be a major international and national (i.e., Greece and Cyprus) concern. International research has documented the employment of PE along with SfA in tackling elements that constitute social disadvantage in young people. Bailey et al. (2009) stated that:

purposeful engagement with the potential to engender positive social behaviours (such as cooperation, personal responsibility and empathy) in young people and to address a number of contemporary social issues relating to problematic youth behaviour [...].

(p. 9)

As such, PE and SfA has attracted much focus in policy agendas relating to issues surrounding youth disadvantage (e.g., Building Canada Fund, 2008; DRASE/CY, 2016; Shedia/Kick-Out-Poverty/GR, 2015; PESSCL and PESSYP-UK, 2003, 2008; PeacePlayers, 2015). Policies employing PE and SfA reflect the strong belief in the role of sport and physical activity along with physical education in addressing, changing, and improving attitudes and ways of elaborating on social disadvantage. Thus, popularised information and shared intergroup definitions should be used in order to enable critical awareness of the personal and socio-cultural reality (Freire, 1974/2010; Freire, 1970/2005). Enhancing PE and SfA should include revising the curriculum and the critical consideration and implementation of PE, physical activities (PA) and youth sport (YS) as Sport-for-All (SfA) always, though, in connection to real life and with an attitude towards tolerance and diversity in society. As Kirk (2010) argued "what comes first should be an investigation of the state of play, of current practices and the residual influence of the past" (p. 24). PE professionals (e.g., teachers, scholars, policymakers) should be expected therefore to collaborate and perhaps, draw upon research projects and scholarly texts, successful and effective past and current policies in order to adapt significant points into everyday practice (as it happens), and/or to create new ones (i.e., in the form of interventions), which could meet the needs of current contemporary social issues of disadvantage (e.g., ethnic minorities/multicultural society, unemployment, the world economic recession, migration and the refugee crisis) (Papadopoulou, 2016; Macrine et al., 2010).

Overall, engagement with PE and SfA has been associated with the development of positive outcomes. Danish et.al. (2005) suggested that physical activities are one of the most significant social arenas after family and school, which influences young people positively. As mentioned earlier, in Cyprus there are PE and SfA programmes (i.e., AGO) and ZEP (=Zone of Educational Priority initiative for disadvantaged young people) as well as DRASE (meaning in English=Initiate action!). The specific policy initiatives are mainly funded by the European Union and are implemented within the school facilities. The European Youth Portal supports 'Sport in Cyprus' and calls for all young people to participate in sports and physical activity that "will allow them to become stronger, not only physically but also mentally". The European Youth Portal describes AGO as "the Cyprus Organisation Programme that aims at healthy occupation of people with sports offering joy, wellness, entertainment, fitness and health"; however, SfA programmes that are exclusively targeted to counter social disadvantage are limited and are mainly delivered through the ZEP and DRASE programmes. Furthermore, the Youth Power organisation, arranges activities to promote peacebuilding and sustain multiculturalism in Cyprus. Youth Power is a network of 12 diverse Greek–Cypriot and Turkish–Cypriot organisations made to promote youth activism. In parallel, PeacePlayers (2015) employ basketball as a 'tool' to promote peace between children from the two communities (i.e., Greek–Cypriots and Turkish–Cypriots). Such camps are supported by the UN and funded through the European Union's Cypriot Civil Society in Action IV financial assistance package. This operates within the framework of the 'Promoting Peace and Wellness in Cyprus' project with the co-funding and support from the Embassy of the United

States in Cyprus, the Laureus Sport for Good Foundation, Adidas, and Jotun. Peace Players particularly advocate that "children who play together, can live together".

In Greece, PE holds a prominent role within the school context with volleyball, basketball, football, athletics, and traditional Greek dance being at the core. At the same time, SfA programmes for socially disadvantaged youth often are not exclusively organised by the Central Authority for Sport and/or the Ministry of Education – the EU also funds relevant projects such Erasmus+ (2024) and ASPIRE (2017). Local municipalities and the private sector organise SfA activities that target elements of social disadvantage; these however, are reported to be limited. SfA initiatives such as the EU-funded 'BE Active/Move Week' are organised once per year, but not with a specific target of addressing and tackling social disadvantage among young people; often it has to do with promoting overall wellbeing. Further, as mentioned earlier, projects such as 'Shedia/Kick-Out-Poverty/Γκολ στη Φτώχεια' employ football to tackle disadvantage whereas 'Κιβωτός του Κόσμου/Ark of the World' employs basketball to tackle disadvantage. Nonetheless, although both Greece and Cyprus are EU countries and employ the same PE curricula, as well as engage with similar PE and SfA policies, there are differences in the policy initiatives that are implemented. Hence, young disadvantaged people experience them differently (Papadopoulou, 2019). Hence, it is crucial for the programmes that are targeted at socially disadvantaged young people to be delivered from specialised teachers and/or coaches/trainers. Their training and professional development on issues that form social disadvantage and ways to tackle and prevent it through PE and SfA should be certainly enriched with contemporary knowledge and practices (Walton-Fisette & Sutherland, 2018).

Conclusion

This chapter has attempted to address issues raised by the international worldwide research (Bailey, 2018; Dagkas, 2018; Hill et al., 2018; Azzarito et al., 2017) and current EU policies and projects such as the Erasmus+ (2024) and the CORDIS-EDUHEALTH (2017–2019). The chapter delves deeper into the elements that constitute social disadvantage in young people and discusses how Sport, PE and SfA can have a positive impact in these young people's lives while bearing in mind negative traits of relevant programmes. The gravity of the phenomenon in youth has become prominent through, for example, forms of severe economic crisis; PE's and SfA's role is of great importance when addressing and dealing with social disadvantage to break down any barriers (Dagkas, 2018; Flintoff et.al., 2008). Nonetheless, the discourse about social disadvantage and about "what policy-makers do to tackle disadvantage" is increasing across the world and education is currently 'under pressure' to follow sport, PE, and SfA policies imposed by neo-liberal governments (Macrine et al., 2010; Penney, 2008) either effectively or not for these young people. Within such a context and within societies that experience severe crisis (i.e., Greece and Cyprus) PE and SfA, we argue, to have a seminal role to play in addressing and tackling social disadvantage while benefiting young people in various psycho-social ways (Zarrett et al., 2008) while benefiting young people in multiple and various ways from a psycho-social perspective. However, the PE curricula and the SfA programmes appear problems in their design, organisation, and implementation. Hence, even when they are implemented, there are significant problems and cannot be delivered to all disadvantaged young people and perhaps at times, they are not exclusively designed for socially disadvantaged young people. It is of utmost importance therefore to bear in mind the powerful impact that PE and SfA can have if designed, managed and delivered appropriately. For example, the staff should be trained appropriately and prepared through their initial training and further during their PE-CPD (continuing professional development) (Timperley, 2011). Key findings of our recent research which was completed right before the pandemic of COVID-19, overall suggests that although young people experience disadvantaged situations in their everyday life, especially related to class, gender, and race/ethnicity, PE and SfA hold a positive and significant role in countering their disadvantage; in other words, PE and SfA improve the quality of their everyday life since it offers them the opportunity. It offers them the opportunity for equal participation in the activities, in socialising with others in equal terms, in free-of-charge physical activity that enhances their physical and mental health. Thus, PE's and SfA's role as explored is definitely positive, yet only under certain circumstances. Furthermore, our research stressed that both generally and explicitly PE and SfA in these two regions can both be described as effective in tackling social disadvantage when they are:

- rooted and linked with modern and inclusive activities 'for all' which are selected especially for these young people;
- school-based, yet with opportunities to visit more and different facilities and with the potential to practise modern and various activities designed for socially disadvantaged young people;
- delivered by teachers and trainers who are exclusively trained for delivering PE and SfA to these young people.

Further, social disadvantage among young people is related to social class in terms of 'available resources' due to the impact of unemployment causing financial concerns; moreover, it is also related to race and ethnicity due to migration and the refugee crisis; last, it is related to the element of gender, that is, although everyone is allowed to participate, the activities available and the structure of the lesson/activity does not always promote participation from all. The notion of gender as socially constructed (Butler, 2004), elements of Bourdieu's theory as capital, taste, and habitus (Bourdieu et al., 2000) along with the ideas of Critical Race Theories (CRT) (Chadderton, 2013) can and perhaps must inform new projects and the overall training and the professional development of PE teachers. Moreover, teamwork, inclusive activities for all, appropriate ways of the professional delivering PE and SfA as well as the manner of the teacher/trainer are inseparable for a project's success. *Effective PE training and CPD for these types of young people were suggested to be collaborative and school-based and additionally, to include modern PE activities so they are informative about current social phenomena.* Last but not least, employing intersectionality as a research paradigm can provide a multidimensional understanding of young people's social disadvantage and PE's and SfA's role for this type of youth (Papadopoulou, 2019).

Concluding, there is a need for more international research to explore the issues discussed in this chapter. However, there have been a few projects tackling social disadvantage through PE and/or SfA activities such as Kick-Out-Poverty in Greece and DRASE in Cyprus. In Greece and Cyprus, research on social disadvantage, sport, PE, and SfA is limited and loaded with severe difficulties in its implementation. Indeed, if social disadvantage is to be considered important and relevant, their examination along with the role (and the provision) of PE and SfA should be centrally incorporated into rather than marginalised within research and educational policies in the two countries. Thus, future research should consider contributing to broader discussions through relating to the multiple dimensions of social disadvantage – not only, for example, to gender, race/ethnicity and class but perhaps on issues of access, ability/disability, assessment and religion. Hence, PE programmes should be designed taking account of current forms of social disadvantage (i.e., refugees; language barriers; gender and, race and social class barriers; modern activities). Further, such programmes should enable change, starting from the roots of the problems that perhaps cause and further reproduce disadvantage, e.g., gender issues, body image, and race/ethnicity. Consequently, the creation, the appropriate design and ultimately the implementation of PE and SfA programmes should meet the needs of young people according to current national and international situations. In particular, we suggest that there should be programmes targeting specific populations (e.g., disaffected young girls), involving PE activities that are of real interest for the young people (e.g., solo or team activities that are not overcompetitive) and in specific contexts. Furthermore, there should be programmes targeting specific problems that enable social disadvantage, such as girls' issues with the PE kit as well as boys engaging in activities other than football. Possibly, girls could themselves design their PE KIT and wear it; hence PE and art could be coupled to eliminate a significant barrier (Chatziefstathiou et al., 2019; Papadopoulou, 2016). Programmes and interventions therefore could enhance and employ the element of young people's creativity giving them voice within the given context and further implemented in order to sustain the programmes' effectiveness and success.

Moreover, it has been argued that PE, SfA, and the overall education contexts are often centrally imposed and determined by political imperatives (Fitz et al., 2006). It is indeed a challenging time for social theory. The employment of intersectional approaches in the field of PE and SfA hold the immense potential to offer new insights in research and future perspectives. Hence, post/decolonial critiques, intersectionality, class, gender, and race have set challenges for us – as scholars – to 'highlight' the so-called sociological imagination and to embrace a broader range of theorists and theoretical perspectives, in addition to those coming from Bourdieusian, Butlerian, CRT, and other feminist, critical realist and poststructuralist positions. Nonetheless, all aspects of social disadvantage in young people certainly need to be researched in depth especially in under-researched regions such as in Greece and Cyprus; with research to be located in relevant educational and social contexts, such as in schools in areas of crisis, in urban (i.e., deprived, high-risk) and, perhaps, in rural areas. We suggest that future projects founded in 'action-research' agendas and collaborations between communities of interest, at local, national, and international levels should be promoted and supported throughout the process. Concluding, future sport, PE, and SfA projects should not only be implemented and researched in Greece and Cyprus but also in other disadvantaged areas of the world; such programmes therefore should be designed and implemented effectively while demonstrating their complexities and interrelations through the lenses of intersectionality (Hankivski et al., 2014; Bourdieu, 2000; Butler, 2004) and CRT (Dagkas et al., 2019; Chadderton, 2013).

References

AGO – *Sports Programme, Cyprus* (2016) Available at: http://ago.org.cy/ (Accessed: 02.02.2016).
Ark of the World/Kivotos tou Kosmou (2019) Available at: https://www.kivotostoukosmou.org/en/ (Accessed: 01.02.2019).
ASPIRE (2017) Sports Programme. Available at: https://www.aspiresport.eu/2017 (Accessed: 25.03.2018).
Assari, S., Nikahd, A., Malekahmadi, M.R., Lankarani, M.M., & Zamanian, H. (2016) 'Race by gender group differences in the protective effects of socioeconomic factors against sustained health problems across five domains', *Journal of Racial and Ethnic Health Disparities*, doi: 10.1007/s40615-016-0291-3. Epub ahead of print. PMID: 27753050

Azzarito, L. & Hill, J. (2013) 'Girls looking for a "second home": bodies, difference and places of inclusion', *Physical Education and Sport Pedagogy*, 18 (4), pp. 351–375.

Azzarito, L. & Solomon, M. (2005) 'A reconceptualization of physical education: the intersection of gender/race/social class', *Sport, Education and Society*, 10 (1), pp. 25–47.

Azzarito, L. & Sterling, J. (2010) 'What it was in my eyes: picturing youths' embodiment in "real" spaces', *Qualitative Research in Sport and Exercise*, 2 (2), pp. 209–228.

Azzarito, L., Macdonald, D., Dagkas, S., & Fisette, J. (2017) 'Revitalizing the physical education social-justice agenda in the global era: where do we go from here?', *Quest*, 69 (2), pp. 205–219.

Bailey, R. (2018) 'Sport, physical education and educational worth', *Educational Review*, 70 (1), pp. 51–66.

Bailey, R., Armour, K.M., Kirk, D., Jess, M., Pickup, I., Sandford, R., & the BERA Physical Education and Sport Pedagogy Special Interest Group (2009) 'The educational benefits claimed for physical education and school sport: an academic review', *Research Papers in Education*, 24 (1), pp. 1–27.

Bauman, Z. (2010) 'Belonging in the age of networks', in Hannon, C. & Tims, C. (eds) *To Tackle the Challenges of Tomorrow, Young People Need Political Capital Today ... An Anatomy of Youth.* London: Demos, pp. 115–121.

BE Active/European Week of Sport (2019). Available at: https://ec.europa.eu/sport/week_en (Accessed: 02.05.2019).

Bhopal, K. (2018) *White Privilege. The Myth of a Post-Racial Society.* Bristol: Policy Press.

Booth, D. (2016) 'Disentangling race: re-narrating apartheid sport?', *The International Journal of the History of Sport*, 33 (15), pp. 1866–1883.

Bourdieu, P. et al. (2000) *The Weight of the World. Social Suffering in Contemporary Society.* France: Editions du Seuil.

British Council in Greece Respecting Diversity (2022) Available at: http://www.Respecting Diversity|BritishCouncilGreece (Accessed 15/06/2022).

Brooks, S.N., Matt, K., & Isais, S. (2017) 'Some kids are left behind: the failure of a perspective, using critical race theory to expand the coverage in the sociology of youth sports', *Sociology Compass*, 11 (2), pp. 1–14.

Building Canada Fund (2008) Available at: http://www.bcfontario.ca/english/about/index.html Accessed: 20/02/2009.

Butler, J. (2004) *Undoing Gender*. Psychology Press: CA Berkeley.

Casey, A. & Larsson, H. (2018) 'It's Groundhog Day: Foucault's governmentality and crisis discourses in physical education', *Quest*, 70 (4), pp. 438–455.

Chadderton, C. (2013) 'Towards a research framework for race in education: critical race theory and Judith Butler', *International Journal of Qualitative Studies in Education*, 26 (1), pp. 39–55.

Chadderton, C. & Edmonds, C. (2015) 'Refugees and access to vocational education and training across Europe: a case of protection of white privilege?', *Journal of Vocational Education & Training*, 67 (2), pp. 136–152.

Chatziefstathiou, D., Iliopoulou, E., & Magkou, M. (2019) 'UrbanDig Project: sport practices and artistic interventions for co-creating urban space', *Sport in Society*, 22 (5), pp. 871–884.

The City at a Time of Crisis: Transformation of Public Spaces in Athens, Greece (2013) ESRC Lead Research Organisation: University of Sussex – Principal investigator: Dalakoglou, D.

Dagkas, S. (2016) 'Problematizing social justice in health pedagogy and youth sport: intersectionality of race, ethnicity, and class', *Research Quarterly for Exercise and Sport*, 87(3), pp. 221–229.

Dagkas, S. (2018) 'Is social inclusion through PE, sport and PA still a rhetoric? Evaluating the relationship between physical education, sport and social inclusion', *Educational Review*, 70 (1), pp. 67–74.

Dagkas, S. & Hunter, L. (2015) '"Racialised" pedagogic practices influencing young Muslims' physical culture', *Physical Education and Sport Pedagogy*, 20 (5), pp. 547–558.

Dagkas, S., Azzarito, L., & Hylton, K. (eds) (2019) *'Race', Youth Sport, Physical Activity and Health.* 1st edn. London: Routledge.

Danish, S. J., Taylor, T. E., & Fazio, R. J. (2005) 'Enhancing adolescent development through sports and leisure', in Adams, G.R. & Berzonsky, M. P. (eds) *Blackwell Handbook of Adolescence.* Oxford: Wiley-Blackwell, pp. 92–108.

Darton, D. & Strelitz, J. (2003) *Tackling UK Poverty and Disadvantage in the Twenty-First Century. An Exploration of the Issues.* York: Joseph Rowntree Foundation.

Dean, H. (2016) 'Chapter 1. Poverty and social inclusion', in Dean, H. & Platt, L. (eds) *Social Advantage and Disadvantage*. Oxford: Oxford University Press, pp. 3–24.

DRASE Platform 2014 – 2020/Cyprus. Available at: https://eacea.ec.europa.eu/national-policies/en/content/youthwiki/44-inclusive-programmes-young-people-cyprus/ (Accessed: 11 June 2016).

EDUHEALTH – EU Research Project (2017–2019). Available at: https://cordis.europa.eu/article/id/418233-slotting-social-justice-into-school-health-and-physical-education (Accessed: 05/12/2018).

ERASMUS+ (2024) Available at: https://ec.europa.eu/programmes/erasmus-plus/node_en (Accessed: 10.01.2024).

Europe 2020 Strategy. Available at: https://ec.europa.eu/eu2020/pdf/COMPLET%20EN%20BARROSO%20%20%20007%20-%20Europe%202020%20-%20EN%20version.pdf (Accessed: 01.03.2016).

EUROPE – Investing in Children (2018) Available at: https://ec.europa.eu/social/main.jsp?catId=1060&langId=en (Accessed: 21.11.2018)

Evans, J. & Davies, B. (2004) 'Pedagogy, symbolic control, identity and health', in Evans, J., Davies, B.,& Wright, J. (eds) *Body Knowledge and Control – Studies in the Sociology of Physical Education and Health*. London: Routledge.

Fitz, J., Davies, B., & Evans, J. (eds) (2006) *Educational Policy and Social Reproduction. Class Inscription and Symbolic Control*. London: Routledge.

Fitzpatrick, K. & Santamaría, L.J. (2015) 'Disrupting racialization: considering critical leadership in the field of physical education', *Physical Education and Sport Pedagogy*, 20 (5), pp. 532–546.

Flintoff, A. (2018) 'Diversity, inclusion and (anti) racism in health and physical education: what can a critical whiteness perspective offer?', *Curriculum Studies in Health and Physical Education*, 9 (3), pp. 207–219.

Flintoff, A., Fitzgerald, H., & Scraton, S. (2008) 'The challenges of intersectionality: researching difference in physical education', *International Studies in Sociology of Education*, 18 (2), pp. 73–85.

FP7 2014-2020. (n.d.). Available at: https://ec.europa.eu/research/fp7/index_en.cfm (Accessed: 21.01.2016).

Freire, P. (1970/2005) *Pedagogy of the Oppressed. 30th Anniversary Edition*. Harmondsworth: Penguin/New York: Continuum.

Freire, P. (1974/2010) *Education for Critical Consciousness*. London: Continuum.

Giddens, A. & Sutton, P.W. (2017) *Sociology*. 8th edn. Cambridge: Polity Press.

Greek Statistics Authority (2018) Available at: http://www.statistics.gr/ (Accessed: 10.07.2018).

Hankivsky, O., Grace, D., Hunting, G., Giesbrecht, M., Fridkin, A., Rudrum, S., Ferlatte, O., & Clark, N. (2014) 'An intersectionality-based policy analysis framework: critical reflections on a methodology for advancing equity', *International Journal for Equity in Health*, 13, (119), pp. 1–17.

Hannon, C. & Tims, C. (2010) *To Tackle the Challenges of Tomorrow, Young People Need Political Capital Today … An Anatomy of Youth*. London: Demos.

HEPA (2014) Available at: http://www.euro.who.int/en/health-topics/disease-prevention/physical-activity/activities/hepa-europe (Accessed: 07.06.2015).

Hill, J. & Azzarito, L. (2012) 'Representing valued bodies in PE: a visual inquiry with British Asian girls', *Physical Education and Sport Pedagogy*, 17 (3), pp. 263–276.

Hill, J., Philpot, R., Walton-Fisette, J., Sutherland, S., Flemons, M., Ovens, A., Phillips, S., & Flory, S. (2018) 'Conceptualising social justice and sociocultural issues within physical education teacher education: international perspectives', *Physical Education & Sport Pedagogy*, 23 (5), pp. 469–483.

Horizon 2020. Available at: https://ec.europa.eu/programmes/horizon2020/en (Accessed: 20.09.2013).

Kirk, D. (2010) 'The practice of physical education and the social construction of aims', in Bailey, R. (ed.), *Physical Education for Learning. A Guide for Secondary Schools*. London: Continuum, pp. 15–25.

Macrine, S.L., McLaren, P., & Hill, D. (eds) (2010) *Revolutionizing Pedagogy. Education for Social Justice within and beyond Global Neo-Liberalism*. New York: Palgrave McMillan

McEvoy, E., MacPhail, A., & Enright, E. (2016) 'Physical activity experiences of young people in an area of disadvantage: there's nothing there for big kids, like us', *Sport, Education and Society*, 21(8), pp. 1161–1175.

Morsy, L. & Rothstein, R. (2015) *Five Social Disadvantages That Depress Student Performance. Why Schools Alone Can't Close Achievement Gaps*. Washington: Economic Policy Institute. Available at: http://www.shankerinstitute.org/sites/shanker/files/Morsey-Rothstein-07-06-2015.pdf (Accessed: 04.12.2016).

Osler, A. (2015) 'Human rights education, postcolonial scholarship, and action for social justice', *Theory & Research in Social Education*, 43 (2), pp. 244–274.

Paechter, C. (2012) 'Bodies, identities and performances: reconfiguring the language of gender and schooling', *Gender and Education*, 24 (2), pp. 229–241.

Pang, B. & Hill, J. (2018) 'Rethinking the "aspirations" of Chinese girls within and beyond health and physical education and physical activity in Greater Western Sydney', *Sport, Education and Society*, 23 (5), pp. 421–434.

Papadopoulou, F. (2016) *Disaffected Youth, Physical Education and School Sport and the Career long Professional Development*. Saarbrucken: Lambert Publishing.

Papadopoulou, F. (2019) *Social Disadvantage and the Role of Physical Education and Sport-for-All in Young People at Cyprus and Greece: Discourse of Social Class, Gender and Race*. PhD thesis. CCCU Research Space.

PeacePlayers [CYPRUS] (2015) Available at: https://www.peaceplayers.org/location/cyprus/ (Accessed: 02.02.2015).

Penney, D. (2008) 'Playing a political game and playing for position: policy and curriculum development in health and physical education', *European Physical Education Review*, 14 (1), pp. 34–49.

PESSCL Strategy (2003) Available at: https://www.education.gov.uk/publications/standard/Physical education/Page1/LTPES (Accessed: 02.10.2007).

PESSYP Strategy (2008) Available at: http://www.lrsport.org/page.asp?section=00010001001000100002&sectionTitle=Physical+Education+and+Sport+Strategy+for+Young+People (Accessed: 03.02.2009).

Price-Robertson, R. (2011) *What Is Community Disadvantage? Understanding the Issues, Overcoming the Problem*. Australia: Australian Institute of Family Studies.

Quarmby, T. & Dagkas, S. (2015) 'Informal mealtime pedagogies: exploring the influence of family structure on young people's healthy eating dispositions', *Sport, Education and Society*, 20 (3), pp. 323–339.

Scraton, S. (2018) 'Feminism(s) and PE: 25 years of shaping up to womanhood', *Sport, Education and Society*, 23 (7), pp. 638–651.

Shedia/Kick-Out-Poverty (2015) Available at: https://www.shedia.gr/kick-out-poverty/ (Accessed: 09.02.2016).

Shilling, C. (2018) 'Embodying culture: body, pedagogics, situated encounters and empirical research', *The Sociological Review*, 66 (1), pp.75–90.

Social Impact Bonds (Published online: 2012/Updated: 2017) Available at: https://www.gov.uk/guidance/social-impact-bonds (Accessed: 15.06.2018).

Spaaij, R., Oxford, S., & Jeanes, R. (2016) 'Transforming communities through sport? critical pedagogy and sport for development', *Sport, Education and Society*, 21 (5), pp. 570–587.

STATISTA CYPRUS (2022) Available at: http://www.statista.com/statistics/811950/youth-unemployment-rate-in-cyprus/ (Accessed: 15/12/2023).

STATISTA GREECE (2022) Available at: http://www.statista.com/statistics/812053/youth-unemployment-rate-in-greece/ (Accessed: 15/12/2023).

Stewart, K. (2016) 'The family and disadvantage', in Dean, H. & Platt, L. (eds) *Social Advantage and Disadvantage*. Oxford: Oxford University Press, pp. 85–111.

Timperley, H. (2011) *Realizing the Power of Professional Learning*. NZ: Open University Press.

Toft, M. (2018) 'Enduring contexts: segregation by affluence throughout the life course', *The Sociological Review*, 66 (3), pp. 645–664.

Wacquant (2013) Available at: http://voidnetwork.gr/wp-content/uploads/2016/08/Symbolic-power-and-group-making-On-Pierre-Bourdieu%E2%80%99s-reframing-of-class-by-Loi%CC%88c-Wacquant.pdf

Wacquant, L. (2018) 'Four transversal principles for putting Bourdieu to work', *Anthropological Theory*, 18 (1), pp. 3–17.

Walton-Fisette, J. & Sutherland, S. (2018) 'Moving forward with social justice education in physical education teacher education', *Physical Education & Sport Pedagogy*, 23 (5), pp. 461–468.

Wellard, I. (2006a) 'Able bodies and sport participation: social constructions of physical ability for gendered and sexually identified bodies', *Sport, Education and Society*, 11 (2), pp. 105–119.

Wellard, I. (2006b) 'Re-thinking abilities', *Sport, Education and Society*, 11(3), pp. 311–315.

Wellard, I. (2012) 'Body-reflexive pleasures: exploring bodily experiences within the context of sport and physical activity', *Sport, Education and Society*, 17 (1), pp. 21–33.

Wellard, I. & Secker, M. (2017) 'Visions for children's health and wellbeing: exploring the complex and arbitrary processes of putting theory into practice', *Sport, Education and Society*, 22 (5), pp. 586–601.

WHO (2013) Available at: https://www.who.int/whr/en/ (Accessed: 17.12.2015).

ZEP (Zones of Educational Priority) (n.d.) Available at: http://www.moec.gov.cy/dde/ep-zep.html (Accessed: 09.08.2015).

Zarrett, N., Lerner, R. M., Carrano, J., Fay, K., Peltz, J. S., & Li, Y. (2008) Variations in adolescent engagement in sports and its influence on positive youth development. In Holt, N. L. (ed.) *Positive Youth Development through Sport*. London: Routledge, p. 124.

Zembylas, M. (2010a) 'Greek-Cypriot teachers' constructions of Turkish-speaking children's identities: critical race theory and education in a conflict-ridden society', *Ethnic and Racial Studies*, 33 (8), pp. 1372–1391.

Zembylas, M. (2010b) 'Negotiating co-existence in divided societies: teachers, students and parents' perspectives at a shared school in Cyprus', *Research Papers in Education*, 25 (4), pp. 433–455.

Zembylas, M. (2011) 'Personal narratives of loss and the exhumation of missing persons in the aftermath of war: in search of public and school pedagogies of mourning', *International Journal of Qualitative Studies in Education*, 24 (7), pp. 767–784.

Zembylas, M. (2014) 'Unmasking the entanglements of violence, difficult knowledge, and schooling', *Religious Education*, 109 (3), pp. 258–262.

Zembylas, M. (2017) 'The contribution of the ontological turn in education: some methodological and political implications', *Educational Philosophy and Theory*, 49 (14), pp. 1401–1414.

Zembylas, M. (2018) 'Political depression, cruel optimism and pedagogies of reparation: questions of criticality and affect in human rights education', *Critical Studies in Education*, 59 (1), pp. 1–17.

Zembylas, M. (2020). 'Re-conceptualizing complicity in the social justice classroom: affect, politics and anti-complicity pedagogy', *Pedagogy, Culture & Society*, 28 (2), pp. 317–331. doi: 10.1080/14681366.2019.1639792

27
SOCIOECONOMIC STATUS IN SPORT AND LEISURE ENGAGEMENT

Adam Gemar

Introduction

Sport and leisure activities form a substantial part of the lives of many in contemporary societies around the world. These activities can be an important component in the collective culture of a place, particularly exemplified by the case of spectator sports, and form core pursuits for physical and mental well-being, affecting the health of both the individual and society. However, the time to participate in leisure activities generally, and the ability to access specific sport and leisure activities, is not evenly distributed. Therefore, the personal and collective benefits are likewise unequally distributed. The reasons for this unequal distribution are often the product of differential socioeconomic resources between people and specific groups of people within a given society and specific policies that underly that distribution.

For instance, the fandom composition of specific sports can be formed by followers from different geographic areas of a city or region that have substantially different socioeconomic conditions or ethnic make-ups that influence their sporting fandom. This can manifest itself in differing actual or reputational social compositions of the respective teams' fanbases, and their subsequent treatment by authorities or other fanbases. Likewise, the degree of economic and cultural barriers to entry greatly affects who engages in sport and leisure, how they do so, and society's reception of this engagement. Indeed, there has been much scholarly work done that affirmatively establishes connections between socioeconomic status (SES) and patterns of leisure engagement. This is the first step towards understanding how we can effectuate social justice in sport and leisure. This chapter seeks to introduce this body of research on SES in leisure engagement and the causes and manifestations of these inequalities found in that research. Starting with the socioeconomic inequalities bound up in the ability to have leisure time generally, this chapter goes on to examine how socioeconomic inequalities affect access to and participation in leisure and especially sporting activities, including spectator sports and the fandom of sport. It therefore generally introduces to readers the role of socioeconomic status in leisure and sport and provides concrete examples and details of SES's influence within a variety of leisure, sporting, and geographical contexts. Social justice in this area requires recognising and analysing these inequalities as socially mediated processes as a pre-requisite task for then forming new ideas by which there can be a more equitable socioeconomic distribution of sport and leisure access and participation (Hocking, 2017). The distribution of socioeconomic resources, such as material and monetary goods or education, rely heavily on such socially mediated processes. This chapter thus approaches social justice regarding socioeconomics in sport and leisure as being the equitable access to both quantity and quality of leisure and sporting engagement regardless of socioeconomic status or economic resources. This chapter ends with a brief overview of scholarship that investigates specific policy interventions which attempt to promote this type of equity and social justice.

Socioeconomic determinants of free (leisure) time

While perhaps not the first thing readers will think of when imagining economic resources, the presence of or ability to have free time is a marker of economic capital and can serve as a type of proxy for monetary resources (Bourdieu, 1984; Sorenson, 2014). This is not a new observation, however. For instance, scholarly work observing the economic determinants of free time and ability to participate in leisure activities extends back well over a century to observations and arguments made by Thorstein Veblen in his seminal work *The Theory of the Leisure Class* ([1899] 1934). For Veblen, the 'leisure class' was constituted by those who did not need to engage in regular paid work in the employment of others. During the time period in which Veblen writes (late nineteenth century), this categorisation is representative of the upper classes of societies around the world. Not only is this upper class the only group able to have leisure time available to them, but their ability to engage in leisure time and activities was a primary driver of social closure for this group. This is to say that by purposefully participating in leisure pursuits, this group was able to draw reinforcing boundaries around leisure activities as exclusive to the upper classes and likewise those in these classes as the only ones able to participate in them. This social closure was reinforced and reproduced by what Veblen ([1899] 1934) called "conspicuous consumption", a term with regards to leisure meant to capture the purposeful way in which the upper classes consumed, that is engaged in, leisure activity and flaunted their free time as distinguishing them from other social classes.

With regards to sport, this was also a time where there was little formal organisation of sport. There was little formalised control or apparatuses of competition as sport during this time, and especially in the Victorian-era Anglosphere and broader British empire where many of the sporting games popular around the globe today originated, sport was exclusively "the prerogative of upper and middle-class men ... to play and to socialize among themselves" (Morrow & Wamsley, 2010: 66). This was bound up in the concept of 'amateurism' in the early years of sport in these contexts. The ethos and codes around amateurism were meant to exclude anyone who participated in or around sport as a way to make a living. But it often extended beyond this focus of making money from participation in sport to exclude those in explicitly working-class occupations. For instance, the British Henley Rowing Club defined an 'amateur' rower who was worthy of membership as "one who is not, among other things, by trade or employment a mechanic, artisan or laborer" (Morrow & Wamsley, 2010: 65).

Beyond Britain, these ideals often became an export of sport through either cultural influence or colonial rule. For instance, in Canada during this period codes of amateurism functioned to "reproduce the social hierarchies of Victorian England and the British Empire and to maintain the primacy of sports as an expression of manly honor" (Kidd, 1996: 27). Those who were deemed to fulfil the values and ethos of amateurism during this period were thus white upper-class men. The element of social closure which amateurism provided was a prominent factor in reproducing ideals of upper-class masculinity in opposition to the traditional, more vulgar, labour of the working classes. Indeed, historians argue that the amateur concept of sport in the late nineteenth and early twentieth century was often used as a tool of class warfare (Morrow & Wamsley, 2010). This social closure was realised explicitly and implicitly by the types of policies described in the codes of sports clubs, the free time and monetary resources necessary to engage in sporting pursuits, the domesticity of middle and upper-class women of the time, and the touted 'superiority' of white values underpinning the ethos of amateurism during this period (Morrow & Wamsley, 2010: 169–171).

In the early part of the twentieth century, and accelerating in the aftermath of the Second World War in industrialised societies, there was a proliferation of the number and types of persons who had sufficient resources to engage in leisure pursuits. This was bolstered by the development of social welfare programs and advantageous labour laws for those employed so as to provide increased and more predictable amounts of free time by which in theory they could engage in leisure activities. In contemporary societies, there has in recent decades and continues to be a proliferation of leisure activities and those engaged in them on a global level, even as in some contexts free time to engage in leisure activities has not linearly increased with industrialisation (Chatzitheochari & Arber, 2012). Today, socioeconomic status continues to highly stratify the free time available to people, especially those of marginalised groups.

Perhaps the most obvious example of this is the free time afforded to women in societies around the world. When we speak of the concept of free time, this refers to the time available to engage in leisure apart from formal and informal work. Much of the informal work that people engage in are domestic obligations in and around the home, including childcare responsibilities. For instance, in a study of Canada and Australia, researchers found that the number of hours per week allocated to childcare responsibilities, both before and during the COVID-19 pandemic that started in 2020, were between 2 (Australia) and 2.5 (Canada) times higher than the number of hours men spent on childcare responsibilities (Johnston, Sheluchin, & van der Linden, 2020). This means substantially lessened free time for those women who are also in full employment, and substantially lessened economic means to pursue leisure for those women who engage in full time domestic work. Likewise, the authors conclude that the increased childcare responsibilities that fell upon women during the COVID-19 pandemic would likely have deleterious career effects for women (Johnston et al., 2020). Indeed, Clark et al. (2019) note that while there is a common perception that these types of childcare responsibilities do not meaningfully hamper economic activity and career prospects of women, they specifically found that "women's childcare responsibilities substantially inhibit their economic activity" (p. 1266) in their study of women in sub-Saharan Africa. Thus while women in some studies have been shown to have more formal leisure time than men in some national contexts, when informal work, such as childcare, is considered, women ultimately have less leisure time, fewer economic resources from which to participate in leisure, and face barriers of less social legitimacy of both their leisure time and the activities they choose (Katz-Gerro & Sullivan, 2010).

Socioeconomic resources therefore pattern both the resources by which one can engage in leisure activities, but also the amount of free time that one has to engage in leisure activities generally. Thus engagement in leisure might be hypothesised to generally reflect the distribution of resources within any given society, with marginalised groups possessing fewer of these resources in societies around the world, particularly based on characteristics such as race and ethnicity (e.g. Akee, Jones, & Porter, 2019; Lessmann & Steinkraus, 2019; Salata, 2020), gender (e.g. Connor & Fiske, 2019; Hong Vo et al., 2021; Fisher & Naidoo, 2016; Katz-Gerro &

Sullivan, 2010; Sullivan & Katz-Gerro, 2007), and immigration status (e.g. Malmberg & Clark, 2021; Tesfai & Thomas, 2019; Wang & Naveed, 2019), among others.

In terms of occupation and the availability of free time, Chatzitheochari and Arber's (2012) study of Britain finds that while during the weekdays those in high earning managerial and professional occupations and shift workers are similarly likely to be deprived of free time, those in the high earning managerial and professional occupations are most likely to have increased free time at the weekends. The availability of free time and socioeconomic position not only patterns how often one is able to participate in leisure, but also which types of activities one can engage in and the way in which they do so (Sullivan & Katz-Gerro, 2007). Thus socioeconomic status patterns more than just the availability and the amount of free time and leisure activity, it also very much influences the kinds of activities that one is attracted to and able to meaningfully access. In other words, these dynamics not only produce social injustices in the quantity of time available to access sport and leisure, but very much also produce injustices by precluding general access to certain activities or specifically excluding certain people from those activities.

Who engages in which types of sport and leisure activities and why?

Both the socioeconomic status of the individual participating in sport and leisure activities and the perceived socioeconomic status and prestige of the activity itself are both important influences that pattern the engagement with these activities and produce social injustices. One pioneering scholar of this perspective was the French sociologist Pierre Bourdieu. Bourdieu found substantial disparities in the kinds of leisure tastes that different social strata of French society had and the types of leisure activities in which they participated. In a broad sense, Bourdieu (1984) found that those of higher socioeconomic status engaged in more culturally venerated 'highbrow' activities, while those of lower socioeconomic status engaged in activities that were considered 'lowbrow'. Similar to the forces of social closure and status differentiation observed by Veblen, the social markers of 'distinction' argued for by Bourdieu (1984) relied upon the types of leisure that one engaged in and how they communicated that engagement. Bourdieu asserted that this patterning of taste and leisure activity choice was in large part influenced and inculcated by the socioeconomic conditions of one's upbringing and socialisation, something that he termed ones 'habitus' (Bourdieu, 1984). From these socioeconomic embedded dispositions towards which types of leisure activity one engages in, Bourdieu asserted 'homologies' of taste and leisure behaviour. This is to say that across the range of leisure activities, one would generally engage in activities congruent with their socioeconomic origins and socialisation on the 'highbrow' and 'lowbrow' spectrum. The patterns of this leisure engagement, and especially the ease with which one could navigate the physical and cultural environments of these activities conveys a type of 'cultural capital', an important component of socioeconomic status (Savage et al., 2013).

In an attempt to explain shifting patterns of leisure engagement and cultural consumption in North America, Richard Peterson and colleagues developed the 'omnivore thesis' of taste and participation (Peterson, 1992, 1997; Peterson & Kern, 1996; Peterson & Simkus, 1992). Within this framework, the omnivore is one who engages in a broad range of leisure activities and likes a broad range of cultural genres across the range of their associated social status, from highbrow to lowbrow. However, this did not mean that socioeconomic delineation faded away. Rather, it was found that those of higher socioeconomic status were the ones able to be omnivorous (Peterson, 1992; Peterson & Kern, 1996). This is both because this group is able to financially access a broad range of activities on a regular basis and culturally navigate the more socially exclusionary environments than those of lower socioeconomic status. Peterson (1992) coined the term 'univore' for many of lower socioeconomic status because they consumed very few or only one (lowbrow) genre of, in Peterson's case, music. Numerous studies since have likewise found that omnivorous patterns of leisure engagement and cultural consumption map strongly onto socioeconomic status (e.g. Gemar, 2019a, 2020a, 2020b; Sintas & Alvarez, 2002, 2004; Sullivan & Katz-Gerro, 2007; Tampubolon, 2008), while others argue that the cultural omnivore may actually be a manifestation of Bourdieu's theories of habitus and homology (e.g. Bennett et al., 2009; Coulangeon & Lemel, 2009; Leguina, 2015; Lizardo & Skiles, 2012). For instance, Jarness (2015) argues that it is the consistent SES based 'how' one consumes, rather than the consistent SES based 'what' one consumes that can also reflect habitus and homology concepts.

While there are relatively few studies that have assessed the concept of the omnivore as it pertains to sports engagement, and the sporting omnivore remains relatively under-researched (Gemar, 2019c; Widdop et al., 2016), there are indeed a handful of studies investigating omnivorous consumption of sport that have generally found that patterns of both omnivorous direct sports participation and professional sport following are characteristic of those from higher socioeconomic positions (e.g. Gemar, 2019b, 2019c, 2021a; Mutz & Müller, 2021; Widdop & Cutts, 2013; Widdop, Cutts, & Jarvie, 2016). There are therefore social injustices in the breadth of activities that people with different socioeconomic positions and economic resources can access. This extends even to areas of leisure, such as sport fandom or following sport, which on the surface might seem to require few resources, but in reality, are highly patterned by socioeconomic position.

Direct sports participation

These conceptions of the relationship between leisure engagement and socioeconomic status, and the social injustices produced thereby, also include the prominent leisure activity of direct participation in sport. Indeed, Bourdieu (1978) highlights the importance of the upper-class origins to a number of sports present in France and Britain during his time and how those origins continue to influence both their cultural (i.e. considered highbrow) and physical location (i.e. elite private schools [Collins, 2016], private members sports clubs, etc.). The lack of cultural capital and economic resources to access these types of activities have strong exclusionary effects (Collins, 2003, 2014) that contribute to social closure around who is able to participate in which types of activities. Indeed, a number of studies find results showing that direct participation in sport generally, or in which types of sport specifically, is stratified by socioeconomic position (e.g. Gemar, 2019a, 2021a, 2021b; Scheerder et al., 2002, 2005; Stempel, 2005, 2020). This is true even as a number of studies have found that those of elevated socioeconomic position participate more in the broad category of sport generally, and also more often attend sporting events (e.g. Hartmann-Tews, 2006; Kahma, 2012; Mehus, 2005; Moens & Scheerder, 2004; Thrane, 2001; White & Wilson, 1999; Wilson, 2002).

In one such foundational study, Wilson (2002) proposes a 'paradox' of social class and sports involvement. This paradox was that although those with higher incomes and education levels (i.e. economic and cultural capital) were more likely to participate in sports generally, those with higher levels of cultural capital were less likely to engage with 'prole' sports, that is sports associated with lower social status, either as a spectator or as a direct participant (Wilson, 2002). This supports Bourdieu's arguments around socioeconomically driven homologies of engagement across different leisure areas, where types of music, art, food, etc. are not just stratified according their engagement generally, but also within each of these domains there are additional hierarchies which are often patterned by the socioeconomic position of those who engage in them and the perceived social status of different genres or activities within a leisure category. Gemar (2019b) refers to these two similar but distinct axes of stratification in leisure activity 'inter-domain' and 'intra-domain', where stratifying patterns in broad categories (or domains) of leisure, such as sport broadly, represent inter-domain patterning and within these categories, such as which types of sport are engaged by those who do, represents intra-domain stratification. Regarding his findings, Wilson concludes that "class-based differences in economic capital enable upper class involvement in expensive sports, leaving "prole" sports largely relegated to the lower classes" (Wilson, 2002: 6).

A few prominent examples of how this stratification occurs, and the economic and cultural barriers by which only the upper socioeconomic bands of society can participate, among many others, include golf, downhill skiing, and particular to a few contexts, ice hockey, which all require specialised locations and equipment to access. Bourdieu (1978, 1984), for his part, often cites the example of golf as an example of a socially stratifying sporting activity and location of social closure. Both the availability of the game and the ability to access it have both been historically and contemporarily restricted, in both *de jure* and *de facto* ways. Historically, access to golf courses and especially golf clubs and organisations have been officially restricted based on physical characteristics. Women, racial and ethnic minorities, and Jewish people, among others, have all been restricted from accessing these spaces in the past, and in some cases the very recent past (Forster, 1951; Kirsch, 2007; Lipman-Blumen, 1976; Sawyer, 1993; Song, 2007). Even after the abolition of these kinds of formally discriminatory policies for access, more tangentially related formal and informal policies, such as housing discrimination and geographical housing segregation continue to inform the intersection between characteristics such as race and ethnicity with socioeconomic status.

Therefore, even beyond these types of historically aggregating barriers of the formal variety, access continues to be limited for a variety of economic and cultural reasons. For one, the geographical availability of golf courses depends on large tracts of land which require substantial monetary investment in themselves, substantial opportunity costs in terms of alternative development options for that land, and substantial upkeep costs. This is especially true in warm arid climates, where water has been and is increasingly in short supply due to climate change and the pervasiveness of drought conditions in many of these locations (Dai, 2013; Vincente-Serrano et al., 2020).

Because of the capital-intensive nature of both the investment and opportunity cost of investment, golf courses are often the product of private investment and ownership. In the United States, for example, there is a substantially higher number of fully private golf course facilities than there are golf course facilities which are publicly owned, with 25 per cent of golf course facilities fully closed to the public and only open for private members (National Golf Foundation, 2022). The other 75 per cent of golf course facilities that are open to the public in the United States, whether publicly or privately owned, require fees to play. These fees are often quite high. In addition, since 2006, there has been a decline in the number of golf courses, with a disproportionate number of these closures being so called 'value' courses – that is courses with greens fees to play a round of golf that fall under US$40 (National Golf Foundation, 2022). The national average and median costs for a round of golf in the United States, however, is higher than this figure (National Golf Foundation, 2021). In addition, between golf clubs, balls, and specialised clothing, start-up costs to participate in the sport run in the hundreds of dollars, and generally cannot be shared amongst a family due to size specificity (Gemar, 2019a). But socioeconomic barriers to this leisure activity, like others, is more than just about money and economics.

More culturally oriented considerations are also prominent barriers to entry to some elite forms of leisure, again with golf being a prominent example cited both in the scholarly literature and popular culture. These more cultural barriers are both in addition to and often linked with economic barriers. They also often revolve around physical comportment and dress, among other factors such as overall cultural fluency within one's surroundings and how well one can engage in relevant conversation in that environment (Gemar, 2019a). For example, Golf Canada, the governing body for golf in Canada, attempts to reassure prospective participants in the sport that they do not have to have the 'latest' golf clothing, and that many courses are 'relaxing' their dress codes (Gemar, 2019a). However, the need to have specialised clothing at all, let alone those which meet these dress codes, many of which are yet to be relaxed, is a substantial barrier to entry and to participation. One must still be able to know what constitutes and purchase the appropriate clothing and be comfortable enough that they are 'golf-appropriate', as well as be able to understand and navigate the historically crafted rules of etiquette that predominate in these environments (Ceron-Anaya, 2010). Even if many golf courses have only started to relax dress codes in recent years in an attempt to widen participation, new participants who take advantage of the more casual forms of dress may still participate along with legacy participants who still adhere to prior codes of dress. This may lead to feeling out of place and not belonging in such an environment. Thus these potential cultural barriers to entry for golf, both in formal and informal rules of dress and etiquette, serve to compound financial barriers and economic incentives by which physical access to these spaces is limited. Golf's both real and popularly conceived status as an elite sport requiring elevated forms of economic and cultural capital is also reinforced by its contemporary and historical connections with the business world and wealthy individuals (Ceron-Anaya, 2010).

Engagement with spectator sports

An arguably even more socially salient and widespread leisure activity than direct sports participation is the following of professional or other spectator sports, or the fandom thereof. Spectator sport is a prominent component of cultures around the world. Unlike direct participatory sport, people of all ages and backgrounds can in theory participate in the following or viewing of spectator sport in similar ways to each other. But is this true? While the financial, and even culture, barriers to access the direct participation in certain sports, especially elite sport, might seem relatively intuitive, the same arguably cannot be said for consuming spectator sport. For instance, there are a number of ostensibly easily accessible mediums (e.g. internet, TV, radio) by which one could follow one or more professional sports teams or leagues. So how does socioeconomic status impact engagement with the leisure form of spectator sport?

For one, the same kind of time constraints that pattern leisure generally applies also to the following of sport. This is especially true for following multiple sports. While the internet has increased the ability to follow sports scores and news more easily, and the proliferation of broadcast rights and streaming options make watching sports more convenient, one must still have the time to do so. This is especially true of watching sports, either on a screen or in person, as the time period of games, and thus the time required to watch them, has not substantially changed with technological advancement. However, Bourdieu (1978) argues that changes in modes of consumption and the increased availability of leisure options can cause "more or less a complete redefinition of the meaning attached to various practices" (p. 833).

One example of this is the English FA's Premier League. After its formation in 1992, there was a substantial uptick in leaguewide revenues, particularly from television rights contracts and corporate sponsorships (Pope, 2011). Match scheduling was substantially adjusted to meet the needs of television partners, global audiences rose, as did player transfer fees and ticket prices in kind (Holt & Mason, 2000). It has been argued that these changes were increasingly likely to disallow access for the traditionally working-class fan contingents of many of these teams (Giulianotti, 1999) as stadia were updated and clubs shifted focus to wealthier fans and families (Cleland & Giulianotti, 2023), something that is perhaps especially true for elite clubs in large metropolitan areas. Indeed, even as early as the late 1990s and early 2000s, studies found that attendance at English Premiership matches consisted disproportionately of those from the highest income groups and social classes, thus resulting also in the exclusion of those fans from lower social classes and with lower incomes (Feehan, Forrest, & Simmons, 2003). While in-person attendance has cost increasing amounts of money, the proliferation of matches available to watch on television or online ostensibly increases the availability for all people, even as some are behind various pay walls. However, while in theory breaking down access barriers, these types of changes in the mode of consumption can also lead to stratification between people who consume spectator sport via these difference modes. As ticket prices for in-person attendance increase, this stratification can entail a socioeconomic divide between in-person and other modes of spectating and following.

Similarly, the introduction of new sports leagues or teams into a context can shift the relative social status of both that league or team and other leagues or teams. This in turn can shift the socioeconomic makeup of fans and followers. For instance, the introduction of new sports leagues and teams to various contexts through the globalisation of the fan profile for elite European football (soccer) club teams and leagues has further decoupled fandom from a traditionally specific socioeconomic profile that is ostensibly working class in many of these contexts and relocated it within these new foreign contexts as a type of 'cosmopolitan' good (Gemar, 2020b). For instance, in the North American context, consuming 'the world's game', and perhaps especially elite European club football located in seemingly glitzy cosmopolitan locations such as Paris, London, Madrid, Barcelona, or Milan, can represent a cultural marker of distinction in the tradition of Bourdieu. It can help signal not only a type of "cosmopolitan cultural capital" (Prieur & Savage, 2013), but also of "openness" (Ollivier, 2008) that likewise confers a cultural marker of distinction and social status. This is also the case in non-Western contexts, where the openness to, and cosmopolitan consumption of, Western cultural products, such as sport, represents a type of cultural capital and is associated with elevated socioeconomic position (Bekesas, Mader, & Riegel, 2016; Lozada, 2008; Rankin, Murat, & Göksen, 2014; Rowe & Gilmour, 2009, 2010; Schwedler, 2010). Indeed, Ollivier (2008) argues that openness reflects "the persisting influence of socioeconomic inequalities and cultural hierarchies in the field of leisure and cultural consumption" (p. 143). Openness, cosmopolitanism, and generally stated appreciation of cultures other than one's own are often embedded in the ethos of the globally mobile classes and highly salient within higher education and other types of elite institutions (Gemar, 2020b). Therefore, these institutions often act to instil this type of cultural capital and serve a reproductive function for this element of socioeconomic position. This is also one reason that higher education is often used as a proxy for cultural capital in studies of socioeconomic engagement with leisure and sport, and why social justice in education likewise has a profound impact on socioeconomic injustices in other realms.

Conclusion

As discussed earlier in this chapter, one of the most fundamental valences of socioeconomic inequality when it comes to leisure activity is the ability to have free leisure time from which to engage those activities. Going back to our definition of social justice with regards to socioeconomic status in sport and leisure, this is an injustice regarding both the quantity and quality of leisure access, especially if certain pursuits require a minimum amount of time to meaningfully access them. Both free leisure time and monetary resources are needed to access desired forms of leisure pattern leisure participation, although neither by themselves are sufficient for leisure engagement (Bittman, 2002). In a public policy context, to promote social justice in this area, Bittman (2002) argues that income-based welfare reforms should consider the cost of leisure as a core component contributing to a 'leisure time poverty line' which is worthy of policy consideration.

Likewise, time considerations are the other core component of such a concept. With a complicated matrix of contributing factors, one prominent one is the fragmentation and decrease in free leisure time (Bittman, 2002), with parents less likely to participate in adult leisure activities (Bittman & Wajcman, 2000), again in a way that is often highly gendered. Public policies regulating the maximum number of paid work hours, providing subsidised childcare, paternity leave, and short to medium-term maternity leave have all been found to contribute to decreased labour time for women, particularly around childcare, although the contribution of these policies to the relative proportion to men's unpaid labour time is more mixed or unclear (Noonan, 2013). However, policies allowing for flexible work schedules and telecommuting may increase the discrepancy in leisure time available to men over women (Noonan, 2013).

Direct participation in sport and exercise activities have been stagnant or decreasing in a number of national contexts (Vail, 2007), especially among youth and in formal sport settings (e.g. Jeanes et al., 2022). It also remains quite low in many other contexts around the world. Both the drop in participation and generally low participation is particularly noticeable in populations that have never had equal access to participation, such as racial and ethnic minorities, gender minorities, sexual minorities, persons with a disability, and those from lower income households (US Department of Health and Human Services, 2019).

There are a number of different levels to sport policy by which participatory access for all socioeconomic groups can be improved. Beyond the individual and interpersonal levels where awareness, education, and positive role models are important, equity in sporting access really occurs at the organisational, community, and public policy levels, where monetary, volunteer, transportation and infrastructure resources help to facilitate equitable access to participation (Collins, 2004; US Department of Health and Human Services, 2019). The involvement of the government in providing these resources, the public policy to facilitate their equitable distribution, and government involvement in supporting and operating sporting facilities can facilitate easier and cheaper access by which socioeconomic barriers to participation can start to be alleviated (Szczepaniak, 2020).

When it comes to spectator sports, there has generally not been a substantial push to increase the socioeconomic diversity of audiences. This is partly due to the fact that spectator sports are fragmented into individual sports clubs that are often for profit and locked in off the field business competition in addition to on-field competition. While programs and policies to be welcoming to marginalised groups in these spaces such as women and racial minorities have become increasingly common at the team, league, and governing body level, the financial costs to access on the field content has continued to increased. Therefore, while there is a slow thawing in the social exclusion of women (Gemar & Pope, 2022), and generally outreach programs to ethnic minority groups or working-class areas which form local fanbases, there has generally not been fundamental socioeconomic shifts in access. Indeed, financial costs to go in-person to sporting matches frequently increase. While there is a proliferation of online and television sporting content, much of this additional content is behind paywalls. These paywalls likewise increase incrementally as broadcasting rights deals increase along with ticket prices and player salaries.

In conclusion, socioeconomic status and its intersections with other social inequalities fundamentally shapes the ability to access leisure time generally, producing injustices in the quantity of leisure access. When leisure time is available, socioeconomic status can likewise pattern leisure tastes and patterns of participation, greatly promoting injustices in the quality of leisure access and engagement. This can happen through either class-based preferences or socioeconomically based exclusionary barriers. With regards to sport, these processes affect both direct participatory sports and spectator sports to a substantial degree. Finally, a number of policy prescriptions have been suggested or shown to work towards social justice in these areas, with some varying success, in the ability for people to have equitable access to the quantity and quality of sport and leisure engagement regardless of socioeconomic position or economic resources.

References

Akee, R., Jones, M. R., & Porter, S. R. (2019). Race matters: Income shares, income inequality, and income mobility for all US races. *Demography*, 56(3), 999–1021.

Bekesas, W. R., Mader, R. V., & Riegel, V. (2016). Media and cultural consumption by young students in the city of São Paulo, Brazil: Evidences of digital divide, possibilities of cosmopolitanism. *Global Media Journal – Canadian Edition*, 9(1), 119–133.

Bennett, T., Savage, M., Silva, E. B., et al. (2009). *Culture, Class, Distinction*. London: Routledge.

Bittman, M. (2002). Social participation and family welfare: The money and time costs of leisure in Australia. *Social Policy & Administration*, 36(4), 408–425.

Bittman, M., & Wajcman, J. (2000). The rush hour: The character of leisure time and gender equity. *Social Forces*, 79(1), 165–189.

Bourdieu, P. (1978). Sport and social class. *Social Science Information*, 17(6): 819–840.

Bourdieu, P. (1984). *Distinction: A Social Critique of the Judgement of Taste*. Cambridge, MA: Harvard University Press.

Ceron-Anaya, H. (2010). An approach to the history of golf: Business, symbolic capital, and technologies of the self. *Journal of Sport and Social Issues*, 34(3), 339–358.

Chatzitheochari, S., & Arber, S. (2012). Class, gender and time poverty: A time-use analysis of British workers' free time resources. *British Journal of Sociology*, 63(3), 451–471.

Clark, S., Kabiru, C. W., Laszlo, S., & Murthuri, S. (2019). The impact of childcare on poor urban women's economic empowerment in Africa. *Demography*, 56(4), 1247–1272.

Cleland, J., & Giulianotti, R. (2023). A sociological analysis of United Kingdom Football Fans: Historical debates and contemporary issues. In: Buarque de Hollanda, B. & Busset, T. (eds) *Football Fandom in Europe and Latin America* (pp. 37–57). Cham: Palgrave Macmillan.

Collins, M. F. (2003). Social exclusion from sport and leisure. In: Houlihan, B (ed.) *Sport and Society: A Student Introduction* (pp. 67–88). London: SAGE.

Collins, M. F. (2004). Sport, physical activity and social exclusion. *Journal of Sports Sciences*, 8, 727–740.

Collins, M. F. (2014). *Sport and Social Exclusion*. New York: Routledge.

Collins, T. (2016). *The Oval World: A Global History of Rugby*. London: Bloomsbury Sport.

Connor, R. A., & Fiske, S. T. (2019). Not minding the gap: How hostile sexism encourages choice explanations for the gender income gap. *Psychology of Women Quarterly*, 43(1), 22–36.

Coulangeon, P., & Lemel, Y. (2009). The homology thesis: Distinction revisited. In: Karen, R. & Chris, S. (eds) *Quantifying Theory: Pierre Bourdieu* (pp. 47–60). Springer.

Dai, A. (2013). Increasing drought under global warming in observations and models. *Nature Climate Change*, 3, 52–58.

Feehan, P., Forrest, D., & Simmons, R. (2003). Premier league soccer: Normal or inferior good? *European Sport Management Quarterly*, 3(1), 31–45.

Fisher, B., & Naidoo, R. (2016). The geography of gender inequality. *Plos One*, 11(3), 1–10.

Forster, A. (1951). America's disadvantaged minorities: The American Jew. *The Journal of Negro Education*, 20(3), 310–319.

Gemar, A. (2019a). *Sport as Culture: Social Class, Styles of Cultural Consumption, and Sports Engagement in Canada*. Durham theses, Durham University. Available at Durham E-Theses Online: http://etheses.dur.ac.uk/13434/

Gemar, A. (2019b). The stratification of professional sports following: Social position and the consumption of major professional sports leagues in Canada. *Leisure Studies*, 38(6), 775–789.

Gemar, A. (2019c). Which sports do you like? Testing intra-domain omnivorousness in Canadian following of professional sport. *International Review for the Sociology of Sport*, 54(7), 813–836.

Gemar, A. (2020a). Sport as culture: Social class, styles of cultural consumption and sports participation in Canada. *International Review for the Sociology of Sport*, 55(2), 186–208.

Gemar, A. (2020b). Sport in broader leisure lifestyles: An analysis of the professional sport consumer's cultural engagement. *International Review for the Sociology of Sport*, 55(3), 291–309.

Gemar, A. (2021a). Social capital networks in sports spectatorship and participation. *International Review for the Sociology of Sport*, 56(7), 813–836.

Gemar, A. (2021b). The social patterning of sport: Dispositions in regular sports participation and stratification in Canada. *World Leisure Journal*, 63(4), 390–410.

Gemar, A., & Pope, S. (2022). Women's consumption of men's professional sport in Canada. Evidence of the 'feminization' of sports fandom and women as omnivorous sports consumers? *International Review for the Sociology of Sport*, 57(4), 552–574.

Giulianotti, R. (1999). *Football: A Sociology of the Global Game*. Cambridge: Polity Press.

Hartmann-Tews, I. (2006). Social stratification in sport and sport policy in the European Union. *European Journal for Sport and Society*, 3(2), 109–124.

Hocking, Clare. (2017). Occupational justice as social justice: The moral claim for inclusion. *Journal of Occupational Science*, 24(1), 29–42.

Holt, R., & Mason, T. (2000). *Sport in Britain 1945-2000*. Oxford: Blackwell Publishing.

Hong Vo, D., Van, L. T.-H., Tran, D. B., Vu, T. N., & Ho, C. M. (2021). The determinants of gender income inequality in Vietnam: A longitudinal data analysis. *Emerging Markets Finance and Trade*, 57(1), 198–222.

Jarness, V. (2015). Modes of consumption: From 'what' to 'how' in cultural stratification research. *Poetics*, 53(1), 65–79.

Jeanes, R., Penney, D., O'Connor, J., Spaaij, R., O'Hara, E., Magee, J., & Lymbery, L. (2022). Spatial justice, informal sport and Australian community sports participation. *Leisure Studies* (online first). https://doi.org/10.1080/02614367.2022.2085772

Johnston, R. M., Sheluchin, A., & van der Linden, C. (2020). Evidence of exacerbated gender inequality in child care obligations in Canada and Australia during the COVID-19 pandemic. *Politics and Gender*, 16(4), 1131–1141.

Kahma, N. (2012). Sport and social class: The case of Finland. *International Review for the Sociology of Sport*, 47(1), 113–130.

Katz-Gerro, T., & Sullivan, O. (2010). Voracious cultural consumption: The intertwining of gender and social status. *Time and Society*, 19(2): 193–219.

Kidd, B. (1996). *Struggle for Canadian Sport*. Toronto: University of Toronto Press.

Kirsch, G. B. (2007). Municipal golf and civil rights in the United States, 1910-1965. *The Journal of African American History*, 92(3), 371–391.

Leguina, A. (2015). Musical distinctions in England – Understanding cultural homology and omnivourism through a methods comparison. *Bulletin of Sociological Methodology/Bulletin de Méthodologie Sociologique*, 126(1), 28–45.

Lessman, C., & Steinkraus, A. (2019). The geography of natural resources, ethnic inequality and civil conflicts. *European Journal of Political Economy*, 59, 33–51.

Lipman-Blumen, J. (1976). Toward a homosocial theory of sex roles: An explanation of the sex segregation of social institutions. *Signs: Journal of Women in Culture and Society*, 1(3), 15–31.

Lizardo, O., & Skiles, S. (2012). Reconceptualizing and theorizing "omnivorousness": Genetic and relational mechanisms. *Sociological Theory*, 30(4), 263–282.

Lozada, E. P. Jr. (2008). Cosmopolitanism and nationalism in Shanghai sports. *City and Society*, 18(2), 207–231.

Malmberg, B., & Clark, W. A. V. (2021). Migration and neighborhood change in Sweden: The interaction of ethnic choice and income constraints. *Geographical Analysis*, 53(2), 259–282.

Mehus, I. (2005). Distinction through sport consumption: Spectators of soccer, basketball, and ski jumping. *International Review for the Sociology of Sport*, 40(3), 321–333.

Moens, M., & Scheerder, J. (2004). Social determinants of sports participation revisited: The role of socialization and symbolic trajectories. *European Journal for Sport and Society*, 1(1), 35–49.

Morrow, D., & Wamsley, K. B. (2010). *Sport in Canada: A History*. Oxford: Oxford University Press.

Mutz, M., & Müller, J. (2021). Social stratification of leisure time exercise activities: Comparison of ten popular sports activities. *Leisure Studies*, 40(5), 597–611.

National Golf Foundation. (2021). *Green fee changes and the cost of golf*. National Golf Foundation. Available at: https://www.ngf.org/green-fee-changes-and-the-cost-of-golf/

National Golf Foundation. (2022). *The Graffis Report 2022: Golf industry 2021 – Year in review*. National Golf Foundation. Available at: https://www.ngf.org/product/the-graffis-report-2022/

Noonan, M. (2013). The impact of social policy on the gendered division of housework. *Journal of Family Theory & Review*, 5(2), 124–134.

Ollivier, M. (2008). Modes of openness to cultural diversity: Humanist, populist, practical, and indifferent. *Poetics*, 36(2–3), 120–147.

Peterson, R. A. (1992). Understanding audience segmentation: From elite and mass to omnivore and univore. *Poetics*, 21(4), 243–258.

Peterson, R. A. (1997). The rise and fall of highbrow snobbery as a status marker. *Poetics*, 25(2–3), 75–92.

Peterson, R. A., & Kern, R. M. (1996). Changing highbrow taste: From snob to omnivore. *American Sociological Review*, 61(5), 900–907.

Peterson, R. A., & Simkus, A. (1992). How musical tastes mark occupational status groups. In: Lamont, M. & Fournier, M. (eds) *Cultivating Differences Symbolic Boundaries and the Making of Inequality* (pp. 152–186). Chicago, IL: University of Chicago Press.

Pope, S. (2011). 'Like pulling down Durham Cathedral and building a brothel': Women as 'new consumer' fans? *International Review for the Sociology of Sport*, 46(4), 471–487.

Prieur, A., & Savage, M. (2013). Emerging forms of cultural capital. *European Societies*, 15(2), 247–267.

Rankin, B., Murat, E., & Göksen, F. (2014). A cultural map of Turkey. *Cultural Sociology*, 8(2), 159–179.

Rowe, D., & Gilmour, C. (2009). Global sport: Where Wembley Way meets Bollywood Boulevard. *Journal of Media and Cultural Studies*, 23(2), 171–182.

Rowe, D., & Gilmour, C. (2010). Sport, media, and consumption in Asia: A merchandised milieu. *American Behavioral Scientist*, 53(10), 1530–1548.

Salata, A. (2020). Race, class and income inequality in Brazil: A social trajectory analysis. *Dados rev. cienc. Sociais*, 63(3), 1–40.

Savage, M., Devine, F., Cunningham, N., Taylor, M., Li, Y., Hjellbrekke, J., Le Roux, B., Friedman, S., & Miles, A. (2013). A new model of social class? Findings from the BBC's Great British class survey experiment. *Sociology*, 47(2), 219–250.

Sawyer, T. H. (1993). Private golf clubs: Freedom of expression and the right to privacy. *Marquette Sports Law Review*, 3(2), 187–213.

Scheerder, J., Vanreusel, B., Taks, M., et al. (2002). Social sports stratification in Flanders 1969-1999: Intergenerational reproduction of social inequalities? *International Review for the Sociology of Sport*, 37(2), 219–245.

Scheerder, J., Vanreusel, B., & Renson, R. (2005). Social stratification patterns in adolescents' active sports participation behaviour: A time trend analysis 1969–1999. *European Physical Education Review*, 11(1), 5–27.

Schwedler, J. (2010). Amman cosmopolitan: Spaces and practices of aspiration and consumption. *Comparative Studies of South Asia, Africa and the Middle East*, 30(3), 547–562.

Sintas, J. L., & Alvarez, E. G. (2002). Omnivores show up again: The segmentation of cultural consumers in Spanish social space. *European Sociological Review*, 18(3), 353–368.

Sintas, J. L., & Alvarez, E. G. (2004). Omnivore versus univore consumption and its symbolic properties: Evidence from Spaniard's performing arts attendance. *Poetics*, 32(6), 471–491.

Song, E. (2007). No women (and dogs) allowed: A comparative analysis of discriminating private golf clubs in the United States, Ireland, and England. *Washington University Global Studies Law Review*, 181, 1–24.

Sorensen, C. (2014). Why Canadian golf is dying. The culprits: Greed, hubris and the demise of free time. *Macleans*. Available at: https://www.macleans.ca/economy/business/the-end-of-golf/

Stempel, C. (2005). Adult participation sports as cultural capital: A test of Bourdieu's theory of the field of sports. *International Review for the Sociology of Sport*, 40(4), 411–432.

Stempel, C. (2020). Sport as high culture in the USA. *International Review for the Sociology of Sport*, 55(8), 1167–1191.

Sullivan, O., & Katz-Gerro, T. (2007). The omnivore thesis revisited: Voracious cultural consumers. *European Sociological Review*, 23(2), 123–137.

Szczepaniak, M. (2020). Public sport policies and health: Comparative analysis across European Union countries. *Journal of Physical Education and Sport*, 20(2), 1022–1030.

Tampubolon, G. (2008). Revisiting omnivores in America circa 1990s: The exclusiveness of omnivores? *Poetics*, 36(2–3), 243–264.

Tesfai, R., & Thomas, K. J. A. (2019). Dimensions of inequality: Black immigrants' occupational segregation in the United States. *Sociology of Race and Ethnicity*, 6(1), 1–21.

Thrane, C. (2001). Sport spectatorship in Scandinavia: A class phenomenon? *International Review for the Sociology of Sport*, 36(2), 149–163.

US Department of Health and Human Services. (2019). *National Youth Sports Survey*. Washington, DC: US Department of Health and Human Services.

Vail, S. E. (2007). Community development and sport participation. *Journal of Sport Management*, 21(4), 571–596.

Veblen, T. ([1899] 1934). *The Theory of the Leisure Class: An Economic Study of Institutions*. New York: Modern Library.

Vincente-Serrano, S. M., Quiring, S. M., Pena-Gallardo, M., Yuan, S., & Dominguez-Castro, F. (2020). A review of environmental droughts: Increased risk under global warming? *Earth Science Reviews*, 201, 1–84.

Wang, C., & Naveed, A. (2019). The social inclusion and inequality nexus: EU versus non-EU migrants. *International Migration*, 57(3), 41–62.

White, P., & Wilson, B. (1999). Distinctions in the stands: An investigation of Bourdieu's 'habitus', socioeconomic status and sport spectatorship in Canada. *International Review for the Sociology of Sport*, 34(3), 245–264.

Widdop, P., & Cutts, D. (2013). Social stratification and sports participation in England. *Leisure Sciences*, 35(2), 107–128.

Widdop, P., Cutts, D., & Jarvie, G. (2016). Omnivorousness in sport: The importance of social capital and networks. *International Review for the Sociology of Sport*, 51(5), 596–616.

Wilson, T. C. (2002). The paradox of social class and sports involvement: The roles of cultural and economic capital. *International Review for the Sociology of Sport*, 37(1), 5–16.

28
ADDRESSING POWER DYNAMICS IN DISABILITY SPORT STUDIES

Emancipatory participatory principles for social justice research

Damian Haslett

In terms of advancing social justice, disability sport research has reached a critical juncture. Up to now, the field has done a valuable job in describing and highlighting the oppression and inequalities that disabled people face in and around various sport and exercise contexts. Nevertheless, as Long, Fletcher, and Watson (2017) said "social justice research is more than simply assessing the existence of disadvantage, it is about embedding and assessing research influence and impact" (p. 1). In this chapter I will argue that while raising awareness of injustices in sport and society is a necessary step, disability sport research to promote social justice needs to focus more on *the advocacy necessary to shift power relations in the production of such research itself*. Moreover, I will suggest some theoretical, methodological, and practical steps to help towards this, as well as discuss challenges involved in addressing power dynamics in the production of research.

Over the last decade, social scientific research interested in disability and sport has experienced a surge of momentum (Brighton, Howe, & Powis, 2023). Although not always explicitly about 'social justice' per se, much of this research engaged with increasingly diverse theories and methodologies to raise awareness and expose issues around disadvantage and inequalities, and the lack of access to rights, opportunities, and resources (see Powis, Brighton, & Howe, 2023). While this body of research has created a useful foundation to think about disability, sport, and social justice, it is evident that the field has now reached a crossroads in terms of producing research to shift social relations in the direction of a more just world. Recognising that there is no one 'right' approach to social justice research, an argument that I and others (e.g. Powis et al., 2023; Smith, Williams, Bone, & the Moving Social Work Co-production Collective, 2022) have made, is that disability sport studies are producing far too much research that talks *about* disabled people people *without* including disabled people across the production of research in meaningful ways. For example, Spencer and Molnár (2022) reviewed paradigmatic trends in the field over the last 40 years and found minimal involvement of people experiencing disability in research in roles other than as a traditional 'participant'.

If this trend continues, we are in danger of producing research that reproduces this 'status quo' at the expense of working towards producing research for transformative justice. The lack of meaningful involvement of disabled people in research has also contributed towards research directions that are creating barriers to producing and advocating for social justice research (Powis et al., 2023). For example, there has been a dominance of positivist scientific work at the expense of research from a critical theory perspective (Spencer & Molnár, 2022). There has also been an overemphasis on research designs exposing the social and political barriers to participation in sport and exercise for disabled people, at the expense of working with disabled people to find suitable ways to challenge such barriers (Ballas, Buultjens, Murphy, & Jackson, 2022). This traditional focus on structural barriers has also led to a lack of research that foregrounds individual experiences of disabled people in sport. Research that connects with disability theory (discussed in the following sub-section) tends to focus more on individual human rights and single identity understandings of disability at the expense of connections to intersectional identities, ableist ideologies, disability justice, and power dynamics in research, sport, and society. The fact that critical theory research tends to focus more on inequalities in and around the elite Paralympic sport systems (see e.g. Howe, 2019) at the expense of recreational sport and exercise contexts, is also a problem towards promoting social justice. All these directions have contributed to the production of undertheorised descriptive journal articles and a failure to engage with innovative theoretical research frameworks required to produce or advocate for social justice research (Howe, Powis, & Brighton, 2023).

While much of this 'traditional' research is indeed high-quality, to change direction and produce disability sport research for transformative justice, the call is now clear for a much stronger connection with disability theory and ideas from the field of critical disability studies. Drawing on writings from disability sport scholars interested in social justice (Adamson, Adamson, Clarke, Richardson, & Sydnor, 2022; Fitzgerald, 2009; Fitzgerald & Long, 2017; Macbeth, 2010; Peers, 2017; Peers, Spencer-Cavaliere, & Eales, 2014; Richard, Joncheray, & Duquesne, 2023; Smith & Perrier, 2015; Stride & Fitzgerald, 2017), I often argue that the problem with the field of disability sport studies, in terms of producing social justice research, is that it looks and feels very different to the wider field of critical disability studies (Goodley, Lawthom, Liddiard, & Runswick-Cole, 2019). With this as my starting point, this chapter will first focus on how scholars and researchers can think about new ways to produce social justice and *disability justice* research through a robust engagement with disability theory and critical disability studies. This chapter goes on to discuss how adopting emancipatory participatory approaches can help to address power differences by producing research that is designed *with* or *by* disabled people, rather than *on*, *about* or *for* disabled people. Then, after highlighting some limitations of participatory terms connected to emancipatory approaches, I will offer some practical guidance for researchers to develop *bespoke participatory principles* to include disabled people in the design and production of their research. This chapter will close by addressing challenges involved in advocating for these social justice principles and approaches within academic systems and structures.

The aim of this chapter therefore is to provide some practical guidance for researchers and scholars, at all stages in their development, to produce and advocate for social justice research required to promote a socially just society. Throughout this chapter I will signpost to helpful literature and draw upon my own experiences in research (e.g. Haslett & Smith, 2022; Haslett, Griffiths, & Lupton, 2024), to help to shift power relations in the production of disability sport research.

Thinking about social justice research with disability theory and critical disability studies

A key purpose of theory is to intervene in the social world (Goodley et al., 2019). Over the last three decades, the field of disability studies – more recently referred to as 'critical disability studies' – produced a body of theoretical work that can help disability sport studies take social justice research seriously. The theoretical foundations of 'disability studies' radically shifted social understandings of disability from dominant notions of individual deficit to a political category around which to mobilise (see Barnes & Mercer, 1997, 2003; Barnes, Mercer, & Shakespeare, 1999; Morris, 1996; Oliver, 1990; Thomas, 1999). Central to these foundations included the development of a social model understanding of disability that has proven to be an incredibly powerful tool for effecting social change and promoting social justice (Griffiths, 2022; Oliver, 2013). The social model understanding of disability was developed by disabled people as a guide for social action. It draws a theoretical distinction between impairment (an individual difference) and disability (the social situation). *Disability* consists of the many barriers that a person with *impairment* experiences because of the way in which society is organised that excludes or devalues them. For example, the United Nations Convention on the Rights for Persons with Disabilities (CRPD) is based on the principles of the social model, including the principles of non-discrimination and full and effective participation and inclusion in society. While disability sport research often connects with social and human rights models of disability (Smith & Bundon, 2018), social justice research requires more theoretical imagination (Brighton et al., 2023), and this can be obtained through engagement in critical disability studies.

Critical disability studies offer a necessary progression from the central theoretical arguments in 'disability studies' (e.g. social and human rights models of disability) including recognition of the intersectionality of disability alongside other important and politicised dimensions of identity, such as gender, sexuality, race, and class (see Feely, 2016; Flynn, 2017; Goodley, 2012, 2014, 2016; Goodley et al., 2019; Liddiard, 2018; Mallett & Runswick-Cole, 2014; Shildrick, 2012). Or as encapsulated by Smith and Perrier (2015) from a disability sport research perspective:

> critical disability studies are committed to exposing injustice through challenging dogmatic theoretical approaches, engaging with thinking from multiple academic disciplines, emphasising community, social change, and well-being, moving "beyond thinking about disabled people to thinking with disabled people" (italics in original) and including culture, the body, impairment, and narrative approaches in exploring the experiences of disabled people.
>
> (p. 97)

In recent years, disability sport scholars who engaged with disability theory and critical disability studies have contributed to research in different ways. For example, Adamson et al. (2022) produced a manifesto for social justice through sport and exercises studies, that considered how injustices along other axes of difference such as class or gender cannot be completely understood without taking disability into account (see also Mladenov, 2016). Macbeth and Powis (2023) advocated that research on disability sport would be richer if more researchers reflected on their status related to disability and how this influenced the decision-making process. Monforte, Gibson, Goodley, and Smith (2023) highlighted critical disability studies uneasy relationship with exercise and rehabilitation and how researchers can reconcile this through Posthumanist thinking. Scholars have also used intersectionality as an analytical tool by connecting disability and sport with experiences of gender (Culver, Shaikh, Alexander, & Fournier, 2022), race (Irish, McDonald, & Cavallerio, 2023), ageing (Brighton, 2023), and sexuality (Wheeler & Peers, 2023). Silva (2023), moreover, explored the possibilities of employing an anti-ableist lens in disability sport research. In addition, drawing on Global South Disability Studies (see e.g. Chataika, 2018; Grech, 2011; Grech & Goodley, 2012), Swartz (2023) critiqued a trend in ambitious 'colonialist' projects, led in the Global North, that make big claims about using Paralympic sport for development in Sub-Saharan Africa, but are based on Eurocentric notions of disability and social change. He urged researchers from the Global North who are interested in social justice to think globally but be prepared to work locally, over time, *with* disabled people and disability activists in the Global South.

While these recent contributions enable scholars to advocate for more social justice research, there is a lack of disability sport studies that centres 'disability justice'. To rethink how research is produced, Fine (2019) challenged researchers to engage in anti-ableist work that centres *disability justice* through the lens of critical disability studies. Disability justice is a social justice movement that employs a cross-disability framework and values access, self-determination, and an expectation of difference (Berne, Morales, Langstaff, & Sins Invalid, 2018). Fine (2019) called for disability justice research to contest normalcy and binaries. For example, disability sport scholars to produce work to challenge categorisations that are grounded on the normativity, such as the classification system in Paralympic sport. Centring disability justice also requires researchers to theorise and organise through intersectionality and an engaged understating of ableism (Fine, 2019). Ableism purports that there is an ideal 'being', intersected by dominant traits of gender, race, sexuality, abledness, and class (Campbell, 2009). For example, scholars should engage with the concept of disability justice to enable critical conversations about ableism in sport and popular discourse, to seeks way to transform sport to be more accessible and inclusive. This can be done through designing critical participatory inquiry projects that centre the experience and expertise of disabled persons, that are led by those most impacted by an ableist ideology.

As discussed, thinking with disability theory and ideas from critical disability studies, such as disability justice, can help scholars to re-imagine and develop new approaches to social justice research. However, we should also be cautious of theory, as over theorisation can muddy the waters of political intent. We should be sceptical of theoretical musings that replace activism and the emancipation of disabled people (Brighton et al., 2023). Therefore, to produce social justice research grounded in theory from critical disability studies, emancipatory participatory approaches are also needed to shift power relations in the production of disability sport research.

Emancipatory participatory approaches for social justice research

An emancipatory disability paradigm is a disrupting and inherently political methodological approach that suits social justice and disability justice research ambitions. As the name implies, it is about facilitating a politics of *possible* by confronting social oppression at whatever level it occurs (Oliver, 1997). Adopting such an approach does not require researchers to have an impairment but it does involve putting research skills, knowledges, and power at the disposal of disabled people or disabled people's movements (Barton, 2005). As Oliver (1992) argued:

> Social relations are built upon a firm distinction between the researcher and the researched; upon the belief that it is the researchers who have specialist knowledge and skills; and that it is they who should decide what topics should be researched and be in control of the whole process of research production. To leave these social relations of

research production unchallenged is to leave the task of setting a research agenda in the hands of these experts. The idea that small groups of 'experts' can get together and set a research agenda for disability is, again, fundamentally flawed. Such an idea is the product of a society which has a positivistic consciousness and a hierarchical social structure which accords experts as an elite role.

(p. 102)

According to Oliver (1992, 1997) and developed by Barnes (1996, 2002) and others (Stone & Priestley, 1996; Zarb 1992) an emancipatory paradigm is a dynamic and engaging process underpinned by core principles, such as:

1. The surrender of claims to objectivity through overt political commitment to the struggles of disabled people for self-emancipation.
2. The evolution of control over research production to ensure full accountability to disabled people and their organisations.
3. Disabled people must actively participate in all stages of the research process.
4. The research process must be transparent, and outcomes should support activism and advocacy or produce knowledge that is useful for disabled people's movements.
5. The willingness only to undertake research where it will be of practical benefit to the self-empowerment of disabled people and/or the removal of disabling barriers.
6. The adoption of a social model understanding of disablement as the epistemological basis for research production.
7. Research must value and foreground lived experience of disability by giving voice to the personal as political, whilst endeavouring to collectivise the political commonality of individual experiences.
8. The willingness to adopt a plurality of methods for data collection and analysis in response to the changing needs of disabled people.

This is a participatory paradigm that involves shifting power relations in the research process, from research traditionally done *on*, *for* or *about* disabled people towards research carried out *with* or dictated *by* disabled people to advance the social and political emancipation *of* disabled people (Griffiths, 2022; Oliver, 1992). The aim of this approach is similar to those advocated by feminists, namely, to produce non-hierarchical and non-manipulative research relationships (Danieli & Woodhams, 2005). Working to change power dynamics in the research production clearly suits disability sport and social justice research because the people who 'live' disabling intersectional barriers (see Thomas, 2014) and who develop strategies to challenge such barriers, will help us better to understand the root causes of oppression and find ways to facilitate a politics of possible. That said, there are arguments against prescribing emancipatory research as the *only* legitimate methodology for social justice research.

To give an example, Danieli and Woodhams (2005) highlighted how policy makers may not take inherently political research seriously if the findings are perceived to support the political viewpoint of the researcher. In addition, not all disabled people agree with the social model of disability and some of those disabled people can hold positions of power in disability sport organisations and/or have different 'social justice' agendas to disability rights movements. Disability is a broad church. Therefore, emancipatory research can end up preaching to the converted and silencing or excluding disabled people who adhere to individualistic understandings of disability (Danieli & Woodhams, 2005).

Moreover, an emancipatory paradigm is just one of many participatory frameworks that claims to work *with*, not *on*, disabled people that are starting to be used in disability sport research, such as 'participatory action research' (Pettican et al., 2022), 'co-production' (Smith et al., 2022), 'public and patient involvement' (Cockcroft, 2020), 'user-centred design research', or 'co-designed research'. For example, in co-produced research (see Smith et al., 2022), equitable partnerships are formed with disabled people and/or their organisations by explicitly addressing inequalities in power so that they can actively contribute to, influence, or even direct the process of research. This approach also values equity of power, lived experience, reciprocity, and respecting the knowledge of all involved in research. However, it is important to know that all these 'participatory' research terms are contested in the sense that all have the potential to included disabled people in meaningful and impactful ways or in problematic tokenistic ways. For example, Smith et al. (2022) highlighted that 'co-production' can be an emancipatory approach when it is equitable and experientially informed but can also involve 'tokenistic' participation in some contexts such as some public and patient involvement research.

As participatory terms connected to emancipatory principles are contested, no one methodological term should be seen as the 'gold-standard'. Also, as Barton (2005) argued, translating these principles into actual practice is far from straightforward as research of this nature entails a time-consuming process. It is also a demanding process in which the emphasis is on self-reflection. As Lloyd et al. (1996), as cited in Barton (2005) said:

> It is centred around openness and trust; being prepared to make ourselves vulnerable rather than disguise mistakes; being prepared to have one's own perspective criticised; being prepared to make one's own skills, knowledge and experience accessible rather than jealously guard expertise; being prepared to share and own results.
>
> (p. 322)

Therefore, in contrast to adhering to a particular methodological approach to achieve political goals, researchers should be sensitive to disability as a fundamental principle of social organisation and be reflexive about the role that their own disability plays on the process of research. To shift power relations in the production of research, where the distribution of privileges involved in knowledge production is fair, it can be helpful for researchers and research teams to develop their own bespoke participatory principles, tailored to their own research contexts.

Developing participatory principles for social justice research

To develop appropriate participatory principles for social justice projects, researchers could first consider the many levers to support including non-academic disabled people across the decision-making process. Drawing reference to participatory principles under the United Nations Convention for the Rights of Persons with Disabilities (CRPD) is a useful start as it was designed by disabled people for disabled people based on the disabled people's movement watchword – *nothing about us, without us!* The CRPD is also informed by the social model understanding of disability. A practical case can also be made by drawing reference to national legal requirements (e.g. the 2010 UK Equality Act www.gov.uk), as well as Equality, Diversity, and Inclusion agendas within academic institutions (Liasidou, 2014). Thinking about the many benefits for disabled people and researchers in developing participatory principles can also help.

For example, principles can facilitate an enjoyable and rewarding experience that can enhance the personal and professional development of both researchers and non-researchers involved. Developing principles can help improve the quality of the data analysis and lead to deeper insights into, and better understanding of, the data. Moreover, including disabled people and their organisations in projects has advantages with relation to the dissemination and impact of research findings. By bringing together teams of collaborators, including those working in policy and practice, this approach can improve and accelerate the active translation of research into policy (Smith et al., 2022). It can help to appreciate how disability policy can impact the lives of approx. 15–20 pe cent of the population (WHO, www.who.int). It also feels right, in my experience.

Towards developing bespoke participatory principles in social justice research, academic and non-academic researchers should consider the means and methods of engagement in the process. A good start towards meaningful participation, and to avoid tokenistic involvement, is to continuously reflect on why disabled people are involved in the research, as well as who is involved, at what stages, where, and for what reasons. For example, working with disability organisations or individual disabled people, or both, can influence how appropriate participatory principles develop. Public health research funders can offer practical advice connecting to patient and public involvement (PPI) principles (see e.g. NIRH, 2020; www.nihr.ac.uk; www.hrb.ie; https://ppinetwork.ie). Access to resources such as funding, connections, networks, experiences, time, spaces, languages, and technology will also make a difference. As not all researchers and projects will have equal access to such resources, it can help to think about the quality rather than quantity of meaningful participation. From my experiences, to develop tailored principles to enhance and advocate for social justice research, here are some broad practical steps researchers may wish to take on board.

The importance of history

It is helpful to recognise that there is a history of non-disabled professionals making research and policy decisions which have not necessarily been in the best interest of disabled people (Barnes, 2007). For example, disabled people have had negative experiences of researchers and policy makers who can be far of the mark with regard to understanding disability issues. In addition, research processes and outcomes have historically been inaccessible to people who communicate in different ways. As a result, from the outset, some disabled people and their organisations can be apathetic and even resistant to participate in traditional forms of research, such as surveys, interviews, focus groups or observations 'on', 'about', or 'for' disabled people, especially when they feel that their experiences, expertise, or time is being used to benefit non-disabled researchers and funders, often at their expense. When researchers are developing participatory principles, it is useful to consider this history in the context of previous published research outputs, academic departments, and institutions, as well as in the context of countries and funders. For example, as Beresford (2021) highlighted, some research contexts can be inherently or meaningfully participatory without claiming to be so, while others claim to be, but are not.

Valuing lived experience

There are many examples of research outcomes that have not worked because of not actively thinking about lived experience. For example, social justice researchers would generally not conduct research that affects women without valuing the lived experience of women in the process. If researchers want the outcomes of research to promote social justice and have effect on disabled people's lives, they should consider ways to show that they are not using disabled people, but that their contribution will be valued. Thinking about lived experience as an *asset* that many non-disabled researchers don't have can help.

People feel valued in different ways but making renumeration (payment) to disabled people who provide their time, experience, and expertise is an increasingly common way to value and acknowledge contributions to research. Importantly, there are different ways of making payment happen, and payment for contribution can be on a sliding scale for various forms of contribution. For example, some disabled people prefer to be paid in vouchers due to social security issues, but a problem with *only* using vouchers is the assumption that disabled people don't work. To develop participatory principles, ask disabled people how they wish to be valued and acknowledged for their contribution to the research process.

Shifting social relations and addressing the perception of power

Social justice research requires explicitly considering power dynamics and the perception of power in research contexts. Some research projects will be easier than others to design so that disabled people have power and control in the production of knowledge. For example, it can be a challenge when there are fewer readily willing and able disabled people available with the relevant knowledge, insights, and ideas. Considering principles related to power relations involves, for example: employing disabled researchers and students; including disabled people in a foundational way in research projects (e.g. inclusion in funding bids); the principle of involvement all the way through a project; and reflecting on how disabled people can see the policy impact of a piece of research. This requires dialog and forethought to consider the methods, channels, and frequency of engagement and feedback in research.

Understanding the difference between genuine and tokenistic forms of participation is an important principle to consider. For example, meaningless and tokenistic consultation is consultation without intent to carry it out or consultation to get the answers researchers want. In contrast, meaningful consultation allows researchers to get answers to make to inform policy decisions rather than seeking answers to confirm decisions. Principles of transparency and honesty are important too because everything is going to have its barriers and boundaries (see next section). For example, a common pitfall to genuine participation in projects is not allowing sufficient time to establish relationships or to upskill non-academic collaborators so that they understand why they are being included (Beresford, 2020, 2021).

Who to engage in research, and why

For decisions about who should be involved in a research project, a common-sense approach is important. Research teams, who wish to inform policy, could work to establish a network or group of disabled experts that includes a broad representation of disabled people (or broadly enough) to provide a genuine voice to the production of knowledge. Considering how to populate a 'network', researchers should consider what they want from it first and what networks already exist. An intersectional lens is an important principle considering multiple identities (gender, race, class and so on) and different disability perspectives and expertise, including those most marginalised by disablement. Seeking representation can be difficult as not everyone self-identifies as disabled. However, representation can be sought through the lens of different types of barriers all people face (communication, social interaction, built environment, socio-economic) in contrast to different impairment types, and/or by allowing space (e.g. in administrative forms) for people to self-identify. The idea is to develop principles to find the best ways to leverage the different values, skills, experiences, time, and insights that different people bring to a project, and to accept and make space for any conflict if it arises, in contrast to avoiding or controlling conflict.

Accessibility

In developing principles to make research accessible to people who communicate in different ways, it's useful to think early about access in research projects, and budget for accessibility costs by asking disabled people involved about access requirements for participation. There are no hard and fast rules for accessibility – access is an ongoing conversation. It could help to scope out in advance what will the research outputs be and who will be the audiences, and what their access needs will be. Consider principles that can help projects adopt a range of methods for data collection and analysis in response to the changing access needs of disabled people. Moreover, considering the benefits to *all* people of making aspects of research accessible (e.g. video reports, easy read reports) is helpful. The more research outputs becomes public, the more access costs there will likely be, and making everything accessible for everyone in all circumstances can be unrealistic and can be a misuse of resources. Responsibility for access lies in what researchers or research teams can control.

Addressing academic barriers to social justice research

As mentioned, implementing these principles in a meaningful way is a challenging process, and will be easier in some research contexts than in others. Also, as disability becomes more of a social justice issue in society (like gender and race) more people are becoming attracted to do disability sport research for social justice. While this development is encouraging, researchers and scholars should be aware of ongoing challenges and barriers involved in advocating and promoting emancipatory participatory principles and approaches. Many of these challenges are rooted within neoliberal and elitist university systems and structures. Let me explain.

One central challenge continues to concern academic ableism. It is safe to say that disability sport research is perceived to be controlled by those who do not experience disability. Although there have been greater numbers of disabled students progressing to higher education in some countries, the number progressing on to academia remains low as the barriers to employment and career progression remain significant (Dolmage, 2017). Accordingly, disability sport research for social justice will continue to be perceived to empower academic institutions, more than disabled people, their organisations, and communities. Engaging with emancipatory participatory principles can, however, help to promote social justice through discovering new and meaningful ways to advocate for more disabled academics to be employed within the field without, of course, assuming that all disabled researchers are interested in disability, sport, or social justice issues.

An associated barrier concerns securing adequate resourcing needed to employ social justice research. Funding applications through academic systems are competitive and often require research questions, designs, costings, and outcomes to be set before funding can be awarded. Neoliberal academic structures also tend to award funding to individual academics to empower their individual careers rather than to emancipatory projects that can help disabled people and disability communities empower themselves. PhDs in institutions of higher education are also awarded to individuals rather than collectives. This can mean that researchers who wish to shift power relations, perversely, must display their expert status to secure funding. Another related challenge involves precarity, such as individual early career academics on short-term contracts trying to secure funding for such long-term participatory projects. In response to such challenges, researchers can take some comfort as some funders in some countries are increasingly taking these principles in research seriously. For example, in Ireland, the ethos of the Health Research Board is becoming consistent with emancipatory principles as funding now requires public involvement in the production of research from the start to the end of the process (see e.g. www.hrb.ie).

Another challenge involves university procedural ethical assumptions. This is universal criteria, assumed to be independent of culture and context, that guide what are the right and wrong decisions to make in the research processes (Sparkes & Smith, 2013). The problem is that procedural ethical assumptions in universities can often imply that disabled people should, at the outset, be considered and treated as vulnerable/passive people and remuneration for participation is coercive. It is therefore important to be aware that decisions across this research process can be guided by a combination of ethical assumptions, including institutional procedures, as well as social justice ethical approaches (Martino & Schormans, 2018; Sparkes & Smith, 2013). Social justice ethical approaches have a political aim of representing the 'voices' and decisions of disabled people in the process of research (Mietola, Miettinen, & Vehmas, 2017). Also, in some counties prior institutional ethical approval is not required to involve the public in decisions about designing and managing the research (see NIRH, 2020).

The trend towards doing social justice research can also be a potential issue. The ever-present potential danger of this scenario is a situation in which ambitious academics who do not necessarily have a research background in critical disability studies, or lived experience of disability, hold significant power in the research process. This development, coupled with the historic norm of researching *on*, *for* or *about* disabled people, means that there is a danger that key underpinning principles of disability theory can get lost in ambitious 'social justice' projects. For example, a social model understanding of disability can become viewed as just one of many theoretical lenses by academics involved in interdisciplinary projects. This is a challenge because a social model understanding of disability (e.g. the principle of doing research to provide information with which disabled people can empower themselves) is a way of thinking that is foundational and core by many critical disability studies scholars and disability activists/advocates (Goodley, 2016). Another major challenge involves trying to persuade the value of an emancipatory participatory principles 'upwards' within academic hierarchies. As Smith et al. (2022) said, due to structural inequalities in academia, those who carry out this kind of work occupy less prestigious academic positions.

I don't unfortunately have solutions to these challenges, but they are useful for scholars and researchers to consider when developing participatory principles in the context of their own social justice research. For example, it might be helpful for scholars in the field of disability sport studies to consider ways to address and rethink what Lau (2019) described as the "academic culture of speed". Think about how the persistent and consistent desire for outputs in academic structures can contribute to disablement rather than emancipation. Think about how early-career academics can be discouraged from engaging in meaningful social justice research due to mounting demands for productivity and competition. Think about how academic careers can be recognised and awarded for engaging in emancipatory approaches that take time. Think about whether big research projects with ambitious goals to change the world for disabled people, that are controlled through hierarchies of knowledge in universities, can really improve the lives of disabled participants or their communities. Lau (2019) suggested to advocate for 'slow scholarship' to allow researchers more time to build relationships and focus on foundational work in disability research projects, as this can help to disrupt rigid structures of academic labour and challenge the status quo.

Conclusion

Disability sport research does an important job raising awareness of disadvantages that disabled people face in sport and society. However, the rapidly growing field is in danger of producing research that talks about disabled people rather than research that is designed with or by disabled people. Challenging the status quo by addressing power dynamics in disability sport studies can help to produce research to find new ways to build a socially just society. Through a robust engagement with disability theory and critical disability studies, disability sport researchers can produce work that is critical, reflexive, scholarly, and political. For example, a critical engagement with the notion of disability justice is a way to re-imagine and develop new approaches to social justice research. Developing bespoke emancipatory participatory principles can help to address power dynamics in research designs, required to value different knowledges and create a disruptive research agenda. Importantly, to develop such principles involves an awareness of the ongoing challenges and barriers found within academic systems and structures. I hope this chapter helps towards the advocacy necessary to shift power relations in the production of disability sport research.

References

Adamson, B., Adamson, M., Clarke, C., Richardson, E. V., & Sydnor, S. (2022). Social justice through sport and exercise studies: A manifesto. *Journal of Sport and Social Issues, 46*(5), 407–444.

Ballas, J., Buultjens, M., Murphy, G., & Jackson, M. (2022). Elite-level athletes with physical impairments: Barriers and facilitators to sport participation. *Disability & Society, 37*(6), 1018–1037.

Barnes, C. (1996). Disability and the myth of the independent researcher. *Disability & Society, 11*(1), 107–112.

Barnes, C. (2002). 'Emancipatory disability research': Project or process? *Journal of Research in Special Educational Needs, 2*(1).

Barnes, C. (2007). Disability activism and the struggle for change: Disability, policy and politics in the UK. *Education, Citizenship and Social Justice, 2*(3), 203–221.

Barnes, C., & Mercer, G. (1997). *Exploring the divide*. Leeds: Disability Press.

Barnes, C., & Mercer, G. (2003). *Disability: Key concepts*. Cambridge: Polity Press.

Barnes, C., Mercer, G., & Shakespeare, T. (1999). *Exploring disability*. London: Polity Press.

Barton, L. (2005). Emancipatory research and disabled people: Some observations and questions. *Educational Review, 3*, 317–327.

Beresford, P. (2020). PPI or user involvement: Taking stock from a service user perspective in the twenty first century. *Research Involvement and Engagement, 6*(1), 1–5.

Beresford, P. (2021). *Participatory ideology: From exclusion to involvement*. Bristol: Policy Press.

Berne, P., Morales, A. L., Langstaff, D., & Invalid, S. (2018). Ten principles of disability justice. *WSQ: Women's Studies Quarterly, 46*(1), 227–230.

Brighton, J. (2023). Disability and aging: Dads, sons, sport and impairment. In B. Powis, J. Brighton, & P. D. Howe (Eds), *Researching disability sport: Theory, method, practice* (pp. 13–40). Routledge.

Brighton, J., Howe, P. D., & Powis, B. (2023). Theorising disability sport. In B. Powis, J. Brighton, & P. D. Howe (Eds), *Researching disability sport: Theory, method, practice* (pp. 13–40). Routledge.

Campbell, F. (2009). *Contours of ableism: The production of disability and abledness*. UK: Springer.
Chataika, T. (2018). *The Routledge handbook of disability in Southern Africa*. London: Routledge.
Cockcroft, E. J. (2020). "Power to the people": The need for more public involvement in sports science for health. *Sport Sciences for Health*, *16*(1), 189–192.
Culver, D. M., Shaikh, M., Alexander, D., & Fournier, K. (2022). Gender equity in disability sport: A rapid scoping review. *Journal of Clinical Sport Psychology*, *16*(4), 383–405.
Danieli, A., & Woodhams, C. (2005). Emancipatory research methodology and disability: A critique. *International Journal of Social Research Methodology*, *8*(4), 281–296.
Dolmage, J. (2017). *Academic ableism: Disability and higher education*. Michigan: University of Michigan Press.
Feely, M. (2016). Disability studies after the ontological turn: A return to the material world and material bodies without a return to essentialism. *Disability & Society*, *31*(7), 863–883.
Fine, M. (2019). Critical disability studies: Looking back and forward. *Journal of Social Issues*, *75*(3), 972–984.
Fitzgerald, H. (2009). Are you a 'parasite' researcher? Researching disability and youth sport. In H. Fitzgerald (Ed.), *Disability and youth sport* (pp. 157–171). London: Routledge.
Fitzgerald, H., & Long, J. (2017). Integration or special provision?: Positioning disabled people in sport and leisure. In J. Long, T. Fletcher, & B. Watson (Eds), *Sport, leisure and social justice* (pp. 126–138). Routledge.
Flynn, S. (2017). Engaging with materialism and material reality: Critical disability studies and economic recession. *Disability & Society*, *32*(2), 143–159.
Goodley, D. (2012). Dis/entangling critical disability studies. *Disability & Society*, *27*(6), 631–644.
Goodley, D. (2014). *Dis/ability studies: Theorising disablism and ableism*. London: Routledge.
Goodley, D. (2016). *Disability studies: An interdisciplinary introduction* (2nd ed.). London: Sage.
Goodley, D., Lawthom, R., Liddiard, K., & Runswick-Cole, K. (2019). Provocations for critical disability studies. *Disability & Society*, *34*(6), 972–997.
Grech, S. (2011). Recolonising debates or perpetuated coloniality? Decentring the spaces of disability, development and community in the global South. *International Journal of Inclusive Education*, *15*(1), 87–100.
Grech, S., & Goodley, D. (2012). Doing disability research in the majority world: An alternative framework and the quest for decolonising methods. *Journal of Human Development, Disability, and Social Change*, *192*(2012), 43–55.
Griffiths, M. (2022). UK social model of disability and the quest for emancipation. In M. Rioux, J. Viera, A. Buettgen, & E. Zubrow (Eds), *Handbook of disability: Critical thought and social change in a globalizing world*. Singapore: Springer.
Haslett, D., Griffiths, M., & Lupton, D. (2024). Shifting power relations in disability sport and social activism research: an emancipatory approach. *Qualitative Research in Sport, Exercise and Health*, *16*(1), 35–52.
Haslett, D., & Smith, B. (2022). Disability, sport and social activism. In R. Magrath (Ed.), *Athlete activism: Contemporary perspectives*. New York: Routledge.
Howe, P. D. (2019). Paralympic sport and social justice: Towards a happy marriage or difficult separation? In B. Watermeyer, J. McKenzie, & L. Swartz (Eds), *The Palgrave handbook of disability and citizenship in the global South*. Cham: Palgrave Macmillan.
Howe, P. D., Powis, B., & Brighton, J. (2023). Conclusion: The future of disability sport research. In B. Powis, J. Brighton, & P. D. Howe (Eds), *Researching disability sport: Theory, method, practice* (pp. 198–201). New York: Routledge.
Irish, T., McDonald, K., & Cavallerio, F. (2023). Race, disability and sport: The experience of black deaf individuals. In B. Powis, J. Brighton, & P. D. Howe (Eds), *Researching disability sport: Theory, method, practice* (pp. 114–125). New York: Routledge.
Lau, T. C. W. (2019). Slowness, disability, and academic productivity: The need to rethink academic culture. In P. Lang (Ed.), *Disability at the university: A disabled students' manifesto* (pp. 11–19). New York: Peter Lang Publishing Group.
Liasidou, A. (2014). Critical disability studies and socially just change in higher education. *British Journal of Special Education*, *41*(2), 120–135.
Liddiard, K. (2018). *The intimate lives of disabled people*. London: Routledge.
Lloyd, M., Preston-Shoot, M., Temple, B., & Wuu, W. R. (1996). Whose project is it anyway? Sharing and shaping the research and development agenda. *Disability & Society*, *11*(3), 301–316.

Long, J., Fletcher, T., & Watson, B. (2017). Introducing sport, leisure and social justice. In J. Long, T. Fletcher, & B. Watson (Eds), *Sport, leisure and social justice* (pp. 1–14). London: Routledge.

Macbeth, J. (2010). Reflecting on disability research in sport and leisure settings. *Leisure Studies*, 29(4), 477–485.

Macbeth, J., & Powis, B. (2023). What are we doing here?: Confessional tales of non-disabled researchers in disability sport. In B. Powis, J. Brighton, & P. D. Howe (Eds), *Researching disability sport: Theory, method, practice* (pp. 55–69). New York: Routledge.

Mallett, R., & Runswick-Cole, K. (2014). *Approaching disability: Critical issues and perspectives*. Abingdon: Routledge.

Martino, A. S., & Schormans, A. F. (2018). When good intentions backfire: University research ethics review and the intimate lives of people labelled with intellectual disabilities. *Qualitative Social Research*, 19(3), 1–18.

Mietola, R., Miettinen, S., & Vehmas, S. (2017). Voiceless subjects? Research ethics and persons with profound intellectual disabilities. *International Journal of Social Research Methodology*, 20(3), 263–274. doi: 10.1080/13645579.2016.1239776

Mladenov, T. (2016). Disability and social justice. *Disability & Society*, 31(9), 1226–1241.

Monforte, J., Gibson, B. E., Smith, B., & Goodley, D. (2023). Exercise, rehabilitation and posthuman disability studies: Four responses. In B. Powis, J. Brighton, & P. D. Howe (Eds), *Researching disability sport: Theory, method, practice* (pp. 171–184). Routledge.

Morris, J. (1996). *Encounters with strangers: Feminism and disability*. London: The Women's Press.

NIRH. (2020). A map of resources for co-producing research in health and social care: A guide for researchers, members of the public and health and social care practitioners (Version 1.2). Retrieved from https://arc-w.nihr.ac.uk/Wordpress/wp-content/uploads/2020

Oliver, M. (1990). *The politics of disablement*. Basingstoke: Macmillan.

Oliver, M. (1992). Changing the social relations of research production? *Disability, Handicap & Society*, 7(2), 101–114.

Oliver, M. (1997). Emancipatory research: Realistic goal or impossible dream. *Doing Disability Research*, 2, 15–31.

Oliver, M. (2013). The social model of disability: Thirty years on. *Disability & Society*, 28(7), 1024–1026.

Peers, D. (2017). Cramping our style: Critical disability studies as axiological affinities. *Disability Studies Quarterly*, 37(3).

Peers, D., Spencer-Cavaliere, N., & Eales, L. (2014). Say what you mean: Rethinking disability language in adapted physical activity quarterly. *Adapted Physical Activity Quarterly*, 31(3), 265–282.

Pettican, A., Goodman, B., Bryant, W., Beresford, P., Freeman, P., Gladwell, V., ... & Speed, E. (2022). Doing together: Reflections on facilitating the co-production of participatory action research with marginalised populations. *Qualitative Research in Sport, Exercise and Health*, 15, 1–18.

Powis, B., Brighton, J., & Howe, P. D. (2023). *Researching disability sport: Theory, method, practice*. New York: Routledge.

Richard, R., Joncheray, H., & Duquesne, V. (2023). Cripping sport and physical activity: An intersectional approach to gender and disability. *Sport, Ethics and Philosophy*, 17, 1–15.

Shildrick, M. (2012). Critical disability studies: Rethinking the conventions for the age of postmodernity. In N. Watson, A. Roulstone, & C. Thomas (Eds), *Handbook of disability studies* (pp. 30–41). London: Routledge.

Silva, C. F. (2023). Confronting Ableism from within: Reflections on anti-Ableism research in disability sport. In B. Powis, J. Brighton, & P. D. Howe (Eds), *Researching disability sport: Theory, method, practice* (pp. 157–170). New York: Routledge.

Smith, B., & Bundon, A. (2018). Disability models: Explaining and understanding disability sport in different ways. In I. Brittain (Ed.), *The Palgrave handbook of Paralympic studies* (pp. 15–34). London: Palgrave Macmillan.

Smith, B., & Perrier, M.-J. (2015). Disability, sport, and impaired bodies: A critical approach. In R. J. Schinke & K. R. McGannon (Eds), *The psychology of sub-culture in sport and physical activity: Critical perspectives* (pp. 95–106). London: Routledge.

Smith, B., Williams, O., Bone, L., & the Moving Social Work Co-production Collective. (2022). Co-production: A resource to guide co-producing research in the sport, exercise, and health sciences. *Qualitative Research in Sport, Exercise and Health*, 15, 1–29.

Sparkes, A. C., & Smith, B. (2013). *Qualitative research methods in sport, exercise and health: From process to product*. New York: Routledge.

Spencer, N., & Molnár, G. (2022). Whose knowledge counts? Examining paradigmatic trends in adapted physical activity research. *Quest*, *74*(1), 1–16.

Stone, E., & Priestley, M. (1996). Parasites, pawns and partners: Disability research and the role of non-disabled researchers. *British Journal of Sociology*, *47*(4), 699–716.

Stride, A., & Fitzgerald, H. (2017). Working towards social justice through participatory research with young people in sport and leisure. In J. Long, T. Fletcher, & B. Watson (Eds), *Sport, leisure and social justice* (pp. 98–110). London: Routledge.

Swartz, L. (2023). Barriers to disability sport research and the global South: A personal view. In B. Powis, J. Brighton, & P. D. Howe (Eds), *Researching disability sport: Theory, method, practice* (pp. 70–82). New York: Routledge.

Thomas, C. (1999). *Female forms: Experiencing and understanding disability*. Buckingham: The Open University Press.

Thomas, C. (2014). Disability and impairment. In J. Swain, S. French, C. Barnes, & C. Thomas (Eds), *Disabling barriers - Enabling environments* (3rd ed., pp. 3–15). London, UK: Sage.

Wheeler, S., & Peers, D. (2023). Playing, passing, and pageantry: A collaborative autoethnography on sport, disability, sexuality, and belonging. In B. Powis, J. Brighton, & P. D. Howe (Eds), *Researching disability sport: Theory, method, practice* (pp. 100–113). New York: Routledge.

Zarb, G. (1992). On the road to Damascus: First steps towards changing the relations of disability research production. *Disability, Handicap & Society*, *7*(2), 125–138.

29
SPORT AND CRIME REDUCTION

Peter R. Harris

Introduction

This chapter critically examines the proposition that sport-based activities can be deployed in response to a perceived social objective, namely the reduction of crime. As a criminologist working predominantly in the field of youth violence prevention, my focus will be on the ways in which participation and involvement in sport may reduce crime through its potential to promote *desistance*, a term used by criminologists to denote the processes behind the cessation of offending behaviour. After briefly defining some key terminology, I discuss some of the paradoxes and tensions that manifest when considering the relationship between sport and crime reduction. I then introduce some 'theories of change' drawn from the disciplines of psychology and sociology to illuminate some of the possible causal relationships, correlations and complexity when considering the relationship between sport and crime reduction, and then illustrate this using an example from my own previous research (Harris & Seal, 2016).

Sport, as a lucrative multi-billion dollar industry, has been implicated in corporate criminal activity (bribery, corruption, match fixing, etc.), and sportsmen and women have been accused of complicity in discrimination, racism, sexism, homophobia, and child abuse. Violence amongst sport spectators, specifically the spectre of hooliganism, is still a feature of football specifically. These aspects of the relationship between sport and crime will have to remain outside the scope of this chapter, but they do form the backdrop to the debate around sport's potential to reduce crime. Here I wish to focus primarily on how certain key concepts (personal identity, morality and values, role models and masculinity) may relate to the crime reduction potential of sporting activity. In doing so, I present an alternative lens through which to see the sport and crime reduction debate, characterised as specifically *psychosocial* and suggest ways that such a lens might enable movement beyond existing research and policy paradigms.

Terminology

Although the terms sport and crime both have porous boundaries, for our purposes here we can define sport as physical activity with some form of bodily movement or fine psychomotor skill that normally includes a competitive dimension but could also include activities taken part in alone, such as weight training and jogging. Criminologists define crime as deviant acts (i.e. those that violate prevailing societal norms) that are detected and punishable by the state. The term *desistance* is a more technical and discipline specific criminological term that may not be as familiar to some readers of this volume and therefore merits some further explanation. Essentially it refers to the psychic and social processes that lie behind the cessation of offending behaviour. Established desistance literature draws a distinction between offenders' initial decision to change their criminal behaviour (termed *primary* desistance) and then to permanently cease offending (*secondary* desistance). The process of desistance is not necessarily unidirectional and can involve 'zig zagging' backwards and forwards through change and relapses on route to permanent or secondary desistance (Healy, 2010). Some desistance scholars such as Maruna (2007) focus more on the internal *psychological* processes which re-orientate the offenders' sense of self. These can involve offenders reconstructing an internal narrative where past events are reinterpreted to suit the new developing self, sometimes at key turning points or 'epiphanies'. At these moments offenders can enter a period of liminality and often try to remove themselves from harmful environments, undesirable companions or even the past itself. Others, such as Laub and Sampson (2003) highlight the *social* transitions in adult life (e.g. employment, marriage and personal relationships, or for that matter change and transitions that arise through involvement in sport) that develop the social bonds that stabilise and sustain new crime-free identities. Maruna et al. (2004) draw on symbolic interactionist theories of identity and labelling (Becker, 1963) to theorise the intersubjective processes that underlie the development of these social bonds and how they relate to desistance, such as the role of the societal on-looker, as captured via Cooley's 'looking-glass (or mirror)-self' metaphor (1902). Labelling theory suggests that deviant acts, when labelled as criminal, can lead to a self-fulfilling prophecy whereby the offender begins to see him/herself as he is seen by others and criminal identity becomes his/her master status. Social recognition of the offender's desistance (de-labelling) is therefore central to the desistance process (Maruna et al., 2004). The role of this social recognition within desistance is given a psychoanalytic twist by Gadd (2006) who suggests that it can be supplemented with an appreciation of unconscious psychodynamics. Drawing on the psychoanalytic work of Benjamin (2017) he outlines how partners or significant others such as peers conferring their recognition on an offender, that is signifying their acceptance, can lead to a slow and often painful process of self-transformation. The causative links and ingredients of this transformation, however, may well remain locked outside the individual's conscious awareness, in a metaphorical 'black box'. This unconscious dimension of personal change has important implications for how we can meaningfully conduct research into desistance and, I suggest, how we can both understand and maximise the crime reduction potential of sport-based activity.

Paradoxes and complexity

Thinking deeply about the crime reduction potential of sport in this way brings to the surface some troubling paradoxes and complexity. First, sport can be seen at one and the same time as both a *cause* and *cure* for crime and criminal behaviour. Sports participation can be viewed as the precursor to, and initiator and reinforcer of, crime and violence as well as an antidote, diversionary or preventative tool. Moreover, many of the qualities and values that are valorised and seen as prerequisites for success in sport, such as discipline, teamwork, a will to win, playing through pain, ruthlessness, toughness and aggression, even violence, gamesmanship and cheating, are often also observable within the behaviour of those involved in criminal activity. Tied up with this are deeper philosophical questions around values, virtues, ethics and morality, and concepts that need to be viewed as socially constructed. Social constructionism, a theoretical sociological framework that points to the importance of subjective perception, essentially argues that all meaning and knowledge is socially created. This perspective suggests that concepts such as success, toughness, masculinity, and even sport itself might be socially constructed in ways that create different meanings at different times and in different places. For example, certain sports might be constructed in classed, gendered or racialised terms. For example, Rugby Union might be perceived as a more middle-class game, tennis as predominantly white and middle-class, and football as more male and working-class. The social construction of sports and how this relates to both personal and social identities such as gender and class is an aspect of the sport and crime reduction debate which merits a more sustained diversion later. At this point it is simply important to observe that sport, and its depiction and portrayal through the media (especially television which brings sport to global audiences) both reflects and produces the social contexts in which it takes place; it is shaped by and shapes the cultural and social forces within which it exists.

There are also some epistemological and methodological questions that bedevil researchers seeking to establish simple causal links or correlations between sport and crime reduction and curtail the production of substantive conclusions. These revolve around what is the best formulation of the question itself; should it be *whether* sport reduces crime or if it does, *how* it does? This is a familiar tension between more positivist and quantitative studies often perceived to be more scientific, rigorous and reliable, versus more qualitative and anecdotal studies that rely on case studies and first hand personal testimonies. In a climate where any crime reduction programmes can come with increased demands for accountability and a sizeable price tag for the taxpayer (especially in an age of austerity) these questions of effectiveness and how to measure it (sometimes coined as the 'what works' debate) come in to sharp focus in policy and public arenas. Again, an extended discussion of this debate is not possible here, except to say that which approach is favoured by policy makers has important implications for how sport programmes with crime reduction objectives are promoted, funded, and evaluated, and how they may be contrasted with alternative 'remedies' for crime and violence, such as punitive measures and incarceration. That is partly why I conclude this chapter with a call for a new approach to how we conceptualise the relationship between sport and crime reduction and a movement towards a new, more meaningful form of research and evaluation.

In order to develop a more meaningful analysis of 'what works' we may need also to begin to draw some finer distinctions within the conceptual space of sport, per se. This involves thinking about varieties of sporting activity, from non-contact, through to contact and combat sports, both individual and team based. Thinking through different forms in which sporting endeavour manifests and the different intra and interpersonal dynamics inherent within them is clearly going to be important if we are to meaningfully identify and differentiate the causal relationships that research into the crime reduction potential of sport study seeks. For example, the crime reduction potential of non-contact sports such as tennis and badminton could operate very differently than contact sports such as rugby, ice hockey, and American football that require and even valorise controlled violence within the game. Combat sports such as boxing and martial arts are predicated on the use of controlled violence, and the identities of boxers are aligned with the idea of violent potential (Jump, 2021). As such, combat sports such as boxing sit at the nexus of the debate around the crime reduction and desistance promotion potential of sport, in that they acutely embody some of the paradoxes and complexity inherent within that debate.

To borrow from a popular cultural resource, the Hollywood film *Karate Kid* epitomises another key variable, with regards to one key interpersonal dynamic – the potential influence of sports leaders and coaches on sportsmen and women and especially younger people. To paraphrase Mr Miyagi, his maxim "there is no such thing as bad pupil, only bad teacher" succinctly captures the central role played by those delivering and facilitating sporting activity, especially in educational and community-based settings. Such popular cultural depictions of sport as a noble pursuit with the power to transform lives, foreground the psychological trope of *role models* in sport, especially as successful sports men and women are so often venerated and elevated to high social status as 'positive' role models and can take on heroic and iconic status in the eyes of younger 'wannabe' sports men and women. The notion of a role model can sometimes be conflated with a normative notion of a *good* role model (e.g. Mr Miyagi) whereas in psychological terms it is possible, of course, for role models to be good and bad, i.e. exert both a positive and negative influence. How sports men and women, coaches, and sports leaders behave both on and off the pitch is therefore a key ingredient when considering how interpersonal influence is related to the attitudinal and behavioural change that lies behind desistance and therefore crime reduction. This question of *'who'* works, along with *'what'* works is therefore highly significant, in the sense that relationships between sports coaches and participants, and the interaction of their respective identities (both personal and social) might actually be one of the key active ingredients in the desistance process. For instance, how coaches, sports leaders, and sports men and women perceive and position each other, and possibly psychologically identify with each other across markers of social difference, needs examination. We need to understand how the psychic and social construction of identities (perhaps most notably gendered identities such as masculinity) and the persistence of personal and social power manifest within those relationships and are implicated within sport and how this relates to processes of personal development and desistance.

Theories of change

Having highlighted the complex and somewhat paradoxical nature of the conceptual terrain, I now turn to set out some broad, theories of change for navigating our understanding of the desistance promoting and crime reduction potential of sport. Building theories of change from available research evidence and the vast array of theoretical frameworks available in this field is a complex task. There is a sizeable back catalogue going back nearly 50 years of studies that seek an answer to the 'whether' question (i.e. does sport reduce crime). Some do indicate that involvement in sports *is* associated with crime reduction and desistance (Begg et al., 1996; Brettschneider & Kleine, 2002; Curry, 1998; Eder et al., 1997; Landers & Landers, 1978; Langbein & Bess, 2002; Mahoney, 2000; Miller et al., 2006; Paetsch & Bertrand, 1997; Segrave & Chu, 1978; Stark et al., 1987). Some others (e.g. Kreager, 2007) distinguish between the desistance promoting potential of contact sports, such as football, and non-contact sports such as tennis. Others maintain there is no relationship at all (Best, 1985; Brettschneider, Brandl-Bredenbeck, & Hofmann, 2005). Some studies do attempt to dig deeper into the specific qualities that organised sports programmes pursuing social objectives should feature if they are to have any effect on desistance, i.e. they ask the *how* question (Eccles & Gootman, 2002; Nichols, 2007). In a wide-ranging meta-analysis of such studies, Mutz and Baur (2009) attempt to amalgamate all of this scholarly activity before concluding that the desistance promoting potential of sport is not inevitable and is entirely contingent on the context in which it is mediated. Their conclusion points to the fundamental centrality of asking the *how* and *who* questions if we are to understand how programmes should be shaped if they are to maximise their crime reduction potential. This requires a clear and broad conceptualisation – a multi-disciplinary hypothetical theoretical framework – of how personal development and change such as desistance is occurring in sporting contexts.

For this we can turn to criminological theories, both classic and more contemporary. Perhaps the most rudimentary way in which sport has been theorised conceived as having crime reduction and desistance promoting potential is in its capacity to simply provide a diversion away from criminal activity. Criminologists use the term incapacitation when discussing traditional criminal justice methods of punishment such as incarceration and how they reduce crime. In essence the premise here is that whilst in prison people cannot commit crime. Classic social control theorists such as Travis Hirschi (1969) move beyond that notion of physical restraint to posit that the social bonds (attachments to others, personal commitments and pro-social beliefs) exert a controlling psychological function on individuals that serves to prevent them from committing crime. The social bonds generated through involvement in sport could therefore be perceived as having the potential to exert a constraining influence on people such that they might not commit crime in the first place or desist from it.

Hirschi's notion of involvement can be applied to view sport as a diversion and controlling influence; put simply, time spent doing something 'positive' and 'constructive' like sport reduces boredom and the possibility that time might be spent involved in criminal activity. This idea can be heard in public and media discourse, often implicitly, to justify supporting diversionary sports based projects, especially with young people, often couched in language such as sport being a means to 'get young people off the streets'. As was noted earlier though, such rationales require much more nuance to be meaningful; encouraging involvement alone must be accompanied by more detailed consideration of how and by whom that involvement is shaped and delivered, as well as how that activity is tailored to the individual.

Considering the 'how and by whom' questions within sport and crime reduction means taking further diversions into several theoretical avenues, including philosophy, psychology and sociology. For example, in sport, and especially in team games, there is often a value placed on the importance of a number of ethical principles and qualities, such as the relegation of self-interest behind some notion of mutual endeavour. Should sporting activity therefore be understood as a practice imbued with ethical and moral values and therefore as a tool for moral development? And if so, what ethical principles can or should it promote? These principles could entail respect for the rules of the game, for opponents, mutual co-operation, fairness, and can be summarised perhaps by the broad concept of 'fair play' (Loland & McNamee, 2000). Van Bottenburg and Schuyt (1996) contend that sporting activity fosters the development of virtues such as team spirit and social responsibility. Coakley (1984) emphasise that it can stimulate social-cognitive competences, such as reciprocity in role-taking. In this way, sport can be promoted as a cultural arena within which the unwritten values and rules of the social contract can engrain the reciprocity required of the citizen in his or her relationship with other citizens and or the state and state actors. Value systems in sport, assuming they are shared, such as allegiance to a common goal and obedience to authority (coaches, umpires and referees) are thus conceived as a means to bring about social cohesion and restore the social contract. Sport requires a strengthening of self-discipline and self-control and sticking to moral codes even in critical situations. A simple cost benefit analysis emerges where transgression of rules results in undesirable effects for the participants. For example, illegitimate fighting could result in being removed from the game and disciplined, both on and off the field of play. This philosophical perspective that emphasises the ethical and moral values imbricated within sport and sporting institutions does require critical engagement as to the legitimacy or equity of the social contract as it exists within the status quo. Bearing in mind the persistent issues with discrimination and corruption within sporting bodies there is also a need to recognise the value of resisting or even usurping traditional power relationships within sporting institutions, and society more widely.

Some studies take more explicitly psychological approaches to suggest participating in sport may facilitate the socially acceptable and cathartic release of aggression. However, the catharsis hypothesis has received minimal empirical support (Bushman, Baumeister, & Stack, 1999; Fitch & Marshall, 2000; Russel, 1983). Although participation in sports in some instances may lead to a reduction in aggressive tendencies (Lamarre & Nosanchuk, 1999; Nosanchuk, 1981; Skelton, Glynn, & Berta, 1991; Zivin et al., 2001), such effects may result from positive socialisation processes in the training milieu rather than from any cathartic effect. Participation in sport may also have negative (criminogenic) effects if the activity in question supports aggressive (physical or verbal) behaviour patterns. Several studies, mainly based on journalistic accounts, have focused on elevated levels of aggressive and violent behaviour among athletes (Messner, 1990; Miedzian, 1991; Rowe, 1998). These studies are mainly based on journalists' accounts of selected violent incidents caused by individual athletes. Some studies suggest that team sports with high levels of physical contact (e.g. ice hockey, football, basketball), and high body contact sports (e.g. boxing, wrestling) are possibly related to enhanced violence outside the sports settings as well as to delinquency (Bloom & Smith, 1996; Nixon, 1997; Rowe, 1998; Watkins, 2000). Nixon (1997) found that for male athletes, hurting someone during sport, accidentally or intentionally, and also having strong beliefs in the value of toughness, was related to aggressive behaviour in everyday life. Several studies have focused on the effects of martial arts training, such as karate, tae kwon do (Korean form of karate), and judo, on aggression. Bjørkqvist and Varhama (2001) found that male students of karate tended to have a more negative attitude towards violent conflict resolution than wrestlers and boxers. However, the results were opposite for females who tended to have a more positive attitude towards violent conflict resolution. Here we see the emergence of a perhaps underdeveloped theme in the sport and crime reduction literature – gender as an important intervening variable – that we will return to later. For now, one useful distinction that can be drawn in this debate is between expressive violence and aggression (which is impulsive, hostile, and reactive) and *instrumental* aggression (Baron, 1977; Berkowitz, 1993, 2000), which is goal-directed and bound to tactical considerations. Despite these paradoxical and somewhat contradictory evidence, it is likely that participation in forms of sport that require physical aggression will continue to be seen as a way as encouraging and engendering instrumental rather than expressive violence, at least in the short term.

Social learning theorists (Bandura, 1977) suggest that more long-lasting changes in behaviour require constant reinforcement, which can be direct or vicarious. Through participation in sport, people can come in contact with people (peers and coaches) who may disapprove of their violent and criminal activities. New patterns of behaviour are learned through imitation and observation and transgression of rules may mean immediate negative consequences that are detrimental to themselves or the team. Sporting clubs could thus be theorised as 'communities of practice' (Lave & Wenger, 1991) where the influence of peers and coaches can come to bear on young people, along with that of fellow participants. As beginners begin to commit to and associate with pro-social groups with norms of high levels of self-control and commitment to fairness, their status shifts and they move from the periphery to the centre of the community of practice.

An influential study by Giordano et al. (2002) that examined the relationship between gender and desistance takes a more explicitly cognitive approach. This suggests that where people are actively engaged in criminal or violent activity, some activities can engage them and act to bring about a 'cognitive transformation' away from crime and violence. Giordano et al. suggest that this process of transformation and personal reinvention requires first an openness to change, followed by the introduction of a 'hook for change'; a factor that initiates some form of motivation to change, allied to a recognition of the value or meaning of the hook, and that is incompatible with continued violent and criminal behaviour. Sporting activity, especially that with 'currency' (i.e. perceived as holding exchange value in terms of the potential for recognition from others) could therefore be meaningfully conceptualised as such a 'hook' for change, with transformative crime reduction potential, enabling engagement with hard to reach communities and exposure to new peer groups with new value systems.

Of central importance in this transformative process is the relationship between leaders/coaches and participants in terms of the norms, morality and values the coaches communicate and how they encourage participants to move through stages of moral reasoning (Weiss et al., 2008). The development of intrinsic, ethical moral reasoning is more likely to occur where there is some discussion or reflection on the significance of values within the sporting context and an effort to build meta-cognitive ability (i.e. the ability to think about how we think and to reflect on our own thought processes and view of the external world). Classic studies of moral development in young people (e.g. Kohlberg, 1984) suggest the possibility of the emergence of new ethical (and potentially non-criminal/violent) moral reasoning is increased when prosocial values are communicated through conversation and dialogue between peers, as opposed to simply transmitted from traditional authority figures such as parents and teachers. When the coach/leader exerting control over the activity is also someone who can facilitate socio-moral dialogue, young people can build moral reasoning skills. Moreover, if the coach/leader is someone with status and respect gained through legitimate means and with whom young people can identify (that is, see themselves in him/her) young people are effectively presented with an embodied road map – a kind of 'blueprint self' which they can then use as a basis for building a new self-identity. This new identity produces new cognitive filters that begin to characterise previous experiences as negative, detrimental and unwanted. For those involved in crime and serious violence, desisting from such activities requires this kind of change in their own self-image; in effect a re-framing of their experiences which leads to the discovery and then on-going commitment to a new (or a return to an old non-criminal and violent) self.

Gender

In some sports, especially those that require the execution of physical force there is arguably a danger of an emergence of so called 'hyper masculinity' (De Garis, 2002) whereby the belief that violence is 'manly' can come to dominate men's self-image and self-esteem. Masculinity and critical feminist scholars contend that the social construction of masculinity should be viewed as a pluralised phenomenon and structured in hierarchical form, with hegemonic masculinity – a cultural pattern of action that allows some men dominance over women and subordinated males – sitting in pole position in terms of status. Work by Connell (1995), Mac an Ghaill and Haywood (2003), Woodward (2004), and Messerschmidt (2000) is particularly relevant here in helping to understand the interplay between these pluralised masculinities, crime, violence and sport. Sport can lead to the internalisation of normative imperatives that legitimate and value the 'win at any price' attitude. Participants (male and female) might behave aggressively within the sport as a means of asserting their identity/self-esteem or confirming their place in the peer group hierarchy. Violent or aggressive behaviour can be rewarded with recognition, respect, and prestige from peers and then be translated to outside the sports arena. Indeed, it could be argued that a disposition towards violence may in fact be necessary for success in such contact or combat sports. Sugden (1996) describes how certain contact and combat sports such as boxing might have particular appeal to young men as a result of how they are gendered. Contact and combat sports such as rugby, football and boxing carry a high degree of what he refers to as 'masculine currency' or 'man-points' which operate at the micro-level, in the form of status differentiating interactions, especially within some youth subcultures. This hyper-masculine discourse (the 'will to win', physical toughness, ability to withstand pain, honour, 'refusing to kneel', etc), combined with the social and psychic rewards possible – money, power, but also belonging, status, respect, is clearly therefore highly attractive to some men, perhaps especially to those whose ability to escape their restricted social and economic circumstances is otherwise limited. Contact and combat sports can provide men with a way of being that is good and bad simultaneously, a route out of economic hardship, as well as assuaging the physic anxiety over vulnerability which simmers under the surface.

Recent work by Gadd and Dixon (2011) has shed further light on how the hostility men express through violent acts has complex and contradictory roots in their own biographies. Feelings of loss, poor self-worth, and weakness often operate at an unconscious level and are triggered by both the dynamics of their early adverse childhood experiences (ACEs) and the structural barriers they face within society. These psychological factors will lead some men in the same social circumstances to react differently to the obstacles they face through social disadvantage. Some young men may not see how their behaviour, often characterised as respect seeking, is triggered by unconscious motivations to gain control and mask their own weaknesses. They may seek to project these unacknowledged feelings onto others who they can then perceive to possess the traits they most fear in themselves (e.g. vulnerability). When these fears are shared by others within their peer group and allowed to take form within fiercely held notions of territoriality on the basis of post codes, or other allegiances, they can become amplified and hardened as the young men invest more and more in their reputations as a form of psychological self-defence. Individual and collective injuries sustained in the low-level violence that ensues further embed such feelings until violent perpetrators can no longer contain them, and serious violence erupts.

There is some evidence (see Harris & Seal, 2016; Jump, 2009, 2021) that for some young men, involvement in combat sports under the supervision of a coach with clearly defined values and social objectives can begin to compensate for these (often unconscious) feelings of inferiority, shame and humiliation (Gilligan, 2000). The extra self-confidence and sense of personal security that participation in sports such as boxing can provide, when delivered within a strong pro-social and value-led framework, mitigate against these feelings and allow young people to sublimate (i.e. release via positive prosocial behaviours) them more successfully. This could then form the basis of them being able to build reflexive ability and recognise themselves in the hitherto unrecognisable 'other' – (the target of their aggression).

Increased self-respect and esteem built through participation in sport can, for people often detrimentally affected by victimisation, poverty, unemployment and educational underachievement, become the means by which they can withstand criticism and provocation by others and more easily walk away from potentially violent scenarios. Notions of masculinity, rather than being tied to physical and sexual power and domination, can be freed up to include self-restraint and responsibility.

This all hangs of course on the ability of the coach/sports leader to contain their own aggression and temporarily forego any attempt to meet their own emotional needs built up within their own life story. The sports leader's own experience of crime, violence, victimisation and desistance, can either be an aid to reciprocal identification (Harris & Seal, 2016) and therefore contribute to desistance and crime reduction or act as a dangerous, exacerbating, criminogenic influence.

A way forward?

These theories of change illustrate the need for an approach to research and evaluation that recognises the internal psychological processes at work in people involved, or at risk of involvement, in crime and violence whilst also locating them in their social worlds. This in turn suggests a need to dig deeper into the specific qualities that organised sports programmes pursuing social objectives such as crime reduction should feature if they are to have any effect on crime and violence. We really do need therefore to explore more deeply *how* sporting activity has crime reduction and desistance promoting potential. Researchers also need to engage in a detailed qualitative analysis of how individuals participating in sport construct meaning and do or do not identify with those seeking to enter into relationships with them; that is, think deeply about the *'who'* question too.

One way to do this is through the methodological medium of case studies (Stake, 1978; Flyvbjerg, 2011) either of specific projects and/or individuals. In our study "Responding to Youth Violence through Youth Work" (2016) Mike Seal and I closely observed a sports-based youth project based in Cologne, Germany. Workers in the project were drawn from a variety of backgrounds, some of whom possess sport-based qualifications and others with social work backgrounds. Rheinflanke's focus is on preventative measures to indirectly or directly counteract a range of social ills (integration, crime, violence, unemployment) using sporting activity (mainly football and boxing). Specific projects include 'Mobile Jugendarbeit' (street based youth-work) within urban and more rural settings focusing with ethnic communities from Russian, Kosovan, Turkish, Moroccan, and other African backgrounds. A major strand of its pedagogical approach revolves around organised football utilising a 'fair play' approach (Pilz, 1982), whereby young people are encouraged to reflect on how they approach the game, and how this is linked to social behaviour. Alongside customary informal education approaches, experienced youth workers also facilitate combat sports such as boxing, sometimes in the street environment. One particularly innovative approach includes the provision of boxing related activities in public space such as car parks or other meeting places. Workers bring sports equipment, including boxing gloves and pads to various sites in the outlying districts of Cologne where young people gather and where there have been reports of nuisance behaviour, sometimes spilling over into petty crime and violence. They then facilitate informal sparring and other boxing related exercises in an atmosphere of banter and light-hearted physical exertion, whilst also providing food and drink from the bus. These informal activities are then developed organically over time into more formalised training sessions in local premises. The mobile provision allows workers to capitalise on young peoples' enthusiasm for activities in the moment and in an environment that they feel comfortable within.

The workers we spoke to stressed that they saw boxing as an effective tool for engaging with young men who might be involved in crime and violence precisely because its combat element is close to their mindsets and existing interests. As such it has 'masculine currency' (Sugden, 1996); a form of sub-cultural street capital that operates in dangerous places (Campbell, 1993) at the micro-level in the form of status differentiating interactions. For the youth workers, boxing provides the arena for these interactions to be explored. We saw young men keen to test their emerging potency, and workers unearthing this in order to then challenge how it might be central to their violent and criminal behaviour, especially spontaneous outbreaks of violence. Workers described how sparring within box training, under tightly controlled conditions, allows those struggling to contain their aggression, to in their words "play with the moment of escalation". They explained how they sought to build recognition of the value of reciprocity into training regimes. Swapping blows with sparring partners facilitated increased awareness of when physical blows became mutually harmful rather than beneficial. Encouraging experimentation with physical contact within controlled boundaries allowed the young people to identify when, or at what point, playful, physical rough and tumble became unwelcome, and when their aggression was becoming expressive rather than instrumental.

Where young peoples' aggression was rooted in earlier biographical experiences, workers claimed that the sublimation of this aggression through boxing helped prevent its manifestation into more harmful and dangerous forms of expressive violence. They sought to reconfigure the 'will to win', an integral part of these young men's masculine identity, so that it could include self-control and restraint, with a tangible benefit in a new sporting, and therefore pro-social context. We interviewed young people who had been engaged by Rheinflanke and had moved from the periphery to the centre of informal groups centred on football and boxing and they reported that as they did so, they began to adopt the norms of the older group members and the boxing coaches. In addition to the opportunity to cathartically release aggression and exposure to new norms of behaviour, young people talked about how boxing in the gym had impacted positively impact on their self-esteem and self-respect. They believed this had led to a decrease in their need to assert dominance in the face of provocation. The inner assurance gained through greater control of (and confidence in) their bodies produced a decreased desire to exert power through their bodies, especially when provoked.

Conclusion

In order to understand the potential for sport to reduce crime and promote desistance, I suggest that research needs to engage in this kind of detailed qualitative analysis of how individuals construct meaning and do or do not identify with those seeking to enter into relationships with them. Through such analysis, research can highlight the central importance of the relationship between sports coaches and participants and the possibility for both negative and positive effects on desistance and crime reduction. The potential of participation in sport to reduce crime rests on the extent to which it can be deployed in such a way as to engender psychological change. For people involved in crime to become receptive to the idea that their behaviour is detrimental to society and themselves, they need to develop a degree of *reflexivity*, i.e. an ability to reflect on their own thought processes and view of the external world. Researchers also need to take into account the impact of social environment on people from deprived communities, as this can help explain why some similarly placed people from those communities become criminal and violent and others do not, or able to desist from such behaviours. The internal processes at work in people involved in crime and violence are always better understood by locating them firmly in a social world. A *psychosocial* conceptual framework is one that can illuminate both the psychological roots of crime and violence in people's biographies – feelings of loss, poor self-worth, and weakness that can operate at an unconscious level – and the structural (social) disadvantages they face. It can also meaningfully inform the shaping, funding and evaluation of sport-based activities with crime reduction objectives. For example, more attention may need to be given to the intersubjective dynamics between sports leaders and participants. Project proposals should foreground certain abilities of the sports trainer/worker as prerequisites, namely the ability to create relationships which are socio-moral in character and to capitalise on the currency generated through sport to both inhabit and disrupt world-views that may include problematic identity constructions such as hyper-masculinity. Supplementing efforts to measure *what* works with questions of *how* and *who* works should remain part of academic and political activity that seeks to understand and promote the crime reduction potential of sport.

References

Bandura, A. (1977). *Social Learning Theory*. New York: General Learning Press.
Baron, R. A. (1977). *Human Aggression*. New York: Plenum Press.
Becker, H. (1963). *Outsiders: Studies in the Sociology of Deviance*. New York: Free Press.
Begg, D. J. et al. (1996). "Sport and delinquency: An examination of the deterrence hypothesis in a longitudinal study". *British Journal of Sports Medicine*, 30 (4), 335–341.
Benjamin, J. (2017). *Beyond Doer and Done to: Recognition Theory, Intersubjectivity and the Third*. London: Routledge.
Berkowitz, L. (1993). *Aggression: Its Causes, Consequences, and Control*. New York: McGraw-Hill.
Berkowitz, L. (2000). *Causes and Consequences of Feelings*. New York: Cambridge University Press.
Best, C. (1985). "Differences in social values between athletes and non-athletes". *Research Quarterly for Exercise and Sport*, 56 (4), 366–369.
Bjørkqvist, K. & Varhama, L. (2001). "Attitudes toward violent conflict resolution among male and female karateka in comparison with practitioners of other sports". *Perceptual and Motor Skills*, 92, 586–588.
Bloom, G. A. & Smith, M. D. (1996). "Hockey violence: A test of cultural spillover theory". *Sociology of Sport Journal*, 13, 65–77.
Brettschneider, W. D. & Kleine, T. (2002). *Jugendarbeit in Sportvereinen*: Anspruch und Wirklichkeit. Schorndorf: Hofmann.
Brettschneider, W. D., Brandl-Bredenbeck, H. P., & Hofmann, J. (2005). *Sportpartizipation und Gewaltbereitschaft bei Jugendlichen*. Aachen: Meyer & Meyer.
Bushman, B. J., Baumeister, R. F., & Stack, A. D. (1999). "Catharsis, aggression, and persuasive influence: Self-fulfilling or self-defeating prophecies?" *Journal of Personality and Social Psychology*, 76, 367–376.
Campbell, B. (1993). *Goliath. Britain's Dangerous Places*. London: Methuen.
Coakley, J. (1984). "Mead's theory on the development of the self: implications for organized youth sport programs". *Paper presented at the Olympic Scientific Congress, Eugene, OR Commission of the European Communities, (2007)*. *White Paper on Sport*. Brussels: EC.
Connell, R. (1995). *Masculinities*. Cambridge: Polity Press.
Cooley, C. H. (1902). *Human Nature and the Social Order*. New York: Scribner's.
Curry, T. J. (1998). "Beyond the locker room: Campus bars and college athletes". *Sociology of Sport Journal*, 15 (3), 205–215.

De Garis, L. (2002). "'Be a buddy to your buddy', male identity, aggression, and intimacy in a boxing gym", in J. McKay, M. Messner, & D. Sabo, eds, *Masculinities, Gender Relations and Sport*, pp. 87–107. London: Sage.

Eccles, J. & Gootman, J., eds, (2002). *Community Programs to Promote Youth Development*. Washington, DC: National Academy Press.

Eder, D., Evans, C. C., & Parker, S. (1997). *School Talk: Gender and Adolescent Culture*. New Brunswick, NJ: Rutgers University Press.

Fitch, T. J. & Marshall, J. L. (2000). "Faces of violence in sports", in D. S. Sandhu, ed., *Faces of Violence: Psychological Correlates, Concepts, and Intervention Strategies*, pp. 87–102. New York: Nova Science Publishers, Inc.

Flyvbjerg, B. (2011). "Case study", in Norman K. Denzin & Yvonna S. Lincoln, eds, *The Sage Handbook of Qualitative Research*, 4th Edition, pp. 301–316. Thousand Oaks, CA: Sage, Chapter 17.

Gadd, D. (2006). "The role of recognition in the desistance process. A case analysis of a former far right activist". *Theoretical Criminology*, 10 (2), 179–202.

Gadd, D. & Dixon, B. (2011). *Losing the Race*. London: Karnac.

Gilligan, J. (2000). *Violence: Reflections on Our Deadliest Epidemic*. London: Jessica Kingsley Publishers.

Giordano, P., Kernkovich, S., & Rudolph, S. (2002). "Gender, crime and desistance: Toward a theory of cognitive transformation". *American Journal of Sociology*, 107 (4), 990–1064.

Harris, P. & Seal, M. (2016) *Responding to Youth Violence through Youth Work*. Bristol: Policy Press.

Healy, D. (2010). *The Dynamics of Desistance: Charting Pathways through Change*. Abingdon: Willan.

Hirschi, T. (1969). *Causes of Delinquency*. London: Routledge.

Jump, D. (2009). *Martial Arts as a Vehicle for Social Change*. Winston Churchill Memorial Funded Research.

Jump, D. (2021). "'Look who is laughing now': Physical capital, boxing, and the prevention of repeat victimisation". *Onati Socio-Legal Series*, 11 (5), 1095–1113. ISSN 2079-5971.

Kohlberg, L. (1984). *The Psychology of Moral Development: The Nature and Validity of Moral Stages (Essays on Moral Development, Volume 2)*. New York: Harper & Row.

Kreager, D. A. (2007). "Unnecessary roughness? School sports, peer networks, and male adolescent violence". *American Sociological Review*, 72 (5), 705–724.

Lamarre, B. W. & Nosanchuk, T. A. (1999). "Judo – The gentle way: A replication of studies on martial arts and aggression". *Perceptual and Motor Skills*, 88, 992–996.

Landers, D. M. & Landers, D. M. (1978). "Socialization via interscholastic athletics: Its effects on delinquency". *Sociology of Education*, 51 (4), 299–303.

Langbein, L. & Bess, R. (2002). "Sports in school: Source of amity or antipathy?". *Social Science Quarterly*, 83 (2), 436–454.

Laub, J. H. & Sampson, R. J. (2003). *Shared Beginnings, Divergent Lives: Delinquent Boys to Age 70*. Cambridge: Harvard University Press.

Lave, J. & Wenger, E. (1991). *Situated Learning. Legitimate Peripheral Participation*. Cambridge: Cambridge University Press.

Loland, S. & McNamee, M. (2000). "Fair play and the ethos of sports: An eclectic philosophical framework". *Journal of Philosophy of Sport*, 27: 63–80.

Mac an Ghaill, M. & Haywood, C (2003). *Men and Masculinities: Theory, Research and Social Practice*. Buckingham: Open University Press.

Mahoney, J. (2000). "School extracurricular activity participation as a moderator in the development of antisocial patterns". *Child Development*, 71 (2), 502–516.

Maruna, S. (2007). *Making Good: How Ex-Convicts Reform and Rebuild Their Lives*. American Psychological Association.

Maruna, S., Lebel, T., Mitchell, N., & Naples, M. (2004). "Pygmalion in the reintegration process. Desistance from crime through the looking glass". *Psychology, Crime and Law*, 10 (3), 271–281.

Messerschmidt, J. (2000). *Nine Lives: Adolescent Masculinities, the Body and Violence*. Colorado: Westview Press.

Messner, M. A. (1990). "When bodies are weapons: Masculinity and violence in sports". *International Review for the Sociology of Sport*, 25, 202–220.

Miedzian, M. (1991). *Breaking the Link between Masculinity and Violence. Boys Will Be Boys*. New York: Anchor Books Doubleday.

Miller, K. E. et al. (2006). "Jocks, gender, binge drinking, and adolescent violence". *Journal of Interpersonal Violence*, 21 (1), 105–120.

Mutz, M. & Baur, J. (2009). "The role of sports for violence prevention: Sport club participation and violent behaviour among adolescents". *International Journal of Sport Policy*, 1 (3), 305–321.

Nichols, G. (2007). *Sport and Crime Reduction. The Role of Sports in Tackling Youth Crime*. London: Routledge.

Nixon, H. L. (1997). "Gender, sport, and aggressive behaviour outside sport". *Journal of Sport and Social Issues*, 21, 379–391.

Nosanchuk, T. A. (1981). "The way of the warrior: The effects of traditional martial arts training on aggressiveness". *Human Relations*, 34, 435–444.

Paetsch, J. J. & Bertrand, L. D. (1997). "The relationship between peer, social, and school factors, and delinquency among youth". *Journal of School Health*, 67 (1), 27–33.

Pilz, G. (1982). *Wandlungen der Gewalt im Sport. Eine entwicklungssoziologische Analyse unter besonderer Berücksichtigung des Frauensports*, Diss. Hannover 1981.

Rowe, C. J. (1998). "Aggression and violence in sports". *Psychiatric Annals*, 28, 265–269.

Russel, G. W. (1983). "Psychological issues in sports aggression", in J. H. Goldstein, ed., *Sports Violence*, pp. 157–181. New York: Springer-Verlag.

Segrave, J. O. & Chu, D. B. (1978). "Athletics and juvenile delinquency". *Review of Sport and Leisure*, 3(2), 3–24.

Skelton, D. L., Glynn, M. A., & Berta, S. M. (1991). "Aggressive behaviour as a function of taekwondo ranking". *Perceptual and Motor Skills*, 72, 179–182.

Stake, R. E. (1978). "The case study method in social inquiry". *Educational Researcher*, 7 (2), 5–8.

Stark, R., Kent, L. & Finke, R. (1987). "Sports and delinquency", in M. R. Gottfredson & T. Hirschi, eds, *Positive Criminology*, pp. 115–124. Newbury Park, CA: SAGE.

Sugden, J. (1996). *Boxing and Society: An International Analysis*. Manchester: Manchester University Press.

Van Bottenburg, M. & Schuyt, K. (1996). *De maatschappelijke betekenis van sport (The Societal Meaning of Sport)*. Arnhem: NOC∗NSF.

Watkins, R. B. (2000). "A social psychological examination of the relationship between athletic participation and delinquent behaviour". *Dissertation Abstracts International*, 60, 4969.

Weiss, M. R., Smith, A. L., & Stuntz, C. P. (2008). "Moral development in sport and physical activity", in T. S. Horn, ed., *Advances in Sport Psychology*, pp. 187–210, 449–452. London: Human Kinetics.

Woodward, K. (2004). "Rumbles in the jungle: Boxing, racialization and the performance of masculinity". *Journal of Leisure Studies*, 23 (1), 5–17.

Zivin, G., Hassan, N. R., DePaula, G. F., Monti, D. A., Harlan, C., Hossain, K. D., & Patterson, K. (2001). "An effective approach to violence prevention: Traditional, martial arts in middle school". *Adolescence*, 36, 443–459.

PART VI

Elite sport, activism, and media

30
ENGLISH FOOTBALL, SAFE STANDING, AND SOCIAL MOVEMENTS

An eventful sociology of fan activism

Mark Turner

Introduction

Whilst there is a plethora of sociological research examining the role of sport in becoming a positive vehicle for social, cultural, and political change, the specific focus on sports activism and sports-based social movements, and their capacity to bring about social justice, remains largely underrresearched and theoretically underdeveloped. Social movements remain important fields of collective action, through which social injustice can be fought and mobilised against. Recently, there has been a proliferation of research into the historical role of sports athletes as *activists*, seeking to raise awareness of social justice, and develop critical consciousness of, important peace, anti-globalisation, anti-racism, anti-sexism, and environmental interventions (Harvey et al., 2013; Boycoff & Carrington, 2020). Through this lens, movements for social justice can be defined as those seeking to break down social, cultural, economic, environmental, or political barriers which limit individual, and collective, rights to place, community, citizenship, and democracy.

Despite this focus on athletes as activists for justice, there remains a dearth of research into the specific micro-level networks, relations and social interactions which produce protests as important social and cultural events (Spracklen & Lamond, 2016), with legacies which have long-term impacts upon their lifeworlds. In this chapter, the relational social worlds of English football are examined to address this gap, and in doing so, this chapter extends research that explores mainstream social justice, through contemporary football social movements. In doing so, this chapter demonstrates that the emergence and mobilizations of movements in football are of interest to general sociology. To do this, this chapter focuses not on athletes but spectator activists, and thus stretches and problematises the creative sociability of football fans in England, in order to theoretically explore their processes of collective action, across the late twentieth and early twenty-first centuries, and the specific historical events through which these networks, interactions, and mobilisations are embedded. By drawing on a high-profile case study in English football, 'Safe Standing', coordinated by the national Football Supporters Association (FSA), this chapter argues that social movements for justice in football, often reinforce the longer-term impact and legacy of important events on, in this case, supporters' rights, and their modern consumption of football as serious leisure.

To operationalise this, this chapter is organised into three parts. First, I introduce Safe Standing and consider the historical, cultural and political conditions from which it emerged across the neoliberal timescape of English football. Second, I conceptualise and apply relational sociology to unpack contemporary football fan activism and mobilisations. And third, I cross-pollinate ideas from sociology and social movement studies on eventful protests and temporality, to show how significant events and ruptures, in this case English football, continue to shape the dynamics of social movements in temporally sensitive ways. By examining the diversity of the associative dynamics of this movement, its national and international networks of influence, and its ability to reverse, to some extent, neoliberal processes of discriminating, and standardising, the rituals, and behaviours of football fans in the long duration after the Hillsborough stadium disaster, attention is thus paid to the complex struggle supporters face over the ritualistic expression of identity and solidarity, which in the case of football, are important markers, of the rights and justices of fans as social actors. This adds theoretical value to our understanding of how social movement meanings are produced across both the political and discursive fields of contention in sociology and sport and leisure studies.

The end of the terraces and the new ritual of watching football

For most English football supporters throughout the twentieth century, the ritual of watching football involved standing on football terraces as a cultural practice. And this became important sociologically because it constituted a public ritual in contemporary British society through which new supporter solidarities emerged. Standing together, football supporters, and the social networks they formed, produced the atmosphere and spectacle which are built into the collective memories and social histories of generations of men, women and children in Britain. What bound them together, according to Wagg (2004), was the mythic sense of freedom to actively express support in ways which were not over-regulated or over-constrained.

Despite this, by 1985, English football was generally played poorly in front of dwindling crowds of violent and often racist men in unsafe and unsanitary football grounds which had little market value (King, 1998). Consequently, the British media and UK government began to increasingly demand that football be brought into line with the direction of broader social and economic change. In order to contextualise the significant social, cultural, and political changes in English football culture and consumption over the past 30 years, it is important to historicise the ways in which an evolution of football stadium legislation, in the wake of a series of disasters on the terraces, further strengthened the role of the state, and ideological commitment to neoliberal, free-market economics (Webber, 2017).

The growing concern over football hooliganism during mid-late twentieth century, resulted in the UK government enacting repressive measures to further prevent spectator violence at matches in England, including the merits of all-seated stadia, the introduction of a national membership scheme, and the installation of perimeter fencing between supporters and the pitch (Taylor, 1991). According to King (1998), these measures echoed then UK Prime Minister Margaret Thatcher's attempt to move the focus of attention from supporter safety to public order, and were characteristic of the government's response to other social disasters which revealed a lax and negligent attitude towards health and safety, and a culture which prioritised profitability (Webber, 2017).

On 29 May 1985, during the UEFA European Cup final between Juventus and Liverpool at Heysel in Brussels, a wall collapsed in section Z of the stadium as a result of a crush created by a group of Liverpool supporters charging towards the Juventus fans (King, 1998). Consequently, 39 Juventus supporters lost their lives and all English football clubs were banned from European competitions for five years by UEFA. According to Taylor (1987), Heysel characterised a changing conjuncture in the development of class relationships in Britain during the 1980s, whereby the bourgeois ethic of competitive market individualism promoted by the radical right and the lack of economic, cultural, or political alternatives, alienated both the bourgeois worker and the mass of unemployed youth. Four years later, the most significant stadium disaster in English football occurred on 15 April 1989 at Hillsborough in Sheffield, resulting in the deaths of 96 Liverpool supporters (Scraton, 2002). According to Taylor (1991, p. 7), the legacy of perimeter fencing and the way in which it acted as a "caged-in pen from which there was no means of escape at a predictable moment of crisis of mass spectator excitement and anxiety", was one of the critical determining causes of the disaster. Immediately after Hillsborough, the UK government set up an inquiry led by Lord Justice Taylor to investigate the causes of the disaster and two reports subsequently emerged. The first interim report published in August 1989 focused on why Hillsborough happened and produced a series of interim recommendations which included "limiting the number of spectators entering each self-contained terraced pen or area to the maximum capacity figure" (Interim Taylor Report, 1989, p. 57). However, the final report published in January 1990, which expanded the post-Hillsborough vision of a 'better future for football', produced a series of more robust recommendations on the need for greater crowd control, including all-seated stadia. As King (1998, p. 99) noted, "Taylor's preference for seating stemmed from his belief that a seated crowd was more controllable" and put together with improved accommodation, better facilities, and better training of police and stewards, these measures would according to Taylor (HM Government, 1990, p. 75) provide the best chance of eliminating or minimising hooliganism. However, whilst the Taylor Report argued that seating offered a safer method of spectating than standing and that "spectators would become accustomed and educated to sitting" (1990, p.14), it also acknowledged that the practice of standing itself at football was "not intrinsically unsafe". Consequently, for King (1998, p. 99), the report must be read within the context of a desire to encourage the attendance of more "disciplined (respectable) families in place of violently disposed young males" but in a way which also recognised Taylor's own concern that some traditional supporters may be excluded as a result of the financial constraints imposed by free market capitalism.

Whilst the Taylor report in many ways was underpinned by social democratic and Keynesian sentiments towards the universal provision of football and public provision of seating, it nonetheless became a catalyst for the restructuring of the leagues' political economy and altering the possibilities for the ritualistic expression of supporter identity and solidarity (King, 1998). In 1990, the UK government enforced Taylor's all-seater recommendations, and a new body, the Football Licensing Authority (now Sports Ground Safety Authority), would operate a licensing system for (all-seated) football grounds used for designated matches and to monitor local authorities' oversight of spectator safety. However, whilst Taylor's interim report was critical of the police officers in charge at Hillsborough, the main thrust of the final report shifted responsibility towards Britain's decaying terraces. The opportunity was missed, therefore, to challenge the prevailing antipathy that existed then, and indeed continues to exist today, towards football fans amongst those responsible for enforcing law and order (Webber, 2017). According to Pearson (2012), the removal of the terraces and the increased regulation within and around football grounds, reduced some capacity for younger fans to experience the carnivalesque nature of home fixtures in traditional ways. Moreover, whilst continuing to expand football's wider public appeal as a modern inclusive game, the imposition of all-seated stadia and the subsequent increases in admission prices and surveillance of supporters represented a significant assault on fan culture and became one of the most important issues which supporters collectively coalesce around. Lord Justice Taylor overstated the extent to which fans would become accustomed to the all-seating legislation. Since 1990, thousands of supporters at games played in the Premier League and Championship have continued to stand, but in areas not designed for them do so. This persistent standing in all-seated stadia has been a sustained source of conflict between football clubs, supporters, stewards, police officers, and various safety bodies.

The imposition of all-seating as an attendance model led, on the other hand, to processes of mobilisation and association of supporters in the new arenas, a reaction to such policies, and to the interruption of traditional ways of supporting clubs. Together, individual supporters, informal supporter groups and formal supporter organisations like the FSA, networked together by way of social ties, built a social movement which now stands to potentially impact and shape the consumption habits of a leisure practice and ritual all over the world. This movement, Safe Standing, seeks to bring about a change to the all-seating legislation by arguing that alternative technologies now allow clubs to create purpose-built Safe Standing areas. Clubs would thus decide, in consultation with supporters, what mix of standing areas or permitted standing in existing seated areas would be most suitable for them (Football Supporters Association [FSA], 2020). Safe Standing was high on the political agenda pre-COVID, and in February 2020, the Sports Grounds Safety Authority (SGSA) reported its emerging findings, namely, the introduction of barrier seating appears to have reduced the potential for conflict and associated risks with fans persistently standing in all-seated areas. In March 2021, Manchester City FC announced plans to install 5,600 Safe Standing 'barrier' seats during the 2021/2022 season, and five months later in August, the Secretary of State for Digital, Culture, Media and Sport announced the government's plan to formally lift the standing ban by allowing a handful of Premier League clubs to use such designated Safe Standing areas in pilot form, as a possible precursor to formal legislation change over the next couple of years (Dowden cited in Winter, 2021).

This case remains sociologically important, because the restriction and partial exclusion of this social group, post-Hillsborough, constitutes a profound social change. Indeed, as a public ritual in contemporary British society, standing at football remains central to the consumption practice and leisure habits of men and women across all parts of society. Moreover, football supporter culture offers sociologists a unique insight into both the origins and consequences of social movements because few other forms of human behaviour are capable of gathering such large crowds on a regular basis. Having contextualised the social, cultural and political conditions from which the all-seating legislation emerged, this chapter turns to understand the complex interplay of cultural and technological dynamics and their manifestations across the compelling timeframes and orientations which make up the consumption of English football in a post-Hillsborough landscape over the past 30 years.

'Football without fans is nothing': Unpacking contemporary fan protests

In sociology, 'traditional' football fandom is often conceptualised as having emerged during the mid-to-late twentieth century, as a predominantly male expression of local identity, and one which developed through standing terrace culture (Taylor, 1971). During the 1970s and 1980s, English football witnessed an intensification of supporter violence, often referred to as 'hooliganism', which became ingrained within British societal consciousness as a social problem (Dunning et al., 1986). Consequently, professional football came to define supporters as 'deviant'. The subsequent moral panic which emerged during a period of economic recession was characterised by an evolution of football safety legislation in the wake of Heysel and Hillsborough (Greenfield & Osborn, 1998). Together, they strengthened the role of the state and an ideological commitment to neoliberal, free market economics (Webber, 2017). And thus, the legacy of Hillsborough became the core conjunctural argument for the reform of football and its supporters (King, 1998), whilst the negative reputation ascribed to them was exploited within popular discourse.

The political economy of English football during the 1990s was, according to King (1998), characterised by the motivation of new entrepreneurial club directors to diversify the consumption of football through the concept of the fan as 'customer'. Whilst this helped attract more women and families to the game, it also encouraged a more restrained form of consumption, thereby acting as a Foucauldian disciplinary measure and governing rubric for the management of supporter behaviour (Pearson, 2012). This, in turn, facilitated increasingly subdued and dispassionate forms of spectating, and less space for collective forms of expression and physicality associated with terrace culture (Crabbe and Brown, 2004).

Consequently, the emergence of the FSA, football fanzines, and Independent Supporter Association (ISA) networks, were according to King (1998), characterised by a culture of 'new football writing' as a distinct style of fandom, informed by boyhood memories of a 'golden age' of football, and founded largely upon socially democratic principles. These memories shaped fanzine writers' response to the neoliberal timescape of football during the late 1980s and 1990s. Central to this was the publication of print fanzines which enabled a supporters' view and often radical interpretation of popular cultural forms to be expressed by fans excluded from mainstream expressions about the new consumption of football (Jary et al., 1991). According to Millward (2008, p. 300), "fanzines sought to provide fans with a liberal voice and were partially created as a form of cultural resistance against the 1980s conflation of football with the racist–hooligan couplet". These were mainly produced by white males, aged 30 years or younger and educated beyond a compulsory educational standard with left wing or liberal political views (Jary et al., 1991).

The reading of fans' interaction with modern football, then, should consider the potentially shared interests between both dominant and subordinate supporter groups, which texture social relations in often complex ways. Indeed, these supporter networks according to King (2003) often consist of a complex and diverse hierarchy of status groups which coalesce and unify at specific clubs to develop relational fan cultures. But whilst some contemporary supporters' groups seek to escalate carnivalesque activity in order to differentiate themselves from more consumer and tourist-based fan networks, their motivations are often at odds with those attempting to manage and control contemporary football crowds (Pearson, 2012).

However, football supporters' social networks are usually divided by established lines of club rivalry (Hill et al., 2018), and thus the mobilisation of club-specific supporter networks is often more effective within increasingly deregulated environments. And whilst these networks continue to be important to the consumption and production of modern football, the integration of such groups, and their capacity to become powerful actors, lies in the collective. Recognising this, sociologists have moved beyond club-based social movement research to consider the ways in which diverse groups unite against the corporate logics of modern football across online and urban spaces (Hill et al., 2018). However, the socio-cultural origins of supporter networks involved in opposition initiatives against the all-seating legislation over three decades remain largely underexplored. Indeed, contemporary movements like *Against Modern Football* (Numerato, 2015) often reference the role of important 'switchers' within supporter groups like the FSA, but do not empirically investigate the histories or mechanisms of the networks seeking to transcend and change contemporary football culture. Switchers, according to Castells (2013), are individuals who are successfully able to connect and ensure the corporation of different networks by sharing common goals and resources.

This chapter addresses this challenge by showing how, whilst contemporary supporter movements continue to articulate reflexivity towards ideas like *Against Modern Football* (that is, a movement which encompasses many different problems supporters have with the game in terms of governance, ownership, atmosphere, cost, etc.), the mobilisations of supporter networks and their consumption of the game are characterised by repeated patterns of social interaction and the legacy of historical events in football, namely the Hillsborough disaster. Across different temporal periods post-1989, the imposition of all-seated stadia, as a key feature of modern football, has agitated a longer-term process of mobilisation. Indeed, recognising this temporal sensitivity, often underexplored in other academic research into football supporter movements, is critical if we are to understand the ways in which networks mobilise, navigate, and negotiate the contours of periods of profound political, economic, and social change. Over the past 30 years, the emergence of a new wave of supporter movements has sought to break down the power of the state in order to achieve more effective involvement and representation in the running of clubs and the game more broadly. Indeed, these actions and demands of supporters and their relationship to broader social, cultural, and political changes must be situated within the wider context of contemporary Britain and social transformations.

Temporality, social movements, and relational sociology

The importance of temporality in sociology has been illustrated by recent case studies on migration (Bass & Yeoh, 2019) and transnational family and long-distance marriages (Acedera & Yeoh, 2019). This body of research captures the importance of recognising how time is constantly negotiated in the lives of people through different, but interdependent, temporal strategies and mobilities. In social movement research, scholars have brought together ideas on temporality and the study of events, by paying attention to the ways in which movements, and the socio-political environments in which they both act and move, and produce moments of protests which 'shock' or 'punctuate' the cultural and material flows of social interaction (Gillan, 2020a; Wagner-Pacifici, 2017). Wagner-Pacifici and Ruggero (2020) highlight how contradictory ideas across different timescales often problematise interaction and coordination among movement actors, whilst Della Porta (2020) shows how particular 'eventful' protests trigger 'critical junctures' which produce abrupt but also long-lasting transformations. At the heart of these analyses is an attempt to understand the intersecting or relational dynamics which are relevant to the study of social movements and time (Haydu, 2020).

This eventful approach to social movements, largely influenced by Sewell's call for an 'eventful sociology' (2005), is useful for considering how mobilisations on sports-based activism like Safe Standing, are relational to the complex temporal sequence of which they are a part. For Sewell (2005), events become significant when they shape and constrain actors' ability to act in the social world, and in doing so, have capacity to produce changes in what he termed, the durable patterns of social relations. This is an important analytical insight when considering both the impact of events on social movements, and moments of protest themselves, as temporal events, because they advance debates on movement mobilisation, by problematising the established importance placed on external political opportunity structures and the role of movement organisations (Edwards, 2014). Embedded within relational sociology, this approach enables us to focus on the socio-political environments of movements as symbolic and discursive spaces in which interactions between activists and other agents, which may include the state, take place (Goldstone, 2004). For Gillan (2020b), this socio-political context is important because it enables us to see more general processes of social change producing certain forms of movements, especially through the construction of new collective identities, rather than solely focusing on political opportunities. This socio-political context is not static but comprises multiple temporal periods and processes. Gillan (2020a) uses the term timescape to capture both the sudden and gradual social changes which, over time, alter the contours and flows of power and counter-power in society.

By focusing on timescape, instead of 'political opportunity' structure, is to "recognise that movements move within an uneven temporality encompassing both repeated patterns of interaction and the contingent unfolding of historical events", which in turn produce interpretations, social action and new events (Gillan, 2020a, p. 519). To make sense of the balance of continuity and change amongst movements over time, Gillan (2020a) introduces the term *vectors*, which signal the important discourses, practices and inter-subjective meanings activists give to such movements and events. By presenting those two different analytical angles on Safe Standing, theoretical and empirical value is added to our understanding of eventful protests and temporality, because by focusing on the storied dimensions of *vectors*, as interdependent actors and action, it becomes clear, that whilst political opportunities remain important structures in English and European football and sport more broadly, the creativity and coordination of small networks are important to the meaning sports activists give to movements and events.

In this discussion, the theoretical and conceptual implications of this work for the study of activism and social justice become clear, because by showing the long-lasting impact of a 30-year conflict, the longer-term empirical significance of events, ruptures and *vectors* to social movements is analytically illuminated. Whilst recent sociological research has considered the ways in which various constituencies within social movements share many values but also disjunctive ideas about compelling timeframes and orientations (Wagner-Pacifici & Ruggero, 2020), the opportunity remains for critical scholars of sport and leisure to deeply profile a movement across a longer-term timescape. What makes English football, and this case, an interesting focus for the study of collective action and temporality, is that as a *lifeworld*, with a rich array of resources and networks, it is characterised by a longstanding historical tribal fan culture as a form of consumption, and a greater focus on club-based fan protests as opposed to national supporter movements (King, 2003). This offers an opportunity to examine the micro-level dynamics of supporter movements as interdependent networks (Crossley, 2015a), and in doing so, provide a rich account of the ways in which events and critical historical moments are played out within movements as networks, and sometimes produce long-lasting social transformations (Della Porta, 2020).

Events and ruptures in the post-Hillsborough neoliberal timescape

In English football, there have been three historically significant events which shaped many of the interpretative practices of football supporter networks and their consumption of the game. Together, they produced the political economic vectors of this neoliberal timescape which have been most relevant to the contemporary wave of football supporter movements, in the generation of grievances against which they move. First, the Heysel disaster in 1985 became a historical event which agitated a small network in Liverpool to form the Football Supporters' Association movement, and in doing so, trigger a wider subjective strain felt by supporters across the various regions of English football.

Second, for those in the FSA and football fanzine movements seeking to "reclaim the game", the Hillsborough disaster became a *rupturing moment* (Wagner-Pacifici, 2017) creating a period of uncertainty and disorientation, at a time when different political ideologies were beginning to emerge. Some activists felt the FSA was becoming a Liverpool-centred network. This period of uncertainty characterised the FSA's response to Hillsborough and the Taylor Report, and whilst there were some attempts to protest through campaigns such as *Stand Up For Your Right to Stand Up*, ultimately, there remained little support in the game politically. This intersected with a vagueness on what the FSA, and those within the fanzine movement, were collectively arguing for. Initially, for some within the FSA, the core rejection of all-seated stadia focused on freedom of choice and the preservation of standing terraces; however, for others, this presented an opportunity to consult engineers on the design of new terracing.

Third, the entry of BSkyB into English football was as symbolic as it was game changing, and in 1991, a proposal by the Football Association (FA) supporting a breakaway Super (Premier) League was accepted by the five biggest clubs who commanded the highest attendance figures. This became the catalyst for a five-year television deal between BSkyB and the newly formed PL worth £304 million (Millward, 2011). For King (1998), it was at this decisive moment where English football, embracing the post-Keynesian free market, came to be irretrievably embodied by Thatcherism and neoliberalism. The formation of the Premier League, after Heysel and Hillsborough, was a significant event which helped diversify the consumption of football and facilitate increasingly subdued and dispassionate forms of spectating, through less space for collective forms of expression and physicality.

However, the micro-level effects of this commercialisation were most obviously felt amongst supporters at individual clubs, and thus the emergence of Independent Supporter Associations (ISAs) were more effective in mobilising fan networks within increasingly deregulated environments (King, 1998). Despite this, ISAs, football fanzines, and the FSA developed shared ways of working and influenced each other indirectly, producing the solidarities which bound core supporter networks together through a shared ideological commitment to a post-Thatcherite social democracy. Yet, together, they actively opposed many of the conjunctural arguments for the reform and regulation of supporters. In doing so, the FSA helped network a critical mass of highly resourced actors who were able to communicate effectively across the various regions of English football, notably from cities such as Liverpool, London, Sheffield, Birmingham, Newcastle, Leeds, Manchester, and Southampton. Together, they constituted a critical mass because, as Crossley (2015b) argued, in larger populations the connecting of resources, communication, capital and collective effervescence is more successful. And many of these supporters, hailing from the middle class, and having attended university, included academics, police officers, trade union activists, business people, and journalists, and held prior social ties to key people inside individual football clubs and the wider industry.

As King (2003) argued, football supporter networks consist of a complex and diverse hierarchy of status groups which coalesce and unify at specific football clubs to develop relational fan cultures. And whilst these cultures do not embody specific 'traditional working class' values, they are in many cases concerned with the 'working class' consumption of the game. During the late 1990s, Safe Standing emerged, from the switching of networked FSA and ISA practices, who together, with the support of fanzines, coordinated small campaigns against the all-seating legislation. These included *Stand Up for Football, Stand Up Like We Used to* and *Bring Back Terracing*. In 1998, a small network of 11 supporters, connected by means of pre-existing networks, formed a 'Coalition of Football Supporters' (CoFS), as a hub-centred network and homophilous cluster.

These standing protests were initially framed in a way which connected to an imagined discourse of authenticity, which in turn helped generate a growing sense of 'moral protest' against the perceived draconian actions of clubs towards the persistent standing of supporters in all-seated areas (Polletta & Jasper, 2001). However, whilst the capacity of fans to build relational collective action was in part due to the creativity and resources within supporters' networks, this must be situated within the wider social transformations of contemporary British society and the Third Way political economy of the New Labour government. Indeed, central figures within the CoFS network became members of the UK government's formal Football Task Force working group in 1997, which aimed to assess the growing impact of football's commercialisation. This was significant for three reasons. First, it ensured that supporters' calls for greater involvement in the regulation of the game became central to ongoing strategic interactions with the state. This was achieved in part through the development of the Supporters' Trust movement, which, with the aid of government funding, encouraged the promotion of democratic supporter ownership. Second, whilst the deregulation of the football industry figured centrally as the economic vector of English football's neoliberal timescape, the significance of Hillsborough as an *event* which reconfigured the ritual of watching football became Safe Standing's core conflict. More importantly, Hillsborough became an unfolding political semiotic process (Wagner-Pacifici, 2017) in which key agents, including supporters, the state, the Premier League, the Football League, and the Football (ground) Licensing Authority, attempted to control interpretation. The performative feature of political semiosis for Wagner-Pacifici (2017) involves the mobilisation of events which are constituted of speech acts, like 'the end of the terraces', which materially change the social or political world. Here, interpretation centred upon the perception of whether all-seated stadia had, or had not, enhanced the safety of supporters and whether modern terracing could be compatible with the Premier League's brand.

Third, as Wagner-Pacifici notes on political semiosis, "it is often in such discursive moments that the interplay of the performatives, the demonstratives, and the representations is at its most elemental and consequential" (2017, p. 31). And thus as 'safety' became the central discourse within those strategic interactions, supporter activists were embedded within such dominant social discourse, employing categories and ideas that itself provided (Steinberg, 1999). Here, the emergence of 'Safe' Terracing or 'Safe' Standing represented the legacy of Hillsborough as a *rupturing moment*, and perhaps more significantly, redirected ongoing *vectors* of critical movement discourse and action in ways which responded directly to the neoliberalisation of modern football. In recognising the long-term vectors of Safe Standing operating both in the domain of culture and through the political and economic realities of English football, this chapter turns to consider how Hillsborough continues to redirect, interrupt and impact these vectors across recent timescales.

'Abandoning the T word': Hillsborough as a restlessness event

The globalisation of English football over the past 20 years is characterised by an economic transnationalism in which the Premier League operates in various 'spaces of flows' (Millward, 2011). Consequently, the contemporary consumption of football is both shaped and constrained by the emergence of a transnational capitalist class, and in turn, many of the movement practices of football supporters are thus characterised by transnational relations within the global network society (King, 2003). Indeed, central players within the CoFS, were, through their former militant tendency networks, tied to supporter activists at Schalke 04 and the Bundniss Aktiver Fußball Fans (BAFF, Association of Active Fans) in Germany. Thus core fan activists were able to successfully switch transnational fan projects in Germany, Holland, Italy, and Switzerland to build a *Football Supporters International* (FSI) network.

In the histories of Safe Standing, German football emerged throughout the course of 2001–2006 as a transformative space producing a critical juncture for future mobilisations. Critical junctures are, according to Della Porta (2020), triggered by eventful protests which produce abrupt changes and develop contingently in ways which become path-dependent. This, in turn, produces a sequence of events which are characterised by ruptures which crack, vibrate and eventually sediment. After Hillsborough, supporter organisations including BAFF, with the support of most German clubs, refused to permanently replace traditional standing terraces with all-seated stadia. Indeed, none of BAFF's arguments, that all-seated stadia would price out many supporters, kill the atmosphere inside grounds and drive many younger fans towards alternative cheaper pastimes, was really contested (Hesse-Lichtenberger, 2002). In July 2000, Germany won the formal bid to host the FIFA 2006 World Cup, which in turn posed a significant threat to the preservation of terracing as all FIFA organised competitions were required to be played in all-seated stadia. Innovatively, German clubs, in liaison with supporter activists, proposed a plan to install removable 'Kombi' or 'rail' seats which, with a removable barrier, allowed a rapid conversion from standing to seating when required for UEFA and FIFA matches.

As clubs like Schalke 04, Hamburg and Werder Bremen began work on ground (re)developments in preparation for the World Cup, core fan activists within the UK-based CoFS, through their own transnational networks, learned of the 'Kombi' and 'rail' seating technology and redirected Safe Standing protests towards German football. These activists, with the help of the FSA, formed a small FSA-coordinated Safe Standing network, with a wider national focus towards German football. However, as Tavory and Eliasoph (2013, p. 909) recognise, "different modes of future movement coordination may conflict with one another during dramatic moments of historical change", which becomes central to the 'puzzling out' of new temporal landscapes (Della Porta, 2020). This was indeed characteristic of Safe Standing's strategic interactions with both the state and wider disparate supporter networks during what was an initial 'irruption' on German 'convertible seating/standing' technology across 2001–2006. Moreover, the reaction of those responsible for the governance of professional football to supporters' excitement at the possibilities for collective action to create something different, only reinforced the power of the all-seating legislation and the long-term safety and securitisation discourse of Hillsborough.

Whilst the key literature on temporality and eventful protests recognises both the immediate and medium-term impacts on activist networks involved in specific moments of contention, what is lacking according to Gillan (2020a, p.520) is "an identification of the ways in which these events form a vital part of the environment in which movements operate". In 2006, the World Cup in Germany became a historical event because it both changed the perception of Safe Standing amongst wider supporter networks across the UK and Europe, and reconfigured future interactions towards understanding the longer-term impact of Hillsborough. This was important because it involved building a longer-term 'ethical definition' of the Taylor Report (Gillan, 2020b), and in doing so, helped sediment Safe Standing protests in ways which reconfigured German 'rail seating' as the *master* frame (Snow & Benford, 1992). Gillan (2020a) argues that such frames or names like *Safe* Standing are themselves deeply political, and in this case, it further highlights the fuzzy temporal boundaries of social movements, in which multiple temporal periods carry different (but relational) meanings, strategic preferences and tactics.

The standing protests coordinated by the CoFS in 1998 moved against the increasing criminalisation of football supporters, and so moved for greater supporter democracy and rights to retain aspects of standing (terraced) culture. However, the critical juncture produced by events within and around German football as a transformative space, moved Safe Standing against the social, cultural and political legacy of Hillsborough and the persistent standing of supporters in all-seated stadia. And in doing so, moved for alternative, technical solutions which could be presented to opponents, as making standing as a modern cultural practice 'safer'. Rail seating thus emerged as a technological *vector* which enabled supporter activists to abandon the T ('terracing') word and change the imagery around standing in ways which made social change visible to those responsible for the governance of professional football. However, whilst this has been tactically important in trying to ensure Hillsborough as a discourse became less dominant in opposition, it characterises the modern consumption of football as paradoxical (Numerato, 2015). And key political mobilisations across the past ten years are characterised by important socio-political ties and networks which further evidence that English football is a lifeworld with a rich array of resources and networks. Together, these mobilisations ensured rail seating became both a complementary and countervailing vector (Gillan, 2020a). However, the sedimentation of rail seating induced by the eventful protests across multiple timescales is, as Della Porta (2020) notes, embedded in the consolidation of collective identities and networks, which together seek to balance and negotiate multiple targets and goals. Moreover, the ends or 'success' of Safe Standing are fundamentally shaped by the means that it employs and thus rail seating, or what has recently been termed 'barrier seating', embodies or 'prefigures' the type of English football culture which activists seek to bring about. Namely, one which advocates a more sustainable form of governance, customer care and greater supporter (stakeholder) choice.

Beyond this, European transnational activism remains important to understanding the wider significance of Safe Standing in ways which are often more direct than the hidden advocacy of supporters in England. However, the hermeneutic tug-of-war over Hillsborough as a *restlessness* event remains a fundamental part of English football culture. Despite this, the tactic to reconfigure rail seating as the *master* frame within a corporate logic of fan (as stakeholder) engagement, has enabled Safe Standing to become internationally significant through the development of supporter networks in Australia, Holland, and the USA. Consequently, PSV Eindhoven, Ajax, CSKA Moscow, SK Sturm Graz, Western Sydney Warriors and Orlando City have all incorporated Safe Standing in new stadium development plans. In England, this technology, which has recently being implemented at high profile clubs in the Premier League, is currently seen as compatible with the current all-seating legislation, and a key method of overcoming the dangers associated with the persistent standing of fans in all-seated areas. However, whilst operating within the parameters of the all-seating legislation, Safe Standing remains embedded within the neoliberalisation of modern football and continues to reinforce the long-term impact and restless indeterminacy of Hillsborough on supporters' modern cultural consumption of the game.

Conclusion

This chapter drew on a high-profile contemporary case of activism in English football, to show how events and ruptures shape the dynamics of a social movement, and how discursive *vectors* indicate the developing understanding of the stakes of the core conflict. In doing so, three conceptual implications for theoretical debates in relational sociology, temporality and eventful protests in sport and leisure are revealed.

First, this case demonstrates the power of long-lasting uncoordinated direct action, such as the persistent standing of supporters in all-seated areas, to be temporally significant, and characteristic of the restless indeterminacy of significant events. Whilst networks and tactics remain important to the emergence, mobilisation and consequences of movements concerned with social democracy and social justice, the everyday lived rituals of consumption, in this case the standing up at football matches, may provide the most radical and powerful source of conflict and counter-power. Second, this case shows the ways in which the employment of dominant social discourse by activists often happens immediately after the significant event, and in some cases, becomes an interpretative struggle lasting 30 years, across a series of interconnected temporal periods. And third, whilst the organisation of horizontal networks is often used to explain the transformation of temporal orientations (Gillan, 2020b; Wagner-Pacifici and Ruggero, 2020), this case reveals the power of small coordination networks and transnational ties to be important to the emergence of multiple social movements, which themselves are embedded within a discourse of an eventful social world. Indeed, the intersections of rituals, consumption, collective action, and temporality reveal social movements to spring into life at specific points in time, and the power of small networks morphing across a timescape which is always in movement. Attention should thus be paid to the ways in which some movements not only move across an uneven fuzzy temporality but produce eventful protests which are embedded within discourse of an eventful world.

Whilst football is an emerging space for social movement research and relational sociology (Cleland et al., 2018), future sport and leisure research should consider the ways in which some contemporary social democratic and social justice movements continue to negotiate with features of political semiosis, but do so across multiple temporal periods which interact economically, culturally and politically (Gillan, 2020b). In the case of Safe Standing in football, the analysis of the storied dimensions of activism and the *vectors* of action reveals a complex and contradictory response to the neoliberal political economy which English football has inhabited over the past 30 years. This matters sociologically because it shows how protests and their discursive practices can both enhance and limit social change in temporally sensitive ways. Locating this in previous debates on eventful protests and temporality, the balanced role between consumerism and activism across time is revealed to be analytically important. Indeed, football supporter networks both produce and consume modern football culture, but subvert the dominant way of watching modern football by persistently standing in all-seated stadia. This complex interplay of cultural and technological *vectors*, and their manifestation across the compelling timeframes and orientations which make up the consumption of English football in a post-Hillsborough timescape, adds both theoretical and empirical value to our understanding of eventual protests and temporality in the sociology of sport and leisure.

References

Acedera, K. & Yeo, B. (2019). 'Making time': Long-distance marriages and the temporalities of the transnational family. *Current Sociology*, 67(2), 250–272.

Bass, M. & Yeoh, B. (2019). Introduction: Migration studies and critical temporalities. *Current Sociology*, 67(2), 161–168.

Boycoff, J. & Carrington, B. (2020). Sporting dissent: Colin Kaepernick, NFL activism, and media framing contests. *International Review for the Sociology of Sport*, 55(7), 829–849.

Castells, M. (2013). A network theory of power. *International Journal of Communications*, 5, 773–787.

Cleland, J., Doidge, M., Millward, P., & Widdop, P. (2018). *Collective Action and Football Fandom: A Relational Sociological Approach*. Basingstoke: Palgrave Macmillan.

Crabbe, T. & Brown, A. (2004). You're not welcome anymore: The football crowd, class and social exclusion. In S. Wagg (Ed.), *Football and Social Exclusion*. London: Routledge, pp. 71–81.

Crossley, N. (2015a). Relational sociology and culture: A preliminary framework. *International Review of Sociology*, 25(1), 65–85.

Crossley, N. (2015b). *Networks of Sound, Style and Subversion: The Punk and Post-Punk Music Worlds of Manchester, London, Liverpool and Sheffield, 1975–1980*. Manchester: Manchester University Press.

Della Porta, D. (2020). Protests as critical junctures: Some reflections towards a momentous approach to social movements. *Social Movement Studies*, 19(5–5), 556–575.

Dunning, E., Murphy, P., & Williams, J. (1986). Spectator violence at football matches: Towards a sociological explanation. *British Journal of Sociology*, 37(2), 221–244.

Edwards, G. (2014). *Social Movements and Protest*. Cambridge: Cambridge University Press.

Football Supporters Association. (2020) Stand up for Choice. Available at: https://thefsa.org.uk/our-work/stand-up-for-choice/

Gillan, K. (2020a). Temporality in social movement theory: Vectors and events in the neoliberal timescape. *Social Movement Studies*, 19(5–6), 516–536.

Gillan, K. (2020b). Social movements: Sequences vs fuzzy temporality. In P. Kivisto (Ed.), *The Cambridge Handbook of Social Theory*. Cambridge: Cambridge University Press, pp. 407–432.

Goldstone, J. A. (2004). More social movements or fewer? Beyond political opportunity structures to relational fields. *Theory and Society*, 33(3), 333–365.

Greenfield, S. & Osborn, G. (1998). Panic law and football fandom. In A. Brown (Ed.), *Fanatics! Power, Identity, and Fandom in football*. London and New York: Routledge.

Harvey, J., Horne, J., Parissa, S., Darnell, S., & Courchesne-O'Neill, S. (2013). *Sport and Social Movements: From the Local to the Global*. London: Bloomsbury.

Haydu, J. (2020). Adding time to social movement diffusion. *Social Movement Studies*, 19(5–6), 625–639.

Hesse-Lichtenberger, U. (2002). *Tor! The Story of German Football*. Essex: When Saturday Comes Books.

Hill, T., Canniford, R., & Millward, P. (2018). Against modern football: Mobilizing protest movements in social media. *Sociology*, 52(4), 688–708.

HM Government. (1989). Interim Report of the Hillsborough Stadium Disaster: 15th April 1989 - Inquiry by the Rt. Hon Lord Justice Taylor, Cmnd. 765. London: HMSO.

HM Government. (1990). Final Report of the Hillsborough Stadium Disaster. 15th April 1989: Inquiry by the Rt. Hon Lord Justice Taylor, Cmnd. 962. London: HMSO.

Jary, D. Horne, J., & Bucke, T. (1991). Football 'fanzines' and football culture: A case of successful 'cultural contestation'. *Sociological Review*, 39(3), 581–597.

King, A. (1998). *The End of the Terraces: The Transformation of English Football in the 1990s*. London: Leicester University Press.

King, A. (2003). *The European Ritual: Football in the New Europe*. Abingdon: Routledge.

Millward, P. (2008). The rebirth of the football fanzine: Using e-zines as data source. *Journal of Sport and Social Issues*, 32(3), 229–310.

Millward, P. (2011). *The Global Football League: Transnational Networks, Social Movements and Sport in the New Media Age*. Basingstoke: Palgrave Macmillan.

Numerato, D. (2015). Who says 'No to modern football'? Italian supporters, reflexivity and neoliberalism. *Journal of Sport and Social Issues*, 39(2), 120–138.

Pearson, G. (2012). *An Ethnography of English Football Fans: Cans, Cops and Carnivals*. Manchester: Manchester University Press.

Polletta, F. & Jasper, J. M. (2001). Collective identity and social movements. *Annual Review of Sociology*, 27, 283–305.

Scraton, P. (2002). Lost lives, hidden voices: 'Truth' and controversial deaths. *Race and Class*, 44(1), 107–118.

Sewell, W. H. (2005). *Logics of History: Social Theory and Social Transformation*. Chicago, IL: University of Chicago Press.

Snow, D. A. & Benford, R. D. (1992). Master frames and cycles of protest. In A. D. Morris & C. M. Mueller (Eds), *Frontiers in Social Movement Theory*. New Haven, CT: Yale University Press, pp. 135–155.

Spracklen, K. & Lamond, I. R. (2016). *Critical Event Studies*. London: Routledge.

Steinberg, M. W. (1999). The talk and back talk of collective action. *American Journal of Sociology*, 105(3), 736–780.

Tavory, I. & Eliasoph, N. (2013). Coordinating futures: Toward a theory of anticipation. *The American Journal of Sociology*, 118(4), 908–942.

Taylor, I. (1971). Football mad: A speculative sociology of soccer hooliganism. In E. Dunning (Ed.), *The Sociology of Sport: A Selection of Readings*. London: Frank Cass.

Taylor, I. (1987). Putting the boot into a working class sport: British soccer after Bradford and Brussels. *Sociology of Sport Journal*, 4, 171–191.

Taylor, I. (1991). English football in the 1990s: Taking Hillsborough seriously? In J. Williams & S. Wagg (Eds), *British Football and Social Change*. Leicester: Leicester University Press.

Wagg, S. (2004). *British Football and Social Exclusion*. Abingdon: Routledge.

Wagner-Pacifici, R. (2017). *What Is an Event?* Chicago and London: University of Chicago Press.

Wagner-Pacifici, R. & Ruggero, C. E. (2020). Temporal blindspots in occupy Philadelphia. *Social Movement Studies*, 19(5–6), 675–696.

Webber, D. (2017). Playing on the break: Karl Polanyi and the double-movement 'against modern football'. *International Review for the Sociology of Sport*, 52(7), 875–893.

Winter, H. (2021). Interview with Oliver Dowden, Secretary of State for the Department for Digital, Culture, Media and Sports. *The Times*. 27 August 2021.

31
BRANDING SOCIAL JUSTICE IN SPORT

Antonio S. Williams, Tanya K. Jones, Kelly J. Brummett, and Zack P. Pedersen

Branding and brand management are critical to differentiating an organisation. Branding are the actions an organisation implements to create and shape perceptions about the organisation and its products or services by the public. Branding should be unique and set the organisation apart from its competitors. A human brand is an individual who is used in marketing and communication efforts, and a celebrity brand constitutes someone who is well known or famous that commercially leverages their unique image (Walsh & Williams, 2017). Celebrities and athletes who are so well-known may be considered brands themselves. The concept of a brand is particularly well suited for athletes given their notoriety and public personas. The athlete brand is "any athlete who has established value in the marketplace through the use of his or her name, likeness, or other brand elements" (Walsh & Williams, 2017, p. 45). Athlete branding can lead to increased fan loyalty, additional revenue streams, and opportunities to leverage brand value post athletic career. Recently, several high-profile athletes have not only used their platforms to advocate for social justice, but they have also incorporated social justice into their personal brands. For example, tennis star Naomi Osaka has unapologetically tied her brand to fighting social injustice. During the 2020 US Open, Osaka wore seven masks that prominently displayed the names of Black victims of injustice (i.e. Tamir Rice, Philando Castile, George Floyd, Trayvon Martin, Ahmaud Arbery, Elijah McClain, and Breonna Taylor), wearing a mask with a different name for every round she advanced in the tournament, for which she made the finals (Porterfield, 2020). In utilising such a stance of solidarity, she cast off any attention aimed at her performance and directed it towards these societal issues. Additionally, Osaka removed herself from a tournament just a month earlier in protest of another injustice (i.e. the shooting of Jacob Blake). Osaka, at the peak of her international stardom, decided to make her personal brand inseparable from the fight for social justice.

Social justice can broadly be defined as justice in terms of the distribution of wealth, opportunities, and privileges within a society. Sport is perceived as an equaliser where wealth, opportunities, and privileges are equally accessible (Brummett & Williams, 2021). Yet, sport is also a microcosm of society, reflecting and reinforcing stereotypes and prejudices (Lee & Cunningham, 2019). Many athletes, who have directly experienced or witnessed injustice and inequity, advocate for social justice either within sport or within the broader context of society. Athletes such as Jesse Owens, Jackie Robinson, John Carlos, Tommie Smith, Muhammad

Ali, Kareem Abdul-Jabbar, and Billie Jean King have gone down in history as athlete activists. While the sportspeople mentioned started participating in their respective sports because of their passion for the game and their athletic ability, each athlete significantly impacted society through the utilisation of the status they accrued during their careers. As athletes continue to use social media for personal branding, the expectations of athletes to address social justice issues continue to rise. Although the relationship between branding and social justice may not at first appear obvious, the merger is powerful, resulting in the desired change we look for in society.

While athlete activism in the United States has occurred since the early twentieth century, in recent years, athletes worldwide are beginning to advocate for marginalised communities. LeBron James, who is one of the leading voices against forms of social injustice, has taken many actions to develop projects and institutions that are able to address and counteract many of the issues he stands for and against. James was the first athlete to create a public school (i.e. the I Promise School in Akron, Ohio) specifically for marginalised youth, allowing at-risk kids access to free uniforms, food, transportation, and tuition to the University of Akron upon graduation (Perano & Muaddi, 2018). This first of its kind brand extension by an athlete into the realm of educational institutions solidifies his precise branding strategy of combining his activism and his personal brand. Some of James' other extensions, such as SpringHill Entertainment and UNINTERUPTED, are also used as conduits for marginalised individuals or people with lesser to no platform as a way to disseminate their stories and situations through short and long form content.

Through the use of social media and with a greater focus on branding, a cultural shift has occurred where a prevalence of athlete activism has influenced companies like Nike, Adidas, and Under Armour, to the point they are now expected to speak out against social injustices (Vredenburg et al., 2020). Athlete activism and the recent trend by some athletes to associate their brand meticulously and unapologetically with social justice initiatives is not fully accepted by sport fans and consumers. However, the ability to bring such issues to the forefront of the sporting landscape has allowed for greater depth and breadth of discussions around these topics. This chapter will examine brand management principles strategically employed by athletes, professional leagues, and their stakeholders to promote public discourse, shape attitudes towards the social justice movement, and bring about change in sport or society.

The pioneer athlete (1900–1960)

Black athletes' participation in sport from the late 1800s through the 1960s was a Herculean effort due to Jim Crow laws that segregated and marginalised African Americans. Black citizens were denied the right to vote, hold a job, seek an education, enter public parks, live in White neighbourhoods, or marry another race. Segregation extended to restrooms, Bibles, textbooks, public pools, phone booths, hospitals, and jails. It was not uncommon to observe signage warning Blacks that they were not welcome in towns or restaurants. One of the early pioneer athletes during this era was Jack Johnson, who was the first Black American world heavyweight boxing champion, a title he won in 1908. Because of prevailing racist sentiment at the time, former world heavyweight boxing champion, James J. Jeffries, a White man, came out of retirement to fight Johnson specifically to prove that "a White man is better than a Negro" (Remnick, 2003). That match, known as "The Fight of the Century" took place on 4 July 1910, with Johnson declared the winner after 14 rounds (Pastorelli-Sosa, 2018).

That would not be the end of Johnson's legacy. Johnson openly flouted Jim Crow laws by marrying White women. In 1912, he was arrested and subsequently convicted of transporting his wife, a White woman, across state lines for 'immoral purposes'. After living as a fugitive for seven years, Johnson surrendered and served almost one year in jail for the crime. Johnson could not even escape racism in death. He died in an automobile accident speeding from a restaurant that refused to serve him. When emergency assistance arrived at the scene, a White ambulance driver refused to render aid, and Johnson was transported to a segregated hospital more than 25 miles away, where he died (Shaffer, 2018). Johnson was 68 years old.

Successful track and field athlete Jesse Owens became famous after participating in the 1936 Berlin Olympic Games, also known as the Nazi Olympics. As a Black man in America, he had minimal rights. He suffered through segregation and discrimination in US society but broke down racial barriers in sport. Owens qualified to compete in the 1936 Olympics, which German dictator Adolf Hitler hoped to use as propaganda to promote the Aryan race (Berkes, 2008). Unfortunately, for Hitler, Jesse Owens outran the German athletes, winning four gold medals in the long jump, the 100- and 200-metre dashes, and the 4 × 100-metre relay (Smith, 1980). US history uses Owens' victory as a commentary against racism and White supremacy. However, when Owens returned to the United States, he received terrible treatment from the same fans who cheered him during the Olympics (Baker, 1986). Unlike his White counterparts, Owens received no invitation to the White House upon returning and faced discrimination in his hometown (Pieper & Linden, 2020). Similarly, Jackie Robinson broke barriers in professional baseball when Branch Rickey, owner of the Brooklyn Dodgers, brought Robinson up from the Negro Leagues to play for the Dodgers organisation (Wiggins, 2014). Although both Owens and Robinson had no intention of becoming historical icons, their tenacity and success in sport began a movement towards promoting social justice through sport.

During this time, sports marketing was in its infancy, and the scholarly review of athlete branding practices had not yet developed. Newspapers and radio were the primary modes of sport consumption, and athletes were just beginning to be employed as product endorsers (Fetchko et al., 2019). Williams et al. (2015) introduced a conceptual framework to assess athlete brand equity. Their model is currently used to address where athletes' brands can find growth in a consumer marketplace. However, it can also be used to evaluate where historical figures, such as Owens and Robinson, were not afforded the opportunity to capitalise on their brand to a greater extent during their careers. Williams et al. discuss the three factors that precede athlete brand equity, namely organisation-induced, market-induced, and athlete-induced antecedents. Each one of these factors describes a way in which athlete brand equity can potentially be influenced. How the athlete's team or league uses them in the marketing mix, and how the media and external entities perceive the athlete to be, cannot be controlled by the athlete. While historically athletes could only attempt to influence teams, fans, and the media by their athletic success and low level of controversy, they had no control over these entities that directly affected their brand equity. Since the advent and growth of social media, athletes have been able to set their own agenda, dispel rumours, define their brand, and fight against false narrative should they so choose. However, historical athletes did not have the ability to access this athlete-induced antecedent in this capacity, therefore stripping them of the control they had of their own narrative, promptly placing the power in the hands of the media and teams/leagues.

Owens and Robinson, because of their skin colour and the ensuing prejudice of teams, leagues, fans, and the media, could not even capitalise on their athletic successes in the endorsement marketplace. Their brands, which were largely developed by external entities (e.g. teams, fans, members of the media) that did not recognise or appreciate their monumental steps towards equality in sports, did not fit with the agenda of the endorsement companies. Despite the accolades they today receive for breaking colour barriers, they lived in a legally segregated America that would not have embraced their marketing efforts.

The revolutionary athlete (1960–1980)

Although the Supreme Court's verdict in *Brown* v. *Board of Education* outlawed segregation in public schools and served as the precursor to desegregation, racism and Jim Crow policies and mentalities persisted through the 1960s as the fight for true civil rights raged. Athlete activism began to make international headlines in the 1960s when US Black athletes began using their platform to express their distaste with policies instilled by the US government. Track and field athletes John Carlos and Tommie Smith wanted to use an international event to highlight the racial injustices occurring within the United States (Bass, 2002). According to historian Amy Bass (2002), they used their platform at the 1968 Mexico City Olympic Games to bring worldwide attention to the mistreatment of Blacks in America. Carlos and Smith's message was made even more powerful through the popularity of television during the 1950s. Television is arguably the most important technology in sport and sports marketing (Fetchko et al., 2019). As more households owned a television, the popularity of sports and athletes grew. Fans could now see athletes play live, rather than simply hearing it on the radio or reading about it the next day in the newspaper. Greater personal and emotional connections were made between fans and athletes. Sponsors began to take notice of the evolving relationship, and many athletes understood this new dynamic and used the platform to voice their concerns about social injustices. Carlos and Smith certainly understood this; imagine reading about the athletes raising their fists in the Black Power salute, then imagine the contrast *seeing* the athletes raising their fists in the Black Power salute. Famous boxer Muhammad Ali fought against the Vietnam War and the US government's mandatory draft into the US Army. Ali stated, "there are two kinds of men, those who compromise and those who take a stand" (Lipsyte, 1968). His religious beliefs conflicted with the United States' involvement in the war, particularly considering the simultaneous civil rights abuses that were rampant on American soil. For US Black athletes in the 1960s, personal branding and economic wealth were not a goal of their activism; they were freedom and equality.

The apolitical athlete (1980–2010)

Following the strife of the Civil Rights era, many minorities progressed by assimilating into the dominant White culture. Assimilation took many forms, including appearance and dress. For instance, Black women would perm their hair to make it straight, resembling that of Europeans, and Black men would not grow full beards lest they look intimidating and dangerous. Athletes were not exempt from following the pathway of assimilation. As a nation, America wanted to forget the turmoil of the previous decades and instead enjoy 'guilt-free Black entertainment'. Notwithstanding his current legal status, the epitome of 'guilt-free Black entertainment' was Bill Cosby and *The Cosby Show*. A successful Black celebrity, athletes included, needed to present as Bill Cosby – funny, wholesome, nonviolent. Athletes who fit this mould were sometimes referred to as "Cosby Jocks" (Brooks et al., 2016). It was the clean-cut, image conscious, high-profile athletes who were introduced as national product endorsers. With this role as a brand ambassador, athlete branding and reputation management took on new meaning. And while some athletes in the US used sport to bring light to injustices against marginalised groups, other athletes like Orenthal James (O. J.) Simpson and Michael Jordan chose to keep their personal and political beliefs away from their athletic career. Simpson's and Jordan's decision helped them break the negative stereotypes of the radical Black athlete from the decades prior and propel them into economic wealth (Walton & Chau, 2018). O. J. Simpson became a pioneer for large brand companies using athletes in campaigns to try and boost sales (Schwab, 2013). Despite his mainstream success, Simpson received backlash from African American community members like Civil Rights activist Harry Edwards. According to Walton and Chau (2018), Edwards stated that through Simpson's silence about racial injustice, O. J. really stated, "I'm not Black, I'm O. J.", attempting to transcend race in America.

Similarly, Michael Jordan utilised his athletic prowess to make his name an international brand. Nike signed Jordan to an endorsement deal in 1984, his first year in the National Basketball Association (NBA). In his debut year, the Jordan brand sold nearly $130 million of shoes and merchandise and elevated Nike's revenues to record levels (Spence, 2009). As Jordan's popularity grew, he expanded Nike's customer base, and by the end of 1998, the Jordan brand earned Nike around $2.6 billion (Spence, 2009). Nike struck gold with Jordan; he was winning on the basketball court, had a clean-cut image, and was likeable, all of which are necessary for a successful brand endorser. Given the "lack of social ills during [this time] when compared with the 1960s and 1970s" (Coombs & Cassilo, 2017, p. 427), many athletes focused on athletic achievement and feared that public comment on social justice issues was too risky and could have a detrimental financial effect (Coombs & Cassilo, 2017). In 1990, the campaign committee for Harvey Gantt, a Black Democrat running for United States Senate, approached Jordan for an endorsement (Kozlowski, 2020). Jordan declined, and when asked his reasoning, he stated, "Republicans buy sneakers, too" (Jones, 2020). His success on the court, coupled with his lack of political commentary, promoted the notion that politics had no place in sports. Harry Edwards (2016) described the decades during Simpson's and Jordan's success as a period of athlete activism immobility. From a marketing and branding perspective, the emphasis was less on social justice and more on sponsors. Taking controversial political and social stances could have damaged both the athlete's and the sponsor's brands.

Since 2016, a shift away from Simpson's and Jordan's apolitical attitude in sports occurred. The promotion of athlete activism began to thrive, precipitated by cause-related marketing commonly employed by large corporations. Cause-related marketing (CRM) is communicating through advertising, packaging, and promotions a company's corporate social responsibility and causes it supports with the intention of attracting consumers to purchase its goods or services (Bronn & Vrioni, 2001). Historically, corporations implement CRM to differentiate themselves in the marketplace, gain goodwill with consumers, and enhance their brand reputation. This marketing tactic is also utilised by athletes, as Kunkel et al. (2020), demonstrated the positive influence of using strategic philanthropy in athlete branding. When shaping their brand, many athletes will utilise a philanthropic logo that incorporates their name, image, and likeness before they create a personal logo that is used on merchandise and other material (Pedersen & Williams, 2022). The consistent practice of athlete strategic philanthropy has given athlete activists a reputable framework on how to incorporate social justice into their brand, much in the same way other athletes incorporate charitable organisations and outreach.

Rarely does a corporation, though, entwine its brand with its philanthropic or charitable endeavours. One such company that has embraced social justice is Nike. In years past, Nike received sharp criticism for perceived unfair labour practices and human rights violations; however, recently, the sports apparel giant has developed advertising campaigns addressing gender, cultural, and racial inequality (Waymer & Logan, 2021). Notably, Nike created a Pro Hijab line; featured an Egyptian and Emirati athlete in its "Dream Crazier" campaign that challenged gender and cultural norms; signed Colin Kaepernick to a sponsorship deal and introduced a new Air Force 1 shoe in his honour; and withdrew a special United States Independence Day shoe featuring the Betsy Ross version of the United States flag after Kaepernick noted the flag is racially offensive (Waymer & Logan, 2021). Nike's actions, considered controversial by many, legitimised its brand as social justice advocate.

The empowered athlete (2010–present)

I'm not a businessman, I'm a business, man.

(West. K, 2005)

These lyrics by entrepreneur and rapper Jay-Z poetically represent the empowered athlete. Athletes are no longer bound by assimilation for success, profit and acceptance; rather, the empowered athlete has created their own clout separate from the team they represent (Chotiner, 2021). Because player empowerment is inextricably linked to race, athletes are taking more control over their careers, which are typically dominated by White commissioners and White owners (Chotiner, 2021). Rejecting the pressure to resemble the dominant European man or woman, empowered athletes embrace and display their full Blackness. This shift of the athletes' consciousness into their own person parallels the millennial generation becoming a key demographic in the marketplace. Corporate and sponsors recognised that the Black athlete was the gatekeeper of a social 'cool' that could marketed, appealing to the youth of White America. At the same time, the value of the Black dollar increased. In 1990, Black buying power, defined as the quantity of goods and services a dollar can buy, was $320 billion, and in 2018, it was $1.3 trillion (Grace & Scott-Aime, 2019). Further, between 2000 and 2018, Black buying power increased 114 per cent compared to an 88 per cent increase in White buying power (Grace & Scott-Aime, 2019). This often resulted in athletes earning more money from endorsements and sponsorships than from playing their sports. Though Tiger Woods may be more comparable to the apolitical athlete than the empowered athlete, Woods played a critical role in the ascendancy of the empowered athlete. Woods' lucrative endorsement deals set the value in the marketplace for future high-profile, elite athletes. Without Woods' multiple eight-figure endorsements, many of today's athletes likely would not be able to command significant endorsement contracts.

No longer are professional athletes figures on a field; fans now have unlimited access to the players' lives. Athletes utilise social media to connect with the public around them, but in doing so, open themselves to extreme scrutiny. Since athletes began to share personal aspects of their lives freely in the twenty-first century, people began to wonder about athlete's stances on social justice issues. Although leaders of the new wave of athlete activism like Colin Kaepernick and LeBron James received significant backlash for using sport to promote social justice ("President Trump Picks Michael Jordan", 2020), sportspersons that have come after them are now expected to speak out against issues plaguing their communities (Loy, 2018). Similar to the athletes of the 1960s, today's athletes welcome the opportunity to use the power of sport to advocate for social justice; and unlike the athletes of the 1980s, many can do so without fear of losing endorsement deals as consumers expect that corporations also have a position on social justice issues, an extension of their corporate social responsibility.

National Football League (NFL) quarterback Colin Kaepernick was the first high-profile professional athlete to publicly spotlight police brutality and anti-Black sentiment when he kneeled during the playing of the United States national anthem at football games. Backlash against Kaepernick was swift and severe, as Kaepernick has not been signed to a professional team since the 2016 season, the year that he kneeled in protest. Kaepernick was undeterred, and continued his advocacy, inspiring other professional athletes to speak out on social justice issues. LeBron James, future Hall of Fame athlete in the NBA, has been vocal about social justice issues, particularly those surrounding race. He has been compared to other well-known athlete-activists Muhammad Ali, Bill Russell, and James Brown (Coombs & Cassilo, 2017). James is an especially compelling voice due to his appeal and marketability to Black, White, Asian, and Hispanic audiences. In 2018, Nike released a limited number of James' 'EQUALITY' LeBron 15 signature shoes (Dodson, 2018). Of the specialty shoes with the word 'equality' embroidered on the heel, James said,

> Us as Americans, no matter the skin color, no matter who you are, I think we all have to understand that having equal rights and being able to stand for something and speak for something and keeping the conversation going.
>
> (Dodson, 2018, para. 4)

Given his popularity with diverse consumers, messages such as these are generally well received, making James an attractive athlete to sponsors.

The significance of the actions these empowered athletes are taking can also be recognised in their forfeiture of other brand associations that they could be building upon, or the substitution of certain athlete brand image components for a greater focus on social justice. Arai et al. (2013), discuss the elements of athlete brand image, and describe three primary factors that influence athlete brand image (i.e. athletic performance, attractive appearance, marketable lifestyle). These factors are the associations that athletes can leverage to make themselves more marketable, such as their personal fitness, their level of success in competition, and the activities they partake in when they are not competing. The combination of how consumers perceive or understand these different associations can influence how an athlete markets and brands themselves. While apolitical athletes such as Michael Jordan and O. J. Simpson focused more on the associations related to their success, charisma, and their competitive spirit, empowered athletes funnel the focus of their brands towards causes they believe in. By specifically utilising their stories, their relationships, and by promoting themselves as role models, they are able to enhance marketable lifestyle capacity. By increasing the significance of this category, which houses associations related to causes athletes are fighting for, athletes are not only spreading awareness about issues they are passionate about, but are beginning to accrue greater endorsement success as well. As previously mentioned, there is a mounting pressure on corporate entities to incorporate CRM to a greater level, while also forcing these entities to take a stance against social injustices as well.

College athletes have also used their collective voices to advocate for social change. Prior to the start of the National Collegiate Athletic Association's (NCAA) Division I men's basketball tournament, hundreds of athletes took to social media using the #NotNCAAProperty hashtag to express their concerns with the NCAA's rules that prohibited them from profiting from their own names, images, and likenesses. The athletes believed that they were being exploited by the arcane rules and demanded a meeting with the NCAA's president to discuss changing the decades-old prohibition. The power of the social media blitz was successful as the NCAA relaxed the rule in July 2021, allowing student–athletes for the first time to enter into sponsorship agreements and endorse commercial products and services.

Women ambassadors

Much like the Black athlete activist that came before her, Billie Jean King wanted to bring attention to discriminatory practices within athletics and society. King used sport to challenge patriarchy and misogyny in athletics in the early 1970s. To combat King's mission, former number one men's tennis player Bobby Riggs challenged King to a tennis match. He boasted that women were inferior to men and that no women could beat him in a competition. King proved him wrong. On 20 September 1973, King beat Riggs in the famous Battle of the Sexes tennis match (Spencer, 2000).

Before Billie Jean King, there was Althea Gibson. Gibson, considered the 'Jackie Robinson of tennis', was the first Black tennis athlete to play in Wimbledon, to be ranked No. 1 in the world, to win a Grand Slam title, and to win both the US Championship and Wimbledon (Jacobs, 2019). Gibson's success was not without struggle and strife. During her first Wimbledon appearance in 1950, she competed gallantly against the backdrop of racists chants. Despite a commanding early lead, Gibson ultimately lost the match to her White counterpart after inclement weather forced suspension of play until the following day (Jacobs, 2019). Gibson would later reflect how far she had come when Queen Elizabeth II presented her with the Wimbledon trophy in 1957. For all her accomplishments, Gibson earned virtually no money from her tennis career, and even her legacy is often overshadowed by subsequent tennis superstars such as King, Venus and Serena Williams, and Naomi Osaka. Although Gibson did not see herself as a representative for African Americans, she nevertheless paved the way for generational talents like the Williams sisters and Osaka. It was not until 2019, with King's involvement, that a statue of Gibson was erected at Arthur Ashe Stadium to honour the reluctant heroine for breaking the colour barrier in tennis.

League leaders

Athletes are not alone in their efforts to effectuate social justice. The NBA and the Women's National Basketball Association (WNBA) have been actively incorporating social justice into their brands. For instance, the NBA is moving away from the term 'owner' to describe those with a controlling interest in teams, instead using the term 'governor' or 'alternate governor' (Kaskey-Blomain, 2019). NBA Commissioner Adam Silver stated that he recognises the racial insensitivity associated with the term 'owner' in a league with predominantly African American players and those with a controlling interest are predominantly White (Kaskey-Blomain, 2019). Following the murder of George Floyd by a Minneapolis police officer in May 2020, both the NBA and WNBA displayed messages of social justice (e.g. Black Lives Matter) on courts and permitted players to wear messages on their jerseys. The NBA also created the annual Kareem Abdul-Jabbar Social Justice Champion award to recognise a current player who pursues social justice and personifies the league's values of equality, respect and inclusion. Kareem Abdul-Jabbar is a six-time NBA champion and member of the Naismith Basketball Hall of Fame who fought for many social justice causes, including racial and religious freedom (Goudsouzian, 2017).

In response to several high-profile incidents of racism in soccer, the Union of European Football Associations (UEFA), adopted guidelines to empower officials to stop play and even abandon the match as a means to addressing racism during competitions. The guidelines outline a three-step procedure: (1) the official will stop play and request an announcement to be made over the public address system that spectators immediately stop the racist behaviour; (2) If the racist behaviour continues, the official will suspend play for a period of time with both teams exiting to their respective dressing rooms and a second announcement made over the public address system; and (3) as a last resort, the official may definitively abandon the match and the case is referred to UEFA for disciplinary action (UEFA, 2019).

These examples of leagues incorporating initiatives and taking stands against forms of racism again demonstrates the magnitude of the athletes throughout history that fought for social justices without the help of teams or leagues. The change agents in sport were/are undoubtedly the athletes in regard to social justice issues, demonstrated by the rise of the utilisation of the athlete-induced antecedent and the prevalence of societal conversations around such issues (Williams et al., 2015). As athletes have accrued a larger audience and greater reach with their branding efforts, through the use of social media, the timing by which certain entities (e.g. teams and members of the media) have taken stances against social injustice is not by mere happenstance.

A global pursuit

During the twentieth century, American athletes led the way in athlete activism; however, the path toward social justice is not uniquely American. While some examples of athletes outside the United States use their sporting platform to promote social justice, the examples are few and far between. Remembering international athletes like Australian track runner Peter Norman is essential. Norman wore the Olympic Project for Human Rights (OPHR) pin during a podium ceremony at the 1968 Mexico City Olympic Games in solidarity with John Carlos and Tommie Smith's protest against racial injustice worldwide (164 Cong. Rec. E1414, 2018). Like his American counterparts, Norman was punished by the Australian National Olympic Committee (NOC) for his efforts and stripped of his Olympic medals (Webster, 2018). From a certain viewpoint in media outlets, the question has been raised as to why is it difficult to find examples of international athlete activists? According to former international basketballer John Amaechi, some international athletes do not involve themselves in politics "because they think it's not their job" (Loy, 2018). The emergence of social media and unlimited access to information on the internet has changed the way athletes use their platforms (Sanderson et al., 2016). In 2014, F. C. Barcelona's centre-back Gerard Piqué posted a photograph of himself on social media at a political demonstration in Barcelona (Dean, 2014). The gathering was concerning the Catalan independence movement, which gained traction in 2014 with the creation of the Catalan independence referendum. According to Guinjoan and Rodon (2016), the referendum asked two questions:

1. Does Catalonia want to become a state?
2. Will that state be independent from Spain?

Piqué received backlash from fans and the Spanish football federation due to his support for Catalonia's independence from Spain ("Barcelona's Gerard Piqué Offers", 2017). While he still plays on the Spanish national team and is still one of F. C. Barcelona's top defenders, Piqué offered to retire early from the sport due to negative reactions he and his family received over his political support ("Barcelona's Gerard Piqué Offers", 2017).

In 2019, Canadian ice hockey star Akim Aliu joined the assembly of athletes fighting for social justice when he spoke out about the culture of racism in the National Hockey League (NHL) (Beaton, 2019). According to sportswriter Terrance Doyle (2020), less than 5 per cent of the players in the NHL are Black, Indigenous, and People of Colour (BIPOC), and an astounding 77 per cent of fans are White. Within the sporting culture of the NHL, BIPOC players and fans feel uncomfortable and unwelcome to participate in the sport (Doyle, 2020; Keating, 2021). Due to the lack of diversity and discrimination that BIPOC hockey players experienced, Aliu created the Hockey Diversity Alliance (HDA) to "eradicate systemic racism and intolerance in hockey" ("Hockey Diversity Alliance", 2021).

References

1 Cong. Rec. E1414 (daily ed. October 16, 2018) (statement of Barbara Lee).
Arai, A., Ko. Y. J., & Kaplanidou, K. (2013). Athlete brand image: Scale development and model test. *European Sport Management Quarterly, 13*(4), 383–403. http://dx.doi.org/10.1080/16184742.2013.811609
Baker, W. J. (1986). *Jesse Owens: An American Life*. Urbana: University of Illinois Press.
Bass, A. (2002). *Not the Triumph but the Struggle: The 1968 Olympics and the Making of the Black Athlete*. Minneapolis: University of Minnesota Press.
Beaton, A. (2019, December 12). Blackface, slurs and the player who brought a racial reckoning to hockey. *The Wall Street Journal*. https://www.wsj.com/articles/blackface-slurs-and-the-player-who-brought-a-racial-reckoning-to-hockey-11576082222
Berkes, H. (2008, June 7). Nazi Olympics tangled politics and sport. *NPR*. https://www.npr.org/templates/story/story.php?storyId=91246674
Bronn, P. S., & Vrioni, A. B. (2001). Corporate social responsibility and cause-related marketing: An overview. *International Journal of Advertising, 20*(2), 207–222.
Brooks, S. N., Cathcart, J., Elias, E., & McKail, M. A. (2016). Whatever happened to the Black (American) athlete? The NBA's cultural renewal and gentrification program. In G. Sailes (Ed.), *Modern Sport & the African-American Experience* (2nd ed.) (pp. 271–291). San Diego: Cognella.
Brummett, K., & Williams, A. S. (2021). *Social Justice. Encyclopedia of Sport Management*. Cheltenham, UK: Edward Elgar Publishing.
CBS Chicago. (2020, August 11). President Trump picks Michael Jordan over LeBron James: 'He wasn't political'. *CBS Chicago*. https://chicago.cbslocal.com/2020/08/11/president-trump-michael-jordan-lebron-james-debate/
Chotiner, I. (2021, May 31). LeBron James's agent is transforming the business of basketball. *The New Yorker*. https://www.newyorker.com/magazine/2021/06/07/lebron-james-agent-is-transforming-the-business-of-basketball
Coombs, D. S. & Cassilo, D. (2017). Athletes and/or activists: LeBron James and Black lives matter. *Journal of Sport and Social Issues, 41*(5), 425–444.
Dean, L. (2014, September 12). Ex-Manchester United defender Gerard Piqué criticised for taking part in pro-Catalonia rally. *International Business Times UK*. https://www.ibtimes.co.uk/ex-manchester-united-defender-gerard-pique-criticised-taking-part-pro-catalonia-rally-1465242
Dodson, A. (2018, August 1). The Nike LeBron 15 'EQUALITY' sneakers find a home at the Smithsonian. *Andscape*. https://andscape.com/features/the-nike-lebron-15-equality-sneakers-find-a-home-at-the-smithsonian/
Doyle, T. (2020, October 19). The NHL says "Hockey is for everyone." Black players aren't so sure. *FiveThirtyEight*. https://fivethirtyeight.com/features/the-nhl-says-hockey-is-for-everyone-black-players-arent-so-sure/
Edwards, H. (2016). The fourth wave: Black athlete protests in the second decade of the 21st century. In *Keynote Address at the North American Society for the Sociology of Sport Conference*, Tampa Bay, FL, 3 November.
Fetchko, M. J., Roy, D.P., & Clow, K. E. (2019). *Sports Marketing* (2nd ed.). New York: Routledge.
Goudsouzian, A. (2017). From Lew Alcindor to Kareem Abdul-Jabbar: Race, religion, and representation in basketball, 1968–1975. *Journal of American Studies, 51*(2), 437–470. https://doi.org/10.1017/S0021875816000621

Grace, C., & Scott-Aime, M. (2019). It's in the bag: Black consumers' path to purchase. Nielsen, Diverse Intelligence Series.

Guinjoan, M., & Rodon, T. (2016). Catalonia at the crossroads: Analysis of the increasing support for secession. In X. Cuadras Morató (Ed.), *Catalonia: A New Independent State in Europe?: A Debate on Secession Within the European Union* (p. 40). London: Routledge.

Hockey Diversity Alliance (2021). Our purpose. Hockey Diversity Alliance. https://hockeydiversityalliance.org/

Jacobs, S.H. (2019, August 26). Althea Gibson, tennis star ahead of her time, gets her due at last. *New York Times*. https://www.nytimes.com/2019/08/26/sports/tennis/althea-gibson-statue-us-open.html

Jones, N. (2020, May 4). The controversy behind Michael Jordan's "Republicans buy sneakers, too' quote". *Vulture*. https://www.vulture.com/2020/05/did-michael-jordan-say-republicans-buy-sneakers-too-yes.html

Kaskey-Blomain, M. (2019, June 24). Adam Silver on NBA using 'governor' in place of 'owner' title: 'We moved away from that term years ago'. *CBS Sports*. https://www.cbssports.com/nba/news/nba-finals-to-limit-chris-pauls-dominance-bucks-must-give-him-a-taste-of-his-own-annoying-medicine/

Keating, S. (2021, February 26). NHL in denial of race issues, says Hockey Diversity Alliance. *Reuters*. https://www.reuters.com/article/us-icehockey-nhl-diversity/nhl-in-denial-of-race-issues-says-hockey-diversity-alliance-idUSKBN2AQ312

Kozlowski, J. (2020, July 29). Michael Jordan is making sure that he doesn't repeat the political mistakes of his past. *Sportscasting*. https://www.sportscasting.com/michael-jordan-is-making-sure-that-he-doesnt-repeat-the-political-mistakes-of-his-past/

Kunkel, T., Doyle, J., & Na, S. (2020). Becoming more than an athlete: Developing an athlete's personal brand using strategic philanthropy, *European Sport Management Quarterly*. Advance online publication. https://doi.org/10.1080/16184742.2020.1791208

Lee, W., & Cunningham, G. (2019). Moving toward understanding social justice in sport organizations: A study of engagement in social justice advocacy in sport organizations. *Journal of Sport and Social Issues*, 43(3), 245–263.

Lipsyte, R. (1968, April 29). Sports of the times: The only real heavyweight champion. *New York Times*. https://www.nytimes.com/1968/04/29/archives/sports-of-the-times-the-only-real-heavyweight-champion.html

Loy, M. (2018, October 16). Beyond the athlete - The role of an international athlete activist today. *Medium*. https://michaelloyusc.medium.com/beyond-the-athlete-the-role-of-an-international-athlete-activist-today-f4711b8a407a

Pastorelli-Sosa, A. (2018, September 21). Jeffries versus Johnson: The fight of the century. *The Met*. https://www.metmuseum.org/blogs/now-at-the-met/2018/on-the-ropes-jeffries-johnson-fight-of-the-century

Pedersen, Z.P., & Williams, A.S. (2022). Advancing the athlete brand: Evaluating the current landscape of athlete logos. *International Journal of Sport Management*, 23(1), 1–22.

Perano, U., & Muaddi, N. (2018, August 4). Lebron James opens elementary school, guarantees college tuition to graduates. *CNN*. https://www.cnn.com/2018/08/04/us/lebron-james-opens-school-trnd/index.html

Pieper, L. P., & Linden, A. D. (2020). Race but not racism: The Jesse Owens story and race. *International Journal of the History of Sport*, 37(10), 853–871. https://doi.org/10.1080/09523367.2020.1842368

Porterfield, C. (2020, September 12). Naomi Osaka wears 7th face mask – this one emblazoned with Tamir Rice's name – for US Open final. *Forbes*. https://www.forbes.com/sites/carlieporterfield/2020/09/12/naomi-osaka-wears-7th-face-mask-this-one-emblazoned-with-tamir-rices-name-for-us-open-final/

Press Association. (2017, October 1). Barcelona's Gerard Piqué offers to end Spain career over Catalan turmoil. *The Guardian*. https://www.theguardian.com/football/2017/oct/01/barcelona-gerard-pique-catalan-independence

Remnick, D. (2003, November 2). Struggle for his soul. *The Observer*. https://www.theguardian.com/observer/osm/story/0,,1072750,00.html

Sanderson, J., Frederick, E., & Stocz, M. (2016). When athlete activism clashes with group values: Social identity threat management via social media. *Mass Communication & Society*, 19(3), 301–322. https://doi.org/10.1080/15205436.2015.1128549

Schwab, F. (2013, June 13). Hertz made advertising history with O. J. Simpson's airport runs. *Yahoo! Finance*. https://finance.yahoo.com/blogs/nfl-shutdown-corner/hertz-made-advertising-history-with-o-j--simpson-s-airport-runs-140015008.html

Shaffer, J. (2018, May 24). Trump pardons heavyweight Jack Johnson, who died in Raleigh's segregated hospital. *The News & Observer*. https://www.newsobserver.com/news/nation-world/article211833674.html

Smith, J. Y. (1980, April 1). Olympic track great Jesse Owens is dead at 66: Jesse Owens, winner of 4 medals in 1936 Olympics. *The Washington Post*. https://www.washingtonpost.com/archive/local/1980/04/01/olympic-track-great-jesse-owens-is-dead-at-66/51f3910e-2d63-4370-991c-151a7e86b076/

Spence, K. (2009). Nike: By the numbers. *Gatton Student Research Publication, 1*(1), Gatton College of Business and Economics, University of Kentucky.

Spencer, N. E. (2000). Reading between the lines: A discursive analysis of the Billie Jean King vs. Bobby Riggs "Battle of the Sexes". *Sociology of Sport Journal, 17*(4), 386–402. https://doi.org/10.1123/ssj.17.4.386

Union of European Football Associations. (2019, October 15). *Empowering referees to act against racism: UEFA's three-step procedure*. https://www.uefa.com/insideuefa/news/0256-0f8e70d1f5fd-c982ef234981-1000--empowering-referees-to-act-against-racism-uefa-s-three-step-pro/

Vredenburg, J., Kapitan, S., Spry, A., & Kemper, J. A. (2020). Brands taking a stand: Authentic brand activism or woke washing? *Journal of Public Policy & Marketing, 39*(4), 444–460. https://doi.org/10.1177/0743915620947359

Walsh, P., & Williams, A. (2017). To extend or not extend a human brand: An analysis of perceived fit and attitudes toward athlete brand extensions. *Journal of Sport Management, 31*(1), 44–60.

Walton, P., & Chau, J. (2018). 'I'm Not Black, I'm O. J.': Constructions, productions, and refractions of Blackness. *Canadian Review of American Studies, 48*(1), 61–76.

Waymer, D., & Logan, N. (2021). Corporate social advocacy as engagement: Nike's social justice communication. *Public Relations Review, 47*(1), 1–9.

Webster, A. (2018, October 20). Finally, the real story about Peter Norman and the black power salute. *The Sydney Morning Herald*. https://www.smh.com.au/sport/finally-the-real-story-about-peter-norman-and-the-black-power-salute-20181018-p50abm.html

West, K. (featuring Jay Z). (2005). Diamonds from Sierra Leone (Remix) [Song]. On Late Registration. Roc-A-Fella Records. Note: Jay Z performs the line "I'm not a businessman, I'm a business, man".

Wiggins, D. K. (2014). Black athletes in White men's games': Race, sport, and American national pastimes. *International Journal of the History of Sport, 31*(1–2), 181–202. https://doi.org/10.1080/09523367.2013.857313

Williams, A. S., Walsh, P., & Rhenwrick, I. (2015). A conceptual framework for assessing brand equity in professional athletes. *International Journal of Sport Management, 16*(1), 77–97.

32
NATIONAL ANTHEMS AND ATHLETE ACTIVISM

Keith D. Parry, Daryl Adair, and Jamie Cleland

Introduction

This chapter explores athlete activism, focussing on its expression via national anthem protests or expressions of solidarity at sport events. We survey this type of activism and map its evolution. In doing so, we highlight three environments – the US, Australia, and Northern Ireland – as epicentres for anthemic protests and expressions of solidarity. In these varying contexts, we explore the bases for, and effectiveness of, these types of athlete activism.

Athlete activism is not a new occurrence, for it can be traced back over time. For instance, in the late 1800s the creation of separate independent and amateur baseball teams for Black baseball players, coaches and officials that had been largely excluded by the White-owned baseball teams and leagues in the US provides an example of how sport was used to pursue legitimacy in society while also creating business opportunities for Black communities. Cooper, Macauley, and Rodriguez (2017, p. 175) term the creation of these teams and leagues "social justice entrepreneurship and economic activism" and situate them within a wider typology of activism that will be detailed below. Yet, as we highlight in this chapter, pervasive discrimination and oppression within society has resulted, and often still does, in considerable backlash to acts of resistance by athletes (Ervine, 2017). Recently, however, the resurgence of athlete activism, combined with the increased media profile of top athletes, have resulted in greater public dialogue around issues pertaining to social justice both on and off the field of play. But, of course, this is not without controversy. Even peaceful activism by athletes during sporting ceremonies has in some instances been met with backlash from other players, administrators, the public, and heads of state (Yan, Pegoraro, & Watanabe, 2021).

In various countries, national anthems with associated tunes and lyrics evolved as part of what Hobsbawm and Ranger (2012) have described as the "invention of tradition" for modernising national states. But there were also pragmatic adaptations. In the United States, for example, the patriotic Star-Spangled Banner was routinely played at sporting events during World War One, though it was not then officially recognised as the country's national anthem. In 1931 that changed, with the Star-Spangled Banner now used to honour the nation's military.

Singing national anthems at the start of international sports matches may have had its genesis with a rugby union match between Wales and New Zealand in 1905 (Volans, 2015). Despite not having a national anthem, the Welsh and New Zealanders, then and now, have a proud tradition of singing en masse at special occasions. The practice also became widespread in the United States for its professional leagues. A catalyst was the prelude to a 1918 baseball game between the Boston Red Sox and the Chicago Cubs. As the band played The Star-Spangled Banner "Players turned to face the centerfield flagpole, and fans, who were already on their feet, began to sing along. By the end, nearly the entire stadium was singing, and the song ended to a chorus of thunderous applause" (Sporcle, 2018).

National anthem activism

Despite claims that sport should be apolitical (Thorson & Serazio, 2018; Zirin, 2013) and should positively distract the masses from their everyday stresses, it also serves as a site for discussions about inclusion, exclusion, and fairness, and thus it has been a high-profile space within which inequalities may be either reinforced or challenged. Indeed, it has long been recognised that major sporting events can be used as propaganda tools for political and ideological regimes, such as with the 1936 Summer Olympic Games, which became a vehicle for Nazi propaganda. International sport is, by its very nature, nationalistic with competitors representing their nations and pre- and post-game rituals frequently involving national anthems and flags that serve as "reminders that nationalism, patriotism, and unquestioning loyalty" are expected components of sport (Smith & Tryce, 2019, p. 172). Yet it is worth bearing in mind Benedict Anderson's (2006) view that nationalism and nationality are merely 'imagined communities'; they are socially constructed, evoked through culture, and "represented through the agencies of ethnicity, language or religion" (Horton, 2012, p. 1670). These myths of national identity can often be laid bare by international competitions where a small group of highly paid and privileged athletes represent the hopes and dreams of a nation. Yet some of these athletes may only be loosely associated with a nation through descent or by having switched allegiances from another nation (often with a financial incentive to do so).

In the early years of the twenty-first century, athlete activism diminished. Cunningham and Regan (2011) offer three reasons why African American athletes were less likely to speak up about social and political issues in the twentieth century. They argue that changes in social norms and legal mandates lessened the social ills prevalent in earlier periods and the need for resistance diminished. Second, the professionalisation of sport meant that athletes focused on athletic excellence alone and not social change. Third, athletes were concerned about losing out financially if they stood up for wider social issues – the inference being that they would be punished.

Indeed, the best-known sporting example of protest during a national anthem – and punishment thereafter – is the so-called Black Power Salute in 1968. The African American runners Tommie Smith and John Carlos made global headlines when they protested during the medal ceremony after the men's 200 metres track event at the Mexico City Olympic Games. As the American national anthem played, Smith and Carlos each raised a fist with a black glove (symbolising Black Power) as they also stood with bare feet (this symbolising the impoverished circumstances of most African Americans). The sprinters also both wore an Olympic Project for Human Rights (OPHR) badge to protest the White-dominated world of American sports administration in the 1960s (Ervine, 2017). This podium protest was part of wider political campaigns that characterised the Civil Rights era. The image of Carlos and

Smith on the medal dais, where they were joined by the Australian silver medallist Peter Norman, is one of the most reproduced and well-known images in sport. It was even included in *Life* magazine's 2003 list of 100 images that changed the world (Osmond, 2010). However, at the time, the protest was met with criticism, ostracism, and even death threats against the American runners (Galily, 2019), not to mention the solitary experiences of ostracism faced by Norman in Australia.

By contrast to Smith and Carlos, an entrepreneurial breed of athletes of colour focused overwhelmingly on their individual pursuits, thereby avoiding difficult conversations of the kind pursued during the 1960s. High-profile athletes, such as golfer Tiger Woods and basketballer Michael Jordan, were careful to avoid political commentary, thereby protecting their endorsements and financial interests (Mudrick, Sauder, & Davies, 2019). Nevertheless, athlete activism, and particularly Black athlete activism, has been a feature of American sporting culture. According to its most astute observer, Harry Edwards, this has been shown to occur in waves, with rises in protests reflecting contemporary struggles against racial discrimination at certain points in history (Edwards, 2016 cited in Cooper, Macauley & Rodriguez, 2017; Yan, Pegoraro & Watanabe, 2021). Cooper, Macauley and Rodriguez (2017) have proposed an African American sport activism typology outlining five categories of activist actions: (1) symbolic activism, (2) scholarly activism, (3) grassroots activism, (4) sport-based activism, and (5) economic activism. Although the current chapter does not focus solely on African American athletes, this typology signposts the importance of connecting sport activism with the broader socio-historical, socio-political, and sociocultural factors that necessitate acts of resistance.

In 2020, the death of George Floyd, an African American man suffocated by the knee of a White police officer in the United States of America (US), was met with widespread horror and condemnation. This murder of Floyd by a Minnesota state official, who was expected to "serve and protect others" (Minneapolis Police Department), gave renewed impetus to Black Lives Matter (BLM). This movement arose in 2013 in response to longstanding and widespread police violence towards coloured communities and, specifically the killing of Trayvon Martin by George Zimmerman. After Floyd's killing, BLM was no longer confined to the US; assertive anti-racism was now a global phenomenon, though most obviously in liberal democracies that allow robust free speech. Here, professional sport has played a pivotal role. Players, club staff, officials, and media organisations have taken part in coordinated shows of solidarity; dropping to one knee before matches, making institutional comments (particularly via social media), and, in the case of Black players, raising fists – doubtless inspired by Carlos and Smith's Black Power Salute. In some instances, these protests have occurred during the playing of national anthems, which has resulted in considerable criticism from some quarters.

During his time as US president, Donald Trump continually attacked athletes who protested during the playing of the national anthem before sport matches. For example, with professional sport matches returning following COVID-19 suspensions, he tweeted "Looking forward to live sports [returning], but any time I witness a player kneeling during the National Anthem, a sign of great disrespect for our Country and our Flag, the game is over for me!" (@realDonaldTrump, 21 July 2020). His responses highlight the tensions that arise when rituals tied to concepts of national identity become contested.

A collective voice among professional athletes has thus recently emerged (Mudrick et al., 2019) whereby sports stars use their celebrity status and/or social media platforms to draw attention to a variety of social movements and campaigns that highlight social injustices.

In this manner, they are able to use their status to act as 'agents of social change' (Smith, 2019). As a result, a recent rise in sport-based activism has been seen in a number of contexts (Galily, 2019), all of which have received substantial media coverage. While these protests have been met with some resistance, those involving national anthems – expressions of patriotic solidarity – have been the most polarising (Smith, 2019).

It is common practice for major sports matches to begin with a short ceremony featuring the playing of the national anthem while the national flag is either raised or flown, along with a variety of ritualised ceremonies (Ward, 2009). This practice was described as 'redundant patriotism' by Spiegel and Spiegel in 1998 but, in the US in particular, sports have since adopted a hyper-patriotic stance, most notably in the wake of the 9/11 terror attacks, (Chaplin & Motez de Oca, 2019) where national symbols and songs have (re)assumed profound significance. Sport organisations such as the National Football League (NFL) and major events like the Super Bowl have been keen to brand themselves as both patriotic and militaristic (Butterworth, 2008; Chaplin & Montez de Oca, 2019; Smith, 2019). The longstanding tradition of anthem singing has thus played an even more powerful role in the symbolic performance of American nationalism (Yan, Pegoraro, & Watanabe, 2021). Under such conditions, patriotism (or patriotic behaviour) risks becoming synonymous with "blind loyalty, staunch allegiance, and inflexible attachment to the country" (Hawkman & Van Horn, 2019, p. 106). Criticising the national anthem or any of these symbols of patriotism, or a refusal to stand or sing the anthem while the national flag is flown, typically results in questioning of someone's ancestry or their commitment to the American nation (Spiegel & Spiegel, 1998). Such activists are often dubbed as unpatriotic, traitors, or even communists (Chaplin & Montez de Oca, 2019). In the US, where professional sport has become increasingly tied to patriotism, athlete activism that calls out racism and racial injustice – especially when expressed by a person of colour – is commonly seen as racially divisive by conservative White Americans. By the process, Black and Brown athletes are labelled as a threat to traditional notions of national identity and community solidarity (Dickerson & Hodler, 2020). By pointing to social injustices according to race, athletes of colour are branded as disloyal to the 'American' dream – a mindset (whether conservative or liberal) within which racial inequities are either ignored or denied (Averbeck, 2018). Donald Trump has, in particular, adopted such a stance. This labelling is mostly applied to racialised minorities to "disqualify them from political citizenship as well as justify state violence and social control" (Chaplin & Montez de Oca, 2019, p. 14).

Colin Kaepernick, the NFL, and anthem protests in the US

Since 2009, the NFL has required players to be on the field for the pre-game playing of the national anthem, apparently after US sports leagues were paid to honour members of the military by the Department of Defence (Berr, 2018) – previously it was typical for them to remain in the locker room (Seri et al., 2019). Colin Kaepernick's anthem protest began in August 2016 and was a response to pervasive police violence and widespread inequality against African Americans (Yan, Pegoraro & Watanabe, 2021). His initial refusal to stand for the national anthem came during an NFL pre-season game when he was the quarterback for the San Francisco 49ers. At the time he was a popular figure with the team's fans; his jersey was the highest selling kit in the NFL ahead of the 2016 season (Mudrick et al., 2019). During his initial protest he sat on the bench and drew little attention (Smith, 2019). However, during the third game his action was captured by a photographer and in a media interview he revealed the reasons behind his move, subsequently generating much more publicity (Daum, 2019). Discussing his protest, Kaepernick said:

> I am not going to stand up to show pride in a flag for a country that oppresses black people and people of color ... To me, this is bigger than football and it would be selfish on my part to look the other way. There are bodies in the street and people getting paid leave and getting away with murder.
> (cited in Murty, Holyfield-moss, Vyas & Roebuck, 2018, p. 46)

To stress that his actions were not aimed at the military, he changed to kneeling after consulting with a friend and military veteran on how best to protest while still respecting the US armed forces (Sevi et al., 2019). Ironically, though, this resulted in a rapid and vitriolic response from many segments of US society, in particular right-wing communities and conservative media (Daum, 2019; Duvall, 2020). Kaepernick's 'stance' was part of a complex racialised cultural moment in the US (Dickerson & Hodler, 2020) that itself is reflective of the privileging of Whiteness and the 'othering' of Black Americans and other minority groups (Johnson, 2019). He followed in the footsteps of a number of other athletes who had protested in support of BLM and earlier movements of resistance to racial discrimination, injustice, and inequality in both law and custom (Chaplin & Montez de Oca, 2019). Given the NFL's influence on American culture (Sevi et al., 2019), Kaepernick's protest was significant as it brought the movement to audiences that had previously remained ignorant of its aim of raising awareness of institutional racism. More so, Kaepernick's protest diverged from other recent protests in that he purposefully protested during the playing of the US national anthem (Duvall, 2020).

Despite the personal sacrifice Kaepernick made (he has been without a playing contract since March 2017 when he opted out of his contract with the San Francisco 49ers), his protest was embraced by a number of Black as well as White players across teams in the NFL. It has been suggested that over 49 NFL players from 13 teams joined Kaepernick in kneeling within two months of him starting this form of protest (Murty et al., 2018) with players in other sports, including the entire Indiana Fever Women's National Basketball Association team, as well as college and high school teams also taking a knee during the anthem (Smith & Tryce, 2019). Subsequently, the league reviewed its policy surrounding the national anthem and decided players could stay in the dressing room if they did not wish to stand for it, but all those on the pitch would be required to stand (Anderson, 2019). Significantly, Kaepernick's protest was well received by some members of the US military and the hashtag *#VeteransForKaepernick* began trending on social media (Murty et al., 2018). Although not violating any league rule, these peaceful anthem protests have met with considerable backlash from other players, administrators, the public, and then President Donald Trump (Yan, Pegoraro & Watanabe, 2021). Kaepernick and fellow protesters have been labelled anti-American, received death threats, and described as "sons of bitches" by Trump, whose criticisms often drew on White nationalist statements (Chaplin & Montez de Oca, 2019; Schmidt et al., 2018). As has been the case with Kaepernick, anyone who protests during traditional US national rituals, such as the playing of the national anthem, quickly has the stigmatising label 'unpatriotic' attached to them by the more right-wing elements of the media due to a perceived lack of respect for tradition or honour for what the anthem symbolises (Sevi et al., 2019).

However, following the public anguish in response to the murder of George Floyd, the NFL revisited its position and permitted players to kneel in protest (Sherwood, 2020). NFL Commissioner Roger Goodell stated that:

> We, the National Football League, condemn racism and the systematic oppression of black people. We, the National Football League admit we were wrong for not listening to NFL players earlier and encourage all to speak out and peacefully protest. We, the National Football League, believe black lives matter. I personally protest with you and want to be part of the much needed change in this country. Without black players, there would be no National Football League. And the protests around the country are emblematic of the centuries of silence, inequality, and oppression of black players coaches, fans, and staff. We are listening, I am listening, and I will be reaching out to players who have raised their voices and others on how we can improve and go forward for a better and more united NFL family.
>
> (Goodell quoted in NFL, 2020)

Again, Trump attacked this decision on Twitter, vehemently arguing that the "Great American Flag" (and the other pre-match rituals such as playing the national anthem) should not be protested, repeating his familiar talking-points that such a stance was disrespecting the country (Murty et al., 2018). Trump's attitude did not deter athletes from their protest; in fact, it may even have encouraged more acts of resistance with NFL players defying Trump via gestures of protest during the anthem, and basketballers Steph Curry and LeBron James speaking out against the President (Siddiqui, 2017).

Of the athletes to kneel in support of Kaepernick, the most vocal was Megan Rapinoe, a star player for the Seattle Reign of the National Women's Soccer League (NWSL) and US Women's National Soccer Team (USWNT). She copied Kaepernick's actions and kneeled during a NWSL match and then two USWNT matches in September 2016 (Schmidt et al., 2018). Rapinoe, a White openly lesbian player who is an outspoken advocate for LGBTI+ rights, stated that kneeling was an act of solidarity and allyship with communities of colour in protest toward police violence toward them (Hawkman & Van Horn, 2019), saying:

> I am disgusted with the way he has [Kaepernick] been treated … and [the] hatred he has received in all of this … We need a more substantive conversation around race relations and the way people of colour are treated.
>
> (McNeal, 2018)

Rapinoe was similarly labelled anti-American by many conservatives, but was also painted as an outlier – acting in isolation (Coombs et al., 2020). Her actions were also minimised as her team's next opponents played the national anthem before Rapinoe had taken the field (Trimbur, 2019) and US Soccer subsequently mandated that players were required to stand during the playing of the anthem. Rapinoe was not to be silenced and took to *The Players' Tribune* (a prominent blog written by athletes) to explain her decision to kneel in detail and to reinforce her respect for the national flag, which she stated represents "the heart of our country's ultimate symbol of freedom" as she faced it during her protests (Rapinoe, 2016). She also played to traditional values and ideals, claiming:

> I am the same woman who has worn the Stars and Stripes across her chest, proud and beaming. I am one of the women you have called an American hero, and not just once.

I look like your sister, your friend, your neighbor or the girl your kids go to school with.
I am the person sitting at your dinner table and coming to your holiday party.

(Rapinoe, 2016, para. 1)

In a move similar to that of the NFL, the USWNT also repealed its rule requiring players to kneel in June 2020, removing the fear of disapproval by the governing body. As a result, the "vast majority of players, coaches, and officials took a knee during the anthem before each game" (Howell, 2021, p. 76). These two decisions can be seen as watershed moments in American sport. For possibly the first time, athletes have been empowered to protest racial discrimination without fear of reprisals – from the governing bodies at least.

Australia

In Australia, Indigenous athletes, who are disproportionately represented in sport, have demonstrated resistance by remaining silent during the national anthems at the start of some high-profile sports matches. These protests were in response to an anthem that, despite popular claims to the notion of a 'fair go' for all, has ignored both the historical and contemporary significance of Indigenous communities to Australia. As has been noted by Cleland, Adair, and Parry (2020), 'fairness', by way of shared opportunity, has typically only applied to opportunities for fair skinned (i.e., White) Australians (Fotinopoulos, 2017). Indeed, far from a 'fair go', Aboriginal peoples have been the subject of a history of institutionalised racial discrimination that has resulted in considerable disadvantages. This discrimination is best highlighted in the forcible removal of Aboriginal children from their families, to be placed in foster care with White families, in many parts of Australia during the early to mid to late twentieth century. The Federal Government issued a national apology for what has become known as the Stolen Generations in 2008 (Murphy, 2011) and committed to a reconciliation process but discrimination, in both overt and covert forms, has remained in wider society and sport (Cleland, Parry & Radford, 2019).

Australia's national anthem, Advance Australia Fair, is, in one sense, relatively new given that it was only made the official anthem via a referendum in 1984. However, the song itself was conceived much earlier, in 1878 by a Scottish migrant – thus reflecting an earlier period in time. The original lyrics have undergone minor adjustments over the years: for example, "Australian sons" was replaced simply by "Australians", thus making the song more gender neutral (Institute of Australian Culture, 2012). Yet, until recently, there had been no effort to acknowledge country's Indigenous peoples. Aboriginal Australians had long criticised the anthem's lyrical claim that Australians are "young and free", citing the historical presence of Aboriginal peoples dating back at least 65,000 years and their subjugated status following the European invasion. In addition, Indigenous critics have (perhaps understandably) construed the title Advance Australia Fair to refer to White skin colour, even if not intended by its author (Welcome to Country, 2019).

Indigenous Australians rose to prominence in professional sport in the late twentieth century, becoming household names in rugby union, rugby league, and Australian Rules football in particular and making up around 10 per cent of contracted players in the latter two sports (Ferrer & Turner, 2017). Recognising this involvement, the National Rugby League (NRL) established a dedicated Indigenous Round of matches every season and more recently introduced a special pre-season rugby league match featuring the 'Indigenous All Stars' against either the (non-Indigenous) 'NRL All Stars' or the (Indigenous New Zealand) 'Māori All

Stars' (Philpott, 2017). Significantly, during the NRL's Indigenous Round in May 2017, alongside Advance Australia Fair, an alternative pre-recorded version of the national anthem was shown on big screens inside the stadiums with the words "young and free" supplanted by "peace and harmony", and "our land abounds in nature's gifts of beauty rich and rare" changed to "our land abounds in nature's gifts to love, respect and share" (Hytner, 2017).

Given that Indigenous Australians comprise around 2.5 per cent of the national population, it may be little surprise that the management of the sport industry and sport media are controlled almost exclusively by non-Indigenous people. We have already seen that Indigenous athletes are prominent, but Indigenous people are much more rarely in off-field positions like coaching, administration, and media commentary. All that said, sport is one of a small number of places where the Indigenous community has some voice and can demonstrate advocacy at a national level (Cleland, Parry & Radford, 2019). Increasingly, sporting bodies have accepted that they need to work with Indigenous people in more profound ways. A key example was the NRL's decision to showcase an alternative national anthem. The initiative recognised that the official song was not deemed appropriate to the history and experiences of First Nations people. That experimental (albeit temporary) step provided a space, in 2019, for a string of high-profile silent protests by key Indigenous rugby league players: they objected to a requirement that the Australian anthem be played at sporting events, and this brought the debate firmly into public consciousness.

The players first used media interviews to openly state their intended refusal to sing Advance Australia Fair ahead of games. Using their privileged positions, the Indigenous rugby players commanded the attention of the national media, compelling them to ask the players why they intended to make this gesture and thus allowing the players to give voice to Indigenous criticisms of the anthem. The media typically provided verbatim statements from the players, significantly allowing Indigenous voices to do the talking and not just be talked about (Cleland, Adair, & Parry, 2020).

Then, during televised games, several players on both teams remained silent during the anthem. The first match was the 'All Stars' game in February 2019. Speaking after this match, Cody Walker, one of the most prominent figures in the protests reflected on the reasons behind his silent protest:

> It just brings back so many memories from what's happened [in Australia's past] …
> I think everyone in Australia needs to get together and work something out [about the national anthem] … It doesn't represent myself and my family.
> (ABC News, 2019)

In the lead up to the three-match State of Origin series between Queensland and New South Wales in June/July 2019, another Indigenous player, Josh Addo-Carr, opined:

> We're Australians too, Indigenous people. We were the first people here … I have full support of Cody's decision and I'll be behind him all the way. The anthem doesn't represent us Indigenous people and I think we've got to change it.
> (Brunsdon, 2019)

During the series, players from both teams remained silent during the national anthem and, significantly, support for the players was tacitly given by the NRL as they were not punished for not singing (Parry & Cleland, 2019). The players also received support from athletes in other sports (Koha, 2019) and in other areas of rugby league. In particular, Indigenous female rugby league players competing in the women's State of Origin in June 2019 also refused to sing the anthem, although this event received less media attention. The coach of the Australian rugby league team, South Sea Islander Mal Meninga, was one prominent individual to speak out in support of the players. In a media interview he stated:

> We expect them [the players] to sing the national anthem, but I'm also in favour of the fact, if it is offensive to Indigenous Australians, let's have a discussion about it. We're a multicultural society, so all of Australia should decide on what our anthem should be. The majority of us are third- and fourth-generation Australians now. What does contemporary Australia want? If it's important to people, why not call for a referendum?
>
> (Nicolussi & Phillips, 2019)

He also drew attention to the fact that it had been over 40 years since Australians had voted on the choice of a national anthem:

> while the Indigenous population has been talking about Advance Australia Fair for a long time, I cannot see why there can't be debate about it again now ... Times have changed since the last decision was made. We've had major decisions around Indigenous Australia, such as native title recognition and cultural heritage being revived. We've had the national Sorry Day so Australians—all Australians—are very aware of our national history, maybe more aware than they were before. So we can have a national debate and let the people of Australia have their say. If we have a national anthem that offends our Indigenous people, let's see what all of Australia thinks.
>
> (Meninga, 2019)

Similarly, an article by Channel Nine (2019) quoted New South Wales coach Brad Fittler (a non-Indigenous Australian) who also indicated his support for the player protests, stating that the national anthem "definitely needs work ... you go to any venue around the country and three-quarters of the people aren't singing". However, the response to these protests was not solely favourable. A small number of Indigenous athletes spoke out against the players. Former Indigenous Queensland rugby league player, Justin Hodges, viewed the national anthem to be about military sacrifice and claimed that he sang the anthem "for the soldiers and those guys that have given us the freedom to play rugby league" (Fox Sports, 2019). The disapproval was led most vocally by rugby union player, Kurtley Beale, who believed that the most appropriate steps towards the ongoing process of reconciliation was to sing the national anthem (Doran, 2019).

What the protests particularly did was to give "oxygen to wider discussions about the appropriateness of the anthem as representative of Australia" (Cleland, Adair, & Parry, 2020, p. 15). Both Indigenous and non-Indigenous journalists and commentators argued that the silent protests had regenerated discussion about changing the anthem and had found support from across the party-political divide. For example, two politicians stated that changing the word "young" in the opening verse containing the lyrics "for we are young and free" would encourage a more inclusive Australia by acknowledging and responding to the criticisms of Aboriginal peoples. In 2020, the state Premier of New South Wales proposed that this line be changed to "for we are one and free". Following approval from a variety of ministers the Prime Minister enacted this change from 1 January 2021.

It is important to note that the athlete voices were not the only ones that championed this change. For instance, The Recognition in Anthem Project in particular, which began in 2017, consulted both Indigenous and non-Indigenous groups to gain support for a change to the lyrics. However, given that professional sport holds a significant place in Australian culture and lends itself to regular media focus and commentary, the athlete protests, with the tacit support of the sport's governing bodies were able to draw media attention to the issue in ways that Aboriginal peoples are not typically afforded. While the Australian government's decision to change the lyrics of the anthem cannot be solely attributed to the action of a small number of rugby league players, they kept debates on its appropriateness in the public eye.

Northern Ireland

The island of Ireland is divided into two nations and so the role of national anthems in sport is complex, particularly given that there are often two separate representative sides for Ireland on the international stage. Athletes from Northern Ireland who are eligible to represent both the Republic of Ireland and the United Kingdom of Great Britain and Northern Ireland (UK) face difficult decisions over which nation to represent (Liston & Moreland, 2009). This identity conflict was highlighted at the Rio 2016 Olympics where Mark and Paul Gleghorne, brothers from Northern Ireland, competed for different national teams (Team GB and Ireland) (Liston & Kitching, 2020).

A number of Association footballers born in Catholic communities in Northern Ireland, where Roman Catholics make up a significant religious group but where the country is aligned to the Protestant UK, have chosen to represent the predominantly Catholic Republic of Ireland rather than their country of birth (Hassan, McCullough & Moreland, 2009). Traditionally, Association football (soccer) has been associated with "those parts of the country that retained support for the union with Britain and less so amongst advocates of Irish national independence movement" (Hassan, 2006, p. 344); i.e., it is linked with unionist Protestants rather than nationalist Catholics. Meanwhile, Catholic players representing Northern Ireland have been targeted for sectarian abuse by sections of the crowd at games (Hassan, 2006) and have even received death threats (Liston & Deighan, 2019). Recently, however, it is claimed that the Northern Irish national team has increasingly been seen as representative of both sides of the ethno-religious divide (Keown, 2020).

As in other nations, matches of representative teams and national cup finals usually begin with the playing of the national anthem, but the anthem itself has unsurprisingly been identified as problematic due to its sectarian connotations (Liston & Deighan, 2019). At this time, in Northern Ireland, God Save the Queen was traditionally played before sports matches – a move that is staunchly unionist and which has been described as demonstrating a "calculated disregard for northern nationalists" (Hassan, McCullough & Moreland, 2009, p. 748). In the Republic of Ireland, the national anthem, Amhrán na bhFiann (The Soldier's Song) is at times replaced with the song Ireland's Call. This was commissioned by the Irish Rugby Football Union ahead of the 1995 World Cup because, although the team represents the Republic of Ireland, players from Northern Ireland are eligible to play for the team and some of these had expressed their unease at the use of the anthem (Fanning, 2016). Nevertheless, nationalists living in Northern Ireland, including footballers, have shown a greater affinity to the anthems of the Republic (and associated ideals) (Murray & Hassan, 2018). In a study of

12 self-declared Irish nationalists and republicans who had represented Northern Ireland at football, Liston and Deighan (2019) found that only one player had developed a level of comfort with the anthem, while the others believed it was an ideological barrier for current and future Catholic players. Despite recommendations for a new anthem to be played at sports matches, the First Minister for Northern Ireland, Arlene Foster refused, expressing a desire to retain what she regarded as the 'depoliticisation' of sport (Liston & Deighan, 2019). The actions of players have again brought this discussion into the public eye.

Football grounds are critical sites of fandom, with allegiances based on religious and political identities. The island has a longstanding ethno-national conflict (known as the Troubles) and Northern Ireland's national Association football venue, Windsor Park, has witnessed violence and religious sectarianism, including sectarian chanting against the Catholic community and denigration of Irish nationalism. In this way, Windsor Park has been 'claimed' by loyalists and unionists from Northern Ireland (Hassan, 2002). The stadium was the site of controversy in 2018 when it played host to the Irish Cup final between Cliftonville, who are identified as being associated with a Catholic/Nationalist tradition, and Coleraine who have Protestant/Unionist ties (Hassan & Ferguson, 2019). During the playing of God Save the Queen before the match, Cliftonville players en masse bowed their heads in protest at the use of this anthem. Their actions divided opinions along predictable political lines with a number of politicians highly critical of their protest, with one claiming that the team "got what their disrespect deserved", as they lost the match (McKeown, 2018).

At international levels, the anthem has not been met with such a coordinated response but individual players at senior and age representative groups have also chosen to bow their heads and not sing. This action has evoked strong responses from unionists, with players criticised and harassed in online public spaces (Liston & Deighan, 2019). Similarly, Republic of Ireland footballer James McLean has received considerable online abuse for his decision to bow his head when the British anthem has been played ahead of matches involving his club side. This abuse even included death threats towards McLean and his family (Kavanagh & Parry, 2021).

It is not only the public that have criticised Northern Irish players for not joining in with the national anthem. Fellow footballers and captains have confronted players that remain silent or bow their heads, claiming that they are disrespecting their team mates along with the anthem (Liston & Deighan, 2019). The notion of shame was also used by coaches in the Northern Irish system to encourage players to keep their heads raised during the anthem, singling out these nationalist players based on ethno-religious bases.

Interestingly, Barry McGuigan, a former boxer from Northern Ireland with a Catholic, nationalist upbringing, adopted a different stance on anthems. He preferred a non-aligned 'anthem' and peace emblems in place of a national flag when he competed and, thus, attempted to avoid some of the issues noted above (Liston & Kitching, 2020). However, while McGuigan's sporting medium meant that he was more accepted by nationalists with an interest in boxing, nationalists interpreted his moves as sporting treachery as he refused to fight under the Irish tricolour (Hassan, 2005). Sugden and Sugden (1997) have similarly noted a degree of flexibility from Irish sports teams when it comes to the flag and anthem by either substituting them with neutral emblems and songs as McGuigan did or by avoiding their use completely. Despite this desire to down-play national symbolism and lower ethno-religious tensions, various European and World sporting authorities continue to insist that a national flag and anthem are included when Irish athletes take part in their competitions (Sugden & Sugden, 1997). The enforced playing of the anthem may also be detrimental to the on-field performance of the Northern Ireland team. Former manager, Michael O'Neil has claimed that it alienated players from a nationalist background, who would typically stand with their head bowed. Speaking in a television documentary, O'Neil stated his belief that the team:

> were at a disadvantage in the anthem, because I could see how other countries would either sing their anthem or display real patriotism, you know, a real togetherness, real emotion during the anthem. And we never really got that.
>
> (Browne, 2021)

He pointed to tensions between the nationalists and those who sang the anthem, seeing it as a representation of their national identity. O'Neil also claimed that such friction and contrasts in body language during the anthem were not present in most other nations where, it is implied, the anthem brought players together.

Conclusion

Despite the opinion of Michael O'Neil that playing national anthems ahead of sports matches can bring players together, the cases discussed in this chapter paint a very different picture. These rituals, utilising songs that are inherently nationalistic, can be marginalising as well as solidifying. Debates around national anthems are not new, yet at a broad level the societies discussed here remain attached to them. The anthems themselves are often problematic as they have been adopted and thus represent the ideals of earlier periods in nations' histories (Parry, Adair, & Cleland, 2020).

In this chapter we have shown athletes across three continents and in a variety of sports have used the combination their celebrity profiles, the media focus on sport, and the desire for sports organisations to associate themselves with nationalistic rituals to draw attention to a variety of social movements and campaigns that highlight social injustices or to challenge the practices of nationalism themselves. Importantly, these protests have revealed that social injustices remain prevalent, even following changes in social norms and legal mandates. Athletes now have platforms and profiles that allow them to highlight areas of society where injustices are most keenly felt.

Through these protests, the roles of anthems in national identity and who they represent have been questioned. In all cases, athletes have challenged the expectation that citizens should passively engage in the hyper-patriotic, militaristic, and ritualistic actions when they are not representative of themselves or all members of the society. These protests have not come without a cost, whether this be to individual players' careers or to team cohesion and performance. However, athletes have also been supported by those within their sport, eventually, even if politicians and governments have been slower to do so.

References

ABC News. (2019). *Indigenous All Stars Captain Cody Walker and Mal Meninga Call for National Anthem to Be Changed.* https://www.abc.net.au/news/2019-02-16/indigenous-allstars-cody-walker-mal-meninga-national-anthem/10818760

Anderson, B. (2006). *Imagined Communities: Reflections on the Origin and Spread of Nationalism* (Rev. ed.). Verso.

Anderson, S. M. (2019). United We Stand, Divided We Kneel: Examining Perceptions of the NFL Anthem Protest on Organizational Reputation. *Communication & Sport, 8*(4–5), 591–610.

Averbeck, R. M. (2018). *Liberalism Is Not Enough: Race and Poverty in Postwar Political Thought.* University of North Carolina Press.

Berr, J. (2018). NFL's Tangled Ties with National Anthem Don't Run Deep. *CBS News*. https://www.cbsnews.com/news/the-nfls-tangled-ties-with-the-national-anthem-dont-run-deep/

Browne, P. J. (2021). O'Neill Believes 'God Save the Queen' Put Northern Ireland at Disadvantage. *Balls.ie*. https://www.balls.ie/amp/football/michael-oneill-northern-ireland-god-save-the-queen-493977

Brunsdon, S. (2019). "We've Got to Change It": Another Blues Star Backs Anthem Boycott. *Fox Sports*. https://www.foxsports.com.au/nrl/state-of-origin/weve-got-to-change-it-bluesstars-back-anthem-boycott/news-story/03de52213a4f569c5c9ccf7b0ca912d5

Butterworth, M. (2008). Fox Sports, Super Bowl XLII, and the Affirmation of American Civil Religion. *Journal of Sport and Social Issues*, *32*(3), 318–323. doi:10.1177/0193723508319715

Channel Nine. (2019). Australian National Anthem "Definitely Needs Work," Says NSW Coach Brad Fittler. *nine.com.au*. https://wwos.nine.com.au/nrl/nrl-news-brad-fittler-australianational-anthem/c5413f3d-9628-462a-95a5-9414d63479c6

Chaplin, K. S., & Montez de Oca, J. (2019). Avoiding the Issue: University Students' Reponses to NFL Players' National Anthem Protests. *Sociology of Sport Journal*, *36*(1), 12–21. doi:10.1123/ssj.2018-0108

Cleland, J., Parry, K., & Radford, D. (2019). "Perhaps She Only Had a Banana Available to Throw": Habitus, Racial Prejudice, and Whiteness on Australian Football League Message Boards. *Sociology of Sport Journal*, *36*(4), 330–338.

Cleland, J., Adair, D., & Parry, K. (2020). Fair Go? Indigenous Rugby League Players and the Racial Exclusion of the Australian National Anthem. *Communication & Sport*. doi:10.1177/2167479520935598

Coombs, D. S., Lambert, C. A., Cassilo, D., & Humphries, Z. (2020). Flag on the Play: Colin Kaepernick and the Protest Paradigm. *Howard Journal of Communications*, *31*(4), 317–336.

Cooper, J. N., Macauley, C., & Rodriguez, S. H. (2017). Race and Resistance: A Typology of African American Sport Activism. *International Review for the Sociology of Sport*, *54*(2), 151–181.

Cunningham, G. B., & Regan, M. R. (2011). Political Activism, Racial Identity and the Commercial Endorsement of Athletes. *International Review for the Sociology of Sport*, *47*(6), 657–669. doi:10.1177/1012690211416358

Daum, C. W. (2019). Taking a Knee: Neoliberalism, Radical Imaginaries, and the NFL Player Protest. *New Political Science*, *41*(4), 514–528.

Dickerson, N., & Hodler, M. (2020). "Real Men Stand for Our Nation": Constructions of an American Nation and Anti-Kaepernick Memes. *Journal of Sport and Social Issues*. doi:10.1177/0193723520950537

Doran, C. (2019, May 30). "Step towards Reconciliation": Why Kurtley Beale Will Sing Anthem and Believes Indigenous Jersey at World Cup is a "Pinnacle Moment" in History. *Fox Sports*. https://www.foxsports.com.au/rugby/wallabies/step-towards-reconciliationwhy-kurtley-beale-will-sing-anthem-and-believes-indigenous-jersey-at-world-cup-is-pinnacle-moment/news-story/1c9fc0bf423b6dce1b0bd7ba976a045f

Duvall, S. S. (2020). Too Famous to Protest: Far-Right Online Community Bonding over Collective Desecration of Colin Kaepernick, Fame, and Celebrity Activism. *Journal of Communication Inquiry*, *44*(3), 256–278. doi:10.1177/0196859920911650

Ervine, J. (2017). Nicolas Anelka and the Quenelle Gesture: A Study of the Complexities of Protest in Contemporary Football. *The International Journal of the History of Sport*, *34*(3–4), 236–250. doi:10.1080/09523367.2017.1359161

Fanning, B. (2016). *Irish Adventures in Nation-building*. Manchester University Press.

Ferrer, J., & Turner, P. (2017). Indigenous Player Inclusion in the Australian Football League. *Equality, Diversity and Inclusion: An International Journal*, *36*(6), 519–532.

Fotinopoulos, C. (2017). It's Advance Australia Fair, Not Fair-Skinned. *Huffington Post*. https://www.huffingtonpost.com.au/chris-fotinopoulos/its-advance-australia-fair-not-fairskinned_a_21658771/

Fox Sports. (2019). Maroons Legend Justin Hodges Weighs in on Anthem Debate. *Fox Sports*. https://www.foxsports.com.au/nrl/state-of-origin/teams/queensland/maroons-legend-justin-hodges-weighs-in-on-anthem-debate/news-story/af1f78f9b55c068afcb24b65ef550c34

Galily, Y. (2019). "Shut Up and Dribble!"?Athletes Activism in the Age of Twittersphere: The Case of LeBron James. *Technology in Society*, *58*, 101109. doi:10.1016/j.techsoc.2019.01.002

Hassan, D. (2002). A People Apart: Soccer, Identity and Irish Nationalists in Northern Ireland. *Soccer & Society*, *3*(3), 65–83. doi:10.1080/714004886

Hassan, D. (2005). 'A Champion Inside the Ring and a Champion Outside it': An Examination of the Socio-political Impact of the Career of Barry McGuigan. *Sport in History*, *25*(2): 221–236.

Hassan, D. (2006). An Opportunity for a New Beginning: Soccer, Irish Nationalists and the Construction of a New Multi-Sports Stadium for Northern Ireland. *Soccer & Society*, *7*(2–3), 339–352. doi:10.1080/14660970600615427

Hassan, D., & Ferguson, K. (2019). Still as Divided as Ever? Northern Ireland, Football and Identity 20 Years after the Good Friday Agreement. *Soccer & Society*, *20*(7–8), 1071–1083. doi:10.1080/14660970.2019.1680504

Hassan, D., McCullough, S., & Moreland, E. (2009). North or South? Darron Gibson and the Issue of Player Eligibility within Irish Soccer. *Soccer & Society*, *10*(6): 740–753.

Hawkman, A. M., & Van Horn, S. E. (2019). What Does It Mean to Be Patriotic? Policing Patriotism in Sports and Social Studies Education. *The Social Studies*, *110*(3), 105–121. doi:10.1080/00377996.2018.1553841

Hobsbawm, E., & Ranger, T. (2012). *The Invention of Tradition*. Cambridge University Press.

Horton, P. A. (2012). Tumultuous Text: The Imagining of Australia through Literature, Sport and Nationalism from Colonies to the Federation. *The International Journal of the History of Sport*, *29*(12), 1669–1686. doi:10.1080/09523367.2012.714930

Howell, C. E. (2021). The 2020 National Women's Soccer League Challenge Cup Anthem Protests: The Limits of Symbolic White Allyship. *The Velvet Light Trap*, *87* (Spring), 76–79.

Hytner, M. (2017). Alternative National Anthem Planned for NRL's Indigenous Round. *Guardian*. https://www.theguardian.com/sport/2017/may/11/alternative-national-anthemplanned-during-nrls-indigenous-round

Institute of Australian Culture. (2012). *Advance Australia Fair: How the Song Became the Australian National Anthem*. http://www.australianculture.org/advance-australia-fair/

Johnson, M. W. (2019). Trump, Kaepernick, and MLK as "Maybe Citizens": Early Elementary African American Males' Analysis of Citizenship. *Theory & Research in Social Education*, *47*(3), 374–395.

Kavanagh, E., & Parry, K. D. (2021). Trolling of Footballers: We All Have the Potential to Be Abused or Become the Abusers. *Irish Examiner*. https://www.irishexaminer.com/sport/soccer/arid-40230161.html

Keown, C. (2020). Translating Sectarianism: Performing Identities in Northern Irish Football. *Translation Studies*, *13*(2), 216–232. doi:10.1080/14781700.2020.1746390

Koha, N. T. (2019). John Steffensen Backs Indigenous Athletes Boycotting Australian National Anthem. *Herald Sun*. https://www.heraldsun.com.au/entertainment/confidential/john-steffensen-backs-indigenous-athletes-boycotting-australian-national-anthem/news-story/b35b16428b7b6ed66bf36b9726cc218f

Liston, K., & Deighan, M. (2019). Whose 'Wee Country'?: Identity Politics and Sport in Northern Ireland. *Identities*, *26*(2), 203–221. doi:10.1080/1070289X.2017.1392103

Liston, K., & Kitching, N. (2020). 'Our Wee Country': National Identity, Golf and 'Ireland'. *Sport in Society*, *23*(5), 864–879. doi:10.1080/17430437.2019.1584186

Liston, K., & Moreland, E. (2009). Hockey and Habitus: Sport and National Identity in Northern Ireland. *New Hibernia Review*, *13*(4), 127–140. doi:10.1353/nhr.0.0115

McKeown, G. (2018). DUP MLA Criticised after Saying Cliftonville 'Got What They Deserved' for Anthem Protest. *The Irish News*. https://www.irishnews.com/news/northernirelandnews/2018/05/07/news/dup-mla-criticised-after-saying-cliftonville-got-what-they-deserved-for-anthem-protest-1323100/

McNeal, L. R. (2018). From Hoodies to Kneeling during the National Anthem: The Colin Kaepernick Effect and Its Implications for K-12 Sports. *Louisiana Law Review*, *78*(8), 145–196.

Meninga, M. (2019). Australia Needs Referendum on National Anthem. *nrl.com*. https://www.nrl.com/news/2019/02/16/mal-meninga-australia-needs-referendum-onnationalanthem/

Mudrick, M., Sauder, M. H., & Davies, M. (2019). When Athletes Don't "Stick to Sports": The Relationship between Athlete Political Activism and Sport Consumer Behavior. *Journal of Sport Behavior*, *42*(2), 177–199.

Murphy, F. (2011). Archives of Sorrow: An Exploration of Australia's Stolen Generations and Their Journey into the Past. *History and Anthropology*, *22*(4), 481–495.

Murray, C., & Hassan, D. (2018). 'They're Just Not My Team': The Issue of Player Allegiances within Irish Football, 2007–2012. *Soccer & Society*, *19*(5–6), 687–703. doi:10.1080/14660970.2017.1399607

Murty, K. S., Holyfield-Moss, B., Vyas, A. G., & Roebuck, J. B. (2018). African American Students' Perceptions toward NFL Kneeling and Trump's Reaction: Racial Justice V. Patriotism. *Journal of Law and Judicial System*, *1*(4), 45–56.

NFL. (2020). *Roger Goodell: NFL 'Wrong' for Not Listening to Protesting Players Earlier*. https://www.nfl.com/news/roger-goodell-nfl-wrong-for-not-listening-to-protesting-players-earlier

Nicolussi, C., & Phillips, S. (2019). "It Doesn't Represent Me or My Family": Indigenous Captain Takes Aim at Anthem. *Sydney Morning Herald*. https://www.smh.com.au/sport/nrl/indigenous-all-stars-captain-takes-aim-at-national-anthem-20190216-p50y7e.html

Osmond, G. (2010). Photographs, Materiality and Sport History: Peter Norman and the 1968 Mexico City Black Power Salute. *Journal of Sport History*, 37(1), 119–137.

Parry, K. D., & Cleland, J. (2019). Our National Anthem Is Non-Inclusive: Indigenous Australians Shouldn't Have to Sing It. *The Conversation*. https://theconversation.com/our-national-anthem-is-non-inclusive-indigenous-australians-shouldnt-have-to-sing-it-118177

Parry, K. D., Adair, D., & Cleland, J. (2020). National Anthems in Sport: Songs of Praise or Memorials that Are Past Their Use-by Date? *The Conversation*. https://theconversation.com/national-anthems-in-sport-songs-of-praise-or-memorials-that-are-past-their-use-by-date-142097

Philpott, S. (2017). Planet of the Australians: Indigenous Athletes and Australian Football's Sports Diplomacy. *Third World Quarterly*, 38(4), 862–881.

Rapinoe, M. (2016). Why I am Kneeling. *The Players' Tribune*. https://www.theplayerstribune.com/articles/megan-rapinoe-why-i-am-kneeling

Schmidt, S. H., Frederick, E. L., Pegoraro, A., & Spencer, T. C. (2018). An Analysis of Colin Kaepernick, Megan Rapinoe, and the National Anthem Protests. *Communication & Sport*, 7(5), 653–677. doi:10.1177/2167479518793625

Sevi, B., Altman, N., Ford, C., & Shook, N. (2019). To Kneel or Not to Kneel: Right-Wing Authoritarianism Predicts Attitudes toward NFL Kneeling Protests. *Current Psychology*. doi:10.1007/s12144-019-00239-4

Sherwood, H. (2020). NFL Decision to Permit Kneeling Protest by Players Enrages Donald Trump. https://www.theguardian.com/us-news/2020/jun/06/nfl-decision-to-permit-kneeling-protest-by-players-enrages-donald-trump

Siddiqui, S. (2017). LeBron James Joins NFL in Hitting Back at Trump: 'The People Run This Country'. *The Guardian*. https://www.theguardian.com/sport/2017/sep/25/nascar-owners-threaten-anthem-protesters-as-presidents-cup-and-nba-prepare-to-start

Smith, L. R. (2019). Stand Up, Show Respect: Athlete Activism, Nationalistic Attitudes, and Emotional Response. *International Journal of Communication (Online)*, 13(2019), 2376–2397.

Smith, B., & Tryce, S. A. (2019). Understanding Emerging Adults' National Attachments and Their Reactions to Athlete Activism. *Journal of Sport and Social Issues*, 43(3), 167–194. doi:10.1177/0193723519836404

Spiegel, A. D., & Spiegel, M. B. (1998). Redundant Patriotism: The United States National Anthem as an Obligatory Sports Ritual. *Culture, Sport, Society*, 1(1), 24–43. doi:10.1080/14610989808721800

Sporcle. (2018). *Why Do We Sing the National Anthem at Sporting Events?* https://www.sporcle.com/blog/2018/08/why-do-we-sing-the-national-anthem-at-sporting-events/

Sugden, J., & Sugden, J. (1997). Sport and Community Relations in Northern Ireland. *Managing Leisure*, 2(1), 39–54.

Thorson, E. A., & Serazio, M. (2018). Sports Fandom and Political Attitudes. *Public Opinion Quarterly*, 82(2), 391–403. doi:10.1093/poq/nfy018

Trimbur, L. (2019). Taking a Knee, Making a Stand: Social Justice, Trump America, and the Politics of Sport. *Quest*, 71(2), 252–265. doi:10.1080/00336297.2018.1551806

Volans, I. (2015). *How the Welsh Introduced National Anthems to International Sporting Fixtures*. http://sportinglandmarks.co.uk/summer-olympic-sports/rugby/how-the-welsh-introduced-national-anthems-to-international-sporting-fixtures/

Ward, T. (2009). The heart of what it means to be Australian. *Soccer & Society*, 10(5), 532–543. doi:10.1080/14660970902955463

Welcome to Country. (2019). *Australia's National Anthem Is a White Supremacist Song*. https://www.welcometocountry.org/australias-national-anthem-is-a-white-supremacist-song/

Yan, G., Pegoraro, A., & Watanabe, N. M. (2021). Examining IRA Bots in the NFL Anthem Protest: Political Agendas and Practices of Digital Gatekeeping. *Communication & Sport*, 9(1), 88–109.

Zirin, D. (2013). *Game Over: How Politics Has Turned the Sports World Upside Down*. New Press.

33
SPORT, THE MEDIA, AND ATHLETE ACTIVISM
'Just shut up and play'

Steph Doehler

Introduction

Despite many organisers and consumers of sport maintaining a belief that sport and politics do not mix, sport has consistently demonstrated itself to be a breeding ground for activism and protest. The argument that sport and politics should remain independent of one another is perhaps most prevalent when it comes to athletes voicing their political opinions (Butterworth, 2016). This reinforces the long-held belief that athletes should concentrate on performance rather than using their platform to engage in activism. Despite this, many athletes express their grievances publicly in a manner that is rarely afforded to others and, thus, sport offers significant opportunity for engagement and debate into social justice issues. We should acknowledge that the concept of activism is complex and can manifest through a range of public and private activities. The term *activism* has caused continued debate over both its definition and differences between similar descriptors such as resistance, rebellion and protest. This chapter characterises activism as confronting apparent repressive hegemonic structures and ideologies by participating in deliberate activities that intend to disturb an inequitable power balance and, in contrast to other similar terms, propose solutions that instigate change.

Kaufman (2008) infers that there is no issue in sport more explosive than race, and this subject provides appropriate context for introducing a chapter on athlete activism. Although anti-racism activism stretches back decades, a new intensity and urgency has developed in recent years as sport has become a prominent site for the Black Lives Matter (BLM) movement, with athletes amongst the campaign's most visible advocates. However, this does not imply that athlete activists are favourably regarded, and it has been suggested by scholars that there is an unwritten understanding in sport that athletes leave their activism off the field of play (Kaufman & Wolff, 2010; Peterson, 2009). Fan responses echo this sentiment, as, despite the country's ethnic diversity, the majority of sports fans in America are white (Thompson, 2014). Therefore, by challenging issues of race, Black athletes are subsequently opposing the powerful position and threatening the distraction that many seek from sport. Supporting this, sportswriter Dave Zirin (2011, para 8) claims that fans want athletes, particularly Black athletes, to just 'shut up and play'.

The debate has become increasingly acrimonious amongst athletes themselves, with a split opinion on NFL's Colin Kaepernick, who was labelled a "renegade national traitor" (Ostler, 2016a) during his 2016 National Anthem protest, and more recently through public debate between basketball superstar LeBron James and Swedish soccer player Zlatan Ibrahimović. James, who has become emblematic of the contemporary athlete activist and one of NBA's leading voices against social injustice, was singled out by the former LA Galaxy player who believes, "Athletes unite the world, politics divide it ... Athletes should be athletes and politicians should do politics" (Rathborn, 2021, para 4). This popular opinion was also demonstrated in 2018 by Fox News host, Laura Ingraham, telling James to "shut up and dribble" following his criticism of President Trump (Bieler, 2018, para 5).

This chapter examines the role of the athlete activist, focusing on American sport, where activism is widespread. It then conceptualises the media's response to activism by introducing the theory of media framing, which forms and modifies public interpretations of stories. After laying a theoretical foundation, Colin Kaepernick's activism is examined as a case study. In this example, the media coverage has been analysed during Kaepernick's 2016 National Anthem protest and, in an innovative departure from other scholars' research on media framing, we return to the reporting of Kaepernick after George Floyd's murder in 2020 to offer insight into the hindsight of a sports protest. This chapter concludes by proposing potential directions for future research into athlete activism.

The four waves of athlete activism

The role and experience of athletes as social activists has been expressly discussed (e.g. Agyemang, Singer, & Weems, 2020; Gill, 2016; Kaufman & Wolff, 2010). Before tracing the development of athlete activists, we should first appreciate why they would enter the realm of activism against social issues and why we, as fans, should not immediately dismiss their worth in doing so. Sport has historically characterised the form and dynamics of social and institutional relationships within and between societies (Butterworth, 2016). Thus, sport is a microcosm of society. As consumers, we invest in sport and let our fandom shape our opinions about institutional politics and culture, reflecting who we are as people and a nation. The question remains, why should we care about what somebody who makes tackles, throws passes, or shoots baskets for a living, thinks about social injustices? The reality is, we care because we have invested in them using the fundamental principles, character and structure that we possess as a society. Whether we agree with them or not is perhaps less relevant; either way we care about what our athletes have to say. Edwards (2016) refers to "powerful personalities" as those who occupy a desire to achieve certain ends, and there are no more powerful personalities in modern society than athletes, and particularly with regards to societal issues and inequalities, Black athletes. As such, Black athletes will be a necessary focal point within this chapter.

Although the proliferation of television and social media allows modern athletes to spread more immediate and widespread messages, the concept of professional athletes using their position to focus on social issues is not a recent development, and to understand the current surge of athlete activists, it must be placed in the context and evolution of those who stood before them in the struggle for freedom, equality, and justice across America. Edwards' (2016) framework, which contextualises the history of athlete activism, suggests that action materialises in waves which consider the broader social movements throughout America coinciding with each respective wave. The first wave (1900–1945) was represented by the likes of Jack

Johnson, Joe Louis, and Jesse Owens, who sought legitimacy through their athletic excellence, often achieving their greatest accomplishments in the international stage, as opposed to the American society which was burdened by racial segregation through law and custom.

The second wave (1946–early 1960s), led by athletes such as Jackie Robinson, Kenny Washington, and Althea Gibson, was focused on gaining positional diversity, gaining advantages by garnering a role, job, or position that makes inroads inside an organisation as well as outside of that organisation. They, amongst others, acted as catalysts to abolish barriers and emerged within the contextual backdrop of America shifting towards desegregation and access across US society.

During the Civil Rights and Black Power movements of the 1960s and 1970s, a new breed of athletic activist arose. Jim Brown, Bill Russell, and Cassius Clay (later known as Muhammad Ali) led a group of athletes who looked beyond the second wave's triumphs and demanded dignity, respect, and social justice. In one of the most iconic images in sports history, Tommie Smith and John Carlos performed the Black Power Salute at the 1968 Mexico Olympics in a political statement against human rights. The responses to these athletes were far from positive; Smith and Carlos were stripped of their Olympic medals for their activism, while Clay was presented as a feared Nation of Islam representative.

Despite the initial three waves of athlete activism, from the mid-1970s until 2005, resistance waned (Cunningham et al., 2021). Ironically, while many athletes were criticised during the first waves, scholars, journalists, and the public bemoaned the subsequent decline (Powell, 2008). Muhammad Ali, who had been maligned in the 1960s, was later championed as a spokesperson for human rights and the prototype against which modern athletes were shamed for their lack of activism (Grano, 2009). Although both Craig Hodges and Mahmoud Abdul-Rauf engaged in political activism in the 1990s, their involvement was the exception rather than the rule. While political and social issues persisted, athletes deliberately distanced themselves from debate, ostensibly to focus solely on performance (Kaufman & Wolff, 2010), as famously emphasised by Michael Jordan, the most well-known athlete of his era, or to avoid the financial consequences of speaking out about contentious issues (Henderson, 2009). The second explanation resonates since Hodges, a two-time NBA champion, never played in the league again after his team's visit to the White House in 1992 during which he wore a dashiki and presented a letter to then-President George Bush detailing racism against Black Americans in the country at the time (Gleeson, 2020). Meanwhile, Abdul-Rauf faced a fine of $31,707 per game for refusing to stand for the National Anthem prior to games. (Denlinger, 1996).

From 2006 onwards a fourth wave of athlete activism emerged, with high-profile athletes forging unprecedented freedom and influence. Megan Rapinoe, Chris Kluwe, and Scott Fujita all expressed support of LGBT+ rights, whilst NBA's Steve Nash was outspoken in his opposition of the Iraq War. Following the New England Patriots' Super Bowl victory in 2017 several members of the team refused President Trump's customary invitation to the White House, and in 2021 Venus Williams wrote an essay on gender equality for *Vogue* magazine. However, the most prevalent topic in the modern resurgence of athlete activism centres on racial injustice. Several Women's NBA players wore t-shirts in demonstration after the killings of Philando Castile and Alton Sterling, whilst their NBA counterparts warmed up with 'I can't breathe' shirts to protest the death of Eric Garner. In August 2020, several MLS, NBA, and MLB games were postponed in protest at Jacob Blake's shooting by a Wisconsin police officer. The resurgence of activism centred on race exemplifies a schism in American society which continues to separate many avenues of diversity from the hegemonic white, heterosexual American male.

The media's response to athlete activism

Despite the principle of objectivity, the media are far from a neutral third party given that their very existence concentrates on circulating ideas to mass audiences. Scholars suggest that the mainstream media persistently struggle to accurately and objectively report on protests that challenge social and political issues (Gamson & Wolfsfeld, 1993), with many outlets outright evading discussion of the subjects (Doehler, 2023). Candaele and Dreier (2004, para 1) infer that being a "jock for justice" is not without consequence, whilst Chan and Lee (1984) suggest that media attention tends to condemn activists for their aberrant behaviour. Although this may be contested today, with the media typically more accepting of an athlete's freedom to protest, evidence suggests that many journalists remain hesitant when tackling topics of activism, notably race (Schmidt, Frederick, & Pegoraro, 2018). In the aftermath of the Black Power Salute at the Mexico City Olympic Games in 1968, much of the sporting world berated Tommie Smith and John Carlos with some reporters refusing to even cover the story (Peterson, 2009), and those who did characterising the athletes as embittered radicals (Coombs, Lambert, Cassilo, & Humphries, 2019). One journalist compared them to Nazis and described the pair as "black-skinned storm-troopers" (Zirin, 2012, para 6). According to Hartmann (2003), the American media attacked the protest because it crossed the barriers between sport and politics, and as a result, Smith and Carlos' action was interpreted as an attack on sport rather than a statement on America's social turmoil. However, over time the likes of Ali, Smith, and Carlos have all been recast more favourably through sentimental reassessments. Considering the media's general response to several examples of athlete activism, somewhat hypocritically in 2008 Lebron James was "ripped from coast to coast by pundits, columnists and social observers" (Smith, 2008, para 2) when he refused to criticise China for its role in the genocide of Darfur. Yet when activists criticise more localised, American issues the same media disparage them for blurring the lines between sport and politics. Academic research has found that coverage of such activism frequently focuses on the method used rather than the issue that instigated it (Boyle, McLeod, & Armstrong, 2012; Doehler, 2023).

The concept of media framing

The recent growth in athlete activism gives an opportunity for scholars to investigate how the media portray this. Goffman (1974) first conceived of framing as a primary framework into which experiences are organised, and was further explored by Entman (2007, p.164) who defined it as, "the process of culling a few elements of perceived reality and assembling a narrative that highlights connections among them to promote a particular interpretation". By raising prominence to specific philosophies, the media can encourage their audience to think and feel in specific ways. Boykoff and Yasuoka (2013) propose that it is through agenda setting that the media tell the public what issues to think about, but it is through framing that the media tell us how to think about the issues. Although Murray, Parry, Robinson, and Goddard (2008) and Cottle (2004) argue that media coverage of activism is more progressive than in the past, others provide evidence to suggest that athletes still face marginalisation through media framing (Angelini, MacArthur, & Billings, 2014; Doehler, 2023; Huang & Fahmy, 2013). I argue that many sports reporters are routinely ill-equipped to examine issues of race and that numerous writers avoid this deficiency by aggressively criticising an activist's behaviour and concentrating on more superficial matters. This will be explored and justified more thoroughly within the case study that follows.

Case study of athlete activism: Colin Kaepernick

Colin Kaepernick: "I am not going to stand up to show pride in a flag for a country that oppresses black people and people of colour. To me, this is bigger than football".

(Wyche, 2016, para 3)

There is no better modern example of sustained athlete activism than former NFL quarterback Colin Kaepernick, who chose to kneel during the American national anthem throughout the 2016 season. For context, Kaepernick had led the San Francisco 49ers to the 2014 Super Bowl and the same year signed a record contract worth up to $126 million. Edwards (2016) suggests that Kaepernick launched an era of Black athlete activism across America, which sets him apart from several other modern athlete activists, many of whom call for peace and justice. Instead, Kaepernick pursued not only reform but an overarching ideological commitment to political transformation, and he continues to use his platform to express a need for systemic change within America's criminal justice system. Thus, there are few more appropriate athletes to explore within this chapter than the bi-racial footballer, both in terms of media coverage and as a representation of the potential implications of being a modern athlete activist. Kaepernick chose to opt out of his contract after a season of activism, becoming a free agent in 2017. Following rumours of being blackballed due to his political statements (despite opting out of his contract), Kaepernick filed a grievance against the league, accusing team owners of conspiracy to keep him out of the sport. In February 2019 Kaepernick reached a confidential agreement with the NFL to withdraw the complaint but has not played professionally since.

This case study analyses the media coverage of Kaepernick in the first weeks of reporting on his protest (August–September 2016) and the coverage regarding Kaepernick in the five weeks following George Floyd's death in May 2020. The articles examined within this investigation were from the *San Francisco Chronicle*, *The Washington Post*, and *The New York Times*.

2016 media coverage

Four key frames are identified through the media's reporting of Kaepernick in the early stages of his activism. The first frame, and perhaps the most predictable when considering media reporting of past activism, is *the action, not the issue*. There was little media attention of Kaepernick's situation. Instead, most headlines focused on kneeling during the National Anthem. Despite repeated assertions to the contrary, Kaepernick was portrayed as anti-American and anti-military in debate. When others were questioned about Kaepernick, the conversation centred on what taking the knee meant to them rather than a talk of social justice. NFL star Drew Brees claimed "there's plenty of other ways that you can do that in a peaceful manner that doesn't involve being disrespectful to the American flag" (Barbash & Andrews, 2016, para 23), Alex Boone called the action "shameful" (Lamothe, 2016, para 5) and Kaepernick's former coach Jim Harbaugh stated, "I don't respect the motivation or the action" (Branch, 2016a, para 3). Even reporters who wrote more favourably towards Kaepernick failed to engage in conversation beyond the method, as acknowledged by Blackistone (2016, para 6), "It wasn't Kaepernick's message that drew so much reaction; it was his method for dissemination" and Somerville (2016, para 11), "It seems like most people are talking about WHAT Kaepernick did. Not WHY he did it". Despite some media acknowledging the subject was skewed, meaningful debate rarely ensued.

Some of the most impassioned dialogue in the media's narrative is highlighted in the second frame, *the military*. Reporters quickly established a connection between Kaepernick's activism and disrespecting the military, for example: "I can understand why some fans, especially ones with friends and relatives in the military, are angry at Kaepernick" (Bowen, 2016, para 7) and "His decision, of course, has inspired plenty of criticism, particularly from those who view his stance as disrespecting the military" (Branch, 2016b, para 10). Even then-President, Barack Obama, acknowledged that the protest was a "tough thing" for military personnel to accept (Wan & Nakamura, 2016, para 1). Media rhetoric of this nature was somewhat expected, after all the NFL has long pursued an agenda to conflate itself with the military. Consequently, when Kaepernick's protest defied the norms and ideals of sport's super-nationalistic setting, particularly post 9/11, the notion that he was a traitor rather than a concerned American was emphasised by reporters asking members of the military for their feelings. "It made me sick" said one Vietnam veteran from Kaepernick's hometown in California (Ostler, 2016b, para 5). Naturally, their views on racial injustice were not sought. On the occasions when NFL personnel commented, positively or negatively, they were often tied with declarations to their own military association, for example Carolina Panther's head coach Ron Rivera remarked "The National Anthem is a very personal thing for me, obviously for specific reasons – my father and my mother's family and their service to this country" (Bieler, 2016a, para 15).

A conflict emerged through the third frame between those who believed Kaepernick's activism was unpatriotic and those who acknowledged his right to protest. As such this frame is termed *patriotism vs freedom of speech*. By taking the knee during the national anthem, Kaepernick immediately challenged two of the most cherished symbols of Americanism, the anthem itself and the American flag. "Here's what bothers me about the 49ers quarterback's protest: its symbolic target. The American flag" wrote Diaz (2016, para 4), whilst Abdul-Jabbar (2016, para 1) suggested that "to some … Kaepernick represents entitled brattish behaviour of a wealthy athlete ungrateful to a country that has given him so much". In contrast, some reporters recognised his right for activism, even if they disagreed in the method, for example: "Whether it's the right way or otherwise, the conduct by Colin Kaepernick is a First Amendment right" (Jackman, 2016, para 18). One reader of *The New York Times* summarised the conflict powerfully, "The very thing that makes America great is our right to free expression, but don't try to use it or you will be called un-American" (Moore & Patel, 2016, para 1).

The final frame uncovered *moral outrage to a discrete action*, typically emphasising Kaepernick as an unsavoury deviant, rather than recognising that his message sparked a wave of similar protests. Reporters described him as "Just a backup quarterback" (Marks, 2016, para 3), "A less-than-perfect football player" (Ross, 2016, para 2) and "ham-fisted" (Saracevic, 2016, para 9). Former NFL star Rodney Harrison called Kaepernick's credibility as an activist into doubt, claiming "He's not black" (Disbrow, 2016, para 2), when citing that Kaepernick was raised by white, adoptive parents. When his legitimacy as a biracial man protesting for Black rights was not called into question, Kaepernick's actions were described in isolation, rather than part of a larger movement; this was *his* activism, not a movement that was duplicated by several amateur and elite athletes across the country. Others endorsed this presentation and discouraged such behaviour, such as NBA star Shaquille O'Neal claiming, "Each to his own … I would never do that" (Bieler, 2016b, para 1). When other athletes took similar action framing still centred on the individual's action despite the increased visibility of the message. Megan Rapinoe, one of America's most recognisable soccer players, who began to take the knee in September 2016 in solidarity with Kaepernick, was similarly condemned for her actions.

2020 media coverage

In the aftermath of George Floyd's murderer by a Minneapolis police officer, Kaepernick, who had spent the interim years continuing his mission for social reformation, was the source of discussion once again by journalists, this time with a more favourable narrative.

Three main frames are identified in this analysis. The first, *It's (largely) not our fault*, showcases an overwhelming account of coverage focused on condemning the NFL and other organisations for failing to acknowledge the sentiment behind Kaepernick's action, rather than taking accountability for their own reporting in 2016. Jenkins (2020a, para 1) wrote, "Two knees. One protesting in the grass, one pressing on the back of a man's neck .... You have to choose which knee you will defend .... NFL owners chose the knee on the neck". This from the same reporter who, in 2016, called Kaepernick "Not the most clarion of dissidents" (Jenkins, 2016, para 3). Meanwhile, whilst much of their 2016 coverage focused on just that, Boren and Bieler (2020, para 10) suggested "Kaepernick and NFL players made it clear that their protest had nothing to do with the flag or ... the military". Nonetheless, a limited number of journalists recognised the role they played in the 2016 rhetoric, for example Jenkins (2020b, para 9) noted the media's "false victory narratives" whilst Killion (2020, para 1) wrote "Maybe if we had listened to Colin Kaepernick four years ago, we wouldn't be here. [We] as a nation – had a chance to have a real conversation about systemic brutality. And we whiffed. He was vilified for it".

The second frame is termed *Colin Kaepernick, the revolutionist*. As with other athletes who engaged in contentious activism, time has been favourable to Kaepernick. A "new appreciation" (Slusser, 2020, para 3) for his decision to kneel was discussed, with Seattle Seahawks Coach Pete Carroll calling him a symbol of courage' (Bieler, 2020a, para 1) and Golden State Warriors Coach Steve Kerr suggesting that Kaepernick would ultimately be considered "a hero" (Boren, 2020, para 2). Others were equally complementary and Kaepernick was described as "a reformer, in the great American tradition" (Jenkins, 2020a, para 12), "simply ahead of his time" (Morris, 2020) and "an unapologetic radical in the best sense of the word" (Zirin, 2020, para 14).

The final frame presented here is the media's consensus that 2020 signified an *opportunity for change*, something Branch (2020, para 11) notes himself by stating "There are signs of change". After Floyd's murder, major firms hastened to condemn racism, bringing racial inequity to the forefront of people's minds and the media quickly acknowledged the issue. "In the past two weeks, more well-known athletes, sports executives and even commissioners, including the NFL's Roger Goodell, have taken strong public stands on societal-political issues" stated Boswell (2020a, para 2). Several NFL players publicly spoke out on the topic, including Eric Reid, who knelt beside Kaepernick in 2016:

> Before we are able to realize impactful change, we must first have the courage and compassion as human beings to come together and acknowledge the problem: black men, women and children and other oppressed minorities continue to be systemically discriminated against.
>
> (Bieler, 2020b, para 14)

This frame also acknowledges the growing perception of Kaepernick with several players declaring their desire to see the NFL reference Kaepernick directly in their communications on athlete activism (see Belson, 2020; Boswell 2020b). When asked if Kaepernick should get another opportunity to play, even President Trump, one of his most ardent critics stated, "If he deserves it, he should" (Bieler, 2020c, para 2). Tom Boswell of *The Washington Post* surmises this frame appropriately:

> I think the times are changing and you will see a significantly different response to kneeling protests. And it will be MUCH harder for those opposed to the protests to say, "They are disrespecting the flag. Or the military. Or the police". Or whatever. We are in a much different place.
>
> (Boswell, 2020b, para 41)

When and what caused this U-turn is unclear. By 2020, America was further divided, and sport continued to represent social and political problems. The killings of Philando Castile, Eric Garner, and Daunte Wright at the hands of police officers brought social justice problems to the forefront for many Americans. With the surge in protests between 2016 and 2020 and some white athletes reflecting on systematic racism in the US, sport became both representative of and responsive to societal circumstances, and the media could no longer remain a bystander or critic of the emerging activism in American sport.

This case study examines how American media portray athletes as activists. During Kaepernick's 2016 protest, the media focused on extraneous topics rather than meaningful discourse that addressed race issues throughout America. Kaepernick's activism cost him his career, and while he continues to live a comfortable life, the ramifications of his acts remain. However, while it was unsophisticated for reporters to focus so fiercely on discussion points that veered away from Kaepernick's intention, it should be acknowledged that ultimately Kaepernick chose both the time and place for his activism with precision, utilising his power as a star footballer to gain critical exposure. While neither the national anthem nor the American flag were the reason for his protest, their representation was a clear target.

Conclusion

Athlete activism continues to influence cultural rhetoric and the research presented within this chapter demonstrates that the ostensible separation of sport and politics is illogical. Sport is closely associated with society and affords significant individuals a unique opportunity to challenge hierarchies that subjugate minority groups. Consequently, when societal injustices or inequities are exposed, sport and its athletes struggle to adopt a passive attitude. Whilst sport is not without criticism, inequality is undeniably prevalent within this arena too, it possesses the opportunity to unite individuals and overcome differences. Whilst this chapter focuses on high-profile sport activism in the US, several local and sub-cultural protests occur frequently which incorporate not only discrete campaigning but also broader community objectives expressed in more nuanced ideologies. In practice, athlete activism has the potential to awaken critical consciousness to social issues. Accordingly, this emboldens action towards addressing injustices and enables connections to broader structural causes that are pursued across a range of agendas and with various outcomes, ranging from enabling dialogue, encouraging reform, transformation of agendas, and even revolutionary progression.

Though activists are inspired by a wide range of topics, many actions focus on racial injustice. The murder of George Floyd globalised the BLM movement, resulting in race-related protests across the world, with sport functioning as a prominent stage for such activism. Convincing athlete activism dispels the myth that sport and politics should not conflate, helping to create confidence that injustices can be confronted and a more equitable society created. Athletes engaged in activism offer inspiration to many through their empowered commitment for change despite the associated risks. The impact of this was highlighted in 2020, during a year when the perceived barriers between sport and politics was breeched repeatedly, as *Sports Illustrated* presented their Sportsperson of the Year award to five athlete activists who they described as "champions on the field, champions for others off it" (Sports Illustrated, 2020, para 4).

Given the diversity of activism occurring internationally, this chapter could be noticeably more detailed to include discussion relating to activism outside the US. However, the examples provided within this chapter are designed to explore how athlete activism has developed throughout America given their long and challenging history with sports protests. Like many scholars, I strongly dispute that American sport, or any sport for that matter, is apolitical. Many sports are clearly willing to connect themselves with political objectives when it fits their philosophy. For example, the NFL swiftly condemned Kaepernick in 2016 for bringing politics into their sport, whilst simultaneously flying military jets over stadiums, unfurling the US flag across fields, and expecting those in attendance to salute their overseas military personnel engaged in political wars.

I have hinted at the promising position of modern athlete activists. During the activism stagnation, athletes were reluctant to speak up on important matters due to fear of repercussions. However, contemporary athletes have a platform at their fingertips that was not available to their predecessors – social media. Here, athletes can create their individual brand through self-marketing and communicate directly with the public. Their activism can be publicised and justified without the necessity for the media to serve as the hierarchical gatekeeper of information. Naturally, this is not to suggest that the media no longer engage in protest discourse; however, their ability to assume exclusive control of narratives has dissipated. Thus, modern athletes are upending the power dynamic that the media has dominated for decades. Of course, there are still very real consequences for athlete activists, as has been explored with Colin Kaepernick.

Scholarly research on this topic is substantial, particularly when it comes to concerns of sport activism and race. However, the unique problems faced by athlete activists have received less attention, particularly with comparisons drawn between high-profile athletes and more localised activism wherein athletes do not possess the same platform or financial security as LeBron James and others. Similarly, there has been limited investigation into the responses of protests on social media. Schmidt et al. (2018) analysed Facebook comments relating to Colin Kaepernick and Megan Rapinoe's national anthem protests; however, the manner in which journalists discuss the issue surrounding protest on social media, where they have opportunity for a more subjective viewpoint compared to their editorials, could offer interesting insight. Another avenue of future research could address the intersectionality of athlete activism, with gender and race the most obvious factors. Female athlete activists receive significantly less media and scholarly attention than male athletes, particularly those men with greater popularity and commercial standing, despite there being significant value in learning about the experiences of those with less celebrity. This casts doubt on who or what is the most noteworthy feature of any protest – if the most prominent athletes receive the most exposure, it is plausible to conclude that the individual is of most significance, not the fundamental issue or even their action. Finally, the athlete's voice is notably absent from scholarly activity on sports activism. With athletes being able to control their rhetoric through social media, there is opportunity to explore the impact of this on the narrative surrounding their activism.

To conclude, let me return to a discussion point that has been prevalent throughout this chapter. Discourse surrounding the place of athlete activists continues to divide. On one hand, activism is almost expected of athletes in modern society, and yet those who threaten the power status quo through methods that are alleged to challenge perceptions of patriotism, particularly in America, are met with criticism and, in more severe cases, loss of employment and/or income. We are, arguably, living in more fractured societies than many will have previously experienced, therefore the notion that athletes should abandon their right for an opinion on social issues purely because of the job they are paid to do must be considered nonsensical.

References

Abdul-Jabbar, K. (2016, August 30). Abdul-Jabbar: Insulting Colin Kaepernick says more about our patriotism than his. *The Washington Post*. Retrieved from www.washingtonpost.com/posteverything/wp/2016/08/30/insulting-colin-kaepernick-says-more-about-our-patriotism-than-his

Agyemang, K., Singer, J., & Weems, A. (2020). 'Agitate! Agitate! Agitate!': Sport as a site for political activism and social change. *Organization*, 27(6), 952–968.

Angelini, J., MacArthur, P., & Billings, A. (2014). Spiralling into or out of stereotypes? NBC's prime-time coverage of male figure skaters at the 2010 Olympic Games. *Journal of Language & Social Psychology*, 33(2), 226–235.

Barbash, F. & Andrews, T. (2016, August 30). A brief history of 'The Star-Spangled Banner' being played at games and getting no respect. *The Washington Post*. Retrieved from www.washingtonpost.com/news/morning-mix/wp/2016/08/30/a-brief-history-of-the-star-spangled-banner-being-played-at-games-and-getting-no-respect

Belson, K. (2020, June 4). Drew Brees's unchanged stance on Kneeling is suddenly out of step. *The New York Times*. Retrieved from www.nytimes.com/2020/06/04/sports/football/drew-brees-apology-comments.html?searchResultPosition=12

Bieler, D. (2016a, August 30). What NFL coaches are saying about the Colin Kaepernick controversy. *The Washington Post*. Retrieved from www.washingtonpost.com/news/early-lead/wp/2016/08/29/what-nfl-coaches-are-saying-about-the-colin-kaepernick-controversy

Bieler, D. (2016b, September 8). Shaquille O'Neal on Colin Kaepernick's protest: 'I would never do that'. *The Washington Post*. Retrieved from www.washingtonpost.com/news/early-lead/wp/2016/09/08/shaquille-oneal-on-colin-kaepernicks-protest-i-would-never-do-that

Bieler, D. (2018, August 7). LeBron James turns 'Shut up and dribble' insult into title of Showtime series. *The Washington Post*. Retrieved from www.washingtonpost.com/news/early-lead/wp/2018/08/07/lebron-james-turns-shut-up-and-dribble-insult-into-title-of-showtime-series/

Bieler, D. (2020a, June 4). Pete Carroll heaps praise on Colin Kaepernick, fails to mention Seahawks' chances to sign QB. *The Washington Post*. Retrieved from www.washingtonpost.com/sports/2020/06/04/pete-carroll-heaps-praise-colin-kaepernick-fails-mention-seahawks-chances-sign-qb/

Bieler, D. (2020b, June 1). Protesting players Eric Reid and Kenny Stills mock NFL's promise to address 'systemic issues'. *The Washington Post*. Retrieved from www.washingtonpost.com/sports/2020/06/01/protesting-players-eric-reid-kenny-stills-mock-nfls-promise-address-systemic-issues/

Bieler, D. (2020c, June 18). Trump in favor of Colin Kaepernick returning to NFL, but 'he has to be able to play well'. *The Washington Post*. Retrieved from www.washingtonpost.com/sports/2020/06/17/trump-favor-colin-kaepernick-returning-nfl-he-has-be-able-play-well/

Blackistone, K. (2016, September 4). Colin Kaepernick challenges sport's nationalism, and our notion of it as safe space. *The Washington Post*. Retrieved from www.washingtonpost.com/sports/colin-kaepernick-challenges-sports-nationalism-and-our-notion-of-it-as-safe-space/2016/09/04/7a312dac-71fd-11e6-be4f-3f42f2e5a49e_story.html

Boren, C. (2020, June 10). Steve Kerr believes Colin Kaepernick will 'ultimately be considered a hero' for protests. *The Washington Post*. Retrieved from www.washingtonpost.com/sports/2020/06/10/steve-kerr-believes-colin-kaepernick-will-ultimately-be-considered-hero-protests/

Boren, C. & Bieler, D. (2020, June 5). Drew Brees says 'I am your ally' in second attempt at an apology. *The Washington Post*. Retrieved from www.washingtonpost.com/sports/2020/06/04/drew-brees-apologizes-is-sick-way-my-comments-were-perceived/

Boswell, T. (2020a, June 15). It's not which sports figures are speaking out that's telling. It's how many. *The Washington Post*. Retrieved from www.washingtonpost.com/sports/2020/06/10/its-not-which-sports-figures-are-speaking-out-thats-telling-its-how-many/

Boswell, T. (2020b, June 15). Ask Boswell: Redskins, Nationals and Washington sports. *The Washington Post*. Retrieved from https://live.washingtonpost.com/ask-boswell-20200615.html

Bowen, F. (2016, September 14). With protest, NFL player is exercising his rights. *The Washington Post*. Retrieved from www.washingtonpost.com/lifestyle/kidspost/with-protest-nfl-player-is-exercising-his-rights/2016/09/14/eed55240-747e-11e6-8149-b8d05321db62_story.html

Boykoff, J. & Yasuoka, M. (2013). Gender and politics at the 2012 Olympics: Media coverage and its implications. *Sport in Society*, 18(2), 219–233.

Boyle, M., McLeod, D., & Armstrong, C. (2012). Adherence to the protest paradigm: The influence of protest goals and tactics on news coverage in US and international newspapers. *The International Journal of Press/Politics*, 17(2), 127–144.

Branch, E. (2016a, August 29). Harbaugh on Kaepernick: 'I don't respect the motivation or the action'. *San Francisco Chronicle*. Retrieved from www.sfchronicle.com/49ers/article/Harbaugh-on-Kaepernick-I-don-t-respect-the-9191072.php

Branch, E. (2016b, August 28). Colin Kaepernick: 'This stand wasn't for me'. *San Francisco Chronicle*. Retrieved from www.sfchronicle.com/49ers/article/Colin-Kaepernick-This-stand-wasn-t-for-me-9189627.php

Branch, E. (2020, June 4). 49ers' Kyle Shanahan speaks passionately on racism: 'Open your eyes'. *San Francisco Chronicle*. Retrieved from www.sfchronicle.com/49ers/article/49ers-Kyle-Shanahan-speaks-passionately-on-15318186.php

Butterworth, M. (2016). Sport and politics in the United States. In A. Bairner, J. Kelly, & J. Lee (Eds), *Routledge Handbook of Sport and Politics* (pp. 150–161). New York, NY: Routledge.

Candaele, K. & Dreier, P. (2004). Where are the jocks for justice?. *The Nation*. Retrieved from www.thenation.com/article/archive/where-are-jocks-justice/

Chan, J. & Lee, C. (1984). Journalistic paradigms on civil protests: A case study of Hong Kong. In A. Arno & W. Dissanayake (Eds), *The News Media in National and International Conflict* (pp. 183–202). Boulder, CO: Westview Press.

Coombs, D., Lambert, C., Cassilo, D., & Humphries, Z. (2019). Flag on the play: Colin Kaepernick and the protest paradigm. *Howard Journal of Communications*, 31(4), 317–336.

Cottle, S. (2004). *The Racist Murder of Stephen Lawrence: Media Performance and Public Transformation*. London: Praeger.

Cunningham, G., Dixon, M., Singer, J., Oshiro, K., Na Young, A., & Weems, A. (2021). A site to resist and persist: Diversity, social justice, and the unique nature of sport. *Journal of Global Sport Management*, 6(1), 30–48.

Denlinger, K. (1996, March 14). Disorder on the court. *The Washington Post*. Retrieved from www.washingtonpost.com/archive/politics/1996/03/14/disorder-on-the-court/9f56fe0d-a7a0-40b6-bc04-e5a6ee682bab/

Diaz, J. (2016, August 29). Flag is wrong symbol for Kaepernick to target. *San Francisco Chronicle*. Retrieved from www.sfchronicle.com/opinion/diaz/article/Flag-is-wrong-symbol-for-Kaepernick-to-target-9191478.php

Disbrow, B. (2016, August 30). Rodney Harrison trying to backtrack after 'Kaepernick, he's not black' comment. *San Francisco Chronicle*. Retrieved from www.sfchronicle.com/sports/article/Rodney-Harrison-trying-to-backtrack-after-9193198.php

Doehler, S. (2023). Taking the star-spangled knee: The media framing of Colin Kaepernick. *Sport in Society*, 26(1), 45–66, doi:10.1080/17430437.2021.1970138

Edwards, H. (2016, November 3). The fourth wave: Black athlete protests in the second decade of the 21st century [Conference presentation]. North American Society for the Sociology of Sport Conference, Tampa, Florida, United States. www.youtube.com/watch?v=Oimoyyx0HpE

Entman, R. (2007). Framing bias: Media in the distribution of power. *Journal of Communication*, 57(1), 163–173.

Gamson, W. & Wolfsfeld, G. (1993). Movements and media as interacting systems. *The Annals of the American Academy of Political and Social Science*, 528(1), 114–125.

Gill, E. (2016). "Hands up, don't shoot" or shut up and play ball? Fan-generated media views of the Ferguson five. *Journal of Human Behavior in the Social Environment*, 26(3–4), 400–412.

Gleeson, S. (2020, August 30). In 1991, ex-NBA player Craig Hodges sought similar game boycott—But had little support. *USA Today*. Retrieved from www.usatoday.com/story/sports/nba/2020/08/30/craig-hodges-nba-player-protest-boycott-1991-finals/5667258002/

Goffman, E. (1974). *Frame Analysis: An Essay on the Organization of Experience*. Cambridge, MA: Harvard University Press.

Grano, D. A. (2009). Muhammad Ali versus the 'modern athlete': On voice in mediated sports culture. *Critical Studies in Media Communication*, 26(3), 191–211.

Hartmann, D. (2003). *Race, Culture, and the Revolt of the Black Athlete*. Chicago: The University of Chicago Press.

Henderson, S. (2009). Crossing the line: Sport and the limits of civil rights protests. *The International Journal of the History of Sport*, 26(1), 101–121.

Huang, Y., & Fahmy, S. (2013). Picturing a journey of protest or a journey of harmony? Comparing the visual framing of the 2008 Olympic torch relay in the US versus Chinese press. *Media, War & Conflict*, 6(3), 191–206.

Jackman, T. (2016, September 21). If Colin Kaepernick has First Amendment rights to protest, do the police too? *The Washington Post*. Retrieved from www.washingtonpost.com/news/true-crime/wp/2016/09/21/if-colin-kaepernick-has-first-amendment-rights-to-protest-do-the-police-too/

Jenkins, S. (2016, September 8). Colin Kaepernick reminds us that dissent is a form of patriotism too. *The Washington Post*. Retrieved from www.washingtonpost.com/sports/redskins/colin-kaepernick-reminds-us-that-dissent-is-a-form-of-patriotism-too/2016/09/08/053830aa-75e4-11e6-8149-b8d05321db62_story.html

Jenkins, S. (2020a, May 30). This is why Colin Kaepernick took a knee. *The Washington Post*. Retrieved from www.washingtonpost.com/sports/2020/05/30/this-is-why-colin-kaepernick-took-knee/

Jenkins, S. (2020b, June 11). From the Civil War to the football field, we have been celebrating the wrong values. *The Washington Post*. Retrieved from www.washingtonpost.com/sports/2020/06/11/civil-war-football-field-weve-been-celebrating-wrong-values/

Kaufman, P. (2008). Boos, bans, and other backlash: The consequences of being an activist athlete. *Humanity & Society*, 32(3), 215–237.

Kaufman, P. & Wolff, E. (2010). Playing and protesting: Sport as a vehicle for social change. *Journal of Sport and Social Issues*, 34(2), 154–175.

Killion, A. (2020, May 30). Colin Kaepernick and George Floyd: Two knees, two reactions, one issue. *San Francisco Chronicle*. Retrieved from www.sfchronicle.com/49ers/annkillion/article/Colin-Kaepernick-and-George-Floyd-Two-knees-two-15305568.php

Lamothe, D. (2016, August 29). The Colin Kaepernick flap highlights the NFL's complex history with the military and patriotism. *The Washington Post*. Retried from www.washingtonpost.com/news/checkpoint/wp/2016/08/29/the-colin-kaepernick-flap-highlights-the-nfls-complex-history-with-the-military-and-patriotism

Marks, G. (2016, September 7). Gene Marks: Sitting and ka-chinging…Many businesses profit from Colin Kaepernick. *The Washington Post*. Retrieved from www.washingtonpost.com/news/on-small-business/wp/2016/09/07/gene-marks-sitting-and-ka-chinging-many-businesses-profit-from-colin-kaepernick/

Moore, L. & Patel, S. (2016, September 3). 'Don't try to use it or you will be called un-American'. *The New York Times*. Retrieved from www.nytimes.com/2016/09/03/nytnow/top-10-comments-dont-try-to-use-it-or-you-will-be-called-un-american.html

Morris, W. (2020, June 3). The videos that rocked America. The song that knows our rage. *The New York Times*. Retrieved from www.nytimes.com/2020/06/03/arts/george-floyd-video-racism.html?searchResultPosition=8

Murray, C. Parry, K., Robinson, P., & Goddard, P. (2008). Reporting dissent in wartime: British press, the anti-war movement and the 2003 Iraq War. *European Journal of Communication*, 23(1), 7–27.

Ostler, S. (2016a, September 7). The new Colin Kaepernick is weathering the storm. *San Francisco Chronicle*. Retrieved from www.sfchronicle.com/49ers/ostler/article/The-new-Colin-Kaepernick-is-weathering-the-storm-9208808.php

Ostler, S. (2016b, September 1). 49ers Kaepernick once a hero, now goat in hometown. *San Francisco Chronicle*. Retrieved from www.sfchronicle.com/sports/ostler/article/49ers-Kaepernick-once-a-hero-now-goat-in-hometown-9199265.php

Peterson, J. (2009). A 'race' for equality: Print media coverage of the 1968 Olympic protest by Tommie Smith and John Carlos. *American Journalism*, 26(2), 99–121.

Powell, S. (2008). *Souled Out? How Blacks are Winning and Losing in Sports*. Champaign, IL: Human Kinetics.

Rathborn, J. (2021, March 2). Zlatan Ibrahimovic reiterates LeBron James criticism with claim 'athletes should be athletes'. *The Independent*. Retrieved from www.independent.co.uk/sport/football/european/lebron-james-zlatan-ibrahimovic-lakers-b1810585.html

Ross, J. (2016, August 29). On Colin Kaepernick and public statements about personal politics in sports. *The Washington Post*. Retrieved from www.washingtonpost.com/news/the-fix/wp/2016/08/29/on-colin-kaepernick-and-public-statements-about-personal-politics-in-sports/

Saracevic, A. (2016, August 27). Kaepernick anthem protest: Wrong place for a noble cause. *San Francisco Chronicle*. Retrieved from www.sfchronicle.com/sports/article/Kaepernick-anthem-protest-Wrong-place-for-a-9188378.php

Schmidt, S., Frederick, E., & Pegoraro, A. (2018). An analysis of Colin Kaepernick, Megan Rapinoe, and the national anthem protests. *Communication & Sport*, 7(5), 563–677.

Slusser, S. (2020, June 3). Ex-A's catcher Bruce Maxwell: 'Where was this support' when he protested racism? *San Francisco Chronicle*. Retrieved from www.sfchronicle.com/athletics/article/Ex-A-s-catcher-Bruce-Maxwell-Where-was-this-15315573.php

Smith, S. (2008, May 16). LeBron speaking out on Darfur. *ESPN*. Retrieved from www.espn.co.uk/nba/news/story?id=3398947

Sommerville, F. (2016, August 30). Somerville: Aren't these stories more important than Kaepernick, Lochte? *San Francisco Chronicle*. Retrieved from www.sfchronicle.com/opinion/article/Somerville-Aren-t-these-stories-more-important-9193010.php

Sports Illustrated (2020, December 6). SI's 2020 Sportsperson of the Year: The activist athlete. *Sports Illustrated*. Retrieved from www.si.com/sportsperson/2020/12/06/sportsperson-2020-james-stewart-mahomes-osaka-duvernay-tardif

Thompson, D. (2014). Which sports have the whitest/richest/oldest fans?. *The Atlantic*. Retrieved from www.theatlantic.com/business/archive/2014/02/which-sports-have-the-whitest-richestoldest-fans/283626

Wan, W. & Nakamura, D. (2016, September 5). Obama: Kaepernick's national anthem protest a 'tough thing' for service members. *The Washington Post*. Retrieved from www.washingtonpost.com/news/post-politics/wp/2016/09/05/obama-kaepernicks-national-anthem-protest-a-tough-thing-for-service-members/

Wyche, S. (2016, August 27). Colin Kaepernick explains why he sat during national anthem. Retrieved from www.nfl.com/news/colin-kaepernick-explains-why-he-sat-during-national-anthem-0ap3000000691077

Zirin, D. (2011, May 4). Shut up and play? Patriotism, jock culture and the limits of free speech. *The Nation*. Retrieved from www.thenation.com/article/archive/shut-and-play-patriotism-jock-culture-and-limits-free-speech

Zirin, D. (2012, June 4). After forty-four years, it's time Brent Musburger apologized to John Carlos and Tommie Smith. *The Nation*. Retrieved from www.thenation.com/article/archive/after-forty-four-years-its-time-brent-musburger-apologized-john-carlos-and-tommie-smith

Zirin, D. (2020, December 7). 'Sports Illustrated' chose the wrong activist athletes. *The Nation*. Retrieved from www.thenation.com/article/society/sports-illustrated-activist-athlete/

34
SOCIAL MEDIA AND ONLINE ACTIVISM IN WOMEN'S RUGBY

From #IAmEnough to #ICare

Ali Bowes and Alex Culvin

Introduction

It is taken as fact that traditional sport media such as radio broadcasts, television coverage, and print news has historically disregarded, downplayed, and trivialised the achievements of women, and continues to do so to this day. Online media – media viewed and distributed on digital devices – and specifically social media has been identified as a space that provides opportunities for female athletes to increase visibility, and to self-represent on their own terms, whilst also presenting sportswomen, fans and commentators a space to share, debate and discuss women's sport (Bruce & Hardin, 2014). In many ways, online media has been co-opted as a space for activism, most notably with the #blacklivesmatter movement in 2013 (Cooky & Antunovic, 2020) but also in challenging the inherent sexism in sport media practices. Given the increasing significance of online media for athletes, it is unsurprising to see a wealth of athletes pushing for social change via this medium. As Cooky and Antunovic (2020, p. 694) note, the world of sport has historically "served as a symbolic site for social justice, ushering change in the wider society and inspiring movements", in which female athletes – especially queer women and women of colour – play a leading role. Using a neoliberal feminist framework, we can understand the significance of female athlete activism in online spaces, in challenging systemic gendered inequalities within specific sport cultures.

One of the most prominent examples of feminist athlete activism in recent times has been the United States Women's National Team (USWNT) gender discrimination lawsuit and fight for equal pay, a high-profile case that has become symbolic for women's struggle for equality in sport globally (Cooky & Antunovic, 2020; Carrick et al., 2021; Culvin et al., 2021). Whilst football has seen a wealth of women athlete activism and increasing recognition and action to address gender inequality at an international level (Carrick et al. 2021), it remains that many historically male-dominated sports are still to catch up. In the United Kingdom and Ireland, although there has been *some* progress in football (for example, both England and Ireland now pay their international players the same) and cricket (for example, the 2021 domestic 'Hundred' tournament offered equal prize money for the men's and women's competitions), it seems that the sport of rugby has been left behind.

Rugby has often been characterised as a typically masculine sport, in both participation and in nature (Nauright & Chandler, 1996; Hardy, 2015), and women's rugby has often existed on the margins globally (Kanemasu & Molnar, 2019). Despite this, women's team sports are experiencing a period of growth internationally, with increasing (semi-)professional opportunities (Taylor et al. 2020; Bowes & Culvin, 2021), and this has extended to women's rugby union in England. An emerging era of professionalisation within women's rugby in the United Kingdom – which has brought investment, player contracts, increased visibility, and improved participation numbers – has not been without gender-specific challenges, though. These challenges have simultaneously not gone unnoticed by the increasing number of women who are playing the game, at all levels, who are often turning to social media to action change and gender equity.

This chapter critically discusses the rise of online activism through the example of rugby union, as women players attempt to challenge their subordinate status in the sport. This chapter will start with a more detailed overview of women in rugby, before focusing on the role of the sport media and online media in the sport. The attention will then shift to two case studies from women's rugby, highlighting how women players and fans have responded to issues of gender inequality using activist hashtag campaigns via social media. The two campaigns, started by women players from within the game, snowballed, reaching the national press in the UK, prompting discussions and – significantly – change. As per Cooky and Antunovic (2020), who challenged the methodological approaches that have dominated sport media research, here we draw upon the collective action of female sports athletes within social media spaces. The analysis of these campaigns will draw upon neoliberal feminist discourse (Toffoletti & Thorpe, 2018a) in making sense of the sociocultural conditions of women's rugby operating in the online media space. This chapter concludes by considering the wider implications of social media activism for women in sport.

Women in rugby

In some of the earliest writing in the field of the sociology of sport, rugby union was identified as being a 'male preserve' (Dunning & Sheard, 1973). The sport of rugby more broadly has a long history in various forms (see Dunning & Sheard, 1976; Raynor, 2018), but currently exists as we know it today in two forms – rugby union and rugby league. The origins of rugby stemmed from various codes of mob and folk football prevalent in the eighteenth and nineteenth centuries, with the individual codified sports of football, rugby union, and rugby league being formed, as well as American football and Australian rules football in their specific geographical locations. The backgrounds of these sports in their modern forms, and prior to, were highly gendered, centring on the boys' public school system in England at the time. The roots of rugby union are inherently tied to then-headmaster of Rugby School, Dr Thomas Arnold, and a formalisation of mob football aligned with his vision of Muscular Christianity – the creation of boys with character and competitive drive, the future leaders of British society (Raynor, 2018). As such, the Rugby School rules of folk football led to the sport of rugby being created, and rugby union was formally codified via the formation of the Rugby Football Union (RFU) in 1871.

The qualities associated with the game of rugby that Dr Arnold wanted to promote are nearly always highlighted as being synonymous with what it means to *be a man*; physicality, competitiveness, strength, and aggression are values central to the sport and strongly associated with notions of masculinity (Schacht, 1996). Schacht (1996, p. 550) identifies rugby football as a quintessential example of how the sport, in both its creation and practice, creates an environment that "both reflects and supports a hierarchical ideology of masculinity and the subordination of women". In ethnographies of men's rugby union in the USA, Schacht (1996) and later Muir and Seitz (2004) highlight how (white, middle-class, male) rugby players *do* masculinity, reproducing rigid images of manhood which involves a subordination of femininity, often manifesting as misogynistic and/or homophobic behaviour. In doing so, the importance of masculinity to the sport is reaffirmed (Muir & Seitz, 2004). Unsurprisingly then, and as Cleary (2000) wrote, the notion of rugby becomes problematic when played by women, and the very marking of *women's* rugby with the qualifier immediately inscribes it as marginal. To this day, the sport is perceived as a masculine sport for male participants, and controversial as an arena for women's participation (Joncheray and Tlili, 2013).

In recent years, there has been an increasing presence of women in the sport of rugby, although Furse (2021) highlights how women and girls have historically been excluded from participating in the sport. However, this is not to say women were not playing the sport, and there has been a sporadic history of women's involvement in the game. This involvement has simultaneously challenged the association of rugby and masculinity as the only way of knowing and understanding the sport and served as evidence of it. In Furse's (2021) documentation of the history of women in rugby, she acknowledges the limited access women had to the sport prior to 1970 but notes that the earliest recorded women's rugby match took place over 80 years previous, in 1887. She then describes the infrequent examples of women's participation in rugby, from charity matches to more sustained participation during the World Wars, with women's involvement in the sport following similar trajectories of other male-dominated sports of that era, namely football.

Furse (2021) identifies 1970 as a watershed year for women's involvement in the sport, and since then there has been a raft of progress. The first World Cup competition was held in 1991. In the UK, the first Home Nations tournament, now known as the Six Nations, was held in 1996.[1] The game has grown at recreational levels too – World Rugby (2015) claimed the sport was one of the world's fastest growing team sports, with 1.77 million taking part in women's rugby in 2014. Rugby Sevens – a shorter, seven-a-side format of the game – was introduced as an Olympic sport for men and women in 2016, which prompted further growth in the 15-a-side version. Heyward et al. (2021) note that the popularity and professionalisation of women's rugby has grown dramatically in recent times, prompting increased financial investment into the sport. This contributed to the launch of a new elite league in England, the Premier 15s, and also manifested into increasing professional opportunities for players. At the top level, England's national team members were awarded full-time professional contracts at the start of 2019, and women players in the Premier 15s were paid for the first time in the following year (Rowan, 2019). In light of this growth, the global organising body for the sport, World Rugby, published its Women's Development Plan in 2017, outlining its ambition for gender equity. This includes becoming a 'global leader', with women involved on and off the field, "making highly valued contributions to participation, performance, leadership and investment in the global game of rugby" (World Rugby, 2017, p. 3). The development plan has five pillars in its strategy: grow sustainable participation, high performance quality competition, inspirational leadership on and off the field, profile with impact inspiring engagement and strategic sustainable investment partners. Since the implementation of the development plan, women's rugby on a global level has experienced unprecedented growth with a reported 2.7 million women playing rugby in 2019 – a 28 per cent increase from 2017 (World Rugby, 2019).

Despite the growth of the game at all levels and increasing professional opportunities and commercial advances in the UK and globally, at the very highest level many women operate on a semi-professional basis where women rugby players balance full- or part- time work with their playing commitments (Taylor et al. 2020; Clarkson et al., 2021; Snyders, 2021). It's apparent that the women's version of the sport remains on the margins of rugby culture more broadly. This was exemplified during the COVID-19 pandemic, especially in the UK (Bowes et al., 2020, 2021; Clarkson et al., 2021). For example, the 2020 Women's Six Nation's tournament was abandoned as the sports inherent amateur status made it 'impossible' to conclude the tournament (Hodges, 2020), while the men's tournament was postponed but later completed. At a domestic level, England's women's Premier 15s competition was also paused in March 2020 at the start of the pandemic, as were their male equivalent leagues (RFU, 2020). The elite men's Premiership competition concluded the 2019–2020 season with COVID-19 testing in place, while the women's Premier 15s 2019–2020 season was declared null and void. To add to the uncertainty, the Premier 15s competition lost its title sponsor in the summer of 2020 (Orchard, 2020a), and the continual struggle of women's rugby to obtain adequate revenue would have no doubt exacerbated concerns for female players on the status of their game. In response to the challenges of the pandemic, the RFU announced a 25 per cent cut in funding to women's Premier 15s teams (totalling £187,500), yet the £25 million distributed per year to men's Premiership rugby remained in place (BBC Sport, 2020). Both competitions restarted in October 2020, although with no funding for testing, the women's Premier 15s league restarted with reduced playing time and rule adaptions (Orchard, 2020b). This highlights the unequal and gendered landscape in the sport, in England and the United Kingdom especially. It is from this position that we can start to comprehend the role of women as athletes, and more recently, activists of change, in the sport. A central piece to this specific discussion, though, is understanding the role of online media in athletes' lives, coupled with an awareness of the media coverage of the sport.

Media coverage, online media and feminist athlete activists

Broadcast visibility was identified by World Rugby (2017) as central in the women's development strategy, for maximising the commercial value of the sport and increasing financial sustainability that can enable or contribute to growth. However, a lack of media coverage of the sport has been a consistent problem, despite increasing numbers of women and girls participating across the world. For example, in Wright and Clarke's (1999) media analysis of women's rugby, they draw on *six* articles collected between 1996 and 1997 on the sport in the UK and Australia. Hardy (2015) notes that the dominant image of rugby in traditional media is men's rugby, which enhances the belief that rugby is a hyper-masculine sport. More recently, writing about the Six Nations championships, Owton (2016) bemoaned that none of the women's matches were broadcast on television, despite the men's event dominating free-to-view broadcast channels. In 2017, the women's Rugby World Cup was hosted in Ireland, with England finishing runners up to New Zealand. In examining media coverage in England at this time, Leflay and Biscomb (2021) were able to draw upon 22 articles across four British newspapers, a notable increase on Wright and Clarke's (1999) work in the 1990s but arguably a limited number nonetheless. Whilst Wright and Clarke (1999) reported that the print media coverage of women in rugby served to trivialise the sport, emphasised femininity, and was distinctly heterosexist, there was a notable difference in Leflay and Biscomb's (2021) findings. They found print media articles celebrated the success of the team, were positive about the performances, but also concluded that the coverage was ambivalent, in that it both celebrated the success of the run to the 2017 final whilst documenting issues behind the scenes regarding the cancellation of player contracts.

Given the limits to coverage in traditional media spaces, it has been noted that the online, digital media environment has increasing importance for women's sport. Sports media academics have often highlighted the potential for digital media to redress the lack of coverage for women's sport and contribute to challenging prevailing hegemonic media representations of female athletes (Antunovic & Hardin, 2012; Bruce & Hardin, 2014; Toffoletti & Thorpe, 2018b; Kitching et al., 2021a, 2021b). Social networking sites such as Twitter, Instagram, and Facebook, alongside sports blogs, now play a central role in the coverage of women's sport, and for female athletes. These social media platforms have created the modern 'accessible athlete' – particularly pertinent for women athletes (Pocock and Skey, 2022) – through a bypassing of traditional media outlets that have been dominated by men's sport and male athletes. As such, some academics note that female athletes can use online media to contest the discourses that devalue sportswomen (Antunovic & Hardin, 2012; Bruce & Hardin, 2014; Sanderson & Gramlich, 2016), with sportswomen recognising the role it can play in both inspiring young girls and engaging with potential sponsors (Pocock & Skey, 2022). However, the use of social media by female athletes is not without its problems.

Pocock and Skey (2022) highlight that with increased visibility in online spaces comes pressure to self-present in overly feminised and sexualised ways. Toffoletti and Thorpe (2018b) identify this as the "athletic labour of femininity". Some (although importantly not all – see, for example, Chase, 2006) research into women's rugby cultures has noted female players portraying a "heterosexy-fit identity" in navigating their involvement in a heavily masculine sports environment (Ezzell, 2009). For female athletes that have to carefully manage their self-presentations in this way, such as emphasising femininity over athleticism, LaVoi and Calhoun (2014) present concerns that while some female athletes may achieve personal benefits – through gaining visibility, promoting their brand, and securing sponsorships – this approach inevitably does little to advance women's sport. Furthermore, many sportswomen have experienced abuse and/or misogyny online, with Mogaji et al. (2022) highlighting the risks associated with using social media, cautioning that sportswomen must be aware of online 'trolls'. The problematic elements of social media are thought to have detrimental effects on sports performance, as well as mental health and well-being, as women navigate and manage their engagements on social media (Pocock & Skey, 2022).

Despite the complex management required by sportswomen in using online spaces, this type of media has enabled a rise in female athlete activism as women have a space to challenge inequalities and injustices (Schmidt et al., 2019; Kitching et al., 2021a, 2021b). There are increasing examples of women athletes using social media either to speak out against broader social justice issues or to enable the proliferation of activist campaigns and ideologies. This has occurred around racism (for example, players in the WNBA supporting the Black Lives Matter movement, McClearen & Fischer, 2021; Williams, 2021) and politics (for example, Megan Rapinoe, Schmidt et al., 2019; Frederick et al., 2020), as well as challenging specific sport-based gender inequality and sexism (for example, Megan MacLaren, Kitching et al., 2021a, 2021b). This is despite recent evidence that informs us that many female athletes are under pressure to feel grateful for the opportunity to compete as professionals, thereby inhibiting them from speaking critically about their involvement (Pavlidis, 2020; Bowes et al., 2021). Antunovic and Hardin (2012) contend that social media harbours feminist potential, and there are continuing examples of sportswomen engaging with social media in this way.

Ahmad and Thorpe (2020) refer to the power of the hashtag (#) on social media sites (specifically Twitter/X and Instagram). They describe how hashtags are used to group communication, with social media users signifying that they are willing to amplify a cause, connect with others and become part of a bigger group when adopting a hashtag on their posts, identifying how hashtags can be used from the "everyday personal politic to contributing to and supporting broader social movements" (Ahmad & Thorpe, 2020, p. 676). Before going on to discuss the ways in which rugby union players have engaged with social media, we first present a brief discussion of the theoretical underpinning to this work.

Neoliberal feminism and female athlete activism

Drawing primarily from Toffoletti and Thorpe's (2018a) writing on the topic, this chapter adopts a neoliberal feminist framework to make sense of this phenomenon. The neoliberal feminist project has highlighted how identifying as a feminist is now seen as a form of cultural capital, and identifies a contemporary rise in feminism (Rottenberg, 2018). However, this is understood as a movement that recognises gender inequality – focusing on women's empowerment and choice – whilst denying the gendered socioeconomic and cultural structures that shape the social world. In relation to sport, Toffoletti and Thorpe (2018a, p. 17) discuss Banet-Weiser's (2015) notion of "economies of visibility" as "a mechanism through which to understand the logics that encourage sportswomen to act as entrepreneurial subjects responsible for the construction and promotion of their online identities as marketable media products". In understanding this in neoliberal feminist terms, it is clear that the subject – the sportswoman – is aware of the inequalities between men and women, is perhaps unaware of the wider social, cultural and economic forces that produce this inequality, yet accepts full responsibility for change, on an individual level (Toffoletti & Thorpe, 2018a). Indeed, social media has provided female athletes with a platform to cultivate visibility, overcoming the tools and logics of the market to promote themselves.

The neoliberal feminist project has enabled women to use their individual voices in challenging gender inequality, yet as Rottenberg (2018) notes, simply drawing attention to these issues will not suffice for cultural and/or institutional change. As such, this approach to *doing* feminism is not the only way to understand how feminist ideologies operate in this space. However, the use of personal social media accounts to challenge inequality that affects athletes on a personal level can be seen as evidence of a neoliberal feminist approach. As such, the next section of this chapter will present two case studies on the ways in which women rugby players in the UK have engaged with social media to challenge inherent gender inequality in their sport.

Online activism in women's rugby: Case studies

The first case study refers to the hashtag #IAmEnough, a social media response popularised by Wasps and Wales player, and founder of sport marketing company The Perception Agency, Flo Williams, following an incident in August 2020. The incident centred on the apparel sponsor of the Ireland national team unveiling the new team playing kit for the 2020/2021 season. The launch featured both men's and women's kit, but the problem lay in who was chosen to promote the kit: the apparel company used three international players to display the men's kit and three models to showcase the women's version. Using her Twitter account, Williams tweeted, alongside pictures of the launch:

SPOT THE DIFFERENCE
2 Jersey Launches
3 Models
3 International Players
3 Profiles lifted
1 HUGE Opportunity Missed
By not using the female players to market THEIR OWN KIT an opportunity to build recognition, fan bases & creating role models for future generations is lost.

(Williams, 2020a)

A follow-up tweet from Williams stated:

A nameless face in the jersey does nothing to represent the women who will be wearing it. Brilliant to inspire the future Robbie Henshaw's and Connor Murray's, but when visibility for the women's game is so key, this is a missed opportunity & thoughtless marketing.

(Williams, 2020b)

Initially, the apparel company – Canterbury of New Zealand – responded to William's tweet the next day, explaining that the COVID-19 pandemic had delayed production of the women's kit. However, William's opening tweet garnered significant attention, with 870 retweets, 187 quote tweets, and 4118 likes at the time of writing. Williams later posted via Instagram:

Because role models are real models. We are more than enough & we've had enough. #enough.

(Perception Agency, 2020)

Shortly after William's tweets on 22 August, women and girls across all levels of the game filled social media with empowering images of themselves in rugby kits, using the #IAmEnough, and with that, the #IAmEnough campaign was born. The premise of this campaign was that female players were worthy of showcasing their own kit, in line with the marketing strategy for the men's kit. #IAmEnough involved individual women rugby players posting active images of themselves playing rugby, in opposition to the use of 'heterosexy' models and marked a backlash from the playing community around the gendered expectations of women in the sport. The campaign was picked up by the popular media, with many leading newspapers in the UK documenting the issue. Fi Tomas of the *Telegraph* referred to it as "the biggest body image movement in the history of women's rugby" (2020, 31 August). After five days, the apparel company in question released the following statement, seven days after the kit launch:

As a brand, we believe in putting our hands up if we get something wrong. To announce that our new Ireland Women's pro jersey was available for pre-order, we super-imposed the jersey's image onto a model to share this exciting development with our dedicated female players and fans. It was always, and remains, our intention to photograph female players in the new jersey and we remain committed to supporting the talented women in our rugby community on and off the field. While the image was primarily designed for our website, which also features male models, it has understandably caused frustration. We accept this was an error and apologise for any upset caused. At Canterbury we believe that rugby is for everyone and we're united by our mutual love of the game. We look forward to sharing our 'A New Horizon' campaign to support the launch of our Ireland Women's Pro jersey in October, with the same commitment and dedication that we have for all our teams.

(Canterbury New Zealand, 2020)

Clearly, the individual campaigning instigated by Williams was a central factor in the backlash to the kit launch. Commiskey (2020, 31 August) reported in the *Irish Times*: "The message is clear now. Male dominated organisations only respond to one method of interaction. The current generation of female athletes are beginning to understand this". The solution to challenging gender inequality in the sport here is clearly framed as an individual problem that relies on the social media nous of female players and their supporters. In this case, the individual entrepreneurship of Williams instigated a collective action movement that critiqued the decision of Canterbury – but arguably did little to recognise the broader social constructs that allowed the issue to occur – and subsequently highlights the neoliberal environment in which these athletes are operating.

Case study two relates to an incident that occurred in 2021. The aforementioned COVID-19 enforced postponement of the women's Six Nations competition, whilst the men's tournament went ahead as planned, was widely reported within the sports media. These stories prompted disparaging comments (such as 'no one cares') from supporters of the men's game about the (lack of) significance of their female counterparts. In response to this, the #ICare campaign was created by Premier 15s player Stef Evans, to challenge the notion – emphasised by both the institutional decisions and the responses from fans of men's rugby – that 'nobody cared' about the women's game. She posted to Instagram:

If you care about the Women's Six Nations, about issues affecting the game, about women's rugby in general – Say it. Post a photo of yourself playing, or your favourite women's player or women's team. Talk about what that photo means to you, what it represents. And use the hashtag #ICare.

(World Rugby, 2021)

The campaign went global, with elite players, recreational players, men, women and fans of the sport using the hashtag to support women's rugby. As Fi Tomas (2021) of the Telegraph noted,

Within hours, the movement took off globally and social media was – for the second time in recent months – flooded with empowering photos of female rugby players and fans from the women's game, telling the world why they cared about their sport.

Fellow Bristol Bears player Elinor Snowsill shared the following tweet, which emphasised the premise of the campaign:

I don't particularly care about mens (sic) football. So when I see a post about mens (sic) football, what do I do? I continue scrolling & don't give it a second thought. I get on with my life. I certainly don't waste precious time commenting on mens (sic) football posts about the fact that I don't care.

Do these men trolling articles about womens (sic) rugby genuinely think we are going to believe them when they say they don't care? Are they really that stupid? The simple act of commenting to declare the statement proves the opposite to be true.

#icare about my sport, as do millions others.

Rugby has truly enriched my life in a way I could never have imagined. It has given me friends for life from all over the world, it has taken me to all corners of the globe, it has given me a full time job, it has given me a purpose and it has taught me life's most important values.

To those men ... can you say the same about your hobby of online trolling?

(BBC Sport, 2021, 17 January)

The postponed Six Nations tournament was later rearranged as a standalone tournament for the first time in its history. Again, we can see evidence of the significance of individual agency and self-representation on social media. The individual voices of the athletes highlight the significance of athletes having an avenue for their personal, unfiltered voice.

Conclusion

This chapter has critically discussed the rise of online activism in rugby union, specifically in the UK, as women players attempt to challenge their subordinate status in the sport. Initially, we can understand this approach as part of a neoliberal shift in feminist attitudes of women, which highlights the role of individual voice in challenging gender inequality that has a direct influence on those speaking out, whilst failing to challenge broader systematic issues. However, as Dabrowski (2021) highlights, feminism has become highly visible and a subject of interest, and its contemporary manifestations go further than neoliberal understandings. As such, it would be remiss to not think of this issue as part of a broader network of feminist action, and as Keller (2015) notes, the online practices of feminists can be seen as part of a thriving contemporary feminist movement, which has the scope to be both culturally and politically significant. The two online hashtag campaigns, started by women players from within the game, can be understood in this way. Initially starting out as individual action, these campaigns snowballed into collective action, reaching the national press in the UK, prompting discussions and, significantly, change.

Whilst academics may be critical of the increasing demand placed on female athletes to carve an online space for themselves to generate media coverage (Toffoletti & Thorpe, 2018a), here the women's rugby community demonstrates the possibility it can create to have voices heard and instigate social justice action, especially in case study one, where the apparel company committed to positive change in regard to its promotion of men's and women's kit. However, the extent to which this has prompted actual, cultural change – either in the company itself, in wider rugby marketing and media practices, or in the game more broadly – remains to be seen. Similarly, it places a great deal of expectation, and additional non-sporting labour, onto female athletes to continue to advocate for change, perhaps extending Toffoletti and Thorpe's (2018b) notion of the athletic labour of femininity to include a feminist agenda as part of that – initially as a form of neoliberal self-empowerment but perhaps also as part of a bigger agenda of collective action.

Note

1 The men's Six Nations started as the Home Nations tournament in 1883, the trophy contested by England, Wales, Scotland and Ireland. It later became the Five Nations Tournament with the addition of France (1910–1931 and 1947–1999). Italy was then added as the competition became the Six Nations from 2000. The Women's Home Nations first featured in 1996 (some 103 years after the men's version of the competition launched), changing to the Five Nations in 1999, and becoming the Six Nations in 2001.

References

Ahmad, N., & Thorpe, H. (2020). Muslim sportswomen as digital space invaders: Hashtag politics and everyday visibilities. *Communication & Sport*, *8*(4–5), 668–691.

Antunovic, D., & Hardin, M. (2012). Activism in women's sports blogs: Fandom and feminist potential. *International Journal of Sport Communication*, *5*(3), 305–322.

Banet-Weiser, S. (2015). Media, markets, gender: Economies of visibility in a neoliberal moment. *The Communication Review*, *18*, 53–70.

BBC Sport (2020, October 1). *Premier 15s: RFU cuts funding for women's elite league by 25%*. www.bbc.co.uk/sport/rugby-union/54381033

BBC Sport (2021, January 17). *#icare: Elinor Snowsill speaks out about trolling of women's rugby players.* www.bbc.co.uk/sport/rugby-union/55694789

Bowes, A., & Culvin, A. (Eds). (2021). *The professionalisation of women's sport: Issues and debates.* Emerald Group Publishing.

Bowes, A., Lomax, L., & Piasecki, J. (2020). The impact of the COVID-19 lockdown on elite sportswomen. *Managing Sport and Leisure*, 1–17 (AOP). https://doi.org/10.1080/23750472.2020.1825988

Bowes, A., Lomax, L., & Piasecki, J. (2021). A losing battle? Women's sport pre-and post-COVID-19. *European Sport Management Quarterly*, *21*(3), 443–461.

Bruce, T., & Hardin, M. (2014). Reclaiming our voices: Sportswomen and social media. In A. C. Billings & M. Hardin (Eds). *The Routledge handbook of sport and new media* (pp. 329–337). Routledge.

Canterbury New Zealand [@CanterburyNZ] (2020, August 27). A short statement [Tweet]. Twitter. https://twitter.com/canterburyNZ/status/1299001317629628416

Carrick, S., Culvin, A., & Bowes, A. (2021). The butterfly effect? Title IX and the USWNT as catalysts for global equal pay. *Journal of Legal Aspects of Sport*, *31*(2), 289–311.

Chase, L. F. (2006). (Un) disciplined bodies: A Foucauldian analysis of women's rugby. *Sociology of Sport Journal*, *23*(3), 229–247.

Clarkson, B. G., Bowes, A., Lomax, L., & Piasecki, J. (2021). The gendered effects of Covid-19 on elite women's sport. In A. Bowes & A. Culvin (Eds). *The Professionalisation of women's sport: Issues and debates* (pp. 229–244). Emerald Publishing Limited.

Cleary, A. (2000). Rugby women. *Annals of Leisure Research*, *3*(1), 21–32.

Commiskey, G. (2020, Aug 31). *The Offload: Canterbury get Ireland women's launch all wrong.* www.irishtimes.com/sport/rugby/the-offload-canterbury-get-ireland-women-s-launch-all-wrong-1.4342328

Cooky, C., & Antunovic, D. (2020). "This isn't just about us": Articulations of feminism in media narratives of athlete activism. *Communication & Sport*, *8*(4–5), 692–711.

Culvin, A., Bowes, A., Carrick, S., & Pope, S. (2021). The price of success: Equal pay and the US women's national soccer team. *Soccer & Society*, 1–12 (AOP).

Dabrowski, V. (2021). 'Neoliberal feminism': Legitimising the gendered moral project of austerity. *The Sociological Review*, *69*(1), 90–106.

Dunning, E. G., & Sheard, K. G. (1973). The rugby football club as a type of "male preserve": Some sociological notes. *International Review of Sport Sociology*, *8*(3), 5–24.

Dunning, E., & Sheard, K. (1976). The bifurcation of rugby union and rugby league: A case study of organizational conflict and change. *International Review of Sport Sociology*, *11*(2), 31–72.

Ezzell, M. B. (2009). "Barbie Dolls" on the pitch: Identity work, defensive othering, and inequality in women's rugby. *Social problems*, *56*(1), 111–131.

Frederick, E. L., Pegoraro, A., & Schmidt, S. (2020). "I'm not going to the f***ing White House": Twitter users react to Donald Trump and Megan Rapinoe. *Communication & Sport*, 1–9 (AOP). 2167479520950778.

Furse, L. J. (2021). A brief history of women in rugby union. In H. Joncheray (Ed). *Women in rugby* (pp. 3–14). Routledge.

Hardy, E. (2015). The female 'apologetic' behaviour within Canadian women's rugby: Athlete perceptions and media influences. *Sport in Society*, 18(2), 155–167.

Heyward, O., Emmonds, S., Roe, G., Scantlebury, S., Stokes, K., & Jones, B. (2021). Applied sport science and medicine of women's rugby codes: A systematic-scoping review and consensus on future research priorities protocol. *BMJ Open Sport & Exercise Medicine*, 7(3), e001108.

Hodges, V. (2020, November 10). Remaining women's Six Nations matches cancelled due to sport's amateur status. *The Telegraph*. www.telegraph.co.uk/womenssport/2020/11/10/remaining-womens-six-nations-matches-cancelleddue-sports-amateur

Joncheray, H., & Tlili, H. (2013). Are there still social barriers to women's rugby? *Sport in Society*, 16(6), 772–788.

Kanemasu, Y., & Molnar, G. (2019). Against all odds: Fijiana's flight from zero to hero in the Rugby World Cup. In J. Harris & N. Wise (Eds). *Rugby in global perspective* (pp. 24–36). Routledge.

Keller, L. (2015). *Girls' feminist blogging in a postfeminist age*. Routledge.

Kitching, N., Bowes, A., & Maclaren, M. (2021a). 'Write when it hurts. Then write till it doesn't': Athlete voice and the lived realities of one female professional athlete. *Qualitative Research in Sport, Exercise and Health*, 13(1), 77–93.

Kitching, N., Bowes, A., & MacLaren, M. (2021b). Online activism and athlete advocacy in professional women's golf: Risk or reward?. In R. McGrath (Ed). *Athlete activism* (pp. 181–192). Routledge.

LaVoi, N. M., & Calhoun, A. S. (2014). Digital Media and Women's Sport: An old view on 'new' media?. In A. C. Billings and M. Hardin (Eds). *Routledge handbook of sport and new media* (pp. 320–330). Routledge.

Leflay, K., & Biscomb, K. (2021). England's summer of sport 2017. *Sport in Society*, 24(9), 1633–1648.

McClearen, J., & Fischer, M. (2021). Maya Moore, Black Lives matter, and the visibility of athlete activism. *The Velvet Light Trap*, 87(1), 64–68.

Mogaji, E., Badejo, F. A., Charles, S., & Millisits, J. (2022). To build my career or build my brand? Exploring the prospects, challenges and opportunities for sportswomen as human brand. *European Sport Management Quarterly*, 22(3), 379–397.

Muir, K. B., & Seitz, T. (2004). Machismo, misogyny, and homophobia in a male athletic subculture: A participant-observation study of deviant rituals in collegiate rugby. *Deviant Behavior*, 25(4), 303–327.

Nauright, J., & Chandler, T. J. L. (Eds). (1996). *Making men: Rugby and masculine identity*. Psychology Press.

Orchard, S. (2020a, May 26). Women's Premier 15s: Tyrrells to end sponsorship of league. *BBC Sport*. www.bbc.co.uk/sport/rugby-union/52807776

Orchard, S. (2020b, October 6). Premier 15s to restart on Saturday with adapted laws and no testing. *BBC Sport*. www.bbc.co.uk/sport/rugby-union/54421879

Owton, H. (2016, February 29). *Blindside of rugby Six Nations: Where are the women?* Open University Sport and Fitness Team Blog. www.open.ac.uk/blogs/OU-Sport/?p=978

Pavlidis, A. (2020). Being grateful: Materialising 'success' in women's contact sport. *Emotion, Space and Society*, 35, 100673.

Perception Agency [@theperceptionagency] (2020, August 27). We are more than enough & we've had enough. #Enough. [Instagram photograph]. *Instagram*. www.instagram.com/p/CEYvlWCAMl0/

Pocock, M., & Skey, M. (2022). 'You feel a need to inspire and be active on these sites otherwise… people won't remember your name': Elite female athletes and the need to maintain 'appropriate distance' in navigating online gendered space. *New Media & Society*, (AOP). 14614448211069343.

Raynor, M. (2018). *Rugby union and professionalisation: Elite player perspectives*. Routledge.

Rottenberg, C. (2018, May 23). How neoliberalism colonised feminism – and what you can do about it. *The Conversation*. https://theconversation.com/how-neoliberalism-colonised-feminism-and-what-you-can-do-about-it-94856

Rowan, K. (2019, September 3). *English women's club rugby players to be paid for the first time*. [Tweet]. www.telegraph.co.uk/rugby-union/2019/09/03/exclusiveenglish-womens-club-rugby-players-paid-first-time

Rugby Football Union (2020, March 20). A message to the rugby union community in England from Bill Sweeney, CEO RFU. www.premier15s.com/news/article/tyrrells-premier-15s-season-cancelled

Sanderson, J., & Gramlich, K. (2016). "You Go Girl!": Twitter and conversations about sport culture and gender. *Sociology of Sport Journal, 33*(2), 113–123.

Schacht, S. P. (1996). Misogyny on and off the "pitch" the gendered world of male rugby players. *Gender & Society, 10*(5), 550–565.

Schmidt, S. H., Frederick, E. L., Pegoraro, A., & Spencer, T. C. (2019). An analysis of Colin Kaepernick, Megan Rapinoe, and the national anthem protests. *Communication & Sport, 7*(5), 653–677.

Snyders, H. (2021). From 'taking a while to settle' to becoming the Imbokodo: Women's Rugby Union in South Africa during the post-Apartheid and professional era, 2001–2020. In A. Bowes & A. Culvin (Eds). *The professionalisation of women's sport* (pp. 37–52). Emerald Publishing Limited.

Taylor, T., O'Connor, D., & Hanlon, C. (2020). Contestation, disruption and legitimization in women's rugby league. *Sport in Society, 23*(2), 315–334. https://doi.org/10.1080/17430437.2019.163180

Toffoletti, K., & Thorpe, H. (2018a). Female athletes' self-representation on social media: A feminist analysis of neoliberal marketing strategies in "economies of visibility". *Feminism & Psychology, 28*(1), 11–31.

Toffoletti, K., & Thorpe, H. (2018b). The athletic labour of femininity: The branding and consumption of global celebrity sportswomen on Instagram. *Journal of Consumer Culture, 18*(2), 298–316.

Tomas, F. (2020, 31 Aug). Irish women's jersey fiasco is a sad indictment of how international women's rugby is still treated. *The Telegraph*. www.telegraph.co.uk/rugby-union/2020/08/28/irish-womens-jersey-fiasco-sad-indictment-international-womens/

Tomas, F. (2021, 21 Jan). Women's rugby 'I care' movement highlights the perennial battle the game has to fight. *The Telegraph*. Women's rugby 'I care' movement highlights the perennial battle the game has to fight (telegraph.co.uk)

Williams, F. [@FlorenceW94] (2020a, August 22). SPOT THE DIFFERENCE. 2 Jersey Launches. 3 Models. 3 International Players. 3 Profiles lifted. 1 HUGE Opportunity Missed. By not using the female players to market THEIR OWN KIT an opportunity to build recognition, fan bases & creating role models for future generations is lost [Tweet]. Twitter. https://twitter.com/FlorenceW94/status/1297155751635492865

Williams, F. [@FlorenceW94] (2020b, August 22). A nameless face in the jersey does nothing to represent the women who will be wearing it. Brilliant to inspire the future Robbie Henshaw's and Connor Murray's, but when visibility for the women's game is so key, this is a missed opportunity & thoughtless marketing [Tweet]. Twitter. https://twitter.com/FlorenceW94/status/1297155969261207552

Williams, A. L. (2021). The heritage strikes back: Athlete activism, Black Lives matter, and the iconic fifth wave of activism in the (W) NBA Bubble. *Cultural Studies ↔ Critical Methodologies*, AOP. 15327086211049718.

World Rugby. (2015, March 8). *More women are playing rugby than ever before*. www.world.rugby/news/60275

World Rugby. (2017). *Women's Development Action Plan 2017–2025*. 2021-Womens_Plan-EN-3.pdf (world.rugby)

World Rugby. (2019, May 21). *World Rugby launches global campaign to revolutionise women's rugby*. www.world.rugby/news/422288

World Rugby. (2021, Jan 20). #icare founder Stef Evans on the online campaign empowering women's rugby. www.world.rugby/news/612332/icare-founder-stef-evans-womens-rugby

Wright, J., & Clarke, G. (1999). Sport, the media and the construction of compulsory heterosexuality: A case study of women's rugby union. *International Review for the Sociology of Sport, 34*(3), 227–243.

35
THE FIVE GROUPS OF ENVIRONMENTAL SPORTS ACTIVISTS

A complex medley

Toby Miller

Professional and elite-level sports have long been popular sites for promoting both progressive and reactionary positions on race, gender, sexuality, disability, politics, capital, nationalism, and the environment (Grano & Butterworth, 2019; Miller, 2018a; Rowe, 2004). This is becoming more and more the case with the Olympics, the men's World Cup of football, and Formula One, which provide this chapter's case studies and demonstrate the need to highlight environmental justice in sports scholarship.

Some of the symbolic freighting accorded to such events is due to sports' elemental claims to incarnate nature and truth – the fastest swimmer, the longest leap, the quickest horse. But these achievements are not only about muscularity, skill, dedication, and coordination. They rely on training, technique, technology, travel, and the transformation of space to create events that showcase athletic prowess and records. Success relies on a host of environmental transformations: everything from human kinesiology to animal enslavement, vitamin supplements to exercise equipment, monumental stadia to mobile horse floats, telecommunications infrastructure to medical facilities, school coaches to betting addicts, and tax arrangements to corporate contracts.

Far from being instantiations of natural ability, these interventions exemplify sports' seemingly inexorable will and sense of entitlement to control and change nature and culture, through the colonial spread of football, cricket, tennis, golf, athletics, and so on; their latter-day governmentalisation, commodification, and televisualisation; and a trans-historical tendency to regard success in nationalistic terms (albeit underwritten by monetary power – gross domestic product is the key predictor of Olympic success).

From traditional golf links to Formula One venues, sports never transcend their ties to the environment. They produce massive carbon footprints, via construction, maintenance, transport, energy, sanitation, water use, and media coverage, all the while endeavouring to promote themselves as good environmental citizens (Warren, 2020). Sports are part of our anthropocentric conjuncture, from the construction of playing fields and stadium stands to the damage done when the flyboys and girls of international competitions trample across time zones in search of glory. The impact is mutual: skiing, hockey, cricket, tennis, and many other sports affect global warming, which in turn affects them (Bonnemains, 2014; Kay, 2019; Martin, 2019). It can be no surprise to learn that the US and Canada's 126 pro sports teams need monumental amounts of energy to power their stadia. Fewer than a third of those buildings deploy renewable energy; the Dallas Cowboys, for example, rely on 750 megawatts on game day, about four times the total power available to Liberia. For its part, the National Hockey League uses 321 million gallons of water a year (McHale, 2019). And these events grow and grow and grow in size and therefore climatic impact – the Olympics and the men's World Cup have increased as 'tourist events' 60 times over in the last half-century, or 13 times the world's economic growth rate (Müller et al., 2023).

So how to confront these horrors? Through activism? The term is historically associated with the left, as broadly defined. It generally refers to volunteer and professional campaigners and analysts struggling against racism, misogyny, war, inequality, and climate change. But today, activism is also the playground of the right, which draws merrily on rejecting state institutions as legitimate representatives of the people and spectacle to make its points, as well as carefully calculated and crafted greenwashing, designed to obscure and legitimise environmental criminality (Miller, 2018b). There has been considerable mendacity on social media over climate science in the recent past, as the right has adopted 'our' tactics of outraged scepticism against voices of expertise and authority (Falkenberg et al., 2022).

There is a lack of compelling evidence about the efficacy of direct action by environmentalists (Gulliver et al., 2022) and little to support the idea that liberals are more positive in their responses than reactionaries (Croco et al., 2023). Regardless of these studies, when we ponder the use of direct action by environmental movements, it's easy to fall into either a critical camp or a celebratory one. The critical camp would say that rationality must be appealed to in discussions of climate change and competition, for emotion will ultimately fail. Why? The silent majority doesn't like the avant-garde, marketing outspends art, such occasions preach to a light-skinned, middle-class eco-choir, media coverage is slender, and crucial decisions are made in golf carts, not galleries. Many people experience activists as militant and eccentric, tree-hugging hippies, dangerous eco-terrorists, anti-growth evangelists, economic ignoramuses, middle-class lay-abouts, vapid vegans, or romantic dreamers. While that otherness may be a core part of some environmentalists' identities (behaving eccentrically in public, grabbing attention, securing column inches) it severely limits their ability to communicate effectively across a range of constituencies, leaving them stuck in a self-fulfilling vanguardist politics (Bashir et al., 2013; M. S., 2019). As *The Economist* (2014) puts it, "reactions to people scaling buildings and unveiling banners range from apathy to mild annoyance. Those tactics seem to belong to another era". Justice will seemingly not arise thanks to taking to the streets.

Conversely, the celebratory camp would argue that a Cartesian distinction between hearts and minds is not sustainable, a sense of humour is crucial to avoid the image of environmentalists as finger-wagging scolds, corporate capital must be opposed in public, the media's need for vibrant textuality can be twinned with serious discussion to alert people who are not activists, and a wave of anti-élite sentiment is cresting (Shenker, 2023). This view argues that only direct action, "putting your body on the line", can "accelerate the global transformations needed to avert environmental catastrophe" (McCarthy, 2021) because climate change "cannot be addressed by traditional party politics. Governing-as-usual is ill-suited to deal with global, complex, interconnected issues that do not respect geographic borders or electoral timetables" (Venzon & Cahen-Salvador, 2019). Instead, "participative democracy, horizontality, inclusiveness, and direct action" (Fians, 2022) can satisfy those "impatient of waiting for the authorities to act on their behalf" (Carter, 2010, pp. 19–20) and who wish to punish the guilty themselves. Sovereignty resides in righteous indignation and universal values that transcend government and represent the popular will in an unmediated way via civil society (Graeber, 2002; McGregor, 2015; Yates, 2015). Hence groups believing that anti-climate change gatherings of a few hundred thousand in a population of two billion signify 'the' people's message (Giacomini & Turner, 2015).

This bifurcation relates to divisions on the left caused by various social transformations of the past half-century. Much of the investment once made in the working class as the next great agent of history after the *bourgeoisie* assumed that 'science' made their uprising and eventual hegemony inevitable. But the break-up of the notion of a single force of change, the discrediting of state socialism, and the identification of rationality with some categories of people and not others militated against progressive investments in traditional labour, and encouraged the intellectual scepticism of post-structuralism and social movements alike – a simultaneous split from the certainties of a united oppositional tendency and grandiloquent forms of thought.

But now the left forms a united front – the need to diminish damage to the planet – and embraces a unified truth – the science of climate change. In this instance, we are on the side of reason (de Coninck, 2021). When very conventional entities such as the United Nations, refereed journals, and the professoriate at fancy schools say something that proves human-generated climate change is authentic, we applaud. Conversely, we deride coin-operated 'sceptics' within think tanks and the *bourgeois* media. Activism pits the right-wing refusal or pseudo-incorporation of environmental critique against a more oppositional, yet scholarly-based, perspective. This is in keeping with a "landscape that ranges from militant tunnel-diggers to the philanthropic arm of corporate giants" (Shenker, 2023).

In the sports world, there is less virulent denial of our climate crisis than in many other industries – and more co-optation. Five, sometimes interlocking, groups engage in environmental sports activism, typifying that landscape and forming a complex medley:

1. Corporate and state actors urging one another, athletes, the *bourgeois* media, and the general public to support events, claiming they are green (Group One – executives)
2. Big non-government environmental organisations arguing for direct action (Group Two – NGOs)
3. Public-interest collectives and scholars producing research reports in opposition to polluters and executives (Group Three– critics)
4. Grassroots fans favouring the environment (Group Four – the public); and
5. Participants supporting environmental priorities (Group Five– athletes)

- *Group One*: Sports have long served as sites for greenwashing by extractive corporations in the petroleum, chemical, gas, transportation, and technology industries (in conjunction with socially-destructive gambling, alcohol, fast-food, tobacco, sugar drinks, and media firms). Sports' 'everyday pleasures' offer effective symbolic cover for sponsorship and branding, projecting an image of commitment to the environment and drawing attention away from activities and industries that display nothing of the sort (Miller, 2018a, p. 2). This unwarranted clean and green image can associate polluting corporations with a 'moderate' pseudo-environmentalism that "no longer represents a hindrance to the economy" (Beck, 2009, p. 103). Big polluters make use of this as part of their search for a 'social license to operate', an invidious concept developed two decades ago by the United Nations Commission on Sustainable Development (1998) that pretends capitalists regard communities as equal 'stakeholders' (Wilburn & Wilburn, 2011). Their executives are from the same oligarchy as the tame politicians and bureaucrats who do their bidding.

- *Group Two*: Many environmental NGOs say they are animated by the truth of science, but claim legitimacy based on grassroots connections, not expertise or representativeness. Organic community ties are asserted at the same time as small numbers of people undertake direct action. Multinational bureaucracies like Greenpeace (Vidal, 2011) stage spectacles at sports events, notably motor racing and football, to disrupt pleasure and attract media attention. The rhetoric is hortatory (Diaz, 2022) but these organisations blend 'wet suits' with 'business suits' (Grant, 2004) and favour popular protest only when orchestrated by their hierarchies (Eden, 2004).
- *Group Three*: Critical scholars and public intellectuals produce an increasing body of knowledge about the environmental criminality of Group One, informing an environmental movement dedicated to influencing states and sports administrators (McCullough & Kellison, 2018). Advocacy groups like the Green Sports Alliance, Sport and Sustainability International, and the Sports Environment Alliance are notable instances (Kay, 2019; Martin, 2019). There is some overlap with Group Two, when entities such as Greenpeace undertake and promote science versus engaging in bureaucratically-driven direct action.
- *Group Four*: There is evidence of organic grassroots opposition to sports' greenwashing and despoliation. Denver citizens voted against hosting the 1976 Winter Olympics due to the rapacious ski industry's environmental destructiveness; progressives successfully opposed Amsterdam bidding for the 1992 Summer Games; and Hamburg and Boston rejected city-government campaigns to gain the 2024 Olympiad (Colorado rejects, 1972; Ramaswamy, 2015; Vaccaro, 2015). Some football supporters criticise corporate control and call for greener bootprints (Davies, 2019; Football Supporters Association, n.d.; Keoghan, 2014). And Protect Our Winters claims over 130,000 supporters dedicated to turning "passionate outdoor people into effective climate advocates" (2019). Group Four works towards environmental justice from the ground up.
- *Group Five*: As Group One executives and owners crave greenwashing, more and more Group Five athletes want real change, for instance North American Stock Car Auto Racing driver Leilani Münter identifying as "a vegan hippie chick with a race car" (n.d.); surfers exhibiting and protesting the doleful impact of polluted oceans (Evers, 2019); 200 downhill skiers insisting that their sport "take the lead in the fight against climate change and make our sport climate neutral as soon as possible" (Protect Our Winters, 2023); and Kiribati weightlifter David Katoatau drawing attention to rising sea levels imperilling his homeland (Friedman, 2016).

The task for groups Two through Five is particularly intense, as they confront executive dominion over the world's most popular sporting fixtures. Those events are directly and indirectly environmentally destructive, via the occasions themselves (construction and tourism in the Olympics and World Cups, engines and their transportation in Formula One) and the promotion of heavy industry and provision of social licenses to operate.

The remainder of this chapter examines the history and contemporaneity of such issues and associated activism. I am operating from the assumption that the rubric of social justice includes – but can sometimes be subsumed by – environmental justice; that the search for equality and fairness must include protection of the planet as much as public health or guaranteed income.

The games

The Olympics are constitutively environmental: their very division between summer and winter contests is climatic. But many sports seek to avoid or alter geography. Pool swimmers and divers are sedulously sheltered from salt and river water and basketballers securely shielded from weather. Skateboarders and motocross riders rely on the evisceration of natural obstacles in their path. Our fellow-animals are largely absent, other than the enslaved horses of equestrianism and the pentathlon, skeet shooting's mimetic birds, and mascots (Sin, 2014).

But the domination of nature is experiencing severe setbacks: because of climate change, within six decades, few world cities will be cool enough to host summer sports safely (Gaind, 2016). Competitors are already falling ill and dying, and distance races in particular are dramatically worsening runners' health (Bernard et al., 2021; Nowak et al., 2022; Wallace et al., 2019).

And the Olympics' environmental impact is dubious (Miller, 2018a; Müller et al., 2021), with notable cases such as the hazards created by abandoned facilities after Athens in 2004 and Rio in 2016 (Evans, 2018). Perhaps the most drastic story is from 50 years ago, when preparations for Tokyo's 1964 Games incarnated despoliation (Whiting, 2014). As with all rapid, massive modernisations (the US, the Soviet Union, and China) Japan's transformation was achieved through violence; in this case, war and its detritus. The flashy welcome to Tokyo modernity[1] in 1964 featured a façade of newness, technology, democracy, and efficiency[2] – a neat lesson in how not to fall prey to socialism when emerging from fascism (Tagsold, 2010; Wilson, 2012). But prior to those Games, construction of a high-speed rail link between Osaka and the capital saw canals, sea, and rivers inundated with concrete and landfill and a centuries-old seaweed field destroyed. Water stagnated, sludge emerged, and marine life perished. Estuaries turned into cesspools and/or became roads. Tramways were largely destroyed in favour of freeways. Sadistic clearances saw hundreds of thousands of homeless cats and dogs killed (Miller, 2018a). There was little resistance to these horrors; they were barely noticed in the bright lights of a seemingly eternal day that blasted war into the past (Jorgenson & Clark, 2016).

Of course, today's dominant Olympian discourse dutifully embraces executive ecological responsibility – rhetorically. Group One's *faux* Carbon Footprint Methodology promises "effective carbon reduction strategies" (International Olympic Committee, 2018, p. 11). But the Games' commercial 'partners' have included such major polluters as MacDonald's, Coca-Cola, Visa, Dow, Toyota, and General Electric, all seeking social licences to operate by appearing green (Samuel & Stubbs, 2013). Group One executives typically claim a high moralism while dodging essential environmental standards; after all, their bureau "issues no hard-and-fast requirement for Games hosts" (Müller, 2015, p. 197). In reality, the Olympics is "an international bacchanal of physical perfection and triumphant will swaddled in human rights abuses and environmental catastrophe" (West, 2016).

It was meant to be different in 2020: a putatively green Games, civilised by environmental science, Group One commitment, Group Two seals of approval, and so on. Five thousand medals were constructed from electronic waste (Nakagawa, 2018). The IOC[3] (trading as the International Olympic Committee, but better known as the International Oligarchy Committee, with its abundance of Royal Highnesses and Sheiks) signed up to that great capitalist oxymoron of our times, the UN's Sustainable Development Goals.[4] Adopting the asininely aspirational slogan "Be better, together, for the planet and the people", it guaranteed a Games characterised by mass transit, renewable energy, and recycled rainwater, making outlandish claims of environmental leadership along the way.[5] But the massive misallocation of public and private resources that embodies the Olympics (Wade, 2020) is predicated on two promises that have rarely been realised: re-useable new infrastructure and ongoing tourism. Despite a pitiful record, those shibboleths have seduced city after exploited city into becoming hosts, oblivious to routine deficits of a billion dollars each time since 1964 (Müller et al., 2022).[6]

Meanwhile, the use of raw materials and accumulation of airmiles compromise any supposed accommodation to our climate crisis.

Tokyo 2020 saw the organisers pillaging rainforests to build their stadium (Rainforest Action Network, 2018); razing public parks and housing and ruining iconic landmarks (Zirin & Boykoff, 2019); and re-imagining Fukushima: don't fear radiation (Boykoff & Gaffney, 2020), it's safer than smoking (Ware, 2021) (apropos, 1964 featured an Olympic cigarette, leading to massive increases in Japanese smoking and lung cancer by the run-up to the 2020 event [Tomizawa, 2016]). Officials estimated 2.73 million tonnes of CO_2 would be emitted courtesy of the 2020 Games – more than many countries produce in a year (Voice of America, 2021), though banning foreign spectators because of the syndemic probably diminished that figure (Tokyo Organising Committee, 2021).

The Games' vacant hotels and spectator-free stadia stood as witless, mute, plastic testimony to the effect of COVID-19 on IOC greenwashing, while the anachronistic invocation of a year that had already passed to describe the Olympics celebrated a pomp and arrogance so thoroughly articulated to marketing that it overdetermined the simplest chronological truth (McDonald, 2020). NBC hegemons complained that a "drumbeat of negativity" dragged down its audience (Hsu, 2021). But those numbers, and the event's physical emptiness, enshrined an ethical void at the core of the movement's very being (Jennings & Sambrook, 2000).

Then there is the question of timing. The 1964 Olympics had been held in October. But a repeat of such a calendar was unacceptable to NBC. Ever since poor ratings for the September 2000 Sydney Games, NBC gets what NBC buys: $7.75 billion worth of influence, if not intellect, competence, or artistry (Armour, 2014; Rutenberg, 2000; Timms, 2021). No matter that a thousand fatalities during the 2018 Japanese summer were declared "The First Undeniable Climate Change Deaths" (Merino, 2020), or that in 2019, the Games period saw Tokyo's daily maximum temperature average 92°F, with 80 per cent humidity, and 20,000 people hospitalised nationwide (Lee, 2019).

During the event itself, host broadcaster NHK's meteorologist Sayaka Mori noted that the weather was "torturing the Olympians and volunteers".[7] Athlete testimony was equally damning.[8] Needless to say, NBC covered the 2021 'heat wave' and typhoon as "another hit of nature's power" (Associated Press, 2021; Siemaszko, 2021). For its part, the International Oligarchy Committee put responsibility onto participants for their health,[9] as if the impact were not the IOC's and NBC's doing (Annear et al., 2021; Lei & Wang, 2021). Nor did it discipline the many federations that failed to care for competitors (Santini & Henderson, 2021). Group One is about activism on its own behalf.

There was some resistance to this institutional irresponsibility. In the years prior to Tokyo, Groups Two to Five targeted the timber trade, which involves illegal logging, dispossession of land, and violence against protestors: Global Witness, the Environmental Investigation Agency, and the Rainforest Action Network, *inter alia*, campaigned with local environmental groups to criticise corporate malfeasance (Global Witness, 2016; Grohmann, 2017; Lester, 2019) and problematised the National Stadium, a veritable 'timber temple' (Hilburg, 2019). Opposition to these activities may not have changed much on-site, but it added to the growing sense that the Games are tarnished by duplicity.

Football

Football is affected by climate change through unprecedented flooding that endangers pitches and buildings (The Climate Coalition, 2018). The sport itself might appear to be among the least ecologically malevolent of pastimes: it requires a ball, space, and people who like to play, as opposed to runways, roads, engines, and petrol heads. But the picture is remarkably different when we take into account where the sport's equipment is made and transported for sale and use, the water and chemicals involved in ground maintenance, the food consumed at games, the electricity required to cover and watch fixtures, and the impact of transportation and tourism (Malhado & Rothfuss, 2013). It has been estimated that football is responsible for 0.3–0.4 per cent of the world's annual emissions – equivalent to Denmark (Ashoo, 2021). English Premier League domestic team travel over the 2016–2017 season generated approximately 1134 tonnes of CO_2-eq (Tóffano Pereira et al., 2019), and clubs insist on flying when this is entirely unnecessary, as Green MEP Karima Delli explains (Rios, 2020). Leading managers and star players are known to treat such criticisms as a joke.[10]

The sport's Group One, its Fédération internationale de football association (FIFA), is unfit to function as a governing body on the climate or any other matter (Conn, 2017; Fruh et al., 2023; Tomlinson, 2014). FIFA represents the ultimate in commodification and governmentalisation, with residual hegemonic membership of greybeards at its highest echelons, where corrupt young technocrats and corrupt old elites commingle.[11] That partial transmogrification, from amateur good-old-boy networks that ran the sport prior to its comprehensive commercialisation, mirrors club history. Western European football teams were once small, city-based businesses, drawing on athletes who had grown up close to their grounds. They were run rather like not-for-profits, representing and regenerating local cultures, albeit sometimes dominated by corporations (in Germany) or *petit-bourgeois machistas* (in Britain). By the 1990s, many clubs had become creatures of exchange. In the course of this radical transformation, they fell prey to fictive capital, sources of asset inflation used by rentiers to service other debts through the cash flow of attendances, television money, and merchandising.

Efforts to expose and counter football's ecological crimes come to naught when Group One's state and capital priorities influence decisions otherwise. For example, Norwegian and South African scientists studying the probable environmental impact of the 2010 men's World Cup Finals issued stern warnings prior to the event (McCarthy, 2009; Republic of South Africa et al., 2009): "A cohort of 12,700 fans flying from Britain would travel more than 232 million kilometres in total, generating more than 53,000 tonnes of CO_2" (McCarthy, 2009).

Contra such materially based knowledge, South Africa's *Accelerated and Shared Growth Initiative* (Republic of South Africa, 2004) successfully argued for the dynamism and equity that would supposedly derive from staging the Finals. Then-President Thabo Mbeki proclaimed a "development World Cup" as part of an "African renaissance" (quoted in Levermore, 2011, p. 887). His administration used traditional economistic and anthropocentric shibboleths about alchemically combining such desires with being green. Government tender documents invited competition to offset aviation footprints, but no contracts were issued. This was hardly surprising, coming as it did from a state that has largely neglected alternative energy sources and statutes mandating environmental assessment of projects (Ahmed & Pretorius, 2010). South Africa lacked adequate stadia and high-speed rail (Estrada, 2010). Improvements were made to mass transit, but freeways received more investment. Excluding construction, the 'development' World Cup had the largest carbon footprint of any commercial event in world history: 1.65 million tonnes, twice the 2008 Beijing Olympics and nine times the 2006 Finals in Germany (Levermore, 2012). Cape Town proposed upgrading its principal stadium, which was rejected by FIFA in favour of new construction (Engar & du Toit, 2023). Cities that engaged in these costly projects appear not to have seen net income benefits, while tax burdens mount to cover stadium upkeep (Coulibaly et al., 2022; Marire, 2022).

Offset programs designed to minimise the 2014 bootprint in Brazil were unsuccessful – 2.72 million tonnes of carbon were emitted (Crabb, 2018; Sturrock, 2018). Estimates of the Cup's environmental impact often exclude construction, but even FIFA's typically self-serving report on the topic acknowledges that 2018 in Russia generated well over 2.1 million tonnes of emissions (FIFA, 2019, p. 68). The 2022 event, held in the anti-democracy Qatar, was characterised by the usual environmental falsehoods. This was achieved via creative accounting, which pretended that the impact of construction, desalination, and water use in an arid climate would be offset by generations of high usage – this despite gate receipts in the hundreds for local matches (Carbon Market Watch, 2022; Raji, 2022). Qatar was responsible for double the carbon bootprint of its immediate predecessors. As usual, the US provided the most international tourists, with travel emissions of 191,055 tonnes. Even the notion of offsets, a problematic concept, found that the small matter of 600 million new trees would be needed to counter Qatar 2022's climate criminality (Hometree, 2022).

On other fronts, fan, club, media, and bureaucratic travel to Europe's 2019 Champions League and Europa League Finals generated 35,000 tonnes of CO_2, while the 2020 Euros could almost have been designed to create maximal ecological chaos – they were scheduled for Germany, Hungary, Scotland, England, Azerbaijan, Holland, Italy, Denmark, Russia, Ireland, and Spain (McKie et al., 2019). Even the tournament's postponement because of the syndemic did not produce an ecologically-rational itinerary based in one country (UEFA, 2020).

Television coverage is another contributor to football's environmental irresponsibility. The UK's National Grid ESO notes the electricity demand created by viewers during half time in the World Cup, when people head for the kitchen and bathroom. As a consequence, audiences are the Grid's biggest drains (Miller, 2018a). Power use surges by as much as 10 per cent in the "TV pick-up" or "half-time kettle effect" (Selectra, 2020). The Grid correlated viewership and energy during England's tragi-comic departure from the 1990 World Cup: "A whopping 2800MW at the end of the penalty shoot-out!" During Brazil's matches in the 2014 competition, UK surges totalled 4348 megawatts, the equivalent of a million and a half kettles being turned on simultaneously. And watching football via mobile telephony multiplies spectators' carbon footprint tenfold in comparison with using television or WiFi (Miller, 2018a).

Attempts by Group Two's Greenpeace to problematise Big Football's impact on the environment have foundered. When it sought to interrupt the 2014 Champions' League Final with a vanguardist protest because Gazprom was a sponsor (saying nothing about the unsustainability of the event itself), its ruse was quickly uncovered and managed. Greenpeace used embarrassingly *macho* corporate language to claim "total domination in the sphere of delivery" (quoted in Miller, 2018a). Prolixity lives, suggesting how close the NGO's bureaucabulary is to its apparent corporate adversaries – and how distant from football fans. This leaves us looking to more organic activism from Group Four, rather than clickocracy, a vital source of Group Two finance. For there is little scholarly evidence that social-media environmental activism reaches beyond chorines. But it's a good fundraiser.

Many fans appreciate that they are contributing to high emissions through travel and television but decline to change their conduct (Sant'Anna School of Advanced Studies, Institute of Management, 2020). In any event, it could be argued that turning to fandom as a source of environmental activism is plutocratic – that it privileges consumption. But football fandom rides a complex frontier between commerce and culture. Many see their commitments as matters of lifelong identity rather than 'rational' purchase (Keoghan, 2014). They seek to transform the sport via popular rather than corporate ownership, based on trusteeship versus profit and campaign against racism and homophobia.[12] The Football Supporters' Association and their cognates are concerned about carbon bootprints and clientelist oligarchs.[13]

Even football hooligans might provide organic forms of environmentalism. Several investigations of such groups reject both their romantic annunciation as working-class scions and their criminalisation via moral panics (Armstrong, 1998; Armstrong & Young, 1997; Giulianotti 1999, pp. 80–82; Schimmel et al., 2007). Such work draws on E.P. Thompson's insight that crowds may be animated by economic conditions, sexual urges, or blind rages, but also by ideological commitments (1971).

We might note the *ultràs* model of Southern European play, with its connotations of carnival or hooliganism, depending on where you sit; the spectacular arena conduct of Argentina's *barras bravas*; the uptake of Latin American chants on British terraces in the 1990s, with fans parading the banner *Cosmopolitanismo Vaincra* [Cosmopolitanism will Triumph]. Consider Gramscian Livorno followers (Pato, 2021); anti-fascist, pro-feminist supporters of Sankt Pauli in Germany (Galbiati, 2013; Montague, 2010; Totten, 2013; Viñas & Parra, 2020); and Turkey's Çarşı aficionados of Beşiktaş opposing both an oppressive state and nuclear power (Erhart, 2014). Their cries for social justice can clearly be articulated to environmental concerns.

Formula One

In 2019, Group Five champion driver Lewis Hamilton acknowledged that "our carbon footprint is higher than the average homeowner who lives in one city" (quoted in Benson, 2019). He spoke in favour of veganism and briefly posted the following on Instagram:

> Honestly, I feel like giving up on everything. Shut down completely. Why bother when the world is such a mess and people don't seem to care. I'm going to take a moment away to gather my thoughts. Thank you to those of you who do give a damn about the world.
>
> (quoted in Lewis Hamilton, 2019)

Hamilton's rival Fernando Alonso shot back with "[w]e all know the lifestyle that Lewis has, and that Formula 1 drivers take 200 planes a year. You can't then say: 'Don't eat meat'" (quoted in Benson, 2019). Some colleagues supported Hamilton's environmentalism, acknowledging their own responsibilities in our climate crisis; others were more sceptical (FIA Thursday, 2019; Ferrisi, 2020; Richards, 2021). Alonso subsequently adopted a greener position (Portillo, 2022).

But these men—and the cars that make them—embody the desire for growth and mobility in a fetishistic blend of economic planning and *bourgeois* liberty. On the one hand, the business drive for regularity, reliability, and control of production, distribution, and consumption is incarnate in Formula One teams. On the other, the drivers exemplify neoliberal subjects, ever ready for adventure. And in 2023, Formula One oligarchs sought to silence their stars on climate change, *inter alia* (Benson, 2023) while the sport's wildly popular Netflix series

Formula 1: Drive to Survive (2018–) steered away from environmental statements (Coleman, 2023).

Group Two Greenpeace has endeavoured to disrupt Grands Prix via people dressing up in bright colours and climbing or mounting things they don't own. This hasn't played well with the significant proportions of Formula One followers fixated on *macho* heroics and the technological sublime of engines, speed, and noise (Cooper, 2013); there is no evidence of success in removing sponsors or changing attitudes among motorsport fans as a consequence of such efforts. Group One takes asymmetric actions against Group Two, based on the strategies of regular armies against *guerrilla*.

Alternatives come from Group Four as well as Five. Australia's Save Albert Park protestors gathered evidence that runs counter to the boosterism that governs Grands Prix (Campbell, 2013), producing kits on the legal, economic, environmental, and traffic implications for birdlife, waterways, trees, public utilisation of the venue, noise, trash, and carbon emissions of the Melbourne event (Miller, 2018a).[14] But legislation exempted it from environmental protection. The state proclaimed that "The Grand Prix Act has been principally designed to ensure that the over 400,000 spectators who attend this event … won't have their fun spoiled by political protest groups" (quoted in Lowes, 2004, p. 80).

The executives triumph, again and again; so when Group One's 2023 racing calendar was released, it might have been designed to maximise flying between destinations, "with the teams and drivers going from Europe to Canada and then back to Europe" (Brinsford, 2023).

Conclusion

This all looks rather grim. But there are positive signs, as we have noted. Group Four's League of Fans *Sports Manifesto* opposes unbridled commodification, in favour of sports' capacity for cultural and civic expression, and calls for citizenship through sports activism. We see similar tendencies in college sports fans' attitudes to the environment (Casper et al., 2014).

Calgary, Innsbruck, Oslo, Bern, and Rome recently rejected hosting the Olympics (Valvur, 2018). Whereas the 2004 Games attracted 11 bids, for 2024 the number was two (Evans, 2018). As we have seen, a few pro football clubs and their supporters are on the ball (Mabon, 2022; Weston, 2022). Most specifically, Football for Future recognises our impending catastrophe.[15] Plans to impose a new Formula One track in Rio were abandoned following opposition to the destruction of native forest, while the disgraceful, but telling, link between the sport and militarism was checked when air-force flybys prior to races were prohibited due to their environmental impact (Benson, 2022).

Within Group Five, footballers Héctor Bellerín promised to pay for three thousand trees to be planted for every game his side won in June 2020 (OneTreePlanted, n.d.) and Morten Throsby founded WePlayGreen, which brings fellow-pros and their followers together to protect the planet.[16] English Football League club Forest Green Rovers has been declared the "world's greenest" sports team (Elder, 2017) and was certified by the UN as the first "carbon neutral club" (Warshaw, 2018). And Ireland's Bohemian FC, owned by its members, has set up an international Football for Climate Justice project.[17]

The struggle remains tough. In this complex medley, Group Three needs to counter Group One's hegemony and quieten Group Two's missteps by researching, criticising, publicising, and learning reciprocally with Groups Four and Five. For significant numbers of the popular classes and athletes are working out that the devastation of big-time sports isn't worth the joy they can bring.

Notes

1. www.youtube.com/watch?v=mGgh4Ii-7Zg&ab_channel=SmithsonianChannel.
2. www.youtube.com/watch?v=WHt0eAdCCns&ab_channel=Olympics.
3. https://olympics.com/ioc/members.
4. https://sdgs.un.org/goals.
5. www.youtube.com/watch?v=-CgvRsX38As&ab_channel=IOCMedia.
6. www.youtube.com/watch?v=0bXJGZgR1BU&t=14s&ab_channel=InsiderBusiness.
7. https://twitter.com/sayakasofiamori?ref_src=twsrc%5Egoogle%7Ctwcamp%5Eserp%7Ctwgr%5Eauthor.
8. www.bbc.co.uk/news/av/world-asia-58110846.
9. https://olympics.com/athlete365/games-time/beat-the-heat/.
10. www.youtube.com/watch?v=ndfGkheP7H4&ab_channel=euronews.
11. www.youtube.com/watch?v=_SPa4zpuC0Y; www.youtube.com/watch?v=S-HA7HKSD9I.
12. http://fsf.org.uk/campaigns/away-fans/twentys-plenty/; www.fcstpauli.com/home/news; www.fanseurope.org/en/news/news-3/1167-add-meeting-eng.html; www.footballvhomophobia.com/.
13. www.fsf.org.uk; www.garethhuwdavies.com/environment/environment_blog/newcastle-united-football-club-top-of-the-green-league/.
14. http://save-albert-park.org.au/sapweb/kits.html.
15. https://footballforfuture.org/.
16. https://weplaygreen.com/.
17. https://bohemianfc.com/?page_id=19070.

References

Ahmed, F. & Pretorius, L. (2010). Mega-events and environmental impacts: The 2010 FIFA World Cup in South Africa. *Alternation 17*(2), 274–96.

Annear, M., Kidokoro, T., & Shimizu, Y. (2021). Existential threats to the Summer Olympic and Paralympic Games? A review of emerging environmental health risks. *Reviews on Environmental Health 36*(2), 159–66.

Armour, N. (2014, May 7). NBC Universal pays $7.75 billion for Olympics through 2032. *USA Today* https://eu.usatoday.com/story/sports/olympics/2014/05/07/nbc-olympics-broadcast-rights-2032/8805989/

Armstrong, G. (1998). *Football hooligans: Knowing the score*. Oxford: Berg.

Armstrong, G. & Young, M. (1997). Legislators and interpreters: The law and 'football hooligans'. In *Entering the field: New perspectives on world football*, edited by Armstrong, G. & Giulianotti, R. 175–91. Oxford: Berg.

Ashoo, S. (2021, December 3). Climate crisis: How can football make a difference? *Euronews*. www.euronews.com/2021/10/28/the-climate-crisis-why-football-can-no-longer-hide

Associated Press. (2021, July 26). Pandemic Olympics endured heat, and now a typhoon's en route. *NBC News* www.nbcnews.com/news/world/pandemic-olympics-endured-heat-now-typhoon-s-en-route-n1274976

Bashir, N. Y., Lockwood, P., Chasteen, A. L., Nadolny, D., & Noyes, I. (2013). The ironic impact of activists: Negative stereotypes reduce social change influence. *European Journal of Social Psychology 43*(7), 614–26.

Beck, U. (2009). *World at risk*. (C. Cronin, trans). Cambridge: Polity.

Benson, A. (2019, October 24). Mexican Grand Prix: Lewis Hamilton defends environmental social media posts. *BBC*. www.bbc.com/sport/formula1/50176037

Benson, A. (2022, January 21). Formula 1 bans military air displays at Grands Prix. *BBC* www.bbc.com/sport/formula1/60082961

Benson, A. (2023, February 7). Formula 1 president Stefano Domenicali says the sport will 'never put a gag on anyone'. *BBC* www.bbc.co.uk/sport/formula1/64563358

Bernard, P., Chevance, G., Kingsbury, C., Baillot, A., Romain, A. J., Molinier, V., Gadais, T., & Dancause, K. N. (2021). Climate change, physical activity and sport: A systematic review. *Sports Medicine 51*, 1041–059.

Bonnemains, A. (2014). Quelle capacité d'adaptation pour les stations de sports d'hiver de haute altitude des Alpes du Nord? Mise en regard de la vulnerabilitié territorial et du plan énergie climat territorial Tarentaise Vanoise. *Sud-Ouest Européen 37*, 29–39.

Boykoff, J. & Gaffney, C. (2020). The Tokyo 2020 Games and the end of Olympic history. *Capitalism Nature Socialism 31*(2), 1–19.

Brinsford, J. (2023, January 18). Formula 1 carbon footprint slammed after 2023 calendar release. *Newsweek* www.newsweek.com/formula-one-carbon-footprint-slammed-2023-calendar-1774806

Campbell, R. (2013). *Blowout! A cost benefit analysis of the Australian Grand Prix*. Economists at Large www.ecolarge.com/wp-content/uploads/2013/03/Blowout-A-cost-benefit-analysis-of-the-Australian-Grand-Prix-Ecolarge-Final.pdf

Carbon Market Watch. (2022, May). *Poor tackling: Yellow card for 2022 FIFA World Cup's carbon neutrality claim* https://carbonmarketwatch.org/wp-content/uploads/2022/05/Poor-tackling_-Yellow-card-for-2022-FIFA-1.pdf

Carter, A. (2010). *Direct action and liberal democracy*. London: Routledge.

Casper, J. M., Pfahl, M. E., & McCullough, B. (2014). Intercollegiate sport and the environment: Examining fan engagement based on athletics department sustainability efforts. *Journal of Issues in Intercollegiate Athletics 7*, 65–91.

The Climate Coalition. (2018). *Game changer: How climate change is impacting sports in the UK* www.theclimatecoalition.org/gamechanger

Coleman, M. (2023, February 25). 'Drive to Survive' season five: Our top five takeaways. *The Athletic* https://theathletic.com/4251298/2023/02/25/drive-to-survive-season-5-takeaways-f1/

Colorado rejects Olympics. (1972, November 8). *Ludington Daily News*, 5.

Conn, D. (2017). *The fall of the house of FIFA*. New York: Nation Books.

Cooper, A. (2013, August 25). Greenpeace launches attack on Shell Oil at Belgian Grand Prix. *Autoweek* www.tirebusiness.com/article/20130826/NEWS/130829930/greenpeace-launches-attack-on-shell-at-belgian-grand-prix

Coulibaly, T. Y., Wakamatsu, M. H., & Managi, S. (2022). The use of geographically weighted regression to improve information from satellite night light data in evaluating the economic effects of the 2010 FIFA World Cup. *Area Development and Policy 7*(4), 463–81.

Crabb, L. A. H. (2018). Debating the success of carbon-offsetting projects at sports mega-events: A case from the 2014 FIFA World Cup. *Journal of Sustainable Forestry 37*(2), 178–96.

Croco, S. E., Cunningham, K. G., & Taylor, V. (2023). Protests and persuasion: Partisanships [*sic*.] effect on evaluating nonviolent tactics in the United States. *Journal of Peace Research* https://journals.sagepub.com/doi/pdf/10.1177/00223433221146577?casa_token=hRXtlZhZdg4AAAAA:58QWGzrpcRAp54UEwUw2g2rIcgYGAudlqQdPvo1aLCL04f4ls0EaBiqrBDEmo0rXFrqlYfAE_UZd71I

Davies, G. H. (2019, February 5). Which football club tops the green league? www.garethhuwdavies.com/environment/environment_blog/which-football-club-top-the-green-league/

de Coninck, H. (2021, November 18). Heleen de Coninck on the value of activists to spur policymakers. *Economist* www.economist.com/by-invitation/2021/11/18/heleen-de-coninck-on-the-value-of-activists-to-spur-policymakers

Diaz, S. (2022, June 15). The art of manipulation: How oil giants are greenwashing with cultural sponsorship. *Greenpeace* www.greenpeace.org/international/story/54285/the-art-of-manipulation-how-oil-giants-are-greenwashing-with-cultural-sponsorship/

The Economist. (2014, October 17). Childish Arguments. www.economist.com/blogs/democracyinamerica/2014/10/greenpeace-lego-and-shell

Eden, S. (2004). Greenpeace. *New Political Economy 9*(4), 595–610.

Elder, A. (2017, September 21). The world's greenest sports team is a century-old football club in a tiny English town. *New Yorker* www.newyorker.com/sports/sporting-scene/the-worlds-greenest-sports-team-is-a-century-old-football-club-in-a-tiny-english-town

Engar, A. & du Toit, J. (2023). Cape Town's 2010 FIFA World Cup stadium location and its spatial and environmental justice implications. In *Sport stadiums and environmental justice*, edited by Kellison, T. 158–71. London: Routledge.

Erhart, I. (2014). United in protest: From 'living and dying with our colours' to 'let all the colours of the world unite'. *International Journal of the History of Sport 31*(14), 1724–738.

Estrada, D. (2010, June 3). World Cup 2010: Climate change fouls and goals. *Guardian* www.theguardian.com/environment/2010/jun/03/climate-change-world-cup

Evans, G. (2018, November 18). Olympic Games: Why cities are snubbing the 'greatest show on Earth'. *BBC News* www.bbc.co.uk/news/world-46236682

Evers, C. W. (2019). Polluted leisure. *Leisure Sciences 41*(5), 423–40.

Falkenberg, M., Galeazzi, A., Torricelli, M., Di Marco, N., Larosa, F., Sas, M., Mekacher, A., Pearce, W., Zollo, F., Quattrociocchi, W., & Baroncheli, A. (2022). Growing polarization around climate change on social media. *Nature Climate Change 12*, 1114–121.

Ferrisi, M. (2020, July 4). La Formule 1 peut-elle vraiment devenir plus écologique? *Ecolosport* https://ecolosport.fr/blog/2020/07/04/la-formule-1-peut-elle-vraiment-devenir-plus-ecologique/

FIA Thursday Press Conference—Mexico. (2019, October 24). www.formula1.com/en/latest/article.fia-thursday-press-conference-mexico-2019.3SPDFzhVfpABUf50XcphLW.html

Fians, G. (2022, March 18). Prefigurative politics. *Open Encyclopedia of Anthropology* www.anthroencyclopedia.com/entry/prefigurative-politics

FIFA. (2019). *2018 FIFA World Cup Russia™ Sustainability Report* https://img.fifa.com/image/upload/ya7pgcyslxpzlqmjkykg.pdf

Football Supporters Association. (n.d.). https://thefsa.org

Friedman, U. (2016, August 17). The saddest Olympic celebration. *The Atlantic* www.theatlantic.com/international/archive/2016/08/david-katoatau-olympics-kiribati/496175/

Fruh, K., Archer, A., & Wojtowicz, J. (2023). Sportswashing: Complicity and corruption. *Sport, Ethics and Philosophy 17*(1), 101–18.

Gaind, N. (2016, August 31). Most cities too hot to host 2088 Summer Olympics. *Nature* www.nature.com/articles/nature.2016.20503

Galbiati, C. (2013, December 16). St. Pauli F. C. de Hamburgo: Una hinchada que ondea la bandera pirate. *El Libertario* http://periodicoellibertario.blogspot.se/2013/12/st-pauli-fc-de-hamburgo-una-hinchada.html

Giacomini, T. & Turner, T. (2015). The 2014 people's climate march and flood Wall Street civil disobedience: Making the transition to a post-fossil capitalist, commoning civilization. *Capitalism Nature Socialism 26*(2), 27–45.

Giulianotti, R. (1999). *Football: A sociology of the global game*. Cambridge: Polity.

Global Witness. (2016). *Wilful ignorance: How Japan's voluntary approach is failing to stop the trade in illegal timber* www.globalwitness.org/en/reports/wilful-ignorance

Graeber, D. (2002). The new anarchists. *New Left Review*, 13 http://newleftreview.org/II/13/david-graeber-the-new-anarchists

Grano, D. A. & Butterworth, M. L., eds (2019). *Sport, rhetoric, and political struggle*. New York: Peter Lang.

Grant, W. (2004). Pressure politics: The changing world of pressure groups. *Parliamentary Affairs 57*(2), 408–19.

Grohmann, K. (2017, September 11). Olympics: NGOs complain to IOC over Tokyo Games environmental record. *Reuters* www.reuters.com/article/us-olympics-tokyo-environment-idUSKCN1BM2AZ

Gulliver, R. E., Star, C., Fielding. K. S., & Louis, W. R. (2022). A systematic review of the outcomes of sustained environmental collective action. *Environmental Science and Policy 133*, 180–92.

Hilburg, J. (2019, January 16). Kengo Kuma is crafting a timber temple to sports for the 2020 Olympics. *The Architect's Paper* www.archpaper.com/2019/01/kengo-kuma-2020-tokyo-olympic-national-stadium/#gallery-0-slide-0

Hometree. (2022). How much will it cost to power the World Cup this winter? www.hometree.co.uk/articles/how-much-will-it-cost-to-power-the-world-cup-this-winter/?referrer=611041&awc=17019_1678021720_6262d94f1cc551a7a7ddc83d0101c338&utm_source=AWIN&utm_medium=affiliate&utm_campaign=Sub+Networks&utm_content=78888-Skimlinks

Hsu, T. (2021, August 5). NBC tries to salvage a difficult Olympics. *New York Times* www.nytimes.com/2021/08/05/business/media/nbc-olympics-tv-ratings.html

International Olympic Committee. (2018). *Carbon footprint methodology for the Olympic Games*. https://library.olympic.org/Default/doc/SYRACUSE/184686/carbon-footprint-methodology-for-the-olympic-games-international-olympic-committee?_lg=fr-FR

Jennings, A. & Sambrook, C. (2000). *The great Olympic swindle: When the world wanted its Games back*. New York: Simon & Schuster.

Jorgenson, A. K. & Clark, B. (2016). The temporal stability and developmental differences in the environmental impacts of militarism: The treadmill of destruction and consumption-based carbon emissions. *Sustainability Science 26*(11), 505–14.

Kay, S. (2019, April 22). Winter is going: How climate change is imperiling outdoor sporting heritage. *Sports Illustrated* www.si.com/nhl/2019/04/22/climate-change-canada-winter-sports-hockey-backyard-rinks

Keoghan, J. (2014). *Punk football: The rise of fan ownership in English football*. Worthing: Pitch Publishing.

Lee, C. W. (2019, October 10). Tokyo braces for the hottest Olympics ever. *New York Times* www.nytimes.com/2019/10/10/sports/tokyo-braces-for-the-hottest-olympics-ever.html

Lei, T-H. & Wang, F. (2021). Looking ahead of 2021 Tokyo Summer Olympic Games: How does humid heat affect endurance performance? Insight into physiological mechanism and heat-related illness prevention strategies. *Journal of Thermal Biology 99*, 1–7.

Lester, L. (2019). *Global trade and mediatised environmental protest: The view from here*. London: Palgrave Macmillan.

Levermore, R. (2011). Sport-for-development and the 2010 Football World Cup. *Geography Compass 5*(12), 886–97.

Levermore, R. (2012). The paucity of, and dilemma in, evaluating corporate social responsibility for development through sport. *Third World Quarterly 32*(3), 551–69.

Lewis Hamilton: Social media post says he feels 'like giving up on everything'. (2019, October 15). *BBC* www.bbc.com/sport/formula1/50061569

Lowes, M. (2004). Neoliberal power politics and the controversial siting of the Australian Grand Prix motorsport event in an urban park. *Loisir et société/Society and Leisure 27*(1), 69–88.

Mabon, L. (2022). Football and climate change: What do we know, and what is needed for an evidence-informed response? *Climate Policy* https://doi.org/10.1080/14693062.2022.2147895

Malhado, A. C. M. & Rothfuss, R. (2013). Transporting 2014 FIFA World Cup to sustainability: Exploring residents' and tourists' attitudes and behaviours. *Journal of Policy Research in Tourism, Leisure and Events 5*(3), 252–69.

Marire, J. (2022). Effect of government spending on total factor productivity in South Africa. *European Journal of Economics, Law and Social Sciences 6*(1), 435–52.

Martin, L. (2019, February 6). Climate change set to disrupt Australia's summer sports calendar. *Guardian* www.theguardian.com/environment/2019/feb/06/climate-change-set-to-disrupt-australias-summer-sports-calendar

McCarthy, J. (2021, December 2). Why is direct action essential for climate justice? *Global Citizen* www.globalcitizen.org/en/content/direct-action-for-the-climate-crisis/

McCarthy, M. (2009, December 8). Football's carbon footprint comes under fire. *Independent* www.independent.co.uk/environment/climate-change/footballs-carbon-footprint-comes-under-fire-1836035.html

McCullough, B. P. & Kellison, T. B. (2018). An introduction to environmental sustainability and sport. *Routledge handbook of sport and the environment*. Ed. McCullough, B. P. & Kellison, T. B. London: Routledge. 3–10.

McDonald, S. (2020, March 25). The reason why Olympics in 2021 will still be called the 2020 Olympic Games. *Newsweek* www.newsweek.com/reason-why-olympics-2021-will-still-called-olympic-2020-games-1494333

McGregor, C. (2015). Direct climate action as public pedagogy: The cultural politics of the Camp for Climate Action. *Environmental Politics 24*(3), 343–62.

McHale, K. (2019). Give the fans what they really want: How professional sports stadiums across the world can positively impact the environment. *Texas Environmental Law Journal 49*(1), 127–58.

McKie, R., Savage, M., & Cornwall, P. (2019, May 11). As English fans get set to cross Europe, anger rises at football's carbon bootprint. *Guardian* www.theguardian.com/environment/2019/may/11/anger-carbon-bootprint-english-football-finals-champions-league-europa-league

Merino, D. (2020, July 23). The first undeniable climate change deaths. *Slate* https://slate.com/technology/2020/07/climate-change-deaths-japan-2018-heat-wave.html

Miller, T. (2018a). *Greenwashing sport*. London: Routledge.

Miller, T. (2018b). We are all activists now. *Workplace 30*, 70–80.

Montague, J. (2010, August 20). Punks, prostitutes and St. Pauli: Inside soccer's coolest club. *CNN* http://edition.cnn.com/2010/SPORT/football/08/18/football.st.pauli.punks/index.html

M. S. (2019, November 14). Youth movements are the fool's gold of politics. *Economist* www.economist.com/open-future/2019/11/14/youth-movements-are-the-fools-gold-of-politics

Müller, M. (2015). (Im-)mobile policies: Why sustainability went wrong in the 2014 Olympics in Sochi. *European Urban and Regional Studies 22*(2), 191–209.

Müller, M., Gogishvili, D., Wolfe, S. D. (2022). The structural deficit of the Olympics and the World Cup: Comparing costs against revenues over time. *EPA: Economy and Space 54*(6), 1200–218.

Müller, M., Gogishvili, D., Wolfe, S. D., Gaffney, C., Hug, M., & Leick, A. (2023). Peak event: The rise, crisis and potential decline of the Olympic Games and the World Cup. *Tourism Management 95*, 104657.

Müller, M., Wolfe, S. D., Gaffney, C., Gogishvili, D., Hug, M., & Leick, A. (2021). An evaluation of the sustainability of the Olympic Games. *Nature Sustainability 4*, 340–48.

Münter, L. (n.d.). www.leilani.green/

Nakagawa, S. (2018, September 2). Criticism grows against gov't 'urban mines' plan for Tokyo 2020 medals. *The Mainchi* https://mainichi.jp/english/articles/20180902/p2a/00m/0na/012000c

Nowak, A. S., Kennelley, G. E., Krabak, B. J., Roberts, W. O., Tenforde, K. M., & Tenforde, A. S. (2022). Endurance athletes and climate change. *Journal of Climate Change and Health 6*, 100118.

OneTreePlanted. (n.d.). https://bellerintrees.raisely.com/

Pato, I. (2021, September 1). In Livorno, Italy's most famous left-wing football club is fighting to survive. *Jacobin* https://jacobin.com/2021/09/livorno-football-club-italy-communism

Portillo, M. (2022, March 4). Alonso: 'Estoy al 100% y hay que ser rápidos en la pista y en la fábrica'. *Forbes España* https://forbes.es/lifestyle/141598/alonso-estoy-al-100-y-hay-que-ser-rapidos-en-la-pista-y-en-la-fabrica%ef%bf%bc/

Protect Our Winters. (2019). https://protectourwinters.org/about-us

Protect Our Winters. (2023, February 27). *Our sport is endangered.* https://protectourwinters.eu/wp-content/uploads/2023/02/open-letter-to-FIS-230209.pdf

Rainforest Action Network. (2018). *Broken promises: A case study on how the Tokyo 2020 Games and Japanese financiers are fueling land-grabbing and rainforest destruction in Indonesia.* www.ran.org/wp-content/uploads/2018/11/BrokenPromises.pdf

Raji, K. (2022, November 17). Qatar 2022: The environmental cost of the FIFA World Cup. *Earth* https://earth.org/qatar-2022/

Ramaswamy, C. (2015, November 30). Hosting the Olympics: The competition noone wants to win. *Guardian* www.theguardian.com/sport/shortcuts/2015/nov/30/hosting-olympics-hamburg-drop-out-2024-games

Republic of South Africa. (2004). *Accelerated and shared growth initiative* www.daff.gov.za/docs/GenPub/asgisa.pdf

Republic of South Africa, Department of Environmental Affairs and Tourism, Norwegian Agency for Development Cooperation, & Norwegian Embassy in South Africa. (2009). *Feasibility study for a carbon neutral 2010 FIFA World Cup in South Africa* www.norway.org.za/NR/rdonlyres/3E6BB1B1FD2743E58F5B0BEFBAE7D958/114457/FeasibilityStudyforaCarbonNeutral2010FIFAWorldCup.pdf

Richards, G. (2021, March 31). Nico Rosberg: 'To do good you need to get out there, you can't sit in a cave'. *Guardian* www.theguardian.com/sport/2021/mar/31/nico-rosberg-to-do-good-you-need-to-get-out-there-you-cant-sit-in-a-cave

Rios, B. (2020, September 7). The French MEP bashing football clubs over their flying habit. *Euractiv* www.euractiv.com/section/health-consumers/news/the-french-mep-bashing-football-clubs-over-their-flying-habit/

Rowe, D. (2004). *Sport, culture and the media: The unruly trinity*, 2nd ed. Maidenhead: Open University Press.

Rutenberg, J. (2000, September 21). Sydney 2000: Television; NBC's ratings for Olympics are worst ever. *New York Times* www.nytimes.com/2000/09/20/sports/sydney-2000-television-nbc-s-ratings-for-olympics-are-worst-ever.html

Samuel, S. & Stubbs, W. (2013). Green Olympics, green legacies? An exploration of the environmental legacies of the Olympic Games. *International Review for the Sociology of Sport, 48*(4), 485–504.

Sant'Anna School of Advanced Studies, Institute of Management. (2020). *The environmental awareness and behaviour of professional football supporters: An empirical survey* https://lifetackle.eu/assets/files/LIFE_TACKLE_Report_on_supporters_survey.pdf

Santini D. & Henderson, H. (2021). The winners and losers in the race to environmental sustainability: A ranking of Summer Olympic International Federation progress. *Emerald Open Research 3*(12). https://doi.org/10.35241/emeraldopenres.14195.1

Schimmel, K. S., Harrington, C. L., & Bielby, D. D. (2007). Keep your fans to yourself: The disjuncture between sport studies' and pop culture studies' perspectives on fandom. *Sport in Society 10*(4), 580–600.

Selectra. (2020, January 22). *What happens when everyone in the UK watches the World Cup at the same time?* https://selectra.co.uk/energy/news/world/world-cup-2018-electricity-surges

Shenker, J. (2023, March 6). The existential question for climate activists: Have disruption tactics stopped working? *Guardian* www.theguardian.com/commentisfree/2023/mar/06/british-eco-activists-disruption-extinction-rebellion

Siemaszko, C. (2021, July 24). Heat wave hits Tokyo as Olympic organizers battle to keep Covid rates down. *NBC News* www.nbcnews.com/news/olympics/heat-wave-hits-tokyo-olympic-organizers-battle-keep-covid-rates-n1274899

Sin, B. (2014, February 12). All the modern Olympic mascots in one adorable infographic. *Sports Illustrated* www.si.com/extra-mustard/2014/02/12/olympics-mascots-infographic

Sturrock, L. (2018, July 12). The environmental impact of the World Cup: Are FIFA scoring sustainability goals? *thegreatProjects* www.thegreatprojects.com/blog/environmental-impact-of-the-world-cup

Tagsold, C. (2010). Modernity, space, and national representation at the Tokyo Olympics 1964. *Urban History 37*(2), 289–300.

Thompson, E. P. (1971). The moral economy of the English crowd in the eighteenth century. *Past & Present 50*, 76–136.

Timms, A. (2021, August 2). NBC paid $7.75bn for its Olympic rights ... And we got televisual vomit. *Guardian* www.theguardian.com/sport/2021/aug/02/nbc-olympic-coverage-peacock-replays-primetime?CMP=Share_iOSApp_Other

Tóffano Pereira, R. P., Filimonau, V., & Mattos Ribeiro, G. (2019). Score a goal for climate: Assessing the carbon footprint of travel patterns of the English Premier League clubs. *Journal of Cleaner Production 227*, 167–77.

Tokyo Organising Committee of the Olympic and Paralympic Games. (2021). *Update to the sustainability pre-Games report* https://gtimg.tokyo2020.org/image/upload/production/cas22cdv09dc0h9yaf5t.pdf

Tomizawa, R. (2016, February 3). Olympia cigarettes: How the 1964 Tokyo Olympics led to increased cases of lung cancer in Japan today. *The Olympians from 1964 to 2020* https://theolympians.co/2016/02/03/olympia-cigarettes-how-the-1964-tokyo-olympics-led-to-increased-cases-of-lung-cancer-in-japan-today/

Tomlinson, A. (2014). *FIFA (Fédération Internationale de Football Association): The men, the myths and the money.* London: Routledge.

Totten, M. (2013). Sport activism and political praxis within the FC Sankt Pauli fan subculture. *Play Left Wing* www.playleftwing.org/wp-content/uploads/2013/10/Fan-Culture-and-Sport-Activism1.pdf

UEFA. (2020). Venues confirmed for EURO 2020 www.uefa.com/uefaeuro-2020/news/025e-0fac6d3ee9e4-85b1a76389ea-1000/

United Nations Commission on Sustainable Development. (1998). Chapeau for business and industry. *Background Paper No. 1* www.un.org/documents/ecosoc/cn17/1998/background/ecn171998-bp1.htm

Vaccaro, A. (2015, April 2). They just don't want the Olympics. *Boston* www.boston.com/news/local-news/2015/04/02/they-just-dont-want-the-olympics

Valvur, A. (2018, November 14). 6 cities that rejected the Olympics. *DW* www.dw.com/en/6-cities-that-rejected-the-olympics/a-46289852

Venzon, A. & Cahen-Salvador, C. (2019, November 1). Party politics is dying, so make citizen movements the new unifier. *Economist* www.economist.com/open-future/2019/11/01/party-politics-is-dying-so-make-citizen-movements-the-new-unifier

Vidal, J. (2011, September 15). Greenpeace at 40: A global brand in good health or an out-of-touch bureaucracy? *Guardian* www.theguardian.com/environment/2011/sep/15/greenpeace-40-year-anniversary

Viñas, C. & Parra, N. (2020). *St. Pauli: Another football is possible* (L. Stobart, trans.). London: Pluto Press.

Voice of America. (2021, July 17). A greener Games? Tokyo's environmental impact. *VoA News.* https://www.voanews.com/a/east-asiapacific_greener-games-tokyos-environmental-impact/6208269.html

Wade, S. (2020, March 25). Tokyo's delayed Olympics: Who pays bills for another year? *AP* https://apnews.com/article/virus-outbreak-ap-top-news-tokyo-sports-general-japan-a882d4bbe66941f9313153e3409ca799

Wallace, J. P., Widenman, E., & McDermott, R. J. (2019). Physical activity and climate change: Clear and present danger? *Health Behavior and Policy Review 6*(5), 534–545.

Ware, A. (2021, July 29). Tokyo's Games are harming the nuclear weapons ban movement. *The Nation* www.thenation.com/article/society/tokyo-olympics-nuclear-weapons/

Warren, G. S. (2020). Mega sports events have mega environmental and social consequences. *Missouri Law Review*, 85(2), 495–524.

Warshaw, A. (2018, August 1). Doing the right thing. Forest Green Rovers are world's first UN-certified carbon neutral club. *Inside World Football* www.insideworldfootball.com/2018/08/01/right-thing-forest-green-rovers-worlds-first-un-certified-carbon-neutral-club

West, L. (2016, August 10). How to talk about female Olympians without being a regressive creep: A handy guide. *Guardian* www.theguardian.com/commentisfree/2016/aug/09/female-olympians-guide-gaffes-athletes-sports-makeup-shorts-marital-status-lindy-west

Weston, B. (2022, May 6). Football must do more to tackle climate change: This is how clubs and fans can help. *Guardian* www.theguardian.com/football/blog/2022/may/06/football-must-do-more-to-tackle-climate-change-this-is-how-clubs-and-fans-can-help

Whiting, R. (2014, October 24). Negative impact of 1964 Olympics profound. *Japan Times* www.japantimes.co.jp/sports/2014/10/24/olympics/olympics-negative-impact-1964-olympics-profound/

Wilburn, K. M. & Wilburn, R. (2011). Achieving social license to operate using stakeholder theory. *Journal of International Business Ethics* 4(2), 3–16.

Wilson, S. (2012). Exhibiting a new Japan: The Tokyo Olympics of 1964 and Expo '70 in Osaka. *Historical Research* 85(227), 159–78.

Yates, L. (2015). Rethinking prefiguration: Alternatives, micropolitics and goals in social movements. *Social Movement Studies: Journal of Social, Cultural and Political Protest* 14(1), 1–21.

Zirin, D. & J. Boykoff. (2019, July 23). These women have lost their homes to the Olympics in Tokyo—Twice. *The Nation* www.thenation.com/article/archive/tokyo-olympics-displacement/

PART VII

Future directions and research methods for social justice

PART VI

36
RESEARCH METHODS FOR SPORT, LEISURE, AND SOCIAL JUSTICE

Ian Jones and Jayne Caudwell

Introduction

As Smith et al. (2023) suggest, research in sport (as well as leisure we would argue) has traditionally been carried out *on* people, doing things *to* them or describing and explaining their experiences *for* them. Such research is then often published in academic journals, often with arguably limited impact beyond that on the immediate academic community. In this chapter, we argue that social justice research involves doing research *with* people, collaborating at all stages of the research process in order to facilitate full and equal participation of all groups in sport, and an equitable allocation of resources (Chapman & Schwartz, 2012). Undertaking social justice research presents a number of theoretical, methodological and personal challenges, especially with regards to issues such as positionality, power relations, and reflexivity (Atkins & Duckworth, 2019). Whilst some of these challenges are to some extent present in most research, this chapter explores some of those specific challenges faced by the researcher with an interest in sport, leisure, and social justice. The focus of this chapter is upon what Atkins and Duckworth (2019) define as "socially just research". By this, they refer to research that is not simply about social justice, but rather research that is socially just in the way that it is undertaken, compared to "research for social justice", which although still seeking to uncover, illuminate, or explain issues of social justice in sport and leisure, will do so with less reflection on the research process. This focus does not imply that socially just research is in any way superior to research for social justice; however, socially just research does have what we would argue to be a unique set of challenges and opportunities for the researcher.

The ethics of social justice research

It is useful to start with a brief discussion of the ethics of socially just research. Whilst all research is (or should be) concerned with ethics, the ethical dimension of social justice research is, we would argue, of paramount importance, and goes beyond the issues that would normally be associated with gaining ethical approval, such as not causing harm, the need for informed consent, voluntary participation, anonymity of participants, and storage of data. Whilst these are, of course, still an essential aspect of the research process for the social justice researcher, it is important to go beyond them, especially given that a mechanistic focus on gaining institutional approval may actually limit a deeper acknowledgement of and reflection upon the ethics of the overall research process (Greenbank, 2003). Traditional ethics approval processes also, it could be argued, lead to the researcher focusing on the ethics of the project, rather than the participants, whereby issues such as those related to data storage take precedence over the concerns, background, and positioning of those participating. As Petit (2020, p. 1) notes, reflection on deeper issues may be subsumed by the need to "neatly package research concerns; locate mitigating solutions before problems emerge through ethics approvals and committees; discuss issues within the confines of short methodology sections before moving on to 'important' discussions of findings". As such, the consideration of ethics for social justice research goes far beyond simplistic 'do no harm' assessments, and instead of separated from the research process become embedded within all aspects, not just as a tool to avoid harm but instead as a means to carefully consider and enhance the chosen methodology so that the research may be seen to instead 'do good'. One key aspect of this lies in the relationships between researcher, and those being researched, and the need for a collaborative, co-produced approach to research.

Epistemic violence and socially just research

Following on from the ethics of social justice research, it is important to introduce the concept of epistemic violence. This concept developed from Foucault's work surrounding the "episteme in Western thought ... as the anonymous codification and structure which determines the knowledge formation of a given epoch" (Bartels et al., 2019, p. 1). In other words, who determines legitimate knowledge and how do they legitimise it? The answers lie with who has power and dominance. Perhaps it is the post-colonial feminist Gayatari Chakravorty Spivak who illuminates the details of epistemic violence best through her work entitled "Can the Subaltern Speak?" (1988). The point she makes concerns who constructs knowledge of the 'other' and how do they construct it. For Spivak, the knowledge created about the 'subaltern', in particular Black and brown women and girls living in countries that are colonised by white people, is produced through the lens of whiteness, imperialism, and the colonial. So, for example, Ratna and Samie (2017) in their work on race, gender, and sport demonstrate "the largely positivistic, androcentric, assimilationist, ethnocentric and Eurocentric thinking which has colonised much of the scholarship in the sociology of sport" (p. 10), vis-à-vis women of colour. As such, women of colour have been denied an episteme – the starting place for knowledge formation – that is free from white Western processes, constructs and production of knowledge.

Critical engagement with the concept epistemic violence does not apply only to social justice research concerned with race, ethnicity, gender, and sport/leisure research; it can be applied to research that involves disability, international relations, sport for development and peace, and potentially sport mega events to name a few. For example, disabled scholars Ymous et al. (2020) write:

> Epistemic violence is violence against one's status as a knower; one's role as a creator and communicator of knowledge. It is the dismissal of people as credible sources of information, because of our presumptions about them, or because of how their communicative means (or what they have to communicate) clashes with how we would like to believe the world works.
>
> (p. 3)

In their paper on disability related technology research, disabled researchers Ymous et al. offer a series of vignettes to demonstrate how they "still face regular ableism" (p. 9) because of ableist ways of knowing and ableist research agendas. Additionally, they argue that in the technology research field:

> the perspectives of disabled people are actively erased in multiple ways: sometimes framed as 'personal' and 'emotional' and 'unscientific', sometimes due to a privileging of "medical expert" knowledge and carer's needs.
>
> (p. 9)

It is their challenge that provides an example of how research that might be deemed social justice research is not necessarily socially just research when it comes to the philosophical ethics underpinning ontology and epistemology.

A similar challenge has been discussed in sport and leisure research, particularly in Sport for Development and Peace (e.g. Darnell & Millington, 2018) in terms of the decolonial (Hayhurst, 2016) and orientalism (Darnell, 2014). Brunner (2021) in her interrogation of International Relations offers a detailed and lengthy account of epistemic violence, demonstrating that it is inherent within the disciplinary field. In her call to "un/doing" epistemic violence (p. 207), she focuses on a delinking from dominant paradigms through "decentring and re-signifying conventional Eurocentric assumptions" (p. 208). Chilisa and Mertens (2021) offer an example of how this can be achieved in regard to the Sustainable Development Goals and the Western cultural lens that determines their evaluation. Chilisa and Mertens (2021) take a Made in Africa Evaluation (MAE) approach because:

> It is a deliberate attempt to adapt evaluation tools, instruments, strategies, and theory models, as well as to develop evaluation practice, theory, and methodologies emanating from local cultures, Indigenous knowledge systems, African philosophies, and African world views ...
>
> (p. 245)

Indigenous epistemologies and methodologies are emerging in sport and leisure research. For example, recent work critically analyses the ways historical narrative and 'the archive'/'Imperial Archive' produce knowledge that reflects the "dominant epistemologies of colonial(ist) sport history" (MacLean, 2019, p. 189).

Epistemic violence is an important concept and process when we think about, devise and design socially just sport and leisure research projects. Ontology and epistemology are the starting places when it comes to the creation of knowledge. It is important that these starting places are socially just and not violating research participants as legitimate knowers, free from tradition and established paradigmatic assumptions of how knowledge can and cannot be produced.

Co-production and socially just research in sport and leisure

The ideas of co-productive, participative and collaborative research are clearly important to social justice research but also to some extent contested in terms of their meaning and application. The idea of co-production is crucial in this regard. As Smith et al. (2023, p. 160) argue:

> how can researchers work with individuals or groups typically referred to in the literature as lay people, stakeholders, value holders, citizens, service users, patients, public

contributors, community members, and (end) knowledge users? How can those with such lived experience be afforded more power in academia to ensure that research agendas and outputs address their needs, concerns, and preferences? How can research be done with or led by partners in ways that are transformative, equitable, and impactful? How can we take more seriously knowledge translation and ensure that evidence informs action and theory informs practice? Whilst not without its complications or challenges, co-production has been put forward as a way of achieving all of this and more.

Rather than aim for a single encompassing definition of co-production, Smith, et al. (2023) go on to suggest that researchers should identify their choice of approach and allow their research to be evaluated against that choice. The two types of co-production that relate most closely to social justice research are first *integrated knowledge translation*, where researchers work collaboratively with stakeholders in a dynamic and iterative way throughout the entire research process, from developing aims and objectives, to collecting analysing and interpreting data, and implementing recommendations emerging from the research, which although having the potential to reduce the time period between research and implementation (Schaillée et al., 2018), may also benefit from being slow and protracted (Ugolotti, 2022).

There are three types of translation practices (Clavier et al., 2012), these being cognitive translation, focusing upon the meanings and content of the research, focusing on developing a shared vision for the aims of the research, strategic translation, focusing upon maintaining stakeholder interest and involvement in the research process, and logistic translation, involving the pragmatics of the research, for example handling budgets, or setting deadlines. Each of these benefit from intensive contact between researcher and stakeholders, allowing trust and shared learning, the dissemination of findings beyond 'traditional' academic outputs, and gaining external, rather than internal funding to undertake the research (Schaillée et al., 2018).

A second type of co-production is *equitable and experientially informed research*, perhaps the most common form within sport based contexts (Brinkley, *et al.*, 2022). Whilst integrated knowledge transfer may include collaborators with a lived experience of the issues being explored, for equitable and experientially informed research their involvement is an absolute necessity. This idea of participative research, and more specifically Participatory Action Research (PAR) emphasises the participation of, and action in research by the community (Atkins & Duckworth, 2019). This should go beyond simply developing relationships with the community so that they may, for example, allow access to data or explanation of key findings. Instead, as Spaaij et al. (2018) argue, it is much more than simply allowing participants to take part in the study. For true participatory research, Spaaij et al. note that there has to be alignment of power and control, positioning participants as "knowledgeable actors" (p. 26) at all stages of the research, from developing research aims to implementing any outcomes from the research. This final element is crucial within participatory research that takes a more activist stance, with participants able to take an active role in addressing the social inequalities that affect their circumstances.

Spaaij et al. (2018) go on to identify a three-dimensional model of participatory research. The three inter-related dimensions are:

1. The degree of participation – this refers to the extent to which participants are actively involved in the research as knowledgeable actors, possessing some power within the research process. Participation may be assessed first by scale, in terms of number of participants involved. When assessing the scale of involvement, it is important to not only

explore numbers involved but also the extent to which those privileged and those marginalised within the community being research have a voice.
2. The reconceptualisation of power relations – unlike more 'traditional' means of research, participants are seen as active and able members of the research team, and as such, researchers become facilitators and collaborators.
3. Reflexivity that goes beyond more common approaches that focus on the researcher's own identity-related characteristics, such as race, gender and so on, to a form of reflexivity that reflect upon the ideas of power and difference, and their role within the research process.

Petican et al. (2023) outline the challenges and opportunities in developing such co-produced research. Some of the key lessons were those of proactively building relationships that reconceptualise existing power relations, developing safe and collaborative spaces where voices that might otherwise not be heard have the opportunity to contribute, and trusting the process, especially in terms of the 'messy' and emergent nature of such collaboration through a discursive approach.

Choosing methods

Although some methods may be more challenging to use in a socially just way, that should neither rule some methods out, nor assign primacy to others. Whilst qualitative approaches dominate, there is still space for more positivist designs, although these tend to be restricted in terms of their ability to lead to truly collaborative and participatory research. They may also have a tendency to rationalise and reproduce existing structures and cultures (Dantley, 2002), and fail to acknowledge individual experiences, in the pursuit of a single 'truth' (Krane & Waldron, 2021) rather than the subjective realities of participants. Interpretative approaches to research are often characterised by their flexible and emergent nature. This should, ideally, be done as a collaborative exercise. Sanford et al. (2021), for example, in their study of sport, disability and an inclusive educational programme worked closely with a charity – Cambridge House – in a co-constructed research programme, where both academics and charity worked "collaboratively with Cambridge House, maintaining an ongoing conversation, with a commitment to sharing information that could assist in refining programme objectives, activities and intended outcomes" (pp. 154–155) to provide critical insights to improve the experience of participants.

The crucial questions for the researcher to ask are:

- What information do we need?
- What methods are able to provide the data to give us this information based on the epistemological and ontological assumptions underpinning the research?
- Are these methods readily accessible to all participants?
- Do these methods allow research to be participatory, rather than one way?
- How should these methods be used to ensure that they do not cause either social or psychological harm to participants?
- Am I making assumptions about participants, for example in terms of their expertise or knowledge?
- What will be the effect of the chosen method on each participant?
- How will participants themselves be involved in the questions that are asked?

If these questions are reflected upon, then it is clear that the choice of methods is something that should emerge through working with the community, rather than determined *a priori*.

Thus, questions could be asked of a researcher who consistently adheres to a single method or design at the expense of a more emergent, flexible design.

Despite growing diversity of methods, research into the sociology of sport and leisure is still dominated by interview, focus group and to a lesser extent, questionnaire based designs. These are also methods that may prove problematic to the socially just researcher. Although questionnaires may be useful to collect qualitative data, for example when they allow greater access to participants, whose voices might be otherwise unheard, for example Ison's (2009) study of 18–25-year-olds with cerebral palsy, or where sensitive topics are discussed, they may still exclude some, for example those with lower levels of literacy, or access to technology, and the data itself may lack the richness or depth (Braun et al., 2020). The advantages of interviews in terms of flexibility, the ability to account for participants with differing characteristics, and ability to follow up and develop key insights have been well documented, but even then, they have a number of concerns to the socially just researcher, specifically in terms of the power balance between interviewer and interviewee. Sometimes this may be addressed, for example using focus groups with children may reduce power issues that would occur with one to one interviews. Alternative methods are becoming increasingly common, and visual methods such as photo elicitation or digital storytelling are seen as beneficial in their ability to address and deconstruct power relations, promote community participation, and promote alternatives to 'traditional' methods rooted in colonial and imperial practices (McSweeney et al., 2023). Ugolotti (2022), for example, in his study of the relevance of parkour to young men of migrant origins in Italy included both photo-elicitation as well as the co-creation and co-production of a documentary film with his participants, allowing a truly rich and collaborative picture to emerge of their experiences. As well as what methods are used, the question of how they are used can also be explored to reduce discomfort, for example Hussain and Cunningham (2021), in their study of marginalised Pakistani women in sport, were able to use Skype interviews. Whilst the often cited benefits of proximity in interviews, such as the ability to develop trust and rapport, were perhaps absent, this was outweighed by the participants being able to be at home, in their "comfort zone" (p. 1058).

Positionality and reflexivity

The socially just researcher will have to reflect on a wide variety of questions regarding the choice and application of methods, as well as their own role as part of the research process. The questions that may be asked include:

- How do I reflect upon each participant, their unique characteristics, histories, experiences and expectations, rather than seeing participants as a homogenous sample?
- How do I act upon that reflection?
- How do my own characteristics, history and attitudes impact upon the research? In what way?
- How do I deal with potential perceived power imbalances between myself as researcher/expert and those being researched? How will such power balances impact participants.

It is also useful to recognise that reflexivity is a multi-layered concept, and this may help frame the researcher's discussion of positionality and reflexivity (Chiu, 2006; Nicholls, 2009). Self-reflexivity refers to the researcher's own position, assumptions, history, and experiences. Inter-personal reflexivity addresses the researcher's role in terms of working with others, the relationships that are formed, and how the characteristics of the research may impact upon the research process. The final layer of reflexivity is that of collective reflexivity, which explores how the collaboration between those researching, and those being researched impacted upon the research aims and the research process, and the subsequent effects upon participants in terms of whether the research was affirming, empowering or transformative.

Hussain and Cunningham (2021) in their research into how less well-known traditional sports offered opportunities for marginalised Pakistani women to participate in physical activity, are an example of how these issues can be explicitly acknowledged. They write, for example, how the primary investigator was a practising Muslim, also from Pakistan with six years' experience of working with marginalised women from the region. They acknowledge that having a male interviewer, female interviewees were reluctant to discuss issues related to sexuality and abuse by men, yet more willing to talk about the negative role of the Western world. Follow up questions were difficult if they addressed issues that were culturally inappropriate. Gender issues were highlighted in the reflexive journal:

> The baggage of false gender superiority is not easy for a Muslim man like me to hide. I have been trained from my birth to dominate women, and the women are being victimized for generations by a man like me, I can feel in their voice tone, the pain caused by men like me. It is difficult to explain in words the emotional tension and unease even in the digital environment that the participants and I go through. I try my level best to make them comfortable. Still, it is an uphill task for a Pakistani Muslim man researcher to create trust.
> (pp. 1056–1057)

It is important to see such a discussion as not having an 'end point'. Here the idea of 'cultural humility' becomes useful. The term 'cultural competence' has long been used within Sport Psychology, developing recognition that their clients should not be considered as a homogenous group, but more as "a mosaic of people with diverse customs and cultures" (Arthur & McMahon, 2005, p. 205). Whilst cultural competence is a useful concept to acknowledge such issues, there is a growing movement towards reframing the idea as cultural humility (Krane & Waldron, 2021), with the argument moving from an assumed end point (as implied by the term 'competence') to an acknowledgement that such reflection is never complete, either in terms of the experiences of the researcher, or those being researched.

Analysing data

Whilst the actual processes of data analysis for social justice research, whether that be through rich description, thematic analysis, or more quantitative forms of analysis will not necessarily differ, there needs to be coherence between the methods, designed to elicit and illuminate participant voices, and the analysis, which should ensure that those voices are both present and accurately presented. This goes beyond the more commonly used approach of 'member checking' (Lincoln & Guba, 1986), whereby conclusions may be 'tested' by participants confirming, or otherwise, the accuracy and interpretations of the data. Instead, it is important that analysis, as with the other elements of the research process, is seen as a collaborative process, with participants actively involved in the analysis of data where possible. In social justice research, however, such a practice may not always be productive, as power relations may lead participants to simply agree with the researcher's conclusions (Buchbinder, 2011), or there may even be the possibility of causing harm to participants (Candela, 2019) depending on the findings. Finally, participants may lack technical knowledge, for example with any quantitative analysis, to have a full role in the analysis of the data. Where participants are able to play an active role in the analysis of the data, however, the benefits are twofold. First, the quality of the research in terms of such concepts as credibility and authenticity may be enhanced. Second, it respects that the data comes from the participants, and that they have had an active role in its production, and thus should, ethically, have a similar role in its analysis to ensure that their voices are accurately represented.

Presenting research

The writing up and dissemination of social justice research goes beyond that normally associated with more traditional academic outputs, notably the journal article, book or conference paper. For example, working with a local organisation called Energise Me, Bournemouth University staff Jayne Caudwell and Daniel Lock completed Sport England-funded research that focused on "Pride in our Workforce", which was designed to explore:

1. The role the workforce plays in the LGBT+ community accessing physical activity and sport, and how the workforce affects and influences their experience as a participant.
2. How the actual and perceived barriers to participation can be identified and overcome by a workforce that has the skills, competencies and behaviours needed to engage the LGBT+ community, to increase participation in high quality physical activity experiences.
3. Whether the current workforce is representative of our local population and, if not, how we can increase the number of people from the LGBT+ community within the workforce.

The results from the on-line survey, focus group and interview research are captured in an industry-type report that is accessible to the local physical activity workforce involved in the study. The research underpins a globally available Internet resource that captures the findings and provides Pride in our Workforce scenario slides. See: www.energiseme.org/funding-support/insight-guides/pride-in-our-workforce-resource/.

It is the animation of the findings through illustrations taken during the focus groups that enables engagement beyond the standard academic output (Figure 36.1).

Issues of 'exit'

The issue of 'exit' from the research process is something that is often overlooked in all research, yet takes on a special resonance in socially just research. Essentially a key question to be asked by the researcher is not just 'how do I collect my data', but that of 'once I have collected my data, how do I exit the relationship between myself and my participants in an ethical and respectful way?'. Too often, this is an overlooked part of the research process, yet is inherently important within socially just research, where 'leaving the field' without careful consideration of the impact upon participants may have considerable ethical implications, especially given our arguments that, by its very nature, socially just research is a collaborative endeavour. Whilst the emergent and flexible nature of qualitative research designs makes it difficult to plan when exit will take place, the question of how it should happen should be considered at the start of the research process. The issues related to exit from the research setting have been outlined by Ortiz (2004) who, although undertaking research from a social justice perspective, has outlined some of the key concerns and strategies. He discussed how he immersed himself almost entirely in the social world of athletes' wives, where "their world

Figure 36.1 Illustrating focus groups – LGBT+ participants focus group.

Source: Courtesy of https://www.energiseme.org/wp-content/uploads/2021/09/Pride-in-Our-Workforce-Resource.pdf

was my world for more than three years" (p. 470). Both the level of long-term immersion and the perceived vulnerability of participants became obstacles to withdrawal, as did the empowerment felt by participants, which motivated them to continue their involvement. As he notes, "Because we worked well together, shared our feelings, and shared a sharp sense of mutuality in our quest for knowledge, the depth of reciprocity in our exchange relationships made it difficult for me to stop the data collection process" (p. 475). This issue is vital for any socially just researcher, who must carefully consider what will happen to the relationships that will form throughout such a collaborative research process.

Developing impact

Praxis refers to a continual process of action and reflection upon the research process to develop a commitment to transformation through bringing to life the relationships between theory and practice to make positive changes to the lives of marginalised people based on the voices and experiences of those people (Blodgett et al., 2008). Thus, the questions asked within a social justice praxis can be summarised as first who benefits from the research, and in what way, second who developed the research design that led to those benefits, and finally who narrates those benefits, and in which format.

Socially just research can develop impact beyond academic outputs through engaging with the community. For example, research with a local transgender group and their participation in recreational swimming involved the production of drawings and illustrations. These visual images were displayed during LGBT+ History Month (2020) at a regional arts centre – the Lighthouse Poole, Dorset – and the public were encouraged to offer their feedback (Figure 36.2).

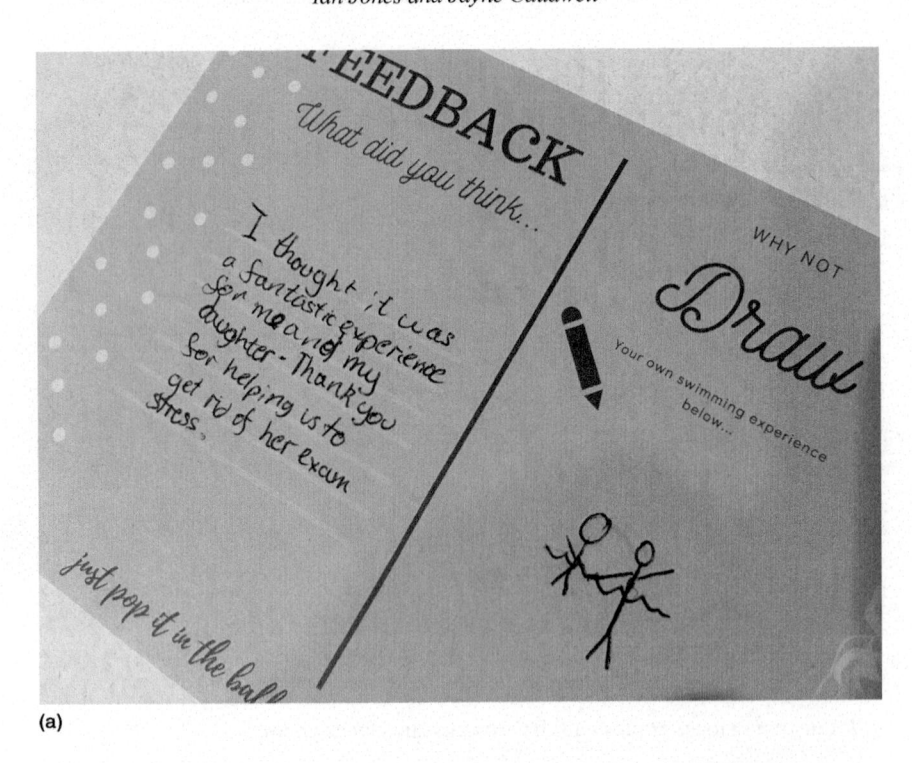

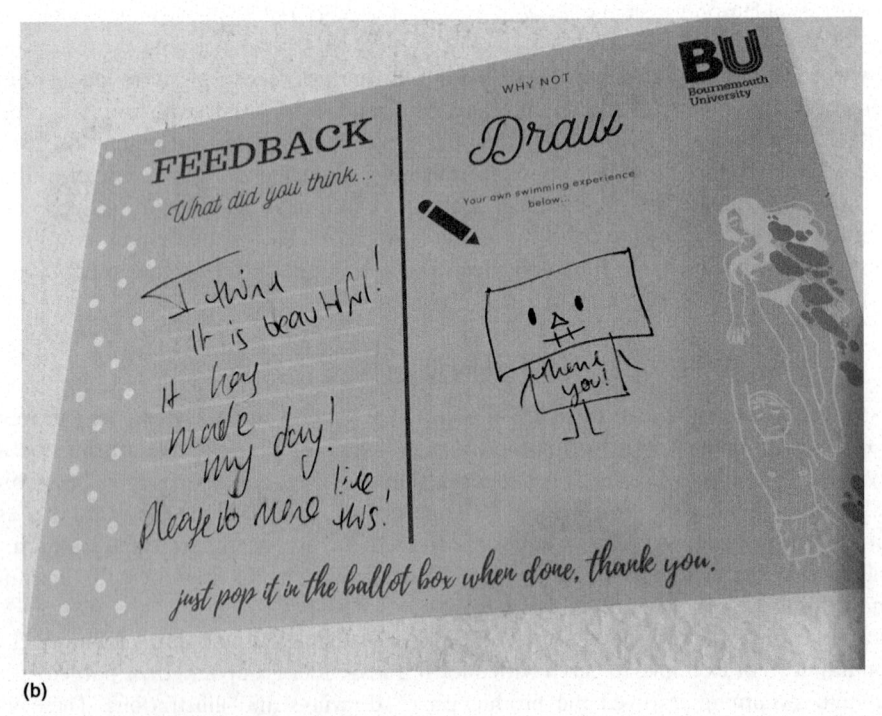

Figure 36.2 Assessing impact with feedback cards. (a) Assessing impact with feedback cards; (b) Assessing impact with feedback cards. (Cont.).

Figure 36.2 (Cont.) (c) Feedback cards exhibition.

Conclusion

Undertaking socially just research is very much a collaborative endeavour, involving the researcher working with participants. As such it requires the researcher to carefully consider issues such as collaboration, co-production, and reflexivity. Whilst there is no 'set' way to successfully undertake such research, or preferred methods, there needs to be a continual acknowledgment of how the research can be undertaken *with* participants, rather than *on* them. This applies to all elements of the research process, from developing the initial aim and objectives, collecting data and analysing data, and disseminating the findings.

References

Arthur, N. & McMahon, M. (2005) Multicultural career counseling: Theoretical applications of the systems theory framework. *The Career Development Quarterly*, 53 (3), 208–222.

Atkins, L. & Duckworth, V. (2019) *Research Methods for Social Justice and Equity in Education*. London: Bloomsbury.

Bartels, A., Eckstein, L., Waller, N., & Wiemann, D. (2019) *Postcolonial Literatures in English*. Stuttgart: J. B. Metzler.

Blodgett, A., Schinke, R., Fisher, L., Wassenego George, C., Peltier, D., Ritchie, S., & Pickard, P. (2008) From practice to praxis: Community-based strategies for Aboriginal youth sport. *Journal of Sport & Social Issues*, (32) (4), 393–414.

Braun, V., Clarke, V., Boulton, E., Davey, L., & McEvoy, C. (2020) The online survey as a qualitative research tool. *International Journal of Social Research Methodology*, 24 (6), 641–654.

Brinkley, A., Sherar, L., & Kinnafick, F. (2022) A sports-based intervention for pupils excluded from mainstream education: A systems approach to intervention acceptability and feasibility. *Psychology of Sport and Exercise*, 61, https://doi.org/10.1016/j.psychsport.2022.102217

Brunner, C. (2021) Conceptualizing epistemic violence: An interdisciplinary assemblage for IR. *International Politics Reviews*, 9, 193–212.

Buchbinder, E. (2011) Beyond checking: Experiences of the validation interview. *Qualitative Social Work*, 10 (1), 106–122.

Candela, A. (2019) Exploring the function of member checking. *The Qualitative Report*, 24 (3), 619–628.

Chapman, S. & Schwartz, J. (2012) Rejecting the null: Research and social justice means asking different questions. *Counseling and Values*, 57 (1), 24–30.

Chilisa, B. & Mertens, D. (2021) Indigenous made in Africa evaluation frameworks: Addressing epistemic violence and contributing to social transformation. *American Journal of Evaluation*, 42 (2), 241–253.

Chiu, L. (2006) Critical reflection: More than nuts and bolts. *Action Research*, 4 (2), 183–203.

Clavier, C., Sénéchal, Y., Vibert, S., & Potvin, L. (2012) A theory-based model of translation practices in public health participatory research. *Sociology of Health & Illness*, 34 (5), 791–805.

Dantley, M. (2002) Uprooting and replacing positivism, the melting pot, multiculturalism, and other impotent notions in educational leadership through an African American perspective. *Education and Urban Society*, 34 (3), 334–352.

Darnell, S. (2014) Orientalism through sport: Towards a Said-ian analysis of imperialism and 'Sport for Development and Peace'. *Sport in Society*, 17 (8), 1000–1014.

Darnell, S. & Millington, R. (2018) Social justice, sport, and sociology: A position statement. *Quest*, 71 (2), 175–187.

Greenbank, P. (2003) The role of values in educational research: The case for reflexivity. *British Educational Research Journal*, 29 (6) 791–801. doi: 10.1080/0141192032000137303

Hayhurst, L. (2016) Sport for development and peace: A call for transnational, multi-sited, postcolonial feminist research. *Qualitative Research in Sport, Exercise and Health*, 8 (5), 424–443.

Hussain, U. & Cunningham, G. (2021) 'These are "our" sports': Kabaddi and Kho-Kho women athletes from the Islamic Republic of Pakistan. *International Review for the Sociology of Sport*, 56 (7) 1051–1069.

Ison, N. (2009) Having their say: Email interviews for research data collection with people who have verbal communication impairment. *International Journal of Social Research Methodology*, 12 (2), 161–172.

Lincoln, Y. & Guba E. (1986) But is it rigorous? Trustworthiness and authenticity in naturalistic evaluation. *New Directions for Program Evaluation*, 30, 73–84.

Krane, V. & Waldron, J. (2021) A renewed call to queer sport psychology. *Journal of Applied Sport Psychology*, 33 (5), 469–490.

MacLean, M. (2019) Engaging (with) indigeneity: Decolonization and indigenous/indigenizing sport history. *Journal of Sport History*, 46 (2), 189–207.

McSweeney, M., Otte, J., Eyul, P., Hayhurst, L., & Parytci, D (2023) Conducting collaborative research across global North-South contexts: Benefits, challenges and implications of working with visual and digital participatory research approaches. *Qualitative Research in Sport, Exercise and Health*, 15 (2), 264–279.

Nicholls, R. (2009) Research and indigenous participation: Critical reflexive methods. *International Journal of Social Research Methodology*, 12 (2), 117–126.

Ortiz, S. (2004) Leaving the private world of wives of professional athletes: A male sociologist's reflections. *Journal of Contemporary Ethnography*, 33 (4), 466–487.

Pettican, A., Goodman, B., Bryant, W., Beresford, P., Freeman, P., Gladwell, V., Kilbride, C., & Speed, E. (2023) Doing together: Reflections on facilitating the co-production of participatory action research with marginalised populations. *Qualitative Research in Sport, Exercise and Health*, 15 (2), 202–219.

Pettit, H. (2020) Uncomfortable ethnography: Navigating friendship and 'cruel hope' with Egypt's disconnected middle-class. *Emotion, Space and Society*, 36, 287–320.

Ratna, A. & Samie, S. F. (2017) *Race, Gender and Sport: The Politics of Ethnic 'Other' Girls and Women*. London: Routledge.

Sanford, R., Beckett, A., & Giulianotti, R. (2021) Sport, disability and (inclusive) education: Critical insights and understandings from the Playdagogy programme. *Sport, Education and Society*, 27 (2), 150–166.

Schaillée, H., Spaaij, R., Jeanes, R., & Theeboom, M. (2018) Knowledge translation practices, enablers, and constraints: Bridging the research–practice divide in sport management. *Journal of Sport Management*, 33 (5) 366–378.

Smith, B., Williams, O., Bone, L., & the Moving Social Work Co-production Collective (2023) Co-production: A resource to guide co-producing research in the sport, exercise, and health sciences. *Qualitative Research in Sport, Exercise and Health*, 15 (2), 159–187.

Spaaij, R., Schulenkorf, N., Jeanes, R., & Oxford, S. (2018) Participatory research in sport-for-development: Complexities, experiences and (missed) opportunities. *Sport Management Review*, 21 (1), 25–37.

Spivak, G. (1988) Can the subaltern speak? In P. Williams & L. Chrisman (Eds) *Colonial Discourse and Post-Colonial Theory. A Reader*. New York: Columbia Press, pp. 66–101/

Ugolotti, N. (2022) Contested bodies in a regenerating city: Post-migrant men's contingent citizenship, parkour and diaspora spaces, *Leisure Studies*, Online First. doi: 10.1080/02614367.2022.2085775

Ymous, A., Spiel, K., Keyes, O., Williams, R., Good, J., Hornecker, E., & Bennett, C. (2020) "I am just terrified of my future" – Epistemic violence in disability related technology research. In *Proceedings of the 38th Annual ACM Conference Extended Abstracts on Human Factors in Computing Systems (CHI EA'20)*. Association for Computing Machinery, New York, NY.

37
ARTS-BASED RESEARCH AND SOCIAL JUSTICE IN SPORT AND LEISURE

David Carless and Kitrina Douglas

Introduction

The importance of social justice research is well recognised in current times, in particular the need for innovative studies that intervene into the complex challenges faced within twenty-first-century societies. Research that makes a difference. Research that works with, on and around the political, economic, and sociocultural obstacles that can conspire to inhibit change where it is most badly needed. As the chapters in this Handbook demonstrate, the importance of social justice scholarship across the field of sport, leisure, and physical activity is recognised. Here, too, researchers, scholars and activists work in ways that strive to make a positive difference.

In this chapter, we consider the utility of arts-based approaches to social justice research and reflect on examples of two film-based projects in sport, leisure, and physical activity. We engage with public responses to these examples, demonstrating the personal, social and cultural meaning and impact of the work, and showing how arts-based research can generate community, solidarity, and personal or social change. We propose that arts-based research offers a means to radically democratise social justice research and scholarship.

Why arts-based research?

Researching human experience – particularly within complex cultural, socioeconomic and political contexts – has never been an easy endeavour. The number of books, journal articles, online resources, and research methods courses produced each year provide testament to just how challenging *doing* socially responsible research can be. Feminist (e.g., Ritchie & Barker, 2005), indigenous (e.g., Kovack, 2010), queer (e.g., Zeeman, Aranda, & Grant, 2014), disability (e.g., Goodley, 2016), and performative (e.g., Denzin, 2003; Gergen & Gergen, 2012) scholars call us to work in ethical ways towards social justice for those who are oppressed or discriminated against on the basis of gender, race, sexuality, disability, or economic disadvantage. These writers, and others, provoke us towards greater awareness of voice, visibility and representation of wide-ranging minority, disadvantaged or oppressed people.

DOI: 10.4324/9781003389682-44

We are challenged to incorporate within our studies what might go unsaid, those aspects of human experience that may be at the borders of what can be expressed (e.g., Butler, 1997) and to avoid excluding felt and spiritual experience (e.g., Dewey, 1934; Freeman, 2014). At the same time, we are asked to ensure our research is accessible, so it may be communicated to wider audiences in engaging ways (e.g., Research Councils UK, 2017). With specific regard to social justice, Koro, Cannella, Huckaby, and Wolgemuth (2022) ask:

> How do we shape our inquiries to call out injustice? How can critical qualitative research call for justice and create possibilities for just transformations? How can critical scholarship be theorized, designed, and practiced with justice as the orienting focus within (en)tangled times, materials and material injustices?
>
> (p. 564)

Together, these are mighty challenges. How might we – as sport and leisure researchers – respond? Arts-based methodologies offer one set of possibilities.

Arts-based research comprises a diverse range of methodological approaches that work in radically different ways in the service of personal, social and cultural understanding, and transformation. It responds to Denzin's (2003) challenge to re-animate the social world by privileging accessibility, engagement and multidimensional sensory interaction. It opens up alternative ways of thinking, feeling, relating and experiencing through diverse creative means of communication.

Although a substantial literature on art-based research now exists (e.g., Bagley & Cancienne, 2002; Barone & Eisner, 2012; Belliveau & Westwood, 2016; Cahnmann-Taylor & Siegesmund, 2007; Foster, 2016; Haywood Rolling, 2013; Jagodzinski & Wallin, 2013; Knowles & Cole, 2008; Leavy, 2009, 2018; Liamputtong & Rumbold, 2008; McNiff, 2008), little had been published when we began our research journeys in the late 1990s. Within our fields, few if any examples of arts-based research were evident. Our methods were not therefore developed from textbooks but instead through exploration, as we creatively responded to challenges faced by participants experiencing mental ill-health (e.g., Douglas & Carless, 2014), homelessness (e.g., Douglas & Carless, 2015), or ageing (e.g., Douglas & Carless, 2005, 2013). Learning through working *with* participants has affected how we live our lives and changed in fundamental ways how we *do* research. It strengthened our commitment to social justice across our work.

Arts-based research for social justice

Like many researchers, arts-based researchers work towards social justice through any number of avenues, which may include education, informing policy, influencing culture, or activism. In practice, however, it is often the case that philosophical differences, paradigmatic controversies, and the relative valuing of different forms of research mean that arts-based work is better suited to striving for social justice through particular channels. While the insights arts-based research offers are certainly research informed, it is often undervalued – seen as secondary or 'lower quality' – within the contexts of evidence-based medicine (EBM) and evidence-based practice (EBP). Arts-based approaches offer something different – something we term *understanding-based medicine* (UBM) and *understanding-based practice* (UBP). We use these terms as an umbrella for the ways arts-based research promotes different kinds of insights than those typical of EBM and EBP.

First, insights from arts-based research tend to be generative (Gergen & Gergen, 2012) rather than prescriptive. EBM and EBP are often directive of a particular course of action, thereby closing down choices. While at times this is useful, at other moments it serves to impoverish an individual's response. Arts-based research is more likely to leave audiences with a question that provokes or suggests possibilities for action, thereby opening up new or context-specific responses.

Second, given the research methodologies that are most highly prized within EBM and EBP (quantitative, positivistic, scientific), the insights that are produced tend to be rational, logical, propositional forms (Chadwick, 2001). Arts-based research offers different kinds of insights. Here, embodied, local, contextual, experiential forms are prevalent, drawing on multiple senses and emotional intelligence. These forms of knowledge, while impossible to pin down or state in words or numbers, can be no less important in working for social justice.

Third, by more highly valuing technical knowledge (Cole & Knowles, 2008), the forms of knowing that support EBM and EBP are often exclusive and inaccessible to non-academic audiences. While academic audiences may be able to put this information to good effect, many members of the public are likely to disengage from the research. It is inaccessible to them. At times, this may cause little harm – technical knowledge is consumed by professionals who process, utilise, or apply it across practical scenarios. At other times, though, it can serve to sustain or deepen the divide between 'professional' and 'Other'. Examples of this polarisation or separation can include 'doctor/patient', 'expert/novice', 'teacher/student', 'rich/poor', 'educated/practical'. This can breed damaging power differentials, entrench inequality, and disenfranchise certain groups from awareness of and power over processes that impact their lives. In the long term, individuals or groups can be enforced into silence or passivity regarding issues that shape their lives.

Fourth, Barone and Eisner (2012) write of how arts-based research is unique as a methodology because it is the only form of research that offers audiences an experience. By, for example, stimulating multisensory engagement, taking audiences into a particular place, activating audience member's memories, or preserving polyvocality through allowing space for multiple and sometimes conflicting voices. These qualities can offer a kind of vicarious experience which encourages us to step outside our preconceptions (e.g., the dominant narratives that constrain thinking), challenge what we think we know, and help us develop empathy, even seeing our own involvement in a new way (e.g., seeing ourselves as 'the bad guy' in a way that is not threatening but enlightening).

While these characteristics may be valuable across a number of domains, within social justice arenas they are of particular importance. Together, the arguably unique qualities of arts-based research can together help promote engagement, inclusion, diversity/plurality, participation, dialogue, respect, empathy, and democracy.

Frank (2000) argued that "more knowledge may be less important than a clearer sense of value" (p. 363). New theories and facts do not help us with the ethical question of what to do with what we know. On this basis, "The challenge for intellectuals is to help people make policy, clinical, corporate, and personal decisions in a milieu of profound dislocation" (p. 363). This is a further way arts-based research can contribute to social justice within sport and leisure. Positioning ourselves, as researchers, in different relationships with 'data', our participants, their experiences, et cetera, has a tendency to open up new ways of seeing and construing appropriate responses. In a similar vein, the ways that arts-based products take audiences into different *kinds* of engagement with participants' lives and the sociocultural contexts where they unfold, can provoke new insights, questions, reflection and/or action in others.

Film and social justice

Given there are so many genres under the arts-based umbrella, we focus in more detail now on one approach – filmmaking. There are several reasons why we consider film to be a particularly fruitful way forward for researchers in sport and leisure who are committed to social justice. First, film is culturally omnipresent in the twenty-first century and, as a result of the technological revolutions of recent years (e.g., YouTube, Vimeo, Instagram), widely accessible. Second, film combines multiple genres (e.g., moving image, sound, music, narrative/story) which can provide high levels of emotional and sensory engagement. Harris (2018) suggests that: "Video-based research offers us the most affective, primal, and thorough rendering of the complexity of human life, which is the core business of all research" (p. 449). Third, social justice concerns are probably more developed in film than in any other art form.

Weaving together multiple genres in myriad ways, films powerfully evoke wide ranging emotional, sensory, and/or intellectual experiences. In some films, it may be the cinematography that accrues recognition. In others, it may be the soundtrack. While in others, it may be the storytelling that takes centre stage. Informing these decisions are costs and preferences of the producer and director, and of course other issues related to the purpose/s of the film.

Within the British film industry, the individual perhaps most recognised for social justice is director Ken Loach. When *I Daniel Blake* won the Palm d'Or at Cannes Film Festival in 2016, Loach said in his acceptance speech: "Cinema has many traditions, one is to be a cinema of dissent and a cinema to represent the interest of the people" (Loach, 2017). Likewise, producer Rebecca O'Brien, said: "You can tackle injustice, by making films. You can be at the heart of politics, without being a politician" (Loach, 2017).

Across a six-decade career, Loach has made a succession of gritty films that tackle social injustice. His film *Cathy Come Home* – a story about homelessness, unemployment and mothers' rights to keep their children – screened for the first time on BBC television on 16 November 1966 to 12 million viewers, a quarter of the UK population at the time. *Cathy Come Home* was voted in a reader's poll in *Radio Times* as the 'best single television programme' ever made and in 2005 it was named by *Broadcast* as the UK's most influential TV programme of all time. Through increasing public awareness of homelessness, it was a catalyst in the formation of the homelessness charity Crisis in 1967.

Like social science research, an idea for a film can begin with one individual being challenged by a social issue. We see this in *Blue Jean* (2023), an example of a commercial film release exploring social justice concerns within sport. Director Georgia Oakley, who self-identifies as queer, was inspired after reading about the bravery of a group of lesbian activists who in 1988 abseiled into the public gallery at the House of Lords to protest Section 28 (a now repealed British law which silenced conversations around homosexuality in schools). Oakley pitched her idea to the commissioning editor/director of BBC Film and was given the go ahead. Oakley and co-director Hélène Sifre then travelled to Newcastle, UK (where the film was shot in 2022), to talk with and interview over 50 people affected by Section 28. "I could tell by speaking to these women that no-one had ever given them the time of day", says Oakley. "They'd been on these personal battles with their own history through their whole lives" (Tabbara, 2022). With financial backing from iFeatures and BBC Film, a six-week shoot took place in Newcastle in 2022, and the film was released in early 2023. Here the director was also the researcher, incorporating first person narratives to weave a compelling story.

Although feature films are a wonderful way to engage audiences with social issues, they come with a hefty price tag that is beyond the budget of most researchers.

Further, screenwriters may rewrite important details in order to create a more commercially successful story; this can create tensions in research contexts. Perhaps the closest form of film to social science research therefore is documentary. Here, there is an expectation that 'real facts' are used and if participants' voices and images can't be used, they are performed by actors. Within the documentary tradition there are numerous experimental forms, blurring of boundaries and weaving together image, sound, and narrative. And some documentaries are made with modest budgets and production costs.

Our filmmaking has been broadly positioned within the experimental documentary tradition given that we incorporate personal narrative, songs/music, poetry and imagery. To illuminate how researchers might move from peer reviewed article to film, we now consider two examples.

Example 1: *The Long Run*

The Long Run began during David's doctoral research (Carless, 2003), created from narrative interviews with Ben, a 36-year-old man with severe and enduring mental health difficulties. We felt from the outset that there was much to be learnt from Ben's accounts of his experiences of physical activity within the context of mental ill health and, on that basis, went on to publish two papers based on his interviews. The first (Carless, 2008), featured a structural narrative analysis which is theoretically dense and inaccessible to all but a limited academic audience. The second (Carless & Sparkes, 2008), used an approach that David developed during his PhD to create a first-person story. Despite featuring an accessible story, to negotiate peer review we were required to present an academic argument for our use of a story form. This made the piece less accessible to most people. In addition, of course, both were published in academic journals which the public are unable to freely access.

The move to film: Our process

We share Saldaña's (2018) view that distilling a first-person narrative into a recorded monologue can be helpful stepping stone into filmmaking. However, film is more than speech. As we have explored elsewhere (see Douglas & Carless, 2020a), music, songs, ambient sound, spoken word and, of course, moving image also matter. Film relies on multiple genres coalescing to tell a story which stimulates the senses to provoke new ways of thinking, feeling, and knowing. This multisensory engagement is perhaps key to the ubiquity and power of film as a medium for entertainment and communication in the twenty-first century.

The first deliberate step in making this film was to move from the *written* word into the texture and sound of *spoken* word through recording David voicing the story. Hearing a story back – as opposed to reading it off the page – takes us into a new level of embodiment, extending felt sense and thereby introducing tone, pitch, and in the process evoking new emotions and meanings.

Having recorded Ben's story, we moved into the visual domain, seeking out appropriate footage to thicken the spoken account. One example of how we achieved this is the sequence of the film shot during a 10K race held in Bristol city centre (Figure 37.1). Despite the challenges of filming in a busy public space, Kitrina had an intuitive sense that footage of this public event might be important. And in the act of *doing the work* – in this case, filming – something profound happened: we gained a sense of the possibilities of life *when you get to join in*, when you aren't stigmatised, discriminated against, or denied access. The runners were

Figure 37.1 A scene from *The Long Run*.

not professional athletes, they were just 'normal' people, all ages and sizes, colours, ethnicities, and abilities, joining together in community. Witnessing, filming, and editing these images began to change how we understood Ben and his running. Like many others, Ben had been *excluded* in numerous ways as a result of his mental health condition: excluded from work, excluded from liberty, excluded from leisure, and excluded from sport.

Crowds packed the final stretch five or six deep, cheering the runners as they crossed the line. Those last few yards of the race were particularly magnetic to us, watching people running alongside others, holding hands and raising their linked arms as they crossed the finish line *together*. It reminded us of how Ben talked about running with his mate, saying: "We done it!" We were unprepared for the intensity of feelings captured in these moments of moving image.

A further stage in our process was the incorporation of music and songs during the editing process. Using one of David's original songs from our music library meant we did not need to record something new or have to negotiate copyright. Once added to the project pane and aligned with the narrative, the piece took on a new integrated form. Put plainly, the physicality in the song recording – a passionate voice and powerful attack on the guitar strings – dovetailed with the story and images. The lyrics ("I've got your needs at the front of my mind/I put your dreams alongside mine") provoke and rouse us to consider our obligations, responsibilities, what comes with privilege and opportunity. The song amplified the images, raised the energy and generated a sense of hope.

Viewer responses

The primary purpose of arts-based research is not, in our view, to create good art. Rather, it is to create art that does good in the world – that achieves something constructive for someone somewhere. The important question for us, then, is not "Is this a good film?" but "What is this film good for?" The way to discern this is by seeking and listening to the responses of others to our work. We have done this for our arts-based research which utilises story, song, and live performance approaches (see Carless & Douglas, 2010, 2011; Douglas & Carless, 2008, 2020b). Here, we share and reflect on some responses to *The Long Run*.

This first response is from Alan (shared through an interview), a soldier on the 'Battle Back' programme for wounded, injured and sick military personnel:

> See if someone has never had a panic attack in their life, they *say* they can understand what it's like, but I don't think they can. If I get a panic attack I get tears streaming down my face, and I can be an emotional wreck, my eyes are welling up. It [*The Long Run*] was quite, my eyes got a bit watery there watching it, stuff like that I can relate to, it means a lot to me. See, being in the army, they can't see what's wrong, people kind-of look down their noses at you. So people with mental health stuff will keep it to themselves and that's the worst thing you can do. You end up just bottling it up inside. What makes me worse is looking at myself in the mirror, and at what I used to look like, but if I can get that thinking through my mind [he points at the screen] like that man on there [pointing again] it's never too late to do something, to get back into it. You see, when you have anxiety and panic attacks it feels like your life is over. Watching that video, it's given me a wee boost to get back running, 'cause if he can do it, I can do it. I like watching stuff like that. The video was good for me, it was powerful, I can relate to it a lot.

Evident in Alan's words is a strong sense of identification with Ben, even across difference. While they are different people, in different situations, who have never met, Alan discerns shared experience around both physical activity and mental health. Perhaps most important is "a wee boost" – motivation, optimism, hopefulness, a sense of possibility which Ben's personal story as shared in the film has unlocked for Alan.

A second response is from Alex (received by email), a mental health service user:

> Its [sic] very true about the right meds. Has a massive difference not only on outlook but in some ways your character or at least behaviour. Which one is cause/effect i'll never know. Very touching vid for me too as i ran a marathon a few years ago with the aim of curing myself. My doctor laughed when i told him that was why and sadly he was very right. At least in my lifetime there'll be no cure, just management. Anyway glad you made it. Always good to teach people the inside story …

Here, Alex's response also demonstrates how another's story told through a film can provoke reflection on one's own experience, in this case medication and healthcare. A film about one person's experience can also be a stimulus for viewers to consider more general political or power issues, evident in this comment (posted on YouTube) about sociocultural attitudes (e.g., stigma) towards those with mental health difficulties:

> Thanks for being the voice of those who are prejudiced and discriminated in the society. this gives us the opportunity to think from the person suffering from mental illness perspective, an idea on how they suffers through a song … i loved the ending so much … simply beautiful …

Finally, what of the ability of *The Long Run* to provoke change? While change – social action, meaningful impact – are outcomes many of us hope from our research, they are not always forthcoming. So too with film. There is, however, evidence that films like *The Long Run* can have effects, albeit small-scale, local-level changes. One example of this was a student who was provoked by the film to pursue a change in his own medication (see Douglas & Carless, 2020a). This change, he informed us, precipitated a sufficient improvement in his health that he was able to pursue postgraduate studies. For us, small-scale personal change is important and is one response to the question "How do we change the world?" Answer: One person at a time. Judging by some responses, this hope is important to many of us researching in areas of social justice:

> Thank you for putting this out there! Your work and research gives me hope that there will be more opportunities to create and study impact through documentary film, particularly for social change. Thank you also for your vulnerability and bravery in sharing your voice and story.
> (YouTube comment)

Example 2: *Gwithian Sands*

Our second example is *Gwithian Sands* (Douglas & Carless, 2013) a 4 minute 36 second song, written by Kitrina, that we used as the basis for a music video (Figure 37.2). Both the song and the film concern the life story of one participant from our research with women in Cornwall commissioned by the Women's Sport & Fitness Foundation (WSFF). The WSFF, as a women's advocacy organisation, were interested to learn about the health and physical activity of women over 60 in areas with health inequalities.

Figure 37.2 A scene from *Gwithian Sands*.

Two areas of England stood out in deprivation indices, the North East and South West. Given we were from the South West, it seemed economically prudent to study the population closest to where we lived, Cornwall. While many people think of Cornwall as being a beautiful tourist destination, it is also an area with some of the lowest incomes and highest house prices. Sport England had some statistics about women's physical activity, but these applied more to women who played sport. Our remit therefore was to learn about the lives of women who did not self-identify as 'sporty'. How was their health? What physically activity were they doing? What barriers and challenges existed for them to being or becoming physically active? We carried out ethnographic research, living in Cornwall for extended periods of time, and as part of the research conducted focus groups and interviews with 30 women aged between 60 and 84.

For Bresler (2006), "The aesthetic inquirer is at the vortex of the movement, actively seeking connections" (p. 94). This description aligns with how we do research: witnessing, experiencing, feeling, thinking and creating in diverse ways and genres, as the topic dictates. However, the WSFF considered that deviating from a traditional research report might be counter-productive to their interests. This was a contentious issue for us, because without an arts-based element, we felt the story we could tell would be less rich, less complex, less evocative and, therefore, less impactful. This was our first commissioned project post-PhD, so we were keen to satisfy the funders. But we also felt a degree of liberty to follow hunches and experiment. As a result, we completed the project with a wonderful resource of poems, songs and stories. Together we shaped these into a performance ethnography and CD titled *Across the Tamar* (Douglas & Carless, 2005).

Our first performance was to a packed village hall of participants and locals. We shared the formal report and a live performance of *Across the Tamar*. And we asked those present for feedback. While WSFF wanted a traditional report, what would the participants feel was appropriate? We had no idea. Unreservedly, we were told that although both forms portrayed women's experiences faithfully, those present preferred *Across the Tamar* as it communicated their emotions in ways that the report could not. The report was therefore, in their eyes, less authentic.

Through numerous performances and analysis of audience responses (see Carless & Douglas, 2010, 2011) we came to understand more fully what an arts-based research product offers over a written report. However, there were two obstacles with performing the research that were difficult to overcome. The first was that a performance required us to be there in person. The second was that touring is expensive and therefore requires significant funding. For this reason, we recorded and produced an audio CD. While the CD became a great resource, it lost an embodied dynamic. Seven years later, though, it was a different story: we had both attended a film making course and were more prepared to try (at least) to explore what film might bring to our embodied understanding and communication.

The move to film: Our process

The processes that comprise filmmaking as research are less well understood than most other forms of qualitative research (Douglas & Carless, 2020a). Gupta (2019) describes six steps behind her filmmaking process: select sociocultural phenomena for conscious raising, collect participants' anecdotes of lived experience, code and thematise the data, translate data into cinematic language, produce a film, promote the film. This kind of preordained procedural approach does not work for us. For example, we do not know before we begin a project how we will move forward and we are much more likely to be led by emergent aspects (such as physical environment, social interactions, soundscapes, etc.) Thus, our films might arise through exploring the stories of participants, by what is provoked in us visually within an environment, or in response to something missing.

In the case of the *Gwithian Sands*, we were provoked to "construct a world" for the viewer that is "cognitive and immersive and sensuous" (Yacavone, 2014, p. xvi). Here, those watching are invited to experience *for themselves* – in this case, how women in Cornwall experience life in Cornwall. This 'world' is of course in part created by our filming, direction and editing, thus is a 'virtual' world. However, it is also an 'actual' world, you can go there and observe it. Our aim was not to literally follow the song's visual cues but, rather, to expand what was an already powerful audio portrayal, by 'thickening' the audience's sensory experience through, for example, introducing visual elements alongside a strong narrative arc. Until we actually shot, edited and produced the film, we did not know what that the end product would look like. It emerged through the *doing*.

On this point Merleau-Ponty (1948) suggested that a carefully crafted film enhances the viewer's perception as aspects of life that can be missed or taken for granted are seen anew. Merleau-Ponty (1948) looked to cinematography to bring out "the fine grain of real life whose aesthetic value may have been lost from sight" (p. 58). The aesthetic quality is both 'felt' and pre-linguistic, and we attempted to become attuned to this by immersing ourselves (yet again) in the environment while being guided by an internal compass which was being evoked by the music and song to create a visual horizon. That is, we allowed the work that had already taken place in our bodies, through doing the research as well as performing the song (see Carless, 2022), to be placed anew within the context, with the particular place the participants lived and described.

Viewer responses

As mentioned above, an important aspect of the films we make is audience response and our confidence comes from viewers telling us the film is meaningful. Many YouTube comments refer to the song being 'catchy', viewers becoming 'caught up' in the film, some listening several times. For example:

> I naturally tend to look at the comments on videos I watch because I like to understand other people's opinions. I think what has been said in the comment section is so true. As I was watching the video, I got very caught up in it. Right at the end when the single line, 'She's just a wife', it really hits home the message. I can only emphasise what has already been said; a great deal has changed but women still face social pressures today. The history of Cornwall is fascinating and I feel that this video pays tribute to that, in wonderful symbolism of those who paid their lives.

For one, this was because the song "stirred something very deep inside me of my own roots and identity". For another, "I wanted to thank you for making this available to listen to here on YouTube. The print copy of the lyrics were helpful, but hearing the song really brought your whole concept together".

A second common response suggests new awareness of women's lives. For example, what women sacrifice to bring up children and how contemporary women should be better off:

> [translation from French] this video and song touches me both by text and by voice. The subject covered is not necessarily easy to deal with and doing it in song is a very original and affordable way for everyone. The condition of women at that time in Cornouaille

was undoubtedly the same here in the Breton countryside. Few of them had access to education. As you say so well, they were above all wives, mothers and sisters whose role was duty. Today, even if the condition of married women is much better, if they have access to education, good jobs and therefore a certain autonomy, they are under a lot of pressure because we are still far from gender equality. Women. Are they freer than before? I doubt it and I wonder about the share of the weight of cultural heritage and this universal notion of natural and visceral attachment that some women have towards their offspring that they accept while acknowledging that this constitutes a "brake" to their personal achievement. But all this is a real debate on the status of women and your song opens a door.

These responses suggest the film opened up conversations about contemporary women's lives. Among the international responses was a man from France who wrote he would like the lyrics and tabs so he could learn the song and play it to his community. As such, the film provided a vehicle to allow the song to take on another life of its own, being sung and shared by others to support advocacy and understanding about women.

Gwithian Sands was the first research film we made. It showed us how, by making a film publicly available via YouTube, multiple impacts can result. It has been used in lectures and seminars, it provides a resource to help people who work in their communities, it opens a door to provoke conversation, and it can motivate others on their social justice journey.

Social justice or social impact?

We conceptualise social justice as a concern with transforming the deepest societal problems of economic, racial, or gendered injustice through critically addressing issues of power and inequality. In short, speaking truth to power. Lessons from filmmakers might, however, offer a more nuanced perspective to inform our work as filmmaker-researchers in sport and leisure. This concerns a distinction between *social justice* and *social impact*. Ortner (2017) describes the difference between these two aims by reflecting on two US-based socially oriented film collectives, Brave New Films and Participant Media:

> The more radical Brave New Films follows what is clearly a social-justice agenda, critically addressing issues of power and inequality, while the more classically liberal Participant Media pursues a social-impact agenda, addressing social problems as technical problems to be fixed.
>
> (p. 531)

For Ortner (2017), a social impact project differs from a social justice project because it "starts from the social and political status quo and asks how people's lives can be improved within the existing limitations" (p. 535). On this basis, social impact may be achieved without serious engagement with existing political, economic and/or power structures. This kind of project, then, is open to criticism for "trying to fix the world without fixing the politics" (p. 534).

At this point in time, having engaged in a series of film-as-research projects over the past decade or so, we take the view that both goals are worthy. Ideally, we work to produce films that are not neutral about social justice issues but, instead, speak truth to power. But we are also pleased to produce films which lead to more practically oriented action, promoting personal or social change within existing political and/or economic structures.

The future of social justice film in sport and leisure

At the core of many researchers' practice is a genuine concern and care for the people and communities we research. Finding ways to communicate what we learn while expanding avenues for social justice requires us to extend our imagination about *how we do research*. Against the philosophy of conveyor-belt research currently flourishing in the neoliberal academy, 'slow science' advocates remind us about the importance of developing and sustaining long-term relationships with the people and communities we research (Koro-Ljungberg & Wells, 2018; Scheurich, 2018). Hitting tight budgets and short time frames can come at the expense of these relationships. Without which, Spooner (2018) suggests, it is impossible to improve social justice.

In our experience, filmmaking is a slow way of doing social research. It is impossible to embrace filmmaking – whether through collaborations with filmmakers or through making films as researchers – and achieve quick results. The processes involved demand time and commitment as the two examples above demonstrate. The rewards of both the process (the diverse skills, aesthetic sensibilities, practical steps) and the outcomes are worthy of this investment. As Harris (2018) notes:

> video is not only a method (a tool, an approach) but also more than that, as it increasingly extends theoretical frames, which means we not only *do* research differently but also *see* the practice, role, and responsibility of research differently. Video-based research can serve different scholarly functions, address different social relations, and suggest new knowledge creation as it goes.
>
> (p. 440)

The need for commitment over time does not only apply to filmmaker-researchers but to professional filmmakers too. According to one Hollywood-based social justice-oriented filmmaker: "Maybe, just maybe, we might make some difference in the world. But it ain't gonna happen overnight" (Ortner, 2017, p. 535).

Producing films that achieve social justice (or, for that matter, social impact) is a tall order – not just for researcher-filmmakers in sport and leisure but also for professional filmmakers. It is from the experiences of these organisations that we might take a final lesson. Ortner (2017) again:

> In an ideal world of socially conscious filmmaking, a film that powerfully addresses a contemporary social or political issue would work as a direct provocation to audiences, causing them to go out and take action … It is increasingly accepted, however, that a film's sociopolitical implications may need to be amplified and driven home by additional mechanisms if it is to bring about some kind of change in the real world.
>
> (p. 530)

While Participant Media began by relying on the persuasive power of the film itself (in line with their motto *a story well told can change the world*), over time their strategy shifted to building more active partnerships to promote impact (Ortner, 2017). In short, creating a campaign. This multistrand approach seems to us to be both realistic and achievable. As researchers, academics, and teachers, we are ideally placed to initiate and run educational, public engagement, and event-based campaigns alongside releasing our research-based films. Indeed, some of us are already doing this through online and face-to-face seminars, conferences and events with students, colleagues, and the general public. By improving and extending this work, the social justice and social impact agendas in sport and leisure can only be strengthened.

References

Bagley, C. & Cancienne, M. B. (2002). *Dancing the Data*. New York: Peter Lang.
Barone, T. & Eisner, E. (2012). *Arts Based Research*. Thousand Oaks, CA: Sage.
Belliveau, G. & Westwood, M. (2016). *Soldiers Performing Self in Contact! Unload: Innovations in Theatre and Counselling*. Vancouver: Faculty of Education, UBC.
Bresler, L. (2006). Toward connectiveness: Aesthetically based research. *Studies in Art Education*, 48(1), 52–69.
Butler, J. (1997). *Excitable Speech: A Politics of the Performative*. New York: Routledge.
Cahnmann-Taylor, M. & Siegesmund, R. (2007). *Arts-Based Research in Education: Foundations for Practice*. Abingdon, UK: Routledge.
Carless, D. (2003). *Mental Health and Physical Activity in Recovery*. Doctoral dissertation, University of Bristol.
Carless, D. (2008). Narrative, identity, and recovery from serious mental illness: A life history of a runner. *Qualitative Research in Psychology*, 5(4), 233–248.
Carless, D. (2022). Where spirit meets bone: A meditation on embodied qualitative inquiry. *International Review of Qualitative Research*. https://doi.org/10.1177/19408447221114848
Carless, D. & Douglas, K. (2010). Performance ethnography as an approach to health-related education. *Educational Action Research*, 18(3), 373–388.
Carless, D. & Douglas, K. (2011). What's in a song? How songs contribute to the communication of social science research. *British Journal of Guidance and Counselling*, 39(5), 439–454.
Carless, D., & Sparkes, A. (2008). The physical activity experiences of men with serious mental illness: Three short stories. *Psychology of Sport and Exercise*, 9(2), 191–210.
Chadwick, P. (2001). *Personality as Art: Artistic Approaches in Psychology*. Ross-on-Wye, UK: PCCS Books.
Cole, A. L. & Knowles, J. G. (2008). Arts-informed research. In J Knowles & A. Cole (eds), *Handbook of the Arts in Qualitative Research*, pp. 55–70. Thousand Oaks, CA: Sage.
Denzin, N.K. (2003). *Performance Ethnography*. Thousand Oaks, CA: Sage.
Dewey, J. (1934). *Art as Experience*. New York: Capricorn Books.
Douglas, K. & Carless, D. (2005). *Across the Tamar: Stories from Women in Cornwall*. Audio CD. Bristol: UK.
Douglas, K. & Carless, D. (2008). Using stories in coach education. *International Journal of Sports Science and Coaching*, 3(1), 33–49.
Douglas, K. and Carless, D. (2013). (Directors/Producers) *Gwithian Sands*. Film, YouTube. www.youtube.com/watch?v=IuUFDMLGfiE
Douglas, K. & Carless, D. (2014). (Directors/Producers) *The Long Run*. Film, YouTube. www.youtube.com/watch?v=v-fprKKUGKo
Douglas, K. & Carless, D. (2015). (Directors/Producers) *The Blue Funnel Line*. Film, YouTube. https://youtu.be/cftAy_SaurY
Douglas, K. & Carless, D. (2020a). The long run: A story about filmmaking as qualitative research. *Qualitative Inquiry*, 26(3–4), 281–290.
Douglas, K. & Carless, D. (2020b). Under one roof: Living together and apart in an urban supported housing scheme. *Departures in Critical Qualitative Research*, 9(3), 3–27.
Foster, E. (2016). *Collaborative Arts-Based Research for Social Justice*. Abingdon, UK: Routledge.
Frank, A. (2000). Standpoint of storyteller. *Qualitative Health Research*, 10(3), 354–365.
Freeman, M. (2014). *The Priority of the Other*. New York, NY: Oxford University Press.
Gergen, M. & Gergen, K. (2012). *Playing with Purpose: Adventures in Performative Social Science*. Walnut Creek, CA: Left Coast Press.
Goodley, D. (2016). *Disability Studies: An Interdisciplinary Introduction*. Thousand Oaks, CA: Sage.

Gupta, N. (2019). The Phenomenological Film Collective: Introducing a cinematic-phenomenological research method for social advocacy filmmaking. *Soc Personal Psychol Compass*, *13*, e12445. https://doi.org/10.1111/spc3.12445

Harris, A. (2018). Ethnocinema and video based research. In P. Leavy (ed.), *Handbook of Arts-Based Research*, pp. 437–452. New York, NY: The Guildford Press.

Haywood Rolling, J. (2013). *Arts-Based Research Primer*. New York: Peter Lang.

Jagodzinski, J. & Wallin, J. (2013). *Arts-Based Research: A Critique and a Proposal*. Rotterdam: Sense Publishers.

Knowles, J. G. & Cole, A. S. (2008). *Handbook of the Arts in Qualitative Research*. Thousand Oaks, CA: Sage.

Koro, M., Cannella, G. S., Huckaby, M. F., & Wolgemuth, J. R. (2022). Critical qualitative inquiry: Justice matters(ings) in (en)tangled times. *International Review of Qualitative Research*, *14*(4), 563–574.

Koro-Ljungberg, M. & Wells, T. (2018). Method ol o gies…that encounter (slowness and) irregular rhythm. In N. K. Denzin & M. D. Giardina (eds), *Qualitative Inquiry in the Public Sphere*, pp. 143–155. New York: Routledge.

Kovack, M. (2010). *Indigenous Methodologies: Characteristics, Conversations, and Contexts*. Toronto: University of Toronto Press.

Leavy, P. (2009). *Method Meets Art: Arts-Based Research Practice*. New York, NY: Guildford Press.

Leavy, P. (2018). *Handbook of Arts-Based Research*. New York, NY: The Guildford Press.

Liamputtong, P. & Rumbold, J. (2008). *Knowing Differently: Arts-Based and Collaborative Research Methods*. New York, NY: Nova Science.

Loach, K. (2017). BAFTA films awards. www.bafta.org/media-centre/transcripts/i-daniel-blake-winner-acceptance-speech-outstanding-british-film-2017 [accessed 1 June 2017].

McNiff, S. (2008). *Art-Based Research*. London, UK: Jessica Kingsley Publishers.

Merleau-Ponty, M. (1948). *The World of Perception*. Abingdon, UK: Routledge.

Ortner, S. B. (2017). Social impact without social justice: Film and politics in the neoliberal landscape. *American Ethnologist*, *44*(3), 528–539.

Research Councils UK. (2017). *What's in it for me? The benefits of public engagement for researchers*. www.rcuk.ac.uk/publications/researchers/initforme/ [digital file] [accessed 10 May 2017].

Ritchie, A. & Barker, M. (2005). Explorations in feminist participant-led research: Conducting focus group discussion with polyamorous women. *Psychology of Women Section Review*, *7*(2), 47–57.

Saldana, J. (2018). Ethnodrama and ethnotheatre: Research as performance. In N. K. Denzin & Y.S. Lincoln (eds), *The Sage Handbook of Qualitative Research*, pp. 565–583. Thousand Oaks, CA: Sage.

Scheurich, J. J. (2018). Research 4 Revolutionaries by ‡jimscheurich. In N. K. Denzin & M. D. Giardina (eds), *Qualitative Inquiry in the Public Sphere*, pp. 125–142. New York, Routledge.

Spooner, M. (2018). Pushing boundaries. In N. K. Denzin & M. D. Giardina (eds), *Qualitative Inquiry in the Public Sphere*, pp. 25–49. New York: Routledge.

Tabbara, M. (2022). Screen Daily. "History, unfortunately, is cyclical": 'Blue Jean' filmmakers on the drama's important warning. www.screendaily.com/features/history-unfortunately-is-cyclical-blue-jean-filmmakers-on-the-dramas-important-warning/5177626.article [accessed 20 January 2023].

Yacavone, D. (2014). *Film Worlds: A Philosophical Aesthetics of Cinema*. New York: Columbia University Press. https://doi.org/10.7312/yaca15768

Zeeman, L., Aranda, K., & Grant, A. (2014). *Queering Health: Critical Challenges to Normative Health and Healthcare*. Ross-on-Wye, UK: PCCS Books.

38
PARTICIPATORY RESEARCH IN SPORT, LEISURE, AND FORCED MIGRATION

Where is the social justice?

Chris Webster and Robyn Smith

Introduction

The so-called 'European Migration Crisis' of the 2010s, characterised by the largest flow of migrants and refugees entering Europe since World War II (UNHCR, 2022), has sparked growing interest from policymakers, sport development practitioners, and sport studies researchers around the role of sport and leisure in refugee resettlement within the Global North. Following a similar trend to mainstream forced migration studies, research in this field has typically been conducted by outsider-researchers, with research aims driven by policy objectives of the Global North rather than the needs of forced migrants (Spaaij et al., 2019), which has led to minimal benefit for communities involved (Pittaway, Bartolomei, & Hugman, 2010).

More recently, there have been calls to conduct research with and for persons from forced migrant backgrounds that is embedded within social justice (Mackenzie, McDowell, & Pittaway, 2007). We conceptualise social justice as a distinct political endeavour concerned with challenging, disrupting, and dismantling hegemonic processes (e.g. 'race', class, gender, sexuality, ability) within societies that serve to maintain the oppression of those who are subordinated. Our conceptualisation of social justice is inspired by a number of radical Left-thinkers ranging from Audre Lorde to Mark Fisher, and David Graeber. Whilst theoretical differences exist between the intellectuals, what unites them is the importance of emancipatory imagination to explore beyond and outside of the existing theoretical paradigms and political orthodoxies towards building alternatives in the present. Therefore, as activists and researchers our pursuit for social justice is not only premised on challenging and resisting the violent symptoms of borders (immigration raids, detention, deportation, and hostile environments), it is also fundamentally concerned with disrupting the top-down epistemological assumptions that serve to construct and fortify borders in the interests of global capitalism as a legacy of empire and colonialism (Mayblin, 2017).

This chapter argues that participatory research approaches, which seek to collaboratively engage stakeholders within the research process and foster a commitment to social change (Cornwall & Jewkes, 1995), may offer a means of challenging hegemonic knowledge production and conducting more socially-just research with and for persons from forced migrant

DOI: 10.4324/9781003389682-45

backgrounds in sport and leisure. Drawing on our experiences of utilising participatory methodologies in sport and leisure contexts with forced migrants in two UK cities (Leeds and London), we highlight the importance of collaborative and meaningful knowledge creation in illuminating the (in)significance of sport and leisure in the lives of forced migrants. To do so, we first provide an introduction to participatory approaches and an overview of our research contexts. We then identify three key interconnected areas of contention in the literature: (1) the scant recognition of the broader complex socio-cultural-political climate in which forced migration and resettlement takes place; (2) the alignment of research agendas to neo-liberal policy objectives of the Global North; and (3) the absence of intersectional approaches, before drawing on our research to suggest how participatory approaches may help overcome some of these challenges. In doing so, we call for a radical sociology of sport and leisure motivated by the pursuit of global social justice for those who are forced to migrate.

Participatory approaches to research

For forced migrant populations, research has historically been a site of exploitation and marginalisation, where dignity and autonomy have been denied, stories stolen, and minimal benefit derived by communities (Mackenzie, McDowell, & Pittaway, 2007; Pittaway, Bartolomei, & Hugman, 2010). Within the traditional research process, predominantly White European or Australian researchers (Spaaij et al., 2019), with their toolkit of academic 'expertise' typically hold ultimate power and control while doing research 'on' the participant (Fine, 2006). Within these approaches, local expertise and alternative ways of knowing are typically devalued in comparison with hegemonic processes of knowledge production as the interests, aims, and intended outcomes of projects that work with marginalised populations are driven by research agendas in the Global North and delivered with minimal consultation from local populations (Tuhiwai Smith, 1999). These deficits in the traditional research process often lead to research that reproduces hegemonic knowledge production, falls short in capturing participants' nuanced lived experiences, and constitutes a site of symbolic violence (Block et al., 2013; Malkki, 1995).

Both authors are methodologically committed to the praxis of participatory approaches as a means of rupturing the epistemological dominance of policymakers in the Global North and conducting meaningful and impactful research alongside community members. 'Participatory approaches' is a catch-all term used to encompass diverse methodologies including Participatory Action Research (PAR), Participatory Research (PR) Action Research (AR), Community Based Participatory Research (CBPR), and co-production. Such approaches can be characterised by a shift in power away from the researcher to other stakeholders throughout the research process (Cornwall & Jewkes, 1995). Both authors have individually utilised a variety of participatory approaches whereby through developing trusting relationships, centring reflexivity and actively working to shift levels of power and participation, participants become partners involved in co-creating knowledge orientated towards challenging social injustices (Cammarota & Fine, 2008; Freire, 1972).

Of particular relevance to the readers of this handbook, participatory approaches have been positioned as a more 'socially just' means of conducting research through actively working to challenge hegemonic knowledge production and fostering mutual benefit to communities involved in research. Our chosen participatory approaches aim to reduce damage derived from traditional oppressive research practises (Tuhiwai Smith, 1999) through dismantling "relations of power and conceptions of knowledge that foment the reproduction of racial, gender, and geo-political hierarchies that came into being or found new and more powerful forms of expression in the modern/colonial world" (Maldonado-Torres, 2007, p. 117). We argue that a methodology concerned with rebelling against the colonialism of research should re-orientate those who were once the 'object' of study to become the knowledge generators (Ndlovu-Gatsheni, 2013). Through adopting participatory approaches that seek to re-position the 'object' of study to a position of 'knowledge-making', it is possible for leisure and migration to be defined on the terms of the 'researched' rather than that of policymakers in the Global North (Mignolo, 2011). As such, in participatory approaches we often see that the research objectives are focused around local issues and the process designed to build capacity, participant skills, and recognise agency; and in turn, this co-produced knowledge is used to transform hegemonic structures (Pittaway, Bartolomei, & Hugman, 2010; Tuhiwai Smith, 1999).

Participatory approaches have gained significant traction over the past five years in sport, leisure, and forced migration studies, and have been utilised predominantly to co-design (Luguetti, Singehebhuye, & Spaaij, 2022a; Robinson et al., 2019; Rosso & McGrath, 2016) and evaluate (Venturini-Trindale, 2021) sport and leisure programmes, and explore meanings attached to sport within wider lived experiences (Mashreghi et al., 2021; Stone, 2018; Webster & Abunaama, 2021). Yet, there are significant challenges in ensuring that participatory approaches are embedded within a social justice framework. Areas of methodological concern involve degrees of stakeholder participation (Enderle & Mashreghi, 2022); researcher reflexivity and positionality (Enderle & Mashreghi, 2022; Luguetti, Singehebhuye, & Spaaij, 2022a; Middleton et al., 2022); and reciprocity and trust (Smith, Mansfield, & Wainwright, 2022). While, participatory methodologies have been positioned as a more ethical means of conducting research (Spaaij et al., 2019), there are well-documented challenges including the reproduction of unequal power hierarchies between researchers and participants (Enderle & Mashreghi, 2022; Luguetti, Singehebhuye, & Spaaij, 2022b), the politics of knowledge production e.g. ownership and representation (Luguetti, Singehebhuye, & Spaaij, 2022b), and the need to move beyond institutional ethical guidelines to ensure that research has reciprocal benefit for communities (McSweeney, Hakiza, & Namukhula, 2022).

Background to research contexts

During her PhD, Robyn employed PAR to explore how community sport and leisure programs are designed for and understood by young people from refugee backgrounds. PAR is a strength-based framework that values the local knowledge of stakeholders and emphasises their agency in facilitating social change through processes of reflection, action, and education (Fals-Borda, 1987). Robyn's research was a collaboration with a London-based charity, BelongHere*, that supports 252 young people from diverse refugee backgrounds (including unaccompanied minors, asylum seekers, and refugees) aged 12–24 years old. The program offers holistic services including case work, therapy, ESOL, alongside sport and leisure activities. In this project, Robyn collaborated with co-researchers and staff to co-design, deliver, and evaluate a new sport and leisure programme that aimed to support wellbeing. Both ethnographic and participatory methods were used to explore the young people's lived experiences inside and outside the program. Robyn spent three years immersed in the research site as a volunteer, researcher, and youth worker. As a white, young, queer, mono-lingual English-speaking British woman, Robyn was considered a cultural outsider to the young people.

Through engaging in critical reflexive practices, spending meaningful time together, and learning to embrace vulnerability, Robyn and the young people came to build relationships based on care, trust, and reciprocity.

As an anti-racist community activist based in Leeds, Chris is involved within a number of social movements and initiatives, from organising radical left-wing football tournaments to resisting and preventing immigration raids in the city. During his PhD research, Chris ethnographically explored the (in)significance of a Leeds-based community football initiative (FFA) in the everyday lives of the forced migrant male participants. The sessions are run by Yorkshire St Pauli, a UK-based supporters club for German professional football team FC St Pauli who are internationally renowned for their commitment to social justice. FFA is an autonomous football space, existing outside the Football Association structure, and funded by the members of Yorkshire St Pauli. As a result, FFA is shaped and reshaped by the experiences and desires of those that inhabit it and remains accountable to the participants rather than the desires of neo-liberal funding providers and policymakers. Chris has been an organiser and participant at FFA since its inception in 2013 which presented him with method(ologically) challenges and possibilities. Chris recognised friendship and emotion as a meaningful way of knowing and exploring the (in)significance of FFA in the everyday lives of those who attend through enabling them to formulate bespoke research methods that were fitting with their individual and collective friendships. Through the decolonial praxis of accompaniment, Chris was able to wander, and wonder, alongside his friends as they explored together the significance of FFA in their everyday lives as forced migrants living in Leeds. Next, we examine three key areas of contention within the literature and examine the potential for participatory methodologies to address these challenges.

Where is the politics?

Under the umbrella term 'forced migrant', we include people who have been forced to flee due to the fear of persecution on the basis of protected characteristics, violence, war, climate change, and natural disasters (UNHCR, 2022). These persons fall under several policy categories including refugees, asylum seekers, and unaccompanied asylum-seeking children (UASC). While refugees are granted protected status and leave to remain in the destination country, asylum seekers arrive at the border of the destination country seeking protection and then undergo the refugee determination process (UNHCR, 2003). As such, these political categories heavily shape lived experiences and trajectories by impacting access to rights and freedoms (Bakewell, 2008). Forced migration, like all other social processes, is inherently political with people forced to flee their country of origin in search of safety and lived experiences being continuously (re)shaped by the ever-changing policies and political discourses of destination countries.

Literature in the field of sport, leisure and migration has historically struggled to reckon with politics in the same way contemporary migration studies has. This is potentially because sport and leisure scholars exploring migration are more likely to focus on 'sport' rather than the wider context of their study. Indeed, in 87 per cent of studies, sport, physical activity, and leisure participation was the main analytical focus (Spaaij et al., 2019). To understand both the significance and limitations of sport and leisure spaces in the lives of forced migrants, it is vital to understand how macro and micro social-political processes affect people's trajectories and ability to navigate everyday life outside of the site of study. As such, we begin by situating our research within the current UK political climate.

Contemporary UK migration policy can be examined and summarised through the 'Hostile Environment policy'. This policy strategy can be described as the formalised embedding of insidious immigration controls across public and private services to make it as difficult as possible for migrants without the correct paperwork to remain in the UK (Goodfellow, 2019). While the Hostile Environment policy was formalised by the Coalition government in the Immigration Act 2014, it should be noted that this policy is an intensification of Labour's Immigration Act 1999, which stated that any person subjected to immigration controls in the UK will have no recourse to public funds and is therefore unable to access welfare services afforded to British citizens (Candappa, 2019). A crucial aspect of the 'Hostile Environment' is the sharing of data across government institutions and the private sector (including banks, doctors, schools, and landlords) to determine whether a person has the correct documentation to access welfare services (Liberty, 2019). As a result, current UK immigration effectively uses the threat or enforcement of destitution as a violent political tool to manipulate people into 'voluntarily' returning to their country of origin. The effect of the Hostile Environment policy is that immigration controls are now centred around everyday interactions. Yuval-Davis, Wemyss, and Cassidy (2018) refer to this as 'everyday bordering' where the function of the state as a public service becomes one of surveillance and violence. Therefore, Back and Sinha (2018) are correct when they argue that immigration controls are situated in the everyday to the extent where all citizens are expected to embody the role of immigration officers.

As researchers interested in the intersections of sport, leisure, and forced migration, it is our social and collective duty to understand how this sociopolitical context (re)shapes the meanings placed on spaces of sport and leisure by those who inhabit them. A handful of papers examine the (in)significance of leisure and sport participation in negotiating the temporal and spatial politics of asylum including liminality, placement in reception centres/hotels, and lack of ontological security (Hartley, Fleay, & Tye, 2017; Schmidt & Palutan, 2021; Waardenburg et al., 2019; Webster & Abunaama, 2021). Sport and leisure may also provide spaces of resistance against hostile asylum regimes through fostering senses of freedom (Lewis, 2015), pleasure (Koopmans & Doidge, 2021), and hope (Stone, 2018). While leisure and sport frequently conjure senses of pleasure, enjoyment, belonging and mental wellbeing, we echo the calls of Stone (2018) and De Martini Ugolotti and Caudwell (2021) that these expressions of agency must not be conflated with dismantling deep-rooted political and social injustices at their sources. Further, with the exception of a handful of scholars (Doidge, 2018; Luguetti, Singehebhuye, & Spaaij, 2022a), few researchers in this field have overtly stood in solidarity with forced migrants against the social injustices experienced through hostile asylum regimes (Spaaij et al., 2019).

(Re)centring politics through participatory approaches

We argue that participatory approaches can provide opportunities for (re)centring politics in forced migration studies and sport. While not all participatory approaches are inherently political (e.g. AR or co-production), PR and PAR are committed to understanding how historically situated structures of oppression have created a reality whereby forced migrants experience oppression and standing in solidarity with communities to transform these realities (Freire, 1972). In our work, we found that this commitment required centring personal politics and emotions, relationship building and immersion, and re-creating collaboratively produced knowledge into action.

Throughout the research process, Chris did not disregard or compromise his personal politics in an attempt to appease positivistic notions of 'objectivism' and research ethics. Instead, through maintaining his political commitment to resisting border violence and racism, Chris built deep and meaningful friendships and senses of solidarity with the 'participants', which enabled knowledge to flow in a fluid and horizontal way. Chris' compassion for the participants and anger at the social and economic conditions created by political institutions is inherent to his study; it would have been impossible (and undesirable) to leave these deeply held, personal emotions at the door of the research site (as might be proposed by a more positivist researcher). Chris conceptualised these emotions as an 'enhancing' tool for the research rather than a hindrance. As explained by Hubbard et al. (2001, p. 135), "Being emotional is a way of knowing about, and acting in, the social world and is just as significant for how we make sense of our respondents' experiences as our cognitive skills". Emotions therefore become the avenue for the researcher and participant to communicate their interpretations of experiences and then forge a sense of empathy and/or solidarity in reaction to these experiences.

To centralise the politics of forced migration in his study, Chris widened the research lens beyond the space of FFA and spent many years immersing himself in everyday spaces, friendships, struggles, and pleasures experienced by the participants to understand how FFA was stitched into the vibrant tapestry of their lives. As Chris was involved with FFA since its inception in 2013, he had developed friendships with the participants before commencing the study. During this three-year project, Chris then accompanied the participants through everyday spaces and struggles. Chris witnessed how the brutal immigration policies of the UK government impacted the lives of his friends as they attempted to establish a sense of belonging in Leeds and shaped the meanings placed on leisure spaces such as FFA and how these were experienced. For example, the pleasures experienced by the participants through playing football were not deemed frivolous and fleeting moments of euphoria, instead they were interpreted as expressions of agency that resisted and defied the biopolitics of the Home Office.

For Robyn and the co-researchers, PAR provided the opportunity to re-centre politics through using co-produced knowledge to foster social change for young people from refugee backgrounds. The co-produced insights from this project directly informed the sport and leisure programme design/delivery at BelongHere, which led to programmes that captured what mattered most to the lives of the young people. The insights were also used to co-create an animated video and workshops for professionals who support young people from refugee backgrounds. For the young people, the action piece of PAR (Fals-Borda, 1987) including creating outputs, delivering sessions, and shaping practice not only allowed them to develop their skills for the future, but also acted as a site of agency and resistance against the hostile asylum system and provided hope of a more socially just system for other young people.

Against the neo-liberal policy objectives of the Global North

The need for greater political analysis of sport and leisure spaces in the lives of forced migrants is inextricably tied to the second call, for sport and leisure scholars exploring migration to be conscious and critical of research agendas that align with the neoliberal policy objectives of the Global North. As researchers we must recognise how histories of empire and colonialism continue to shape forced migration patterns and the lived experiences of those who navigate the 'post-colonial' cities of the Global North. Recognising histories of colonialism must not be limited to subject matters but must also be interrogated in the production of knowledge. It is not enough to just provide a 'platform' for forced migrant's leisure experiences to be heard, instead we must attempt to radically disrupt and resist the epistemic violences of the Global North through approaching research in a way that allows the production of knowledge generation from the bottom-up. As the esteemed Indian author, Arundhati Roy, declared in her 2004 Sydney Peace Prize Lecture, "there is really no such thing as the voiceless. There are only the deliberately silenced and preferably unheard".

Within sport, leisure, and forced migration studies, many of these voices have indeed been 'deliberately silenced and preferably unheard' in favour of appeasing the policy agendas of the Global North. This is because, first, researchers tasked with concocting research questions are often ladened with the hegemonic assumptions concerning forced migration, and second, because research aims and objectives are often stipulated by research funders who, particularly in the field of sport, leisure, and migration are frequently policymakers (Spaaij et al., 2019). Therefore, all too often research in this field is conducted from the same epistemological position of policymakers and fails to explore the complexities of different lifeworlds, thus leaving aspects of people's lived experience invisible (Bakewell, 2008).

Indeed, Spaaij et al. (2019) found that 49 per cent of papers in the field focused on sport/physical activity/dance interventions that may facilitate policy goals of the Global North such as health and wellbeing promotion, social inclusion, and integration. Reflecting neo-liberal healthism discourses, studies examined how physical activity and sport may enhance wellbeing, in particular through reducing traumatic stress (Harris, 2007; Ley, Rato Barrio, & Koch, 2018; Richards et al., 2014). Further, reflecting policy-level concerns around the socio-cultural-economic costs of resettlement, there is an over-representation of integration or acculturation frameworks which examine how leisure/sport can be a means and marker of integration through developing the desired cultural and social capital in the destination country (Block & Gibbs, 2017; Doidge, Keech, & Sandri, 2020; Spaaij, 2012; Stura, 2019). These theoretical frameworks are often posited on the assumption that forced migrants are traumatised 'deficits' to be 'fixed', rather than challenging how dehumanising policies negatively impact freedoms and mobilities in the first place (Malkki, 1995).

Participatory approaches and moving beyond neo-liberal policy goals

In the spirit of Mallki (1995), Bakewell (2008), and De Martini Ugolotti and Caudwell (2021), we call researchers to move beyond policy driven themes to explore sport and leisure in relation to the lived experiences, emotions, embodied dimensions, thoughts, and opinions of people who have experienced forced migration themselves. Participatory approaches may hold promise in achieving this goal. We found that involving community members within research design provided opportunities to shift power away from ourselves and conduct locally-driven research shaped by the needs of the communities we were working alongside.

Chris felt that it was important that the methods used in his study recognised and spoke to his existing individual and collective friendships with the participants. By asking the participants the critical, yet open-ended question "What does FFA mean in the context of your everyday life?", participants were provided with the initiative and freedom to explore the research question in a way that was meaningful to themselves and their friendship with Chris. As a result, each participant co-created a bespoke research method tailored to their needs. For example, Chris often spent multiple hours a day 'hanging out' with his participants in their asylum accommodation or at the local park. In response to his friend expressing their frustration and anger at their state of enforced idleness (due to strict immigration control), Chris provided his friend with notebooks to help fill his time. The notebooks enabled him to record daily experiences whilst practising his writing skills in the absence of much desired English classes. Chris and his friend would then sit in the local cafe and mutually explore the drawings and stories.

As early career researchers in positions of precarity, subject to institutional authorities, it is important to note that participatory approaches are still subject to challenges in resisting policy-driven research agendas. Robyn's research objectives' broadly aligned to the policy goals of the Global North. Her PhD studentship stipulated that the project should examine wellbeing, diversity, and sport/leisure. Further, the research objectives were co-produced by staff at BelongHere, and as such, were influenced heavily by programme funders, who stipulated that the outcomes of the sport and leisure programme should (1) improve mental health and wellbeing; (2) reduce risky behaviours; and (3) foster social inclusion. The funders' conceptualisations of wellbeing aligned with neo-liberal policy goals and captured dimensions of wellbeing valued in the Global North including social capital, social inclusion, subjective wellbeing, and integration (Spaaij et al., 2019) Within the funder's desired outcomes, we also saw that wellbeing was pathologised and often reduced to measuring indicators of depression, anxiety, and PTSD and typically overlooked the lived experiences and needs of the young people.

Despite the broad alignment of research objectives to neo-liberal policy goals in Robyn's project, involving the young people in co-designing the research methods allowed local and contextual understandings of wellbeing, sport, and leisure to emerge. Participatory methods were co-designed and delivered by the young co-researchers at BelongHere and informed by local practices, values, and ways of understanding the world (Tuhiwai Smith, 1999). To facilitate flexibility and reflect the young people's shifting needs, interests and time commitments (Cammarota & Fine, 2008), methods were designed iteratively as the project progressed and included digital storytelling, digital diaries, photo voice, WhatsApp photo challenges, and art. These methods utilised digital spaces and storytelling/sharing techniques that the young people already used in their day to day lives. Through these approaches, the young people generated knowledge that did not align with dominant frameworks, but rather, was relevant to their lives inside and outside the programme. While we recognise that the neo-liberal policy agenda is so deeply woven into funding grants and research proposals and challenging to circumvent, we argue that participatory approaches offer flexible, collaborative and creative tools to foster bottom-up knowledge production within these structures.

Yet, despite participatory approaches holding promise in challenging the hegemony of expertise (Fine, 2006), we urge scholars to be cautious of glorifying participatory methods as a means to decolonise hegemonic knowledge production (Ozkul, 2020). Participatory approaches are still typically conducted by 'outsider' researchers within communities who have experienced oppression (Ozkul, 2020). As such, the researcher and structures of authority still possess ultimate power in initiating research, decision making, and ultimately have the most to gain (Ozkul, 2020). We do not claim to have uncovered perceived utopian research processes where each stakeholder automatically benefits equally and all knowledge is organically generated from the bottom-up. Instead, our experiences are centred on methodological struggle and hope. A struggle to be committed to the decolonial praxis and a hope of doing reflexive, inclusive research with progressive possibilities that rupture the epistemological dominance of the Global North.

The absences or lack of intersectionality approaches

Finally, we argue that in forced migration, sport, and leisure studies there is a dearth of intersectional approaches that not only recognise the heterogeneity of forced migrant communities but actively research these differences. It is vital for scholars to recognise that "displacement and resettlement are differently lived and negotiated by people seeking asylum across different and overlapping markers of gender, sexuality, ethnicity, religion, and legal status" (De Martini Ugolotti, 2021, p. 5). These markers of identity can impact resource allocation, freedoms, social networks, resilience, and community attitudes/perceptions, of which can significantly impact access to and experiences within sport and leisure (Spaaij et al., 2019).

Calls for intersectional approaches in sport, leisure, and social justice research are far from new (Watson & Scraton, 2013). However, because there is a temptation to homogenise the experiences of forced migrants, we argue that the need to adopt intersectional approaches is more acute than ever. This is particularly the case in the field of forced migration and sport where there are a wealth of studies concerning the participation of able-bodied, young asylum seeking or refugee men in football projects within resettlement countries in the Global North (Dukic, McDonald, & Spaaij, 2017; McDonald et al., 2019; Spaaij, 2015; Stone, 2018; Stura, 2019; Webster & Abunaama, 2021; Woodhouse & Conricode, 2017). We argue that researchers should seek to respond to a lack of gender diversity in football spaces by adopting theoretical and methodological approaches that explore (re)constructions of gender (alongside 'race', age, (dis)ability, and sexuality).

Within forced migration studies and sport/leisure, we see that the experiences of people who identify as women, non-gender conforming, and queer, have been marginalised. This is particularly problematic considering that many forced migrants have fled their home country due to persecution on the basis of these identity markers (United Nations, 1951). While a growing number of studies examine the impacts of forced migrant women's physical activity and sport programmes and barriers/facilitators to participation, many of these studies reproduce the neo-liberal policy goals of the Global North as they focus on the outcomes that can be derived to cisgendered, straight, able-bodied forced migrant women through sport/physical activity. However, there are a handful of exceptions with scholars examining how intersections of gender, ethnicity, culture, and religion (re)shape sport and physical activity experiences within resettlement countries (Agergaard et al., 2021; Collison & De Martini Ugolotti, 2021; Gulamhusein, 2021; Mohammadi, 2019; Palmer, 2009). Further, Venturini-Trindade (2021) is the only scholar to examine the lived experiences of transgender asylum-seeking individuals within a sport and leisure program and found that their unique lived experiences and needs were often overlooked within funding aims and outcomes. We argue that through not taking an intersectional focus, sport and leisure programmes for forced migrant populations may overlook the needs and lived experiences of individuals, thus further marginalising groups (De Martini Ugolotti & Caudwell, 2021).

Participatory approaches and examining intersectionality

We argue that participatory methodologies may offer promise in capturing intersectionality in action in everyday life, generating local insights that shape sport and leisure programmes to meet people's diverse and intersecting needs, and moving beyond top-down identity constructions.

When Robyn first started at BelongHere, 92 per cent of participants self-identified as male and all programs were mixed-gendered. Through the use of digital diaries, the young women discussed how the mixed-gendered sport and leisure programmes were a site of creating, negotiating, and resisting their multiple identities as a young Muslim refugee living in London. In particular, they also noted how they experienced harassment from young male participants for participating in sport and leisure activities as young Muslim women and did not feel safe. We used these participatory insights to develop safer, more inclusive practises within the mixed-gendered program and co-create a girls-only sport and leisure program. Through this bottom-up knowledge generation process, we were better positioned to meet the unique needs of refugee girls from Muslim backgrounds, and nearly tripled the number of participants who identified as women. However, despite the promises around participatory research and enhanced intersectionality, it is important to note the overrepresentation of participatory approaches with young people from forced migrant backgrounds in sport and leisure. Indeed, alongside Chris, only a couple of participatory studies examined the experiences of adult forced migrants (see Stone, 2018).

Echoing the calls of Bakewell (2008) we encourage researchers to avoid fixating on top-down identity constructions (such as 'asylum seeker' and 'refugee') to explore how (multiple) identities are constructed and reconstructed throughout spaces of sport and leisure. Indeed, in their systematic literature review of the field, Spaaij et al. (2019) found that only two studies used participants' self-identification as a form of reference. Participatory methodologies may offer promise here. Indeed, in their separate studies, Chris and Robyn found that the terms 'forced migrant', 'refugee', and 'asylum seeker' held little relevance to the people they worked with beyond marking their legal status. In Chris' case, his friends chose to collectively identify as 'footballers' rather than migrants as this is the marker by which their myriad individual identities were united. In the same spirit, Robyn's co-researchers identified themselves as 'young people' rather than UASC, refugees, or asylum seekers as they believed that these labels were stigmatising and failed to capture their collective identities. Therefore, intersectional approaches are vital to explore how these different individual and collective identities shape, and are shaped by, sport and leisure spaces as people navigate asylum systems.

Conclusion

In response to the increased attention on the (in)significance of spaces of sport and leisure in the lives of forced migrants, we have identified three key areas of contention within the literature (1) the lack of attention to the broader complex socio-cultural-political climate in which forced migration takes place; (2) the alignment of research agendas with the neo-liberal policy objectives of the Global North; and (3) the limited use of intersectional approaches. In response to these three intertwined challenges identified, we have offered our experiences of being politically committed to the praxis of decolonising research methodologies through the vehicle of participatory approaches as a means of co-producing knowledge from the bottom-up. We argue that participatory approaches may offer promise in conducting more socially just research through reorienting those who were once the 'object' of study as the knowledge generator who has the ability to foster social change around issues meaningful to them. Considering the last decade of intensifying nationalistic sentiments and hostility to migrants globally, now more than ever, if researchers are serious about pursuing social justice, they must rid themselves of the shackles of the perceived 'neutrality' and 'objectivism' championed in positivistic research and stand in unequivocal solidarity with their participants, co-researchers, and friends as they navigate increasingly hostile and violent asylum and settlement processes.

References

Agergaard, A., Lenneis, V., Simonsen, C.B., & Ryom, K. (2021). Granted asylum and healthy living?: Women newcomers experiences of options for accessing leisure time physical activity. In N. De Martini Ugolotti, & J. Caudwell (Eds), *Leisure and Forced Migration: Lives Lived in Asylum Systems*. 105–120. Abingdon: Routledge.

Back, L., & Sinha, S. with Bryan, C., Baraku, V., & Yembi, M. (2018). *Migrant City*. Routledge: London.

Bakewell, O. (2008). Research beyond the categories: The importance of policy irrelevant research into forced migration. *Journal of Refugee Studies, 21*, 432–453.

Block, K., & Gibbs, L. (2017). Promoting social inclusion through sport for refugee-background youth in Australia: Analysing different participation models. *Social Inclusion, 5*(2), 91–100.

Block, K., Warr, D., Gibbs, L., & Riggs, E. (2013). Addressing ethical and methodological challenges in research with refugee-background young people: Reflections from the field. *Journal of Refugee Studies, 26* (1), 69–87.

Cammarota, J., & Fine, M. (2008). *Revolutionizing Education: Youth Participatory Action Research in Motion*. New York, NY: Routledge.

Candappa, M. (2019). Border politics, the "hostile environment" for migration, and education in the UK. *Hungarian Educational Research Journal, 9* (3), 414–433.

Collison, C., & De Martini Ugolotti, N. (2021). Pain, faith and yoga: An intersectional-phenomenological perspective of Syrian Muslim womens experiences of yoga and resettlement in Sweden. In N. De Martini Ugolotti, & J. Caudwell (Eds), *Leisure and Forced Migration: Lives Lived in Asylum Systems*. 121–138. Abingdon: Routledge.

Cornwall, A., & Jewkes, R. (1995). What is participatory research? *Social Science and Medicine, 41* (12), 1667–1676.

De Martini Ugolotti, N., & Caudwell, J. (2021). *Leisure and Forced Migration Lives Lived in Asylum Systems*. Abingdon: Routledge. 1–18.

Doidge, M. (2018). Refugees united: the role of activism and football in supporting refugees. In Carter, T., Burdsey, D., & Doidge, M. (Eds), *Transforming Sport: Knowledges, Practices, Structures*. 25–33. London: Routledge.

Doidge, M., Keech, M., & Sandri, E. (2020). 'Active integration': Sport clubs taking an active role in the integration of refugees. *International Journal of Sport Policy and Politics, 12*(2), 305–319.

Dukic, D., McDonald, B., & Spaaij, R. (2017). Being able to play: Experiences of social inclusion and exclusion within a football team of people seeking asylum. *Social Inclusion, 5*, 101–110. https://doi.org/10.17645/si.v5i2.892

Enderle, S., & Mashreghi, S. (2022). Methodological challenges and opportunities in working within a participatory paradigm in the context of sport, forced migration and settlement: An insider perspective. *Sport in Society, 25* (3), 469–484.

Fals-Borda, O. (1987). The application of participatory action-research in Latin America. *International Sociology, 2* (4), 329–347.

Fine, M. (2006). Bearing witness: Methods for researching oppression and resistance: A textbook for critical research. *Social Justice Research, 19* (1), 83–108.

Freire, P. (1972). *Pedagogy of the Oppressed*. London: Penguin.

Goodfellow, M. (2019). *Hostile Environment*. London: Verso.

Gulamhusein, S. (2021). A Shia Ismaili Muslims ringette experiences on and off the ice: An autoethnography. In N. De Martini Ugolotti, & J. Caudwell (Eds), *Leisure and Forced Migration: Lives Lived in Asylum Systems*. 191–204. Abingdon: Routledge.

Harris, D.A. (2007). Dance/movement therapy approaches to fostering resilience and recovery among African adolescent torture survivors. *Torture: Quarterly Journal on Rehabilitation of Torture Victims and Prevention of Torture, 17*(2), 134–155.

Hartley, L., Fleay, C., & Tye, M.E. (2017). Exploring physical activity engagement and barriers for asylum seekers in Australia coping with prolonged uncertainty and no right to work. *Health and Social Care in the Community, 25*(3), 1190–1198.

Hubbard, G., Backett-Milburn, K., & Kemmer, D. (2001). Working with emotion: Issues for the researcher in fieldwork and teamwork. *International Journal of Social Research Methodology, 4*(2), 119–137.

Koopmans, B., & Doidge, M. (2021). 'They play together, they laugh together': Sport, play and fun in refugee sport projects. *Sport in Society*, ahead of print.

Lewis, H. (2015). Music, dancing and clothing as belonging and freedom among people seeking asylum in the UK. *Leisure Studies*, *34* (1), 42–58.

Ley, C., Rato Barrio, M., & Koch, A. (2018). "In the sport I am here": Therapeutic processes and health effects of sport and exercise on PTSD. *Qualitative Health Research*, *28*, 491–507.

Liberty (Ed.). (2019). *A Guide to the Hostile Environment*. London: Liberty.

Luguetti, C., Singehebhuye, L., & Spaaij, R. (2022a). 'Stop mocking, start respecting': An activist approach meets African Australian refugee-background young women in grassroots football." *Qualitative Research in Sport, Exercise and Health*, *14* (1), 119–136.

Luguetti, C., Singehebhuye, L., & Spaaij, R. (2022b). A collaborative self-study of ethical issues in participatory action research with refugee-background young people in grassroots football. *Sport in Society*, *25* (3), 453–468.

Mackenzie, C., McDowell, C., & Pittaway, E. (2007). Beyond 'do no harm': The challenge of constructing ethical relationships in refugee research. *Journal of Refugee Studies*, *20*, 299–318.

Maldonado-Torres, N. (2007). On the coloniality of being: Contributions to the development of a concept. *Cultural Studies*, *21* (23), 240–270.

Malkki, L. (1995) *Purity and Exile: Violence, Memory and National Cosmology among Hutu Refugees in Tanzania*. Chicago: University of Chicago Press.

Mashreghi, S., Yasmin, H., & Mohammed, A. (2021). Decolonial stories of forced migrants in physical activity and sport: We are the Afghan kids. In N. De Martini Ugolotti, & J. Caudwell (Eds), *Leisure and Forced Migration: Lives Lived in Asylum Systems*. 157–175. Abingdon: Routledge.

Mayblin, L. (2017). *Asylum after Empire*. New York: Rowman and Littlefield.

McDonald, B., Spaaij, R., & Dukic, D. (2019). Moments of social inclusion: Asylum seekers, football and solidarity. *Sport Sociology*, *22*, 935–949.

McSweeney, M., Hakiza, R., & Namukhula, J. (2022). Participatory action research and visual and digital methods with refugees in Kampala, Uganda: Process, ethical complexities, and reciprocity. *Sport in Society*, *25* (3), 485–505.

Middleton, T., Schinke, R., Lefebvre, D., Habra, B., Coholic, B., & Giffin, C. (2022). Critically examining a community-based participatory action research project with forced migrant youth. *Sport in Society*, *25* (3), 418–433.

Mignolo, W.D. (2011). *The Darker Side of Western Modernity: Global Futures, Decolonial Options*. North Carolina: Duke Press.

Mohammadi, S. (2019). Social inclusion of newly arrived female asylum seekers and refugees through a community sport initiative: The case of Bike Bridge. *Sport Sociology*, *22*, 1082–1099.

Ndlovu-Gatsheni, S.J. (2013). Why decoloniality in the 21st century? *The Thinker*. February 2013, *48*, 11–15.

Ozkul, D. (2020). Participatory research: Still a one-sided research agenda? *Migration Letters*, *17* (2), 229–237. doi: https://doi.org/10.33182/ml.v17i2.804

Palmer, C. (2009). Soccer and the politics of identity for young Muslim refugee women in South Australia. *Soccer in Society*, *10*, 27–38.

Pittaway, E., Bartolomei, L., & Hugman. R., (2010). 'Stop stealing our stories': The ethics of research with vulnerable groups. *Journal of Human Rights Practice*, *2* (2), 229–251.

Richards, J., Foster, C., Townsend, N., & Bauman, A. (2014). Physical fitness and mental health impact of a sport-for-development intervention in a post-conflict setting: Randomised controlled trial nested within an observational study of adolescents in Gulu, Uganda. *BMC Public Health*, *14* (619), 1–13.

Robinson, D.B., Robinson, I.M., Currie, V., & Hall, N. (2019). The Syrian Canadian sports club: A community-based participatory action research project with/for Syrian youth refugees. *Social Sciences*, *8*, 163.

Rosso, E., & McGrath, R. (2016). Promoting physical activity among children and youth in disadvantaged South Australian CALD communities through alternative community sport opportunities. *Health Promotion Journal of Australia*, *27* (2), 105–110.

Schmidt, D., & Palutan, G. (2021). Thick leisure: Waiting time in a migratory context. In N. De Martini Ugolotti, & J. Caudwell (Eds), *Leisure and Forced Migration: Lives Lived in Asylum Systems*. 52–66. Abingdon: Routledge.

Smith, R., Mansfield, L., & Wainwright, E. (2022). 'Should I really be here?': Problems of trust and ethics in PAR with young people from refugee backgrounds in sport and leisure. *Sport in Society, 25* (3), 434–452.

Spaaij, R. (2012). Beyond the playing field: Experiences of sport, social capital, and integration among Somalis in Australia. *Journal of Ethnic Racial Studies, 35,* 1519–1538.

Spaaij, R. (2015). Refugee youth, belonging and community sport. *Leisure Studies, 34,* 303–318.

Spaaij, R., Broerse, J., Oxford, S., Luguetti, C., McLachlan, F., McDonald, B., Klepac, B., Lymbery, L., Bishara, J., & Pankowiak, A. (2019). Sport, refugees, and forced migration: A critical review. *Frontiers in Sport and Active Living, 1* (89), 1–18.

Stone, C. (2018). Utopian community football? Sport, hope and belongingness in the lives of refugees and asylum seekers. *Leisure Studies, 37,* 171–183.

Stura, C. (2019). "What makes us strong": The role of sports clubs in facilitating integration of refugees. *European Journal Sport Sociology, 16,* 128–145.

Tuhiwai Smith, L. (1999). *Decolonizing Methodologies: Research and Indigenous People.* London: Zed Books.

UN General Assembly. (1951). *Convention Relating to the Status of Refugees*, 28 July 1951, United Nations, Treaty Series, 189, 137, available at: www.refworld.org/docid/3be01b964.html

UNHCR. (2003). *Procedural Standards for Refugee Status Determination under UNHCR's Mandate*, 20 November 2003, www.refworld.org/docid/42d66dd84.html

UNHCR (2022). Refugee data finder. Available at: www.unhcr.org/refugee-statistics/ (accessed on 21 November 2022).

Venturin-Trinade, N. (2021). Leisure provision for LGBTIQ + refugees: Opportunities and constraints on building solidarity and citizenship across differences in Brazil. In N. De Martini Ugolotti, & J. Caudwell (Eds), *Leisure and Forced Migration: Lives Lived in Asylum Systems.* 86–104. Abingdon: Routledge.

Waardenburg, M., Visschers, M., Deelen, I., & van Liempt, I. (2019). Sport in liminal spaces: The meaning of sport activities for refugees living in a reception centre. *International Review for the Sociology of Sport, 54* (8), 938–956.

Watson, B., & Scraton, S. (2013). Leisure studies and intersectionality. *Leisure Studies, 32* (1), 35–47.

Webster, C., & Abunaama, K. (2021). Informal football spaces and the negotiation of temporal politics in the lives of forced migrants. In N. De Martini Ugolotti, & J. Caudwell (Eds), *Leisure and Forced Migration: Lives Lived in Asylum Systems.* 21–35. Abingdon: Routledge.

Woodhouse, D., & Conricode, D. (2017). In-ger-land, In-ger-land, In-ger-land! Exploring the impact of soccer on the sense of belonging of those seeking asylum in the UK. *International Review for the Sociology of Sport, 52,* 940–954.

Yuval-Davis, N., Wemyss, G., & Cassidy, K. (2018). Everyday bordering: Belonging and the reorientation of British immigration legislation. *Sociology, 52*(2), 228–244.

39
INDIGENOUS METHODOLOGIES FOR SPORT, LEISURE AND SOCIAL JUSTICE RESEARCH

A Pacific studies perspective

Gina Hawkes

Introduction

Research methodologies that are ethically just, culturally aware, and flexibly attuned to those they seek to engage, are paramount in social analyses of sport and leisure. As spaces that are often understood to be liminal, embodied, symbolic, and where racialised and similar 'othering' narratives have wide appeal and influence, sport and leisure provide salient places for Western paradigms of categorisation, separation, and objectivity to be critiqued and replaced with more nuanced understandings, where Indigenous and other minority experiences can be centred (Nabobo-Baba 2008; Smith 1999; Thaman 2003; Uperesa 2016).

This chapter argues that *how* one researches sport and leisure is just as important as the *subject* of sport and leisure research. It does this with a particular emphasis on Indigenous epistemologies and decolonial practices in sports studies, particularly those from the Pacific, where leaders in the fields of Indigenous methodologies (e.g. Linda Tuhiwai-Smith), and critical sports studies (e.g. Brendan Hokowhitu and Lisa Uperesa), show both Indigenous and non-Indigenous people how to do research that is not only socially just, but that corrects historical biases, and more accurately presents the nuance and complexity within sporting spaces. The growing body of literature focused on Indigenous sports engagement across the Pacific addresses a paradox facing many Indigenous groups across the world – being over-researched yet under-valued and misunderstood, and many of its proponents are moving away from 'deficit' narratives towards models for flourishing.

This chapter begins by briefly outlining the influences and theories of social justice research (SJR) in sports and leisure that connect to critical Indigenous and Pasifika[1] studies, arguing that at the core of Indigenous and Pasifika methodologies is a social justice ethos. Next, it introduces the framework: 'from surviving to thriving' and sets out a few key methodological and subject-matter concerns to think about when attempting to do socially just research in sport and leisure with Indigenous and other minoritised groups. An important part of this research is reflexivity, and the final part of the chapter critically reflects on the very nature of doing research with a moral agenda. I argue that Indigenous frameworks, such as those from the Pacific, can help researchers see outside the myth of objectivity so prevalent in Western positivist paradigms, and illuminate how high-quality evidence-based scientific research can be done with a commitment to social justice and equality.

This chapter brings together key theories and arguments on important relational aspects of: identity; masculinity; spaces outside of the Western paradigms of individuality and separated genders; community; and the quotidian joys of sport in the everyday lives of Indigenous and other historically marginalised people. By synthesising and presenting these key arguments, it makes a case for future research to continue with this socially just focus on decolonial methodologies, Indigenous (and by extension other minority) thriving, and engagement with the everyday experiences of sport and leisure.

Critical Indigenous studies meets social justice research in sport and leisure

Social justice research in the sport and leisure space takes many shapes, and has been influenced by critical race theory (CRT), feminist and postcolonial studies, and many other approaches. Fields like social justice research (SJR) can therefore be hard to define due to the sheer size and complexity of the approaches and influences within. Like in other areas of social inquiry, SJR, CRT, feminist, and postcolonial critiques largely arose in response to flaws inherent in positivist paradigms resulting in outcomes that did not always help, and oftentimes hindered, minoritised groups (Crenshaw 1989). Yet despite the differences and tensions between these movements, each share some form of an emancipatory commitment, which is often based on lived experience, or a deep understanding of people's lived experiences, often relying on a closeness formed through, and sometimes outside, research partnerships (Parry, Johnson, & Stewart 2013). In 2000, Denzin posited that social justice work articulates a 'politics of hope' – that things will not only be critiqued but imagined how they could be different (Denzin 2000: 262). Denzin, drawing on mid-century African American cultural critics, argued that methodological, artistic, and political elements could never be neatly separated (2000: 261). Instead, we must use all the resources available to us – as humans and researchers – to understand and dismantle injustices. Similarly, Riches, Rankin-Wright, Swain, & Kuppan (2017) draw on Trussell (2014), Parry (2014), and Denzin (2000), to argue for moving beyond simply understanding how people live and negotiate their leisure experiences, to challenging and breaking down hegemonic social structures (2017: 218). Parry argues that 'it is not enough to interpret the world – one must change it as well' (2014: 353, drawing on Denzin 2000). But how do we know what change is good, helpful, wanted, or needed? And when do we go from interpreting to changing?

The field of critical Indigenous studies can help us answer these questions and provide examples of how research can be done with a socially just emancipatory commitment. From looking at the historical atrocities performed in the name of 'helping' – such as the 'civilising' and missionary ethos, and white saviourism, and exploring how things can be done better through partnership, consultation, and connection – social justice through sport and leisure can be a space of real positive change for all. Having preconceived notions of what people need, or what is socially just, without taking the time to listen and learn and understand, can be just as damaging (and often even more so) than doing nothing or upholding inequalities and injustices (Moreton-Robinson 2016). It is therefore paramount to work from a critically informed place that takes decolonial and other minoritised frameworks seriously. Social justice scholars, like Denzin (2000), Trussell (2014), and Parry (2014) argue for the importance of what are stalwarts of many Indigenous epistemologies, including those from the Pacific – connection, a critique of binaries, the need for mixed-methods, and the inclusion of lived experiences, senses, and emotions. Social studies of sport and leisure that only rely on Western neoliberal knowledge systems, and attempt to remove the researcher from the research, or focus on macro-social structures only, run counter to both Pasifika epistemologies and to socially just research ethics in sport and leisure studies more broadly.

Most recent scholarship in the critical leisure and sports studies fields is based in the UK and the US, and so perhaps understandably, the CRT, feminist, and postcolonial work from these regions has been particularly influential (Riches et al. 2017). The connections and similarities between this literature and the growing body of work in Indigenous sports studies, particularly from the Pacific, is significant, and can add much to the critical debates on how to do socially ethical research in sport and leisure. Like the UK/US-centred social justice research, Pasifika studies has, at its core, a commitment to the social justice ethos – particularly working with (not for) historically minoritised[2] peoples (Nabobo-Baba 2008; Parry et al. 2013). Like social justice studies more broadly, Pasifika studies demonstrates a common critique of, and desire to change and break down, dichotomies, and to move away from the deficit language so often used when discussing Indigenous and other minoritised groups, to focus on higher standards of thriving.

From surviving to thriving: A framework

There is a growing call within both Indigenous and social sports and leisure studies to move away from the common focus on deficits with minoritised peoples, and focus on higher standards of thriving, sometimes referred to as 'from surviving to thriving' (Durie 2016; Rua 2016). Much Indigenous sports scholarship focuses on the important relational aspects of identity (Stewart-Withers, Sewabu, & Richardson 2017), masculinity (Chen 2014), spaces outside the Western paradigms of individuality and separated genders (Tengan 2008), identity markers and communities (Panapa & Phillips 2014), as well as on the quotidian joys and mundaneness of sports (Teaiwa 2016). Much of this research considers the socially just research ethics needed to address these key concerns in sport and leisure studies (Uperesa & Mountjoy 2014), utilising frameworks that move away from deficit models and move towards opportunities for thriving.

For example, Stewart-Withers et al. (2017), in their work on Pasifika sports management, argue for the importance of utilising *talanoa* with Pasifika participants. *Talanoa* is a respected form of communication that centres around kinship, the group setting, the lack of an agenda, and reciprocal engagement and sharing of stories (Vaioleti 2006). Rather than conducting one-on-one interviews, with structured questions, and asking people to read written consent forms, the methods of *talanoa* show respect to a researcher's participants and can help make them feel comfortable. Stewart-Withers et al.'s work (2017, among others) set a precedent for researchers in the field of Pasifika sports studies, including Hawkes (2018), Lakisa, Adair, and Taylor (2014), and Borell (2022), who have each used *talanoa* to some degree, in their work with Pasifika rugby league players.

Long, Fletcher, and Watson, in their 2017 book on sport, leisure and social justice, also argue for the need to move away from deficit models. They acknowledge how policy often casts disadvantaged groups as a problem and argue for the need for more 'fundamental research that will introduce to the policy arena a nuanced understanding of the lives of disadvantaged people, problematising disadvantage without using a deficit model that makes them the problem' (2017: 5). Similarly, Riches et al. (2017, drawing on Aitchison 2007), in the same volume, encourage future scholars in leisure and sport to move 'from *marking* differences to *making* a difference' through inclusive and participatory research practices.

David Lakisa (2020) has done this in his work, utilising appropriate methodologies for working with Pasifika people, and has subsequently been contracted by the Australian National Rugby League (NRL) to work with all clubs on best practice management and cultural awareness for and of Pasifika players (Edwards 2023).

Many Indigenous scholars are also urging researchers to be wary of uncritical 'development' language (Hallinan & Judd 2013). Sport studies which concern themselves with the ways sport can 'help' Indigenous people to 'develop', can be in danger of assuming that Indigenous people need to develop, and with this focus on sport as a means to another end, can ignore the experiential, playful and quotidian elements of sport. There are possibilities for adding something different to the popular sport development discourse, where sport and minoritised groups can be studied together to explore what sport brings to people's lives on an everyday level, both good and bad, and what sport offers in and of itself rather than as a means to an end. I suggest that to do this we should take the role of joy seriously, and critique Western-centric sport for development discourses, which can place undue emphasis on the role of sport in developing external factors, such as achieving educational or economic goals (Jeanes, Magee, Kay, & Banda 2013). Instead, focusing on the cultural and creative elements of sports engagement, allows us to foreground alternative knowledges and ways of being, and move away from Western binaries and dichotomies. In Aotearoa/New Zealand Māori research, this is called *Mauri Ora* (Durie 2016), and it includes moving away from past struggles to future opportunities, among other things. Table 39.1 synthesises some of the core movements scholars have identified to make research more socially just – both methodologically, and in the subject of one's research.

The mundane joy of sport and leisure for minoritised people: Unpacking dichotomies

While sport can be implicated in reproducing inequalities, it also offers opportunities to challenge and transform them (Hawkes 2018; Long, Fletcher, & Watson 2017). Unlike many other subjects of research, sport and leisure offer spaces for joy and play, and present a special opportunity to explore and strengthen human feelings of belonging, as well as a sense of self and identity. Sport offers joy in its ability to create meaning, community, belonging, happiness and opportunities, and it is just as important to acknowledge the role of joy in sports as it is the continuing problems, especially for people from historically and structurally marginalised groups. As Phipps argues,

> Enjoyment can ... be an act of resistance against the dominant global culture and its preferences for productivity and commodified pleasures. Pleasure in the experience of specific, collective cultural difference really matters to people – most urgently to groups facing adversity.
>
> (2016: 252–253)

For the world's Indigenous peoples, and other minoritised groups, sport's quotidian, almost taken-for-granted presence can play a profound role in helping shape and make sense of their lived identities. A focus on quotidian lifeworlds, including the joy and sense of belonging sport can foster, as opposed to macro-social structures of 'economic determinism' (Hau'ofa 1994), is an approach many Pasifika and sports scholars have recognised the need for in recent years (e.g. Dewey Jr 2014; Lakisa et al. 2014; Molnar and Kanemasu 2014). These scholars bring to light the skilful negotiations Indigenous people in sport make between seemingly

Table 39.1 A social justice framework for research with minoritised groups[3]

	Move away from	To include more
Methodology	Conducting research on issues the researcher thinks are important to a certain group of people	Research that is relevant, responsible, and respectful to those with whom it engages
	Minoritised people as the object of study	Minoritised people as active agents and producers of discourse
	Incorporating scholarly protocols	Incorporating appropriate cultural protocols and practices
	Interpreting the world	Changing the world
	Fixing a problem	Sustaining wellness
	Working for	Working with
	Marking difference	Making a difference
	Giving back	Standing with
	Addressing disadvantage	Unleashing potential
Subject	Determinants of languishing	Pathways to flourishing
	Minoritised peoples' disadvantages	Minoritised peoples' strengths
	Past struggles	Future opportunities
	Legislation that contradicts minoritised groups	Legislation that endorses minoritised groups' rights
	Minoritised models of treatment and care	Minoritised models of wellness and safety
	Surviving	Thriving

disparate worlds. Through sport they enable a world of competing identities, of relational understandings of kin, space, liminality, service, of the aesthetics and senses in life. While sport can be, and has been, damaging and oppressive, it has also been a space of connection, belonging, and identity formation, and has ample potential in positively affecting the practices and perceptions of not only Indigenous peoples, but all peoples across the globe.

A growing body of scholars argue that it is important to seriously consider the positives of sport in the everyday lives of a minoritised group of peoples (Teaiwa 2016). Marsters and Tiatia-Seath (2019) offer one of the few studies on the mental health of Pasifika athletes that focuses on 'pleasant emotions' as opposed to unpleasant ones, showing how sport interconnects with other important aspects of Pasifika athletes' lives to enhance their mental wellbeing. Acknowledging the joy in sport and the playing of sport for its own sake has been seen by some scholars as a form of decolonisation in itself. Jeanes et al. argue that macro-social development agendas, as well as common attacks on sports development programs as neocolonialist, often ignore complex and actual experiences for local peoples, and they argue the need to "decolonise methodologies within sport for development research to prioritise local knowledge and experience" (2013: 135).

Decolonial frameworks have been championed by Aotearoa/New Zealand based scholars such as Smith (1999) and Hokowhitu (2004), and influenced other scholars across the Pacific and beyond (Besnier 2015). Within this movement, Western paradigms of categorisation, separation, and 'objectivity' are critiqued and replaced with more nuanced local understandings where Indigenous experiences are centred (see Nabobo-Baba 2008; Smith 1999; Thaman 2003; Uperesa 2016). Renowned Māori scholar, Linda Tuhiwai Smith notes that in racial debates "'Authorities'" and outside experts are often called in to … give judgements about the validity of indigenous claims to … ways of knowing" and that these debates "frequently have the effect … of silencing … the presence of other groups within the indigenous society like women, the urban non-status tribal person and those whose ancestry or 'blood quantum' is 'too white'" (1999: 72–73). While Smith is talking specifically about Indigenous knowledge claims, we can apply her arguments to other minoritised groups, such as gender-diverse people or people with a disability, whose 'ways of knowing' are often called into question based on Western preoccupations with objectivity and distance.

Another leading Māori scholar, Brendan Hokowhitu, uses a postcolonial lens to argue for the importance of local knowledges in sport studies. He argues that:

> any analysis of indigeneity and sport must be firstly cognisant of "local knowledges" and place, the dispossessing nature of colonialism, the role sport played in assimilating the Indigenous population within the nation state, the complexity that is the indigenous athlete as both indigenous hero and dupe, the possibilities that sport holds as a spectacle of indigenous resistance and, more than anything, the relationship between sport and indigenous postcolonial corporeality.
>
> (Hokowhitu 2013: xvii)

While Hokowhitu's work seriously considers the destruction caused by colonialism for the world's Indigenous people, and how this has been inflected in sports, he also acknowledges the paradoxes inherent within the Indigenous sporting space, such as the glorification and demonisation of Indigenous and black athletes, and how sport can exploit and oppress, as well as offer possibilities for emancipation (Hokowhitu 2013).

This ties in with the growing calls to move away from minoritised struggle and survival narratives, to focus more on thriving and flourishing (Durie 2016; Rua 2016). While violent, spectacular, and mega events are often the focus of sports studies and sports media, most sporting experiences are far less sensational. There is an immediate tangibility to sports, whether it be through watching or participating, making it a desirable space for many minoritised peoples, who may struggle with feelings of belonging, and even joy and purpose in places historically levelled against them through discriminatory policies and structural disadvantage. As Phipps and Slater note, "Belonging – being and feeling at home, safe, nurtured and responsible for, and to, people and place – is fundamental to not only individual but also social wellbeing" (2010: 41). The exceptions of sport have been the traditional focus of sport studies, whereas the quotidian experiences of sport, which are so incredibly pervasive across the world, are surprisingly neglected, particularly sports that are seen to be 'lower-class', like rugby league (Spracklen, Timmins, & Long 2010).

I will give an example from my own area of study, with the Pasifika diaspora in Australia and Aotearoa/New Zealand. In these nations, Pasifika men are couched in discourses of problems, issues and struggles, much like their Indigenous Australian brothers. They are overrepresented in the justice system and have lower socioeconomic status than the white majority populations (Ravulo 2015). Sports like rugby league, despite all their problems, provide, at times a very rare, opportunity for both mundane quotidian joy as well as spectacular livelihood building opportunities. A major reason for playing rugby league for young Pasifika men in Sydney is simply to enjoy it, with this enjoyment coming from a sense of belonging and camaraderie, which in turn heightens self-esteem. As one of my Australian-Tongan participants said about why so many Pasifika people love rugby league: "it's a very team-oriented sport, and we do community so well, we live in communities, we were brought up by communities" (Hawkes 2018). For the world's Indigenous and other minoritised peoples, such as those diasporic Pasifika peoples engaged in rugby league with whom I have worked, sport's quotidian presence can play a profound role in helping shape and make sense of lived identities. It is therefore important to seriously consider sports' power and potential, not just as a means to some other end, such as financial or social capital, but as something important in and of itself, as something joyful, meaningful and fulfilling in life.

In Grainger's 2009 article on the racialisation of athletic performance in the Pacific Islands, he argues that "all too frequently the intellectual and the physical are assumed as antithetical and antagonistic" (2009: 53). He says this in reference to the discourse on 'Islander' styles of play and the importance of seeing them in the context of a long history of racialised athletic ability. This quote speaks to key methodological concerns of social justice research in sport and leisure – it highlights the importance of qualitative research; Indigenous epistemologies of relationality; and deep engagement with decolonial perspectives and practices. In this argument Grainger expresses a modern conundrum – that of the continuing binary oppositional assumption of the intellectual and the physical introduced through colonisation and perpetuated to this day. Grainger's quote both pertains to the historical exclusion of serious engagement with sports and other corporeal practices in social science scholarship, and makes us think about the separation of body and mind and how this manifests in sporting discourse, particularly around black and brown peoples, whose physicality is often highlighted at the expense of their intellectual and other abilities (Hawkes 2018; McDonald & Rodriguez 2014; Zakus & Horton 2009).

In drawing attention to the ways the intellectual and the physical are separated in sports, scholars highlight that despite the physical quality of sports, there are always intellectual, and socio-cultural components to it (Grainger 2008). These components are also often highly historically and structurally inscribed (Besnier 2014). For example, the way Pasifika men are lauded for particular styles of play which are highly physical, natural, and biological, instead of styles of play that are smart, disciplined, and showing leadership, is a view that comes from a history of colonisation based on racial stratification and assumes the physicality of Pasifika peoples to be their greatest asset and in lieu of other capabilities (Hawkes 2018; Hokowhitu 2004). The ways in which Pasifika peoples are popularly framed, and have at times internalised – as brawn over brain, as half-and-halves but authentically neither, as hyper-physical, hyper-masculine, warriors or undisciplined – are based on categories aimed at colonising Pasifika bodies and minds (Tengan & Markham 2009). They rely on Western binaries and taking things out of context in order to test them 'scientifically'. Riches et al. (2017) argue that we need to unpack dichotomies to integrate social justice well into our research agendas, e.g. those between theory/practice, personal/professional, and scholar/activist, which create divisions and isolation from each other and from the "empowering potential of reflexive inquiry" (2017: 211). These dichotomies work in direct contrast to many Indigenous and social justice-focused frameworks, which not only acknowledge the need to unpack research dichotomies but those apparent in sports as well, such as the intellectual and physical being antithetical.

Gina Hawkes

Ethical responsibility: Letting the research change you

Pacific Studies scholar Lisa Uperesa, argues that it is not your position as outsider or insider that makes your work good but how you do that research (Uperesa 2010). Critical reflexive research, in order to be socially just, needs to recognise the relationship between researcher(s) and researched, and move beyond simple positionality statements in one's finished work, to consider the concerns outlined in Table 39.1 from the very beginning of a research project – is this research wanted and needed by the people it engages with? Is it consultative, working with and not simply for? Will it help create positive change, and if not, will it aid understanding that can lead to positive change for future scholars? As UK-based rugby league scholars, Spracklen, Timmins, and Long said, as ethnographers of rugby league it is our job to "try and make the game more equal", but if we are unable to do that, we must at least "expose the game's failings in understanding 'race', racism and racialised discourse (and gender and sexuality)" (Spracklen, Timmins, & Long 2010: 410). Leisure studies scholar Trussell makes her position explicit, recognising that her position "as a white, heterosexual, and able-bodied woman who is a mother, and as a feminist, starts from a privileged position of power (academically and personally)" (2014: 343), and that with this privilege comes responsibility. She draws on Watson and Scraton, who argue that "Those who hold a central position in the dominant discourse have a responsibility to engage in critical, reflexive research to support both theoretical and political change" (2001, as cited in Trussell 2014: 343).

Pasifika scholars have an excellent understanding of the need for critical reflexive scholarship, as their identities are embedded in the connections between people, as well as non-human elements. Aotearoa/New Zealand Māori people for instance, introduce themselves through their relationship to *iwi* (tribe), not who they are as an individual. They reveal their identity through relationships to environmental signifiers, such as their *waka* (canoe), and their *maunga* (mountain), and to their ancestors, which may change depending on who they are talking to, choosing to emphasise the ones most relevant to their interlocutors. Similarly, people from Samoa have status and place-based indicators in their name, which will give their interlocutors a sense of their relationship. An Aotearoa/New Zealand psychological study in 2005 found that Samoan sense of self was not individual, starting from a sense of 'I', but only had meaning in relation to others (Tamasese, Peteru, Waldegrave, & Bush 2005). The High Court of New Zealand's Justice Joe Williams explains how Māori science works in opposition to Western science, comparing the Cartesian dualism of 'I *think* therefore I am', to the Polynesian understanding of 'I *belong* therefore I am', claiming that 'kinship explains everything' for Polynesian people and that 'if you get this, you get the whole system' (Williams 2016). Relationships between people and groups are where strength and identity are created, and it is important to make this information accessible and not hide or obfuscate who you are.

This is why I, and other scholars committed to social justice, do not try to hide the different experiences and feelings we have through our research, whether they be feelings of white privilege, awkwardness, ease, guilt, insider worries, familial or community responsibilities, but instead choose to make them an explicit part of the process and critically analyse them. I have become increasingly aware that the awkwardness, guilt, and non-belonging I feel at times during my research is but a miniscule fraction of the difficulties and complexities most of my Indigenous and other minoritised peers face in their research journeys (see Uperesa 2010). In the early days of my research career, I wished I was Indigenous, to have some special claim to what I considered a deeper 'culture', to have a claim to a communal suffering, to feel the pride of survival and have a deep connection with my fellow group members. I share this incredibly naïve and embarrassing confession because I think it is a more common sentiment than many of us would like to admit, and the ignorance it implies is something that takes acknowledgment and understanding of the continuing historical legacy of Indigenous oppression the world over. In other words, I share it because there is something deeply troubling and actually dangerous about the desire to co-opt what appear to be the positive parts of an Indigenous culture without understanding the quotidian historical and structural racism your own position as the legacy of genocide and oppression privileges from. Linda Tuhiwai Smith (1999), Ty P. Kawika Tengan (2008), and Lisa Uperesa (2010) are three Indigenous Pasifika scholars who highlight the complexities of straddling the worlds of academia and their cultural and familial responsibilities. They remind non-Indigenous scholars of some of the individualistic freedoms we often have. Uperesa notes that the legitimacy of minority and Indigenous scholars' research is often questioned because it does not fit neatly within canonised frameworks, or is suspect because it does not sustain the fiction of objectivity (2016: n.p.). As more scholars critique this fiction, and find new ways to conduct research, the legitimacy of minoritised ways of doing things will continue to be enhanced. Closeness, not distance, can produce good research.

Feminist scholar Judith Butler argues that the ethical stance means permitting the other to live in its alterity in the full knowledge that one's notions of self-coherence and self-identity will be interrupted by the difference that one embraces (Salih & Butler 2004: 3). This reminds us of the imperativeness of taking the time to understand before rushing in to 'try and help', particularly those of us with a social justice ethos. We need to acknowledge difference, spend time and work hard to understand as best we can, allowing ourselves to be challenged and changed. Only after that, and the consideration of the methods and theories discussed in this chapter and in Table 39.1, should we begin to seek change. By acknowledging the power of the spaces and relationships between selves and environments, a more holistic sense of our shared identities and differential experiences can begin to take shape.

In my PhD thesis (Hawkes 2019), I discuss my own journey of slowly removing my rose-coloured glasses from what we could call the fashionable 'neo-paternal collection' – that which frames the researcher as a sort of 'proto-parent' wanting to 'help' the 'vulnerable' (see Hawkes, Pollock, Judd, Phipps, & Assoulin 2017 for more on this term) – and replacing them with a complex weathered view that sees flaws and incongruences, and most importantly, sees these within my own self and my own socio-cultural habits. For all researchers, and particularly if you are not a member of the minoritised group(s) you research, a 'kind yet critical' focus can be very helpful – both on the content of your work, and on your relationship with your self. It is not enough to include an introduction or token references to your self in your work, and call it reflexivity. There needs to be a constantly evolving critical engagement with your positionality, and the relationship/s between your self and those with whom your work engages. Because this can be incredibly uncomfortable and confronting, a kindness is also necessary. You can fail, you can get things wrong, and you can let these teach you how to be a better researcher, and ultimately a better person. Only then will the truly emancipatory possibilities of our research as sports and leisure practitioners and scholars committed to social justice be realisable. Vulnerability, humility, and humour also go a long way! As Parry notes of her own research journey, she has learned "to be respectful of silences, to read body language, to probe through eye contact, and gentle questions, the value of humour at the right moment, and to carry facial tissues" (Parry 2014: 355).

Conclusion

Indigenous North American feminist scholar, Kimberley Tallbear, argues that we should engage more deeply with feminist and Indigenous scholarship and positions, not in order to simply invert traditional binaries, to see things from an Indigenous or feminist standpoint but to become more attuned to the particular histories of privilege and denial and to create greater insight and responsibility (Tallbear 2013: 25). In sport and leisure studies, this is paramount for the pursuit of social justice.

By combining the literature on critical social justice research in sport and leisure, with the ground-breaking research coming out of the growing Indigenous and Pasifika studies realms, we see the need for open and engaged studies of local nuances that address social justice issues and tie in with larger discursive and historical considerations. The way we teach and value methodologies and ethics are two places where sport and leisure studies can make meaningful contributions. Because sport and leisure offer opportunities for joy, play, belonging, community, and other forms of flourishing, the growing call to move away from deficit models when it comes to minoritised peoples has a natural home in socially just sport and leisure studies.

In recognising that knowledge is always positional, we can acknowledge (and embrace) that our research can, and sometimes must, draw on relationships, and that it can be oral, visual, embodied, and somewhere in between (Hawkes 2023). As the scholars referenced in this chapter attest, far from being too unspecific or unscientific, these approaches correct historical bias, and in turn create more accurate science as they engage with many rules and protocols to gain better knowledge; they are just rules that have gone unrecognised by dominant Western research paradigms. If we focus on the lived experiences, feelings, and emotions of sport, we may be able to better understand what it adds to people's lives on an everyday basis and shape it in ways that are beneficial for historically minoritised groups. The myth of objectivity in scientific research has no place in sport and leisure studies committed to social justice.

Notes

1. A term used to encompass both ideas and people from the Pacific Islands as well as their dispersed global diaspora.
2. This is not a commonly used word in Pasifika studies; however, it is common in UK-based leisure studies where this book is being published. I use it to refer to groups of people who are generally considered outside the mainstream and have been oppressed in some way because of this – including Indigenous people, people of colour, members of the LGBTQ+ community, neurodivergent, and physically disabled people. I acknowledge the complexity of these identities and that no one word can encapsulate such a diverse group of people.
3. Synthesised from numerous studies in Pacific, Indigenous, sports, and social justice research, most notably Durie (2016), Ka'ili (2017); Tallbear (2014), and White and Tengan (2001).

References

Aitchison, C. (2007). Marking difference or making a difference: Constructing places, policies and knowledge of inclusion, exclusion and social justice in leisure, sport and tourism. In I. Ateljevic, A. Pritchard, & N. Morgan (Eds), *The Critical Turn in Tourism Studies: Innovation Research Methodologies*. Elsevier: 77–90.

Besnier, N. (2014). Pacific Island rugby: Histories, mobilities, comparisons. *Asia Pacific Journal of Sport and Social Science* 3(3): 268–276.

Besnier, N. (2015). Sports mobilities across borders: Postcolonial perspectives. *The International Journal of the History of Sport* 32(7): 849–861.

Borell, P. J. (2022). *Polysaturated: Illuminating the experiences of Polynesian athletes in professional rugby league*. PhD dissertation. University of Canterbury, Christchurch. Available at: https://ir.canterbury.ac.nz/bitstream/handle/10092/104767/Borell%2C%20Phillip_Final%20phd%20Thesis.pdf?Sequence=1

Chen, C. H. (2014). Prioritizing hyper-masculinity in the Pacific region. *Culture, Society and Masculinities* 6(1): 69–90.

Crenshaw, K. (1989). Demarginalizing the intersection of race and sex: A black feminist critique of antidiscrimination doctrine, feminist theory and antiracist politics. *University of Chicago Legal Forum* 1(8): 139–167.

Denzin, N. K. (2000). Aesthetics and the practices of qualitative inquiry. *Qualitative Inquiry* 6(2): 256–265.

Dewey Jr, R. F. (2014). Fiji and Pacific rugby research: The state of the game. *Asia Pacific Journal of Sport and Social Science* 3(3): 186–201.

Durie, M. (2016). *Mauri Ora, indigenous human flourishing*. Ngā Pae o te Māramatanga conference, November 16. Auckland University.

Edwards, C. (2023). New advisory group helping highlight Pasifika perspectives. NRL. Available at: www.nrl.com/news/2023/03/19/new-advisory-group-helping-highlight-pasifika-perspectives/

Grainger, A. (2008). *The browning of the All Blacks: Pacific peoples, rugby, and the cultural politics of identity in New Zealand*. PhD dissertation, University of Maryland. Available at: https://drum.lib.umd.edu/bitstream/handle/1903/8202/umi-umd-5398.pdf?sequence=1&isAllowed=y

Grainger, A. (2009). Rugby island style: Paradise, Pacific people, and the racialisation of athletic performance. *Junctures* 12: 45–63.

Hallinan, C., & B. Judd. (2013). *Native Games: Indigenous Peoples and Sports in the Post-Colonial World*. UK: Emerald Group Publishing.

Hau'ofa, E. (1994). Our sea of islands. *The Contemporary Pacific* 6(1): 148–161.

Hawkes, G. L. (2018). Indigenous masculinity in sport: The power and pitfalls of rugby league for Australia's Pacific Island diaspora. *Leisure Studies* 37(3): 318–330.

Hawkes, G. L. (2019). *Diasporic Belonging, Masculine Identity and Sports: How Rugby League Affects the Perceptions and Practices of Pasifika Peoples in Australia*. PhD dissertation. RMIT University, Melbourne. Available at: https://researchrepository.rmit.edu.au/esploro/outputs/doctoral/%20Diasporicbelonging-masculine-identity-and-sports-how-rugbyleague-affects-theperceptions-and-practices-of-Pasifika-peoples-inaustralia/9921864288401341

Hawkes, G. L. (2023). Football, faith and family for the Australian Pacific Island diaspora: The role of the vā (space between) in rugby league, *Sport in Society* 26(9): 1530–1548. http://dx.doi.org/10.1080/17430437.2022.2160708

Hawkes, G. L., Pollock, D., Judd, B., Phipps, P., & Assoulin, E. (2017). Ngapartji Ngapartji: Finding ethical approaches to research involving indigenous peoples. Australian Perspectives. *Ab-Original 1*: 17–41.

Hokowhitu, B. (2004). Tackling Maori masculinity: A colonial genealogy of savagery and sport. *The Contemporary Pacific* 16(2): 259–284.

Hokowhitu, B. (2013). Foreword. In C. Hallinan & B. Judd. (Eds), *Native Games: Indigenous Peoples and Sports in the Postcolonial World*. UK: Emerald Group Publishing: xvxxi.

Jeanes, R., J. Magee, T. Kay, & D. Banda. (2013). Sport for development in Zambia: The new or not so new colonisation? In C. Hallinan, & B. Judd (Eds), *Native Games: Indigenous Peoples and Sports in the Post-Colonial World*. UK: Emerald Group Publishing: 127–146.

Ka'ili, T. O. (2017). *Marking Indigeneity: The Tongan Art of Sociospatial Relations*. Tucson: University of Arizona Press.

Lakisa, D. (2020). *Managing Pasifika Diaspora in Australian Rugby League*. PhD dissertation. University of Technology Sydney. Available at: http://hdl.handle.net/10453/144109

Lakisa, D., D. Adair, & T. Taylor (2014). Pasifika diaspora and the changing face of Australian Rugby League. *The Contemporary Pacific* 26(2): 347–367.

Long, J., Fletcher, T., & Watson, B. (2017). *Sport, Leisure and Social Justice*. London, UK: Taylor & Francis Group.

Marsters, C., & Tiatia-Seath, J. (2019). Young pacific male rugby players' perceptions and experiences of mental wellbeing. *Sports 7*(4), 83.

Mcdonald, B., & L. Rodriguez. (2014). 'It's our meal ticket': Pacific bodies, labour and mobility in Australia. *Asia Pacific Journal of Sport and Social Science 3*(3): 236–249.

Molnar, G., & Y. Kanemasu (2014). Playing on the global periphery: Social scientific explorations of rugby in the Pacific Islands. *Asia Pacific Journal of Sport and Social Science 3*(3): 175–185.

Moreton-Robinson, A. (2016). *Critical Indigenous Studies: Engagement in First World Locations.* Tucson: The University of Arizona Press.

Nabobo-Baba, U. (2008). Decolonising framings in Pacific research: Indigenous Fijian Vanua research framework as an organic response. *Alternative: An International Journal of Indigenous Peoples 4*(2): 141–154.

Panapa, L., & M. Phillips. (2014). Ethnic persistence: Towards understanding the lived experiences of Pacific Island athletes in the National Rugby League. *The International Journal of the History of Sport 31*(11): 1374–1388.

Parry, D. C. (2014). My transformative desires: Enacting feminist social justice leisure research. *Leisure Sciences 36*(4): 349–364.

Parry, D. C., Johnson, C. W., & Stewart, W. (2013). Leisure research for social justice: A response to Henderson. *Leisure Sciences 35*(1): 81–87.

Phipps, P. (2016). Performing Indigenous sovereignties across the Pacific. In K. Alexeyeff, & J. Taylor (Eds), *Touring Pacific Cultures.* ACT: ANU Press: 245–265.

Phipps, P., & L. Slater. (2010). *Indigenous Cultural Festivals: Evaluating Impact on Community Health and Wellbeing.* Melbourne: Globalism Research Centre, RMIT.

Ravulo, J. (2015). *Pacific Communities in Australia.* University of Western Sydney.

Riches, G., Rankin-Wright, A. J., Swain, S., & Kuppan, V. (2017). Moving forward: Critical reflections on doing social justice research. In Long, J., Fletcher, T., & Watson, B. (Eds), *Sport, Leisure and Social Justice.* London: Taylor & Francis Group: 209–221.

Rua, M. (2016). *Māori men's positive and interconnected sense of self, being and place. NAISA conference,* May 18. University of Hawai'i.

Salih, S., & J. Butler. (2004). *The Judith Butler Reader.* Malden: Blackwell Publishing.

Smith, L. T. (1999). *Decolonizing Methodologies: Research and Indigenous Peoples.* London, New York, Dunedin: Zed Books Ltd, University of Otago Press.

Spracklen, K., S. Timmins, & J. Long. (2010). Ethnographies of the imagined, the imaginary and the critically real: Blackness, whiteness, the north of England and rugby league. *Leisure Studies 29*(4): 397–414.

Stewart-Withers, R., K. Sewabu, & S. Richardson. (2017). Talanoa: A contemporary qualitative methodology for sport management. *Sport Management Review 20*: 55–68.

Tallbear, K. (2013). *Native American DNA: Tribal Belonging and the False Promise of Genetic Science.* Minneapolis: University of Minnesota Press.

Tallbear, K. (2014). Standing with and speaking as faith: A feminist-indigenous approach to inquiry. *Journal of Research Practice 10*(2): 1–6.

Tamasese, C., C. Peteru, C. Waldegrave, & A. Bush. (2005). O le Taeao Afua, the New Morning: A qualitative investigation into Samoan perspectives on mental health and culturally appropriate services. *Australian and New Zealand Journal of Psychiatry 39*(4): 300–309.

Teaiwa, K. M. (2016). Niu Mana, sport, media and the Australian diaspora. In M. Tomlinson, & T. P. K. Tengan (Eds), *New Mana: Transformations of a Classic Concept in Pacific Languages and Cultures.* The Australian National University, Canberra: ANU Press: 107–130.

Tengan, T. P. K. (2008). *Native Men Remade: Gender and Nation in Contemporary Hawai'i.* Durham and London: Duke University Press.

Tengan, T. P. K., & J. M. Markham. (2009). Performing Polynesian masculinities in American football: From 'rainbows to warriors'. *The International Journal of the History of Sport 26*(16): 2412–2431.

Thaman, K. H. (2003). Decolonizing Pacific studies: Indigenous perspectives, knowledge, and wisdom in higher education. *The Contemporary Pacific 15*(1): 1–17.

Trussell, D. E. (2014). Dancing in the margins. *Journal of Leisure Research 46*(3): 342–352.

Uperesa, F. L. (2010). A different weight: Tension and promise in 'indigenous anthropology'. *Pacific Studies 33*(2): 280.

Uperesa, F. L. (2016). A decolonial turn in anthropology? A view from the Pacific. *Savage Minds*. June 7. Available at: http://savageminds.org/2016/06/07/a-decolonialturn-in-anthropology-a-view-from-the-pacific/. Accessed June 2016.

Uperesa, F. L., & T. Mountjoy. (2014). Global sport in the Pacific: A brief overview. *The Contemporary Pacific 26*(2): 263–279.

Vaioleti, T. M. (2006). Talanoa research methodology: A developing position on Pacific research. *Waikato Journal of Education 12*: 21–34.

White, G. M., & T. P. K. Tengan. (2001). Disappearing worlds: Anthropology and cultural studies in Hawai'i and the Pacific. *The Contemporary Pacific 13*(2): 381–416.

Williams, J. (2016). *Te Reo me Ngā Tikanga Māori: Thriving indigenous languages*. Ngā Pae o te Māramatanga conference, 15 November. Auckland University.

Zakus, D., & P. Horton. (2009). Pasifika in Australian rugby: Eminent cultural, social and economic issues. *Sporting Traditions 26*(2): 67–86.

40
RESEARCH INTEGRITY AND ETHICS IN SPORT SOCIAL JUSTICE RESEARCH
Safe practice

Christina Philippou

Introduction

From Colin Kaepernick's confrontations with the NFL over racial inequality and social injustice (Graham, 2019), to Alysia Montaño's public shaming of sponsor Nike over their maternity policy (Montaño, 2019), to government investment decisions involving sporting entities (Næss, 2019), to human rights abuses in pursuit of sport mega-events (Byrne, Ludvigsen, & Andre, 2022), sport has often found itself in the midst of a very broad range of social justice controversies. And controversies breed debate, both internally and externally to academia, which is when researchers often step in to provide evidence so as to support or refute arguments put forward. The 2022 FIFA World Cup is a prime example of this, with researchers providing an array of evidence from interdisciplinary perspectives as part of the multiple debates arising (Philippou, 2022).

Literature on social justice is, by its nature, often emotive and linked to social causes. And researcher motivation for investigating areas related to particular social causes often means that the subject covered is likely to be close to the researcher's heart, leaving it open to accusations of moralism (Hammersley & Traianou, 2011). Alternatively, funding by lobby groups reluctant to change the status quo – a change that could (and does) arise from evidence-based concerns raised by advocates of the relevant social cause – could also leave the research itself open to accusations of unethical behaviour.

So, just as ethics is at the core of research motivation for literature on social justice topics, so should it be at the core of the research itself. Thus, when tackling social justice topics, the ethics of the research itself always needs to be a focus of the researcher from the very start of a project, from design through to dissemination.

From a practical perspective, too, strong research ethics are key to ensuring that any outputs are robust when subjected to greater scrutiny (as they are likely to be) than other less emotive topics by both those within and outside academia. If research is used, as it should be, to support calls for action in respect of social causes and social injustices based on evidence, it needs to ensure that its robustness will not be compromised by potentially unethical practices at some point within the research journey.

This chapter therefore charts the research journey from a research ethics perspective, highlighting the philosophical and practical challenges of social justice work. It covers the notion of integrity, before going on to outline how practitioners can maintain integrity while working to (often) neoliberal agendas. The chapter also covers requirements for research ethics in the research design, data collection, analysis of data and final outputs, and the research integrity of post-publication dissemination.

The notion of integrity

The notion of integrity plays a crucial role in the study of social justice in sport. Integrity is an important concept not just in the academic world but also in politics (Council of Europe & UEFA, 2018, Article 2), sport governance (see, for example, World Athletics, 2019, Article 3.34), sponsors of sporting events or entities (Hughes, 2018), monitoring (in bodies like WADA (Howman, 2013)), and law enforcement (Interpol, 2020). The concept of integrity is becoming increasingly relevant to consumers, particularly those who are concerned about social justice in sport. It therefore stands to reason that one cannot research social justice in sport without having a clear spine of integrity running through the work itself. However, the definition of integrity is not universally agreed upon and can vary in its conceptual and theoretical foci.

So what is the notion of integrity? 'Integrity of sport' is a concept of multi-disciplinary and interdisciplinary importance and one that, via the notion of public concern (Carroll, 1979), is becoming important to consumers (Rodgers, Söderbom, & Guiral, 2015), particularly those with a leaning towards social justice agendas in sport. As such, the notion of integrity is directly compatible with that of social justice.

In the same way that 'integrity' is often at the heart of any discussions around controversy in sport both on (Harvey & McNamee, 2019) and off the field/court/pitch (Philippou, 2019), it is also subject to differing opinions when it comes to a definition.

Integrity has a number of theoretical and conceptual foci, such as the concept of replication in research integrity (Savolainen & VanEseltine, 2018) and ethical underpinnings in general understandings of the term in relation to sport (Philippou & Hines, 2021). For example, Breivik (2000) splits out different ethical considerations affecting sporting outcomes, such as 'ontological chance' (the idea of factors brought about by chance including biology) and 'epistemological uncertainty' (where uncertainty of outcomes exist, e.g. lotteries for groups in tournaments). These different ethical considerations thus also play a role in determining the definition of integrity and ethics in sport. For example, Skillen (1998) shows how the competitive environments in existence around most sports are not necessarily incompatible with the concept of sporting values and therefore the notion of integrity as social benefits could arise if viewed through a utilitarian ethical lens.

The existence of varied definitions of integrity can create tensions – between theory and practice, and within the conceptual and theoretical foci themselves. For example, integrity breaches are often at the core of the creation of social justice causes, but if the definitions of integrity vary between stakeholders, then whether or not an integrity breach has indeed even occurred may become a topic of debate.

So integrity is arguably integral to sport in its various guises. With the notion of integrity deeply embedded in sport, it is unsurprising that social justice in sport is also steeped in the notion. And when a topic is infused then so, too, does the research underpinning it need to be.

The notion of research ethics

It is of course not a coincidence that a lot of the discussions and debates around the concept of integrity actually centre around points of ethics. In fact, the two terms are often interchangeable in discourses in sport (McNamee & Parry, 1998). In a similar vein to the variety of definitions of the term integrity as applied to sport, there are multiple definitions of the term 'research ethics'.

Ethics is a very wide and diverse field of study (Simon, 2011), and the breadth of ontological positions in relation to sport ethics mirrors that of its wider parent field (Arthur & Brendan, 2017). Research ethics define all elements of a study project, from inception through to post-publication discussions and use. As such, research ethics as a definition has to be fairly broad to encompass all these aspects in its coverage.

Research ethics is defined by social norms (Rawls, 1971), which vary over time and space, and as such create much debate around what exactly constitutes moral behaviour. For example, definitions of research ethics can incorporate elements from a fair and reasonable standard of care in clinical and medical trials (Benatar & Singer, 2000) to the concept of vulnerability when assessing sources of data for projects (Bracken-Roche, Bell, Macdonald, & Racine, 2017). The definition of research ethics thus is broad and wide-ranging, but is concerned with conducting research in the right way. In academic discourse, research ethics as a topic has historically concerned itself with reputation and trust (Nunan, 2021), although the shifts in method applied by researchers over time (including a move towards more big data and online research (Nunan & Di Domenico, 2013)), has unsurprisingly also affected the direction of the study agenda.

As a result of its reach, research ethics envelops the whole research project – from the very beginnings of a kernel of an idea of something to investigate in the area of social justice in sport all the way to the post-publication discussions that often arise from studies so steeped in the social narrative of sport.

How can practitioners maintain integrity while working to (often) neoliberal agendas?

As discussed above, so as to maintain integrity while working to social justice agendas, scholars and practitioners need to be mindful of ethics throughout the research project journey, from design to dissemination. Throughout the process, reputational concerns and pressure from external sources, be they funding or organisations whose actions may come under scrutiny from a particular social justice collaboration, to follow particular theoretical or methodological paths must be resisted in line with research ethics norms. For example, researchers have faced reputational damage when linked to topics such as tobacco and cancer (Proctor, 2012) or climate change denial (Dunlap & McCright, 2010) as a result of biases brought about through funding or pressures.

This is also where reflexivity and positionality come into the topic of research ethics. Where researchers occupy multiple different roles or positions that overlap (Alshallaqi, 2022), positionality of the researcher needs to be clarified. This is particularly important as both ethics and fieldwork relations are affected by positionality (Hausermann & Adomako, 2022). Thus, there needs to be clarity around the positionality of the researcher to ensure ethical accountability ensues and thus protects the integrity of the project.

Reflexivity, or the assessment of positionality's effect on research, is linked to the concept of influence and intervention, with positive moral outcomes ensuing from open-endedness in these instances (van Wijngaarden, Leget, & Goossensen, 2018). Reflexivity with regards to research ethics can also change depending on whether research ethics is procedural or practical in nature (Guillemin & Gillam, 2004).

Ethics codes and ethical requirements

Establishing research as a profession of experts came with the need for compliance against a set of rules to ensure 'confidence in data' (Nunan, 2021), bringing with it a structure to be followed by researchers. It is for this reason that ethical conduct by researchers is aided by the existence and requirements of Codes of Ethics for research. There are a number of regional and national codes and concordats that those engaging in research need to abide by, such as the Code of Conduct for Research (UK Research Integrity Office, 2021). Of course, most researchers inevitably go through their institutions' internal ethical control procedures prior to commencing a research project. And it is particularly important that institutional and regional ethics procedures are followed and continuously adhered to throughout the project to ensure that the research output is robust.

However, despite most researchers being fully aware of basic ethical research conduct requirements, it is how these conduct requirements apply at all stages of the research project that adds potential complications to social justice projects. For that, one needs to split the research into its various component parts and consider the ethical implications at each stage, both before commencing the research, and then revisiting and, if required, readjusting during the research process itself.

Topic selection

Every piece of research starts off as an idea, before a research question is formulated and research design agreed. As stated both earlier in this chapter, and indeed throughout this book, social justice research in sport has a large potential of relevant projects and topics from which a researcher can choose to focus. And with these ideas comes risk.

While ethical considerations often come into play at the research design stage, given the concerns discussed previously in this chapter, it is worth starting the research ethics journey with choosing a particular research question. For example, some research questions may intrinsically come with a requirement for unethical conduct or association with unethical components of industry, which may in itself bring the ethics of the researcher into question. Needless to say, these should be avoided.

Historical examples of unethical research strongly interlink with the social justice theme. World War II medical testing on concentration camp prisoners (Christianto, 2021) and the American Tuskegee Syphilis study on black males (Brandt, 1978) are oft-cited examples of unethical research where the subjects' human rights were disregarded. International codes of ethics such as the Helsinki code and the European Declaration of Human Rights cover protection for research participants (Robson & McCartan, 2016). And it is imperative that researchers follow these codes throughout the entire duration of their studies.

It is important to remember that unethical 'labels' on researchers or projects do not necessarily come about through unethical behaviour itself. Given the level of scrutiny of social justice projects, a perception of unethical conduct is sufficient to cause reputational damage for both researcher and project. This can, in turn, lead to robust and useful findings being rejected by policymakers and stakeholders. For example, an anti-corruption expert was convicted of money-laundering in 2021, which inevitably repudiated much of his own research on corruption (Patel, 2021).

Topic selection can be posed as an ethical dilemma in itself and can therefore create further need for ethical considerations before the research design requirements are even approached. Michler, Masters, and Josephson (2021) posit that changing incentives can determine topic selection as demonstrated by the principle of induced innovation. This is intertwined with the concept of selection bias, and considering this element in the selection process at least establishes a baseline from which to understand the researchers' own biases and philosophical position when it comes to topics of social justice.

Research design

Once the research question has been agreed, the traditional requirements of considering the research design of the project need to be implemented. Here, too, the ethical considerations of a particular project can have direct bearing on the perception of the project itself. A classic example of controversial research from an ethical perspective includes the Milgram studies in the 1960s, where participants were asked to administer electric shocks to others in a bid to ascertain the lengths to which individuals would go to for figures of perceived authority (Griggs, Blyler, & Jackson, 2020). This example clearly demonstrates the need for ethical considerations at the design phase of a research project and a clear ethical decision-making approval process.

At the research design stage, a focus on transformational research with an aim to influence social policy is common (Mertens, 2011) and, indeed, sometimes valued from an impact perspective, as institutional researchers have increasingly come under pressure to ensure that their research provides impact for local, regional, national or international communities. For example, in the UK, institutional research is assessed in the Research Excellence Framework model which includes a number of impact case studies, and thus in turn influences the requirements internally at institutions undergoing this assessment process.

However, care must be taken that the methodological pressures stemming from this need for creating impact are not simultaneously jeopardising research ethics such as those set out in various researcher Codes of Conduct (see, for example, European Science Academy & ALL European Academies, 2011; UK Research Integrity Office, 2021). For example, designing research with a specific impact case study outcome in mind could jeopardise objectivity throughout the project. And thus social justice researchers may be faced with ethical dilemmas relating to their professional ethics at the very start of the research project.

It is for these reasons that social justice research, particularly in sport, often requires quite extensive ethical clearance. To avoid issues around judgement of one's own project on ethical grounds and thus to avoid ethical dilemma resolution being undertaken by researchers themselves when assessing their own research design in what would be a conflict of interest, the research community structure has created ethical review boards and committees to take responsibility for this decision-making process (Robson & McCartan, 2016).

A discussion of ethical structures would be remiss without the inclusion of a warning. While research ethics committees are there to take responsibility for making ethical decisions where a dilemma or potential dilemma arises, it is important for researchers to remember that no structure is foolproof. Ethics review boards and committees can be under-funded and under-resourced, which in turn may affect their abilities to monitor projects adequately (Ángeles-Llerenas, Thrasher, Domínguez-Esponda, López-Ridaura, & Macklin, 2022) or adequately protect research participants when it comes to ensuring the practice of informed consent through a focus on process above outcome (Josephson & Smale, 2021).

Participatory studies, designed with stakeholder involvement to enable participant engagement to address concerns with authority, power and voice within socially just research designs, can also impact the ethics process through the researcher's participation as an 'insider' within the movement being analysed. As true participatory action research involves a close collaborative relationship with insider stakeholders, taken to extremes this can lead to loss of decision-making power by the researcher (Robson & McCartan, 2016), which can in turn affect the ethical robustness of the study or lead to required changes to the ethics process where traditional ethics processes and systems might struggle to deal with participatory and emergent designs. Milligan (2016) conceptualised participatory methods to include the 'inbetweener' researcher, taking aspects of both action and independence, which both allowed for knowledge (co-)construction and academic independence, something that would facilitate the ethics process, particularly with regards informed consent. The issue of informed consent is also of course an issue at the data collection stage, and it is to this that we turn to next.

Data collection

Once the research topic and the research design have been both decided and undergone a successful ethics review process, the next ethical hurdle encountered by researchers is that of data collection. In researching the social justice elements in sport, the methods of data collection are themselves intrinsically interlinked with the notion of integrity and the requirements for ethical conduct as previously discussed.

Issues relating to research integrity can be encountered at the data collection stage in relation to engagement with (Murphy, 2022) and access to participants and data. Given the scope and ideological underpinnings of much of social justice research, particular care must be taken with qualitative data to not pressure participants to engage with, or to voice views aligning to those of, the researcher. With quantitative data, integrity of source information is similarly key to ethical robustness.

The type of data collection will inevitably influence the ethical requirements for robust research practice, and this is influenced by the research question itself. Social justice research in sport can often include investigations in cases of vulnerability and discrimination, both of which need care from both the legal and ethical perspective. Athletes and former athletes, sports officials, grassroots participants, consumers of sport, and other stakeholders often form the subjects of data collection in this field, and so the nuances attached to each specific type of data collection needs to be taken into account from an ethical perspective when considering your own research. This applies to both quantitative and qualitative research.

Children and vulnerable adults can be subjects, and particular caution and care must be taken under these circumstances. While children are often treated as a special case when it comes to human rights, the social and cultural evolution of research using children as subjects has led to a growth in techniques used, and thus an increased need for ethical frameworks around things like sensitivity and confidentiality is key to maintaining integrity in research involving children (Nairn & Clarke, 2012).

Another area of growth is the use of online research techniques or tapping into online communities. For example, conducting ethnographic research using electronic communities can raise a number of ethical dilemmas, including the philosophical basis for the ethical framework used by the researcher, deontological issues such as whether to adopt specific codes of ethics, teleological and utilitarian dilemmas around 'the greatest good for the greatest number', and whether different social sciences should interpret matters differently (Hair & Clark, 2007).

Continuing the online trend, web surveys have also seen a growth in the use for research purposes. This method of data collection may see efficiency improvements in both time and financial value through incentivisation which may differ from that of more traditional surveys (Cobanoglu & Cobanoglu, 2003), but the ethical implications of any form of incentivisation in social justice remain. For example, there have been ethical issues in the past with undue inducements, potential for exploitation, and biased enrolment on projects (Resnik, 2015).

On the qualitative side, the use of digital media for conducting interviews online may create 'barriers to disclosure', although the limited (in terms of usefulness) mitigating factor of familiarity between interviewer and interviewee may improve matters (Van Zeeland, Van den Broeck, Boonen, & Tintel, 2021). There is also some evidence of differences between answers provided by children in online versus face-to-face interviews in qualitative studies (Enochsson, 2011), while Meherali and Louie-Poon (2021) found that challenges in conducting online interviews with adolescents increase as a result of the inability of the researchers to control the environment in which the interviewee is located for the duration of the interview.

Whether online or off, interviews or electronically collected data also pose the perennial problem of anonymity for the participants, particularly with regards to sensitive projects or topics that require confidentiality due to the vulnerability of participants or emotiveness of topic. Anonymity is traditionally used to safeguard the participants as well as the researchers, and allows for topics that would otherwise require a large legal resource to manage or would result in far fewer participants coming forward (or both). However, the move towards increased use of electronically acquired or online data increases the problems associated with potential re-identification following reverse engineering of raw data despite its anonymisation (Nunan & Di Domenico, 2016).

On the quantitative side, there are numerous ethical concerns around the concepts of validity and objectivity which can be improved through contextual relevance (Zyphur & Pierides, 2017). With regards online quantitative research, issues around confidentiality, anonymity, and robustness of data (including verifying sources) can present some ethical dilemmas to compound general research ethics concerns of social justice projects.

Another common method used in social justice research, particularly due to the rise in availability of thought resulting from this, is the use of social media. From a research ethics perspective, the wealth of interpersonal communication available should not detract from the need to ensure that consent is granted for use in research. The need to differentiate between informed and uninformed consent, particularly when using social media networks, may require realignment of norms in obtaining consent. Nunan and Yenicioglu (2013) argue for the use of participative consent, whereby the dynamic settings of social media networks allow knowledge exchange and are conceptualised within a dynamic research paradigm, which in turn allows the application of the substance of off-line ethics codes to the differing requirements of an online world. This 'participatory trend' has implications for action research in areas such as customer relationship management in marketing research (Maklan, Knox, & Ryals, 2008), which has similarities to action research in the areas of social justice and sport.

Action research and ethical concerns have also been the topic of conceptualisation, with the two areas of persistence and consent (Davison, Martinsons, & Wong, 2022) being particularly pertinent to social justice research. Specifically when collaborating with organisations, the duration of action research projects may lead to undue pressure for a swift conclusion of the project, which may be problematic as time pressure can affect decision-making (Santos & Cunha, 2021) and lead to initially incomplete data (Male, 2021). This can also lead to the misrepresentation of participants, a lack of voice and not being truly transformative. A transformative method is one focused on social justice with respectful inclusion of stakeholders throughout the process, leading to ethical collaboration and engagement (Mertens, 2018), but can fail for the reasons indicated above. In summary, external pressure, whether or not intentional or via a collaborative approach imbalance) can affect the next stages of the research project too: analysis and write-up.

Analysis and write-up

The final stages of the research project are usually considered to be analysis and write-up. In line with other aspects of the research project, the analysis of data and write-up of findings need an ethical stance throughout, ensuring that both sides of the research question argument are considered and the objectivity that academic writing is renowned for is adhered to despite the often emotive and possibly neoliberal topic of research. As previously discussed, social justice research is often emotive, may affect the researcher directly, and can be linked to the ideological positioning of the researcher. As such, extra care needs to be taken to control for internal biases (see positionality and reflexivity covered earlier in this chapter) when analysing the data and concluding.

It is also important not to succumb to pressures stemming from having a policy focus resulting from transformational research axioms (Mertens, 2011) or external influences, such as funding bodies or government stakeholders. The need to maintain objectivity throughout is interwoven with the notion of integrity previously discussed and the need to ensure that the ideological standing of the work is in line with the often moral reasoning that motivated the research in the first place. There is also a need to maintain the space and time required to complete the project to its full potential, without having to face ethical dilemmas in relation to external pressures to complete before full analysis has been undertaken, something which Davison et al. (2022) referred to as persistence in their 'four issues of concern' in relation to ethics integrity in action research.

Research misconduct is a surprisingly common phenomenon (Craig, Cox, Tourish, & Thorpe, 2020) but could be particularly harmful to the social justice campaign or policy linked with neoliberal research that would be detrimental to more than the researchers. As social justice research is often used as evidence to secure change through legal or regulatory means by organisations, policymakers, social actors, and government, so it needs to ensure that the research is grounded in ethical conduct. The case of ethical breaches by Paul McRory has been cited as being detrimental to the cause for change in regards to concussion protocols in football (Davey, Convery, & Kemp, 2022), and should be taken as a warning example of how poor ethical conduct at the research phase (in this case, on concussions) may actively endanger the social justice cause itself (in this case, the welfare of athletes).

Anonymisation has already been covered in the data collection section, but the risk to participants of identification through digital means (Nunan & Di Domenico, 2016) can also be exacerbated at the write-up stage. Therefore, extra care needs to be taken where sensitive data is used, particularly where quotations of research participants' online interactions are incorporated in the final published work. Anonymity is not guaranteed solely by removing someone's name: identifying information can be garnered by other means, particularly where gender pronouns or race is disclosed in an industry where few have the positions referred to in the "anonymised" work. As an example, the identification of the whistleblower as female in the FIFA investigations concerning World Cup bid-rigging allegations allowed for the identification of the individual in question despite their name being omitted from the report (Mersiades, 2018).

Ethical issues in relation to analysis of data and final outputs can also include the positionality of the researcher and the transparency with which this is dealt with in the final published paper(s), particularly in relation to social justice narratives and moralism (Hammersley & Traianou, 2011). The positionality of the researcher may be characterised by a more fluid and changing nature compared to that of the researcher's identity (Medzani, 2021), and this may also affect the integrity of the research if it is not carefully considered and adequately disclosed.

Post-publication

With most research, the ethical considerations often end at publication. However, social justice research is often leaned on by external stakeholders to use as evidence for enacting change. This increases the length of ethical consideration in relation to a particular social justice project to include any post-publication discussion or sharing of work.

It is not just the philosophical challenges of social justice work that require constant vigilance with respect to ethics, but the practical ones as well. Smith (2022) invokes the trade-off between 'reportability and tellability' in media dialogical networking when addressing communication ethics arising in the interactions between academic experts and interviewing journalists. This interlinks with the idea of avoidance of "media ethics anomie" (Wen, 2021), with the researcher's involvement in a media article where the latter's ethics may be questioned by other stakeholders creates a difficult ethical scenario. The researcher may have to weigh up between the need to aid a social justice campaign by providing relevant evidence via the media against the potential to be caught up in others' narratives that may be at odds with the researcher's own.

Conclusion

Integrity and research ethics are heavily intertwined in research projects of this nature. The philosophical challenges of social justice work need to be considered from a variety of ethical standpoints, while the practical implications of conducting such research need to be imbibed in every nook and cranny of the research project.

Social justice research, because of its usefulness and potential for impact in wider communities beyond that of academia, requires a very robust ethical stance. While the deontological approach to ethics with regards research may be a good starting point, the need to deliver a project whose ethical grounding is as robust as its research findings is key. As set out in both this chapter and this book as a whole, social justice research is more than the sum of its parts. This makes the topics interesting, useful, and a strong crutch for decision-makers and policy-makers to enact change, but it also opens up the research to more scrutiny than some other areas of research. And as researchers, it is our duty to ensure that our research does not fall short of the standards required.

References

Alshallaqi, M. (2022). Cultural practices and organizational ethnography: Implications for fieldwork and research ethics. *Journal of Organizational Ethnography*, *11*(3), 259–274. doi: 10.1108/JOE-06-2021-0036

Ángeles-Llerenas, A., Thrasher, J. F., Domínguez-Esponda, R., López-Ridaura, R., & Macklin, R. (2022). Operation of research ethics committees in Colombia, Costa Rica, Guatemala, and Mexico: Mesoamerican Project. *Salud Pública de México, 64*(1), 66–75. doi: 10.21149/12588

Arthur, L. C., & Brendan, P. (2017). *The ethics of sport: Essential readings*. New York, NY: Oxford University Press.

Benatar, S. R., & Singer, P. A. (2000). A new look at international research ethics. *BMJ, 321*(7264), 824–826.

Bracken-Roche, D., Bell, E., Macdonald, M. E., & Racine, E. (2017). The concept of 'vulnerability' in research ethics: An in-depth analysis of policies and guidelines. *Health Research Policy and Systems, 15*(1), 1–18.

Brandt, A. M. (1978). Racism and research: The case of the Tuskegee Syphilis Study. *The Hastings Center Report, 8*(6), 21–29. doi: 10.2307/3561468

Breivik, G. (2000). Against chance: A causal theory of winning in sport. In T. Tännsjö & C. M. Tamburrini (Eds), *Values in sport: Elitism, nationalism, gender equality and the scientific manufacture of winners*: London: E & FN Spon.

Byrne, S., Ludvigsen, L., & Andre, J. (2022). Sport mega-event governance and human rights: The 'Ruggie Principles', responsibility and directions. *Leisure Studies*, 1–16. doi: 10.1080/02614367.2022.2094998

Carroll, A. B. (1979). A three dimensional conceptual model of corporate social responsibility. *Academy of Management Review, 4*, 497–505.

Christianto, V. (2021). Rethinking medical ethics from Hyppocratic Oath to Nuremberg Code. *Bio Science Research Bulletin-Biological Sciences, 37*(2), 88–91. doi: 10.5958/2320-3161.2021.00013.4

Cobanoglu, C., & Cobanoglu, N. (2003). The effect of incentives in web surveys: Application and ethical considerations. *International Journal of Market Research, 45*(4), 1–13. doi: 10.1177/147078530304500406

Council of Europe, & UEFA. (2018). *Memorandum of understanding between the Council of Euope and the Union of European Football Associations (UEFA)*. Retrieved from www.uefa.com/MultimediaFiles/Download/uefaorg/General/02/56/17/27/2561727_DOWNLOAD.pdf

Craig, R., Cox, A., Tourish, D., & Thorpe, A. (2020). Using retracted journal articles in psychology to understand research misconduct in the social sciences: What is to be done? *Research Policy, 49*(4), 103930. doi: 10.1016/j.respol.2020.103930

Davey, M., Convery, S., & Kemp, E. (2022, 22 September). New plagiarism claims against sport concussion guru Paul McCrory. *The Guardian*. Retrieved from www.theguardian.com/sport/2022/sep/23/new-plagiarism-claims-against-sport-concussion-guru-paul-mccrory#:~:text=The%20world%2Drenowned%20concussion%20expert,research%20grants%20he%20has%20received

Davison, R. M., Martinsons, M. G., & Wong, L. H. M. (2022). The ethics of action research participation. *Information Systems Journal, 32*(3), 573–594. doi: 10.1111/isj.12363

Dunlap, R. E., & McCright, A. M. (2010). Climate change denial: Sources, actors and strategies. In C. Lever-Tracy (Ed.), *Routledge handbook of climate change and society* (pp. 240–259). Abingdon: Routledge.

Enochsson, A.-B. (2011). Who benefits from synchronous online communication?: A comparison of face-to-face and synchronous online interviews with children. *Procedia – Social and Behavioral Sciences, 28*, 15–22. doi: 10.1016/j.sbspro.2011.11.004

European Science Academy, & ALL European Academies. (2011). *The European Code of Conduct for Research Integrity*. Retrieved from http://archives.esf.org/index.php?eID=tx_nawsecuredl&u=0&g=0&t=1664636342&hash=0e870cd367ac879728798ea54f656eed5e9c417d&file=/fileadmin/be_user/CEO_Unit/MO_FORA/MOFORUM_ResearchIntegrity/Code_Conduct_Research Integrity.pdf

Graham, B. A. (2019, 15/02/2019). Colin Kaepernick reaches settlement with NFL over kneeling protest fallout. *The Guardian*. Retrieved from www.theguardian.com/sport/2019/feb/15/colin-kaepernick-reaches-settlement-with-nfl-over-kneeling-protest-fallout

Griggs, R. A., Blyler, J., & Jackson, S. L. (2020). Using research ethics as a springboard for teaching Milgram's obedience study as a contentious classic. *Scholarship of Teaching and Learning in Psychology, 6*(4), 350–356. doi: 10.1037/stl0000182

Guillemin, M., & Gillam, L. (2004). Ethics, reflexivity, and 'ethically important moments' in research. *Qualitative Inquiry, 10*(2), 261–280. doi: 10.1177/1077800403262360

Hair, N., & Clark, M. (2007). The ethical dilemmas and challenges of ethnographic research in electronic communities. *International Journal of Market Research*, *49*(6), 1–13. doi: 10.1177/147078530704900609

Hammersley, M., & Traianou, A. (2011). Moralism and research ethics: A Machiavellian perspective. *International Journal of Social Research Methodology*, *14*(5), 379–390. doi: 10.1080/13645579.2011.562412

Harvey, A., & McNamee, M. (2019). Sport integrity: Ethics, policy and practice: An introduction. *Journal of Global Sport Management*, *4*(1), 1.

Hausermann, H., & Adomako, J. (2022). Positionality, 'the field', and implications for knowledge production and research ethics in land change science. *Journal of Land Use Science*, *17*(1), 211–225. doi: 10.1080/1747423X.2021.2015000

Howman, D. (2013). Supporting the integrity of sport and combating corruption. *Marquette Sports Law Review*, 23, 245–248.

Hughes, A. (2018). Why some Western companies are distancing themselves from the World Cup brand. *The Conversation*. Retrieved from https://theconversation.com/why-some-western-companies-are-distancing-themselves-from-the-world-cup-brand-96989

Interpol. (2020). Corruption in sport. Retrieved from www.interpol.int/Crimes/Corruption/Corruption-in-sport

Josephson, A., & Smale, M. (2021). What do you mean by 'informed consent'? Ethics in economic development research†. *Applied Economic Perspectives and Policy*, *43*(4), 1305–1329. doi: https://doi.org/10.1002/aepp.13112

Maklan, S., Knox, S., & Ryals, L. (2008). New trends in innovation and customer relationship management. *International Journal of Market Research*, *50*(2), 221–240. doi: 10.1177/147078530805000206

Male, V. (2021). Menstrual changes after Covid-19 vaccination. *BMJ*, *374*, n2211. doi: 10.1136/bmj.n2211

McNamee, M., & Parry, S. J. (1998). *Ethics and sport*. London: E & FN Spon.

Medzani, J. M. (2021). Positionality statement on studying male victims of intimate partner abuse in Zimbabwe: A research note. *International Journal of Social Research Methodology*, *24*(3), 387–392. doi: 10.1080/13645579.2020.1798682

Meherali, S. M., & Louie-Poon, S. (2021). Challenges in conducting online videoconferencing qualitative interviews with adolescents on sensitive topics. *Qualitative Report*, *26*(9), 2851–2856. doi: 10.46743/2160-3715/2021.4906

Mersiades, B. (2018). *Whatever it takes: The inside story of the FIFA way*. Sydney: Fair Play Publishing.

Mertens, D. M. (2011). Integrating pathways: Research and policy making in pursuit of social justice. *International Review of Qualitative Research*, *4*(2), 149–169. doi: 10.1525/irqr.2011.4.2.149

Mertens, D. M. (2018). Transformative mixed methods and policy evaluation. *Diritto & Questioni Pubbliche: Rivista di Filosofia del Diritto e Cultura Giuridica*, *18*(1), 250–269.

Michler, J. D., Masters, W. A., & Josephson, A. (2021). Research ethics beyond the IRB: Selection bias and the direction of innovation in applied economics. *Applied Economic Perspectives & Policy*, *43*(4), 1352–1365. doi: 10.1002/aepp.13132

Milligan, L. (2016). Insider-outsider-inbetweener? Researcher positioning, participative methods and cross-cultural educational research. *Compare*, *46*(2), 235–250. doi: 10.1080/03057925.2014.928510

Montaño, A. (2019). Nike told me to dream crazy, until I wanted a baby. *The New York Times*. Retrieved from www.nytimes.com/2019/05/12/opinion/nike-maternity-leave.html

Murphy, D. (2022). Walking, talking, imagining: Ethical engagement with sex workers. *Ethics & Social Welfare*, *16*(2), 219–234. doi: 10.1080/17496535.2022.2033809

Næss, H. E. (2019). Investment ethics and the global economy of sports: The Norwegian oil fund, Formula 1 and the 2014 Russian Grand Prix. *Journal of Business Ethics*, *158*(2), 535–546. doi: 10.1007/s10551-017-3751-8

Nairn, A., & Clarke, B. (2012). Researching children: Are we getting it right?: A discussion of ethics. *International Journal of Market Research*, *54*(2), 177–198. doi: 10.2501/IJMR-54-2-177-198

Nunan, D. (2021). Collection: Privacy and research ethics. *International Journal of Market Research*, *63*(3), 271–274. doi: 10.1177/14707853211015445

Nunan, D., & Di Domenico, M. (2013). Market research and the ethics of big data. *International Journal of Market Research*, *55*(4), 505–520. doi: 10.2501/ijmr-2013-015

Nunan, D., & Di Domenico, M. (2016). Exploring reidentification risk: Is anonymisation a promise we can keep? *International Journal of Market Research*, *58*(1), 19–34. doi: 10.2501/ijmr-2016-004

Nunan, D., & Yenicioglu, B. (2013). Informed, uninformed and participative consent in social media research. *International Journal of Market Research*, *55*(6), 791–808. doi: 10.2501/ijmr-2013-067

Patel, V. (2021, 17 November). Professor cited as corruption expert is sentenced for money laundering, *The New York Times*. Retrieved from www.nytimes.com/2021/11/17/us/bruce-bagley-money-laundering-venezuela.html

Philippou, C. (2019). Towards a unified framework for anti-bribery in sport governance. *International Journal of Disclosure & Governance*, *16*(2/3), 83–99. doi: 10.1057/s41310-019-00058-w

Philippou, C. (2022). World Cup: Fifa needs Qatar 2022 to leave a legacy of progress against corruption. *The Conversation*. Retrieved from https://theconversation.com/world-cup-fifa-needs-qatar-2022-to-leave-a-legacy-of-progress-against-corruption-196331

Philippou, C., & Hines, T. (2021). Anti-bribery and corruption policies in International Sports Governing Bodies. [Policy and Practice Reviews]. *Living*, *3*(93). doi: 10.3389/fspor.2021.649889

Proctor, R. N. (2012). The history of the discovery of the cigarette–lung cancer link: Evidentiary traditions, corporate denial, global toll. *Tobacco Control*, *21*(2), 87. doi: 10.1136/tobaccocontrol-2011-050338

Rawls, J. (1971). *A theory of justice*. [electronic resource]. Belknap Press of Harvard University Press.

Resnik, D. B. (2015). Bioethical issues in providing financial incentives to research participants. *Medicoleg Bioeth*, *5*, 35–41. doi: 10.2147/mb.s70416

Robson, C., & McCartan, K. (2016). *Real world research: A resource for users of social research methods in applied settings* (4th ed.). Chichester, West Sussex, United Kingdom: Wiley.

Rodgers, W., Söderbom, A., & Guiral, A. (2015). Corporate social responsibility enhanced control systems reducing the likelihood of fraud. *Journal of Business Ethics*, *131*(4), 871–882.

Santos, C., & Cunha, P. (2021). Influence of trust, time pressure and complexity factors in judgment and decision-making in auditing. *Brazilian Business Review (Portuguese Edition)*, *18*(6), 605–623. doi: 10.15728/bbr.2021.18.6.1

Savolainen, J., & VanEseltine, M. (2018). Replication and research integrity in criminology: Introduction to the special issue. *Journal of Contemporary Criminal Justice*, *34*(3), 236–244.

Simon, R. (2011). The ethics of sport: A reader. *Sports, Ethics & Philosophy*, *5*, 88–89.

Skillen, A. (1998). Sport is for losers. In M. J. McNamee & S. J. Parry (Eds), *Ethics and sport*: London: E & FN Spon.

Smith, S. (2022). 'Sharing expertise with the public': The production of communicability and the ethics of media dialogical networking. *Discourse, Context & Media*, *45*. doi: 10.1016/j.dcm.2021.100560

UK Research Integrity Office. (2021). Code of Practice for research: Promoting good practice and preventing misconduct. Retrieved from https://ukrio.org/wp-content/uploads/UKRIO-Code-of-Practice-for-Research.pdf

Van Zeeland, I., Van den Broeck, W., Boonen, M., & Tintel, S. (2021). Effects of digital mediation and familiarity in online video interviews between peers. *Methodological Innovations*, 1–15. doi: 10.1177/20597991211060743

van Wijngaarden, E., Leget, C., & Goossensen, A. (2018). Ethical uneasiness and the need for open-ended reflexivity: The case of research into older people with a wish to die. *International Journal of Social Research Methodology*, *21*(3), 317–331. doi: 10.1080/13645579.2017.1399621

Wen, Y. (2021). How to use new media technology to avoid media ethics anomie. *Procedia Computer Science*, *183*, 833–836. doi: 10.1016/j.procs.2021.03.006

World Athletics. (2019). Integrity Code of Conduct. Retrieved from https://worldathletics.org/about-iaaf/documents/book-of-rules

Zyphur, M. J., & Pierides, D. C. (2017). Is quantitative research ethical? Tools for ethically practicing, evaluating, and using quantitative research. *Journal of Business Ethics*, *143*(1), 1–16.

41
INTERSECTIONAL SCHOLARSHIP ON SPORT AND LEISURE
Trends, tensions, and promising directions

Prisca Bruno Massao and Mari Haugaa Engh

Introduction: From women in sport to intersectionality in sport

Critical engagement with sport and gender emerged in the United States, Canada, and England in the late 1960s and was influenced by the development of a discipline for the study of physical education in the previous decade (Bandy, 2005). Most of the research and writing produced in this early stage was concerned only with the female sporting experiences (Bandy, 2005; Markula, 2005) and was later criticised for simplified analyses by presenting gender (or sex) as a "variable or distributive category" (Birrell, 2000, cited in Markula, 2005: 3). In the 1980s, however, through what is referred to as feminist cultural studies, analyses became more sophisticated and feminist writings on sport became "a theoretically informed, critical analysis of the cultural forces that work to produce the ideological practices that influence the relations of sport and gender" (Birrell, 1988: 492 cited in Markula, 2005: 3). Following this development, the scope of research widened and in 1986 Helen Lenskyj was the first feminist to offer a critical analysis of sport and sexuality (in Bandy, 2005). This ground-breaking work fostered the development of arguments concerning masculine superiority, compulsory heterosexuality, and the dangers associated with "the lesbian bogeywoman" in sports (Markula, 2005). Through the 1990s, feminist sports studies continued to examine the ways in which hegemonic ideals of gender and sexuality functioned to position the female athlete as an oxymoron (Kolnes, 1995).

Hence, the argument *could* be made that studies of/on gender in sport and leisure have had an intersectional perspective since the beginning. Yet, the extent of the intersectionality was limited given that, the mutual imbrication of gender, sexuality, and embodiment was at the centre of the analyses (cf. Griffin, 1992; Lenskyj, 1994), these studies almost exclusively focused on queer and straight women racialised as White. This was critiqued by scholars like Susan Birrell (1990 cited in Scraton, 2001), who warned about the absence of Black women's voices and experiences in Western sport scholarship. In this chapter we navigate through the trends, tensions, and the promising directions of intersectionality. We aim to shed light on the unfolding nature of intersectionality and its ability to produce cross-disciplinary, cross-sectoral, and global feminist conversations. Doing so, however, we argue would require that we take seriously the history and trajectories of intersectionality itself, and endeavour to

DOI: 10.4324/9781003389682-48

return to a conceptualisation that does not gloss over the heterosexist, masculinist, White normative, and colonial logics of modern competitive sports. We end this chapter by pointing to recent and ongoing work that we believe will deliver on the need to 'decentre the normative subject' of modern sport.

Intersectionality

While the conceptual and political history of the concept of intersectionality is rooted in the history of Black feminist activism and scholarship across the Global North *and* in the anti-colonial struggles of women of colour in the (post)colonial south, the concept intersectionality itself is commonly attributed to the Black American legal and feminist scholar Kimberlé Crenshaw (1989, 1991). She coined the term as a tool for analysing and addressing the interaction of racism and patriarchy, the results of which are made invisible by single-axis analyses of either gender or race. Subsequently, the term has been employed to describe and account for a wider range of social inequalities, such as gender, race, class, sexuality/sexual orientations, (dis)abilities, nationalities. Although Crenshaw is known for coining the term, the political history of the concept is also often traced to the 1970s and the Combahee River Collective, of Black lesbian feminists in Boston, who critiqued White feminist movements for ignoring the racism, heterosexism, and classism experienced by Black women. Their statement has had a key influence on Black feminism and on critical theories on race, gender, sexuality, and class. Their assertion that the "major systems of oppression are interlocking" (Combahee River Collective, 1977: 272) laid the groundwork for later articulations of intersectionality.

While intersectionality in North America emerged as a tool to interrogate structural racism, its development in Europe, and in sport, took place in the context of blooming postmodern and post structural feminism. These feminisms aimed to avoid essentialising the categories that they claimed critical scholars perpetuated and instead encouraged the recognition of differences and diversities. In sport, scholars like Heywood (2018: 474) argued that such an approach aided the development of a framework that could account for a multiplicity of body images, identities, and ideals, and could help "in making sense of contradictions in current representations, which tend to contain a mix of residual, dominant and emergent codings. The dualistic 'pretty or powerful' form of representation is now residual, while 'pretty and powerful' is more dominant".

As the history of intersectionality often centres on the concepts' roots in Black feminist movements and theorisation in North America and Europe, we want to point to how feminist struggles, and writing from outside the Global North have also played a key – albeit overlooked – part in intersectional scholarship. We argue that a full account of the history and trajectory of intersectionality cannot ignore the influence and contributions of postcolonial and decolonial feminists from both the Global North and South, such as Oyeronke Oyewumi (1997) and Ifi Amadiume (1997). Both critiqued the presumed universality of Western gendered norms and provided detailed accounts of African gender systems, that were not rooted in a White supremacist and masculinist bio-logic alone (Tamale, 2020). According to Oyewumi "The racial and gender oppressions experienced by African women should not be seen in terms of addition, as if they were piled one on top of the other" (Oyewumi, 1997: 123). Hence, African conceptualisations of gender illustrate the impossibility of understanding gender as a single axis of domination, given that global, imperial, and postcolonial forces co-constitute gender with local, cultural, economic, and racial positionings. Another good example of the Southern and African roots of intersectionality is Anne McClintock's (1995) scholarship. She argued that:

race, gender and class are not distinct realms of experience, existing in splendid isolation from each other; nor can they be simply yoked together retrospectively like armatures of Lego. Rather, they come into existence in and through relation to each other ...
(McClintock, 1995: 5)

The Ugandan feminist legal scholar Sylvia Tamale continues this work and has provided a clear call for decolonial and African-centred analyses of the co-operations of heterosexism, patriarchy, racism, and capitalist imperialism. According to her, the modern sex/gender system (Lugones, 2007) must be seen in light of the fact that "race always intersects with gender and sexuality, so we have to speak of a racialized gendered sexuality" (Tamale, 2020: 105). Tamale poses a decolonial understanding of intersectionality by emphasising that; "there is no 'race' without colonial constructions of a binary, hierarchical, sex/gender system, incorporating all 'women' into one 'racialized' group or another" (Tamale, 2020: 6). Tamale brings together (North American) Black feminist theory, Latin American decolonial interventions, with African feminist epistemologies, to show the "intersectional dynamics between forces such as racialism, capitalism and patriarchy" (2020: 39).

Intersectionality and social justice in sport

Citing intersectionality as a product of Black feminist politics and movements, Sirma Bilge, argues that the concept encompasses a knowledge project oriented toward social justice (Bilge, 2014: 2). Yet despite its political ancestry, she argues, intersectionality has been neutralised, and 'whitened'; a neoliberal normative understanding in which intersectionality is conflated with multiple identities (Bilge, 2014). This neutralising, or whitening, removes social justice, and material politics, from the analysis, and produces scholarship that is more concerned with 'seeing' complex identities than addressing social transformation. Key in this approach, according to Bilge, is a refusal to let intersectionality be disciplinarily bound to gender/feminist studies, and accounting for its postcolonial, anti-colonial and race-critical roots and histories. In sporting contexts social justice frameworks demand working against colour-blind racism and the persistent White colonial frame (Love, Deeb, & Waller, 2020). Sport is often regarded as meritocratic and apolitical but also at the periphery of society (especially in the Global South), thus sport is often left out of everyday concerns with inequality, power, and discrimination in society (Carrington, 2010).

While historically the heteronormative binary gender division has been regarded as stable and as the foundation of the binary division of sport into women's and men's sports, Lenskyj and Greey (2022) has provided powerful arguments of why that division is becoming more and more irrelevant if sport truly lives or aspire to live up to its fair play vision. This aligns with the main "intersectional critique" of feminism's focus on gender as a primary factor determining a woman's fate (hooks, 2014). Whitened intersectionality enables the increasing resistance toward transgender and gender diverse athletes, and in particular transgender women in sport, as it supports single-axis gender equality legislation that denies the rights of participation for women who do not fit in the traditional binary gender categories set by White supremacist heteropatriarchal systems. This ranges from everyday regulations such as sports uniforms, using testosterone level to assess 'femaleness' in sport, and indirect and direct denial of participation for women who do not fit into the White, able-bodied, heterosexual gender/sex parameters in sport (Karkazis et al., 2012; Limoochi & Le Clair, 2011). (Re)actions such as testosterone panic indicates the destabilisation transgender movements, and their allies pose to the White supremacist heteropatriarchal assemblages of power and privilege in general and the sex-segregated structure of sport in particular. Researchers and practitioners need to engage in transformative visions for sport, in which those who are marginalised "participate in their own struggles for justice, both individually and collectively" (Darnell & Millington, 2019: 181).

Integration of intersectionality in sport is necessary to achieve social justice in and through sport. However, we argue that, if sport is to live up the spirit of fair play, radical transformative changes are required that will undo (Butler, 2004) and disrupt (McSweeney et al., 2019) gender categories and the gender binary system that remains at the core of sport organising today. By disruption we mean to centre those who experience injustice in sport, and place them at the centre of the social (in)justice narratives in modern sport. Those who are marginalised need to "participate in their own struggles for justice, both individually and collectively" (Darnell & Millington, 2019: 181). By doing so, sport will be able to provide space for the marginalised groups to be active agents who challenge socially unjust practices within contemporary sport organisations and policies. Although it is not our intention to a give detailed account of how such undoing and disruption should be achieved, scholars like Travers suggested as early as 2006 as a part of a long-term transition to 'all-gender sport', having two transitional categories – 'female' and 'open' or 'universal' – with the caveat that participation in the 'female' category be based on gender self-determination (in Travers, 2022).

Opening intersectionality up to undoing, disruption, and decoloniality entails grasping the present-day neutralising of intersectionality within the neoliberal knowledge governance in an era deemed post-racial, a time in which racial neoliberalism expands by building silently on the structural conditions of racism while evaporating the very categories of their recognisability. It entails disrupting the hegemony of the Global North in sport (McSweeney et al., 2019). Pursuing a social justice agenda in sports research, then, does not merely entail a focus on equitable participation, access, and representation, but also address the fundamental problems and structures and system of inequity in sport. It requires a critical engagement with, and effort to transform, the heteropatriarchal coloniality of sport, past and present.

Trends and tensions in intersectional studies in sport

As intersectionality 'hit' feminist theorisation in the 1990s, sport was not an exception. Feminist sport scholars began to re-conceptualise gender and race (or the euphemistic ethnicity), and Black feminist theory and concepts began to be employed in mainstream sport feminism (Scraton, 2001). This late inclusion of intersectionality into sport was addressed as a feminist setback, as the field failed to sufficiently address the marginalisation of Black women and women from the Global South, as well as the effects of White normativity and privilege (Scraton, 2001). Sheila Scraton pointed out how the dearth of race critical feminist scholarship contradicted the very fundamental definition of feminism as an anti-oppressive theory and movement committed to challenging the marginalisation of 'all' women, and in the early 2000s, there was a marked increase in studies of Black women's experiences in sport. In their race-critical, feminist, and sociological work on Black sporting experiences in the United States, Adjepong and Carrington (2014) situate the marking of Black women as transgressive and invasive within the history of 'mainstream' feminist sporting narratives. Referencing Sojourner Truth, they illustrated that the ongoing marginalisation of Black women's bodies in sporting worlds is not a new phenomenon and doing so they situate current responses to Black women's sporting lives within a long history of overdetermining and "controlling images" (Collins, 2000) of Black women's bodies and social roles (Adjepong & Carrington, 2014). Black women continue to be positioned as space invaders in sport as they disrupt the normative White gender order in sport. As such, their presence in sport exposes the heterosexist and racist exclusivity in sport (Adjepong & Carrington, 2014). This scholarship echoes the conceptualisation of intersectionality that requires engagement with how identities are "processes constituted in and through power relations" (Brah & Phoenix, 2004: 77).

Although intersectionality helped to highlight the marginalisation of Black women in sport, the presence of Black women's bodies in Western sport continued to be met with extra control and surveillance by both sport cultures and media, governance and institutional bodies, and other athletes (Adjepong & Carrington, 2014; Brown, 2015; McDonald, 2005). Extending the concept of space invaders to sports, allowed examination of the structural constraints that Black women but also queer, gender-diverse, and transgender athletes must simultaneously navigate in sport. Significantly, it enables us to hear the subjective knowledge developed by these groups to locate and counter the dominant narratives at different levels. Engh, Agergaard, and Settler (2017), in their work on African women footballers working in Scandinavia, also illustrate the mutual imbrication of gender, race, and imperial legacies in the way that African women footballers are understood and positioned as having muscles and rhythm but lacking discipline and being in need of benevolent assistance to become 'true' professionals.

We assert, alongside scholars such as Adjepong (2019, 2020, 2022), Bruening (2005), McDonald (2005), and Scraton et al. (2005) that by utilising intersectional analyses sport scholarship could start to engage more meaningfully with the complexity of Black women's experiences in sport, without essentialising difference(s), and/or reducing Black women's experiences to victimhood. This, however, requires a keen awareness of the political histories of the concept itself, lest we reproduce the de-politicisation and White normativity that shapes sections of existing intersectional work.

Delia Douglas' (2005) analysis of whiteness moves the focus from victimhood to the structures that contribute to those victimisations, such as racism, patriarchy, and heteronormativity. She has explored how White normativity and everyday practices of racialisation give rise to dehumanising and humiliating representations of Black women athletes. The privileges afforded to whiteness through racial ideologies in sport often signify that whiteness is equated to normalcy and/or citizenship (Skogvang & Massao, forthcoming; Zenquis & Mwaniki, 2019). While Black feminism facilitated the exposure of whiteness as sporting norm, it has done less to expose the colonial legacy and impact on diverse groups of women in the Global North and South. This includes a lack of analysis on how local, global, traditional, and modern systems of power position some sportswomen in political struggles without genuine local or international allies. Examples of the latter is particularly evident in existing research on Muslim immigrant women in Europe, which given their political position in 'othered' religion, race/ethnicity and gender, make their struggle invisible and contribute to cementing the existing stereotypes of Muslim and immigrant women of colour as passive due to restrictions they experience from their immigrant communities. Similarly, women from the Global South are made near invisible in sport participation and scholarship, despite a widespread Sport for Development and Peace (SDP) interventions in these regions. In SDP movements and research, scholars have drawn attention to how contextual differences generate alternative engagements, political, and methodological debates, and they have provided critical assessment of the formulations and impacts of SDP programmes (Darnell & Hayhurst, 2013).

This is because trends in SDP are underpinned by a heteronormative foundation, sometimes connected to Christianity, and have failed to highlight diverse forms of gender and sexual expressions, particularly in the Global South (Hayhurst et al., 2021: 25; Oxford & Spaaij, 2019). Oxford (2019) argues that the modernity and aid discourses that intersect in SDP reproduce colonial logics. This involves the way sport (aid) recipients/project participants, who are girls and marginalised youths, are supposed to document their achievements in sport projects through providing the proof of their participation using pictures that are displayed in different documents such as websites, reports, etc. Hayhurst (2015) elaborated further how language, particularly English, is a technology of colonisation, and translating the experiences of research participants into English works to reaffirm 'linguicide' as a hegemonic dialect in social sciences and sport research.

As discussed, there have been different trajectories of development for intersectional conceptualisation, within and beyond sport scholarship. This is because intersectionality has always functioned as a work-in-progress, allowing reflection of nuances that expose the complexities of marginalisation and privilege in different contexts. However, if we can agree that the key feature of intersectionality is a concern with social justice (Collins & Bilge, 2016) and a "decentring of the normative subject" of feminism (Brah & Phoenix, 2004: 78), sport scholarship should not be exceptional.

In a recent review of intersectionality in sport scholarship, Aarti Ratna (2018) argues that despite the work done in the last two decades there is still a lack of critical knowledge and scholarship in sport and leisure. Ratna makes it clear how African and Indigenous communities and athletes remain largely invisible in sport scholarship. She concludes that despite claims to be conducting so-called 'critical studies' the trend is nevertheless one of presenting Black women's sporting lives through "homogenising and false narratives" (Ratna, 2018: 9, 1–2). By reproducing limited accounts, such scholarship also fails to consider "other aspects of people of colour's relationships to sport including bodily pleasures, desires, and affects" (Ratna, 2018: 9, 1–2). These misrepresentations and silences, she argues, can be challenged and rectified using critical and decolonial feminist approaches that are attentive to the structural dimensions of domination and oppression (Ratna, 2018: 1–3).

Ratna's critique of the current application of intersectionality in sport exposes the tensions between how de/postcolonial and Black feminists (what she categorises as transnational feminism) think *with* intersectionality – as a way of understanding interlocking axes, histories, and structures of dominations – and the European poststructuralist use of intersectionality to count and account for various aspects of 'difference'. Like Ratna (2018), Chawansky and Itani (2017), and Oxford and Spaaij (2019) we are concerned about the dearth of decolonial, and Indigenous feminist, perspectives in sports scholarship, and thus dedicate the remainder of this chapter to highlighting existing work that employs these perspectives. They do so in numerous ways, and in diverse settings, yet finding fruitful connections between the consequences of colonial pasts and presents in diverse locales. It is our belief that the future of intersectional scholarship in sport and leisure, lies in a committed effort to decentering Eurocentric and colonial gender perspectives.

Promising directions for sport and leisure scholarship

In this section, we direct our attention towards some of the branches and avenues of intersectional scholarship that we believe have the greatest potential to decentre the normative subjects and epistemologies of sport and leisure scholarship. The research we include does not constitute an exhaustive list but should be seen as a selective presentation of perspectives that we believe are underrepresented and underutilised in sports scholarship.

As articulated by bell hooks (2014), the emergence of intersectionality challenged the notion that 'gender' was the primary factor determining a woman's fate. Depending on their context and situation, women across the world might experience post-colonial relations, migration status and/or their gendered embodiment as having more impact on their sport participation than gender does. Race, class, sexuality, coloniality, religion and/or migration status all determine experiences of marginality and privilege in sport both locally and internationally.

We align with the contention of Cho, Crenshaw, and McCall (2013: 785) that one of the fields of intersectionality is the application of an intersectional frame of analysis "to attend to a variety of context-specific inquires". We see the need of capitalising on the contextual approach insofar as it will provide analytical lenses to show how 'race', gender, and ability intersect with respect for sport both locally and globally. For instance, approaching the feminisation of netball intersectionally will require not only to examine how men and women are positioned in netball locally but also how such positioning aligns with the British postcolonial, Victorian imperial legacy.

De-centring Europe: African feminist trajectories

While scholarship centring African women's sporting lives and experiences remains marginal in sports scholarship, this field of research is by no means new or recent. Jennifer Hargreaves (1994), already in the 1990 included an empirical focus on African sport to highlight how women's access to sports was mediated also by race and class. Through investigating Olympic sports in Zimbabwe and South Africa, she showed that the 'culture of sport' was more dominant and well-resourced in White communities, leading to opportunities for White women to participate in sport on a higher level than Black women, leaving their sporting potentials "untapped" (Hargreaves, 1994: 232). These early engagements with sport in Africa, while limited in geographic scope, nevertheless illustrated the importance, and intellectual contribution, of centring intersectional analysis in contexts outside the Global North.

In 2014, almost 30 years after Hargreaves, a full-length volume on women's sport in Africa was finally published, and contributions were made from a range of sporting codes and contexts across the continent. In the introduction, Sikes and Bale (2014) point out the invisibility of African sporting women in international scholarship, and state that in addition to challenging the reigning Eurocentrism in sports scholarship, the issue aimed at challenging the dominant image of the African woman as victim. Alongside the work done by Denise Jones (2001, 2003), Cheryl Roberts (1992, 1993), Cynthia Pelak (2009, 2010), Martha Saavedra (2004), Cassandra Ogunniyi (2014), and Mari H. Engh (2010, 2011; 2020; Engh & Potgieter, 2015) on women's netball, football, and athletics, a sizeable corpus of intersectional scholarship now exists concerning African sports. While this work reinforces the 'exceptional status' of South Africa and employs various versions of intersectionality – not all of which deliver on the aspiration to 'decentre the normative subject' of modern sports – the scholarship nevertheless contributes to rupturing the Eurocentrism in sport scholarship, and to expose locally sensitive applications of intersectional analysis.

In the last few years, several important contributions have been made, as African feminist engagements with sport have expanded further across the continent, and African epistemologies and intersectional theorisations of gender have increasingly been employed.

Zenquis and Mwaniki (2019) have produced an excellent example of the analysis of gender, race and nationality/ethnicity in sports media representations of the Nigerian American Oqwumike sisters. Centring their analysis on two African athletes, they examine how the reception and representation of the sisters was shaped by "a nexus of crisscrossing power relations" (Zenquis & Mwaniki, 2019: 23). Their intersectional analysis of media portrayals illustrates that what at first glance may appear to be "acceptance or praise for highly skilled Black African migrants (here in the context of U.S. sport) is liminal at best and influenced by stereotypes of Africa" (Zenquis & Mwaniki, 2019: 24), thus reinforcing Western-centric and White normativities in sport. Similarly, Engh and Potgieter (2015), have examined how gender, sexuality, and race intersect in South African popular discourses about sportswomen, constituting representational practices that stifle productive engagement with gender and sexuality and marginalize South African women athletes that are not seen 'fit' with hetero- and White-normative ideals of sporting femininity. In her contribution to the *Handbook of Queer African Studies*, Beth Packer employs an intersectional lens to explore how Senegalese women footballers fashion and take pride in their transgressive identities as *fotballeuse*; "an embodied performance that publicly blurs the lines between masculinity and femininity" (Packer, 2019: 130). Rather than a narrative of pain and suffering, Packer's (2019) chapter offers an intersectional narrative of Black, queer, and Muslim self-fashioning in African sport.

Particularly notable among this recent work are the writings of Anima Adjepong (2019, 2020, 2022). Their work spans the Black Atlantic and provides a sensitive application of Black feminist and African feminist theories that chart opportunities for (intersectional) gender justice in and through sport. Through a study of popular understandings of women's football in Ghana, Adjepong illustrates that despite efforts among the governing bodies of football to heterosexualise the national women's football team in the service of a heteropatriarchal state, "football's popularity in Ghana paradoxically challenges the gendering of the nation by creating a space for women to be celebrated as unequivocal representatives of the hetero-masculine nation" (Adjepong, 2022: 17). Through this, Adjepong highlights the necessity of an intersectional perspective when examining women's sport, but they also write against the Eurocentric presentation of African women as particularly underdeveloped and in need of rescue and/or support. Adjepong's work illustrates the liberatory potentials of women's football on the African continent and illustrates how decolonial, Queer African epistemology enables imagining a more inclusive gender and sexual terrain within and beyond sport (Adjepong, 2019). Adjepong's work opens a promising trajectory for engagements with sports, that begin with African realities, and utilise African theories and concept in the pursuit of gender justice in and through sport. Through exploring the complex visibilities of queer, Black and African sportswomen such as Caster Semenya, their work poses a challenge to "heteropatriarchal narratives that seek to rewrite African geographies and histories as devoid of queer genders and sexuality, through 'homosexuality is un-African' discourses" (Adjepong, 2020: 870).

This work connects directly to that of Sylvia Tamale. First, it shows the productive potential of decolonial African feminist analyses of sport as "[it] offers a lens to understand the hidden-from-view interconnections between race and gender and the relation of each to normative heterosexuality" (Tamale, 2020: 7). Second, Tamale's (2020) work illustrates how the gender-binary system imposed across the world through various colonial projects and sustained through institutions such as modern pro-lympic sport, is founded on polarised dualisms in which female and male, man and woman, are always already locked in a rigid, oppositional, biologically determined, and unequal relation. Through the imposition of this system, pre-colonial forms of gender- expansiveness, gender-bending, and/or gendered flexibilities were made undesirable, and to a large extent, illegal (Tamale, 2020). This is the coloniality of gender; a gender system that created very different arrangements for colonised males and females than for White Bourgeoise colonisers (Lugones, 2007: 186). Intersectional studies of sports offer an excellent arena for exploring the past, present, and incompleteness of the coloniality of gender.

De-centring sport: Decolonial and Indigenous conceptualisations

In the neo-liberal era both traditional and Westernised structures merge and consolidate the combined effects of race, gender, sexuality, language, and religion from both local and global contexts. Contemporary narratives of Black and Indigenous female bodies in sport and leisure are still tied to the legacy of slavery and/or colonial epistemologies which intersect with the traditional cultures and structures that combined still uphold whiteness, patriarchies and heterosexuality. However, this is not to say that women, Queer communities, and persons with disabilities are the only victims of these structures. Men and other groups who do not conform to these structures also become marginalised.

Using decolonial feminist analysis Oxford and Spaaij (2019: 3) analyse SDP in Colombia to address who can play and why they can play. Hence, they explore the multiple relations that shape subject formation in contradictory ways and draw attention to the complex interplay between agency and structure and how the coloniality of gender operates in SDP context. This decolonial feminist approach sheds light on how colonial structures did not automatically disappear when the European political and judicial systems were ceremonially handed over to the natives (Grosfoguel, 2009 in Oxford & Spaaij, 2019). Referred to as invisible threads of constraints, the women are connected to traces of colonialism creating multiple exclusions regardless of their participation in the SDP projects in the Global South. As also expressed by Oxford and Spaaij (2019), there exists a false sense of agency claimed to be entangled in diverse oppressions that lie at the junction of the coloniality of gender causing these young women to accept a multitude of socially constructed restrictions as they consider them to be normal and part of their culture.

Moreover, the settler-colonial lens deficit approach to Indigenous peoples' and rural culture and lifestyle constructs them as passive, unfit and even ill, and sets the stage for eventual stereotyping, eliminating, and marginalising them. Indigenous and rural women's connection to the land is foundational to their cultural identity. McGuire-Adams (2020) shows how colonialism, genocide, and forced removal of Indigenous peoples from their lands and marginalisation in the mainstream culture continues to impact Indigenous peoples' health identities. To turn this deficit-based approach, Indigenous scholars such as Tricial Magurie Adams (2020) in Canada employ Indigenous feminist Gikendassowin (knowledge) and research paradigms such as the Anishinaabeg research paradigm to understand how Indigenous women are creating wellbeing for themselves, their families, and communities through engaging in various cultural, physical, and outdoors activities. While under modernity structures of leisure/sport and work, as well as family and work, are separated, Indigenous epistemologies do not necessarily have the same demarcations, and work mainly performed outdoors is integrated as part of family as well as leisure life (Skogvang & Massao, forthcoming). In her more than ten years of field work at Indigenous Riddu Riđđu festival in Troms in Northern Norway, Bente Skogvang, who herself is sami (Indigenous people in *Sapmi* land that spreads from Norway, Sweden, Finland and Russia), a Norwegian physical education (PE) teacher educator and top international football referee, found that the Norwegian popular concept of outdoor leisure activities known as *friluftsliv* and a part of PE teacher education in Norway did not exist in Sami language or culture. This is because the outdoor activities are directly connected to free time from work. At the same time, Sami's reindeer herding, fishing/coastal, and/or forestry traditions were not always strictly gendered and separated from family and work life as is the case in modern society (Skogvang, 2021). Contextualising sport, leisure and physical activities in this way allows an understanding that can explain the underrepresentation of certain groups in modern sports in better and more nuanced ways, which could eventually empower the groups concerned. This holistic experience and performance of leisure and sporting activities can be explored more in the Indigenous festival such as Riḋḋu Riḋḋu or Indigenous games such as 'Alaska Native Games' or 'Inuit Games' (Skogvang, 2021).

The Indigenous sport, physical activity, and knowledge described by these scholars is not very different from the experiences of many rural men and women around the world, whose livelihoods and leisure depend on the land and environment around them rather than a football pitch. Decentering the understanding of leisure, sport, fitness, and health (physical and mental) requires stepping out of a Eurocentric epistemology of modern sport (Lavallée, 2007) and exploring leisure and sporting epistemologies from different cultural and geographic positions.

De-centring 'the female' – transfeminist perspectives

Sport is among the institutions that still perpetuate a binary system of gender, which results in the gendered segregation of most sport codes (Sullivan, 2011). Even though transgendered and gender non-normative athletes have been admitted to participation at the highest level of sport since at least 2004, it is particularly the last ten years that concerns with so-called gender 'testing' or verification has that become a source of debate. Sex-segregated sports are regulated by the governing bodies to clearly and, they claim, accurately place athletes in the right sex/gender category; 'boys/men' or 'girls/women' (Erikainen, 2019). Gender verification is an attempt to control the athletic bodies that deviate from western femininity and heteronormativity; it enforces suspicion towards 'female masculinity' and non-binary gendered embodiment. Sporting women are placed in a gender-bind: "femininity and athleticism are oxymoronic and inappropriate, whereas masculinity and athleticism are natural and correct" (Pieper, 2016: 185).

The gender verification praxis of institutions such as World Athletics presumes that atypical sexual development is more common in underdeveloped parts of the world and has caused "a targeted concern about black and brown women from the Global South" (Karkazis & Jordan-Young, 2018: 21). Rather than being purely objective and clinical assessments of human physiology, the practice of gender testing rests on subjective and visual assessments of athletic bodies, and evaluations of gendered 'averages' and deviance that has its roots in imperial and racist science. There is a long and violent history in 'white science' (Engh, 2020) for seeing and assessing the Black female body as different from the White western woman's body (McClintock, 1995).

The suspicion raised towards Black women from the postcolonial South illustrates the ongoing effects of the coloniality of gender, and requires examination from a historically sensitive, race-critical, and gender-expansive perspective. Such a lens can be found in various de-colonial feminist approaches, as well as in race-critical transfeminist scholarship (Andersson & Travers, 2017; Travers, 2011). In the introduction to the first volume on transgender lives in sport, Eric Andersson and Travers (2017: 5) outline how:

sport remains a largely unexamined bastion of sex segregation in Western cultures ... our culture predominantly believes in the rightfulness of men's and women's segregation via athletic teams; even when it comes at the expense of women's participation and cultural and economic equality.

Revealing that the central concern of their analysis is the institutionalisation and perpetuation of a colonial, gender binary system. Rupturing the power and reach of this gender-system in sport should thus be considered a key task of critical sports scholarship, one that would require the use of intersectional perspectives that are attuned to how the sex/gender binary is foundationally racialised and locally articulated.

Conclusion

As insisted by Collins (2019), intersectionality as a form of critical inquiry and praxis, has not yet realised its potential as a critical social theory, nor has it adequately democratised its own processes for producing knowledge. But the foundation is there. It is precisely this foundation, and potentials, we have navigated in this chapter. We believe that the future of critical intersectional scholarship in sport is best served by conceptual openness and curiosity, rather than rigid taxonomies and definitions. What has remained at the centre of our overview, is our desire to open-up a more "meaningful and liberatory sporting feminist project" (Ratna, 2018: 2) that does not rely solely on Eurocentric analyses and theories. This requires careful local examination and conceptualisation of the past and present of gendered, heterosexist, racist, and colonial discrimination in and through sport.

What is made possible through a decolonial Indigenous perspective is not merely an accounting for the ways in which the modern pro-Olympic sporting system disciplines and de-humanises the bodies and achievements of Black women, how it strips them of womanhood, but, importantly, it enables the formulation of counter-narratives, of stories of how nonnormative embodiment is *possible*, even joyful and unproblematic. It makes it possible to place 'the problem' of discrimination in sport where it belongs: not in the deviant gender and sexualities of Black, Indigenous or trans bodies, but in the histories, institutions and gazes that are arrested and stuck in rigid and inflexible blueprints for gendered life. This is what it entails to employ a critical intersectional vision for justice. Producing pluriversal and decolonial social science analyses if sport, may also enable sporting institutions to access the gender expansive and joyful embodiment that Black, Indigenous, queer, trans, and other groups and athletes already *know* and *live*.

References

Adjepong, A. (2019). Are you a footballer?: The radical potential of women's football at the national level. In Routledge *Handbook of Queer African Studies* (pp. 76–89). New York: Routledge.
Adjepong, A. (2020). Voetsek! Get [ting] lost: African sportswomen in 'the sporting Black diaspora'. *International Review for the Sociology of Sport*, 55(7), 868–883.
Adjepong, A. (2022). Playing for Oman Ghana: Women's football and gendered nationalism. *Contemporary Journal of African Studies*, 9(2), 1–24.
Adjepong, A. & Carrington, B. (2014). Black female athletes as space invaders. In J. Hargreaves, & E. Anderson (Eds), *Routledge Handbook of Sport, Gender and Sexuality* (pp. 169–178). Abingdon: Routledge.
Amadiume, I. (1997). *Re-inventing Africa: Matriarchy, Religion and Culture*. London and New York: Zed Books.

Andersson, E. & Travers, A. (2017). *Transgender Athletes in Competitive Sport*. London and New York: Routledge.

Bandy, S. J. (2005). From women in sport to cultural critique: A review of books about women in sport and physical culture. *Women's Studies Quarterly*, 33(1/2), 246–261.

Bilge, S. (2014). Whitening intersectionality. *Racism and Sociology*, 5, 175.

Brah, A. & Phoenix, A. (2004). Ain't I a woman? Revisiting intersectionality. *Journal of International Women's Studies*, 5(3), 75–86.

Brown, L. E. C. (2015). Sporting space invaders: Elite bodies in track and field, a South African context. *South African Review of Sociology*, 46 (1), 7–24, DOI: 10.1080/21528586.2014.989666

Bruening, J. (2005). Gender and racial analysis in sport: Are all the women White and all the Blacks men? *Quest*, 57(3), 330–349, DOI: 10.1080/00336297.2005.10491861

Butler, J. (2004). *Undoing Gender* (1st ed.). London: Routledge.

Carrington, B. (2010). *Race, Sport and Politics: The Sporting Black Diaspora*. London, UK: Sage.

Chawansky, M. & Itani, S. (2017). Sexualized/sexed bodies. In M. Silk, D. Andres & H. Thorpe (Eds), *The Routledge Handbook of Physical Cultural Studies*. London: Routledge.

Cho, S., Crenshaw, K. W., & McCall, L. (2013). Toward a field of intersectionality studies: Theory, and praxis. *Signs*, 38(4), 785–810, DOI: 10.1086/669608

Collins, P. H. (2000). *Black Feminist Thought: Knowledge, Consciousness, and the Politics of Empowerment* (2nd ed.). New York, NY: Routledge.

Collins, P. H. (2019). *Intersectionality as Critical Social Theory*. Durham: Duke University Press.

Collins, P. H. & Bilge, S. (2016). *Intersectionality*. Cambridge, UK: John Wiley & Sons.

Combahee River Collective. (1977). 'A Black feminist statement' Reprinted in Linda Nicolson (Ed.), (1997). *The Second Wave: A Reader in Feminist Theory*. New York: Routledge.

Crenshaw, K. W. (1989). *Demarginalizing the Intersection of Race and Sex: A black Feminist Critique of Antidiscrimination Doctrine, Feminist Theory, and Antiracist Politics*. Chicago: University of Chicago Legal Forum.

Crenshaw, K. (1991). Mapping the margins: Intersectionality, identity politics, and violence against women of color. *Stanford Law Review*, 43(6), 1241–1299, DOI: 10.2307/1229039

Darnell, S. & Hayhurst, L. M. C. (2013). De-colonising the politics and practice of sport-for-development: Critical insights from post-colonial feminist theory and methods. In Schulenkorf, N., & Adair, D. (Eds), *Global Sport-for-Development*. Global Culture and Sport Series. London: Palgrave Macmillan, DOI: 10.1057/9781137289636_3

Darnell, S. C. & Millington, R. (2019). Social justice, sport, and sociology: A position statement. *Quest*, 71(2), 175–187, DOI: 10.1080/00336297.2018.1545681

Douglas, D. D. (2005). Venus, Serena, and the Women's Tennis Association: When and where 'race' enters. *Sociology of Sport Journal*, 22(3), 256–282.

Engh, M. H. (2010). The battle for centre stage: Women's football in South Africa. *Agenda: Empowering Women for Gender Equity*, 85, 97–104.

Engh, M. H. (2011). Tackling femininity: The heterosexual paradigm and women's football in South Africa. *International Journal for the History of Sport*, 28(1), 137–152

Engh, M. H. (2020). 'Gjennomsnittskvinnen', kjønnstesting og det hvite blikket: rasialiserte forestillinger om kjønn i eliteidrett. *Tidsskrift for Kjønnsforskning*, 44(3), 187–201.

Engh, M. H., Agergaard, S., & Settler, F. G. (2017). 'The ball and the rhythm in her blood': Racialised imaginaries and football migration from Nigeria to Scandinavia. *Ethnicities*, 17(1), 66–84.

Engh, M. H. & Potgieter, C. (2015). Social cohesion, sexuality, homophobia and women's sport in South Africa. *African Journal on Conflict Resolution*, 15(3), 37–60.

Erikainen, S. (2019). *Gender Verification and the Making of the Female Body in Sport: A History of the Present*. London: Routledge.

Griffin, P. (1992). Changing the game: Homophobia, sexism, and lesbians in sport. *Quest*, 44(2), 251–265, DOI: 10.1080/00336297.1992.10484053

Hargreaves, J. (1994). *Sporting Females: Critical Issues in the History and Sociology of Women's Sports*. London: Routledge, DOI: 10.4324/9780203221945

Hayhurst, L. M. C. (2015). Sport for development and peace: a call for transnational, multi-sited, postcolonial feminist research. *Qualitative Research in Sport, Exercise and Health*. DOI: 10.1080/2159676X.2015.1056824

Hayhurst, L. M. C., Thorpe, H., & Chawansky, M. (2021). 'Introducing Sport, Gender and Development: A Critical Intersection', *Sport, Gender and Development (Emerald Studies in Sport and Gender)*. Bingley: Emerald Publishing Limited, pp. 1–32, DOI: 10.1108/978-1-83867-863-020211001

Heywood, L. (2018). Third-wave feminism and representation. In L. Mansfield, J. Caudwell, B. Wheaton & B. Watson (Eds), *The Palgrave Handbook of Feminism and Sport, Leisure and Physical Education* (pp. 463–477). London: Palgrave Macmillan UK.

hooks, b. (2014) [first published 1984]. *Feminist Theory: From Margin to Centre* (3rd ed.). New York: Routledge.

Jones, D. E. M. (2001). In pursuit of empowerment: Sensei Nellie Kleinsmidt, race and gender challenges in South Africa. In F. Hong & J. A. Mangan (Eds), *Freeing the Female Body: Inspirational Icons*. London: Frank Cass.

Jones D. E. M. (2003). Women and sport in South Africa: Shaped by history and shaping sporting history. In I. Hartman-Tews & G. Pfister (Eds), *Sport and Women: Social Issues in International Perspective*. London: Routledge.

Karkazis, K. & Jordan-Young, R. (2018). The powers of testosterone: Obscuring race and regional bias in the regulation of women athletes. *Feminist Formations*, 30(2), 1–39.

Karkazis, K. et al. (2012). Out of bounds? A critique of the new policies on hyperandrogenism in elite female athletes. *The American Journal of Bioethics*, 12(7), 3–16, DOI: 10.1080/15265161.2012.680533

Kolnes, L.-J. (1995). Heterosexuality as an organizing principle in women's sport. *International Review for the Sociology of Sport*, 30(1).

Lavallée, L. (2007). Physical activity and healing through the medicine wheel. *Pimatisiwin*, 5(1), 127–153.

Lenskyj, H. J. (1994). Sexuality and femininity in sport contexts: Issues and alternatives. *Journal of Sport and Social Issues*, 18(4), 356–376, DOI: 10.1177/019372394018004005

Lenskyj, H. J. & Greey, A. D. (2022). Introduction: The Binary World of Sport. In A. D. Greey & H. J. Lenskyj (Eds) *Justice for Trans Athletes* (pp. 3–15). Leeds: Emerald Publishing Limited. DOI: 10.1108/978-1-80262-985-920221001

Limoochi, S., & Le Clair, J. M. (2011). Reflections on the participation of Muslim women in disability sport: Hijab, Burkini, modesty and changing strategies. *Sport in Society*, 14(9), 1300–1309.

Love, A., Deeb, A., & Waller, S. N. (2020). Social justice, sport, and racism: A position statement. In Nick J. Watson, Grant Jarvie, Andrew Parker (Eds) *Sport, Physical Education, and Social Justice* (pp. 131–144). New York: Routledge.

Lugones, M. (2007). Heterosexualism and the colonial/modern gender system. *Hypatia*, 22(1), 186–219.

Markula, P. (2005). *Feminist Sport Studies: Sharing Experiences of Joy and Pain*. New York: SUNY Press.

McClintock, A. (1995). *Imperial Leather: Race, Gender and Sexuality in the Colonial Context*. New York: Routledge

McDonald, M. (2005). Mapping whiteness and sport: An introduction. *Sociology of Sport Journal*, 22(3), 245–255, DOI: 10.1123/ssj.22.3.245

McGuire-Adams, T. (2020). *Indigenous Feminist Gikendaasowin: Decolonization through Physical Activity*. Cham: Springer International Publishing.

McSweeney, M., Kikulis, L., Thibault, L., Hayhurst, L., & van Ingen, C. (2019). Maintaining and disrupting global-North hegemony/global-South dependence in a local African sport for development organisation: The role of institutional work. *International Journal of Sport Policy and Politics*, 11(3), 521–537, DOI: 10.1080/19406940.2018.1550797

Ogunniyi, C. (2014). Perceptions of the African Women's Championships: Female footballers as anomalies. *Sport in Society*, 17(4), 537–549.

Oxford, S. (2019). 'You look like a machito!': A decolonial analysis of the social in/exclusion of female participants in a Colombian sport for development and peace organization. *Sport in Society*, 22(6), 1025–1042, DOI: 10.1080/17430437.2019.1565389

Oxford, S. & Spaaij, R. (2019). Gender relations and sport for development in Colombia: A decolonial feminist analysis. *Leisure Sciences*, 41(1/2), 54–71.

Oyewumi, O. (1997). *The Invention of Women: Making an African Sense of Western Gender Discourses*. Minneapolis: University of Minnesota Press.

Packer, B. D. (2019). Moral agency and the paradox of positionality: Disruptive bodies and queer resistance in Senegalese women's soccer. In *Routledge Handbook of Queer African Studies* (pp. 129–141). New York: Routledge.

Pelak, C. F., (2009). Women's sport as a site for challenging racial and gender inequalities in post-apartheid South Africa. In F. Britton, J. N. Fish & S. Meintjies (Eds), *Women's Activism in South Africa: Working Across Divides*. Scottsville: University of KwaZulu Natal Press.

Pelak, C. F. (2010). Women and gender in South African soccer: A brief history. *Soccer and Society*, 11(1–2), 63–78.

Pieper, L. (2016). *Sex Testing: Gender Policing in Women's Sports*. Urbana-Champaign: University of Illinois Press, DOI: 10.5406/illinois/9780252040221.001.0001

Ratna, A. (2018). Not just merely different: Travelling theories, post-feminism and the racialized politics of women of color. *Sociology of Sport Journal*, 35 (3). ISSN 1543-2785, DOI: https://doi.org/10.1123/ssj.2017-0192

Roberts, C. (1992). *Against the Grain: Women and Sport in South Africa*. Cape Town: Township Publishing Cooperative.

Roberts, C. (1993). "Black women, recreation and organised sport", Agenda, Number 17.

Saavedra, M. (2004). Football feminine- development of the African game: Senegal, Nigeria and South Africa. In F. Hong and J. A. Mangan (Eds), *Soccer, Women, Sexual Liberation; Kicking Off a New Era*. London: Frank Cass Publishers.

Scraton, S. (2001). Reconceptualizing race, gender and sport: The contribution of Black feminism. In B. Carrington & I. McDonald (Eds), *'Race' Sport and British Society* (pp. 170–187). London: Routledge.

Scraton, S., Caudwell, J., & Holland, S. (2005). 'BEND IT LIKE PATEL' centring 'Race', ethnicity and gender in feminist analysis of women's football in England. *International Review for the Sociology of Sport*, 40(1), 71–88.

Sikes, M. & Bale, J. (2014). Introduction: Women's sport and gender in sub-Saharan Africa. *Sport in Society*, 17(4), 449–465.

Skogvang, B. O. (2021). Sámi sports and outdoor life at the Indigenous Riddu Riđđu festival. *Journal of Adventure Education and Outdoor Learning*, 21(4), 357–370, DOI: 10.1080/14729679.2020.1838934

Skogvang, B. O. & Massao, P. B. (forthcoming). Kulturelle og politiske betydninger av Aktivitetstilbud for barn og unge på urfolksfestivalen Riddu Riđđu – en helhetlig tilnærming, i: Isak Lidström & Helge Chr. Pedersen (red.) Idrott, historia & samhälle '*Etniska minoriteter i idrottsperiferin – Historiska studier från Nordkalotten*'.

Sullivan, C. F. (2011). Gender verification and gender policies in elite sport: Eligibility and 'fair play'. *Journal of Sport and Social Issues*, 35(4), 400–419, DOI: 10.1177/0193723511426293

Tamale, S. (2020). *Decolonization and Afro-Feminism*. Ottawa: Daraja Press.

Travers, A. (2011). Women's ski jumping, the 2010 Olympic Games and the deafening silences of sex segregation, whiteness and wealth. *Journal of Sport and Social Issues*, 35(2), 126–145.

Travers, A. (2022). 'Female' sport and testosterone panic. In A. D. Greey & H. J. Lenskyj (Eds), *Justice for Trans Athletes: Challenges and Struggles*. Leeds: Emerald Publishing Limited.

Zenquis, M. R., & Mwaniki, M. F. (2019). The intersection of race, gender, and nationality in sport: Media representation of the Ogwumike sisters. *Journal of Sport and Social Issues*, 43(1), 23–43, DOI: 10.1177/0193723518823338

INDEX

Note: Pages in *italics* refer to figures, pages in **bold** refer to tables, and pages followed by "n" refer to notes.

Aartun, I. 238
Abdul-Rauf, M. 448
Abelson, M. 92–94
ableism 210, 379, 384
Abolition of the British Slave Trade Act 33
Abooali, S. 163
Abrahão, B. O. L. 151
accreditation process 136–137
Action Sport 338, 340
Active Communities Development Fund (ACDF) 340
activism 446; allies 64–65; athletes 59–67, 405, 431–442, 446–455; collective 5; environmental sports 471–481; eventful sociology 405–417; goals 60–61; location 62–63; non-confrontational and confrontational tactic 63; online 459–468; outcomes 65–66; pedagogy approach 226, 229; political 12, 304, 448; tactics 63–64; women athletes' 59–67
activist-scholarship 8–9; audience 11; barriers 11; challenges for 3–15; methodologies 10; in neoliberal moment 9–10; searching for integrity 13–14
Adair, D. 309, 437, 533
Adamson, B. 378
Addo-Carr, J. 438
Adelman, M. 324
adiaphorization 53–54
Adjepong, A. 559–560, 563
Advance Australia Fair 437–439
advocacy: active, pedagogy approach 272–273; anti-racist 153–154; in youth sport 205–214

affirmative action 219, 271
African American: athletes 171, 432; branding social justice 420, 423, 426; children's leisure geographies 198–199; cultural critics 532; National Anthems 433–434
African feminist theory 558, 562–564
age of precarity 45–54
Agergaard, S. 560
Aguilar, S. J. 273
Ahmad, N. 464
Alfrey, L. 225, 286
Ali, M. 59, 66, 422, 448
Aliu, A. 428
all-or-nothing model 75
Alonso, F. 479
Amadiume, I. 557
Amaechi, J. 427
Amhrán na bhFiann (The Soldier's Song) 440
Anarchy, State and Utopia (Nozick) 24
Anderson, B. 432
Anderson, E. 73, 75–77, 79, 81, 119, 565; *Inclusive masculinity: the changing nature of masculinities* 75
Andre, A. 72
androgen insensitivity syndrome (AIS) 103
anonymisation 550–552
anti-Blackracism 146, 148–150, 152, 155
anti-racism 41, 132, 140; *see also* racism; activism 446; assertive 433; awareness 196; community activist 521; and cultural assertion 199; defence of 145–155; in physical education 284
anti-transgender movement 95, 123

Antonio, A. L. 328
Antunovic, D. 459, 463
apolitical athletes 422–425; *see also* athletes
Apple, M. 225
Arai, A. 425
Arai, S. 197
Arber, S. 366
Arcelus, J. 211
Arellano, A. 299, 302–304
Armour, K. M. 222
Armstrong, G. 315
Arts and Humanities Research Council (AHRC) 35
arts-based research 504–505; film *see* film, social justice and; for social justice 505–506; substantial literature on 505
Aspire (2017) 353, 356
Assumpção, L. O. T. 155
athletes; *see also* sport; achievements 267; activism 59–67, 405, 431–442, 446–455; African American 171, 432; apolitical 422–425; Black athletes 149, 153–154, 171, 173, 175–176, 420, 422, 446–447; branding 419–428; celebrity 300, 419; elite 47, 51, 53, 59–61, 72, 208; empowered 424–426; in England 38; gay and lesbian 81; high-profile 59–60, 419, 422, 433, 448, 454; Indigenous *see* Indigenous athletes; intersex 104–105, 107, 110; LGBTQ 72; LGBTQI2S 211; Pasifika 535; performance-enhancing drugs 53; personal branding 419–428; on personal level 464; pioneer 420–422; polarising effect 323; professional 18, 424–425, 433, 447, 509; revolutionary 422; social justice 181; training of teen 252; transgender 88, 91, 95, 101, 103–105, 110–111, 123, 211, 219; treatment of 109; violent incidents 395
Atkins, L. 491
Atkinson, D. 170–176
Atlanta Olympic Games 340
audience 11–12
austerity 7, 37, 342–343, 349–350
Australian National Olympic Committee (NOC) 427

Back, L. 5, 522
Bagelman, J. 12
Bailey, R. 350, 354
Bairner, A. 11
Baker, C. 36
Baker, M. 182
Bakewell, O. 524, 527
Bale, J. 562
Banet-Weiser, S. 464
Barber, J. 41
Barber, W. 273

Barnes, C. 380
Barnes, J. 173
Barone, T. 506
Barreto, L. 148
Bass, A. 422
Bastide, R. 151
Bauman, Z. 46–47, 50–52, 54
Beale, K. 439
Beijing Games 2008 12
Belfast Telegraph 79
Bellerín, H. 480
bell hooks 225, 562
Benjamin, J. 391
Benjamin, R. 141
Ben & Jerry's 6
Bennett, G. 327
Bennett, M. 176n1
Benn, T. 224
Bentham, J. 49
Beresford, P. 382
Berggren, K. 75
Berlin Olympic Games 37, 421
Bhopal, K. 351
bicultural pedagogy 272
Bieler, D. 452
Big Society 342
Bilge, S. 558
Bindel, J. 86
Birrell, S. 556
Biscomb, K. 462
Bittman, M. 371
Bjørkqvist, K. 395
Black athletes 149, 153–154, 171, 173, 175–176, 420, 422, 446–447
Black, D. R. 299, 301, 303
Black, Indigenous, and People of Colour (BIPOC) 428
Black Lives Matter (BLM) 3, 27, 38, 46, 61, 181, 321, 433, 435, 446, 454, 459
Black Power movement 183, 199
Black Power Salute 432, 448–449
Black reasoning by Whites 152–153
Blackshear, T. B. 284
A Black Theology of Liberation (Cone) 183
Blake, J. 448
Blau, G. 72
Blázquez, F. 240
blitz campaign, social media 425–426
Bloomfield, S. 172
Blue Jean 507
Blue Plaque Rebellion 38
Bocarro, J. N. 194
bodily practices: physical education (PE) 237–239, 241–245; school physical education 280–281, 285
Bolt, U. 267

571

Bonilla-Silva, E. 132
Boone, A. 450
Borell, P. J. 533
Boren, C. 452
Boswell, T. 453
Boulmerka, H. 64
Bouman, W. P. 211
Bourdieu, P. 366–367, 370
Bowling Alone (Putnam) 186
#BoycottNike movement 27
Boykoff, J. 449
Boyle, D. 36
Bracht, V. 281
Bradford's National Science and Media Museum 35
Branch, E. 452
branding social justice 419–428
Brave New Films 514
Brazilian sport: anti-Blackracism 146, 148–150, 152, 155; anti-racist advocacy 153–154; bourgeois distribution of 150; civilising process and 148; globalisation problem 152–153; late slavery abolishment in 146–148; modern 147–152, 155; physical education 153–154; political life *versus* 150–152; racism in 145–155; recognition policy 155; school physical education 280–287
Breen, O. 91
Brees, D. 450
Bresler, L. 512
British Museum 40
The British Olympics and Played in Liverpool (Polley and Physick) 36
Brohm, J.-M. 150, 153
Brown, A. A. 198
Brown, D. 222
The Brownies' Book 199
Brown, J. 448
Brown v. Board of Education 422
Bruening, J. E. 327, 560
Brunner, C. 493
Bruno, F. 174
Bryan, N. 197
Bullingham, R. 81
Bundniss Aktiver Fußball Fans (BAFF) 414
Burawoy, M. 11
Bush, G. 448
Bush, K. A. 327
Butler, J. 539

Calhoun, A. S. 463
Campbell, P. I. 36
Campbell, T. 23
Candaele, K. 449
Cannella, G. S. 505

capitalism 6–7, 33, 518; contemporary financial 186; free market 407; in liquid modernity 51; modern sports to 245; pedagogical approach 285; post-industrial 236, 240
caring teaching strategies 222–223, 228
Carlisle, C. 174
Carlos, J. 21, 59, 66, 267, 422, 427, 432–433, 448
Carney, A. 314
Carney, M. 186; *Values(s): Building a Better World for All* 186
Carrington, B. 559
Carter Report 341
Cartwright, S. 170–172
Cassidy, K 522
Castells, M. 410
Cathy Come Home 507
Caudwell, J. 72–73, 89, 91, 498, 522, 524
cause-related marketing (CRM) 423, 425
Cavallo, J. 72
Centre for Social Justice 5
Chan, J. 449
Channel Nine 439
Channon, A. 119
Chatzitheochari, S. 366
Chau, J. 423
Chawansky, M. 314, 561
Chelladurai, P. 324
children's leisure geographies 192–200; adult-centric lenses 193–194; antiracist resistance 198–199; barriers and experiences 196–198; cultural heritage 198–199; racialised minority 194–196
Chilisa, B. 493
China: elite sport system 251–260; gender inequality 251; government's management 251–260; hybrid rationality 252–255; racially minoritised children's leisure 198
Cho, S. 562
Christianity 178–190; Catholic documents 183–186; cultural backdrop 179–180; gender and sexuality 188–190; inherent dangers 180; racial justice 181–188; solidarity 186; sport *versus* social justice 180–181
Chung, E. 139
CIPPEFE (2020) 281–287
cisgender; *see also* gender; female athletes, impact on 107; individuals 99; research community 88, 95
cisnormative masculinity 89
citizenship education 273
Civil Rights Act 135
civil rights movements 46, 134, 172, 181, 269, 274, 422–423, 432
Clarke, G. 462
Clark, L. 223, 284
Clark, S. 365

Clarkson, W. 173
Cleary, A. 461
Cleary, B. 326
Cleland, J. 79, 81, 437
closure, sociology 364–368
Coakley, J. 131, 158, 394
Coalition government in the Immigration Act 2014 522
coalition of football supporters (CoFS) 413–415
Coalter, F. 298, 317, 335, 338
co-educational groups, physical education (PE) 118–120
Coleby, J. 312
collective activism 5; *see also* activism
Collins, P. H. 566
Collison, C. 162
Collymore, S.: *Tackling My Demons* 174
Colston, E. 38–39
combat sports 392, 397–398; *see also* sport
Commiskey, G. 466
Commission for Accreditation of Park and Recreation Agencies (CAPRA) 136–137
commodification 8, 30, 36, 51, 477, 480, 534
Commonwealth Games 35, 40–41
community sport development (CSD) 334–345; alleviating barriers to participation 335; challenges 342; emergence of 338–339; milestones in **337**; new era for 343–344; new labour 340–341; 'no compromise' approach 342; policy and practice 344–345; Positive Futures 341; pre-CSD 336–338; sport for sports sake 339–340; in United Kingdom 336–338, 344–345
Community Treatment Orders 172
competing theories, social justice 22–27, 29; fairness and 22; libertarian 24–25; Rawlsian approach 25–26; sceptics 23–24
compulsory competitive tendering (CCT) 50, 54n3, 339
Cone, J.: *A Black Theology of Liberation* 183
confrontational tactics, women elite athletes 63–64
Connell, R. W. 76, 94, 397
conspicuous consumption 364
contact sports 100–101, 196, 392–393, 395, 397; *see also* sport
contemporary society 18, 53, 239–240, 350–351, 354, 363, 365
contrasting approaches, to social justice 18–30
Cooky, C. 9, 11, 459
cooperative learning 121, 224, 228
Cooper, J. N. 431, 433
Corinthians, London 40
corporate museums 36, 40
corporate social responsibility 330, 423–425
Corrêa, L. H. 149
Cosby, B. 422

The Cosby Show 422
Cottle, S. 449
Cottrell Boyce, F. 36–37
de Coubertin, B. P. 159
Court, M. 66
Court of Arbitration for Sport (CAS) 106
COVID-19 164, 284, 344, 349–350, 353, 357, 365, 433, 462, 465–466, 476
Crenshaw, K. W. 557, 562
crime reduction 390–391, 399–400; gender 396–398; masculine currency 399; paradoxes and complexity 391–393; theories of change 393–396
criminal justice system 49, 197, 450
Crisor, V. R. 281
critical disability studies 376–379
critical feminist theory 313, 328
critical pedagogy 280, 282; *see also* pedagogy approach; aspects of 207; in Brazil 281; in higher education 325; knowledge 9; physical education (PE) 238; reflective processes 213; in school physical education 280, 282–284, 286–287; social 220–221, 225, 228–229; Sport for Development and Peace (SDP) 317
critical race theory (CRT) 3, 10, 27, 139, 192, 197, 532; PE teacher education (PETE) programmes 284; US legislation and policies against 264–275
Crossley, N. 412
Croston, A. 118, 120
Crow, J. 46, 135, 420–421
CSD *see* community sport development
Csikszentmihalyi, M. 164
Culp, B. 284
cultural difference 196; collective 534; influence of 27; recognition of 28
culturally responsive pedagogy (CRP) approach 271–272
culture: celebrity impact 53; in Christian community 184–186; competence 223, 270, 497; corporate 14; discrimination 183; Drapetomania and 172–173; Fanonian critique of 153; of football 189, 408; heritage 198–199; humility 497; inclusive theories 175–176; injustices 206, 209; intercultural education 224; LGBTIQ+ 79; omnivore 367; predatory 236, 240; significance of sport 30; of social advocacy 330; theoretical foundation based on 282
The Culture, Sport and Media Committee 81
Cunha Júnior, H. A. 154
Cunningham, G. B. 324, 432, 495, 497
Curry, S. 436

Dabrowski, V. 467
Dagkas, S. 224, 351

Daily Mail 86
Dallas Cowboys 472
Damatta, R. 150
Danieli, A. 380
Danish, S. J. 355
Darnell, S. C. 22, 146, 298–300, 311–312, 315
Davies, A. 164
Davis, K. 324
Davison, E. 21
Davison, R. M. 551
Day, D. 38
Declaration of Human Rights 296, 308
deficit-based approach 312, 564
Deighan, M. 441
Delale-O'Connor, L. 199
Deleuze, G. 73
Delgado, R. 197
Della Porta, D. 410, 414–415
DeLuca, C. 224
De Martini Ugolotti, N. 162, 522, 524
Demers, G. 211
democratic pedagogy approach 225–227; *see also* pedagogy approach
Denison, E. 78, 210
Denzin, N. K. 74, 505, 532
Depression and suicide: Football's Secret Uncovered 174
desistance process 390–391, 393–394, 396, 398–399
Devís-Devís, J. 10
Dewey, J. 225, 322, 325
Diagnostic and Statistical Manual of Mental Disorders 82n2
DiAngelo, R. 132
differences of sexual development (DSD) 105
dilemma: ethical 548–551; theory of 171
Dillard, C. B. 8
Dingle, S. 326
disability sport 251; *see also* sport; embodiment 241–242; inclusion of 281, 284–285; power dynamics in 376–386; youth sport 209–210
discipline: methods 51; panopticon system 52; to seduction 50–51; of sociology 158
Discourse on the Origins and the Foundations of Inequality Among Men (Rousseau) 179
discrimination 210; patterns of 172; physical education *see* physical education; prejudice and 211; racial 322; social/cultural 183; in sport 99–111
Disraeli, B. 186
distributive justice 20, 22, 27, 335; *see also* social justice
diversity: activism 454; conservatism 5; culture *see* cultural difference; decision-making perspectives 270; equity, and inclusion (DEI) *see* equity, diversity, and inclusion; gender-typing process 118; human rights and 266; sexualities 72–73, 76; young people's involvement 209
Dixon, B. 397
Dixon, M. 324
'doing gender' theory 114–115, 117, 123
Donaldson, M. 75
Donnelly, J. 188–189
Donnelly, P. 11
Donnor, J. K. 8
Douglas, D. 560
Dowling, F. 284
Downey, A. 299, 302–304
Doyle, T. 428
Drane, D. 327
Drapetomania 170–176
Dreier, P. 449
Drury, S. 122
Duany, A.: *Suburban Nation: The Rise and Decline of the American Dream* 135
Du Bois, W. E. B. 158, 199
Duckworth, V. 491
Dumaresq, M. 101

economic determinism 534
EDI *see* equity, diversity, and inclusion
Edwards, H. 423, 433, 447, 450
Eisner, E. 381
Elias, N. 47
elite athletes, women 47, 51, 53, 67n2, 72, 208; *see also* gender; sex; activism 59–67; cisgender impact on 107; intersex impact on 105–107; physically weaker and less athletic 100–101; transgender impact on 103–105; youth sport *see* youth sport
Ellison, R.: *Invisible Man* 181
Emancipation Proclamation 140, 322
emancipatory participatory approaches 377, 379–381, 384–386
embodiment: pedagogy approach 238–239; in physical education 236–245
Empire Café 41
empowered athletes 424–426; *see also* athletes
Engh, M. H. 560, 563
England's Rugby Football Union (RFU) 37
English football: BSkyB into 412; clubs 24; drapetomania 172–174; grounds 38; Heysel disaster 407, 412; in Hillsborough 406, 412–416; ritual of watching football 406–408; Safe Standing 405–417; temporality in sociology 410–411; unpacking contemporary fan protests 409–410
English Premier League (EPL) 6, 24, 50, 370, 414, 477
Enlightenment 47, 54n2
Enright, E. 225

Entine, J. 146
Entman, R. 449
environmental sports activism, five groups of 471–481
epistemic violence 492–493; *see also* violence
Eppler, M. 326
Epson Derby 21
Equal Employment Opportunity Commission 62
equality: gender 65; social 21, 25, 180; sport consensus 21; in Sport for Development and Peace (SDP) 295–304
Equality Act 4, 86
Equal pay 64
Equity Action Plan 137
equity, diversity, and inclusion (EDI) 13–14, 132, 136–139; impression management 139; National Football League (NFL) 138–139; National Recreation and Park Association (NRPA) 136–137; US Olympic and Paralympic Committee (USOPC) 132, 138–139
equity, in sport 134–136
Erevelles, N. 285
Errickson, M. 326
Eschmann, R. 27
Esptein, D. 101
ethical responsibility 538–539
ethics: codes 547; integrity and 544–552; media ethics anomie 552; requirements 547; of social justice research 491–492
ethnographic research 36, 196, 212, 254, 461, 512, 520, 538, 549
Eurocentrism 176, 238, 562, 566; of African women 563; disability and social change 379; discourses 311, 313; education implications 267; epistemology of modern sports 565; structural inequality 314
European Convention on Human Rights (ECHR) 4, 547
European Court of Human Rights 61
European Youth Portal 355
Evans, J. 182, 222
eventful sociology, of fan activism 405–417
evidence-based medicine/practice (EBM/EBP) 505–506
exclusionary power, social justice 53–54
experiential learning 322, 325–326

Fairground Park 134
fairness and social justice 22, 25–26
Falcous, M. 10–11
families, in youth sport 205–214
Fan, H. 252
Fanon, F. 147, 149, 153, 155, 173
Farber, R. 89–90, 94
Farias, L. G. S. 148
Farquharson, K. 209, 213

Fashanu, J. 174
F. C. Barcelona 427
Fédération Internationale de Football Association (FIFA) 296–297, 316, 414, 477–478, 552
female elite athletes *see* women elite athletes
femininity: cisnormative masculinity and 89; inclusive masculinity theory 71, 75, 77; performance 71; White 108–109, 557
feminism 4; African feminist theory 558, 562–564; cultural studies 556; Fraser's idea 29; gender critical 85–96; intersectionality 556–566; trans-exclusionary cultures 123
feminist theory 313, 328, 559, 563
Ferdinand, R. 173
Fernandes, F. 151
feudalism 47–48
Filgueiras, I. P. 281
film, social justice and: filmmaking process 509, 512–513; future of 515–516; *Gwithian Sands 511*, 511–514; *The Long Run* 508–511, *509*; social impact 514; viewer responses 509–511, 513–514
Fine, M. 379
Finneran, M. 179
Fittler, B. 439
Fitzgerald, H. 284
Fitzpatrick, K. 122, 271–272, 286
Fletcher, T. 25, 376, 533
Flintoff, A. 284
Floyd, G. 21, 38, 46, 433, 436, 447, 450, 452, 454
Floyd, M. F. 194
Flunker, L. 326
Foley, M. 35
football 476–479; culture of 189; English football *see* English football; Leeds-based community 521; professional 172–174
Football for Hope project 316
Football in the Community schemes 338
Football Licensing Authority 407
Football Supporters Association (FSA) 405, 410, 412–413
forced migration, participatory research 518–527
Forde, S. D. 314
formal education, legitimate embodiment in 236–245
Formula One 471, 479–480
Fortune, M. 7
Forty-million-dollar Slave (Rhoden) 171
Foucault, M. 45, 47–50, 73, 237–238, 256, 258
Frank, A. 506
Fraser, N. 19, 23, 206, 209–210, 212, 236, 259–260; academic applications 33; integrated approach to social justice 28–29; *Justice Interruptus: Critical Reflections on the "Postsocialist" Condition* 28

575

Freebody, K. 179
Freeman, C. 67
free societies 147
Freidman, M. 50
Freire, P. 117, 207, 213, 220, 225, 274, 280, 282, 286, 317, 326
Freitas Junior, M. A. 149
French National Convention 48
Freud, S. 51
Friedman, M. 5
Frisby, W. 314
Fromm, E. 48, 52
Fuentes-Miguel, J. 122
Fukuyama, F. 180, 189
Furse, L. J. 461

Gadd, D. 391, 397
Games of the New Emerging Forces (GANEFO) 296
Gantt, H. 423
Garner, E. 448
Garratt, D. 273
Garvey, M. 46
Gemar, A. 368
gender; *see also* sex; activism 59–67; Christianity 188–190; critical feminists 85–96; efforts at inclusion 109–110; equality 65; historical assumptions about 100–101; and homosexuality 71–82; identity 93, 99, 105; inequality 89, 92, 251; non-conformity 103, 107, 110–111, 117, 123; normativity 93, 96; physical education (PE) 114–123, 267; recognition process 85; school physical education 285–286; segregation 61; self-identification system 85; and sexualities 71; social disadvantage 351; socialisation 89, 93; sport and 91–95; verification 565; violence 396–398; in youth sport 114–123
Gender Recognition Act (GRA) 85
gender-typing process 117–118
General Assembly Report 308
The Geographies of Threat and the Production of Violence: The State and the City Between Us (Mowatt) 135
Gerdin, G. 116, 120
Gerwirtz, S. 158
Gibson, A. 426, 448
Gibson, B. E. 378
Giddens, A. 45, 351
Gide, A. 188–189
Giles, A. R. 312, 314
Gillan, K. 411, 415
Gillborn, D. 197
Giordano, P. 396
Giroux, H. A. 317
Giulianotti, R. 48, 298, 309, 315

Gleitze, M. 38
Goddard, P. 449
God Save the Queen, Northern Ireland 440–441
Goffman, E. 449
Goffman, I. 139
golf, in Canada 368–369
Goodell, R. 436, 452
Goodley, D. 378
Grace, E. J. 285
Grainger, A. 537
Gramsci, A. 317
Grand Prix Act 480
Great Sport Myth 131
Greek Olympic Winners organisation 353
Green, M. 336
Greenpeace 474, 478, 480
Greey, A. D. 558
Gruden, J. 133
The Guardian 79–80, 95
Guattari, F. 73
Gubby, L. 119
Guerin, R. 240
Guinjoan, M. 427
Gwithian Sands 511, 511–514

Halberstam, J. 94
Hallaitken 341
Hall, S. 74
Haltom, T. M. 118
Hamilton, L. 479
Handbook of Queer African Studies 563
Harbaugh, J. 450
Hardin, M. 463
Hardy, E. 462
Hargreaves, J. 49
Harris, A. 515
Harrison, R. 451
Hartmann, D. 295, 297, 299, 301, 303–304, 309, 449
Harwood, C. G. 208
Hasson, R. 344
Hawkes, G. L. 533
Haycraft, E. 211
Hayek, F. 20, 23–24, 50
Hayhurst, L. M. 212, 298–299, 311–312, 314, 561
Haywood, C. 397
health: critical studies on 286; homonegativism 72; medical interventions 106, 109; mental 170–176; school physical education 286; sport *see* sport
Hegel, G.: *Phenomenology of Spirit* 180
hegemonic masculinity 74–76, 86, 91–96, 120, 396
Henderson, J. 178
Henderson, K. A. 192

Henley Rowing Club 364
Henson, R. 327
Heritage Lottery Fund 35
heritage, sport 33–41; Australia's Aboriginal communities 33; Everton and Liverpool FCs 40; honouring of 40; intangible 36; leisure and 33–41; 'past' in present 38–40; performance of 36–37; public history 40–41; tangible immovable/movable 34; trans 94; in United Kingdom 35–36; University of Glasgow 40–41
heteropatriarchy 558–559, 563
heterosexual masculinity 89, 92
Heysel stadium disaster 407, 412
Heyward, O. 461
Heywood, A. 557
Highland Park 135
High-Performance Management Organisations (HPMOs) 138
high-profile athletes *see* women elite athletes
Hill, D. 173
Hill, J. 206
Hillsborough stadium disaster, English football 406, 412–416
Hills, L. A. 118–120
Hirschi, T. 394
Historically Black Colleges and Universities (HBCUs) 269–270
Hitler, A. 421
HIV/AIDS education 297, 308–309, 314
Hobsbawm, E. 431
Hockey Diversity Alliance (HDA) 428
Hodge, C. J. 194
Hodges, C. 448
Hodges, J. 439
Hokowhitu, B. 536
homohysteria 76–77, 79
homonegativism 71–73, 77, 80, 82n1
homosexuality 71–82
homosexuality obsessive-compulsive disorder (HOCD) 82n2
homosociality 76–79
hooliganism 338, 390, 406–407, 409, 479
Hope, L. B. 199
hostile environment policy 522
Houlihan, B. 335–336, 339
How the Word is Passed (Smith) 136
Hubbard, G. 523
Hubbard, L. 219
Huckaby, M. F. 505
Hudson, W. W. 82n1
Humphrey, K. 95
Hunter, L. 351
"hunting for racists" strategy 132, 134, 140–141
Hurtado, D. 238
Hussain, U. 495, 497

Hylton, K. 10, 53, 342
hyper masculinity 396–397, 400

#IAmEnough 464–465
Ibrahimović, Z. 447
#ICare 466–467
identity politics 27–28, 41, 179–180
impression management 139
IMT *see* inclusive masculinity theory
Inclusive masculinity: the changing nature of masculinities (Anderson) 75
inclusive masculinity theory (IMT) 71–75; empirical concerns 77–80; political promotion of queer people 80–81; researchers 80–82; theoretical concerns 75–76
Independent Supporter Associations (ISAs) 412–413
Indigenous athletes 437–440; epistemology 493, 531–532, 537, 564; intersectionality 564–565; school physical education, in Brazil 283–284; social justice research (SJR) 531–540
industrial capitalism 51; *see also* capitalism
inequality: gender 89, 92, 251; social 24–25, 236; structural *see* structural inequality
integrity approach 14, 544; challenges for 3–15; data analysis and write-up 551–552; data collection 549–551; Fraser's idea 28; knowledge translation 494; neoliberal agendas 546–552; notion of 545; online quantitative research 550; post-publication 552; searching 13–14; of social justice 19, 28–30; topic selection 547–548
International Criminal Court (ICC) 266
International Olympic Academy 185
International Olympic Committee (IOC) 37, 103, 163, 180, 296–297
International Olympic Movement 152
International Quidditch Association (IQA) 109
intersectionality 556–566; de-centring Europe 562–564; decolonial and indigenous conceptualisations 564–565; normative subjects and epistemologies 561–562; in North America 557; social justice 558–559; Sport for Development and Peace (SDP) 560–561, 564; transfeminist perspectives 565; trends and tensions in 559–561
intersex: athletes 104–105, 107, 110–111; female athletes, impact on 105–107; variations 108
Inuit Games 565
invisibility of trans men, in sport/sporting spaces 85–96
Invisible Man (Ellison) 181
Ireland's Gaelic Athletic Association (GAA) 37
Irish Rugby Football Union 440
Ironsmith, M. 326

Ison, N. 495
Itani, S. 561

Jackson, D. 12
Jakubowska, H. 29
James, L. 46, 322, 420, 424, 436, 447, 454
Jaramillo, L. 238
Jarness, V. 367
Jawad, H. 224
Jeanes, R. 212, 225, 313
Jeffreys, K. 336
Jeffries, J. J. 420
Jesus, G. M. 148
Johnson, J. 420–421
Jones, B. A. 211
Jones, R. L. 222
Jordan, M. 423, 425, 433, 448
Jordan-Young, R. M. 103
Josephson, A. 548
Justice and the Politics of Difference (Young) 26
justice, equity, diversity, and inclusion (JEDI) 13–14
Justice Interruptus: Critical Reflections on the "Postsocialist" Condition (Fraser) 28

Kaepernick, C. 46, 59, 65, 322–323, 451, 544; branding social justice 424–425; media and athlete activism 447, 450–453; national anthems 434–437
Kant, I. 163
Karate Kid (film) 393
Kareem Abdul-Jabbar Social Justice Champion award 426
Karkazis, K. A. 103
Kaufman, P. 446
Kaufman, Z. 316
Keddie, A. 206, 208
Keller, L. 467
Kelley, R. 34
Kelvingrove Museum 40
Kendi, I. X. 133
Kendrick, J. R. 326
Kennedy, D. 40
Kerr, S. 452
Kessel, A. 38
Keynesian welfare strategy 50
Keyser-Verreault, A. 211
Kicking AIDS out 297
Kick-out-Poverty 353, 356–357
killings of Castile and Sterling 448
King, A. 406–407, 409, 412–413
King, B. J. 59, 61–62, 65, 426
King, C. 175, 176n2
King, M. L. 179, 181–188
Kirk, D. 49, 229, 355
Kivel, B. D. 197

Klitschko, V. 51
Knight, C. J. 208
knowledge: critical pedagogy 9; integrity approach 494; non-subjugated 238; production 8–9, 300, 381, 518–520, 525; social justice 10; of socially marginalised groups 285; subjugated 237–238; and teaching 9–12
Kohn, K. 72
Koro, M. 505
Koss, J. O. 297
Kournikova, A. 109
Kuh, G. D. 325
Kumar, S. 273
Kunkel, T. 423
Kunz, E. 282
Kuppan, V. 532
Kwauk, C. 295, 297, 299, 301, 303–304, 309

Labour's Immigration Act 522
Ladson-Billings, G. 8
laissez-faire neoliberalism 22, 24; *see also* neoliberalism
Lakisa, D. 533–534
Lalik, R. 227, 229
Landi, D. 117
Lange, A. C. 328
Lan, P. 198
Larson, A. 222
Larsson, H. 118, 121
late slavery abolishment 146–148
Laub, J. H. 391
Laureus Lifetime Achievement Award 131
Lau, T. C. W. 385–386
LaVoi, N. M. 463
Lawrence, S. 51, 53
learning: cooperative 121, 224, 228; democratic school process 273; physical education *see* physical education; sport *see* sport; transformative critical educator 207; vocational 8
Lee, C. 449
Lee, I. 240
Leflay, K. 462
the leftist approaches 4–5, 472–473
left libertarianism 4, 15n1
legitimate embodiment, in formal education 236–245
leisure: activities as basic human need 157–165; adult-centric definitions 193–194; in age of precarity and prosumption 45–54; in Brazil 145–155; children's geographies 192–200; heritage in 33–41; history of 35; Indigenous methodologies for 531–540; intersectional scholarship 556–566; at neoliberal moment 3–15; panoptic power structures 49; participatory research in 518–527; public history in 33–41; for refugees and asylum seekers

157–165; research methods for 491–501; as site of discipline 48–50; social justice in 33–41; socioeconomic status (SES) 363–372; in United States 131–141
Lenskyj, H. J. 558
Lentillon-Kaestner, V. 116
Lester, S. W. 326
LGBTIQ+ 72, 79, 82n1, 207, 210, 213–214
LGBTQ 72
LGBTQIAPN+ 280–281, 286
liberation; *see also* neoliberalism; interpretation of racism 154; pedagogy approach 311, 315; theology 182
libertarianism: left 4, 15n1; radical 23; Rawls' conception elements 25–26; social justice 24–25
Lighthouse Poole, Dorset 499
Light, R. 324
liquid modernity 50–51
Liston, K. 441
Little Rock Nine 136
Li, W. 222–223
Li, Y. 223
Li Ying 251
Lleixà, T. 224
Lloyd, M. 381
Loach, K. 507
Local Delivery Pilots (LDPs) 343–345
Lock, D. 498
Long, J. 206, 376, 533, 538
The Long Run 508–511, *509*
Louie-Poon, S. 550
Lovell, T. 28
Luengo, M. 240
Lu, X. 198

Mac an Ghaill, M. 397
Macauley, C. 431, 433
Macbeth, J. 378
Macgrath, R. 81
Machiavelli, N. 45
Mackintosh, C. 336
Maclean, C. 119
Made in Africa Evaluation (MAE) approach 493
Magee, J. 212, 313
Mahatma Gandhi 182
Major, J. 339
Maldonado, D. T. 281
Malkki, L. 164, 524
Mandela, N. 131
Manuel, P. 88
Manzo, K. 316
Māori research 534
Marsters, C. 535
Maruna, S. 391

Marx, K. 158; critique of social justice theories 23; social theory 23; *Thesis on Feuerbach* 158
Marylebone Cricket Club 35
masculinity 71–82; cisnormative 89; currency 397, 399; gay men and 93; hegemonic 74–76, 86, 91–96, 120, 396; hyper 396–397, 400; inclusive masculinity theory *see* inclusive masculinity theory
Mason, J. 323
Masters, W. A. 548
Mathare Youth Sport Association 297
Mathiesen, T. 52
Maxwell, H. 213
Mbeki, T. 477
Mbembe, A. 146, 151–153
McCall, L. 562
McClintock, A. 557
McConnell, F. 86
McCormack, M. 76–77
McCuaig, L. A. 10, 222
McDonald, M. 560
McGhee, H. 135
McGlashan, H. 122
McGoldrick, K. 328
McGovern, R. A. 194
McGuigan, B. 441
McGuire-Adams, T. 564
McLaren, P. 240, 285
McLean, J. 441
McPherson, G. 35
McRory, P. 551
media, athlete activism 446; case study 450; coverage 450–453; four waves 447–448; framing 449; responses 449; women's rugby 459–468
Meherali, S. M. 550
Meir, D. 25
men athletes' activism 59–67; *see also* women elite athletes
Men's Roller Derby Association (MRDA) 110
mental health 72, 170–176
meritocracy 131, 187
Merleau-Ponty, M. 238, 513
Mertens, D. 493
Messerschmidt, J. 397
Michler, J. D. 548
Michon, C. 211
Milgrim, M. 117
Millennium Development Goals (MDGs) 297, 308
Miller, D. 19–20, 334
Miller, T. 75
Milligan, L. 549
Millington, R. 22, 146
Mills, C. W. 133
Millward, P. 409

misrecognition 28, 206, 259; *see also* recognition
Mitchell, K. 174
mixed (co-educational) groups, physical education (PE) 118–120
Mixed Marital Arts 26
Mobile Jugendarbeit 398
modern sports 54, 159, 165; in Brazil 147–152, 155; to capitalism 245; decentre normative subject 557, 562; Eurocentric epistemology of 565; feudalism to 47–48; liquid 50–51; and panopticon 48–50; roots of 161; social (in)justice narratives in 559
Mogaji, E. 463
Mohanty, C. T. 311
Molina, V. A. B. 281
Molnár, G. 376
Monforte, J. 378
Moore, G. 316
Morality. Restoring the Common Good in Divided Times (Sacks) 186
Mordal Moen, K. 222–223
Moreno-Doña, A. 245n1
Morsy, L. 354
Mosier, C. 88
Movimento journal 281
Mowatt, R. A.: *The Geographies of Threat and the Production of Violence: The State and the City Between Us* 135
Muir, K. B. 461
multiculturalism 285, 355
Munich Olympic Games 21
Münter, L. 474
Murray, C. 449
muscular Christianity 159, 165, 181, 296, 460
Museum of Childhood, Edinburgh 35
Mwaanga, O. 309, 315, 317
Mwaniki, M. F. 563
Mwansa, K. 309

Nash, S. 448
Nassib, C. 72
national anthems 431–442; Advance Australia Fair 437–439; Amhrán na bhFiann (The Soldier's Song) 440; in Australia 437–440; God Save the Queen 440–441; in Northern Ireland 440–442; protests in United States 434–437; The Star-Spangled Banner 431–432
National Association for the Advancement of Colored People (NAACP) 135
National Basketball Association (NBA) 59, 131–132, 423, 426
National Collegiate Athletic Association (NCAA) 103, 139, 425–426
National Demonstration Projects 338, 340
National Football League (NFL) 6, 132–133, 138–139, 322–323, 425, 434, 436–437, 447
National Football Museum 35
National Governing Bodies (NGBs) 138, 341
National Hockey League (NHL) 428, 472
National Horse Racing Museum 35
National Lottery 35, 339
National Museum of African American History and Culture 136
National Recreation and Park Association (NRPA) 132, 136–137
National Rugby League (NRL) 437–438, 534
National Traditional Games of Ethnic Minorities 251
National Women's Soccer League (NWSL) 436
Nazi Olympics 421
Neale, B. 193
Neill, A. S. 225
neo-colonialism 108, 298, 303, 311–313
neoliberalism: activist-scholarship in 9–10; China *see* China; integrity approach 546–552; interpretation of racism 154; laissez-faire 22; 'new right' politics 23; participatory approaches, policy objectives 523–524; in public education policies 281; social justice 6–8, 13; sport at 3–15; Sport for Development and Peace (SDP) 315–316; women elite athletes 464
New Labour, sports 160, 340–341
Newman, J. H. 163
Nicholls, S. 299
Nieva, C. 224
Nike 6
Nixon, H. L. 395
Nobis, T. 162
Noddings, N. 222–223
non-binary adults 86–87; methods 87–88; youth sport in 210
non-confrontational tactics, women elite athletes 63–64
nonracism 133, 146; *see also* racism
non-subjugated knowledge 238; *see also* knowledge
North American Society for the Sociology of Sport (NASSS) 9
Northern Ireland, national anthems in 440–442
not-for-profit organisations (NGOs) 297, 315, 474, 478
#NotNCAAProperty 425
Nozick, R.: *Anarchy, State and Utopia* 24
Nunan, D. 550

Oakley, G. 507
Obama, B. 40
O'Connor, J. 225, 286
Office of the United Nations High Commissioner for Human Rights (OHCHR) 106
Okazawa-Rey, M. 9
de Oliveira, V. J. M. 286

Oliver, K. L. 227, 229
Oliver, M. 379–380
Ollivier, M. 370
Olschewski, E. 194
Olusoga, D. 39
Olympic education prorgamme 260n1
Olympic Games 219, 341–343; in Atlanta 340; in Berlin 37, 421; Greek Olympic Winners organisation 353; in London 36, 65; Mexico City 427, 432; in Munich 21; Summer Olympic Games 432; in Tokyo 61, 65, 190
Olympic Project for Human Rights (OPHR) 427, 432
Olympic Truce organisation 353
Olympism 159, 163, 181
Oncescu, J. 7
O'Neal, S. 451
O'Neil, M. 441–442
one-size-fits-all approach 312, 335
online activism 459–468
On the Duty of Civil Disobedience (Thoreau) 182
Ortiz, S. 498
Ortner, S. B. 514
Osaka, N. 419
O'Sullivan, M. 225
Otele, O. 40
Outley, C. W. 198
Owens, J. 421
Owton, H. 462
Oxford, S. 561, 564
Oyewumi, O. 557

Pacific/Pasifika studies, social justice research 531–532, 540, 540n2; critical race theory 532–533; decolonial frameworks 535–536; ethical responsibility 538–539; minoritised groups 534–537, **535**; pleasant emotions 535; from surviving to thriving 533–534
Packer, D. 563
Pacquaio, M. 51
Painter, K. R. 72
Palmer v Thompson (1971) 135
panopticism 48–50
paradoxes 107, 163, 367, 391–393
Paralympic Games 185, 243, 341–342
Parekh, G. 285
parity of participation *see* participatory parity
Parker, K. 330
Parry, D. C. 532, 539
Parry, K. 437, 449
Participant Media 514–515
participatory action research (PAR) 10, 161, 494, 520, 522–523
participatory approaches: accessibility 384; (re) centring politics through 522–523; emancipatory 377, 379–381, 384–386; and equity 265–266; integrity 549; intersectionality 526–527; lived experience 382–383; neo-liberal policy 523–525; participatory research (PR) 518–527; to research 519–521; for social justice research 381–384, 518–527; three-dimensional model of 494
participatory parity 28–29, 206
The Pass 188–189
Patagonia 6
Paterno, J. 39
patient and public involvement (PPI) principles 382
Paton, G. 324
patriarchal ideas: gender differences 100–101; heteropatriarchal 558–559, 563; power 206; Sport for Development and Peace 313–315
Paul, A. 185
PeacePlayers 353
Pearson, G. 408
Pearson's chi-squared test 245n2
pedagogy approach 9, 221, 274; *see also* critical pedagogy; active advocacy 272–273; activism 226, 229; bicultural 272; of care 222–223, 228; citizenship education 273; critical *see* critical pedagogy; culturally responsive 271–272; democratic 225–227, 273; direct/explicit teaching strategies 271; embodiment 238–239; on health and beauty standards 286; Historically Black Colleges and Universities (HBCUs) 269; of inclusion 223–225; liberation 311, 315; queering 121–122; for reflection and inquiry 120–121; within schools and communities 220–221; social justice 118, 120–121; sport-for-all (SfA) programmes 350; student-centred 122, 228; Tinning's idea 10; transformative critical educator 207
Peirats, J. 245
Penney, D. 224–225
people with disabilities *see* disability sport
The Perception Agency 464
Pericot, J. 240
Perrier, M.-J. 378
Peterson, R. A. 366–367
Petrie, K. 225
Pettican, A. 495
Pettit, H. 492
Phelps, M. 102
Phenomenology of Spirit (Hegel) 180
philanthropy 38–39, 66–67, 163, 423–424, 473
Phillips, M. 36
Philosophy at the University of Sussex 86
Philpot, R. 280, 282
Phipps, P. 534, 536
physical education (PE) 9, 219–229; addressing disparities 270–271; adversity 274–275; age and ability 268–269; age-biased embodiment 242; bodily practices 237–239; branded

apparel 244; Brazilian sport 153–154; challenge 245, 270; citizenship 273; democratic school process 273; disability embodiment 242–243; doing gender 114–115, 117, 123; embodiment in 236–245; gender in 114–123; historical contexts and influences 269–270; leadership body 238; male/female embodiment 241, *241*; mixed (co-educational) groups 118–120; participation in physical exercise 243–244; pedagogical approaches/strategies *see* pedagogy approach; racial homogeneity 242; religion and language 268; research example 122; school, in Brazil 280–287; sex integration 118–120; shaping inclusive environments 271; single-sex 115–117; and sport-for-all (SfA) programmes 349–358; temperature of schools 239–240; textbooks images 240–244; theoretical background 220–221; trick of reality 240; undoing gender 114–115, 117–122; US legislation and policies, critical race theory (CRT) 264–275
physical education teacher education (PETE) 284, 564–565
Physick, R.: *The British Olympics and Played in Liverpool* 36
Pielichaty, H. 212
Piqué, G. 427
Piscopo, J. 65
Pittaway, E. 160–161
Plan of Health China 2030 251
The Players' Tribune 436
Playing for Scotland: The Making of Modern Sport 40
'Playing to Win' strategy 341
pleasure principle 51
plus sport/sport plus 162, 309, 335–336
Pocock, M. 463
police brutality 46, 61, 322, 425
Policy Action Team 10, 340
political activism 12, 304, 448; *see also* activism
political movement 28, 54n1
political semiosis 413, 416
Polley, M. 38; *The British Olympics and Played in Liverpool* 36
Posadas, B. M. 198
Positive Futures approach 341
post-COVID 3, 304
Potgieter, C. 563
power 45, 54, 73; as authority 47–48; dynamics in disability sport studies 376–386; exclusionary 53–54; in industrial society 47; liquid modernity 50–51; modernity and panopticon 48–50; panopticism 48–50, 52; pleasure principle 51; reality principle 51; synopticism 51–53; technologies of 48

Powis, B. 378
precarization 52
predatory culture 236, 240; *see also* culture
Premier League Kickz 342
Prince, S. 315, 317
Pringle, R. 10–12, 78
production-based economy 51
professional football 172–174
professional sport 4, 13, 21, 24, 50, 149, 154, 323–324, 342, 345, 369, 433–434, 437, 440
prosumption 45–54
public history: performance of 37; in sport and leisure 33–41
Public Investment Fund (PIF) 187
public–political campaign 6
public sociology 8–9, 11; *see also* sociology
Putnam, R.: *Bowling Alone* 186

Qatar FIFA World Cup 2022 6, 12
quasi-structuralist model, inclusive masculinity theory (IMT) 74, 76, 81
Queen's Park, Glasgow 40
queering pedagogy approach 121–122
Quidditch game 109

race: children's leisure geographies 192–200; ethnicity and 266–267
racialisation: compensatory cultivation 199; and sex-testing 108–109; social disadvantage 351
racism; *see also* anti-racism; binary framing of 132; in Brazil 145–155; Christianity and 181–188; clinical approach 132; decoupling 139; democracy myth 151; discrimination 322; hunting for 132, 134, 140–141; Indigenous and Black ethnic-racial relations **283**, 284; inequity 139–140; injustice 27; King's study 176n2; liberal interpretation of 154; microaggression 197–198; minority children's leisure 194–196; physical violence 135; and police brutality 46, 61, 322; product of individual bias 133; science 145–146; in sport and leisure 132–134; structural 37, 46, 132–134, 137, 140, 148, 195, 539, 557; in United States 131–141; violence 147, 149
radical libertarian 23
Rainbow Laces 3
Ralph, B. 78–79
Ramshaw, G. 34
Ranger, T. 431
Rankin-Wright, A. 532
Rapinoe, M. 59, 65, 72, 436, 451, 454
Ratna, A. 492, 561
Ravenhill, J. P. 93
Rawls, J. 25, 158; distributive justice-as-fairness 22; feminist critique 26–27; social justice 25–26; *A Theory of Justice* 25

Ray, V. 139
Reagan, R. 5, 7, 23
reality principle 51
recognition 259; Brazilian sport 155; Fraser's perspective 206; gender 85; progressive policies of 149; public 180; social justice through 26–27
Recognition in Anthem Project 440
reconciliation process 153, 437, 439
recreation spaces: equitable sport and 134–136; social justice in 140
re-democratisation process 281
Refugee Olympic Team 159
refugees, sport/social justice for 157–165; centralising ethics 165; crisis 159–160, 352; and forced migrants 160; UN Convention Relating to the Status of Refugees 159
Refugees Welcome 3
Regan, M. R. 432
Reid, E. 452
Reilly, J. 35
Reisch, M. 206
relational sociology 410–411; *see also* sociology
representational justice 20; *see also* social justice
research design 377, 386, 498–499, 524, 545, 547–549
research ethics 533, 544–548, 550, 552
research, social justice *see* social justice research
Restore Trust 39
Rethinking Recognition 28
Reveries of the Solitary Walker (Rousseau) 179
revolutionary athletes 422; *see also* athletes
Rey-Cao, A. 244
Rhode Island District Court 101
Rhoden, W. C. 171, 175; *Forty-million-dollar Slave* 171
Ribeiro, L. C. 149
Richards, K. A. 273
Riches, G. 532–533, 537
Ricketts, W. A. 82n1
Rickey, B. 421
Riggs, B. 426
right libertarianism 15n1
Rio 2016 games 159
Ritchie Report 175
Roberts, S. 78–79
Robinson, J. 41, 421, 426, 448
Robinson, P. 449
Robinson, T. 39
Rodon, T. 427
Rodriguez, S. H. 431, 433
Roe vs Wade 4
Ronaldo, C. 53
Rooney Rule 138–139
Rose, J. 7
Rosenbauer, B. P. 316

Rosenoir, L. 174
Rosen, R. 196
Rothstein, R. 354
Rottenberg, C. 464
Roure, C. 116
Rousseau, J.-J.: *Discourse on the Origins and the Foundations of Inequality Among Men* 178; *Reveries of the Solitary Walker* 179
Roy, A. 524
Rozaitul, M. 29
Rugby Sevens 461
rugby union 37, 74–75, 392, 432, 437; women's involvement 459–468
Rugby World Cup 37
Ruggero, C. E. 410
Ruiz-Montero, P. J. 327
Russell, B. 448
Russell, D. 286

Sacks, J.: *Morality. Restoring the Common Good in Divided Times* 186
Sacks, R. 186
Safe Standing, English football 405–417
Saini, A. 145
St Mary's Stadium 39
Saldaña, J. 509
Samie, S. F. 492
Sampson, R. J. 391
Sanches Neto, L. 154
Sánchez-Hernández, N. 121, 224
Sandel, M. J. 22, 187
Sanford, R. 495
SARS-Cov-2 (Covid-19) pandemic 284
Save Albert Park 480
Save Our Statues 39
Savile, J. 39
Sayer, F. 34
Scannapieco, M. 72
scepticism, social justice 23–24, 108, 317, 379, 472–473, 479
Schacht, S. P. 460–461
Schalke 04 414
Schenker, K. 207
Schilt, K. 92, 94
Schinke, R. 214
Schmidt, S. H. 454
school physical education, in Brazil 280–281, **283**; *see also* physical education; critical studies, on health and beauty standards 286; findings 283; gender and sexuality issues 285–286; inclusive bodily practices 285; Indigenous and Black ethnic-racial relations **283**, 284; knowledge of socially marginalised groups 285; method 282–283; people with disabilities 284–285
schools of thought, social justice 19, 22, 24, 29

school sports, China: authoritarianism 252–255; social justice in 251–260; special permission 255–256; students' unequal access 258–259; unequal distribution 256–258
Schulenkorf, N. 309
Schuster, L. 160
Schuyt, K. 394
Schweiger, G. 25
Scoats, R. 77
Scotland Act 85
Scottish Football Museum 40–41
Scraton, S. 29, 120, 559–560
Seal, M. 398
Second Vatican Council 183–186
Sedgwick, E. K. 72, 94
seduction, discipline to 50–51
Seifried, C. 324
Seitz, T. 461
self-actualisation 115, 117
self-fulfilling prophecy 391
self-harm 72, 80
self-identification system 85, 89, 123, 383–384, 507, 512, 527
self-perpetuating phenomenon 107
Semenya, C. 61, 100, 563
service-learning 321–330; best practices of implementation 327–329; components 325; experiential education and 325–326; to promote social justice awareness 326–327
Settler, F. G. 560
Sewell, W. H. 411
sex; *see also* gender; activism 59–67; and gender 100; integration 110–111, 118–120; in male sporting spaces 91; re-assignment surgery 104; segregation 111, 115; spectrum 101; testing 99–111
sexual abuse 10, 39, 49
sexuality: Christianity 188–190; homosexuality 71–82; issues 285–286
sexual orientation 189, 211, 267–268, 314
Sheffield, E. 324
Shelley, K. 10
Shindana Toys 199
Sifre, H. 507
Sigley, G. 259
Sikes, M. 562
Silva, I. C. C. 154
Silva, M. 281
Silver, A. 426
Silverman, S. J. 222
Simmel, G. 164
Simons, L. 326
Simpson, O. J. 423, 425
single-sex physical education (PE) 115–117; *see also* physical education
Sinha, S. 522

Sisjord, M. K. 116
Skey, M. 463
Skillen, A. 545
Skogvang, B. 564
Slater, L. 536
Smart Water 6
Smith, A. 174
Smith, B. 378, 381, 385, 491, 493
Smith, C.: *How the Word is Passed* 136
Smith, D. 536
Smith, L. T. 536, 539
Smith, S. 552
Smith, T. 21, 59, 66, 422, 427, 432–433, 448
Smits, F. 210
Snowsnill, E. 466
Soares, A. J. 151
Sobal, J. 117
Sochi Games 2014 12
social activism 7, 67, 229, 304; *see also* activism
social change 11, 321–330
social class 150, 351–352, 357, 364, 367
social consciousness 269, 326–327, 329–330
social disadvantage 349–350; issues 356; policy perspectives 352–356; racialisation 351; unemployment 351; in young people 356–358
social equality 21, 25, 180
Social Exclusion Unit 340
social inequality 24; inevitability of 24–25; physical education (PE) 236
social injustice 46, 266; in modern sports 559; physical education *see* physical education; youth sport 207–212
socialisation process: gender 89, 93; Sport for Development and Peace (SDP) 298; in training milieu 395
social justice 3–6; *see also* transformative justice; academic barriers to 384–386; in age of precarity and prosumption 45–54; branding 419–428; in Brazil 145–155, 280–287; children's leisure geographies 192–200; Christianity 178–190; competing theories of 22–27; contrasting approaches to 3–15; emancipatory participatory approaches 377, 379–381, 384–386; exclusionary power 53–54; fairness and 22, 25–26; integrated theory 19, 28–30; intersectionality 558–559; issue of 149; libertarian 24–25; at neoliberal moment 6–8; participatory research in 518–527; pedagogy approach 120–121; physical education (PE) 219–229; principles 265–266; Rawlsian approach 25–26; for refugees 157–165; research methods for *see* social justice research; sceptics 23–24; schools of thought 19, 22, 24, 29; in school sports 251–260; in sport and leisure 33–41; in Sport for Development and Peace (SDP) 295–304;

through recognition 26–27; in and through sport 21–22; 'undoing' gender in physical education (PE) 117–122; in United States 131–141; in youth sport 205–214
social justice education (SJE) 118
social justice research (SJR) 491–501; challenges 495–496; co-production 493–495; data analysis 497–498; epistemic violence 492–493; ethics of 491–492; impact 499, *500–501*; Indigenous methodologies for 531–540; issues of 'exit' 498–499; minoritised groups 534–537, **535**; positionality and reflexivity 496–497; presenting research 498; self-reflexivity 496
social life 29, 46–47, 52, 93, 164
social majority and minority 311–313, 315–316
social media 53, 63, 65, 454–455, 550; environmental activism 478; gender critical feminism 87; over climate science 472; for personal branding 420–421, 424–425, 427; #*VeteransForKaepernick* on 435; in women's rugby 459–468
social movements 433, 442, 447, 464, 473, 521; #BlackLivesMatter *see* Black Lives Matter; development of 62; fan activism 405–417; literature on 67; pitfalls 29; resistance of 280
social recognition 180, 391; *see also* recognition
social reproduction 297–298, 300, 302–303
social structure, sport 45, 53–54, 76, 220, 264, 298, 303–304, 380, 532
social theory 23, 50, 358, 566
social welfare 7, 53, 365
socio-economic injustices 206, 208
socioeconomic status (SES) 363–372
sociology: closure 364–368; discipline of 158; of fan activism 405–417; imagination 358; public 8–9, 11; relational 410–411; temporality in 410–411
The Soldier's Song (Amhrán na bhFiann) 440
solidarity 419, 451, 523; in Christian community 180–181, 184–186, 190; expressions of 431; with forced migrants 522; Hillsborough stadium disaster 406; identity and 406–407; networks of 164; patriotic expressions 434; to racial justice 21; with trans community 88; unequivocal 527
Sousa Santos, B. 285
Southampton Football Club 39
Spaaij, R. 158, 160, 162, 212–213, 494, 524, 527, 561, 564
Sparkes, A. C. 10
spectator sport 369–371; *see also* sport
Spencer, N. 376
Spiegel, A. D. 434
Spiegel, M. B. 434
Spivak, G. C. 492
Spooner, M. 515

sport 87; *see also* athletes; in age of precarity and prosumption 45–54; biological advantage in 102; branding social justice 419–428; in Brazil 145–155; Christianity 178–190; contrasting approaches to social justice in 3–15; and crime reduction 390–400; cultural significance of 30, 46; for development sector 161, 163; direct participation 367–369; discrimination in 99–111; environmental activists, five groups of 471–481; equality consensus 21; fair play 99; and gender 91–95; heritage *see* heritage, sport; high-profile 59, 67, 437, 453; inclusive masculinity theory 71–82; Indigenous methodologies for 531–540; intersectional scholarship 556–566; management education 323–325; media framing 446–455; at neoliberal moment 3–15; participatory research in 518–527; plus 162, 309, 335–336; policy discourse 18; problematic consensus 22; public history in 33–41; public sociology 8–9; qualitative methods 10; for refugees 157–165; research methods 491–501; service-learning 321–330; sex-testing in 99–111; sexualities *see* sexuality; as site of discipline 48–50; social change 321–330; social justice *see* social justice; social structure 45, 53–54, 76, 220, 264, 298, 303–304, 380, 532; socioeconomic status 363–372; transgender in 88; in United States 131–141; and virtue 179; women activism 59–67
Sport Action Zones (SAZ) 340–341, 344
Sport England 340–343, 345, 512
sport-for-all (SfA) programmes 30, 349–358; community sport development (CSD) 334–338, 342, 344; hierarchies of the body 354; pedagogy approach 350; physical education (PE) and 349–358; social disadvantage *see* social disadvantage
Sport for Development and Peace (SDP) 295–304, 336, 493; advancing neoliberalism 315–316; in Burundi 311; conceptualising social justice 300–301; criticisms 297–300; data-driven analyses 304; deficit approach 312; features of 303; future 308–317; impact 309–316; imperial foundations 311–313; intersectionality 560–561, 564; liberation pedagogy approach 311, 315; limitations 302; main tenets of 296–297; neo-colonial critique 312; organisations 309; patriarchal ideologies 313–315; planning, design, and implementation of 312; practical sporting activities 309; Right to Play's activities 297, 299; social justice 300–304; soft employability skills 316; theoretical analyses 310; top-down *versus* bottom-up approaches 299–301

sporting spaces 85–96
Sports Council 336
Sports Grounds Safety Authority (SGSA) 408
Spracklen, K. 538
The Star-Spangled Banner (national anthems) 431–432
Stefancic, J. 197
Stephens, A. C. 12
Sterling, D. 132
Stewart, D.-L. 328
Stewart, K. 354
Stewart, W. 192
Stewart-Withers, R. 533
Stockholm Consensus 108
Stock, K. 86
Stolen Generations 437
Stone, C. 522
Stronach, M. 213
structural inequality 200, 274; in academia 385; challenges 315–316; in Eurocentric society 314
structural racism 37, 46, 132–134, 137, 140, 148, 195, 539, 557
subjugated knowledges 237–238; see also knowledge
Suburban Nation: The Rise and Decline of the American Dream (Duany) 135
Sudbury, J. 9
Sugden, J. 397, 441
suicide 72, 80–82, 174, 312
Summer Olympic Games 432; Tokyo 36, 72
Super Bowl 434, 448, 450
Sustainable Development Goals (SDGs) 297, 308
Sutherland, S. 118
Sutton, P. W. 351
Swain, S. 51, 532
Swartz, L. 379
Sweep Curling Club 255
Swiss Federal Court (SFC) 106
Sykes, H. J. 121
synopticism 51–53

Táboas-Pais, M. I. 244
Tackling My Demons (Collymore) 174
Talburt, T. 40
Tallbear, K. 540
Tamale, S. 558, 563
tangible immovable/movable heritage 34
Taylor, B. 46
Taylor, C. 188
Taylor, I. 407
Taylor, L. 36, 38
Taylor, T. 213, 533

technology of dominance 49
Tengan, P. K. 539
territorial sovereignty 47
Thatcher, M. 5, 7, 23, 338–339, 406
Theoharis, G. 132
theories of change 390, 393–396
A Theory of Justice (Rawls) 25
The Theory of the Leisure Class (Veblen) 364
Thesis on Feuerbach (Marx) 158
Third Winter Sports Games 257
Thompson, E. P. 479
Thompson, T. D. 194
Thoreau, H. D.: *On the Duty of Civil Disobedience* 182
Thorjussen, I. M. 116
Thorpe, H. 463–464, 467
Thuram, L. 173, 175
Tiatia-Seath, J. 535
Tiessen, R. 312–313
Timken, G. 116
Timmins, S. 538
Timothy, D. 34
Tinning, R. 10
Toffler, A. 52
Toffoletti, K. 463–464, 467
Tokyo Olympic Games 36, 61, 65, 72, 91, 190, 475
Tolgfors, B. 224
Tomas, F. 465–466
Tomillero, J. 79–80
Tomkovick, C. 326
Tomlinson, A. 75
top-ranked athletes see women elite athletes
Totten, M. 342
trans-exclusionary radical feminist (TERF) 87, 123
transformative justice 120, 122, 551; see also social justice; disability sport studies 376–377; pedagogy approach see pedagogy approach; sport for development and peace 295, 297–298, 300–304
transgender: in Abelson's research 92; athletes 88, 91, 95, 101, 103–105, 110–111, 123, 211, 219; co-educational groups 120; impact on women athletes 103–105; individuals 99; masculinity see masculinity; moral panic 123, 409; and non-binary 86–87; in sporting spaces 90–91; youth sport in 210–211
Travers, A. 559, 565
Tredway, K. 67
Trudeau, D. 135
Trump, D. 433–436, 448
Trussell, D. E. 211, 213–214, 532, 538
Truth, S. 559
Tuskegee Syphilis study 547

2SLGBTQIA+ 4–6
Tyson, M. 174

Ubuntu 315–316
Ugolotti, N. 495
uncertainty 47, 52, 54, 412, 462, 545
understanding-based medicine/practice (UBM/UBP) 505
'undoing' gender 114–115, 117–123; gender-typing with diverse activities 118; mixed (co-educational) groups 118–120; pedagogies for reflection and inquiry 120–121; queering pedagogy 121–122; research example 122; sex integration 118–120
unemployment, social disadvantage 351
UNIA movement 46
Union of European Football Associations (UEFA) 426–427
United Kingdom (UK): Centre for Social Justice 5; community sport development (CSD) in 336–338, 344–345; Conservative and Unionist Party 5; Equality Act 4, 86; Equality Standard for Sport 21; heritage 35–36; House of Commons 81; Illegal Immigration Bill 160; 'Levelling-up' 343; National Grid ESO 478
United Nations (UN): Commission on Sustainable Development 473; Convention on the Rights for Persons with Disabilities (CRPD) 378, 381; Convention on the Rights of the Child (UNCRC) 193; Declaration of Human Rights 296, 308; General Assembly Report 308; Rights of the Child Convention 208
United Negro Improvement Association 54n1
United States (US/USA): Civil War 40; Golf Association (USGA) 101; national anthems protests in 434–437; National Association of Social Workers 300; Olympic and Paralympic Committee (USOPC) 132, 138–139; racism in 131–141; Soccer Federation 62, 64; Supreme Court 4, 135; Tennis Association (USTA) 101; Women's National Soccer Team (USWNT) 62, 64, 436–437, 459
University of Brighton's Football 4 Peace versus Homophobia project 11
Uperesa, L. 538–539
UrbanDig 353

Values(s): Building a Better World for All (Carney) 186
Van Bottenburg, M. 394
Varhama, L. 395
Vatican's sport 183–186; see also sport
Veblen, T. 364; The Theory of the Leisure Class 364
Venturin-Trindade, N. 526
#VeteransForKaepernick 435

Vicente, M. 244
violence: epistemic 492–493; gender 396–398; incidents 395; physical 135; racial 147, 149
de Visser, O. R. 93
vocational learning 8

Wagg, S. 406
Wagner-Pacifici, R. 410, 413
Walker, M. F. 322
Walton-Fisette, J. L. 118
Walton, P. 423
Washington, K. 448
The Washington Post 453
Waterton, E. 34
Watson, A. 40–41
Watson, B. 29, 206, 376, 533
Watson, S. 34
Webb Ellis, W. 37
Weber 187
Webster, C. 165
Wells, T. A. 326
Welsh, L. 41
Welsing, C. 173
Wemyss, G. 522
West, C. 114
#WeThe15 3
Wetherly, P. 18, 22, 25, 206
White, A. 335, 339
White femininity 108–109, 557
White Paper on Sport and Recreation 336
Whole Sport Plans 342
Wilberforce, W. 33
de Wilde, A. 324
Williams, A. S. 421
Williams, B. 5
Williams, F. 464–466
Williams, J. 538
Williams, S. 59, 61–62, 64, 109, 426, 448
Williams, V. 59, 61–62, 64, 109, 426, 448
Wilson, M. 207
Wilson, T. C. 367
Wimbledon All England Tennis Club 35
window dressing 132, 136–139
Windsor Park 441
Wink, J. 317
Winkler, E. N. 198
Winter Olympics 180, 257–259
Wolfenden Report 336
Wolgemuth, J. R. 505
women elite athletes 59–60, 67n2, 419, 422, 433, 448, 454; *see also* gender; sex; activism 59–67; cisgender impact on 107; intersectional scholarship 556–566; intersex impact on 105–107; media in 459–468; neoliberal feminism and 464; physically weaker and less

athletic 100–101; rugby 459–468; transgender impact on 103–105
Women's Flat Track Derby Association (WFTDA) 109–110
Women's Home Nations 468n1
Women's National Basketball Association (WNBA) 59, 61, 426–427
Women's Sport & Fitness Foundation (WSFF) 511–512
Wood, C. A. 101
Woodhams, C. 380
Wood, S. 174
Woodson, C. G. 134
Woods, T. 424, 433
Woodward, K. 397
World Athletics 61, 104–106, 108–109, 565
World Championships 100
world-class athletes *see* women elite athletes
World Rugby 103, 461–462
World Rugby Museum 35, 37
Wright, J. 314, 462

Yasuoka, M. 449
Yenicioglu, B. 550
Ymous, A. 492
Young, I. M. 27–28; *Justice and the Politics of Difference* 26
Youth Power organisation 355
youth sport 205–214; advocacy in 212–213; conceptualising social justice 206–207; family and 207–213; gender in 114–123; social injustice 207–212; transgender 210
Yull, D. 207
Yuval-Davis, N. 522

Zeigler, E. F. 324
Zenquis, M. R. 563
Zhang, H. L. 256, 259
Zhao, Q. 222
Ziegert, A. 328
Zimmerman, D. 114
Zimmerman, G. 433
Zirin, D. 446